TIGRINYA

Student Dictionary

English-Tigrinya / Tigrinya-English

Compiled by
Wondmagegn Hunde

Hippocrene Books, Inc.
New York

Hippocrene Books, Inc. edition, 2022.

ISBN: 978-0-7818-1403-4

For information, address:
HIPPOCRENE BOOKS, INC.
171 Madison Avenue
New York, NY 10016
www.hippocrenebooks.com

Published by arrangement with
Star Foreign Language Books, a unit of ibs Books (UK)
56, Langland Crescent, Stanmore HA7 1NG, U.K.

Printed at Everest Press, New Delhi-110 020 (India)

Introduction to the Tigrinya Language

Tigrinya (also written as Tigrigna) is an Afro-Asiatic language spoken by about 7 million people, primarily in Eritrea and Ethiopia. Tigrinya is written in the same Ge'ez script used for the Ethiopic language Amharic, but Tigrinya grammar and usage differs significantly from Amharic.

This comprehensive bilingual student dictionary includes **over 25,000 Word-to-Word dictionary entries** and is perfect for ESL/ELL students to use for standardized testing. This dictionary is also useful to English speakers (students, travelers, businesspeople, and aid workers) who need to communicate in Tigrinya, as it includes simple Romanization/phonetic pronunciation for all Tigrinya words.

English - Tigrinya

A

a *(a.)* ኤ *eh*
aback *(adv.)* ንድሕሪት *ndḧrit*
abandon *(v.t.)* ራሕረሐ *raḧreḧe*
abase *(v.)* ኣዋረደ *'awarede*
abash *(adj.)* ኣሕነኸ *'aḧneḱe*
abate *(v.t.)* ሃድአ *had'e*
abate *(v.t.)* ሃድአ *had'e*
abbey *(n.)* ገዳም *gedam*
abbot *(n.)* ኣበ-ገዳም *'abegedam*
abbreviate *(v.t.)* ኣሕጸረ *'aḧxere*
abbreviation *(n.)* ምሕጻር *mḧxar*
abdicate *(v.t,)* ወረደ *werede*
abdication *(n.)* ምሕዳግ *mḧdag*
abdomen *(n.)* ከብዲ *kebdi*
abdominal *(a.)* ናይ ከብዲ *nay aberration*
abduct *(v.t.)* ጨወየ *čeweye*
abduction *(n.)* ጨወየ *čeweye*
aberrant *(adj.)* ዝንቡል *znbul*
aberration *(n.)* ስሕታን *sḧtan*
abet *(v.)* ኣደፋፈረ *adefafere*
abeyance *(n.)* ዉንዛፈ *wunzafe*
abhor *(v.)* ፈንፈነ *fenfene*
abhorrence *(n.)* ክርሃት *krhat*
abhorrent *(adj.)* ክሩህ *kruh*
abide *(v.i)* ጸንዐ *xen'ë*
abiding *(adj.)* ዘይውዳእ *zeywda'è*
ability *(n.)* ዓቕሚ *'äq̈mi*
abject *(adj.)* ሕርቱም *ḧrtum*
abjure *(v.)* መሓለ *meḧale*
ablaze *(adv.)* ዘንጸባርቕ *zenxebarq̈*
able *(adj.)* ክኢላ *k'ila*
ablution *(n.)* ሕጽበት *ḧxbet*
abnormal *(adj.)* ምዝቡል *mzbul*
aboard *(adv.)* ኣብ ልዕሊ *'ab l'ëli*
abode *(n.)* ገዛ *geza*
abolish *(v.t)* ሰረዘ *sereze*
abolition *(v.)* ምውጋድ *mwgad*
abominable *(adj.)* ዚጽላእ *zixla'è*
abominate *(v.)* ጸልአ *xel'e*
aboriginal *(adj.)* ጥንታዊ *ẗntawi*
abort *(v.i)* ተወግረ *tewegre*
abortion *(n.)* ምንጻል *mnxal*
abortive *(adj.)* ውጉር *wgur*
abound *(v.i.)* ፈድፈደ *fedfede*
about *(adv.)* ብዛዕባ *bza'ëba*
about *(prep.)* ኣብ ዙርያ *'ab zurya*
above *(adv.)* ላዕሊ *la'ëli*
above *(prep.)* ብዝያዳ *bzyada*
abrasion *(n.)* ልሕላሐ *lḧlaḧe*
abrasive *(adj.)* ፋሕፋሒ *faḧfaḧi*
abreast *(adv.)* ጎድነ-ጎድኒ *godnegodni*
abridge *(v.t)* ኣሕጸረ *aḧxere*
abroad *(adv.)* ወጻኢ *wexa'i*
abrogate *(v.)* ሰረዘ *sereze*
abrupt *(adj.)* ሃንደበታዊ *handebetawi*
abscess *(n.)* ሓገል *ḧagel*
abscond *(v.)* ጸለቑ *xeleq̈Wu*
absence *(n.)* ብኩራት *bkurat*
absent *(adj.)* ብኹር *bḱur*
absentee *(n.)* ትሩፍ *truf*
absolute *(adj.)* ፍጹም *fxum*
absolution *(n.)* ስሬት *sreet*
absolve *(v.)* መሓረ *meḧare*
absorb *(v.)* መጸየ *mexeye*
abstain *(v.)* ተቐጠበ *teq̈eẗebe*
abstinence *(n.)* ዛህዲ *zahdi*
abstract *(adj.)* ረቒቕ *req̈iq̈*
abstruse *(adj.)* ጥሉቕ *ẗluq̈*
absurd *(adj.)* ሃዚል *hazil*
absurdity *(n.)* ትርጉም ኣልቦነት *trgum 'albonet*

abundance *(n.)* ምልኣት *ml'at*
abundant *(v.t.)* ፍድፉድ *fdfud*
abuse *(v.)* ዓመጸ *ämexe*
abusive *(adj.)* ተጻራፊ *texarafi*
abut *(v.)* ተዳወበ *tedawebe*
abysmal *(adj.)* ደልሃመታዊ *delhametawi*
abyss *(n.)* ደልሃመት *delhamet*
academic *(adj.)* ኣካደሚያዊ *akademiyawi*
academy *(n.)* ኣካደሚ *akademi*
accede *(v.)* መጸ *mexe*
accelerate *(v.)* ነሃረ *nehare*
accelerator *(n.)* ኣንሃሪ *anhari*
accent *(n.)* ምጉላሕ *mgulaḧ*
accentuate *(v.)* ኣጉለሐ *aguleḧe*
accept *(v.)* ተቐበለ *teq̈ebele*
acceptable *(adj.)* ተቐባልነት ዘለዎ *teq̈ebalnet zelewo*
acceptance *(n.)* ቅባለ *qbale*
access *(n.)* ኣኽእሎ *'ak'èlo*
accessible *(adj.)* ክእቶ ዝከኣል *k'èto zke'al*
accession *(n.)* ብጽሓት *bxḧat*
accessory *(n.)* መሳርሒ *mesarḧi*
accident *(n.)* ሓደጋ *ḧadega*
accidental *(adj.)* ናይ ሓደጋ *nay ḧadega*
acclaim *(v.)* ኣጨብጨበ *ačebčebe*
accolade *(n.)* ሞሳ *mosa*
accommodate *(v.)* ኣጣጥሓ *'aẗaẗḧa*
accommodation *(n.)* መጣጥሒ *meẗaẗḧi*
accompaniment *(n.)* መሰነይቲ *meseneyti*
accompany *(v.)* ዓጀበ *äĵebe*
accomplice *(n.)* ግብረ-ኣበር *gbre'aber*
accomplish *(v.)* ፈጸመ *fexeme*
accomplished *(adj.)* ክኢላ *k'ila*
accomplishment *(n.)* ፍጻሜ *fxamee*
accord *(v.)* ውዕል - *w'ël*
accordance *(n.)* ተውህዶ *tewhdo*
according *(adv.)* ብመሰረት *bmeseret*
accordingly *(adv.)* ስለዚ *slezi*
accost *(v.)* ጐነፈ *gWanefe*
account *(n.)* ሕሳብ *ḧsab*
accountable *(adj.)* ተሓታቲ *teḧatati*
accountancy *(n.)* ናይ ተጸባጻቢ ሞያ *nay texabaxabi moya*
accountant *(n.)* ተጸባጻቢ *texebaxabi*
accoutrement *(n.)* ተውሳኸ-ዕጥቂ *tewsak̈e'ëtqi*
accredit *(v.)* ብወግዒ ለኣኸ *bweg'ï le'ak̈e*
accredited *(adj.)* ወግዓዊ *weg'äwi*
accretion *(n.)* ዕብየት *ëbyet*
accrue *(v.t.)* ደለበ *delebe*
accumulate *(v.)* ኣዋህለለ *awahlele*
accumulation *(n.)* ውህለላ *whlela*
accurate *(adj.)* ልክዕ *lk'ë*
accusation *(n.)* ግዚ *gzi*
accuse *(v.)* ከሰሰ *kesese*
accused *(v.t.)* ክሱስ *ksus*
accustom *(v.)* ለመደ *lemede*
accustomed *(adj.)* ልሙድ *lmud*
ace *(n.)* ብልጫዊ *blčawi*
acerbic *(adj.)* አረቢክ *arebik*

acetate ***(n.)*** **መጺጽ** *mexix*
acetone ***(n.)*** **ነታጉ** *qememawi*
ache ***(n.)*** **ቀመማዊ** *nafeq̈e*
achieve ***(v.)*** **ተጎናጸፈ** *tegonaxefe*
achievement ***(n.)*** **ፍጻሜ** *fxamee*
acid ***(n.)*** **መጺጽ** *mexix*
acidity ***(n.)*** **መጭቋር** *mečqWAr*
acknowledge ***(v.)*** **ተኣመነ** *te'amene*
acknowledgement ***(n.)*** **ምቕጻል** *mq̈xal*
acme ***(n.)*** **ጫፍ** *čaf*
acne ***(n.)*** **ዕንፍሩር** *ënfrur*
acolyte ***(n.)*** **ኣናጎንስጤስ** *anagonsẗees*
acorn ***(n.)*** **ውጽኢት** *wx'it*
acoustic ***(adj.)*** **ምስማዓዊ** *msma'äwi*
acquaint ***(v.)*** **ኣፋለጠ** *afaleẗe*
acquaintance ***(n.)*** **ሌላ** *leela*
acquiesce ***(v.)*** **ተሰማምዐ** *tesemam'e*
acquiescence ***(n.)*** **ምስምማዕ** *msmma'e*
acquire ***(v.)*** **ረኸበ** *rek̔ebe*
acquisition ***(n.)*** **ቅስመት** *qsmet*
acquit ***(v.)*** **ፈትሐ** *fetḧe*
acquittal ***(n.)*** **ናጻ ምልቃቕ** *naxa mlqaq̈*
acre ***(n.)*** **ኣክር** *'akr*
acrid ***(adj.)*** **በዳን** *bedan*
acrimony ***(n.)*** **ምረት** *mret*
acrobat ***(n.)*** **ኣክሮባት** *akrobat*
acrobatic ***(adj.)*** **ን ኣክሮባት** *n 'akrobat*
across ***(adv.)*** **ስግር** *sgr*
acrylic ***(adj.)*** **ኣክሪሊክ** *'akrilik*
act ***(v.)*** **ምግባር** *mgbar*
acting ***(n.)*** **ምውሳእ** *mwsa'è*
acting ***(adj.)*** **ወኪል** *wekil*
actinium ***(n.)*** **ቀመማዊ** *qememawi*
action ***(n.)*** **ምግባር** *mgbar*
actionable ***(adj.)*** **ዘኽስስ** *zek̔ss*
activate ***(v.)*** **ኣንጠፈ** *anẗefe*
active ***(adj.)*** **ንጡፍ** *nẗuf*
activist ***(n.)*** **ምንቅስቓስ** *mnqsq̈as*
activity ***(n.)*** **ንጥፈት** *nẗfet*
actor ***(n.)*** **ተዋናይ** *tewanay*
actress ***(a.)*** **ተዋሳኢት** *tewasa'it*
actual ***(adj.)*** **ህሉው** *hluw*
actually ***(adv.)*** **ብሓቂ** *bḧaqi*
actuary ***(n.)*** **ገምጋሚ** *gemgami*
actuate ***(v.)*** **ኣንጠፈ** *anẗefe*
acumen ***(n.)*** **ትኩርና** *tkurna*
acupuncture ***(n.)*** **ኣኩፓንክቸር** *akupankcher*
acute ***(adj.)*** **ንሱር** *nsur*
adamant ***(adj.)*** **ተሪር** *terir*
adapt ***(v.)*** **ኣልዘበ** *alzebe*
adaptation ***(n.)*** **ምውህሃድ** *mwhhad*
add ***(v.)*** **ቀጸለ** *qexele*
addendum ***(n.)*** **መመላእታ** *memela'èta*
addict ***(n.)*** **ተወለፈ** *tewelefe*
addicted ***(adj.)*** **ዉሉፍ** *wuluf*
addiction ***(n.)*** **ወልፊ** *welfi*
addition ***(n.)*** **ወሰኽ** *wesek̔*
additional ***(adj.)*** **ተወሳኺ** *tewesak̔i*
additive ***(n.)*** **ንምዕቃብ** *nm'ëqab*
addled ***(adj.)*** **ዝተናወጸ** *ztenawexe*
address ***(n.)*** **ኣድራሻ** *adrasha*
addressee ***(n.)*** **ተቐባላይ** *teq̈ebalay*
adduce ***(v.)*** **ጠቐሰ** *ẗeq̈ese*

adept ***(adj.)*** **ክኢላ** *k'ila*
adequacy ***(n.)*** **እኹልነት** *èḱulnet*
adequate ***(adj.)*** **እኹል** *èḱul*
adhere ***(v.)*** **ሰዓበ** *se'äbe*
adherence ***(n.)*** **ምድጋፍ** *mdgaf*
adhesive ***(n.)*** **ላጋቢ** *lagabi*
adieu ***(n.)*** **ላጋቢደሓን ኩን** *deḧan kun*
adjacent ***(adj.)*** **ጐረቤት** *gWarebeet*
adjective ***(n.)*** **ቅጽል** *qxl*
adjoin ***(v.)*** **ተጋወረ** *tegawere*
adjourn ***(v.)*** **ኣቋረጸ** *aqWArexe*
adjournment ***(n.)*** **ኣመሓላለፈ** *ameḧalalefe*
adjudge ***(v.t.)*** **በየነ** *beyene*
adjudicate ***(v.)*** **ፈረደ** *ferede*
adjunct ***(n.)*** **ጥብቆ** *ẗbqo*
adjust ***(v.)*** **ኣመዓራረየ** *ame'ärareye*
adjustment ***(n.)*** **ምውዳድ** *mwdad*
administer ***(v.)*** **ኣመሓደረ** *ameḧadere*
administration ***(n.)*** **ምምሕዳር** *mmḧdar*
administrative ***(adj.)*** **ምምሕዳራዊ** *mmḧdarawi*
administrator ***(adj.)*** **ኣመሓዳሪ** *ameḧadari*
admirable ***(adj.)*** **ዚነኣድ** *zine'ad*
admiral ***(n.)*** **ኣድሚራል** *admiral*
admiration ***(n.)*** **ኣድናቖት** *adnaq̈ot*
admire ***(v.)*** **ኣድነቐ** *adneq̈e*
admissible ***(adj.)*** **ዚፍቀድ** *zifqed*
admission ***(n.)*** **ቅበላ** *qbela*
admit ***(v.)*** **ተኣመነ** *te'amene*
admittance ***(n.)*** **ቅበላ** *qbela*
admonish ***(v.)*** **ገሰጸ** *gesexe*
ado ***(n.)*** **ሸቐልቀል** *sheq̈elqel*
adobe ***(n.)*** **ጥረ-ሕጡብ** *ẗreḧẗub*
adolescence ***(n.)*** **ብጽሕና** *bxḧna*
adolescent ***(adj.)*** **በጽሒ** *bexḧi*
adopt ***(v.)*** **ወሰደ** *wesede*
adoption ***(n.)*** **ምርዓም** *mr'äm*
adoptive ***(adj.)*** **ረዓሚ** *re'ämi*
adorable ***(adj.)*** **ተፈታዊ** *tefetawi*
adoration ***(n.)*** **ፍቕሪ** *fq̈ri*
adore ***(v.t.)*** **ኣምለኸ** *amleḱe*
adorn ***(v.)*** **ኣሰወነ** *asewene*
adrift ***(adj.)*** **ፋሉል** *falul*
adroit ***(adj.)*** **ጨሌ** *čele*
adsorb ***(v.)*** **አድሶረብ** *adserb*
adulation ***(n.)*** **ውዳሰ-ከንቱ** *wdasekentu*
adult ***(n.)*** **እኹል** *èḱul*
adulterate ***(v.)*** **ኣመራሰሐ** *ameraseḧe*
adulteration ***(n.)*** **ምምርሳሕ** *mmrsaḧ*
adultery ***(n.)*** **ዝሙት** *zmut*
advance ***(v.)*** **ሰጐመ** *segWame*
advance ***(n.)*** **ለዓለ** *le'äle*
advancement ***(n.)*** **ምምዕባል** *mm'ëbal*
advantage ***(v.t.)*** **ብልጫ** *blča*
advantage ***(n.)*** **ረብሓ** *rebḧa*
advantageous ***(adj.)*** **ጠቓሚ** *ẗeq̈ami*
advent ***(n.)*** **ምጽኣት** *mx'at*
adventure ***(n.)*** **ዕንደራ** *ëndera*
adventurous ***(adj.)*** **ሓደገ'ኛ** *ḧadegeḧa*
adverb ***(n.)*** **ተወሳከ-ግሲ** *tewesakegsi*
adversary ***(n.)*** **ተጻይ** *texay*
adverse ***(adj.)*** **ኣሉታዊ** *alutawi*

adversity *(n.)* **ሽግር** *shgr*
advertise *(v.)* **ኣፋለጠ** *afaleṫe*
advertisement *(n.)* **ረክላም** *reklam*
advice *(n.)* **ምዕዶ** *m'ëdo*
advisable *(adj.)* **ዝሓሽ** *zḧashe*
advise *(v.)* **መዓደ** *me'äde*
advocate *(n.)* **ደጋፊ** *degafi*
advocate *(v.)* **ተሓላቒ** *teḧalaq̈i*
aegis *(n.)* **ዑቕባ** *üq̈ba*
aeon *(n.)* **ኣዩን** *ayun*
aerial *(n.)* **ሰፋፊ** *sefafi*
aerobatics *(n.)* **ኣይሮባቲክስ** *ayrobatiks*
aerobics *(n.)* **ኤሮቢካ** *'eerobika*
aerodrome *(n.)* **መዓርፎ ነፈርቲ** *me'ärfo neferti*
aeronautics *(n.)* **ስነ-ምንፋር** *snemnfar*
aeroplane *(n.)* **ኣይሮፕላን** *ayroplan*
aerosol *(n.)* **ፍሊት** *flit*
aerospace *(n.)* **ጠፈረ-ህዋ** *ṫeferehwa*
aesthetic *(adj.)* **ጽባቐኣዊ** *xbaq̈e'awi*
aesthetics *(n.)* **ስነ-ጽባቐ** *snexbaq̈e*
afar *(adv.)* **ንርሑቕ** *nrḧuq̈*
affable *(adj.)* **ፍሕሹው** *fḧshuw*
affair *(n.)* **ፍጻሜ** *fxamee*
affect *(v.)* **ጸለወ** *xelewe*
affectation *(n.)* **ምስሉይነት** *msluynet*
affected *(adj.)* **ኣምሳሊ** *amsali*
affection *(n.)* **ፍትወት** *ftwet*
affectionate *(adj.)* **ርህሩህ** *rhruh*
affidavit *(n.)* **ቃለ-ማሕላ** *qalemaḧla*
affiliate *(v.)* **ተጸግዐ** *texeg'ë*
affiliation *(n.)* **ምጽጋዕ** *mxga'ë*
affinity *(n.)* **ተማስሎ** *temaslo*
affirm *(v.)* **ኣረጋገጸ** *aregagexe*
affirmation *(n.)* **ምርግጋጽ** *mrggax*
affirmative *(adj.)* **ኣወንታዊ** *awentawi*
affix *(v.t.)* **ልቃ'በ** *lqabe*
afflict *(v.)* **ጐድአ** *gWad'e*
affliction *(n.)* **ጭንቂ** *čnqi*
affluence *(n.)* **ሃብቲ** *habti*
affluent *(adj.)* **ሃብታም** *habtam*
afford *(v.t.)* **ኣተኻኸለ** *ateḱaḱele*
afforestation *(n.)* **ምግራብ** *mgrab*
affray *(n.)* **ናዕቢ** *na'ëbi*
affront *(n.)* **ዘለፈ** *zelefe*
afield *(adv.)* **ኣብ ርሑቕ** *'ab rḧuq̈*
aflame *(adj.)* **ዝተቓጸለ** *zteq̈axele*
afloat *(adj.)* **ዘንሳፍፍ** *zensaff*
afoot *(adv.)* **ኣብ ምቅርራብ** *'ab mqrrab*
afraid *(adj.)* **ዝፈርሀ** *zferhe*
afresh *(adv.)* **እንደገና** *'èndegena*
African *(adj.)* **አፍሪቃ** *afriqa*
aft *(adv.)* **ንድሕሪት** *ndḧrit*
after *(adv.)* **ድሕሪ** *dḧri*
after *(conj.)* **ድሕረ** *dḧre*
after *(prep.)* **ከም ናይ** *kem nay*
again *(adv.)* **እንደገና** *'èndegena*
against *(prep.)* **ኣንጻር** *anxar*
agate *(n.)* **ተሪር ክቡር እምኒ** *terir kbur 'èmni*
age *(n.)* **ዕድመ** *ëdme*
aged *(adj.)* **ሽማግለታት** *shmagletat*
ageism *(n.)* **dndena 'aregawyan** *dndena 'aregawyan*

ageless *(adj.)* **ዘይሓርር** *zeyḧarr*
agency *(n.)* **wanin** *wanin*
agenda *(n.)* **ኣጀንዳ** *aĵenda*
agent *(n.)* **ሰላይ** *selay*
agglomerate *(v.)* **ኣከበ** *akebe*
aggravate *(v.)* **ኣግደደ** *agdede*
aggravation *(n.)* **ዘቑጥዕ** *zeq̈uẗ'ë*
aggregate *(n.)* **ደመረ** *demere*
aggression *(n.)* **መጥቃዕቲ** *meẗqa'ëti*
aggressive *(adj.)* **ዓማጺ** *ämaxi*
aggressor *(n.)* **ኣጥቃዒ** *aẗqa'ï*
aggrieve *(v.)* **ኣቐየመ** *aq̈eyeme*
aghast *(adj.)* **ዝሰምበደ** *zsembede*
agile *(adj.)* **ስሉጥ** *sluẗ*
agility *(n.)* **ሶፕራኖ** *soprano*
agitate *(v.)* **ቀስቀሰ** *qesqese*
agitation *(n.)* **ምኳስ** *mḱWas*
agnostic *(n.)* **ኢፈሊጣዊ** *ifeliẗawi*
ago *(adv.)* **ይገብር** *ygebr*
agog *(adj.)* **ርቡጽ** *rbux*
agonize *(v.)* **ሃወኸ** *haweḱe*
agony *(n.)* **መሪር ሓዘን** *merir ḧazen*
agrarian *(adj.)* **መሬታዊ** *mereetawi*
agree *(v.)* **ተሰማምዐ** *tesemam'ë*
agreeable *(adj.)* **ዚሰማማዕ** *zisemama'ë*
agreement *(n.)* **ስምምዕ** *smm'ë*
agricultural *(adj.)* **ሕርሻዊ** *ḧrshawi*
agriculture *(n.)* **ሕርሻ** *ḧrsha*
aground *(adj.)* **ኣብ ባይታ** *'ab bayta*
ahead *(adv.)* **ኣብ ቅድሚ** - *'ab qdmi*
aid *(n.)* **ረድእ** *red'e*
aide *(n.)* **ደጋፊ** *degafi*
aids *(n.)* **ረድኢ** *red'i*
ail *(v.)* **ኣጨነቐ** *ačeneq̈e*
ailing *(adj.)* **ኣጨነቕኢ** *ačeneq̈e'i*
ailment *(n.)* **ሕማም** *ḧmam*
aim *(v.i.)* **ዕላማ** *ëlama*
aim *(n.)* **ሸቶ** *shto*
aimless *(adj.)* **ሰሓተ** *seḧate*
air *(n.)* **ኣየር** *ayer*
aircraft *(n.)* **ነፋሪት** *nefarit*
airy *(adj.)* **ነፋሻ** *nefasha*
aisle *(n.)* **ኮሪደዮ** *korideyo*
ajar *(adv.)* **ዝተገፍተነ** *ztegeftene*
akin *(adj.)* **ዚዛመድ** - *zizamed*
alacritous *(n.)* **ስሉጥ** *sluẗ*
alacrity *(n.)* **ቅሩብነት** *qrubnet*
alarm *(n)* **መጠንቀቕታ** *meẗenqeq̈ta*
alarm *(v)* **ስግኣት** *sg'at*
alas *(conj.)* **ዋይ ኣነ** *way 'ane*
albeit *(conj.)* **ሸሕ'ኳ** *shḧkWa*
album *(n)* **ኣልቡም** *'album*
albumen *(n.)* **ኣልቡመን** *albumen*
alchemy *(n.)* **ኣልከሚ** *alkemi*
alcohol *(n.)* **ኣልኮል** *alkol*
alcoholic *(adj.)* **ሰታይ** *setay*
alcove *(n.)* **ስብሳብ** *sbsab*
ale *(n.)* **ኣይል=ዓይነት ቢራ** *'ayl'äynet bira*
alert *(adj.)* **ጥንቁቕ** *ẗnquq̈*
algebra *(n.)* **ኣልጀብራ** *alĵebra*
alias *(adv.)* **ሳጓ** *sagWa*
alias *(n.)* **ልውጢ-ስም** *lwẗesm*
alibi *(n.)* **መውጽኢ-ነፍሲ** *mewx'inefsi*
alien *(adj.)* **ba'ëdi** *ባዕዲ*
alienate *(v.i.)* **ነጸለ** *nexele*
alight *(v.t.)* **ዚነድድ** *zinedd*
align *(v.)* **ሰርዐ** *ser'ë*

alignment ***(n.)*** **ኣሳላልፋ** *asalalfa*
alike ***(adj.)*** **ተመሳሳሊ** *temesasali*
alimony ***(n.)*** **ክፍሊት ፍትሕ** *kflit ftḧ*
alive ***(adj.)*** **ህያው** *hyaw*
alkali ***(n.)*** **ኣልካሊ** *alkali*
all ***(adj.)*** **ኩሉ** *kulu*
allay ***(v.)*** **ኣፋኰሰ** *afakWase*
allegation ***(n.)*** **ብህሎ** *bhlo*
allege ***(v.)*** **ኣለ** *ale*
allegiance ***(n.)*** **ተኣማንነት** *te'amannet*
allegory ***(n.)*** **ምስሌኣዊ ዛንታ** *mslee'awi zanta*
allergen ***(n.)*** **ስራይ ድጋም** *sray dgam*
allergic ***(adj.)*** **ተቖጣዒ** *teq̈oẗa'ï*
allergy ***(n.)*** **ቁጥዐ** *quẗ'ë*
alleviate ***(v.)*** **'aqalele** *ኣቃለለ*
alleviation ***(n.)*** **ምቕላል** *mq̈lal*
alley ***(n.)*** **መሸጐራጉር** *meshgWaragur*
alliance ***(n.)*** **ኪዳን** *kidan*
allied ***(adj.)*** **ተጸግዐ** *texeg'ë*
alligator ***(n.)*** **ዓንጎግ** *ängog*
alliterate ***(v.)*** **ደምሰሰ** *demsese*
alliteration ***(n.)*** **ድግመተ-ኣፈና** *dgmete'afena*
allocate ***(v.)*** **ኣካፈለ** *akafele*
allocation ***(n.)*** **ምምቕራሕ** *mmq̈raḧ*
allot ***(v.)*** **ኣማስሐ** *amasḧe*
allotment ***(n.)*** **ምስሒት** *msḧit*
allow ***(v.)*** **ፈቐደ** *feq̈ede*
allowance ***(n.)*** **መውዕሎ** *mew'ëlo*
alloy ***(n.)*** **ቆርቆሮ** *qorqoro*
allude ***(v.t.)*** **ኣመተ** *amete*
allure ***(n.)*** **ኣወናወነ** *awenawene*
alluring ***(adj.)*** **ኣወናወኒ** *awenaweni*
allusion ***(n.)*** **ኣመት** *amet*
ally ***(n.)*** **ሽርካ** *shrka*
almanac ***(n.)*** **ኣልማናክ** *almanak*
almighty ***(adj.)*** **ኩሉ ዚከኣሎ** *kulu zike'alo*
almond ***(n.)*** **ሉዝ** *luz*
almost ***(adv.)*** **ዳርጋ** *darga*
alms ***(n.)*** **ምጽ'ዋት** *mxwat*
aloft ***(adv.)*** **ዝተሰቕለ** *zteseq̈le*
alone ***(adv.)*** **በይኑ** *beynu*
along ***(prep.)*** **ኣብ ጐድኒ** *ab gWadni*
alongside ***(prep.)*** **ኣብ ጐድነኒ** *ab gWadneh*
aloof ***(adj.)*** **ግሉል** *glul*
aloud ***(adv.)*** **ብዓውታ** *b'äwta*
alpha ***(n.)*** **ኣልፋ** *alfa*
alphabet ***(n.)*** **ፊደል** *fidel*
alphabetical ***(adj.)*** **ብናይ ፊደላት ተርታ** *bnay fidelat terta*
alpine ***(adj.)*** **ከረናዊ** - *kerenawi*
already ***(adv.)*** **ዛጊት** *zagit*
also ***(adv.)*** **ከምኡ'ውን** *kem'uwn*
altar ***(n.)*** **መንበረ-ታቦት** *menberetabot*
alter ***(v.)*** **ጠረጴዛ ቁርባን** *ẗereṕeeza qurban*
alteration ***(n.)*** **ምልዋጥ** *mlwaẗ*
altercation ***(n.)*** **ቈይቍ** *qWeyqWi*
alternate ***(v.t.)*** **ምርጫ** *mrča*
alternative ***(adj.)*** **ቅያር** *qyar*
although ***(conj.)*** **ምንም'ኳ** *mnmkWa*
altitude ***(n.)*** **ብራኸ** *braḱe*
altogether ***(adv.)*** **ኩሉኹሉ** *kuluḱulu*
altruism ***(n.)*** **ልግስነት** *lgsnet*

aluminium *(n.)* አሉሚኒዮም *aluminiyom*
alumnus *(n.)* ተማሃራይ ዩኒቨርሲቲ ነበር *yuniversiti neber*
always *(adv.)* ኩሉ ግዜ *kulu gzee*
amalgam *(n.)* ሕዋስ ባዚቃ *ḧwas baziqa*
amalgamate *(v.)* ደብለቐ *debleq̈e*
amalgamation *(n.)* ምሕባር *mḧbar*
amass *(v.)* ኣከበ *akebe*
amateur *(n.)* ኣማተር *amater*
amateurish *(adj.)* ዘይክኢላ *zeyk'ila*
amatory *(adj.)* መስተፋቅር *mestefaqr*
amaze *(v.)* ኣገረመ *agereme*
amazement *(n.)* ኣድናቖት *adnaq̈ot*
Amazon *(n.)* ኣማዘን *amazen*
ambassador *(n.)* ኣምባሳደር=ልኡኽ *ambasaderl'uḱ*
amber *(n.)* ዕንዲዳ ጌጽ *ëndida geex*
ambient *(adj.)* ዙርያዊ *zuryawi*
ambiguity *(n.)* ዘይንጹርነት *zeynxurnet*
ambiguous *(adj.)* ዘይንጹር *zeynxur*
ambit *(n.)* ደረት *deret*
ambition *(n.)* ህርፋን *hrfan*
ambitious *(adj.)* ህንጡይ *hnẗuy*
ambivalent *(adj.)* ማንታዊ *mantawi*
amble *(v.)* ተሳለየ *tesaleye*
ambrosia *(n.)* ምቁር *mqur*
ambulance *(n.)* ኣምቡላንስ *ambulans*
ambush *(n.)* ድብያ *dbya*
ameliorate *(v.)* ኣመሓየሸ *ameḧayeshe*
amelioration *(n.)* ምምሕያሽ *mmḧyash*
amenable *(adj.)* ተሓታቲ *teḧatati*
amend *(v.)* ኣመሓየሸ *ameḧayeshe*
amendment *(n.pl.)* መኣረምታ *me'aremta*
amiable *(adj.)* ተፈታዊ *tefetawi*
amicable *(adj.)* ምሕዝነታዊ *mḧznetawi*
amid *(prep.)* ኣብ መንጎ *'ab mengo*
amiss *(adj.)* ግጉይ *gguy*
amity *(n.)* ዕርክነት *ërknet*
ammunition *(n.)* ተተኳሲ *tetekWasi*
amnesia *(n.)* ርሳዕ *rsa'ë*
amnesty *(n.)* ምሕረት *mḧret*
amok *(adv.)* ብዕብድብድ *b'ëbdbd*
among *(prep.)* ኣብ መንጎ *ab mengo*
amoral *(adj.)* ብዕሉግ *b'ëlug*
amorous *(adj.)* ፍቕራዊ *fq̈rawi*
amorphous *(adj.)* ቅርጸ-ኣልቦ *qrxe'albo*
amount *(n.)* ማዕረ ኮነ *ma'ëre kone*
ampere *(n.)* ኣምፐር *amper*
ampersand *(n.)* ፍሉጥ ሰብ *fluẗ seb*
amphibian *(n.)* ምድረ-ማያዊ *mdremayawi*
amphitheatre *(n.)* ኣምፊትያትር *amfityatr*
ample *(adj.)* ሰፊሕ *sefiḧ*
amplification *(n.)* ተወሳኺ *tewesaḱi*

amplifier *(n.)* **መጉልሒ** *megulḧi*
amplify *(v.)* **ኣጉልሐ** *agulḧe*
amplitude *(n.)* **ስፍሓት** *sfḧat*
amulet *(n.)* **ክታብ** *ktab*
amuse *(v.)* **ኣዘናግዐ** *azenag'ë*
amusement *(n.)* **ምዝንጋዕ** *mznga'ë*
an *(adj.)* **ሓደ** *ḧade*
anachronism *(n.)* **ዕለቱ ዝሰሓተ** *ëletu zseḧate*
anaemia *(n.)* **ዋሕዲ ደም** *waḧdi dem*
anaesthesia *(n.)* **ድንዛዘ** *dnzaze*
anaesthetic *(n.)* **መደንዘዚ** *medenzezi*
anal *(adj.)* **ቆይቋም** *qoyqWAm*
analgesic *(n.)* **ጸረ-ቃንዛ** *xereqanza*
analogous *(adj.)* **ተመሳሳሊ** *temesasali*
analogue *(adj.)* **ተመሳሳልነት** *temesasalnet*
analogy *(n.)* **ተመሳሳልነት** *temesasalnet*
analyse *(v.)* **ምትንታን** *mtntan*
analysis *(n.)* **ምርምር** *mrmr*
analyst *(n.)* **ተንታኒ** *tentani*
analytical *(adj.)* **ትንታነኣዊ** *tntane'awi*
anarchism *(n.)* **ፋሉልነት** *falulnet*
anarchist *(n.)* **ፋሉላዊ** *falulawi*
anarchy *(n.)* **ፋሉልነት** *falulnet*
anatomy *(n.)* **ስነ-ቅርጺ ኣካል** *sneqrxi 'akal*
ancestor *(n.)* **ኣበው** *abew*
ancestral *(adj.)* **ውርሻዊ** *wrshawi*
ancestry *(n.)* **ኣበው** *abew*
anchor *(n.)* **መልህቕ** *melhq̈*
anchorage *(n.)* **ተዓሻገ** *te'äshage*
ancient *(adj.)* **ጥንታዊ** *ẗntawi*
ancillary *(adj.)* **ጽግዕተኛ** *xg'ëteṅa*
and *(conj.)* **ድማ** *dma*
android *(n.)* **ጽግዕተኛ** *xg'ëteṅa*
anecdote *(n.)* **ጽዋ** *xwa*
anew *(adv.)* **እንደገና** *èndegena*
angel *(n.)* **ፍቱው** *ftuw*
anger *(n.)* **ቁጥዐ** *quẗ'ë*
angina *(n.)* **ሕማም** *ḧmam*
angle *(n.)* **ኩርናዕ** *kurna'ë*
angry *(adj.)* **ሕሩቕ** *ḧruq̈*
anguish *(n.)* **ጓሂ** *gWahi*
angular *(adj.)* **ኩርናዓዊ** *kurna'äwi*
animal *(n.)* **እንስሳ** *ènssa*
animate *(v.)* **ህያው** *hyaw*
animated *(adj.)* **ሕያው** *ḧyaw*
animation *(n.)* **ህያውነት** *hyawnet*
animosity *(n.)* **ጽልኢ** *xl'i*
aniseed *(n.)* **ሸለን** *shelen*
ankle *(n.)* **ዓንካር-ዓንካሪቶ** *änkar'änkarito*
anklet *(n.)* **ኣንባር** *anbar*
annals *(n.)* **መዝገበ-ፍጻሜታት** *mezgebefxameetat*
annex *(v.)* **ጎበጠ** *gobeẗe*
annexation *(n.)* **ጐበጣ** *gWabeẗa*
annihilate *(v.)* **ኣጽነተ** *axnete*
annihilation *(n.)* **ድምሰሳ** *dmsesa*
anniversary *(n.)* **ዝክረ-ዓመት** *zkre'ämet*
annotate *(v.)* **ኣመልከተ** *amelkete*
announce *(v.)* **ገለጸ** *gelexe*
announcement *(n.)* **መግለጺ** *meglexi*
annoy *(v.)* **ሸወዘ** *ṣheweze*
annoyance *(n.)* **ቁጥዐ** *quẗ'ë*

annual *(adj.)* በብዓመት *beb'ämet*
annuity *(n.)* በብዓመት *beb'ämet*
annul *(v.)* ሰረዘ *sereze*
anode *(n.)* ኤለትሮድ *'eeletrod*
anoint *(v.)* ቀብአ *qeb'e*
anomalous *(adj.)* ዘይስሩዕ *zeysru'ë*
anomaly *(n.)* ዘይስተ *zeyst*
anonymity *(n.)* ስመ-ስውርነት *smeswrnet*
anonymous *(adj.)* ስመ-ስውር *smeswr*
anorexia *(n.)* ምንማነ *mnmane*
another *(adj.)* ካልእ *kal'è*
answer *(n.)* መልሲ *melsi*
answerable *(adj.)* ኪምለስ ዚከኣል *kimles zike'al*
ant *(n.)* ጻጸ *xaxe*
antacid *(adj.)* ጻጸ መጺጽ *xaxe mexix*
antagonism *(n.)* ተጻራርነት *texararnet*
antagonist *(n.)* ተጻራሪ *texarari*
antagonize *(v.)* ተጻረረ *texarere*
Antarctic *(adj.)* ኣንታርክቲክ *antarktik*
antecedent *(n.)* ቅድመ ፍጻመ *qdme fxame*
antedate *(v.)* ኣቐደመ *aquadme*
antelope *(n.)* ዓጋዜን *ägazeen*
antenna *(n.)* ኣንተና *antena*
anthem *(n.)* ኣንቴማ *anteema*
anthology *(n.)* እኩብ ዛንታታት *'èkub zantatat*
anthrax *(n.)* ነፍሪ *nefri*
anthropology *(n.)* ስነ-ሰብ *sneseb*
anti *(n.)* ጸረ *xere*
antibiotic *(n.)* ጸረ-ነፍሳት *xerenefsat*
antibody *(n.)* ጸረ-ኣካል *xere'akal*
antic *(n.)* ወጀሃላይ *weĵehalay*
anticipate *(v.)* ተጸበየ *texebeye*
anticipation *(n.)* ትጽቢት *txbit*
anti-climax *(n.)* ምንቁልቋል *mnqulqWAl*
antidote *(n.)* ጸረ-መርዚ *xeremerzi*
antioxidant *(n.)* ጸረ-መርዚ *xeremerzi*
antipathy *(n.)* ክርሃት *krhat*
antiperspirant *(n.)* ኩሕለ-ምሕሊ *kuḧlemḧli*
antiquarian *(adj.)* ዘጥንቲ *zeẗnti*
antiquated *(adj.)* ድሑር *dḧur*
antique *(n.)* ጥንታዊ *ẗntawi*
antiquity *(n.)* ጥንቲ *ẗnti*
antiseptic *(adj.)* ጸረ-ረኽሲ *xerereḱsi*
antisocial *(adj.)* ጸረ-ማሕበራዊ *xeremaḧberawi*
antithesis *(n.)* ኣንጻር *anxar*
antler *(n.)* ጭንፋር ቀርኒ *čnfar qerni*
antonym *(n.)* ኣሉታ *aluta*
anus *(n.)* መሃንቱስ *mehantus*
anvil *(n.)* ናውቲ *nawti*
anxiety *(n.)* ጭንቀት *čnqet*
anxious *(adj.)* ሃረርተኛ *harerteṅa*
any *(adj.)* ዝኾነ *zḱone*
anyhow *(adv.)* ብዘይተገዳስነት *bzeytegedasnet*
anyone *(pron.)* ዝኾነ ሰብ *zḱone seb*
anything *(pron.)* ዝኾነ ነገር *zḱone neger*
anywhere *(adv.)* ዝኾነ ቦታ *zḱone bota*

apace *(adv.)* ብቕልጡፍ *bq̈lẗuf*
apart *(adv.)* ዝተፈላለየ *ztefelaleye*
apartheid *(n.)* ኣፓርታይድ *apartayd*
apartment *(n.)* ክፍሊ-ገዛ *kfligeza*
apathy *(n.)* ዘይተገዳስነት *zeytegedasnet*
ape *(n.)* ቀዳሒ *qedaḧi*
aperture *(n.)* ጮርታ *črta*
apex *(n)* ጫፍ *čaf*
aphorism *(n.)* ምስላ *msla*
apiary *(n.)* መንህብ *menhb*
aplomb *(n.)* ርእሰ-ርጉጽነት *r'èserguxnet*
apocalypse *(n.)* ራእይ - *ra'èy*
apologize *(v.)* ይቕሬታ ሓተተ *yq̈reeta ḧatete*
apology *(n.)* ይቕሬታ *yq̈reeta*
apoplectic *(adj.)* ኣፖፕለቲካዊ *apopletikawi*
apostate *(n.)* ከሓዲ እምነት *keḧadi 'èmnet*
apostle *(n.)* ሃዋርያ *hawarya*
apostrophe *(n.)* ጮረት *čret*
appal *(v.)* ኣስካሕከሐ - *askaḧkeḧe*
apparatus *(n.)* መሳርሒ *mesarḧi*
apparel *(n.)* ክዳን *kdan*
apparent *(adj.)* ብሩህ *bruh*
appeal *(v.t.)* ብሩህ *bruh*
appear *(v.)* ተራእየ *tera'èye*
appearance *(n.)* ምቕልቃል *mq̈lqal*
appease *(v.)* ኣዝሓለ *azḧale*
append *(v.)* መልአ *mel'e*
appendage *(n.)* መመላእታ *memela'èta*
appendicitis *(n.)* ነድሪ ጥብቆ *nedri ẗbqo*
appendix *(n.)* መመላእታ *memela'èta*
appetite *(n.)* ሸውሃት *shewhat*
appetizer *(n.)* ከፋት ሸውሃት *kefat shewhat*
applaud *(v.)* ኣጨብጨበ *ačebčebe*
applause *(n.)* ጨብጨባ *čebčeba*
apple *(n.)* ቱፋሕ *tufaḧ*
appliance *(n.)* መሳርያ *mesarya*
applicable *(adj.)* ብቑዕ *bq̈u'ë*
applicant *(n.)* ኣመልካቲ *amelkati*
application *(n.)* ምሕታት *mḧtat*
apply *(v.t.)* ተጠቕመ *teẗeq̈me*
appoint *(v.)* ወሰነ *wesene*
appointment *(n.)* ቈጸራ *qWexera*
apportion *(v.t.)* ጐዘየ *gWazeye*
apposite *(adj.)* ዚሰማማዕ *zisemama'ë*
appraise *(v.)* ገምገመ *gemgeme*
appreciable *(adj.)* እኹል *èḱul*
appreciate *(v.)* ተገንዘበ *tegenzebe*
appreciation *(n.)* ኣስተያየት *asteyayet*
apprehend *(v.)* ተረድአ *tered'e*
apprehension *(n.)* ምርዳእ *mrda'è*
apprehensive *(adj.)* ዝተሻቐለ *zteshaq̈ele*
apprentice *(n.)* ተልመዴን *telmedeen*
apprise *(v.)* ኣፍለጠ *afleẗe*
approach *(v.)* ቀረበ *qerebe*
appropriate *(adj.)* ብቑዕ *bq̈u'ë*
appropriation *(n.)* ምንዛዐ *mnza'ë*
approval *(n.)* ቅባለ *qbale*
approve *(v.)* ተቐበለ *teq̈ebele*

approximate *(adj.)* ዳርጋ *darga*
apricot *(n.)* ሚሽሚሽ *mishmishe*
apron *(n.)* ግርምብያለ *grmbyale*
apt *(adj.)* በሊሕ *beliḧ*
aptitude *(n.)* ተውህቦ *tewhbo*
aquarium *(n.)* ጥርሙዝ ፍስቶ *ṫrmuz fsto*
aquatic *(adj.)* ማያዊ *mayawi*
aqueous *(adj.)* ማያዊ *mayawi*
Arab *(n.)* አረብ *areb*
Arabian *(n.)* አረቢያን *arebian*
Arabic *(n.)* አረቢክ *arebik*
arable *(adj.)* ገድላ *gedla*
arbiter *(n.)* ፈራዲ *feradi*
arbitrary *(adj.)* ሃውሪ *hawri*
arbitrate *(v.)* ዳነየ *daneye*
arbitration *(n.)* ዳኘነት *daṅnet*
arbitrator *(n.)* ዳኛ *daṅa*
arbour *(n.)* ዳስ *das*
arc *(n.)* ቀስቲ *qesti*
arcade *(n.)* ቀልደዳዊ *qeldedawi*
arch *(n.)* ቀልደድ *qelded*
archaeology *(n.)* ስነ ጥንቲ *sne ṫnti*
archaic *(adj.)* ጥንታዊ *ṫntawi*
archangel *(n.)* ሊቀ መላእክት *liqe mela'èkt*
archbishop *(n.)* ሊቀ-ጳጳሳት *liqep̈ap̈asat*
archer *(n.)* መንታጋይ *mentagay*
architect *(n.)* ስነ-ሃናጺ *snehanaxi*
architecture *(n.)* ስነ-ህንጻ *snehnxa*
archives *(n.)* ኣርቺብ *archiv*
Arctic *(adj.)* ኣርክቲክ *arktik*
ardent *(adj.)* ውዕውዕ *w'ëw'ë*
ardour *(n.)* ብርቱዕ ድሌት *brtu'ë dleet*
arduous *(adj.)* ኣድካሚ *adkami*
area *(n.)* ስፍሓት *sfḧat*
arena *(n.)* መድረኽ *medreḱ*
argue *(v.)* ተማጎተ *temagote*
argument *(n.)* መጎተ *megote*
argumentative *(adj.)* መጎቲና *megotina*
arid *(adj.)* ኣጻምእ *axam'è*
arise *(v.)* ተላዕለ *tela'ële*
aristocracy *(n.)* ኣሪስቶክራሲ *aristokrasi*
aristocrat *(n.)* ኣሪስቶክራታዊ *aristokratawi*
arithmetic *(n.)* ቊጽሪ *quxri*
arithmetical *(adj.)* ቊጽሪና *quxrina*
ark *(n.)* ታቦት *tabot*
arm *(n.)* ምናት *mnat*
armada *(n.)* ኣርመደ *armede*
Armageddon *(n.)* ኣርማጌዶን *armagedon*
armament *(n.)* ኣጽዋር *axwar*
armistice *(n.)* ግዝያዊ ተኹሲ-ዕጸ *gzyawi teḱusi'ëxo*
armour *(n.)* ድርዒ ሓጺን *dr'ï ḧaxin*
armoury *(n.)* ድርዒ ሓጺኒ *dr'ï ḧaxini*
army *(n.)* ሰራዊት *serawit*
aroma *(n.)* መዓዛ *me'äza*
aromatherapy *(n.)* መዓዛ - ፍወሳ *me'äza fwesa*
around *(adv.)* ኣብ ዙርያ *'ab zurya*
arouse *(v.)* ኣበራበረ *aberabere*
arrange *(v.)* ሰርዐ *ser'ë*
arrangement *(n.)* ኣሰራርዓ *aserar'ä*
arrant *(adj.)* ምሒር *mḧir*

array *(n.)* ተሰለፈ *teselefe*
arrears *(n.)* ተሰለፈን *teselefin*
arrest *(v.)* ኣሰረ *asere*
arrival *(n.)* እትወት *ètwet*
arrive *(v.)* መጸ *mexe*
arrogance *(n.)* ኣትሒቱ ረኣየ *'atḧitu re'aye*
arrogant *(adj.)* ትዕቢተኛ *t'ëbiteňa*
arrogate *(v.)* መንዘዐ *menze'ë*
arrow *(n.)* ፍላጻ *flaxa*
arsenal *(n.)* እንዳብረት *èndabret*
arsenic *(n.)* ብርቱዕ ስሚ *brtu'ë smi*
arson *(n.)* ብውሳይ ምቅጻል *bwsay mqxal*
art *(n.)* ጥበብ *ẗbeb*
artefact *(n.)* ጥንቲ *ẗnti*
artery *(n.)* ኣርተሪ *arteri*
artful *(adj.)* ብልሂ *blhi*
arthritis *(n.)* ሪሕ *riḧ*
artichoke *(n.)* ካርቾፊ *karchofi*
article *(n.)* ኣቕሓ *aq̈ḧa*
articulate *(adj.)* ኣነጸረ *anexere*
artifice *(n.)* ክእለት *k'èlet*
artificial *(adj.)* ስኑ'ዕ *snu'ë*
artillery *(n.)* ከቢድ ብረት *kebid bret*
artisan *(n.)* ክኢላ *k'ila*
artist *(n.)* ስነ-ጠቢብ *sneẗebib*
artistic *(adj.)* ስነ-ጥበባዊ *sneẗbebawi*
artless *(adj.)* ባህርያዊ *bahryawi*
as *(adv.)* ከም *kem*
asbestos *(n.)* ማዕድን *ma'ëdn*
ascend *(v.)* ደየበ *deyebe*
ascendant *(adj.)* ደያቢ *deyabi*
ascent *(n.)* ዕርገት *ërget*
ascertain *(v.)* ኣረጋገጸ *aregagexe*
ascetic *(adj.)* መናን *menan*
ascribe *(v.)* ሃበ *habe*
aseptic *(adj.)* ጽዱይ *xduy*
asexual *(adj.)* ግብረ-ሰዶመኛ *gbresedomeňa*
ash *(n.)* ኣሽ *ash*
ashamed *(adj.)* ዝሓፈረ *zḧafere*
ashore *(adv.)* መሬት *mereet*
Asian *(adj.)* ኤሽያዊ *eshiyawi*
aside *(adv.)* ገጽ *gex*
asinine *(adj.)* ዓንጃል *änĵal*
ask *(v.)* ሓተተ *ḧatete*
askance *(adv.)* ብጥርጣረ *bẗrẗare*
askew *(adv.)* ዘባል *zebal*
asleep *(adj.)* ጽሙው *xmuw*
asparagus *(n.)* ሻሞት *shamot*
aspect *(n.)* መልክዕ *melk'ë*
asperity *(n.)* ጎነጽ *gonex*
aspersions *(n.)* ምክፋእ *mkfa'è*
asphyxiate *(v.)* ዓበሰ *äbese*
aspirant *(n.)* ደላዪ *delayi*
aspiration *(n.)* ትምኒት *tmnit*
aspire *(v.)* ተመነየ *temeneye*
ass *(n.)* ኣድጊ *adgi*
assail *(v.)* ኣጥቀዐ *aẗqe'ë*
assassin *(n.)* ቀታል-ነፍሲ *qetalnefsi*
assassinate *(v.)* ቀተለ *qetele*
assassination *(n.)* ቀተለሊ *qeteli*
assault *(n.)* ኣጥቀዐ *aẗqe'ë*
assemblage *(n.)* ምግጥጣም *mgẗẗam*
assemble *(v.)* ኣጋጠመ *agaẗeme*
assembly *(n.)* ኣኼባ *aḱeeba*
assent *(n.)* ስምምዕ *smm'ë*
assert *(v.)* ጸዓደ *xe'äde*

assess ***(v.)*** **ኣማኸረ** *amaḱari*
assessment ***(n.)*** **መርመራ** *mermera*
asset ***(n.)*** **ንብረት** *nbret*
assiduous ***(adj.)*** **ጻዕረኛ** *xa'ërena*
assign ***(v.)*** **ረተበ** *retebe*
assignation ***(n.)*** **ምደባ** *mdeba*
assignment ***(n.)*** **ምዱብ ስራሕ** *mdub sraḧ*
assimilate ***(v.)*** **ተዋሃደ** *tewahade*
assimilation ***(n.)*** **ተዋህዶ** *tewahdo*
assist ***(v.)*** **ሓገዘ** *ḧageze*
assistance ***(n.)*** **ሓገዝ** *ḧagez*
assistant ***(n.)*** **ረዳት** *redat*
associate ***(v.)*** **ተሓባበረ** *teḧababari*
association ***(n.)*** **ማሕበር** *maḧber*
assonance ***(n.)*** **ስምምዕ** *smm'ë*
assorted ***(adj.)*** **ዝተፋላለየ** *ztefalaleye*
assortment ***(n.)*** **በብዓይነቱ** *beb'äynetu*
assuage ***(v.)*** **ኣጸናንዐ** *axenan'ë*
assume ***(v.)*** **ገመተ** *gemete*
assumption ***(n.)*** **ግምት** *gmt*
assurance ***(n.)*** **መረጋገጺ** *meregagexi*
assure ***(v.)*** **ኣረጋገጸ** *aregagexe*
assured ***(adj.)*** **ዋሕስ** *waḧs*
asterisk ***(n.)*** **ኣስትሪስክስ** *astrisks*
asteroid ***(n.)*** **ዓለም** *älem*
asthma ***(n.)*** **ኣዝማ** *azma*
astigmatism ***(n.)*** **ነበዐ** *nebe'ë*
astonish ***(v.)*** **ኣደነቐ** *adeneq̈e*
astonishment ***(n.)*** **ድንጽዉና** *dnxwuna*
astound ***(v.)*** **ኣስደመመ** *asdememe*
astral ***(adj.)*** **ኮኾባዊ** *koḱobawi*
astray ***(adv.)*** **ህውቱት** *hwtut*
astride ***(prep.)*** **ብምግሕታን** *bmgḧtan*
astrologer ***(n.)*** **ብልጹግ** *blxug*
astrology ***(n.)*** **ቌጸራ ከዋኽብቲ** *qWexera kewaḱbti*
astronaut ***(n.)*** **ጠፈርተኛ** *ṫeferteṅa*
astronomer ***(n.)*** **ስነ-ኮኾቢ** *snekoḱobi*
astronomy ***(n.)*** **ስነ-ኮኾብ** *snekoḱob*
astute ***(adj.)*** **ትኩር** *tkur*
asunder ***(adv.)*** **ዝተፈላለየ** *ztefelaleye*
asylum ***(n.)*** **ዑቕባ** *üq̈ba*
at ***(prep.)*** **ኣብ** *ab*
atavistic ***(adj.)*** **የዋህ** *yewah*
atheism ***(n.)*** **ኢዚሀርነት** *izihernet*
atheist ***(n.)*** **ኢዚሄራዊ** *iziheerawi*
athlete ***(n.)*** **ስፖርተኛ** *sporteṅa*
athletic ***(adj.)*** **ስፖርታዊ** *sportawi*
atlas ***(n.)*** **ኣትላስ** *atlas*
atmosphere ***(n.)*** **ሃዋህው** *hawahw*
atoll ***(n.)*** **ደሴት** *deseet*
atom ***(n.)*** **ኣቶም** *atom*
atomic ***(adj.)*** **ኣቶማዊ** *atomawi*
atone ***(v.)*** **ከሓሰ** *keḧase*
atonement ***(n.)*** **ድሕነት** *dḧnet*
atrium ***(n.)*** **ክፍሊ** *kfli*
atrocious ***(adj.)*** **ኣሰቃቒ** *aseqaq̈i*
atrocity ***(n.)*** **ገፍዐ** *gef'ë*
attach ***(v.)*** **ኣጣበቐ** *aṫabeq̈e*
attaché ***(n.)*** **ኣታሽ** *atash*
attachment ***(n.)*** **ጥብቀት** *ṫbqet*

attack *(v.)* **አጥቅዐ** *aẗq'ë*
attain *(v.)* **ምሉእ** *mlu'è*
attainment *(n.)* **ሰመረ** *semere*
attempt *(v.)* **ፈተ'ነ** *fetene*
attempt *(v.)* **ጀመረ** *ĵemere*
attend *(v.)* **ተኸታተለ** *teḱetatele*
attendance *(n.)* **ተሳትፎ** *tesatfo*
attendant *(n.)* **ኣገልጋሊ** *agelgali*
attention *(n.)* **ኣቓልቦ** *aq̈albo*
attentive *(adj.)* **ጥንቑቕ** *ẗnquq̈*
attest *(v.)* **ኣረጋገጸ** *aregagexe*
attic *(n.)* **ዋልድቢት** *waldbit*
attire *(n.)* **ልብሲ** *lbsi*
attitude *(n.)* **ኣቃጫጭ** *aqačač*
attorney *(n.)* **ጠበቓ** *ẗebeq̈a*
attract *(v.)* **ሰሓበ** *seḧabe*
attraction *(n.)* **ስሕበት** *sḧbet*
attractive *(adj.)* **ማራኺ** *maraḱi*
attribute *(v.)* **ባህርይ** *bahry*
aubergine *(n.)* **ማርጋሪን** *margarin*
auction *(n.)* **ሓራጅ** *ḧaraĵ*
audible *(adj.)* **ኪስማዕ ዚከኣል** *kisma'ë zike'a*
audience *(n.)* **ነባሮ** *nebaro*
audio *(n.)* **ደሃይ** *dehay*
audit *(n.)* **ጸብጻብ** *xebxab*
audition *(n.)* **ምስማዕ** *msma'ë*
auditorium *(n.)* **ኣውዲቶርዩም ኣዳራሽ** *'awditoryum 'adarash*
augment *(v.)* **ወሰኸ** *ወሰኸ*
August *(n)* **ነሓሰ** *neḧase*
aunt *(n.)* **ሓትኖ** *ḧatno*
aura *(n.)* **ኣኽሊል** *aḱlil*
auspicious *(adj.)* **ተስፋኣዊ** *tesfa'awi*
austere *(adj.)* **ጥብቒ** *ẗbqi*
Australian *(n.)* **አዎስትራልያ** *awustraliya*
authentic *(adj.)* **ሓቀኛ** *ḧaqeňa*
authenticity *(n.)* **ልክዕነት** *lk'ënet*
author *(n.)* **ደራሲ** *derasi*
authoritative *(adj.)* **ምዙዝ** *mzuz*
authority *(n.)* **መዚ** *mezi*
authorize *(v.)* **መዘዘ** *mezeze*
autism *(n.)* **አዉቲዝም** *awutizim*
autobiography *(n.)* **ርእሰ-ታሪኽ** *r'èsetariḱ*
autocracy *(n.)* **ኣውቶክራሲ** *awtokrasi*
autocrat *(n.)* **ውልቀ-መላኺ** *wlqemelaḱi*
autocratic *(adj.)* **ኣውቶክራቲክ** *wlqemelaḱ*
autograph *(n.)* **ርእሰ-ጽሑፍ** *r'èsexḧuf*
automatic *(adj.)* **ኣውቶማቲክ** *awtomatik*
automobile *(n.)* **ኣውቶሞቢል=መኪና** *awtomobilm ekina*
autonomous *(adj.)* **ርእሰ-ምምሕዳራዊ** *r'èsemmḧdarawi*
autopsy *(n.)* **ምርምረ-ሬሳ** *mrmrereesa*
autumn *(n.)* **ቀውዒ** *qew'ï*
auxiliary *(adj.)* **ሓጋዚ** *ḧagazi*
avail *(v.)* **ተጠቕመ** *teẗeq̈me*
available *(adj.)* **ክትጥቀመሉ ትኽእል** *ktẗqemelu tḱ'èl*
avalanche *(n.)* **መደረጋሕ** *mederegaḧ*
avarice *(n.)* **ስስዐ** *ss'ë*
avenge *(v.)* **ሕነ ፈደየ** *ḧne fedeye*
avenue *(n.)* **ጐደና** *gWadena*

average *(n.)* ማእከላይ *ma'èkelay*
averse *(adj.)* ኣንጻር *anxar*
aversion *(n.)* ጽልኣት *xl'at*
avert *(v.)* ኣለየ *aleye*
aviary *(n.)* እንዳ ኣዕዋፍ *'ènda 'a'ëwaf*
aviation *(n.)* ስነ-ምንፋር *snemnfar*
aviator *(n.)* ፓይሎት *paylot*
avid *(adj.)* ህንጡይ *hnẗuy*
avidly *(adv.)* ህንጡዪ *hnẗuyi*
avocado *(n.)* ኣቮካዶ *avokado*
avoid *(v.)* ወገደ *wegede*
avoidance *(n.)* ጉስያ *gusya*
avow *(v.)* ኣመነ *amene*
avuncular *(adj.)* ኣኮኣዊ *'ako'awi*
await *(v.)* ተጸበየ *texebeye*
awake *(v.)* ነቕሐ *neq̈ḧe*
awaken *(v.)* ነቕሐ *neq̈ḧe*
award *(v.)* ሰለመ *seleme*
aware *(adj.)* ገንዘብ *genzeb*
away *(adv.)* ናብ ርሑቕ *nab rḧuq̈*
awe *(n.)* ተምሳጥ *temsaẗ*
awesome *(adj.)* ዘርዕድ *zer'ëd*
awful *(adj.)* ዘስካሕክሕ *zeskaḧkḧ*
awhile *(adv.)* ንሓጺር ግዜ *nḧaxir gzee*
awkward *(adj.)* ጋሕማጥ *gaḧmaẗ*
awry *(adv.)* ብልሽው *blshw*
axe *(n.)* ፋስ *fas*
axis *(n.)* መቐለሲ *meq̈elesi*
axle *(n.)* መቐለስ *meq̈eles*

B

babble *(v.)* ኣዕዘምዘመ *a'ëzemzeme*
babe *(n.)* ህጻን *hxan*
Babel *(n.)* ዘይምስምማዕ *zeymsmma'ë*
baboon *(n.)* ህበይ *hbey*
baby *(n.)* ህጻን *hxan*
bachelor *(n.)* ቤተ'ልቦ - *beetelbo*
back *(n.)* ዝባን *zban*
backbone *(n.)* ዓንዲ-ሕቖ *ändiḧq̈o*
backdate *(v.)* ሓለፈ *ḧalefe*
backdrop *(n.)* ትዕይንቲ *t'ëynti*
backfire *(v.)* ምጉሳዕ *mgusa'ë*
background *(n.)* ተመኩሮ *temekuro*
backhand *(n.)* ኣሸሙራዊ *ashmurawi*
backing *(n.)* ረድኢ *red'e*
backlash *(n.)* መልሰ-ግብሪ *melsegbri*
backlog *(n.)* መሃዚ *mehazi*
backpack *(n.)* ማህደር *mahder*
backside *(n.)* ብድሕሪት *bdḧrit*
backstage *(adv.)* ዝባን መድረኽ *zban medreḱ*
backtrack *(v.)* ዝባን ኣሰር *zban aser*
backward *(adj.)* ንድሕሪት *ndḧrit*
backwater *(n.)* ዝባን ማይ *zban may*
bacon *(n.)* ቤኮን *beekon*
bacteria *(n.)* ባክተሪያ *bakteriya*
bad *(adj.)* ሕማቕ *ḧmaq̈*
badge *(n.)* ኣርማ *arma*
badly *(adv.)* ብሕማቕ *bḧmaq̈*

badminton *(n.)* ባድሚንተን *badminten*
baffle *(v.)* ኣገረመ *agereme*
bag *(n.)* መልአ *mel'e*
baggage *(n.)* ጋዓዝ *ga'äz*
baggy *(adj.)* ገፍላው *geflaw*
baguette *(n.)* ሕቡር ስልማት *ḧbur slmat*
bail *(n.)* ዋሕስ *waḧs*
bailiff *(n.)* ፖሊስ *polis*
bait *(n.)* መስሓቢ *mesḧabi*
bake *(v.)* ደረቐ *dereq̈e*
baker *(n.)* ሰንካቲ *senkati*
bakery *(n.)* እንዳ ባኒ *ènda bani*
balance *(n.)* ተረፍ *teref*
balcony *(n.)* ሰገነት *segenet*
bald *(adj.)* በራሕ *beraḧ*
bale *(n.)* ጥቕላል *ẗq̈lal*
ball *(n.)* ኩዕሶ *ku'ëso*
ballad *(n.)* ግጥሚ ወይ ደርፊ *gẗmi wey derfi*
ballet *(n.)* ባለ *bale*
balloon *(n.)* ባሉን *balun*
ballot *(n.)* ምርጫ *mrča*
balm *(n.)* በለሳን *belesan*
balsam *(n.)* በለሳን *belesan*
bamboo *(n.)* ኣርቃይ *arqay*
ban *(v.)* ኣገደ *agede*
banal *(adj.)* ተራ *tera*
banana *(n.)* ባናና *banana*
band *(n.)* መእሰሪ *me'èseri*
bandage *(n.)* መጀነኒ *meĵeneni*
bandit *(n.)* ሽፍታ ወረበላ *shfta werebela*
bane *(n.)* መርዚ ስሚ *merzi smi*
bang *(n.)* ገውታ *gewta*
banger *(n.)* ገውት *gewtat*
bangle *(n.)* በናጅር *benaĵr*
banish *(v.)* ሓየረ *ḧayere*
banishment *(n.)* ጥርዝያ *ẗrzya*
banisters *(n.)* መደንደል *medendel*
banjo *(n.)* ባንጆ *banĵo*
bank *(n.)* ባንኪ *banki*
banker *(n.)* መኰነን *mekWanen*
bankrupt *(adj.)* ጥፉሽ *ẗfush*
bankruptcy *(n.)* ጥፈሻ *ẗfesha*
banner *(n.)* ሰንደቕ *sendeq̈*
banquet *(n.)* በዓል *be'äl*
banter *(n.)* ተዋዘየ *tewazeye*
baptism *(n.)* ጥምቀት *ẗmqet*
Baptist *(n.)* መጥምቓዊ *meẗmq̈awi*
baptize *(v.)* ኣጠመቐ *aẗemeq̈e*
bar *(n.)* መታወር *metawer*
barb *(n.)* ዓንቃሪቦ *änqaribo*
barbarian *(n.)* ባርባራዊ *barbarawi*
barbaric *(adj.)* ባርባራዊ *barbarawi*
barbecue *(n.)* ጥብሲ ቦታ *ẗbsi bota*
barbed *(adj.)* ወጋኢ *wega'i*
barber *(n.)* ቀምቃማይ *qemqamay*
bard *(n.)* ግጥሚ ወይ ደርፊ *gẗmi wey derfi*
bare *(adj.)* ጥርሑ *ẗrḧu*
barely *(adv.)* ብቕሉዕ *bq̈lu'ë*
bargain *(n.)* ዋጋ ዕዳጋ *waga 'ëdaga*
barge *(n.)* ባርጅ *barĵ*
bark *(n.)* ቅራፍ *qraf*
barley *(n.)* ስገም *sgem*
barn *(n.)* መኽዘን *meḱzen*
barometer *(n.)* ባሮሜተር *baromeeter*

baron *(n.)* ባላባት *balabat*
barrack *(n.)* ባራካ *baraka*
barracuda *(n.)* መሸኒት *meshenit*
barrage *(n.)* ግድብ *gdb*
barrel *(n.)* በርሚል *bermil*
barren *(adj.)* መኻን *meḱan*
barricade *(n.)* መደንደል *medendel*
barrier *(n.)* ዕንቅፋት *ënqfat*
barring *(prep.)* ግድብ *gdb*
barrister *(n.)* ጠበቓ *ẗebeq̈a*
barter *(v.)* በደላ *bedela*
base *(n.)* ሰረተ *serete*
baseless *(adj.)* ሰረትኣልቦ *seret'albo*
basement *(n.)* ትሕተ-ቤት *tḧtebeet*
bashful *(adj.)* ሓፋር *ḧafar*
basic *(n.)* ሰረታዊ *seretawi*
basil *(n.)* ሪሓን *riḧan*
basilica *(n.)* ባዚሊካ *bazilika*
basin *(n.)* ስሓኒ - *sḧani*
basis *(n.)* ሰረት *seret*
bask *(v.)* ተጸልወ *texelwe*
basket *(n.)* ዘንቢል *zenbil*
bass *(n.)* ባስ ዓይነት ዓሳ *bas 'äynet 'äsa*
bastard *(n.)* ድቓላ *dq̈ala*
baste *(v.)* ሸለለ *shelele*
bastion *(n.)* ዕርዲ *ërdi*
bat *(n.)* መንካዕ *menka'ë*
batch *(n.)* እኩብ *èkub*
bath *(n.)* ምሕጻብ *mḧxab*
bathe *(v.)* ኣለኸ *aleḱe*
bathos *(n.)* ህውተታ *hwteta*
batik *(n.)* ባቲክ *batik*
baton *(n.)* በትሪ ፖሊስ *betri polis*
battalion *(n.)* ቦጦሎኒ *boẗoloni*
batten *(n.)* ተገዳም *tegedam*
batter *(n.)* ከትከተ *ketkete*
battery *(n.)* ባተሪ *bateri*
battle *(n.)* ውግእ *wg'è*
bauble *(n.)* ሕቡር ስልማት *ḧbur slmat*
baulk *(v.)* መሰናኽል *mesenaḱl*
bawl *(v.)* ወጨጨ *wečeče*
bay *(n.)* ፉርዳ *furda*
bayonet *(n.)* ሳንጃ *sanĵa*
bazaar *(n.)* ባዛር ሹቕ *bazar shuq̈*
bazooka *(n.)* ባዙቃ *bazuqa*
be *(v.)* ኮነ *kone*
beach *(n.)* ገምገም ባሕሪ *gemgem baḧri*
beacon *(n.)* መና *mena*
bead *(n.)* ዕንቆ *ënqo*
beady *(adj.)* ቆርቋር *qorqWAr*
beagle *(n.)* ቢግል *bigl*
beak *(n.)* መትኮብ *metkob*
beaker *(n.)* ብርጭቆ *brčqo*
beam *(n.)* ገመል *gemel*
bean *(n.)* ባልዶንጓ *baldongWa*
bear *(v.t)* ድቢ *dbi*
bear *(n.)* ተሸከመ *teshekeme*
beard *(n.)* ጭሕሚ *čḧmi*
bearing *(n.)* ማእዝን *ma'èzn*
beast *(n.)* እንስሳ *ènssa*
beastly *(adj.)* እንስሳዊ *ènssawi*
beat *(v.)* ላጸየ *laxeye*
beatitude *(n.)* ደስታ *desta*
beautician *(n.)* ላጸየ *laxeye*
beautiful *(adj.)* ማራኺ *maraḱi*
beautify *(v.)* ኣመልክዐ *amelk'ë*
beauty *(n.)* መልክዕ *melk'ë*
beaver *(n.)* ቢቨር *biver*
becalmed *(adj.)* ኣህድአ *ahd'e*
because *(conj.)* ስለ *sle*

beck ***(n.)*** ምልክት *mlkt*
beckon ***(v.)*** ኣመልከተ *amelkete*
become ***(v.)*** ኮነ *kone*
bed ***(n.)*** መዕረፊ *me'ërefi*
bedding ***(n.)*** መንጸፍ *menxef*
bedlam ***(n.)*** ዕግርግር *ëgrgr*
bedraggled ***(adj.)*** ኣጨፈቐ *ačefeq̈e*
bee ***(n.)*** ንህቢ *nhbi*
beech ***(n.)*** ዋዕሮ *wa'ëro*
beef ***(n.)*** ስጋ ከብቲ *sga kebti*
beefy ***(adj.)*** ረጒድ *regWid*
beep ***(n.)*** ምልክት *mlkt*
beer ***(n.)*** ቢራ *bira*
beet ***(n.)*** ብንጅር *bnĵr*
beetle ***(n.)*** ማሳ *masa*
beetroot ***(n.)*** ሓምሊ *ḧamli*
befall ***(v.)*** ወረደ *werede*
befit ***(v.)*** በቕዐ *beq̈'ë*
before ***(adv.)*** ቅድሚ *qdmi*
beforehand ***(adv.)*** ኣቐዲሙ *ኣቐዲሙ*
befriend ***(v.)*** መዓደ *me'äde*
befuddled ***(adj.)*** ኣገረመ *agereme*
beg ***(v.)*** ለመነ *lemene*
beget ***(v.)*** ወለደ *welede*
beggar ***(n.)*** ለማኒ *lemani*
begin ***(v.)*** ጀመረ *ĵemere*
beginning ***(n.)*** መጀመርታ *meĵemerta*
beguile ***(v.)*** ኣዘናገዐ *azenage'ë*
behalf ***(n.)*** ኣብ ክንዲ *ab kndi*
behave ***(v.)*** ገበረ *gebere*
behaviour ***(n.)*** ጠባይ *ẗebay*
behead ***(v.)*** ቈረጸ *qWerexe*
behemoth ***(n.)*** ጨካን *čekan*
behest ***(n.)*** ትእዛዝ *t'èzaz*
behind ***(prep.)*** ብድሕሪት *bdḧrit*
behold ***(v.)*** ተመልከተ *temelkete*
beholden ***(adj.)*** ኣመስጋኒ *amesgani*
beige ***(n.)*** ፋሕራይ *faḧray*
being ***(n.)*** ህላወ *hlawe*
belabour ***(v.)*** ቀጥቀጠ *qeẗqeẗe*
belated ***(adj.)*** ድንጉይ *dnguy*
belay ***(v.)*** ጠመረ *ẗemere*
belch ***(v.)*** ተፍአ *tef'e*
beleaguered ***(adj.)*** ኣጨነቐ *ačeneq̈e*
belie ***(v.)*** ብጌጋ ኣርኣየ *bgeega 'ar'aye*
belief ***(n.)*** እምነት *èmnet*
believe ***(v.)*** ኣመነ *amene*
belittle ***(v.)*** ኣቈናጸበ *aqWenaxebe*
bell ***(n.)*** ቃጭል *qačl*
belle ***(n.)*** ጽብቕቲ *xbq̈ti*
bellicose ***(adj.)*** ተባኣሳይ *teba'asay*
belligerent ***(adj.)*** ባእሲ ምድላይ *ba'èsi mdlay*
bellow ***(v.)*** ነቀወ *neqewe*
bellows ***(n.)*** መናፍሕ *menafḧ*
belly ***(n.)*** ከብዲ *kebdi*
belong ***(v.)*** ተኣሳሰረ *te'asasere*
belongings ***(n.)*** ግላዊ ኣቕሑ *glawi 'aq̈ḧu*
beloved ***(adj.)*** ፍቑር *fq̈ur*
below ***(prep.)*** ትሕቲ *tḧti*
belt ***(n.)*** ቁልፊ *qulfi*
bemoan ***(v.)*** ጓሃየ *gWahaye*
bemused ***(adj.)*** ኣቃልቦ ኣዘንበለ *'aqalbo 'azenbele*
bench ***(n.)*** ርቦ *rbo*
bend ***(v.)*** ለወየ *leweye*
beneath ***(adv.)*** ትሕቲ *tḧti*

benediction *(n.)* ቡራኬ *burakee*
benefactor *(n.)* ገቢረ-ሰናይ *gebiresenay*
benefice *(n.)* ገዛ ቀሺ *geza qeshi*
beneficent *(adj.)* ግብረ-ሰናይ *gbresenay*
beneficial *(adj.)* ለዋህ *lewah*
benefit *(n.)* ሓጋዚ *ḧagazi*
benevolence *(n.)* ግብረ-ሰናይ *gbresenay*
benevolent *(adj)* ግብረ-ሰናያዊ *gbresenayawi*
benign *(adj.)* ለዋህ *lewah*
bent *(adj.)* ተውህቦ *tewhbo*
bequeath *(v.)* ኣውረሰ *awrese*
bequest *(n.)* ውርሻ *wrsha*
berate *(v.)* ወቐሰ *weq̈ese*
bereaved *(v.)* ዘረፈ *zerefe*
bereavement *(n.)* ሓዘን *ḧazen*
bereft *(adj.)* ለማኒ *lemani*
bergamot *(n.)* ከውሒ በረድ *kewḧi bered*
berk *(n.)* ደንቆሮ *denqoro*
berry *(n.)* ፍረ *fre*
berserk *(adj.)* ዕብድብድ *ëbdbd*
berth *(n.)* መደቀሲ *medeqesi*
beseech *(v.)* ለመነ *lemene*
beset *(v.)* ኣሸገረ *ashegere*
beside *(prep.)* ኣብ ጥቓ *ab ẗq̈a*
besiege *(v.)* ከበበ *kebebe*
besmirch *(v.)* ኣመራሰሐ *ameraseḧe*
besom *(n.)* መኾስተር *mek̈oster*
besotted *(adj.)* ዕኑድ *ënud*
bespoke *(adj.)* ዓውዲ ጸቐጠ *äwdi xeq̈eẗe*
best *(adj.)* ብዝበለጸ *bzbelexe*
bestial *(adj.)* ኣራዊታዊ *'arawitawi*
bestow *(v.)* ሸለመ *sheleme*
bestride *(v.)* ተጋሕተነ *tegaḧtene*
bet *(v.)* ተጣልዐ *teẗal'ë*
betake *(v.)* ከደ *kede*
betray *(v.)* ከድዐ *ked'ë*
betrayal *(n.)* ቅጥፈት *qẗfet*
better *(adj.)* ዝሓሸ *zḧashe*
between *(adv.)* ኣብ መንጎ *'ab mengo*
bevel *(n.)* ስያፍ *syaf*
beverage *(n.)* መስተ *meste*
bevy *(n.)* ኣኼባ *ak̈eeba*
bewail *(v.)* ኣልቀሰ *alqese*
beware *(v.)* ጥንቁቕ *ẗnquq̈*
bewilder *(v.t)* ደንጸዎ *denxewo*
bewitch *(v.)* ሰረየ *sereye*
beyond *(adv.)* ክንየው *knyew*
bi *(comb.)* ኣብ ከክልተ *'ab keklte*
biannual *(adj.)* ፍርቂ በብዓመት *frqi beb'ämet*
bias *(n.)* ምቕናን *mq̈nan*
biased *(adj.)* መቕናን *meq̈nan*
bib *(n.)* ሳልቤታ *salbeeta*
Bible *(n.)* መጽሓፍ ቅዱስ *mexḧaf qdus*
bibliography *(n.)* ዝርዝረ-ጽሑፋት *zrzrexḧufat*
bibliophile *(n.)* ፈታው መጽሓፍ *fetaw mexḧaf*
bicentenary *(n.)* ካልኣይ ዘመን *kal'ay zemen*
biceps *(n.)* ጩዋዳምናት *čwadamnat*
bicker *(v.)* ተቛየቘ *teq̈WAyeq̈We*
bicycle *(n.)* ብሽክለታ *bshkleta*
bid *(v.)* ሰመየ *semeye*
biddable *(adj.)* ተሓታቲ *teḧatati*

bidder *(n.)* **ስማይ** *smay*
bide *(v.)* **ኣኽበረ** *aḱbere*
bidet *(n.)* **ምምሻጥ** *mmshaẗ*
biennial *(adj.)* **ክልተ ዓመታዊ** *klte 'ämetawi*
bier *(n.)* **ቃሬዛ** *qareeza*
bifocal *(adj.)* **ጽምደ-ትኹረታዊ** *xmdetḱuretawi*
big *(adj.)* **ዓቢ** *äbi*
bigamy *(n.)* **ድርብ መርዓ** *drb mer'ä*
bigot *(n.)* **ሕሉ'ፍ** *ḧluf*
bigotry *(n.)* **ምቕናን** *mq̈nan*
bike *(n.)* **ብሽክለታ** *bshkleta*
bikini *(n.)* **ቢኪኒ** *bikini*
bilateral *(adj.)* **ክልተ ጐድናዊ** *klte gWadnawi*
bile *(n.)* **ሓሞት** *ḧamot*
bilingual *(adj.)* **ድርብ-ልሳናዊ** *drblsanawi*
bill *(n.)* **ጎዞሞ** *gozomo*
billet *(n.)* **መኣንገድ ድርጎኛ** *me'anged drgoňa*
billiards *(n.)* **ቢልያርዶ** *bilyardo*
billion *(n.)* **ቢልዮን** *bilyon*
billionaire *(n.)* **ሃብታም** *habtam*
billow *(v.)* **ዓቢ ማዕበል** *'äbi ma'ëbel*
bin *(n.)* **ቆፎ** *qofo*
binary *(adj.)* **ዕጽፊ** *ëxfi*
bind *(v.)* **ጠመረ** *ẗemere*
binding *(n.)* **መዛዘሚ** *mezazemi*
binge *(n.)* **ፈንጠዝያ** *fenẗezya*
binocular *(adj.)* **በዓል ለዓት መነጽር** *be'äl le'ät menexr*
biochemistry *(n.)* **ስነ-ቅመም ህይወታውያን** *sneqmem hywetawyan*

biodegradable *(adj.)* **ኢኮሎጂ** *ikoloĵi*
biodiversity *(n.)* **ባዮዳይቨርስቲ** *bayidayiversiti*
biography *(n.)* **ሂወት ጽውጽዋይ** *hiwet xwxway*
biologist *(n.)* **ኢኮሎጂ** *ikoloĵi*
biology *(n.)* **ስነ-ህይወት** *snehywet*
biopsy *(n.)* **ምርምረ-ሬሳ** *mrmrereesa*
bipartisan *(adj.)* **ጽምደ-ሰልፋዊ** *xmdeselfawi*
birch *(n.)* **ኮመዲኖ** *komedino*
bird *(n.)* **ዑፍ** *üf*
bird flu *(n.)* **ኢንፍሉወንዛ** *influwenza*
birth *(n.)* **ምውላድ** *mwlad*
biscuit *(n.)* **ብሽኮቲ** *bshkoti*
bisect *(v.)* **ገመሰ** *gemese*
bisexual *(adj.)* **ግብረ-ሰዶመኛ** *gbresedomeňa*
bishop *(n.)* **ኣቡን** *abun*
bison *(n.)* **ብዕራይ በረኻ** *b'ëray bereḱa*
bit *(n.)* **ልጓም** *lgWam*
bitch *(n.)* **ዋዕሮ** *wa'ëro*
bite *(v.)* **ነኸሰ** *neḱese*
biting *(adj.)* **ወጋኢ** *wega'i*
bitter *(adj.)* **መሪር** *merir*
bizarre *(adj.)* **ፈንጠጋር** *fenẗegar*
blab *(v.)* **ሃተ'ፈ** *hatefe*
black *(adj.)* **ጸሊም** *xelim*
blackberry *(n.)* **ብላክቤሪ** *blakberi*
blackboard *(n.)* **ሰሌዳ** *seleeda*
blacken *(v.)* **ኣጸለመተ** *axelemete*
blacklist *(n.)* **ጸሊም መዝገብ** *xelim mezgeb*

blackmail *(n.)* **ታህዲደ-ምቕላዕ** *tahdidemq̈la'ë*
blackout *(n.)* **ጽልማተ** *xlmate*
blacksmith *(n.)* **ሓጓዲ ኣንጠረኛ ሓጺን** *ḧagWadi 'anẗereṅa ḧaxin*
bladder *(n.)* **ፍሕኛ** *fḧṅa*
blade *(n.)* **ግላዝ** *glaz*
blain *(n.)* **ኣብ ከክልተ** *'ab keklte*
blame *(v.)* **ከሰሰ** *kesese*
blanch *(v.)* **ጻዕደወ** *xa'ëdewe*
bland *(adj.)* **ልዙብ** *lzub*
blank *(adj.)* **ጥርሑ** *ẗrḧu*
blanket *(n.)* **ኮበርታ** *koberta*
blare *(v.)* **ድምጺ** *dmxi*
blarney *(n.)* **ኣተዓሻሸወ** *ate'äshashewe*
blast *(n.)* **ነትጒ** *netgWi*
blatant *(adj.)* **ቅሉዕ** *qlu'ë*
blaze *(n.)* **ሃልሃልታ** *halhalta*
blazer *(n.)* **ጃኬት** *ĵakeet*
bleach *(adj.)* **ኣጻዕደወ** *axa'ëdewe*
bleak *(adj.)* **ቀዛሒ** *qezaḧi*
bleat *(v. i)* **እምቤዕ** *èmbee'ë*
bleed *(v.)* **ደመየ** *demeye*
bleep *(n.)* **ቃና** *qana*
blemish *(n.)* **ኣበር** *aber*
blench *(v.)* **ምዩቕ በለ** *myuq̈ bele*
blend *(v. t)* **ሓዋወሰ** *ḧawawese*
blender *(n.)* **ሕውስ** *ḧws*
bless *(v.)* **ባረኸ** *bareḱe*
blessed *(adj.)* **ብሩኽ** *bruḱ*
blessing *(n.)* **ምርቓ** *mrq̈a*
blight *(n.)* **ዋግ** *wag*
blind *(adj.)* **ዕዉር** *ëwur*
blindfold *(v.)* **ዓመተ** *ämete*
blindness *(n.)* **ጉድለት** *gudlet*
blink *(v.)* **ሰምሰም ኣበለ** *semsem 'abele*
blinkers *(n.)* **ጋራዲ** *garadi*
blip *(n.)* **መቓልሕ** *meq̈alḧ*
bliss *(n.)* **ታሕጓስ** *taḧgWas*
blister *(n.)* **ማይ ምዕጎ** *may m'ëgo*
blithe *(adj.)* **ሕጉስ** *ḧgus*
blitz *(n.)* **ደቡብ** *debub*
blizzard *(n.)* **ህቦብላ ውርጪ** *hbobla wrči*
bloat *(v.)* **ነፍሐ** *nefḧe*
bloater *(n.)* **ቋንጣ ዓሳ** *qWanẗa 'äsa*
blob *(n.)* **ንጣብ** *nẗab*
bloc *(n.)* **ቀጽሪ** *qexri*
block *(n.)* **ግላዕ** *gla'ë*
blockade *(n.)* **ድንደላ** *dndela*
blockage *(n.)* **ዕግታ** *ëgta*
blog *(n.)* **ሳይት** *sayit*
bloke *(n.)* **ቈንደፈ** *qWendefe*
blonde *(adj.)* **ጨዓይ ጸጉሪ ዘለዎ** *če'äy xeguri zelewo*
blood *(n.)* **ደም** *dem*
bloodshed *(n.)* **ደም ምፍሳስ** *dem mfsas*
bloody *(adj.)* **ደማዊ** *demawi*
bloom *(v.)* **ዕምባባ** *ëmbaba*
bloomers *(n.)* **ስረ-ግትር** *sregtr*
blossom *(n.)* **ዕምባባ** *ëmbaba*
blot *(n.)* **ንጣብ ቀለም** *nẗab qelem*
blotch *(n.)* **ትኳዕ** *tkWa'ë*
blouse *(n.)* **ካምቻ** *kamcha*
blow *(v.)* **ነፈሰ** *nefese*
blowsy *(adj.)* **ቈንደፈ** *qWendefe*
blub *(v.)* **ተነኽነኸ** *teneḱneḱe*
bludgeon *(n.)* **ጓመድ** *gWamed*

blue *(adj.)* ሰማያዊ ሕብሪ *semayawi ḧbri*
bluff *(v.)* መጻድፎ *mexadfo*
blunder *(n.)* ጠምበርበር በለ *ẗemberber bele*
blunt *(adj.)* ጎዲም *godim*
blur *(v.)* ጽያቕ *xyaq̈*
blurb *(n.)* ትሕዝቶ መጽሓፍ *tḧzto mexḧaf*
blurt *(v.)* ኣምለቑ *amleq̈We*
blush *(v.)* ሓፈረ *ḧafere*
blusher *(n.)* ቀንዲ *qendi*
bluster *(v.)* ኣሸምበበ *ashembebe*
boar *(n.)* መፍለስ *mefles*
board *(n.)* ጣውላ *ẗawla*
boast *(v.)* ጃህራ *ĵahra*
boat *(n.)* ጃልባ *ĵalba*
bob *(v.)* ሓፍ ኮፍ በለ *ḧaf kof bele*
bobble *(n.)* ገልተው *geltew*
bode *(v.)* ሓበረ *ḧabere*
bodice *(n.)* ጅለ-ሰበይቲ *ĵlesebeyti*
bodily *(adv.)* ኣካላዊ *akalawi*
body *(n.)* ኣካል *akal*
bodyguard *(n)* ዘብዐኛ *zeb'ën̈a*
bog *(n.)* ዓዘቕቲ *äzeq̈ti*
bogey *(n.)* ጋኔን *ganeen*
boggle *(v.)* ተወላወለ *tewelawele*
bogus *(adj.)* ሓቂ ዘይብሉ *ḧaqi zeyblu*
boil *(v.i.)* ምጉሊ ኣንጬዋ *mguli 'ančwa*
boiler *(n.)* መፍልሒ *meflḧi*
boisterous *(adj.)* ናውጼን *nawxeen*
bold *(adj.)* ተባዕ ደፋር *teba'ë defar*
boldness *(n.)* ድምቀት *dmqet*
bole *(n.)* ጉንዲ *gundi*
bollard *(n.)* ገመል *gemel*
bolt *(n.)* መሸጐር *meshegWar*
bomb *(n.)* ቦምብ *bomb*
bombard *(v.)* ደብደበ *debdebe*
bombardment *(n.)* ደብዳብ *debdab*
bomber *(n.)* ቦምብር *bomber*
bona fide *(adj.)* ሓቀኛ *ḧaqen̈a*
bonanza *(n.)* ኣኸዘ *ak̈eze*
bond *(n.)* ውዕል *w'ël*
bondage *(n.)* ጊልያነት ከዳሚነት *gilyanet kedaminet*
bone *(n.)* ዓጽሚ *äxmi*
bonfire *(n.)* መጋርያ *megarya*
bonnet *(n.)* ልስሉስ ቆብዕ *lslus qob'ë*
bonus *(n.)* መቑሹሽ *meq̈ushush*
bony *(adj.)* ዓጻም *äxam*
book *(n.)* መጽሓፍ *mexḧaf*
bookish *(adj.)* መጽሓፋዊ *mexḧafawi*
booklet *(n.)* ንእሽቶ መጽሓፍ *n'èshto mexḧaf*
booklet *(n.)* ንእሽቶ መጽሓፍ *n'èshto mexḧaf*
bookmark *(n.)* መቓቐር *meq̈aq̈er*
bookseller *(n.)* መጽሓፍ ሸያጢት *mexḧaf sheyaẗit*
boom *(n.)* ፊሕታ *fiḧta*
boon *(n.)* ሕቶ *ḧto*
boor *(n.)* ጠገለ-ኣልቦ *ẗegele'albo*
boost *(v.)* ምስፋሕ *msfaḧ*
booster *(n.)* ሰንካቲ *senkati*
boot *(n.)* ነዊሕ ሳእኒ *newiḧ sa'èni*
booth *(n.)* ጎጆ *goĵo*
bootleg *(adj.)* ኮንትሮባንድ *kontroband*

booty *(n.)* ምርኮ *mrko*
border *(n.)* ዶብ *dob*
bore *(v.)* ጐርጐሐ *gWargWaḧe*
born *(adj.)* ወልደ *tewelde*
borough *(n.)* ወረደ *werede*
borrow *(v.)* ተለቅሐ *teleqḧe*
bosom *(n.)* ሕጽöኒ *ḧxni*
boss *(n.)* ሓለቓ *ḧaleq̈a*
bossy *(adj.)* ኣውቶክራት *'awtokrat*
botany *(n.)* ስነ-ኣትክልቲ *sne'atklti*
both *(adj. & pron.)* ክልቲኡ *klti'u*
bother *(v.)* ኣሸገረ *ashegere*
bottle *(n.)* ጥርሙዝ *ẗrmuz*
bottom *(n.)* ታሕቲ *taḧti*
bough *(n.)* ቃራና *qarana*
boulder *(n.)* ዓረ *äre*
boulevard *(n.)* ጐደና *gWadena*
bounce *(v.)* ነጠረ *neẗere*
bouncer *(n.)* መሰነዪ *meseneyi*
bound *(v.)* ሓጸረ *ḧaxere*
boundary *(n.)* ዶብ *dob*
boundless *(adj.)* ደረት-ኣልቦ *deret'albo*
bountiful *(adj.)* ለጋስ *legas*
bounty *(n.)* ልግሲ *lgsi*
bouquet *(n.)* ሕቑፊ-ዕምባባ *ḧq̈ufi'ëmbaba*
bout *(n.)* ግጥ'ም *gẗm*
boutique *(n.)* ባዛር *bazar*
bow *(n.)* ቀስቲ *qesti*
bow *(v.)* ሰገደ *segede*
bowel *(n.)* መዓናጡ *me'änaẗu*
bower *(n.)* ዳስ *das*
bowl *(n.)* ጭሖሎ *čḧolo*
box *(n.)* ሳንዱቕ *sanduq̈*
boxer *(n.)* ተጋዳላይ *tegadalay*
boxing *(n)* ጉስጢ *gusẗi*
boy *(n.)* ወዲ *wedi*
boycott *(v.)* ኣደመ *ademe*
boyhood *(n)* ንእስነት *n'èsnet*
bra *(n.)* ቢኪኒ *bikini*
brace *(n.)* ድጋፍ *dgaf*
bracelet *(n.)* በናጅር *benaĵr*
bracket *(n.)* መደገፍ *medegef*
brag *(v.)* ተጀሃረ *teĵehari*
Braille *(n.)* ብረይል *breyl*
brain *(n.)* ሓንጎል *ḧangol*
brake *(n.)* ልጓም *lgWam*
branch *(n.)* ጨንፈር *čenfer*
brand *(n.)* ዕላመት *ëlamet*
brandish *(v.)* ኣንበልበለ *anbelbele*
brandy *(n.)* ብራንዲ *brandi*
brash *(adj.)* ደረቖኛ *dereq̈eǹa*
brass *(n.)* ኣስራዚ *asrazi*
brave *(adj.)* ተባዕ *teba'ë*
bravery *(n.)* ትብዓት *tb'ät*
brawl *(n.)* ቈየቛ *qWeyeq̈WA*
bray *(v.)* ህላ *hla*
breach *(v.)* ምጥሓስ *mẗḧas*
bread *(n.)* እንጀራ *ènĵera*
breadth *(n.)* ውርዲ *wrdi*
break *(v.)* ሰበረ *sebere*
breakage *(n.)* ስብረት *sbret*
breakfast *(n.)* ቁርሲ *qursi*
breast *(n.)* ጡብ *ẗub*
breath *(n.)* ትንፋስ *tnfas*
breathe *(v.)* ኣተንፈሰ *atenfese*
breech *(n.)* ዓንቀር ጠበንጃ *änqer ẗebenĵa*
breeches *(n.)* ስረ-ግትር *sregtr*
breed *(v.)* ኣራብሐ *arabḧe*
breeze *(n.)* ህዱእ ንፋስ *hdu'è nfas*

brevity *(n.)* ሕጽረት ሓጺርነት *ḧxret ḧaxirnet*
brew *(v.)* ጸመቘ *xemeq̈We*
brewery *(n.)* እንዳ ቢራ *'ènda bira*
bribe *(v. t.)* ጉቦ *gubo*
brick *(n.)* ሕጡብ ማቶኒ *ḧẗub matoni*
bridal *(adj.)* ናይ መርዓ *nay mer'ä*
bride *(n.)* መርዓት *mer'ät*
bridegroom *(n.)* መርዓዊ *mer'äwi*
bridge *(n.)* ድልድል *dldl*
bridle *(n.)* ልጓም *lgWam*
brief *(adj.)* ሓጺር *ḧaxir*
briefing *(n.)* ሓጺር መግለጺ *ḧaxir meglexi*
brigade *(n.)* ጉጅለ *guĵle*
brigadier *(n.)* መራሕ ብርጌድ *meraḧ brgeed*
bright *(adj.)* ድሙቕ *dmuq̈*
brighten *(v.)* ደመቐ በርሀ *demeq̈e berhe*
brilliance *(n.)* ብልጫ *blča*
brilliant *(adj.)* ድሙቕ *dmuq̈*
brim *(n.)* ጫፍ *čaf*
brindle *(adj.)* ሓበጀራይ *ḧabeĵeray*
brine *(n.)* ማይ ጨው *may čew*
bring *(v.)* ኣምጸአ *amxe'e*
brinjal *(n.)* ብሪንጃል *birinjal*
brink *(n.)* ጠረፍ *ẗeref*
brisk *(adj.)* ስሉጥ *sluẗ*
bristle *(n.)* ነደ'ረ *nedere*
British *(adj.)* ብሪቲሽ *biritish*
brittle *(adj.)* ተሰባሪ *tesebari*
broach *(adj.)* ኣንኰለ *ankWale*
broad *(adj.)* ሰፊሕ *sefiḧ*
broadcast *(v. t)* ዘርግሐ *zergḧe*
brocade *(n.)* በዘቕዘቕ *bezeq̈zeq̈*
broccoli *(n.)* ካውሎ ፍዮሪ *kawlo fyori*
brochure *(n.)* መንሹር *menshur*
broke *(adj.)* ሰበረ *sebere*
broken *(adj.)* ስቡር *sbur*
broker *(n.)* ደላ'ላይ *delalay*
bronchial *(adj.)* ቃራየ ጉርጉማ *qaraye gurguma*
bronze *(n.)* ብሮንዞ *bronzo*
brood *(n.)* ጨቓዊት *čeq̈awit*
brook *(n.)* ዛራ *zara*
broom *(n.)* መኽስተር *meḱoster*
broth *(n.)* መረቕ *mereq̈*
brothel *(n.)* እንዳ ኣመንዝራ *ènda 'amenzra*
brother *(n.)* ሓው *ḧaw*
brotherhood *(n.)* ሕውነት *ḧwnet*
brow *(n.)* ሽፋሽፍቲ *shefashfti*
brown *(n.)* ቡናዊ *bunawi*
browse *(v.)* ገሃጸ *gehaxe*
browser *(n.)* ማእረረ *ma'èrere*
bruise *(n.)* ስንብራት *snbrat*
brunch *(n.)* ኩላሶ *kulaso*
brunette *(n.)* ጸሊም ጸጉሪ *xelim xeguri*
brunt *(n.)* ቀንዲ ክብደት *qendi kbdet*
brush *(n.)* ኣስባስላ *asbasla*
brusque *(adj.)* ኣሻኹ *ashaḱWi*
brutal *(adj.)* ዘይምሕር *zeymḧr*
brute *(n.)* እንስሳ *ènssa*
bubble *(n.)* ዓፍራ *äfra*
buck *(n.)* ኮናዕ *kona'ë*
bucket *(n.)* መገለል *megelel*
buckle *(n.)* መቑለፍ *meq̈Welef*
bud *(n.)* ኣጓም *agWam*
budge *(v.)* ምንቕ በለ *mnq̈ bele*

budget *(n.)* ባጀት *baĵet*
buffalo *(n.)* ጎባይ *gobay*
buffer *(n.)* ወሓጥ ጐንጺ *weḧaẗ gWanxi*
buffet *(n.)* ጉስጢ *gusẗi*
buffoon *(n.)* መስሓቕ *mesḧaq̈*
bug *(n.)* ትኺን *tḱWan*
buggy *(n.)* ካሮሳ *karosa*
bugle *(n.)* ጥሩምባ *ẗrumba*
build *(v.)* ሃነጸ *hanexe*
building *(n.)* ህንጻ *hnxa*
bulb *(n.)* ሽጉርቶ *shgurto*
bulge *(n.)* ሕበጥ *ḧbeẗ*
bulimia *(n.)* ቡሊምያ *bilimiya*
bulk *(n.)* ብብዝሒ *bbzḧi*
bulky *(adj.)* ደጐላጽ *degWalax*
bull *(n.)* ኣርሓ *arḧa*
bulldog *(n.)* ገዚፍ ዓይነት ከልቢ *gezif 'äynet kelbi*
bullet *(n.)* ዓረር *ärer*
bulletin *(n.)* ቡለቲን *buletin*
bullion *(n.)* ሕጡብ ወርቂ *ḧtub werqi*
bullish *(adj.)* ኣዛዚ *azazi*
bullock *(n.)* ቅጥቁጥ ብዕራይ *qẗquẗ b'ëray*
bully *(n.)* ዓላቕ *älaq̈*
bulwark *(n.)* ዕርዲ *ërdi*
bum *(n.)* መዓኮር *me'äkor*
bumble *(v.)* ተዓንቀፈ *te'änqefe*
bump *(n.)* ተናጐጸ *tenagWaxe*
bumper *(n.)* ዋልጋ ጐንጺ *walga gWanxi*
bumpkin *(n.)* ሁጉሬ *huguree*
bumpy *(adj.)* ተናጐጸ *tenagWaxe*
bun *(n.)* ምቁር ባኒ *mqur bani*
bunch *(n.)* ጥማር *ẗmar*
bundle *(n.)* ጠቕለለ *ẗeq̈lele*
bung *(n.)* ቡሽ *bush*
bungalow *(n.)* ሓደ ዝደርቡ ገዛ *ḧade zderbu geza*
bungle *(v.)* ገልተው *geltew*
bunk *(n.)* ሃደመ *hademe*
bunker *(n.)* መኽዘን ነዳዲ ናይ መርከብ *meḱzen nedadi nay merkeb*
buoy *(n.)* ሓባ'ር መርከብ *ḧabar merkeb*
buoyancy *(n.)* ምንስፋፍ *mnsfaf*
buoyant *(adj.)* ተንሳፋፊ *tensafafi*
burble *(v.)* ጐራዕራዕ በለ *gWara'ëra'ë bele*
burden *(n.)* ሸከም *shekem*
bureau *(n.)* ሰደቓ *sedeq̈a*
bureaucracy *(n.)* ቢሮክራሲ *birokrasi*
bureaucrat *(n.)* ቢሮክራታዊ *birokratawi*
burgeon *(v.)* ኣጐመ *agWame*
burger *(n.)* በርገር *berger*
burglar *(n.)* ሰራቒ *seraq̈i*
burglary *(n.)* ገበን *geben*
burial *(n.)* ቀብሪ *qebri*
burlesque *(n.)* ላግጺ *lagxi*
burn *(v.)* ምንዳድ *mndad*
burner *(n.)* ኣንዳዲ *andadi*
burning *(adj.)* ርሱን *rsun*
burrow *(n.)* ጉድጓድ *gudgWad*
bursar *(n.)* ተሓዝ ገንዘብ *teḧaz genzeb*
bursary *(n.)* ሓገዝ *ḧagez*
burst *(v.)* ነተጐ *netegWa*
bury *(v.)* ቀበረ *qebere*
bus *(n.)* ኣውቶቡስ *awtobus*
bush *(n.)* ቈጥቋጥ *qWeẗqWAẗ*
bushy *(adj.)* ጎፍጓፍ *gofgWaf*

business *(n.)* ዋኒን *wanin*
businessman *(n.)* ነጋዳይ *negaday*
bust *(n.)* ደረት *deret*
bustle *(v.)* ኣሽበድበደ *ashbedbede*
busy *(adj.)* ተጸምደ *texemde*
but *(conj.)* ግን *gn*
butcher *(n.)* ሓራድ ስጋ *ḧarad sga*
butler *(n.)* ባልጠጂ *balẗeĵi*
butter *(n.)* ጠስሚ *ẗesmi*
butterfly *(n.)* ጽምብላሊዕ *xmblali'ë*
buttock *(n.)* ዶሶ *doso*
button *(n.)* መልጎም *melgom*
buy *(v.)* ገዝአ *gez'e*
buyer *(n.)* ዓዳጊ *ädagi*
buzz *(n.)* ዚዝ በለ *ziz bele*
buzzard *(n.)* ሽላ *shla*
buzzer *(n.)* ሲረና *sirena*
by *(prep.)* ብ *b*
by-election *(n.)* ጎድናዊ-ምርጫ *godnawimrča*
bygone *(adj.)* ቀደም *qedem*
by-line *(n.)* ብ ሕንጻጽ *bḧnxax*
bypass *(n.)* ጎድናዊ መንገዲ *godnawi mengedi*
byre *(n.)* ደምበ *dembe*
bystander *(n.)* ተመልካቲ *temelkati*
byte *(n.)* ባይት *bayit*

C

cab *(n.)* ጋቢ'ና *gabina*
cabaret *(n.)* ካባረ *kabare*
cabbage *(n.)* ካውሎ *kawlo*
cabin *(n.)* ጋቢና *gabina*
cabinet *(n.)* ከብሒ *kebḧi*
cable *(n.)* መዳወር *medawer*
cacao *(n.)* ካካው *kakaw*
cache *(n.)* ሓብአ *ḧab'e*
cachet *(n.)* ክታም *ktam*
cackle *(n.)* ቃቓ *qaq̈a*
cactus *(n.)* ቈልቋል *qWelqWAl*
cad *(n.)* ነውራም *newram*
cadaver *(n.)* ሬሳ *reesa*
cadaver *(n.)* ሬሳ *reesa*
caddy *(n.)* ካዲ *kadi*
cadet *(n.)* ካደት *kadet*
cadmium *(n.)* ካድምዩም *kadmyum*
cadre *(n.)* ኣስከሬን *askereen*
caesarean *(n.)* ቄሳር *qeesar*
cafe *(n.)* ካፈ *kafe*
cafeteria *(n.)* ካፈተርያ *kafeterya*
cage *(n.)* ጎብያ *gobya*
cahoots *(n.)* ኪዳን *kidan*
cajole *(v.)* ሸሓጠ *sheḧaẗe*
cake *(n.)* ዶልሺ *dolshi*
calamity *(n.)* መዓት *me'ät*
calcium *(n.)* ካልስዩም *kalsyum*
calculate *(v.)* ቀመረ *qemere*
calculation *(n.)* ቀመር *qemer*
calculator *(n.)* መተሓሳሰቢ *meteḧasasebi*
calendar *(n.)* ዓውደ-ኣዋርሕ *äwde'awarḧ*
calf *(n.)* ምራኽ *mraḱ*
calibrate *(v.)* ኣተኸኸለ *ateḱaḱele*

calibre *(n.)* ውሽጣዊ ሰንጣቒት *wshťawi senťaq̈it*
call *(v.)* ደወለ *dewele*
calligraphy *(n.)* ጽባቐ ጽሒፈት *xbaq̈e xȟfet*
calling *(n.)* ሞያ *moya*
callous *(adj.)* ጽዖታዊ *x'ötawi*
callow *(adj.)* ጥረ *ťre*
calm *(adj.)* ህዱእ *hdu'è*
calorie *(n.)* ካሎሪ *kalori*
calumny *(n.)* ምጽላም *mxlam*
camaraderie *(n.)* ብጻይነት *bxaynet*
camber *(n.)* ጐብጓበ *gWabgWabe*
cambric *(n.)* ሻሽ *shash*
camcorder *(n.)* ካምኮርደር *kamkorder*
camel *(n.)* ገመል *gemel*
cameo *(n.)* ካምዮ *kamyo*
camera *(n.)* ካመራ *kamera*
camp *(n.)* መዓስከር *me'äsker*
campaign *(n.)* ዘመተ *zemete*
camphor *(n.)* ካምፎራ *kamfora*
campus *(n.)* ካምፓስ *kampas*
can *(n.)* ታኒካ *tanika*
can *(v.)* ኣብ ታኒካ ሓተመ *'ab tanika ȟateme*
canal *(n.)* መትረብ *metreb*
canard *(n.)* ናይ ሓሶት ጸብጻብ *nay ȟasot xebxab*
cancel *(v.)* ሰረዘ *sereze*
cancellation *(n.)* ምጥፋእ *mťfa'è*
cancer *(n.)* መንሽሮ *menshro*
candela *(n.)* ብራሃን *brahan*
candid *(adj.)* ግሁድ *ghud*
candidate *(n.)* ሕጹይ *ȟxuy*
candle *(n.)* ሽምዓ *shm'ä*
candour *(n.)* ጋህዲ *gahdi*
candy *(n.)* ካራመላ *karamela*
cane *(n.)* ከረዛን *kerezan*
canine *(adj.)* ከልባዊ *kelbawi*
canister *(n.)* ሳጹን *saxun*
cannabis *(n.)* ሀምፕ *hemp*
cannibal *(n.)* በላዕ ሰብ *bela'ë seb*
cannon *(n.)* መድፍዕ *medf'ë*
canny *(adj.)* ጒራሕ *gWaraȟ*
canoe *(n.)* ታንኳ *tankWa*
canon *(n.)* ቀኖና *qenona*
canopy *(n.)* ድባብ *dbab*
cant *(n.)* ግብዝና *gbzna*
cantankerous *(adj.)* ሓራቕ *ȟaraq̈*
canteen *(n.)* ካንቲና *kantina*
canter *(n.)* ህዱእ ጋልቢት *hdu'è galbit*
canton *(n.)* ወረዳ *wereda*
cantonment *(n.)* ቀዋሚ መዓስከር *qewami me'äsker*
canvas *(n.)* ጅርባ *ĵrba*
canvass *(v.)* ብምሉ'እ ተዛተየ *bmlu'è tezateye*
canyon *(n.)* ዓሚቕ ስንጭሮ *ämiq̈ sněro*
cap *(n.)* ቈብዕ *qWeb'ë*
capability *(n.)* ዓቕሚ *äq̈mi*
capable *(adj.)* ክኢላ *k'ila*
capacious *(adj.)* ሰፊሕ *sefiȟ*
capacitor *(n.)* ካፓሲተር *kapaciter*
capacity *(n.)* ዓቕሚ *äq̈mi*
caparison *(v.)* ሰለመ *seleme*
cape *(n.)* መንጠሊና *menťelina*
capital *(n.)* ርእሰ-ማል *r'èsemal*
capitalism *(n.)* ርእሰ-ማልነት *r'èsemalnet*

capitalist ***(n. &adj.)*** **ርእሰ-ማላዊ** *r'èsemalawi*
capitalize ***(v.)*** **ርእሰ-ማል ገበረ** *r'èsemal gebere*
capitation ***(n.)*** **ግብሪ** *gbri*
capitulate ***(v.)*** **ተምበርከኸ** *temberkeḱe*
caprice ***(n.)*** **ቅበጥ** *qbeẗ*
capricious ***(adj.)*** **ቀባጥ** *qebaẗ*
capsicum ***(n.)*** **ካፕሲከም** *kapsikem*
capsize ***(v.)*** **ገልበጠ** *gelbeẗe*
capstan ***(n.)*** **ጠምጣሚ መስሕብ** *ẗemẗami meshb*
capsule ***(n.)*** **ለቖታ-ፍረ** *leq̈otafre*
captain ***(n.)*** **ግብጣን** *gbẗan*
captaincy ***(n.)*** **ግብጣኒ** *gbẗani*
caption ***(n.)*** **ኣርእስቲ** *ar'èsti*
captivate ***(v.)*** **መሰጠ** *meseẗe*
captive ***(n.)*** **ምሩኽ** *mruḱ*
captivity ***(n.)*** **ምሩኽነት** *mruḱnet*
captor ***(n.)*** **ሓላው ምሩኽ** *ḧalaw mruḱ*
capture ***(v.)*** **ኣሰረ** *asere'*
car ***(n.)*** **ማኪና** *makina*
caramel ***(n.)*** **ካራሜል** *karame' el*
carat ***(n.)*** **ካራት** *kara 't*
caravan ***(n.)*** **ቃፍላይ** *qaflay*
carbohydrate ***(n.)*** **ሽኮር መሰል** *shkor mesel*
carbon ***(n.)*** **ሕመት** *hemete*
carbonate ***(adj.)*** **ባይካርቦነት** *baykarbonet*
carboy ***(n.)*** **ጥርሙዝ** *terimuz*
carcass ***(n.)*** **ገምቢ** *ge'mbi*
card ***(n.)*** **ካርዲ** *ka'ardi*
cardamom ***(n.)*** **ጠጠው አቢሉ** *tte'ttew aa'billu*
cardboard ***(n.)*** **ካርቶን** *kartoon*
cardiac ***(adj.)*** **ናይ ልቢ** *na' ae lebii*
cardigan ***(n.)*** **ጎልፎ** *gole 'foo*
cardinal ***(n.)*** **ጳጳስ** *papase'*
cardiograph ***(n.)*** **ካርድዮግራፍ** *kardyograf*
cardiology ***(n.)*** **ካርድዮሎጂ** *kardyoloĵi*
care ***(n.)*** **ክንክን** *kinkin*
career ***(n.)*** **ስራሕ** *sir'ahh*
carefree ***(adj.)*** **ዘይአጅቦ** *they'aa jibo*
careful ***(adj.)*** **ጥንቁቅ** *tinkuq*
careless ***(adj.)*** **ዘየስተውዕል** *ze yestewu 'el*
carer ***(n.)*** **ኣብ** *aa'b*
caress ***(v.)*** **ተናኸፈ** *tenahe'fe*
caretaker ***(n.)*** **ወኪል** *wekil*
cargo ***(n.)*** **ኣብ መርከብ** *aa'b merkeb*
caricature ***(n)*** **ምስሊ** *mesili*
carmine ***(n.)*** **ቀይሕ ሕብሪ** *qeyiha hib're*
carnage ***(n.)*** **ጭፍጨፋ** *Chif'chefa*
carnal ***(adj.)*** **ስጋዊ** *segawi*
carnival ***(n.)*** **ካርኒቫል** *karnival*
carnivore ***(n.)*** **በላዕ ስጋ** *bela'ë sga*
carol ***(n.)*** **ደርፊ** *derfi*
carpal ***(adj.)*** **ኣዕበርበረ** *zz'ebere bere*
carpenter ***(n.)*** **ፀራቢ** *tserabi*
carpentry ***(n.)*** **ፅርበት** *tsirbet*
carpet ***(n.)*** **መንፀፍ** *mentseff*
carriage ***(n.)*** **ባቡር** *babur*
carrier ***(n.)*** **ብነፋሪት** *binefarit*
carrot ***(n.)*** **ካሮት** *carrot*
carry ***(v.)*** **ተሸከመ** *teshekeme*
cart ***(n.)*** **ዓረብያ** *arebia*
cartel ***(n.)*** **ካርተል** *kartel*

cartilage *(n.)* ቆርጠምጠማ *qorẗemẗema*
carton *(n.)* ባኮ *bako*
cartoon *(n.)* ካርቱን *kartun*
cartridge *(n.)* ቀልሃ *qeliha*
carve *(v.)* ቀረፀ *qeretse*
carvery *(n.)* ጠበሰ ስጋ *ẗebese sga*
Casanova *(n.)* ወዲ *wedi*
cascade *(n.)* መንጫ ጫዕታ *mencha chaeta*
case *(n.)* ኩነት *kunet*
casement *(n.)* መስኮት *mesekote*
cash *(n.)* ቅርሺ *qeriishe*
cashew *(n.)* ኦም *ome*
cashier *(n.)* ተቀባሊት ቅርሺ *teqebalit qereshi*
cashmere *(n.)* ሱፍ *suf*
casing *(n.)* ዝተለበጠ *zetelebte*
casino *(n.)* ህንፀት *hintsete*
cask *(n.)* ፊስቶ *fiseto*
casket *(n.)* ሳፁን ሬሳ *satsun resa*
casserole *(n.)* ምግቢ *megebi*
cassock *(n.)* ጁባ *juba*
cast *(v.)* ተመልከተ *temeleket*
castaway *(n.)* ውጻእ መዓት *wxa'è me'ät*
caste *(n.)* ማሕበራዊ ደረጃ *mahiberawi dereja*
castigate *(v.)* ነቀፈ *neqefe*
casting *(n.)* ደርበየ *derebye*
castle *(n.)* ቤት ነገስታት *bete negestat*
castor *(n.)* ወሃብ ቅርጺ *wehab qrxi*
castor oil *(a.)* ጎማ ዘይት *goma zeite*
castrate *(v.)* ቀጥቀጥ *qeteqetw*
casual *(adj.)* ዘይተሓሰበሉ *zeytehasebelo*
casualty *(n.)* ዝሞተ *zemote*
cat *(n.)* ድሙ *demu*
cataclysm *(n.)* መቕዘፍቲ *meq̈zefti*
catalogue *(n.)* ብስሩዕ መዝገብ *bsru'ë mezgeb*
catalyse *(v.)* ኣቀፃፀለ *aqetsatsele*
catalyst *(n.)* ኣቀፃፃሊ *aqetsatseli*
cataract *(n.)* ሓበላ *habela*
catastrophe *(n.)* መቕዘፍቲ *meq̈zefti*
catch *(v.)* ቆበለ *qobl*
catching *(adj.)* ተላጋቢ *telagabi*
catchy *(adj.)* ተዛካሪ *tezakari*
catechism *(n.)* ትምህርተ-ሃይማኖት *tmhrtehaymanot*
categorical *(adj.)* ፍጹም *fxum*
categorize *(v.)* ጎጀለ *goje-le*
category *(n.)* ጉጅለ *guge-le*
cater *(v.)* ሰርዐ *sere'aa*
caterpillar *(n.)* ኣባጨጓራ *aaba'che'guara*
catharsis *(n.)* ምሕራእ *mḧra'è*
cathedral *(n.)* ደብሪ *debri*
catholic *(adj.)* ካቶሊክ *catholic*
cattle *(n.)* ከብቲ *kebtei*
catty *(n.)* ሓሜተኛ *hametegna'*
Caucasian *(adj.)* ካውካዝያዊ *kawkazyawi*
cauldron *(n.)* በራድ *beradd*
cauliflower *(n.)* ካዉሎ ፍዮሪ *kawulo fiyorii*
causal *(adj.)* ጠንቃዊ *ẗenqawi*
causality *(n.)* ጠንቅነት *ẗenqnet*
cause *(n.)* መንቀሊ *mneqsi*
causeway *(n.)* ኣዉራ መንገዲ *awra mnegedeei*
caustic *(adj.)* መፂፅ *matsiee.e*

caution *(n.)* **መጠንቀቕታ** *metenqekta*

cautionary *(adj.)* **ኣጠንቀቐ** *aa'tenqeqe*

cautious *(adj.)* **ጥንቁቕ** *tenquqk*

cavalcade *(n.)* **ናይ ፈረሳት** *nayei feresat*

cavalier *(adj.)* **ዘይግደስ** *zeyg des*

cavalry *(n.)* **ፈረሰኛ** *fresenga*

cave *(n.)* **በዓቲ** *beaa'ti*

caveat *(n.)* **መዘካከሪ** *mezkakrii*

cavern *(n.)* **ገፊሕ በዓቲ** *gefihe beatii*

cavernous *(adj.)* **ብጣዕሚ ገፊሕ** *betaemi gefihei*

cavity *(n.)* **ዝጎድጎደ ስኒ** *zgodedod sieni*

cavort *(v.)* **ተሰራሰረ** *teserasere*

cease *(v.)* **ደው ኣበለ** *dwuo aabele*

ceasefire *(n.)* **ተኹሲ ኣቋረጸ** *tekusi 'aqWArexe*

ceaseless *(adj.)* **ዘየቋርጽ** *zeyeqWArx*

cedar *(n.)* **ኦም ሲዳር** *oom cidar*

cede *(v.)* **ኣስተለመ** *'asteleme*

ceiling *(n.)* **ሰንቀ** *senqe*

celandine *(n.)* **ዕምባባ** *embaba*

celebrant *(n.)* **ቀዳሲ** *qedasi*

celebrate *(v.)* **ኣብዓለ** *'ab'äle*

celebration *(n.)* **በዓል** *beaal*

celebrity *(n.)* **ስሙይ ሰብ** *semuyei sebe*

celestial *(adj.)* **ሰማያዊ** *semayawii*

celibacy *(n.)* **ድንግልና** *denegelena*

celibate *(adj.)* **ድንግላይ** *denegelaye*

cell *(n.)* **ዋህዮ** *waheyo*

cell phone *(n.)* **ተንቀሳቓሲ ስልኪ** *teneqesaqasi seliki*

cellar *(n.)* **ናይ እሱራት ክፍሊ** *naye esurat kiflii*

cellular *(adj.)* **ልኡክ ጉጀለ** *leuuke gujelle*

cellulite *(n.)* **ስብሒ** *sebehi*

celluloid *(n.)* **ዝነድድ ረብሓ** *zenededei rehehaa*

cellulose *(n.)* **ሓይሊ ወሃቢ ንጥረ ምግቢ** *hayeli wehabi netere megebi*

Celsius *(n.)* **ሴልሲየስ** *celcius*

Celtic *(adj.)* **ሴልቲክ ቋንቋ** *celtik quaniqua*

cement *(n.)* **ስሚንቶ** *seminito*

cemetery *(n.)* **መካነ መቓብር** *mekne mekabir*

censer *(n.)* **ሸሓነ** *shehane*

censor *(n.)* **መርማሪ** *meremari*

censorious *(adj.)* **ነቓፊ** *neqkafi*

censorship *(n.)* **ቅድመ ምርመራ** *qedeme meremra*

censure *(v.)* **ብርቱዕ ነቀፌታ** *beretiee' neqefeta*

census *(n.)* **ቆፀራ** *qoxera*

cent *(n.)* **ሳንቲም** *sanetim*

centenary *(n.)* **ዝክረ-ዘመን** *zkrezemen*

centennial *(n.)* **ኣብ ርእ** *ab reaa'*

centigrade *(adj.)* **ሙቀት መጠን** *muqete metene*

centimetre *(n.)* **ርቐት መጠን** *reqete metene*

centipede *(n.)* **ዘርኢ ሰብ ዝመስል** *zereii sebe zemsle*

central *(adj.)* **ኣዉራ/ቀንዲ** *aawura/qenedi*

centralize *(v.)* **ኣማእከለ** *zamaeekele*
centre *(n.)* **ማዕከል** *meee'kele*
century *(n.)* **ዘበን** *zbene*
ceramic *(n.)* **ጣሳ** *tasa*
cereal *(n.)* **ጥራጥረ** *teraterre*
cerebral *(adj.)* **ናይ ሓንጎል** *nayei hanegole*
ceremonial *(adj.)* **ስነ ስርዓታዊ** *sene sereaa'tawii*
ceremonious *(adj.)* **ስነ ስርዓት ዘለዎ** *senei sereat zelewoo*
ceremony *(n.)* **በዓል/ፅምብል** *beaal/xeembil*
certain *(adj.)* **ርጉፅ** *reguxee*
certainly *(adv.)* **ብዘይጥርጥር** *bethzey tiritir*
certifiable *(adj.)* **ዕቡድ/ፅሉል** *eebudd/xelule*
certificate *(n.)* **ምስክር ወረቐት** *mesekir wereqet*
certify *(v.)* **ምስክር ወረቐት ሃበ** *meseker wereqket habe*
certitude *(n.)* **ርግፀኝነት** *regexegninet*
cervical *(adj.)* **ናይ ክሳድ** *nay ksad*
cessation *(n.)* **ምቁራፅ** *mekuraxee*
cession *(n.)* **ውህበት** *whbet*
chain *(n.)* **ሰንሰለት** *seneselet*
chair *(n.)* **ወንበር** *weneber*
chairman *(n.)* **ኣቦወንበር** *abo' weneber*
chaise *(n.)* **ሰብ ተጓዕዝ** *sebe tegwaeeze*
chalet *(n.)* **ባራካ** *barakaa*
chalice *(n.)* **ፅዋዕ** *xewaee*
chalk *(n.)* **በረቕ** *bereqqe*
challenge *(n.)* **ፈተነ** *fetene*
chamber *(n.)* **አዳራሽ** *adarashe*
chamberlain *(n.)* **ኣጋፋሪ** *'agafari*
champagne *(n.)* **ሻምፓኝ** *shampagne*
champion *(n.)* **ዕዉት/ሰዓራይ** *eewuut/seaarayi*
chance *(n.)* **ዕድል** *eedil*
chancellor *(n.)* **መራሒ መንግስቲ** *merahi menegeseti*
Chancery *(n.)* **ቤት ፅሕፈት** *bete xehifeti*
chandelier *(n.)* **ልሻን ሽለመ** *leshane' shelem'e*
change *(v.)* **ለወጠ/ተለወጠ** *lewete/telewete*
channel *(n.)* **ጣቢያ ቴሌቪዥን** *tabiya television*
chant *(n.)* **ዜማ** *zema*
chaos *(n.)* **ህዉከት** *hewuuket*
chaotic *(adj.)* **ዕግርግር ዘለዎ** *egereger zelewo*
chapel *(n.)* **ንእሽተይ ቤተክርስቲያን** *neeshtey betekerestian*
chaplain *(n.)* **ካህን** *kahiN'*
chapter *(n.)* **ምዕራፍ** *mee'eraf*
char *(v.)* **ሓረር/ኣሕረረ** *harer/aaehi'rere*
character *(n.)* **ባሕርይ/ፀባይ** *bahereyei/xebayii*
characteristic *(n.)* **ባሕርይ** *bahereyei*
charcoal *(n.)* **ፋሓም/ሕመት** *fahame/hemeute*
charge *(n.)* **ክፍሊት ሓተተ** *kefelit hatete*
charge *(v.)* **ክፍሊት** *kefelite*
charger *(n.)* **ብርጭቆ መልአ** *bereCheqo melea'a*

chariot *(n.)* **ዓረብያ/ሰረገላ** *arebiya/seregela*
charisma *(n.)* **ግርማ ሞገስ** *gerima moges*
charismatic *(adj.)* **በዓል ሞገስ** *beal moges*
charitable *(adj.)* **ናይ ገባሪ ሰናይ** *nayei gebari senayei*
charity *(n.)* **ትካል ገባሪ ሰናይ** *tekaal gebarii senayei*
charlatan *(n.)* **መምሰሊ** *memeiseli*
charm *(n.)* **ሰሓባይነት** *sehabayineet*
charming *(adj.)* **ሰባሓይ/ማራኪ** *sebahaayi/marakii*
chart *(n.)* **ሰንጠረዥ** *seneterezjj*
charter *(n.)* **መምርሒ** *memerehii*
chartered *(adj.)* **ተኮናተረ** *tekonateree*
chary *(adj.)* **ስግኣት** *segeaa'te*
chase *(v.)* **አጓየየ** *aaguwayeye*
chassis *(n.)* **ሞተር** *mote'R'*
chaste *(adj.)* **ዘየዝሙዉ** *zeyezemuwue*
chasten *(v.)* **ወቐሰ** *weqqese*
chastise *(v.)* **ኣደብ** *A'deb*
chastity *(n.)* **ዘይምዝማዉ** *zeymzemawu*
chat *(v. i.)* **ኣዕለለ/ኣዉገዐ** *aae'lele/aawugeaa'*
chateau *(n.)* **ቤት ነገስታት** *bete' negeseta't*
chattel *(n.)* **ንብረት/ንዋይ** *neberet/newaye*
chatter *(v.)* **ሃተፈ/ለፈለፈ** *hatefe/lefelefe*
chauffeur *(n.)* **ኣውቲስታ** *aawutiseta*
chauvinism *(n.)* **ትምክሕቲ** *temekeheti*
chauvinist *(n. &adj.)* **ምኩሕ** *mekuhh*
cheap *(adj.)* **ሕሳር** *hesaree*
cheapen *(v. t.)* **ኣዋረደ** *aawarede*
cheat *(n.)* **ኣሕሰረ** *aa'hesere*
cheat *(v.)* **ኣታለለ** *aatalele*
check *(v.)* **ኣፃረየ** *axareyee*
checkmate *(n)* **ዝተዛዘመ** *ziteza'zeme'*
cheek *(n.)* **ምዕጉርቲ** *meaegurtii*
cheeky *(adj.)* **ባዕለገ** *bae'leGe'*
cheep *(n.)* **ጩቅ በለ** *Chuqk' bele*
cheer *(v. t.)* **ታሕጓስ** *taheGua'ss*
cheerful *(adj.)* **ወትሩ ሕጉስ** *wetru higus*
cheerless *(adj.)* **ዘየሕጉስ** *zyehiGus'*
cheery *(adj.)* **ሕጉስ** *Higus'*
cheese *(n.)* **ኣጅቦ** *Ajobo*
cheetah *(n.)* **ጭኮንበሳ** *ChikonbeSa*
chef *(n.)* **ዋና ከሻኒ** *wana Kesha'ni*
chemical *(adj.)* **ኬሚካል** *kemikal*
chemist *(n.)* **ቐማሚ** *Qe'mami*
chemistry *(n.)* **ቕመም** *qE'mem*
chemotherapy *(n.)* **ሕክምና** *hikiM'NA*
cheque *(n.)* **ቸክ** *chek*
cherish *(v.)* **ኣፍቀረ** *Af'Qere*
chess *(n.)* **ቼዝ** *Chezz'*
chest *(n.)* **ኣፍልቢ** *Aflebi*
chestnut *(n.)* **ሳንዱቕ** *saneduqQ*
chevron *(n.)* **መለለይ ምልክት** *Me'Leleyei milikit*
chew *(v.)* **ሓየከ** *HayYeke*
chic *(adj.)* **ስብቁል** *sbqul*
chicanery *(n.)* **ሸፍጢ** *Shefe'Ti*

chicken *(n.)* ደርሆ *Dereho*
chickpea *(n.)* ዓይኒ ዓተር *Ayni Ater*
chide *(v.)* ነቐፈ *NeQefe*
chief *(n.)* ኣዉራ/ቀንዲ *Auwra/Qendi'*
chiefly *(adv.)* ሓላፊ/ሓለቓ *Halafi/HaleQa*
chieftain *(n.)* መሪሕነት *MerihNet'*
child *(n.)* ቆልዓ *QoleA'*
childhood *(n.)* ቁልዕነት *Qole'eneT'*
childish *(adj.)* ናይ ቆልዓ *Nayei QoleA'*
chill *(n.)* ቁሪ/ቀዝሒ *Quri/Qezhi*
chilli *(n.)* ሽርባ/በርበረ *Shirba/berebre*
chilly *(adj.)* ቆራር *qorare*
chime *(n.)* ሰዓት ደወለት *seAt' dwle't*
chimney *(n.)* ቆንቆር *QonQkor*
chimpanzee *(n.)* ህበይ *HeBeyei*
chin *(n.)* መንከስ *Menkes'*
china *(n.)* በረቕ *BereqQe'*
chip *(n.)* ሽርፍራፍ *Sherifrafe*
chirp *(v.)* ጩቕ በለ *CchUQ' Bel'le*
chisel *(n.)* መንደል *Mendel*
chit *(n.)* ንእሽቶ ቈልዓ *n'èshto qWel'ä*
chivalrous *(adj.)* ድጊ *dgi*
chivalry *(n.)* ዳጌት *dageet*
chlorine *(n.)* ክሎሪን *kilorin*
chloroform *(n.)* መርዚ *merzi*
chocolate *(n.)* ቸኮላታ *checolata*
choice *(n.)* መረፃ *meretsa*
choir *(n.)* መዘምራን *mezemeran*
choke *(v.)* ሓነቐ *haneqe*
cholera *(n.)* ሕማም ሽሮኽ *hemam sheroke*
choose *(v. t)* መረፀ *meretse*
chop *(v.)* ከተፈ *ketefe*
chopper *(n.)* ሴፍ *sefe*
chopstick *(n.)* ጥሕሎ *telohe*
choral *(adj.)* ክፋል መዝሙር *kefale mezemur*
chord *(n.)* ደመርቲ *dmreti*
chorus *(n.)* ተደጋጊሙ ዝዝመር *tedegagimu zezemre*
Christ *(n.)* ክርስቶስ *keresetos*
Christian *(adj.)* ክርስቲያን *keresitiyane*
Christianity *(n.)* ክርስትና ሃይማኖት *keresetena hayimanot*
Christmas *(n.)* በዓል ልደት *beal lidet*
chrome *(n.)* ቀምቀመ *qemeqme*
chronic *(adj.)* ነባር *nebar*
chronicle *(n.)* ዜና መዋልዕ *zena mewalee*
chronograph *(n.)* ሰዓት *seat*
chronology *(n.)* ስነ-ዕለታት *sne'ëletat*
chuckle *(v.)* ክምስ *kemese*
chum *(n.)* ቀረባ ፈታሒ *qereba fetahi*
chunk *(n.)* ቁርማም *qurmame*
church *(n.)* ቤተ ክርስቲያን *bete kiristian*
churchyard *(n.)* መካነ መቓብር *mekane meqabere*
churn *(v.)* ዓምጠቑ *ameteqku*
chutney *(n.)* ፀብሒ *xebhi*
cider *(n.)* ሲደር *cider*
cigar *(n.)* ሲጋር *sigar*
cigarette *(n.)* ሽጋራ *shegara*
cinema *(n)* ቤት ስኒማ *bet ciniema*
cinnamon *(n.)* ቐረፋ *qerefa*
circle *(n.)* ክቢ *kebi*

circuit *(n.)* ዑደት *'üdet*
circular *(adj.)* ክቢብ *kbibe*
circulate *(v.)* ተሰራጨወ *tsrachew*
circulation *(n.)* ዑደት *xudet*
circumcise *(v.)* ገረዘ *gereze'*
circumference *(n.)* ዶብ *dobe*
circumscribe *(v.)* ገደበ *gedebe*
circumspect *(adj.)* ኣዝዩ ጥንቑቕ *azeyu tenequqe*
circumstance *(n.)* ሃዋህዉ *hawahewu*
circus *(n.)* ሰርከስ *serekse*
cist *(n.)* ሳንዱቕ *sanaduqe*
cistern *(n.)* ማይ መዋህለሊ *maye mwaheleli*
citadel *(n.)* ዕርደ-ከተማ *'ërdeketema*
cite *(v.)* ጠቐሰ *tekese*
citizen *(n.)* ዜጋ *zega*
citizenship *(n.)* ዜግነት *zegenet*
citric *(adj.)* ሲትሪክ *citric*
citrus *(n.)* ተኽል *tekil*
city *(n.)* ከተማ *ketema*
civic *(adj.)* ናይ ከተማ *nayei ketema*
civics *(n.)* ናይ ስነ ዜጋ ትምሕርቲ *nayei sine zega temehereti*
civil *(adj.)* ማሕበረሰባዊ *mahebresebawi*
civilian *(n.)* ስቪል ሰብ *sevil sebe*
civilization *(n.)* ስልጣነ *seletan*
civilize *(v.)* ኣሰልጠነ *aseltene*
clad *(adj.)* ዝተኸደነ *zetkdn*
cladding *(n.)* ኽዳን *Kedan*
claim *(v.)* ሓቂዩ በለ *haqiyu bele*
claimant *(n.)* ይግበኣኒ በሃላይ *yigbeani behalayi*
clammy *(adj.)* ርሁድ *rehude*
clamour *(n.)* ብኣዉያት ሓተተ *beawyat hattete*
clamp *(n.)* ኣጣበቕ *atabeqe*
clan *(n.)* ዓሌት *alet*
clandestine *(adj.)* ሕቡእ *hibuea'*
clap *(v.)* ኣጣቐዐ *atabeqe*
clarification *(n.)* ክለሰ *keles*
clarify *(v.)* ኣብራህረሀ *abrahereh*
clarion *(adj.)* መልእኽቲ *mleekti*
clarity *(n.)* ግልፅነት *geletsinet*
clash *(v.)* ባእሲ *baesii*
clasp *(v.)* ጨበጠ *chebete*
class *(n.)* ክፍሊ *kifeli*
classic *(adj.)* ሕሩይ *heruyei*
classical *(adj.)* ቀንደኛ *qenedegna*
classification *(n.)* ምጉጃል *megujak*
classify *(v.)* ጎጀለ *gojele*
clause *(n.)* ዓንቀፅ *aneqetse*
claustrophobia *(n.)* ኣብ ፀቢብ ቦታ *ab tsebib bota*
claw *(n.)* ፅፍሪ *txefri*
clay *(n.)* ጭቃ *chiqa*
clean *(adj.)* ፅሩይ *tsxeruye*
cleanliness *(n.)* ፅሬት *tsxerete*
cleanse *(v.)* ሓፀበ *hatsxebe*
clear *(adj.)* ንፁር *netsxur*
clearance *(n.)* ምእላይ *meaelayi*
clearly *(adv.)* ፅሩይ *tsxeruyi*
cleave *(v.)* ጨደደ *chedede*
cleft *(n.)* ጨዳድ *cdade*
clemency *(n.)* ምሕረት *meherte*
clement *(adj.)* መሓሪ *mhari*
Clementine *(n.)* ክሌምንታይን *klemintaine*
clench *(v.)* ነኸሰ *nKes*
clergy *(n.)* ካህናት *kahenat'*

cleric *(n.)* ካህን *kahin*
clerical *(adj.)* ቀሺ *qshi*
clerk *(n.)* ፀሓፊ *tsehafi*
clever *(adj.)* ብልሂ *bilihi*
click *(n.)* ድምፂ ፈጠረ *dimtsi ftre'*
client *(n.)* ዓሚል *Amil*
cliff *(n.)* ፀድፊ *Tsxdefi*
climate *(n.)* ኩነታት ኣየር *kunetat ayer'*
climax *(n.)* መዛዘሚ ወሳናይ *mzammi wsanaye*
climb *(v.i)* ደየበ *deYebe*
clinch *(v.)* ተዓወተ *tAwte'*
cling *(v.)* ተለጠፈ *tlTefe'*
clinic *(n.)* ክሊኒክ *kliniqk*
clink *(n.)* ኣጋጨዉ *agachewu*
clip *(n.)* መንቀርቀር *menqerker*
cloak *(n.)* መንጠሊና *mentelina*
clock *(n.)* ሰዓት *seat'*
cloister *(n.)* ናይ ገዳም ሕይወት *nayei gedam hiwot*
clone *(n.)* ምድቃል *mdqal*
close *(adj.)* ዓፀወ *atsewe*
closet *(n.)* ውሻጠ *wushate'*
closure *(n.)* ዝተቓረበ *zitqarebe*
clot *(n.)* ዝረገአ ደም *ziregeaA' deM'*
cloth *(n.)* ክዳን *kidan*
clothe *(v.)* ከደነ *kedeNe'*
clothes *(n.)* ክዳዉንቲ *kidawunti'*
clothing *(n.)* ክዳውንቲ *kdawnti*
cloud *(n.)* ደበና *debNa'*
cloudy *(adj.)* ዕስለ ኣናሕብ *esil anahib*
clove *(n.)* ሸኾና *shekona*
clown *(n.)* ኣዘናግእ *azenagiaa*
cloying *(adj.)* ኣዝዩ ጥዑም ግን ዝመርር *aziyu teum gin zemrer*
club *(n.)* ጋንታ *ganeta*
clue *(n.)* ኣፋፍኖት *afafenote*
clumsy *(adj.)* ላህዛዝ *lahezaZ'*
cluster *(n.)* ዝተኣከቡ ነገራት *ziteakebu negerat*
clutch *(v. t.)* ኣጥቢቑ ሓዘ *atbiqu haze'*
coach *(n.)* ኣሰልጣኒ *aseltani*
coal *(n.)* ሕመት *himet*
coalition *(n.)* ሓድነት *hatnet*
coarse *(adj.)* ሻሕኻር *shahikar*
coast *(n.)* ገምገም ባሕሪ *gemgem bahiriyi*
coaster *(n.)* ኣብ ገምገም ባሕሪ ዝርከብ *ab gemgem bahiri zirkeb*
coat *(n.)* ጁባ *juba*
coating *(n.)* ለፀመ *ltseme'*
coax *(v.)* ሸሓረ *shehare*
cobalt *(n.)* ኣገደዳሲ ኣካል *agededasi akal'*
cobble *(n.)* ኮረት *koret*
cobbler *(n.)* ሰራሒ ሳእኒ *serahi saeni'*
cobra *(n.)* ኮብራ ተመን *korabe tmN'*
cobweb *(n.)* ዓለባ ሳሬት *aleba saret*
cocaine *(n.)* ኮኬን *kocain*
cock *(n.)* ኩኩናይ መኮንን *kukunai mekonin*
cockade *(n.)* ቁፃር *qutsar*
cockpit *(n.)* ሰፈር ኣብራሪ ኣየር *sefer abrar ayer*
cockroach *(n.)* ድዱዕ *diduee'*
cocktail *(n.)* ሕዉስዋስ መስተ *hiwuswas meste*
cocky *(adj.)* ዕቡይ *eebuY;*
cocoa *(n.)* ክእለት *keeileT*
coconut *(n.)* ኮኮናት *coconat*

cocoon *(n.)* ኮኩን *cocoon*
code *(n.)* ምስጢራዊ ፅሑፍ *mesetirawi tsihuf*
co-education *(n.)* ኣወዳትን ኣጓላትን ዝማሃርሉ *awedatin agwalatene zemayarelu*
coefficient *(n.)* ቀዋሚ *qewami*
coerce *(v.)* ኣገደደ *agedded*
coeval *(adj.)* ኣምረሓ *amreha*
coexist *(v.)* ተሳነየ ተስማዕሞያም ነበሩ *tesanY' tesmaemoom neberu*
coexistence *(n.)* ሓቢርካ ምንባር *habireka menebare*
coffee *(n.)* ቡን *bun*
coffer *(n.)* ካዝና *kazina*
coffin *(n.)* ሳፁን ሬሳ *satsun resa*
cog *(n.)* ቅልጣፈ *qiltafe*
cogent *(adj.)* ዘዕግብ *heigib*
cogitate *(v.)* ኣስተንተነ *astentene*
cognate *(adj.)* ተመሳሳሊ *temesasali*
cognizance *(n.)* ግንዛበ *ginizabe*
cohabit *(v.)* ከይተመርዓዉ ሓቢሮም ነበሩ *keyitemerawu habirom neberu*
cohere *(v.)* ተሳነየ *tesaneyei*
coherent *(adj.)* ዝሳነይን ዘእተዋደድን *zisaneyin etewadedin*
cohesion *(n.)* ሓድነት *hadinet*
cohesive *(adj.)* ሓድነት ዝፈጠረ *hadinet zifetere*
coil *(n.)* ዓኹለለ *qkulele*
coin *(n.)* ሳንቲም *sanetime*
coinage *(n.)* ሳንቲም ሰርሐ *sanetime sereha*
coincide *(v.)* ተገጣጠመ *tegetateme*
coincidence *(n.)* ተጓንፎ *tegwanefo*
coir *(n.)* ዓለባ *aleba*
coke *(n.)* ቀፀላይ *qetselayi*
cold *(adj.)* ቆራር *qorare*
colic *(n.)* ቁርፀት ከብዲ *quretset kebedi*
collaborate *(v.)* ተሓባበረ *tehababere*
collaboration *(n.)* ትህብብር *tehibiberi*
collage *(n.)* ናይ ስራሕ ቦታ *nayei serahe bota*
collapse *(v.)* ተደርዓመ *tederame*
collar *(n.)* ኳሌታ *kwaleta*
collate *(v.)* ኣከበ *akebe*
collateral *(n.)* ትሕጃ *tihija*
colleague *(n.)* መሳርሕቲ *mesarḧti*
collect *(v.)* ኣከበ *akebe'*
collection *(n.)* ተዋሕለለ *tewahilwlw*
collective *(adj.)* ተጠራቕመ *teteraqeme*
collector *(n.)* ኣምፀአ *amtseA'*
college *(n.)* ኮሌጅብርኪ ትምህርቲ *co;ege berki temihereti*
collide *(v.)* ተጋጨወ *tegachewe*
colliery *(n.)* ናይ ማዕድን *nayi maeidin*
collision *(n.)* ናይ ምግጫዉ ሓደጋ *nayei megechaw hadega*
colloquial *(adj.)* ናይ ዘረባ *nay zereba*
collusion *(n.)* ምሽጥራዊ ስምምዕ *mishtirawi simemeeh*
cologne *(n.)* ሽቶ *shito*
colon *(n.)* ዓብይ መኣንጣ *abiy meanta*

colonel *(n.)* ኮሎኔል *kolonele*
colonial *(adj.)* ባዕዳዊ *baeedawi*
colony *(n.)* ግዝኣት *gz'at*
colossal *(adj.)* ገዚፍ *gezife*
colossus *(n.)* ሓወልቲ *hawelti*
colour *(n.)* ሕብሪ *hibri*
colouring *(n.)* ፅልዋ ኣሕደረ *tsilwa ahdere*
colourless *(n.)* ዝተሕብረ *zitehibri*
column *(n.)* ዓንዲ *anedi*
coma *(n.)* ሕሊና ምስሓት *hilina mesehate*
comb *(n.)* ሚዶ/መመሸጥ *mido/memesheti*
combat *(n.)* ኹናት *kunaṭ*
combatant *(n)* ተዋጋኢ *tewagaei*
combination *(n.)* ጥማር *timar*
combine *(v.)* ፀንበረ *tsenber*
combustible *(adj.)* ነዳዲ *nedadi*
combustion *(n.)* ተቐፃፃላይ *teqetsatsalaye*
come *(v.)* ናዓ *na'ä*
comedian *(n.)* መስሓቕ *mesḧaq̈*
comedy *(n)* መስሓቕ *mesḧaq̈*
comet *(n.)* ጅራታም ኮኾብ *ĵratam*
comfort *(n.)* ምቾት *mchot*
comfort *(v.)* ጥጣሐ *ẗtaḧe*
comfortable *(adj.)* ምቹእ *mchu'è*
comic *(adj.)* ተዋዛዪ *tewazayi*
comma *(n.)* ጭሕጋር *čḧgar*
command *(v.)* ኣዘዘ *azeze*
commandant *(n.)* ኣዛዚ *azazi*
commander *(n.)* ኮማንደር *komander*
commando *(n.)* ኮማንዶ *komando*
commemorate *(v.)* ኣኽበረ *ak̈bere*
commemoration *(n.)* ዝክር *zkr*
commence *(v.)* ጀመረ *ĵemere*
commencement *(n.)* ምጅማር *mĵmar*
commend *(v.)* ነኣደ *ne'ade*
commendable *(adj.)* ዚነኣድ *zine'ad*
commendation *(n.)* ናእዳ *na'èda*
comment *(n.)* ርእይቶ *r'èyto*
commentary *(n.)* ታዕሊቕ *ta'ëliq̈*
commentator *(n.)* ዓላቒ *älaq̈i*
commerce *(n.)* ንግድ *ngd*
commercial *(adj.)* ንግዳዊ *ngdawi*
commiserate *(v.)* ራህርሀ *rahrhe*
commission *(n.)* ውክልና *wklna*
commissioner *(n.)* ኮሚሽነር *komishner*
commissure *(n.)* መጋጠሚ *megatmi*
commit *(v.)* ፈጸመ *fexeme*
commitment *(n.)* መብጽዓ *mebx'ä*
committee *(n.)* ሽማግለ *shmagle*
commode *(n.)* ተመዛዚ ከብሒ *temezazi kebḧi*
commodity *(n.)* ኣቕሓ *'aq̈ḧa*
common *(adj.)* ሓባራዊ *ḧabarawi*
commoner *(n.)* ሓፋሽ *ḧafash*
commonplace *(adj.)* ልሙድ *lmud*
commonwealth *(n.)* ናይ ሓባር ብልጽግና *nay ḧabar blxgna*
commotion *(n.)* ህውከት *hwket*
communal *(adj.)* ኮማዊ *komawi*
commune *(n.)* ተዋህደ *tewahde*

communicable *(adj.)* ተማሓላለፊ *temaȟalalefi*
communicant *(n.)* ቈራቢ *qWerabi*
communicate *(v.)* ሃበሬታ ተለዋወጠ *habereta*
communication *(n.)* ርክብ *rkb*
communion *(n.)* ምክፋል *mkfal*
communism *(n.)* ዴስነት *deesnet*
community *(n.)* ማሕበረ ሰብ *maȟbere seb*
commute *(v.)* ለወጠ *leweẗe*
compact *(adj.)* ጥርኑፍ *ẗrnuf*
companion *(n.)* ብጻይ *bxay*
company *(n.)* መሰነይታ *meseneyta*
comparative *(adj.)* ተነጻጸሪ *tenexaxeri*
compare *(v.)* ኣነጻጸረ *anexaxere*
comparison *(n.)* ምንጽጻር *mnxxar*
compartment *(n.)* ክፍሊ *kfli*
compass *(n.)* ቡሶላ *busola*
compassion *(n.)* ድንጋጸ *dngaxe*
compatible *(adj.)* ተቓዳዊ *teq̈adawi*
compatriot *(n.)* ወዲ ሃገር *wedi hager*
compel *(v.)* ቀሰ'በ *qesebe*
compendious *(adj.)* ቁንጩል *qunčul*
compendium *(n.)* ቁንጩል *qunčul*
compensate *(v.)* ከሓሰ *keȟase*
compensation *(n.)* ካሕሳ *kaȟsa*
compère *(n.)* ኣላ'ላዪ *alalayi*
compete *(v.)* ተቐዳደመ *teq̈edademe*
competence *(n.)* ክእለት *k'èlet*
competent *(adj.)* ክኢላ *k'ila*
competition *(n.)* ምውድዳር *mwddar*
competitive *(adj.)* ውድድራዊ *wddrawi*
competitor *(n.)* ተዋዳዳሪ *tewadadari*
compile *(v.)* ጠርነፈ *ẗernefe*
complacent *(adj.)* ዕጉብ *ëgub*
complain *(v.)* ተጣርዐ *teẗar'ë*
complaint *(n.)* ዝበልዎ ሕራይ ዝብል *zibeliwo hirayi zibil*
complaisant *(adj.)* ምቕሉል *mq̈lul*
complement *(n.)* መልአ *meleA'*
complementary *(adj.)* መላኢ *mela'i*
complete *(adj.)* ምሉእ *mlu'è*
completion *(n.)* ምፍጻም *mfxam*
complex *(adj.)* ዝተሓላለኸ *zteȟalalek̇e*
complexion *(n.)* ወጅሂ *weĵhi*
complexity *(n.)* ሕልኽልኽ *ȟlk̇lk̇*
compliance *(n.)* እሺታ *èshita*
compliant *(adj.)* ምቕሉል *mq̈lul*
complicate *(v.)* ሓላለኸ *ȟalalek̇e*
complication *(n.)* ሕልኽልኽ *ȟlk̇lk̇*
complicit *(adj.)* ምስ ግበነኛ *mis gibenegna*
complicity *(n.)* ምሽባን *mshban*
compliment *(n.)* ናእዳ *na'èda*
compliment *(v. i)* ናእዳ *na'èda*
comply *(v.)* ተኣዘዘ *te'azeze*
component *(n.)* ክፋል *kifale*
comport *(v.)* ኣኽበረ *ak̇bere*
compose *(v.)* ኣቈመ *aq̈Weme*
composer *(n.)* ደራሲ ወራቢ *derasi werabi*

composite *(adj.)* ዝተዋሃሃደ *ztewahahade*
composition *(n.)* ምድላው *mdlaw*
compositor *(n.)* ለቓም ፊደል *leq̈am fidel*
compost *(n.)* ድኹዒ *dḱu'ï*
composure *(n.)* ቅሳነት *qsanet*
compound *(n.)* ውሁድ *whud*
comprehend *(v.)* ተረድአ *tered'e*
comprehensible *(adj.)* ኪርዳእ ዚከኣል *kirda'è zike'al*
comprehension *(n.)* ምርዳእ *mrda'è*
comprehensive *(adj.)* ኣጠቓላሊ *aẗeq̈alali*
compress *(v.)* ጨበጠ *čebeẗe*
compression *(n.)* ምጭባጥ *mčbaẗ*
comprise *(v.)* ሓዘ *ḧaze*
compromise *(n.)* ግድድፍ *gddf*
compulsion *(n.)* ምግዳ'ድ *mgdad*
compulsive *(adj.)* ግዴታዊ *gdeetawi*
compulsory *(adj.)* ግድነታዊ *gdnetawi*
compunction *(n.)* ስክፍታ *skfta*
computation *(n.)* ምቕማር *mq̈mar*
compute *(v.)* ቈጸረ *qWexere*
computer *(n.)* ኮምፕዩተር *kompyuter*
computerize *(v.)* ኣራጠበ *aratebe*
comrade *(n.)* ብጻይ *bxay*
concatenation *(n.)* ምትእስሳር *mt'èssar*
concave *(adj.)* ሃጓም *hagWam*
conceal *(v.)* ሓብአ *ḧab'e*
concede *(v.)* ኣመነ *amene*
conceit *(n.)* ትዕቢት *t'ëbit*
conceivable *(adj.)* ተኣማኒ *te'amani*
conceive *(v. t)* ተረድአ *tered'e*
concentrate *(v.)* ኣጽዓቐ *ax'äq̈e*
concentration *(n.)* ምጽዓቕ *mx'äq̈*
concept *(n.)* ኣምር *amr*
conception *(n.)* ምእማር *m'èmar*
concern *(v.)* ተመልከተ *temelkete*
concerning *(prep.)* ብዛዕባ *bza'ëba*
concert *(n.)* ሙዚቃዊ ምርኢት *muziqawi mr'it*
concerted *(adj.)* ውሁድ *whud*
concession *(n.)* ሕድገት *ḧdget*
conch *(n.)* ዛዕጎል *za'ëgol*
conciliate *(v.)* ደገፍ ረኸበ *degef reḱebe*
concise *(adj.)* ሓጺርን ብሩህን *ḧaxirn bruhn*
conclude *(n.)* ወድአ *wed'e*
conclusion *(n.)* መወዳእታ *meweda'èta*
conclusive *(adj.)* ደካሊ *dekali*
concoct *(v.)* ኣቃመመ *aqameme*
concoction *(n.)* ፈጠራ *feẗera*
concomitant *(adj.)* መኻይድቲ *meḱaydti*
concord *(n.)* ስምምዕ *smm'ë*
concordance *(n.)* ስምምዕ *smm'ë*
concourse *(n.)* ብሓባር ምኻድ *bḧabar mḱad*
concrete *(n.)* ጭቡጥ *čbuẗ*
concubine *(n.)* ውሽማ *wshma*
concur *(v.)* ተሰማምዐ *tesemam'ë*

concurrent *(adj.)* ተቓዳዊ *teq̈adawi*
concussion *(n.)* መውቃዕቲ *mewqa'ëti*
condemn *(v.)* ኰነነ *kWanene*
condemnation *(n.)* ምኹናን *mḱunan*
condense *(v.)* ሓፈሰ *ḧafese*
condescend *(v.)* ተበርጠጠ *tebertete*
condiment *(n.)* ቀመመ *qememe*
condition *(n.)* ኩነት *kunet*
conditional *(adj.)* ኩነታዊ *kunetawi*
conditioner *(n.)* ኩነታት ጥዕና *kunetate tiena*
condole *(v.)* ደበ'ሰ *debese*
condolence *(n.)* ምጽንናዕ *mxnna'ë*
condom *(n.)* ኮንዶም *condom*
condominium *(n.)* ሓበራዊ መንበሪ ህንፃ *haberawi menberi hintsa*
condone *(v.)* መሓረ *meḧare*
conduct *(n.)* ጠባይ *ẗebay*
conduct *(v.)* ኣደብ *adeb*
conductor *(n.)* መራሒ *meraḧi*
cone *(n.)* ኮኖ *kono*
confection *(n.)* ሕዋስ ምቁራን *ḧwas mquran*
confectioner *(n.)* ናይ ዶልሺ *naydolshi*
confectionery *(n.)* እንዳ-ዶልሺ *èndadolshi*
confederate *(adj.)* ተሓባባሪ *teḧababari*
confederation *(n.)* ማሕበር *maḧber*
confer *(v.)* ዓደለ *ädele*
conference *(n.)* ዘተ *zete*
confess *(v.)* ተናዘዘ *tenazeze*
confession *(n.)* ኑዛዜ *nuzazee*
confidant *(n.)* ኣማኒት *amanit*
confide *(v.)* ምስጢር ኣካፈለ *msẗir 'akafele*
confidence *(n.)* እምነት *èmnet*
confident *(adj.)* ተኣማማኒ *te'amamani*
confidential *(adj.)* ምስጢራዊ *msẗirawi*
configuration *(n.)* ኣሰራርዓ *aserar'ä*
confine *(v.)* ወሰነ *wesene*
confinement *(n.)* ማእሰርቲ *ma'èserti*
confirm *(v.)* ኣረጋገጸ *aregagexe*
confirmation *(n.)* ምርግጋጽ *mrggax*
confiscate *(v.)* ወረሰ *werese*
confiscation *(n.)* ውርሳ *wrsa*
conflate *(v.)* ፀንበረ *tsenbere*
conflict *(n.)* ግጭት *gčt*
confluence *(n.)* መራኽበ *meraḱbo*
confluent *(adj.)* ሓባሪ *ḧabari*
conform *(v.)* ተሰማምዐ *tesemam'ë*
conformity *(n.)* ስምምዕ *smm'ë*
confront *(v.)* ተጋተረ *tegatere*
confrontation *(n.)* ቅርሕንቲ *kiri hinti*
confuse *(v.)* ኣደናገረ *adenagere*
confusion *(n.)* ዕግርግር *ëgrgr*
confute *(v.)* ረትዐ *ret'ë*
congenial *(adj.)* ዚወሃሃድ *ziwehahad*
congenital *(adj.)* ውርሻዊ *wrshawi*

congested ***(adj.)*** **ቅጽጽ ዝበለ** *qxx zbele*
congestion ***(n.)*** **ጸዕቂ** *xa'ëqi*
conglomerate ***(n.)*** **ኣኻኸበ** *aḱaḱebe*
conglomeration ***(n.)*** **እኽብካብ** *èḱbkab*
congratulate ***(v.)*** **እንቋዕ ኣሓጐሰካ በለ** *ènqWA'ë 'aḧagWaseka bele*
congratulation ***(n.)*** **መግለጺ ሓጐስ** *meglexi ḧagWas*
congregate ***(v.)*** **ተኣከበ** *te'akebe*
congress ***(n.)*** **ጉባኤ** *guba'ee*
congruent ***(adj.)*** **ዝስማዕማዕ** *zismaemae tsemaexmeaa*
conical ***(adj.)*** **ተሰስማዕመዐ** *tsemaexmeaa*
conjecture ***(n. &v.)*** **ግምታዊ ሓሳብ** *gemetawi hasabe*
conjugal ***(v.t. & i.)*** **መወስቦኣዊ** *mewesbo'awi*
conjugate ***(v.)*** **ግጥሚ ኣንበበ** *geTemi anebbb*
conjunct ***(adj.)*** **መስተፃምር** *,mestetsamire*
conjunction ***(n.)*** **ጠራፊ መሳርዕ** *Terafi ms*
conjunctivitis ***(n.)*** **ናይ ቁስለት ዓይኒ** *nay'l qusele't aa'yeni*
conjuncture ***(n.)*** **ዋኒን/ጉዳይ** *maniein/guda'yi*
conjure ***(v.)*** **ምትሃተኛ** *meteha'te'gna*
conker ***(n.)*** **ኮራዕ** *kora'ee*
connect ***(v.)*** **ኣራኸበ** *aara'EH'kebe*
connection ***(n.)*** **ርክብ** *re'KE'be*
connive ***(v.)*** **ተመሻጠረ** *temeSHA'tere*
conquer ***(v.)*** **ወረረ** *were're*
conquest ***(n.)*** **ወረራ** *we're'ra*
conscience ***(n.)*** **ሕሊና** *hi'lina*
conscious ***(adj.)*** **ግንዛበ ዘለዎ** *giniza'be zelewo*
consecrate ***(v.)*** **ቀደሰ** *qede'se*
consecutive ***(adj.)*** **ተኸታታሊ** *teHE'tata'li*
consecutively ***(adv.)*** **ዝተሓተ** *zi'te'hat'ee*
consensus ***(n.)*** **ሓበራዊ ምርድዳእ** *haberawi merederaoo*
consent ***(v.t.)*** **ስምምዕ** *se'memeee*
consent ***(n.)*** **ፍቓድ** *feqa'de*
consequence ***(n.)*** **ሳዕቤን** *saee'bene*
consequent ***(adj.)*** **ውፅኢት** *wutsieiit*
conservation ***(n.)*** **ሓለዋ ተፈጥሮ** *haalewa tefetero*
conservative ***(adj.)*** **ፀረ ለዉጢ** *tsere lewuti*
conservatory ***(n.)*** **ሰርዐ** *sereaa'*
conserve ***(v. t)*** **ብቑጠባ ተጠቐመ** *b'quteba te'teqe'mu*
consider ***(v.)*** **ኣስተንተነ** *aa' seten'tene*
considerable ***(adj.)*** **ብዙሕ** *bezuHi'h*
considerate ***(adj.)*** **ሓሳቢ** *ha'sabi*
consideration ***(n.)*** **ኣብ ግምት ኣእተወ** *hab' gimit aaetewe*
considering ***(prep.)*** **ኣተኩሩ ረኣየ** *aa' tekuru rexayee*
consign ***(v.)*** **ሰንደወ** *senedwwe*

consignment *(n.)* ዝተለኣኹ ኣቑሑት *zetelezaaHu aaqkuhut*
consist *(v.)* ኣካተተ *aakate'te*
consistency *(n.)* ተኸታታሊ *te'KHE'tatali*
consistent *(adj.)* ዘይቕየር *zey'qeyer*
consolation *(n.)* መፅናዕንዒ *mexenaee'neeeii*
console *(v. t.)* ኣፀናንዐ *a'txennea*
consolidate *(v.)* ኣሐየለ *ahayl'e*
consolidation *(n.)* ፀንበረ *xeneber*
consonant *(n.)* ስምምዕ *sememe'*
consort *(n.)* ሰብኣይ ንግስቲ *sebeaayi negeseti*
consortium *(n.)* ኮንሰርትዮም *konsertyom*
conspicuous *(adj.)* ብቐሊሉ ዝረኣይ *beqlilu zereaayii*
conspiracy *(n.)* ሻራ *shara*
conspirator *(n.)* ዉዲት *wudit*
conspire *(v.)* ተመሻጠረ *temeshatere*
constable *(n.)* ኮንስታብል *konstablee*
constabulary *(n.)* ኮንስታብል ሰብነት *konstable sebenet'*
constant *(adj.)* ዘየቋርፅ *zeye'qereXe'*
constellation *(n.)* ናይ ከዋኽብቲ *naye kKe'wakib'ti*
consternation *(n.)* ድንጋፀ *denegaXE'*
constipation *(n.)* ድርቀት *dere'qe'T*
constituency *(n.)* ክፋል *kefale*
constituent *(adj.)* ኣድማፂ *adma'txi*
constitute *(v.)* ተሓሰበ *teha'sebe*
constitution *(n.)* ሕገ መንግስቲ *hige mengistii*
constitutional *(adj.)* ቅዋማዊ *qwamawi*
constrain *(v.)* ኣጋደደ *aagadede*
constraint *(n.)* ገደብ *gedbb*
constrict *(v.)* ኣፅበበ *axebebbe'*
construct *(v.)* ሃነፀ *hanXE'*
construction *(n.)* ህንፀት *hintsxet'*
constructive *(adj.)* ሃናፂ *hanatxi'*
construe *(v.)* ተረደአ *teredeA'*
consul *(n.)* ቆንስል *qonesele*
consular *(n.)* ቆንፅላ *qonexela*
consulate *(n.)* ናይቆንስል ገዛ *nayi qonsele geza*
consult *(v.)* ኣማኸረ *aAmaHe're*
consultant *(n.)* ኣማኻሪ *amaHa'ri*
consultation *(n.)* ተመማኻኸረ *temeHaHere'*
consume *(v.)* ተመቓመ *temeQeme'*
consumer *(n.)* ሸማቲ *shemati*
consummate *(v.)* ምሉ'እ *mlu'è*
consumption *(n.)* ምጥቓም *miT; Qqam'*
contact *(n.)* ርክብ *rikib*
contagion *(n.)* ምልጋብ *milgab*
contagious *(adj.)* ተላጋቢ *telagabi*
contain *(v.t.)* ሓዘ *haze'*
container *(n.)* ኮንቴነር *konte'ner*
containment *(n.)* ምዕጋት *meegat*
contaminate *(v.)* በከለ *bekele*
contemplate *(v.)* ሓሰበ *haseb*

contemplation *(n.)* ኣትኹሩ ረኣየ *xteKuru reAaye'*
contemporary *(adj.)* እዋናዊ *eewanawi*
contempt *(n.)* ንዕቐት *neeeiqet*
contemptuous *(adj.)* ሸለልታ *shelelta*
contend *(v.)* ተኸራኸረ *teHerakere*
content *(adj.)* ዝዓገበ *zea'gebe*
content *(n.)* ትሕዝቶ *tihizeto*
contention *(n.)* ቅርሕንቲ *kqir'hinti*
contentious *(adj.)* ዘቀሓሕር *zeqkeha'hir*
contentment *(n.)* ዕግበት *qeig'bet*
contest *(n.)* ዉድድር *wudi'dir*
contestant *(n.)* ተወዳዳሪ *te'we'dada'Rei*
context *(n.)* ሃዋህው *hawahewu'*
contiguous *(adj.)* ጥቓንጥቓ *tQAneTeQA'*
continent *(n.)* ክፍለ አለም *kefele ale'm*
continental *(adj.)* ክፍለ አለማዊ *kefele alemawii*
contingency *(n.)* ወዝቢ *wezbi*
continual *(adj.)* ተደጋጋሚ *tedegagami*
continuation *(n.)* ተደጋጋሚ *tedegagami*
continue *(v.)* ቀፀለ *qeTsele'*
continuity *(n.)* ዝተቐፃፀለ *zeteqaTsaTse'le*
continuous *(adj.)* ቀፃላይ *qetsetay*
contort *(v.)* እስርስር በለ *esir'sir bele*
contour *(n.)* ወሰናወሰን *wesena'wesen*
contra *(prep.)* ምፅባዕ *mitsbaee*
contraband *(n.)* ኮንትሮባንድ *kontroband*
contraception *(n.)* ምክልኻል ጥንሲ *meihil'hal tinsi*
contraceptive *(n.)* መከላኸሊ ጥንሲ *mekelaḱeli ẗnsi*
contract *(n.)* ናይ ዉዕሊ *nayei wueili'*
contract *(n)* ውዕል *w'ël*
contraction *(n.)* ኣሕፀረ *had'e*
contractor *(n.)* ተኾናታሪ *awarede*
contractual *(adj.)* ዉዕሊ ፈፀመ *raḧreḧe*
contradict *(v.)* ተፃበአ *ztegedfe*
contradiction *(n.)* ተፃረረ *gedam*
contrary *(adj.)* ተቓራኒ *abegedam*
contrast *(n.)* ኣፈላላይ *mḧxar*
contravene *(v.)* ሕጊ ጠሓሰ *werede*
contribute *(v.)* ኣዋፅአ *mwrad*
contribution *(n.)* ወፈየ *neq̈ele*
contrivance *(n.)* ኢ-ተኣማኒነት *ḧamed*
contrive *(v.)* ገበረ *kebdi*
control *(n.)* ቁፅፅር *nay kebdi*
controller *(n.)* ተቖፃፃሪ *zerefe*
controversial *(adj.)* ኣከራኻሪ *zerefe*
controversy *(n.)* ኽርክር *mzbul*
contusion *(n.)* ስምብራት *sḧtan*
conundrum *(v. t)* ሽግር *adefafere*
conurbation *(n.)* ምኽታ'ም *mḱtam*

convene *(v.)* **ኣኼባ ፀወዐ** *fenfene*
convenience *(n.)* **ምቾት** *krhat*
convenient *(adj.)* **ምችዊ** *kruh*
convent *(n.)* **ናይ ደናግል ገዳም** *xen'ë*
convention *(n.)* **ባህሊ/ልምዲ** *zeywda'è gedam*
converge *(v.)* **ተኣኻኸበ** *'äq̈mi*
conversant *(adj.)* **ፍልጠት ዘለዎ** *ḧrtum zelwo*
conversation *(n.)* **ወግዒ** *meḧale*
converse *(v.)* **ኣዋግዐ** *lbu'ë*
conversion *(n.)* **ምቕያር** *nfu'ë bq̈u'ë*
convert *(n.)* **ቀየረ** *me'änaẗu*
convert *(v.)* **ተቐየረ** *mzbul*
convey *(v.)* **ገለፀ** *'ab l'ëli*
conveyance *(n.)* **አጓጓዘ** *geza*
convict *(n.)* **ገበነኛ** *'aẗfe'e*
convict *(v.)* **ገበነኛ እዩ በለ** *mïfa'è bele eyik*
conviction *(n.)* **ገበነኝነት** *zixla'è*
convince *(v.)* **ኣእመነ** *xel'e*
convivial *(adj.)* **ምሑእ/ደስ ዝብል** *ẗntawi*
convocation *(n.)* **ኣኼባ** *tewegre*
convoy *(n.)* **ተዓጂበን ብሓባር ዝኸዳ** *mwgad*
convulse *(n.)* **ኣንቀጥቀጠ** *wgur*
convulsion *(n.)* **ምንቅጥቃጥ** *fedfede*
cook *(n.)* **ከሻኒ** *bza'ëba*
cook *(v.)* **ኣብሰለ** *'ab zurya*
cooker *(n.)* **ዘበናዊ እቶን** *'ab l'ëli*
cookie *(n.)* **ኬክ** *bzyada*
cool *(adj.)* **ዝሑል** *lḧlaḧe*
coolant *(n.)* **ዛሕሊ** *faḧfaḧi*
cooler *(n.)* **ዝሕልቱ** *godnegodni*
cooper *(n.)* **ምሕዳስ** *aḧxere*
cooperate *(v.)* **ተሓባበረ** *wexa'i*
cooperation *(n.)* **ትሕብብር** *sereze*
cooperative *(adj.)* **ተሓጋገዘ** *handebetawi*
coordinate *(v. t)* **ኣተሓባበረ** *ḧagel*
coordination *(n.)* **ሓቢሩ ከደ** *xeleq̈Wu*
cope *(v.)* **ተፃወረ** *bkurat*
copier *(n.)* **ብማሽን ዝተገልበጠ ቅዳሕ** *bḱur*
copious *(adj.)* **ኣዝዩ ብዙሕ** *bḱur*
copper *(n.)* **መዳብ** *fxum*
copulate *(v.)* **ሰረረ** *sreet*
copy *(n.)* **ቅዳሕ** *meḧare*
copy *(v.)* **ናይ ሓንቲ ሓባ** *seteye*
coral *(n.)* **ደረቕ ተሪር** *teq̈eẗebe*
cord *(n.)* **ፍሕሶ** *zahdi*
cordial *(adj.)* **ልባዊ** *req̈iq̈*
cordon *(n.)* **ዝተስለፉ ፖላይስ** *ẗluq̈*
core *(n.)* **ወዉሽጣዊ ኣካ** *trgum 'albo*
coriander *(n.)* **ተኽሊ ቅመቃ ቕመም** *trgum 'albonet*
cork *(n.)* **ኮረኪ** *ml'at*
corn *(n.)* **ሱማ** *fdfud*
cornea *(n.)* **ፃዕዳ አይኒ** *ämexe*
corner *(n.)* **ኹርናዕ** *texarafi*
cornet *(n.)* **ዘዛንሙሎ** *tedawebe*
coronation *(n.)* **ስርዓተ ንግስና** *delhametawi*
coroner *(n.)* **መርማሪ** *delhamet*
coronet *(n.)* **ኣኽሊል** *akademiyawi*
corporal *(n.)* **ኣካላዊ** *akademi*
corporate *(adj.)* **ዓብይ** *mexe*
corporation *(n.)* **ዓብይ ትካል ንግዲ** *nehare*

corps *(n.)* ብርጌድ *anhari*
corpse *(n.)* ሬሳ *mgulaḧ*
corpulent *(adj.)* ሃዝራጥ *aguleḧe*
correct *(adj.)* ልክዕ *teq̈ebele*
correct *(v.)* ኣረመ *teq̈ebalnet zelewo*
correction *(n.)* እርማት *qbale*
corrective *(adj.)* መቕፃዕቲ *me'ètewi*
correlate *(v.)* ተዛመደ *kirkeb zike'al*
correlation *(n.)* ዝምድና *bxḧat*
correspond *(v.)* ተመሳሰለ *mesarḧi*
correspondence *(n.)* ስምምዕ *smm'ë*
correspondent *(n.)* ፀብፃቢ *nay ḧadega*
corridor *(n.)* ናይ ህንፃ መተሓላለፊ *ačebčebe*
corroborate *(v.)* መረዳእታ ኣቕረበ *a'ënewe*
corrode *(v.)* ኣበላሸወ *selamta*
corrosion *(n.)* መበላሸቲ *tesemam'ë*
corrosive *(adj.)* ዝጎድእ *me'ëref 'agaysh*
corrugated *(adj.)* ዕፅፍፃፍ *meseneyti*
corrupt *(adj.)* ግዕዙይ *äĵebe*
corrupt *(n.)* ጋዕዞየ *gbre'aber*
corruption *(n.)* ግዕይዝና *fexeme*
cortisone *(n.)* ኮርቲሶን *k'ila*
cosmetic *(adj.)* መፀባበቒ *fxamee*
cosmetic *(n.)* መፀባበቂ ቕብኣት *w'ël*
cosmic *(adj.)* ምስ ሃዋህዉ *tewhdo*
cosmology *(n.)* ጠፈር ዝተዛመደ *bmeseret*
cosmopolitan *(adj.)* ቆዝሞፖሊታዊ *qozmopolitawi*
cosmos *(n.)* ሃዋህዉ *gWanefe*
cost *(v.)* ዋጋ ኣዉፃኢ *ḧsab*
costly *(adj.)* ክቡር *teḧatati*
costume *(n.)* ክዳን ሰበይቲ *kdan sebeyti*
cosy *(adj.)* ምዉቕን ምቹዊን *sneẗebib*
cosy *(adj.)* ምዉቕን ምቹዊን *texebaxabi*
cot *(n.)* ዓራት ቆልዓ *bweg'ï le'ak̍e*
cottage *(n.)* ጐጆ *bweg'ï le'ak̍e*
cotton *(n.)* ተኽሊ ጡጥ *weg'äwi*
couch *(n.)* ወንበር *ëbyet*
couchette *(n.)* ዝዝርጋሕ ዓራት *delebe*
cough *(v.)* ሰዓለ *awahlele*
council *(n.)* ቤት ምኽሪ *whlela*
councillor *(n.)* ኣባል ቤት ምኽሪ *lk'ë*
counsel *(n.)* ምኽሪ/ማዕዳ *gzi*
counsel *(v.)* ኣማኸረ *kesese*
counsellor *(n.)* ጠበቃ *teḧatatnet*
count *(v.)* ቆፀረ *lemede*
countenance *(n.)* ገፅ ሰብ *lmud*
counter *(n.)* ባንኮኒ *ḧade*
counter *(v.t.)* መልሲ ሃበ *arebik*
counteract *(v.)* ተጻረረ *texarere*
counterfeit *(adj.)* ተመሳሰሲሉ ዝተሰርሐ *netagWi*
counterfoil *(n.)* ቅዳሕ ቅብሊት *qdaḧ qblit*
countermand *(v.)* ትእዛዝ ለወጠ *tegonaxefe*
counterpart *(n.)* መዘና *fxamee*

countless *(adj.)* **መዓት/ማእለያ ሀይብሉ** *mexix*
country *(n.)* **ሃገር/ዓዲ** *mečqWAr*
county *(n.)* **መዲና** *amesgene*
coup *(n.)* **ዕልዋ መንግስቲ** *mq̈xal*
coupe *(n.)* **ሽሓነ** *čaf*
couple *(n.)* **ፅምዲ/ክልተ** *ënfrur*
couplet *(n.)* **ዉሑዳት** *anagonsẗees*
coupon *(n.)* **ኩፖን** *fre 'ok nay ḧade 'ok zisme gereb fre*
courage *(n.)* **ጅግንነት** *ms msma'ë zte'asasere*
courageous *(adj.)* **ጅግና** *afaleẗe*
courier *(n.)* **ኣቒሑ ዘብፅሕ ሰብ** *leela*
course *(n.)* **ዓይነት ትምህርቲ** *tesemam'e*
court *(n.)* **ቤት ፍርዲ/መጋባእያ** *msmma'e*
courteous *(adj.)* **ምእዙዝ** *reḱebe*
courtesan *(n.)* **ፋይቶት** *qsmet*
courtesy *(n.)* **ትሕትና** *fetḧe*
courtier *(n.)* **ተቐባሊ ጋሻ** *naxa mlqaq̈*
courtly *(adj.)* **ኣዝዩ ምእዙዝ** *akr*
courtship *(n.)* **ኣርገፀ/ጀነጀነ** *bedan*
courtyard *(n.)* **ካንሸሎ** *mret*
cousin *(n.)* **ወዲኣኮ/ወዲሓዉቦ** *akrobat*
cove *(n.)* **ዕረፍቲ** *bariton*
covenant *(n.)* **ቃል ኪዳን** *sgr*
cover *(n.)* **መሸፈኒ** *zer'ëd*
cover *(v.)* **ሸፈነ/ከወለ** *mgbar*
covert *(adj.)* **ሕቡእ/ምሽጢራዊ** *gzeeyawi fexami*
covet *(v.)* **ተሃቀወ** *mwsa'è*
cow *(n.)* **ላሕሚ** *zefrh*
coward *(n.)* **ጃጃዊ** *mgbar*
cowardice *(n.)* **ፍርሓት** *'ab ḧgawi mesrḧ ze'ètu*
cower *(v.)* **ተጎንበሓ** *anẗefe*
coy *(adj.)* **ሓፋር** *nẗuf*
crab *(n.)* **ሽርጣን** *nẗfet*
crack *(n.)* **ነቓዕ/ጭዳድ** *tewanay*
crack *(v.)* **ነቐዐ/ጨደደ** *tewasa'it*
cracker *(n.)* **ብሽኩቲ** *hluw*
crackle *(v.)* **ጠራዕራዕ ዝብል ደምፂ** *bḧaqi*
cradle *(n.)* **ዓራት ህፃን** *gemgami*
craft *(n.)* **እደጥበብ** *anẗefe*
craftsman *(n.)* **ጥበበኛ** *tkurna*
crafty *(adj.)* **ለመጭ** *meridyan*
cram *(v.)* **ጠቕጠቐ** *nsur*
cramp *(n.)* **ስትራፖ** *terir*
crane *(n.)* **ሰፍሳፊት** *alzebe*
crank *(v.)* **ዘወረ** *mwhhad*
crash *(v.)* **ተጋጨወ** *demere*
crass *(adj.)* **ተቐባልነት ዘይብሉ** *memela'èta*
crate *(n.)* **ካሳ/ናይ ጥርሙዝ ሳንዱቕ** *tewelefe*
cravat *(n.)* **ክራባት** *mwlaf*
crave *(v. t)* **ተሃንቀወ/ሃረር በለ** *welfi*
craven *(adj.)* **ፈራሕ/ጃጃዊ** *mdmar*
crawl *(v.)* **ታተ በለ** *tewesaḱi*
crayon *(n.)* **ሕብሪ/ኩሩሽ** *äqabi*
craze *(n.)* **ዝምነዉ ድልየት** *dngur*
crazy *(adj.)* **ዓንጃል/ሃላይ** *adrasha*
creak *(n.)* **ፂፅ በለ** *teq̈ebali 'èti 'adrasha'u ztexaḧfe seb*
creak *(v.)* **ፂፅ ዝብል ድምፂ** *ẗeq̈ese*
cream *(n.)* **ላህመት/ላመት** *k'ila*

crease *(n.)* **ሽምራር** *èḱulnet*
create *(v.)* **ፈጠረ/ሰርሐ** *èḱul*
creation *(n.)* **ምፍጣር** *se'äbe*
creative *(adj.)* **መሃዛይ** *mdgaf*
creator *(n.)* **ፈጣሪ** *lagabi*
creature *(n.)* **ፍጥረት** *deḧan kun*
crèche *(n.)* **መዉዓሊ ህፃናት** *gWarebeet*
credentials *(n.)* **ብቕዓት፤ ስልጠናን ተመክሮን** *qxl*
credible *(adj.)* **እሙን** *texeg'ë 'ab gWadni kone*
credit *(n.)* **ኣዉድ** *aqWArexe*
creditable *(adj.)* **ተኣማኒነት** *ameḧalalefe*
creditor *(n.)* **ኣወፋይ** *beyene*
credulity *(adv.)* **ናይ ምእማን ክእለት/ድልየት** *ferede*
creed *(n.)* **እምነት** *ïbqo*
creek *(n.)* **ፍሰት** *ame'ärareye*
creep *(v.)* **መሎቑ** *mwdad*
creeper *(n.)* **ሓረግ** *ameḧadere*
cremate *(v.)* **ሬሳ ኣቃፀለ** *mmḧdar*
cremation *(n.)* **ሬሳ ማቃፀል** *mmḧdarawi*
crematorium *(n.)* **ሬሳ ኣቃፀለ ቦታ/ከባቢ** *ameḧadari*
crescent *(n.)* **ሓዳሽ ናይ ዝተወለደት ወርሒ ቅርፂ** *zine'ad*
crest *(n.)* **ወሳናይ/ዘሐጉስ** *admiral*
crew *(n.)* **ሓቢሮም ዝሰርሑ ኪኢላታት** *adnaq̈ot*
crib *(n.)* **ዓራ ቆልዓ** *adneq̈e*
cricket *(n.)* **ክሪኬት** *zifqed*
crime *(n.)* **ገበን** *qbela*
criminal *(n.)* **ገበነኛ** *te'amene*
criminology *(n.)* **ናይ ገበነኛ መፅናዕቲ** *qbela*
crimson *(n.)* **ቀይሕ** *gesexe*
cringe *(v.)* **ሸለገ** *sheq̈elqel*
cripple *(n.)* **ልሙስ ሰብ** *ẗreḧẗub*
crisis *(n.)* **ቅልዉላዉ** *bxḧna*
crisp *(adj.)* **ተሪርን ነቓፅን** *bexḧi*
criterion *(n.)* **ረቋሕ መለክዒ** *wesede*
critic *(n.)* **ናይ መፅሓፍ ተዋስኦ/ገምጋሚ** *mr'äm*
critical *(adj.)* **ነቓፊ** *re'ämi*
criticism *(n.)* **ነቐፌታ** *tefetawi*
criticize *(v.)* **ነቐፈ** *fq̈ri*
critique *(n.)* **ነቓፊ ዝኾነ ሰብ** *amleḱe*
croak *(n.)* **ብኽያት** *asewene*
crochet *(n.)* **ኹረሽ** *falul*
crockery *(n.)* **ብልቃጥ ስራ** *čele*
crocodile *(n.)* **ሓርገፀ** *adserb*
croissant *(n.)* **ኩራሳ** *wdasekentu*
crook *(n.)* **መልቲ** *èḱul*
crooked *(adj.)* **ቄባዕ** *ameraseḧe*
crop *(n.)* **ዘራእቲ** *mmrsaḧ*
cross *(n.)* **መስቀል** *zmut*
crossing *(n.)* **ተሳገረ/ሓለፈ** *segWame*
crotchet *(n.)* **ቀራጺቶ** *le'äle*
crouch *(v.)* **ተኾደመ/ተኾደጨ** *mm'ëbal*
crow *(n.)* **ንቅዋ** *blča*
crowd *(n.)* **ዝተኣከቡ ሰባት** *rebḧa*
crown *(n.)* **ኣኽሊል** *ẗeq̈ami*
crown *(v.)* **ኣንገሰ** *mx'at*
crucial *(adj.)* **ኣዝዩ ወሳናይ** *ëndera*
crude *(adj.)* **ሓፈሻዊ** *ḧadegeḧa*
cruel *(adj.)* **ጨካን** *tewesakegsi*

cruelty *(adv.)* ጭካነ *texay*
cruise *(v.)* ብመርከብ ተጓጓዓዘ *alutawi*
cruiser *(n.)* መርከብ *shgr*
crumb *(n.)* ቁራስ ባኒ/ፓስተ *afaleẗe*
crumble *(v.)* ቆረሰ/መቖለ *reklam*
crumple *(v.)* ዓምጠረ/ሓምተለ *m'ëdo*
crunch *(v.)* ፀገም *zḧashe*
crusade *(n.)* ቃልሲ/ተጋድሎ *me'äde*
crush *(v.)* ፀቐጠ/ዓምጠረ *degafi*
crust *(n.)* ላዕለዋይ *teḧalaq̈i*
crutch *(n.)* ምርኩስ *üq̈ba*
crux *(n.)* አዉራ ሽግር/ዋኒን *sefafi*
cry *(n.)* ብኽያት *ayun*
cry *(v.)* በኸየ *ayrobatiks*
crypt *(n.)* ሕቡእ *mariwana*
crystal *(n.)* ዓካር *me'ärfo neferti*
cub *(n.)* ኩርኩር ኣንበሳ *snemnfar*
cube *(n.)* ኪዩብ *ayroplan*
cubical *(adj.)* ኪዩቢካል *flit*
cubicle *(n.)* ዝተኸፈለ ፀቢብ ክፍሊ *nay neferti*
cuckold *(n.)* ሰብኣይ *xbaq̈e'awi*
cuckoo *(n.)* ዒፍ/ርግቢት *snexbaq̈e*
cucumber *(n.)* ዝኩኒ *kab rḧuq̈*
cuddle *(v.)* ሓቖፈ *fḧshuw*
cuddly *(adj.)* ምሕቛፍ *fxamee*
cudgel *(n.)* ጎመድ *xelewe*
cue *(n.)* ፍንጪ *msluynet*
cuff *(n.)* ታሕተዋይ ክፋል እጅገ *amsali*
cuisine *(n.)* ኣከሻሽና ፀብሒ/ምግቢ *ftwet*
culinary *(adj.)* ለኸተተ *rhruh*
culminate *(v.)* ዛዘመ *qalemaḧla*
culpable *(adj.)* ዝኾነን *texeg'ë*
culprit *(n.)* ገበነኛ ሰብ *mxga'ë*
cult *(n.)* ዉሩይ/ፍሉጥ *temaslo*
cultivate *(v.)* ሓረሰ *aregagexe*
cultural *(adj.)* ባህላዊ *mrggax*
culture *(n.)* ባህሊ *awentawi*
cumbersome *(adj.)* ኣዝዩ ረዚን *lqabe*
cumin *(n.)* ተኽሊ *gWad'e*
cumulative *(adj.)* በብእዋኑ ዝዉስኽ *čnqi*
cunning *(adj.)* ተበላፂ/መታለሊ *habti*
cup *(n.)* ኩባያ *habtam*
cupboard *(n.)* ጣዉላ *atek̇ak̇ele*
cupidity *(n.)* ስስዐ *mgrab*
curable *(adj.)* ዝሓዊ/ዝፍወስ *na'ëbi*
curative *(adj.)* ኣረጋግአ *zelefe*
curator *(n.)* ኣመሓዳሪ *'ab rḧuq̈*
curb *(v. t)* ተቖፃፀረ/ዓገተ *zteq̈axele*
curd *(n.)* ኣጅቦ *zensaff*
cure *(v. t.)* ኣሕወጠ/ፈወሰ *'ab mqrrab*
curfew *(n.)* ሕላፍ ሰዓት *zferhe*
curiosity *(n.)* ሃንቀዉታ ፍልጠት *kem bḧadsh*
curious *(adj.)* ንምፍላጥ ዝህንቀው *afriqa*
curl *(v.)* ተዓኹለለ *'ab ritemerkeb*
currant *(n.)* ዘቢብ *dḧri*
currency *(n.)* ገንዘብ *dḧre*
current *(adj.)* ናይ ሕጂ/ሎሚ *dḧri*
current *(n.)* ምንቅስቓስ ባሕሪ/ዉሕጅ *'èndegena*
curriculum *(n.)* ስርዓተ ትምህርቲ *anxar*
curry *(n.)* ሕሩጭ *terir kbur 'èmni*

curse *(n.)* መርገም *ëdme*
cursive *(adj.)* ናይ ኢድ ፅሑፍ *shmagletat*
cursor *(n.)* ሽተት ኣበለ *qdmefrdi*
cursory *(adj.)* ብህፁፅ ዝተሰርሓ *zel'alemawi*
curt *(adj.)* ሓጺር *nay wklna tkal*
curtail *(v.)* ዓገተ *aĵenda*
curtain *(n.)* መጋረጃ *glul*
curve *(n.)* ጎባጥ *akebe*
cushion *(n.)* መተርኣስ/መኸዳ *agdede*
custard *(n.)* መወራረዲ ምቁር ምግቢ *zeq̈uẗ'ë*
custodian *(n.)* ኣበብ ቀይዲ ምዉዕል ሰብ *demere*
custody *(n.)* ቅዳሕ ቅብሊት *qdaḧ qblit*
custom *(n.)* ባህሊ *ämaxi*
customary *(adj.)* ልሙድ *aẗqa'ï*
customer *(n.)* ዓሚል *aq̈eyeme*
customize *(v.)* ለዉጢ ገበረ *zsembede*
cut *(v.)* ሓረድ/ተለዘ *sluẗ*
cute *(adj.)* ዉቅብቲ *soprano*
cutlet *(n.)* ፍረ ነገር *qesqese*
cutter *(n.)* ምቕምቃም *mḱWas*
cutting *(n.)* ቁራፀ *ifeliẗawi*
cyan *(n.)* ሲያን *ygebr'abilu yḱewn*
cyanide *(n.)* ሲያናይድ *rbux*
cyber *(comb.)* ሳይበር *haweḱe*
cyberspace *(n.)* ሳይበርስፔስ *merir ḧazen*
cycle *(n.)* ብሽክሌታ *mereetawi*
cyclic *(adj.)* ዑደት *tesemam'ë*
cyclist *(n.)* ቱግቱግ ሰብ *zisemama'ë*
cyclone *(n.)* ኣባኸበራ *smm'ë*
cylinder *(n.)* ሲሊንደር *ḧrshawi*
cynic *(n.)* ተጠራጣሪ ሰብ *ḧrsha*
cynosure *(n.)* መስሕብ *'ab bayta*
cypress *(n.)* ተኽሊ *'ab qdmi*
cyst *(n.)* ማይ ዝማያገ ሕብጠት *red'e*
cystic *(adj.)* ፍሕኛ *degafi*

D

dab *(v.)* ለኸየ *ačeneq̈e*
dabble *(v.)* ተሳተፈ *ačeneq̈e'i*
dacoit *(n.)* ገበነኛ *ḧmam*
dad *(n)* ኣቦ *ëlama*
daffodil *(n.)* ተኽሊ *shto*
daft *(adj.)* ዓንጃል *seḧate*
dagger *(n.)* ሰንጢ *ayer*
daily *(adj.)* ዕለታዊ *nefarit*
dainty *(adj.)* ንእሽተይን ማራኺን *nefasha*
dairy *(n.)* ምፍራይ ፀባ *korideyo*
dais *(n.)* ኣትራኖስ *ztegeftene*
daisy *(n.)* ኣትራኖሳዊ *zizamed*
dale *(n.)* ሽንጥሮ *sluẗ*
dalliance *(n.)* ኣዕጠይጠየ *meẗenqeq̈ta*
dally *(v.)* ቀሰይ ኢሉ ሰርሐ *qrubnet*
dam *(n.)* ሓፀቢ *sg'at*
damage *(n.)* መጉዳእቲ *way 'ane*
dame *(n.)* ሰበይቲ *shḧkWa*
damn *(v.)* ኮነነ *'album*
damnable *(adj.)* ተኮናኚ *albumen*
damnation *(n.)* ኩነኔ *alkemi*
damp *(adj.)* ርሑስ/ትርኩስ *alkol*
dampen *(v.)* ኣጠልቀየ *setay*
damper *(n.)* ጠየቀ *sbsab*
dampness *(n.)* ኣዛሕተለ *'ayl'äynet bira*

damsel *(n.)* ዘይተመርዓወት ጓል *ïnquq̈*
dance *(v.)* ሳዕሰዐ *alǰebra*
dancer *(n.)* መምስዕሳዕ ሰብ *sagWa*
dandelion *(v.)* ተኽሊ *lwïesm*
dandle *(v.)* ኣሰራሰረ *aserasere*
dandruff *(n.)* ፎረፎር *mewx'inefsi*
dandy *(n.)* ስብቁል *sbqul*
danger *(n.)* ሓደጋ *zinedd*
dangerous *(adj.)* ሓደገኛ *ser'ë*
dangle *(v. i.)* ዓነጠልጠለ *asalalfa*
dank *(adj.)* ርሑስን ቆራርን *temesasali*
dapper *(adj.)* ፅፉፍ *kflit ftḧ*
dapple *(v.)* ዕንፍሩር *hyaw*
dare *(v.)* ደፈረ/ተብዐ *alkali*
daring *(adj.)* ጅግና/ደፋር *kulu*
dark *(adj.)* ዝፀልመተ *afakWase*
darken *(v.)* ፀልመተ *ale*
darkness *(n.)* ፀልማት *bhlo*
darling *(n.)* መዓረይ *te'amannet*
darn *(v.)* ለገበ *mslee'awi zanta*
dart *(n.)* ቀስቲ *aḧreq̈e*
dash *(v.)* ሸዉ ምበል *teq̈oẗa'ï*
dashboard *(n.)* ጣዉላ *quẗ'ë*
dashing *(adj.)* ፅቡቕ *afaḱWase*
dastardly *(adj.)* ፈራሕ *mq̈lal*
data *(n.)* ሓበሬታ *meshgWaragur*
database *(n.)* ሓበሬታ *kidan*
date *(n.)* ዕለት *texeg'ë*
date *(n.)* እዋን *ängog*
datum *(n.)* ተምሪ *demsese*
daub *(v.)* ለመፀ *dgmete'afena*
daughter *(n.)* ጓል *akafele*
daughter-in-law *(n.)* ሰበይቲ ወዲ *mmq̈raḧ*
daunt *(v.)* ኣፈራረሐ *amasḧe*
dauntless *(adj.)* ዘይፈርሕ *msḧit*
dawdle *(v.)* ኣዕጠይጠየ *feq̈ede*
dawn *(n.)* ወጋሕታ *mew'ëlo*
day *(n.)* መዓልቲ *qorqoro*
daze *(v.)* ዝዓዘመ *amete*
dazzle *(v. t.)* ሕዉዝዉዝ ኣበለ *awenawene*
dead *(adj.)* ዝማተ *awenaweni*
deadline *(n.)* መዕፀዊ ዕለት *amet*
deadlock *(n.)* ኣብ ስምምዕ ዘይምብፃሕ *shrka*
deadly *(adj.)* ዝቕትል *almanak*
deaf *(adj.)* ፀማም *kulu zike'alo*
deafening *(adj.)* ዘፅምም *luz*
deal *(n.)* ብዙሕ *darga*
deal *(v. i)* ጠልዕ ዓደለ *mxwat*
dealer *(n.)* ነጋዳይ *zteseq̈le*
dean *(n.)* ሓለቓ ደብሪ *beynu*
dear *(adj.)* ተፈታዊ/ፍትዊ *ab gWadni*
dearly *(adv.)* ክባር *ab gWadneh*
dearth *(n.)* ዋሕዲ *glul*
death *(n.)* ሞት *b'äwta*
debacle *(n.)* ስዕረት *alfa*
debar *(v. t.)* ኽለከለ *fidel*
debase *(v.)* ኣርከሰ *bnay fidelat terta*
debatable *(adj.)* ክትዕ *kerenawi*
debate *(v. t.)* ተላዘበ *kem'uwn*
debate *(n.)* ምይይጥ/ዘተ *zagit*
debauch *(v.)* ዕዋላ *menberetabot*
debauchery *(n.)* ዕዋላዊ *ẗereṕeeza qurban*
debenture *(n.)* ዘመስግን *mlwaẗ*
debilitate *(v.)* ኣዳኸመ *qWeyqWi*
debility *(n.)* ማማንማን *mrča*
debit *(n.)* ዕዳ *qyar*

debonair *(adj.)* **ዘበናዊን ብዓርሱ ዝተኣማመንን** *mnmkWa*
debrief *(v.)* **ሓተተ** *brake*
debris *(n.)* **ፈፍርስራስ** *kulukulu*
debt *(n.)* **ዕዳ** *lgsnet*
debtor *(n.)* **ናይ ወፃኢ ሰብ** *aluminiyom*
debunk *(v.)* **ሓሶት ከምዝኾነ ኣርኣየ** *yuniversiti neber*
debut *(n.)* **ናይ መፈለምታ መድረኽ** *kulu gzee*
debutante *(n.)* **ተቓላዒት** *teqala'ït*
decade *(n.)* **ዓሰርተ ዓመት** *debleqe*
decadent *(adj.)* **ጥፉሽ** *ïfashe*
decaffeinated *(adj.)* **ብዘይ ካፈይን** *bzey kafeyn*
decamp *(v.)* **ጠፍአ/መለስ በለ** *amater*
decant *(v.)* **ኣገማድሐ** *zeyk'ila*
decanter *(n.)* **ኣገማድሒ** *mestefaqr*
decapitate *(v.)* **ቀንዘፈ/ሰየፈ** *agereme*
decay *(v. i)* **በስበሰ** *adnaqot*
decease *(n.)* **ሞት** *amazen*
deceased *(adj.)* **ምዉት** *'ambasaderl'uk*
deceit *(n.)* **ቅጥፈት** *'ëndida geex*
deceitful *(adj.)* **መታለሊ** *zuryawi*
deceive *(v.)* **ኣታለለ/ሓበለ** *zeynxurnet*
decelerate *(v.)* **ናህሪ ቀነሰ** *zeynxur*
December *(n.)* **ታሕሳስ** *deret*
decency *(n.)* **ትሕትና** *hrfan*
decent *(adj.)* **ፅቡቕ/ግሩም** *hnïuy*
decentralize *(v.)* **ስልጣኑ ኣካፈለ** *mantawi*
deception *(n.)* **ምትላል** *tesaleye*
deceptive *(adj.)* **መደናገሪ** *mqur*
decibel *(n.)* **ዴሲቤል** *ambulans*
decide *(v.)* **ወሰነ** *dbya*
decided *(adj.)* **ዝተረጋገፀ** *amehayeshe*
decimal *(adj.)* **ዴሲማል** *mmhyash*
decimate *(v.)* **ረፍረፈ** *amehayeshe*
decipher *(v.)* **ትርጉሙ ረኸበ** *me'aremta*
decision *(n.)* **ዉሳነ** *tehatati*
decisive *(adj.)* **ወሳናይ** *tefetawi*
deck *(n.)* **ላዕለዋይ ደብሪ መርከብ** *mhznetawi*
deck *(n)* **ደብሪ** *'ab mengo*
declaim *(v.)* **ዓዉ ኢሉ ተዛረበ** *gguy*
declaration *(v. t.)* **መግለፂ** *ërknet*
declare *(n)* **ኣወጀ** *tetekWasi*
declassify *(v.)* **ዕላዊ** *rsa'ë*
decline *(v. t.)* **ምንቁልቋል/ምንካይ** *mhret*
declivity *(n.)* **ንታሕቲ/ንቑልቑል** *b'ëbdbd*
decode *(v.)* **ትርጉሙ ፈልፈለ** *ab mengo*
decompose *(n.)* **በስበሰ** *b'ëlug*
decomposition *(v. t)* **መቓቐለ** *fqrawi*
decompress *(v.)* **ድፍኢት ኣየር ነከየ** *qrxe'albo*
decongestant *(n.)* **ንጥረ ነገር** *ma'ëre kone*
deconstruct *(v.)* **ዘይተሃነፀን** *amper*
decontaminate *(v.)* **ዝተመረዘ ከባቢ/ነገር ኣፅረየ** *fluï seb*

decor *(n.)* **ኣገያይፃ/ኣሸላልማ** *mdremayawi*
decorate *(v.)* **ኣፀባበቐ/ሸለመ** *amfityatr*
decoration *(n.)* **ሽልማት** *sefiḧ*
decorative *(adj.)* **ኣፀባበቒ** *tewesak̓i*
decorous *(adj.)* **ቅቡል** *megulḧi*
decorum *(n.)* **ትሕትና** *agulḧe*
decoy *(n.)* **መተዓሻሸዊ ሰብ/ነገር** *sfḧat*
decrease *(v.)* **ነከየ** *ktab*
decree *(n.)* **ኣዋጅ** *azenag'ë*
decrement *(v. t.)* **ኣንቆልቆለ** *mznga'ë*
decrepit *(adj.)* **ዝቖንቖነ** *ḧade*
decriminalize *(v.)* **ሕጋዊ ንክኸዉን ገበረ** *ëletu zseḧate*
decry *(v.)* **ኮነነ** *waḧdi dem*
dedicate *(v.)* **ወፈየ** *dnzaze*
dedication *(n.)* **ዉፋይነት** *medenzezi*
deduce *(v.)* **ተገንዘበ** *qoyqWAm*
deduct *(v.)* **ቆርፁ ወሰደ** *xereqanza*
deduction *(n.)* **ግንዛበ** *temesasali*
deed *(n.)* **መግብር** *temesasalnet*
deem *(v.)* **ርእይቶ ሓዘ** *temesasalnet*
deep *(adj.)* **ዉሸጢ** *mtntan*
deer *(n.)* **ዓጋዜን/ርኤም** *mrmr*
deface *(v.)* **ፀየቐ** *tentani*
defamation *(n.)* **ዝጠቀነ** *tntane'awi*
defame *(v.)* **ጠቀነ/ሽም ሰብ ኣጥፈአ** *falulnet*
default *(n.)* **ዕዳኻ ዘይምኽፋል** *falulawi*
defeat *(v. t.)* **ሰዓረ/ተዓወተ** *falulnet*
defeatist *(n.)* **ሰዓሪ** *sneqrxi 'akal*
defecate *(v.)* **ሓርአ/ቀልቀል ወፀ** *abew*
defect *(n.)* **ጉድለት/ሕፍቲ** *wrshawi*
defective *(adj.)* **ከድዐ** *abew*
defence *(n.)* **ምክልኻል** *melhq̈*
defend *(v.)* **ተኸላኸለ** *te'äshage*
defendant *(n.)* **ተኸሳሲ** *ïntawi*
defensible *(adj.)* **ተኸላኸለ ዝሕለፍ** *xg'ëteṅa*
defensive *(adj.)* **መካተ** *dma*
defer *(v.)* **ኣመሓላለፈ** *xg'ëteṅa*
deference *(n.)* **ኽብሪ** *xwa*
defiance *(n.)* **እምቢታ** *èndegena*
deficiency *(n.)* **ዋሕዲ** *ftuw*
deficient *(adj.)* **ዉሑድ** *quẗ'ë*
deficit *(n.)* **ክሳራ** *ḧmam*
defile *(v. t)* **ኣርኸሰ** *kurna'ë*
define *(v.)* **ተርጎመ** *ḧruq̈*
definite *(adj.)* **ዝተረጋገፀ** *gWahi*
definition *(n.)* **ገለፃ** *kurna'äwi*
deflate *(v.)* **ኣንፈሰ** *ènssa*
deflation *(n.)* **ኣብ ጥቅሚ ዝዉዕል ናይ ዘንዘብ መጠን ምንካይ** *hyaw*
deflect *(v.)* **ኣንፈት ቀየረ** *hyawnet*
deforest *(v.)* **ዱር ኣብረሰ** *hyawnet*
deform *(v.)* **ኣዛበዐ** *xl'i*
deformity *(n.)* **ጉድኣት ኣካል** *shelen*
defraud *(v.)* **ኣታለለ** *änkar'änkarito*
defray *(v.)* **ወፃኢኡ ከኣለ/ሸፈነ** *anbar*
defrost *(v.)* **ኣዉዓየ/ወዓየ** *mezgebefxameetat*
deft *(adj.)* **ክእለት ዘለዎ** *gobeẗe*

defunct *(adj.)* **ዝበረሰ/ኣብ ጥቕሚ ዘይዉዕል** *gWabeẗa*
defuse *(v.)* **ዓገተ/ኣለዘበ** *axnete*
defy *(v.)* **እምቢ በለ** *dmsesa*
degenerate *(v.)* **ተዳኸመ** *zkre'ämet*
degrade *(v.)* **ኣራኸሰ** *amelkete*
degree *(n.)* **መለክዒ ኩርናዕ** *gelexe*
dehumanize *(v.)* **ሰብኣዊነት ዘጥፍእ** *meglexi*
dehydrate *(v.)* **ኣፅለለ** *sheweze*
deify *(v.)* **ኣጥዐመ** *quẗ'ë*
deign *(v.)* **ተኣነነ** *beb'ämet*
deity *(n.)* **ጣኦት** *beb'ämet*
déjà vu *(n.)* **ሓደ ዓይነት ምኽን** *sereze*
deject *(v.)* **ኣሕዘነ** *'aḧzene*
dejection *(n.)* **ጓሂ/ሕርቃን** *qeb'e*
delay *(v. t)* **ኣደንጎየ** *zeysru'ë*
delectable *(adj.)* **መኣዛ ዘለዎ** *zeyst*
delectation *(n.)* **ራህዋ/ፍስሃ** *smeswrnet*
delegate *(n.)* **ልኡኽ/ተወካሊ** *smeswr*
delegation *(n.)* **ልኡኽንት** *mnmane*
delete *(v. i)* **ደምሰሰ** *kal'è*
deleterious *(adj.)* **ጉዳኢ** *kimles zike'al*
deletion *(n.)* **ሰረዘ** *melsi*
deliberate *(adj.)* **ዝተሃነቀ** *xaxe*
deliberation *(n.)* **ምኽክር/ዘተ** *xaxe mexix*
delicacy *(n.)* **ተነቃፊነት** *texararnet*
delicate *(adj.)* **ተነቃፊ/ተሰባሪ** *texarari*
delicatessen *(n.)* **ዓብይ ሹቕ** *texarere*
delicious *(adj.)* **ምቁር/ስፋጥ** *antarktik*
delight *(v. t.)* **ፍስሃ/ታሕጓስ** *qdme fxame*
delightful *(adj.)* **ዘሕጉስ** *aquadme*
delineate *(v.)* **ገለፀ/ኣርኣየ** *ägazeen*
delinquent *(adj.)* **ገበነኛ/በደለኛ** *antena*
delirious *(adj.)* **ስሚዒታዊ** *anteema*
delirium *(n.)* **ዘተሓጎስ** *'èkub zantatat*
deliver *(v.)* **ኣብፀሐ** *sneseb*
deliverance *(n.)* **ምርካብ** *nefri*
delivery *(n.)* **ምርካብ** *xere*
dell *(n.)* **ሸንጥሮ** *xerenefsat*
delta *(n.)* **ዴልታ** *xere'akal*
delude *(v.)* **ኣታለለ** *weĵehalay*
deluge *(n.)* **ከቢድ ዝናም** *texebeye*
delusion *(n.)* **ምትላል** *mtlal*
deluxe *(adj.)* **ኣዝዩ ፅፉፍን ክባርን** *mnqulqWAl*
delve *(v.)* **ኣለሸ በለ** *xeremerzi*
demand *(n.)* **ጥብቂ ሕቶ** *xeremerzi*
demanding *(adj.)* **ብዙሕ ክእለት /ትዕግስቲ/ፃዕሪ** *krhat*
demarcation *(n.)* **ምጥራር/ጥሪ** *kuḧlemḧli*
demean *(v.)* **ኣዋረደ** *zeẗnti*
demented *(adj.)* **ዕቡድ/ፅሉል** *dḧur*
dementia *(n.)* **ዝዓበደ** *ẗntawi*
demerit *(n)* **ጌጋ** *ẗnti*
demise *(n.)* **ውድቀት** *xerereḱsi*

demobilize *(v.)* ረፈተ *xeremaḧberawi*
democracy *(n.)* ዲሞክራሲ *anxar*
democratic *(adj.)* ደዲሞክራሲያዊ *čnfar qerni*
demography *(n.)* ቁፅራዊ ሐበሬታ *aluta*
demolish *(v.)* ኣዕነወ *mehantus*
demon *(n.)* ርኹስ መንፈስ *wexeq̈a meter'as nay ziq̈ẗqeẗ ḧaxin*
demonize *(v.)* ዘጨንቕ ነገር *čnqet*
demonstrate *(v.)* ሰላማዊ ሰልፈኛ *harerteħa*
demonstration *(n.)* ሰላማዊ ሰልፊ *zḱone*
demoralize *(v.)* ደሃለ *bzeytegedasnet*
demote *(v.)* ኣዉረደ *zḱone seb*
demur *(v.)* ተቓወመ/ተፃረረ *zḱone neger*
demure *(adj.)* ህድእቲ *zḱone bota*
demystify *(v.)* ኣብራህረህ *bq̈lẗuf*
den *(n.)* ገዛ እንስሳ ዘገዳም *ztefelaleye*
denationalize *(v.)* ትካል ሸጠ *apartayd*
denial *(n.)* ክሕደት *kḧdet*
denigrate *(v.)* ኣናሸወ *zeytegedasnet*
denomination *(n.)* ስም *sm*
denominator *(n.)* ረቋሒ *črta*
denote *(v. t)* ኣመላኸተ *čaf*
denounce *(v.)* ኣዉገዘ *msla*
dense *(adj.)* ፅዑቕ *menhb*
density *(n.)* ፃዕቒ *r'èserguxnet*
dent *(n.)* ኣጠንበቐ *ra'èy*
dental *(adj.)* ናይ ስኒ *q̈reeta ḧatete*
dentist *(n.)* ናይ ስኒ ሓኪም *yq̈reeta*
denture *(n.)* ሰብሰርሖ ስኒ *apopletikawi*
denude *(v.)* ቀንጠጠ *keḧadi 'èmnet*
denunciation *(n.)* ነቐፈ *hawarya*
deny *(v. i.)* ኣሉ በለ *čret*
deodorant *(n.)* ክሕደት *askaḧkeḧe*
depart *(v.)* ነቐለ *mesarḧi*
department *(n.)* መምርሒ *kdan*
departure *(n.)* መምልቃቕ *bruh*
depend *(v.)* ተደረኸ *bruh*
dependant *(n.)* ፅግዕተኛ ዝኾነ ቆልዓ *tera'èye*
dependency *(n.)* ፅግዕተኛነት *mq̈lqal*
dependent *(adj.)* ዉሉፍ *azḧale*
depict *(v.)* ሰኣለ *mel'e*
depilatory *(adj.)* ኣጥፋእ ጸጉሪ *'aẗfa'è xeguri*
deplete *(v.)* ኣዉሓደ *nedri ẗbqo*
deplorable *(adj.)* ዘሰቅ ቕ *memela'èta*
deploy *(v.)* ኣዋፈረ *shewhat*
deport *(v. t)* ጠረዘ *kefat shewhat*
depose *(v.)* ኣዉረደ *ačebčebe*
deposit *(n.)* ዕቋር *čebčeba*
depository *(n.)* ትሕጃ *tufaḧ*
depot *(n.)* መኻዚኖ *mesarya*
deprave *(v.)* ኣባዕለገ *bq̈u'ë*
deprecate *(v.)* ኣናሸወ *amelkati*
depreciate *(v.)* ዋግኡ ነከየ *mḧtat*
depreciation *(n.)* ድሕሪ እዋን *teẗeq̈me*
depress *(v.)* ኣተከዘ *wesene*
depression *(n.)* ትካዘ *qWexera*
deprive *(v.)* ከልከለ *gWazeye*

depth *(n.)* **ዕምቁት** *zisemama'ë*
deputation *(n.)* **ተወከልቲ** *gemgeme*
depute *(v.)* **ወከለ** *èḱul*
deputy *(n.)* **ምኽትል** *tegenzebe*
derail *(v. t.)* **ካብ መስመሩ ኣስሓተ** *asteyayet*
deranged *(adj.)* **ኣእምሩኡ ዝተቓወሰ** *tered'e*
deregulate *(v.)* **ካብ ደምቢን ቁፅፅርናን ናፃ ገበረ** *mrda'è*
deride *(v.)* **ኣላገፀ** *zteshaq̈ele*
derivative *(adj.)* **መበቆል** *telmedeen*
derive *(v.)* **ረኸበ** *afleẗe*
derogatory *(adj.)* **ክብሪ ዝነክእ** *qerebe*
descend *(v.)* **ተሓተ/ወረደ** *bq̈u'ë*
descendant *(n.)* **ትዉልዲ** *mnza'ë*
descent *(n.)* **ጭምት** *qbale*
describe *(v.)* **ገለፀ** *teq̈ebele*
description *(n.)* **ገለፃ** *darga*
desert *(v.)* **ደርበየ** *mishmishe*
deserve *(v. t.)* **ተገነኦ** *grmbyale*
design *(n.)* **ኣሰራርሓ** *beliḧ*
designate *(v.)* **ሰየመ** *tewhbo*
desirable *(adj.)* **ተደላዪ** *tedelayi*
desire *(n.)* **ድልየት** *mayawi*
desirous *(adj.)* **ህንቁዉ** *mayawi*
desist *(v.)* **አቋረፀ** *areb*
desk *(n.)* **ሰደቓ** *arebian*
desolate *(adj.)* **ፅምዋ ዝኾነ** *arebik*
despair *(n.)* **ቅብፀት ምቁራፅ** *gedla*
desperate *(adj.)* **ቀባፅ ዝቖረፅ** *feradi*
despicable *(adj.)* **ርጉም** *hawri*
despise *(v.)* **ነዓቐ** *daneye*
despite *(prep.)* **እንትርፊ** *dan̈net*
despondent *(adj.)* **ዝጎሃየ** *dah̀a*
despot *(n.)* **ዉልቀ መላኺ መራሒ** *das*
dessert *(n.)* **መወራረዲ ምቁር ምግቢ** *qesti*
destabilize *(v.)* **ቅልዉላዉ ፈጠረ** *qeldedawi*
destination *(n.)* **መብፅሒ ቦታ** *qelded*
destiny *(n.)* **ዕድል** *sne ẗnti*
destitute *(adj.)* **ስኡን** *ẗntawi*
destroy *(v.)* **ኣዕነወ** *liqe mela'èkt*
destroyer *(n.)* **ኣጥፊእ ሰብ** *liqeṕaṕasat*
destruction *(n.)* **ብርሰት** *mentagay*
detach *(v.)* **ፈለየ** *snehanaxi*
detachment *(n.)* **ዕሽሽታ** *snehnxa*
detail *(n.)* **ዝርዝር** *archiv*
detain *(v. t)* **ኣሰረ** *arktik*
detainee *(n.)* **ናይ ፓለቲካ እሱር** *w'ëw'ë*
detect *(v.)* **ኣሊሹ ረኸበ** *brtu'ë dleet*
detective *(n.)* **መርማሪ ፖሊስ** *adkami*
detention *(n.)* **ማእሰርቲ** *sfḧat*
deter *(v.)* **ዓቀበ** *medreḱ*
detergent *(n.)* **መሕፀቢ** *temagote*
deteriorate *(v.)* **ተጋደደ** *megote*
determinant *(n.)* **ዉሱንን ንፁርን** *megotina*
determination *(v. t)* **ፅንዓት** *axam'è*
determine *(v. t)* **መርመረ** *tela'ële*
deterrent *(n.)* **መዐቀቢ** *aristokrasi*
detest *(v.)* **ፀልአ** *aristokratawi*
dethrone *(v.)* **ኣዉረደ** *quxri*
detonate *(v.)* **ነተጉ** *quxrina*

detour *(n.)* **ኣኳላል መንገዲ** *tabot*
detoxify *(v.)* **መርዚ ኣወገደ** *mnat*
detract *(v.)* **ኣዛሕተለ** *čfra meraḱb wg'è*
detriment *(n.)* **ዕንወት ምስዓብ** *armagedon*
detritus *(n.)* **ተረፈ ምህርቲ** *axwar*
devalue *(v.)* **ሸርፌ ወፃኢ ነኸየ** *gzyawi teḱusi'ëxo*
devastate *(v.)* **ኣባደመ** *dr'ï ḧaxin*
develop *(v.)* **ዓበየ** *dr'ï ḧaxini*
development *(n.)* **ዕብየት** *serawit*
deviant *(adj.)* **ፍሉይ** *me'äza*
deviate *(v.)* **ተፈለየ** *me'äza fwesa*
device *(n.)* **መሳርሒ** *'ab zurya*
devil *(n.)* **ሰይጣን** *aberabere*
devious *(adj.)* **ሸፋጢ** *ser'ë*
devise *(v.)* **መሃዘ** *aserar'ä*
devoid *(adj.)* **ኣልቦ ዘይብሉ** *mḧir*
devolution *(n.)* **ውክልና** *wklna*
devolve *(v.)* **ሓላፍነት ሃበ** *teselefin*
devote *(v.)* **ወፈየ** *asere*
devotee *(n.)* **ፈታዊ** *ètwet*
devotion *(n.)* **ፍቕሪ** *mexe*
devour *(v.)* **ዉሕጥሕጥ ኣበለ** *'atḧitu re'aye*
devout *(adj.)* **ሃይማኖተኛ** *t'ëbiteṅa*
dew *(n.)* **ዛዕዛዕታ** *menze'ë*
dexterity *(n.)* **ናይ ኢድ ጥበብ** *flaxa*
diabetes *(n.)* **ሽኮርያ** *èndabret*
diagnose *(v.)* **መርሚሩ ፈለጠ** *brtu'ë smi*
diagnosis *(n.)* **ምርመራ** *bwsay mqxal*
diagram *(n.)* **ሰደቓ** *ïbeb*
dial *(n.)* **መዘወሪ** *ïnti*

dialect *(n.)* **ከባቢያዊ ቋንቋ** *arteri*
dialogue *(n.)* **ቃለ ምልልስ** *blhi*
dialysis *(n.)* **ሕክምና** *riḧ*
diameter *(n.)* **ስፋቲ** *karchofi*
diamond *(n.)* **ኣልማዝ** *aq̈ḧa*
diaper *(n.)* **ጨርቂ ሽንቲ** *anexere*
diarrhoea *(n.)* **ዉፅኣት** *k'èlet*
diary *(n.)* **ዕለታዊ ማስታወሻ** *snu'ë*
Diaspora *(n.)* **ናይ ኣይሁዳዊያን ስደት** *kebid bret*
dice *(n.)* **ሓደገኛ** *k'ila*
dictate *(adj.)* **ብልቃ ኣፅሓፈ** *sneïebib*
dictation *(n.)* **ብቓል ምፅሓፍ** *sneïbebawi*
dictator *(n.)* **ዉልቂ መላኺ መራሒ** *bahryawi*
diction *(n.)* **ኣነባበብ ቃላት** *kem*
dictionary *(n.)* **መዝገበ ቃላት** *mezgebeqalat*
dictum *(n.)* **ብሂል** *deyebe*
didactic *(adj.)* **ትምሕርታዊ** *deyabi*
die *(v.)* **ሞተ** *ërget*
diesel *(n.)* **በንዚን** *aregagexe*
diet *(n.)* **ምግቢ** *menan*
dietician *(n.)* **ዉሱን ምግቢ ተመጋቢ ሰብ** *habe*
differ *(v.)* **ተፈላለየ** *xduy*
difference *(n.)* **ኣፈላላይ** *gbresedomeṅa*
different *(adj.)* **ፍሉይ** *ash*
difficult *(adj.)* **ኣሸጋሪ** *zḧafere*
difficulty *(n.)* **ሽግር** *'ab gemgem baḧri*
diffuse *(v.)* **ዝተጋፍሐ** *eshiyawi*
dig *(v.)* **ኮዓተ** *'ab wey nab gWadni*

digest *(v.)* ሓቖቖ *änĵal*
digestion *(n.)* ምሕቓቕ ምግቢ *ḧatete*
digit *(n.)* ቁፅሪ *bïrïare*
digital *(adj.)* ኣፃብዕቲ *zebal*
dignified *(adj.)* ግርማ ሞገስ ዘለዎ *xmuw*
dignify *(v.)* ኣማዕረገ *shamot*
dignitary *(n.)* ሰበ ስልጣን መዚ *melk'ë*
dignity *(n.)* ክብሪ *gonex*
digress *(v.)* ካብ ኣርእስቲ ወዘ *mkfa'è*
dilapidated *(adj.)* ዑና *äbese*
dilate *(v.)* ኣግፈሐ *delayi*
dilemma *(n.)* ሰንፈላል *tmnit*
diligent *(adj.)* ትጉሕ *temeneye*
dilute *(v.)* በፅበፀ *adgi*
dim *(adj.)* ዘይድሙቕ *aïqe'ë*
dimension *(n.)* መለክዒ *qetalnefsi*
diminish *(v.)* ነከየ *qetele*
diminution *(n.)* ምንካይ *qeteli*
din *(n.)* ጫዉጫዉታ *aïqe'ë*
dine *(v.)* ተደረረ *mgïïam*
diner *(n.)* ተመጋቢ *agaïeme*
dingy *(adj.)* ፀልማትን ረሳሕን *aḱeeba*
dinner *(n.)* ድራር *smm'ë*
dinosaur *(n.)* ዳይኖሰር *daynoser*
dip *(v. t)* ጠምዐ *amaḱari*
diploma *(n.)* ዲፕሎማ *diploma*
diplomacy *(n.)* ብልሃት *blhat*
diplomat *(n.)* ቆንስል *xa'ërèna*
diplomatic *(adj.)* ቆንስላዊ *retebe*
dipsomania *(n.)* ሰታይ *mdeba*
dire *(adj.)* ጥብቂ *mdub sraḧ*
direct *(adj.)* ቀጥታዊ *tewahade*
direction *(n.)* ኣንፈት *tewahdo*
directive *(n.)* መምርሒ *ḧageze*
directly *(adv.)* ቀጥ ዝበለ *ḧagez*
director *(n.)* ሓላፊ/ኣመሓዳሪ *redat*
directory *(n.)* መሓበሪ *meḧaberi*
dirt *(n.)* ረስሓት *maḧber*
dirty *(adj.)* ረሳሕ *smm'ë*
disability *(n.)* ድኽመት *ztefalaleye*
disable *(v.)* ሃሰየ *beb'äynetu*
disabled *(adj.)* ዝተሃሰየ *axenan'ë*
disadvantage *(n.)* ጉድኣት *gemete*
disaffected *(adj.)* ዘይዓገበ *gmt*
disagree *(v.)* ተፈላለየ ተረፈ *meregagexi*
disagreeable *(adj.)* ዘፅልእ *aregagexe*
disagreement *(n.)* ዘይምስምዕማዕ *waḧs*
disallow *(v.)* ነፀገ *astrisks*
disappear *(v.)* ተኸወለ *älem*
disappoint *(v.)* ኣሕዘነ *azma*
disapproval *(n.)* ተቓዉሞ *nebe'ë*
disapprove *(v.)* ተቓወመ *adeneq̈e*
disarm *(v.)* ዕጥቂ ኣፍተሓ *dnxwuna*
disarmament *(n.)* ምንካይ ቁፅሪ ሰራዊት ዉግዕ *asdememe*
disarrange *(v.)* ኣጋዕዘየ *koḱobawi*
disarray *(n.)* ዕግርግር *hwtut*
disaster *(n.)* ከቢድ ሓደጋ/መዓት *bmgḧtan*
disastrous *(adj.)* ሕማቕ *blxug*

disband *(v.)* በተነ *qWexera kewaḱbti*
disbelief *(n.)* ጥርጣረ *ẗeferteȟa*
disburse *(v.)* ገንዘብ ዓደለ *snekoḱobi*
disc *(n.)* ዲስክ *snekoḱob*
discard *(v.)* ሰንደወ *tkur*
discern *(v.)* ተረደአ *ztefelaleye*
discharge *(v.)* ፍቓድ ሃበ *üq̈ba*
disciple *(n.)* ተኸታሊ *ab*
discipline *(n.)* ስነ ስርዓት *yewah*
disclaim *(v.)* ኣሉ በለ/ከሓደ *izihernet*
disclose *(v.)* ዕላዊ ገበረ *iziheerawi*
disco *(n.)* ዲስኮ *sporteȟa*
discolour *(v.)* ፈሰመ ሃሰሰ *sportawi*
discomfit *(v.)* ኣደናገረ *atlas*
discomfort *(n.)* ቃንዛ *hawahw*
disconcert *(v.)* ኣሕፈረ *deseet*
disconnect *(v.)* ነቐለ *atom*
disconsolate *(adj.)* ዝጎሃየ *atomawi*
discontent *(n.)* መረረት *keȟase*
discontinue *(v.)* ኣቋረፀ *dȟnet*
discord *(n.)* ቅርሕንቲ *kfli*
discordant *(adj.)* ዘይስማማዕ *aseqaq̈i*
discount *(n.)* ንካይ *gef'ë*
discourage *(v.)* ንምክልኻል ፀዓረ *aẗabeq̈e*
discourse *(n.)* መደረ *atash*
discourteous *(adj.)* ብዕሉግ *ẗbqet*
discover *(v.)* ሓድሽ ነገር ረኸበ *aẗq'ë*
discovery *(n.)* ሓበሬታ ረኽቦ *mlu'è*
discredit *(v.)* ኣዋረደ *semere*
discreet *(adj.)* ጠጥንቁቕ *fetene*
discrepancy *(n.)* ኣፈላላይ *ĵemere*
discrete *(adj.)* ዓርሱ ዝኸኣለ *tek̃etatele*
discriminate *(v.)* ፈለየ *tesatfo*
discursive *(adj.)* ሃውታቲ *agelgali*
discuss *(v.)* ተዛተየ *aq̈albo*
discussion *(n.)* ዘተ/ምይይጥ *ẗnquq̈*
disdain *(n.)* ንዕቐት *aregagexe*
disease *(n.)* ሕማም *waldbit*
disembark *(v.)* ወረደ *lbsi*
disembodied *(adj.)* ካ ዘይተፈለጠ በታ ዝመፀዕ *aqačač*
disempower *(v.)* ዝሓይሊ *ẗebeq̈a*
disenchant *(v.)* ዝተሰላቸወ *seȟabe*
disengage *(v.)* ኣላቐቐ *sȟbet*
disentangle *(v.)* መመየ *maraḱi*
disfavour *(n.)* ፅልኢ *bahry*
disgrace *(n.)* ዉርደት *margarin*
disgruntled *(adj.)* ዝተበሳጨ *ȟaraĵ*
disguise *(v.)* መልክዑ ቀየረ *kisma'ë zike'a*
disgust *(n.)* ፅልኢ *nebaro*
dish *(n.)* ሸሓነ *dehay*
dishearten *(v.)* ደሃለ *xebxab*
dishonest *(adj.)* ሸፋጢ *nay msma'ë fetena*
dishonour *(n.)* ዉርደት *'oditoryomme'akebi 'aderash*
disillusion *(v.)* እምነት ሰብ ኣፍረሰ *ወሰኸ*
disincentive *(n.)* ተስፋ ዘቑርፅ ነገር *neȟase*

disinfect *(v.)* **ብፀረ ታሕዋሲያን ፀረገ** *ḧatno*
disingenuous *(adj.)* **መምሰሊ** *aḱlil*
disinherit *(v.)* **ንኸይወርስ ከልከለ** *tesfa'awi*
disintegrate *(v.)* **ሓምሸሸ** *ïbqi*
disjointed *(adj.)* **ዘይተሓሓዝ** *awustraliya*
dislike *(v.)* **ፀልኣ** *ḧaqeḧa*
dislocate *(v.)* **ቆፀየ** *lk'ënet*
dislodge *(v.)* **ፈንቀለ** *derasi*
disloyal *(adj.)* **ከሓዲ** *mzuz*
dismal *(adj.)* **ዘሕዝን** *mezi*
dismantle *(v.)* **ፈታተሐ** *mezeze*
dismay *(n.)* **ሓዘን** *awutizim*
dismiss *(v.)* **ዕሽሽ በለ** *r'èsetariḱ*
dismissive *(adj.)* **ሰደደ/ፈነወ** *awtokrasi*
disobedient *(adj.)* **እምቢተኛ** *wlqemelaḱi*
disobey *(v.)* **እምቢ በለ** *wlqemelaḱ*
disorder *(n.)* **ሕንፍሽፍሽ** *r'èsexḧuf*
disorganized *(adj.)* **ብደንቢ ዘይተተለመ** *awtomatik*
disorientate *(v.)* **ኣጋገየ** *awtomobilmekina*
disown *(v.)* **ኣግለለ** *r'èsemmḧdarawi*
disparity *(n.)* **ኣፈላላይ** *mrmrereesa*
dispassionate *(adj.)* **ፍትሓዊ** *qew'ï*
dispatch *(v.)* **ለኣኸ** *ḧagazi*
dispel *(v.)* **ስሚዒቱ ኣጥፈአ** *teïeq̈me*
dispensable *(adj.)* **ዘየድሊ** *ktïqemelu tḱ'èl*
dispensary *(n.)* **ግልጋሎት** *mederegaḧ*
dispense *(v.)* **ኣዉፂኡ ሃበ** *ss'ë*
disperse *(v.)* **ተበታተነ** *ḧne fedeye*
dispirited *(adj.)* **ድሁል** *gWadena*
displace *(v. t)* **ኣመዛበለ** *ma'èkelay*
display *(v.)* **ኣርኣየ** *anxar*
displease *(v.)* **ኣበሳጨወ** *xl'at*
displeasure *(n.)* **ሕርቃን** *aleye*
disposable *(adj.)* **ተጠምቒምካሉ ዝድርበ** *'ènda 'a'ëwaf*
disposal *(n.)* **ምእላይ** *snemnfar*
dispose *(v. t)* **ኣመዓራረየ** *paylot*
dispossess *(v.)* **መንጠለ** *hnïuy*
disproportionate *(adj.)* **ዘይመጣጠን** *hnïuyi*
disprove *(v.)* **ጌጋ ከምዝኾነ ኣርኣየ** *avokado*
dispute *(v. i)* **ክትዕ** *wegede*
disqualification *(n.)* **ብቕዓት-ማጣት** *gusya*
disqualify *(v.)* **ንኸይተሳተፍ ከልከለ** *amene*
disquiet *(n.)* **ንኸይተሳተፍ** *'ako'awi*
disregard *(v. t)* **ሸለል በለ** *texebeye*
disrepair *(n.)* **ዝተበላሸወ ህንፃ ወዘተ** *neq̈ḧe*
disreputable *(adj.)* **መታለሊ** *neq̈ḧe*
disrepute *(n.)* **ንዕቐት** *seleme*
disrespect *(n.)* **ንዕቐት** *genzeb*
disrobe *(v.)* **ክዳኑ ኣዉፀአ** *nab rḧuq̈*

disrupt *(v.)* አቋረፀ *temsaï*
dissatisfaction *(n.)* ቅርታ *zer'ëd*
dissect *(v.)* በጢሑ ተመራመረ *zeskaḧkḧ*
dissent *(v.)* ተፈለየ *nḧaxir gzee*
dissertation *(n.)* መመረቒ ፅሑፍ *gaḧmaï*
dissident *(n.)* ብርቱዕ ተቓዋሚ *blshw*
dissimulate *(v.)* ትክክለኛ ስሚዒቱ ሓብአ *fas*
dissipate *(v.)* ኣዳኸመ *meq̈elesi*
dissolve *(v. t)* ሓቐቐ *meq̈eles*
dissuade *(v.)* ኣታረፈ *'atarefe*
distance *(n.)* ርሕቀት *rḧqet*
distant *(adj.)* ርሑቕ *a'ëzemzeme*
distaste *(n.)* ፅልኢ *hxan*
distil *(v.)* ፅረየ *zeymsmma'ë*
distillery *(n.)* ኣፅረየ መሻሸሒ *hbey*
distinct *(adj.)* ብቐሊሉ ዝስማዕ *hxan*
distinction *(n.)* አኣፈላይ/ፍልልይ *beetelbo*
distinguish *(v. t)* ፈለየ *zban*
distort *(v.)* ኣዛነዐ *ändiḧq̈o*
distract *(v.)* ኣቓልበ ሰብ ሃወኸ *ḧalefe*
distraction *(n.)* ዝርብሽ ነገር *t'ëynti*
distress *(n.)* ከቢድ ጭንቀት *mgusa'ë*
distribute *(v.)* ዓደለ *temekuro*
distributor *(n.)* ዕደላ ሰብ *ashmurawi*
district *(n.)* ክልል *red'e*
distrust *(n.)* ጥርጣረ *melsegbri*
disturb *(v.)* ረበሸ *mehazi*
ditch *(n.)* መትረብ *mahder*
dither *(v.)* ኣመንተወ *bdḧrit*
ditto *(n.)* ከምኡ *zban medrek̗*
dive *(v.)* ቲፎ ኣተወ *zban aser*
diverge *(v.)* ኣንፈቱ ቀየረ *ndḧrit*
diverse *(adj.)* ዝተፈላዩ *zban may*
diversion *(n.)* ኣንፈት ምቕያር *beekon*
diversity *(n.)* ፍልልይ *bakteriya*
divert *(v. t)* ኣንፈት ቀየረ *ḧmaq̈*
divest *(v.)* ኣዉፀአ *arma*
divide *(v.)* መቐለ *bḧmaq̈*
dividend *(n.)* ኽፍፍሊ *badminten*
divine *(adj.)* ኣምላኻዊ *agereme*
divinity *(n.)* ኣምላኽነት *mel'e*
division *(n.)* ክፍፍል *ga'äz*
divorce *(n.)* ፍትሕ *geflaw*
divorcee *(n.)* ዝተፋትሐ *ḧbur slmat*
divulge *(v.)* ምሽጥር ነገር *waḧs*
do *(v.)* ገበረ *polis*
docile *(adj.)* ምእዙዝ *mesḧabi*
dock *(n.)* ፉርዳ *dereq̈e*
docket *(n.)* ሓጺር ጽሑፍ *ḧaxir xḧuf*
doctor *(n.)* ሓኪም *ènda bani*
doctorate *(n.)* ደረጃ *dereĵa*
doctrine *(n.)* እምነት *segenet*
document *(n.)* ሰነድ *beraḧ*
documentary *(n.)* ዶኩመንታዊ *dokumentawi*
dodge *(v. t)* ተመኹለየ *ku'ëso*
doe *(n.)* ኣንስተይቲ ማንቲለ *g̈tmi wey derfi*
dog *(n.)* ከልቢ *bale*
dogma *(n.)* ሕጊ *balun*
dogmatic *(adj.)* ሕጋዊ *nay medmexi wereq̈et*
doldrums *(n.)* ሓዘን *belesan*
doll *(n.)* ባምቡላ *belesan*

dollar *(n.)* **ዶላር** *arqay*
domain *(n.)* **ዓይነት ፍልጠት** *agede*
dome *(n.)* **ጉልላት** *tera*
domestic *(adj.)* **ናይ ዉሽጢ ዓዲ** *banana*
domicile *(n.)* **አድራሻ** *me'èseri*
dominant *(adj.)* **ዓብላላይ** *meĵeneni*
dominate *(v.)* **ዓብለለ** *shfta werebela*
dominion *(n.)* **ስልጣን** *merzi smi*
donate *(v.)* **ለገሰ** *gewta*
donkey *(n.)* **አድጊ** *gewtat*
donor *(n.)* **ለጋሲ ሰብ** *benaĵr*
doom *(n.)* **ሞት** *ḧayere*
door *(n.)* **ማዕፆ** *ïrzya*
dormitory *(n.)* **መደቀሲ ክፍሊ** *medendel*
dose *(n.)* **ዓቐን** *banĵo*
dossier *(n.)* **መዝገብ** *banki*
dot *(n.)* **ነጥቢ** *mekWanen*
dote *(v.)* **አፍቀረ** *ïfush*
double *(adj.)* **ድርብ** *ïfesha*
doubt *(n.)* **ጥርጣረ** *sendeq̈*
dough *(n.)* **ብሒቍ** *be'äl*
down *(adv.)* **ኣብ ታሕቲ** *tewazeye*
downfall *(n.)* **ዉድቀት** *ïmqet*
download *(v.)* **ዝጫነ** *meïmq̈awi*
downpour *(n.)* **ዝፈሰሰ** *aïemeq̈e*
dowry *(n.)* **ገዝሚ** *metawer*
doze *(v. i)* **ሰለም አበለ** *änqaribo*
dozen *(n.)* **ደርዘን** *barbarawi*
drab *(adj.)* **ዘአይስሕባ ዘይብል** *barbarawi*
draft *(n.)* **ንድፊ** *ndfi*
drag *(v. t)* **ጎተተ** *wega'i*
dragon *(n.)* **ሓላዉ** *qemqamay*
drain *(v. t)* **አፅረረ** *gïmi wey derfi*
drama *(n.)* **ተዋስኦ** *ïrḧu*
dramatic *(adj.)* **ዘርገም** *bq̈lu'ë*
dramatist *(n.)* **ፀሓፊ ተዋስኦ** *waga 'ëdaga*
drastic *(adj.)* **ጥብቂ** *tegačewe telag'ë*
draught *(n.)* **ንፋስ** *qraf*
draw *(v.)* **ሰኣለ** *sgem*
drawback *(n.)* **መሰናኽል** *mek̈zen*
drawer *(n.)* **ትሬቶ** *baromeeter*
drawing *(n.)* **ዝወቀለ** *balabat*
dread *(v.t)* **ሰግአ** *baraka*
dreadful *(adj.)* **ኣዝዩ ሕማቕ** *meshenit*
dream *(n.)* **ሕልሚ** *gdb*
dreary *(adj.)* **ዘሕዝን** *bermil*
drench *(v.)* **ኣጠልቀየ** *mek̈an*
dress *(v.)* **ተኸደነ** *medendel*
dressing *(n.)* **ናይ ሰላጣ መመቀሪ** *ënqfat*
drift *(v.)* **ዘገምታ** *gdb*
drill *(n.)* **መንደል** *ïebeq̈a*
drink *(v. t)* **መስተ ፈሳሲ** *bedela*
drip *(v. i)* **ጥብጥብ በለ** *serete*
drive *(v.)* **ዘወረ** *seret'albo*
driver *(n.)* **ዘዋሪ ማኪና** *tḧtebeet*
drizzle *(n.)* **ኣኻፈየ** *ḧafar*
droll *(adj.)* **ኣዘናጋዒ** *seretawi*
droop *(v.)* **ደነነ** *riḧan*
drop *(v.)* **ወደቐ** *bazilika*
dross *(n.)* **ዘይረብሕ** *sḧani*
drought *(n.)* **ድርቂ** *seret*
drown *(v.)* **ጥሒሊ ሞተ ቀተለ** *texelwe*
drowse *(v.)* **ተታኸሰ** *zenbil*
drug *(n.)* **ሓሽሽ** *bas 'äynet 'äsa*
drum *(n.)* **ከበሮ** *dq̈ala*

drunkard *(adj.)* ሰኽራም *shelele*
dry *(adj.)* ደረቕ *ërdi*
dryer *(n.)* አድራቒ *menka'ë*
dual *(adj.)* ፅምዲ *èkub*
dubious *(adj.)* ዝተጠራጠረ *mḧxab*
duck *(n.)* ደርሆ ማይ *aleḱe*
duct *(n.)* ቱቦ *hwteta*
dudgeon *(n.)* ሕርቃን *batik*
due *(adj.)* ዝሰዓበ *betri polis*
duel *(n.)* ቅልስ *boẗoloni*
duet *(n.)* ክልተ *tegedam*
dull *(adj.)* ዘፅልእ *ketkete*
dullard *(n.)* ዘይርደኦ *'ahadu kebid bret*
duly *(adv.)* ብትኽኽል *wg'è*
dumb *(adj.)* ዓባስ/በሃም *ḧbur slmat*
dummy *(n.)* ክዳን መርኣይ ባንቡላ *mesenaḱl*
dump *(n.)* ደርበየ *wečeče*
dung *(n.)* ዒባ *furda*
dungeon *(n.)* ትሕቲ መሬት ዝርከብ ክፍሊ *sanĵa*
duo *(n.)* ብሕባር ዝደርፉ ክልተ ሰባት *bazar shuq̈*
dupe *(v.)* ኣታለለ *bazuqa*
duplex *(n.)* ክልተ *kone*
duplicate *(adj.)* ኣብዝሐ *nab dendes 'axege'ë*
duplicity *(n.)* ሽፍጢ *mena*
durable *(adj.)* ንብዙሕ እዋን ዝፀንሕ *ënqo*
duration *(n.)* ዉሱን እዋን *qorqWAr*
during *(prep.)* ኣብ እዋን *bigl*
dusk *(n.)* ኣጋ ምሸት *metkob*
dust *(n.)* ደሮና *brčqo*
duster *(n.)* መወልወሊ ጨርቂ *gemel*
dutiful *(adj.)* ሰብ መኽበሪ *baldongWa*
duty *(n.)* ሓላፍነት *dbi*
duvet *(n.)* ኮበርታ *teshekeme*
dwarf *(n.)* ደኽዳኽ *čḧmi*
dwell *(v.)* ነበረ *ma'èzn*
dwelling *(n.)* መንበሪ ቦታ *ènssa*
dwindle *(v. t)* ወሓደ/ነኣሰ *ènssawi*
dye *(n.)* ቀለም ለኸየ *laxeye*
dynamic *(adj.)* ሓያል/ጥንኩር *laxeye*
dynamics *(n.)* ሰጓማይ *maraḱi*
dynamite *(n.)* ደማሚት *amelk'ë*
dynamo *(n.)* ዲናሞ *desta*
dynasty *(n.)* ስርወ መንግስቲ *melk'ë*
dysentery *(n.)* ሕመም *biver*
dysfunctional *(adj.)* ብልሽዊ *ahd'e*
dyslexia *(n.)* ዝኣንበቢ *mḱnyatu bmknyat*
dyspepsia *(n.)* ብቐሊሉ ዘይሓቅቕ ምግቢ *mlkt*

E

each *(adj.)* ሕድሕድ *kone*
eager *(adj.)* ህንጡዉ *me'ërefi*
eagle *(n.)* ንስሪ *menxef*
ear *(n.)* እዝኒ *me'ëqob snkulane'a'èmro*
earl *(n.)* ምዕሩግ *ačefeq̈e*
early *(adj.)* መጀመርታ *nhbi*
earn *(v.)* ሰሪሑ ረኸበ *wạ'ëro*
earnest *(adj.)* ቅኑዕ *sga kebti*
earth *(n.)* ዓለም *regWid*

earthen *(adj.)* **ብጭቃ ዝተሰርሐ** *mlkt*
earthly *(adj.)* **ምድራዊ** *bira*
earthquake *(n.)* **ራዕዲ መሬት** *bnĵr*
ease *(n.)* **ቅለት** *masa*
east *(n.)* **ምብራቕ** *mbraq̈*
Easter *(n.)* **ትንሳኤ** *werede 'agaẗeme*
eastern *(adj.)* **ኣብ ምብራቕ ዝርከብ** *beq̈'ë*
easy *(adj.)* **ቀሊል** *qdmi*
eat *(v.)* **በልዐ** *ሓቓዲሙ*
eatable *(adj.)* **ዝብላዕ** *agereme*
eatery *(n.)* **በቤት ብልዒ** *me'äde*
ebb *(n.)* **ዳሕረዋይ** *lemene*
ebony *(n.)* **ደረቕ** *welede*
ebullient *(adj.)* **ልበ ምሉእ** *lemani*
eccentric *(adj.)* **ዘይልሙድ** *ĵemere*
echo *(n.)* **መቓልሕ** *meĵemerta*
eclipse *(n.)* **ግርደት** *grdet*
ecology *(n.)* **ስነ ምሕዳር** *ab kndi*
economic *(adj.)* **ቁጠባዊ** *gebere*
economical *(adj.)* **ቆጣቢ** *ẗebay*
economics *(n.)* **መፅናዕቲ ሃብቲ ቁጠባ** *qWerexe*
economy *(n.)* **ሃብቲ ቁጠባ** *čekan*
ecstasy *(n.)* **ፍሰሃ** *t'èzaz*
edge *(n.)* **ወሰናወሰን** *bdḧrit*
edgy *(adj.)* **ቁጡዕ** *temelkete*
edible *(adj.)* **ዝብላዕ** *amesgani*
edict *(n.)* **ኣዋጅ** *faḧray*
edifice *(n.)* **ህንጻ** *hnxa*
edit *(v.)* **ንኽሕተም ኣሰናደአ** *qeẗqeẗe*
edition *(n.)* **መሰናድኦ** *dnguy*
editor *(n.)* **ኣሰናዳኢ** *ẗemere*
editorial *(adj.)* **ናይ ኣሰናዳኢ መልእኽቲ** *tef'e*
educate *(v.)* **ኣማሃረ** *ačeneq̈e*
education *(n.)* **ትምህርቲ** *bgeega 'ar'aye*
efface *(v.)* **ኣጥፈአ** *èmnet*
effect *(n.)* **ሳዕቤን** *amene*
effective *(adj.)* **ዉፅኢታዊ** *aqWenaxebe*
effeminate *(adj.)* **ሰበይታይ** *qačl*
effete *(adj.)* **ዝተዳኸመ** *xbq̈ti*
efficacy *(n.)* **ፈዋሳይነት** *teba'asay*
efficiency *(n.)* **ብቕዓት** *ba'èsi mdlay*
efficient *(adj.)* **ብቑዕ** *neqewe*
effigy *(n.)* **ሓወልቲ** *menafḧ*
effort *(n.)* **ፃዕሪ** *kebdi*
egg *(n.)* **እንቋቑሖ** *te'asasere*
ego *(n.)* **ባዕሊ** *ba'ëli*
egotism *(n.)* **ተጀሃሪ ዝኾነ ሰብ** *fq̈ur*
eight *(adj. & n.)* **ሸሞንተ** *tḧti*
eighteen *(adj. & n.)* **ዓሰርተ ሸሞንተ** *qulfi*
eighty *(adj. & n.)* **ሰማንያ** *gWahaye*
either *(adv.)* **ወይ** *'aqalbo 'azenbele*
ejaculate *(v.)* **ኣምነወ** *rbo*
eject *(v. t)* **ኣባረረ** *leweye*
elaborate *(adj.)* **ዘዝተሓላለኸን ዝርዝርን** *tḧti*
elapse *(v.)* **ግዜ ሓለፈ** *burakee*
elastic *(adj.)* **ላስቲክ** *gebiresenay*
elbow *(n.)* **ኵርናዕ ኢድ** *geza qeshi*
elder *(adj.)* **ዓብይ** *gbresenay*
elderly *(adj.)* **ኣረጊት/ሽማግሌ** *lewah*
elect *(v.)* **መረፀ** *ḧagazi*

election *(n.)* **መረፃ** *gbresenay*
elective *(adj.)* **ብመረፃ ዝተመረፀ** *gbresenayawi*
electorate *(n.)* **መራፂ ህዝቢ** *lewah*
electric *(adj.)* **ኮረንቲ ዝጥቀም** *tewhbo*
electrician *(n.)* **ኪኢላ ኮረንቲ** *awrese*
electricity *(n.)* **ኮረንቲ መብራሕቲ** *wrsha*
electrify *(v.)* **ዝለዓለ ስሚዒት** *weq̈ese*
electrocute *(v.)* **ብኮረንቲ ኣቑሰለ** *zerefe*
electronic *(adj.)* **ኤልክትሮኒክስ** *ḧazen*
elegance *(n.)* **ግሩምት** *lemani*
elegant *(adj.)* **ግርማ ሞገስ ዘለዎ** *kewḧi bered*
element *(n.)* **ኣገዳሲ ኣካል** *denqoro*
elementary *(adj.)* **ናይ ቀዳማይ ብርኪ ጀመርቲ** *fre*
elephant *(n.)* **ሓርማዝ** *ëbdbd*
elevate *(v.)* **ደረጃ ሃበ** *medeqesi*
elevator *(n.)* **ናይ ባላሶ መደየቢት** *lemene*
eleven *(adj. & n.)* **ዓሰርተ ሓደ** *ashegere*
elf *(n.)* **ፀይቂ/ርጉም** *'ab ẗq̈a*
elicit *(v.)* **ሓበሬታ ረኸበ** *kebebe*
eligible *(adj.)* **ብቑዕ** *ameraseḧe*
eliminate *(v.)* **ኣልገሰ** *mek̇oster*
elite *(n.)* **እንቋቑሖ መሰል** *'ènqWAq̈uḧo mesel*
ellipse *(n.)* **ሞልሟል** *äwdi xeq̈eẗe*
elocution *(n.)* **ክእለት ዘረባ** *bzbelexe*
elongate *(v.)* **ነዉሐ** *newḧe*
elope *(v.)* **ኮብለለ** *sheleme*
eloquence *(n.)* **መዳሪ ሰብ** *tegaḧtene*
else *(adv.)* **ብተወሳኺ** *teẗal'ë*
elucidate *(v. t)* **ኣብራህረህ** *kede*
elude *(v.)* **ተኸወለ** *ked'ë*
elusion *(n.)* **ምርካብ** *q̈ẗfet*
elusive *(adj.)* **ንምርካብ** *zḧashe*
emaciated *(adj.)* **ማሕቋቑ** *'ab mengo*
email *(n.)* **መልእኽቲ** *syaf*
emancipate *(v. t)* **ሓራ ኣዉፀአ** *meste*
emasculate *(v.)* **ኣዳኸመ** *ak̇eeba*
embalm *(v.)* **በልሰነ** *belsene*
embankment *(n.)* **ገምገም** *gemgem*
embargo *(n.)* **እገ'ዳ** *'ègeda*
embark *(v. t)* **ደየበ** *sereye*
embarrass *(v.)* **ኣሕፈረ** *knyew*
embassy *(n.)* **ኢምባሲ** *'ab keklte*
embattled *(adj.)* **ብሽግር ዝኸበበ** *frqi beb'ämet*
embed *(v.)* **ኣጣበቐ** *mq̈nan*
embellish *(v.)* **ኣፀባበቐ** *meq̈nan*
embitter *(v.)* **ኣበሳጨወ** *salbeeta*
emblem *(n.)* **ኣርማ** *mexḧaf qdus*
embodiment *(v. t.)* **ኣርኣያ** *zrzrexḧufat*
embolden *(v.)* **ኣደፋፈረ** *fetaw mexḧaf*
emboss *(v.)* **ኣጉለሐ** *'aguleḧe*
embrace *(v.)* **ሓቖፈ** *čwadamnat*
embroidery *(n.)* **ጥልፊ** *teq̈WAyeq̈We*
embryo *(n.)* **ድቂ** *bshkleta*
emend *(v.)* **ኣረመ** *semeye*
emerald *(n.)* **ስመራግድ** *teḧatati*

emerge *(v.)* **ተቐልቐለ** *smay*
emergency *(n.)* **ሓደጋ** *aḱbere*
emigrate *(v.)* **ተሰደደ** *mmshaï*
eminence *(n.)* **ዝና/ክብሪ** *klte 'ämetawi*
eminent *(adj.)* **ስሙይ** *qareeza*
emissary *(n.)* **ልኡኽ** *l'uḱ*
emit *(v.)* **ድምፂ ፈነወ** *äbi*
emollient *(adj.)* **ዘረጋግእ** *drb mer'ä*
emolument *(n.)* **ክስቢ** *ḧluf*
emotion *(n.)* **ብርቱዕ ስሚዒት** *mq̈nan*
emotional *(adj.)* **ናይ ስሚዒት** *bshkleta*
emotive *(adj.)* **ስምዒታዊ** *sm'ïtawi*
empathy *(n.)* **ተደናጋጽነት** *tedenagaxnet*
emperor *(n.)* **ሃፀይ** *ḧamot*
emphasis *(n.)* **ጠመተ** *drblsanawi*
emphasize *(v.)* **ጠመተ ሃበ** *gozomo*
emphatic *(adj.)* **ዘየማትእ** *zeyemat'è*
empire *(n.)* **ግዝኣት** *bilyardo*
employ *(v.)* **ቆፀረ** *bilyon*
employee *(n.)* **ሰራሕተኛ** *habtam*
employer *(n.)* **ቖፃሪ** *'äbi ma'ëbel*
empower *(v.)* **ስልጣን ሃበ** *qofo*
empress *(n.)* **ንግስቲ ነገስት** *ëxfi*
empty *(adj.)* **ጥርሑ** *ẗemere*
emulate *(v. t)* **ተወዳደረ** *tewedadere*
enable *(v.)* **ኣኽኣለ** *fenẗezya*
enact *(v.)* **ሓገገ** *be'äl le'ät menexr*
enamel *(n.)* **ኣናመል** *'anamel*
enamour *(v. t)* **ኣዝዩ ዝፈተወ** *ikoloĵi*
encapsulate *(v.)* **ኣብ ካፕሱላ ዓጸወ** *'ab kapsula 'äxewe*
encase *(v.)* **ሓፀረ ጠቕለለ** *tarik̔ hywet bkal'è seb ztexaḧfe nay ḧade*
enchant *(v.)* **ምሒር ማረኸ** *ikoloĵi*
encircle *(v. t)* **ከበበ ሓዘ** *snehywet*
enclave *(n.)* **ከተማ** *mrmrereesa*
enclose *(v.)* **ኪነየ ሰርሐ** *xmdeselfawi*
enclosure *(n.)* **ምኽላል** *mḱlal*
encode *(v.)* **ኣሸፈረ** *'ashefere*
encompass *(v.)* **ብዙሕ ነገር ኣጠቓለለ** *influwenza*
encore *(n.)* **ተወሳኺ ምርኢት** *mwlad*
encounter *(v.)* **ኣጓነፈ ኣጋጠመ** *bshkoti*
encourage *(v.)* **ኣተባብዐ** *gemese*
encroach *(v.)* **በዝበዘ** *gbresedomeṅa*
encrypt *(v.)* **ነዝዐ** *abun*
encumber *(v.)* **ኣፃገመ** *b'ëray bereḱa*
encyclopaedia *(n.)* **eensayklopidya** *ኢንሳይክሎፒድያ*
end *(n.)* **ጫፍ** *wa'ëro*
endanger *(v.)* **ንሓደጋ ኣሳጠሐ** *neḱese*
endear *(v.)* **ስሙይ ገበረ** *wega'i*
endearment *(n.)* **ፍቕሪ መግለፂ ቃል** *merir*
endeavour *(v.)* **ፀዓረ** *fenẗegar*
endemic *(adj.)* **በብርቂ** *hatefe*
endorse *(v.)* **ደገፈ** *xelim*
endow *(v.)* **ገንዘብ ወፈየ** *blakberi*
endure *(v.)* **ተፃወረ** *seleeda*
enemy *(n.)* **ፀላኢ** *axelemete*

energetic *(adj.)* ሓያል *xelim mezgeb*
energy *(n.)* ጉልበት *tahdidemq̈la'ë*
enfeeble *(v.)* ኣዳኸመ *xlmate*
enfold *(v.)* ሓቖፈ *ḧaq̈ofe*
enforce *(v.)* ኣኽበረ *fḧna*
enfranchise *(v.)* ለቐቐ *leq̈eq̈e*
engage *(v.)* ኣድሕቦ *'ab keklte*
engagement *(n.)* ሕፀ *kesese*
engine *(n.)* ሞተር *xa'ëdewe*
engineer *(n.)* መሃንዲስ *lzub*
English *(n.)* እንግሊዝኛ *ïrḧu*
engrave *(v.)* ፀሑፍ/ቅርፂ ቀረፀ *koberta*
engross *(v.)* መሰጠ *dmxi*
engulf *(v.)* ወሓጠ *weḧaïe*
enigma *(n.)* ምሽጥር *netgWi*
enjoy *(v.)* ኣዘዘ *qlu'ë*
enlarge *(v.)* ኣዐበየ *halhalta*
enlighten *(v.)* ሓበሬታ ሃበ *ĵakeet*
enlist *(v.)* ደፋፍአ *axa'ëdewe*
enliven *(v.)* ከምዝስሕብ ገበረ *qezaḧi*
enmity *(n.)* ፅልኢ *èmbee'ë*
enormous *(adj.)* ገዚፍ *demeye*
enough *(adj.)* እኹል *qana*
enquire *(v.)* ሓተተ *aber*
enquiry *(n.)* ምፅራይ *myuq̈ bele*
enrage *(v.)* ኣገሃየ *ḧawawese*
enrapture *(v.)* ብሓጐስ ፈንጨሐ *bḧagWas fenčeḧe*
enrich *(v.)* ኣማዕበለ *bareḱe*
enrol *(v.)* ተመዝገበ *bruḱ*
enshrine *(v.)* ኣኽበረ *mrq̈a*
enslave *(v.)* ባርያ ገበረ ገዝአ *wag*
ensue *(v.)* ሰዓበ *ëwur*
ensure *(v.)* ኣረጋገፀ *ämete*
entangle *(v. t)* ሓለኸ *gudlet*
enter *(v.)* ኣተወ *semsem 'abele*
enterprise *(n.)* ትካል *garadi*
entertain *(v.)* ኣአንገደ *meq̈alḧ*
entertainment *(n.)* መዘናግዒ *taḧgWas*
enthral *(v.)* መሰጠ *may m'ëgo*
enthrone *(v.)* ኣብ ዙፋን ኮፍ በለ *ḧgus*
enthusiasm *(n.)* ውዕውዕ ስምዒት *w'ëw'ë sm'ït*
enthusiastic *(n.)* ኣፍቃሪ *hbobla wrči*
entice *(v.)* ኣሀረፈ *nefḧe*
entire *(adj.)* ሙሉእ *qWAnïa 'äsa*
entirety *(n.)* ሙሉእ ብሙሉእ *nïab*
entitle *(v.)* መሰል ሃበ *qexri*
entity *(n.)* ዓርሱ ዝኸኣለ ነገር *gla'ë*
entomology *(n.)* ባልዕ ምርምሪ *dndela*
entourage *(n.)* ዓጀብቲ *ëgta*
entrails *(n.)* ዛንጡ መዓንጡ *sayit*
entrance *(n.)* መእተዊ *qWendefe*
entrap *(v. t.)* ሓለኸ *'a'äshewe*
entreat *(v.)* ተማሕፀነ *dem*
entreaty *(v. t)* ምሕፅንታ *dem mfsas*
entrench *(v.)* ኣስረፀ *demawi*
entrepreneur *(n.)* ስራሀ ፈጣሪ ሰብ *ëmbaba*
entrust *(v.)* ሓላፍነት ሃበ *sregtr*
entry *(n.)* ምእታዉ *ëmbaba*
enumerate *(v. t)* ዘርዘረ *nïab qelem*
enunciate *(v.)* ቃላት አንበበ *tkWa'ë*
envelop *(v.)* ሸፈነ *kamcha*
envelope *(n.)* ቡስጣ *nefese*
enviable *(adj.)* ዘቕንእ *qWendefe*

envious *(adj.)* ቀናእ *qena'è*
environment *(n.)* ከበቢ *gWamed*
envisage *(v.)* ተንበየ *semayawi ḧbri*
envoy *(n.)* ልኡኽ *mexadfo*
envy *(n.)* ቅንኣት *ẗemberber bele*
epic *(n.)* ነዊሕ ግጥሚ *godim*
epicure *(n.)* ኣስተማቓሪ *'astemaq̈ari*
epidemic *(n.)* ለበዳ ሕማም *tḧzto mexḧaf*
epidermis *(n.)* ላዕለዋይ ክፋል ቆርበት *amleq̈We*
epigram *(n.)* መበእታ *ḧafere*
epilepsy *(n.)* ትግርትያ *tgrtya*
epilogue *(n.)* ድሕረ-ጽሑፍ *dḧrexḧuf*
episode *(n.)* ፍፃመ/ተዳንፎ *mefles*
epistle *(n.)* መልእኽቲ *mel'èḱti*
epitaph *(n.)* ጽሑፈ-መቓብር *xḧufemeq̈abr*
epitome *(n.)* ጽማቑ *xmaq̈Wi*
epoch *(n.)* ዘበን *ḧaf kof bele*
equal *(adj.)* ማዕረ *geltew*
equalize *(v. t)* ማዕረ ገበረ *ḧabere*
equate *(v.)* ማዕረ ጌሩ ረኣየ *ĵlesebeyti*
equation *(n.)* ማዕረ ጌሩ ሃበ *akalawi*
equator *(n.)* ንፍቀ ምድሪ መሬት *akal*
equestrian *(adj.)* ፈረስ ጋለቢ *zeb'ëḧa*
equidistant *(adj.)* ማዕረ ዝርሕቀቱ *ma'ëre zrḧqetu*
equilateral *(adj.)* ማዕረ-ጐድናዊ *ma'ëregWadnawi*
equilibrium *(n.)* ሚዛን *tewelawele*
equip *(v.)* ኣማልአ *ḧaqi zeyblu*
equipment *(n.)* መሳርሒ *mguli 'ančwa*
equitable *(adj.)* ሚዛናዊ *meflḧi*
equity *(n.)* ፍትሓዊነት *nawxeen*
equivalent *(adj.)* ማዕረ *ma'ëre*
equivocal *(adj.)* ማንታ ቃል *manta qal*
era *(n.)* ዘበን *gundi*
eradicate *(v.)* መሓወ *meḧawe*
erase *(v.)* ደምሰሰ *demsese*
erect *(adj.)* ቅኑዕ ዝበለ *bomb*
erode *(v.)* ሸርሸረ *debdebe*
erogenous *(adj.)* ኤሮሳዊ *eerosawi*
erosion *(n.)* ፍግረት *fgret*
erotic *(adj.)* ፍቕራዊ *fq̈rawi*
err *(v.)* ተጋገየ *aḱeze*
errand *(n.)* መልኣኽቲ *w'ël*
errant *(adj.)* ግጉይ *gguy*
erratic *(adj.)* ዘይስሩዕ *äxmi*
erroneous *(adj.)* ግጉይ *gguy*
error *(n.)* ጌጋ *geega*
erstwhile *(adj.)* ቀደም *qedem*
erudite *(adj.)* ምሁር *äxam*
erupt *(v.)* ነቶገ *netoge*
escalate *(v.)* ኣዕረገ *'a'ërege*
escalator *(n.)* ኣደያቢ *'adeyabi*
escapade *(n.)* ጽልቋ *xlqWA*
escape *(v.i)* ኣምለጠ *mexḧafawi*
escort *(n.)* መሰነዪ *meseneyi*
esoteric *(adj.)* ናይ ክቲ *nay kti*
especial *(adj.)* ዝበለፀ *ḧto*
especially *(adv.)* ብፍላይ *ẗegele'albo*
espionage *(n.)* ስለላ *msfaḧ*

espouse *(v.)* ድጋፍ ሃበ *senkati*
espresso *(n.)* ስፕሬሶ *newiḧ sa'èni*
essay *(n.)* ሓጺር ፅሁፍ *goĵo*
essence *(n.)* ፍረ ነገር *kontroband*
essential *(adj.)* ዝኣዩ ነገር *mrko*
establish *(v.)* ኣጣየሸ *dob*
establishment *(n.)* ትካል *gWargWaḧe*
estate *(n.)* ርስቲ *tewelde*
esteem *(n.)* ኽብሪ *werede*
estimate *(v. t)* ግምት *teleqḧe*
estranged *(adj.)* ነጸለ *nexele*
et cetera *(adv.)* ወዘተረፈ *ḧaleq̈a*
eternal *(adj.)* ዘልኣለማዊ *zel'alemawi*
eternity *(n.)* ዘልኣለማዊነት *sne'atklti*
ethic *(n)* ስነ ምግባር *klti'u*
ethical *(n.)* ስነ ምግባራዊ *ashegere*
ethnic *(adj.)* ናይ ዓሌት *ïrmuz*
etiquette *(n.)* ደምቢ *qarana*
etymology *(n.)* ፍልቀተ-ቃል *flqeteqal*
eunuch *(n.)* ስሉብ *gWadena*
euphoria *(n.)* ጡብላሕታ *neẗere*
euro *(n.)* ገንዘብ *genzeb*
European *(n.)* ናይ ኣዉሮፓ *ḧaxere*
euthanasia *(n.)* ምሕረተ-ቅትለት *mḧreteqtlet*
evacuate *(v.)* ኣልቀቐ *deret'albo*
evade *(v. t)* ኣምለጠ *legas*
evaluate *(v. i)* ገምገመ *lgsi*
evaporate *(v.)* ሃፈፈ *ḧq̈ufi'ëmbaba*
evasion *(n.)* ምዝንጋዕ *mznga'ë*
evasive *(adj.)* ጉስያዊ *gusyawi*
eve *(n.)* ድሮ *qesti*
even *(adj.)* ለሚፅ *segede*
evening *(n.)* ምሸት *me'änaẗu*
event *(n.)* ፍፃመ *das*
eventually *(adv.)* ኣብ መወዳእታ *čḧolo*
ever *(adv.)* ዋላ ሓደሻዕ *sanduq̈*
every *(adj.)* ሕድሕድ *tegadalay*
evict *(v.)* ኣባረረ *gusẗi*
eviction *(n.)* ዝባረረ *wedi*
evidence *(n.)* መረዳእታ *ademe*
evident *(adj.)* ብንፁር *n'èsnet*
evil *(adj.)* ጨካን *bikini*
evince *(v.)* ብጋህዲ ኣርኣየ *dgaf*
evoke *(v.)* ኣዘከረ *benaîr*
evolution *(n.)* ኣዝጋሚ ዕብየት *medegef*
evolve *(v.)* ቀስ ብቐስ ዓበየ *teĵehari*
exact *(adj.)* ትኽክለኛ *breyl*
exaggerate *(v.)* ኣጋነነ *ḧangol*
exaggeration *(n.)* ግነት *lgWam*
exalt *(v.)* ልዕል ኣበለ *čenfer*
exam *(n.)* ፈተና *ëlamet*
examination *(n.)* ምርመራ *anbelbele*
examine *(v.)* ኣፅነዐ *brandi*
examinee *(n.)* ተመርማሪ *dereq̈eḧa*
example *(n.)* ኣብነት *asrazi*
exasperate *(v.)* ኣበሳጨወ *teba'ë*
excavate *(v.)* ኮዓተ *tb'ät*
exceed *(v.)* በለፀ *qWeyeq̈WA*
excel *(v.)* ነፍዐ *hla*
excellence *(n.)* ዝለዓለ ፅሬት *mẗḧas*
Excellency *(n.)* ክቡር *ènĵera*
excellent *(adj.)* ኣዝዩ ፅቡቕ *wrdi*

except *(prep.)* ብጀካ *sebere*
exception *(n.)*
ተቓውሞ *teq̈awmo*
excerpt *(n.)* ጥቕሲ *qursi*
excess *(n.)* ተረፍ ነገር *ẗub*
excessive *(adj.)* ዕዙዝ ዝበዝሐ
tnfas
exchange *(v. t)* ልዉዉጥ
atenfese
exchequer *(n.)* ዓቃቢ ንዋይ
änqer ẗebenĵa
excise *(n.)* ቀረፅ *sregtr*
excite *(v.i)* ኣሐጎሰ *arabḧe*
excitement *(n.)* ታሕጓስ *hdu'è*
nfas
exclaim *(v.)* ኣንሃርሃር *ḧxret*
ḧaxirnet
exclamation *(n.)* ኣንሃርሃር ሃበ
xemeq̈We
exclude *(v.)* ኣትረፈ *'ènda bira*
exclusive *(adj.)* ብሕታዊ *gubo*
excoriate *(v.)* ኣቖጥዐ *ḧẗub*
matoni
excrete *(v.)* ምውጻእ *mwxa'è*
excursion *(n.)* ሽርሽር *mer'ät*
excuse *(v.)* ምኽኒት *mer'äwi*
execute *(v.)* ቀተለ *dldl*
execution *(n.)* መቕተልቲ *lgWam*
executive *(n.)* ናይ ምፍጻም *nay*
mfxam
executor *(n.)* ወዳኢ *weda'i*
exempt *(adj.)* ምሒር *mḧir*
exercise *(n.)* ምዉስዋስ ኣካላት
meraḧ brgeed
exert *(v.)* ስልጣኑ ተጠቐመ *dmuq̈*
exhale *(v.)* ኣተንፈሰ *demeq̈e*
berhe
exhaust *(v.)* ኣድከመ *blča*
exhaustive *(adj.)* ዝተማልአ
dmuq̈
exhibit *(v.)* ንህዝቢ ኣርእየ *čaf*
exhibition *(n.)* ምርኢት *mr'it*
exhilarate *(v.)* 'aḧagWase
'aḧagWase
exhort
(v.) ኣተሓሳሰበ *'ateḧasasebe*
exigency *(n.)* ህፀፅ *birinjal*
exile *(n.)* ስደት *ẗeref*
exist *(v.)* ሃለወ *sluẗ*
existence *(n.)* ህልዉና *nedere*
exit *(n.)* መዉፅኢ በሪ *biritish*
exonerate *(v.)* ተሓታታይ ኣይኮነን
በለ *tesebari*
exorbitant *(adj.)* ኣዝዩ ብጣዕሚ
ዝለዓለ *ankWale*
exotic *(adj.)* ካብ ካልእ ሃገር *sefiḧ*
expand *(v.)* ገፈሐ *zergḧe*
expanse *(n.)* ለጥ ዝበለ *bezeq̈zeq̈*
expatriate *(n.)* ወዲ ወፃእ *kawlo*
fyori
expect *(v.)* ትፅቢት ገበረ *menshur*
expectant *(adj.)* ተፀባይ *sebere*
expedient *(adj.)* ጠቓሚ *ẗeq̈ami*
expedite *(v.)* ኣሳለጠ *delalay*
expedition *(n.)* ወፍሪ *wefri*
expel *(v. t)* ለጎጉ *bronzo*
expend *(v.)* ኣዉፀአ *čeq̈awit*
expenditure *(n.)* ወፃኢ *zara*
expense *(n.)* ወፃኢ *meḱoster*
expensive *(adj.)* ክቡር *mereq̈*
experience *(n.)* ልምዲ *temekro*
experiment *(n.)* ሳይንሳዊ ፈተነ
ḧaw
expert *(n.)* በዓልሞያ *ḧwnet*
expertise *(n.)* ሞያ *shefashfti*
expiate *(v.)* ዓደየ *ädeye*
expire *(v.)* ወደቐ *wedeq̈e*

expiry *(n.)* **መፈጸምታ** *mefexemta*
explain *(v.)* **ኣብራህረሀ** *snbrat*
explicit *(adj.)* **ንፁር** *kulaso*
explode *(v.)* **ነተጉ** *bunawi čeguri 'äyni gex zelewa xa'ëda sebeyti*
exploit *(v. t)* **ተበለፀ** *qendi kbdet*
exploration *(n.)* **ብዝበዛ** *asbasla*
explore *(v.)* **ዳህሰሰ** *ashaḱWi*
explosion *(n.)* **ነትጉ** *zeymḧr*
explosive *(adj.)* **ነታጉ** *ènssa*
exponent *(n.)* **ደጋፊ** *äfra*
export *(v. t.)* **ናብ ወፃዕ ለኣኸ** *kona'ë*
expose *(v.)* **ኣቃልዐ** *megelel*
exposure *(n.)* **ምቅላዕ** *meq̈Welef*
express *(v.)* **ገለፀ** *agWam*
expression *(n.)* **መግለፂ** *mnq̈ bele*
expressive *(adj.)* **ሓሳብ ዝገልፅ** *baĵet*
expropriate *(v.)* **ሃገረ** *gobay*
expulsion *(n.)* **ምብራር** *weḧaẗ gWanxi*
extant *(adj.)* **እስካዕ ሕጂ ዘሎ** *gusẗi*
extend *(v.)* **ኣንወሐ** *mesḧaq̈*
extension *(n.)* **ምስፍሕፋሕ** *tḱWan*
extent *(n.)* **ክብደት** *karosa*
exterior *(adj.)* **ደገ** *ẗrumba*
external *(adj.)* **ግዳማይ ወፃኢ** *hanexe*
extinct *(adj.)* **ዝፃነተ** *hnxa*
extinguish *(v.)* **ኣጥፈአ** *shgurto*
extirpate *(v.)* **ኣልገሰ** *ḧbeẗ*
extort *(v.)* **ብሓይሊ ወሰደ** *bḧayli wesede*
extra *(adj.)* **ተወሳኺ** *bbzḧi*
extract *(v. t)* **ኣወፃፀአ** *degWalax*
extraction *(n.)* **መበቆል** *arḧa*
extraordinary *(adj.)* **ፍሉይ** *fluy*
extravagance *(n.)* **ምሕንሻሽ** *ärer*
extravagant *(adj.)* **ሓሻሺ** *buletin*
extravaganza *(n.)* **ሸንዳሕዳሕ** *shendaḧdaḧ*
extreme *(adj.)* **ምሒር ዝለዓለ** *azazi*
extremist *(n.)* **ፅንፈኛ ዝኮነ ሰብ** *qẗquẗ b'ëray*
extricate *(v.)* **ኣምለጠ** *älaq̈*
extrovert *(n.)* **ሕዉስ** *ërdi*
extrude *(v.)* **ደፈኡ ኣዉፀአ** *me'äkor*
exuberant *(adj.)* **ዉዕዉዕ** *te'änqefe*
exude *(v.)* **ኣርኣየ** *tenagWaxe*
eye *(n.)* **ዓይኒ** *walga gWanxi*
eyeball *(n.)* **ኩዕሶ ዓይኒ** *huguree*
eyesight *(n.)* **ናይ ምርኣይ ዓቕሚ** *nay mr'ay 'äq̈mi*
eyewash *(n.)* **እጥበት ዓይኒ** *mqur bani*
eyewitness *(n.)* **ምስክር** *ẗmar*

F

fable *(n.)* **ነበረያ** *bush*
fabric *(n.)* **እሉም** *èlum*
fabricate *(v.)* **ኣለመ** *'aleme*
fabulous *(adj.)* **ዘይእመን** *zey'èmen*
facade *(n.)* **ገጽ** *gex*
face *(n.)* **ገፅ** *ḧabar merkeb*
facet *(n.)* **ጐድኒ** *gWadni*
facetious *(adj.)* **ናይ ቀልዲ** *mnsfaf*
facial *(adj.)* **ናይ ገጽ** *nay gex*
facile *(adj.)* **ቀሊል** *qelil*

facilitate *(v.)* ኣሳለጠ *sedeq̈a*
facility *(n.)* ስሉጥነት *sluẗnet*
facing *(n.)* ገፃዊ *birokratawi*
facsimile *(n.)* ቅዳሕ *qdaḧ*
fact *(n.)* ክውንነት *kwnnet*
faction *(n.)* ተቓዉሞ *seraq̈i*
factitious *(adj.)* ልብ ወለዳዊ *geben*
factor *(n.)* ምኽንያት *qebri*
factory *(n.)* ፋብሪካ *lagxi*
faculty *(n.)* ክእለት *mndad*
fad *(n.)* መሐደሲ *andadi*
fade *(v.i)* ሃሰሰ *rsun*
Fahrenheit *(n.)* ፋሐረናይት *gudgWad*
fail *(v.)* ተረፈ *terefe*
failing *(n.)* ድኽመት *ḧagez*
failure *(n.)* ዉድቀት *netegWa*
faint *(adj.)* ብንፁር ዘይረአ *qebere*
fair *(adj.)* ሚዛናዊ *awtobus*
fairing *(n.)* ብቕንዕና *bq̈n'ëna*
fairly *(adv.)* ብመጠኑ *gofgWaf*
fairy *(n.)* ስንድሮ *wanin*
faith *(n.)* እምነት *negaday*
faithful *(adj.)* ተኣማኒ *deret*
faithless *(adj.)* ዘይእመን *ashbedbede*
fake *(adj.)* ተምያን *temyan*
falcon *(n.)* ሊላ *lila*
fall *(v.)* ወደቐ *ḧarad sga*
fallacy *(n.)* ግጉይ ሓሳብ *balẗeĵi*
fallible *(adj.)* ክጋገ ዝኽእል *ẗesmi*
fallow *(adj.)* ቃድሬ *xmblali'ë*
false *(adj.)* ሓሶት *doso*
falsehood *(n.)* ምሕሳዉ *melgom*
falter *(v.)* ተዳኸመ *gez'e*
fame *(n.)* ዝና *ädagi*
familiar *(adj.)* ልሙድ *ziz bele*
family *(n.)* ስድራ ቤት *shla*
famine *(n.)* ጥሜት *sirena*
famished *(adj.)* ኣዝዩ ዝጠመየ *'azyu zẗemeye*
famous *(adj.)* ስሙይ *godnawimrča*
fan *(n.)* ኣድናቒ *qedem*
fanatic *(n.)* ኣፍቃሪ *bḧnxax*
fanciful *(adj.)* ሓላሚ *ḧalami*
fancy *(n.)* ደለየ *dembe*
fanfare *(n.)* ኣርኣየ *temelkati*
fang *(n.)* ስኒ ተመን *bayit*
fantasize *(v.)* ቀረጸ *qerexe*
fantastic *(adj.)* ዘገርም *zegerm*
fantasy *(n.)* ትምኒት *kawlo*
far *(adv.)* ርሑቕ *gabina*
farce *(n.)* መስሓቕ *mesḧaq̈*
fare *(n.)* ዋጋ *waga*
farewell *(interj.)* ቻዉ *kakaw*
farm *(n.)* ሕርሻ *ḧab'e*
farmer *(n.)* ሓረስታይ *ktam*
fascia *(n.)* መእሰሪ ነገር *qaq̈a*
fascinate *(v.)* መሰጠ *qWelqWAl*
fascism *(n.)* ፋሽስትነት *fashstnet*
fashion *(n.)* ዘበናይነት *reesa*
fashionable *(adj.)* ዘበናይ *kadi*
fast *(adj.)* ቅልጡፍ *reesa*
fasten *(v.)* ቆለፈ *kadet*
fastness *(n.)* ጠንካታ ትሕዞ *kadmyum*
fat *(n.)* ሃዝራጥ *askereen*
fatal *(adj.)* ቀታሊ *qeesar*
fatality *(n.)* ሞት *kafe*
fate *(n.)* መጨረሽታ *kafeterya*
fateful *(adj.)* **xḧftawi** *ጽሕፍታዊ*
father *(n.)* ኣቦ *kidan*
fathom *(n.)* ተረደአ *sheḧaẗe*

fatigue *(n.)* ብርቱዕ ድኻም *dolshi*
fatuous *(adj.)* ብስለት ዘይብሉ *me'ät*
fault *(n.)* ስሕተት *kalsyum*
faulty *(adj.)* ፍፁም ዘይኮነ *qemere*
fauna *(n.)* እንስሳታት *meteḧasasebi*
favour *(n.)* ድጋፍ *qemer*
favourable *(adj.)* ቅንዕና ዘለዎ *äwde'awarḧ*
favourite *(adj.)* ተፈታዊ *mraḱ*
fax *(n.)* ጽሑፍ *xḧuf*
fear *(n.)* ፈርሀ *ferhe*
fearful *(adj.)* ዝፈረሐ *dewele*
fearless *(adj.)* ዘይፈርሕ *xbaq̈e xḧfet*
feasible *(adj.)* ክኸውን ዝኽእል *kḱewn zḱ'èl*
feast *(n.)* ድግስ *x'ötawi*
feat *(n.)* ክእለት *ïre*
feather *(n.)* ክንቲት *hdu'è*
feature *(n.)* መልክዕ *melk'ë*
febrile *(adj.)* ጭኑቕ *mxlam*
February *(n.)* ለካቲት *bxaynet*
feckless *(adj.)* ዋጋ ዘይብሉ *waga zeyblu*
federal *(adj.)* ፌደራላዊ *shash*
federate *(v.)* ፎደራ *fodera*
federation *(n.)* ፈደረሽን *federeshn*
fee *(n.)* ክፍሊት *kamyo*
feeble *(adj.)* ድኹም *kamera*
feed *(v.)* መገበ *me'äsker*
feeder *(n.)* ተመጋቢ *zemete*
feel *(v.)* ተሰምዩ *kamfora*
feeling *(n.)* ስምዒት *kampas*
feign *(v.)* ኣምሰለ *amsele*
feisty *(adj.)* መዕለበጢ *me'ëlebeẗi*
felicitate *(v.)* ኣዳለወ *'adalewe*
felicitation *(n.)* መግለጺ ሓጐስ *meglexi ḧagWas*
felicity *(n.)* ፍሰሃ *sereze*
fell *(v.)* ኦም ቆረፀ *mẗfa'è*
fellow *(n.)* ሰብኣይ *menshro*
fellowship *(n.)* ብፃይነት *brahan*
felon *(n.)* ገበነኛ *ghud*
female *(adj.)* ኣንስታያዊ *anstayawi*
feminine *(adj.)* ኣንስታያዊ *'anstayawi*
feminism *(n.)* ኣንስታይነት *'anstaynet*
fence *(n.)* ሓፁር *karamela*
fencing *(n.)* መሕፀሪ *kerezan*
fend *(v.)* ዓርሱ ተኸናኸነ *kelbawi*
feng shui *(n.)* ፌንግ ሽዊ *saxun*
fennel *(n.)* ተኽሊ *hemp*
feral *(adj.)* ቀይዲ በተኽ *bela'ë seb*
ferment *(v.)* በኹዐ *medf'ë*
fermentation *(n.)* ቡኾዕ *gWaraḧ*
fern *(n.)* ተክሊ *tankWa*
ferocious *(adj.)* ጨካን *qenona*
ferry *(n.)* መርከብ *dbab*
fertile *(adj.)* ልሙዕ *gbzna*
fertility *(n.)* ልሙዕነት *ḧaraq̈*
fertilize *(v.)* ኣጽገየ *axgeye*
fertilizer *(n.)* ድኹዒ *dḱu'ï*
fervent *(adj.)* ውዕውዕ *w'ëw'ë*
fervid *(adj.)* ምውቕ *mwq̈*
fervour *(n.)* ብርቱዕ ተምሳጥ *brtu'ë temsaẗ*
fester *(v.)* ረኾሰ *reḱWase*
festival *(n.)* በዓል *ämiq̈ snčro*
festive *(adj.)* ናይ በዓል *qWeb'ë*
festivity *(n.)* ምድሳት *mdsat*
fetch *(v.)* ኣምፀአ *k'ila*

fete *(n.)* **ፅንብል** *sefiḧ*
fetish *(n.)* **ጣኦት** *kapaciter*
fettle *(n.)* **ጥዕና** *äq̈mi*
feud *(n.)* **ቅርሕንቲ** *seleme*
feudalism *(n.)*
መስፍንነት *mesfnnet*
fever *(n.)* **ረስኒ** *r'èsemal*
few *(adj.)* **ዉሑድ** *r'èsemalnet*
fey *(adj.)* **ስሚዒታዊ** *r'èsemalawi*
fiancé *(n.)* **ሕፁይ** *r'èsemal gebere*
fiasco *(n.)* **ዉድቀት** *gbri*
fibre *(n.)* **ቃንጫ** *temberkeḱe*
fickle *(adj.)* **ተለዋዋጣይ** *qbeẗ*
fiction *(n.)* **ልቢ ወለድ** *qebaẗ*
fictitious *(adj.)* **ናይ ምህዞ** *kapsikem*
fiddle *(n.)* **ተናኸፈ** *gelbeẗe*
fidelity *(adj.)*
ተኣማኒነት *ẗemẗami mesḧb*
field *(n.)* **ግራት** *leq̈otafre*
fiend *(n.)* **ጨካን ሰብ** *gbẗan*
fierce *(adj.)* **ሐያል** *gbẗani*
fiery *(adj.)* **ሓዊ ዝመስል** *ar'èsti*
fifteen *(adj. & n.)* **ዓሰርተ ሓሙሽተ** *'äserte ḧamushte*
fifty *(adj. & n.)* **ሓምሳ** *ḧamsa*
fig *(n.)* **ተኸሊ** *mruḱnet*
fight *(v.t)* **ተበኣሰ** *tebe'ase*
fighter *(n.)* **ተጋዳላይ** *tegadalay*
figment *(n.)* **ምህዞ** *makina*
figurative *(adj)* **ምስላዊ** *karame' el*
figure *(n.)* **ቁፀሪ** *kara 't*
figurine *(n.)* **ንእሽቶ ምስሊ** *n'èshto msli*
filament *(n.)* **ቀጢን ስልኪ** *qeẗin slki*
file *(n.)* **ፋይል** *fayl*
filings *(n.)* **ብራድ** *brad*
fill *(v.)* **መልአ** *terimuz*
filler *(n.)* **መወተፊ** *ge'mbi*
filling *(n.)* **መምልኢ** *meml'i*
fillip *(n.)* **ጦፍታ** *ẗofta*
film *(n.)* **ፊልሚ** *kartoon*
filter *(n.)* **መፅለሊ** *na' ae lebii*
filth *(n.)* **ግዕጋዕ** *gole 'foo*
filtrate *(n.)* **ዝፀለለ** *papase'*
fin *(n.)* **ክንፊ** *knfi*
final *(adj.)*
መወዳእታዊ *meweda'ètawi*
finalist *(n.)* **መጨረሻ** *mečeresha*
finance *(n.)* **ገንዘብ** *sir'ahh*
financial *(adj.)* **ናይ ገንዘብ** *they'aa jibo*
financier *(n.)* **ናይ ገንዘብ ሰብ** *tinkuq*
find *(v.)* **ረኸበ** *ze yestewu 'el*
fine *(adj.)* **ፅቡቕ** *aa'b*
finesse *(n.)* **ኣኸእሎ** *tenahe'fe*
finger *(n.)* **ኣፃብዕት** *wekil*
finial *(n.)* **መጠቓለሊ** *aa'b merkeb*
finicky *(adj.)* **መማረፂ** *mesili*
finish *(v.)* **ዛዘመ** *qeyiha hib're*
finite *(adj.)* **ዉሱን** *Chif'chefa*
fir *(n.)* **ተኸሊ** *segawi*
fire *(n.)* **ባርዕ** *bar'ë*
firewall *(n.)* **ባርዕ ምሕላው** *bar'ë mḧlaw*
firm *(adj.)* **ትካል** *derfi*
firmament *(n.)* **ሰማይ** *zz'ebere bere*
first *(adj. & n.)* **ፈለማ** *tserabi*
first aid *(n.)* **ቀዳማይ ረድኤት** *qedamay red'eet*
fiscal *(adj.)* **ናይ ግብሪ** *mentseff*
fish *(n.)* **ዓሳ** *babur*

fisherman *(n.)* ገፋፍ ዓሳ *binefarit*
fishery *(n.)* ምርባሕ ዓሳ *carrot*
fishy *(adj.)* አጠራጣሪ *teshekeme*
fissure *(n.)* ቋቚራ *arebia*
fist *(n.)* ዕምኹ *'ëmkWa*
fit *(adj.)* በቐዐ *beq̈'ë*
fitful *(adj.)* ዝተቖራረፀ *bako*
fitter *(n.)* ቀዳዳይ *qedaday*
fitting *(n.)* ምዕቃን *m'ëqan*
five *(adj. & n.)* ሓሙሽተ *qeretse*
fix *(v.)* ኣጥበቐ *'aẗbeq̈e*
fixture *(n.)* ጥባቕ *ẗbaq̈*
fizz *(v.)* ፈጨጭ በለ *kunet*
fizzle *(v.)* ድምጺ *mesekote*
fizzy *(adj.)* ጋዝ ዘለዎ *qeriishe*
fjord *(n.)* ወሽመጥ *ome*
flab *(n.)* ለምባእ *lemba'è*
flabbergasted *(adj.)* አዝዩ ዝተደነቐ *suf*
flabby *(adj.)* ሃጥሃጥ ዝብል *zetelebte*
flaccid *(adj.)* ልስሉስን ድኹምን *hintsete*
flag *(n.)* ባንዴራ *fiseto*
flagellate *(v.)* ብጭጉራፍ ወቐዐ *satsun resa*
flagrant *(adj.)* ግሁድ *megebi*
flair *(n.)* ተዉህቦ *juba*
flake *(n.)* ቅራፍ *temeleket*
flamboyant *(adj.)* መብለጭለጪ *meblečleči*
flame *(n.)* ነበልባል *ameteqku*
flammable *(adj.)* ብቐሊሉ ዝነድድ *xebhi*
flank *(n.)* ጎኒ ሕንፃ *cider*
flannel *(n.)* ላና *lana*
flap *(v.)* ጸፍዐ *xef'ë*
flapjack *(n.)* ኬክ *bet ciniema*
flare *(n.)* ተወለዐ *qerefa*
flash *(v.)* ማሕ በለ *kebi*
flashlight *(n.)* ላምባዲና *lampadina*
flask *(n.)* ብርጭቆ *kbibe*
flat *(adj.)* ፀፊሕ *tsrachew*
flatten *(v.t.)* ኣፅፈሐ *xudet*
flatter *(v.)* ኣተዓሻሸወ *gereze'*
flatulent *(adj.)* ዝተቖብቀበ *dobe*
flaunt *(v.)* ተበርጠጠ *gedebe*
flavour *(n.)* መቐረት *meq̈eret*
flaw *(n.)* ጉድለት *hawahewu*
flea *(n.)* ቁንጪ *serekse*
flee *(v.)* ሃደመ *sanaduqe*
fleece *(n.)* ጸምሪ *xemri*
fleet *(n.)* ጭፍራ *čfra*
flesh *(n.)* ስጋ *tekese*
flex *(v.)* ኣማወቐ *zega*
flexible *(adj.)* ተቐያያራይ *zegenet*
flexitime *(n.)* እዋን ምርጫ *tekil*
flick *(v.)* ነፀገ *citric*
flicker *(v.t)* ዉልዕ ጥፍእ በለ *ketema*
flight *(n.)* ንፍረት *nfret*
flimsy *(adj.)* ምህሙን *mhmun*
flinch *(v.)* ሰገጥ በለ *segeẗ bele*
fling *(v.)* ሰንደወ *sevil sebe*
flint *(n.)* ፅንፅሕላ *seletan*
flip *(v.)* ተጠወየ *aseltene*
flippant *(adj.)* ደረቓኛ *dereq̈eňa*
flipper *(n.)* ተጣወቒ *Kedan*
flirt *(v.i)* ኣኺሸመ *tenaḱefe*
flit *(v.)* ተናፈረ *tenafere*
float *(v.)* ተንሳፈፈ *tensafefe*
flock *(n.)* መጓሰ *megWase*
floe *(n.)* በረድ *atabeqe*
flog *(v.)* ገረፈ *alet*
flood *(n.)* ዉሕጅ *hibuea'*

floodlight *(n.)* ባዉዛ *atabeqe*
floor *(n.)* ባይታ ቤት *abrahereh*
flop *(v.)* ዘፍ በለ *keles*
floppy *(adj.)* ወደቐ *mleekti*
flora *(n.)* ተኽልታት *geletsinet*
floral *(adj.)* ዕምባባዊ *'ëmbabawi*
florist *(n.)* ሸያጢ ዕምበባ *chebete*
floss *(n.)* ተኽሊ ጡጥ *kifeli*
flotation *(n.)* ሰፈፍ ምባል *heruyei*
flounce *(v.)* ቁጡዕ *qenedegna*
flounder *(v.)* ሓሰበ *megujak*
flour *(n.)* ሕሩጭ *gojele*
flourish *(v.)* ደንፈዐ *aneqetse*
flow *(v.i)* ፈሰሰ *fesese*
flower *(n.)* ዕምበባ *txefri*
flowery *(adj.)* ን ፍዮሪ *n fyori*
flu *(n.)* ጉንፋዕ *tsxeruye*
fluctuate *(v.)* ተለዋዋጢ *telewawaẗi*
fluent *(adj.)* መላኽ ቋንቋ *melaḱ qWAnqWA*
fluff *(n.)* ልስሉስ *netsxur*
fluid *(n.)* ፈሳሲ ነገር *meaelayi*
fluke *(n.)* ፍሉክ *fluk*
fluorescent *(adj.)* ፍሎረሸንት *floreshent*
fluoride *(n.)* ፍሎራይድ *cdade*
flurry *(n.)* ጭንቅንቕ *meherte*
flush *(v.)* ኣኹርዐ *'aḱur'ë*
fluster *(v.)* ኣጨናነቐ *klemintaine*
flute *(n.)* ሻምብቆ *nKes*
flutter *(v.)* ኣንበልበለ *kahenat'*
fluvial *(adj.)* ሩባ *kahin*
flux *(n.)* ዋሕዚ *waḧzi*
fly *(v.i)* ነፈረ *tsehafi*
foam *(n.)* ሰፍነግ *bilihi*
focal *(adj.)* ማእኸላይ *dimtsi ftre'*
focus *(n.)* ኣድሃበ ገበረ *Amil*
fodder *(n.)* ፍሩሽካ ንፋይ *Tsxdefi*
foe *(n.)* ድርቋ *xela'i*
fog *(n.)* ጸላኢ *gme*
foil *(v.)* ኣፈሸለ *deYebe*
fold *(v.t)* ዓፀፈ *tAwte'*
foliage *(n.)* ኣቑፅልቲ *tlTefe'*
folio *(n.)* ቆጽሊ ወረቐት *qoxli wereq̈et*
folk *(n.)* ህዝቢ *agachewu*
follow *(v.)* ሰዓበ *menqerker*
follower *(n.)* ተኽታሊ *mentelina*
folly *(n.)* ዕሽነት *seat'*
fond *(adj.)* ኣፍቃሪ *'afqari*
fondle *(v.)* ደረዘ *dereze*
font *(n.)* ጽዋእ *xwa'è*
food *(n.)* ምግቢ *wushate'*
fool *(n.)* ዓንጃል *zitqarebe*
foolish *(adj.)* ዓንጃል *änĵal*
foolproof *(adj.)* ዘይጋገ *zeygage*
foot *(n.)* መርገፂ እግሪ *kedeNe'*
footage *(n.)* ቀረፃ *kidawunti'*
football *(n.)* ኩዕሶ እግሪ *ku'ëso 'ègri*
footing *(n.)* መርገፂ *debNa'*
footling *(adj.)* ርክብ *esil anahib*
for *(prep.)* ን *n*
foray *(n.)* ፈተነ *azenagiaa*
forbear *(v.)* ወገደ *wegede*
forbid *(v.)* ኸልከለ *ganeta*
force *(n.)* ሓይሊ *afafenote*
forceful *(adj.)* ዘእምን *lahezaZ'*
forceps *(n.)* ወረጦ *wereẗo*
forcible *(adj.)* ናይ ሓይሊ *nay ḧayli*
fore *(adj.)* ቕዲሙ *aseltani*
forearm *(n.)* ቅልፅም *himet*
forebear *(n.)* ኣያታት *hatnet*
forecast *(v.t)* ተንበየ *shahikar*

forefather *(n.)* **አቦሓጎ** *'abohago*
forefinger *(n.)* **ኣመልካቲቶ** *'amelkatito*
foregoing *(adj.)* **ዝሓለፈ** *zḧalefe*
forehead *(n.)* **ግንባር** *juba*
foreign *(adj.)* **ናይ ወፃእ** *shehare*
foreigner *(n.)* **ባዕዲ** *ba'ëdi*
foreknowledge *(n.)* **ብኣጋ ኣፍልጦ** *b'aga 'aflïo*
foreleg *(n.)* **ኢድ** *id*
foreman *(n.)* **ሓለቓ** *ḧaleq̈a*
foremost *(adj.)* **ብቐዳሚ** *aleba saret*
forename *(n.)* **ስዕሚ** *kocain*
forensic *(adj.)* **beet frdawi** *ቤት ፍርዳዊ*
foreplay *(n.)* **ናይ ፍቕሪ ዛንታ** *nay fq̈ri zanta*
forerunner *(n.)* **ተነባዪ** *tenebayi*
foresee *(v.)* **ተንበየ** *diduee'*
foresight *(n.)* **ሳዛ** *saza*
forest *(n.)* **ዱር** *dur*
forestall *(v.)* **ኣበርዓነ** *'aber'äne*
forestry *(n.)* **ስነ-ዱር** *snedur*
foretell *(v.)* **ተንበየ** *cocoon*
forever *(adv.)* **ንዘልኣለም** *nzel'alem*
foreword *(n.)* **መቕድም** *meq̈dm*
forfeit *(v.)* **ኣሀገረ** *qewami*
forge *(v.t)* **ፀዓረ** *agedded*
forgery *(n.)* **temyan** *ተምያን*
forget *(v.)* **ረስዐ** *res'ë*
forgetful *(adj.)* **ረሳዒ** *resa'ï*
forgive *(v.)* **መሓረ** *meḧare*
forgo *(v.)* **ሓደገ** *kazina*
fork *(n.)* **ፋርኬታ** *farkeeta*
forlorn *(adj.)* **ብሕታዊ** *qiltafe*
form *(n.)* **ዓይነት** *heigib*
formal *(adj.)* **ስሩዕ** *astentene*
formality *(n.)* **ኣገባብ** *temesasali*
format *(n.)* **መልኺ** *ginizabe*
formation *(n.)* **ኣቀዋውማ** *'aqewawma*
former *(adj.)* **ናይ ቀደም** *tesaneyei*
formerly *(adv.)* **ቅድም** *qdm*
formidable *(adj.)* **ዘይድፈር** *hadinet*
formula *(n.)* **ቅዋመ** *qwame*
formulate *(v.)* **ዘመወ** *qkulele*
forsake *(v.)* **ሓደገ** *sanetime*
forswear *(v.)* **ነጸገ** *nexege*
fort *(n.)* **ዕርዲ** *tegetateme*
forte *(n.)* **ጩኸት** *tegwanefo*
forth *(adv.)* **ቀረባ** *aleba*
forthcoming *(adj.)* **ዝስዕብ** *zs'ëb*
forthwith *(adv.)* **ቅፅበታዊ** *qorare*
fortify *(v.)* **ዓረደ** *'ärede*
fortitude *(n.)* **ትብዓት** *tehababere*
fortnight *(n.)* **ክልተ ቕነ** *tehibiberi*
fortress *(n.)* **ዕርዲ** *'ërdi*
fortunate *(adj.)* **ዕድለኛ** *tederame*
fortune *(n.)* **ዕድል** *kwaleta*
forty *(adj.& n.)* **ኣርባዓ** *akebe*
forum *(n.)* **መድረኽ** *tihija*
forward *(adv. &adj.)* **ንቕድሚት** *nq̈dmit*
fossil *(n.)* **ኣሰር ህይወት** *'aser hywet*
foster *(v.)* **ኣጎልበተ** *tewahilwlw*
foul *(adj.)* **ጋዕጋዕ** *teteraqeme*
found *(v.)* **ኣጣየሸ** *amtseA'*
foundation *(n.)* **መሰረት** *meseret*
founder *(n.)* **መስራቲ** *tegachewe*
foundry *(n.)* **ቤት ንህበት** *beet nhbet*

fountain *(n.)* ምንጪ *mnči*
four *(adj.& n.)* ኣርባዕተ *'arba'ëte*
fourteen *(adj.& n.)* ዓሰርተ ኣርባዕተ *'äserte 'arba'ëte*
fourth *(adj.& n.)* ራብዓይ *shito*
fowl *(n.)* ዑፍ *abiy meanta*
fox *(n.)* በኋርያ *kolonele*
foyer *(n.)* ኣዳራሽ *baeedawi*
fraction *(n.)* ጉዚ *guzi*
fractious *(adj.)* ተኣፋፊ *te'afafi*
fracture *(v.t)* መንቃዕቲ *hawelti*
fragile *(adj.)* ተሰባሪ *anedi*
fragment *(n.)* ስባር *hibri*
fragrance *(n.)* መኣዛ *me'aza*
fragrant *(adj.)* ምዑዝ *zitehibri*
frail *(adj.)* ድኹም *dḱum*
frame *(n.)* መቃን *meqan*
framework *(n.)* መዋቕር *kunat*
franchise *(n.)* ፈቓድ *tewagaei*
frank *(adj.)* ግልፂ *timar*
frankfurter *(n.)* ስጋ ከፍቲ *tsenber*
frantic *(adj.)* ህውፅ *nedadi*
fraternal *(adj.)* ሕውነታዊ *ḧwnetawi*
fraternity *(n.)* ማሕበር *na'ä*
fraud *(n.)* ገበን ሽፍጢ *mesḧaq̈*
fraudulent *(adj.)* መታለሊ *metaleli*
fraught *(adj.)* ዝተመልአ *ĵratam*
fray *(v.)* ተዘርዘረ *mchot*
freak *(n.)* ፈታዊ *ẗtaḧe*
freckle *(n.)* ፈፀጋ *mchu'è*
free *(adj.)* ናፃ *tewazayi*
freebie *(n.)* ናጻ *naxa*
freedom *(n.)* ናፅነት *azeze*
freeze *(v.)* ደስከለ *deskele*
freezer *(n.)* መዝሓሊት *mezḧalit*
freight *(n.)* ፅዕነት *komando*
freighter *(n.)* ተጻዓኒት *texe'änit*
French *(adj.)* ናይ ፈረንሳይ *zkr*
frenetic *(adj.)* ዘይተዋደደ *ĵemere*
frenzy *(n.)* ናዕዋ *na'ëwa*
frequency *(n.)* **dggm** *dggm*
frequent *(adj.)* ተደጋጋሚ *zine'ad*
fresh *(adj.)* ትኩስ *na'èda*
fret *(v.t.)* ተጨናነቐ *r'èyto*
fretful *(adj.)* ዝተጨናነቐ *ta'ëliq̈*
friable *(adj.)* ፍርትት ዝብል *älaq̈i*
friction *(n.)* ፍግፍግ *ngd*
Friday *(n.)* ዓርቢ *'ärbi*
fridge *(n.)* መዝሓሊ *mezḧali*
friend *(n.)* ዓርኪ *wklna*
fright *(n.)* ፍርሒ *komishner*
frighten *(v.)* ኣፍረሐ *megatmi*
frigid *(adj.)* ቆራር *fexeme*
frill *(n.)* ሽንሽን *mebx'ä*
fringe *(n.)* ዘፈር *zefer*
frisk *(v.)* ዓንደረ *'ändere*
fritter *(v.)* ኣባኸነ *'aq̈ḧa*
frivolous *(adj.)* ዘይዕቱብ *zey'ëtub*
frock *(n.)* ቀምሽ *ḧafash*
frog *(n.)* ጭንቁራዕ *lmud*
frolic *(v.i.)* ተጻወተ *texawete*
from *(prep.)* ካብ *hwket*
front *(n.)* ቅድሚት *komawi*
frontbencher *(n.)* ቅድሚት ተሳኣሊ *qdmit tesa'ali*
frontier *(n.)* ዶብ *temaḧalalefi*
frost *(n.)* ዉርጪ *qWerabi*
frosty *(adj.)* ዉርጨም ቆራር *habereta*
froth *(n.)* ዓፍራ *rkb*
frown *(v.i)* ተፀወገ *mkfal*
frowsty *(adj.)* ዳህናዉ *deesnet*
frugal *(adj.)* ጥንቁቕ *ẗnquq̈*

fruit *(n.)* **ፍሬምረ** *leweṫe*
fruitful *(adj.)* **ዕዉት** *ïrnuf*
frump *(n.)* **ገዋድ** *gewad*
frustrate *(v.)* **ኣበሳጨወ** *meseneyta*
fry *(v.)* **ጠበሰ** *tenexaxeri*
fudge *(n.)* **ሽፋፈነ** *anexaxere*
fuel *(n.)* **ነዳዲ** *mnxxar*
fugitive *(n.)* **ሃዲም** *hadim*
fulcrum *(n.)* **ደገፊ** *busola*
fulfil *(v.)* **ኣዐወተ** *dngaxe*
fulfilment *(n.)* **ናብ ተግባር** *teq̈adawi*
full *(adj.)* **ሙሉእ** *wedi hager*
fulsome *(adj.)* **ሸሕጣን** *shḧṫan*
fumble *(v.)* **ባእባእ በለ** *qunčul*
fume *(n.)* **ተበሳጨወ** *qunčul*
fumigate *(v.)* **ዓጠነ** *keḧase*
fun *(n.)* **ታሕጓስ** *kaḧsa*
function *(n.)* **ተግባር** *alalayi*
functional *(adj.)* **ተግባራዊ** *tegbarawi*
functionary *(n.)* **ሓላፊ** *k'èlet*
fund *(n.)* **ገንዘብ** *k'ila*
fundamental *(adj.)* **መሰረታዊ** *mwddar*
funeral *(n.)* **ስርዓት ቀብሪ** *wddrawi*
fungus *(n.)* **ሳባ** *tewadadari*
funky *(adj.)* **ዘበናይ** *ṫernefe*
funnel *(n.)* **መንቆርቆር** *ëgub*
funny *(adj.)* **ዘስሕቕ** *teṫar'ë*
fur *(n.)* **ጸምሪ** *xemri*
furious *(adj.)* **ኣዝዩ ዝተቖጥዐ** *mq̈lul*
furl *(v.)* **ዓፂፉ ጠቕለለ** *meleA'*
furlong *(n.)* **ራሕቒ** *mela'i*
furnace *(n.)* **መምከኺ ቦታ** *mlu'è*
furnish *(v.)* **ብኣቕሑት ኣማልአ** *mfxam*
furnishing *(n.)* **ኣቕረበ ኣበ** *zteḧalaleḱe*
furniture *(n.)* **ኣቕሑ ገዛ** *ḧlḱlḱ*
furore *(n.)* **ህዝባዊ ቁጠዐ** *weĵhi*
furrow *(n.)* **ትልሚ** *èshita*
further *(adv.)* **ርሑቕ** *mq̈lul*
furthermore *(adv.)* **ብተወሳኺ** *ḧalaleḱe*
furthest *(adj.& adv.)* **ተወሳኺ** *ḧlḱlḱ*
fury *(n.)* **ቁጠዐ** *mis gibenegna*
fuse *(v.)* **ፀንበረ** *mshban*
fusion *(n.)* **ዉህደት** *na'èda*
fuss *(n.)* **ጭንቀት** *na'èda*
fussy *(adj.)* **መማረፂ** *te'azeze*
fusty *(adj.)* **ህድሁድ** *kifale*
futile *(adj.)* **ከንቱ** *aḱbere*
futility *(n.)* **ብልሹነት** *aq̈Weme*
future *(n.)* **መፃኢ እዋን** *derasi werabi*
futuristic *(adj.)* **ኣዝዩ ዘበናይ** *ztewahahade*

G

gab *(v.)* **ብዙሕ ምዝራብ** *bzuh-mzrab*
gabble *(v.t.)* **ከየገናዘብካ ብቕልጡፍ ምዝራብ** *ke-ye-gena-zebka bkil-tuf m-z-rab*
gadget *(n.)* **ናይ ኤሌትሪክ መሳርሒ** *nay electric me-sar-hi*
gaffe *(n.)* **ኣብ ኣደባባይ ዝተሰርሐ ዘሕፍር ስሕተት** *ab ade-ba-bay z-te-ser-he ze-h-fr se-h-tet*

gag *(n.)* ቅድሚ ተምላስ ዘሎ ናይ ምምላስ ስምዒት *kidmi temlas zelo nay me-mlas sem-eit*

gaga *(adj.)* ምዕባድ፣ ኣብ ሽማግለታት ናይ ኣእምሮ ዘይምርግጋዕ *m-ae-bad*

gaiety *(n.)* ሕጉስ ምኳን *h-gus me-kua-n*

gaily *(adv.)* ኣብ ዓይኒ ዉሽጢ ዝኣትው፣ ሕጉስ፣ ሰሓቒ፣ ተጫዋቲ *ab ayini wushti z-at-ew*

gain *(v.)* ምትራፍ፣ ዝኾነ ነገር ምርካብ *m-traf*

gainful *(adj.)* ኣትራፍን ጠቓምን ዝኾነ ነገር *atraf-en tekami z-kone neger*

gait *(n.)* ኣካይዳ፣ ናይ ፈረስ ኣካይዳ *akayida*

gala *(n.)* ፅምብል በዓል *tse-m-bel be-al*

galaxy *(n.)* ናይ ከዋኽብቲ ስብስብ *nay kewakbti sebseb*

gale *(n.)* ህቦብላ *h-bo-b-la*

gall *(n.)* ናይ ሰውነት ስቓይ *nay sewnet se-kay*

gallant *(adj.)* ጀግና *jegna*

gallantry *(n.)* ጅግንነት *jegninet*

gallery *(n.)* ኣደራሽ *adarash*

gallon *(n.)* ናይ ማይ መጠን መለክዒ *nay ma-y me-ten*

gallop *(n.)* ምግላብ *m-glab*

gallows *(n.)* ንመሕነቒ ዝጥቀምዎ ዕንጨይቲ *n-mehneqi z-tkemwo enchei-ti*

galore *(adj.)* ብዙሕ *bzuh*

galvanize *(v.i.)* ብረት ንከይዝዕግ ብዚንክ ምሽፋን *bret zkeyiz-eg b-zinc m-shfan*

gambit *(n.)* መመሰስታ ነገር *memesesta neger*

gamble *(v.)* ቁማር *kumar*

gambler *(n.)* ቁማር ዝጫወት ሰብ *kumar z-chawet*

gambol *(v.)* ዓንደረ *andere*

game *(n.)* ግጥም፣ ፀዋታ *g-tim*

gamely *(adj.)* ብትብዓት *b-tb-at*

gammy *(adj.)* ዝተበላሸወ፣ ዘይሰርሕ *z-tebela-shewe*

gamut *(n.)* ማዕቐፍ *ma-ekef*

gang *(n.)* ናይ ገበነኛታት፣ሰባት ስብስብ *nay gebenegnatat sebeseb*

gangling *(adj.)* ቀዉላል *kewlal*

gangster *(n.)* ገበነኛ *geben-egna*

gangway *(n.)* መስገር *mesg-er*

gap *(n.)* ኽፍተት *k-ftet*

gape *(v.)* ሃነነ *hane-ne*

garage *(n.)* ጋራጅ *gara-j*

garb *(n.)* መደናገር *mede-nager*

garbage *(n.)* ጎሓፍ *go-haf*

garble *(v.)* ዝተደናገረ *z-tedenagere*

garden *(n.)* ገደና *ge-de-na*

gardener *(n.)* ገደና ሰብ *ge-de-na seb*

gargle *(v.)* ተጉመፅመፀ *tegume-tse-me-tse*

garish *(adj.)* ኣመና ድሙቕ *amena dmu-que*

garland *(n.)* ናይ ዕምበባ ጌፀ *nay embaba ge-tse*

garlic *(n.)* ፃዕዳ ሽጉርቲ *tsa-e-da sh-gur-ti*

garment *(n.)* ክዳን *kdan*

garner *(v.)* ኣምፀኣ *am-tse-a*

garnet *(n.)* ማዕድን *ma-e-den*

garnish *(v.)* ሸለመ *she-leme*

garret *(n.)* ንላዕሊ ቀልዐ *nla-e-li que-le-ea*
garrulous *(adj.)* ዓዛፍ *a-zaf*
garter *(n.)* ክዳን *kdan*
gas *(n.)* ሃፋ *hafu*
gasket *(n.)* ጎማ *goma*
gasp *(v.i)* ላህለሀ *lahle-he*
gastric *(adj.)* ከስዓዊ *kes-a-wi*
gastronomy *(n.)* ስነ-መግቢ *sin-e meg-bi*
gate *(n.)* በሪ *beri*
gateau *(n.)* ኬክ *kek*
gather *(v.)* ኣከበ *akebe*
gaudy *(adj.)* ምርኡይ *mruy*
gauge *(n.)* ዓቐን *aken*
gaunt *(adj.)* ዕባራ *ebara*
gauntlet *(n.)* ጓንቲ ብረት *gua-nti bret*
gauze *(n.)* ጋርዘ *garze*
gawky *(adj.)* ቀዉላል *kewlal*
gay *(adj.)* ሕጉስ *hgus*
gaze *(v.)* ኣትኩሩ ረኣየ *atkuru re-aye*
gazebo *(n.)* መዋቕር *mewaker*
gazette *(n.)* ጋዜጣ *gazeta*
gear *(n.)* ማርሽ *marsh*
geek *(n.)* ደርጋፍ *dergaf*
gel *(n.)* ዓይነት ቕብኣት *aynet kibat*
geld *(v.)* ቀጥቀጠ *ketkete*
gem *(n.)* ክቡር እምኒ *kbur emni*
gender *(n.)* ስርዓተ ፆታ *srate tsota*
general *(adj.)* ሓፈሻዊ *hafeshawi*
generalize *(v.)* ኣጠቓላሊ *atekalali*
generate *(v.)* ፈጠረ *fetere*
generation *(n.)* ትዉልዲ *te-wle-di*
generator *(n.)* ጀነረተር *generater*
generosity *(n.)* ልግስና *legesena*
generous *(adj.)* ለጋስ *legas*
genesis *(n.)* መፈለምታ *mefelemta*
genetic *(adj.)* ናይ ዘር *nay zer*
genial *(adj.)* ምእዙዝ *me-ezuz*
genius *(n.)* ዝለዓለ ፍልጠት *ze-le-ale feltet*
genteel *(adj.)* ሱቕተኛን ትሑት *suktegnan tehut*
gentility *(n.)* ግሩም ፀባይ *gerum tse-bay*
gentle *(adj.)* ህዱእ *he-du-e*
gentleman *(n.)* ወረጃ ዝኮነ ሰብ *wereja zekone seb*
gentry *(n.)* ደቀባት *dekebat*
genuine *(adj.)* ሓቐኛ *hakegna*
geographer *(n.)* ክኢላ *k'ila*
geographical *(adj.)* ስፍራ *sefra*
geography *(n.)* ጀኦግራፍ *ĵe'ograf*
geologist *(n.)* መርማሪ ሰብ *mermari seb*
geology *(n.)* ምድር ምርመራ *meder mermera*
geometric *(adj.)* ጂኦሜትሪክ *geo-met-eric*
geometry *(n.)* ጂኦሜትሪ *geo-met-ery*
germ *(n.)* ታሕዋስያን *tahwas-eyan*
German *(n.)* ጀርመን *ger-man*
germane *(adj.)* ኣድላይ *adlay*
germinate *(v.)* በቖለ *bekole*
germination *(n.)* በቑል ሃበ *bekul habe*
gerund *(n.)* ቅርጺ *kirtsi*
gestation *(n.)* ጥንሲ *tensi*
gesture *(n.)* ወስታ *westa*

get *(v.)* **ተቐበለ** *tekebele*
geyser *(n.)* **ዓይኒ ማይ** *ayni may*
ghastly *(adj.)* **ዘሰቅቕ** *zesekek*
ghost *(n.)* **ረቒቕ** *rekik*
giant *(n.)* **ኪኢላ** *ki-ila*
gibber *(v.)* **ብረውምረው በለ** *briwmriw bele*
gibe *(v.)* **ኣላገፀ** *alagetse*
giddy *(adj.)* **ዘንፀራረዎ** *zentserarewo*
gift *(n.)* **ዉህብቶ** *wuhbto*
gifted *(adj.)* **ተዉህቦ ዘለዎ** *tewuhbo zelewo*
gigabyte *(n.)* **ምዕቃን** *m'ëqan*
gigantic *(adj.)* **ገዚፍ** *gezif*
giggle *(v.t.)* **ኪርኪር በለ** *kir kir bele*
gild *(v.)* **ኮልዐ** *kole'ea*
gilt *(adj.)* **ደሚቕ ብጫ** *demiq bicha*
gimmick *(n.)* **መተዓሻሸዊ ነገር** *m-ete-a-sha-she-wi neger*
ginger *(n.)* **ዝንጅብል** *zenjebel*
gingerly *(adv.)* **ብዝዓለ ጥንቃቕ** *beze-le-a-le tenkake*
giraffe *(n.)* **ዘራፍ** *zeraf*
girder *(n.)* **ጩራ** *chu-ra*
girdle *(n.)* **ቅናት** *qnat*
girl *(n.)* **ጓል** *qede'se*
girlish *(adj.)* **ናይ ጓል** *teHE'tata'li*
giro *(n.)* **ምምሕልላፍ** *mmḧlla*
girth *(n.)* **ማዕጠቕ** *ma'ëteq̈*
gist *(n.)* **ጽሟቕ** *tsemWaq̈*
give *(v.)* **ሃበ** *habe*
given *(adj.)* **የቕረበ** *yeq̈rebe*
glacial *(adj.)* **በረዳዊ** *beredawi*
glacier *(n.)* **ከውሒ-በረድ** *kewḧibered*
glad *(adj.)* **ሕጉስ** *ḧgus*
gladden *(v.)* **ኣሓጕሰ** *'aḧagWase*
glade *(n.)* **ቃልዕ** *qal'ë*
glamour *(n.)* **ውበት** *wbet*
glance *(v.i.)* **ቍሊሕ በለ** *quliḧ bele*
gland *(n.)* **ጽኪ** *tseki*
glare *(v.i)* **ደጕሐ** *deguḧe*
glass *(v.t.)* **ጥርሙዝ፣ መስተዋት** *ẗrmuz*
glaze *(v.)* **ፈዘዘ** *fezeze*
glazier *(n.)* **ቀባኢ ብረቕረቕ** *qeba'i briq̈riq̈*
gleam *(v.)* **ጸዳል** *tsedal*
glean *(v.)* **ቀረመ** *qereme*
glee *(n.)* **ደስታ** *desta*
glide *(v.)* **ሰለል በለ** *selel bele*
glider *(n.)* **ሰፋፊቶ** *sefafito*
glimmer *(v.)* **ብልጭ ብልጭ** *blč blč*
glimpse *(n.)* **ቈላሕታ** *qWelaḧta*
glisten *(v.)* **ኣንጸባረቐ** *antsebareq̈e*
glitch *(n.)* **ኢንታ** *'inta*
glitter *(v.)* **ብልጭልጭ** *berhe*
gloat *(v.)* **ብህርፋን ነፈገ** *bhrfan nefege*
global *(adj.)* **ዓለምለኻዊ** *'älemleḱawi*
globalization *(n.)* **ስልጣነ** *mrbaḧ*
globe *(n.)* **ዓለም** *glob*
globetrotter *(n.)* **ዳህሳሲ** *dahsasi*
gloom *(n.)* **ደበንገረ** *debengere*
gloomy *(adj.)* **ጽልሙት** *tselmut*
glorification *(n.)* **ክብሪ** *kbr*
glorify *(v.)* **ኣኽበረ** *'aḱbere*
glorious *(adj.)* **ምስጉን ክቡር** *msgun kbur*
glory *(n.)* **ዝና ክብሪ** *zna kbri*
gloss *(n.)* **ብረቕረቕታ** *briq̈riq̈ta*

glossary *(n.)* ማህደረ ቃላት *mahdere qalat*
glossy *(adj.)* ኣስተንታኒ *astentani*
glove *(n.)* ጓንቲ *gWanti*
glow *(v.)* ጐሃረ *gWahare*
glucose *(n.)* ግሉኮዝ *glukoz*
glue *(n.)* መጣበቒ *telaḥage*
glum *(adj.)* ትኩዝ *tkuz*
glut *(n.)* መልአ *mel'e*
glutton *(n.)* ውሒጣ *wḥiṭa*
gluttony *(n.)* ሃረርታ *harerta*
glycerine *(n.)* ግሊሰሪን *gliserin*
gnarled *(adj.)* ሓባጥ ጎባጥ *ḥabaṭ gobaṭ*
gnat *(n.)* ጽንጽያ *tsentseya*
gnaw *(v.)* ገሃጸ *gehatse*
go *(v.t)* ኪድ *kede*
goad *(v.)* ደፍአ *def'e*
goal *(n.)* ዕላማ *ëlama*
goalkeeper *(n.)* ሓላዊ ማዕጾ *ḥalawi-ma'ëxo*
goat *(n.)* ጤል *ṭeel*
gob *(n.)* ኣፍ *af*
gobble *(v.)* ሰነገ *senege*
goblet *(n.)* መለኪያ *melekiya*
god *(n.)* ኣምላኽ *amlaḱ*
godchild *(n.)* ጓል ኣበ ኣልገ *gWal blgna*
goddess *(n.)* ኣምላኽ *amlḱo*
godfather *(n.)* ኣቦ ኣልገ *abalge*
godly *(adj.)* ሃይማኖተኛ *haymanoteña*
godmother *(n.)* ኣልገ እኖ *'ènolge*
goggle *(n.)* ጉልሓጥሓጥ በለ *gulḥaṭḥaṭ bele*
going *(n.)* መንገዲ *mengedi*
gold *(n.)* ወርቂ *werqi*
golden *(adj.)* ወርቃዊ *werqawi*
goldsmith *(n.)* ወርቂ ሰሪ *werqi-serri*
golf *(n.)* ጎልፍ *golf*
gondola *(n.)* ጎንዶላ *gondola*
gong *(n.)* ብረታዊ ነጋሪት *bretawi negarit*
good *(adj.)* ጽቡቕ *tsebuq̈*
goodbye *(excl.)* ደሓን ኩን *deḥan kun*
goodness *(n.)* የዋህነት፣ ፅቡቕነት *lewhat*
goodwill *(n.)* ፅቡቕ ስራሕ *meftḧ*
goose *(n.)* ዓዓ *'ä'ä*
gooseberry *(n.)* ክሽምሽ *kshmsh*
gore *(n.)* ርጉእ ደም *rgu'è dem*
gorgeous *(adj.)* ቖንጆ *dmuq̈*
gorilla *(n.)* ህበይ *gorila*
gory *(adj.)* ደማዊ *demawi*
gospel *(n.)* ወንጌል *wengeel*
gossip *(n.)* ሓሜት *ḥmeeta*
gouge *(v.)* መንደል *mendel*
gourd *(n.)* ሓምሓም *ḥamḥam*
gourmand *(n.)* ፈታው መግቢ *fetaw megbi*
gourmet *(n.)* ቀማሲ *qemasi*
gout *(n.)* ድሌት *dleet*
govern *(v.)* ምግዛእ *gez'e*
governance *(n.)* ኣገዛዝኣ *mgza'è*
governess *(n.)* መራሒት *'alayt qWel'ä*
government *(n.)* መንግስቲ *mengsti*
governor *(n.)* መመሓደሪ፣ ገዛኢ *geza'i*
gown *(n.)* ቀሚሽ ክዳን *qemish kdan*
grab *(v.)* ምሓዝ *m-ha-z*
grace *(n.)* ጸጋ *tsega*
graceful *(adj.)* ምዕሩግ *m'ërug*

gracious *(adj.)* ጥዑም *ṭ'üm*
gradation *(n.)* መዓርግ *me'ärg*
grade *(n.)* ደረጃ *dereğa*
gradient *(n.)* ቀነነ *qenene*
gradual *(adj.)* ደፋእታዊ *defa'ètawi*
graduate *(n.)* ምምራቕ *temereq̈e*
graffiti *(n.)* ምጽያቕ *mtseyaq̈*
graft *(n.)* ጨንገር ምድ'ቓል *čhenger mdq̈al*
grain *(n.)* እኽሊ *'èḱli*
gram *(n.)* ግራም *gram*
grammar *(n.)* ሰዋስው *sewasw*
gramophone *(n.)* ባዚቃ *baziqa*
granary *(n.)* ማዕከን *ma'èken*
grand *(adj.)* ኣዝዩ ኣገዳሲ *azyu 'agedasi*
grandeur *(n.)* ዕቤት *ëbeet*
grandiose *(adj.)* ኣዝዩ ሰፊሕ *azyu sefiḥ*
grandmother *(n.)* ዓባይ *'äbay*
grange *(n.)* ገዛ ገጠር *geza geṭer*
granite *(n.)* ጸሊም እምኒ *tselim 'èmni*
grant *(v.)* ሃበ *habe*
granule *(n.)* ዓንካር *änkar*
grape *(n.)* ወይኒ *fre weyni*
graph *(n.)* ስእላዊ መግለፂ *graf*
graphic *(adj.)* ስእላዊ *s'èlawi*
graphite *(n.)* ፈኲሽ ጸሊም *fekWish tselim*
grapple *(v.t.)* ተጠማጠመ *teṭemaṭeme*
grasp *(v.)* ተረድአ *tered'e*
grass *(n.)* ሳዕሪ *sa'ëri*
grasshopper *(n.)* ኩብኩብታ *kubkubta*
grate *(v.t)* መንፊት ፈርኔሎ *menfit ferneelo*
grateful *(n.)* ኣመስጋኒ *amesgani*
grater *(n.)* መፋሕፍሒ *mefaḥfḥi*
gratification *(n.)* ምሕጓስ *mḥgWas*
gratify *(v.)* ኣሐጐሰ *aḥegWase*
grating *(n.)* ማዕጾ ርባ *ma'ëtso rba*
gratis *(adv. &adj.)* ብነጻ *bnetsa*
gratitude *(n.)* ታሕጓስ *mosa*
gratuitous *(adj.)* ብናጻ *bnatsa*
gratuity *(n.)* እስትሕጋግ *'èsthgag*
grave *(n.)* መቓብር *meq̈abr*
gravel *(n.)* ብጉዑር ሽፈነ *bgu'ür shefene*
graveyard *(n.)* መካነ-መቓብር *mekanemeq̈abr*
gravitas *(n.)* ክብረት *kbret*
gravitate *(v.)* ተሳሕበ *tesaḥbe*
gravitation *(n.)* ናይ ስሕበት ኩነት *sḥbet*
gravity *(n.)* ስሕበት *sḥbet*
gravy *(n.)* መረቕ *mereq̈*
graze *(v.)* ሳዕሪ ኣብልዐ *sa'ëri 'abl'ë*
grease *(n.)* ስብሒ *sbḥi*
great *(adj.)* ዓቢ *'äbi*
greatly *(adv.)* ኣዝዩ ብብዝሒ *azyu bbzḥi*
greed *(n.)* ስስዐ *ses'ë-a*
greedy *(adj.)* ህሩፍ *hruf*
green *(adj. & n.)* ቆፃል *qotsal*
greenery *(v.t.)* ቈጽለ መጽሊ *qoetsele metseli*
greengrocer *(n.)* በዓል ድኳን *be'äl dkWan*
greet *(n.)* ሰላም በለ *selam bele*
greeting *(n.)* ሰላምታ *selamta*

grenade *(a.)* ንእሽቶ ቦምባ *n'èshto bomba*
grey *(n.)* ሓሙኽሽታይ *ḥamuḱshtay*
greyhound *(n.)* ከልቢ ሃድን *kelbi hadn*
grid *(n.)* መስርዕ *mesr'ë*
griddle *(n.)* መቑሎ *meq̈Wulo*
grief *(n.)* ጓሂ *gWahi*
grievance *(n.)* ቅርታ *qrta*
grieve *(v.)* ኣጉሃየ *aguhaye*
grievous *(adj.)* ዘጉሂ *zeguhi*
grill *(v.)* ሚሒ-ጥብሲ *miḥeṭbsi*
grim *(adj.)* ጥብቂ *ṭebqi*
grime *(n.)* ምርሳሕ *arsḥe*
grin *(v.)* ፍሽኽታ *fshḱ bele*
grind *(v.)* ምጥሓን *me-tha-n*
grinder *(n.)* መጥሐኒ *meṭḥani*
grip *(v.)* ጭበጠ *ç̣hebeṭe*
gripe *(v.)* ሓዘ *ḧaze*
grit *(n.)* ሑጻ *ḥutsa*
groan *(v.)* ተኣነነ *te'anene*
grocer *(n.)* በዓል ኣስቤዛ *be'äl 'asbeza*
grocery *(n.)* ኣስቤዛ *asbeza*
groggy *(adj.)* ዘይርጉእ *zeyrgu'è*
groin *(n.)* ሽምጢ *shmṭi*
groom *(v.)* መርዓዊ *alay feres*
groove *(n.)* ፍሓ'ር *fḥar*
grope *(v.)* ሃሰው በለ *hasew bele*
gross *(adj.)* ዓሰርተ ክልተ ደርዘን፣ ዝቐፍፍ ነገር *äserte klte derzen*
grotesque *(adj.)* ዘደንቕ *zedenq̈*
grotto *(n.)* በዓቲ *be'äti*
ground *(n.)* ባይታ *bayta*
groundless *(adj.)* መሰረት ኣልቦ *meseret 'albo*
group *(n.)* ጉጅለ *gujele*
grouping *(n.)* ምጉጃል፣ ምክፍፋል *mgujal*
grout *(n.)* ዘፍታ *zefta*
grovel *(v.)* ሰገደ *segede*
grow *(v.i.)* ምዕባይ፣ ምምዕባል *denfe'ë ma'ëbele*
growl *(v.)* ሕኒን በለ *ḥenin bele*
growth *(n.)* ዕቤት *'ëbeet*
grudge *(n)* ቂም *qim*
grudging *(adj.)* ዘይረደየ *zeyredeye*
gruel *(n.)* ቦጅቦጅ *bojboj*
gruesome *(adj.)* ዘፈንፍን *zefenfn*
grumble *(v.)* ተጣርዐ *teṭar'ë*
grumpy *(adj.)* ተነጫናጪ *tenecha na chi*
grunt *(v.i.)* ምጉርምራም *mgurmram*
guarantee *(v.t)* ተዋሓሰ *tewaḥase*
guarantor *(n.)* ዋሕስ *waḥs*
guard *(v.)* ዘብዐኛ *zeb-egna*
guarded *(adj.)* ዝተሓለወ *ztehalewe*
guardian *(n.)* ሓላዊ *halawi*
guava *(n.)* ዘይቱን *zeytun*
gudgeon *(n.)* ብቐሊሉ ዝታለል ሰብ፣ ኣብ ንእሽተን ማይ ዘሎ ዓሳ *gağeyon*
guerrilla *(n.)* ደባይ ኲናት *debay kWinat*
guess *(v.i)* ገመተ *gemet*
guest *(n.)* ጋሻ *gasha*
guffaw *(n.)* ካዕካዕ በለ *ka'ëka'ë bele*
guidance *(n.)* ኣመራርሓ *amerarha*

guide *(n.)* ሓባሪ፣ መራሒ *ḥabari meraḥi*
guidebook *(n.)* ሓባሪ መፅሓፍ *habari metsehaf*
guild *(n.)* ማሕበር *maḥbe*
guile *(n.)* ተንኰል *tenkWal*
guillotine *(n.)* መቑረጽ ወረቐት *meq̈uretsi wereq̈et*
guilt *(n.)* ገበን *geben*
guilty *(adj.)* ፀፀት *tse tse t*
guise *(n.)* ቅዲ ክዳን *qdi kdan*
guitar *(n.)* ጊታር *gitar*
gulf *(n.)* ወሽመጥ *weshmeṭ*
gull *(n.)* ሮብራ *robra*
gullet *(n.)* ጎሮሮ *gororo*
gullible *(adj.)* ብቐሊሉ ተጎዳኢ *bkelilu tegoda-ei*
gully *(n.)* መትረብ፣ ዝተሸርሸረ መንገዲ *metreb*
gulp *(v.)* ወሓጠ *weḥaṭe*
gum *(n.)* ድርፃን፣ ድዲ *drtsan*
gun *(n.)* ጠበንጃ፣ መሳርሒ *ṭebenja mesarhi*
gurdwara *(n.)* ናይ ኣምልኾት ቦታ *nay amlkot bota*
gurgle *(v.)* በቕ በቕ ምባል *beq̈beq̈ mbal*
gust *(n.)* ሓያል ንፋስ *hayal nefas*
gut *(n.)* መዓንጣ *me'änta*
gutsy *(adj.)* ጅግና *ĵgna*
gutter *(n.)* ንረስሓት መሕለፊ ዝተሰርሐ መንገዲ *ne resahat mehlefi mengedi*
guy *(n.)* ወዲ ተባዕታይ *wedi teba-etay*
guzzle *(v.)* ብፍጥነት ምብላዕ *b-ftnet mebla-e*
gymnasium *(n.)* ናይ ኣካል ብቕዓት እንቅስቃሰ ዝስርሓሉ ቦታ *nay akal bqat enkeskase zserehelu bota*
gymnast *(n.)* ናይ ኣካል ብቕዓት እንቅስቃሰ ዝሰርሕ ሰብ *nay akal bqat enkeskase zserh*
gymnastic *(n.)* ናይ ኣካል ብቕዓት እንቅስቃሰ *nay akal bqat enkeskase*
gynaecology *(n.)* ብዛዕባ ማህፀን ዘፀንዕ ትምህርቲ *bzaeba mahtsen zetsene-e temerti*
gypsy *(n.)* ብሌብነት ዝመሓደር ሰብ *blebnet zmehader*
gyrate *(v.)* ሕምብሊል በለ *ḥmblil bele*

H

habit *(n.)* ልማድ *le-mad*
habitable *(adj.)* ክትነብረሉ ዚበቅዕ *ktnebrelu zibeq'ë*
habitat *(n.)* መቓምጦ *meq̈amṭo*
habitation *(n.)* ምቕማጥ *mq̈maṭ*
habituate *(v.t.)* ኣልመደ *almede*
hack *(v.)* ቆረጸ *qoretse*
hackneyed *(adj.)* ኣመና ልሙድ *amena lmud*
haemoglobin *(n.)* ሀሞግሎቢን *hemoglobin*
haemorrhage *(n.)* ድምያ *dmya*
haft *(n.)* ለዓት *le'ät*
hag *(n.)* ጠንቋሊት *ṭenqWAlit*
haggard *(adj.)* ዓዝዓዝ *äz'äz*
haggle *(v.)* ተዋገየ *tewageye*

hail *(n.)* በረድ ሃረመ *bered hareme*
hair *(n.)* ጸጉሪ *tseguri*
haircut *(n.)* ምቕሶ *mq̈so*
hairstyle *(n.)* ኣመሻሽጣ ጸጉሪ *ameshashẗa tseguri*
hairy *(adj.)* ጨጓር *čheguar*
hajji *(n.)* ዝሓጀጀ *zḧaĵeĵe*
halal *(adj.)* ዝተቐደሰ *zteq̈edese*
hale *(adj.)* ጨጠለ *čheṭele*
halitosis *(n.)* ብስናው *b-snaw*
hall *(n.)* ኣደራሽ መጋበእያ *'aderash megabe'èya*
hallmark *(n.)* ዕላመት *ëlamet*
hallow *(v.)* ባረኸ *bareḱe*
hallucinate *(v.)* ኣህተፍተፈ *ahteftefe*
halogen *(n.)* ጠባይ *ẗebay*
halt *(v.)* ጠጠው በለ *ṭeṭew bele*
halter *(n.)* መወጠጢ ፈረስ *meweṭeṭi feres*
halting *(adj.)* መጠጠው *maṭeṭew*
halve *(v.)* ፈረቐ *fereq̈e*
halyard *(n.)* ገመድ ባንዴራ *gemed bandeera*
ham *(n.)* ሰለፍ ሓሰማ *selef ḥasema*
hamburger *(n.)* ሃምበርገር *hamberger*
hamlet *(n.)* ንእሽቶ ቁሸት *n'èshto qushet*
hammer *(n.)* ማርተሎ *martelo*
hammock *(n.)* ሃለለ *halele*
hamper *(n.)* ኣሰናኸለ *asenaḱele*
hamster *(n.)* ሃምስተር *hamster*
hamstring *(n.)* ቁና *quna*
hand *(n.)* ኢድ *e-i-d*
handbag *(n.)* ቦርሳ ኢድ *borsa e-i-d*
handbill *(n.)* ፎልዮ *folyo*
handbook *(n.)* ማኑዋል *manuwal*
handcuff *(n.)* መቑሕ ኢድ *mequḧ 'id*
handful *(n.)* ዕታሮ *ëtaro*
handicap *(n.)* ዕንቅፋት ጸገም *ënqfat tsegem*
handicapped *(n.)* ዕንቅፋት ጸገም *ënqfat tsegem*
handicraft *(n.)* ኢደ-ጥበብ *ideṭbeb*
handiwork *(n.)* ኢደ-ስራሕ *idesraḧ*
handkerchief *(n.)* መንዲል *mendil*
handle *(v.t)* ሓዘ *ḥaze*
handout *(n.)* ምምጽዋት *meme tse wat*
handshake *(n.)* ሰላምታ ኢድ *selamta 'id*
handsome *(adj.)* ምልኩዕ *mlku'ë*
handy *(adj.)* ስሉጥ *sluṭ*
hang *(v.i.)* ተንጠልጠለ *tenṭelṭele*
hangar *(n.)* ሰፈር ነፈርቲ *sefer neferti*
hanger *(n.)* መንጠልጠሊ *menṭelṭeli*
hanging *(n.)* ምሕናቕ *mḥnaq̈*
hangover *(n.)* ቅርሲ *qrsi*
hank *(n.)* ጥቕላል ፈትሊ *ṭq̈lal fetli*
hanker *(v.)* ብብርቱዕ ሃረፈ *bbrtu'ë harefe*
haphazard *(adj.)* ሃንደበታዊ *handebetawi*
hapless *(adj.)* ዘይዕድለኛ *zey'ëdleña*
happen *(v.)* ኰነ *kone*
happening *(n.)* ፍጻመ *ftsame*

happiness *(n.)* ሓጐስ *ḥagos*
happy *(adj.)* ደስታ *desta*
harass *(v.)* ኣጨነቐ *ačheneq̈e*
harassment *(n.)* መጨነቕ *mečheneq̈e*
harbour *(n.)* መርሳ *mersa*
hard *(adj.)* ብትሪ ብብርታዕ *btri bbrta'ë*
hard drive *(n.)* መሰርሒ *mesarḧi*
hardback *(n.)* መጥመሪ *meẗmeri*
harden *(v.)* ተረረ *terere*
hardly *(adv.)* ሳሕቲ *saḥtị*
hardship *(n.)* ሽግር *shgr*
hardy *(adj.)* ጠንካራ *ṭenkara*
hare *(n.)* ማንቲለ *mantile*
harelip *(n.)* ጎነፈ *gonefe*
harem *(n.)* ሓሪም *ḥarim*
hark *(v.)* ሰምዐ *sem'ë*
harlequin *(n.)* ተዋዛዪ *tewazayi*
harm *(n.)* ጉድኣት *gud'at*
harmful *(adj.)* ተጓዳኢ *tegoda'i*
harmless *(adj.)* ዘይጎድእ *zeygod'è*
harmonious *(adj.)* ዝተወሃሃደ *ztewehahade*
harmonium *(n.)* ሃርሞኑዮም *harmunyem*
harmonize *(v.)* ተወሃሃደ *tewehahade*
harmony *(n.)* ውህደት *whdet*
harness *(n.)* ስርዒት ፈረስ *sr'ït feres*
harp *(n.)* በገና *begena*
harpy *(n.)* ጨካን ፍጥረት *čekan fţret*
harrow *(n.)* ጨካን ፍጥረት *ḉekan fţret*
harrowing *(adj.)* ጨካን ፍጥረት *ḉekan fţret*
harsh *(adj.)* ዘይምእሙእ *zeym'èmu'è*
harvest *(n.)* ጸማ *tsama*
harvester *(n.)* ዓጻዲ *ätsadi*
hassle *(n.)* መትከር *metker*
hassock *(n.)* መተርኣስ ብርኪ *meter'as brki*
haste *(n.)* ሃወኸ *haweḱe*
hasten *(v.)* ተሃወኸ *tehaweḱe*
hasty *(adj.)* ህውኽ *hwḱ*
hat *(n.)* ቆብዕ *qob'ë*
hatch *(n.)* ነቒሓ *neq̈uḥe*
hatchet *(n.)* ፋስ *fas*
hate *(v.t.)* ጸልአ *tsel'e*
hateful *(adj.)* ጽሉእ *tselu'è*
haughty *(adj.)* ዕቡይ *ëbuy*
haulage *(n.)* ምጉዕዓዝ *mgu'ë'äz*
haulier *(n.)* ኣጓዓዚ *agWa'ä'äzi*
haunch *(n.)* ጎሎ *golo*
haunt *(v.)* ኣሻቐለ *'ashaq̈ele*
haunted *(adj.)* ኣሻቐለ *'ashaq̈ele*
have *(v.)* ኣሎዎ... *'alowo*
haven *(n.)* መድሕን *medḥn*
havoc *(n.)* ዕንወት *ënwet*
hawk *(n.)* ተገዳር ሓረስታይ *tegedar ḥarestay*
hawker *(n.)* ኣዝዋሪ *azwari*
hawthorn *(n.)* ቆጥቋጥ *qoṭqoat*
hay *(n.)* ሓሰር *ḥaser*
hazard *(n.)* ሓደጋ *ḥadega*
hazardous *(adj.)* ድንገተኛ *dngeteňa*
haze *(n.)* ፈኰስ ግመ *fokis gme*
hazy *(adj.)* ግመኣዊ *gme'awi*
he *(pron.)* ተባዕታይ *teba'ëtay*
head *(n.)* ርእሲ *r'èsi*
headache *(n.)* ርእሲ ቃንዛ *r'èsi qanza*

heading *(n.)* አርእስቲ *ar'èsti*
headlight *(n.)* መኪና ብርሃን *mekina brhan*
headline *(n.)* አርእስተ-ዜና *ar'èstezeena*
headmaster *(n.)* ሓለቓ መማህራን *ḥaleq̈a memahran*
headphone *(n.)* መስምዒ ራድዮ *mesm'ï radyo*
headquarters *(n.)* ምሉእ ስልጣን *mlu'è slṫan*
headstrong *(adj.)* ነቓጽ *neq̈atse*
heady *(adj.)* ነዳሪ *nedari*
heal *(v.)* ሓከመ *ḥakeme*
health *(n.)* ጥዕና *ṭ'ëna*
healthy *(adj.)* ጥዑይ *ṭ'üy*
heap *(n.)* ከመረ ደበራ *kemere debera*
hear *(v.)* ሰምዐ *sem'ë*
hearing *(n.)* ምስማዕ *msma'ë*
hearse *(n.)* መኪና ቀብሪ *mekina qebri*
heart *(n.)* ልቢ *lebi*
heartache *(n.)* ጓሂ *guahi*
heartbreak *(n.)* ሓዘን *ḧazen*
heartburn *(n.)* ቀሓር *qeḧar*
hearten *(v.)* አተባብዐ *'atebab'ë*
heartening *(adj.)* አተባብዐ *'atebab'ë*
heartfelt *(adj.)* ልባዊ *lebawi*
hearth *(n.)* መጋርያ *megarya*
heartless *(adj.)* ጨካን * çhekan*
hearty *(adj.)* ልባዊ *lebawi*
heat *(n.)* ዋዒ *wa'ï*
heater *(n.)* መሞቒ *memoq̈i*
heath *(n.)* ቃድራ *qadra*
heathen *(n.)* አምላኽ ጣኦት *amlak̈ ṭa'ot*
heather *(n.)* ኮሎና *koloṅa*
heating *(n.)* መውዓይ *mew'äy*
heave *(v.)* አልዓለ *'al'äle*
heaven *(n.)* መንግስተ-ሰማያት *mengstesemayat*
heavenly *(adj.)* ሰማያዊ *semayawi*
heavy *(adj.)* ከቢድ *kebid*
heckle *(v.)* ወጠረ *we-ṭe-re*
hectare *(n.)* ሄክታር *hektar*
hectic *(adj.)* ዕረፍቲ ዘይብሉ *'ërefti zeyblu*
hector *(v.)* አጉባዕብዐ *aguba'ëb'ë*
hedge *(n.)* ተኽሊ ሓጹር *tek̈li ḥatsur*
hedonism *(n.)* ሄዶንነት *heedonnet*
heed *(v.)* አቃልቦ *'aqalbo*
heel *(n.)* ሸኾና *shek̈Wana*
hefty *(adj.)* ገዚፍን ብርቱዕን n *gezifn brtu'ë*
hegemony *(n.)* ዕብላለ *'ëblale*
height *(n.)* ቁመት *qumet*
heighten *(v.)* ለዓለ *le'äle*
heinous *(adj.)* ጭካነአዊ *chkane-awi*
heir *(n.)* ወራሲ *werasi*
helicopter *(n.)* ሄሊኮፕተር *heelikopter*
heliport *(n.)* መዕረፍ ሄሊኮፕተር *me'ëref heelikopter*
hell *(n.)* ገሃነም *gehanem*
helm *(n.)* መዛወሪ መርከብ *mezaweri merkeb*
helmet *(n.)* ሃልመት *halmet*
help *(v.)* ሓገዘ ረድአ *ḥageze red'e*
helpful *(adj.)* ሓጋዚ *ḥagazi*
helping *(n.)* መአዲ *me'adi*
helpless *(adj.)* ሓጋዚ አልቦ *ḥagazi 'albo*

hem *(n.)* ክፉፍ *kfuf*
hemisphere *(n.)* ንፍቀ-ክቢ *nfqekbi*
hen *(n.)* ደርሆ *derho*
hence *(adv.)* ካብዚ *kabzi*
henceforth *(adv.)* ካብ ሕጂ ንደሓር *kab ḥği ndeḥar*
henchman *(n.)* እሙን ደጋፊ *èmun degafi*
henpecked *(adj.)* ኮረየ *koreye*
hepatitis *(adj.)* ወይቦ *weybo*
heptagon *(n.)* ስቡዕ ጐኖ *sbu'ë guano*
her *(pron.)* ንዓኣ *n'ä'a*
herald *(n.)* ተለኣኣኺ *tele'a'aḱi*
herb *(n.)* ንእሽቶ ተኽሊ *n'èshto teḱli*
herculean *(adj.)* ንእሽቶ ተኽሊ *n'èshto teḱli*
herd *(n.)* መጓሰ *meguase*
here *(adv.)* ኣብዚ *'abzi*
hereabouts *(adv.)* ኣብዚ ከባቢ'ዚ *abzi kebabizi*
hereafter *(adv.)* ድሕሪ ሕጂ *dḥri ḥği*
hereby *(adv.)* በዚ ገይሩ *bezi geyru*
hereditary *(adj.)* ተወርሶኣዊ *tewerso'awi*
heredity *(n.)* ዓሌት *ae-leet*
heritage *(n.)* ውርሲ *wersi*
hermetic *(adj.)* ኣየር ዘየሕልፍ *'ayer zeyeḥlf*
hermit *(n.)* ባሕታዊ *baḥtawi*
hermitage *(n.)* ኣግልሎ *agllo*
hernia *(n.)* ኤርንያ *eernya*
hero *(n.)* ጅግና *jegna*
heroic *(adj.)* ጅግንነታዊ *jegn-netawi*
heroine *(n.)* ፍርሰት *frset*
herpes *(n.)* ሕማም *ḧmam*
herring *(n.)* ገፈፈ *gefefe*
hers *(pron.)* ናታ *nata*
herself *(pron.)* ባዕላ *ba'ëla*
hesitant *(adj.)* ሰጋእ መጋእ በሃሊ *sega'è mega'è behali*
hesitate *(v.)* ተወላወለ *tewelawele*
heterogeneous *(adj.)* ዝተፈላለየ *ztefelaleye*
heterosexual *(adj.)* ልዩ-ጾተኛ *lyu tsoteňa*
hew *(v.)* ቆረጸ *qoretse*
hexogen *(n.)* ጠባይ *ẗebay*
heyday *(n.)* ጥዑም ግዜ *ṭ'üm gzee*
hibernate *(v.)* ነወመ *neweme*
hiccup *(n.)* ጥዑም ግዜ *ṭ'üm gzee*
hide *(v.t)* ሓብአ *ḥab'e*
hideous *(adj.)* ግናይ *gnay*
hierarchy *(n.)* መስርዕ-መዓርግ *mesr'ëme'ärg*
high *(adj.)* ላዕሊ *la'ëli*
highlight *(v.)* ኣጉልሐ *'agulḥe*
highly *(adv.)* ብዝለዓለ *bzle'äle*
Highness *(n.)* ልዑልነት *l'ülnet*
highway *(n.)* ጽርግያ *tsergya*
hijack *(v.)* ጨውያ *chewya*
hike *(n.)* ዙረት *zuret*
hilarious *(adj.)* ካዕካዕታዊ *ka'ëka'ëtawi*
hilarity *(n.)* ካዕካዕታ *ka'ëka'ëta*
hill *(n.)* ኮረብታ *korebta*
hillock *(n.)* ኩጀት *kujet*
hilt *(n.)* ልዓት-ሴፍ *le-a-t seef*
him *(pron.)* ንዓኡ *ne-a-u*
himself *(pron.)* ባዕሉ *ba-e-lu*

hinder ***(v.)*** **ዓንቀጸ** *anqe-tse*
hindrance ***(n.)*** **ዕንቅፋት** *enqefat*
hindsight ***(n.)*** **ተረድአ** *tered'e*
hinge ***(n.)*** **መፍሰል** *mefsel*
hint ***(n.)*** **ኣንፈት** *anfet*
hip ***(n.)*** **ምሕኵልቲ** *mḥkulti*
hire ***(v.t)*** **ተኻረየ** *teḱareye*
hirsute ***(adj.)*** **ጸጓር** *tseguar*
his ***(adj.)*** **ናቱ** *natu*
hiss ***(v.i)*** **ጺጽ በለ** *tsi-tse bele*
histogram ***(n.)*** **ቍጽራዊ** *qutserawi*
historian ***(n.)*** **ተራኺ** *teraki*
historic ***(adj.)*** **ታሪኸኛ** *tariḱeña*
historical ***(adj.)*** **ታሪኻዊ** *tariḱawi*
history ***(n.)*** **ታሪኽ** *tariḱ*
hit ***(v.)*** **ሃረመ** *hareme*
hitch ***(v.)*** **ቋጸረ** *qua-tse-re*
hither ***(adv.)*** **ክሳብ ሕጂ** *ksab ḧĵi*
hitherto ***(adv.)*** **ክሳብ ሕጂ** *ksab ḥğı*
hive ***(n.)*** **ጎጆ ንህቢ** *gojo nehbi*
hoard ***(n.)*** **ኣከበ** *'akebe*
hoarding ***(n.)*** **ምዕቋር** *me-e-qua-r*
hoarse ***(adj.)*** **ላሕታት** *laḥtat*
hoax ***(n.)*** **ኣዐሸወ** *aeshewe*
hob ***(n.)*** **መጽሎ** *metselo*
hobble ***(v.)*** **ደርገፍገፍ በለ** *dergefgef bele*
hobby ***(n.)*** **ፍሉይ ግዳሰ** *fluy gdase*
hobgoblin ***(n.)*** **ጋኔን** *ganeen*
hockey ***(n.)*** **ቃርሳ** *qarsa*
hoist ***(v.)*** **ሰቐለ** *seq̈ele*
hold ***(v.t)*** **ሓዘ** *ḥaze*
holdall ***(n.)*** **ማህደር** *mahder*
hole ***(n.)*** **ነኳል** *neḱual*
holiday ***(n.)*** **በዓል** *be-al*
holistic ***(adj.)*** **መለኮታዊ** *melekotawi*
hollow ***(adj.)*** **ዘይሓቂ** *zeyḧaqi*
holly ***(n.)*** **ንኡድ** *n'ud*
holmium ***(n.)*** **ባእታ** *ba'èta*
holocaust ***(n.)*** **ህልቂት** *hlqit*
hologram ***(n.)*** **ብምሳሌ ምጥቃም** *bmsalee mẗqam*
holster ***(n.)*** **ሰፈር ሽጉጥ** *sefer shguṭ*
holy ***(adj.)*** **ቅዱስ** *qdus*
homage ***(n.)*** **ኣኽብሮት** *aḱbrot*
home ***(n.)*** **ገዛ** *geza*
homely ***(adj.)*** **ምቕሉል** *mq̈lul*
homeopathy ***(n.)*** **ኣተሓሕዛ** *ateḧaḧza*
homicide ***(n.)*** **ቅትለተ-ሰብ** *qtleteseb*
homoeopath ***(n.)*** **ሕክምናዊ** *ḧkmnawi*
homogeneous ***(adj.)*** **ባህረ-ሓደ** *bahreḥade*
homogeneous ***(a.)*** **ባህረ-ሓደ** *bahreḥade*
homophobia ***(n.)*** **ፈርሀ ግብረ-ሰዶመኛ** *ferhe gbresedomeňa*
homosexual ***(n.)*** **ግብረ-ሰዶመኛ** *gbresedomeña*
honest ***(adj.)*** **ቅኑዕ** *qnu'ë*
honesty ***(n.)*** **ቅንዕና** *qn'ëna*
honey ***(n.)*** **መዓር** *me'är*
honeycomb ***(n.)*** **ስፈ ንህቢ** *sfe nhbi*
honeymoon ***(n.)*** **ሕጽኖት** *ḥxnot*
honk ***(n.)*** **ድምጺ ደርሆ ማይ** *dmxi derho may*
honorary ***(adj.)*** **ክብራዊ** *kbrawi*
honour ***(n.)*** **ክብሪ** *kbri*

honourable *(adj.)* መዓርግ ዘለዎ *me'ärg zelewo*
hood *(n.)* ቆብዕ *qob'ë*
hoodwink *(v.)* ኣታለለ *atalele*
hoof *(n.)* ሽኾና *shḱona*
hook *(n.)* ዓይነት ማዕጺድ *äynet ma'ëxid*
hooked *(adj.)* ዓይነት ማዕጺድ *äynet ma'ëxid*
hooligan *(n.)* ዕዋላ *ëwala*
hoop *(n.)* ዕንክሊል *'ënklil*
hoopla *(n.)* ዕዋላ *ëwala*
hoot *(n.)* ድምጺ ጉንዃ *dmxi gungWa*
Hoover *(n.)* መስመር መኾስተር *mesmer meḱoster*
hop *(v.)* ነጠረ ምንጣር *neṭere mnṭar*
hop *(v.t.)* ነጠረ ምንጣር *neṭere mnṭar*
hope *(n.)* ተስፋ *tesfa*
hopefully *(adv.)* ብተስፋ *btesfa*
hopeless *(adj.)* ተስፋ ኣልቦ *tesfa 'albo*
horde *(n.)* ጭፍራ *çfra*
horizon *(n.)* ደረት ትርኢት *deret tr'it*
horizontal *(adj.)* ጋድም *gadm*
hormone *(n.)* ሆርሞን *hormon*
horn *(n.)* ጥሩምባ *ṭrumba*
hornet *(n.)* ዕኮት *ëkot*
horoscope *(n.)* ስነ ከዋኽብቲ *sene kewakbti*
horrendous *(adj.)* ዘሰንብድ *zesenbd*
horrible *(adj.)* ሕማቕ *ḥmaq̈*
horrid *(adj.)* ዘስገድግድ *zesgedgd*
horrific *(adj.)* ኣፍራሒ *'afraḥi*
horrify *(v.)* ኣፍርሐ *'afrḥe*
horror *(n.)* ፍርሒ *frḥi*
horse *(n.)* ፈረሰኛ *fereseña*
horsepower *(n.)* ሓይሊ ፈረስ *ḥayli feres*
horticulture *(n.)* እጽዳት *ètsedat*
hose *(n.)* ቱቦ ማይ *tubo may*
hosiery *(n.)* ሶል ጫማ *sol chama*
hospice *(n.)* መዕረፊ *me'ërefi*
hospitable *(adj.)* ኣእንጋዲ *'a'èngadi*
hospital *(n.)* ሆስፒታል *hospital*
hospitality *(n.)* ኣእንጋዲነት *a'engadinet*
host *(n.)* ኣእንጋዲ *a'engadi*
hostage *(n.)* ጀሆ *ğeho*
hostel *(n.)* ሆስተል *hostel*
hostess *(n.)* ኣእንጋዲት *a'engadit*
hostile *(adj.)* ተጻባኢ *tetsaba'i*
hostility *(n.)* ጽልኢ *tsel-ei*
hot *(adj.)* ውዑይ *w'üy*
hotchpotch *(n.)* ሕንፍጽፋጽ *ḥnftsefatse*
hotel *(n.)* ሆቴል *hoteel*
hound *(n.)* ከልቢ ሃድን *kelbi hadn*
hour *(n.)* ሰዓት *se'ät*
house *(n.)* ገዛ *geza*
housewife *(n.)* በዓልቲ ሓዳር *bealti hadar*
housing *(n.)* መዕቆቢ *me-ekobi*
hovel *(n.)* ዑና *üna*
hover *(v.)* ዘንበየ *zenbeye*
how *(adv.)* ከመይ *kemey*
however *(adv.)* ሽሕኳ *she-h-kua*
howl *(n.)* ጨደረ *che-dere*
hub *(n.)* ሕምብርቲ *h-m-brti*
hubbub *(n.)* ዕግርግር *e-gerger*

huddle *(v.)* ተደጎለ *tedegole*
hue *(n.)* ሕብሪ *he-bri*
huff *(n.)* ቁጥዐ *qute-e*
hug *(v.)* ሓቖፈ *haqo-fe*
huge *(adj.)* ገዚፍ *gezif*
hulk *(n.)* ደርጓጎ መርከብ *derguag merkeb*
hull *(n.)* ቅርፍቲ *qerefti*
hum *(v.)* ዚዝ *ziz*
human *(adj.)* ሰብኣዊ *seb'awi*
humane *(adj.)* ሕያዋይ *heya-way*
humanism *(n.)* ሰብኣውነት *seb'awnet*
humanitarian *(adj.)* ሰብኣዊ *seb'awi*
humanity *(n.)* ወዲ ሰብ *wedi seb*
humanize *(v.)* ሰብኣዊ ኮነ *seb'awi kone*
humble *(adj.)* ትሑት *tehut*
humid *(adj.)* ርጡብ *retub*
humidity *(n.)* ጠሊ *ṭeli*
humiliate *(v.)* ኣዋረደ *awarede*
humility *(n.)* ትሕትና *tehtena*
hummock *(n.)* ኩጀት *kujet*
humorist *(n.)* ተዋዛዪ *tewazayi*
humorous *(adj.)* መስሓቕ *mesḥaq̈*
humour *(n.)* ዋዛ *waza*
hump *(n.)* መንጉድ *mengud*
hunch *(v.)* ቍራስ ግናድ *mi-eti*
hundred *(adj.& n.)* ሚእቲ *mi-eti*
hunger *(n.)* ጠመየ *ṭemeye*
hungry *(adj.)* ጥሙይ *temuy*
hunk *(n.)* ግማ'ድ *gmad*
hunt *(v.)* ደወረ *dewere*
hunter *(n.)* ሃዳናይ *hadanay*
hurdle *(n.)* መሰናኽል *mesenaḱl*
hurl *(v.)* ወርወረ *werwere*
hurricane *(n.)* ህቦብላ *hebobla*
hurry *(v.)* ሃወኽ ኣቐልጠፈ *haweḱe 'aq̈elṭefe*
hurt *(v.)* ጎድአ *god'e*
hurtle *(v.)* ወንጨፈ *wenchefe*
husband *(n.)* በዓል ቤት *beal bet*
husbandry *(n)* ሕርሻ *hersha*
hush *(v.i)* ኣህድአ *ah-dea*
husk *(n.)* ቅቃሕ *qe-qah*
husky *(adj.)* ንቑጽ *nequtse*
hustle *(v.)* ጐናነጸ *gonanetse*
hut *(n.)* ኣጉዶ *agudo*
hutch *(n.)* ጋቢያ *gabiya*
hybrid *(n.)* ድቓላ *deqala*
hydrant *(n.)* ማፋ ማይ *mafa may*
hydrate *(v.)* በጽበጸ *betse betse*
hydraulic *(adj.)* ሓይለ-ማያዊ *ḥaylemayawi*
hydrogen *(n.)* ሃይድሮጅን *haydrogen*
hyena *(n.)* ዝብኢ *zeb-ei*
hygiene *(n.)* ስነ-ጥዕና *sene te-ena*
hymn *(n.)* ማህለት *mahlet*
hype *(n.)* ኣምሲልካ ምቕራብ *amsilka mq̈rab*
hyperactive *(adj.)* ኣመና ንጡፍ *amena nṫuf*
hyperbole *(n.)* ዝተጋነነ መግለጺ *zteganene meglexi*
hypertension *(n.)* ጸቕጢ-ደም *tseqti dem*
hyphen *(n.)* መፈላለዪ ሕንጻጽ *mefelaleyi hentsatse*
hypnosis *(n.)* ዕንዛዘ *ënzaze*
hypnotize *(v.)* ኣዐንዘዘ *ae-nzeze*
hypocrisy *(n.)* ምስሉይነት *mesluynet*
hypocrite *(n.)* ምስሉይ *meslu*

hypotension *(n.)* **ጸቕጢ-ደም** *tseqti dem*
hypothesis *(n.)* **ጥንሰ-ሓሳብ** *tebse hasab*
hypothetical *(adj.)* **ጽንሰ-ሓሳባዊ** *tsnsehasabawi*
hysteria *(n.)* **ዓበድበድ** *aebedbed*
hysterical *(adj.)* **ዕቡድ** *ebud*

I

I *(pron.)* **ኣነ** *'ane*
ice *(n.)* **በረድ** *bered*
iceberg *(n.)* **ከውሒ በረድ** *kewḥi bered*
ice-cream *(n.)* **በረድ ሽኮር** *bered shkor*
icicle *(n.)* **ጭራሮ በረድ** *çraro bered*
icing *(n.)* **መመላኸዒ ኬክ** *memelakh'e cake*
icon *(n.)* **ምስሊ ቅዱሳን** *msli qdusan*
icy *(n.)* **በረዳዊ** *beredawi*
idea *(n.)* **ሓሳብ** *ḥasab*
ideal *(n.)* **ብ ሓሳብ ደረጃ** *b hasab dereja*
idealism *(n.)* **ሓሳባዊነት** *hasabawinet*
idealist *(n.)* **ሓሳባዊ** *hasabawi*
idealize *(v.)* **ከም ፍጹም ምቑፃር** *kem fxum mqutsar*
ideally *(adv.)* **ብሓሳብ** *b hasab*
identical *(adj.)* **ሓደ ዓይነት** *hade aynet*
identification *(n.)* **መለለዪ** *meleleyi*
identify *(v.)* **ምልላይ** *mllay*
identity *(n.)* **ሓደ ምኳን** *ḥade mḱWan*
ideology *(n.)* **ስነ-ሓሳብ** *sneḥasab*
idiocy *(n.)* **ዕሽነት** *'ëshnet*
idiom *(n.)* **ቋንቋኛ** *qWAnqWAgna*
idiomatic *(adj.)* **ቛንቋኛዊ** *qunquñawi*
idiosyncrasy *(n.)* **ፍሉይ ጠባይ** *fluy ṭebay*
idiot *(n.)* **ዓሻ** *'äsha*
idiotic *(adj.)* **ናይ ዓሻ ስራሕ** *nay ash srah*
idle *(adj.)* **ዘይ ምስራሕ** *zey msrah*
idleness *(n.)* **ስንፍነት** *snfnet*
idler *(n.)* **ሰነፍ** *senef*
idol *(n.)* **ጣኦት** *ṭa'ot*
idolatry *(n.)* **ጣኦት ኣምልኾ** *ṭa'ot 'amlḱo*
idolize *(v.)* **ምምላኽ** *mmlak*
idyll *(n.)* **ቐሊል** *qhlil*
if *(conj.)* **እንድሕር** *endhr*
igloo *(n.)* **ኢግሎ** *'iglo*
igneous *(adj.)* **እሳተ ጐሞራዊ** *'èsate gWamorawi*
ignite *(v.)* **ወልዐ** *wel'ë*
ignition *(n.)* **ምውላዕ** *mwla'ë*
ignoble *(adj.)* **ዘይውርዙይ** *zeywrzuy*
ignominious *(adj.)* **ውርደተኛ** *wrdeteña*
ignominy *(n.)* **ውርደት** *wrdet*
ignoramus *(n.)* **ደንቆሮ** *denqoro*
ignorance *(n.)* **ዘይምፍላጥ** *zeymflaṭ*
ignorant *(adj.)* **ዘይፈልጥ** *zeyfeleṭe*
ignore *(v.)* **ዘይ ምድማፅ** *zeymdmats*

ill *(adj.)* **ሕሙም** *ḥmum*
illegal *(adj.)* **ዘይሕጋዊ** *zeyḥgawi*
illegibility *(n.)* **ተቐባልነት** *teqhebalnet*
illegible *(adj.)* **ተቐባልነት ዘለዎ** *teqhbalnet zelewo*
illegitimate *(adj.)* **ዘይሕጋዊ** *zeyḥgawi*
illicit *(adj.)* **ዘይሕጋዊ፣ ዘይንቡር** *zeyḥgawi, zeynubur*
illiteracy *(n.)* **መሃይምነት** *mehaymnet*
illiterate *(n.)* **መሃይም** *mehaym*
illness *(n.)* **ሕማም** *ḥmam*
illogical *(adj.)* **ዘይስነ-መጐታዊ** *zeysnemegWatawi*
illuminate *(v.)* **ኣብርሀ፣ ግልጺ ገበረ** *abrhe, gltsi gebere*
illumination *(n.)* **ምብራህ፣ ግልጺ ምግባር** *mbrah, gltsi mgbar*
illusion *(v.t.)* **መሕላም** *meḥlam*
illusory *(adj.)* **መሕልማዊ** *meḥlmawi*
illustrate *(n.)* **ኣረድአ** *'ared'e*
illustration *(n.)* **መረዳእታ መግለጺ** *mereda'èta meglexi*
illustrious *(adj.)* **ክቡር** *kbur*
image *(n.)* **ምስሊ** *msli*
imagery *(n.)* **ብምሳሌ ምጥቃም** *bmsalee mṭqam*
imaginary *(adj.)* **ዘይጭቡጥ ፣ ሓሳባዊ** *zeychubut, hasabawi*
imagination *(n.)* **ምሕሳብ** *mhsab*
imaginative *(adj.)* **ብልሂ** *blhi*
imagine *(v.t.)* **ቀረጸ ፣ ሓሰበ** *qerexe, hasebe*
imbalance *(n.)* **ዘይምምጣን** *zeymmṭan*
imbibe *(v.)* **ሰተየ** *seteye*
imbroglio *(n.)* **ኸቢድ ኩነታት** *kebid kuknetat*
imbue *(v.)* **መልአ** *mel'e*
imitate *(v.)* **ቀድሐ** *qedḥe*
imitation *(n.)* **ምቕዳሕ** *mqdaḥ*
imitator *(n.)* **ቐዳሒ** *kedahi*
immaculate *(adj.)* **ፁሩይ** *tsury*
immanent *(adj.)* **ህልው** *hlw*
immaterial *(adj.)* **ዘይረብሕ** *zeyrebḥ*
immature *(adj.)* **ጥረ፣ ዘይ በሰለ** *ṭre, zeybesele*
immaturity *(n.)* **ቈልዓዊ** *qWel'äwi*
immeasurable *(adj.)* **ኪዕቀን ዘይከኣል** *ki'ëqen zeyke'al*
immediate *(adj.)* **ቀጥታዊ፣ ብፍጥነት** *qeṭtawi, b ftnet*
immemorial *(adj.)* **ኣዝዩ ጥንታዊ** *'azyu ṭntawi*
immense *(adj.)* **ኣዚዩ ዓቢዩ** *aziyu abyi*
immensity *(n.)* **ግዝፊ** *gzfi*
immerse *(v.)* **ኣጥሓለ** *'aṭḥale*
immersion *(n.)* **ምጥሓል** *mṭḥal*
immigrant *(n.)* **ፈላሲ** *felasi*
immigrate *(v.)* **ፈለሰ** *felese*
immigration *(n.)* **ፍልሰት** *flset*
imminent *(adj.)* **ስሩብ** *srub*
immoderate *(adj.)* **ተቐባልነት ዘይብሉ** *teqhbalnet zeyblu*
immodest *(n.)* **ዕቡ'ይ** *'ëbuy*
immodesty *(a.)* **ዕቡ'ይ** *'ëbuy*
immolate *(v.)* **ሰወአ** *sewe'e*
immoral *(adj.)* **ዘይሞራላዊ** *zeymoralawi*
immorality *(n.)* **ብዕልግና** *be'älegna*

immortal *(adj.)* **ዘይርሳዕ፣ ዘይመውት** *zeyrsa'ë, zeymewut*
immortality *(n.)* **ህያውነት** *hyawnet*
immortalize *(v.)* **ህያው ገበረ** *hyaw gebere*
immovable *(adv.)* **ቀዋሚ፣ ዘይቀሳቀስ** *qewami, zeynqesaqhes*
immune *(adj.)* **ዉሑስ** *wuhus*
immunity *(n.)* **ዉሑስነት** *wuhsnet*
immunize *(v.)* **ውሕስነት ሃበ** *wuhsnet habe*
immunology *(n.)* **ስነ-ዉሕስና** *sne- wuhsna*
immure *(n.)* **ሕዋስ** *hwas*
immutable *(adj.)* **ዘይቅየር** *zeyqyer*
impact *(n.)* **ምንካእ** *mnka'e*
impair *(v.)* **ኣድከመ** *adkeme*
impalpable *(adj.)* **ዘይተሓዝ** *zeyteḥaz*
impart *(v.)* **ኣካፈለ** *'akafele*
impartial *(adj.)* **ኣድልዎ ዘይብሉ** *'adlwo zeyblu*
impartiality *(n.)* **ፍትሒ** *fthi*
impassable *(adj.)* **ዘየሕልፍ** *zeyeḥlf*
impasse *(n.)* **ዓጋቲ** *'ägati*
impassioned *(adj.)* **ስምዒታዊ** *sm'ïtawi*
impassive *(adj.)* **ድንዙዝ** *dnzuz*
impatient *(adj.)* **ዘይዕጉስ፣ ችኩል** *zey'ëgus, chkul*
impeach *(v.)* **ጠርጠረ** *ṭerṭere*
impeachment *(n.)* **ክሲ** *ksi*
impeccable *(adj.)* **ኣበር ዘይብሉ** *'aber zeyblu*
impede *(v.)* **ዓንቀፈ** *'änqefe*
impediment *(n.)* **ዕንቅፋት** *'ënqfat*
impel *(v.)* **ኣተባብዐ** *'atebab'ë*
impending *(adj.)* **ሕዚ ዝኾነ ነገር ክፍጠር እዩ ዝብል ስሚዒት** *hzi zkone neger kfter eyu zbel smiet*
impenetrable *(adj.)* **ኸቢድ** *khebid*
imperative *(n.)* **ብጣዕሚ ጠቓሚ** *bta'emi tqhami*
imperfect *(adj.)* **ኣበር ዘለዎ** *aber zelewo*
imperfection *(n.)* **ኣበር ምህላው** *aber mhlaw*
imperial *(adj.)* **ኑጉሳዊ ስሚዒት ዘለዎ** *nugusawi smi'et zelewo*
imperialism *(n.)* **ኑጉሳዊ** *nugusawi*
imperil *(v.)* **ኣብ ሓደጋ ጠሓለ** *ab hadega tehale*
impersonal *(adj.)* **ምሳኻ ርክብ ዘይብሉ ነገር** *msakha rkb zeyblu neger*
impersonate *(v.)* **ምምሳል፣ ዘይኮንካዮ እየ ምባል** *mmsal, zeykonkayo eye mbal*
impersonation *(n.)* **ምምሳል** *mmsal*
impertinence *(n)* **ቕንዕና ዘይብሉ ፀባይ** *qhn'ena zeyblu tebay*
impertinent *(adj.)* **ቑኑዕ ዘይ ምኧን** *qhhunu;e zeymkhuan*
impervious *(adj.)* **ምክልኻል** *mklkhal*
impetuous *(adj.)* **ችኩል ዘየስተውዕል** *chkul zeyestew'el*
impetus *(n.)* **ምፍጣን** *mftan*

impious *(adj.)* ን ሃይማኖታዊ ነገር ክብሪ ዘይብሉ *n haymanotawi neger kbri zeyblu*
implacable *(adj.)* ኸቢድ ቑጠዐ *khbid qhute'e*
implant *(v.)* ኣብ ውሽጢ ስውነት መቐማጥ ምቕባር *ab wushti ssewunet m'etaw*
implausible *(adj.)* ሓቒ ክኾውን ዘይኽእል *haqi kkha=wun zeykh'el*
implement *(n.)* ምትግባር *mtgbar*
implicate *(v.)* ምኽሳስ *mkhsas*
implication *(n.)* ኽሲ *khsi*
implicit *(adj.)* ዝርዝረ-ጽሑፋት *zrzrexḧufat*
implode *(v.)* ብድንገት ምጭፍላቕ *bdnget mchflak*
implore *(v.t.)* ምግዳድ *mgdada*
imply *(v.)* ምሕባር *mhbar*
impolite *(adj.)* ዘይቑኑዕ *zeyqhunu'e*
import *(v.)* ምምፃእ *mmtsa'e*
importance *(n.)* ጠቓምነት *teqhamnet*
important *(adj.)* ጠቓሚ *teqhami*
importer *(n.)* ኣምፃኢ *amtsa'e*
impose *(v.)* ምግዳድ *mgdad*
imposing *(v.)* ምግዳድ *mgdad*
imposition *(n.)* ምግዳድ *mgdad*
impossibility *(n.)* ዘይምኽኣል *zeymkh'al*
impossible *(adj.)* ዘይከኣል *zeymkh'al*
imposter *(n.)* መመሰሊ *memeseli*
impotence *(n.)* ስንፈተ ግብረስጋ *snfete gebresga*
impotent *(adj.)* ስንፈተ ግብረስጋ ዘለዎ *snfete gebresga zelewo*
impound *(v.)* ብሕጊ ምዉራስ *bhgi mwuras*
impoverish *(v.)* ምድኻም *mdkham*
impracticable *(adj.)* ክትግበር ዘይክእል *ktgeber zeyk'el*
impractical *(adj.)* ዘይ ተግበራዊ *zey tegberawi*
impress *(v.)* ምድናቕ *mdnaqh*
impression *(n.)* ናይ ሰብ ባህሪ ምምሳል *nay sb bahri mmsal*
impressive *(adj.)* ዝድነቕ *zeneqh*
imprint *(n.)* ዓሸራ *ashara*
imprison *(n.)* ምእሳር *m'esar*
improbable *(adj.)* ክኾን ዘይኽእል *kkhon zeykh'eal*
improper *(adj.)* ኣግባብ ዘይብሉ *agbaba zeybl·ı*
ı.ı̂propriety *(n.)* ኣግባብ ዘይብሉ ፀባይ *agbaba zeyblu tsebay*
improve *(v.)* ኣስተኻክል *astekhakl*
improvement *(n.)* ምስትኽካል *mstkhkal*
improvident *(adj.)* ጠመረ *ẗemere*
improvise *(v.)* ዘለካ ተጠቒም ምስራሕ *zeleka tetqhimka m.. ıh*
imprudent *(adj.)* ጥንቃቔ ዘይፈልጥ *tnqaqhie zeyfelt*
impudent *(adj.)* ትሕትና ዘይፈልጥ *thtna zeyfelt*
impulse *(n.)* ሃንደፍታ *handefta*
impulsive *(adj.)* ሁንድፍ *hunduf*
impunity *(n.)* ክቕፃዕ ዘለዎ *kqhtsa'e zelewo*
impure *(adj.)* ዘይንጹህ *zeynutsuh*
impurity *(n.)* ዘይንጹህ *zeynutsuh*
impute *(v.)* ኢድ ምጡቋም *ed mtuquam*

in *(prep.)* **ዉሽጢ** *wusht.*
inability *(n.)* **ብዓቕሚ** *b'aqmi*
inaccurate *(adj.)* **ትኽክል ዘይኮነ** *tkhkl zeylone*
inaction *(n.)* **ምንም ዘይምግባር** *mnm zetmgbar*
inactive *(adj.)* **ንቑሕ ዘይኮነ** *nuqhuh zeykone*
inadequate *(adj.)* **ዘይኣክል** *zeyakl*
inadmissible *(adj.)* **ኣብ ቤት ፈርዲ ተቐባልነት ዘይብሉ** *ab bet frdi teqhebalnet zeyblu*
inadvertent *(adj.)* **ተይፈልጥኻ ዝግበር** *teyfeltka zgber*
inane *(adj.)* **ሃሳስ፣ ደደብ** *hasas, dedeb*
inanimate *(adj.)* **ሂወት ዘይብሉ ነገር** *hiwet heyblu neger*
inapplicable *(adj.)* **ክትግበር ዘይኽእል** *ktgber zeykh'el*
inappropriate *(adj.)* **ኣግባብነት ዘይብሉ** *agbabnet zeyblu*
inarticulate *(adj.)* **ምዝራብ ዘይኽእል** *mzrab zeykh'el*
inattentive *(adj.)* **ትኹረት ዘይሀብ** *tkhret zeyhb*
inaudible *(adj.)* **ዘይስማዕ** *zeysma'e*
inaugural *(adj.)* **መኽፈቲ መደረ** *mekhfeti medere*
inaugurate *(v.)* **ስራሕ ምጅማር** *srah mjmar*
inauspicious *(adj.)* **ዘይሰኻዕ** *zeyssakha'e*
inborn *(adj.)* **መፋጥርቲ** *mefatrti*
inbred *(adj.)* **ድቃል** *dqal*
incalculable *(adj.)* **ክስላሕ ዘይኽእል** *kslah zykh'el*
incapable *(adj.)* **ዓቕሚ ዘይብሉ** *aqmi zeyblu*
incapacity *(n.)* **ብዓቕሚ** *b'aqmi*
incarcerate *(v.)* **ምእሳር** *m'esar*
incarnate *(adj.)* **ምስለ መልኣኽ** *msle mle'akh*
incarnation *(n.)* **ኣፀቢቕካ ምውካል** *atsebiqhka mwukal*
incense *(n.)* **ዕጣን** *etan*
incentive *(n.)* **መተባበዒ** *metebab'e*
inception *(n.)* **መጀመርታ** *mejemerta*
incest *(n.)* **ኣብመንጎ ቤተሰብ ዝግበር ግብረ ስጋ** *ab mengo beteseb zgber gbre-sga*
inch *(n.)* **ኢንች** *inch*
incidence *(n.)* **ናይ ምግላፅ ዕድል** *nay mglatz edl*
incident *(n.)* **ብ ኣጋጣሚ ዝፈጠር ሓደጋ** *b agatammi zfter hadega*
incidental *(adj.)* **ብ ኣጋጣሚ ዝፈጠር ሓደጋ** *b agatammi zfter hadega*
incisive *(adj.)* **ብግልፂ ሓሳብካ ምግላፅ** *b gltsi hasbka mglats*
incite *(v.)* **ምድፍፋእ** *mdffa'e*
inclination *(n.)* **ግበር ዝብል ስምዒት** *gber zbl smi'et*
incline *(v.)* **ምፅፃፍ** *metsaf*
include *(v.)* **ምክታት** *mktat*
inclusion *(n.)* **ምክታት** *mktat*
inclusive *(adj.)* **ኣካታቲ** *akatati*
incoherent *(adj.)* **ባዕሉ ንባዕሉ ዘይስማዕማዕ** *ba'elu n ba'elu zeysma'ema'e*
income *(n.)* **ኣታዊ** *atawi*
incomparable *(adj.)* **ዘይወዳደሩ** *zeywedaderu*

incompatible *(adj.)* **ዘይስማዕማዑ** *zeysma'ema'u*
incompetent *(adj.)* **ዓቕሚ ዘይምህላው** *aqhmi zeymhlaw*
incomplete *(adj.)* **ዘይተወደአ** *zeytewede'e*
inconclusive *(adj.)* **መደምደምታ ዘይብሉ** *medemdemta zeyblu*
inconsiderate *(adj.)* **ብዛዕባ ካልኦት ዘይሓስብ** *bza'eba kal'ot zeyhasb*
inconsistent *(adj.)* **ቀፃልነት ዘይብሉ** *qhetsalnet zeyblu*
inconsolable *(adj.)* **ካብ ዓቕን ብላዕሊ ምሕዛን** *kab aqhen bla'eli mhzan*
inconspicuous *(adj.)* **ትኹረት ዘይምስሓብ** *tkhuret zeymhsab*
inconvenience *(n.)* **ችግር ምፍጣር** *chger mftar*
incorporate *(v.)* **ምክታት** *mktat*
incorporation *(n.)* **ብምክታት** *bmktat*
incorrect *(adj.)* **ስሕተት** *s'htet*
incorrigible *(adj.)* **ክቕየር ዘይኽእል ሕመቕ** *kqhyer zeykh'el hmeqh*
incorruptible *(adj.)* **ብላዕ ዘይበልዕ** *bla'e zeybel'e*
increase *(v.)* **ምዉሳኽ** *mwusakh*
incredible *(adj.)* **ገራሚ** *gerammi*
increment *(n.)* **ዘዉስኸሉ መጠን** *zwusekhelu metn*
incriminate *(v.i.)* **ምዉንጃል** *mwunjal*
incubate *(v.)* **ምብሳል** *mbsal*
inculcate *(v.)* **ብምድግጋም ምምሃር** *bmdggam mmhar*
incumbent *(adj.)* **ብዓል ስልጣን** *b'al sltan*
incur *(v.)* **ዋጋ ስራሕካ ምርካብ** *waga srahka mrkab*
incurable *(adj.)* **ክድሕን ዘይኽእል** *kdhn zeykh'el*
incursion *(n.)* **ምጥሓስ** *mthas*
indebted *(adj.)* **ኣብ ዕዳ ምእታው** *ab eda m'etaw*
indecency *(n.)* **ፆታዊ ስርዓት ኣልብኘነት** *tsotawi sr'at albegneet*
indecent *(adj.)* **ፆታዊ ስርዓት ኣልቦ** *tsotawi sr'at albo*
indecision *(n.)* **ውሳኔ ምኡዉሳን ዘይምኽኣል** *wusanie mwusan zeykh'el*
indeed *(adv.)* **ብደንቢ** *bdenbi*
indefensible *(adj.)* **ካብ መጥቃዕቲ ንምክልኻል ኣፀጋሚ** *kab metka'et nmklkhal zetsgm*
indefinite *(adj.)* **ግልፂ ዘይኮነ** *gltsi zeykone*
indemnity *(n.)* **ሓለዋ** *halewa*
indent *(v.)* **ዉፅእ ኢልካ ምጅማር** *wts'e elka mjmar*
indenture *(n.)* **ተገዲድካ ንስብ ምስራሕ** *tegedidka nseb msrah*
independence *(n.)* **ነፃነት** *netanet*
independent *(adj.)* **ነፃ** *netsa*
indescribable *(adj.)* **ንምግላፅ ዘፀግም** *nmglats zetsegm*
index *(n.)* **ኢንዴክስ** *index*
Indian *(n.)* **ህንዳዊ** *hndawi*
indicate *(v.)* **ምምልካት** *mmlkat*
indication *(n.)* **ኣምልካቲ** *amlkati*
indicative *(adj.)* **ኣምልካቲ** *amlkati*
indicator *(n.)* **ኣምልካቲ** *amlkati*

indict *(v.)* **ምጥቃም** *mtkoum*
indictment *(n.)* **ኽሲ** *khsi*
indifference *(n.)* **ድልየት ዘይምህላው** *dlyet zeymhlaw*
indifferent *(adj.)* **ድልየት ዘይምህላው** *dlyet zeymhlaw*
indigenous *(adj.)* **ናይ ሓደ ሃገር በዓል ዋና** *nay hade hager be'el wana*
indigestible *(adj.)* **ብቐሊሉ ዘይሓቅቕ** *bqhelilu zwyhaqqh*
indigestion *(n.)* **ብዘይ ምሕቓቕ ምግቢ ዝመፅእ ቓንዛ ኸብዲ** *bzey mhqaqh mgbi zmets'e qhanza kebdi*
indignant *(adj.)* **ቑጠዐ** *qhute'e*
indignation *(n.)* **ቑጠዐ** *qhute'e*
indignity *(n.)* **ምሕፋር** *mhfar*
indigo *(n.)* **ፀሊም ሊላዊ ዕንቆዋይ** *tselim lilawi enqoway*
indirect *(adj.)* **ብተዘዋዋሪ** *btezewawari*
indiscipline *(n.)* **ስርዓት ዘይተምሃረ** *sr'at zeytemhare*
indiscreet *(adj.)* **ሕፍረት ዘይብሉ** *hfret zeyblu*
indiscretion *(n.)* **ሕፍረት ዘይምህላይ** *hfret zeymhlay*
indiscriminate *(adj.)* **ብዘይ ኣፍላላይ** *bzey afelalay*
indispensable *(adj.)* **ወሳኒ** *wsani*
indisposed *(adj.)* **ዘይምህላው** *zeymhlaw*
indisputable *(adj.)* **ዘየከራኽር** *zeyekerakr*
indistinct *(adj.)* **ንፁር ዘይኮነ** *ntsur zeykone*
individual *(adj.)* **ዉልቀ** *wlqe*
individualism *(n.)* **ዉልቃዊነት** *wlqawinet*
individuality *(n.)* **ዉልቃዊነት** *wlqawinet*
indivisible *(adj.)* **ዘይኽፈል** *zeykhfel*
indolent *(adj.)* **ሰነፍ** *senef*
indomitable *(adj.)* **ተስፋ ዘይምቑራፅ** *tesfa zeymuqhurats*
indoor *(adj.)* **ኣብ ውሽጢ ገዛ** *ab wushti geza*
induce *(v.)* **ምፍጣር ምግባር** *mftr mgbar*
inducement *(n.)* **መተባብዒ** *metebab'e*
induct *(v.)* **ስልጣን ወይ ስራህ ምሃብ** *sltan wey srah mhab*
induction *(n.)* **ስልጣን ወይ ስራህ ምሃብ** *sltan wey srah mhab*
indulge *(v.)* **ዘደለዮ ንክገብር ምፍቃድ፣ ስዲ ሰዲድዎ** *zdeleyo neger kgebr mfqhad, sdi msdada*
indulgence *(n.)* **ስዲ ምስዳድ** *sdi msdada*
indulgent *(adj.)* **ስዲ ምስዳድ** *sdi msdada*
industrial *(adj.)* **ኢንዱስትርያላዊ** *industryalawi*
industrious *(adj.)* **ፃዕራም** *tsa'eram*
industry *(n.)* **ኢንዱስትሪ** *industri*
ineffective *(adj.)* **ስክዒታማ ዘይኮነ መንግዲ** *sk;etama zeykone megedi*
inefficient *(adj.)* **ጊዚኡ ብኣግባብ ዘይጥቀም** *gizi'u b agbab zeytkem*
ineligible *(adj.)* **ብቑዕ ዝይኮነ** *buqhu'e zeykone*

inequality ***(n.)*** **ኢ_ማዓርነት** *e-ma'arnet*
inert ***(adj.)*** **ዘይስሕብ** *zeyshb*
inertia ***(n.)*** **ኢነርሻ** *inertia*
inescapable ***(adj.)*** **ክምለጥ ዘይክእል** *kmlet zyk'el*
inevitable ***(adj.)*** **ዘይቐሪ ነገር** *zeyqheri neger*
inexact ***(adj.)*** **ትኽክል ዘይኮነ** *tkhkl zeykone*
inexcusable ***(adj.)*** **ተቐባልነት ዘይብሉ** *teqhebalnet zeyblu*
inexhaustible ***(adj.)*** **ዘይውዳእ** *zeywda'e*
inexorable ***(adj.)*** **ክቋረፅ ዘይኽእል** *kquarets zeykh'el*
inexpensive ***(adj.)*** **ርካሽ** *rkash*
inexperience ***(n.)*** **ልምዲ ዘይብሉ** *lmdi zeyblu*
inexplicable ***(adj.)*** **ዘይፍለጥ ምኽንያት** *zeyflet mknyat*
inextricable ***(adj.)*** **ክፈላለዩ ዘይኽእሉ** *kfelaleyu zeykh'elu*
infallible ***(adj.)*** **ተሰሓሒቱ ዘይፈልጥ** *tesehahitu zeyfelt*
infamous ***(adj.)*** **ተፈላጥ** *tefelati*
infamy ***(n.)*** **ተፈላጢ ምኽን** *tefelati mkhan*
infancy ***(n.)*** **ቈልዕነት** *qhul'enet*
infant ***(n.)*** **ዕሸል** *eshel*
infanticide ***(n.)*** **ዕሸል ምቕታል** *eshel mqhtal*
infantile ***(adj.)*** **ቖልዓ** *qhol'a*
infantry ***(n.)*** **እግረኛ ወታደር** *egregna wetader*
infatuate ***(v.)*** **ምፍታው** *mftaw*
infatuation ***(n.)*** **ምፍታው** *mftaw*
infect ***(v.)*** **ምብካል** *mbkal*
infection ***(n.)*** **ብኽለት** *bkhlet*
infectious ***(adj.)*** **ተመሓላለፊ** *temhalallefi*
infer ***(v.)*** **ካብ ዝበሎ ተላዒለ** *kab zbelo tela'ele*
inference ***(n.)*** **ካብ ዝበሎ ተላዒለ** *kab zbelo tela'ele*
inferior ***(adj.)*** **ትሑት** *thut*
inferiority ***(n.)*** **ታሕተዋይነት** *tahtewaynet*
infernal ***(adj.)*** **ደስ ዘይብል** *deszeyble*
infertile ***(adj.)*** **መኻን** *mkhan*
infest ***(v.)*** **ብብዝሓት ምህላው** *bbzhat mhlaw*
infidelity ***(n.)*** **ካብ ሕዳርካ ወፃኢ ዝግበር ግብረ ሰጋ** *kab hadarka wetsa'e zgber gbre-sga*
infighting ***(n.)*** **ቃራና** *qarana*
infiltrate ***(v.)*** **እብ ውሽጢ ኣቲኻ ምስላል** *ab wshti atikha mslal*
infinite ***(adj.)*** **ብጣዕሚ ቡዙሕ** *bta'emi buzuh*
infinity ***(n.)*** **ብጣዕሚ ቡዙሕ** *bta'emi buzuh*
infirm ***(adj.)*** **ብሕማም ዝመፅእ ድኻም** *b hmam zmets'e hmam*
infirmity ***(n.)*** **ብሕማም ዝመፅእ ድኻም** *b hmam zmets'e hmam*
inflame ***(v.)*** **ምውዕዋዕ** *mw'ewa'e*
inflammable ***(adj.)*** **ተዋዓዋዒ** *tewa'awa'i*
inflammation ***(n.)*** **ምኩሳሕ** *mkusah*
inflammatory ***(adj.)*** **ተኧሳሒ** *tekhuasahi*
inflate ***(v.)*** **ምውሳኽ** *mwusakh*
inflation ***(n.)*** **ወሰኽ ዋጋ** *weskh waga*
inflect ***(v.)*** **ምምልካት** *mmlkat*

inflexible *(adj.)* ዘይቕየር ደረቕ *zyqhyer dereqh*
inflict *(v.)* ክስመያ ምግባር *ksme'o mgbar*
influence *(n.)* ተሰማዒነት *tesema'enet*
influential *(adj.)* ተሰማዒ *tesema'e*
influenza *(n.)* ኢንፉሉዌንዛ *influenza*
influx *(n.)* ብበዝሒ ምምፃእ *bbezhi mmtsa'e*
inform *(v.)* ምሕባር *mhbar*
informal *(adj.)* ዘይኣግባባዊ *zeyagbabawi*
information *(n.)* ሓበሬታ *haberieta*
informative *(adj.)* ኣደመ *ademe*
informer *(n.)* ሓባሪ *habari*
infrastructure *(n.)* መሰረተ ልምዓት *meserete lm'at*
infrequent *(adj.)* ሓሓሊፉ *hahalifu*
infringe *(v.)* ምጥሓስ *mthas*
infringement *(n.)* ጥሕሰት *thset*
infuriate *(v.)* ምቑጣዕ *mqhuta'e*
infuse *(v.)* ምምላእ *mmla'e*
infusion *(n.)* ምልኢት *el'it*
ingrained *(adj.)* ዝፀነሐ *ztsenehe*
ingratitude *(n.)* ምስጋና ቢስ *msgana bis*
ingredient *(n.)* ቕመም *qhmem*
inhabit *(v.)* ይንብር/ሩ *ynebr/ru*
inhabitable *(adj.)* ንምምባር ዘይኾን *nmmbar zeykhon*
inhabitant *(n.)* ነበርቲ *neberti*
inhale *(v.)* ኣየር ምስሓብ *ayer mshab*
inhaler *(n.)* መተንፈሲ *btenfesi*
inherent *(adj.)* ካብ ወሎዶ ናብ ወሎዶ ዝመሓላለፉ *kab welodo nab welodo zmehlalef*
inherit *(v.)* ወረሰ *werese*
inheritance *(n.)* ውርሲ *wursi*
inhibit *(v.)* ምክልኻል *mklkhal*
inhibition *(n.)* ሕፍረት *hfret*
inhospitable *(adj.)* ክሕከም ዘይኽእል *khkem zeykh'el*
inhuman *(adj.)* ኢ_ስብኣዊ *e-sb'awi*
inimical *(adj.)* ዘተባብዕ *zetebab'e*
inimitable *(adj.)* ፉሉይ *fuluy*
initial *(adj.)* መጀመርታ *mejemerta*
initiate *(v.)* ጀምር *jemr*
initiative *(n.)* ምልዕዓል *ml'ë'äl*
inject *(v.)* ምውጋእ *mwga'e*
injection *(n.)* መርፌእ ምውጋእ *merfi'e mwga'e*
injudicious *(adj.)* ዕሽነት ዝትምሎኦ ዉሳኔ *arabħe*
injunction *(n.)* ናይ ፍርዲ ቤት ኽልከላ *nay bet ferdi khlkela*
injure *(v.)* ምጉዳእ *mguda'e*
injurious *(adj.)* ጎዳኢ *goda'e*
injury *(n.)* ጉድኣት *gudu'at*
injustice *(n.)* ኢ_ፍትሓዊ *e-fthawi*
ink *(n.)* ቐለም *qhelem*
inkling *(n.)* ምቕላም *mqhlam*
inland *(adj.)* ሃገራዊ *hagerawi*
inmate *(n.)* እስረኛ *esregna*
inmost *(adj.)* ውሽጣዊ *wshtawi*
inn *(n.)* ኑኡሽተይ ኣረጊት ሆቴል *nu'eshtey aregit hotel*
innate *(adj.)* ሒዝካዮ እትውልድ ኽእለት *hizkayo etwled kh'elet*
inner *(adj.)* ውሽጣዊ *wushtawi*

innermost *(adj.)* **ውሽጣዊ** *wushtawi*
innings *(n.)* **ተፃወቲ ክርኬት ኩዑሶ ዝወቕዐሉ ግዘ** *ttsaweti krikate ku'eso zewek'elu gizie*
innocence *(n.)* **ዘይምፍላጥ ዘይምግባር** *zeymflat zeymegbar*
innocent *(adj.)* **ዘይፈልጥ ዘይገበረ** *zeyfelt zeygeber*
innovate *(v.)* **ምፍጣር** *mftar*
innovation *(n.)* **ፈጠራ** *fetari*
innovator *(n.)* **ፈጣሪ** *fetari*
innumerable *(adj.)* **ብዙሕ** *bzuh*
inoculate *(v.)* **ምኽታብ** *mkhtab*
inoculation *(n.)* **ኽትባት** *khtbat*
inoperative *(adj.)* **ዘይሰርሕ** *zeyserh*
inopportune *(adj.)* **ዘይሙቹ** *zeymuchu*
inpatient *(n.)* **ድቂሱ ዝሕከም** *dekisu zhkem*
input *(n.)* **ኣታዊ** *atawi*
inquest *(n.)* **ናይ ሓደጋ ምርመራ** *nay hadega mrmera*
inquire *(v.)* **ሓበሬታ ምሕታት** *haberieta mhtat*
inquiry *(n.)* **ሓበሬታ ንምግናይ ዝሕተት ሕቶ** *haberieta nmgnay zhtet hto*
inquisition *(n.)* **ፖሊሳዊ ምርመራ** *polisawi mrmera*
inquisitive *(adj.)* **ሚስጥራት ምምርማር ዘፈቱ** *mistrat mmrmar zefetu*
insane *(adj.)* **ዑብድ** *ebud*
insanity *(n.)* **ዕብደት** *ebdt*
insatiable *(adj.)* **ዓቕን ዘይብሉ ድልየት** *aqhen zeyblu dlyet*
inscribe *(v.)* **ፁሑፍ ምቕራፅ** *tsuhuf mqhrats*
inscription *(n.)* **ዝተቐረፀ ፁሑፍ** *zteqhretse tsuhuf*
insect *(n.)* **ደቐቕቲ እንስሳት** *deqheqhti enssat*
insecticide *(n.)* **ፀረ_ባልዕ** *tsere-bal'e*
insecure *(adj.)* **ዘየተኣማምን** *zeyte'amamen*
insecurity *(n.)* **ዘየተኣማምን** *zeyete'amamn*
insensible *(adj.)* **ትርጉም ዘይህብ** *trgum zeyhb*
inseparable *(adj.)* **ዘይነፃፀል** *zeynetsatsel*
insert *(v.)* **ሰኹዐ** *seḱu'ë*
insertion *(n.)* **ምስኳዕ** *mskWa'ë*
inside *(n.)* **ውሽጢ** *wshẗi*
insight *(n.)* **ስውጠት** *swṭet*
insignificance *(n.)* **ዘይረብሕ** *zeyrebḥ*
insignificant *(adj.)* **ዘይረብሕ** *zeyrebḥ*
insincere *(adj.)* **ናይ ዉሽጡ ዘይዛረብ** *nay wushtu zeyzareb*
insincerity *(adv.)* **ናይ ውሽጥኻ ዘይምዝራብ** *nay wushtkha zeymzrab*
insinuate *(v.)* **ሰለኹ** *seleḱWa*
insinuation *(n.)* **ምስላኽ** *mslakh*
insipid *(adj.)* **ዘይጥዕም** *zeyt'em*
insist *(v.)* **ኣትሪሩ ተዛረበ** - *atriru tezarebe*
insistence *(n.)* **ፅኑዕ** *tsnu'ë*
insistent *(adj.)* **ተደጋጋሚ** *tedegagami*
insolence *(n.)* **ዘይምኽባር** *zeymkbar*

insolent *(adj.)* ዘይምኽባር *zeymkbar*
insoluble *(adj.)* ዘይሓቅቕ *zeyḥaqq̈*
insolvency *(n.)* ዕዳኻ ንምኽፋል ዓቕሚ ምስኣን *edaka nmkhfakl akmi ms'an*
insolvent *(adj.)* ዕዳኡ ኪኽፍል ዘይከኣለ *ed'u kkefel zeyke'ale*
inspect *(v.)* መርመረ *mermere*
inspection *(n.)* ቍጽጽር *qutstsr*
inspector *(n.)* ተቘጻጻሪ *teq̈Wetsatsari*
inspiration *(n.)* መተባበዒ *temsaṭ*
inspire *(v.)* ኣተባብዐ *'atebab'ë*
instability *(n.)* ዘይቀዋሚነት *zeyqewaminet*
install *(v.)* ኣብ ስልጣን ኣደየበ *'ab slṭan 'adeyebe*
installation *(n.)* ቦታ ምሓዝ *bota mḥaz*
instalment *(n.)* ክፋል *kfal*
instance *(n.)* ኣብነት መረዳእታ *'abnet mereda'èta*
instant *(adj.)* ቅፅበት *qtsbetawi*
instantaneo 's *(adj.)* ቅፅበታዊ *qtsbetawi*
instead *(adv.)* ኣብ ክንዲ *ab kndi*
instigate *(v.)* ቀስቀሰ *qesqese*
instil *(v.)* በብቑሩብ ኣእተወ *bebq̈urub 'a'ètewe*
instinct *(n.)* ባህረት *bahret*
instinctive *(adj.)* ባህረታዊ *bahretawi*
institute *(n.)* ኣቘመ *'aq̈Weme*
institution *(n.)* ተቛም *tqhuam*
instruct *(v.)* መሃረ *mehare*
instruction *(n.)* መምርሒ *memrhi*
instructor *(n.)* መምህር *memhr*
instrument *(n.)* መሳርሒ *mesarhi*
instrumental *(adj.)* መሳርሒያዊ *mesarhawi*
instrumentalist *(n.)* ተጻዋቲ መሳርሒ *texawati mesarhi*
insubordinate *(adj.)* ምሕንጋድ *mhngad*
insubordination *(n.)* ምሕንጋድ *mḥngad*
insufficient *(adj.)* ዘይእኹል *zey'èḱul*
insular *(adj.)* ሓዱሽ ስብ ወይ ሓሳብ ዘይቕበል *hadish sb wey hasab zeyqqhbel*
insulate *(v.)* ካብ ኤልክትሪክ ወይ ካብ ሙቐት ምክልኻል *kab electric wey muqhet mklkhal*
insulation *(n.)* ካብ ኤልክትሪክ ወይ ሙቐት ዝከላኸል ሽፋን *kab electric wey muqhet zkelakhel shfan*
insulator *(n.)* ኤልክትሪክ ወይ ካብ ሙቐት ዘይመሓላልፍ *electric wey muqhet zeyemehalalf*
insulin *(n.)* ኢንሱሊን *'insulin*
insult *(v.t.)* ፀረፈ;ኣዋረደ *tserefe;awarede*
insupportable *(adj.)* ክትጽመሞ ዘይከኣል *ktsmemo zeyke'al*
insurance *(n.)* መድሕን *medḧn*
insure *(v.)* ኣውሓሰ *'awḧase*
insurgent *(n.)* ፀረ ምንግስቲ *tse-mengsti*
insurmountable *(adj.)* ክስተኽኽል ዘይኽእል ፀገም *kstekhakel zeylh'el tsegem*
insurrection *(n.)* ዓምፅ *ametse*

intact *(adj.)* ዘይተጎደአ *zeytegode'e*
intake *(n.)* መምልኢ *meml'i*
intangible *(adj.)* ኪጭበጥ ዘይከኣል *kičbeť zeyke'al*
integral *(adj.)* ዘይንፀል ኣካል *zeyntsel 'akal*
integrity *(n.)* ቅንዕና *qn'ëna*
intellect *(n.)* ሊቅ *liq*
intellectual *(adj.)* ምሁር በሊሕ ሊቅ *mhur beliḧ liq*
intelligence *(n.)* ክእለት; ኣስተውዕሎ *k'èlet; astew'ëlo*
intelligent *(adj.)* ኣስተውዓሊ *'astew'äli*
intelligible *(adj.)* ብሩህ *bruh*
intend *(v.)* ወጠነ *weťene*
intense *(adj.)* ስምዒታዊ *sm'ïtawi*
intensify *(v.)* ፀዓቐ *tse'äq̈e*
intensity *(n.)* ፀዕቂ *tsa'ëqi*
intensive *(adj.)* ፅዑቕ *ts'üq̈*
intent *(n.)* ዕላማ *ëlama*
intention *(n.)* ምውጣን *mwťan*
intentional *(adj.)* ዉጡን *wutun*
interact *(v.)* ምትእትታው *mt'ettaw*
intercede *(v.)* ይቕር ንክብል ምእማን *yker nkbl m'eman*
intercept *(v.)* ኣቋረጸ *'aqWArexe*
interception *(n.)* ምቁራጽ *mqurats*
interchange *(v.)* ተለዋወጠ *telewaweťe*
intercom *(n.)* ውሽጣዊ መዘራረቢ *wshťawi mezerarebi*
interconnect *(v.)* ዝተረኻኸቡ *ztelkhakhebu*
intercourse *(n.)* ግብረ ስጋ *gbre sga*
interdependent *(adj.)* ተማራኺሲ *temarak̇Wasi*
interest *(n.)* ድልየት ወይ ዝንባለ *dlyet wey znbale*
interesting *(adj.)* ማራኺ *marak̇i*
interface *(n.)* ሽርካ *shrka*
interfere *(v.)* ኢዱ ኣእተወ *'idu 'a'ètewe*
interference *(n.)* ኢድ ምእታው *id m'ètaw*
interim *(n.)* ጊዜዊ *gizawi*
interior *(adj.)* ውሽጣዊ *wshťawi*
interject *(v.)* ዝዛረብ ሰብ ኣቋረፀ *zzareb seb aqaretse*
interlink *(v.)* ተኣሳሰረ *te'asasere*
interlock *(v.)* ተገጣጠመ *tegeťaťeme*
interlocutor *(n.)* መዋግዕቲ *mewag'eti*
interloper *(n.)* ጦብሎቕ በሃሊ *ťobloq̈ behali*
interlude *(n.)* ዕረፍቲ *'ërefti*
intermediary *(n.)* መንጎኛ *mengoṅa*
intermediate *(adj.)* ማእከላይ *ma'èkelay (ንግዜ ቦታ፣ ደረጃ... ወዘተ)*
interminable *(adj.)* መወዳእታ ዘይብሉ *meweda'èta zeyblu*
intermission *(n.)* ዕረፍቲ *'ërefti*
intermittent *(adj.)* ሓሓሊፉ ዝድጋገም *hahalifu zdegagem*
intern *(v.)* ሰልጣኒ *seltani*
internal *(adj.)* ውሽጣዊ *wshťawi*
international *(adj.)* ዓለም-ለኻዊ *'älemlek̇awi*
interplay *(n.)* ርክብ *rkb*
interpret *(v.)* ተረጎመ *teregome*

interpreter *(n.)* አስተርጓሚ *'astergWami*
interracial *(adj.)* በየነ-ዓሌታዊ *beyene'äleetawi*
interrelate *(v.)* ተዘማመደ *tezemamede*
interrogate *(v.)* ሓተተ *ḧatete*
interrogative *(adj.)* ናይ ሕቶ ቃል *nay ḧto qal*
interrupt *(v.)* ኣቋረፀ *aqaretse*
interruption *(n.)* ምቁራፅ *mqurats*
intersect *(v.)* ሰንጠቐ *senẗeq̈e*
interstate *(n.)* በየነ-መንግስታዊ *beyenemengstawi*
interval *(n.)* ካብ እስካብ *kab eskab*
intervene *(v.)* ጣልቃ ኣተወ *ẗalqa 'atewe*
intervention *(n.)* ኢድ ምእታው *'id m'ètaw*
interview *(n.)* ቃለ-መጠይቕ *qalemeẗeyq̈*
intestine *(n.)* መዓንጣ *me'änẗa*
intimacy *(n.)* ምትዕርራኽ *mt'ërraḱ*
intimate *(adj.)* ቀንዲ *qendi*
intimidate *(v.)* ኣፈራረሐ *aferarehe*
intimidation *(n.)* ምፍርራሕ *mfrrah*
into *(prep.)* ናብ *nab*
intolerable *(adj.)* ዘይፅወር *zeytswer*
intolerant *(adj.)* ዘይፅወር *zeytswer*
intone *(v.)* ኣዜመ *'azeeme*
intoxicate *(v.)* መረዘ *mereze*
intoxication *(n.)* ምምራዝ *mmraz*
intractable *(adj.)* ዘይእዱብ ዘይግራሕ *zey'èdub zeygraḧ*
intranet *(n.)* መርበብ *merbeb*
intransitive *(adj.)* ዘይሳገር *zeysager*
intrepid *(adj.)* ተባዕ *teba'ë*
intricate *(adj.)* ክትርድኦ ዘሸግር *ktrd'o zeshegr*
intrigue *(v.)* ምሽባን ምምሽጣር ምድናቕ *mshban mmshẗar mdnaqh*
intrinsic *(adj.)* ባህርያዊ *bahryawi*
introduce *(v.)* ኣፋለጠ ኣላለየ *'afaleẗe 'alaleye*
introduction *(n.)* ምፍላጥ ምልላይ *mflaẗ mllay*
introductory *(adj.)* መፋለጢ *mefaleẗi*
introspect *(v.)* መፈለጢ ሓተታ *mefelaleti hateta*
introspection *(n.)* ነብስኻ ምምርማር *nebsḱa mmrmar*
introvert *(n.)* ግልፂ ዘይኮነ ሰብ *gltsi zeykone seb*
intrude *(v.)* ህሩግ በለ ጠብሎቕ በለ *hrug bele ẗebloq̈ bele*
intrusion *(n.)* ህሩግ ምባል *hrug mbal*
intrusive *(adj.)* ህሩግ በሃሊ *hrug behali*
intuition *(n.)* ገምሪ *gemri*
intuitive *(n.)* ገምራዊ *gemrawi*
inundate *(v.)* ኣዕለቕለቐ *'a'ëleq̈leq̈e*
invade *(v.)* ወረረ *werere*
invalid *(n.)* ምግዱር ኣካለ-ስንኩል *mgdur 'akalesnkul*
invalidate *(v.)* ዘይቅቡል ገበረ ኣፍረሰ *zeyqbul gebere 'afrese*

invaluable *(adj.)* **አዝዩ ክቡር ዕዙዝ** *azyu kbur 'ëzuz*
invariable *(adj.)* **ዘይለዋወጥ** *zeylewaweẗ*
invasion *(n.)* **ምውራር** *mwrar*
invective *(n.)* **ነውሪ; ፅያፍ** *newri; tsyaf*
invent *(v.)* **መሃዘ** *mehaze*
invention *(n.)* **ምምሃዝ** *mmhaz*
inventor *(n.)* **መሃዚ** *mehazi*
inventory *(n.)* **ዝርዝራዊ ፍቕዲ** *zrzrawi fq̈di*
inverse *(adj.)* **ግምጡል** *gmẗul*
invert *(v.)* **ገምጠለ** *gemẗele*
invest *(v.t.)* **ኣውዓለ** *aw'ale*
investigate *(v.)* **ኣፅንዐ መርመረ** *atsn'ë mermere*
investigation *(n.)* **መርመራ** *mermera*
investment *(n.)* **ምውዓል** *mw'al*
invigilate *(adj.)* **ሓለወ** *ḧalewe*
invigilator *(n.)* **ሓላዊ** *ḧalawi*
invincible *(adj.)* **ዘይስዓር** *zeys'är*
inviolable *(adj.)* **ኪጠሓስ ዘይብሉ** *kiẗeḧas zeyblu*
invisible *(adj.)* **ዘይረአ** *zeyre'e*
invitation *(n.)* **መፀዋዕታ** *metsewa'ëta*
invite *(v.)* **ፀወዐ ዓደመ** *tsewe'ë ademe*
inviting *(adj.)* **ማራኺ** *marak̍i*
invocation *(n.)* **ፀሎት** *tselot*
invoice *(n.)* **ዝርዝር ናይ ዝተሸጡ ኣቕሑ** *zrzr nay ztesheẗu 'aq̈ḧu*
invoke *(v.)* **ብሕጊ መሰረት ገበረ** *b hgi meseret gebere*
involuntary *(adj.)* **ዘይእዙዝ** *zey'èzuz*
involve *(v.)* **ኣእተወ** *a'ètewe*
invulnerable *(adj.)* **ዘይህሰ ዘይድፈር** *zeyhse zeydfer*
inward *(adj.)* **ውሽጣዊ** *wshẗawi*
irate *(adj.)* **ሓራቕ** *ḧaraq̈*
ire *(n.)* **ሕርቃን** *ḧrqan*
iris *(n.)* **ጸላም-ዓይኒ** *tselam'äyni*
irksome *(v.)* **መናደዲ መሕረቒ** *menadedi mehreqhi*
iron *(n.)* **ሓፂን** *ḧatsin*
ironical *(adj.)* **ሓጫጪ ኣሽሙረኛ** *ḧačači 'ashmureňa*
irony *(n.)* **ሕጫጨ ኣሽሙር** *ḧčače 'ashmur*
irradiate *(v.)* **ብርሃን ሃበ** *brhan habe*
irrational *(adj.)* **መሰረት ዘይብሉ ዘይርትዓዊ** *meseret zeyblu zeyrt'äwi*
irreconcilable *(adj.)* **ዘይተዓረቕ** *zeyte'äreq̈*
irredeemable *(adj.)* **ዘይስተኻኸል** *zeystekhakel*
irrefutable *(adj.)* **ዘይርታዕ** *zeyrta'ë*
irregular *(adj.)* **ዘይስሩዕ** *zeysru'ë*
irregularity *(n.)* **ዘይስሩዕነት** *zeysru'ënet*
irrelevant *(adj.)* **ዘይዛመድ** *zeyzamed*
irreplaceable *(adj.)* **ኪትካእ ዘይከኣል** *kitka'è zeyke'al*
irresistible *(adj.)* **ይኣኽለኒ ዘይብሃል** *y'akleni zeybhal*
irresolute *(adj.)* **ተጠራጣሪ ዘይዉስን** *teẗeraẗari zeywsen*
irrespective *(adj.)* **ኣብ ግምት ብዘይምእታው** *'ab gmt bzeym'ètaw*

irresponsible *(adj.)* **ሓላፍነት ዘይስምዖ** *ḧalafnet zeysm'ö*
irreversible *(adj.)* **ናብ ዝነበሮ ክምለስ ዘይኽእል** *nab znebro kmles zeyk'el*
irrevocable *(adj.)* **ዘይልወጥ** *zeylweẗ*
irrigate *(v.)* **ብመስኖ ማይ ኣስተየ** *bmesno may 'asteye*
irrigation *(n.)* **መስኖ** *mesno*
irritable *(adj.)* **ሓራቕ** *ḧaraq̈*
irritant *(n.)* **ኣትካሪ** *'atkari*
irritate *(v.)* **ኣትከረ** *'atkere*
irruption *(n.)* **ፈንጢስካ ምእታው** *fenẗiska m'ètaw*
Islam *(n.)* **እስልምና** *islmna*
island *(n.)* **ደሴት** *deseet*
isle *(n.)* **ደሴት** *deseet*
islet *(n.)* **ንእሽቶ ደሴት** *n'èshto deseet*
isobar *(n.)* **ኣይሶባር** *'aysobar*
isolate *(v.)* **ኣግለለ** *'aglele*
isolation *(n.)* **ምግላል** *mglal*
issue *(n.)* **ሃበ** *habe*
it *(pron.)* **ንሱ ንሳ** *nsu nsa*
italic *(adj.)* **ኢታሊክ ቄናን** *italik qeenan*
itch *(v.i.)* **ህርፋን ቀሊል ቃንዛ** *hrfan qelil qanza*
itchy *(adj.)* **ኣስሓዪ ምሕከኺ** *asḧayi mehkeki*
item *(n.)* **ኣቑሑ** *aqhhu*
iterate *(v.)* **ደጋገመ** *degageme*
itinerary *(n)* **ናይ ጉዕዞ ዉጥን** *nay go'ezo wutn*
itself *(pron.)* **ንባዕሉ** *nba'ëlu*
ivory *(n.)* **ስኒ ሓርማዝ** *sni ḧarmaz*
ivy *(n.)* **ኣይቪ** *ayvi*

J

jab *(v.)* **ኣጕረጠ** *'agureẗe*
jabber *(v.)* **ኣዝዩ ቅልጡፍ ዘረባ** *'azyu qlẗuf zereba*
jack *(n.)* **መልዓሊ መኪና ዓሻ** *mel'eli mekina 'äsha (ንሰብ)*
jackal *(n.)* **ከልቢ ዝመስል እንስሳ** *kelbi zmesl 'ènssa*
jackass *(n.)* **ተባዕታይ ኣድጊ** *teba'ëtay 'adgi*
jacket *(n.)* **ጃኬት** *ĵakeet*
jackpot *(n.)* **ዝለዓለ ሽልማት** *zle'ale shlmat*
Jacuzzi *(n.)* **ጃኩዚ** *ğakuzii*
jade *(n.)* **ቆፃል ኹብር እምኒ** *qhotsal khubr emni*
jaded *(adj.)* **ምድባር** *mdbar*
jagged *(adj.)* **በሊሕ** *belih*
jail *(n.)* **ቤት ማእሰርቲ** *beet ma'èserti*
jailer *(n.)* **ኣላዪ** *'alayi*
jam *(v.t.)* **ምትዕፅፃይ** *mt'etstsaw*
jam *(n.)* **ዓገተ** *'ägete (ንድምጺ)*
jamboree *(n.)* **ፌስታዊ ኣኼባ** *feestawi 'aḱeeba*
janitor *(n.)* **ዓቃበ-ህንጻ** *äqabehntsa*
January *(n.)* **ጥሪ** *ẗri*
jar *(n.)* **ስልጣንያ** *sltanya*
jargon *(n.)* **ፉሉይ ቃል** *fuluy kal*
jasmine *(n.)* **ሓቢ ጸሊም** *ḧabi xelim (ዓይነት ተኽሊ)*
jaundice *(n.)* **ዓይኒን ቆርበትን ቢጫ ዝገብር ሕማም** *aynen korbetn bicha zgebr hmam*
jaunt *(n.)* **ጉብኝት** *ḧaxir zuret*
jaunty *(adj.)* **ክዩፍ በዓል_ዓርሰእምነት** *kyuf*

javelin *(n.)* ነዊሒ ጦር *čmara*
jaw *(n.)* ምንጋጋ *mngaga*
jay *(n.)* ናይ ዒፍ ዓይነት *bzuḧ zzareb*
jazz *(n.)* ያዕያዕታ ጃዝ *ya'ëya'ëta ĵaz*
jazzy *(adj.)* ሕብራዊ ዘመናዊ *muziqawi*
jealous *(adj.)* ቀናእ *qena'è*
jealousy *(n.)* ቅንኣት *qn'at*
jeans *(n.)* ጂንስ *ĵins*
jeep *(n.)* መኪና በረኻ *mekina bereḱa*
jeer *(v.)* ኣባጨወ *'abačewe*
jelly *(n.)* መለግለጋ *meleglega*
jellyfish *(n.)* መለግለጋይ ዓሳ *meleglegay 'äsa*
jeopardize *(v.)* ኣብ ሓደጋ ኣውደቐ *'ab ḧadega 'awdeq̈e*
jeopardy *(n.)* ግድዓት ኣብ ሓደጋ ምውዳቕ *gd'ät*
jerk *(n.)* ነው ኣበለ ሃሳስ *new 'abele*
jerkin *(n.)* እጀገ ኣልቦ *'èĵege 'albo*
jersey *(n.)* ጎልፎ ማልያ *golfo*
jest *(n.)* መስሓቕ *mesḧaq̈*
jester *(n.)* ተዋዛይ *tewazay*
jet *(n.)* ፍሊልታ *flilta*
jet lag *(n.)* ንፍረት ሕማም *ḥmam-nfret*
jewel *(n.)* ገይጺ መጋየጺ *ĵewhar*
jeweller *(n.)* ገይጺ ፈጣሪ *ĵewhar feẗari*
jewellery *(n.)* ገይጺ መጋየጺ *ĵewhar*
jibe *(n.)* ምልጋፀ *'alagexe*
jig *(n.)* ቅልጡፍ ሳዕስዒት *qlẗuf sa'ës'ït*
jiggle *(v.)* ሓቘነ *ḧaq̈Wene*
jigsaw *(n.)* ምጥዋይን ምስሓብን *mṭwayn msḥabn*
jingle *(n.)* ጫሕጫሕ ኣበለ *čaḧčaḧ 'abele*
jinx *(n.)* ቑርሱስ *qruḧ qrsus*
jitters *(n.)* ራዕዲ *ra'ëdi*
job *(n.)* ስራሕ *sraḧ*
jockey *(n.)* ብፈረስ ተቐዳደመ *bferes teq̈edademe*
jocose *(adj.)* ተዋዛዪ *tewazayi*
jocular *(v.t.)* ተዋዛዪ ተጫዋቲ *tewazayi*
jog *(v.)* ሳምሶማ ጉያ *ḧagWaxgWax 'abele*
joggle *(v.)* ተነውነወ *tenewnewe*
join *(v.)* ኣባል ኮነ *'abal kone*
joiner *(n.)* ኣግጣሚ *agẗami*
joint *(n.)* መሓውር መጋጥም *meḧawr*
joist *(n.)* ሙራለ *murale*
joke *(n.)* ቀልዲ *'asḧaq̈e*
joker *(n.)* ቐልዲ *tewazayi*
jolly *(adj.)* ሕጉስ *ḧgus*
jolt *(v.t.)* ሓጎፅጎፅ ኣበለ *ḧagWaxgWax 'abele*
jostle *(v.t.)* ነውነወ *newnewe*
jot *(v.t.)* ቅንጣብ ፁሑፍ *qnẗab*
journal *(n.)* ጋዜጣ *gazeeẗa*
journalism *(n.)* ጋዜጠኛነት *gazeeẗeňanet*
journalist *(n.)* ጋዜጠኛ *gazeeẗeňa*
journey *(n.)* ጉዕዞ *gu'ëzo*
jovial *(adj.)* ሑጉስ *mesḧaq̈*
joviality *(adv.)* ብሓጎስ *teḥagWase*
joy *(n.)* ደስታ *desta*
joyful *(adj.)* ሕጉስ *dsut*
joyous *(adj.)* ሕጉስ *ḥgus*
jubilant *(adj.)* ሕጉስ *dsut*

jubilation ***(n.)*** **ሓጐስ** *ḧagWas*
jubilee ***(n.)*** **ኢዮበልዩ** *iyobelyu*
judge ***(n.)*** **ዳኛ** *feradi*
judgement ***(n.)*** **ምፍራድ** *mfrad*
judicial ***(adj.)*** **ፍርዳዊ** *frdawi*
judiciary ***(n.)*** **ፍርዳዊ** *ferado*
judicious ***(adj.)*** **መስተውዓሊ** *mestew'äli*
judo ***(n.)*** **ጁዶ** *ĵudo (ናይ ምክል ኽልን ምጥቃዕን ቃልሲ)*
jug ***(n.)*** **ብራኳ** *brakWa*
juggle ***(v.)*** **ኣደናገረ ካብቲናብቲ ምባል** *'adenagere*
juggler ***(n.)*** **ምርኢት ኣቕራቢ** *mr'it 'aq̈rabi*
juice ***(n.)*** **ፅማቝ** *xmaq̈Wu*
juicy ***(adj.)*** **ጡዑም** *texemaq̈Wi*
July ***(n.)*** **ሓምለ** *ḧamle*
jumble ***(n.)*** **ድብልቕላቕ** *debaleq̈e*
jumbo ***(adj.)*** **ገጅፍ ዝዓይነቱ** *geĵf z'äynetu*
jump ***(v.i)*** **ነጠረ ዘለለ** *neťere*
jumper ***(n.)*** **ዘላሊ** *zelali*
jumper ***(n.)*** **ጎልፎ** *termin*
junction ***(n.)*** **መራኸቢ** *meraḱebi*
juncture ***(n.)*** **መራኸቢ** *meraḱebi*
June ***(n.)*** **ሰነ** *sene*
jungle ***(n.)*** **ጫካ** *čaka*
junior ***(adj.)*** **ታሕታዋይ መባእታ** *salsay 'ämet*
junior ***(n.)*** **ንኡስ** *n'us*
junk ***(n.)*** **ጐሓፍ** *gWaḧaf*
Jupiter ***(n.)*** **ጁፒተር** *ĵupiter*
jurisdiction ***(n.)*** **ሕጋዊ ስልጣን** *ḧgawi slťan*
jurisprudence ***(n.)*** **ስነ-ሕጊ** *sneḧgi*
jurist ***(n.)*** **ክኢላ ሕጊ** *k'ila ḧgi*
juror ***(n.)*** **ኣባል ፈራዶ** *daṅa*
jury ***(n.)*** **ፈራዶ** *ferado*
just ***(adj.)*** **ልክዕ** *lk'ë*
justice ***(n.)*** **ፍትሒ** *ftḧi*
justifiable ***(adj.)*** **ቑቡል** *bq̈Wu'ë*
justification ***(n.)*** **መመኽነይታ** *memeḱneyta*
justify ***(v.)*** **ኣረጋገጸ** *'aregagexe*
jute ***(n.)*** **ጁት** *ĵut*
juvenile ***(adj.)*** **ትሕቲ ዕድመ** *men'èsey*

K

kaftans ***(n.)*** **ካፍታን** *kaftan*
kaleidoscope ***(n.)*** **ተቐያያሪ ሕብርታት** *teq̈eyayari ḧbrtat*
kangaroo ***(n.)*** **ካንጋሩ** *kangaru*
karma ***(n.)*** **ካርማ** *karma*
kebab ***(n.)*** **ከቢብ** *kebib*
keel ***(n.)*** **ናይ ገልባ ታሕታዋይ ኣካል** *nay jelba tahtaway alkal*
keen ***(adj.)*** **ምህንጣይ** *mhntay*
keenness ***(n.)*** **ድልየት** *dlyet*
keep ***(v.)*** **ሓለወ** *ḧalewe*
keeper ***(n.)*** **ሓላዊ** *ḧalawi*
keeping ***(n.)*** **ምሕላው** *mhlaw*
keepsake ***(n.)*** **መዘከርታ** *mezekerta*
keg ***(n.)*** **ንእሽቶ በርሚል** *n'èshto bermil*
kennel ***(n.)*** **ጋቢያ ሰፈር ከልቢ** *gabiya sefer kelbi*
kerb ***(n.)*** **ናይ እግረኛ መንግዲ ጫፍ** *nay egregna mengedi chaf*
kernel ***(n.)*** **ፍረ ዓካት** *fre 'äkat*
kerosene ***(n.)*** **ላምባ** *lamba*

ketchup *(n.)* ከቻፕ *kechap*
kettle *(n.)* በራድ *berad*
key *(n.)* መፍትሕ *mefth̩*
keyboard *(n.)* ሰሌዳ መፋትሕ *seleeda mefath̩*
keyhole *(n.)* ዓይኒ መፍትሕ *'äyni mefth*
kick *(v.)* ሃረመ ወቐዐ *hareme weqh'e*
kid *(n.)* ማሕስእ ህፃን *maḥs'è htsan*
kidnap *(v.)* ጨወየ *čewey*
kidney *(n.)* ኵሊት *kulit*
kill *(v.)* ቀተለ *qetele*
killing *(n.)* ቅትለት *qtlet*
kiln *(n.)* እቶን *'èton*
kilo *(n.)* ኪሎ *kilo*
kilobyte *(n.)* ኪሎ ባይት *kilo-byt*
kilometre *(n.)* ኪሎሜተር *kilomeeter*
kilt *(n.)* ከሽከሽ ቐሚሽ *keshkesh qhemish*
kimono *(n.)* ጀለብያ ዚመስል ናይ ጃፓን ክዳን *ğelebya zimesl nay japan kdan*
kin *(n.)* ዘመድ *zemed*
kind *(n.)* ዓይነት የዋህ *äynet yewah*
kindergarten *(n.)* ቤት-ትምህርቲ ሕጻናት *beettmhrti ḥxanat*
kindle *(v.)* ተወለዐ *tewele'ë*
kindly *(adv.)* ብሕያውነት *bḥyawnet*
kinetic *(adj.)* ምንቅስቓሳዊ *mnqsq̈asawi*
king *(n.)* ንጉስ *ngus*
kingdom *(n.)* ስርወ መንግስቲ *srwe-mengsti*
kink *(n.)* ጠዋይ ለዋይ *ṭeway leway*
kinship *(n.)* ዝምድና *zmdna*
kiss *(v.t.)* ስዕመት *s'ëmet*
kit *(n.)* መሳርሒ ኣቕሑ *mesarḥi 'aq̈ḥu*
kitchen *(n.)* ክሽነ *kshne*
kite *(n.)* ኣብ ኣየር ዝበርር ናይ መረቀት መፃወቲ *ab ayer zeberr nay werqet metsaweti*
kith *(n.)* ዓርከይ *arkey*
kitten *(n.)* ውላድ ድሙ *wlad dmu*
kitty *(n.)* መዋጮ *mewacho*
knack *(n.)* ብልሓት *blḥat*
knacker *(v.)* ዝኣረጉ ኣፍራስ ዚገዝእን ዚሓርድን ሰብ *z'aregu 'afras zigez'èn ziḥardn seb*
knave *(n.)* ዘይቅኑዕ *zeyqnu'ë*
knead *(v.)* ለወሰ ኣብኮዐ *lewese abko'e*
knee *(n.)* ብርኪ *brki*
kneel *(v.)* ተንበርከኸ *tenberkeḱe*
knickers *(n.)* ናይ ደቂ ኣንስትዮ ስረ ብርኪ *nay deki- anstyo sre brki*
knife *(n.)* ካራ *kara*
knight *(n.)* ፈረሰኛ ወተሃደር *fereseña wetehader*
knit *(v.)* ረከመ *rekeme*
knob *(n.)* ለዓት *le'ät*
knock *(v.)* ኳሕኵሐ *kWaḥkuḥe*
knot *(n.)* ቍጻር *quxar*
knotty *(adj.)* ዝተሓላለኸ *zteḥalaleḱe*
know *(v.)* ፈለጠ *feleṭe*
knowing *(adj.)* መፍለጥ *meflet*
knowledge *(n.)* ፍልጠት *flṭet*
knuckle *(n.)* መላግቦ ኣጻብዕቲ *melagbo 'axab'ëti*
kudos *(n.)* ክብሪ *kbri*

L

label *(n.)* ናይ ኣቕሓ መለለይ መንነት *nay aqha meleleyi mennet*
labial *(adj.)* ከንፈራዊ *kenferawi*
laboratory *(n.)* ቤተ-ፈተነ *biete-fetene*
laborious *(adj.)* ኣድካሚ *'adkam*
labour *(n.)* ዕዮ *'ëyo*
labyrinth *(n.)* ጥንግንግ *ṭngng*
lace *(n.)* ዘረፍረፍ *zerefref*
lacerate *(v.)* ተርብዐ *terb'ë*
lachrymose *(adj.)* ነባዒ *neba'ï*
lack *(n.)* ምስኣን *ms'an*
lackey *(n.)* ዓሽከር *'äshker*
laconic *(adj.)* ቁጡብ ቡዙሕ ዘይዛረብ *qhutub buzuh zey zareb*
lacquer *(n.)* በርኒሽ *bernich*
lacuna *(n.)* ዋጋ ዘይብሉ *waga zeyblu*
lacy *(adj.)* ታንቴላዊ *tanteelawi*
lad *(n.)* ወዲ *wedi*
ladder *(n.)* መሳልል *mesall*
laden *(n.)* ዝተፅዓነ *ztets'ane*
ladle *(n.)* መንጨለፍ *menchelef*
lady *(n.)* ወይዘሮ *weyzero*
lag *(v.)* ዘሓጠ *zeḧaẗe*
lager *(n.)* ፈኰስ ቢራ *fekWis bira*
laggard *(n.)* ድሕሪት ምቕራይ *dhrit mqhray*
lagging *(n.)* ናይ ቱቦ ሽፋን *nay tubo shfan*
lagoon *(n.)* ላጉን *lagun*
lair *(n.)* ሰፈር ኣራዊት *sefer 'arawit*
lake *(n.)* ቐላይ *qhelay*
lamb *(n.)* ማሕሲእ *mahsi'e*
lame *(adj.)* ሓንካስ *ḧankas*
lament *(n.)* ሓዘን ምግላፅ *hazen mglats*
lamentable *(adj.)* ዘሕዝን *zehzn*
laminate *(v.)* ናይ ላስቲክ ሽፋን *nay lastik shfan*
lamp *(n.)* ፋኑስ *fanus*
lampoon *(v.)* ቐልዳዊ ወቐሳ *qheldawi weqhesa*
lance *(n.)* ዓብዪ ጦር *abyi tor*
lancet *(n.)* ላንሰት ናይ መጥባሕቲ ክልተ ዝኣፉ ካራ *lanset nay meẗbaḧti klte z'afu kara*
land *(n.)* መሬት *mereet*
landing *(n.)* ምውራድ ምዕራፍ *mwrad m'eraf*
landlady *(n.)* በዓልቲ ገዛ *be'älti geza*
landlord *(n.)* በዓል ገዛ *be'äl geza*
landscape *(n.)* ስእሊ መሬት *s'èli mereet*
language *(n.)* ቋንቋ *qWAnqWA*
languid *(adj.)* ጎታት *gotat*
languish *(v.)* ማሰነ *masene*
lank *(adj.)* ለማሽ *lemash*
lanky *(adj.)* ቐጢን ነዊሕ *qhetin newih*
lantern *(n.)* ፋኑስ *fanus*
lap *(n.)* ሽለፍ *shelef*
lapse *(n.)* ጊዜዊ ሕማቕ ባህሪ *gizawi hmaqh bahri*
lard *(n.)* ካብ ሓሰማ ዝርከብ ስብሒ *kab hasama zrkeb sbhi*
larder *(n.)* ክፍሊ መመገቢ ምግቢ *kfli memegebi mgbi*
large *(adj.)* ገዚፍ *gezife*
largesse *(n.)* ናይ የዋህነት ተግባር *nay yewahnet tegbar*
lark *(n.)* ሓመዳዊት ዒፍ *hamedawit if*

larva *(n.)* **ላርቫ** *larva*
larynx *(n.)* **ደባዒቶ** *deba'eto*
lasagne *(n.)* **ላሳኛ** *lasagna*
lascivious *(adj.)* **ናይ ግብረ ስጋ ሉዑል ድልየት ዘለዎ** *nay gbre sga l'eul dlyet zelewo*
laser *(n.)* **ናይ ብርሃን ጨረር** *nay brhan cherer*
lash *(v.)* **ቕንድብ** *qhndb*
lashings *(n.)* **ምግራፍ** *mgraf*
lass *(n.)* **ጓል** *gWal*
last *(adj.)* **መጨረሻ** *mečeresha*
lasting *(adj.)* **ንነዊሕ ግዜ ዝፀንሕ** *nnewi gzie ztsenh*
latch *(n.)* **ባልና ሚስት** *balna mist*
late *(adj.)* **ምድንጓይ** *mdnguay*
lately *(adv.)* **ሐዚታት** *hezitat*
latent *(adj.)* **ዘይረአ** *mezemeran*
lath *(n.)* **ሓነቐ** *haneqe*
lathe *(n.)* **ተርንዮ ማሽን** *hemam sheroke*
lather *(n.)* **ምቕባእ** *mqhba'e*
latitude *(n.)* **ናይ ምግባር ነፃነት** *nay mgbar netsanet*
latrine *(n.)* **ሽንቲ ቤት** *shnti biet*
latte *(n.)* **ካብ ፃባ ዝስራሕ ጠንካራ ቡን** *kab tsaba zsrah tenkara bun*
latter *(adj.)* **ዳሕራዋይ** *dahraway*
lattice *(n.)* **ናይ ዓውዲ አካል ውሽጣዊ ቕርፂ** *nay awdi akal wshtawi qhrtsi*
laud *(v.)* **ምድናቕ** *mdnaqh*
laudable *(adj.)* **ክድነቕ ዝግቦኦ** *kdneqh zgbo'e*
laugh *(v.)* **ሰሓቐ** *sehqhe*
laughable *(adj.)* **መስሓቒ** *meshaqhi*
laughter *(n.)* **ሰሓቕ** *sehqh*
launch *(v.)* **ምቱኳስ** *mtukuas*
launder *(v.)* **ምሕፃብ** *mhtsab*
launderette *(n.)* **ቤት ሕፅቦ** *bet htsbo*
laundry *(n.)* **ዝሕፀቡ ክዳውንቲ** *zhtsebu kdawnti*
laureate *(n.)* **ናይ አርቲስት ሉዑል ማዓርግ** *nay artist lu'ul ma'arg*
laurel *(n.)* **ቖፃል ተኽሊ** *qhotsal tekhli*
lava *(n.)* **ላቫ** *lava*
lavatory *(n.)* **ሽንቲ ቤት** *shnti biet*
lavender *(n.)* **ዕንቆዋይ ሊላ ዕንበባ ዘለዎ ተኽሊ** *e'nqhoway lila e'nbaba zelewo tekhli*
lavish *(adj.)* **ገራሚ** *gerami*
law *(n.)* **ሕጊ** *hgi*
lawful *(adj.)* **ሕጋዊ** *hgawi*
lawless *(adj.)* **ሕጊ አልቦ** *hgi albo*
lawn *(n.)* **አብ እፍደገ ገዛ ዝርከብ ዝተኸርከመ ሳዕሪ** *ab afdege geza zrkeb ztkhrkeme sa'eri*
lawyer *(n.)* **ጠበቓ** *tbeqha*
lax *(adj.)* **ፍትሕ ዝበለ** *fth zbele*
laxative *(n.)* **ቐልቐል ንክትብል ዝውሰድ መድሓኒ ወይ ምግቢ** *kelkel n ktble zwsed medhanit wey mgbi*
laxity *(n.)* **ኸቢድ ቑፅፅር ዘይምህላይ** *khebid kutstsr zymhlaw*
lay *(v.)* **ምቕማጥ ምውዳቕ** *mqhmat mwdaqh*
layer *(n.)* **ሽፋን** *shfan*
layman *(n.)* **ሞያ ዘይብሉ** *moya zeyblu*
laze *(v.)* **ምዝንጋዕ** *mznga'e*
lazy *(adj.)* **ሰነፍ** *senef*
leach *(v.)* **ደፈአ** *defe'e*
lead *(n.)* **ምምራሕ** *mmrah*

lead *(v.)* **መረሐ** *meleh*
leaden *(adj.)* **ደስ ዘይብል** *des zeybl*
leader *(n.)* **መራሒ** *merahi*
leadership *(n.)* **መሪሕነት** *merihnet*
leaf *(n.)* **ቆፅሊ** *qhotsli*
leaflet *(n.)* **ብዛዕባ ዝኾነ ነገር ሓበሬታ ዘሓዘ ንእሽተይ መፅሓፍ** *bza'eba zkhone neger haberieta zheze neshtey metshaf*
league *(n.)* **ሊግ** *lig*
leak *(v.)* **ኣንጠብጢቡ** *antebtibu*
leakage *(n.)* **ምንጥብጣብ** *mntbtab*
lean *(v.)* **ተደጊፉ** *tdegifu*
leap *(v.)* **ምዝላል** *mzlal*
learn *(v.)* **ምምሃር** *mmhar*
learned *(adj.)* **ምምሃር** *mmhar*
learner *(n.)* **ተምሃሪ** *temhari*
learning *(n.)* **ምምሃር** *mmhar*
lease *(n.)* **ናይ ክራይ ስምምዕነት** *nay kray smm'enet*
leash *(n.)* **መእሰሪ ኸልቢ** *me'eseri kebi*
least *(adj.& pron.)* **መወዳእታ** *meweda'eta*
leather *(n.)* **ኣንጋረ** *angare*
leave *(v.t.)* **ኽድ ልቐቕ** *khd lqheqh*
lecture *(n.)* **ትምህርቲ** *tmhrti*
lecturer *(n.)* **መምህር** *memhr*
ledge *(n.)* **ጫፍ** *chaf*
ledger *(n.)* **መዝገብ** *mezgeb*
leech *(n.)* **ኣብ ዉሽጢ ማይ ዝነብር ንኡሽተይ እንስሳ** *ab wshti may znebr nu'ushtey enssa*
leek *(n.)* **ሹንጉርቲ ዝመስል ተኽሊ** *sunkurti zmesl tekhli*
left *(n.)* **ፀጋም** *tsegam*
leftist *(n.)* **ኮሚኒስት** *cominist*
leg *(n.)* **እግሪ** *egri*
legacy *(n.)* **ዉርሲ** *wursi*
legal *(adj.)* **ሕጋዊ** *hgawi*
legality *(n.)* **ሕጋዊነት** *hgawnet*
legalize *(v.)* **ሕጋዊ ምግባር** *hgawi mgbar*
legend *(n.)* **ዛnta** *zanta*
legendary *(adj.)* **ዛንታዊ ተፈላጢ** *zantawi teflati*
leggings *(n.)* **ጥርንቕ ዘብል ስረ** *trnqh zble sre*
legible *(adj.)* **ተነባቢ** *tenbabi*
legion *(n.)* **ብርጌድ** *brgied*
legislate *(v.)* **ሕጊ ኣፅደቐ** *hgi atsdqh*
legislation *(n.)* **ሕጊ ምፅዳቕ** *hgi mtsdaqh*
legislative *(adj.)* **ሕጊ ኣፅዳቒ** *higi atzdaqhi*
legislator *(n.)* **ኣባል ሕጊ ኣፅዳቒ** *abal higi atsdaqhi*
legislature *(n.)* **ሕጊ መፅደቕቲ** *hgi metsdeqhti*
legitimacy *(n.)* **ሕጋዊነት** *hgawinet*
legitimate *(adj.)* **ሕጋዊነት** *hgawinet*
leisure *(n.)* **ትርፊ ግዘ** *trfi gize*
leisurely *(adj.)* **እናተዘናጋዕካ** *enatezenag'eka*
lemon *(n.)* **ለሚን** *lemin*
lemonade *(n.)* **ናይ ለሚን መስተ ወይ ፁማቕ** *nay lemin meste wey tsumaqh*
lend *(v.)* **ምልቓሕ** *mlqh'h*
length *(n.)* **ንውሓት** *nwhat*

lengthy *(adj.)* ንነዊሕ ግዜ ዝፀንሕ *nnewih gzie ztsenh*
leniency *(n.)* ጡንኩር ዘይኮነ ኣተሓሳስባ *tunkur zeykone atehasasba*
lenient *(adj.)* ጡንኩር ዘይኮነ *tunkur zeykone*
lens *(n.)* ሌንስ *lienis*
lentil *(n.)* ባሎንጓ *balongua*
Leo *(n.)* ሊዮ *lio*
leopard *(n.)* ኣባ ሸማኔ *aba shemanie*
leper *(n.)* ዱዉይ *dwuy*
leprosy *(n.)* ዱውየት *duwyet*
lesbian *(n.)* ኣንስተይቲ ን ኣንተይቲ ፆታዊ ፍትወት *ansteyti n ansteyti tsotawi ftwet*
less *(adj. & pron.)* ቑሩብ *qhurub*
lessee *(n.)* ተኻራዪ *tekharayi*
lessen *(v.)* እናንኣሰ *enan'ase*
lesser *(adj.)* ዝነኣሰ *zne'ase*
lesson *(n.)* ትምህርቲ *tmhrti*
lessor *(n.)* ኣካራዪ *akarayi*
lest *(conj.)* ከይ *k*
let *(v.)* እንበል *enbel*
lethal *(adj.)* ዝቕትል ነገር *zqhtl neger*
lethargic *(adj.)* ምድኻም *mdkham*
lethargy *(n.)* ድኻም *dkham*
letter *(n.)* ድብዳቤ *dbdabie*
level *(n.)* ደረጃ *dereja*
lever *(n.)* 14 ሓንዶቛዱቕ *ħandoqWAduq̈*
leverage *(n.)* ትሕጃ *thja*
levity *(n.)* ኣብ ዘይቅለድ ምቕላድ *ab zeyqhed mqhlad*
levy *(v.)* ምኽፋል *mkhfal*
lewd *(adj.)* ፆታዊ ፅያፍ *tsotawi tsyaf*
lexical *(adj.)* ናይ ዝተፈላለዩ ቋንቋታት ቃላት ምዝማድ *nay ztefelaleyu quanquatat qalt mzmad*
lexicon *(n.)* ናይ ዓይነት ቃላት *nay aynet qalt*
liability *(n.)* ጠቕላላ ዕዳ *tklala eda*
liable *(adj.)* ተዓዳዩ *te'ad'u*
liaise *(v.)* ብሓደ ምስራሕ *bhade msrah*
liaison *(n.)* ብሓደ ምስራሕ *bhade msrah*
liar *(n.)* ሓሳዊ *hasawi*
libel *(n.)* ናይ ሓሶት ክሲ *nay hasot ksi*
liberal *(adj.)* ነፃ *netsa*
liberate *(v.)* ነፃ ኣውፀአ *netsa mwtsa'e*
liberation *(n.)* ነፃነት *netsanet*
liberator *(n.)* ነፃ ኣውፃኢ *netsa awtsa'e*
liberty *(n.)* ነፃነት *netsanet*
libido *(n.)* ናይ ፆታዊ ስሚዒት ኣካል *nay tsotawi smi'et akal*
Libra *(n.)* ሊብራ *lbra*
librarian *(n.)* ሓላዊ ቤተ_መፃሕፍቲ *halwi biete-metsahft*
library *(n.)* ቤተ_መፃሕፍቲ *biete-metsahft*
licence *(n.)* ፍቓድ *fqhad*
licensee *(n.)* ዝተፈቐደሉ *ztefeqhedelu*
licentious *(adj.)* ካብ ማሕበረሰብ ዝወፀ ናይ ግበረ_ስጋ ፀባይ *kab mahbere seb zewetse nay gbre-sga tsebay*

lick *(v.)* **ምልሓስ** *mlhas*
lid *(n.)* **ኽዳን** *khdan*
lie *(v.)* **ሓሱ** *hasu*
liege *(n.)* **ጋንታ** *ganta*
lien *(n.)* **ትሕጃ ምሓዝ** *thja mhaz*
lieu *(prep.)* **ኽንዲ** *k̇hndi*
lieutenant *(n.)* **ሌተናንት** *letenant*
life *(n.)* **ሂወት** *hiwet*
lifeless *(adj.)* **ሂወት ዘይብሉ** *hiwet zeyblu*
lifelong *(adj.)* **ሙሉእ ሂወት** *mlu'e hiwet*
lift *(v.t.)* **ምልዓል** *ml'al*
ligament *(n.)* **ኣዕፅምቲ ዘራኽብ ጠንካራ ቲሹ/ጨዋዳ** *a'etsmti zerakhb tenkara tish/chwada*
light *(n.)* **ብርሃን** *brhan*
lighten *(v.)* **ብርሀ ምባል** *brh mbal*
lightening *(n.)* **መበረቕ እንትበርቕ** *mbreqh entberqh*
lighter *(n.)* **መወለዒ** *mwel'e*
lighting *(n.)* **መብረቕ** *mbreqh*
lightly *(adv.)* **ብቐሊሉ** *bqhelilu*
lignite *(n.)* **ምስጢራዊ ፅሑፍ** *mistrawi tsuhuf*
like *(prep.)* **ምፍታው** *mftaw*
likeable *(adj.)* **ተፈታዊ** *teftawi*
likelihood *(n.)* **ናይ ሙኳን ዕድል** *nay mkhuan edl*
likely *(adj.)* **ክኾን ትኽእል** *kkhon tkh'el*
liken *(v.)* **ተመሳሳሊ** *temesasali*
likeness *(n.)* **ተመሳሳሊነት** *temesasalinet*
likewise *(adv.)* **ተመሳሰልቲ እዮም** *temesaselti eyom*
liking *(n.)* **ምፍታው** *mftaw*
lilac *(n.)* **ናይ ዕንበባ ተኽሊ ዓይነት** *nay enbeba tkhli*
lily *(n.)* **ናይ ዕንበባ ዓይነት** *nay enbeba aynet*
limb *(n.)* **መሓውር** *mehawr*
limber *(v.)* **ምሙዋቕ** *mmuwaqh*
limbo *(n.)* **እብ መንጎ** *ab mengo*
lime *(n.)* **ናይ ካልሲየም ዉሁድ** *nay kalisiom wuhud*
limelight *(n.)* **ትኹረት ዝተውሃበሉ** *tkhuret ztwhableu*
limerick *(n.)* **በዓል ሓሙሽተ መስመር መስሕቒ ግጥሚ** *be'al hamushte mesmer msheqhi gtmi*
limit *(n.)* **ገደብ** *gdeb*
limitation *(n.)* **ገደብ** *gdeb*
limited *(adj.)* **ዝተገደበ** *ztegedebe*
limousine *(n.)* **ናይ መርዓ ንውሕ መኪና** *nay mer'a newih mekina*
limp *(v.)* **ምሕንካስ** *mhnkas*
line *(n.)* **መስመር** *msmer*
lineage *(n.)* **ናይ ትውልዲ መስመር** *nay twlide mesmer*
linen *(n.)* **ናይ ክዳን ዓይነት** *nay kdan aynet*
linger *(v.)* **ቐሊጢፉ ዘይጠፍእ** *qhlitifu zey tef'e*
lingerie *(n.)* **ናይ ድቂ እንስትዮ ክዳን ዉሽጢ** *nay dqi anstyo kdan wushti*
lingo *(n.)* **ዘይትርድኦ ቋንቋ** *zeytrd'o quanqua*
lingua *(n.)* **ተወሳኺ ቋንቋ** *tewsakhi quanqua*
lingual *(n.)* **ኣፋዊ** *afawi*
linguist *(adj.)* **ናይ ቋንቋ ሙሁር** *nay quanqua muhur*
linguistic *(adj.)* **ናይ ቋንቋ ትምህርቲ** *nay quanqua tmhrti*
lining *(n.)* **መራጎዲ ሽፋን** *meragodi shfan*

link *(n.)* **መራኸቢ** *mrakhebi*
linkage *(n.)* **መራኸቢ** *mreakhebi*
linseed *(n.)* **ትሕጃ** *thja*
lintel *(n.)* **ኣብ ልዕሊ ማዕፆ ዝግበር ሞራለ** *ab l'eli ma'etso zgber morale*
lion *(n.)* **ኣንበሳ** *anbesa*
lip *(n.)* **ከንፈር** *kenfer*
liposuction *(n.)* **ናይ ቑንጅና ቅዶ ፅገና ሕክምና** *nay qhunjna qhedo tsgena hkmna*
liquefy *(v.)* **ምምካኽ** *mwsakh*
liquid *(n.)* **ፈሳሲ** *fesasi*
liquidate *(v.)* **ንብረት ምሻጥ** *nbret mshat*
liquidation *(n.)* **ንብረት ምሻጥ** *nbret mshat*
liquor *(n.)* **ናይ ኣልኮል መስተ** *nay alkol meste*
lisp *(n.)* **ናይ s እና z ኩልትፍና** *nay s enn z kultfna*
lissom *(adj.)* **ምሽጥራዊ ስምምዕ** *mshtrawi smm'e*
list *(n.)* **መዝገብ ዝርዝር** *mzgeb zrzr*
listen *(v.)* **ምስማዕ** *msma'e*
listener *(n.)* **ሰማዒ** *sema'e*
listless *(adj.)* **ዱኹም** *dukhum*
literal *(adj.)* **ብቐጥታ** *bqhetta*
literary *(adj.)* **ብፁሑፍ** *btsuhuf*
literate *(adj.)* **ሙሁር** *muhur*
literature *(n.)* **ድርሰት** *drset*
lithe *(adj.)* **ተዓፃፃፊ** *te'atsatsefi*
litigant *(n.)* **ናይ ማሕበራዊ ፍርዲ ቤት ከሳኢ ወይተከሳሲ** *nay mahbeawi frdi biet kesaki wey tekesasi*
litigate *(v.)* **ምኽሳስ** *mkhsas*
litigation *(n.)* **ኽሲ ምክልኻል ኣብ ማሕበራዊ ቤት ፍርዲ** *khsi mklkhal ab mhberawi frdi biet*
litre *(n.)* **መዐቐኒ ትሕዝቶ** *m'eqeni thzto*
litter *(n.)* **ዝወዳደቐ ጓሓፍ** *zwedeqe guahaf*
little *(adj.)* **ኑኡሽተይ** *nu/eshtey*
live *(v.)* **ንበር** *nber*
livelihood *(n.)* **ናይ ኣታዊ ምንጪ** *nay atawi mnchi*
lively *(adj.)* **ሑጉስ ደስተኛ** *hugus destegna*
liven *(v.)* **ምድምማቅ** *mdmmaqh*
liver *(n.)* **ፀላም ኸብዲ** *tselam kebdi*
livery *(n.)* **ናይ ገዛ ሰራሕተኛ ዲቢዛ** *nay geza serahtegna dibiza*
living *(n.)* **ምንባር** *mnbaar*
lizard *(n.)* **ጠበቕ** *tebeqh*
load *(n.)* **ኽብደት** *khbdet*
loaf *(n.)* **ዓብዩ ሕንባሻ/ባኒ** *abyi hnbash/bani*
loan *(n.)* **ልቓሕ** *lqhah*
loath *(adj.)* **እምቢ በሃልነት** *embi behalnet*
loathe *(v.)* **ብጣዕሚ ምፅላእ** *bta'emi mtsla'e*
loathsome *(adj.)* **መፅልኢ** *metsl'e*
lobby *(n.)* **ኣፍደገ** *afdege*
lobe *(n.)* **ናይ እዝኒ ሉስሉስ ኣካል** *nay ezni luslus akal*
lobster *(n.)* **ሎብስተር** *lobster*
local *(adj.)* **ናይ እቲ ዓዲ** *nay eti adi*
locale *(n.)* **ኑኡሽተይ ቦታ** *nu'ushtey bota*
locality *(n.)* **ኣብ ሓድ ሃገር ዝርከብ ቦታ** *ab hade hager zrkeb bota*

localize *(v.)* **ሃገራዊ ምግባር** *hagerawi mgbar*
locate *(v.)* **ዘለዎ ቦታ ምፍላጥ** *zelewo bota mflat*
location *(n.)* **ኣድራሻ** *adrash*
lock *(n.)* **ቑልፊ** *qhulfi*
locker *(n.)* **መሸገጥ** *meshget*
locket *(n.)* **ኣብ ክሳድ ዝእሰር ፎቶ ዝሓዘ መጋይፂ** *ab ksasd zeseer foto zelowo mgayetsi*
locomotion *(n.)* **ነገራት ሙጉዕዓዝ** *negerat mugu'e'az*
locomotive *(n.)* **መጓዓዓዚ** *megua'a'azi*
locum *(n.)* **ተተካኢ ሓኪም** *teteka'e hakim*
locus *(n.)* **ማእኸል** *ma'ekhel*
locust *(n.)* **ባርኖስ** *barnos*
locution *(n.)* **ኮሚሽነር** *komishner*
lodge *(n.)* **መናፈሻ** *menafesh*
lodger *(n.)* **ተኻራዪ ገዛ** *tekharayi geza*
lodging *(n.)* **ጊዜዊ መምበሪ** *gizawi menberi*
loft *(n.)* **ኣብ ቆርቆሮ ዝስራሕ ክፍሊ** *ab qorqoro zsrah kfli*
lofty *(adj.)* **ጠቓሚ** *tkami*
log *(n.)* **ቁራፅ ዕንፀይቲ** *qhurats entseyti*
logarithm *(n.)* **ሎጋሪዝም** *logarizm*
logic *(n.)* **ስነ ሞጎት** *sne-mogot*
logical *(adj.)* **ምኽንያታዊ** *mkhnyatawi*
logistics *(n.)* **ኣቑሑ** *aqhuhu*
logo *(n.)* **ኣርማ** *arma*
loin *(n.)* **ፆታዊ ክፍሊ ኣካል** *tsotawi kfli akal*
loiter *(v.)* **ብዘይ ምኽንያት ኣብ ሓደ ቦታ ዘወርወር ምባል** *bzey mkhnyat ab hade bota zewerwer mbal*
loll *(v.)* **ተዝናኒካ ኮፍ ምባል** *teznanika kof mbal*
lollipop *(n.)* **ለካሌካ** *liekalieka*
lolly *(n.)* **ለካሌካ** *liekalieka*
lone *(adj.)* **ብሕታዊ** *bhtawi*
loneliness *(n.)* **ብሕታዊነት** *bhtawinet*
lonely *(adj.)* **ብሕታዊ** *bhtawi*
loner *(n.)* **ብሕትኡ ምኹን ዝመርፅ** *bht'u mukhun zmerts*
lonesome *(adj.)* **ብሕታዊ** *bhtawi*
long *(adj.)* **ነዊሕ** *newih*
longevity *(n.)* **ነዊሕ ሂወት** *niweh hiwet*
longing *(n.)* **ብምስኣን ዝመፅእ ሓዘን** *bms'an zmets'e hazen*
longitude *(n.)* **ሎንጊቱደ** *longitud*
loo *(n.)* **ሽንቲ ቤት** *shnti biet*
look *(v.)* **ረአ** *re'e*
look *(n)* **ምርኣይ** *mr'ay*
lookalike *(n.)* **ምምስሳል** *mmsal*
loom *(n.)* **ሽመና ማሽን** *shmena mashn*
loop *(n.)* **ዓንኬል** *ankiel*
loose *(adj.)* **ሰፊሕ** *sefih*
loosen *(v.)* **ኣስፈሐ** *asfehe*
loot *(n.)* **ምስራቕ** *msraqh*
lop *(v.)* **ምንቃል** *mnqal*
lope *(v.)* **ምስዳር** *msdar*
lopsided *(adj.)* **ዘይመጣጠን** *zeymetaten*
lord *(n.)* **ጎይታ** *goyta*
lordly *(adj.)* **ብኹርዓት** *bkhur'at*
lore *(n.)* **ባህላዊ ዛንታ** *bahlawi zanta*

lorry *(n.)* ናይ ፅዕንት መኪና *nay ts'ent mekina*
lose *(v.)* ምስዓር *ms'ar*
loss *(n.)* ምስኣን *ms'an*
lot *(pron.)* ብዙሕ *bzuh*
lotion *(n.)* ቕብኣት *qhb'at*
lottery *(n.)* ሎተሪ *loteri*
lotus *(n.)* ናይ ዕንበባ ዓይነት *nay enbeba aynet*
loud *(adj.)* ዓው ዝበለ *aw zbl*
lounge *(v.)* ምዝንጋዕ *mznga'e*
lounge *(n.)* ማእኸል መዛናግዒ *ma'ekhel mezanag'e*
louse *(n.)* ናይ ምድሪ ሓሰኻ *nay mdri hassekh*
lousy *(adj.)* ሱሩ ሑ ብኣግባብ ዘይሰርሕ *suruhu b'agbab zeyserh*
lout *(n.)* ብቑጠዐ እና ብ ሓይሊ ዝኣምን *buqhte'e ena bhayli z'amn*
Louvre *(n.)* ሱሉስ ኩርናዕ ዘለዎ ሞስኮት ወይ ማዕፆ *sulus kurna'e zelewo moskot wey ma'etso*
lovable *(adj.)* ተፈቃሪ *tefqari*
love *(n.)* ፍቕሪ *fqhri*
lovely *(adj.)* ተፈቃሪ *tefeqari*
lover *(n.)* ኣፍቃሪ *afqari*
low *(adj.)* ትሑት *thut*
lower *(adj.)* ትሕት ዝበለ *tht zbele*
lowly *(adj.)* ታሕተዎት *tahtaway*
loyal *(adj.)* ኡሙን *umun*
loyalist *(n.)* ብምትእምማን ዝኣምን *bmt'eman z'amn*
lozenge *(n.)* ናይ ሰዓል ከረሜላ *nay se'al keremiela*
lubricant *(n.)* ቕብኣት *qhb'at*
lubricate *(v.)* ቕብኣት ቆበአ *qhb'at qhbe'e*
lubrication *(n.)* ቕብኣት *qhb'at*
lucent *(adj.)* ኣቈመ *aqhome*
lucid *(adj.)* ብቐሊሉ ዝርዳእ ፁሑፍ ወይ መደረ *bqhelilu zrda'e tsuhuf wey medere*
lucidity *(adv.)* ብቕሊሉ ክርዳእ ምኽኣል *bqhlilu krda'e zkh'el*
luck *(n.)* ዕድል *edl*
luckless *(adj.)* ዕድል ኣልባ *edl albo*
lucky *(adj.)* ዕድለኛ *edlegna*
lucrative *(adj.)* ትርፋማ *trfama*
lucre *(n.)* ብዘይቑንዕ መንገዲ ዝተረኸበ ገንዘብ *bzey qhunu'e mengedi ztrekhebe genzeb*
ludicrous *(adj.)* ምኽንያታዊ ዘይኮነ *mkhnyatawi zeykone*
luggage *(n.)* ናይ ጉዕዞ ሻንጣ *nay gu'ezo shanta*
lukewarm *(adj.)* ለብ ዝበለ ፈሳሲ *lb zbele fesasi*
lull *(v.)* ፀጥ ዘብለ ግዜ *tset zbele gzie*
lullaby *(n.)* ናይ ህፃናት መደቀሲ ሙዚቃ *nay htssanat medeqeesi muziqa*
luminary *(n.)* ብዛዕባ ሓደ ነገር ሰፊሕ ፍልጠት ዘሎዎ *bza'eba hade neger sefih fltet zelewo*
luminous *(adj.)* መንፀባረቒ *mntsebareqhi*
lump *(n.)* ኣምፖል *ampol*
lunacy *(n.)* ሃሳስ *hasas*
lunar *(adj.)* ወርሓዊ *werhawi*
lunatic *(n.)* ዕብድ *ebud*
lunch *(n.)* ምሳሕ *msah*
luncheon *(n.)* ናይ ምሳሕ ዝግጅት *nay msah zgjt*
lung *(n.)* ሳምባ *samba*

lunge *(n.)* ብፍጥነት ኣንፈት ምቕያር *bftnet anfet mqhyar*
lurch *(n.)* ሃንደፍደፍ *handefdef*
lure *(v.)* ምትላል *mtlal*
lurid *(adj.)* ግጭት፣ ግብረ ስጋ እና መደንገፂ ትሕዝቶ ዘካተተ *gcht, gbre-sga ena medengetsi thzto zekatette*
lurk *(v.)* ተሓቢእካ ምፅባይ *tehbi'eka mtsbay*
luscious *(adj.)* ሰሓቢ *sehabi*
lush *(adj.)* ደስ ዝብል ኣታክልቲ ዘለዎ ቦታ *des zbl ataklti zelewo bota*
lust *(n.)* ግብረ ስጋዊ ድልየት *gbre-sgawi dlyet*
lustful *(adj.)* ግብረ ስጋዊ ድልየት *gbre-sgawi dlyet*
lustre *(n.)* ድብዝዝ ዘበለ ተንፀባራቒ ብርሃን *dbzz zbele tentsebaraqhi brhan*
lustrous *(adj.)* ደሚቕ ተንፀባራቒ ብርሃን *demiqhi tentsebara qhi brhan*
lusty *(adj.)* በዓል ሙሉእ ጥዕና *beal mulu'e t'ena*
lute *(n.)* ጊታር ዝመስል መሰርሒ ሙዚቃ *gitar zmesl mesarhi muziqa*
luxuriant *(adj.)* ፁብቕ *tsubuqh*
luxurious *(adj.)* ቑኑጡ *qhetinu*
luxury *(n.)* ቑኑጡ *qhetinu*
lychee *(n.)* ናይ ቻይና ፈረምረ *nay chayna fremre*
lymph *(n.)* ፃዕዳ ዋህዮ ደም ዘፈጠርሉ ኣካል *tsa'eda wahyo dem zfterlu akal*
lynch *(n.)* ብዘይ ፍርዲ ሓኒቕካ ምቕታል *bzey frdi haniqhka mqhtal*
lyre *(n.)* ናይ ገመድ ሙዚቃ መሰርሒ *nay gemd muziqa mesarhi*
lyric *(n.)* ናይ ሙዚቃ ግጥሚ *nay muziqa gtmi*
lyrical *(adj.)* ግጥማዊ *gtmawi*
lyricist *(n.)* ናይ ሙዚቃ ግጥሚ ገጣሚ *nay muziqa gtmi getami*

M

macabre *(adj.)* ዘርዕድ *zer'ëd*
machine *(n.)* መኪና *mekina*
machinery *(n.)* ተንቀሳቓሲ ኣካል ናይ መኪና መካይን *tenqesaq̈asi 'akal nay mekina mekayn*
mackintosh *(n.)* ናይ ዝናብ ክዳን *nay znab kdan*
mad *(adj.)* ፁሉል *tsulul*
madam *(n.)* ወይዘሮ *weyzero*
madcap *(adj.)* ዘይሳኽዕ ዉጡን *zeysakha'e wutun*
magazine *(n.)* መፂሄት *metsihiet*
magenta *(n.)* ማጀንታ *maĵenta*
magic *(n.)* ስራሕ ሰራይ *srah seray*
magician *(n.)* ሰራዪ *serayi*
magisterial *(adj.)* ሉዑል በዓል ስልጣን *lu'el be'al sltan*
magistrate *(n.)* ታሕታዋይ ዳኛ *tahtaway dagna*
magnanimous *(adj.)* ይቕር በሃሊ *yqhr behali*
magnate *(n.)* ኣዚዩ ሃፍታም *aziyu haftam*
magnet *(n.)* ማግኔት *magnet*

magnetic *(adj.)* ማግኔታዊ *magnetawi*
magnetism *(n.)* ማግኔታዊነት *magnetawinet*
magnificent *(adj.)* ብጣዕሚ ፁብቕ *bta'emi tsubqh*
magnify *(v.)* ምጉላሕ *mgulah*
magnitude *(n.)* ዓቕን *aqhen*
magpie *(n.)* ኒዊሕ ጭራ ዘለዋ ዒፍ *newih chra zelewa ef*
mahogany *(n.)* ናይ ጣውላ ዕንፀይቲ *nay tawla entseyti*
mahout *(n.)* ጠባይ *ṫebay*
maid *(n.)* ሰራሕተኛ ገዛ *serahtegna geza*
maiden *(n.)* መንእሰይ ስብይቲ *men'esey sebyti*
mail *(n.)* ፖስታ *posta*
mail order *(n.)* ብፖስታ ዝተገዙኡ *bposta ztegez'u*
maim *(v.)* ኸብድ መጥቃዕቲ ኣብፀሐ *khebid metqh'eti eabtsehe*
main *(adj.)* ዋና *wana*
mainstay *(n.)* ዋና ኣካል *wana alkal*
maintain *(v.)* ፀገነ *tsegene*
maintenance *(n.)* ምፅጋን ምዕራይ *mtsgan m'eray*
maisonette *(n.)* ናይ ደገ ማዕፆ ዘለዎ ክፍሊ ገዛ *nay dege ma'etso zelewo kfli geza*
majestic *(adj.)* ቖንጆ *qhonjo*
majesty *(n.)* ኽብርነትዎ *khbrnetwo(ልኡኡስ ወይ ንግስቲ)*
major *(adj.)* ዋና *wana*
majority *(n.)* ብዝሓት *bzhat*
make *(v.)* ምስራሕ *msrah*
make-up *(n.)* ምስራሕ *msrah*
making *(n.)* ምስራሕ *msrah*
maladjusted *(adj.)* ናይ ኣእምሮ ሑሙም *nay a'emro humum*
maladministration *(n.)* ትኽክል ዘይኮነ መሕድራ *tkhkl zeykone mehdra*
malady *(n.)* ሕማም *hmam*
malaise *(n.)* ቐሊል መፍትሒ ዘይብሉ ናይ ማሕበረ ሰብ ፀገም *qhelil meftihi zeyblu nay mahbere seb tsegem*
malaria *(n.)* ዓሶ *aso*
malcontent *(n.)* ዘይዓገቡ *zey'agebu*
male *(n.)* ተባዕታይ *teba'ëtay*
malediction *(n.)* እርግማን *ergman*
malefactor *(n.)* ሕጊ ዝጠሓሰ *hgi ztehase*
malformation *(n.)* ዝተበላሸየ ቕርፂ ኣካልሰውነት ካብ ትውልዲ ጀሚሩ *ztebelasheye qhrtsi akalsewnet kab teldi jemiru*
malfunction *(v.)* ምብልሻው *mblshaw*
malice *(n.)* ምውራድ *mwrad*
malicious *(adj.)* ምውራድ *mwrad*
malign *(adj.)* ብሕማቕ ምልዓል *bhmaqh ml'al*
malignant *(adj.)* ካብ ቑፅፅር ዝወፀ ሕማም መንሽሮ *kab qhutstsr zwets hmam menshro*
mall *(n.)* ናይ ዕዳጋ ማእኸል *nay edaga ma'ekhel*
malleable *(adj.)* ተዓፃፃፊ *te'atsatsafi*
mallet *(n.)* ካብ ዕንፀይቲ ዝተሰረሐ መዶ ሻ *kab entseyti ztesreh medisha*

malnutrition *(n.)* ሕፀረት ምግቢ *htsret mgbi*
malpractice *(n.)* ኣግባባ ዘይብሉ ኣሰራርሓ *agbab zeyblu aserarha*
malt *(n.)* ጉዑሽ *gu'ush*
maltreat *(v.)* ምጉዳእ *mguda'e*
mammal *(n.)* መጥበውቲ *mtbeewti*
mammary *(adj.)* ምስ ጡብ ዝተተሓሓዘ *ms tub ztetehahaze*
mammon *(n.)* ቕርሺ *qhrsh*
mammoth *(n.)* ዓብዪ *abiyi*
man *(n.)* ሰብኣይ *sb'ay*
manage *(v.)* ምምሕዳር *mmhdar*
manageable *(adj.)* ክስራሕ ዝኽእል *ksrah zkh'el*
management *(n.)* ምምሕዳር *mmhdar*
manager *(n.)* ስራሕ ኣፈፃሚ *srah asfetsami*
managerial *(adj.)* ምምሕዳራዊ *mmhdarawi*
mandate *(n.)* ግዴታ *gdieta*
mandatory *(adj.)* ግዴታ *gdieta*
mane *(n.)* ጨጉሪ ኣምበሳ ወይ ፈረስ *cheguri ambesa wey feres*
manful *(adj.)* ተባዕ *teba'e*
manganese *(n.)* ማንጋኔዝ *manganiez*
manger *(n.)* መብልዒ እንስሳ ጋቢያ *mbl'e anbesa gabiya*
mangle *(v.)* ምጭፍላቕ *mchflaqh*
mango *(n.)* ማንጎ *mango*
manhandle *(n.)* ምጉስቓል *mgusqhal*
manhole *(n.)* መፈተሺ *mefeteshi*
manhood *(n.)* ስብኣይነት *sb'aynet*
mania *(n.)* ሕማም ጭንቀት *hmam chnqet*
maniac *(n.)* ፁሉል *tsulul*
manicure *(n.)* ኢድ ወይ ኣፅፋርካ ምክንካን *eid wey atsfarka*
manifest *(adj.)* ብግልፂ ዝረአ ሓቒ *gltsi zre'e haqhi*
manifestation *(n.)* ዝግለፀሉ መንገዲ *zgletselu mengedi*
manifesto *(n.)* ዕላማ እና ፖሊሲ ዝሓዘ ፁሑፍ *elama ena polisi zhaze tsuhuf*
manifold *(adj.)* ማኒፎልድ *manifold*
manipulate *(v.)* ኣታለለ *atalele*
manipulation *(n.)* ምትላል *mtlal*
mankind *(n.)* ሰብ *seb*
manly *(adj.)* ናይ ሰብኣይ ስራሕ *nay sb'ay srah*
manna *(n.)* ኣብቲ ዝተደለየ ግዜ ዝተፈጠረ ፁብቕ ነገር *abti ztedeleye gzie ztetere tsubuqh neger*
mannequin *(n.)* ናይ ቡቲክ ኣሻንጉሊት *nay butik ashangulit*
manner *(n.)* ስርዓት *sr'at*
mannerism *(n.)* ስርዓት *sr'at*
manoeuvre *(n.)* ምግናሕ *mgnah*
manor *(n.)* ዓብዪ ገዛ *abyi geza*
manpower *(n.)* ሓይሊ ሰብ *hayli seb*
mansion *(n.)* ዓብዪ ገዛ *abyi geza*
mantel *(n.)* ናይ መሞቒ ሓዊ ጠርዚ *nay mmaqhi hawi terzi*
mantle *(n.)* ቕርፊት መሬት *qhrfit meriet*
mantra *(n.)* ቡዱሂስት እና ሂንዱ ኣብ እዋን ፀሎት ዘደጋግምዎ ቃል *buduhist ena hindu ab ewan tselot zdegagmwo kal*

manual *(adj.)* ዝርዝር መስርሕ *zrzr mesrh*
manufacture *(v.)* ምምራት *mmrat*
manufacturer *(n.)* ኣምራቲ *amrati*
manumission *(n.)* ተጻራፊ *texarafi*
manure *(n.)* ዒባ *eba*
manuscript *(n.)* ናይ ፊልሚ ድርሰት *nay flmi drset*
many *(adj.)* ብዝሕ *buzh*
map *(n.)* ካርታ *karta*
maple *(n.)* ሓሙሽተ ጫፍ ዘለዎ ቆፅሊ ዘለዎ ተኽሊ *hamushte chaf zelwo qhotsli zelwo tekhli*
mar *(v.)* ምብላሻው *mblshaw*
marathon *(n.)* ማራቶን *maraton*
maraud *(v.)* ኣንሃሪ *anhari*
marauder *(n.)* ሊያቡ ወይ ቐተልቲ *lieyabu wey qhetelti*
marble *(n.)* እምኒ በረድ *emni bered*
march *(n.)* ወታደራዊ ሰልፊ *wetaderawi selfi*
march *(v.)* ምስዳር *msdar*
mare *(n.)* ዓባይ ተንስተይቲ ፈረስ *abay tnsteyti feres*
margarine *(n.)* ካብ ኣትክልቲ እና ካብ እንስሳ ስብሒ ዝስራሕ ናይ ምግቢ ተስሚ *kab atklti ena kab enssa sbhi zsrah nay mgbi tesmi*
margin *(n.)* ኣብመንጎ ክልተ ቑፅርታት ዘሎ ኣፈላላይ *ab mengo klte qhutsrtat zelo afelalay*
marginal *(adj.)* ኑኡሹተይ *nu'ushtey*
marigold *(n.)* ቢጫ ዕንበባ *bich enbeba*
marina *(n.)* ናይ ኣናእሽተይ ጀልባ መዕረፊ *nay ana'ushtey jelba me'erefi*
marinade *(n.)* ኣብ ስጋ ዝቕባእ ዘይቲ *ab sga zqhba'e zeyti*
marinate *(v.)* ስጋ ኣብ ዝተፈላለዩ ዘይቲ ምቕማጥ *sga ab ztefelaleye zeyti mqhmat*
marine *(adj.)* ባሕረኛ ወታደር *bahregna wetader*
mariner *(n.)* ሓምባሲ *hambasi*
marionette *(n.)* ብገምደ ዝንቀሳቐስ ኣሻንጉሊት *b gemed znqesaqhes ashangulit*
marital *(adj.)* ምስ ሓዳር ዝተተሓሓዘ *ms hadar ztetehahaze*
maritime *(adj.)* ምስ ባሕሪ ዝተተሓሓዘ *ms bahri ztetehahaze*
mark *(n.)* ምልክት *mlkt*
marker *(n.)* ምልክት መግበሪ *mlkt megberi*
market *(n.)* ዕዳጋ *edega*
marketing *(n.)* ስነ ዕዳጋ *sne edaga*
marking *(n.)* ምልክት ምግባር *mlkt mgbar*
marksman *(n.)* ጎበዝ ጨማቲ *gobez chemati*
marl *(n.)* ተውህዶ *tewhdo*
marmalade *(n.)* *bmeseret*
maroon *(n.)* በዚ ምኽንያት'ዚ *bezi mḱnyatzi*
marquee *(n.)* ጐነፈ *gWanefe*
marriage *(n.)* ሕሳብ *ḧsab*
marriageable *(adj.)* ተሓታቲ *teḧatati*
marry *(v.)* ተመርዓወ *temer'äwe*
Mars *(n.)* ተጸባጸቢ *texebaxabi*

marsh *(n)* ብወግዒ ለአኸ *bweg'ï le'aḱe*
marshal *(n.)* ብወግዒ ለአኸ *bweg'ï le'aḱe*
marshmallow *(n.)* ወግዓዊ *weg'äwi*
marsupial *(n.)* ዕብየት *ëbyet*
mart *(n.)* ደለበ *delebe*
martial *(adj.)* ኣዋህለለ *awahlele*
martinet *(n.)* ውህለላ *whlela*
martyr *(n.)* ልክዕ *lk'ë*
martyrdom *(n.)* ግዚ *gzi*
marvel *(v.i)* ከሰሰ *kesese*
marvellous *(adj.)* ተሓታትነት *teḧatatnet*
Marxism *(n.)* ለመደ *lemede*
marzipan *(n.)* ልሙድ *lmud*
mascara *(n.)* ሓደ *ḧade*
mascot *(n.)* አረቢክ *arebik*
masculine *(adj.)* ተባዕታይ *teba'ëtay*
mash *(v.t)* ነታጕ *netagWi*
mask *(n.)* ቃንዛ *qanza*
masochism *(n.)* ተጎናጸፈ *tegonaxefe*
mason *(n.)* ፍጻሜ *fxamee*
masonry *(n.)* መጺጽ *mexix*
masquerade *(n.)* መጮቋር *mečqWAr*
mass *(n.)* ኣመስገነ *amesgene*
massacre *(n.)* ምቕጻል *mq̈xal*
massage *(n.)* ጫፍ *čaf*
masseur *(n.)* ዕንፍሩር *ënfrur*
massive *(adj.)* ኣናጎንስጤስ *anagonsẗees*
mast *(n.)* ስኻን *sḱan*
master *(n.)* ኣቦ ገዛ *abo geza*
mastermind *(n.)* ኣፋለጠ *afaleẗe*
masterpiece *(n.)* ሌላ *leela*
mastery *(n.)* ተሰማምዐ *tesemam'e*
masticate *(v.)* ምስምማዕ *msmma'e*
masturbate *(v.)* ረኸበ *reḱebe*
mat *(n.)* ቅስመት *qsmet*
matador *(n.)* ፈትሖ *fetḧe*
match *(n.)* ናጻ ምልቃቕ *naxa mlqaq̈*
matchmaker *(n.)* ኣክር *akr*
mate *(n.)* በዳን *bedan*
material *(n.)* ምረት *mret*
materialism *(n.)* ኣክሮባት *akrobat*
materialize *(v.)* ባሪቶን *bariton*
maternal *(adj.)* ስግር *sgr*
maternity *(n.)* ዘርዕድ *zer'ëd*
mathematical *(adj.)* ምግባር *mgbar*
mathematician *(n.)* ግዜያዊ ፈጻሚ *gzeeyawi fexami*
mathematics *(n.)* ምውሳእ *mwsa'è*
matinee *(n.)* ዘፍርህ *zefrh*
matriarch *(n.)* ምግባር *mgbar*
matricide *(n.)* ቅትለተ-ኣደ *qtlete'ade*
matriculate *(v.)* ኣንጠፈ *anẗefe*
matriculation *(n.)* ንጡፍ *nẗuf*
matrimonial *(adj.)* ስነ-ጠቢብ *sneẗebib*
matrimony *(n.)* ንጥፈት *nẗfet*
matrix *(n.)* ተዋናይ *tewanay*
matron *(n.)* ተዋሳኢት *tewasa'it*
matter *(n.)* ህሉው *hluw*
mattress *(n.)* ብሓቂ *bḧaqi*
mature *(adj.)* ገምጋሚ *gemgami*
maturity *(n.)* ኣንጠፈ *anẗefe*
maudlin *(adj.)* ትኩርና *tkurna*

maul *(v.)* መሪድያን *meridyan*
maunder *(v.)* ንሱር *nsur*
mausoleum *(n.)* ተሪር *terir*
maverick *(n.)* ኣልዘበ *alzebe*
maxim *(n.)* ምውህሃድ *mwhhad*
maximize *(v.)* ደመረ *demere*
maximum *(n.)* መመላእታ *memela'èta*
May *(n.)* ተወለፈ *tewelefe*
may *(v.)* ምውላፍ *mwlaf*
maybe *(adv.)* ወልፊ *welfi*
mayhem *(n.)* ምድማር *mdmar*
mayonnaise *(n.)* ተወሳኺ *tewesaḱi*
mayor *(n.)* ዓቃቢ *äqabi*
maze *(n.)* ድንጉር *dngur*
me *(pron.)* ኣድራሻ *adrasha*
mead *(n.)* ሸካ *sheḱa*
meadow *(n.)* ጠቐሰ *ẗeq̈ese*
meagre *(adj.)* ክኢላ *k'ila*
meal *(n.)* እኹልነት *èḱulnet*
mealy *(adj.)* እኹል *èḱul*
mean *(v.)* ሰዓበ *se'äbe*
meander *(v.)* ምድጋፍ *mdgaf*
meaning *(n.)* ላጋቢ *lagabi*
means *(n.)* ላጋቢደሓን ኩን *dehan kun*
meantime *(adv.)* ጐረቤት *gWarebeet*
meanwhile *(adv.)* ቅጽል *qxl*
measles *(n.)* ተጸግዐ ኣብ ጐድኒ ኮነ *texeg'ë 'ab gWadni kone*
measly *(adj.)* ኣቋረጸ *aqWArexe*
measure *(a.)* በየነ *beyene*
measure *(v.)* ኣመሓላለፈ *amehalalefe*
measured *(adj.)* ፈረደ *ferede*
measurement *(n.)* ጥብቆ *ẗbqo*
meat *(n.)* ኣመዓራረየ *ame'ärareye*
mechanic *(n.)* ምውዳድ *mwdad*
mechanical *(adj.)* ኣመሓደረ *amehadere*
mechanics *(n.)* ምምሕዳር *mmhdar*
mechanism *(n.)* ምምሕዳራዊ *mmhdarawi*
medal *(n.)* ኣመሓዳሪ *amehadari*
medallion *(n.)* ዚነኣድ *zine'ad*
medallist *(v.i.)* ኣድሚራል *admiral*
meddle *(v.)* ኣድናቖት *adnaq̈ot*
media *(n.)* ኣድነቐ *adneq̈e*
median *(adj.)* ዚፍቀድ *zifqed*
mediate *(v.)* ቅበላ *qbela*
mediation *(n.)* ተኣመነ *te'amene*
mediation *(n.)* ተፈታዊ *tefetawi*
medic *(n.)* ቅበላ *qbela*
medical *(adj.)* ገሰጸ *gesexe*
medication *(n.)* ሸቐልቀል *sheq̈elqel*
medicinal *(adj.)* ጥረ-ሕጡብ *ẗrehẗub*
medicine *(n.)* ብጽሕና *bxhna*
medieval *(adj.)* በጽሒ *bexhi*
mediocre *(adj.)* ወሰደ *wesede*
mediocrity *(n.)* ምርዓም *mr'äm*
meditate *(v.)* ረዓሚ *re'ämi*
meditative *(adj.)* ፍቕሪ *fq̈ri*
Mediterranean *(adj.)* ኣምለኸ *amleḱe*
medium *(n.)* ኣሰወነ *asewene*
medley *(n.)* ፋሉል *falul*
meek *(adj.)* ጨለ *čele*
meet *(v.)* ኣድሶረብ *adserb*
meeting *(n.)* ውዳሰ-ከንቱ *wdasekentu*

mega *(adj.)* **እኹል** *èḱul*
megabyte *(n.)* **ኣመራሰሐ** *ameraseḧe*
megahertz *(n.)* **ምምርሳሕ** *mmrsaḧ*
megalith *(n.)* **ዝሙት** *zmut*
megalithic *(adj.)* **ሰጐመ** *segWame*
megaphone *(n.)* **ለዓለ** *le'äle*
megapixel *(n.)* **ምምዕባል** *mm'ëbal*
melamine *(n.)* **ብልጫ** *blča*
melancholia *(n.)* **ረብሓ** *rebḧa*
melancholy *(n.)* **ጠቓሚ** *ṫeq̈ami*
melange *(n.)* **ምጽኣት** *mx'at*
meld *(n.)* **ዕንደራ** *ëndera*
melee *(n.)* **ሓደገ'ኛ** *ḧadegeǹa*
meliorate *(v.)* **ተወሳከ-ግሲ** *tewesakegsi*
mellow *(adj.)* **ተጸይ** *texay*
melodic *(adj.)* **ኣሉታዊ** *alutawi*
melodious *(adj.)* **ሽግር** *shgr*
melodrama *(n.)* **ኣፋለጠ** *afaleṫe*
melodramatic *(adj.)* **ረክላም** *reklam*
melody *(n.)* **ምዕዶ** *m'ëdo*
melon *(n.)* **ዝሓሸ** *zḧashe*
melt *(v.)* **መዓደ** *me'äde*
member *(n.)* **ደጋፊ** *degafi*
membership *(n.)* **ተሓላቒ** *teḧalaq̈i*
membrane *(n.)* **ውቕባ** *üq̈ba*
memento *(n.)* **ሰፋፊ** *sefafi*
memo *(n.)* **ኣዩን** *ayun*
memoir *(n.)* **ኣይሮባቲክስ** *ayrobatiks*
memorable *(adj.)* **ማሪዋና** *mariwana*
memorandum *(n.)* **መዓርፎ ነፈርቲ** *me'ärfo neferti*
memorial *(n.)* **ስነ-ምንፋር** *snemnfar*
memory *(n.)* **ኣይሮፕላን** *ayroplan*
menace *(n.)* **ፍሊት** *flit*
mend *(v.)* **ናይ ነፈርቲ** *nay neferti*
mendacious *(adj.)* **ጽባቐኣዊ** *xbaq̈e'awi*
mendicant *(adj.)* **ስነ-ጽባቐ** *snexbaq̈e*
menial *(adj.)* **ካብ ርሑቕ** *kab rḧuq̈*
meningitis *(n.)* **ፍሕሹው** *fḧshuw*
menopause *(n.)* **ፍጻሜ** *fxamee*
menstrual *(adj.)* **ጸለወ** *xelewe*
menstruation *(n.)* **ምስሉይነት** *msluynet*
mental *(adj.)* **ኣምሳሊ** *amsali*
mentality *(n.)* **ፍትወት** *ftwet*
mention *(v.)* **ርህሩህ** *rhruh*
mentor *(n.)* **ቃለ-ማሕላ** *qalemaḧla*
menu *(n.)* **ተጸግዐ** *texeg'ë*
mercantile *(adj.)* **ምጽጋዕ** *mxga'ë*
mercenary *(adj.)* **ተማስሎ** *temaslo*
merchandise *(n.)* **ኣረጋገጸ** *aregagexe*
merchant *(n.)* **ምርግጋጽ** *mrggax*
merciful *(adj.)* **ኣወንታዊ** *awentawi*
mercurial *(adj.)* **ልቃ'በ** *lqabe*
mercury *(n.)* **ጐድእ** *gWad'e*
mercy *(n.)* **ጭንቂ** *čnqi*
mere *(adj.)* **ሃብቲ** *habti*
meretricious *(adj.)* **ሃብታም** *habtam*

merge *(v.)* **ኣተኻኸለ** *atek̒ak̒ele*
merger *(n.)* **ምግራብ** *mgrab*
meridian *(n.)* **ናዕቢ** *na'ëbi*
merit *(n.)* **ዘለፈ** *zelefe*
meritorious *(adj.)* **ኣብ ርሑቕ** *'ab rḧuq̈*
mermaid *(n.)* **ዝተቓጸለ** *zteq̈axele*
merry *(adj.)* **ዘንሳፍፍ** *zensaff*
mesh *(n.)* **ኣብ ምቅርራብ** *'ab mqrrab*
mesmeric *(adj.)* **ዝፈርሀ** *zferhe*
mesmerize *(v.)* **ከም ብሓድሽ** *kem bḧadsh*
mess *(n.)* **አፍሪቃ** *afriqa*
message *(n.)* **ኣብ ሪተ-መርከብ** *'ab ritemerkeb*
messenger *(n.)* **ድሕሪ** *dḧri*
messiah *(n.)* **ድሕረ** *dḧre*
messy *(adj.)* **ድሕረ** *dḧri*
metabolism *(n.)* **እንደገና** *'èndegena*
metal *(n.)* **ኣንጻር** *anxar*
metallic *(adj.)* **ተሪር ክቡር እምኒ** *terir kbur 'èmni*
metallurgy *(n.)* **ዕድመ** *ëdme*
metamorphosis *(n.)* **ሽማግለታት** *shmagletat*
metaphor *(n.)* **ቅድመ-ፍርዲ** *qdmefrdi*
metaphysical *(adj.)* **ዘልኣለማዊ** *zel'alemawi*
metaphysics *(n.)* **ናይ ውክልና ትካል** *nay wklna tkal*
mete *(v.)* **ኣጀንዳ** *aĵenda*
meteor *(n.)* **ግሉል** *glul*
meteoric *(adj.)* **ኣከበ** *akebe*
meteorology *(n.)* **ኣግደደ** *agdede*
meter *(n.)* **ዘቑጥዕ** *zeq̈uẗ'ë*
method *(n.)* **ደመረ** *demere*
methodical *(adj.)* **መጥቃዕቲ** *meẗqa'ëti*
methodology *(n.)* **ዓማጺ** *ämaxi*
meticulous *(adj.)* **ኣጥቃዒ** *aẗqa'ï*
metre *(n.)* **ኣቐየመ** *aq̈eyeme*
metric *(adj.)* **ዝሰምበደ** *zsembede*
metrical *(adj.)* **ስሉጥ** *sluẗ*
metropolis *(n.)* **ሶፕራኖ** *soprano*
metropolitan *(adj.)* **ቀስቀሰ** *qesqese*
mettle *(n.)* **ምኽስ** *mk̒Was*
mettlesome *(n.)* **ኢፈሊጣዊ** *ifeliẗawi*
mew *(v.)* **ኛው** *ǹaw*
mews *(n.)* **ርቡጽ** *rbux*
mezzanine *(n.)* **ሃወኸ** *hawek̒e*
miasma *(n.)* **መሪር ሓዘን** *merir ḧazen*
mica *(n.)* **መሬታዊ** *mereetawi*
microbiology *(n.)* **ተሰማምዐ** *tesemam'ë*
microchip *(n.)* **ዚሰማማዕ** *zisemama'ë*
microfilm *(n.)* **ስምምዕ** *smm'ë*
micrometer *(n.)* **ሕርሻዊ** *ḧrshawi*
microphone *(n.)* **ሕርሻ** *ḧrsha*
microprocessor *(n.)* **ኣብ ባይታ** *'ab bayta*
microscope *(n.)* **ኣብ ቅድሚ** *'ab qdmi*
microscopic *(adj.)* **ረድአ** *red'e*
microsurgery *(n.)* **ደጋፊ** *degafi*
microwave *(n.)* **ረድኢ** *red'i*
mid *(adj.)* **ኣጨነቐ** *ačeneq̈e*
midday *(n.)* **ኣጨነቕኢ** *ačeneq̈e'i*
middle *(adj.)* **ሕማም** *ḧmam*
middleman *(n.)* **ዕላማ** *ëlama*
middling *(adj.)* **ሽቶ** *shto*

midget *(n.)* ሰሓተ *sehate*
midnight *(n.)* ኣየር *ayer*
midriff *(n.)* ነፋሪት *nefarit*
midst *(adj.)* ነፋሻ *nefasha*
midsummer *(adj.)* ኮሪደዮ *korideyo*
midway *(adv.)* ዝተገፍተነ *ztegeftene*
midwife *(n.)* ዚዛመድ - *zizamed*
might *(v.)* ስሉጥ *sluẗ*
mighty *(adj.)* ቅሩብነት *qrubnet*
migraine *(n.)* መጠንቀቕታ *meẗenqeq̈ta*
migrant *(n.)* ስግኣት *sg'at*
migrate *(v.)* ዋይ ኣነ *way 'ane*
migration *(n.)* ሽሕ'ኳ *shḧkWa*
mild *(adj.)* ኣልቡም *'album*
mile *(n.)* ኣልቡመን *albumen*
mileage *(n.)* ኣልከሚ *alkemi*
milestone *(n.)* ኣልኮል *alkol*
milieu *(n.)* ሰታይ *setay*
militant *(adj.)* ስብሳብ *sbsab*
militant *(n.)* ኣይል=ዓይነት ቢራ *'ayl'äynet bira*
military *(adj.)* ጥንቁቕ *ẗnquq̈*
militate *(v.)* ኣልጀብራ *alĵebra*
militia *(n.)* ሳጓ *sagWa*
milk *(n.)* ልውጠ-ስም *lwẗesm*
milkshake *(n.)* መውጽኢ-ነፍሲ *mewx'inefsi*
milky *(adj.)* መውጽኢ-ነፍሲ *mewx'inefsi*
mill *(n.)* ነጸለ *nexele*
millennium *(n.)* ዚነድድ *zinedd*
millet *(n.)* ሰርዐ *ser'ë*
milligram *(n.)* ኣሳላልፋ *asalalfa*
millimetre *(n.)* ተመሳሳሊ *temesasali*
milliner *(n.)* ክፍሊት ፍትሒ *kflit ftḧ*
million *(n.)* ህያው *hyaw*
millionaire *(n.)* ኣልካሊ *alkali*
millipede *(n.)* ኩሉ *kulu*
mime *(n.)* ኣፋኰሰ *afakWase*
mime *(n.)* ብህሎ *bhlo*
mimic *(n.)* ኣለ *ale*
mimicry *(n.)* ተኣማንነት *te'amannet*
minaret *(n.)* ምስሌኣዊ ዛንታ *mslee'awi zanta*
mince *(v.)* ኣሕረቐ *aḧreq̈e*
mind *(n.)* ተቖጣዒ *teq̈oẗa'ï*
mindful *(adj.)* ቁጥዐ *quẗ'ë*
mindless *(adj.)* ኣፋዅሰ *afaḱWase*
mine *(pron.)* ምቕላል *mq̈lal*
mine *(n.)* መሽጎራጉር *meshgWaragur*
miner *(n.)* ኪዳን *kidan*
mineral *(n.)* ተጸግዐ *texeg'ë*
mineralogy *(n.)* ዓንጎግ *ängog*
minestrone *(n.)* ደምሰሰ *demsese*
mingle *(v.)* ድግመተ-ኣፈና *dgmete'afena*
mini *(adj.)* ኣካፈለ *akafele*
miniature *(adj.)* ምምቕራሕ *mmq̈raḧ*
minibus *(n.)* ኣማስሐ *amasḧe*
minicab *(n.)* ምስሒት *msḧit*
minim *(n.)* ፈቐደ *feq̈ede*
minimal *(adj.)* መውዕሎ *mew'ëlo*
minimize *(v.)* ቆርቆሮ *qorqoro*
minimum *(n.)* ኣመተ *amete*
minion *(n.)* ኣወናወነ *awenawene*
miniskirt *(n.)* ኣወናወኒ *awenaweni*

minister *(n.)* **አመት** *amet*
ministerial *(adj.)* **ሽርካ** *shrka*
ministry *(n.)* **አልማናክ** *almanak*
mink *(n.)* **ኩሉ ዚከኣሎ** *kulu zike'alo*
minor *(adj.)* **ሉዝ** *luz*
minority *(n.)* **ዳርጋ** *darga*
minster *(n.)* **ምጽ'ዋት** *mxwat*
mint *(n.)* **ዝተሰቕለ** *zteseq̈le*
minus *(prep.)* **በይኑ** *beynu*
minuscule *(adj.)* **ኣብ ጐድኒ** *ab gWadni*
minute *(n.)* **ኣብ ጐድነኒ** *ab gWadneh*
minute *(adj.)* **ግሉል** *glul*
minutely *(adv.)* **ብዓውታ** *b'äwta*
minx *(n.)* **ኣልፋ** *alfa*
miracle *(n.)* **ፊደል** *fidel*
miraculous *(adj.)* **ብናይ ፊደላት ተርታ** *bnay fidelat terta*
mirage *(n.)* **ከረናዊ** *kerenawi*
mire *(n.)* **ዛጊት** *zagit*
mirror *(n.)* **ከምኡ'ውን** *kem'uwn*
mirth *(n.)* **መንበረ-ታቦት** *menberetabot*
mirthful *(adj.)* **ጠረጴዛ ቁርባን** *ẗerep̈eeza qurban*
misadventure *(n.)* **ምልዋጥ** *mlwaẗ*
misalliance *(n.)* **ቈይቍ** *qWeyqWi*
misapply *(v.)* **ምርጫ** *mrča*
misapprehend *(v.)* **ቅያር** *qyar*
misapprehension *(n.)* **ምንም'ኳ** *mnmkWa*
misappropriate *(v.)* **ብራኽ** *braḱe*
misappropriation *(v.)* **ኩሉኹሉ** *kuluḱulu*
misbehave *(v.)* **ልግስነት** *lgsnet*
misbehaviour *(n.)* **ኣሉሚኒዮም** *aluminiyom*
misbelief *(n.)* **ተማሃራይ ዩኒቨርሲቲ ነበር** *yuniversiti neber*
miscalculate *(v.)* **ኩሉ ግዜ** *kulu gzee*
miscalculation *(n.)* **ሕዋስ ባዚቃ** *ḧwas baziqa*
miscarriage *(n.)* **ደብለቐ** *debleq̈e*
miscarry *(v.)* **ምሕባር** *mḧbar*
miscellaneous *(adj.)* **ኣከበ** *akebe*
mischance *(n.)* **ኣማተር** *amater*
mischief *(n.)* **ዘይክኢላ** *zeyk'ila*
mischievous *(adj.)* **መስተፋቅር** *mestefaqr*
misconceive *(v.)* **ኣገረመ** *agereme*
misconception *(n.)* **ኣድናቖት** *adnaq̈ot*
misconduct *(n.)* **ኣማዘን** *amazen*
misconstrue *(v.)* **ኣምባሳደር=ልኡኽ** *'ambasaderl'u ḱ*
miscreant *(n.)* **ዕንዲዳ ጌጽ** *'ëndida geex*
misdeed *(n.)* **ዙርያዊ** *zuryawi*
misdemeanour *(n.)* **ዘይንጹርነት** *zeynxurnet*
misdirect *(v.)* **ዘይንጹር** *zeynxur*
miser *(n.)* **ደረት** *deret*
miserable *(adj.)* **ህርፋን** *hrfan*
miserly *(adj.)* **ህንጡይ** *hnẗuy*
misery *(n.)* **ማንታዊ** *mantawi*
misfire *(v.)* **ተሳለየ** *tesaleye*
misfit *(n.)* **ምቁር** *mqur*
misfortune *(n.)* **ኣምቡላንስ** *ambulans*
misgive *(v.)* **ድብያ** *dbya*

misgiving *(n.)* ኣመሓየሽ *amehayeshe*
misguide *(v.)* ምምሕያሽ *mmhyash*
mishandle *(v.)* ኣመሓየሽ *amehayeshe*
mishap *(n.)* መአረምታ *me'aremta*
misinform *(v.)* ተሓታቲ *tehatati*
misinterpret *(v.)* ተፈታዊ *tefetawi*
misjudge *(v.)* ምሕዝነታዊ *mhznetawi*
mislay *(v.)* ኣብ መንጎ *'ab mengo*
mislead *(v.)* ግጉይ *gguy*
mismanagement *(n.)* ዕርክነት *ërknet*
mismatch *(n.)* ተተኳሲ *tetekWasi*
misnomer *(n.)* ርሳዕ *rsa'ë*
misplace *(v.)* ምሕረት *mhret*
misprint *(n.)* ብዕብድብድ *b'ëbdbd*
misquote *(v.)* ኣብ መንጎ *ab mengo*
misread *(v.)* ብዕሉግ *b'ëlug*
misrepresent *(v.)* ፍቕራዊ *fqrawi*
misrule *(n.)* ቅርጸ-ኣልቦ *qrxe'albo*
miss *(n.)* ኣምፐር *amper*
miss *(v.)* ማዕረ ኮነ *ma'ëre kone*
missile *(n.)* ፍሉጥ ሰብ *fluṫ seb*
missing *(adj.)* ምድረ-ማያዊ *mdremayawi*
mission *(n.)* ኣምፊትያትር *amfityatr*
missionary *(n.)* ሰፊሕ *sefih*
missive *(n.)* ተወሳኺ *tewesaḱi*
misspell *(v.)* መጉልሒ *megulhi*
mist *(n.)* ኣጉልሐ *agulhe*
mistake *(n.)* ስፍሓት *sfhat*
mistaken *(adj.)* ክታብ *ktab*
mistletoe *(n.)* ኣዘናግዐ *azenag'ë*
mistreat *(v.)* ምዝንጋዕ *mznga'ë*
mistress *(n.)* ሓደ *hade*
mistrust *(v.)* ዕለቱ ዝሰሓተ *ëletu zsehate*
misty *(adj.)* ዋሕዲ ደም *wahdi dem*
misunderstand *(v.)* ድንዛዘ *dnzaze*
misunderstanding *(n.)* መደንዘዚ *medenzezi*
misuse *(v.)* ቆይቋም *qoyqWAm*
mite *(n.)* ጸረ-ቃንዛ *xereqanza*
mitigate *(v.)* ተመሳሳሊ *temesasali*
mitigation *(n.)* ተመሳሳልነት *temesasalnet*
mitre *(n.)* ተመሳሳልነት *temesasalnet*
mitten *(n.)* ምትንታን *mtntan*
mix *(v.)* ምርምር *mrmr*
mixer *(n.)* ተንታኒ *tentani*
mixture *(n.)* ትንታነኣዊ *tntane'awi*
moan *(n.)* ፋሉልነት *falulnet*
moat *(n.)* ፋሉላዊ *falulawi*
mob *(n.)* ፋሉልነት *falulnet*
mobile *(adj.)* ስነ-ቅርጺ ኣካል *sneqrxi 'akal*
mobility *(n.)* ኣበው *abew*
mobilize *(v.)* ውርሻዊ *wrshawi*
mocha *(n.)* ኣበው *abew*
mock *(v.)* መልሀቕ *melhq*
mockery *(n.)* ተዓሻገ *te'äshage*
modality *(n.)* ጥንታዊ *ṫntawi*
mode *(n.)* ጽግዕተኛ *xg'ëteña*

model *(n.)* ድማ *dma*
modem *(n.)* ጽግዕተኛ *xg'ëteňa*
moderate *(adj.)* ጽዋ *xwa*
moderation *(n.)* እንደገና *èndegena*
moderator *(n.)* ፍቱው *ftuw*
modern *(adj.)* ቁጥዐ *quť'ë*
modernism *(n.)* ሕሩቕ *ḧruq̈*
modernity *(n.)* ሕማም *ḧmam*
modernize *(v.)* ኩርናዕ *kurna'ë*
modest *(adj.)* ጓሂ *gWahi*
modesty *(n.)* ኩርናዓዊ *kurna'äwi*
modicum *(n.)* እንስሳ *ènssa*
modification *(n.)* ህያው *hyaw*
modish *(adj.)* ህያውነት *hyawnet*
modulate *(v.)* ጽልኢ *xl'i*
module *(n.)* ሽለን *shelen*
moil *(v.)* ዓንካር-ዓንካሪቶ *änkar'änkarito*
moist *(adj.)* ኣንባር *anbar*
moisten *(v.)* መዝገበ-ፍጻሜታት *mezgebefxameetat*
moisture *(n.)* ጎበጠ *gobeťe*
moisturize *(v.)* ጐበጣ *gWabeťa*
molar *(n.)* ኣጽነተ *axnete*
molasses *(n.)* ድምሰሳ *dmsesa*
mole *(n.)* ዝክረ-ዓመት *zkre'ämet*
molecular *(adj.)* ኣመልከተ *amelkete*
molecule *(n.)* ገለጸ *gelexe*
molest *(v.)* መግለጺ *meglexi*
molestation *(n.)* ሸወዘ *sheweze*
mollify *(v.)* ቁጥዐ *quť'ë*
molten *(adj.)* ምካኽ *mkak*
moment *(n.)* በብዓመት *beb'ämet*
momentary *(adj.)* ሰረዘ *sereze*
momentous *(adj.)* ኣገዳሲ *'agedasi*
momentum *(n.)* ቀብአ *qeb'e*
monarch *(n.)* ዘይስሩዕ *zeysru'ë*
monarchy *(n.)* ዘይስተ *zeyst*
monastery *(n.)* ስመ-ስውርነት *smeswrnet*
monastic *(adj.)* ስመ-ስውር *smeswr*
monasticism *(n.)* ምንማነ *mnmane*
Monday *(n.)* ካልእ *kal'è*
monetarism *(n.)* መልሲ *melsi*
monetary *(adj.)* ኪምለስ ዚከኣል *kimles zike'al*
money *(n.)* ጻጸ *xaxe*
monger *(n.)* ጻጸ መጺጽ *xaxe mexix*
mongoose *(n.)* ተጻራርነት *texorarnet*
mongrel *(n.)* ተጻራሪ *texarari*
monitor *(n.)* ተጻረረ *texarere*
monitory *(adj.)* ኣንታርክቲክ *antarktik*
monk *(n.)* ቅድመ ፍጻመ *qdme fxame*
monkey *(n.)* ኣቐደመ *aquadme*
mono *(n.)* ዓጋዜን *ägazeen*
monochrome *(n.)* ኣንተና *antena*
monocle *(n.)* ኣንቴማ *anteema*
monocular *(adj.)* እኩብ ዛንታታት *'èkub zantatat*
monody *(n.)* ስነ-ሰብ *sneseb*
monogamy *(n.)* ነፍሪ *nefri*
monogram *(n.)* ጸረ *xere*
monograph *(n.)* ጸረ-ነፍሳት *xerenefsat*

monolatry *(n.)* ጸረ-ኣካል *xere'akal*
monolith *(n.)* ወጀሃላይ *weĵehalay*
monologue *(n.)* ተጸበየ *texebeye*
monophonic *(adj.)* ትጽቢት *txbit*
monopolist *(n.)* ምንቁልቋል *mnqulqWAl*
monopolize *(v.)* ጸረ-መርዚ *xeremerzi*
monopoly *(n.)* ጸረ-መርዚ *xeremerzi*
monorail *(n.)* ክርሃት *krhat*
monosyllable *(n.)* ኩሕለ-ምሕሊ *kuȟlemȟli*
monotheism *(n.)* ዘጥንቲ *zeẗnti*
monotheist *(n.)* ድሑር *dȟur*
monotonous *(adj.)* ጥንታዊ *ẗntawi*
monotony *(n.)* ጥንቲ *ẗnti*
monsoon *(n.)* ጸረ-ረኽሲ *xerereḱsi*
monster *(n.)* ጸረ-ማሕበራዊ *xeremaȟberawi*
monstrous *(n.)* ኣንጻር *anxar*
monstrous *(adj.)* ጭንፋር ቀርኒ *čnfar qerni*
montage *(n.)* ኣሉታ *aluta*
month *(n.)* መሃንቱስ *mehantus*
monthly *(adj.)* ወርሓዊ *werȟawi*
monument *(n.)* ጭንቀት *čnqet*
monumental *(adj.)* ሃረርተኛ *harerteňa*
moo *(v.)* ዝኾነ *zḱone*
mood *(n.)* ብዘይተገዳስነት *bzeytegedasnet*
moody *(adj.)* ዝኾነ ሰብ *zḱone seb*
moon *(n.)* ዝኾነ ነገር *zḱone neger*
moonlight *(n.)* ዝኾነ ቦታ *zḱone bota*
moor *(n.)* ብቕልጡፍ *bq̈lẗuf*
moorings *(n.)* ዝተፈላለየ *ztefelaleye*
moot *(adj.)* ኣፓርታይድ *apartayd*
mop *(n.)* ክፍሊ-ገዛ *kfligeza*
mope *(v.)* ዘይተገዳስነት *zeytegedasnet*
moped *(n.)* ቀዳሒ *qedaȟi*
moraine *(n.)* ጭርታ *črta*
moral *(adj.)* ጫፍ *čaf*
morale *(n.)* ምስላ *msla*
moralist *(n.)* መንህብ *menhb*
morality *(n.)* ርእሰ-ርጉጽነት *r'èserguxnet*
moralize *(v.)* ራእይ - *ra'èy*
morass *(n.)* ይቕሬታ ሓተተ *q̈reeta ȟatete*
morbid *(adj.)* ይቕሬታ *yq̈reeta*
morbidity *(adv.)* ኣፖፕለቲካዊ *apopletikawi*
more *(n.)* ከሓዲ እምነት *keȟadi 'èmnet*
moreover *(adv.)* ሃዋርያ *hawarya*
morganatic *(adj.)* ጭረት *čret*
morgue *(n.)* ኣስካሕከሐ - *askaȟkeȟe*
moribund *(adj.)* መሰርሒ *mesarȟi*
morning *(n.)* ክዳን *kdan*
moron *(n.)* ብሩህ *bruh*
morose *(adj.)* ብሩህ *bruh*
morphine *(n.)* ተራእየ *tera'èye*
morphology *(n.)* ምቕልቃል *mq̈lqal*
morrow *(n.)* ኣዝሓለ *azȟale*
morsel *(n.)* መልእ *mel'e*

mortal *(adj.)* መመላእታ *memela'èta*
mortality *(n.)* ነድሪ ጥብቆ *nedri ẗbqo*
mortar *(n.)* መመላእታ *memela'èta*
mortgage *(n.)* ሸውሃት *shewhat*
mortgagee *(n.)* ከፋት ሸውሃት *kefat shewhat*
mortgagor *(n.)* ኣጨብጨበ *ačebčebe*
mortify *(v.)* ጨብጨባ *čebčeba*
mortuary *(n.)* ቱፋሕ *tufaḧ*
mosaic *(n.)* መሳርያ *mesarya*
mosque *(n.)* ብቑዕ *bq̈u'ë*
mosquito *(n.)* ኣመልካቲ *amelkati*
moss *(n.)* ምሕታት *mḧtat*
most *(n.)* ተጠቕመ *teẗeq̈me*
mote *(n.)* ወሰነ *wesene*
motel *(n.)* ቈጸራ *qWexera*
moth *(n.)* ጕዘየ *gWazeye*
mother *(n.)* ገምገመ *gemgeme*
mother *(n.)* ዚሰማማዕ *zisemama'ë*
motherboard *(n.)* እኹል *èḱul*
motherhood *(n.)* ተገንዘበ *tegenzebe*
mother-in-law *(n.)* ኣስተያየት *asteyayet*
motherly *(adj.)* ተረድአ *tered'e*
motif *(n.)* ምርዳእ *mrda'è*
motion *(n.)* ዝተሻቐለ *zteshaq̈ele*
motionless *(adj.)* ተልመዴን *telmedeen*
motivate *(v.)* ኣፍለጠ *afleẗe*
motivation *(n.)* ቀረበ *qerebe*
motive *(n.)* ብቑዕ *bq̈u'ë*
motley *(adj.)* ምንዛዐ *mnza'ë*
motor *(n.)* ቅባለ *qbale*
motorcycle *(n.)* ተቐበለ *teq̈ebele*
motorist *(n.)* ዳርጋ *darga*
motorway *(n.)* ሚሽሚሸ *mishmishe*
mottle *(n.)* ግርምብያለ *grmbyale*
motto *(n.)* በሊሕ *beliḧ*
mould *(n.)* ተውህቦ *tewhbo*
moulder *(v.)* ቦኽቦኽ *boḱboḱe*
moulding *(n.)* ማያዊ *mayawi*
moult *(v.)* ማያዊ *mayawi*
mound *(n.)* ኣረብ *areb*
mount *(v.)* ኣረቢያን *arebian*
mountain *(n.)* ኣረቢክ *arebik*
mountaineer *(n.)* ገድላ *gedla*
mountaineering *(n.)* ፈራዲ *feradi*
mountainous *(adj.)* ሃውሪ *hawri*
mourn *(v.)* ዳነየ *daneye*
mourner *(n.)* ዳኘነት *daǹnet*
mournful *(adj.)* ዳኛ *daǹa*
mourning *(n.)* ዳስ *das*
mouse *(n.)* ቀስቲ *qesti*
mousse *(n.)* ቀልደዳዊ *qeldedawi*
moustache *(n.)* ቀልደድ *qelded*
mouth *(n.)* ስነ ጥንቲ *sne ẗnti*
mouthful *(n.)* ጥንታዊ *ẗntawi*
movable *(adj.)* ሊቀ መላእክት *liqe mela'èkt*
move *(v.)* ሊቀ-ጳጳሳት *liqep̈ap̈asat*
movement *(n.)* መንታጋይ *mentagay*
mover *(n.)* ስነ-ሃናጺ *snehanaxi*
movies *(n.)* ስነ-ህንጻ *snehnxa*
moving *(adj.)* ኣርቺቭ *archiv*
mow *(v.)* ኣርክቲክ *arktik*
mozzarella *(n.)* ውዕውዕ *w'ëw'ë*

much *(pron.)* ብርቱዕ ድሌት *brtu'ë dleet*
mucilage *(n.)* ኣድካሚ *adkami*
muck *(n.)* ስፍሓት *sfḧat*
mucous *(adj.)* መድረኽ *medreḱ*
mucus *(n.)* ተማጎተ *temagote*
mud *(n.)* መጎተ *megote*
muddle *(v.)* መጎቲና *megotina*
muesli *(n.)* ኣጻምእ *axam'è*
muffin *(n.)* ተላዕለ *tela'ële*
muffle *(v.)* ኣሪስቶክራሲ *aristokrasi*
muffler *(n.)* ኣሪስቶክራታዊ *aristokratawi*
mug *(n.)* ቍጽሪ *quxri*
muggy *(adj.)* ቍጽሪና *quxrina*
mulatto *(n.)* ታቦት *tabot*
mulberry *(n.)* ምናት *mnat*
mule *(n.)* ጭፍራ መራኽብ ውግእ *čfra meraḱb wg'è*
mulish *(adj.)* ኣርማጌዶን *armagedon*
mull *(v.)* ኣጽዋር *axwar*
mullah *(n.)* ግዝያዊ ተኹሲ-ዕጾ *gzyawi teḱusi'ëxo*
mullion *(n.)* ድርዒ ሓጺን *dr'ï ḧaxin*
multicultural *(adj.)* ድርዒ ሓጺኒ *dr'ï ḧaxini*
multifarious *(adj.)* ሰራዊት *serawit*
multiform *(adj.)* መዓዛ *me'äza*
multilateral *(adj.)* መዓዛ - ፍወሳ *me'äza fwesa*
multimedia *(n.)* ኣብ ዙርያ *'ab zurya*
multiparous *(adj.)* ኣበራበረ *aberabere*
multiple *(adj.)* ሰርዐ *ser'ë*
multiplex *(n.)* ኣሰራርዓ *aserar'ä*
multiplication *(n.)* ምሒር *mḧir*
multiplicity *(n.)* ተሰለፈ *teselefe*
multiply *(v.)* ተሰለፊን *teselefin*
multitude *(n.)* ኣሰረ *asere*
mum *(n.)* እትወት *ètwet*
mumble *(v.)* መጸ *mexe*
mummer *(n.)* ኣትሒቱ ረኣየ *'atḧitu re'aye*
mummify *(v.)* ትዕቢተኛ *t'ëbiteṅa*
mummy *(n.)* መንዘዐ *menze'ë*
mumps *(n.)* ፍላጻ *flaxa*
munch *(v.)* እንዳብረት *èndabret*
mundane *(adj.)* ብርቱዕ ስሚ *brtu'ë smi*
municipal *(adj.)* ብውሳይ ምቅጻል *bwsay mqxal*
municipality *(n.)* ጥበብ *ẗbeb*
munificent *(adj.)* ጥንቲ *ẗnti*
muniment *(n.)* ኣርተሪ *arteri*
munitions *(n.)* ብልሂ *blhi*
mural *(n.)* ሪሕ *riḧ*
murder *(n.)* ካርቾፊ *karchofi*
murderer *(n.)* ኣቕሓ *aq̈ḧa*
murk *(n.)* ኣነጸረ *anexere*
murky *(adj.)* ክእለት *k'èlet*
murmur *(v.)* ስኑ'ዕ *snu'ë*
muscle *(n.)* ከቢድ ብረት *kebid bret*
muscovite *(n.)* ክኢላ *k'ila*
muscular *(adj.)* ስነ-ጠቢብ *sneẗebib*
muse *(n.)* ስነ-ጥበባዊ *sneẗbebawi*
museum *(n.)* ባህርያዊ *bahryawi*
mush *(n.)* ከም *kem*
mushroom *(n.)* ቃንጥሻ *qanẗsha*
music *(n.)* ደየበ *deyebe*
musical *(adj.)* ደያቢ *deyabi*

musician *(n.)* ዕርገት *ërget*
musk *(n.)* ኣረጋገጸ *aregagexe*
musket *(n.)* መናን *menan*
musketeer *(n.)* ሃበ *habe*
Muslim *(n.)* ጽዱይ *xduy*
muslin *(v.)* ግብረ-ሰዶመኛ *gbresedomeňa*
mussel *(n.)* ኣሽ *ash*
must *(v.)* ዝሓፈረ *zḧafere*
mustang *(n.)* ኣብ ገምገም ባሕሪ *'ab gemgem baḧri*
mustard *(n.)* ኤሽያዊ *eshiyawi*
muster *(v.)* ኣብ ወይ ናብ ጐድኒ *'ab wey nab gWadni*
musty *(adj.)* ዓንጃል *änĵal*
mutable *(adj.)* ሓተተ *ḧatete*
mutate *(v.)* ብጥርጣረ *bťrťare*
mutation *(n.)* ዘባል *zebal*
mutative *(v.)* ጽሙው *xmuw*
mute *(adj.)* ሻሞት *shamot*
mutilate *(v.)* መልክዕ *melk'ë*
mutilation *(n.)* ጎነጽ *gonex*
mutinous *(adj.)* ምክፋእ *mkfa'è*
mutiny *(n.)* ዓበሰ *äbese*
mutter *(v.)* ደላዪ *delayi*
mutton *(n.)* ትምኒት *tmnit*
mutual *(adj.)* ተመነየ *temeneye*
muzzle *(n.)* ኣድጊ *adgi*
muzzy *(adj.)* ኣጥቀዐ *aťqe'ë*
my *(adj.)* ቀታል-ነፍሲ *qetalnefsi*
myalgia *(n.)* ቀተለ *qetele*
myopia *(n.)* ቀተሊ *qeteli*
myopic *(adj.)* ኣጥቀዐ *aťqe'ë*
myosin *(n.)* ምግጥጣም *mgťťam*
myriad *(n.)* ኣጋጠመ *agaťeme*
myrrh *(n.)* ኣኼባ *ak̍eeba*
myrtle *(n.)* ስምምዕ *smm'ë*
myself *(pron.)* ጸዓደ *xe'äde*
mysterious *(adj.)* ኣማኻሪ *amak̍ari*
mystery *(n.)* መርመራ *mermera*
mystic *(n.)* ንብረት *nbret*
mystical *(adj.)* ጻዕረኛ *xa'ëreňa*
mysticism *(n.)* ረተበ *retebe*
mystify *(v.)* ምደባ *mdeba*
mystique *(n.)* ምዱብ ስራሕ *mdub sraḧ*
myth *(n.)* ተዋሃደ *tewahade*
mythical *(adj.)* ተዋህዶ *tewahdo*
mythological *(adj.)* ሓገዘ *ḧageze*
mythology *(n.)* ሓገዝ *ḧagez*

N

nab *(v.)* ተሓባባሪ *teḧababari*
nabob *(nabob)* ማሕበር *maḧber*
nacho *(n.)* ስምምዕ *smm'ë*
nadir *(n.)* ዝተፋላለየ *ztefalaleye*
nag *(v.t.)* በብዓይነቱ *beb'äynetu*
nail *(n.)* ኣጸናንዐ *axenan'ë*
naivety *(n.)* ገመተ *gemete*
naked *(adj.)* ግምት *gmt*
name *(n.)* መረጋገጺ *meregagexi*
namely *(n.)* ኣረጋገጸ *aregagexe*
namesake *(n.)* ዋሕስ *waḧs*
nanny *(n.)* ኣስትሪስክስ *astrisks*
nap *(n.)* ዓለም *älem*
nape *(n.)* ኣዝማ *azma*
naphthalene *(n.)* ነበዐ *nebe'ë*
napkin *(n.)* ኣደነቐ *adeneq̈e*
nappy *(n.)* ድንጽዉና *dnxwuna*
narcissism *(n.)* ኣስደመመ *asdememe*

narcissus *(n.)* ኮኾባዊ *kok̓obawi*
narcotic *(n.)* ህውቱት *hwtut*
narrate *(v.)* ብምግሕታን *bmgḧtan*
narration *(n.)* ብልጹግ *blxug*
narrative *(n.)* ቈጸራ ከዋኽብቲ *qWexera kewak̓bti*
narrator *(n.)* ጠፈርተኛ *ẗeferteṅa*
narrow *(adj.)* ስነ-ኮኾቢ *snekok̓obi*
nasal *(adj.)* ስነ-ኮኾብ *snekok̓ob*
nascent *(adj.)* ትኩር *tkur*
nasty *(adj.)* ዝተፈላለየ *ztefelaleye*
natal *(adj.)* ዑቕባ *üq̈ba*
natant *(adj.)* ኣብ *ab*
nation *(n.)* የዋህ *yewah*
national *(adj.)* ኢዚሀርነት *izihernet*
nationalism *(n.)* ኢዚሄራዊ *iziheerawi*
nationalist *(n.)* ስፖርተኛ *sporteṅa*
nationality *(n.)* ስፖርታዊ *sportawi*
nationalization *(n.)* ኣትላስ *atlas*
nationalize *(v.)* ሃዋህው *hawahw*
native *(n.)* ደሴት *deseet*
nativity *(n.)* ኣቶም *atom*
natty *(adj.)* ኣቶማዊ *atomawi*
natural *(adj.)* ከሓሰ *keḧase*
naturalist *(n.)* ድሕነት *dḧnet*
naturalization *(n.)* ኣሰቃቒ *aseqaq̈i*
naturalize *(v.)* ክፍሊ *kfli*
naturally *(adv.)* ገፍዐ *gef'ë*
nature *(n.)* ኣጣበቐ *aẗabeq̈e*
naturism *(n.)* ኣታኽ *atash*
naughty *(adj.)* ጥብቀት *ẗbqet*
nausea *(n.)* ኣጥቅዐ *aẗq'ë*
nauseate *(v.)* ምሉእ *mlu'è*
nauseous *(adj.)* ሰመረ *semere*
nautical *(adj.)* ፈተ'ነ *fetene*
naval *(adj.)* ጀመረ *ĵemere*
nave *(n.)* ተኸታተለ *tek̓etatele*
navigable *(adj.)* ተሳትፎ *tesatfo*
navigate *(v.)* ኣገልጋሊ *agelgali*
navigation *(n.)* ኣቓልቦ *aq̈albo*
navigator *(n.)* ጥንቁቕ *ẗnquq̈*
navy *(n.)* ኣረጋገጸ *aregagexe*
nay *(adv.)* ዋልድቢት *waldbit*
near *(v.i.)* ጠበቓ *ẗebeq̈a*
near *(adv.)* ልብሲ *lbsi*
nearby *(adv.)* ኣቃጫጭ *aqačač*
nearest *(adj.)* ሰሓበ *seḧabe*
nearly *(adv.)* ስሕበት *sḧbet*
neat *(adj.)* ማራኺ *marak̓i*
nebula *(n.)* ባህርይ *bahry*
nebulous *(adj.)* ማርጋሪን *margarin*
necessarily *(adv.)* ሓራጅ *ḧaraĵ*
necessary *(adj.)* ኪስማዕ ዚከኣል *kisma'ë zike'a*
necessitate *(v.)* ነባሮ *nebaro*
necessity *(n.)* ደሃይ *- dehay*
neck *(n.)* ጸብጻብ *xebxab*
necklace *(n.)* ናይ ምስማዕ ፈተና *nay msma'ë fetena*
necklet *(n.)* ጌጽ ወይ ስልማት ናይ ክሳድ *geex wey slmat nay ksad*
necromancy *(n.)* ወሰኸ *ወሰኸ*
necropolis *(n.)* ነሓሰ *neḧase*
nectar *(n.)* ሓትኖ *ḧatno*
nectarine *(n.)* ኣኽሊል *ak̓lil*
need *(v.)* ተስፋኣዊ *tesfa'awi*
needful *(adj.)* ጥብቂ *ẗbqi*

needle *(n.)* **አዎስትራልያ** *awustraliya*
needless *(adj.)* **ሓቀኛ** *ḧaqeḧa*
needy *(adj.)* **ልክዕነት** *lk'ënet*
nefarious *(adj.)* **ደራሲ** *derasi*
negate *(v.)* **ምዙዝ** *mzuz*
negation *(n.)* **መዚ** *mezi*
negative *(adj.)* **መዘዘ** *mezeze*
negativity *(n.)* **አዉቲዝም** *awutizim*
neglect *(v.)* **ርእሰ-ታሪኽ** *r'èsetariḱ*
negligence *(n.)* **ኣውቶክራሲ** *awtokrasi*
negligent *(adj.)* **ውልቀ-መላኺ** *wlqemelaḱi*
negligible *(adj.)* **ኣውቶክራቲክ** *wlqemelaḱ*
negotiable *(adj.)* **ርእሰ-ጽሑፍ** *r'èsexḧuf*
negotiate *(v.)* **ኣውቶማቲክ** *awtomatik*
negotiation *(n.)* **ኣውቶሞቢል=መኪና** *awtomobilm ekina*
negotiator *(n.)* **ርእሰ-ምምሕዳራዊ** *r'èsemmḧdarawi*
negress *(n.)* **ምርምረ-ሬሳ** *mrmrereesa*
negro *(n.)* **ቀውዒ** *qew'ï*
neigh *(n.)* **ሓጋዚ** *ḧagazi*
neighbour *(n.)* **ተጠቕመ** *teẗeq̈me*
neighbourhood *(n.)* **ክትጥቀመሉ ትኽእል** *ktẗqemelu tḱ'èl*
neighbourly *(adj.)* **መደረጋሕ** *mederegaḧ*
neither *(adj.)* **ስስዐ** *ss'ë*
nemesis *(n.)* **ሕነ ፈደየ** *ḧne fedeye*
neoclassical *(adj.)* **ጐደና** *gWadena*
Neolithic *(adj.)* **ማእከላይ** *ma'èkelay*
neon *(n.)* **ኣንጻር** *anxar*
neophyte *(n.)* **ጽልኣት** *xl'at*
nephew *(n.)* **ኣለየ** *aleye*
nepotism *(n.)* **እንዳ ኣዕዋፍ** *'ènda 'a'ëwaf*
Neptune *(n.)* **ስነ-ምንፋር** *snemnfar*
nerd *(n.)* **ፓይሎት** *paylot*
Nerve *(n.)* **ህንጡይ** *hnẗuy*
nerveless *(adj.)* **ህንጡዪ** *hnẗuyi*
nervous *(adj.)* **ኣቮካዶ** *avokado*
nervy *(adj.)* **ወገደ** *wegede*
nest *(n.)* **ጉስያ** *gusya*
nestle *(v.)* **ኣመነ** *amene*
nestling *(n.)* **ኣኮኣዊ** *'ako'awi*
net *(n.)* **ተጸበየ** *texebeye*
nether *(adj.)* **ነቕሐ** *neq̈ḧe*
netting *(n.)* **ነቕሐ** *neq̈ḧe*
nettle *(n.)* **ሰለመ** *seleme*
network *(n.)* **ገንዘብ** *genzeb*
neural *(adj.)* **ናብ ርሑቕ** *nab rḧuq̈*
neurologist *(n.)* **ተምሳጥ** *temsaẗ*
neurology *(n.)* **ዘርዕድ** *zer'ëd*
neurosis *(n.)* **ዘስካሕክሕ** *zeskaḧkḧ*
neurotic *(adj.)* **ንሓጺር ግዜ** *nḧaxir gzee*
neuter *(adj.)* **ጋሕማጥ** *gaḧmaẗ*
neutral *(adj.)* **ብልሽው** *blshw*
neutralize *(v.)* **ፋስ** *fas*
neutron *(n.)* **መቐለሲ** *meq̈elesi*
never *(adv.)* **መቐለስ** *meq̈eles*

new *(adj.)* ሓድሽ *ḧadsh*
newly *(adv.)* ኣዕዘምዘመ *a'ëzemzeme*
news *(n.)* ህጻን *hxan*
next *(adj.)* ዘይምስምማዕ *zeymsmma'ë*
nexus *(n.)* ህበይ *hbey*
nib *(n.)* ህጻን *hxan*
nibble *(v.)* ቤተ'ልቦ *beetelbo*
nice *(adj.)* ዝባን *zban*
nicety *(n.)* ዓንዲ-ሕቖ *ändiḧqo*
niche *(n.)* ሓለፈ *ḧalefe*
nick *(n.)* ትዕይንቲ *t'ëynti*
nickel *(n.)* ምጉሳዕ *mgusa'ë*
nickname *(n.)* ተመኩሮ *temekuro*
nicotine *(n.)* ኣሽሙራዊ *ashmurawi*
niece *(n.)* ረድኣ *red'e*
niggard *(n.)* መልሰ-ግብሪ *melsegbri*
niggardly *(adj.)* መሃዚ *mehazi*
nigger *(n.)* ማህደር *mahder*
niggle *(v.)* ብድሕሪት *bdḧrit*
nigh *(adv.)* ዝባን መድረኽ *zban medreḱ*
night *(n.)* ዝባን ኣሰር *zban aser*
nightie *(n.)* ቤኮን *beekon*
nightingale *(n.)* ንድሕሪት *ndḧrit*
nightmare *(n.)* ዝባን ማይ *zban may*
nihilism *(n.)* ባክተሪያ *bakteriya*
nil *(n.)* ሕማቕ *ḧmaq̈*
nimble *(adj.)* ኣርማ *arma*
nimbus *(n.)* ብሕማቕ *bḧmaq̈*
nine *(adj. & n.)* ባድሚንተን *badminten*
nineteen *(adj. & n.)* ኣገረመ *agereme*
nineteenth *(adj. & n.)* መልኣ *mel'e*
ninetieth *(adj. & n.)* ጋዓዝ *ga'äz*
ninety *(adj. & n.)* ሕቡር ስልማት *ḧbur slmat*
ninth *(adj. & n.)* ገፍላው *geflaw*
nip *(v.)* ዋሕስ *waḧs*
nipple *(n.)* ፖሊስ *polis*
nippy *(adj.)* መስሓቢ *mesḧabi*
nirvana *(n.)* ደረቐ *dereq̈e*
nitrogen *(n.)* ሰንካቲ *senkati*
no *(adj.)* እንዳ ባኒ *ènda bani*
nobility *(n.)* ተረፍ *teref*
noble *(adj.)* ሰገነት *segenet*
nobleman *(n.)* በራሕ *beraḧ*
nobody *(pron.)* ጥቕላል *ẗq̈lal*
nocturnal *(adj.)* ኩዕሶ *ku'ëso*
nod *(v.)* ግጥሚ ወይ ደርፊ *gẗmi wey derfi*
node *(n.)* ባለ *bale*
noise *(n.)* ባሉን *balun*
noisy *(adj.)* ናይ መድመጺ ወረቐት *nay medmexi wereq̈et*
nomad *(n.)* በለሳን *belesan*
nomadic *(adj.)* በለሳን *belesan*
nomenclature *(n.)* ኣርቃይ *arqay*
nominal *(adj.)* ኣገደ *agede*
nominate *(v.)* ተራ *tera*
nomination *(n.)* ባናና *banana*
nominee *(n.)* መእሰሪ *me'èseri*
non-alignment *(n.)* መጀነኒ *meĵeneni*
nonchalance *(n.)* ሽፍታ ወረበላ *shfta werebela*
nonchalant *(adj.)* መርዚ ስሚ *merzi smi*
nonconformist *(n.)* ገውታ *gewta*

none *(pron.)* ገውት *gewtat*
nonentity *(n.)* በናጅር *benaĵr*
nonetheless *(a.)* ጥርዝያ *ïrzya*
nonpareil *(adj.)* መደንደል *medendel*
nonplussed *(adj.)* ሓየረ *ḧayere*
nonplussed *(adj.)* ባንጆ *banĵo*
nonsense *(n.)* ባንኪ *banki*
nonstop *(adj.)* መኰነን *mekWanen*
noodles *(n.)* ጥፉሽ *ïfush*
nook *(n.)* ጥፈሻ *ïfesha*
noon *(n.)* ሰንደቕ *sendeq̈*
noose *(n.)* በዓል *be'äl*
nor *(conj.&adv.)* ተዋዘየ *tewazeye*
Nordic *(adj.)* ጥምቀት *ïmqet*
norm *(n.)* መጥምቓዊ *meïmq̈awi*
normal *(adj.)* ነቐለ ከደ ተሰናበተ *neq̈ele kede tesenabete*
normalcy *(n.)* ሓመድ *ḧamed*
normalize *(v.)* ከብዲ *kebdi*
normative *(adj.)* ናይ ከብዲ *nay kebdi*
north *(n.)* ዘረፈ *zerefe*
northerly *(adj.)* ዘረፈ *zerefe*
northern *(adj.)* ምዝቡል *mzbul*
nose *(n.)* ስሕታን *sḧtan*
nostalgia *(n.)* ኣደፋፈረ *adefafere*
nostril *(n.)* ዉንዛፈ *wunzafe*
nostrum *(n.)* ፈንፈነ *fenfene*
nosy *(adj.)* ክርሃት *krhat*
not *(adv.)* ክሩህ *kruh*
notable *(adj.)* ጸንዐ *xen'ë*
notary *(n.)* ዘይውዳእ *zeywda'è*
notation *(n.)* ዓቕሚ *'äq̈mi*
notch *(n.)* ሕርቱም *ḧrtum*
note *(n.)* መሓለ *meḧale*
notebook *(n.)* ልቡዕ *lbu'ë*
noted *(adj.)* ንፉዕ ብቑዕ *nfu'ë bq̈u'ë*
noteworthy *(adj.)* መዓናጡ *me'änaïu*
nothing *(pron.)* ምዝቡል *mzbul*
notice *(n.)* ኣብ ልዕሊ *'ab l'ëli*
noticeable *(adj.)* ገዛ *geza*
noticeboard *(n.)* ኣጥፈአ *'aïfe'e*
notifiable *(adj.)* ምጥፋእ *mïfa'è*
notification *(n.)* ዚጽላእ *zixla'è*
notify *(v.)* ጸልአ *xel'e*
notion *(n.)* ጥንታዊ *ïntawi*
notional *(adj.)* ተወግረ *tewegre*
notoriety *(n.)* ምውጋድ *mwgad*
notorious *(prep.)* ውጉር *wgur*
notwithstanding *(prep.)* ፈድፈደ *fedfede*
nougat *(n.)* ብዛዕባ *bza'ëba*
nought *(n.)* ኣብ ዙርያ *'ab zurya*
noun *(n.)* ኣብ ልዕሊ *'ab l'ëli*
nourish *(v.)* ብዝያዳ *bzyada*
nourishment *(n.)* ልሕላሓ *lḧlaḧe*
novel *(n.)* ፋሕፋሒ *faḧfaḧi*
novelette *(n.)* ጎድነ-ጎድኒ *godnegodni*
novelist *(n.)* ኣሕጸረ *aḧxere*
novelty *(n.)* ወጻኢ *wexa'i*
November *(n.)* ሰረዘ *sereze*
novice *(n.)* ሃንደበታዊ *handebetawi*
now *(adv.)* ሓገል *ḧagel*
nowhere *(adv.)* ጸለቝ *xeleq̈Wu*
noxious *(adj.)* ብኩራት *bkurat*
nozzle *(n.)* ብኹር *bḱur*
nuance *(n.)* ብኹር *bḱur*
nubile *(a.)* ፍጹም *fxum*

nuclear ***(adj.)*** **ስሬት** *sreet*
nucleus ***(n.)*** **መሓረ** *meȟare*
nude ***(adj.)*** **ሰተየ** *seteye*
nudge ***(v.)*** **ተቐጠበ** *teq̈eṫebe*
nudge ***(v.)*** **ጥሉቕ** *ṫluq̈*
nudist ***(n.)*** **ዛህዲ** *zahdi*
nudity ***(n.)*** **ረቒቕ** *req̈iq̈*
nugatory ***(adj.)*** **ትርጉም ኣልቦ** *trgum 'albo*
nugget ***(n.)*** **ትርጉም ኣልቦነት** *trgum 'albonet*
nuisance ***(n.)*** **ምልኣት** *ml'at*
null ***(adj.)*** **ፍድፉድ** *fdfud*
nullification ***(n.)*** **ዓመጸ** *ämexe*
nullify ***(v.)*** **ተጻራፊ** *texarafi*
numb ***(adj.)*** **ተዳወበ** *tedawebe*
number ***(n.)*** **ደልሃመታዊ** *delhametawi*
numberless ***(adj.)*** **ደልሃመት** *delhamet*
numeral ***(n.)*** **ኣካደሚያዊ** *akademiyawi*
numerator ***(n.)*** **ኣካደሚ** *akademi*
numerical ***(adj.)*** **መጸ** *mexe*
numerous ***(adj.)*** **ነሃረ** *nehare*
nun ***(n.)*** **ኣንሃሪ** *anhari*
nunnery ***(n.)*** **ምጉላሕ** *mgulaȟ*
nuptial ***(adj.)*** **ኣጉለሐ** *aguleȟe*
nurse ***(n.)*** **ተቐበለ** *teq̈ebele*
nursery ***(n.)*** **ተቐባልነት ዘለዎ** *teq̈ebalnet zelewo*
nurture ***(v.)*** **ቅባለ** *qbale*
nut ***(n.)*** **መእተዊ** *me'ètewi*
nutrient ***(n.)*** **ኪርከብ ዚከኣል** *kirkeb zike'al*
nutrition ***(n.)*** **ብጽሓት** *bxȟat*
nutritious ***(adj.)*** **መሰርሒ** *mesarȟi*
nutritive ***(adj.)*** **ሓደጋ** *ȟadega*
nutty ***(adj.)*** **ናይ ሓደጋ** *nay ȟadega*
nuzzle ***(v.)*** **ኣጨብጨበ** *ačebčebe*
nylon ***(n.)*** **ኣዕነወ** *a'ënewe*
nymph ***()*** **ሰላምታ** *selamta*

O

oaf ***(n.)*** **halay** *ሃላይ*
oak ***(n.)*** **daEro** *ዳዕሮ*
oar ***(n.)*** **nay jelba betri** *ናይ ጀልባ በትሪ*
oasis ***(n.)*** **lmu'E meriet** *ለሙዕ መሬት*
oat ***(n.)*** **Aynet Teremer** *ዓይነት ጥረምረ*
oath ***(n.)*** **meHala** *መሓላ*
oatmeal ***(n.)*** **kab Teremer zsraH Aynet mgbi** *ካብ ጥረምረ ዝስራሕ ዓይነት ምግቢ*
obduracy ***(n.)*** **dfret** *ድፍረት*
obdurate ***(adj.)*** **Kbur** *ክቡር*
obedience ***(n.)*** **teazaznet** *ተኣዛዝነት*
obedient ***(adj.)*** **m'ezuz** *ምእዙዝ*
obeisance ***(n.)*** **segede** *ሰገደ*
obese ***(adj.)*** **regiud** *ረጉድ*
obesity ***(n.)*** **lEli AQn mizan sebnet** *ልዕሊ ዓቐን ሚዛን ሰብነት*
obey ***(v.)*** **m'ezaz** *ምእዛዝ*
obfuscate ***(v.)*** **Hbu'e** *ሕቡእ*
obituary ***(n.)*** **Hmum** *ሕሙም*
object ***(n.)*** **neger** *ነገር*
objection ***(n.)*** **mqwam** *ምቅዋም*
objectionable ***(adj.)*** **mKHad zK'el** *ምኽሓድ ዝኽእል*
objective ***(adj.)*** **Oe'lama** *ዕላማ*

objectively ***(adv.)*** **zeyedalw** *ዘየዳልው*
oblation ***(n.)*** meswa'eti *መስዋእቲ*
obligated ***(v.)*** **tegedede** *ተገደደ*
obligation ***(n.)*** **gdeta** *ግዴታ*
obligatory ***(adj.)*** **gdeta** *ግዴታ*
oblige ***(v.)*** **zegeded** *ዘገድድ*
obliging ***(adj.)*** **Hagazi** *ሓጋዚ*
oblique ***(adj.)*** **zembal** *ዘምባል*
obliterate ***(v.)*** **demsese** *ደምሰሰ*
obliteration ***(n.)*** **mdemsas** *ምድምሳስ*
oblivion ***(n.)*** **Hbu'e** *ሕቡእ*
oblivious ***(adj.)*** **zres'o** *ዚረስዕ*
oblong ***(adj.)*** **zelela** *ዘለላ*
obloquy ***(n.)*** **shem mxfa'e** *ስም ምጥፋእ*
obnoxious ***(adj.)*** **zeyeHegus** *ዘየሕጉስ*
obscene ***(adj.)*** **boalege** *ባዓለገ*
obscenity ***(n.)*** **zetsl'e neger** *ዘጽልእ ነገር*
obscure ***(adj.)*** **bruh zeykone** *ብሩህ ዘይኮነ*
obscurity ***(n.)*** **Hebu'e** *ሕቡእ*
observance ***(n.)*** **Kdri** *ኽብሪ*
observant ***(adj.)*** **z'Ezeb** *ዝዕዘብ*
observation ***(n.)*** **t'Ezebti** *ትዕዝብቲ*
observatory ***(n.)*** **mekane-t'Ezebti** *መካነ-ትዕዝብቲ*
observe ***(v.)*** **te'azebe** *ተዓዘበ*
obsess ***(v.)*** **bHasab wehate** *ብሓሳብ ወሓጠ*
obsession ***(n.)*** **chenqet** *ጭንቀት*
obsolescent ***(adj.)*** **zemenawi** *ዘመናዊ*
obsolete ***(adj.)*** **gziu zhalefe** *ግዚኡ ዝሓለፈ*
obstacle ***(n.)*** **Enqfat** *ዕንቅፋት*
obstinacy ***(n)*** **dereqnet** *ደረቕነት*
obstinate ***(adj.)*** **dereq** *ደረቕ*
obstruct ***(v.)*** **Agete** *ዓገተ*
obstruction ***(n.)*** **tsegem** *ጸገም*
obstructive ***(adj.)*** **zAgt** *ዝዓግት*
obtain ***(v.)*** **reKibu** *ረኺቡ*
obtainable ***(adj.)*** **krkeb zKel** *ክርከብ ዝኽእል*
obtrude ***(v.)*** **zteKefle** *ዝተኸፍለ*
obtuse ***(adj.)*** **gaHtat** *ጋሕጣጥ*
obverse ***(n.)*** **m'Ezab** *ምዕዛብ*
obviate ***(v.)*** **zeyntsur** *ዘይንጹር*
obvious ***(adj.)*** **gltsi** *ግልጺ*
occasion ***(n.)*** **agatami** *ኣጋጣሚ*
occasional ***(adj.)*** **halhalifu** *ሓልሓሊፉ*
occasionally ***(adv.)*** **halhalifu** *ሓልሓሊፉ*
occident ***(n.)*** **m'Erab** *ምዕራብ*
occidental ***(adj.)*** **m'Erabawi** *ምዕራባዊ*
occlude ***(v.)*** **dqas** *ድቃስ*
occult ***(n.)*** **menafstawi ftsame** *መንፈስታዊ ፍጻመ*
occupancy ***(n.)*** **mHaz** *ምሓዝ*
occupant ***(n.)*** **tHazay** *ተሓዛይ*
occupation ***(n.)*** **moya** *ሞያ*
occupational ***(adj.)*** **moyawi** *ሞያዊ*
occupy ***(v.)*** **Haze** *ሓዘ*
occur ***(v.)*** **metse** *መጸ*
occurrence ***(n.)*** **kstet** *ክስተት*
ocean ***(n.)*** **wqyanos** *ውቅያኖስ*

oceanic *(adj.)* wqyanosawi ውቅያኖሳዊ
octagon *(n.)* shemonte wegen ሸሞንተ ወገን
octave *(n.)* ney muziqa 8notatat bebi 2 nota zfelaleyu ናይ ሙዚቃ 8ኖታታት በቢ 2 ኖታ ዝፈላለዩ
octavo *(n.)* 16 gets zelewo metsHaf 16 ገፅ ዘለዎ መፅሓፍ
October *(n.)* Tkemti ጥቅምቲ
octogenarian *(n.)* kab 80-89 Edme zelewo seb ካብ 80-89 ዕድመ ዘለዎ ሰብ
octopus *(n.)* oktapos ኦክታፑስ
octroi *(n.)* tsuret ጹረት
ocular *(adj.)* emut እሙት
odd *(adj.)* zeylmud ዘይልሙድ
oddity *(n.)* gasha ጋሻ
odds *(n.)* flly ፍልልይ
ode *(n.)* bza'Eba Hade neger zzareb gTmi ብዛዕባ ሓደ ነገር ዝዛረብ ግጥሚ
odious *(adj.)* mesHaQ መስሓቕ
odium *(n.)* tsl'at ፅልኣት
odorous *(adj.)* shta ሽታ
odour *(n.)* chena ጨና
odyssey *(n.)* nay grik gTmi ናይ ግሪክ ግጥሚ
of *(prep.)* nay ናይ
off *(adv.)* Tefiu ጠፊኡ
offence *(n.)* mesenakl መሰናኽል
offend *(v.)* bedele በደለ
offender *(n.)* bedali በዳሊ
offensive *(adj.)* tetsela'i ተጻላኢ
offer *(v.)* mQrab ምቕራብ
offering *(n.)* meswa'eti መስዋእቲ
office *(n.)* biet-tshfet ቤት-ጽሕፈት
officer *(n.)* mekonen መኮንን
official *(adj.)* be'Al mezi በዓል መዚ
officially *(adv.)* b'Eli ብዕሊ
officiate *(v.)* mekonen መኮንን
officious *(adj.)* fluT ፍሉጥ
offset *(v.)* mkeHaHasi ምክሓሓሲ
offshoot *(n.)* nkaye ንካየ
offshore *(adj.)* gemgem baHri ገምገም ባሕሪ
offside *(adj.)* Tf'ategna ጥፍኣተኛ
offspring *(n.)* wlad ውላድ
oft *(adv.)* tera ተራ
often *(adv.)* btedegagami ብተደጋጋሚ
ogle *(v.)* gulbet ጉልበት
oil *(n.)* zeyti ዘይቲ
oil *(v.)* mlkay zeyti ምልካይ ዘይቲ
oily *(adj.)* zeyti ztebekele ዘይቲ ዝተበከለ
ointment *(n.)* lKay ልኻይ
okay *(adj.)* Heray ሓራይ
old *(adj.)* aregit ኣረጊት
oligarchy *(n.)* hager zemeHadr gujele ሃገር ዘመሓድር ጉጅለ
olive *(n.)* awli'E ኣውሊዕ
Olympic *(adj.)* olompiyawi ኦሊምፕያዊ
omelette *(n.)* omliet ኦምሌት
omen *(n.)* fal ፋል
ominous *(adj.)* atseyafi ኣፀያፊ
omission *(n.)* mgdaf ምግዳፍ
omit *(v.)* mgdaf ምግዳፍ
omnibus *(n.)* eKbkab እኽብካብ
omnipotence *(n.)* kulu mK'al ኩሉ ምኽኣል

omnipotent ***(adj.)*** **kulu keali** ኩሉ ከኣሊ
omnipresence ***(n.)*** **kab kulu nla'Eli** ካብ ኩሉ ንላዕሊ
omnipresent ***(adj.)*** **kab kulu nla'Eli** ካብ ኩሉ ንላዕሊ
omniscience ***(n.)*** **kulu mflaT** ኩሉ ምፍላጥ
omniscient ***(adj.)*** **kulu felaTi** ኩሉ ፈላጢ
on ***(prep.)*** **ab l'Eli** ኣብ ልዕሊ
once ***(adv.)*** **Hade gizie** ሓደ ግዜ
one ***(n. & adj.)*** **Hade** ሓደ
oneness ***(n.)*** **Hadnet** ሓድነት
onerous ***(adj.)*** **brtu'E** ብርቱዕ
oneself ***(pron.)*** **Arse** ዓርሰ
onion ***(n.)*** **shegurti** ሽጉርቲ
onlooker ***(n.)*** **temelkati** ተመልካቲ
only ***(adv.)*** **Tray** ጥራይ
onomatopoeia ***(n.)*** **kab dmtsu zemetse qal** ካብ ድምፁ ዝመፀ ቃል
onset ***(n.)*** **mejemerya** መጀመርያ
onslaught ***(n.)*** **Tfatat** ጥፍኣታት
ontology ***(n.)*** **nay sne hiwet tmrti** ናይ ስነ ሂወት ትምርቲ
onus ***(n.)*** **nay Hade seb gdieta** ናይ ሓደ ሰብ ግዴታ
onward ***(adv.)*** **nQdmit** ንቕድሚት
onyx ***(n.)*** **Aynet ma'Adn** ዓይነት ማዓድን
ooze ***(v.i.)*** **Hafis fesasi** ሓፊስ ፈሳሲ
opacity ***(n.)*** **brhal albanet** ብርሃን-ኣልባነት
opal ***(n.)*** **Aynet ma'Adn** ዓይነት ማዓድን
opaque ***(adj.)*** **brhal zeyeHelf** ብርሃን ዘየሕልፍ
open ***(adj.)*** **kfut** ክፉት
opening ***(n.)*** **kftet** ክፍተት
openly ***(adv.)*** **bgahdi** ብጋህዲ
opera ***(n.)*** **opiera** ኦፔራ
operate ***(v.)*** **zserH** ዝሰርሕ
operation ***(n.)*** **mTbaHti tsgena** መጥባሕቲ ጽገና
operational ***(adj.)*** **ab sraH zwe'Ale** ኣብ ስራሕ ዝወዓለ
operative ***(adj.)*** **tenaHanaHi** ተናሓናሒ
operator ***(n.)*** **asraHi** ኣስራሒ
opine ***(v.)*** **r'eyto mhab** ርእይቶ ምሃብ
opinion ***(n.)*** **r'eyto** ርእይቶ
opium ***(n.)*** **Hshsh** ሓሽሽ
opponent ***(n.)*** **tenaHanaHi** ተናሓናሒ
opportune ***(adj.)*** **mchuw** ምቹው
opportunism ***(n.)*** **Edl** ዕድል
opportunity ***(n.)*** **Edl** ዕድል
oppose ***(v.)*** **teQaweme** ተቓወመ
opposite ***(adj.)*** **b'antsaru** ብኣንጻሩ
opposition ***(n.)*** **mqwam** ምቅዋም
oppress ***(v.)*** **deQose** ደቖሰ
oppression ***(n.)*** **cheqona** ጨቆና
oppressive ***(adj.)*** **chequani** ጨቛኒ
oppressor ***(n.)*** **chequani** ጨቛኒ
opt ***(v.)*** **mmrts** ምምራፅ
optic ***(adj.)*** **ms Ayni wey mr'ay zmlket** ምስ ዓይኒ ወይ ምርኣይ ዝምልከት
optician ***(n.)*** **nay Ayni Hakim** ናይ ዓይኒ ሓኪም

optimism *(n.)* awentawi are'a'eya ኣወንታዊ ኣረኣእያ
optimist *(n.)* bruh ብሩህ
optimistic *(adj.)* Qnu'e Hasab zelewo ቅኑዕ ሓሳብ ዘለዎ
optimize *(v.)* mt'eKKal ምትእኽኻል
optimum *(adj.)* eKul እኹል
option *(n.)* amaratsi ኣማራጺ
optional *(adj.)* gdieta zeykone ግዴታ ዘይኮነ
opulence *(n.)* udet ዑደት
opulent *(adj.)* habtam ሃብታም
or *(conj.)* wey ወይ
oracle *(n.)* Tenquali ጠንቋሊ
oracular *(adj.)* mTnqual ምጥንቋል
oral *(adj.)* bQal ብቓል
orally *(adv.)* bQal ብቓል
orange *(n.)* aranshi ኣራንሺ
oration *(n.)* mdlaw ምድላው
orator *(n.)* medalewi መዳለዊ
oratory *(n.)* tsbuQ mKuan ፅቡቕ ምኳን
orb *(n.)* kbawi akal ክባዊ ኣካል
orbit *(n.)* qnate zuret ቅናት-ዙረት
orbital *(adj.)* Udetawi ዑደታዊ
orchard *(n.)* atsede fratat ኣጸደ-ፍረታት
orchestra *(n.)* muziqawi qnat ሙዚቃዊ ቅናት
orchestral *(adj.)* muziqawi qnat ሙዚቃዊ ቅናት
orchid *(n.)* nay Embaba Aynet ናይ ዕምበባ ዓይነት
ordeal *(n.)* mekera መከራ
order *(n.)* mesr'E መስርዕ
orderly *(adj.)* bsr'At ብስርዓት
ordinance *(n.)* dngage ድንጋገ
ordinarily *(adv.)* lmudawi ልሙዳዊ
ordinary *(adj.)* lmud ልሙድ
ordnance *(n.)* nay kuinat mieda ናይ ኲናት ሜዳ
ore *(n.)* ma'Adn ማዕድን
organ *(n.)* akal ኣካል
organic *(adj.)* organik ኦርጋኒክ
organism *(n.)* sne hywet ስነ ሕይወት
organization *(n.)* kubanya ኩባንያ
organize *(v.)* adalew ኣዳለዉ
orgasm *(n.)* Trzi sm'It ጥርዚ-ስምዒት
orgy *(n.)* tfg'et ትፍግእት
orient *(n.)* bniew mbraQ ብነው ምብራቕ
oriental *(adj.)* mbraQawi ምብራቓዊ
orientate *(v.)* meteHababeri መተሓባበሪ
origami *(n.)* bjapanawyan zsraH nay wereQet qrtsaqrtsi ብጃፓናውያን ዝስራሕ ናይ ወረቐት ቕርፃቕርፂ
origin *(n.)* felami ፈላሚ
original *(adj.)* Qdamawi ቀዳማዊ
originality *(n.)* mebeqolawinet መበቈላውነት
originate *(v.)* mnchuw ምንጩው
originator *(n.)* mejemeri መጀመሪ
ornament *(n.)* tr'it ትርኢት
ornamentation *(n.)* tr'itawi ትርኢታዊ
ornate *(adj.)* zuret ዙረት
orphan *(n.)* zeKtam ዘኽታም

orphanage ***(n.)*** meHebHebi zeKtam htsanat መሐብሐቢ ዘኽታም ህፃናት
orthodox ***(adj.)*** qbul ቅቡል
orthodoxy ***(n.)*** qbul ቅቡል
orthopaedics ***(n.)*** Aynet Hkmna ዓይነት ሕክምና
oscillate ***(v.)*** mzwar ምዝዋር
oscillation ***(n.)*** zuret ዙረት
ossify ***(v.)*** nab Atsmi mQyar ናብ ዓፅሚ ምቕያር
ostensible ***(adj.)*** zeygltsi ዘይግልፂ
ostentation ***(n.)*** zeygltsi ዘይግልፂ
osteopathy ***(n.)*** nay Atsmn megeTaTemin Hkmna ናይ ዓፅምን መግጣጠምን ሕክምና
ostracize ***(v.)*** aglele ኣግለለ
ostrich ***(n.)*** segen ሰገን
other ***(adj. & pron.)*** kal'e ካልእ
otherwise ***(adv.)*** tezeykone gn ተዘይኮነ ግን
otiose ***(adj.)*** heTeqm ዘይጠቅም
otter ***(n.)*** Asa zmgb ensesa ዓሳ ዝምግብ እንስሳ
ottoman ***(n.)*** dkua ድኳ
ounce ***(n.)*** me'Eqeni fesasi መዐቀኒ ፈሳሲ
our ***(adj.)*** natna ናትና
ourselves ***(pron.)*** nHna ንሕና
oust ***(v.)*** segon ሰጎገ
out ***(adv.)*** dege ደገ
outbid ***(v.)*** zle'Ale kflit mQrab ዝለዓለ ክፍሊት ምቕራብ
outboard ***(adj.)*** kab dege ካብ ደገ
outbreak ***(n.)*** werershgn ወረርሽኝ
outburst ***(n.)*** ntuag ንትጓ
outcast ***(n.)*** ntsug ንጹግ
outclass ***(v.)*** l'Ul ልዑል
outcome ***(n.)*** wts'it ውፅኢት
outcry ***(n.)*** bKyat ብኽያት
outdated ***(adj.)*** gizie zHalefo ጊዜ ዝሓለፎ
outdo ***(v.)*** m'Eblal ምዕብላል
outdoor ***(adj.)*** dege ደገ
outer ***(adj.)*** degawi ደጋዊ
outfit ***(n.)*** Kdan ኽዳን
outgoing ***(adj.)*** tetsawati ተፃዋቲ
outgrow ***(v.)*** m'Ebay ምዕባይ
outhouse ***(n.)*** shQaQ ሽቓቕ
outing ***(n.)*** shrshr ሽርሽር
outlandish ***(adj.)*** gdamawi ግዳማዊ
outlast ***(v.)*** b'Edme beletse ብዕድመ በለፀ
outlaw ***(n.)*** zeyHgawi mgbar ዘይሕጋዊ ምግባር
outlay ***(n.)*** wetsieu mbal ወጺኡ ምባል
outlet ***(n.)*** mesheTi መሸጢ
outline ***(n.)*** ndfi ንድፊ
outlive ***(v.)*** b'Edme beletse ብዕድመ በለፀ
outlook ***(n.)*** r'eyot ርእዮት
outlying ***(adj.)*** wetsieu mbal ወጺኡ ዝበለ
outmoded ***(adj.)*** bahlawi ባህላዊ
outnumber ***(v.)*** bQutsri beletse ብቑፅሪ በለፀ
outpatient ***(n.)*** Arat zeyHaze teHakami ዓራት ዘይሓዘ ተሓካሚ
outpost ***(n.)*** Erdi ዕርዲ
output ***(n.)*** wts'it ውፅኢት
outrage ***(n.)*** Abi wenjel ዓቢ ወንጀል

outrageous ***(adj.)*** **zedengts** ዘደንግጽ
outrider ***(n.)*** **Ajabi** ዓጃቢ
outright ***(adv.)*** **meweda'eta** መወዳእታ
outrun ***(v.)*** **bguya Qedeme** ብጉያ ቐደመ
outset ***(n.)*** **mejemeri** መጀመሪ
outshine ***(v.)*** **zentsebarq** ዘንፀባርቕ
outside ***(n.)*** **dege** ደገ
outsider ***(n.)*** **guana** ጓና
outsize ***(adj.)*** **Abyi** ዓብዪ
outskirts ***(n.)*** **edub gemgem** እዱብ ገምገም
outsource ***(v.)*** ካብ ደገ ዕዳጋ ግልጋሎት ምርካብ
outspoken ***(adj.)*** **gltsi r'eyto** ግልፂ ርእይቶ **kab dege Edaga glgalot mrkab**
outstanding ***(adj.)*** **bTa'Emi tsbuQ** ብጣዕሚ ፅቡቕ
outstrip ***(v.)*** **goyKa mQdam** ጎይኻ ምቕዳም
outward ***(adj.)*** **nab dege** ናብ ደገ
outwardly ***(adv.)*** **degawi** ደጋዊ
outweigh ***(v.)*** **bKbdet beletse** ብኽብደት በለፀ
outwit ***(v.)*** **btsaweta beletse** ብፃወታ በለፀ
oval ***(adj.)*** **nay enquaQuHo qrtsi** ናይ እንቋቑሖ ቅርጺ
ovary ***(n.)*** **maHdere enquaQuHo** ማሕደረ እንቋቑሖ
ovate ***(adj.)*** **nay enquaQuHo qrtsi** ናይ እንቋቑሖ ቅርጺ
ovation ***(n.)*** **dKnet** ድኽነት
oven ***(n.)*** **forno** ፎርኖ
over ***(prep.)*** **nla'Eli** ንላዕሊ
overact ***(v.)*** **l'Eli meTen mtgbar** ልዕሊ መጠን ምትግባር
overall ***(adj.)*** **bTeQlala** ብጠቕላላ
overawe ***(v.)*** **akenawene** ኣወናወነ
overbalance ***(v.)*** **l'Eli mizan** ልዕሊ ሚዛን
overbearing ***(adj.)*** **l'El l'El** ልዕል ልዕል
overblown ***(adj.)*** **zteleTefe** ዝተለጠፈ
overboard ***(adv.)*** **ab merkeb** ኣብ መርከብ
overburden ***(v.)*** **sraH abzaHe** ስራሕ ኣብዘሐ
overcast ***(adj.)*** **shfan** ሽፋን
overcharge ***(v.)*** **trfi kflit** ትርፊ ክፍሊት
overcoat ***(n.)*** **mederebi Kdan** መደረቢ ኽዳን
overcome ***(v.)*** **se'Are** ሰዓረ
overdo ***(v.)*** **l'Eli meTen mTQam** ልዕሊ መጠን ምጥቃም
overdose ***(n.)*** **medHanit l'Eli meTen mwsad** መድሓኒት ልዕሊ መጠን ምውሳድ
overdraft ***(n.)*** **lQaH** ልቓሕ
overdraw ***(v.)*** **kab gbu'e nla'Eli m'emat** ካብ ግቡእ ንላዕሊ ምእማት
overdrive ***(n.)*** **kab AQmi nl'Eli msraH** ካብ ዓቕሚ ንላዕሊ ምስራሕ
overdue ***(adj.)*** **gizie zeHlefe** ጊዜ ዘሕለፈ
overestimate ***(v.)*** **bziH m'emat** ብዙሕ ምእማት

overflow ***(v.)*** **bTa'Emi meli'u** *ብጣዕሚ መሊኡ*
overgrown ***(adj.)*** **bTa'emi Abyi** *ብጣዕሚ ዓብዪ*
overhaul ***(v.)*** **mt'Ereray** *ምትዕርራይ*
overhead ***(adv.)*** **kab r'esi nla'Eli** *ካብ ርእሲ ንላዕሊ*
overhear ***(v.)*** **b'agaTami sem'E** *ብኣጋጣሚ ሰምዐ*
overjoyed ***(adj.)*** **kebid Hagos** *ከቢድ ሓጎስ*
overlap ***(v.)*** **chafatu tederarebe** *ጫፋቱ ተደራረበ*
overleaf ***(adv.)*** **bdHrit** *ብድሕሪት*
overload ***(v.)*** **kebit ts'Enet** *ከቢድ ፅዕነት*
overlook ***(v.)*** **mermere** *መርመረ*
overly ***(adv.)*** **kab lk'E nla'eli** *ካብ ልክዕ ንላዕሊ*
overnight ***(adv.)*** **bHade leyti** *ብሓደ ለይቲ*
overpass ***(n.)*** **dldl** *ድልድል*
overpower ***(v.)*** **se'Are** *ሰዓረ*
overrate ***(v.)*** **kab lk'E nla'eli** *ካብ ልክዕ ንላዕሊ*
overreach ***(v.)*** **arkebe** *ኣርከበ*
overreact ***(v.)*** **bTa'emi astemasele** *ብጣዕሚ ኣስተማሰለ*
override ***(v.)*** **Ablele** *ዓብለለ*
overrule ***(v.)*** **teKelkele** *ተኸልከለ*
overrun ***(v.)*** **werere** *ወረረ*
overseas ***(adv.)*** **gdamawi hager** *ግዳማዊ ሃገር*
oversee ***(v.)*** **te'Azebe** *ተዓዘበ*
overseer ***(n.)*** **l'uK** *ልኡኽ*
overshadow ***(v.)*** **antselalewe** *ኣንጸላለወ*
overshoot ***(v.)*** **ambza asrHe** *እምብዛ ኣስርሐ*
oversight ***(n.)*** **znga'E** *ዝንጋዐ*
overspill ***(n.)*** **ksab zfess zmel'e** *ክሳብ ዝፈስስ ዝምልእ*
overstep ***(v.)*** **kab meTen nla'eli** *ካብ መጠን ንላዕሊ*
overt ***(adj.)*** **Adakie nla'Eli** *ዓዳኺ ንላዕሊ*
overtake ***(v.)*** **Qedeme** *ቐደመ*
overthrow ***(v.)*** **gelbeTe** *ገልበጠ*
overtime ***(n)*** **tewesaKi se'At** *ተወሳኺ ሰዓት*
overtone ***(n.)*** **Hbu'e trgum zelewo** *ሕቡእ ትርጉም ዘለዎ*
overture ***(n.)*** **Kbri** *ኽብሪ*
overturn ***(v.)*** **mglbaT** *ምግልባጥ*
overview ***(n.)*** **TeQlala r'eyot** *ጠቕላላ ርእዮት*
overweening ***(adj.)*** **kab meTen nla'eli Arse mt'emman** *ካብ መጠን ንላዕሊ ዓርሰ ምትእምማን*
overwhelm ***(v.)*** **chenqi** *ጩንቂ*
overwrought ***(adj.)*** **zKerere** *ዝኸረረ*
ovulate ***(v.)*** **mfTar enquaQHo** *ምፍጣር እንቋቕሖ*
owe ***(n.)*** **m'ewad** *ምእዋድ*
owing ***(adj.)*** **m'ewad** *ምእዋድ*
owl ***(n.)*** **gungua** *ጉንጓ*
own ***(adj. & pron.)*** **mwnan** *ምውናን*
owner ***(n.)*** **wana** *ዋና*
ownership ***(n.)*** **wannet** *ዋንነት*
ox ***(n.)*** **b'Eray** *ብዕራይ*

oxide *(n.)* **oksayd** ኦክሳይድ
oxygen *(n.)* **oksjn** ኦክስጅን
oyster *(n.)* **ab may znebr ensesa** ኣብ ማይ ዝነብር እንስሳ
ozone *(n)* **ozon** ኦዞን

P

pace *(n.)* **መተሓላለፊ መንገዲ** *mtehalalefi mengedi*
pacemaker *(n.)* **መራሕ መንገዲ** *merah mengedi*
pacific *(n.)* **ሰላማዊ** *selamawi*
pacifist *(n.)* **ደጋፊ ሰላም** *degafi selam*
pacify *(v.)* **ኣህድአ** *ahd'e*
pack *(n.)* **ጾዕነት** *xëinet*
package *(n.)* **መጠቕለሊ** *meëeqleli*
packet *(n.)* **ጥቕላል** *ẗqlal*
packing *(n.)* **ምጥርናፍ** *mẗrnaf*
pact *(n.)* **ምስምማዕ** *msm'maë*
pad *(n.)* **ፍርናሽ** *frnash*
padding *(v.)* **ኣዘናግዐ** *mesrhi meteras*
paddle *(n.)* **መጀለቢ** *mejelebi*
paddock *(n.)* **ጎልጎል ሳዕሪ** *golgol saëri*
paddy *(n.)* **ነድሪ** *nedri*
padlock *(n.)* **ሊኬቶ** *likieto*
paediatrician *(n.)* **ናይ ህጻናት ዶክቶር** *nay hxanat doctor*
paediatrics *(n.)* **ጨንፈር ሕክምና ህጻናት** *čenfer hkmna hxanat*
paedophile *(n.)* **ምስ ህጻናት ጾታዊ ርክብ ምፍጻም ዝማረኽ በጽሒ** *ms hixanat xotawi rkb mfxam zmarek bexhi*
pagan *(n.)* **ኣረሚን** *aremien*
page *(n.)* **ምዕራፍ** *m'ëraf*
pageant *(n.)* **ስነ-ስርዓት በዓል** *sne-srät beäl*
pageantry *(n.)* **ሕብራዊ ምረኢት** *hbrawi mreit*
pagoda *(n.)* **ብውወርቂ ተሰርሐ ሳንቲም** *bwerqi teserhe santim*
pail *(n.)* **ሰንኬሎ** *senkielo*
pain *(n.)* **ቃንዛ** *qanza*
painful *(adj.)* **ዘቀንዙ** *zeqenzu*
painkiller *(n.)* **ቀታሊ ቃንዛ** *qetali qanza*
painstaking *(adj.)* **ጥንቁቕ** *ẗnquq*
paint *(n.)* **ምቅባእ** *mqbaè*
painter *(n.)* **ቀብኣይ** *qebeay*
painting *(n.)* **ቅብኣ** *qba*
pair *(n.)* **ጽምዲ** *xmdi*
paisley *(n.)* **ኣበው//////** *abew*
pal *(n.)* **መሓዛ** *mehaza*
palace *(n.)* **ቤተ መንግስቲ** *biete mengsti*
palatable *(adj.)* **ምቁር** *mqur*
palatal *(adj.)* **ናይ ናሕሲ ኣፍ** *nay nahsi af*
palate *(n.)* **ናሕሲ ኣፍ** *nahsi af*
palatial *(adj.)* **ቤተ መንግስታዊ** *biete mengstawi*
pale *(adj.)* **ጽምሉው** *xmluw*
palette *(n.)* **መስርዕ ሕብርታት ናይ ዝተዋህበ ስራሕ** *msrie hbrtat nay ztewahbe srah*
paling *(n.)* **ዝበልሖ ዕንጸይቲ ሓጹር** *zbelhe enxeyti haxur*
pall *(n.)* **ግሩም ልብሲ** *grum lbsi*
pallet *(n.)* **መሳርሒ ካይላ** *msarhi kayla*

palm *(n.)* ስየ *sye*
palmist *(n.)* ጠንቋሊ *meqali*
palmistry *(n.)* ናይ ጻዕዳ ኢድ ጥንቁልና *nay xaeda eid tnqulna*
palpable *(adj.)* ዝጭበጥ *zchbet*
palpitate *(v.)* ተደጋጋሚ ምውቃዕ ልቢ *tedagagami mwqae lbi*
palpitation *(n.)* ዘይንቡር መውቃዕቲ ልቢ *zeynbur wqaeti lbi*
palsy *(n.)* መልመስቲ *melmesti*
paltry *(adj.)* ዘይበቅዕ *zeybeqe*
pamper *(v.)* ምሕንቃቕ *mhnqaq*
pamphlet *(n.)* መንሹር *menshur*
pamphleteer *(n.)* ዓዳሊ መንሹር *adali menshur*
pan *(n.)* ባዴላ/ድስቲ *badela/dsti*
panacea *(n.)* መድሓኒ *mdhani*
panache *(n.)* ኳዕናን *kuae'nan*
pancake *(n.)* ፓንኬክ *pankek*
pancreas *(n.)* ሓሞት *hamot*
panda *(n.)* ድቢ *dbi*
pandemonium *(n.)* ናዕቢ *naebi*
pane *(n.)* ኣንሶላ መስኮት *ansola mskot*
panegyric *(n.)* መደረ ዝህብ *medere zhb*
panel *(n.)* ጓዳ *guada*
pang *(n.)* ውግኣት *wgat*
panic *(n.)* ራዕዲ *raedi*
panorama *(n.)* ኣጠቓላሊ ኣቀማምጣ መሬት *ataqalali aqmamta meriet*
pant *(v.)* ምልህላህ *mlhlah*
pantaloons *(n.)* ፓንታሎኒ *pantaloni*
pantheism *(n.)* ኣብ ኩሎም ኣማልኽቲ ምእማን *ab kulom amalkti meman*
pantheist *(adj.)* ኣብ ኩሎም ኣማልኽቲ ዝኣምን *ab kulom amalkti zamn*
panther *(n.)* ዓባይ ድሙ *abay dmu*
panties *(n.)* ኮስትሞታት *kostmotat*
pantomime *(n.)* ትያትር ቆልዑ *tyatr qoleu*
pantry *(n.)* ከብሒ ክሽነ *kebhi kshne*
pants *(n.)* ስረ *sre*
papacy *(n.)* ናይ ፓፓስ ኦፊስ *nay papas ofis*
papal *(adj.)* ናይ ፓፓስ *nay papas*
paper *(n.)* ወረቐት *werqet*
paperback *(n.)* ተዓጻጻፊ ገበር ዘለዎ መጽሓፍ *taxaxafi geber zelewo mxhaf*
par *(n.)* ማዕርነት ኩነታት *maernet kunetat*
parable *(n.)* ሓጺር ትረኻ *haxir traka*
parachute *(n.)* ጃንጥላ *jantla*
parachutist *(n.)* ብጃንጥላ ዝንቆት *bjantla znqot*
parade *(n.)* ሰልፊ *selfi*
paradise *(n.)* ገነት *genet*
paradox *(n.)* ምግጫው/ስግንጢር *mgchaw/sgntir*
paradoxical *(adj.)* ተጋጫዊ/ስግንጢራዊ *tegachawi sgintrawi*
paraffin *(n.)* ላምባ *lamba*
paragon *(n.)* ካልኣይ/ማዕረ *kaleay/maere*
paragraph *(n.)* ዓንቀጽ *anqex*
parallel *(n.)* ጎኒጎኒ *gonigoni*

parallelogram *(n.)* ጎኒጎኒ ዝከይድ ጎብጋብ ርቡዕጎናዊ *gni goni zkeyd gobgab rubue kurnawi*
paralyse *(v.)* ምልማስ *mlmas*
paralysis *(n.)* ምልምስና *mlmsna*
paralytic *(adj.)* ብምልምስና ዝሳቐ ሰብ *bmlmsna zsaqe seb*
paramedic *(n.)* ሓኪም መረጋግኢ ሕሙማት *hakim meregagi hmumat*
parameter *(n.)* ፐራመተር *parameter*
paramount *(adj.)* ዝለዓለ *zleale*
paramour *(n.)* ፍቕራዊ *fqrawi*
paraphernalia *(n.)* ካብ ገዝሚ ወጻኢ ንብረት መርዓት *kab gezmi weai nbret mrat*
paraphrase *(v.)* ትርጉም ምንጻር *trgum mnxar*
parasite *(n.)* ኣብ ነፍሳት ዝነብሩ ፍጥረት *ab nefsat znebru ftret*
parasol *(n.)* ጽላል *xlal*
parcel *(n.)* ፓርሰል ደሴት *parsel deset*
parched *(adj.)* ዝነቐጸ *zenqexe*
pardon *(n.)* ምሕረት *mhretawi*
pardonable *(adj.)* ምሕረታዊ *mhretawi*
pare *(v.)* ቀኒሱ *qenisu*
parent *(n.)* ወላዲ *weladi*
parentage *(n.)* ስድራቤት *sdrabetawi*
parental *(adj.)* ስድራቤታዊ *sdrabetawi*
parenthesis *(n.)* ቅንፍ *qnf*
pariah *(n.)* ዝተሰደደ ሰብ *zteedede seb*
parish *(n.)* ደብሪ *debri*
parity *(n.)* ማዕርነት/ምንጽጻር ሓይሊ *maernet/mnxxar hayl*
park *(n.)* መናፍፈሲ ቦታ *menafesi bota*
parky *(adj.)* ዝሑል *zhul*
parlance *(n.)* ኣገባብ ኣዘራርባ *agebab azerarba*
parley *(n.)* ኣኼባ ዕርቂ *akeba eirqi*
parliament *(n.)* ፓርላማ *parlma*
parliamentarian *(n.)* ኣባል ፓርላማ *abal parlama*
parliamentary *(adj.)* ፓርላማዊ *parlamawi*
parlour *(n.)* መዘናግዒ ክፍሊ(ሳሎን) *mezenagei kfli*
parochial *(adj.)* ደብራዊ *debrawi*
parody *(n.)* ጭርቃን *chrqan*
parole *(n.)* ብዋሕስ ምውጻእ *bwahs mwxae*
parricide *(n.)* ወለዱ ዝቐተለ *weledu zqetele*
parrot *(n.)* ፓፓጋሎ *papagalo*
parry *(v.)* ክትዕ ምውጋድ *ktie mwgad*
parse *(v.)* ተንቲኑ *tentu*
parsimony *(n.)* ስስዐ *ssie*
parson *(n.)* ካህን *kahn*
part *(n.)* ክፋል *kfal*
partake *(v.)* ምክፋል *mkfal*
partial *(adj.)* ዘይምሉእ *zeymulue*
partiality *(n.)* ምድላው/ምፍታው *mdlaw/mftaw*
participant *(n.)* ትሳታፋይ *tsatafay*
participate *(v.)* ተስሳተፈ *tesatefe*
participation *(n.)* ምስታፍ *mstaf*
particle *(n.)* ንእሽተይ በቕሊ *neshtey beqli*

particular *(adj.)* ፍሉይ *fluy*
parting *(n.)* ምፍልላይ *mfllay*
partisan *(n.)* ደጋፊ *degafi*
partition *(n.)* ምክፍፋል *mkffal*
partly *(adv.)* ፍርቂ *frqu*
partner *(n.)* ተሻራኺ *tesharaki*
partnership *(n.)* ሽርክነት *shrket*
party *(n.)* ውድብ *wdb*
pass *(v.)* ምሕላፍ/ምቕባል *mhlaf/mkbal*
passable *(adj.)* ተሓላፊ *tehalafi*
passage *(n.)* መተሓላለፊ *metehalalefi*
passenger *(n.)* ተሳፋሪ *tsafari*
passing *(adj.)* ምስጋር *msgar*
passion *(n.)* ብርቱዕ ስምዒት *brtue smeit*
passionate *(adj.)* ስምዒታዊ/ተምሳጣዊ *smeitawi/temsatawi*
passive *(adj.)* ብዘይ ምኽንያት *bzeymknyat*
passport *(n.)* ፓስፖርት *pasport*
past *(adj.)* ሕሉፍ *hluf*
pasta *(n.)* ባስታ *basta*
paste *(n.)* ለጠፈ *letefe*
pastel *(n.)* ባህላዊ መግቢ ላቲን ኣመሪካ *bahlawi megbi latin amrica*
pasteurized *(adj.)* ምውዓይ መግቢ ባክተርያ ንምጥፋእ *mwuay megbi bakteriya nmtfae*
pastime *(n.)* ሕሉፍ ሰዓት *hluf seat*
pastor *(n.)* ካህን *kahn*
pastoral *(adj.)* መንፈሳዊ *menfesawi*
pastry *(n.)* ቤት ሕብስቲ *biet hbsti*
pasture *(n.)* ግራት መቐለቢ ጥሪት *grat meqlebi trit*
pasty *(n.)* ብሑቕ መሰል *bque mesl*
pat *(v.)* ፍኩስ ጽፍዒት *fkus xfeit*
patch *(n.)* ምልጋብ/ምስፋይ *mlab/msfay*
patchy *(adj.)* ልጋባዊ/ስፋይምፋይ *lgabwi/sfaymfay*
patent *(n.)* መኽበሪ መሰል ሰነድ *mekberi mesel sened*
paternal *(adj.)* ኣቦኣዊ *aboawi*
paternity *(n.)* ኣቦነት *abonet*
path *(n.)* ኣጋር መንገዲ *agar mengedi*
pathetic *(adj.)* ዘደንግጽ *zedengx*
pathology *(n.)* ስርዓተ መጽናዕቲ ሕማም *srate mxnaeti hmam*
pathos *(n.)* ስምዒት ሓዘን *smeit hazen*
patience *(n.)* ትዕግስቲ *tegsti*
patient *(n.)* ሕሙም *hmum*
patient *(adj.)* ዕጉስ *egus*
patio *(n.)* መረባ *mereba*
patisserie *(n.)* ቤት ሕብስቲ *biet hbsti*
patriarch *(n.)* ዝለዓለ ክፋል ቅሽነት *zleale kfal qshnet*
patricide *(n.)* ቅትለተ-ኣቦ *qtlet abo*
patrimony *(n.)* ዝተወርሰ መሰል *ztewerse mesel*
patriot *(n.)* ሓርበኛ *harbena*
patriotic *(adj.)* ሓርበኛዊ *harbenawi*
patriotism *(n.)* ሓርበኛነት *harbenanet*
patrol *(v.)* ቃፊር/ዋርድያ *qafir/wardiya*
patron *(n.)* ዕሚል/ደጋፊ ተኸራኻሪ *amil/degafi tekerakari*
patronage *(n.)* ዓማዊል *amawil*

patronize *(v.)* **ደጋፊ/ዓሚል ሙኻን** *degafi/amil mkan*
pattern *(n.)* **ሓረግ/ቅዲ** *hareg/qdi*
patty *(n.)* **ክቢ** *kbi*
paucity *(n.)* **ምናስ** *mnas*
paunch *(n.)* **ጉስጢ** *gusti*
pauper *(n.)* **ድኻ/በተኽ** *dka/betek*
pause *(n.)* **ሓጺር ዕረፍቲ** *haxir erefti*
pave *(v.)* **ጽሪጉ** *xerigu*
pavement *(n.)* **ምጽራግ** *mxrag*
pavilion *(n.)* **ዳስ** *das*
paw *(n.)* **ግናዕ ኢድ** *gnae ide*
pawn *(n.)* **ትሕጃ ምትሓዝ** *thja mthaz*
pawnbroker *(n.)* **ተሓዚ ትሕጃ** *tehazi thja*
pay *(v.)* **ምኽፋል** *mkfal*
payable *(n.)* **ተኽፋሊ** *tekefali*
payee *(n.)* **ከፋሊ** *kefali*
payment *(n.)* **ክፍሊት** *kflit*
pea *(n.)* **ዓይኒ ዓተር** *ayni ater*
peace *(n.)* **ሰላም** *selam*
peaceable *(adj.)* **ሰላማዊ** *selamawi*
peaceful *(adj.)* **ሰላማዊ** *selamawi*
peach *(n.)* **ኩኽ** *kuk*
peacock *(n.)* **ተባዕታይ ጣዎስ** *tabaetay taewa*
peahen *(n.)* **ኣንስተይቲ ጣዎስ** *ansteyti taewa*
peak *(n.)* **ጥርዚ** *trzi*
peaky *(adj.)* **ጥርዛዊ** *trzawi*
peal *(n.)* **ድምጺ ደወል** *dmxi dewel*
peanut *(n.)* **ፋል** *ful*
pear *(n.)* **ናይ ሜለ ገረብ** *nay mele gereb*
pearl *(n.)* **ሉል** *lul*
peasant *(n.)* **ሃገረሰብ** *hagereseb*
peasantry *(n.)* **ገባሮ** *gebaro*
pebble *(n.)* **ጸጸር** *xexer*
pecan *(n.)* **ፔካን** *pekan*
peck *(v.i.)* **ወጋእ** *wge*
peculiar *(adj.)* **ፍሉይ** *fluy*
pedagogue *(n.)* **መምህር ቆልዑ** *memher qoleu*
pedagogy *(n.)* **ምምህርና** *mmhrna*
pedal *(n.)* **ዝርገጽ መቆጻጸሪ ማሺን** *zrgex mekoxaxeri mashen*
pedant *(n.)* **ሰራዊት** *serawit*
pedantic *(adj.)* **ፈለጥኩ በሃሊ** *feletku bhali*
peddle *(v.)* **ቤላሮባ/እንዳዘረ ዝሸቅጥ** *beilaroba*
pedestal *(n.)* **ናይ ክብሪ ቦታ** *nay kbri bota*
pedestrian *(n.)* **ኣጋር** *agar*
pedicure *(n.)* **ኣላዪ ኣእጋርን ኣጻብዕቲ ኣእጋርን** *alayi aearnaxabetn aegarn*
pedigree *(n.)* **ዝርዝር ዓሌት** *zrzr alet*
pedlar *(n.)* **እንዳዘረ ዝሸቅጥ** *enazere zshket*
pedometer *(n.)* **ርሕቀት ጉዕዞ ዓቃኒት** *rhket guezo aqanit*
peek *(v.)* **ሰረቕካ ምራይ** *seriqka mray*
peel *(n.)* **ምቕላጥ/ምቕራፍ** *mqlat/mqrf*
peep *(v.)* **ሕሹኽሹኽ** *hshukshuk*
peer *(n.)* **መዘና** *mzena*
peer *(v.)* **ቅልቅል ምባል** *qlql mbal*
peerage *(n.)* **ምድብ መዘና** *mdb mezena*
peerless *(adj.)* **መዘና ኣንበ** *mezena albo*

peg *(n.)* ተካባኖ *tekabano*
pejorative *(adj.)* ኣንነኣኣሲ *aneaasi*
pelican *(n.)* ዘርኢ ዑፍ *zrei euf*
pellet *(n.)* ዕኳር *ekuar*
pelmet *(n.)* መጋረጃ *megareja*
pelt *(v.)* ቆርበት ወዲ ሰብ *qorbet wedi seb*
pelvis *(n.)* ጎሎ *golo*
pen *(n.)* ቢሮ *biro*
penal *(adj.)* ገበናዊ *gebenawi*
penalize *(v.)* ምቕጻዕ *mqxae*
penalty *(n.)* መቕጻዕቲ *mqxaeti*
penance *(n.)* ንስሓ *nsha*
penchant *(n.)* ፍትወት/መቀረት *ftwet/meqeret*
pencil *(n.)* ርሳስ *rsas*
pendant *(n.)* መንጠልጥሎ *menteltlo*
pendent *(adj.)* ዝተጠልጠለ *ztenteltele*
pending *(adj.)* ይጽናሕ ዝተባህለ *yxnah ztebahle*
pendulum *(n.)* ምንጥልጣል *mntltal*
penetrate *(v.)* ውሽጢ ምእታው *wshti metaw*
penetration *(n.)* ንውሽጢ ምእታው *nwsheti metw*
penguin *(n.)* ውሽጢ ምእታው *wsheti metaw*
peninsula *(n.)* ወሽመጥ *weshmt*
penis *(n.)* መሸሊት ወዲ ተባዕታይ *mesheit nay wedi tebaetay*
penitent *(adj.)* ተናሳሒ *tenasahi*
penniless *(adj.)* ሳንቲም ዘይብሉ *santim zeyblu*
penny *(n.)* ሳንቲም *santim*
pension *(n.)* ኣበል ጥሮታ/መዕረፍ ኣጋይሽ *abel trota/meref agaysh*
pensioner *(n.)* ጥሮተኛ *trotena*
pensive *(adj.)* ምትካዝ *mtkaz*
pentagon *(n.)* በዓል ሓሙሽተ መኣዝን *beal hamushte meazn*
penthouse *(n.)* ኣፓርታማ ኣብ ዝለዓለ ደርቢ ዝርከብ *apartama ab zleale derbi*
penultimate *(adj.)* ዳርጋ/ኣብ መወዳእታ *darga/ab mewedet a*
people *(n.)* ሰባት *sebat*
pepper *(n.)* ፐፐሮኒ *peperoni*
peppermint *(n.)* ሜንታ ፐፐሮኒ *mienta peperoni*
peptic *(adj.)* ሓጋዚ ምሕቃቕ መግቢ *hagazi mhqaq megbi*
per *(prep.)* ንነፍሲ ወከፍ *nnefsi wekef*
perambulate *(v.t.)* ጅረሎ *jerelo*
perceive *(v.)* ምርዳእ *mrdae*
percentage *(n.)* ሚእታዊት *mietawit*
perceptible *(adj.)* ዝርዳእ *zrdae*
perception *(n.)* ርደኢት *rdeit*
perceptive *(adj.)* ተረዳኢ *teredaei*
perch *(n.)* ልዕል ዝበለ *lel zbele*
percipient *(adj.)* መስተውዓሊ *mestewali*
percolate *(v.)* ልሒኹ *lhiku*
percolator *(n.)* ዘቋቒት ቡን *zequaqit bun*
perdition *(n.)* ሴኦል *sieol*
perennial *(adj.)* ጸናሒ *xenahi*
perfect *(adj.)* ፍጹም *fxum*
perfection *(n.)* ፍጹምነት *fxumnet*
perfidious *(adj.)* መታለሊ *metaleli*

perforate *(v.)* በሳሲው *besasieu*
perforce *(adv.)* ናይ ንግዲ *nay ngdi*
perform *(v.)* ምትግባር *mtgbar*
performance *(n.)* ትግባሬ *tgbarie*
performer *(n.)* ኣተግባሪ/ምረኢት ኣርኣዪ *ategbari/mreit arayi*
perfume *(n.)* ጨና *chena*
perfume *(adv.)* ጨና ምልካይ *chena mlkay*
perfunctory *(adj.)* ካብ ክሳድ ንላዕሊ *kab ksad nlaeli*
perhaps *(adv.)* ምናልባሽ *mnalbash*
peril *(n.)* ሓደጋ *hadega*
perilous *(adj.)* ሓደገኛ *hadegena*
period *(n.)* እዋን/ዘበን *ewan/zeben*
periodic *(adj.)* እዋናዊ/ዘበናዊ *ewanawi/zebenawi*
periodical *(adj.)* እዋናዊ/ዘበናዊ *ewanawi/zebenawi*
periphery *(n.)* ጨጫፍ *chechaf*
perish *(v.)* ሞይቱ/መሽሚሹ *moytu/meshmishu*
perishable *(adj.)* ተበላሻዋይ *tebalashaway*
perjure *(v.)* ብሓሶት ምምስካር *bhasot mmskar*
perjury *(n.)* ብሓሶት ምምሓል *bhasot mmhal*
perk *(v.)* ምስራሕ *msrah*
perky *(adj.)* ንቑሕ *nquh*
permanence *(n.)* ቀዋምነት *qewamnet*
permanent *(adj.)* ቀዋሚ *qwami*
permeable *(adj.)* ማይ ዝወጥጥ *may zwett*
permissible *(adj.)* ዝፍቀድ *zfqed*
permission *(n.)* ፍቓድ *fqad*
permissive *(adj.)* ዝናሕነሐ *znahnehe*
permit *(v.)* ኣፍቀደ *afqede*
permutation *(n.)* ኣለዋዊጥካ ምቕማጥ *alewawitka mqmat*
pernicious *(adj.)* ጠንቂ *tenqi*
perpendicular *(adj.)* ቀጥ በለ *qet bele*
perpetrate *(v.)* ገበን ምፍጻም *geben mfxam*
perpetual *(adj.)* መፈጸምታ ዘይብሉ *mefexemta zeyblu*
perpetuate *(v.t.)* ሓሊኻ ምጽናሕ *halika mxnae*
perplex *(v.)* ኣደናጊሩ *adenagiru*
perplexity *(n.)* ምድንጋር *mdngar*
perquisite *(n.)* ካብ መሃያ ወጻኢ ዝርከብ *kab mehaya wexaei zrkeb*
Perry *(n.)* ስም ከተማ *sm ketema*
persecute *(v.)* ምጽቃጥ *mxqat*
persecution *(n.)* ቈጸራ ከዋኽብቲ *qoxera kewakbti*
perseverance *(n.)* ድሕር ዘይምባል *dhr zeymbal*
persevere *(v.i.)* ንድሕሪት ዘይብል *ndhrit zeybl*
persist *(v.)* ጸንዐ *xene*
persistence *(n.)* ምጽናዕ *mxnae*
persistent *(adj.)* ጽኑዕ *xnue*
person *(n.)* ሰብ *seb*
persona *(n.)* ገጸ ባህሪ *gexe bahri*
personage *(n.)* ህቡብ ሰብ *hbub seb*
personal *(adj.)* ብሕታዊ *bhtawi*
personality *(n.)* ጠባይ *tebay*
personification *(n.)* ኣብነትነት *abnetnet*
personify *(v.)* ኣብነታዊ *abnetawi*

personnel *(n.)* ሰራሕተኛታት *serahtenatat*
perspective *(n.)* ሓሳባት *hasabat*
perspicuous *(adj.)* ርዱእ *rdue*
perspiration *(n.)* ርሃጽ *rhax*
perspire *(v.t.)* ምርሃጽ *mrhax*
persuade *(v.)* ኣእመነ *aemene*
persuasion *(n.)* ምእማን *meman*
pertain *(v.)* ጠቓሚ/ኣባል ሙኳን *teqami/abal mukuan*
pertinent *(adj.)* ኣድላዪ *adlayi*
perturb *(v.)* ሃዊኹ *hawiku*
perusal *(n.)* ብጥንቃቐ ምንባብ *btnqaqe mnbab*
peruse *(v.)* ብጥንቃቐ ኣንቢቡ *btnqaqe anbibu*
pervade *(v.)* በኪሉ *bekilu*
perverse *(adj.)* ህልኽ *hlk*
perversion *(n.)* ምውራድ *mwrad*
perversity *(n.)* ህልኸኛ *hlkena*
pervert *(v.)* መገዲ ምቕያር *megedi mqyar*
pessimism *(n.)* ቅኑዕ ዘይምሕሳብ *qnue zeymhsab*
pessimist *(n.)* ቅኑዕ ዘይሓስብ *qnuo hasab*
pessimistic *(adj.)* ተስፋ ዘይምግባር *tesfa zeymgbar*
pest *(n.)* ባልዕ *ble*
pester *(v.)* ምርባሽ *mrbash*
pesticide *(n.)* ጸረ ባልዕ *xere ble*
pestilence *(n.)* ተላባዒ *telabaei*
pet *(n.)* ናይ ገዛ እንስሳ *nay geza enssa*
petal *(n.)* ክፋል ዕንባባ *kfal onbaba*
petite *(adj.)* ቀጣን/ነእሽቶ *qetan/neshto*
petition *(n.)* ጥርዓን *tran*
petitioner *(n.)* ጠራዓይ *teraay*
petrify *(v.)* ኣንቂጹ *anqixu*
petrol *(n.)* በንዚን *benzin*
petroleum *(n.)* ነዳዲ ዘይቲ *nedadi zyti*
petticoat *(n.)* ንይ ውሽጢ ክዳን *nay wshti kdan*
pettish *(adj.)* ሕማቕ ጠባይ *hmaq tebay*
petty *(adj.)* ዘይረብሕ *zeyrebh*
petulance *(n.)* ኲራ *kuara*
petulant *(adj.)* ኮርፋፍ *korfaf*
phantom *(n.)* ረቂቕ መንፈስ *reqiq menfes*
pharmaceutical *(adj.)* መድሃኒታዊ *medhanitawi*
pharmacist *(n.)* ቀማሚ መድሃኒት *qemami medhanit*
pharmacy *(n.)* ቤት መድሃኒት *biet medhanit*
phase *(n.)* ደረጃ *dereja*
phenomenal *(adj.)* ክስተታዊ *kstetawi*
phenomenon *(n.)* ክስተት *kstet*
phial *(n.)* ብልቃጥ *blqat*
philanthropic *(adj.)* ወሃቢ *wehabi*
philanthropist *(n.)* ግብረ ሰናያዊ *gbresenayawi*
philanthropy *(n.)* ግብረ ሰናይ *gbre senay*
philately *(n.)* ቴንብር ዓቃቢ *tienbr aqabi*
philological *(adj.)* ናይ ዛንታ ስነ ጽሑፍ *nay zanta sne xhuf*
philologist *(n.)* ስነ ጽሑፋዊ ዛንታ *sne xhufawi zanta*
philology *(n.)* ስነ ጽሑፍ ዛንታ *sne xhufawi zanta*

philosopher *(n.)* ተፈላሳፊ *tefelasafi*
philosophical *(adj.)* ፍልስፍናዊ *flsfnawi*
philosophy *(n.)* ፍንስፍና *flsfna*
phlegmatic *(adj.)* ግዲ ዘይብሉ *gdi zeyblu*
phobia *(n.)* ፍቭያ *fovya*
phoenix *(n.)* ፊነክስ *fneks*
phone *(n.)* ስልኪ *seli*
phonetic *(adj.)* መጽናዕቲ ድምጺ ልሳን *mexnaeti dmxi lsan*
phosphate *(n.)* ፎዝፌት *fozfeyet*
phosphorus *(n.)* ናይ ንግሆ ኮኾብ *nay ngho kokob*
photo *(n.)* ስእሊ *seli*
photocopy *(n.)* ፍቶ ኮፒ *foto kopi*
photograph *(n.)* ስእሊ *seli*
photographer *(n.)* ሰኣሊ *seali*
photographic *(adj.)* ስእላዊ *selawi*
photography *(n.)* ጥበብ ስእሊ *tbeb seli*
photostat *(n.)* ፎቶ ኮፒ *foto kopi*
phrase *(n.)* ሓረግ *hareg*
phraseology *(n.)* ኣዘራርባ *azerarba*
physical *(adj.)* ኣካላዊ ተፈጥሮ *akalawi tefetro*
physician *(n.)* ፈዋሲ *fewasi*
physics *(n.)* ፊዚክስ *fizkis*
physiognomy *(n.)* ደጋዊ ትረኢት *degawi treit*
physiotherapy *(n.)* ፊዝዮተራፒ *fizyoterapi*
physique *(n.)* መሸከል *meshekel*
pianist *(n.)* ተጻዋታይ ፒያኖ *texawatay piyano*
piano *(n.)* ፒያኖ *piyano*
piazza *(n.)* በረንዳ *beranda*
pick *(v.)* ኣልዓለ *alale*
picket *(n.)* ሰላማዊ ሰልፊ ጌሩ *selemawi selfi gieru*
pickings *(n.)* ምልዓል *mlal*
pickle *(n.)* ከቢድ ኩነታት *kebidkunetat*
picnic *(n.)* ኣብ ደገ ዝብላዕ መኣዲ *ab dege zblae meadi*
pictograph *(n.)* ስእላዊ መግለጺ *selawi meglexi*
pictorial *(adj.)* ንስእሊ ዝምልከት *asali zmlket*
picture *(n.)* ስእሊ/ፊልም *seli/filmi*
picturesque *(adj.)* ምሩጽ ስእሊ *mrux seli*
pie *(n.)* ፓይ *pay*
piece *(n.)* ጩራም *chram*
piecemeal *(adv.)* በብቁሩብ *bebequrub*
pier *(n.)* ናይ ወደብ መድረኽ *nay wedeb mdreke*
pierce *(v.)* ሱቕሬን *suqren*
piety *(n.)* ሃይማኖተኛ *haymanotena*
pig *(n.)* ሓሸማ *hashema*
pigeon *(n.)* ርግቢት *rgbit*
pigeonhole *(n.)* ናይ ደብዳበ መግለጺ *nay debdabe mglexi*
piggery *(n.)* መፍረ ሓሰማ *mfre hasema*
pigment *(n.)* ሕብሪ ዋሃዮ *hbri wahiyo*
pigmy *(n.)* ድንኪ *dnki*
pike *(n.)* ጬማራ *čmara*
pile *(n.)* ኩምራ *kumra*
pilfer *(v.)* ምስራቕ *msraq*

pilgrim *(n.)* **ሃይማኖታዊ ቦታታት ዝበጽሕ** *haymanotawi botatat zbxh*
pilgrimage *(n.)* **ንግደት** *ngdet*
pill *(n.)* **ከኒና** *kenina*
pillar *(n.)* **ዓምዲ** *amdi*
pillow *(n.)* **መተርኣስ** *meteras*
pilot *(n.)* **ፓይሎት** *paylot*
pimple *(n.)* **ፈጸጋ** *fexega*
pin *(n.)* **ዓይኒ ዘይብሉ መርፍእ** *ayni zeyblu mefe*
pincer *(n.)* **ወረጦ** *wereto*
pinch *(v.)* **ቆንጠጠ** *qontete*
pine *(v.)* **ሃረፈ** *harefe*
pineapple *(n.)* **ኣናናስ** *ananas*
pink *(adj.)* **ሮዛ** *roza*
pinnacle *(n.)* **ሓፍ ዝበለ ብርኪ** *ḧaf zbele brki*
pinpoint *(v.)* **ብልክዕ ምምልካት** *bmelke mmlkat*
pint *(n.)* **1/8 ጃሎን** *1/8 jalon*
pioneer *(n.)* **ቀዳምነት ዝሓዘ** *qedamnety zhaze*
pious *(adj.)* **ዘይሰምር** *zeysemr*
pipe *(n.)* **ትቦ** *tubo*
pipette *(n.)* **ምንቅስቃስ ፈሳሲ ዝጠቅም መሳርሒ** *mnqsqas fesasi zṫekm mesarḧi*
piquant *(adj.)* **ሰሓቢ** *seḧabi*
pique *(n.)* **ስምዒት ሕማም** *smeit hmam*
piracy *(n.)* **ኣብ ባሕሪ ስርቂ** *ab bahri srqi*
pirate *(n.)* **ገበንነኛ ኣብ ባሕሪ ዝዝርፍ** *gebenña ab baḧri zzrf*
pistol *(n.)* **ሽጉጥ** *shguẗ*
piston *(n.)* **ፒስቶን** *piston*
pit *(n.)* **ጉድጓድ** *gudgad*
pitch *(n.)* **ኣገዳሲ ኣካል** *agedasi akal*
pitcher *(n.)* **የእታዊ** *yeètawi*
piteous *(adj.)* **ዘሕዝን** *zeḧzn*
pitfall *(n.)* **ዘይፍለጥ ጸገም** *zeyflet xegem*
pitiful *(adj.)* **ዘደንግጽ** *zedengx*
pitiless *(adj.)* **ድንጋጸ ዘይብሉ** *dngaxe zeyblu*
pity *(n.)* **ድንጋጸ** *dngaxe*
pivot *(n.)* **ተሽከርኪሩ** *teshkerkiru*
pivotal *(adj.)* **ተሽከርካሪ** *teshkerkari*
pixel *(n.)* **ስእሊ ዝፈጥር ንሽተይ ነጠብጣብ ኣብ ኮምፒተር** *sèli zfeẗr nèshtey neẗebẗab nay kompiter*
pizza *(n.)* **ፒሳ** *pisa*
placard *(n.)* **ሓበሬታ** *ḧberieta*
placate *(v.)* **ምዝሓል** *maḧzel*
place *(n.)* **መንበሪ ቦታ** *menberi bot*
placement *(n.)* **መቀመጢ** *meqemeẗ*
placid *(adj.)* **ሰላማዊ** *selamawi*
plague *(n.)* **ለበዳ** *lebeda*
plain *(adj.)* **ጎልጎል** *golgol*
plaintiff *(n.)* **ከሳሳይ** *kesasy*
plaintive *(adj.)* **ናይ ሓዘን** *nay hazen*
plait *(n.)* **ቁኖ** *quno*
plan *(n.)* **መደብ** *medeb*
plane *(n.)* **ነፋሪት** *nefarit*
planet *(n.)* **ፕላኔት** *planiet*
planetary *(adj.)* **ናይ ፕላኔታት** *nay planatan*
plank *(n.)* **ደጋፊ** *degafi*
plant *(n.)* **ተኽሊ** *teḱli*
plantain *(n.)* **ፕላንተይን** *planteyn*

plantation *(n.)* ተኽሊ ዝተተኽለሉ ቦታ *teḱli zteteḱlelu bota*

plaque *(n.)* ብእምኒ ዝተቐርጸ መጋየጺ *bèmni zteq̈erexe megayexi*

plaster *(n.)* መለጠፊ *meleẗfi*

plastic *(n.)* ፕላስቲክ *plastik*

plate *(n.)* ቢያቲ *biyati*

plateau *(n.)* ሮራ *rora*

platelet *(n.)* ፕላተሌት *planiet*

platform *(n.)* መድረኽ *medreḱ*

platinum *(n.)* ሕብሪ ሓጺን *ḧbri ḧxin*

platonic *(adj.)* ዘይጾታዊ ርክብ *zeyxotawi ckb*

platoon *(n.)* ሰብ ኣልቦ ተሽከርከርቲ *seb anbo teshkerkerti*

platter *(n.)* ጸፊሕ ሸሓኒ *xefiḧ sheḧani*

plaudits *(n.)* ምንጭብጫብ *mnčbčab*

plausible *(adj.)* ብቑዕ *bq̈uë*

play *(v.i.)* ጸወታ *xeweta*

player *(n.)* ተጻዋታይ *texawatay*

playground *(n.)* መጽጻወቲ ቦታ *mexaweti bota*

playwright *(n.)* ጸሓፊ ቲያትር *xeḧafi tyatr*

plaza *(n.)* ክፉት መአከቢ ቦታ *kfut makebi bota*

plea *(n.)* ምኽንያት *mḱnyat*

plead *(v.)* ምግላጽ ምጉት *mglax mgut*

pleasant *(adj.)* ፍሕሹው *fḧshuwnet*

pleasantry *(n.)* ናይ ቀልዲ ኣዘራርባ *nay qeldi azerazba*

please *(v.)* ብኽብረት *bḱbret*

pleasure *(n.)* ፍስሃ *fsha*

pleat *(n.)* ሸንሸነ *shenshene*

plebeian *(adj.)* ናይ ሓባር ሰብ *nay ḧabar seb*

plebiscite *(n.)* ሪፈረንዶም *riferendom*

pledge *(n.)* ቃል ምእታው *qal mètaw*

plenty *(n.)* ዕጽፊ *ëxfi*

plethora *(n.)* ምልኡነት *mleunet*

pliable *(adj.)* ተዓጻጻፊ *teëaxaxafi*

pliant *(adj.)* ተዓጻፊ *teëaxaxafi*

pliers *(n.)* ፒንሳ *pinsa*

plight *(n.)* ጽቡቅ ጥዕና *xbuq̈ ẗëna*

plinth *(n.)* ሰረት *seret*

plod *(v.)* ዝሑል ምንቅስቓስ *zḧul mnqsqas*

plot *(n.)* ምስእጢራዊ መደብ *msẗirawi medeb*

plough *(n.)* ምሕራስ *mḧrasq̈a*

ploughman *(n.)* ሓረስታይ *ḧarestay*

ploy *(n.)* ስርሒት *srḧit*

pluck *(v.)* መሽጎጥ/ብሓይሊ ምውጻእ *meshgoẗ /bḧayli*

plug *(n.)* ሶኬት *sokiet*

plum *(n.)* ካብ ክንቲት ዝተሰርሐ መጋየጺ *kab kntit zteserḧe*

plumage *(n.)* ክንቲት ዑፍ *kntit ëuf*

plumb *(v.)* ዓረር *ärer*

plumber *(n.)* ድራውሊኮ *drawliko*

plume *(n.)* ሓፋር *ḧafar*

plummet *(v.)* ምንቛት *mnq̈uat*

plump *(adj.)* ረጕድ *reguied*

plunder *(v.)* ዘረፋ *zerefa*

plunge *(v.)* ተደቕደቐ *tedeq̈deq̈e*

plural *(adj.)* ካብ ሓደ ንላዕሊ *kab ḧde alaëli*

plurality *(n.)* ድራብነት *drabnet*
plus *(n.)* ተደመሮ *tedemero*
plush *(n.)* ክቡር *kbur*
ply *(n.)* ቀጸላ *qexela*
pneumatic *(adj.)* ኣየር ዝመስል *ayer zmesl*
pneumonia *(n.)* ነድሪ ሳንቡእ *nedri sanbuè*
poach *(v.)* ልስሉስ ሙኳን *lslus muḱuan*
pocket *(n.)* ጁባ *ĵuba*
pod *(n.)* ለቆታ *leqota*
podcast *(n.)* ፖድካስት *podkast*
podium *(n.)* መድረኽ *medreḱ*
poem *(n.)* ግጥሚ *gẗmi*
poet *(n.)* ገጣሚ *geẗami*
poetry *(n.)* ፍርያት ግጥሚ *fryat gẗmi*
poignancy *(n.)* ኣደንጋጽነት *adengaxnet*
poignant *(adj.)* ስምዒት ዘንቀሳቕስ *smëit zenqesaqs*
point *(n.)* ነጥቢ/ኣመልክት *neẗbi/amelkt*
pointing *(n.)* ምምልካት *mmlkat*
pointless *(adj.)* ትርጉም ዘይብሉ *trgum zeyblu*
poise *(n.)* ብዘይ ምንቅስቓስ *bzey mnqsq̈as*
poison *(n.)* መርዚ *wečeče merzi*
poisonous *(adj.)* መርዛም *merzam*
poke *(v.)* ምውጋእ *mwgai*
poker *(n.)* ወጋኢ *weraei*
poky *(adj.)* ጸቢብ *xebib*
polar *(adj.)* ናይ ዕንጨይቲ *nay ënčeyti*
pole *(n.)* ፓሎ/ዕንጨይቲ *palo/ënčeyti*
polemic *(n.)* ምጉት *mgut*
police *(n.)* ፖሊስ *polis*
policeman *(n.)* ፖሊስ *polis*
policy *(n.)* መምርሒ *memrḧi*
polish *(n.)* ምውልዋል/ፖላንዳዊ *mwlwal/polandawi*
polite *(adj.)* ምቕሉል *mq̈lul*
politeness *(n.)* ምቕልልና *gemel*
politic *(adj.)* ናይ ፖለቲካ *nay polotika*
political *(adj.)* ፖለቲካዊ *polotikawi*
politician *(n.)* ፖለቲከኛ *poletikeňa*
politics *(n.)* ፖለቲክስ *poletiks*
polity *(n.)* ፖለቲቻዊ ጥርናፈ *poletikeňawi ẗrnafe*
poll *(n.)* መምረጺ ቦታ *memrexi bota*
pollen *(n.)* ጽገ ዕንባባ *xge ënbaba*
pollster *(n.)* ምርጫ ዘካይድ *mrča zekayd*
pollute *(v.)* ምብካል *mbkal*
pollution *(n.)* ብከላ *bkela*
polo *(n.)* ፖሎ *palo*
polyandry *(n.)* ብሓደ ግዜ ልዕሊ ሓደ ሰብኣይ ትምርያ ሰበይቲ *bḧde gzie lëli ḧade gzie sebay tmräw sebeyti*
polygamous *(adj.)* ብሓደ ግዜ ልዕሊ ሓደ ሰብኣይ/ሰበይቲ ተመርዓዊ *bḧde gzie lëli ḧade gzie sebay/sebeti temeräwi*
polygamy *(n.)* ብሓደ ግዜ ልዕሊ ሓደ ሰብኣይ/ሰበይቲ ምምርዓው *bḧde gzie lëli ḧade gzie sebay/sebeti mmräw*
polyglot *(adj.)* ብዙሕ ቋንቋ ዝዛረብ *bzuḧ quanq̈a zzareb*

polygraph *(n.)* ፖሊግራፍ *poligraf*
polytechnic *(n.)* ትምህርቲ ቴክኖሎጂ *tmhrti tieknoloĵi*
polytheism *(n.)* ንዝዙሓት ኣማልኽቲ ምምላኽ *nbzuḧat amalḱti mmlaḱ*
polytheistic *(adj.)* ንብዙሓት ኣማልኽቲ ዘምልኽ *nbzuḧat amalḱti zemlḱ*
pomegranate *(n.)* ጸሊም ቀይሕ ሕብሪ *xelim qeyḧ ḧbri*
pomp *(n.)* ድሙቕ ውራይ *dmuq̈ wray*
pomposity *(n.)* ጃህራ *ĵhra*
pompous *(adj.)* ምጅሃር *mĵhar*
pond *(n.)* ራህያ *rahya*
ponder *(v.)* ኣመዛዘነ *amezazene*
pontiff *(n.)* ቀሺ *qeshi*
pony *(n.)* ቅንጹብ ፈረስ *qnxub feres*
pool *(n.)* ንእሽተይ ቐላይ *mlkt neshtey q̈lay*
poor *(adj.)* ድኻ *dḱa*
poorly *(adv.)* ዘይእኹል ናብራ *zeyèḱul nabra*
pop *(v.)* ተጉ ምባል *tegiue mbal*
pope *(n.)* ጳጳስ *ṕaṕas*
poplar *(n.)* ፖፕላር *potlar*
poplin *(n.)* ዓይነት ጨርቂ *äynet čerqi*
populace *(n.)* ደቂ ባት *deqi bat*
popular *(adj.)* ተፈታዊ *tefetawi*
popularity *(n.)* ተፈታውነት *tefetawnet*
popularize *(v.)* ተፈታዊ ምግባር *tefetawi mgbar*
populate *(v.)* ምብዛሕ *mbzaḧ*
population *(n.)* ብዝሒ ህዝቢ *bzḧi hzbi*
populous *(adj.)* ብዙሕ ህዝቢ ዘለዎ *bzuḧ hzbi zelewo*
porcelain *(n.)* ሰራሕ ሸኽላ *sraḧ shḱla*
porch *(n.)* በረንዳ *berenda*
porcupine *(n.)* ቅንፍዝ *qnfz*
pore *(n.)* ናይ ቆርበት ኖኳል *nay qorbet noḱual*
pork *(n.)* ስጋ ሓሰማ *sga ḧasema*
pornography *(n.)* ፖርኖግራፊ *pornografi*
porridge *(n.)* ገዓት *geät*
port *(n.)* ወደብ *wedeb*
portable *(adj.)* ቀሊል *qelil*
portage *(n.)* ፖርቴጅ *portieĵ*
portal *(n.)* ኣፍደገ *afdege*
portend *(v.)* መጠንቀቒ *meẗenqeq̈i*
portent *(n.)* ምልክት *mlkt*
porter *(n.)* ረፋዕ *refaë*
portfolio *(n.)* መትሓዚ ገንዘብ *metḧazi genzeb*
portico *(n.)* መእተዊ ማዕጾ *meètewi maëxo*
portion *(n.)* ብጽሒት *bẗḧit*
portrait *(n.)* ቅብኣ *qba*
portraiture *(n.)* ቅብኣ ምቅባእ *qba mqbaè*
portray *(v.)* ቀብአ *qeba*
portrayal *(n.)* ምቅባእ *mqbaè*
pose *(v.)* ጠጠው ምባል *ẗeẗew mbal*
posh *(adj.)* ግሩም *grum*
posit *(v.)* ምቕማጥ *mq̈maẗ*
position *(n.)* ኣቀማምጣ *aqemamẗ*
positive *(adj.)* ኣወንታዊ *awentawi*
possess *(v.)* ወነነ *wenene*

possession *(n.)* ዋንነት *wannet*
possessive *(adj.)* ኣጋናዛቢ *aganazabi*
possibility *(n.)* ዝከኣል *zkeal*
possible *(adj.)* ተኽእሎ *teḱèlo*
post *(n.)* ምልጣፍ *mlẗaf*
post office *(n.)* ፖስጣ ቤት *posẗa biet*
postage *(n.)* ዋጋ ቴንብር *waga tienbr*
postal *(adj.)* ብፖስጣ *bposẗa*
postcard *(n.)* ካርተሊና *kartelina*
postcode *(n.)* ቁጽሪ ፖስጣ *quxri posẗ*
poster *(n.)* ፖስተር *poster*
posterior *(adj.)* መቐመጫ *meq̈emeča*
posterity *(n.)* ሰዓብቲ ወለዶ *seäabti weledo*
postgraduate *(n.)* ሕላፍ መመረቕታ *ḧlaf memereq̈ta*
posthumous *(adj.)* ደድሕሪ ሞት *dedḧri mot*
postman *(n.)* እንዳ ፖስጣ ዝሰርሕ *ènda posẗ zserḧ*
postmaster *(n.)* ምሕደራ እንዳ ፖስጣ *mḧdera ènda posẗa*
post-mortem *(n.)* መርመራ ኣስከሬን *mermera askegrien*
postpone *(v.)* ኣተሓላሊፉ *ateḧalalifu*
postponement *(n.)* ምትሕልላፍ *mtḧllaf*
postscript *(n.)* ድሕሪ መወዳእታ ዛንታ *dḧri mewedaèta zanta*
posture *(n.)* ኣቃውማ *aqawma*
pot *(n .)* ዕትሮ *ëtro*
potato *(n.)* ድንሽ *dnsh*
potency *(n.)* ዓቕሚ *ääq̈mi*
potent *(adj.)* ዘተኣማምን *zeteamamn*
potential *(adj.)* ዓቕሚ *ääq̈mi*
potentiality *(n.)* ዝብጻሕ ነገር *zbxaḧ neger*
potter *(v.)* ሰራሕ ካይላ *sraḧ kayla*
pottery *(n.)* ስርሓት ካይላ *srḧat kayla*
pouch *(n.)* ከረጢት *kereẗit*
poultry *(n.)* መፍረ ኣዕዋፍ *mefre aëwaf*
pounce *(v.)* ሃንደበት ምንጣር *handebet mnẗar*
pound *(n.)* ባጤራ እንግሊዝ *baẗiera èngliz*
pour *(v.)* ምቕዳሕ *mq̈daḧ*
poverty *(n.)* ድኽነት *dḱnet*
powder *(n.)* ሕሩጭ *ḧruč*
power *(n.)* ሓይሊ *ḧyli*
powerful *(adj.)* ሓያል *ḧeyal*
practicability *(n.)* ግብራውነት *gbrawnet*
practicable *(adj.)* ግብራዊ ዝኾነ *gbrawi zḱone*
practical *(adj.)* ግብራዊ *gbrawi*
practice *(n.)* ተግባር *tegbar*
practise *(v.)* ተላመደ *telamede*
practitioner *(n.)* ተላማዲ *telamadi*
pragmatic *(adj.)* ብእምነት ዘይኮነ ብኩነታት ዝሰርሕ *bèmnet zeykone bkunetat zserḧ*
pragmatism *(n.)* ፕራግማውነት *pragmawnet*
praise *(v.t.)* ምስጋና *msgana*
praline *(n.)* ፕራላይን *pralayn*
pram *(n.)* ጅረሎ *ĵrelo*
prank *(n.)* ምዝንጋዕ *mzngaë*
prattle *(v.)* ሃተፍተፍ *hateftef*

pray *(v.)* **ምጽላይ** *mxlay*
prayer *(n.)* **ጸሎት** *xelot*
preach *(v.)* **ምስባኽ** *msbaḱ*
preacher *(n.)* **ሰባኺ** *sebaḱi*
preamble *(n.)* **መቕድም** *meq̈dm*
precarious *(adj.)* **ዘየተኣማምን** *zeyeteamamn*
precaution *(n.)* **ጥንቃቐ** *ẗnqaq̈e*
precautionary *(adj.)* **ጥንቃቓዊ** *ẗnqaq̈awi*
precede *(v.)* **ኣቐዲሙ** *aq̈edimu*
precedence *(n.)* **ቀዳምነት** *qedemanet*
precedent *(n.)* **ምሳሌ ዘረኢ** *msalie zereei*
precept *(n.)* **ምኽሪ** *mḱri*
precinct *(n.)* **ክልል** *kll*
precious *(adj.)* **ብርቂ** *brqi*
precipitate *(v.)* **ኣንከባሊሉ** *ankebalilu*
precis *(n.)* **ኩምራ ማይን በረድን** *kumra mayn beredn*
precise *(adj.)* **ልክዕ** *lkë*
precision *(n.)* **ልክዕነት** *lkënet*
precognition *(n.)* **ናይ መጻኢ ፍልጠት** *nay mexaei flẗet*
precondition *(n.)* **ቅድመ ኹነት** *qdme kunet*
precursor *(n.)* **ዘበስር** *zebesr*
predator *(n.)* **ሃዳኒ እንስሳ** *hadali ènssa*
predecessor *(n.)* **ናይ ቀደም** *nay qedem*
predestination *(n.)* **ጽሕፍቶ** *xḧfto*
predetermine *(v.)* **ቅድመ ውሳነ** *qdme wsane*
predicament *(n.)* **ኣሸጋሪ ኩነታት** *ashegari kunetat*
predicate *(n.)* **ኣንቀጸ** *anqexe*
predict *(v.)* **ተነበየ** *tenebeye*
prediction *(n.)* **ትንቢት** *tnbit*
predominance *(n.)* **ቅድመ ዓብላልነት** *qdme äblalnet*
predominant *(adj.)* **ቅድመ ዓብላላዊ** *qdme äblalawi*
predominate *(v.)* **ቅድመ ምዕብላል** *qdme mëblal*
pre-eminence *(n.)* **ብልጫዊ** *blčawi*
pre-eminent *(adj.)* **ብልጫ** *blča*
pre-empt *(v.)* **ቀዲሙ ሒዙ** *qedimu ḧizu*
prefabricated *(adj.)* **ቀዲሙ ዝተሰርሐ** *qedimu zteserḧe*
preface *(n.)* **መባእታ** *mebaèta*
prefect *(n.)* **ኮማንደር** *komander*
prefer *(v.)* **መረጸ** *merexe*
preference *(n.)* **ምርጫ** *mrča*
preferential *(adj.)* **ምርጫዊ** *mrčawi*
preferment *(n.)* **ሹመት** *shumet*
prefix *(n.)* **ለቀበ** *leqebe*
pregnancy *(n.)* **ጥንሲ** *ẗnsi*
pregnant *(adj.)* **ጥንስቲ** *ẗnsti*
prehistoric *(adj.)* **ቅድመ ታሪኽ** *qdme tarik̈i*
prejudge *(v.)* **ቅድመ ፍርዲ** *qdme frdi*
prejudice *(n.)* **ኣገባብ ዘይብሉ ጽለኢ** *agebab zeyblu xlei*
prejudicial *(adj.)* **ሃሳዪ** *hasayi*
prelate *(n.)* **ላዕለዋይ ቀሺ** *laëleway qeshi*
preliminary *(adj.)* **ኣገዳሲ/ኣላላዪ** *agedasi/alalayi*
prelude *(n.)* **ድሮ** *dro*
premarital *(adj.)* *qdme merä*

premature *(adj.)* **ግዜኡ ዘይበጽሐ** *gzieeu zeybexḧe*
premeditate *(v.)* **ኣቀዲምካ ምሕሳብ** *aqedimka mḧsab*
premeditation *(n.)* **ቀዲምካ ምምዳብ** *qedimka mmdab*
premier *(adj.)* **ቀዳማይ /ላዕለዋይ** *qedamay/laëleway*
premiere *(n.)* **ቀዳማይ ፈነወ ፊልሚ** *qedamay felewe filmi*
premise *(n.)* **ኣቐዲሙ ዝተረቚሐ መሰረት ምጉት** *aq̈edimu ztereq̈uḧ meseret mgut*
premises *(n.)* **ኣቐዲሞም ዝተረቚሑ መሰረት ምጉት** *aq̈edimom ztereq̈uḧ meseret mgut*
premium *(n.)* **ዝለዓለ ሽልማት** *zleäale shlmat*
premonition *(n.)* **ሕማቅ ስምዒት** *ḧmaq smëit*
preoccupation *(n.)* **ዘሕስብ ነገር** *zeḧsb neger*
preoccupy *(v.)* **ምርስሳዕ** *mrssaë*
preparation *(n.)* **ምድላው** *mdlaw*
preparatory *(adj.)* **ቅድመ ምድላው** *qdme mdlaw*
prepare *(v.)* **ኣዳለወ** *adalewe*
preponderance *(n.)* **ካብ ኩሉ ዝበለጸ** *kab kulu zbelexe*
preponderate *(v.)* **ካብ ኩሉ በሊጹ** *kab kulu belixu*
preposition *(n.)* **መስተዋድድ** *mestewadd*
prepossessing *(adj.)* **ተፈታዊ** *tefetawi*
preposterous *(adj.)* **ዓንጀንጀል** *änĵelĵel*
prerequisite *(n.)* **ቅድመ ኹነት** *qdmi ḱunet*
prerogative *(n.)* **ስልጣን** *qdme*
presage *(v.)* **ከም ዝመጽእ ሓበረ** *kem zmexè ḧbere*
prescience *(n.)* **ፍልጠት ቅድመ ፍጻሜ** *flẗet qdme fxamie*
prescribe *(v.)* **ኣዘዘ** *azeze*
prescription *(n.)* **መአዘዚ መድሃኒት** *meazezi medhanit*
presence *(n.)* **ህላዌ** *hlawe*
present *(adj.)* **ናይ ሕጂ** *nay ḧĵi*
present *(n.)* **ህሉው** *hluw*
present *(v.)* **ኣቕረበ** *aq̈rebe*
presentation *(n.)* **ምቕራብ** *mq̈rab*
presently *(adv.)* **ኣብዚ እዋን** *abzi èwan*
preservation *(n.)* **ዕቃበ** *ëqabe*
preservative *(n.)* **ዓቃባዊ** *ëqabawi*
preserve *(v.)* **ዕቃበ** *ëqabe*
preside *(v.)* **ተቆጻጺሩ** *teqoxaxiru*
president *(n.)* **ፕረዘንት** *prezent*
presidential *(adj.)* **ፕረዘንታዊ** *prezentawi*
press *(v.)* **ጸቒጡ** *xeẗiẗu*
pressure *(n.)* **ጸቕጢ** *xeq̈iẗu*
pressurize *(v.)* **ጸቕጣዊ** *xeq̈ẗawi*
prestige *(n.)* **ክብረት/ፍሉጥ** *kbret/fluẗ*
prestigious *(adj.)* **ውሩይ** *wruy*
presume *(v.)* **ግምት** *gmt*
presumption *(n.)* **ግምታዊ** *gmtawi*
presuppose *(v.)* **ብግምት ምውሳን** *bgmt mwsan*
presupposition *(n.)* **ብግምት ውሳኔ** *bgmt wusalie*

pretence *(n.)* ምምሳል *mmsal*
pretend *(v.)* ኣምሰሉ *amselu*
pretension *(n.)* ኣለኹ ኣለኹ ኢሉ *aleḱu aleḱu eilu*
pretentious *(adj.)* ኣምሳሊ *amsali*
pretext *(n.)* ምስምስ *msms*
prettiness *(n.)* ጽባቐ *xbaq̈*
pretty *(adj.)* መልክዐኛ *melkäňa*
pretzel *(n.)* ጠዋይ *ẗway*
prevail *(v.)* ልዕሊ ኹሉ ሙኧን *lëli ḱulu muḱuan*
prevalence *(n.)* ኩነታት ልዕሊ ኹሉ ሙኧን *kunetat lëli ḱulu muḱuan*
prevalent *(adj.)* ዓብላሊ *äblali*
prevent *(v.)* ዓገተ *gete*
prevention *(n.)* ምዕጋት *mägat*
preventive *(adj.)* ዓጋታዊ *gatawi*
preview *(n.)* ፈተነ *fetene*
previous *(adj.)* ዝሓለፈ *zḧalefe*
prey *(n.)* ተሃዳኒ *tehadani*
price *(n.)* ዋጋ *waga*
priceless *(adj.)* ተበሃጊ ዘይሸየጥ ብዝኮነ ዋጋ *tebehagi zeyshyeẗ bzkone waga*
prick *(v.)* ንእሽቶ ነኺል *nèshto neḱual*
prickle *(n.)* ወግአ *wega*
pride *(n.)* ሓበን *ḧaben*
priest *(n.)* ቀሺ *qeshi*
priesthood *(n.)* ቀሽነት *qexri qeshnet*
prim *(adj.)* ፈራሕ *feraḧ*
primacy *(n.)* ቀዳማይ ምስራዕ *qedamay msraë*
primal *(adj.)* ቀዳማይ *qedamay*
primarily *(adv.)* ቀዳምነት *qedamnet*
primary *(adj.)* መባእታዊ *mebaètawi*
primate *(n.)* ሊቀ ፓፓስ *liqe papas*
prime *(adj.)* ብግዜ ቀዳማይ *brzie qedamay*
primer *(n.)* መጽሓፍ ንጀመርቲ *mexḧaf*
primeval *(adj.)* ቀዳማይ ዕድመ *qedamay ëdme*
primitive *(adj.)* ናይ ድሕሪት *nay dḧrit*
prince *(n.)* ወድ ንጉስ *wedi ngus*
princely *(adj.)* ናይ ወዲ ንጉሳዊ *nay wedi ngusawi*
princess *(n.)* ጓል ንጉስ *gual ngus*
principal *(adj.)* ዳይረክተር *dayrekter*
principal *(n.)* ጀማሪ *ĵemari*
principle *(n.)* መትከል *metkel*
print *(v.)* ሓተመ *ḧateme*
printer *(n.)* ሓታሚት *ḧatamit*
printout *(n.)* ዝተሓትመ ወረቐት *zteḧatme wereq̈et*
prior *(adj.)* ቅድሚ *qdmi*
priority *(n.)* ቀዳምነት *qedamnet*
priory *(n.)* ገዳም *gedam*
prism *(n.)* ፕሪዝም *prizm*
prison *(n.)* ቤት ማሕቡስ *biet maḧbus*
prisoner *(n.)* እሱር *èsur*
pristine *(adj.)* ዘይመጽጽ *zeymexx*
privacy *(n.)* ውልቃውነት *wlqawnet*
private *(adj.)* ውልቃዊ *wlqawi*
privation *(n.)* ድኽነት *dḱnet*
privatize *(n.)* መንግስታዊ ምቁጽጻር ናብ ብሕታዊ ምቅያር *mengsatawi mquxxar nab bḧtawi mq̈yar*

privilege *(n.)* ሓለፋታት *ḧlefatat*
privy *(adj.)* ጃህራ *ḧalefatat*
prize *(n.)* ሽልማት *shlmat*
pro *(n.)* ጥቕሚ *ẗq̈mi*
proactive *(adj.)* ገልተው *geltew*
probability *(n.)* ናይ ሙኳን ዕድል *nay muḱuan ëdl*
probable *(adj.)* ምናልባት *mnalbat*
probably *(adv.)* ምናልባት *mnalbat*
probate *(n.)* ኣጣለለ *aẗalele*
probation *(n.)* ኣመክሮ *amekro*
probationer *(n.)* ኣመኩሮኣዊ *amkuroawi*
probe *(n.)* ምቱኳይ *mtukuay*
probity *(n.)* ሓቅነት *ḧaqnet*
problem *(n.)* ሽርግ *shgr*
problematic *(adj.)* ሽርራዊ *shgrawi*
procedure *(n.)* ስርዓት *sräat*
proceed *(v.)* ንቅድሚት ኣምርሐ *nqdmit amrḧe*
proceedings *(n.)* ሜላ ኣሰራርሓ *miela aserarḧa*
proceeds *(n.)* ትርፊ ሰልዲ *trfi seldi*
process *(n.)* ምድላው *mdlaw*
procession *(n.)* ሰልፊ *selfi*
proclaim *(v.)* ኣፍሊጡ *afliẗu*
proclamation *(n.)* ኣዋጅ *awaĵ*
proclivity *(n.)* ዝንባለ *znbalie*
procrastinate *(v.)* ኣደናጎየ *adenagueye*
procrastination *(n.)* ምድንጓይ *mdnguay*
procreate *(v.)* ሓድጊ ገደፈ *ḧdgi gedefe*
procure *(v.)* ረኺቡ *reḱibu*
procurement *(n.)* ምዕዳግ *mëdag*
prod *(v.)* ውግእ ውግእ ኣቢሉ *wgè wgè abilu*
prodigal *(adj.)* ኣባኺኑ *abaḱinu*
prodigious *(adj.)* ገዚፍ *gezif*
prodigy *(n.)* ዘደንጹ *zedenxu*
produce *(v.)* ኣፍርዩ *afryu*
producer *(n.)* ኣፍራዪ *afrayi*
product *(n.)* ፍርያት *fryat*
production *(n.)* ምህርቲ *mhrti*
productive *(adj.)* ጠቓሚ *ẗeq̈ami*
productivity *(n.)* ውጽኢት /ምህርቲ *wxeit/mhrti*
profane *(adj.)* ኣርኪሱ *arkisu*
profess *(v.)* ኣሚኑ *amilu*
profession *(n.)* ሞያ *moya*
professional *(adj.)* በዓል ሞያ *beäl moya*
professor *(n.)* ፕሮፌሰር *profieser*
proficiency *(n.)* ጣቋ *ẗaq̈ua*
proficient *(adj.)* ጥቁው *ẗquw*
profile *(n.)* ትርፊ *trfi*
profit *(n.)* መኽሰብ *meḱseb*
profitable *(adj.)* መኽሰባዊ *meḱsebawi*
profiteering *(n.)* ሓድሕዳዊ መኽሰብ *ḧadḧdawi meḱseb*
profligacy *(n.)* ዘይተገዳስነት *zeytegedasnet*
profligate *(adj.)* ኣባኻኒ *abaḱani*
profound *(adj.)* ከቢድ *kebid*
profundity *(n.)* ክብደት *kbdet*
profuse *(adj.)* ብጣዕሚ ብዙሕ *bẗaëmi bzuḧ*
profusion *(n.)* ብርካተ *brkate*
progeny *(n.)* ትውልዲ *twldi*
prognosis *(n.)* ዕድል ናይ ምሕዋይ *ëdl nay mḧway*

prognosticate *(v.)* ምትንባይ *mtnbay*
programme *(n.)* መደብ *medeb*
progress *(n.)* ምምሕያሽ *mmḧyash*
progressive *(adj.)* ምምሕያሻዊ *mmḧyashawi*
prohibit *(v.)* ኣገደ *agede*
prohibition *(n.)* ምእጋድ *mègad*
prohibitive *(adj.)* ክቡር *kbur*
project *(n.)* ትልሚ *tlmi*
projectile *(n.)* ንቅድሚት ተደርበየ *nqdmit tederbeye*
projection *(n.)* በሊሕ ነገር *beliḧ neger*
projector *(n.)* ፕሮጀክቶር *proĵecter*
prolapse *(n.)* ካብ ቦታ ወጻኢ ምንቅስቓስ *kab bot wexaei mnqsq̈as*
proliferate *(v.)* ተራብሐ *terabḧe*
proliferation *(n.)* ምርባሕ *mrbaḧ*
prolific *(adj.)* ፈራዩ *ferayi*
prologue *(n.)* መቕድም *meq̈dm*
prolong *(v.)* ኣናውሐ *anawḧe*
prolongation *(n.)* ምንዋሕ *mnwaḧ*
promenade *(n.)* መሸራሸሪ ህዝቢ *mesherasheri hzbi*
prominence *(n.)* ጠቓሚ *ẗq̈ami*
prominent *(adj.)* በይኑ ዝወጸ *beynu zmexe*
promiscuous *(adj.)* ልኽስክስ *lḱsks*
promise *(n.)* ምምብጻዕ *mmbxaë*
promising *(adj.)* ተስፋ ዝወሃቦ *tesfa zwehabo*
promote *(v.)* ሹመት *shumet*
promotion *(n.)* ሽመት *shmet*
prompt *(v.)* ኣፍሊቑ *afliq̈u*
prompter *(n.)* ኣፍላቒ *aflaq̈i*
promulgate *(v.)* ኣውጺኡ *awxieu*
prone *(adj.)* ዝንባሌ *znbalie*
pronoun *(n.)* ኣፍሊጡ *afliẗu*
pronounce *(v.)* ኣድመጸ *admexe*
pronunciation *(n.)* ኣደማምጻ *ademamxa*
proof *(n.)* መረጋገጺ *meregagexi*
prop *(n.)* ዳጌፋ *dagiefa*
propaganda *(n.)* ስብከት *sbket*
propagate *(v.)* ምርብባሕ *mrbaḧ*
propagation *(n.)* ምንቅስቓስ ማዕበል *mnqsq̈as*
propel *(v.)* ሰደደ *sedede*
propeller *(n.)* ሽኽርክሪት *shḱrkrit*
proper *(adj.)* ግቡእ *gbuè*
property *(n.)* ርስቲ *rsti*
prophecy *(n.)* ትንቢት *tnbit*
prophesy *(v.)* ተነበየ *tenebeye*
prophet *(n.)* ነቢይ *nebie*
prophetic *(adj.)* ትንቢታዊ *tnbitawi*
propitiate *(v.)* ኣዝሒሉ *azḧilu*
proportion *(n.)* ማዕረ ምቅሊት *maëre mqlit*
proportional *(adj.)* ማዕራዊ ምቅሊት *maërawi mqlit*
proportionate *(adj.)* ብማዕረ *bmaëre*
proposal *(n.)* ሓሳብ *ḧsab*
propose *(v.)* ሓሳብ ምቕራብ *ḧsab mq̈rab*
proposition *(n.)* ሓሳብ *ḧsab*
propound *(v.)* ኣቕረቡ *aq̈ribu*
proprietary *(adj.)* በዓል ገዛ *beäl geza*
proprietor *(n.)* ዋና *wana*

propriety *(n.)* ናይ ሰብ ርስቲ *nay seb rsti*
prorogue *(v.)* ምንኳል *mnkual*
prosaic *(adj.)* ተራ *tera*
prose *(n.)* ጽሑፍ *xḧuf*
prosecute *(v.)* ናብ ሕጊ ኣቕሪቡ *nab ḧgi aq̈ribu*
prosecution *(n.)* ናብ ሕጊ ምቕራብ *nab ḧgi mq̈rab*
prosecutor *(n.)* ኣኽባር ሕጊ *ak̈bar ḧgi*
prospect *(n.)* ተስፋዊ *tesfawi*
prospective *(adj.)* ትጽቢታዊ *txbitawi*
prospectus *(n.)* መዝገብ መግለጺ ሓሳባት *mezgeb meglexi ḧasabat*
prosper *(v.)* በልጸገ *belxege*
prosperity *(n.)* ብልጽግና *blxgna*
prosperous *(adj.)* ብልጽግናዊ *blxgnawi*
prostate *(n.)* ፕሮስተይት *prosteyt*
prostitute *(n.)* ኣመንዝራ *amenzra*
prostitution *(n.)* ምንዝርና *mnzrna*
prostrate *(adj.)* ፕሮስተይት *prosteyt*
prostration *(n.)* ምሕሳው *mḧsaw*
protagonist *(n.)* ቀንዲ ተዋሳኢ *qendi tewasai*
protect *(v.)* ተኸላኸለ *tek̈lak̈ele*
protection *(n.)* ምክልኻል *mklk̈al*
protective *(adj.)* ተኸላኻላይ *tek̈elak̈alay*
protectorate *(n.)* ተኸላኻሊ *tek̈elak̈ali*
protein *(n.)* ፕሮቲን *protin*
protest *(n.)* ተቓውሞ *teq̈awmo*
protestation *(n.)* ተቓዋምነት *teq̈awamnet*
protocol *(n.)* እኩብ ሕግታት *èkub ḧgtat*
prototype *(n.)* መርኣዪ ፈተነ ምድላው *merayi fetene mdlaw*
protracted *(adj.)* ንለዊሕ ዝጸንሕ *newiḧ zxeniḧ*
protractor *(n.)* ነዊሕ ጸናሒ *newiḧ xenaḧi*
protrude *(v.)* ተወጥወጠ *teweẗweẗe*
proud *(adj.)* ኩሩዕ *kuruë*
prove *(v.)* ኣእመነ *aèmene*
provenance *(n.)* ኣውራጃነት *awraĵanet*
proverb *(n.)* እተባህለ *tebahle*
proverbial *(adj.)* ጽውጽዋይ *xwxway*
provide *(v.)* ምምጻእ *amxaè*
providence *(n.)* ፍቓድ ኣምላኽ *fq̈d amlak̈*
provident *(adj.)* መስተውዓሊ *mestewäli*
providential *(adj.)* ዕድለኛ *ëdleňa*
province *(n.)* ኣውራጃ *awraĵa*
provincial *(adj.)* ኣውራጃዊ *awraĵawi*
provision *(n.)* ኣስነቐ *asneq̈e*
provisional *(adj.)* ንእዋኑ ግን ምስ ግዜ ቖዋሚ *nèwanu gn ms gzie q̈owami*
proviso *(n.)* ምምጻእ *mmxaè*
provocation *(n.)* ሳዕቤን *saäbien*
provocative *(adj.)* ሳዕቤናዊ *saäbienawi*
provoke *(v.)* ኣስዓበ *asäbe*
prowess *(n.)* ብልሓት *blḧat*
proximate *(adj.)* ቅርበት *qrbet*
proximity *(n.)* ቅርበትነት *qrbetnet*

proxy *(n.)* ወኪል *wekil*
prude *(n.)* ጉርሒ *gurȟi*
prudence *(n.)* ምጉራሕ *mguraȟ*
prudent *(adj.)* ጥንቃቐ *mẗnqaq̈*
prudential *(adj.)* ጥንቁቕ *ẗnquq̈*
prune *(n.)* ዝዘነቐጸ ፕሮኞ *zneq̈eẗe proňo*
pry *(v.)* ኣቕሪብካ ምዕዛብ *aqribka mëzab*
psalm *(n.)* መዝሙር ዳዊት *mezmur dawit*
pseudo *(adj.)* ሓሳዊ *ȟasawi*
pseudonym *(n.)* ሳጓ *sagua*
psyche *(n.)* መንፈስ ሰብ *menfes seb*
psychiatrist *(n.)* ሓኪም ኣእምሮ *ȟakim aèmro*
psychiatry *(n.)* ስነ ኣእምሮ *sne aèmro*
psychic *(adj.)* ናይ መጸኢ ዝጥንቁል *nay mexaei zẗnqul*
psychological *(adj.)* ሳይኮሎጂካል *saykoloĵikal*
psychologist *(n.)* ሳይኮሎጂካዊ *saykoloĵikawi*
psychology *(n.)* ሳይኮሎጂ *saykoloyĵi*
psychopath *(n.)* መደናጋሪ *medenagari*
psychosis *(n.)* ኽማም ኣእምሮ *ȟmam aèmro*
psychotherapy *(n.)* ፍወሳ ሕማም ኣእምሮ *fwesa ȟmam aèmro*
pub *(n.)* ባርን ሬስቶራንትን *barn giestorantn*
puberty *(n.)* ግርዝውና *grzwna*
pubic *(adj.)* ኣብ ግርዝውና ዝበቁል ጸጉሪ *ab grzwna zboqul xeguri*
public *(adj.)* ህዝባዊ *hzbawi*
publication *(n.)* ሕትመት *ȟtmet*
publicity *(n.)* ተፈላጥነት *tefelaẗnet*
publicize *(v.)* ምፍላጥ *mflaẗ*
publish *(v.)* ምሕታም *mȟtam*
publisher *(n.)* ሓታሚ *ȟtami*
pudding *(n.)* ዝፈልሐ ጠስሚ *zfelȟ ẗesmi*
puddle *(n.)* ንእሽተይ ጉድጓድ ማይ *nèshtey gudguad may*
puerile *(adj.)* ቁልዕነት *qulënet*
puff *(n.)* ምርሽራሽ *mrshrash*
puffy *(adj.)* ምንፋሕ *mnfaȟ*
pull *(v.)* ሰሓበ *seȟabe*
pulley *(n.)* መስሓቢ ማሽን *mesȟabi mashn*
pullover *(n.)* ብርእሲ ስሒብካ ዝኽደን ኽዳን *brèsi sȟibka zḱden ḱdan*
pulp *(n.)* ልስሉስ ክፋል ስኒ *lslus kfal sni*
pulpit *(n.)* መስበኽያ *mesbeḱya*
pulsar *(n.)* ዘዋሪ ኮኾብ *zewari koḱob*
pulsate *(v.)* ምህራም *mhram*
pulsation *(n.)* ትርግታ *trgta*
pulse *(n.)* ድምጺ ትርግታ *dmxi trgta*
pummel *(v.)* ብተደጋጋሚ ምህራም *btedegagami mhram*
pump *(n.)* ምጭንጓዕ *mčnguaë*
pumpkin *(n.)* ዱባ *duba*
pun *(n.)* ሓይሊ ምጉዳል *ȟayli mgudal*
punch *(v.)* ጉስጢ *gusẗi*
punctual *(adj.)* ኣብ ሰዓቱ *ab seätu*

punctuality *(n.)* **ኣብ ሰዓቱ ዝርከብ** *ab seätu zrkeb*
punctuate *(v.)* **ምውሳኽ(")** *mwsaḱ(")*
punctuation *(n.)* **ምልክት መግለጺ ትርጉም (")** *mlkt meglexi qal(")*
puncture *(n.)* **ብበለሕ ነገር ዝፍጠር ቀዳድ** *bbeli neger zfẗer qedad*
pungency *(n.)* **ብርቱዕ ጨና ምህላው** *brtuë čena mhlaw*
pungent *(adj.)* **ብርቱዕ ጨና** *brtuë čena*
punish *(v.)* **ምቕጻዕ** *mq̈xaë*
punishment *(n.)* **መቕጻዕቲ** *meq̈xaëti*
punitive *(adj.)* **ቖጻዒ** *q̈exaë*
punter *(n.)* **ዓሚል ኣመንዝራ** *ämil amenzra*
puny *(adj.)* **ድኹም** *dḱum*
pup *(n.)* **ንእሽቶ፣ተመኩሮ ዘይብሉ** *neshto,temekuro zeyblu*
pupil *(n.)* **ዘኽታም ብመንግስቲ ዝናበ** *zeḱtam bmengsti znabe*
puppet *(n.)* **ብነብሱ ዘይምራሕ** *bnebsu zeymraḧ*
puppy *(n.)* **ኩርኩር** *kurkur*
purblind *(adj.)* **ፍርቂ ዕዉር** *frqi ëwur*
purchase *(v.)* **ምዕዳግ** *mëdag*
pure *(adj.)* **ንጹህ** *nxuh*
purgation *(n.)* **ካብ ሓጥያት ምንጻህ** *kab ḧaẗyat mnxah*
purgative *(adj.)* **ካብ ሓጥያት ክነጽህ ኽእል** *kab ḧaẗyat knexh zḱèl*
purgatory *(n.)* **ስቓይ ናይ ምድሓን** *sq̈ay nay mdḧan*
purge *(v.)* **ካብ ሓጥያት ኣንጻሀ** *kab ḧaẗyat anxehe*
purification *(n.)* **ምንጻህ** *mnxah*
purify *(v.)* **ኣጻረየ** *axareye*
purist *(n.)* **ንጹህነት** *nxuhnet*
puritan *(n.)* **ምቕሉል** *mq̈lul*
puritanical *(adj.)* **ነተጎ** *netegue*
purity *(n.)* **ኣጹህነት** *axuhnet*
purple *(n.)* **ሊላ** *lila*
purport *(v.)* **ደገፍ** *degef*
purpose *(n.)* **ዕላማ** *ëlama*
purposely *(adv.)* **ኮነ ኢልካ** *kone eilka*
purr *(v.)* **ናይ ደስታ ድምጺ** *nay desta dmxi*
purse *(n.)* **ቦርሳ** *borsa*
purser *(n.)* **ሰራሕ ቦርሳ** *seraḧ borsa*
pursuance *(n.)* **ምድላይ** *mdlay*
pursue *(v.)* **ንክጎድእ ሰዓበ** *nkgodè seäbe*
pursuit *(n.)* **ንክጎድእ ምስዓብ** *nkgodè msäb*
purvey *(v.)* **ምቕራብ** *mq̈rab*
purview *(n.)* **ርደኢት** *rdeit*
pus *(n.)* **ሙጉሊ** *muguili*
push *(v.)* **ደፍአ** *defae*
pushy *(adj.)* **ቖራጽነት** *qoraxnet*
puss *(n.)* **ንእሽቶ ዓል** *nèshto gual*
put *(v.)* **ኣቐመጠ** *aq̈emeẗe*
putative *(adj.)* **ግምት** *gmt*
putrid *(adj.)* **ብልሹው** *blshw*
puzzle *(v.t.)* **መስቀላዊ** *mesqelawi*
pygmy *(n.)* **ድንኪ** *dnki*
pyjamas *(n.)* **ብጃማ** *bĵama*
pyorrhoea *(n.)* **ምፍሳስ መጉሊ** *mfsas meguili*
pyramid *(n.)* **ፒራሚድ** *piramid*
pyre *(n.)* **ዝርዝር ቐብሪ** *zrzr q̈ebri*

pyromania *(n.)* ሕማም ሓዊ *ḧmam ḧawi*
python *(n.)* ናይ ዓዲ እንግሊዝ ኮሚዳውያን *nay ädi èngliz commiedawyan*

Q

quack *(n)* ጋቢ'ና *gabina*
quackery *(n.)* ካባረ *kabare*
quad *(n.)* ካውሎ *kawlo*
quadrangle *(a.)* ጋቢና *gabina*
quadrangular *(n.)* ከብሒ *kebḧi*
quadrant *(n.)* መዳወር *medawer*
quadrilateral *(n.)* ካካው *kakaw*
quadruped *(n.)* ሓብእ *ḧab'e*
quadruple *(adj.)* ክታም *ktam*
quadruplet *(n.)* ቃቓ *qaq̈a*
quaff *(v.)* ቈልቋል *qWelqWAl*
quail *(n.)* ነውራም *newram*
quaint *(adj.)* ሬሳ *reesa*
quaintly *(adv.)* ካዲ *kadi*
quake *(v.)* ሬሳ *reesa*
Quaker *(n.)* ካደት *kadet*
qualification *(n.)* ካድምዩም *kadmyum*
qualify *(v.)* አስከሬን *askereen*
qualitative *(adj.)* ቄሳር *qeesar*
quality *(n.)* ካፈ *kafe*
qualm *(n.)* ካፈተርያ *kafeterya*
quandary *(n.)* ጎብያ *gobya*
quango *(n.)* ኪዳን *kidan*
quantify *(v.)* ሸሓጠ *sheḧaẗe*
quantitative *(adj.)* ዶልሺ *dolshi*
quantity *(n.)* መዓት *me'ät*
quantum *(n.)* ካልስዩም *kalsyum*
quarantine *(n.)* ቀመረ *qemere*
quark *(n.)* መተሓሳሰቢ *meteḧasasebi*
quarrel *(n.)* ቀመር *qemer*
quarrelsome *(adj.)* ዓውደ-አዋርሕ *äwde'awarḧ*
quarry *(n.)* ምራኽ *mraḱ*
quart *(n.)* ደረጃታት መጠነ ወይ ሓንጸጸ *dereĵatat meẗene wey ḧanxexe*
quarter *(n.)* ውሽጣዊ ሰንጣቒት *wshẗawi senẗaq̈it*
quarterly *(adj.)* ደወለ *dewele*
quartet *(n.)* ጽባቐ ጽሕፈት *xbaq̈e xḧfet*
quartz *(n.)* ሞያ *moya*
quash *(v.)* ጽዖታዊ *x'ötawi*
quaver *(v.)* ጥረ *ẗre*
quay *(n.)* ህዱእ *hdu'è*
queasy *(adj.)* ካሎሪ *kalori*
queen *(n.)* ምጽላም *mxlam*
queer *(adj.)* ብጸይነት *bxaynet*
quell *(v.)* ጐብጓበ *gWabgWabe*
quench *(v.)* ሻሽ *shash*
querulous *(adj.)* ካምኮርደር *kamkorder*
query *(n.)* ገመል *gemel*
quest *(n.)* ካምዮ *kamyo*
question *(n.)* ካመራ *kamera*
questionable *(adj.)* መዓስከር *me'äsker*
questionnaire *(n.)* ዘመተ *zemete*
queue *(n.)* ካምፎራ *kamfora*
quibble *(n.)* ካምፓስ *kampas*
quick *(adj.)* ታኒካ *tanika*
quicken *(v.)* ኣብ ታኒካ ሓተመ *'ab tanika ḧateme*
quickly *(adv.)* መትረብ *metreb*

quid *(n.)* ናይ ሓሶት ጸብጻብ *nay ḧasot xebxab*
quiescent *(adj.)* ሰረዘ *sereze*
quiet *(adj.)* ምጥፋእ *mẗfa'è*
quieten *(v.)* መንሽሮ *menshro*
quietude *(n.)* ብራሃን *brahan*
quiff *(n.)* ግሁድ *ghud*
quilt *(n.)* ሕጹይ *ḧxuy*
quilted *(adj.)* ሽምዓ *shm'ä*
quince *(n.)* ካራመላ *karamela*
quinine *(n.)* ከረዛን *kerezan*
Quinn *(n.)* ጋህዲ *gahdi*
quintessence *(n.)* ከልባዊ *kelbawi*
quip *(n.)* ሳጹን *saxun*
quirk *(n.)* ሀምፕ *hemp*
quit *(v.)* በላዕ ሰብ *bela'ë seb*
quite *(adv.)* መድፍዕ *medf'ë*
quits *(adj.)* ጐራሕ *gWaraḧ*
quiver *(v.)* ታንኳ *tankWa*
quixotic *(adj.)* ቀኖና *qenona*
quiz *(n.)* ድባብ *dbab*
quizzical *(adj.)* ግብዝና *gbzna*
quondam *(adj.)* ሓራቕ *ḧaraq̈*
quorum *(n.)* ካንቲና *kantina*
quota *(n.)* ህዱእ ጋልቢት *hdu'è galbit*
quotation *(n.)* ወረዳ *wereda*
quote *(v.)* ቀዋሚ መዓስከር *qewami me'äsker*
quotient *(n.)* ጅርባ *ĵrba*

R

rabbit *(n.)* ዓሚቕ ስንጭሮ *ämiq̈ snčro*
rabble *(n.)* ቈብዕ *qWeb'ë*
rabid *(adj.)* ዓቕሚ *äq̈mi*
rabies *(n.)* ክኢላ *k'ila*
race *(v.)* ካፓሲተር *kapaciter*
race *(n.)* ሰፊሕ *sefiḧ*
racial *(adj.)* ዓቕሚ *äq̈mi*
racialism *(n.)* ሰለመ *seleme*
rack *(n.)* መንጠሊና *menẗelina*
racket *(n.)* ርእሰ-ማል *r'èsemal*
racketeer *(n.)* ርእሰ-ማልነት *r'èsemalnet*
racy *(adj.)* ርእሰ-ማላዊ *r'èsemalawi*
radar *(n.)* ርእሰ-ማል ገበረ *r'èsemal gebere*
radial *(adj.)* ግብሪ *gbri*
radiance *(n.)* ተምበርከኸ *temberkeḱe*
radiant *(adj.)* ቅበጥ *qbeẗ*
radiate *(v.)* ቀባጥ *qebaẗ*
radiation *(n.)* ካፕሲከም *kapsikem*
radical *(adj.)* ገልበጠ *gelbeẗe*
radio *(n.)* ጠምጣሚ መስሕብ *ẗemẗami meshḧb*
radioactive *(adj.)* ለቖታ-ፍረ *leq̈otafre*
radiography *(n.)* ግብጣን *gbẗan*
radiology *(n.)* ግብጣኒ *gbẗani*
radish *(n.)* ኣርእስቲ *ar'èsti*
radium *(n.)* መሰጠ *meseẗe*
radius *(n.)* ምሩኽ *mruḱ*
raffle *(n.)* ምሩኽነት *mruḱnet*
raft *(n.)* ሓላው ምሩኽ *ḧalaw mruḱ*
rag *(n.)* ኣሰረ *asere'*

rage *(n.)* ማኪና *makina*
ragged *(adj.)* ካራሜል *karame' el*
raid *(n.)* ካራት *kara 't*
rail *(n.)* ሓዲድ *ḧadid*
railing *(n.)* መደንደል *medendel*
raillery *(n.)* ሕመት *hemete*
railway *(n.)* መገዲ ባቡር *megedi babur*
rain *(n)* ጥርሙዝ *terimuz*
rainbow *(n.)* ገምቢ *ge'mbi*
raincoat *(n.)* ካርዲ *ka'ardi*
rainfall *(n.)* ጠጠው አቢሉ *tte'ttew aa'billu*
rainforest *(n.)* ካርቶን *kartoon*
rainy *(adj.)* ናይ ልቢ *na' ae lebii*
raise *(v.)* ጎልፎ *gole 'foo*
raisin *(n.)* ጳጳስ *papase'*
rake *(n.)* ልብ ሓኪም መሳርሒ *lib hakim mesarehi*
rally *(n.)* ሓኪም ሕመም ልቢ *hakim himem le'bi*
ram *(n.)* ክንክን *kinkin*
ramble *(v.)* ስራሕ *sir'ahh*
ramification *(n.)* ዘይአጅቦ *they'aa jibo*
ramify *(v.)* ጥንቁቅ *tinkuq*
ramp *(n.)* ዘየስተውዕል *ze yestewu 'el*
rampage *(v.)* ኣብ *aa'b*
rampant *(adj.)* ተናኸፈ *tenahe'fe*
rampart *(n.)* ወኪል *wekil*
ramshackle *(adj.)* ኣብ መርከብ *aa'b merkeb*
ranch *(n.)* ምስሊ *mesili*
rancid *(adj.)* ቀይሕ ሕብሪ *qeyiha hib're*
rancour *(n.)* ጭፍጨፋ *Chif'chefa*
random *(adj.)* ስጋዊ *segawi*
range *(n.)* ተርታ ኣትሓዘ *terta 'atḧaze*
ranger *(n.)* ፎረስታለ *forestale*
rank *(v.)* ኣዕበርበረ *zz'ebere bere*
rank *(n.)* ደርፊ *derfi*
rankle *(v.)* ፀራቢ *tserabi*
ransack *(v.)* ፅርበት *tsirbet*
ransom *(n.)* መንፀፍ *mentseff*
rant *(v.)* ባቡር *babur*
rap *(v.)* ብነፋሪት *binefarit*
rapacious *(adj.)* ካሮት *carrot*
rape *(v.)* ተሸከመ *teshekeme*
rapid *(adj.)* ዓረብያ *arebia*
rapidity *(n.)* ፍጥነት *fṫnet*
rapier *(n.)* ልስሉስ ዓፅሚ *leseluse aa'tsmi*
rapist *(n.)* ባኮ *bako*
rapport *(n.)* ስኒት *snit*
rapprochement *(n.)* ቀልሃ *qeliha*
rapt *(adj.)* ቀረፀ *qeretse*
rapture *(n.)* ምሳጠ *msaẗe*
rare *(adj.)* ወዲ *wedi*
raring *(adj.)* መንጫ ጫዕታ *mencha chaeta*
rascal *(n.)* ኩነት *kunet*
rash *(adj.)* መስኮት *mesekote*
rasp *(n.)* ቅርሺ *qeriishe*
raspberry *(n.)* ኦም *ome*
rat *(n.)* ተቀባሊት ቅርሺ *teqebalit qereshi*
ratchet *(n.)* ሱፍ *suf*
rate *(n.)* ዝተለበጠ *zetelebte*
rather *(adv.)* ህንፀት *hintsete*
ratify *(v.)* ፊስቶ *fiseto*
rating *(n.)* ሳፁን ሬሳ *satsun resa*
ratio *(n.)* ምግቢ *megebi*
ration *(n.)* ጁባ *juba*

rational *(adj.)* **ተመልከተ** *temeleket*
rationale *(n.)* **ስነ-መጎታዊ መሰረት** *snemegotawi meseret*
rationalism *(n.)* **ማሕበራዊ ደረጃ** *mahiberawi dereja*
rationalize *(v.)* **ነቀፈ** *neqefe*
rattle *(v.)* **ደርበየ** *derebye*
raucous *(adj.)* **ቤት ነገስታት** *bete negestat*
ravage *(v.t.)* **ዝሸክርከር ጎማ ወንበር** *zeShekirker goma wenber*
rave *(v.)* **ቀጥቀጥ** *qeteqetw*
raven *(n.)* **ጎማ ዘይት** *goma zeite*
ravenous *(adj.)* **ዘይተሓሰበሉ** *zeytehasebelo*
ravine *(n.)* **ዝሞተ** *zemote*
raw *(adj.)* **ድሙ** *demu*
ray *(n.)* **ብርሰት ዘስዕብ ሓደጋ** *bereset zsee'b hadega*
raze *(v.)* **ነንኣብነት መፃሕፍቲ** *nenabinet metsahifti*
razor *(n.)* **ኣቀፃፀለ** *aqetsatsele*
reach *(v.)* **ኣቀፃፃሊ** *aqetsatseli*
react *(v.)* **ሓበላ** *habela*
reaction *(n.)* **ከቢድ ሃንደበታዊ ሓደጋ** *kebid hanedbtawi a'adega*
reactionary *(adj.)* **ቆበለ** *qobl*
reactor *(n.)* **ብቀሊሉ ዝላገብ** *newlilunzehegden beqlilu zezekren*
read *(v.)* **ኣንበበ** *'anbebe*
readily *(adv.)* **ንፁርን ርጉፅን** *nitsurin regutsin*
reading *(n.)* **ጎጀለ** *goje-le*
readjust *(v.)* **ጉጅለ** *guge-le*
ready *(adj.)* **ሰርዐ** *sere'aa*
reaffirm *(v.)* **ኣባጨጓራ** *aaba'che'guara*
real *(adj.)* **ናይ ብሓቂ** *nay bḧaqi*
realism *(n.)* **ደብሪ** *debri*
realistic *(adj.)* **ካቶሊክ** *catholic*
reality *(n.)* **ከብቲ** *kebtei*
realization *(n.)* **ሓሜተኛ** *hametegna'*
realize *(v.)* **ፃዕዳ ዘርኢ ሰብ** *tsaeda' zereei sebe'*
really *(adv.)* **በራድ** *beradd*
realm *(n.)* **ካዉሎ ፍዮሪ** *kawulo fiyorii*
ream *(n.)* **ናይ ምክንያትን ዉፅኢትን** *nayei mikneyatene wutsieitin*
reap *(v.)* **ዓጸደ** *'äxede*
reaper *(n.)* **መንቀሊ** *mneqsi*
reappear *(v.)* **ኣዉራ መንገዲ** *awra mnegedeei*
reappraisal *(n.)* **መፂፅ** *matsiee.e*
rear *(n.)* **መጠንቀቅታ** *metenqekta*
rearrange *(v.)* **ኣጠንቀቀ** *aa'tenqeqe*
reason *(n.)* **ጥንቁቅ** *tenquqk*
reasonable *(adj.)* **ናይ ፈረሳት** *nayei feresat*
reassess *(v.)* **ዘይግደስ** *zeyg des*
reassure *(v.)* **ፈረሰኛ** *fresenga*
rebate *(n.)* **በዓቲ** *beaa'ti*
rebel *(v.)* **መዘካከሪ** *mezkakrii*
rebellion *(n.)* **ገፊሕ በዓቲ** *gefihe beatii*
rebellious *(adj.)* **ብጣዕሚ ገፊሕ** *betaemi gefihei*
rebirth *(n.)* **ዝጎድጎደ ስኒ** *zgodedod sieni*
rebound *(v.)* **ብታሕጓስ ዓንደረ** *bitahegwas aanede're*
rebuff *(v.)* **ደዉ ኣበለ** *dwuo aabele*

rebuild *(v.)* **ተኩሲ ደው ናይ ምግባር ስምምዕ** *tekusi dwu nayi megebare sememea 'e*
rebuke *(v.t.)* **ኦም ሲዳር** *oom cidar*
recall *(v.)* **ሓይሊ/መሰል ሃበ** *hailyii/msele habee*
recap *(v.)* **ሰንቀ/ጣርያ ገዛ** *seneqe/tareya geza*
recapitulate *(v.)* **ዕምባባ** *embaba*
recapture *(v.)* **ቅዳሴ ዝመርሕ ቀሺ** *qwedase zemrehe qeshi*
recede *(v.)* **ኣብዓለ/በዓል ኣከበረ** *aab'ale/bea'eal akebere*
receipt *(n.)* **በዓል** *beaal*
receive *(v.)* **ስሙይ ሰብ** *semuyei sebe*
receiver *(n.)* **ሰማያዊ** *semayawii*
recent *(adj.)* **ድንግልና** *denegelena*
recently *(adv.)* **ድንግላይ** *denegelaye*
receptacle *(n.)* **ዋህዮ** *waheyo*
reception *(n.)* **ናይ እሱራት ክፍሊ** *naye esurat kiflii*
receptionist *(n.)* **ተንቀሳቃሲ ስልኪ** *teneqesaqasi seliki*
receptive *(adj.)* **ልኡክ ጉጀለ** *leuuke gujelle*
recess *(n.)* **ስብሒ** *sebehi*
recession *(n.)* **ዝነድድ ረብሓ** *zenededei rehehaa*
recessive *(adj.)* **ዕብሉል** *'ëblul*
recharge *(v.)* **ሴልሲየስ** *celcius*
recipe *(n.)* **ሴልቲክ ቋንቋ** *celtik quaniqua*
recipient *(n.)* **ስሚንቶ** *seminito*
reciprocal *(adj.)* **መከነ መቃብር** *mekne mekabir*
reciprocate *(v.)* **ሸሓነ** *shehane*
recital *(n.)* **መርማሪ** *meremari*
recite *(v.)* **ቅድመ ምርመራ** *qedeme meremra*
reckless *(adj.)* **ነቃፊ** *neqkafi*
reckon *(v.t.)* **ብርቲዕ ነቀፌታ** *beretiee' neqefeta*
reclaim *(v.)* **ቆፀራ** *qoxera*
reclamation *(n.)* **ሳንቲም** *sanetim*
recline *(v.)* **ተገምበወ** *tegembewe*
recluse *(n.)* **ኣብ ርእ** *ab reaa'*
recognition *(n.)* **ማዕከል** *maeekele*
recognize *(v.i.)* **ሙቀት መጠን** *muqete metene*
recoil *(v.)* **ርቐት መጠን** *reqete metene*
recollect *(v.)* **ዘርኢ ሰብ ዝመሰል** *zereii sebe zemsle*
recollection *(n.)* **ኣዉራ/ቀንዲ** *aawura/qenedi*
recommend *(v.)* **ኣማእክለ** *zamaeekele*
recommendation *(n.)* **ማዕከል** *meee'kele*
recompense *(v.)* **ዘበን** *zbene*
reconcile *(v.)* **ጣሳ** *tasa*
reconciliation *(n.)* **ጥራጥረ** *teraterre*
recondition *(v.)* **ናይ ሓንጎል** *nayei hanegole*
reconsider *(v.)* **ስነ ስርዓታዊ** *sene sereaa'tawii*
reconstitute *(v.)* **ስነ ስርዓት ዘለዎ** *senei sereat zelewoo*
reconstruct *(v.)* **በዓል/ፅምብል** *beaal/xeembil*
record *(n.)* **ርጉፅ** *reguxee*
recorder *(n.)* **ብዘይጥርጥር** *bethzey tiritir*

recount *(v.)* **ዕቡድ/ፅሉል** *eebudd/xelule*
recoup *(v.)* **ምስክር ወረቐት** *mesekir wereqet*
recourse *(n.)* **ምስክር ወረቐት ሃበ** *meseker wereqket habe*
recover *(v.)* **ርግፀኝነት** *regexegninet*
recovery *(n.)* **ምሕዋይ** *mḧway*
recreate *(v.)* **ምቑራፅ** *mekuraxee*
recreation *(n.)* **ምዝንጋዕ** *mznga'ë*
recrimination *(n.)* **ሰንሰለት** *seneselet*
recruit *(v.)* **ወንበር** *weneber*
rectangle *(n.)* **ኣቦወንበር** *abo' weneber*
rectangular *(adj.)* **ሰብ ተጓዕዝ** *sebe tegwaeeze*
rectification *(n.)* **ባራካ** *barakaa*
rectify *(v.)* **ፅዋዕ** *xewaee*
rectitude *(n.)* **በረቕ** *bereqqe*
rectum *(n.)* **ፈተነ** *fetene*
recumbent *(adj.)* **አዳራሽ** *adarashe*
recuperate *(v.)* **ናይ በዓል ስልጣን** *naye beeal seletane*
recur *(v.)* **ሻምፓኝ** *shampagne*
recurrence *(n.)* **ዕዉት/ሰዓራይ** *eewuut/seaarayi*
recurrent *(adj.)* **ዕድል** *eedil*
recycle *(v.)* **መራሒ መንግስቲ** *merahi menegeseti*
red *(adj.)* **ቤት ፅሕፈት** *bete xehifeti*
reddish *(adj.)* **ልሻን ሸለመ** *leshane' shelem'e*
redeem *(v.)* **ለወጠ/ተለወጠ** *lewete/telewete*
redemption *(n.)* **ጣቢያ ጤሌቪዥን** *tabiya television*
redeploy *(v.)* **ዜማ** *zema*
redolent *(adj.)* **ህዉከት** *hewuuke*
redouble *(v.)* **ዕግርግር ዘለዎ** *egereger zelewo*
redoubtable *(adj.)* **ንእሽተይ ቤተክርስቲያን** *neeshtey betekerestian*
redress *(v.)* **ካህን** *kahiN'*
reduce *(v.)* **ምዕራፍ** *mee'eraf*
reduction *(n.)* **ሓረር/ኣሕረረ** *harer/aaehi'rere*
reductive *(adj.)* **ባሕርይ/ፀባይ** *bahereyei/xebayii*
redundancy *(n.)* **ባሕርይ** *bahereyei*
redundant *(adj.)* **ፋሓም/ሕመት** *fahame/hemeute*
reef *(n.)* **ክፍሊት** *kefelite*
reek *(v.)* **ክፍሊት ሓተተ** *kefelit hatete*
reel *(n.)* **ብርጭቆ መልአ** *bereCheqo melea'a*
refer *(v.)* **ዓረብያ/ሰረገላ** *arebiya/seregela*
referee *(n.)* **ግርማ ሞገስ** *gerima moges*
reference *(n.)* **በዓል ሞገስ/ምዕሩግ** *beal moges/mee'erug*
referendum *(n.)* **ናይ ገባሪ ሰናይ** *nayei gebari senayei*
refill *(v.)* **ትካል ገባሪ ሰናይ** *tekaal gebarii senayei*
refine *(v.)* **መምሰሊ/መታለሊ ሰብ** *memeiseli/metalelei sebe'e*
refinement *(n.)* **ሰሓባይነት** *sehabayineet*

refinery ***(n.)*** **ሰባሓይ/ማራኪ** *sebahaayi/marakii*
refit ***(v.)*** **ሰንጠረዥ** *seneterezjj*
reflect ***(v.)*** **መምርሒ** *memerehii*
reflection ***(n.)*** **ተኮናተረ** *tekonateree*
reflective ***(adj.)*** **ስግኣት** *segeaa'te*
reflex ***(n.)*** **አጓየየ/አባረረ** *aaguwayeye/aabarere*
reflexive ***(adj.)*** **ሞተር** *mote'R'*
reflexology ***(n.)*** **ዘየዝሙዉ/ዘይትዝሙዉ** *zeyezemuwue/zeyitzemuwu*
reform ***(v.)*** **ወቐሰ** *weqqese*
reformation ***(n.)*** **ኣደብ** *A'deb*
reformer ***(n.)*** **ዘይምዝማዉ** *zeymzemawu*
refraction ***(n.)*** **ኣዕለለ/ኣዉገዐ** *aae'lele/aawugeaa'*
refrain ***(v.t.)*** **ቤት ነገስታት** *bete' negeseta't*
refresh ***(v.)*** **ንብረት/ንዋይ** *neberet/newaye*
refreshment ***(n.)*** **ሃተፈ/ለፈለፈ** *hatefe/lefelefe*
refrigerate ***(v.)*** **ኣውቲስታ/ዘዋሪማኪና** *aawutiseta/zewarimeckina*
refrigeration ***(n.)*** **ትምክሕቲ** *temekeheti*
refrigerator ***(n.)*** **ምኩሕ** *mekuhh*
refuge ***(n.)*** **ሕሰር** *hesaree*
refugee ***(n.)*** **ኣዋረደ** *aawarede*
refulgence ***(adj.)*** **ኣታለለ** *aatalele*
refulgent ***(adj.)*** **ኣሕሰረ** *aa'hesere*
refund ***(v.)*** **ኣፃረየ** *axareyee*
refund ***(v.)*** **ዝተዛዘመ** *ziteza'zeme'*
refurbish ***(v.)*** **ምዕጉርቲ** *meaegurtii*
refusal ***(n.)*** **ባዕለገ** *bae'leGe'*
refuse ***(v.)*** **ጩቕ በለ** *Chuqk' bele*
refuse ***(n.)*** **ታሕጓስ** *taheGua'ss*
refutation ***(n.)*** **ወትሩ ሕጉስ** *wetru higus*
refute ***(v.)*** **ዘየሕጉስ** *zyehiGus'*
regain ***(v.)*** **ሕጉስ** *Higus'*
regal ***(adj.)*** **ኣጅቦ** *Ajobo*
regard ***(v.)*** **ጭኮንበሳ** *ChikonbeSa*
regarding ***(prep.)*** **ዋና ከሻኒ** *wana Kesha'ni*
regardless ***(adv.)*** **ኬሚካል** *kemikal*
regenerate ***(v.)*** **ቐማሚ** *Qe'mami*
regeneration ***(n.)*** **ቕመም** *qE'mem*
regent ***(n.)*** **ሕክምና** *hikiM'NA*
reggae ***(n.)*** **ናይ ባንኪ ቼክ** *naYei banki' Cheqk*
regicide ***(n.)*** **ኣፍቀረ** *Af'Qere*
regime ***(n.)*** **ቼዝ** *Chezz'*
regiment ***(n.)*** **ኣፍልቢ** *Aflebi*
region ***(n.)*** **ሳንዱቕ** *saneduqQ*
regional ***(adj.)*** **መለለይ ምልክት** *Me'Leleyei milikit*
register ***(n.)*** **ሓየክ** *HayYeke*
registrar ***(n.)*** **ዘበናይ ሰሓባይን** *Zebenayei Sehabayin*
registration ***(n.)*** **ሸፍጢ** *Shefe'Ti*
registry ***(n.)*** **ደርሆ** *Dereho*
regress ***(v.)*** **ዓይኒ ዓተር** *Ayni Ater*
regret ***(n.)*** **ነቐፈ** *NeQefe*
regrettable ***(adj.)*** **ኣዉራ/ቀንዲ** *Auwra/Qendi'*
regular ***(adj.)*** **ሓላፊ/ሓለቓ** *Halafi/HaleQa*
regularity ***(n.)*** **መሪሕነት** *MerihNet'*
regularize ***(v.)*** **ቆልዓ** *QoleA'*

regulate *(v.)* ቁልዕነት *Qole'eneT'*
regulation *(n.)* ናይ ቆልዓ *Nayei QoleA'*
regulator *(n.)* ቁሪ/ቀዝሒ *Quri/Qezhi*
rehabilitate *(v.)* ሽርባ/በርበረ *Shirba/berebre*
rehabilitation *(n.)* ቆራር *qorare*
rehearsal *(n.)* ሰዓት ደወለት *seAt' dwle't*
rehearse *(v.)* ቆንቆር *QonQkor*
reign *(v.)* ሀበይ *HeBeyei*
reimburse *(v.)* መንከስ *Menkes'*
rein *(n.)* በረቕ *BereqQe'*
reincarnate *(v.)* ሽርፍራፍ *Sherifrafe*
reinforce *(v.)* ጩቕ በለ *CchUQ' Bel'le*
reinforcement *(n.)* መንደል *Mendel*
reinstate *(v.)* ናብ ስልጣን መለሰ *nab slťan melese*
reiterate *(v.)* ደጋገመ *degageme*
reiteration *(n.)* ክሎሪን *kilorin*
reject *(v.)* መርዚ *merzi*
rejection *(n.)* ቸኮላታ *checolata*
rejoice *(v.)* መረፃ *meretsa*
rejoin *(v.)* መዘምራን *mezemeran*
rejoinder *(n.)* ሓነቐ *haneqe*
rejuvenate *(v.)* ሕማም ሽሮኽ *hemam sheroke*
rejuvenation *(n.)* መረፀ *meretse*
relapse *(v.)* ከተፈ *ketefe*
relate *(v.)* ሴፍ *sefe*
relation *(n.)* ጥሕሎ *telohe*
relationship *(n.)* ክፋል መዝሙር *kefale mezemur*
relative *(adj.)* ደመርቲ *dmreti*
relativity *(n.)* ተደጋጊሙ ዝዝመር *tedegagimu zezemre*
relax *(v.)* ክርስቶስ *keresetos*
relaxation *(n.)* ክርስቲያን *keresitiyane*
relay *(n.)* ክርስትና ሃይማኖት *keresetena hayimanot*
release *(v.)* በዓል ልደት *beal lidet*
relegate *(v.)* ቀምቀመ *qemeqme*
relent *(v.)* ነባር *nebar*
relentless *(adj.)* ዜና መዋልዕ *zena mewalee*
relevance *(n.)* ርክብ *rkb*
relevant *(adj.)* ሰዓት *seat*
reliable *(adj.)* ክምስ/ፍሽክ በለ *kemese/feshek bele*
reliance *(n.)* ቀረባ ፈታሒ *qereba fetahi*
relic *(n.)* ቁርማም *qurmame*
relief *(n.)* ቤተ ክርስቲያን *bete kiristian*
relieve *(v.)* መካነ መቓብር *mekane meqabere*
religion *(n.)* ዓምጠቑ *ameteqku*
religious *(adj.)* ፀብሒ *xebhi*
relinquish *(v.)* ሲደር *cider*
relish *(v.)* መቐረት *meq̈eret*
relocate *(v.)* ሽጋራ *shegara*
reluctance *(n.)* ቤት ስኒማ *bet ciniema*
reluctant *(adj.)* ቐረፋ *qerefa*
rely *(v.)* ክቢ *kebi*
remain *(v.)* ተረፈ *terefe*
remainder *(n.)* ክቢብ *kbibe*
remains *(n.)* ተሰራጨወ *tsrachew*
remand *(v.)* ዑደት *xudet*
remark *(v.)* ገረዘ *gereze'*
remarkable *(adj.)* ዶብ *dobe*
remedial *(adj.)* ገደበ *gedebe*

remedy *(n.)* አዝዩ ጥንቁቕ *azeyu tenequqe*
remember *(v.)* ሃዋህዉ *hawahewu*
remembrance *(n.)* ሰርከስ *serekse*
remind *(v.)* ሳንዱቕ *sanaduqe*
reminder *(n.)* ማይ መዋህለሊ *maye mwaheleli*
reminiscence *(v.)* ኣስተንትኖ *'astentno*
reminiscent *(adj.)* ጠቐሰ *tekese*
remiss *(adj.)* ዜጋ *zega*
remission *(n.)* ዜግነት *zegenet*
remit *(n.)* ተኽል *tekil*
remittance *(n.)* ሲትሪክ *citric*
remnant *(n.)* ከተማ *ketema*
remonstrate *(v.)* ናይ ከተማ *nayei ketema*
remorse *(n.)* ናይ ስነ ዜጋ ትምሕርቲ *nayei sine zega temehereti*
remote *(adj.)* ማሕበረሰባዊ *mahebresebawi*
removable *(adj.)* ስቪል ሰብ *sevil sebe*
removal *(n.)* ስልጣነ *seletan*
remove *(v.)* ኣሰልጠነ *aseltene*
remunerate *(v.)* ዝተኸደነ *zetkdn*
remuneration *(n.)* ኽዳን *Kedan*
remunerative *(adj.)* ሓቂዩ በለ *haqiyu bele*
renaissance *(n.)* ይግበኣኒ በሃላይ *yigbeani behalayi*
render *(v.)* ርሁድ *rehude*
rendezvous *(n.)* ብኣዉያት ሓተተ *beawyat hattete*
renegade *(n.)* ኣጣበቐ *atabeqe*
renew *(v.)* ዓሌት *alet*
renewal *(adj.)* ሕቡእ *hibuea'*
renounce *(v.t.)* ኣጣቐ0 *atabeqe*
renovate *(n.)* ኣብራሀረሀ *abrahereh*
renovation *(n.)* ከለሰ *keles*
renown *(n.)* መልእኽቲ *mleekti*
renowned *(adj.)* ግልፀነት *geletsinet*
rent *(n.)* ባእሲ *baesii*
rental *(n.)* ጨበጠ *chebete*
renunciation *(n.)* ክፍሊ *kifeli*
reoccur *(v.)* ሕሩይ *heruyei*
reorganize *(v.)* ቀንደኛ *qenedegna*
repair *(v.)* ምጉጃል *megujak*
repartee *(n.)* ጎጀለ *gojele*
repatriate *(v.)* ዓንቀፀ *aneqetse*
repatriation *(n.)* ኣብ ፀቢብ ቦታ *ab tsebib bota*
repay *(v.)* ፅፍሪ *txefri*
repayment *(n.)* ጭቃ *chiqa*
repeal *(v.)* ፅሩይ *tsxeruye*
repeat *(v.)* ፅሬት *tsxerete*
repel *(v.)* ሓፀበ *hatsxebe*
repellent *(adj.)* ንፁር *netsxur*
repent *(v.)* ምእላይ *meaelayi*
repentance *(n.)* ፅሩይ *tsxeruyi*
repentant *(adj.)* ጨደደ *chedede*
repercussion *(n.)* ጨዳድ *cdade*
repetition *(n.)* ምሕረት *meherte*
replace *(v.)* መሓሪ *mhari*
replacement *(n.)* ክሌምንታይን *klemintaine*
replay *(v.)* ነኽሰ *nKes*
replenish *(v.)* ካህናት *kahenat'*
replete *(adj.)* ካህን *kahin*
replica *(n.)* ቀሺ *qshi*
replicate *(v.)* ፀሓፊ *tsehafi*

reply *(v.)* ብልሂ *bilihi*
report *(v.)* ድምጺ ፈጠረ *dimtsi ftre'*
reportage *(n.)* ዓሚል *Amil*
reporter *(n.)* ፀድፊ *Tsxdefi*
repose *(n.)* ኩነታት ኣየር *kunetat ayer'*
repository *(n.)* መዛዘሚ ወሰናይ *mzammi wsanaye*
repossess *(v.)* ደየበ *deYebe*
reprehensible *(adj.)* ተዓወተ *tAwte'*
represent *(v.)* ተለጠፈ *tlTefe'*
representation *(n.)* ክሊኒክ *kliniqk*
representative *(adj.)* ኣጋጨዉ *agachewu*
repress *(v.)* መንቀርቀር *menqerker*
repression *(n.)* መንጠሊና *mentelina*
reprieve *(v.)* ሰዓት *seat'*
reprimand *(v.)* መግናሕቲ *megnaȟti*
reprint *(v.)* እንደገና ሓተመ *'èndegena ȟateme*
reprisal *(n.)* ዓፀወ *atsewe*
reproach *(v.)* ውሻጠ *wushate'*
reprobate *(n.)* ዝተቓረበ *zitqarebe*
reproduce *(v.)* ዝረገአ ደም *ziregeaA' deM'*
reproduction *(n.)* ክዳን *kidan*
reproductive *(adj.)* ከደነ *kedeNe'*
reproof *(n.)* ክዳዉንቲ *kidawunti'*
reprove *(v.)* ወቐሰ *weq̈ese*
reptile *(n.)* ደበና *debNa'*
republic *(n.)* ዕስለ ኣናሕብ *esil anahib*
republican *(adj.)* ሸኾና *shekona*
repudiate *(v.)* ኣዘናግአ *azenagiaa*
repudiation *(n.)* ኣዝዩ ጥዑም ግን ዝመርር *aziyu teum gin zemrer*
repugnance *(n.)* ጋንታ *ganeta*
repugnant *(adj.)* ኣፋፍኖት *afafenote*
repulse *(v.)* ላህዛዝ *lahezaZ'*
repulsion *(n.)* ዝተኣከቡ ነገራት *ziteakebu negerat*
repulsive *(adj.)* ኣጥቢቑ ሓዘ *atbiqu haze'*
reputation *(n.)* ኣሰልጣኒ *aseltani*
repute *(n.)* ሕመት *himet*
request *(n.)* ሓድነት *hatnet*
requiem *(n.)* ሻሕኻር *shahikar*
require *(v.)* ገምገም ባሕሪ *gemgem bahiriyi*
requirement *(n.)* ኣብ ገምገም ባሕሪ ዝርከብ *ab gemgem bahiri zirkeb*
requisite *(n.)* ለፀመ *ltseme'*
requisite *(adj.)* ጁባ *juba*
requisition *(n.)* ሸሓረ *shehare*
requite *(v.t.)* ኣገደዳሲ ኣካል *agededasi akal'*
rescind *(v.)* ኮረት *koret*
rescue *(v.)* ሰራሒ ሳእኒ *serahi saeni'*
research *(n.)* ኮብራ ተመን *korabe tmN'*
resemblance *(n.)* ዓለባ ሳሬት *aleba saret*
resemble *(v.)* ኮኬን *kocain*
resent *(v.)* ኩኩናይ መኮንን *kukunai mekonin*
resentment *(n.)* ቁፃር *qutsar*
reservation *(n.)* ሰፈር ኣብራሪ ኣየር *sefer abrar ayer*
reserve *(v.)* ድዱዕ *diduee'*

reservoir *(n.)* ሕዉስዋስ መስተ *hiwuswas meste*
reshuffle *(v.)* ዕቡይ *eebuY;*
reside *(v.)* ክእለት *keeileT*
residence *(n.)* ኮኮናት *coconat*
resident *(n.)* ኮኩን *cocoon*
residential *(adj.)* ምስጢራዊ ፅሑፍ *mesetirawi tsihuf*
residual *(adj.)* ትራፍ *traf*
residue *(n.)* ቀዋሚ *qewami*
resign *(v.)* ኣገደደ *agedded*
resignation *(n.)* ኣምረሓ *amreha*
resilient *(adj.)* ተመላሲ *temelasi*
resist *(v.)* ተቓወመ *teq̈aweme*
resistance *(n.)* ቡን *bun*
resistant *(adj.)* ካዝና *kazina*
resolute *(adj.)* ሳፁን ሬሳ *satsun resa*
resolution *(n.)* ቅልጣፈ *qiltafe*
resolve *(v.)* ዘዕግብ *heigib*
resonance *(n.)* ኣስተንተነ *astentene*
resonant *(adj.)* ተመሳሳሊ *temesasali*
resonate *(v.)* ግንዛበ *ginizabe*
resort *(n.)* ከይተመርዓዉ ሓቢሮም ነበሩ *keyitemerawu habirom neberu*
resound *(v.)* ተሳነየ *tesaneyei*
resource *(n.)* ዝሳነይን ዘእተዋደድን *zisaneyin etewadedin*
resourceful *(adj.)* ሓድነት *hadinet*
respect *(n.)* ሓድነት ዝፈጠረ *hadinet zifetere*
respectable *(adj.)* ዓኹለለ *qkulele*
respectful *(adj.)* ሳንቲም *sanetime*
respective *(adj.)* ሳንቲም ሰርሐ *sanetime sereha*
respiration *(n.)* ተገጣጠመ *tegetateme*
respirator *(n.)* ተጓንፎ *tegwanefo*
respire *(v.)* ዓለባ *aleba*
respite *(n.)* ቀፀላይ *qetselayi*
resplendent *(adj.)* ቆራር *qorare*
respond *(v.)* ቁርፀት ከብዲ *quretset kebedi*
respondent *(n.)* ተሓባበረ *tehababere*
response *(n.)* ትህብብር *tehibiberi*
responsibility *(n.)* ናይ ስራሕ ቦታ *nayei serahe bota*
responsible *(adj.)* ተደርዓመ *tederame*
responsive *(adj.)* ኳሌታ *kwaleta*
rest *(v.)* ኣከበ *akebe*
restaurant *(n.)* ትሕጃ *tihija*
restful *(adj.)* ኣከበ *akebe'*
restitution *(n.)* ተዋሕለለ *tewahilwlw*
restive *(adj.)* ተጠራቐመ *teteraqeme*
restoration *(adj.)* ኣምፀአ *amtseA'*
restore *(v.)* ኮሌጅብርኪ ትምህርቲ *co;ege berki temihereti*
restrain *(v.)* ተጋጨወ *tegachewe*
restraint *(n.)* ናይ ማዕድን *nayi maeidin*
restrict *(n.)* ናይ ምግጫዉ ሓደጋ *nayei megechaw hadega*
restriction *(n.)* ቀያዲ *qeyadi*
restrictive *(adj.)* ምሽጥራዊ ስምምዕ *mishtirawi simemeeh*

result *(n.)* ሽቶ *shito*
resultant *(adj.)* ዓብይ መእንጣ *abiy meanta*
resume *(v.)* ኮሎኔል *kolonele*
resumption *(n.)* ባዕዳዊ *baeedawi*
resurgence *(a.)* ብባእዳዉያን ትግዛዕ ሃገር *bibaedawiyane tegezaze hager*
resurgent *(adj.)* ገዚፍ *gezife*
resurrect *(v.)* ሓወልቲ *hawelti*
retail *(n.)* ዓንዲ *anedi*
retailer *(n.)* ሕብሪ *hibri*
retain *(v.i.)* ፅልዋ ኣሕደረ *tsilwa ahdere*
retainer *(n.)* ዝተሕብረ *zitehibri*
retaliate *(v.)* ሕሊና ምስሓት *hilina mesehate*
retaliation *(n.)* ሚዶ/መመሸጥ *mido/memesheti*
retard *(v.)* ኹናት *kunat*
retardation *(n.)* ተዋጋኢ *tewagaei*
retarded *(adj.)* ጥማር *timar*
retch *(v.)* ፀንበረ *tsenber*
retention *(n.)* ነዳዲ *nedadi*
retentive *(adj.)* ተቐፃፃላይ *teqetsatsalaye*
rethink *(v.)* ናዓ *na'ä*
reticent *(adj.)* መስሓቕ *meshaq̈*
retina *(n.)* መስሓቕ *meshaq̈*
retinue *(n.)* ጅራታም ኮኾብ *ĵratam*
retire *(v.)* ምቾት *mchot*
retirement *(n.)* ጥጣሐ *ẗtahe*
retiring *(adj.)* ምቹእ *mchu'è*
retort *(v.)* ተዋዛዪ *tewazayi*
retouch *(v.)* ጭሕጋር *čhgar*
retrace *(v.t.)* ኣዘዘ *azeze*
retract *(v.)* ኣዛዚ *azazi*
retread *(v.)* ኮማንደር *komander*
retreat *(v.t.)* ኮማንዶ *komando*
retrench *(v.)* ኣኽበረ *ak̈bere*
retrenchment *(n.)* ዝክር *zkr*
retrial *(n.)* ጀመረ *ĵemere*
retribution *(n.)* ምጅማር *mĵmar*
retrieve *(v.)* ነኣደ *ne'ade*
retriever *(n.)* ዚነኣድ *zine'ad*
retro *(adj.)* ናእዳ *na'èda*
retroactive *(adj.)* ርእይቶ *r'èyto*
retrograde *(adj.)* ታዕሊቕ *ta'ëliq̈*
retrospect *(n.)* ዓላቒ *älaq̈i*
retrospective *(adj.)* ንግድ *ngd*
return *(v.)* ንግዳዊ *ngdawi*
return *(n.)* ራህርሀ *rahrhe*
reunion *(n.)* ውክልና *wklna*
reunite *(v.)* ኮሚሽነር *komishner*
reuse *(v.)* መጋጠሚ *megatmi*
revamp *(v.)* ፈጸመ *fexeme*
reveal *(v.)* መብጽዓ *mebx'ä*
revel *(v.)* ሽማግለ *shmagle*
revelation *(n.)* ተመዛዚ ከብሒ *temezazi kebḧi*
revenge *(n.)* ኣቕሓ *'aq̈ḧa*
revenue *(n.)* ሓባራዊ *ḧabarawi*
reverberate *(v.)* ሓፋሽ *ḧafash*
revere *(v.)* ልሙድ *lmud*
revered *(adj.)* ናይ ሓባር ብልጽግና *nay ḧabar blxgna*
reverence *(n.)* ህውከት *hwket*
reverend *(adj.)* ኮማዊ *komawi*
reverent *(adj.)* ተዋህደ *tewahde*
reverential *(adj.)* ተማሓላለፊ *temaḧalalefi*
reverie *(n.)* ቈራቢ *qWerabi*
reversal *(n.)* ሃበሬታ ተለዋወጠ *habereta*

reverse *(v.)* ርክብ *rkb*
reversible *(adj.)* ምክፋል *mkfal*
revert *(v.)* ዴስነት *deesnet*
review *(n.)* ማሕበረ ሰብ *mahbere seb*
revile *(v.)* ለወጠ *leweṫe*
revise *(v.)* ጥርኑፍ *ṫrnuf*
revision *(n.)* ብጸይ *bxay*
revival *(n.)* መሰነይታ *meseneyta*
revivalism *(n.)* ተነጸጸሪ *tenexaxeri*
revive *(v.)* ኣነጸጸረ *anexaxere*
revocable *(adj.)* ምንጽጻር *mnxxar*
revocation *(n.)* ክፍሊ *kfli*
revoke *(v.)* ቡሶላ *busola*
revolt *(v.)* ድንጋጸ *dngaxe*
revolution *(n.)* ተቓዳዊ *teq̈adawi*
revolutionary *(adj.)* ወዲ ሃገር *wedi hager*
revolutionize *(v.)* ቀሰ'በ *qesebe*
revolve *(v.)* ቁንጩል *qunčul*
revolver *(n.)* ቁንጩል *qunčul*
revulsion *(n.)* ከሓሰ *keḧase*
reward *(n.)* ካሕሳ *kaḧsa*
rewind *(v.)* ኣላ'ላዪ *alalayi*
rhapsody *(n.)* ተቐዳደመ *teq̈edademe*
rhetoric *(n.)* ክእለት *k'èlet*
rhetorical *(adj.)* ክኢላ *k'ila*
rheumatic *(adj.)* ምውድዳር *mwddar*
rheumatism *(n.)* ውድድራዊ *wddrawi*
rhinoceros *(n.)* ተዋዳዳሪ *tewadadari*
rhodium *(n.)* ጠርነፈ *ṫernefe*
rhombus *(n.)* ዕጉብ *ëgub*
rhyme *(n.)* ተጣርዐ *teṫar'ë*
rhythm *(n.)* ዝበልዎ ሕራይ ዝብል *zibeliwo hirayi zibil*
rhythmic *(adj.)* ምቕሉል *mq̈lul*
rib *(n.)* መልአ *meleA'*
ribbon *(n.)* መላኢ *mela'i*
rice *(n.)* ምሉእ *mlu'è*
rich *(adj.)* ምፍጻም *mfxam*
richly *(adv.)* ዝተሓላለኸ *zteḧalaleḱe*
richness *(n.)* ሕልኽልኽ *ḧlḱlḱ*
rick *(n.)* ወጅሂ *weĵhi*
rickets *(n.)* እሺታ *èshita*
rickety *(adj.)* ምቕሉል *mq̈lul*
rickshaw *(n.)* ሓላለኸ *ḧalaleḱe*
rid *(v.)* ሕልኽልኽ *ḧlḱlḱ*
riddance *(n.)* ምስ ግበነኛ *mis gibenegna*
riddle *(n.)* ምሽባን *mshban*
riddled *(adj.)* ናእዳ *na'èda*
ride *(v.)* ናእዳ *na'èda*
rider *(n.)* ተኣዘዘ *te'azeze*
ridge *(n.)* ክፋል *kifale*
ridicule *(n.)* ኣኽበረ *aḱbere*
ridiculous *(adj.)* ኣቔመ *aq̈Weme*
rife *(adj.)* ደራሲ ወራቢ *derasi werabi*
rifle *(n.)* ዝተዋሃሃደ *ztewahahade*
rifle *(v.)* ምድላው *mdlaw*
rift *(n.)* ለቓም ፊደል *leq̈am fidel*
rig *(v.)* ድኹዒ *dḱu'ï*
rigging *(n.)* ቅሳነት *qsanet*
right *(adj.)* ውሁድ *whud*
right *(n)* ተረድአ *tered'e*
righteous *(adj.)* ኪርዳእ ዚከኣል *kirda'è zike'al*
rightful *(adj.)* ምርዳእ *mrda'è*
rigid *(adj.)* ኣጠቓላሊ *aṫeq̈alali*
rigmarole *(n.)* ጨበጠ *čebeṫe*

rigorous *(adj.)* ምጭባጥ *mčbaṫ*
rigour *(n.)* ሓዘ *ḧaze*
rim *(n.)* ግድድፍ *gddf*
ring *(n.)* ምግዳ'ድ *mgdad*
ring *(v.)* ግዴታዊ *gdeetawi*
ringlet *(n.)* ግድነታዊ *gdnetawi*
ringworm *(n.)* ስክፍታ *skfta*
rink *(n.)* ምቕማር *mq̈mar*
rinse *(v.)* ቌጸረ *qWexere*
riot *(n.)* ኮምፕዩተር *kompyuter*
rip *(v.)* ኣራጠበ *aratebe*
ripe *(adj.)* ብጻይ *bxay*
ripen *(v.)* ምትእስሳር *mt'èssar*
riposte *(n.)* ሃጓም *hagWam*
ripple *(n.)* ሓብአ *ḧab'e*
rise *(v.)* ኣመነ *amene*
risible *(adj.)* ትዕቢት *t'ëbit*
rising *(n.)* ተኣማኒ *te'amani*
risk *(n.)* ተረድአ *tered'e*
risky *(adj.)* ኣጽዓቕ *ax'äq̈e*
rite *(n.)* ምጽዓቕ *mx'äq̈*
ritual *(n.)* ኣምር *amr*
rival *(n.)* ምእማር *m'èmar*
rivalry *(n.)* ተመልከተ *temelkete*
rive *(v.)* ብዛዕባ *bza'ëba*
river *(n.)* ሙዚቃዊ ምርኢት *muziqawi mr'it*
rivet *(n.)* ውሁድ *whud*
rivulet *(n.)* ሕድገት *ḧdget*
road *(n.)* ዛዕጎል *za'ëgol*
roadster *(n.)* ወድአ *wed'e*
roadwork *(n.)* ደገፍ ረኸበ *degef rek̗ebe*
roadworthy *(adj.)* ሓጺርን ብሩህን *ḧaxirn bruhn*
roam *(v.)* መወዳእታ *meweda'èta*
roar *(n.)* ደካሊ *dekali*
roar *(v.)* ኣቃመመ *aqameme*

roast *(v.)* ፈጠራ *feṫera*
rob *(v.)* መኻይድቲ *mek̗aydti*
robber *(n.)* ስምምዕ *smm'ë*
robbery *(n.)* ስምምዕ *smm'ë*
robe *(n.)* ብሓባር ምኻድ *bḧabar mk̗ad*
robot *(n.)* ጭቡጥ *čbuṫ*
robust *(adj.)* ውሽማ *wshma*
rock *(n.)* ተሰማምዐ *tesemam'ë*
rocket *(n.)* ተቓዳዊ *teq̈adawi*
rocky *(adj.)* መውቃዕቲ *mewqa'ëti*
rod *(n.)* ኰነነ *kWanene*
rodent *(n.)* ምኹናን *mk̗unan*
rodeo *(n.)* ሓፈሰ *ḧafese*
roe *(n.)* ተበርጠጠ *tebertete*
rogue *(n.)* ቀመመ *qememe*
roguery *(n.)* ኩነት *kunet*
roguish *(adj.)* ኩነታዊ *kunetawi*
roister *(v.)* ኩነታት ጥዕና *kunetate tiena*
role *(n.)* ደበ'ሰ *debese*
roll *(v.i.)* ምጽንናዕ *mxnna'ë*
roll *(n.)* ኮንዶም *condom*
roll-call *(n.)* ኣስማት ምጽዋዕ *'asmat mxwa'ë*
roller *(n.)* መሓረ *meḧare*
rollercoaster *(n.)* ጠባይ *ṫebay*
romance *(n.)* ኣደብ *adeb*
romantic *(adj.)* መራሒ *meraḧi*
romp *(v.)* ኮኖ *kono*
roof *(n.)* ሕዋስ ምቁራን *ḧwas mquran*
roofing *(n.)* ናይ ዶልሺ *naydolshi*
rook *(n.)* እንዳ-ዶልሺ *èndadolshi*
rookery *(n.)* ተሓባባሪ *teḧababari*
room *(n.)* ማሕበር *maḧber*
roomy *(adj.)* ዓደለ *ädele*
roost *(n.)* ዘተ *zete*

rooster *(n.)* **ተናዘዘ** *tenazeze*
root *(n.)* **ኑዛዜ** *nuzazee*
rooted *(adj.)* **ኣማኒት** *amanit*
rope *(n.)* **ምስጢር ኣካፈለ** *msẗir 'akafele*
rosary *(n.)* **እምነት** *èmnet*
rose *(n.)* **ተኣማማኒ** *te'amamani*
rosette *(n.)* **ምስጢራዊ** *msẗirawi*
roster *(n.)* **ኣሰራርዓ** *aserar'ä*
rostrum *(n.)* **ወሰነ** *wesene*
rosy *(adj.)* **ማእሰርቲ** *ma'èserti*
rot *(v.)* **ኣረጋገጸ** *aregagexe*
rota *(n.)* **ምርግጋጽ** *mrggax*
rotary *(adj.)* **ወረሰ** *werese*
rotate *(v.)* **ውርሳ** *wrsa*
rotation *(n.)* **ፀንበረ** *tsenbere*
rote *(n.)* **ግጭት** *gčt*
rotor *(n.)* **መራኽቦ** *meraḱbo*
rotten *(adj.)* **ሓባሪ** *ḧabari*
rouge *(n.)* **ተሰማምዐ** *tesemam'ë*
rough *(adj.)* **ስምምዕ** *smm'ë*
roulette *(n.)* **ተጋተረ** *tegatere*
round *(adj.)* **ቅርሕንቲ** *kiri hinti*
roundabout *(n.)* **ኣደናገረ** *adenagere*
rounded *(adj.)* **ዕግርግር** *ëgrgr*
roundly *(adv.)* **ረትዐ** *ret'ë*
rouse *(v.)* **ዚወሃሃድ** *ziwehahad*
rout *(n.)* **ውርሻዊ** *wrshawi*
route *(n.)* **ቅጽጽ ዝበለ** *qxx zbele*
routine *(n.)* **ጻዕቂ** *xa'ëqi*
rove *(v.)* **ኣኻኽበ** *aḱaḱebe*
rover *(n.)* **እኽብካብ** *èḱbkab*
roving *(adj.)* **ተንቀሳቓሲ** *tenqesaq̈asi*
row *(n.)* **መግለጺ ሓጐስ** *meglexi ḧagWas*
rowdy *(adj.)* **ተኣከበ** *te'akebe*
royal *(n.)* **ጉባኤ** *guba'ee*
royalist *(n.)* **ዝስማዕማዕ** *zismaemae tsemaexmeaa*
royalty *(n.)* **ተሰስማዕመዐ** *tsemaexmeaa*
rub *(n.)* **ግምታዊ ሓሳብ** *gemetawi hasabe*
rub *(v.)* **ፋሕፍሐ** *faḧfḧe*
rubber *(n.)* **ግጥሚ አንበበ** *geTemi anebbb*
rubbish *(n.)* **መስተፃምር** *,mestetsamire*
rubble *(n.)* **ጠራፊ መሳርዕ** *Terafi ms*
rubric *(n.)* **ናይ ቁስለት ዓይኒ** *nay'l qusele't aa'yeni*
ruby *(n.)* **ዋኒን/ጉዳይ** *manien/guda'yi*
rucksack *(n.)* **ምትሃተኛ** *meteha'te'gna*
ruckus *(n.)* **ኮራዕ** *kora'ee*
rudder *(n.)* **ኣራኽበ** *aara'EH'kebe*
rude *(adj.)* **ርክብ** *re'KE'be*
rudiment *(n.)* **ተመሻጠረ** *temeSHA'tere*
rudimentary *(adj.)* **ወረረ** *were're*
rue *(v.)* **ወረራ** *we're'ra*
rueful *(adj.)* **ሕሊና** *hi'lina*
ruffian *(n.)* **ግንዛበ ዘለዎ** *giniza'be zelewo*
ruffle *(v.)* **ቀደሰ** *qede'se*
rug *(n.)* **ተኸታታሊ** *teHE'tata'li*
rugby *(n.)* **ዝተሓተ** *zi'te'hat'ee*
rugged *(adj.)* **ሓበራዊ ምርድዳእ** *haberawi merederaoo*
ruin *(n.)* **ፍቓድ** *feqa'de*
ruinous *(adj.)* **ስምምዕ** *se'memeee*
rule *(n.)* **ሳዕቤን** *saee'bene*

rule *(v.)* ውፅኢት *wutsieiit*
ruler *(n.)* ሓለዋ ተፈጥሮ *haalewa tefetero*
ruling *(n.)* ፀረ ለዉጢ *tsere lewuti*
rum *(n.)* ሰርዐ *sereaa'*
rumble *(v.)* ብቑጠባ ተጠቐመ *b'quteba te'teqe'mu*
rumbustious *(adj.)* ኣስተንተነ *aa' seten'tene*
ruminant *(n.)* ብዙሕ *bezuHi'h*
ruminate *(v.)* ሓሳቢ *ha'sabi*
rumination *(n.)* ኣብ ግምት ኣእተወ *hab' gimit aaetewe*
rummage *(v.)* ኣተኩሩ ረኣየ *aa' tekuru rexayee*
rummy *(n.)* ሰንደወ *senedwwe*
rumour *(n.)* ዝተለኣኹ ኣቑሑት *zetelezaaHu aaqkuhut*
rumple *(v.)* ኣካተተ *aakate'te*
rumpus *(n.)* ተኸታታሊ *te'KHE'tatali*
run *(n.)* ዘይቕየር *zey'qeyer*
run *(v.)* መፅናዕንዒ *mexenaee'neeeii*
runaway *(adj.)* ኣፀናንዐ *a'txennea*
rundown *(adj.)* ኣሐየለ *ahayl'e*
rung *(n.)* ስምምዕ *sememe'*
runnel *(n.)* ሰብኣይ ንግስቲ *sebeaayi negeseti*
runner *(n.)* ጐያዪ *gWayayi*
runny *(adj.)* ብቐሊሉ ዝረኣይ *beqlilu zereaayii*
runway *(n.)* ፀንበረ *xeneber*
rupture *(v.t.)* ሻራ *shara*
rural *(adj.)* ዉዱት *wudit*
ruse *(n.)* ተመሻጠረ *temeshatere*
rush *(v.)* ኮንስታብል *konstablee*
Rusk *(n.)* ኮንስታብል ሰብነት *konstable sebenet'*
rust *(n.)* ዘየቐርፅ *zeye'qereXe'*
rustic *(adj.)* ናይ ከዋኽብቲ *naye kKe'wakib'ti*
rusticate *(v.)* ድንጋፀ *denegaXE'*
rustication *(n.)* ድርቀት *dere'qe'T*
rusticity *(n.)* ክፋል *kefale*
rustle *(v.)* ኣድማፂ *adma'txi*
rusty *(adj.)* ተሓሰበ *teha'sebe*
rut *(n.)* ሕገ መንግስቲ *hige mengistii*
ruthless *(adj.)* ኩነታት ጥዕና ውልቀሰብ *kunetat tieiina wulkeseb*
rye *(n.)* ኣጋደደ *aagadede*

S

Sabbath *(n.)* ኣፀበበ *axebebbe'*
sabotage *(v.)* ሃነፀ *hanXE'*
sabre *(n.)* ህንፀት *hintsxet'*
saccharin *(n.)* ሃናፂ *hanatxi'*
saccharine *(adj.)* ተረደአ *teredeA'*
sachet *(n.)* ቆንስል *qonesele*
sack *(n.)* ቆንፅላ *qonexela*
sack *(v.)* ናይቆንስል ገዛ *nayi qonsele geza*
sacrament *(n.)* ኣማኸረ *aAmaHe're*
sacred *(adj.)* ኣማኻሪ *amaHa'ri*
sacrifice *(n.)* ተመማኻኸረ *temeHaHere'*
sacrifice *(v.)* ተመቐመ *temeQeme'*
sacrificial *(adj.)* ሸማቲ *shemati*
sacrilege *(n.)* ርክብ ግብረ ስጋ ፈፀመ *rekib gibre siga fetxem'e*

sacrilegious *(adj.)* **ምጥቓም** *miT; Qqam'*
sacrosanct *(adj.)* **ርክብ** *rikib*
sad *(adj.)* **ምልጋብ** *milgab*
sadden *(v.)* **ተላጋቢ** *telagabi*
saddle *(n.)* **ሓዘ** *haze'*
saddler *(n.)* **ኮንቴነር** *konte'ner*
sadism *(n.)* **ምዕጋት** *meegat*
sadist *(n.)* **መራዚ ንጥረ ነገር** *merazi netire negere'*
safari *(n.)* **ሓሰበ** *haseb*
safe *(adj.)* **ኣትኹሩ ረኣየ** *xteKuru reAaye'*
safe *(n.)* **እዋናዊ** *eewanawi*
safeguard *(n.)* **ንዕቐት** *neeeiqet*
safety *(n.)* **ሸለልታ** *shelelta*
saffron *(n.)* **ተኸራኸረ** *teHerakere*
sag *(v.)* **ዝዓገበ** *zea'gebe*
saga *(n.)* **ትሕዝቶ** *tihizeto*
sagacious *(adj.)* **ቅርሕንቲ** *kqir'hinti*
sagacity *(n.)* **ዕግበት** *qeig'bet*
sage *(n.)* **ዘቀሓሕር** *zeqkeha'hir*
sage *(adj.)* **ዉድድር** *wudi'dir*
sail *(v.)* **ሃዋህው** *hawahewu'*
sail *(n.)* **ተወዳዳሪ** *te'we'dada'Rei*
sailor *(n.)* **ጥቓንጥቓ** *tQAneTeQA'*
saint *(n.)* **ክፍለ አለም** *kefele ale'm*
saintly *(adj.)* **ክፍለ አለማዊ** *kefele alemawii*
sake *(n.)* **ሳክ** *sak*
salad *(n.)* **ተደጋጋሚ** *tedegagami*
salary *(n.)* **ቀፀለ** *qeTsele'*
sale *(n.)* **ዝተቐፃፀለ** *zeteqaTsaTse'le*
saleable *(adj.)* **ተደጋጋሚ** *tedegagami*
salesman *(n.)* **ቀፃላይ** *qetsetay*
salient *(adj.)* **እስርስር በለ** *esir'sir bele*
saline *(adj.)* **ወሰናወሰን** *wesena'wesen*
salinity *(n.)* **ምፅባዕ** *mitsbaee*
saliva *(n.)* **ጥፍጣፍ** *ẗfẗaf*
sallow *(adj.)* **ምክልኻል ጥንሲ** *meihil'hal tinsi*
sally *(n.)* **ፍንጣሰ** *fnẗase*
salmon *(n.)* **ናይ ዉዕሊ** *nayei wueili'*
salon *(n.)* **ሳሎን** *salon*
saloon *(n.)* **ዉዕሊ ፈፀመ** *raḧreḧe*
salsa *(n.)* **ተኾናታሪ** *awarede*
salt *(n.)* **ኣሕፀረ** *had'e*
salty *(adj.)* **ተፃበአ** *ztegedfe*
salutary *(adj.)* **ተፃረረ** *gedam*
salutation *(n.)* **ተቓራኒ** *abegedam*
salute *(n.)* **ኣፈላላይ** *mḧxar*
salvage *(v.)* **ሕጊ ጠሓሰ** *werede*
salvation *(n.)* **ኣዋፅአ** *mwrad*
salver *(n.)* **ወፈየ** *neq̈ele*
salvo *(n.)* **ኢ-ተአማኒነት** *ḧamed*
Samaritan *(n.)* **ገበረ** *kebdi*
same *(adj.)* **ቁፅፅር** *nay kebdi*
sample *(n.)* **ተቖፃፃሪ** *zerefe*
sampler *(n.)* **ኣከራኻሪ** *zerefe*
sanatorium *(n.)* **ኽርክር** *mzbul*
sanatorium *(n.)* **ገበነኛ እዩ በለ** *mẗfa'è bele eyik*
sanctification *(n.)* **ስምብራት** *sḧtan*
sanctify *(v.)* **ሽግር** *adefafere*
sanctimonious *(adj.)* **ጭዋ** *wunzafe*
sanction *(v.)* **ኣኼባ ፀወዐ** *fenfene*
sanctity *(n.)* **ምኾት** *krhat*
sanctuary *(n.)* **ምችዊ** *kruh*

sanctum ***(n.)*** **ናይ ደናግል ገዳም** *xen'ë*
sand ***(n.)*** **ባህሊ/ልምዲ** *zeywda'è gedam*
sandal ***(n.)*** **ተኣኻኸበ** *'äq̈mi*
sandalwood ***(n.)*** **ፍልጠት ዘለዎ** *ḧrtum zelwo*
sander ***(n.)*** **ወግዒ** *meḧale*
sandpaper ***(n.)*** **ኣዋግዐ** *lbu'ë*
sandwich ***(n.)*** **ምቕያር** *nfu'ë bq̈u'ë*
sandy ***(adj.)*** **ቀየረ** *me'änaẗu*
sane ***(adj.)*** **ተቐየረ** *mzbul*
sangfroid ***(n.)*** **ገለፀ** *'ab l'ëli*
sanguinary ***(adj.)*** **አጓጓዘ** *geza*
sanguine ***(adj.)*** **ገበነኛ** *'aẗfe'e*
sanitary ***(adj.)*** **ገበነኛነት** *zixla'è*
sanitation ***(n.)*** **ኣእመነ** *xel'e*
sanitize ***(v.)*** **ምሹእ/ደስ ዝብል** *ẗntawi*
sanity ***(n.)*** **ኣኼባ** *tewegre*
sap ***(n.)*** **ተዓጂበን ብሓባር ዝኸዳ** *mwgad*
sapling ***(n.)*** **ኣንቀጥቀጠ** *wgur*
sapphire ***(n.)*** **ምንቅጥቃጥ** *fedfede*
sarcasm ***(n.)*** **ከሻኒ** *bza'ëba*
sarcastic ***(adj.)*** **ኣብሰለ** *'ab zurya*
sarcophagus ***(n.)*** **ዘበናዊ እቶን** *'ab l'ëli*
sardonic ***(adj.)*** **ኬክ** *bzyada*
sari ***(n.)*** **ዝሑል** *lḧlaḧe*
sartorial ***(adj.)*** **ዛሕሊ** *faḧfaḧi*
sash ***(n.)*** **ዝሕልቱ** *godnegodni*
Satan ***(n.)*** **ምሕዳስ** *aḧxere*
satanic ***(adj.)*** **ተሓባበረ** *wexa'i*
Satanism ***(n.)*** **ትሕብብር** *sereze*
satchel ***(n.)*** **ተሓጋገዘ** *handebetawi*
sated ***(adj.)*** **ኣተሓባበረ** *ḧagel*
satellite ***(n.)*** **ሓቢሩ ከደ** *xeleq̈Wu*
satiable ***(adj.)*** **ተፃወረ** *bkurat*
satiate ***(v.)*** **ብማሽን ዝተገልበጠ ቅዳሕ** *bḱur*
satiety ***(n.)*** **ኣዝዩ ብዙሕ** *bḱur*
satin ***(n.)*** **መዳብ** *fxum*
satire ***(n.)*** **ሰረረ** *sreet*
satirical ***(adj.)*** **ቅዳሕ** *meḧare*
satirist ***(n.)*** **ናይ ሓንቲ ሓባ** *seteye*
satirize ***(v.)*** **ደረቕ ተረር** *teq̈eẗebe*
satisfaction ***(n.)*** **ፍሕሶ** *zahdi*
satisfactory ***(adj.)*** **ልባዊ** *req̈iq̈*
satisfy ***(v.)*** **ዝተስለፉ ፖላይስ** *ẗluq̈*
saturate ***(v.)*** **ወዉሽጣዊ ኣካ** *trgum 'albo*
saturation ***(n.)*** **ተኽሊ ቅመቃ ቕመም** *trgum 'albonet*
Saturday ***(n.)*** **ኮረኺ** *ml'at*
saturnine ***(adj.)*** **ሱማ** *fdfud*
sauce ***(n.)*** **ፃዕዳ አይኒ** *ämexe*
saucer ***(n.)*** **ኹርናዕ** *texarafi*
saucy ***(adj.)*** **ዘዛንመሎ** *tedawebe*
sauna ***(n.)*** **ስርዓተ ንግስና** *delhametawi*
saunter ***(v.)*** **መርማሪ** *delhamet*
sausage ***(n.)*** **ኣኽሊል** *akademiyawi*
savage ***(adj.)*** **ኣካላዊ** *akademi*
savagery ***(n.)*** **ዓብይ** *mexe*
save ***(v.)*** **ዓብይ ትካል ንግዲ** *nehare*
savings ***(n.)*** **ብርጌድ** *anhari*
saviour ***(n.)*** **ነቐለ ከደ ተሰናበተ** *neq̈ele kede tesenabete*
savour ***(v.t.)*** **ሓመድ** *ḧamed*
savoury ***(adj.)*** **ከብዲ** *kebdi*
saw ***(n.)*** **ናይ ከብዲ** *nay kebdi*

saw *(v.)* ዘረፈ *zerefe*
sawdust *(n.)* ዘረፈ *zerefe*
saxophone *(n.)* ምዝቡል *mzbul*
say *(n.)* ስሕታን *sḧtan*
saying *(n.)* ኣደፋፈረ *adefafere*
scab *(n.)* ዉንዛፈ *wunzafe*
scabbard *(n.)* ፈንፈነ *fenfene*
scabies *(n.)* ክርሃት *krhat*
scabrous *(adj.)* ክሩህ *kruh*
scaffold *(n.)* ጸንዐ *xen'ë*
scaffolding *(n.)* ዘይውዳእ *zeywda'è*
scald *(v.)* ዓቕሚ *'äq̈mi*
scale *(n.)* ሕርቱም *ḧrtum*
scallop *(n.)* መሓለ *meḧale*
scalp *(n.)* ልቡዕ *lbu'ë*
scam *(n.)* ንፉዕ ብቑዕ *nfu'ë bq̈u'ë*
scamp *(n.)* መዓናጡ *me'änaẗu*
scamper *(v.t.)* ምዝቡል *mzbul*
scan *(v.)* ኣብ ልዕሊ *'ab l'ëli*
scandal *(n.)* ኣጥፈአ *'aẗfe'e*
scandalize *(v.)* ምጥፋእ *mẗfa'è*
scanner *(n.)* ገዛ *geza*
scant *(adj.)* ዚጽላእ *zixla'è*
scanty *(adj.)* ጸልአ *xel'e*
scapegoat *(n.)* ጥንታዊ *ẗntawi*
scar *(n.)* ተወግረ *tewegre*
scarce *(adj.)* ምውጋድ *mwgad*
scarcely *(adv.)* ውጉር *wgur*
scare *(v.)* ፈድፈደ *fedfede*
scarecrow *(n.)* ብዛዕባ *bza'ëba*
scarf *(n.)* ኣብ ዙርያ *'ab zurya*
scarlet *(n.)* ኣብ ልዕሊ *'ab l'ëli*
scarp *(n.)* ብዝያዳ *bzyada*
scary *(adj.)* ልሕላሐ *lḧlaḧe*
scathing *(adj.)* ፋሕፋሒ *faḧfaḧi*
scatter *(v.)* ጎድነ-ጎድኒ *godnegodni*
scavenge *(v.)* ኣሕጸረ *aḧxere*
scenario *(n.)* ወጻኢ *wexa'i*
scene *(n.)* ሰረዘ *sereze*
scenery *(n.)* ሃንደበታዊ *handebetawi*
scenic *(adj.)* ሓገል *ḧagel*
scent *(n.)* ጸለቝ *xeleq̈Wu*
sceptic *(n.)* ብኩራት *bkurat*
sceptical *(adj.)* ብዅር *bḱur*
sceptre *(n.)* ብዅር *bḱur*
schedule *(n.)* ፍጹም *fxum*
schematic *(adj.)* ስሬት *sreet*
scheme *(n.)* መሓረ *meḧare*
schism *(n.)* ሰተየ *seteye*
schizophrenia *(n.)* ተቐጠበ *teq̈eẗebe*
scholar *(n.)* ዛህዲ *zahdi*
scholarly *(adj.)* ረቒቕ *req̈iq̈*
scholarship *(n.)* ጥሉቕ *ẗluq̈*
scholastic *(adj.)* ትርጉም ኣልቦ *trgum 'albo*
school *(n.)* ትርጉም ኣልቦነት *trgum 'albonet*
sciatica *(n.)* ምልኣት *ml'at*
science *(n.)* ፍድፉድ *fdfud*
scientific *(adj.)* ዓመጸ *ämexe*
scientist *(n.)* ተጸራፊ *texarafi*
scintillating *(adj.)* ተዳወበ *tedawebe*
scissors *(n.)* ደልሃመታዊ *delhametawi*
scoff *(v.i.)* ደልሃመት *delhamet*
scold *(v.)* ኣካደሚያዊ *akademiyawi*
scoop *(n.)* ኣካደሚ *akademi*
scooter *(n.)* መጸ *mexe*
scope *(n.)* ነሃረ *nehare*
scorch *(v.)* ኣንሃሪ *anhari*

score *(n.)* ምጉላሕ *mgulaḧ*
score *(v.)* ኣጉለሐ *aguleḧe*
scorer *(n.)* ተቐበለ *teq̈ebele*
scorn *(n.)* ተቐባልነት ዘለዎ *teq̈ebalnet zelewo*
scornful *(adj.)* ቅባለ *qbale*
scorpion *(n.)* መእተዊ *me'ètewi*
Scot *(v.)* ኪርኪብ ዚከኣል *kirkeb zike'al*
scot-free *(adv.)* ብጽሓት *bxḧat*
scoundrel *(n.)* መሳርሒ *mesarḧi*
scour *(v.)* ሓደጋ *ḧadega*
scourge *(n.)* ናይ ሓደጋ *nay ḧadega*
scout *(n.)* ኣጨብጨበ *ačebčebe*
scowl *(n.)* ኣዕነወ *a'ënewe*
scrabble *(v.)* ሰላምታ *selamta*
scraggy *(adj.)* ተሰማምዐ *tesemam'ë*
scramble *(v.)* መዕረፍ ኣጋይሽ *me'ëref 'agaysh*
scrap *(n.)* መሰነይቲ *meseneyti*
scrape *(v.)* ዓጀበ *äĵebe*
scrappy *(adj.)* ግብረ-ኣበር *gbre'aber*
scratch *(v.t.)* ፈጸመ *fexeme*
scrawl *(v.)* ክኢላ *k'ila*
scrawny *(adj.)* ፍጻሜ *fxamee*
scream *(v.)* ተውህዶ *tewhdo*
screech *(n.)* ውዕል - *w'ël*
screech *(n.)* ብመሰረት *bmeseret*
screed *(n.)* በዚ ምኽንያት'ዚ *bezi mḱnyatzi*
screen *(n.)* ጐነፈ *gWanefe*
screw *(n.)* ሕሳብ *ḧsab*
screwdriver *(n.)* ተሓታቲ *teḧatati*
scribble *(v.)* ናይ ተጻባጻቢ ሞያ *nay texabaxabi moya*
scribe *(n.)* ተጸባጸቢ *texebaxabi*
scrimmage *(n.)* ብወግዒ ለኣኸ *bweg'ï le'aḱe*
scrimp *(v.)* ብወግዒ ለኣኸ *bweg'ï le'aḱe*
script *(n.)* ወግዓዊ *weg'äwi*
scripture *(n.)* ዕብየት *ëbyet*
scroll *(n.)* ደለበ *delebe*
scrooge *(n.)* ኣዋህለለ *awahlele*
scrub *(v.)* ውህለላ *whlela*
scruffy *(adj.)* ልክዕ *lk'ë*
scrunch *(v.)* ግዚ *gzi*
scruple *(n.)* ከሰሰ *kesese*
scrupulous *(adj.)* ተሓታትነት *teḧatatnet*
scrutinize *(v.)* ለመደ *lemede*
scrutiny *(n.)* ልሙድ *lmud*
scud *(v.)* ሓደ *ḧade*
scuff *(v.)* ኣረቢክ *arebik*
scuffle *(n.)* እምባ-ጋሮ *'èmbagaro*
sculpt *(v.)* ነታጐ *netagWi*
sculptor *(n.)* ቃንዛ *qanza*
sculptural *(adj.)* ተጎናጸፈ *tegonaxefe*
sculpture *(n.)* ፍጻሜ *fxamee*
scum *(n.)* መጺጽ *mexix*
scurrilous *(adj.)* መጭቋር *mečqWAr*
scythe *(n.)* ኣመስገነ *amesgene*
sea *(n.)* ምቕጻል *mq̈xal*
seagull *(n.)* ጫፍ *čaf*
seal *(n.)* ዕንፍሩር *ënfrur*
sealant *(n.)* ኣናጎንስጤስ *anagonsẗees*
seam *(n.)* ጭምዳድ *čmdad*
seamy *(adj.)* ኣፋለጠ *afaleẗe*
sear *(v.)* ሌላ *leela*

search *(v.)* **ተሰማምዐ** *tesemam'e*
seaside *(n.)* **ምስምማዕ** *msmma'e*
season *(n.)* **ረኸበ** *reḱebe*
seasonable *(adj.)* **ቅስመት** *qsmet*
seasonal *(adj.)* **ፈትሐ** *fetḧe*
seasoning *(n.)* **ናጻ ምልቃቕ** *naxa mlqaq̈*
seat *(n.)* **ኣክር** *akr*
seating *(n.)* **በዳን** *bedan*
secede *(v.)* **ምረት** *mret*
secession *(n.)* **ኣክሮባት** *akrobat*
seclude *(v.)* **ባሪቶን** *bariton*
secluded *(adj.)* **ስግር** *sgr*
seclusion *(n.)* **ዘርዕድ** *zer'ëd*
second *(adj.)* **ምግባር** *mgbar*
secondary *(adj.)* **ግዜያዊ ፈጻሚ** *gzeeyawi fexami*
secrecy *(n.)* **ምውሳእ** *mwsa'è*
secret *(adj.)* **ዘፍርህ** *zefrh*
secretariat *(n.)* **ምግባር** *mgbar*
secretary *(n.)* **ጸሓፊ** *xeḧafi*
secrete *(v.)* **ኣንጠፈ** *anẗefe*
secretion *(n.)* **ንጡፍ** *nẗuf*
secretive *(adj.)* **ስነ-ጠቢብ** *sneẗebib*
sect *(n.)* **ንጥፈት** *nẗfet*
sectarian *(adj.)* **ተዋናይ** *tewanay*
section *(n.)* **ተዋሳኢት** *tewasa'it*
sector *(n.)* **ህሉው** *hluw*
secular *(adj.)* **ብሓቂ** *bḧaqi*
secure *(adj.)* **ገምጋሚ** *gemgami*
security *(n.)* **ኣንጠፈ** *anẗefe*
sedan *(n.)* **ትኩርና** *tkurna*
sedate *(adj.)* **መሪድያን** *meridyan*
sedation *(n.)* **ንሱር** *nsur*
sedative *(n.)* **ተሪር** *terir*
sedentary *(adj.)* **ኣልዘበ** *alzebe*
sediment *(n.)* **ምውህሃድ** *mwhhad*
sedition *(n.)* **ደመረ** *demere*
seditious *(adj.)* **መመላእታ** *memela'èta*
seduce *(v.)* **ተወለፈ** *tewelefe*
seduction *(n.)* **ምውላፍ** *mwlaf*
seductive *(adj.)* **ወልፊ** *welfi*
sedulous *(adj.)* **ምድማር** *mdmar*
see *(v.)* **ተወሳኺ** *tewesaḱi*
seed *(n.)* **ዓቃቢ** *äqabi*
seedy *(adj.)* **ድንጉር** *dngur*
seek *(v.i.)* **ኣድራሻ** *adrasha*
seem *(v.)* **መሰለ** *mesele*
seemly *(adj.)* **ጠቐሰ** *ẗeq̈ese*
seep *(v.)* **ክኢላ** *k'ila*
seer *(n.)* **እኹልነት** *èḱulnet*
see-saw *(n.)* **እኹል** *èḱul*
segment *(n.)* **ሰዓበ** *se'äbe*
segregate *(v.)* **ምድጋፍ** *mdgaf*
segregation *(n.)* **ላጋቢ** *lagabi*
seismic *(adj.)* **ላጋቢ ደሓን ኩን** *deḧan kun*
seize *(v.)* **ጕረቤት** *gWarebeet*
seizure *(n.)* **ቅጽል** *qxl*
seldom *(adv.)* **ሳሕቲ** *saḧti*
select *(v.)* **ኣቋረጸ** *aqWArexe*
selection *(n.)* **ኣመሓላለፈ** *ameḧalalefe*
selective *(adj.)* **በየነ** *beyene*
self *(n.)* **ፈረደ** *ferede*
selfish *(adj.)* **ጥብቆ** *ẗbqo*
selfless *(adj.)* **ኣመዓራረየ** *ame'ärareye*

self-made ***(adj.)*** **ምውዳድ** *mwdad*
sell ***(v.)*** **አመሓደረ** *amehadere*
seller ***(n.)*** **ምምሕዳር** *mmhdar*
selvedge ***(n.)*** **ምምሕዳራዊ** *mmhdarawi*
semantic ***(adj.)*** **ኣመሓዳሪ** *amehadari*
semblance ***(n.)*** **ዚነኣድ** *zine'ad*
semen ***(n.)*** **ኣድሚራል** *admiral*
semester ***(n.)*** **ኣድናቖት** *adnaq̈ot*
semicircle ***(n.)*** **ኣድነቐ** *adneq̈e*
semicolon ***(n.)*** **ዚፍቀድ** *zifqed*
seminal ***(adj.)*** **ቅበላ** *qbela*
seminar ***(n.)*** **ተኣመነ** *te'amene*
Semitic ***(adj.)*** **ቅበላ** *qbela*
senate ***(n.)*** **ገሰጸ** *gesexe*
senator ***(n.)*** **ሸቐልቀል** *sheq̈elqel*
senatorial ***(adj.)*** **ጥረ-ሕጡብ** *ẗrehẗub*
send ***(v.)*** **ብጽሕና** *bxhna*
senile ***(adj.)*** **በጽሒ** *bexhi*
senility ***(n.)*** **ወሰደ** *wesede*
senior ***(adj.)*** **ምርዓም** *mr'äm*
seniority ***(n.)*** **ረዓሚ** *re'ämi*
sensation ***(n.)*** **ተፈታዊ** *tefetawi*
sensational ***(adj.)*** **ፍቕሪ** *fq̈ri*
sensationalize ***(v.)*** **ኣምለኸ** *amleḱe*
sense ***(n.)*** **ኣሰወነ** *asewene*
senseless ***(adj.)*** **ፋሉል** *falul*
sensibility ***(n.)*** **ጨለ** *čele*
sensible ***(adj.)*** **ኣድሶረብ** *adserb*
sensitive ***(adj.)*** **ውዳሰ-ከንቱ** *wdasekentu*
sensitize ***(v.)*** **እኹል** *èḱul*
sensor ***(n.)*** **ኣመራሰሐ** *amerasehe*
sensory ***(adj.)*** **ምምርሳሕ** *mmrsah*
sensual ***(adj.)*** **ዝሙት** *zmut*
sensualist ***(n.)*** **ሰጐመ** *segWame*
sensuality ***(n.)*** **ለዓለ** *le'äle*
sensuous ***(adj.)*** **ምምዕባል** *mm'ëbal*
sentence ***(n.)*** **ብልጫ** *blča*
sententious ***(adj.)*** **ረብሓ** *rebha*
sentient ***(adj.)*** **ጠቓሚ** *ẗeq̈ami*
sentiment ***(n.)*** **ምጽኣት** *mx'at*
sentimental ***(adj.)*** **ዕንደራ** *ëndera*
sentinel ***(n.)*** **ሓደገ'ኛ** *hadegeǹa*
sentry ***(n.)*** **ተወሳከ-ግሲ** *tewesakegsi*
separable ***(adj.)*** **ተጻይ** *texay*
separate ***(v.)*** **ኣሉታዊ** *alutawi*
separation ***(n.)*** **ሽግር** *shgr*
separatist ***(n.)*** **ኣፋለጠ** *afaleẗe*
sepsis ***(n.)*** **ረክላም** *reklam*
September ***(n.)*** **ምዕዶ** *m'ëdo*
septic ***(adj.)*** **ዝሓሸ** *zhashe*
sepulchral ***(adj.)*** **መዓደ** *me'äde*
sepulchre ***(n.)*** **ደጋፊ** *degafi*
sepulchre ***(n.)*** **ተሓላቒ** *tehalaq̈i*
sequel ***(n.)*** **ዑቕባ** *üq̈ba*
sequence ***(n.)*** **ሰፋፊ** *sefafi*
sequential ***(adj.)*** **ኣዩን** *ayun*
sequester ***(v.)*** **ኣይሮባቲክስ** *ayrobatiks*
serene ***(adj.)*** **ማሪዋና** *mariwana*
serenity ***(n.)*** **መዓርፎ ነፈርቲ** *me'ärfo neferti*
serf ***(n.)*** **ስነ-ምንፋር** *snemnfar*
serge ***(n.)*** **ኣይሮፕላን** *ayroplan*
sergeant ***(n.)*** **ፍሊት** *flit*
serial ***(adj.)*** **ናይ ነፈርቲ** *nay neferti*

serialize *(v.)* **ጽባቐኣዊ** *xbaq̈e'awi*
series *(n.)* **ስነ-ጽባቐ** *snexbaq̈e*
serious *(adj.)* **ካብ ርሑቕ** *kab rḧuq̈*
sermon *(n.)* **ፍሕሹው** *fḧshuw*
sermonize *(v.)* **ፍጻሜ** *fxamee*
serpent *(n.)* **ጸለወ** *xelewe*
serpentine *(adj.)* **ምስሉይነት** *msluynet*
serrated *(adj.)* **ኣምሳሊ** *amsali*
servant *(n.)* **ፍትወት** *ftwet*
serve *(v.)* **ርህሩህ** *rhruh*
server *(n.)* **ቃለ-ማሕላ** *qalemaḧla*
service *(n.)* **ተጸግዐ** *texeg'ë*
serviceable *(adj.)* **ምጽጋዕ** *mxga'ë*
serviette *(n.)* **ተማስሎ** *temaslo*
servile *(adj.)* **ኣረጋገጸ** *aregagexe*
servility *(n.)* **ምርግጋጽ** *mrggax*
serving *(n.)* **ኣወንታዊ** *awentawi*
sesame *(n.)* **ልቃ'በ** *lqabe*
session *(n.)* **ጐድአ** *gWad'e*
set *(n)* **ሃብቲ** *habti*
set *(v.)* **ጬንቂ** *čnqi*
settee *(n.)* **ሃብታም** *habtam*
setter *(n.)* **ኣተኻኸለ** *atek̗ak̗ele*
setting *(n.)* **ምግራብ** *mgrab*
settle *(v.)* **ናዕቢ** *na'ëbi*
settlement *(n.)* **ዘለፈ** *zelefe*
settler *(n.)* **ኣብ ርሑቕ** *'ab rḧuq̈*
seven *(adj. & n.)* **ዝተቓጸለ** *zteq̈axele*
seventeen *(adj. & n.)* **ዘንሳፍፍ** *zensaff*
seventeenth *(adj. & n.)* **ኣብ ምቅርራብ** *'ab mqrrab*
seventh *(adj. & n.)* **ዝፈርሀ** *zferhe*
seventieth *(adj. & n.)* **ከም ብሓድሽ** *kem bḧadsh*
seventy *(adj. & n.)* **ኣፍሪቃ** *afriqa*
sever *(v.)* **ኣብ ሪተ-መርከብ** *'ab ritemerkeb*
several *(adj. & pron.)* **ድሕሪ** *dḧri*
severance *(n.)* **ድሕረ** *dḧre*
severe *(adj.)* **ድሕረ** *dḧri*
severity *(n.)* **እንደገና** *'èndegena*
sew *(v.)* **ኣንጻር** *anxar*
sewage *(n.)* **ተሪር ክቡር እምኒ** *terir kbur 'èmni*
sewer *(n.)* **ዕድመ** *ëdme*
sewerage *(n.)* **ሽማግለታት** *shmagletat*
sex *(n.)* **ቅድመ-ፍርዲ** *qdmefrdi*
sexism *(n.)* **ዘልኣለማዊ** *zel'alemawi*
sexton *(n.)* **ናይ ውክልና ትካል** *nay wklna tkal*
sextuplet *(n.)* **ኣጀንዳ** *aĵenda*
sexual *(adj.)* **ግሉል** *glul*
sexuality *(n.)* **ኣከበ** *akebe*
sexy *(adj.)* **ኣግደደ** *agdede*
shabby *(adj.)* **ዘቁጥዕ** *zeq̈uẗ'ë*
shack *(n.)* **ደመረ** *demere*
shackle *(n.)* **መጥቃዕቲ** *meẗqa'ëti*
shade *(v.)* **ኣጥቃዒ** *aẗqa'ï*
shade *(n.)* **ዓማጺ** *ämaxi*
shadow *(a.)* **ዝሰምበደ** *zsembede*
shadow *(n.)* **ኣቐየመ** *aq̈eyeme*
shadowy *(adj.)* **ስሉጥ** *sluẗ*
shady *(adj.)* **ሶፕራኖ** *soprano*
shaft *(n.)* **ቀስቀሰ** *qesqese*
shag *(n.)* **ምኳስ** *mk̗Was*
shake *(v.)* **ኢፈሊጣዊ** *ifeliẗawi*
shaky *(adj.)* **ድኹም ቀይቃይ** *dk̗um qeyqay*

shall *(v.)* **ርቡጽ** *rbux*
shallow *(adj.)* **ሃወኸ** *haweḱe*
sham *(n.)* **መሪር ሓዘን** *merir ḧazen*
shamble *(v.)* **መሬታዊ** *mereetawi*
shambles *(n.)* **ተሰማምዐ** *tesemam'ë*
shame *(n.)* **ዚሰማማዕ** *zisemama'ë*
shameful *(adj.)* **ስምምዕ** *smm'ë*
shameless *(adj.)* **ሕርሻዊ** *ḧrshawi*
shampoo *(n.)* **ሕርሻ** *ḧrsha*
shank *(n.)* **ኣብ ባይታ** *'ab bayta*
shanty *(n.)* **ኣብ ቅድሚ** - *'ab qdmi*
shape *(n.)* **ረድአ** *red'e*
shapeless *(adj.)* **ደጋፊ** *degafi*
shapely *(adj.)* **ረድኢ** *red'i*
shard *(n.)* **ኣጨነቐ** *ačeneq̈e*
share *(n.)* **ኣጨነቐኢ** *ačeneq̈e'i*
shark *(n.)* **ሕማም** *ḧmam*
sharp *(adj.)* **ዕላማ** *ëlama*
sharpen *(v.)* **ሽቶ** *shto*
sharpener *(n.)* **ሰሓተ** *seḧate*
shatter *(v.t.)* **ኣየር** *ayer*
shattering *(adj.)* **ነፋሪት** *nefarit*
shave *(v.)* **ነፋሻ** *nefasha*
shaven *(adj.)* **ኮሪደዮ** *korideyo*
shaving *(n.)* **ዝተገፍተነ** *ztegeftene*
shawl *(n.)* **ዚዛመድ** - *zizamed*
she *(pron.)* **ስሉጥ** *sluẗ*
sheaf *(n.)* **ቅሩብነት** *qrubnet*
shear *(v.)* **መጠንቀቕታ** *meẗenqeq̈ta*
sheath *(n.)* **ስግኣት** *sg'at*
shed *(n.)* **ዋይ ኣነ** *way 'ane*
sheen *(n.)* **ሽሕ'ኳ** *shḧkWa*
sheep *(n.)* **ኣልቡም** *'album*
sheepish *(adj.)* **ኣልቡመን** *albumen*
sheer *(adj.)* **ኣልከሚ** *alkemi*
sheet *(n.)* **ኣልኮል** *alkol*
shelf *(n.)* **ሰታይ** *setay*
shell *(n.)* **ስብሳብ** *sbsab*
shelter *(n.)* **መጽለሊ** *mexleli*
shelve *(v.)* **ጥንቁቕ** *ẗnquq̈*
shepherd *(n.)* **ኣልጀብራ** *alĵebra*
shield *(n.)* **ሳጓ** *sagWa*
shift *(v.)* **ልውጠ-ስም** *lwẗesm*
shiftless *(adj.)* **ሓከየ** *ḧakeye*
shifty *(adj.)* **ምያ ዘሎዎ** *mya zelowo*
shimmer *(v.)* **ነጸለ** *nexele*
shin *(n.)* **ዚነድድ** *zinedd*
shine *(v.)* **ሰርዐ** *ser'ë*
shingle *(n.)* **ኣሳላልፋ** *asalalfa*
shiny *(adj.)* **ተመሳሳሊ** *temesasali*
ship *(n.)* **ክፍሊት ፍትሕ** *kflit ftḧ*
shipment *(n.)* **ህያው** *hyaw*
shipping *(n.)* **ኣልካሊ** *alkali*
shipwreck *(n.)* **ኩሉ** *kulu*
shipyard *(n.)* **ኣፋኰሰ** *afakWase*
shire *(n.)* **ብህሎ** *bhlo*
shirk *(v.)* **ኣለ** *ale*
shirker *(n.)* **ተኣማንነት** *te'amannet*
shirt *(n.)* **ምስሌኣዊ ዛንታ** *mslee'awi zanta*
shiver *(v.)* **ኣሕረቐ** *aḧreq̈e*
shoal *(n.)* **ተቖጣዒ** *teq̈oẗa'ï*
shock *(n.)* **ቁጥዐ** *quẗ'ë*
shock *(v.)* **ኣፋኸሰ** *afaḱWase*
shocking *(adj.)* **ምቕላል** *mq̈lal*
shoddy *(adj.)* **መሽጕራጕር** *meshgWaragur*
shoe *(n.)* **ኪዳን** *kidan*

shoestring *(n.)* ተጸግዐ *texeg'ë*
shoot *(v.)* ዓንጎግ *ängog*
shooting *(n.)* ደምሰሰ *demsese*
shop *(n.)* ድግመተ-ኣፈና *dgmete'afena*
shopkeeper *(n.)* ኣካፈለ *akafele*
shoplifting *(n.)* ምምቕራሕ *mmq̈raḧ*
shopping *(n.)* ኣማስሐ *amasḧe*
shore *(n.)* ምስሒት *msḧit*
short *(adj.)* ፈቐደ *feq̈ede*
shortage *(n.)* መውዕሎ *mew'ëlo*
shortcoming *(n.)* ቆርቆሮ *qorqoro*
shortcut *(n.)* ኣመተ *amete*
shorten *(v.)* ኣወናወነ *awenawene*
shortfall *(n.)* ኣወናወኒ *awenaweni*
shortly *(adv.)* ኣመት *amet*
should *(v.)* ሽርካ *shrka*
shoulder *(n.)* ኣልማናክ *almanak*
shout *(v.i.)* ኩሉ ዚከኣሎ *kulu zike'alo*
shove *(v.)* ሉዝ *luz*
shovel *(n.)* ዳርጋ *darga*
show *(v.)* ምጽ'ዋት *mxwat*
showcase *(n.)* ዝተሰቕለ *zteseq̈le*
showdown *(n.)* በይኑ *beynu*
shower *(n.)* ኣብ ጐድኒ *ab gWadni*
showy *(adj.)* ኣብ ጐድነኒ *ab gWadneh*
shrapnel *(n.)* ግሉል *glul*
shred *(n.)* ብዓውታ *b'äwta*
shrew *(n.)* ኣልፋ *alfa*
shrewd *(adj.)* ፊደል *fidel*
shriek *(v.)* ወጨጨ *wečeče*
shrill *(adj.)* ከረናዊ *kerenawi*
shrine *(n.)* ዛጊት *zagit*
shrink *(v.)* ከምኡ'ውን *kem'uwn*
shrinkage *(n.)* መንበረ-ታቦት *menberetabot*
shrivel *(v.)* ጠረጴዛ ቁርባን *ťerep̈eeza qurban*
shroud *(n.)* ምልዋጥ *mlwaẗ*
shrub *(n.)* ቈይቈ *qWeyqWi*
shrug *(v.)* ምርጫ *mrča*
shudder *(v.)* ቅያር *qyar*
shuffle *(v.t.)* ምንም'ኳ *mnmkWa*
shun *(v.t.)* ብራኽ *braḱe*
shunt *(v.)* ኩሉኹሉ *kulukulu*
shut *(v.)* ልግስነት *lgsnet*
shutter *(n.)* ኣሉሚኒዮም *aluminiyom*
shuttle *(n.)* መደርብዮ *shuttle*
shuttlecock *(n.)* ኩሉ ግዜ *kulu gzee*
shy *(adj.)* ሕዋስ ባዚቃ *ḧwas baziqa*
sibilant *(adj.)* ደብለቐ *debleq̈e*
sibling *(n.)* ምሕባር *mḧbar*
sick *(adj.)* ኣከበ *akebe*
sickle *(n.)* ኣማተር *amater*
sickly *(adj.)* ዘይክኢላ *zeyk'ila*
sickness *(n.)* መስተፋቅር *mestefaqr*
side *(n.)* ኣገረመ *agereme*
sideline *(n.)* ኣድናቖት *adnaq̈ot*
siege *(n.)* ኣማዘን *amazen*
siesta *(n.)* ሓጺር ድቃስ *ḧaxir dqas*
sieve *(n.)* ዕንዲዳ ጌጽ *'ëndida geex*
sift *(v.)* ዙርያዊ *zuryawi*
sigh *(v.i.)* ዘይንጹርነት *zeynxurnet*
sight *(n.)* ዘይንጹር *zeynxur*
sighting *(n.)* ደረት *deret*

sightseeing *(n.)* ህርፋን *hrfan*
sign *(n.)* ህንጡይ *hnẗuy*
signal *(n.)* ማንታዊ *mantawi*
signatory *(n.)* ተሳለየ *tesaleye*
signature *(n.)* ምቁር *mqur*
significance *(n.)* ኣምቡላንስ *ambulans*
significant *(n.)* ድብያ *dbya*
signification *(n.)* ኣመሓየሸ *amešayeshe*
signify *(v.)* ምምሕያሽ *mmḧyash*
silence *(n.)* ኣመሓየሸ *amešayeshe*
silencer *(n.)* መኣረምታ *me'aremta*
silent *(adj.)* ተሓታቲ *teḧatati*
silhouette *(n.)* ተፈታዊ *tefetawi*
silicon *(n.)* ምሕዝነታዊ *mḧznetawi*
silk *(n.)* ኣብ መንጎ *'ab mengo*
silken *(adj.)* ግጉይ *gguy*
silkworm *(n.)* ዕርክነት *ërknet*
silky *(adj.)* ተተኳሲ *tetekWasi*
sill *(n.)* ርሳዕ *rsa'ë*
silly *(adj.)* ምሕረት *mḧret*
silt *(n.)* ብዕብድብድ *b'ëbdbd*
silver *(n.)* ኣብ መንጎ *ab mengo*
similar *(adj.)* ብዕሉግ *b'ëlug*
similarity *(n.)* ፍቕራዊ *fq̈rawi*
simile *(n.)* ቅርጸ-ኣልቦ *qrxe'albo*
simmer *(v.)* ማዕረ ኮነ *ma'ëre kone*
simper *(v.)* ኣምፐር *amper*
simple *(adj.)* ፍሉጥ ሰብ *fluẗ seb*
simpleton *(n.)* ምድረ-ማያዊ *mdremayawi*
simplicity *(n.)* ኣምፊትያትር *amfityatr*
simplification *(n.)* ሰፊሕ *sefiḧ*
simplify *(v.)* ተወሰኺ *tewesak̈i*
simulate *(v.)* መጉልሒ *megulḧi*
simultaneous *(adj.)* ኣጉልሐ *agulḧe*
sin *(n.)* ስፍሓት *sfḧat*
since *(prep.)* ክታብ *ktab*
sincere *(adj.)* ኣዘናግዐ *azenag'ë*
sincerity *(n.)* ምዝንጋዕ *mznga'ë*
sinecure *(n.)* ሓደ *ḧade*
sinful *(adj.)* ዕለቱ ዝሰሓተ *ëletu zseḧate*
sing *(v.)* ዋሕዲ ደም *waḧdi dem*
singe *(v.)* ድንዛዘ *dnzaze*
singer *(a.)* መደንዘዚ *medenzezi*
single *(adj.)* ቆይቋም *qoyqWAm*
singlet *(n.)* ጸረ-ቃንዛ *xereqanza*
singleton *(n.)* ተመሳሳሊ *temesasali*
singular *(adj.)* ተመሳሳልነት *temesasalnet*
singularity *(n.)* ተመሳሳልነት *temesasalnet*
singularly *(adv.)* ምትንታን *mtntan*
sinister *(adj.)* ምርምር *mrmr*
sink *(n.)* ትንታነኣዊ *tntane'awi*
sink *(v.)* ተንታኒ *tentani*
sinner *(n.)* ፋሉልነት *falulnet*
sinuous *(adj.)* ፋሉላዊ *falulawi*
sinus *(n.)* ፋሉልነት *falulnet*
sip *(v.)* ስነ-ቅርጺ ኣካል *sneqrxi 'akal*
siphon *(n.)* ኣበው *abew*
sir *(n.)* ውርሻዊ *wrshawi*
siren *(n.)* ኣበው *abew*
sissy *(n.)* መልህቕ *melhq̈*
sister *(n.)* ተዓሻገ *te'äshage*
sisterhood *(n.)* ጥንታዊ *ẗntawi*
sisterly *(adj.)* ጽግዕተኛ *xg'ëteǹa*

sit *(v.)* ድማ *dma*
site *(n.)* ጽግዕተኛ *xg'ëteňa*
sitting *(n.)* ጽዋ *xwa*
situate *(v.)* እንደገና *èndegena*
situation *(n., a)* ፍቱው *ftuw*
six *(adj.& n.)* ቁጥዐ *quť'ë*
sixteen *(adj. & n.)* ሕማም *ḧmam*
sixteenth *(adj. & n.)* ኩርናዕ *kurna'ë*
sixth *(adj. & n.)* ሕሩቕ *ḧruq̈*
sixtieth *(adj. & n.)* ጓሂ *gWahi*
sixty *(adj. & n.)* ኩርናዓዊ *kurna'äwi*
size *(n.)* እንስሳ *ènssa*
sizeable *(adj.)* ህያው *hyaw*
sizzle *(v.)*
skate *(n.)* ህያውነት *hyawnet*
skateboard *(n.)* ጽልኢ *xl'i*
skein *(n.)* ሸለን *shelen*
skeleton *(n.)* ዓንካር-ዓንካሪቶ *änkar'änkarito*
sketch *(n.)* ኣንባር *anbar*
sketchy *(adj.)* ዘይምሉእ *zeymlu'è*
skew *(v.)* ጎበጠ *gobeťe*
skewer *(n.)* ጐበጣ *gWabeťa*
ski *(n.)* ኣጽነተ *axnete*
skid *(v.)* ድምሰሳ *dmsesa*
skilful *(adj.)* ዝክረ-ዓመት *zkre'ämet*
skill *(n.)* ኣመልከተ *amelkete*
skilled *(adj.)* ገለጸ *gelexe*
skim *(v.)* መግለጺ *meglexi*
skimp *(adj.)* ሸወዘ *sheweze*
skin *(n.)* ቁጥዐ *quť'ë*
skinny *(adj.)* በብዓመት *beb'ämet*
skip *(v.)* በብዓመት *beb'ämet*
skipper *(n.)* ሰረዘ *sereze*
skirmish *(n.)* ግጥም *gťm*
skirt *(n.)* ቀብአ *qeb'e*
skirting *(n.)* ዘይስሩዕ *zeysru'ë*
skit *(n.)* ዘይስተ *zeyst*
skittish *(adj.)* ስመ-ስውርነት *smeswrnet*
skittle *(n.)* ስመ-ስውር *smeswr*
skull *(n.)* ምንማነ *mnmane*
sky *(n.)* ካልእ *kal'è*
skylight *(n.)* መልሲ *melsi*
skyscraper *(n.)* ኪምለስ ዚከኣል *kimles zike'al*
slab *(n.)* ጻጸ *xaxe*
slack *(adj.)* ጻጸ መጺጽ *xaxe mexix*
slacken *(v.)* ተጻራርነት *texararnet*
slag *(n.)* ተጻራሪ *texarari*
slake *(v.t.)* ተጻረረ *texarere*
slam *(v.)* ኣንታርክቲክ *antarktik*
slander *(n.)* ቅድመ ፍጻመ *qdme fxame*
slanderous *(adj.)* ኣቐደመ *aquadme*
slang *(n.)* ዓጋዜን *ägazeen*
slant *(v.)* ኣንተና *antena*
slap *(v.t.)* ኣንቴማ *anteema*
slash *(v.)* እኩብ ዛንታታት *'èkub zantatat*
slat *(n.)* ስነ-ሰብ *sneseb*
slate *(n.)* ነፍሪ *nefri*
slattern *(n.)* ጸረ *xere*
slatternly *(adj.)* ጸረ-ነፍሳት *xerenefsat*
slaughter *(n.)* ጸረ-ኣካል *xere'akal*
slave *(n.)* ወጀሃላይ *weĵehalay*
slavery *(n.)* ተጸበየ *texebeye*
slavish *(adj.)* ትጽቢት *txbit*
slay *(v.)* ምንቁልቋል *mnqulqWAl*
sleaze *(n.)* ጸረ-መርዚ *xeremerzi*

sleazy *(adj.)* **ጸረ-መርዚ** *xeremerzi*
sledge *(n.)* **ክርሃት** *krhat*
sledgehammer *(n.)* **ኩሕለ-ምሕሊ** *kuḧlemḧli*
sleek *(adj.)* **ዘጥንቲ** *zeẗnti*
sleep *(n.)* **ድሑር** *dḧur*
sleeper *(n.)* **ጥንታዊ** *ẗntawi*
sleepy *(adj.)* **ጥንቲ** *ẗnti*
sleet *(n.)* **ጸረ-ረኽሲ** *xerereḱsi*
sleeve *(n.)* **ጸረ-ማሕበራዊ** *xeremaḧberawi*
sleigh *(n.)* **ኣንጻር** *anxar*
sleight *(n.)* **ጭንፋር ቀርኒ** *čnfar qerni*
slender *(adj.)* **ኣሉታ** *aluta*
sleuth *(n.)* **መሃንቱስ** *mehantus*
slice *(n.)* **ጽላት** *xlat*
slick *(adj.)* **ጭንቀት** *čnqet*
slide *(v.)* **ሃረርተኛ** *harerteṅa*
slight *(adj.)* **ዝኾነ** *zḱone*
slightly *(adv.)* **ብዘይተገዳስነት** *bzeytegedasnet*
slim *(adj.)* **ዝኾነ ሰብ** *zḱone seb*
slime *(n.)* **ዝኾነ ነገር** *zḱone neger*
slimy *(adj.)* **ዝኾነ ቦታ** *zḱone bota*
sling *(n.)* **ብቕልጡፍ** *bq̈lẗuf*
slink *(v.)* **ዝተፈላለየ** *ztefelaleye*
slip *(v.)* **ኣፓርታይድ** *apartayd*
slipper *(n.)* **ክፍሊ-ገዛ** *kfligeza*
slippery *(adj.)* **ዘይተገዳስነት** *zeytegedasnet*
slit *(v.t.)* **ቀዳሒ** *qedaḧi*
slither *(v.)* **ጭርታ** *črta*
slob *(n.)* **ጫፍ** *čaf*
slobber *(v.)* **ምስላ** *msla*
slogan *(n.)* **መንህብ** *menhb*
slope *(v.)* **ርእሰ-ርጉጽነት** *r'èserguxnet*
sloppy *(adj.)* **ራእይ** - *ra'èy*
slot *(n.)* **ይቕሬታ ሓተተ** *q̈reeta ḧatete*
sloth *(n.)* **ይቕሬታ** *yq̈reeta*
slothful *(adj.)* **ኣፖፕለቲካዊ** *apopletikawi*
slouch *(v.)* **ከሓዲ እምነት** *keḧadi 'èmnet*
slough *(n.)* **ሃዋርያ** *hawarya*
slovenly *(adj.)* **ጭረት** *čret*
slow *(adj.)* **ኣስካሕከሐ** - *askaḧkeḧe*
slowly *(adv.)* **መሳርሒ** *mesarḧi*
slowness *(n.)* **ክዳን** *kdan*
sludge *(n.)* **ብሩህ** *bruh*
slug *(n.)* **ብሩህ** *bruh*
sluggard *(n.)* **ተራእየ** *tera'èye*
sluggish *(adj.)* **ምቕልቃል** *mq̈lqal*
sluice *(n.)* **ኣዝሓለ** *azḧale*
slum *(n.)* **መልአ** *mel'e*
slumber *(v.)* **መመላእታ** *memela'èta*
slump *(v.)* **ነድሪ ጥብቆ** *nedri ẗbqo*
slur *(v.)* **መመላእታ** *memela'èta*
slurp *(v.)* **ሸውሃት** *shewhat*
slush *(n.)* **ከፋት ሸውሃት** *kefat shewhat*
slushy *(adj.)* **ኣጨብጨበ** *ačebčebe*
slut *(n.)* **ጨብጨባ** *čebčeba*
sly *(adj.)* **ቱፋሕ** *tufaḧ*
smack *(n.)* **መሳርያ** *mesarya*
small *(adj.)* **ብቑዕ** *bq̈u'ë*
smallpox *(n.)* **ኣመልካቲ** *amelkati*
smart *(adj.)* **ምሕታት** *mḧtat*
smarten *(v.)* **ተጠቕመ** *teẗeq̈me*
smash *(v.)* **ወሰነ** *wesene*
smashing *(adj.)* **ቈጸራ** *qWexera*

smattering *(n.)* ጒዘየ *gWazeye*
smear *(v.)*
ዚሰማማዕ *zisemama'ë*
smell *(n.)* ገምገመ *gemgeme*
smelly *(adj.)* እኹል *èḱul*
smidgen *(n.)* ተገንዘበ *tegenzebe*
smile *(v.)* ኣስተያየት *asteyayet*
smirk *(v.)* ተረድአ *tered'e*
smith *(n.)* ምርዳእ *mrda'è*
smock *(n.)* ዝተሻቐለ *zteshaq̈ele*
smog *(n.)* ተልመዴን *telmedeen*
smoke *(n.)* ኣፍለጠ *afleẗe*
smoky *(adj.)* ቀረበ *qerebe*
smooch *(v.)* ብቑዕ *bq̈u'ë*
smooth *(adj.)* ምንዛዐ *mnza'ë*
smoothie *(n.)* ቅባለ *qbale*
smother *(v.)* ተቐበለ *teq̈ebele*
smoulder *(v.)* ዳርጋ *darga*
smudge *(v.)*
ሚሽሚሸ *mishmishe*
smug *(adj.)*
ግርምብያለ *grmbyale*
smuggle *(v.)* በሊሕ *beliḧ*
smuggler *(n.)* ተውህቦ *tewhbo*
snack *(n.)* ጠዓሞት *ẗe'ämot*
snag *(n.)* ማያዊ *mayawi*
snail *(n.)* ማያዊ *mayawi*
snake *(n.)* አረብ *areb*
snap *(v.)* አረቢያን *arebian*
snapper *(n.)* አረቢክ *arebik*
snappy *(adj.)* ገድላ *gedla*
snare *(n.)* ፈራዲ *feradi*
snarl *(v.t.)* ዳነየ *daneye*
snarl *(v.)* ሃውሪ *hawri*
snatch *(v.)* ዳኘነት *daṅnet*
snazzy *(adj.)* ዳኛ *daṅa*
sneak *(v.)* ዳስ *das*
sneaker *(n.)* ቀስቲ *qesti*
sneer *(n.)* ቀልደዳዊ *qeldedawi*
sneeze *(v.i.)* ቀልደድ *qelded*
snide *(adj.)* ስነ ጥንቲ *sne ẗnti*
sniff *(v.)* ጥንታዊ *ẗntawi*
sniffle *(v.)* ሊቀ መላእክት *liqe mela'èkt*
snigger *(n.)* ሊቀ-ጳጳሳት *liqep̣ap̣asat*
snip *(v.)* መንታጋይ *mentagay*
snipe *(v.)* ስነ-ሃናጺ *snehanaxi*
snippet *(n.)* ስነ-ህንጻ *snehnxa*
snob *(n.)* ኣርቺቭ *archiv*
snobbery *(n.)* ኣርክቲክ *arktik*
snobbish *(adj.)* ውዕውዕ *w'ëw'ë*
snooker *(n.)* ብርቱዕ ድሌት *brtu'ë dleet*
snooze *(n.)* ኣድካሚ *adkami*
snore *(n.)* ስፍሓት *sfḧat*
snort *(n.)* መድረኽ *medreḱ*
snout *(n.)* ተማጎተ *temagote*
snow *(n.)* መጎተ *megote*
snowball *(n.)* መጎቲና *megotina*
snowy *(adj.)* ኣጻምእ *axam'è*
snub *(v.)* ተላዕለ *tela'ële*
snuff *(v.)* ኣሪስቶክራሲ *aristokrasi*
snuffle *(v.)*
ኣሪስቶክራታዊ *aristokratawi*
snug *(adj.)* ቍጽሪ *quxri*
snuggle *(v.)* ቍጽሪና *quxrina*
so *(adv.)* ታቦት *tabot*
soak *(v.)* ምናት *mnat*
soap *(n.)* ሳሙና *samuna*
soapy *(adj.)* ኣርማጌዶን *armagedon*
soar *(v.i.)* ኣጽዋር *axwar*
sob *(v.)* ተነኽነኸ *teneḱneḱe*
sober *(adj.)* ድርዒ ሓጺን *dr'ï ḧaxin*

sobriety *(n.)* ድርዒ ሓጺነ *dr'ï ḧaxini*
soccer *(n.)* ሰራዊት *serawit*
sociability *(n.)* መዓዛ *me'äza*
sociable *(adj.)* መዓዛ - ፍወሳ *me'äza fwesa*
social *(adj.)* ኣብ ዙርያ *'ab zurya*
socialism *(n.)* ኣበራበረ *aberabere*
socialist *(n. & adj.)* ሰርዐ *ser'ë*
socialize *(v.)* ኣሰራርዓ *aserar'ä*
society *(n.)* ምሒር *mḧir*
sociology *(n.)* ተሰለፈ *teselefe*
sock *(n.)* ተሰለፈን *teselefin*
socket *(n.)* ኣሰረ *asere*
sod *(n.)* እትወት *ètwet*
soda *(n.)* መጸ *mexe*
sodden *(adj.)* ኣትሒቱ ረኣየ *'atḧitu re'aye*
sodomy *(n.)* ትዕቢተኛ *t'ëbiteña*
sofa *(n.)* መንዘዐ *menze'ë*
soft *(adj.)* ፍላጸ *flaxa*
soften *(v.)* እንዳብረት *èndabret*
soggy *(adj.)* ብርቱዕ ስሚ *brtu'ë smi*
soil *(n.)* ብውሳይ ምቅጻል *bwsay mqxal*
sojourn *(n.)* ጥበብ *ẗbeb*
solace *(n.)* ጥንቲ *ẗnti*
solar *(adj.)* ኣርተሪ *arteri*
solder *(n.)* ብልሂ *blhi*
soldier *(n.)* ሪሕ *riḧ*
sole *(n.)* ካርቾፊ *karchofi*
solely *(adv.)* ኣቕሓ *aq̈ḧa*
solemn *(adj.)* ኣነጸረ *anexere*
solemnity *(n.)* ክእለት *k'èlet*
solemnize *(v.)* ስኑ'ዕ *snu'ë*
solicit *(v.)* ከቢድ ብረት *kebid bret*
solicitation *(n.)* ክኢላ *k'ila*
solicitor *(n.)* ስነ-ጠቢብ *sneẗebib*
solicitous *(adj.)* ስነ-ጥበባዊ *sneẗbebawi*
solicitude *(n.)* ባህርያዊ *bahryawi*
solid *(adj.)* ከም *kem*
solidarity *(n.)* ሓድነት *solidarity*
soliloquy *(n.)* ደየበ *deyebe*
solitaire *(n.)* ደያቢ *deyabi*
solitary *(adj.)* ዕርገት *ërget*
solitude *(n.)* ኣረጋገጸ *aregagexe*
solo *(n.)* መናን *menan*
soloist *(n.)* ሃበ *habe*
solubility *(n.)* ጽዱይ *xduy*
soluble *(adj.)* ግብረ-ሰዶመኛ *gbresedomeña*
solution *(n.)* ኣሽ *ash*
solve *(v.)* ዝሓፈረ *zḧafere*
solvent *(n.)* ኤሽያዊ *eshiyawi*
sombre *(adj.)* ጽልሙት *xlmut*
some *(adj.)* ዓንጃል *änĵal*
somebody *(pron.)* ሓተተ *ḧatete*
somehow *(adv.)* ብጥርጣረ *bẗrẗare*
someone *(pron.)* ዘባል *zebal*
somersault *(n.)* ጽሙው *xmuw*
something *(pron.)* መልክዕ *melk'ë*
somewhat *(adv.)* ጎነጽ *gonex*
somewhere *(adv.)* ምክፋእ *mkfa'è*
somnambulism *(n.)* ዓበሰ *äbese*
somnambulist *(n.)* ደላዪ *delayi*
somnolence *(n.)* ትምኒት *tmnit*
somnolent *(adj.)* ሻሞት *shamot*
somnolent *(adj.)* ተመነየ *temeneye*
son *(n.)* ኣድጊ *adgi*

song *(n.)* አጥቀዐ *aẗqe'ë*
songster *(n.)* ቀታል-ነፍሲ *qetalnefsi*
sonic *(adj.)* ቀተለ *qetele*
sonnet *(n.)* ቀተለሊ *qeteli*
sonority *(n.)* አጥቀዐ *aẗqe'ë*
soon *(adv.)* ምግጥጣም *mgẗẗam*
soot *(n.)* አጋጠመ *agaẗeme*
soothe *(v.)* አኼባ *aḱeeba*
sophism *(n.)* ስምምዕ *smm'ë*
sophist *(n.)* ጸዓደ *xe'äde*
sophisticate *(n.)* አማኻሪ *amaḱari*
sophisticated *(adj.)* መርመራ *mermera*
sophistication *(n.)* ንብረት *nbret*
soporific *(adj.)* ጻዕረኛ *xa'ëreňa*
sopping *(adj.)* ረተበ *retebe*
soppy *(adj.)* ምደባ *mdeba*
sorbet *(n.)* ምዱብ ስራሕ *mdub sraḧ*
sorcerer *(n.)* ተዋሃደ *tewahade*
sorcery *(n.)* ተዋህዶ *tewahdo*
sordid *(adj.)* ሓገዘ *ḧageze*
sore *(adj.)* ሓገዝ *ḧagez*
sorely *(adv.)* ረዳት *redat*
sorrow *(n.)* ተሓባባሪ *teḧababari*
sorry *(adj.)* ማሕበር *maḧber*
sort *(n.)* ስምምዕ *smm'ë*
sortie *(n.)* ዝተፋላለየ *ztefalaleye*
sough *(v.)* በብዓይነቱ *beb'äynetu*
soul *(n.)* አጸናንዐ *axenan'ë*
soul mate *(n.)* መረጋገጺ *meregagexi*
soulful *(adj.)* ገመተ *gemete*
soulless *(adj.)* ግምት *gmt*
sound *(n.)* አረጋገጸ *aregagexe*
soundproof *(adj.)* ዋሕስ *waḧs*
soup *(n.)* ኣስትሪስክስ *astrisks*
sour *(adj.)* ዓለም *älem*
source *(n.)* ኣዝማ *azma*
souse *(v.)* ነበዐ *nebe'ë*
south *(n.)* ኣደነቐ *adeneq̈e*
southerly *(adj.)* ድንጽዉና *dnxwuna*
southern *(adj.)* ኣስደመመ *asdememe*
souvenir *(n.)* ኮኾባዊ *koḱobawi*
sovereign *(n.)* ህውቱት *hwtut*
sovereignty *(n.)* ብምግሕታን *bmgḧtan*
sow *(n.)* ብልጹግ *blxug*
spa *(n.)* ቈጸራ ከዋኽብቲ *qWexera kewaḱbti*
space *(n.)* ጠፈርተኛ *ẗeferteňa*
spacious *(adj.)* ስነ-ኮኾቢ *snekoḱobi*
spade *(n.)* ስነ-ኮኾብ *snekoḱob*
spam *(n.)* ትኩር *tkur*
span *(n.)* ዝተፈላለየ *ztefelaleye*
Spaniard *(n.)* ዑቕባ *üq̈ba*
spaniel *(n.)* ኣብ *ab*
Spanish *(n.)* የዋህ *yewah*
spank *(v.)* ኢዚሀርነት *izihernet*
spanking *(adj.)* ኢዚሄራዊ *iziheerawi*
spanner *(n.)* ስፖርተኛ *sporteňa*
spare *(adj.)* ስፖርታዊ *sportawi*
sparing *(adj.)* ኣትላስ *atlas*
spark *(n.)* ሃዋህው *hawahw*
sparkle *(v.)* ደሴት *deseet*
sparkling *(n.)* ኣቶም *atom*
sparrow *(n.)* ኣቶማዊ *atomawi*
sparse *(adj.)* ከሓሰ *keḧase*
spasm *(n.)* ድሕነት *dḧnet*
spasmodic *(adj.)* ክፍሊ *kfli*

spastic *(adj.)* **አሰቃቒ** *aseqaq̈i*
spat *(n.)* **ገፍዐ** *gef'ë*
spate *(n.)* **ኣጣበቐ** *aẗabeq̈e*
spatial *(adj.)* **ኣታሽ** *atash*
spatter *(v.)* **ጥብቀት** *ẗbqet*
spawn *(v.)* **ኣጥቅዐ** *aẗq'ë*
spay *(v.)* **ምሉእ** *mlu'è*
speak *(v.)* **ሰመረ** *semere*
speaker *(n.)* **ፈተ'ነ** *fetene*
spear *(n.)* **ጀመረ** *ĵemere*
spearhead *(n.)* **ተኸታተለ** *teḱetatele*
spearmint *(n.)* **ተሳትፎ** *tesatfo*
special *(adj.)* **ኣገልጋሊ** *agelgali*
specialist *(n.)* **ኣቓልቦ** *aq̈albo*
speciality *(n.)* **ጥንቁቕ** *ẗnquq̈*
specialization *(n.)* **ኣረጋገጸ** *aregagexe*
specialize *(v.)* **ዋልድቢት** *waldbit*
species *(n.)* **ልብሲ** *lbsi*
specific *(adj.)* **ኣቃጫጭ** *aqačač*
specification *(n.)* **ጠበቓ** *ẗebeq̈a*
specify *(v.)* **ሰሓበ** *seḧabe*
specimen *(n.)* **ስሕበት** *sḧbet*
specious *(adj.)* **ማራኺ** *maraḱi*
speck *(n.)* **ባህርይ** *bahry*
speckle *(n.)* **ማርጋሪን** *margarin*
spectacle *(n.)* **ሓራጅ** *ḧaraĵ*
spectacular *(adj.)* **ኪስማዕ ዚከኣል** *kisma'ë zike'a*
spectator *(n.)* **ነባሮ** *nebaro*
spectral *(adj.)* **ደሃይ** - *dehay*
spectre *(n.)* **ጸብጻብ** *xebxab*
spectrum *(n.)* **ናይ ምስማዕ ፈተና** *nay msma'ë fetena*
speculate *(v.)* **ኦዲቶርዮም** *'oditoryomme'akebi 'aderash*
speculation *(n.)* **ወሰኸ** *ወሰኸ*
speech *(n.)* **ነሓሰ** *neḧase*
speechless *(adj.)* **ሓትኖ** *ḧatno*
speed *(n.)* **ኣኽሊል** *aḱlil*
speedway *(n.)* **ተስፋኣዊ** *tesfa'awi*
speedy *(adj.)* **ጥብቂ** *ẗbqi*
spell *(v.t.)* **አዎስትራልያ** *awustraliya*
spellbound *(adj.)* **ሓቀኛ** *ḧaqeña*
spelling *(n.)* **ልክዕነት** *lk'ënet*
spend *(v.)* **ደራሲ** *derasi*
spendthrift *(n.)* **ምዙዝ** *mzuz*
sperm *(n.)* **መዚ** *mezi*
sphere *(n.)* **መዘዘ** *mezeze*
spherical *(n.)* **አዉቲዝም** *awutizim*
spice *(n.)* **ርእሰ-ታሪኽ** *r'èsetariḱ*
spicy *(adj.)* **ኣውቶክራሲ** *awtokrasi*
spider *(n.)* **ውልቀ-መላኺ** *wlqemelaḱi*
spike *(n.)* **ኣውቶክራቲክ** *wlqemelaḱ*
spiky *(adj.)* **ርእሰ-ጽሑፍ** *r'èsexḧuf*
spill *(v.)* **ኣውቶማቲክ** *awtomatik*
spillage *(n.)* **ኣውቶሞቢል** *awtomobilmekina*
spin *(v.)* **ርእሰ-ምምሕዳራዊ** *r'èsemmḧdarawi*
spinach *(n.)* **ምርምረ-ሬሳ** *mrmrereesa*
spinal *(adj.)* **ቀውዒ** *qew'ï*
spindle *(n.)* **ሓጋዚ** *ḧagazi*
spindly *(adj.)* **ተጠቕመ** *teẗeq̈me*
spine *(n.)* **ክትጥቀመሉ ትኽእል** *ktẗqemelu tḱ'èl*
spineless *(adj.)* **መደረጋሕ** *mederegaḧ*
spinner *(n.)* **ስስዐ** *ss'ë*

spinster *(n.)* ሕነ ፈደየ *ḧne fedeye*
spiral *(adj.)* ጐደና *gWadena*
spire *(n.)* ማእከላይ *ma'èkelay*
spirit *(n.)* ኣንጻር *anxar*
spirited *(adj.)* ጽልኣት *xl'at*
spiritual *(adj.)* ኣለየ *aleye*
spiritualism *(n.)* እንዳ ኣዕዋፍ *'ènda 'a'ëwaf*
spiritualist *(n.)* ስነ-ምንፋር *snemnfar*
spirituality *(n.)* ፓይሎት *paylot*
spit *(n.)* ህንጡይ *hnẗuy*
spite *(n.)* ህንጡዪ *hnẗuyi*
spiteful *(adj.)* ኣቮካዶ *avokado*
spittle *(n.)* ወገደ *wegede*
spittoon *(n.)* ጉስያ *gusya*
splash *(v.)* ኣመነ *amene*
splatter *(v.)* ኣኮኣዊ *'ako'awi*
splay *(v.)* ተጸበየ *texebeye*
spleen *(n.)* ነቕሐ *neq̈ḧe*
splendid *(adj.)* ነቕሐ *neq̈ḧe*
splendour *(n.)* ሰለመ *seleme*
splenetic *(adj.)* ገንዘብ *genzeb*
splice *(v.)* ናብ ርሑቕ *nab rḧuq̈*
splint *(n.)* ተምሳጥ *temsaẗ*
splinter *(n.)* ዘርዕድ *zer'ëd*
split *(v.)* ዘስካሕክሕ *zeskaḧkḧ*
splutter *(v.)* ንሓጺር ግዜ *nḧaxir gzee*
spoil *(v.)* ጋሕማጥ *gaḧmaẗ*
spoiler *(n.)* ብልሸው *blshw*
spoke *(n.)* ፋስ *fas*
spokesman *(n.)* መቐለሲ *meq̈elesi*
sponge *(n.)* መቐለስ *meq̈eles*
sponsor *(n.)* ሓላዪ ሰብ *ḧalayi seb*
spontaneity *(n.)* ኣዕዘምዘመ *a'ëzemzeme*
spontaneous *(adj.)* ህጻን *hxan*
spool *(n.)* ዘይምስምማዕ *zeymsmma'ë*
spoon *(n.)* ህበይ *hbey*
spoonful *(n.)* ህጻን *hxan*
spoor *(n.)* ቤተ'ልቦ - *beetelbo*
sporadic *(adj.)* ዝባን *zban*
spore *(n.)* ዓንዲ-ሕቖ *ändiḧq̈o*
sport *(n.)* ሓለፈ *ḧalefe*
sporting *(adj.)* ትዕይንቲ *t'ëynti*
sportive *(adj.)* ምጉሳዕ *mgusa'ë*
sportsman *(n.)* ተመኩሮ *temekuro*
spot *(n.)* ኣሽሙራዊ *ashmurawi*
spotless *(adj.)* ረድእ *red'e*
spousal *(n.)* መልሰ-ግብሪ *melsegbri*
spouse *(n.)* መሃዚ *mehazi*
spout *(n.)* ማህደር *mahder*
sprain *(v.t.)* ብድሕሪት *bdḧrit*
sprat *(n.)* ዝባን መድረኽ *zban medreḱ*
sprawl *(v.)* ዝባን ኣሰር *zban aser*
spray *(n.)* ንድሕሪት *ndḧrit*
spread *(v.)* ዝባን ማይ *zban may*
spreadsheet *(n.)* ቤኮን *beekon*
spree *(n.)* ባክተሪያ *bakteriya*
sprig *(n.)* ሕማቕ *ḧmaq̈*
sprightly *(adj.)* ኣርማ *arma*
spring *(v.)* ብሕማቕ *bḧmaq̈*
sprinkle *(v.i.)* ባድሚንተን *badminten*
sprinkler *(n.)* ኣገረመ *agereme*
sprinkling *(n.)* መልእ *mel'e*
sprint *(v.)* ጋዓዝ *ga'äz*
sprinter *(n.)* ገፍላው *geflaw*

sprout *(v.)* **ሕቡር ስልማት** *ḧbur slmat*
spry *(adj.)* **ዋሕስ** *waḧs*
spume *(n.)* **ፖሊስ** *polis*
spur *(n.)* **መስሓቢ** *mesḧabi*
spurious *(adj.)* **ደረቐ** *dereq̈e*
spurn *(v.)* **ሰንካቲ** *senkati*
spurt *(v.)* **እንዳ ባኒ** *ènda bani*
sputum *(n.)* **ተረፍ** *teref*
spy *(n.)* **ሰገነት** *segenet*
squabble *(n.)* **በራሕ** *beraḧ*
squad *(n.)* **ጥቕላል** *ẗq̈lal*
squadron *(n.)* **ኩዕሶ** *ku'ëso*
squalid *(adj.)* **ገስረጥ** *gesreẗ*
squall *(n.)* **ባለ** *bale*
squander *(v.)* **ባሉን** *balun*
square *(n.)* **ትርብዒት** *trb'ït*
squash *(v.)* **በለሳን** *belesan*
squat *(v.i.)* **በለሳን** *belesan*
squawk *(v.)* **ኣርቃይ** *arqay*
squeak *(n.)* **ኣገደ** *agede*
squeal *(n.)* **ተራ** *tera*
squeeze *(v.)* **ባናና** *banana*
squib *(n.)* **መእሰሪ** *me'èseri*
squid *(n.)* **መጀነኒ** *meĵeneni*
squint *(v.)* **ሽፍታ ወረበላ** *shfta werebela*
squire *(n.)* **መርዚ ስሚ** *merzi smi*
squirm *(v.)* **ገውታ** *gewta*
squirrel *(n.)* **ገውት** *gewtat*
squirt *(v.)* **በናጅር** *benaĵr*
squish *(v.)* **ሓየረ** *ḧayere*
stab *(v.)* **ጥርዝያ** *ẗrzya*
stability *(n.)* **መደንደል** *medendel*
stabilization *(n.)* **ባንጆ** *banĵo*
stabilize *(v.)* **ባንኪ** *banki*
stable *(adj.)* **መኰነን** *mekWanen*
stable *(n.)* **ጥፉሽ** *ẗfush*
stack *(n.)* **ጥፈሻ** *ẗfesha*
stadium *(n.)* **ሰንደቕ** *sendeq̈*
staff *(n.)* **በዓል** *be'äl*
stag *(n.)* **ተዋዘየ** *tewazeye*
stage *(n.)* **ጥምቀት** *ẗmqet*
stagecoach *(n.)* **መጥምቓዊ** *meẗmq̈awi*
stagger *(v.)* **ኣጠመቐ** *aẗemeq̈e*
staggering *(adj.)* **መታወር** *metawer*
stagnant *(adj.)* **ዓንቃሪቦ** *änqaribo*
stagnate *(v.)* **ባርባራዊ** *barbarawi*
stagnation *(n.)* **ባርባራዊ** *barbarawi*
staid *(adj.)* **rezin** *rezin*
stain *(v.t.)* **ወጋኢ** *wega'i*
stair *(n.)* **ቀምቃማይ** *qemqamay*
staircase *(n.)* **ግጥሚ ወይ ደርፊ** *gẗmi wey derfi*
stake *(n.)* **ጥርሑ** *ẗrḧu*
stale *(adj.)* **ብቕሉዕ** *bq̈lu'ë*
stalemate *(n.)* **ዋጋ ዕዳጋ** *waga 'ëdaga*
staleness *(n.)* **ተጋጨወ ተላግዐ** *tegačewe telag'ë*
stalk *(n.)* **ቅራፍ** *qraf*
stalker *(n.)* **ስገም** *sgem*
stall *(n.)* **መኽዘን** *meḱzen*
stallion *(n.)* **ባሮሜተር** *baromeeter*
stalwart *(adj.)* **ባላባት** *balabat*
stamen *(n.)* **ባራካ** *baraka*
stamina *(n.)* **መሸኒት** *meshenit*
stammer *(v.)* **ግድብ** *gdb*
stamp *(n.)* **በርሚል** *bermil*
stamp *(v.)* **መኻን** *meḱan*

stampede *(n.)* መደንደል *medendel*
stance *(n.)* ዕንቅፋት *ënqfat*
stanchion *(n.)* ግድብ *gdb*
stand *(v.)* ጠበቓ *ťebeq̈a*
standard *(n.)* በደላ *bedela*
standardization *(n.)* ሰረተ *serete*
standardize *(v.)* ሰረትኣልቦ *seret'albo*
standing *(n.)* ትሕተ-ቤት *tḧtebeet*
standpoint *(n.)* ሓፋር *ḧafar*
standstill *(n.)* ሰረታዊ *seretawi*
stanza *(n.)* ሪሓን *riḧan*
staple *(v.)* ስሓኒ - *sḧani*
staple *(n.)* ባዚሊካ *bazilika*
stapler *(n.)* ሰረት *seret*
star *(n.)* ተጸልወ *texelwe*
starch *(n.)* ዘንቢል *zenbil*
starchy *(adj.)* ባስ ዓይነት ዓሳ *bas 'äynet 'äsa*
stare *(v.)* ድቓላ *dq̈ala*
stark *(adj.)* ሸለለ *shelele*
starlet *(n.)* ዕርዲ *ërdi*
starry *(adj.)* እኩብ *èkub*
start *(v.)* ምሕጻብ *mḧxab*
starter *(n.)* ኣለኸ *aleḱe*
startle *(v.)* ህውተታ *hwteta*
startling *(n.)* መንካዕ *menka'ë*
starvation *(n.)* ባቲክ *batik*
starve *(v.)* በትሪ ፖሊስ *betri polis*
stash *(v.)* ቦጦሎኒ *boťoloni*
state *(n.)* ተገዳም *tegedam*
stateless *(adj.)* ከትከተ *ketkete*
statement *(n.)* ውግእ *wg'è*
statesman *(n.)* ሕቡር ስልማት *ḧbur slmat*
static *(adj.)* መሰናኽል *mesenaḱl*
statically *(adv.)* ወጨጨ *wečeče*
station *(n.)* ፉርዳ *furda*
stationary *(adj.)* ሳንጃ *sanĵa*
stationer *(n.)* ባዛር ሹቕ *bazar shuq̈*
stationery *(n.)* ባዙቃ *bazuqa*
statistical *(adj.)* ኮነ *kone*
statistics *(n.)* መና *mena*
statuary *(n.)* ዕንቆ *ënqo*
statue *(n.)* ቆርቋር *qorqWAr*
statuesque *(adj.)* ቢግል *bigl*
statuette *(n.)* መትኮብ *metkob*
stature *(n.)* ብርጭቆ *brčqo*
status *(n.)* ገመል *gemel*
statute *(n.)* ባልዶንጓ *baldongWa*
statutory *(adj.)* ድቢ *dbi*
staunch *(adj.)* ተሸከመ *teshekeme*
stave *(n.)* ጭሕሚ *čḧmi*
stay *(v.)* ማእዝን *ma'èzn*
stead *(n.)* እንስሳ *ènssa*
steadfast *(adj.)* እንስሳዊ *ènssawi*
steadiness *(n.)* ላጸየ *laxeye*
steady *(adj.)* ላጸየ *laxeye*
steak *(n.)* ማራኺ *maraḱi*
steal *(v.)* ኣመልክዐ *amelk'ë*
stealth *(n.)* ደስታ *desta*
stealthily *(adv.)* መልክዕ *melk'ë*
stealthy *(adj.)* ቢቨር *biver*
steam *(n.)* ኣህድአ *ahd'e*
steamer *(n.)* ምኽንያቱ ብምክንያት *mḱnyatu bmknyat*
steed *(n.)* ምልክት *mlkt*
steel *(n.)* ኣመልከተ *amelkete*
steep *(adj.)* ኮነ *kone*
steeple *(n.)* መዕረፊ *me'ërefi*

steeplechase *(n.)* መንጸፍ *menxef*
steer *(v.)* መዕቆብ ስንኩላነ-ኣእምሮ *me'ëqob snkulane'a'èmro*
stellar *(adj.)* ኣጨፈቐ *ačefeq̈e*
stem *(n.)* ንህቢ *nhbi*
stench *(n.)* ዋዕሮ *wa'ëro*
stencil *(n.)* ስጋ ከብቲ *sga kebti*
stenographer *(n.)* ረጕድ *regWid*
stenography *(n.)* ምልክት *mlkt*
stentorian *(adj.)* ቢራ *bira*
step *(n.)* ብንጅር *bnĵr*
steppe *(n.)* ማሳ *masa*
stereophonic *(adj.)* ወረደ ኣጋጠመ *werede 'agaẗeme*
stereoscopic *(adj.)* በቕዐ *beq̈'ë*
stereotype *(n.)* ቅድሚ *qdmi*
sterile *(adj.)* ኣቐዲሙ *ኣቐዲሙ*
sterility *(n.)* መዓደ *me'äde*
sterilization *(n.)* ኣገረመ *agereme*
sterilize *(v.)* ለመነ *lemene*
sterling *(n.)* ወለደ *welede*
stern *(adj.)* ለማኒ *lemani*
sternum *(n.)* ጀመረ *ĵemere*
steroid *(n.)* መጀመርታ *meĵemerta*
stertorous *(adj.)* ኣዘናገዐ *azenage'ë*
stethoscope *(n.)* ኣብ ክንዲ *ab kndi*
stew *(n.)* ገበረ *gebere*
steward *(n.)* ጠባይ *ẗebay*
stick *(n.)* ቈረጸ *qWerexe*
sticker *(n.)* ጨካን *čekan*
stickleback *(n.)* ትእዛዝ *t'èzaz*
stickler *(n.)* ብድሕሪት *bdḧrit*
sticky *(adj.)* ተመልከተ *temelkete*
stiff *(adj.)* ኣመስጋኒ *amesgani*
stiffen *(v.)* ፋሕራይ *faḧray*
stifle *(v.)* ህላወ *hlawe*
stigma *(n.)* ቀጥቀጠ *qeẗqeẗe*
stigmata *(n.)* ድንጉይ *dnguy*
stigmatize *(v.)* ጠመረ *ẗemere*
stile *(n.)* ተፍአ *tef'e*
stiletto *(n.)* ኣጨነቐ *ačeneq̈e*
still *(adj.)* ብጌጋ ኣርኣየ *bgeega 'ar'aye*
stillborn *(n.)* እምነት *èmnet*
stillness *(n.)* ኣመነ *amene*
stilt *(n.)* ኣቈናጸበ *aqWenaxebe*
stilted *(adj.)* ቃጭል *qačl*
stimulant *(n.)* ጽብቕቲ *xbq̈ti*
stimulate *(v.)* ተባኣሳይ *teba'asay*
stimulus *(n.)* ባእሲ ምድላይ *ba'èsi mdlay*
sting *(n.)* ነቀወ *neqewe*
stingy *(adj.)* መናፍሕ *menafḧ*
stink *(v.)* ከብዲ *kebdi*
stint *(n.)* ተኣሳሰረ *te'asasere*
stipend *(n.)* ግላዊ ኣቕሑ *glawi 'aq̈ḧu*
stipple *(v.)* ፍቑር *fq̈ur*
stipulate *(v.)* ትሕቲ *tḧti*
stipulation *(n.)* ቁልፊ *qulfi*
stir *(v.)* ጓሃየ *gWahaye*
stirrup *(n.)* ኣቃልቦ ኣዘንበለ *'aqalbo 'azenbele*
stitch *(v.)* ለወየ *leweye*
stitch *(n.)* ርቦ *rbo*
stock *(n.)* ትሕቲ *tḧti*
stockade *(n.)* ገቢረ-ሰናይ *gebiresenay*
stockbroker *(n.)* ቡራኬ *burakee*
stocking *(n.)* ገዛ ቀሺ *geza qeshi*

stockist *(n.)* ግብረ-ሰናይ *gbresenay*
stocky *(adj.)* ለዋህ *lewah*
stoic *(n.)* ሓጋዚ *ḧagazi*
stoke *(v.)* ግብረ-ሰናይ *gbresenay*
stoker *(n.)* ግብረ-ሰናያዊ *gbresenayawi*
stole *(n.)* ለዋህ *lewah*
stolid *(adj.)* ተውህቦ *tewhbo*
stomach *(n.)* ኣውረሰ *awrese*
stomp *(n.)* ውርሻ *wrsha*
stone *(n.)* ወቐሰ *weq̈ese*
stony *(adj.)* ዘረፈ *zerefe*
stooge *(n.)* ሓዘን *ḧazen*
stool *(n.)* ለማኒ *lemani*
stoop *(v.)* ከውሒ በረድ *kewḧi bered*
stop *(v.)* ደንቆሮ *denqoro*
stoppage *(n.)* ፍረ *fre*
stopper *(n.)* ዕብድብድ *ëbdbd*
storage *(n.)* መደቀሲ *medeqesi*
store *(n.)* ለመነ *lemene*
storey *(n.)* ኣሸገረ *ashegere*
stork *(n.)* ኣብ ጥቓ *'ab ẗq̈a*
storm *(n.)* ከበበ *kebebe*
stormy *(adj.)* ኣመራሰሐ *ameraseḧe*
story *(n.)* መኾስተር *meḱoster*
stout *(adj.)* ዕኑድ *ënud*
stove *(n.)* ዓውዲ ጸቐጠ *äwdi xeq̈eẗe*
stow *(v.)* ብዝበለጸ *bzbelexe*
straddle *(v.)* ኣራዊታዊ እንስሳዊ ጨካን *'arawitawi 'ènssawi čekan*
straggle *(v.)* ሸለመ *sheleme*
straggler *(n.)* ተጋሕተነ *tegaḧtene*
straight *(adj.)* ተጣልዐ *teẗal'ë*
straighten *(v.)* ከደ *kede*
straightforward *(adj.)* ከድዐ *ked'ë*
straightway *(adv.)* ቅጥፈት *qẗfet*
strain *(n.)* ኣብ መንጎ *'ab mengo*
strain *(v.)* ዝሓሸ *zḧashe*
strained *(adj.)* ስያፍ *syaf*
strait *(n.)* መስተ *meste*
straiten *(v.i.)* ኣኼባ *aḱeeba*
strand *(v.)* ኣልቀሰ *alqese*
strange *(adj.)* ተጠንቀቕ! ወይልኻ! *teẗenqeq̈ weylḱa*
stranger *(n.)* ደንጸዎ *denxewo*
strangle *(v.)* ሰረየ *sereye*
strangulation *(n.)* ክንየው *knyew*
strap *(n.)* ኣብ ከክልተ *'ab keklte*
strapping *(adj.)* ፍርቂ በብዓመት *frqi beb'ämet*
stratagem *(n.)* ምቕናን *mq̈nan*
strategic *(adj.)* መቕናን *meq̈nan*
strategist *(n.)* ሳልቤታ *salbeeta*
strategy *(n.)* መጽሓፍ ቅዱስ *mexḧaf qdus*
stratify *(v.)* ዝርዝረ-ጽሑፋት *zrzrexḧufat*
stratum *(n.)* ፈታው መጽሓፍ *fetaw mexḧaf*
straw *(n.)* ዝክረ ክልተ ሚእቲ ዓመት *zkre klte mi'èti 'ämet*
strawberry *(n.)* ጭዋዳምናት *čwadamnat*
stray *(v.)* ተቛየቜ *teq̈WAyeq̈We*
streak *(n.)* ብሽክለታ *bshkleta*
streaky *(adj.)* ሰመየ *semeye*
stream *(n.)* ተሓታቲ *teḧatati*
streamer *(n.)* ስማይ *smay*
streamlet *(n.)* ኣኽበረ *aḱbere*
street *(n.)* ምምሻጥ *mmshaẗ*

strength *(n.)* ክልተ ዓመታዊ *klte 'ämetawi*
strengthen *(v.)* ቃሬዛ *qareeza*
strenuous *(adj.)* ጽምደ-ትኹረታዊ *xmdetḱuretawi*
stress *(v.t.)* ድርብ መርዓ *drb mer'ä*
stress *(n.)* ዓቢ *äbi*
stretch *(n.)* ምቕናን *mq̈nan*
stretch *(v.)* ሕሉ'ፍ *ḧluf*
stretcher *(n.)* ብሽክለታ *bshkleta*
strew *(v.)* ቢኪኒ *bikini*
striation *(n.)* ክልተ ጐድናዊ *klte gWadnawi*
stricken *(adj.)* ሓሞት *ḧamot*
strict *(adj.)* ድርብ-ልሳናዊ *drblsanawi*
strictly *(adv.)* ጎዞሞ *gozomo*
stricture *(n.)* መአንገድ ድርጎኛ *me'anged drgoǹa*
stride *(v.)* ቢልያርዶ *bilyardo*
strident *(adj.)* ቢልዮን *bilyon*
strife *(n.)* ሃብታም *habtam*
strike *(v.)* ዓቢ ማዕበል *'äbi ma'ëbel*
striker *(n.)* ቆፎ *qofo*
striking *(adj.)* ዕጽፊ *ëxfi*
string *(n.)* ጠመረ *ẗemere*
stringency *(n.)* መዛዘሚ *mezazemi*
stringent *(adj.)* ፈንጠዝያ *fenẗezya*
stringy *(adj.)* በዓል ለዓት መነጽር *be'äl le'ät menexr*
strip *(v.t.)* ስነ-ቅመም ህይወታውያን *sneqmem hywetawyan*
stripe *(n.)* ኢኮሎጂ *ikoloĵi*
stripling *(n.)* ባዮዳይቨርስቲ *bayidayiversiti*
strive *(v.)* ኢኮሎጂ *ikoloĵi*
strobe *(n.)* ስነ-ህይወት *snehywet*
stroke *(n.)* ምርምረ-ሬሳ *mrmrereesa*
stroll *(v.)* ጽምደ-ሰልፋዊ *xmdeselfawi*
strong *(adj.)* ኮመዲኖ *komedino*
stronghold *(n.)* ዑፍ *üf*
strop *(n.)* ኢንፍሉወንዛ *influwenza*
stroppy *(adj.)* ምውላድ *mwlad*
structural *(adj.)* ብሽኮቲ *bshkoti*
structure *(n.)* ገመሰ *gemese*
strudel *(n.)* ግብረ-ሰዶመኛ *gbresedomeǹa*
struggle *(v.)* ኣቡን *abun*
strum *(v.)* ብዕራይ በረኸ *b'ëray bereḱa*
strumpet *(n.)* ልጓም *lgWam*
strut *(n.)* ዋዕሮ *wa'ëro*
Stuart *(adj.)* ነኸሰ *neḱese*
stub *(n.)* ወጋኢ *wega'i*
stubble *(n.)* መሪር *merir*
stubborn *(adj.)* ፈንጠጋር *fenẗegar*
stucco *(n.)* ሃተ'ፈ *hatefe*
stud *(v.)* ብላክቤሪ *blakberi*
stud *(n.)* ጸሊም *xelim*
student *(n.)* ሰሌዳ *seleeda*
studio *(n.)* ኣጸለመተ *axelemete*
studious *(adj.)* ጸሊም መዝገብ *xelim mezgeb*
study *(v.)* ጽልማተ *xlmate*
study *(n.)* ታህዲደ-ምቕላዕ *tahdidemq̈la'ë*

stuff *(n.)* ሓጓዲ ኣንጠረኛ ሓጺን *ḧagWadi 'anẗereḧa ḧaxin*
stuffing *(n.)* ፍሕኛ *fḧḧa*
stuffy *(adj.)* ግላዝ *glaz*
stultify *(v.)* ኣብ ከክልተ *'ab keklte*
stumble *(v.)* ከሰሰ *kesese*
stump *(n.)* ጸዕደወ *xa'ëdewe*
stun *(v.)* ልዙብ *lzub*
stunner *(n.)* ጥርሑ *ẗrḧu*
stunning *(adj.)* ኮበርታ *koberta*
stunt *(v.)* ድምጺ *dmxi*
stupefy *(v.)* ኣተዓሻሸወ *ate'äshashewe*
stupendous *(adj.)* ነትጉ *netgWi*
stupid *(adj.)* ቅሉዕ *qlu'ë*
stupidity *(n.)* ሃልሃልታ *halhalta*
stupor *(n.)* ጃኬት *ĵakeet*
sturdy *(adj.)* ኣጸዕደወ *axa'ëdewe*
stutter *(v.)* ቀዛሒ *qezaḧi*
sty *(n.)* እምቤዕ *èmbee'ë*
stygian *(adj.)* ደመየ *demeye*
style *(n.)* ቃና *qana*
stylish *(adj.)* ኣበር *aber*
stylist *(n.)* ምዩቕ በለ *myuq̈ bele*
stylistic *(adj.)* ሓዋወሰ *ḧawawese*
stylized *(adj.)* መግቢ ሓዋሲ ኣደባላቒ *megbi ḧawasi 'adebalaq̈i*
stylus *(n.)* ባረኸ *bareḱe*
stymie *(v.)* ብሩኽ *bruḱ*
styptic *(adj.)* ምርቓ *mrq̈a*
suave *(adj.)* ዋግ *wag*
sub judice *(adj.)* ሕጉስ *ḧgus*
subaltern *(n.)* ዕዉር *ëwur*
subconscious *(adj.)* ዓመተ *ämete*
subcontract *(v.)* ጉድለት *gudlet*
subdue *(v.)* ሰምሰም ኣበለ *semsem 'abele*
subedit *(v.)* ጋራዲ *garadi*
subject *(n.)* መቓልሕ *meq̈alḧ*
subjection *(n.)* ታሕጓስ *taḧgWas*
subjective *(adj.)* ማይ ምዕጎ *may m'ëgo*
subjugate *(v.)* በርቃዊ መጥቃዕቲ *berqawi meẗqa'ëti*
subjugation *(n.)* ሀቦብላ ውርጪ *hbobla wrči*
subjunctive *(adj.)* ነፍሐ *nefḧe*
sublet *(v.t.)* ቋንጣ ዓሳ *qWAnẗa 'äsa*
sublimate *(v.)* ንጣብ *nẗab*
sublime *(adj.)* ቀጽሪ *qexri*
subliminal *(adj.)* ግላዕ *gla'ë*
submarine *(n.)* ድንደላ *dndela*
submerge *(v.)* ዕግታ *ëgta*
submerse *(v.)* ሳይት *sayit*
submersible *(adj.)* ቈንደፈ *qWendefe*
submission *(n.)* ጨዓይ ጸጉሪ ዘለዎ *če'äy xeguri zelewo*
submissive *(adj.)* ደም *dem*
submit *(v.)* ደም ምፍሳስ *dem mfsas*
subordinate *(adj.)* ደማዊ *demawi*
subordination *(n.)* ዕምባባ *ëmbaba*
suborn *(v.)* ስረ-ግትር *sregtr*
subscribe *(v.)* ዕምባባ *ëmbaba*
subscript *(adj.)* ንጣብ ቀለም *nẗab qelem*
subscription *(n.)* ትኳዕ *tkWa'ë*
subsequent *(adj.)* ካምቻ *kamcha*
subservience *(n.)* ነፈሰ *nefese*

subservient *(adj.)* **ቈንደፈ** *qWendefe*
subside *(v.)* **ተነኽነኸ** *teneḱneḱe*
subsidiary *(adj.)* **ጓመድ** *gWamed*
subsidize *(v.)* **ሰማያዊ ሕብሪ** *semayawi ḧbri*
subsidy *(n.)* **መጻድፎ** *mexadfo*
subsist *(v.)* **ጠምበርበር በለ** *ṫemberber bele*
subsistence *(n.)* **ጎዲም** *godim*
subsonic *(adj.)* **ጽያቕ** *xyaq̈*
substance *(n.)* **ትሕዝቶ መጽሓፍ** *tḧzto mexḧaf*
substantial *(adj.)* **ኣምለቜ** *amleq̈We*
substantially *(adv.)* **ሓፈረ** *ḧafere*
substantiate *(v.)* **ቀንዲ** *qendi*
substantiation *(n.)* **ኣሸምበበ** *ashembebe*
substantive *(adj.)* **መፍለስ** *mefles*
substitute *(n.)* **ጣውላ** *ṫawla*
substitution *(n.)* **ጃህራ** *ĵahra*
subsume *(v.)* **ጃልባ** *ĵalba*
subterfuge *(n.)* **ሓፍ ኮፍ በለ** *ḧaf kof bele*
subterranean *(adj.)* **ገልተው** *geltew*
subtitle *(n.)* **ሓበረ** *ḧabere*
subtle *(adj.)* **ጅለ-ሰበይቲ** *ĵlesebeyti*
subtlety *(n.)* **ኣካላዊ** *akalawi*
subtotal *(n.)* **ኣካል** *akal*
subtract *(v.)* **ዘብዐኛ** *zeb'ëňa*
subtraction *(n.)* **ዓዘቕቲ** *äzeq̈ti*
subtropical *(adj.)* **ጋኔን** *ganeen*
suburb *(n.)* **ተወላወለ** *tewelawele*
suburban *(adj.)* **ሓቂ ዘይብሉ** *ḧaqi zeyblu*
suburbia *(n.)* **ምጉሊ ኣንጭዋ** *mguli 'ančwa*
subversion *(n.)* **መፍልሒ** *meflḧi*
subversive *(adj.)* **ናውጼን** *nawxeen*
subvert *(v.i.)* **ተባዕ ደፋር** *teba'ë defar*
subway *(n.)* **ድምቀት** *dmqet*
succeed *(v.)* **ጉንዲ** *gundi*
success *(n.)* **መእሰር ናይ መርከብ** *me'èser nay merkeb*
successful *(adj.)* **መሸጐር** *meshegWar*
succession *(n.)* **ቦምብ** *bomb*
successive *(adj.)* **ደብደበ** *debdebe*
successor *(n.)* **ደብዳብ** *debdab*
succinct *(adj.)* **ቦምብር** *bomber*
succour *(n.)* **ሓቀኛ** *ḧaqeňa*
succulent *(adj.)* **ኣኸዘ** *aḱeze*
succumb *(v.)* **ውዕል** *w'ël*
such *(adj.)* **ጊልያነት ከዳሚነት** *gilyanet kedaminet*
suck *(v.)* **ዓጽሚ** *äxmi*
sucker *(n.)* **መጋርያ** *megarya*
suckle *(v.)* **ልስሉስ ቆብዕ** *lslus qob'ë*
suckling *(n.)* **መቜሹሽ** *meq̈ushush*
suction *(n.)* **ዓጻም** *äxam*
sudden *(adj.)* **መጽሓፍ** *mexḧaf*
suddenly *(adv.)* **ንእሽቶ መጽሓፍ** *n'èshto mexḧaf*
Sudoku *(n.)* **መቓቐር** *meq̈aq̈er*

sue *(v.t.)* መጽሓፍ ሸያጢት *mexḧaf sheyaẗit*
suede *(n.)* መጽሓፋዊ *mexḧafawi*
suffer *(v.i.)* ንእሽቶ መጽሓፍ *n'èshto mexḧaf*
sufferance *(n.)* ፊሕታ *fiḧta*
suffice *(v.)* ሕቶ *ḧto*
sufficiency *(n.)* ጠገለ-ኣልቦ *ẗegele'albo*
sufficient *(adj.)* ምስፋሕ *msfaḧ*
suffix *(n.)* ሰንካቲ *senkati*
suffocate *(v.)* ነዊሕ ሳእኒ *newiḧ sa'èni*
suffocation *(n.)* ጎጆ *goĵo*
suffrage *(n.)* ኮንትሮባንድ *kontroband*
suffuse *(v.)* ምርኮ *mrko*
sugar *(n.)* ዶብ *dob*
suggest *(v.)* ጕርጕሐ *gWargWaḧe*
suggestible *(adj.)* ወልደ *tewelde*
suggestion *(n.)* ወረደ *werede*
suggestive *(adj.)* ተለቅሐ *teleqḧe*
suicidal *(adj.)* ሕጽöኒ *ḧxni*
suicide *(n.)* ሓለቓ *ḧaleq̈a*
suit *(n.)* ምሉእ ክዳን *mlu'è kdan*
suitability *(n.)* ስነ-ኣትክልቲ *sne'atklti*
suitable *(adj.)* ክልቲኡ *klti'u*
suite *(n.)* ኣሸገረ *ashegere*
suitor *(n.)* ጥርሙዝ *ẗrmuz*
sulk *(v.)* ታሕቲ *taḧti*
sullen *(adj.)* ቃራና *qarana*
sully *(v.)* ዓረ *äre*
sulphur *(n.)* ጐደና *gWadena*
sultana *(n.)* ነጠረ *neẗere*
sultry *(adj.)* መሰነዪ *meseneyi*
sum *(n.)* ሓጸረ *ḧaxere*
summarily *(adv.)* ዶብ *dob*
summarize *(v.)* ደረት-ኣልቦ *deret'albo*
summary *(n.)* ለጋስ *legas*
summer *(n.)* ልግሲ *lgsi*
summit *(n.)* ሕቑፊ-ዕምባባ *ḧq̈ufi'ëmbaba*
summon *(v.)* ግጥ'ም *gẗm*
summons *(n.)* ባዛር *bazar*
sumptuous *(adj.)* ቀስቲ *qesti*
sun *(v.)* መዓናጡ *me'änaẗu*
sun *(n.)* ሰገደ *segede*
sundae *(n.)* ዳስ *das*
Sunday *(n.)* ጭሖሎ *čḧolo*
sunder *(v.)* ሳንዱቕ *sanduq̈*
sundry *(adj.)* ተጋዳላይ *tegadalay*
sunken *(adj.)* ጉስጢ *gusẗi*
sunny *(adj.)* ወዲ *wedi*
super *(adj.)* ኣደመ *ademe*
superabundance *(adj.)* ንእስነት *n'èsnet*
superabundant *(adj.)* ቢኪኒ *bikini*
superannuation *(n.)* ድጋፍ *dgaf*
superb *(adj.)* በናጅር *benaĵr*
supercharger *(n.)* መደገፍ *medegef*
supercilious *(adj.)* ተጀሃሪ *teĵehari*
superficial *(adj.)* ብረይል *breyl*
superficiality *(n.)* ሓንጎል *ḧangol*
superfine *(adj.)* ልጓም *lgWam*
superfluity *(n.)* ጨንፈር *čenfer*
superfluous *(adj.)* ዕላመት *ëlamet*
superhuman *(adj.)* ኣንበልበለ *anbelbele*
superimpose *(v.)* ብራንዲ *brandi*

superintend *(v.)* ደረቐኻ *dereq̈eh̊a*
superintendence *(n.)* ኣስራዚ *asrazi*
superintendent *(n.)* ተባዕ *teba'ë*
superior *(adj.)* ትብዓት *tb'ät*
superiority *(n.)* ቈየቛ *qWeyeq̈WA*
superlative *(adj.)* ህላ *hla*
supermarket *(n.)* ምጥሓስ *mẗḧas*
supernatural *(adj.)* እንጀራ *ènĵera*
superpower *(n.)* ውርዲ *wrdi*
superscript *(adj.)* ሰበረ *sebere*
supersede *(v.)* ምስባር ስባር መስበርቲ *msbar sbar mesberti*
supersonic *(adj.)* ቁርሲ *qursi*
superstition *(n.)* ጡብ *ẗub*
superstitious *(adj.)* ትንፋስ *tnfas*
superstore *(n.)* ኣተንፈሰ *atenfese*
supervene *(v.)* ዓንቀር ጠበንጃ *änqer ẗebenĵa*
supervise *(v.)* ስረ-ግትር *sregtr*
supervision *(n.)* ኣራብሐ *arabḧe*
supervisor *(n.)* ህዱእ ንፋስ *hdu'è nfas*
supper *(n.)* ሕጽረት ሓጺርነት *ḧxret ḧaxirnet*
supplant *(v.)* ጸመቔ *xemeq̈We*
supple *(adj.)* እንዳ ቢራ *'ènda bira*
supplement *(n.)* ጉቦ *gubo*
supplementary *(adj.)* ሕጡብ ማቶኒ *ḧẗub matoni*
suppliant *(n.)* ናይ መርዓ *nay mer'ä*
supplicate *(v.)* መርዓት *mer'ät*
supplier *(n.)* መርዓዊ *mer'äwi*
supply *(v.)* ድልድል *dldl*
support *(n.)* ሓጺር *ḧaxir*
support *(v.)* ልጓም *lgWam*
suppose *(v.)* ሓጺር መግለጺ *ḧaxir meglexi*
supposition *(n.)* ምግማት *mgmat*
suppository *(n.)* መራሕ ብርጌድ *meraḧ brgeed*
suppress *(v.)* ድሙቕ *dmuq̈*
suppression *(n.)* ደመቐ በርሀ *demeq̈e berhe*
suppurate *(v.)* ብልጫ *blča*
supremacy *(n.)* ድሙቕ *dmuq̈*
supreme *(adj.)* ጫፍ *čaf*
surcharge *(n.)* ሓበጀራይ *ḧabeĵeray*
sure *(adj.)* ማይ ጨው *may čew*
surely *(adv.)* ኣምጸአ *amxe'e*
surety *(n.)* ብሪንጃል *birinjal*
surf *(n.)* ጠረፍ *ẗeref*
surface *(n.)* ስሉጥ *sluẗ*
surfeit *(n.)* ነደ'ረ *nedere*
surge *(n.)* ብሪቲሽ *biritish*
surgeon *(n.)* ተሰባሪ *tesebari*
surgery *(n.)* ኣንኰለ *ankWale*
surly *(adj.)* ሰፊሕ *sefiḧ*
surmise *(v.t.)* ዘርግሐ *zergḧe*
surmount *(v.)* በዘቕዘቕ *bezeq̈zeq̈*
surname *(n.)* ካውሎ ፍዮሪ *kawlo fyori*
surpass *(v.)* መንሹር *menshur*
surplus *(n.)* ሰበረ *sebere*
surprise *(n.)* ስቡር *sbur*
surreal *(adj.)* ደላ'ላይ *delalay*

surrealism *(n.)* ቃራየ ጉርጉማ *qaraye gurguma*
surrender *(n.)* ጨቓዊት *čeq̈awit*
surrender *(v.)* ብሮንዞ *bronzo*
surreptitious *(adj.)* ዛራ *zara*
surrogate *(n.)* መኾስተር *mek̇oster*
surround *(v.)* መረቕ *mereq̈*
surroundings *(n.)* እንዳ ኣመንዝራ *ènda 'amenzra*
surtax *(n.)* ሓው *ḧaw*
surveillance *(n.)* ሕውነት *ḧwnet*
survey *(v.t.)* ሸፋሽፍቲ *shefashfti*
surveyor *(n.)* ቡናዊ *bunawi*
survival *(n.)* ገሃጸ *gehaxe*
survive *(v.)* ማእረረ *ma'èrere*
susceptible *(adj.)* ስንብራት *snbrat*
suspect *(v.)* ኵላሶ *kulaso*
suspect *(n)* ťerťere *ťerťere*
suspend *(v.)* ቀንዲ ክብደት *qendi kbdet*
suspense *(n.)* ኣስባስላ *asbasla*
suspension *(n.)* ኣሻኹ *ashak̇Wi*
suspicion *(n.)* ዘይምሕር *zeymḧr*
suspicious *(adj.)* እንስሳ *ènssa*
sustain *(v.)* ዓፍራ *äfra*
sustainable *(adj.)* ኮናዕ *kona'ë*
sustenance *(n.)* መገለል *megelel*
suture *(n.)* መቈለፍ *meq̈Welef*
svelte *(adj.)* ኣጓም *agWam*
swab *(n.)* ምንቕ በለ *mnq̈ bele*
swaddle *(v.)* ባጀት *baĵet*
swag *(n.)* ጎባይ *gobay*
swagger *(v.)* ወሓጥ ጐንጺ *weḧaẗ gWanxi*
swallow *(v.)* ጉስጢ *gusẗi*
swamp *(n.)* መስሓቕ *mesḧaq̈*
swan *(n.)* ትኳን *tk̇Wan*
swank *(v.)* ካሮሳ *karosa*
swanky *(v.)* ጥሩምባ *ẗrumba*
swap *(v.)* ሃነጸ *hanexe*
swarm *(n.)* ህንጻ *hnxa*
swarthy *(adj.)* ሽጉርቶ *shgurto*
swashbuckling *(adj.)* ሕበጥ *ḧbeẗ*
swat *(v.)* ቡሊምያ *bilimiya*
swathe *(n.)* ብብዝሒ *bbzḧi*
sway *(v.)* ደጐላጽ *degWalax*
swear *(v.)* ኣርሓ *arḧa*
sweat *(n.)* ገዚፍ ዓይነት ክልቢ *gezif 'äynet kelbi*
sweater *(n.)* ዓረር *ärer*
sweep *(v.)* ቡለቲን *buletin*
sweeper *(n.)* ሕጡብ ወርቂ *ḧẗub werqi*
sweet *(n.)* ቅጥቊጥ ብዕራይ *qẗquẗ b'ëray*
sweet *(adj.)* ኣዛዚ *azazi*
sweeten *(v.)* ዓላቕ *älaq̈*
sweetener *(n.)* ተዓንቀፈ *te'änqefe*
sweetheart *(n.)* ዕርዲ *ërdi*
sweetmeat *(n.)* መዓኮር *me'äkor*
sweetness *(n.)* ተናጐጸ *tenagWaxe*
swell *(n.)* ሁጉሬ *huguree*
swell *(v.)* ዋልጋ ጐንጺ *walga gWanxi*
swelling *(n.)* ተናጐጸ *tenagWaxe*
swelter *(v.)* ምቁር ባኒ *mqur bani*
swerve *(v.)* ጥማር *ẗmar*
swift *(adj.)* ጠቕለለ *ẗeq̈lele*
swill *(v.)* ቡሽ *bush*
swim *(v.)* ሓደ ዝደርቡ ገዛ *ḧade zderbu geza*
swimmer *(n.)* ገልተው *geltew*

swindle *(v.)* **ሃደመ** *hademe*
swine *(n.)* **ሓባ'ር መርከብ** *ḧabar merkeb*
swing *(v.)* **ምንስፋፍ** *mnsfaf*
swing *(n.)* **ተንሳፋፊ** *tensafafi*
swingeing *(adj.)* **ጕራዕራዕ በለ** *gWara'ëra'ë bele*
swipe *(v.)* **ሸከም** *shekem*
swirl *(v.)* **ሰደቓ** *sedeq̈a*
swish *(adj.)* **ቢሮክራሲ** *birokrasi*
switch *(n.)* **ቢሮክራታዊ** *birokratawi*
swivel *(v.)* **ኣጐመ** *agWame*
swoon *(v.)* **በርገር** *berger*
swoop *(v.)* **ሰራቒ** *seraq̈i*
sword *(n.)* **ገበን** *geben*
sybarite *(n.)* **ቀብሪ** *qebri*
sycamore *(n.)* **ላግጺ** *lagxi*
sycophancy *(n.)* **ምንዳድ** *mndad*
sycophant *(n.)* **ኣንዳዲ** *andadi*
syllabic *(adj.)* **ርሱን** *rsun*
syllable *(n.)* **ጉድጓድ** *gudgWad*
syllabus *(n.)* **ተሓዝ ገንዘብ** *teḧaz genzeb*
syllogism *(n.)* **ሓገዝ** *ḧagez*
sylph *(n.)* **ነተጐ** *netegWa*
sylvan *(adj.)* **ቀበረ** *qebere*
symbiosis *(n.)* **ኣውቶቡስ** *awtobus*
symbol *(n.)* **ቈጥቋጥ** *qWeẗqWAẗ*
symbolic *(adj.)* **ጎፍጓፍ** *gofgWaf*
symbolism *(n.)* **ዋኒን** *wanin*
symbolize *(v.)* **ነጋዳይ** *negaday*
symmetrical *(adj.)* **ደረት** *deret*
symmetry *(n.)* **ኣሽበድበደ** *ashbedbede*
sympathetic *(adj.)* **ተጸምደ** *texemde*
sympathize *(v.)* **ግን** *gn*
sympathy *(n.)* **ሓራድ ስጋ** *ḧarad sga*
symphony *(n.)* **ባልጠጂ** *balẗeĵi*
symposium *(n.)* **ጠስሚ** *ẗesmi*
symptom *(n.)* **ጽምብላሊዕ** *xmblali'ë*
symptomatic *(adj.)* **ዶሶ** *doso*
synchronize *(v.)* **መልጎም** *melgom*
synchronous *(adj.)* **ገዝአ** *gez'e*
syndicate *(n.)* **ዓዳጊ** *ädagi*
syndrome *(n.)* **ዚዝ በለ** *ziz bele*
synergy *(n.)* **ሽላ** *shla*
synonym *(n.)* **ሲረና** *sirena*
synonymous *(adj.)* **ብ** *b*
synopsis *(n.)* **ጎድናዊ-ምርጫ** *godnawimrča*
syntax *(n.)* **ቀደም** *qedem*
synthesis *(n.)* **ብ ሕንጻጽ** *bḧnxax*
synthesize *(v.)* **ጎድናዊ መንገዲ** *godnawi mengedi*
synthetic *(adj.)* **ደምበ** *dembe*
syringe *(n.)* **ተመልካቲ** *temelkati*
syrup *(n.)* **ባይት** *bayit*
system *(n.)* **ጋቢ'ና** *gabina*
systematic *(adj.)* **ካባረ** *kabare*
systematize *(v.)* **ካውሎ** *kawlo*
systemic *(adj.)* **ጋቢና** *gabina*

T

tab *(n.)* መፈላልጦ *mefelalto*
table *(n.)* ጣውላ፣ሰንጠረዥ *terebeza*
tableau *(n.)* ብዘይ ምንጋር ብዘይ ምንቅስቃስ ዝግበር ዉደደር *bzey-mangar bzey-manqsqas zgeber wudder*
tablet *(n.)* ክንኒንያ፣ *knnya*
tabloid *(n.)* ኣማሙቅ ጋዘጠግኛ *amawuq gazitegna*
taboo *(n.)* ዝተኸልከለ ነገር፣ሕማቅ ነገር *ztekelkele neger*
tabular *(adj.)* ብሰንጠረዥ ዝተሰርሐ *bsenterez zteserhe*
tabulate *(v.)* ብሰንጠረዥ ኣዘጋጅዩ ተዳልዩ *bsenterz ztezagajeye*
tabulation *(n.)* ብሰንጠረዥ ምስራሕ ምምዳብ *bsenterez msrah mzgjay*
tabulator *(v.)* ሰንጠረዥ ዝሰርሕ ሰብ *kadet*
tachometer *(n.)* ካድምዩም *kadmyum*
tacit *(adj.)* ሱቅ ኣልካ ምስምዕማዕ *suq ailka msm'amaa*
taciturn *(adj.)* ሱቅ በሃሊ፣ሕቱም *su behali,htum*
tack *(n.)* ሓባጠ ጎባጥ ቦታ *habate gobat bota*
tackle *(v.t.)* ኲዕሾ ምምንጣል *kuausho mmntal*
tacky *(adj.)* ዘይጥዕም ዘይረብሕ *zeyt'am zeyrebh*
tact *(n.)* ብልሓት ጥንቃቀ *blhat tnkak*
tactful *(adj.)* ብልሓት ጥንቃቀ *blhat tnkak*
tactic *(n.)* ዜዴ ብልሓት *zede blhat*
tactical *(adj.)* ብሞያ ዝተሓገዘ *bmoya ztehageze*
tactician *(n.)* በሊሕ መለኛ *belih melegna*
tactile *(adj.)* ዝድህሰስ ነገር *zdhses neger*
tag *(n.)* ምልክት ዝልጠፍ ወይ ዝእሰር *mlkt ztef'o wey z'aser*
tail *(n.)* ጭራ *chra*
tailor *(n.)* ሰፋዩ ክዳን *sefayi kdan*
taint *(v.)* ተበኪሉ፣ሸቲቱ *tebelilu shetitu*
take *(v.)* ምዉሳድ ምሓዝ *mwusad mhaz*
takeaway *(n.)* ምውሳድ *mwusad*
takings *(n.)* ትርፊ፣ምህርቲ *trfi , mhrti*
talc *(n.)* ጽባቐ ጽሕፈት *tsibuq tsuhuf*
tale *(n.)* ትረኻ *treka*
talent *(n.)* ሞያ *moya*
talented *(adj.)* ብዓል ሞያ *bal moya*
talisman *(n.)* ክታብ *ktab*
talk *(v.)* ምንጋር *mnggar*
talkative *(adj.)* ለፍላፊ፣ተናጋሪ *leflefi, tenagari*
tall *(adj.)* ነዊሕ *newih*
tallow *(n.)* ኣንግዕ *angu'a*
tally *(n.)* ተስማዕሚዑ *tesmaamiu*
talon *(n.)* ጠንካራ ናይ ኣሞራ ጭፍሪ *tenkara na amora chifri*
tame *(adj.)* ለማዳ እንስሳ *lemada enssa*
tamely *(adv.)* መዓስከር *measker*

tamp *(v.)* ጠቅጢቁ፣መሊኡ *tnqiqu meliu*
tamper *(v.)* ጣልቃ *talya*
tampon *(n.)* ፐሪድ ዝመጽሉ ግዘ *pered zmetselu gze*
tan *(n.)* ቆርበት ኣልፊዑ *qorbet alfi'u*
tandem *(n.)* ብክልተ ሰብ ትዝወር ሳይክል *bklte seb etzwer siykle*
tang *(n.)* ሓያል ሽታ ንኣፍንጫ ዝርብሽ *hayal shta naafncha zrbish*
tangent *(n.)* ተጽጊዑ ዝሓልፍ መስመር *tetsegiuzhalf mesmer*
tangerine *(n.)* መንደሪኒ *menderini*
tangible *(adj.)* ኣካል ዘለዎ ዝጨበጥ *akal zelewo zchbet*
tangle *(v.t.)* ኣጠላሊፉ *atalalafi*
tank *(n.)* ታንኪ *tanki*
tanker *(n.)* ናይ ማይ መትሓዚ ዓብዪ ጎማ *naymay methazi abuyi goma*
tanner *(n.)* ቆርበት ፍሓቂ *qorbet fehaqi*
tannery *(n.)* ናይ ቆርበት ፋብሪካ *nay qorbet fabrika*
tantalize *(v.)* ኣጎምጅዩ፣ኣቁለጭሊጬ *agomjyu aqulech lichu*
tantamount *(adj.)* ተመጣጣኒ *temetatani*
tantrum *(n.)* ምክንያት ዘይብሉ ቁጥዐ *mknyat zeyblu qutea*
tap *(n.)* መኽፈቲ ቡምባ፣ዳንሲ ዓይነት *makfeti bunba,dansi aynet*
tape *(v.i.)* ናይ ካሴት ክሪ *nay kaset kri*
tape *(n.)* ብላዕሊ ቅርሺ ምሃብ *blaali qrshi mhab*
taper *(v.)* ጢፍ *twaf*
tapestry *(n.)* ስግዳን *sgdan*
tappet *(n.)* ናይ ሞተር መጫወቲ *nay moter mechaweti*
tar *(n.)* ኣስፓልት መንገዲ፣ብቦምቢ ዝተሓጸረ መንገዲ *aspalt mengedi,bbonbi ztehasere mengedi*
tardy *(adj.)* ፈዛዝ፣ዘገምተግኛ *fezaz,zegemtagna*
target *(n.)* ዕላማ *alama*
tariff *(n.)* ቀረፅ *qeres*
tarn *(n.)* ፈዚዙ *fezizu*
tarnish *(v.)* ፈዛዝ *fezaz*
tarot *(n.)* ጥንቆላ *tnkola*
tarpaulin *(n.)* ናይ ዝናብ ክዳን *nay znab kdan*
tart *(n.)* ጥዑም ነገር ዝሓዘ ብያቲ *t'um neger zhaze byati*
tartar *(n.)* ምስ ሰብ ክረዳዳእ ዘይክእል ሰብ *ms seb kredadaA zeyekAl seb*
task *(n.)* ስራሕ፣ሞያ *srah moya*
tassel *(n.)* ምንስናስ *mnsnas*
taste *(v.)* ኣማራፂ *amaratsi*
taste *(n.)* ጣዕሚ *taami*
tasteful *(adj.)* ጥዑም *t'um*
tasteless *(adj.)* ጣዕሚ ዘይብሉ *taami zeyblu*
tasty *(adj.)* ጥዑም *t'um*
tattle *(n.)* ቅርሪታ ኣቅሪቡ *qreta aqribu*
tattoo *(n.)* ዉቃጦ *wuqato*
tatty *(adj.)* ኣረጊት፣ዝተቀደደ *aregit,zteqdede*
taunt *(n.)* ምዝንባል፣ዘንቢሉ *mznbal,zenbilu*

taut *(adj.)* ዝተወጠረ *ztewetere*
tavern *(n.)* ናይ መሸት ቡና ቤት *nay mshet buna bet*
tawdry *(adj.)* ብልጭልጭ ርካሽ *blchlich rkash*
tax *(n.)* ግብሪ *gbri*
taxable *(adj.)* ግብሪ ዝክፈለሉ *gbri zkfelelu*
taxation *(n.)* ናይ ግብሪ ኣከፋፍላ *ney gbri akefafla*
taxi *(n.)* ታክሲ *taksi*
taxonomy *(n.)* ናይ እንስሳትን ኣትክልትን ዘፅንዕ *nay enssat atkltn zesn'a*
tea *(n.)* ሻሂ *shahi*
teach *(v.)* ምምሃር *mmhar*
teacher *(n.)* መምህር *memhr*
teak *(n.)* ናይ ሰሊጥ ዘርኢ *nay selit zer'i*
team *(n.)* ቡዱን *budun*
tear *(n.)* ንብዕት *nb'at*
tear *(v.)* ንብዕት *nb'at*
tearful *(adj.)* መሕዘኒ *mehzeni*
tease *(v.)* መብሸቂ *mebsheqi*
teat *(n.)* ናይ እንስሳ ጫፍ ጡብ *nay anssa chaf tub*
technical *(adj.)* ሞያዊ *moyawi*
technician *(n.)* በዓል ሞያ *beal moya*
technique *(n.)* ብልሓት *blhat*
technological *(adj.)* ብተክኖሎጅይ ዝተሓገዘ *bteknology ztehageze*
technologist *(n.)* በዓል ሞያ *beal moya*
technology *(n.)* ሞያዊ ስልጣነ ቴክኖሎጂ *moyawi sltena teknology*
tedious *(adj.)* መሰልቸዪ *meselchyi*
teem *(v.)* መሊኡ፣ሸፊኑ *meliu shefinu*
teenager *(n.)* ወጣት ዕድሚኡ 13-19 ዝኾነ *wetat admiu kab 13-19 zkone*
teens *(adj.)* ካብ 13-19 ዝርከብ *kab 13-19 zrkeb*
teeter *(v.)* ተንጎድጊዱ *tengedagidu*
teethe *(v.)* ስኒ ኣውፂኡ ን ህፃን *sni awsiau nhsan*
teetotal *(adj.)* ምንም መስተ ዘይሰቲ *mnm meste zeyseti*
teetotaller *(n.)* ምንም መስተ ዘይሰቲ *mnm meste zeyseti*
telecommunications *(n.)* ስልኪ፣ቲቪ፣ኢንተርኔት *slki,tivi,ainternet*
telegram *(n.)* ቴሌግራም *telegaram*
telegraph *(n.)* ቴሌግራም *telegaram*
telegraphic *(adj.)* ቴሌግራም ናይ ምኣላክ ሒደት *telegram nay melak hidet*
telegraphy *(n.)* ቴሌግራም ናይ ምኣላክ ሒደት *telegram nay melak hidet*
telepathy *(n.)* ናይ መንፈስ(ኣእምሮ) ርክብ *nay menfes aemro rkb*
telephone *(n.)* ስልኪ *slki*
telescope *(n.)* ኣቅሪቡ ዘርኢ መነፀር *aqribu zerai meneser*
televise *(v.)* ብቴሌቪዥን ተሓላሊፉ *btelevizn tehalalifu*
television *(n.)* ቴሌቪዥን *televizion*

tell *(v.)* **ምንጋር** *mngar*
teller *(n.)* **ገንዘብ ከፋሊ** *genzeb kefali*
telling *(adj.)* **ዉጺኢታማ** *wusieitama*
telltale *(adj.)* **ሚስጥረኛ** *mistregna*
temerity *(n.)* **ዘየድሊ ድፍረት** *zeyedli dfret*
temper *(n.)* **ተናዳዲ** *tenadadi*
temperament *(n.)* **ኣመል** *amel*
temperamental *(adj.)* **ቀልጢፉ ቀልጢፉ ዝኹሪ** *qltifu qltifu zkuri*
temperance *(n.)* **ንእሽተይ ዝበልዕ** *nashtey zbl'a*
temperate *(adj.)* **ወይና ደጋ** *weyna dega*
temperature *(n.)* **ሙቀት መጠን** *muqet meten*
tempest *(n.)* **ኣዉሎ ንፋስ** *awulo nfas*
tempestuous *(adj.)* **ዉዝምበሩ ዝዎፆ** *wuzmbru zwese*
template *(n.)* **ዝኮነ ነገር ንምስራሕ ዝተዛጋጀየ ኣቅሓ** *zkone neger nmsrah ztezgajeye aqha*
temple *(n.)* **ቤተ መቅደስ** *bet mekdes*
tempo *(n.)* **ናይ ሙዚቃ ስልቲ** *ney muzika slti*
temporal *(adj.)* **ግዜያዊ** *giziyawi*
temporary *(adj.)* **ግዜያዊ** *giziyawi*
temporize *(v.)* **ግዜ ንምግናይ ውሳኒኡ ኣደንጉዩ** *gze nmgnay wusanau adenguyu*
tempt *(v.)* **ንምፅላእ ምሙካር** *nmslaá mumukar*
temptation *(n.)* **ብጣዕሚ ናይ ምድላይ ስሚዒት** *btaami namdlay smiait*
tempter *(n.)* **ተፈታታኒ ሰብ** *tefetatani seb*
ten *(adj. & adv.)* **ዓሰርተ** *asert*
tenable *(adj.)* **ዝተረጋገፀ** *zteregagese*
tenacious *(adj.)* **ዘይረብሕ** *zeyrebh*
tenacity *(n.)* **ጥንካረ** *tenkara*
tenancy *(n.)* **ሓሪፍ ትኮነሉ ግዘ** *harif tkonelu gze*
tend *(v.)* **ሃዋህው** *hawahwu*
tendency *(n.)* **ዝንባለ** *znbale*
tendentious *(adj.)* **ዝንባለ** *znbale*
tender *(n.)* **የዋህ** *yewah*
tender *(adj.)* **ጨረታ** *chereta*
tendon *(n.)* **ናይ ሰዉነት ጅማት** *nay sewunet jmat*
tenement *(n.)* **ኣብ ፎቅ ዝካረ ቦታ** *ab foq zkare bota*
tenet *(n.)* **መምርሒ** *memrhi*
tennis *(n.)* **ናይ ሜዳ ተንስ ጨዋታ** *nay meda tens chewata*
tenor *(n.)* **ወዲ ደራፊ ፅብቅ ድምፂ ዘለዎ** *wedi derafi sbuk dmsi zelewo*
tense *(adj.)* **ናይ ግዘታት ስብስብ** *nay gizetat sbsb*
tensile *(adj.)* **ናይ ዉጥረት ስብስብ** *nay wutret sbsb*
tension *(n.)* **ናይ ሓይሊ መብራህቲ መጠን** *nay hayli mebrahti meten*
tent *(n.)* **ኬንዳ** *kenda*
tentacle *(n.)* **ኣከርካሪ ዘይብሎም እንስሳታት** *akerkari zeyblom anssatat*
tentative *(adj.)* **ዘየተኣማምን ገ ዘ ክቅየር ዝክእል** *zeyeteamamn geza kqyer zkal*

tenterhook *(n.)* ብጣዕሚ ምህንጣይ *btaami mhntay*
tenth *(adj. & n.)* ዓስራይ *asray*
tenuous *(adj.)* ቀጢን ብቀሊሉ ዘይስበር *qetin bkelilu zeysber*
tenure *(n.)* ናይ ፖሎቲካ ስልጣን ዝሃዘ *nay pletika sltan zhaze*
tepid *(adj.)* ብዙሕ ዘይሞቀ ማይ *bzuh zeymoke may*
term *(n.)* ናይ ሓደ ክፍለ ግዘ መጀመሪ/መወድ ኢ *nay hadekfle gze mjemeri/mewedei*
termagant *(n.)* ነገረኛ ሰበይቲ *negeregna sebeyti*
terminal *(adj.)* ና መጨረሻ ደረጃ *na mecheresha dereja*
terminate *(v.)* ኣቋሪፁ *aqarisu*
termination *(n.)* ትኣጊዱ *t'agidu*
terminological *(adj.)* ና ሓደ ስራሕ መረዳድኢ ቋንቋ *na hade srah meredadei kanka*
terminology *(n.)* ና ሓደ ስራሕ መረዳድኢ ቋንቋ *na hade srah meredadei kanka*
terminus *(n.)* ናይ ኣየር መስተኣናገዲ ቦታ *nay ayer msteanagedi bota*
termite *(n.)* ምሳጠ *msat*
terrace *(n.)* ዕብዪ መርየት *abyi meret*
terracotta *(n.)* ቀይሕ ሓመድ *keyh hamed*
terrain *(n.)* ምልክዐ ምድሪ *melka mdri*
terrestrial *(adj.)* ናይ የብስ ነባሪ *nay yebs nebari*
terrible *(adj.)* ከቢድ ሓዘን *kebid hazen*
terrier *(n.)* ና ሃደን ከልቢ *nahaden kelbi*
terrific *(adj.)* ከቢድ *kebid*
terrify *(v.)* ምስቃቅ *msqay*
territorial *(adj.)* ብሂራዊ ጦር ኣባል *bherawi tor abal*
territory *(n.)* ግዝኣት *gzat*
terror *(n.)* መፍርሒ ሰብ *mefrhi seb*
terrorism *(n.)* ሽብርተኝነት *shbrtegnnet*
terrorist *(n.)* ሽብርኛ *shbrtegna*
terrorize *(v.)* ኣሸቢሩ *ashebiru*
terry *(n.)* ዘርፍ *zerefa*
terse *(adj.)* ሕፅር ምጥን ዝበለ *hsr mtn zbele*
tertiary *(adj.)* ስኣልሳይ ደረጃ *salsay derja*
test *(n.)* ፈተና/ሙኮራ *fetena/mukera*
testament *(n.)* ንዛዘ *nzaze*
testate *(adj.)* ዘይ ምንዛዝ *zey mnzaz*
testicle *(n.)* ፍረ ነብሲ *frenebsi*
testify *(v.)* ምምስካር *mmskar*
testimonial *(n.)* ናይ ምስክር ወረቀት *ney mskr werket*
testimony *(n.)* ናይ ቃል መሓላ *nay kal mehala*
testis *(n.)* ፍረ ነብሲ *frenebsi*
testy *(adj.)* ተናዳዲ *tenadadi*
tetchy *(adj.)* ምግላል *mglal*
tether *(v.t.)* ና እንስሳት መእሰሪ ሰንሰለት *naanssat meseri senselet*
text *(n.)* ፅሑፍ *shuf*
textbook *(n.)* ደፍተር *defter*
textile *(n)* ጨርቃ ጨርቅ *cherka cherki*
textual *(adj.)* ካብ ፅሑፍ *kab shuf*

textual *(adj.)* ካብ ፅሑፍ *kab shuf*
texture *(n.)* ኩነታት ናዞ ነገር ሓርፋፍ/ለማፅ *kunetat nazu neger*
thank *(v.)* ኣመስጊኑ *amesginu*
thankful *(adj.)* ኣመስጋኒ *amesginu*
thankless *(adj.)* ዉለታ ቢስ *wuleta bis*
that *(pron. & adj.)* እቲ *ati*
thatch *(n.)* ኩምር ዝበለ ፀጉሪ *kumur zbele seguri*
thaw *(v.)* ሙውቅ ኣየር *muwuq ayer*
the *(adj.)* ፉሉጥ ዘኮነ ነገር ንምግላፅ እንጥቀመሉ *flut zkone neger nmflat entkemelu*
theatre *(n.)* ተውኒት *tewunet*
theatrical *(adj.)* ተውኒታዊ *tewunitawi*
theft *(n.)* ስርቂ *srki*
their *(adj.)* ናዮም *nayom*
theism *(n.)* ብእግዛቢሄር ምንባር ምእማን *magzabher mnbar m'eman*
them *(pron.)* እሶም *asom*
thematic *(adj.)* ዝተጨበጠ ነገር *ztechebet neger*
themselves *(pron.)* ባዕሎም *baalom*
then *(adv.)* ብድሕ ሪኡ *bdhriu*
thence *(adv.)* ብድሕ ሪኡ *bdhriu*
theocracy *(n.)* ብቀሺ ዝምራሕ ዓዲ *bqeshi zmrah adi*
theodolite *(n.)* ናይ ቅየሳ መሳርሒ *nay kyesa mesarhi*
theologian *(n.)* ናይ ሃይማኖት ጠቢብ *nay haymanot tebib*
theology *(n.)* ስነ-ሃይማኖት *sne haymanot*
theorem *(n.)* መላ ምት *melamt*
theoretical *(adj.)* ብፅሑፍ ዘሎ/ ዘይተሞከረ *bsuhuf zelo/zeytmokere*
theorist *(n.)* ሓሳብ ዘመንጪ *hasab zemenchi*
theorize *(v.)* ሓሳብ ኣመንጭዩ *hasab amenchiyu*
theory *(n.)* ፅንሲ ሓሳብ *tnsi hasab*
theosophy *(n.)* ብፆሎት ብምምሳጥ ምስ እግዛቢሄር ብቀጥታምንግጋር *bsolot bmmsat ms egzabher mgnay*
therapeutic *(adj.)* ሕማም ናይምድሓን ዕቅሚ *hmam namdhan aqmi*
therapist *(n.)* ሓኪም *hakim*
therapy *(n.)* ናይ ሕማም መድሓኒ ሕክምና *nahmam medheni hkmna*
there *(adv.)* ኣብ ኡ *abuu*
thermal *(adj.)* ሙቅ *muk*
thermometer *(n.)* ናይ ሙቀት መለክዒ መሳርሒ *nay muket melekai mesarhi*
thermos *(n.)* ፔርሙዝ *permuz*
thermosetting *(adj.)* ብሙቀት ዝጥንክር ፕላስቲክ *bmuqet ztnker plastik*
thermostat *(n.)* ሙቀት መቆፃፀሪ መሳርሒ *muqet meqosaseri meserhi*
thesis *(n.)* ና ዲግሪ መማልኢ ፁሑፍ *nadgri memalai shuf*
they *(pron.)* እሶም *Asom*
thick *(adj.)* ረጊድ *regid*
thicken *(v.)* ኣርጊዱ *argidu*

thicket *(n.)* በዕቲ *bati*
thief *(n.)* ሰራቂ *seraqi*
thigh *(n.)* ዳንጋ *dabga*
thimble *(n.)* ጓንቲ *ganti*
thin *(adj.)* ቀጢን *qetin bkelilu zeysber*
thing *(n.)* ስም ዝይብሉ ኣቅሓ *sm zeyblu aqh*
think *(v.)* ምሕሳብ *Mhsab*
thinker *(n.)* ሓሳቢ/ፋላስፋ *hasabi falasfa*
third *(adj.)* ሲሶ *siso*
thirst *(n.)* ማይ ምፅማእ *may msmaa*
thirsty *(adj.)* ማይ ምፅማእ *may msmaa*
thirteen *(adj. & n.)* ዕሰር ሰለስተ *aserte seleste*
thirteen *(adj. & n.)* ዕሰር ሰለስተ *aserte seleste*
thirteenth *(adj. & n.)* መበል ዕሰር ሰለስተ *mebel aserte seleste*
thirtieth *(adj. & n.)* መበል ሰላሳ *mebel selasa*
thirtieth *(adj. & n.)* መበል ሰላሳ *mebel selasa*
thirty *(adj. & n.)* ሰላሳ *selasa*
thirty *(adj. & n.)* ሰላሳ *selasa*
this *(pron.& adj.)* ኡዚ *azi*
thistle *(n.)* ሓሽክሾኽ ምባል *hashekushok mbal*
thither *(adv.)* ርሕቕ ዝበለ ቦታ *rhik zebele bota*
thong *(n.)* ናየ ቆዳ መሰርሒ *nay koda mesrhi*
thorn *(n.)* ዕሾክ *ashok*
thorny *(adj.)* ዕሾክ መዉፅኢ *ashok mewusai*
thorough *(adj.)* ጥብቂ *tebeka*
thoroughfare *(n.)* ዋና ጎዳና *wana godana*
though *(conj.)* ዋላካ እንተኮነ *walaka entekone*
thoughtful *(adj.)* ሓሳቢ *hasbi*
thoughtless *(adj.)* ዘይሓስብ *zeyhasb*
thousand *(adj. & n.)* ሽሕ *shih*
thrall *(n.)* ባርነት *barnet*
thrash *(v.)* ገረፋ *gerefe*
thread *(n.)* ክሪ *kri*
threat *(n.)* ፍርሒ *frhi*
threaten *(v.)* ፈሪሑ *ferisu*
three *(adj. & n.)* ሰለስተ *seste*
thresh *(v.)* ስንዳይ ካብ ሓሰሩ ምፍላይ *snday hasitu mflay*
threshold *(n.)* መእተዊ በሪ *matewi beri*
thrice *(adv.)* ሰለስተ ግዜ *seleste gze*
thrift *(n.)* ምቁጣብ *mqutab*
thrifty *(adj.)* ቆጣቢ *qotabi*
thrill *(n.)* ኣነቃቂሑ *ane kaki hu*
thriller *(n.)* ልቢ ሰቃሊ ታሪክ *lbisekali tarik*
thrive *(v.)* ተስፋሕፊሑ *tesfahfihu*
throat *(n.)* ጎሮሮ *gororo*
throaty *(adj.)* ዝተዓፈነ ድምፂ *zteafene dmsi*
throb *(v.)* ልቢ ብፍጥነት ክወቂዑ *lbu bftnet weqiau*
throes *(n.)* ከቢድ ስቃይ *kebid skay*
throne *(n.)* ዙፋን *zefen*
throng *(n.)* ብሓደ ኪዱ ግር ኢሉ *bhade kidu ger ailu*
throttle *(n.)* ሓነቂ *hanaki*
through *(prep. &adv.)* ነዳዲ መቆፃፀሪ *naedadi mekosasaeri*

throughout *(prep.)* ሙሉእ ብሙሉእ *mulua bmulua*
throw *(v.)* ደርብዩ/ምድርባይ *derbyu mdrbay*
thrush *(n.)* ሕብሪ ዝበዝሓ ዒፍ *hbri zbezha af*
thrust *(v.)* ምዉጋእ *mwudae*
thud *(n.)* ሃተፈ/ለፈለፈ *hatafe/leflafi*
thug *(n.)* ዓመፀኛ *amesegna*
thumb *(n.)* ዓባይ ኢድ *anay ad*
thunder *(n.)* ነጎድጋድ *negodgad*
thunderous *(adj.)* ነጎድጓዳዊ *negodgadawo*
Thursday *(n.)* ሓሙስ *hamus*
thus *(adv.)* ብዚ ምክንያት *bzi mknyat*
thwart *(v.)* ኣሰናኪሉ/ከልኪሉ *asenakilu/kelkilom*
thyroid *(n.)* ዕብየት ዝቆፃፀር *abyet zqossaser*
tiara *(n.)* ናይ ጳጳስ ዘዉዲ *nay papas zewudi*
tick *(n.)* ጨረት *cherk*
ticket *(n.)* ቲኬት *tket*
ticking *(n.)* ምቁፃር *mksat*
tickle *(v.)* ምኩርካዕ *kurkaa*
ticklish *(adj.)* ኮርኪዕካዮ ዝስሕቅ *korkiakayo zshk*
tidal *(adj.)* ማዕበል *maabel*
tidally *(n.)* ማዕበላዊ *maabelawi*
tide *(n.)* ማዕበል ባሕሪ *maobrl hahi*
tidiness *(n.)* ንፅህና *nshna*
tidings *(n.)* ዜና/ወረ *zena were*
tidy *(adj.)* ዝተስተካከለ *ztekelkele*
tie *(v.)* ካራባታ *karabota*
tie *(n.)* ጠንካራ ግኑኙነት *tenkar*ɩ*atenkara gnugnnet*
tied *(adj.)* ዝተኣሳሰረ *z'atesasere*
tier *(n.)* ብደረጃ ዝተደርደሩ *bdereja ztederaderu*
tiger *(n.)* ነብሪ *nebri*
tight *(adj.)* ሰጢሙ ዝተኣሰረ *setimu zete asere*
tighten *(v.)* ኣስጢሙ ሒዙ *astimu hizu*
tile *(n.)* ሸክላ ቆርቆሮ *shekla qorqoro*
till *(prep.)* እስካብ/ቀደደ *eskab/qdede*
tiller *(n.)* ሓረስታይ፣መቅዘፊ *harestay,mkzefi*
tilt *(v.)* ናብሓደ ምዝንባል *nab hade mznbal*
timber *(n.)* ኣፅኒዑ *as'ainu*
time *(n.)* ስዓት *seat*
timely *(adj.)* ብሰዓቱ *bseat*
timid *(adj.)* ሓፋር *hafar*
timidity *(n.)* ፍርሒ *hrhi*
timorous *(adj.)* ሓፋር *hafar*
tin *(n.)* ታንኒካ፣ቆርቆሮ *tanika,qorqoro*
tincture *(n.)* ብኣልኮል ዝብፅበፅ መድሓኒት *balkol zbsbes medhanit*
tinder *(n.)* ሓዊ ምቅፅፃል *hawi mks'al*
tinge *(n.)* ንእሽተይ ንምምሳል ምቅባእ *nAshtey nmmsal mkbae*
tingle *(n.)* መጠነኛ ናይ ምዉጋእ ስምዕት *metenegna nay mugae samet*
tinker *(v.)* ንእሽተይ ምዕራይ *nAshtey m'aray*
tinkle *(v.)* ተደዊሉ *tedewilu*
tinsel *(n.)* መጋየፂ ወረቀታት *megayesi werketat*
tint *(n.)* ንእሽተይ ንምምሳል ምቅባእ *n'ashtey nmmsal mkbae*

tiny *(adj.)* **ንእሽተይ፣ብጣዕሚ ንእሽተይ** *n'ashtey,btaami n'eshtey*

tip *(n.)* **ኣፍሲሱ፣ገልቢጡ** *afsisu,gelbitu*

tipple *(v.)* **ኣልኮል መስተ** *alkol meste*

tipster *(n.)* **ናፈርስ ዉድድር ቅርሺ ኣናተቀበለ ዝግምት** *naferes wudder qrshi enateqebele zgmt*

tipsy *(n.)* **ሞቅ ዝበሎ** *mok zbelo*

tiptoe *(v.)* **ብኣፃብዕቲ እግርካ ምካድ** *basabati egrka mkad*

tirade *(n.)* **ነዊሕ ጭቅጭቅ ዝተሓወሰ ንግግር** *newih chikchik ztehaweso nggr*

tire *(v.)* **ተስፋ ቆረፀ** *taesfa kors*

tired *(adj.)* **ድኻም** *dekam*

tireless *(adj.)* **ዘይፅዕር** *zeys'r*

tiresome *(adj.)* **ኣድካሚ ፣ኣሰልቻዪ** *adkami aselchayi*

tissue *(n.)* **ሶፍቲ** *softi*

titanic *(adj.)* **ብጣዕሚ ዓቡዪ ኣድላዪ** *btaemi abyi adlayi*

tithe *(n.)* **ቃል ሓደ እስረኛ ን ቤተ-ክርስትያን ዝወሃብ** *kal hade esregna nbetekrstyan zwehab*

titillate *(v.)* **ን ግብረ ስጋዊ ግኑኝነት ስሚዕት ምልዕዓል** *ngbre ssgawi gnugnunet smiait mlal*

titivate *(v.)* **ተቆናጅዩ** *tekonajyu*

title *(n.)* **ኣርእስቲ** *arasti*

titled *(adj.)* **በዓል መኣርግ** *beal mearg*

titular *(adj.)* **ንስም ብቻ ዝወሃብ መኣርግ** *nsm bcha zwehab mearg*

to *(prep.)* **ናብ** *nab hade mznbal*

toast *(n.)* **ዝተጠበሰ** *ztetbese*

toaster *(n.)* **ፎርኖ/ባኒ መብሰሊ ማሺን** *forno/bani mebseli mashion*

tobacco *(n.)* **ትምባኮ** *tmbako*

today *(adv.)* **ለሞዕንቲ** *lemaanti*

toddle *(v.)* **ኣለክሊኩ** *alkliku*

toddler *(n.)* **ታተ ዝብለ ህፃን** *tate zble hsan*

toe *(n.)* **ዓባይ ኣፃብዕቲ እግሪ** *abay asabati egry*

toffee *(n.)* **ካብ ፀባ ዝተሰርሐ ከረሜላ** *kab seba zteserhe kerimela*

tog *(n.)* **ዝተፈለየ ናይ በዓል ክዳን ምክዳን** *ztefely nay beal kdan mkdan*

toga *(n.)* **ናይ ሮማውያን ና ኣወዳት ጃኪት** *na romawuyan na awedat jaket*

together *(adv.)* **ብሓደ** *bhade*

toggle *(n.)* **ሞልጎሙ ብዕንጨይቲ ዝኮነ ክዳን** *molgomu bancheyti zteserhe kedean*

toil *(v.i.)* **ከቢድ ስራሕ ብርትዐ ዘድልዮ** *kebid srah brtea zdlyo*

toilet *(n.)* **ሽቃቅ፣ሽንቲ ቤት** *shqaq ,shnti bet*

toiletries *(n.)* **መተሓፃፀቢ ኣቁሑት** *metehasasebi akuhut*

toils *(n.)* **ከቢድ ስራሕ ብርትዐ ዘድልዮ** *kebid srah brtea zdlyo*

token *(n.)* **ምልክት መስታወሻ** *mlkt mestawesha*

tolerable *(adj.)* **ክትዕገሶ ዝካኣል** *ktageso tk'al*

tolerance *(n.)* **ትዕግስቲ** *tagsti*

tolerant *(adj.)* **ትዕግስተኛ** *tagstegna*

tolerate *(v.)* **ታዓጊሱ** *taagisu*

toleration *(n.)* **ትዕግስተኛነት** *t'agstegninet*
toll *(n.)* **ና ሓዘን ደወል፣ኣብ ኪላ ዝቁራፅ ቀርፅ** *nahazen dewel,ab kelazqures qeres*
tomato *(n.)* **ኮሚደረ** *komidere*
tomb *(n.)* **መቃብር** *mekabr*
tomboy *(n.)* **ፋሉይ ሎቶሪ** *fluy loteri*
tome *(n.)* **ዝዓበየ ና ምርምር መፅሓፍ** *zabeye namrmr meshaf*
tomfoolery *(n.)* **ዕብዳን** *abdan*
tomorrow *(adv.)* **ናጋ/ፅባሕ** *naga/sbah*
ton *(n.)* **ናይ ክብደት መለክዒ** *nakbdet melekai*
tone *(n.)* **ናይ ድምፂ ቃና** *na dmsi kana*
toner *(n.)* **ና ፕሪንተር ቀለም** *na printer kelem*
tongs *(n.)* **መቆንጠጢ** *mekonteti*
tongue *(n.)* **መልሓስ** *melhas*
tonic *(n.)* **ዘነቃቅሕ መድሓኒ** *zenekakh medhanit*
tonight *(adv.)* **ለሞዓንቲ ምሸት** *lemoanti mshet*
tonnage *(n.)* **ናይ መርከብ ፅዕነት ጠቅላላ ክብደት** *na merkeb teklala s'anet*
tonne *(n.)* **ሓደ ሺሕ ኪሎ ግራም** *hade shih kilogram*
tonsil *(n.)* **ቶንሲል** *tonsil*
tonsure *(n.)* **ብቡድሃ ሃይማኖት መላጥ** *bbudha haymanot melat*
too *(adv.)* **ብጣዕሚ፣ድጋሜ** *btaemi, dgame*
tool *(n.)* **ናይ ኢድ መሳርሒ** *ḧrtum*
tooth *(n.)* **ስኒ** *sni*
toothache *(n.)* **ናይ ስኒ ሕማም** *nay sni hmm*
toothless *(adj.)* **ሸራፍ** *sheraf*
toothpaste *(n.)* **ናይ ስኒ ሳሙና** *nay sni samuna*
toothpick *(n.)* **ና ስኒ መጎርገሪ ዕንጨይቲ** *nasni megorgori anchyti*
top *(n.)* **ኣብ ልዕሊ** *ab laali*
topaz *(n.)* **ፋሉጥ** *flut*
topiary *(n.)* **ኣትክልቲ ብመልክዕ ምቁራፅ** *atklti bmelka mkuras*
topic *(n.)* **ኣርእስቲ** *are'esti*
topical *(adj.)* **ወቅታዊ** *weqtawi*
topless *(adj.)* **ካብ መዓንጣ ንልዕሊ ጥራሕካ ምካን** *kab meantanlaali trahka mukan*
topographer *(n.)* **ናይ መሬት ኣቀማምጣ ዝፅንዕ ሙሁር** *nay meret akemamta zesna muhur*
topographical *(adj.)* **ናይ መሬት ኣቀማምጣ ዘርኢ ካርታ** *nay meret akemamta zerei karta*
topography *(n.)* **ናይ መሬት ኣቀማምጣ** *nay meret akemamta*
topping *(n.)* **ብልዕሊ ዝግበር** *blaeli zgber*
topple *(v.)* **ገልቢጡ ካብ ስልጣን** *gelbitu kab sltan*
tor *(n.)* **ና ከዉሒ ጎቦ** *na kewuhi gobo*
torch *(n.)* **ኣቃፂሉ** *akasilu*
toreador *(n.)* **ተመልካቲ** *temelkati*
torment *(n.)* **ከቢድ ስቃይ** *kebid skay*
tormentor *(n.)* **ኣቸጋሪ ሰብ** *achegari seb*
tornado *(n.)* **ብጣዕሚ ሓያል ንፋስ** *btaemi hayal nfas*

torpedo *(n.)* ብዉሽጢ ማይ ዝጎዓዝ ቦምብ *bwushti may zgoaz bomb*
torpid *(adj.)* ፈዛዝ *fezaz*
torrent *(n.)* ፅሕፉ፣ዉሑጅ *shfa ,wuhj*
torrential *(adj.)* ከቢድ ብጣዕሚ ሓያል *kebid btaami hayal*
torrid *(adj.)* ብጣዕሚ ሓያል ፀሎ *kebid btaami hselo*
torsion *(n.)* ምጥምዛዝ *mtmzaz*
torso *(n.)* ኢድ እግሪ ርእሲ ዘይብሉ አካል *aid agri resi zeyblu akal*
tort *(n.)* ፍትሒ ን ብሄር ወንጀል *fthi n bher wenjel*
tortoise *(n.)* ኣቦ ጋቡየ *abo gabuye*
tortuous *(adj.)* ዝተጠምማዘዘ *ztetemazeze*
torture *(n.)* ስቃይ *skay*
toss *(v.)* ወርዊሩ አፈንጢሩ *werwiru afentiru*
tot *(n.)* ጠንካራ ና አልኮል መስተ *tenkara alkol meste*
total *(n.)* ድምር፣ጠቅላላ *dmer,teklala*
total *(adj.)* ድምር፣ጠቅላላ *dmer,teklala*
totalitarian *(adj.)* ኣምባገነንነት ና ሓደ ፓርቲ መንግስቲ *ambagenennet na hade parti mengsti*
totality *(n.)* ብጠቅላላ *bteqlala*
tote *(v.)* ብምትሓዝ ዝግነ ቅርሺ *bmthaz zgne qrshi*
totter *(v.)* ደኪሙ መንግስቲ ወዲቁ *dekimu mensti wediqu*
touch *(v.)* ነኪኡ፣ምንካእ *nekiau mnkae*
touching *(adj.)* ልቢ ዝነክእ *lbiznekea*
touchy *(adj.)* ተናዳዲ *tenadadi*
tough *(adj.)* ጠንካራ *tenkaara*
toughen *(v.)* ኣበርቲዑ፣አጠንኪሩ *abertiau,atenkiru*
toughness *(n.)* ጥንካሬ *tenkara*
tour *(n.)* ጉዕዞ *guazo*
tourism *(n.)* ጎብነይቲ ምስትእንጋድ *gobneyti mstengad*
tourist *(n.)* ጎብናዪ *gobnayi*
tournament *(n.)* ዉድድር *wuddr*
tousle *(v.)* ዝረስሐ ፀጉሪ *zreshe seguri*
tout *(v.)* ኣሻይጡ *ashaytu*
tow *(v.)* ስሒቡ፣ጎቲቱ *sihibu gotitu*
towards *(prep.)* ናብ፣ብዝምልከት *nab bzmlket*
towel *(n.)* ፎጣ *fota*
towelling *(n.)* ፎጣ መስርሒ ጨርቂ *fota mesrhi cherki*
tower *(n.)* ፎቅ *foq*
town *(n.)* ከተማ *ketema*
toxic *(adj.)* መርዛማ *merzama*
toxicology *(n.)* ናይ መርዚ ፅንዓት *nay merzi snat*
toxin *(n.)* መርዛማ *merzama*
toy *(n.)* ቧምብላ *bwambula*
trace *(v.t.)* ለጢፉ ኮሪጁ፣ተከታቲልካ ምብፃሕ *letifu koriju,teketatilka mhaz*
traceable *(adj.)* ምስ ዝተተሓሓዘ ዝመፀ *ms ztetehahaze zmese*
tracing *(n.)* ዝተገልበጠ ካርታ *ztegelbete karta*
track *(n.)* ዝበፅሖ፣ናይ እግሪ መንገዲ *zbeshwo,nay egrimengedi*

tract *(n.)* በራሪ ወረቀት *berari wereket*
tractable *(adj.)* ብቀሊሉ ክቆፃፀርዎ ዝክእሉ *bqelilu kqosaserwa zk'al*
traction *(n.)* ዝንቀሳቀስ ሕይሊ *znqesaqes hyli*
tractor *(n.)* ናይ ሕርሻ መኪና *nay hrsha mekina*
trade *(n.)* ንግዲ *ngdi*
trademark *(n.)* ናይ ንግሪ ምልክት *nay ngdimlkt*
trader *(n.)* ነጋዴ *negade*
tradesman *(n.)* ነጋዴ *negade*
tradition *(n.)* ባህሊ፣ልምዲ *bahli,lmdi*
traditional *(adj.)* ብህላዊ *bahlawi*
traditionalist *(n.)* በዚ ምኽንያት'ዚ *bezimknyat ezi*
traduce *(v.)* ኣብሺቁ *abshiqu*
traffic *(n.)* ኣብ ሓደ ቦታ ብምንቅስቃስ ዘሎ መኪና *ab hade bota ab mnkskas zelo mekina*
tragedian *(n.)* መሕዘኒት ተዋናዪት፣መሕዘኒ ተውኒት *mehzednit tewanayit,mehzeni tewnit*
tragedy *(n.)* መሕዘኒ ኩነታት/ድርጊት *mehzeni kunetat/drgit*
tragic *(adj.)* መሕዘኒ *mehzeni*
trail *(n.)* ተከታቲሉ *teketatilu*
trailer *(n.)* ትእስሓቢ መኪና *teshabi mekina*
train *(v.)* ኣለማሚዱ፣ምልምማድ *alemamidu,mlmmad*
train *(n.)* ደቂኑ *deqinu*
trainee *(n.)* ሰልጣኒ *seltani*
trainer *(n.)* ኣሰልጣኒ *aseltani*
training *(n.)* ስልጠና *sltena*
traipse *(v.)* ምንቅርፋፍ *mnkrfaf*
trait *(n.)* ባህሪ *bhri*
traitor *(n.)* ካሕዳም *kahdam*
trajectory *(n.)* ዝንቀሳቀስ ነገር ምልክት ዳሓደገ ዝከድ *znqesaqes neger mlkt na hadege zked*
tram *(n.)* ና ከተማ ኤለትሪክ ባቡር *na ketema electric babur*
trammel *(v.)* ስራሕ ዝክልክል ነገር *srah zklkl neger*
tramp *(v.)* ደፍጢጡ፣ገሊፁ *deftitu,gelisu*
trample *(v.)* ተርጋጊፁ *teregagisu*
trampoline *(n.)* ጅምናስቲክ መስርሒ ዕራት *jmnastic mesrhi arat*
trance *(n.)* ብዕልካ ለይምፍላጥ *baalka zeymflat*
tranquil *(adj.)* ፀጥ ዝበለ ነገር *set zbele neger*
tranquillity *(n.)* ፀጥታ *settaa*
tranquillize *(v.)* ኣረጋጊያም፣ፀጥ ኣቢልዎም *aregagiaom,set abilowom*
transact *(v.)* ዕዳጋ ገይሮም፣ትሸዋዊጦም *adaga girom teshewawitom*
transaction *(n.)* ናይ ንግዲ ዉዕሊ *nay ngdi wualo*
transatlantic *(adj.)* ዉቅያኖስ ዘቋርፅ *wuqyanos zeqars*
transcend *(v.)* ሒሹ *hishu*
transcendent *(adj.)* ሕሽ ዝበለ ኣተሓሳስባ ዘለዎ *hish zbele atehasasba zelwo*
transcendental *(adj.)* ዝሓሸ ኣተሓሰስባ *zhashe atehasasba*

transcontinental *(adj.)* **አህጉር መቋረጺ** *ahugur meqaresi*
transcribe *(v.)* **ብካሊእ ቋንቋ ፂሒፉ** *bkakie qanqa sihifu*
transcript *(n.)* **ፅሑፍ ንንግግር ን ቃለ መጠይቅ** *shuf ngger nkale meteyik*
transcription *(n.)* **ምስምማዕ** *msm'emae*
transfer *(v.)* **ምልኣክ፣ምምሕልላፍ** *mleake mmhllaf*
transferable *(adj.)* **ተመሓላለፊ** *temehalalafi*
transfiguration *(n.)* **ምልክዕ ምቅያር/ምቁንጃይ** *melka mkyar mkunjay*
transfigure *(v.)* **ምልክዑ ቀይሩ/ትቋናጅዩ** *melk'u keyru tekoonajyu*
transform *(v.)* **ልዉጢ፣ናብ ካሊእ ነገር ምቅያር** *lewtinab kalia neger mkyar*
transformation *(n.)* **ምልዋጥ** *mlwat*
transformer *(n.)* **ናይ ኢኤለትሪክ ሓይሊ ዝቅይር መሰርሒ** *na eletric hayli zqyir mesarhi*
transfuse *(v.)* **ደም ምሃብ** *dem mhab*
transfusion *(n.)* **ደም ና ምሃብ ተግባር፣ልኮነ ፈሳሲ ናብ ካሊእ ምግልባጥ** *dem na mhab tegbar*
transgress *(v.)* **ደንቢሩ ጢሒሱ** *denbiru thisu*
transgression *(n.)* **ድንበር ምጥሓስ** *dnber mthas*
transient *(adj.)* **ግዜያዊ/ሓላፊ** *gziywi halafi*
transistor *(n.)* **ንእሽተይ ናይ ኤሊትሪክ ፍሰት መቆፃፀሪ መሳርሒ** *nAshtey nay eletric hayli mokosaseri*
transit *(n.)* **መሸጋገሪ ቦታ** *meshegageri bota*
transition *(n.)* **መሸጋገሪ ፣ናይ ሽግግር ወቅቲ/ግዜ** *meshegageri,na mshiggar gze*
transitive *(adj.)* **ተሻጋሪ ግስ** *teshagari gs*
transitory *(adj.)* **ግዜያዊ** *gziyawi*
translate *(v.)* **ተርጊሙ** *tergimu*
translation *(n.)* **ትርጉም** *trgum*
transliterate *(v.)* **ሓድ ቋንቋ ብካሊእ ቋንቋ ክፀሓፍ ከሎ** *hade qnaqa bkalie qanqa ksehaf kelo*
translucent *(adj.)* **ብርሃን ዘሕልፍ** *brhan zehlf*
transmigration *(n.)* **ናይ ሂወት ካብ ሞት ናብ ህያው ምዝዉዋር** *nay hiwet hab mot nab hyab mshiggar*
transmission *(n.)* **ዝመሓላለፍ ነገር፣ምምሕልላፍ** *zmehalalef neger mmhllaf*
transmit *(v.)* **ኣመሓላሊፉ** *amehalalifu*
transmitter *(n.)* **መመሓላለፊ መሳርሒ** *memahalalefi mesarhi*
transmute *(v.)* **ለዉጢ ቅርፂ ተፈጥሮ** *lewuti qrsi tefetro*
transparency *(n.)* **ብዉሽጢ ኣመሓላሊፍካ ምርኣይ** *bwushty amehalalifka mray*
transparent *(adj.)* **ብዉሽጡ ዘርኢ** *bwushti zer,i*

transpire *(v.)* ብቆርብት ቀዳድ ርስሓት ምውጋድ *bkorbet kedda dshat mray*

transplant *(v.)* ኣብ ሓደ ቦታ ዝተተከለ ናብ ካሊእ ቦታ ነቂልካ ምትካል *ab hade bota ztetekele nab kalie bota neklka mtkal*

transport *(v.)* መጉዑዓዝ *megueaz*

transportation *(n.)* መጓዓዝያ *megaazya*

transporter *(n.)* መጓዓዝያ *megaazya*

transpose *(v.)* ኣለዋዊጡ ፂሒፉ *alewawitu sihifu*

transsexual *(n.)* ፆታ ምቕያር *sota mkyar*

transverse *(adj.)* ኣግድም ዝተቀመጠ ኣግድማ *agdm ztekemete agdami*

transvestite *(n.)* ና ተቕራኒ ክዳን ክክደን ዝፎቲ *na teqarani sota kdan kkden zufoti*

trap *(n.)* ምፅመድ *mdmas*

trapeze *(n.)* ሽለውሊዋ መጫወቲ ኮፍ መበሊኡ *shelewliwa mechaeti kef mebeliu*

trash *(n.)* ጓሓፍ *gahaf*

trauma *(n.)* መደንገፂ ተሞክሮ *medengesi temokkuro*

travel *(v.)* ጉዕዞ *guazo*

traveller *(n.)* ተጉዕዚ *tegaizu*

travelogue *(n.)* ስለ ጉዕዞ ዘርኢ ፊልሚ *sleguazo zerai filmi*

traverse *(v.)* ተሻጊሩ/ኣቋሪፁ *teshagiru /aqarisu*

travesty *(n.)* ብዘስሕቕ መልክዑ ምምሳል *bzeshq melkau mmsal*

trawler *(n.)* ጃልባ መትሓዚ ዓሳ *jalba methazi asa*

tray *(n.)* ብያቲ፣ሸሓነ *bati,shehanee*

treacherous *(adj.)* ብምክሓድ/ብምሽዋድ *bmkhad bmshwad*

treachery *(n.)* ክሕደት *khdet*

treacle *(n.)* ሓፊስ ፈሳሲ ሽኮር *hafis fesasi sukor*

tread *(v.)* ኣካይዳ *akayda*

treadle *(n.)* ና ስፈት መኪና ፒዳል *nasfyet mekina pedal*

treadmill *(n.)* ኣሰልቻዩ በዓልታዊ ተግባር *aselchyi mealtawi tegbr*

treason *(n.)* ሃገር ክሒድካ ምስ ፀላኢ ምሕባር *hager kihidka ms selai mhbar*

treasure *(n.)* ሃፍቲ *hafti*

treasurer *(n.)* ምስምማዕ *msmame*

treasury *(n.)* ና ንብርት ሓላፊ *nanbret halefi*

treat *(v.)* ጋቢዙ *gabigu*

treatise *(n.)* ብሓደ ነገር ዘተኮረ ነዊሕ ፁሑፍ *bhade neger zetekore newih suhuf*

treatment *(n.)* ሕክምና *hkmna*

treaty *(n.)* ናይ ፁሑፍ ስምምዕነት *nay suhuf smm'a*

treble *(adj.)* ብሓደ መዓልቲ ሰለስተ ዉድድር ምሽናፍ *bhade mealti seleste gze mshnaf*

tree *(n.)* በህርዛፍ፣ጫዓ *baharzaf,chaa*

trek *(n.)* ነዊሕ ጉዕዞ ብእግሪ *newih guazo b'ageri*

trellis *(n.)* ናሓረግ መደገፊ ዕንጨይቲ *nahareg medegefi anseyti*
tremble *(v.)* ተንቀጥቂጡ፣ተዋዛዊዙ *tenqetkitu*
tremendous *(adj.)* ብጣዕሚ ቡዙሕ *btaami bzuh*
tremor *(n.)* ንእሽተይ መሬት ምንቅጥቃጥ *n'ashtey merit mnqtqat*
tremulous *(adj.)* ዘይተርጋገዐ *zeyteregageae*
trench *(n.)* ቦይ *boy*
trenchant *(adj.)* ግልፂ ዝኮነ ተግሳፅ *glsi zkone tegsas*
trend *(n.)* ዝንባለ *znbale*
trendy *(adj.)* ብወቅታዊ ፋሽን ዝክተል *bwuqtawi fashn zktel*
trepidation *(n.)* ዝሰርሕዎ ስራሕ ምፍራሕ *zserhwo srah mfrah*
trespass *(v.)* ሕጊ ጢሒሱ *higi tihisu*
tress *(n.)* ንቆርቆሮ ዝኮን ዕንጨይቲ *nqorqoro zkon anseyti*
trestle *(n.)* ተነቃሊ ና ጠረቢዛ እግሪ *teneqali naterebiza egri*
trial *(n.)* ሙኮራ *mukora*
triangle *(n.)* ሰለስተ መኣዝን *seleste meazen*
triangular *(adj.)* በዓል ሰለስተ መኣዝን *beal seleste meazn*
tribal *(adj.)* ና ጎሳ *nagosa*
tribe *(n.)* ጋሳ *gasa*
tribulation *(n.)* ላዕሊ ታሕቲይ ቺገር መከራ *laaliy tahty mekera chigr*
tribunal *(n.)* ፍሉይ ቤት ፍርዲ *fluy bet frdi*
tributary *(n.)* ዝተገደበ ዉሕጅ *ztegedebe wuhj*
tribute *(n.)* ናምስጋና ንግግር *namsgana nggr*
trice *(n.)* ብፍጥነት *bftnet*
triceps *(n.)* ና ማእገር ጨዋዳ *na maager chwada*
trick *(n.)* ምሸዋድ፣ምትላል *mshwad mtlal*
trickery *(n.)* ተንኮል *tenkol*
trickle *(v.)* ጥብ ጥብ ተንጠብጢቡ *tentebtibu*
trickster *(n.)* ተንኮለኛ *tenkolegna*
tricky *(adj.)* መሰሓሓቲ *mesahahati*
tricolour *(n.)* በዓል ሰለስተ ሕብሪ ባንደራ *beal seleste hbri bandera*
tricycle *(n.)* በዓል ሰለስተ ጎማ ሳይክል *beal seleste goma sycle*
trident *(n.)* በዓል ሰለስተ እግሪ መሰርሒ *beal seleste agri mesarhi*
Trier *(n.)* ፋሕጠርጠር ዝብለ ጎበዝ ሰራሕተኛ *fahterter zble tenkara serahtegna*
trifle *(n.)* ኣመል ኮይንዎ *amel koynuwo*
trigger *(n.)* መልሓስ ሽጉጥ *melhas shugut*
trigonometry *(n.)* ኩርናዓት ዝፅንዐሉ ናይ ሒሳብ ዘርፍ *kurnaat zesnalu na hisab zerfi*
trill *(n.)* ናይ ሙዚቃ ድምፂ *namuziqa*
trillion *(adj & n.)* ዓሰርተ ክልተ ዜሮ ዘለዋ ቁፅሪ/1,000,000,000,000 *dmsi*
trilogy *(n.)* ሰለስተ ተመሳሳሊ ሓሳብ ዘለዎ ነገር ተከታቲሉ

ክመፀእ ከሎ *seleste temesasali hasab zelewom*
trim *(v.)* ቆሪፁ *qorisu*
trimmer *(n.)* ሸንቃጣ *shenkata*
trimming *(n.)* ጌይሲ *geysi*
trinity *(n.)* ስላሴ *slasi*
trinket *(n.)* ርካሽ ግን ደስ በሃሊ *rkash gn des behali*
trio *(n.)* ሰለስቲኦም ሰለስተ ሙዚቃ *selestiaom seleste muziqa*
trip *(v.)* ጉዕዞ *guazo*
tripartite *(adj.)* ደጋፊ *degafi*
triple *(n.)* ሰለስተ ዕፀፊ፣ሰለስተ ጊዘ *seleste asfi,seleste gze*
triplet *(n.)* ብሓደ ግዘ ሰለስተ ቆልዑ ምዉላድ *bhade gze seleste kol'u mwulad*
triplicate *(adj.)* ሰለስተ ቅድሕታት *seleste kdhtat*
tripod *(n.)* ብዓል ሰለስተ እግሪ ጠጠው መበሊ *beal seleste egri tetew mebeli*
triptych *(n.)* ብሰለስተ ዕንጨይቲ ዝተስኣለ ስእሊ *bseleste ansyti ztesale seli*
trite *(adj.)* ዘይረብሕ *zeyrebh*
triumph *(n.)* ናዓወት ደስታ ኩነታት *nawet dsta knetat*
triumphal *(adj.)* ናዓወት መዓልቲ *naawet mealti*
triumphant *(adj.)* ናዓወት ስሚዒት *naawet smait*
trivet *(n.)* ጉልቻ *gulch*
trivia *(n.)* ዘየድሊ ትንተና *zeyedli tntena*
trivial *(adj.)* ዋጋ ቢስ የማይረባ *waga bis yemayreba*
trolley *(n.)* ጋሪ ጠረጴዛ *gari terebiza*
troop *(n.)* ብጉሩፕ ዝጓዓዙ ሰባት *bgurup zgaazu sebat*
trooper *(n.)* ናይ ክልል ፖሊስ *nay kll plis*
trophy *(n.)* ዋንጫ ሽልማት *wanch shlmat*
tropic *(n.)* ሙቀት እና ደርቅ ኣየር *muket ena derq ayer*
tropical *(adj.)* ሙቀት እና ደርቅ ኣየር *muket ena derq ayer*
trot *(v.)* ጋሊቡ *ebashi/zesqi seb*
trotter *(n.)* ግልባ ዝሰልጠነ *glba zseltene*
trouble *(n.)* እስቸጋሪ *aschegari*
trouble-shooter *(n.)* ሜላ ደላዪ ሰብ *mela delayi seb*
troublesome *(adj.)* ረባሺ/ዘሳቂ ሰብ *rebashi/seb zesaki seb*
trough *(n.)* ገንዳ/መሕመሲ *genda mehwesi*
trounce *(v.)* ኣጉል ቅጸዓት *agul qsat*
troupe *(n.)* ትተኣማመነሉ ሰብ *tteamamenelu seb*
trousers *(n.)* ስረ *sre*
trousseau *(n.)* ሓዳሽ መርዓት ናብ ስብኣያ ትወስዶ ኣቁሑ *hadash merat nab sbaya etwosddo aquhu*
trout *(n.)* ልብላዕ ዓሳ *lblaa asa*
trowel *(n.)* ና ነዳቂ ማንካ *na nedaqi manka*
truant *(n.)* ስርሑ ዘይሰርሕ ሰብ *srhu zeyserh seb*
truck *(n.)* ናፅዕነት መኪና *nas'anet mekina*
trucker *(n.)* ናፅዕነት መኪና ሹፈር *nas'anet mekina shuifer*
truculent *(adj.)* ተብኣሲ ለከፍ *tebaeisu lekef*

trudge *(v.)* ሙጉታት ምርማድ *mugutat*
true *(adj.)* ትኽክል /ሓቂ *tkkl/haqi*
truffle *(n.)* እንጉዳይ *anguday*
trug *(n.)* ናኣትክልተኛ ዘምቢል *naatkeltegna zenbil*
truism *(n.)* ፍሉጥ ሓቂ ምንጋር ዘየድልዮ *flut haki mngar zeyedlyo*
trump *(n.)* ፈጠራ *fetera*
trumpet *(n.)* ዓው ኢሉ ተናጊሩ *awu elu tenagiru*
truncate *(v.)* ቀንጢቡ *kentibu*
truncheon *(n.)* ና ፖሊስ ዱላ *na polis dula*
trundle *(v.)* ደፊኡ /ጎቲቱ *defiau/gotitu*
trunk *(n.)* ጉንዲ፣ና ሰዉነት ኣካል *gundi,nasewunet akal*
truss *(n.)* ድጋፍ *degafi*
trust *(n.)* እምነት ምግባር *amnet mgbar*
trustee *(n.)* ብዓል ሓደራ *beal hadera*
trustful *(adj.)* ኩሉ ዝኣምን *kulu zamn*
trustworthy *(adj.)* እምነት ዝግበረሉ *amnet zgberelu*
trusty *(adj.)* እሙን እስረኛ *amun esregna*
truth *(n.)* ሓቂ *haki*
truthful *(adj.)* ሓቀኛ *hakegna*
try *(v.)* ሞክር *mokr*
trying *(adj.)* ሙኮራ *mukera*
tryst *(n.)* ሞካሪ *mokari*
tub *(n.)* ጎድጋድ ሸሓነ *godgad shehane*
tube *(n.)* ቱቦ *tubo*
tubercle *(n.)* ና ሳንባ መንቀርሳ ምልክት *nasanba menkersa mlkt*
tuberculosis *(n.)* ና ሳንባ መንቀርሳ *nasanba menkersa*
tubular *(adj.)* ብሳንባ መንቀርሳ ዝሳቀ *basanba menkersa zsaqe*
tuck *(v.)* ኣእትዩ *aatyu*
Tuesday *(n.)* ሰሉስ *selus*
tug *(v.)* መንጪቁ/ጎቲቱ *menchiqu/gotitu*
tuition *(n.)* ናመምሃሪ ክፍሊት *namemhari kflit*
tulip *(n.)* ና ዕንበባ ዓይነት *na anbeba aynet*
tumble *(v.)* ሱቅ ኢሉ ወዲቁ *suq ilu wediqu*
tumbler *(n.)* ብርጭቆ *brchiqo*
tumescent *(adj.)* ኣብ ግብረ ስጋዊ ግኑኙነት ምሕባጥ *ab gbre sgawi gnugnnet mhbat*
tumour *(n.)* እጢ *ati*
tumult *(n.)* ረበሻ ጫውጫው ዝበለ ቦታ *rebesha chawchaw zbele bota*
tumultuous *(adj.)* ዝተረጋግዐ ረበሻ *zteregagea rebesha*
tun *(n.)* ና ወይኒ በርሚን *na weyni brmin*
tune *(n.)* ዜማ ቅኝት *zema qgnt*
tuner *(n.)* መመሓላለፊ ጣብያ *memehalalefe tabya*
tunic *(n.)* ና ወታደር ጃኬት *nawetader jaket*
tunnel *(n.)* በዓቲ *beati*
turban *(n.)* ና ሙስሊም ጥምጥም *na muslim tmtam*
turbid *(adj.)* ዘይተዘረገ *zeytzerege*
turbine *(n.)* ብኣየር ብማይ ብጋዝ ዝሽክርከር ሞተር *bmay bayer ngaz zshkrker moter*

turbulence *(n.)* ረበሻ ብጥብጥ ብና ፖለቲካ *rebesh btbt bna poletica*

turbulent *(adj.)* ሓድደገግና ነዉፅ ኣየር ባሕሪ *hdhdna newase ayer bahri*

turf *(n.)* ሳዕሪ ምግባር ምትካል *saeri mgbar*

turgid *(adj.)* ምንም ዘይርደአካ ቋንቋ *mnm zeyrdeeka qanqa*

turkey *(n.)* ና ኤሜሪካ ደርሆ *na america derho*

turmeric *(n.)* ዕርዲ *ardi*

turmoil *(n.)* ብፅብፅ ዓመፅ *bsbs ames*

turn *(v.)* ተዓፅፉ *teasifu*

turner *(n.)* ብ መሳርሒ ቅርፂ ዘዋፅእ *bmesarhi qrsi zwese*

turning *(n.)* መዕፀፊ ቦታ *measefi bota*

turnip *(n.)* ቀይ ስር *key sr*

turnout *(n.)* ብሓደ ኩነታት ዝተራከቡ ሰባት *bhade kunetat zterakebu sebat*

turnover *(n.)* ብዝተወሰነ ግዘ ዝተሰርሐ ንግዲ *bztewesene gze zteserhe ngdi*

turpentine *(n.)* ና ቀለም መቅጠኒ ኬሚካል *qelem meqteni kemikal*

turquoise *(n.)* ቆፃል ድይመንድ *qosal dymend*

turtle *(n.)* ና ባሕሪ ኣባ ጋዉየ *nabahri aba gabuye*

tusk *(n.)* ና ሓርማዝ ስኒ *naharmaz sni*

tussle *(n.)* ንምዉሳድ ምልፋዕ *nmwusad mlfae*

tutelage *(n.)* ካብ ጎበዝ ተፅጊዕካ ምምሃር *kab gobez tesegiaka mmhar*

tutor *(n.)* ና ግሊ መምህር *nagli memhr*

tutorial *(n.)* ና መምህር እና ተምሃሪ ና ዉይዪት መፅሓፍ *na memher ena temhari na wuyyt meshaf*

tuxedo *(n.)* ናድራር ክዳን *nadrar kdan*

tweak *(v.)* ምምንጫቅ *mmnchq*

twee *(adj.)* ደካማ ስምዕታዊ ሰባት ዝፈትዉዎ *dekama smiaitawi sebat zfetwuwo*

tweed *(n.)* ረጊድ ዝንጉርጉር ክዳን *regid zngurgur kdan*

tweet *(v.)* ና ንእሽተይ ዒፍ ድምፂ *naneshtey aif dmsi*

tweeter *(n.)* ንእሽተይ ድምፂ መጋዉሒ *neshtey dmsi megawuhi*

tweezers *(n.)* ወረንጦ *werento*

twelfth *(adj.&n.)* ጥቅምቲ *tkmti*

twelfth *(adj.&n.)* ጥቅምቲ *tkmti*

twelve *(adj.&n.)* ዓሰርተ ክልተ *aserte klte*

twentieth *(adj.&n.)* መበል ዒስራ *mebel aisra*

twentieth *(adj.&n.)* መበል ዒስራ *mebel aisra*

twenty *(adj.&n.)* ዒስራ *aisra*

twice *(adv.)* ክልተ ግዘ *glte gze*

twiddle *(v.)* ብዘይ ጥቅሚ ዘዊሩ *bzey tkmi zewiru*

twig *(n.)* ቅርንጫፍ *qrnchaf*

twilight *(n.)* ናፀሓይ ምዕራብ *nasahay marab*

twin *(n.)* ማንታ *manta*

twine *(n.)* ገመድ *gemed*

twinge *(n.)* ሕማቅ ስምዒት ንሓፅር ግዘ *hmaq smiet nhasir gze*
twinkle *(v.)* ኣብለጭሊጩ *ablechlichu*
twirl *(v.)* ተሽከርካሪ *teshkerkari*
twist *(v.)* ዝተጠምዘዘ *ztetemazeze*
twitch *(v.)* ምንቅጥቃጥ *mnktkat*
twitter *(v.)* ናይ ኣዕዋፍ ፍፆት *naeawaf fsot*
two *(adj.&n.)* ክልተ *klte*
twofold *(adj.)* ኣጥፊኡ *atfiu*
tycoon *(n.)* ሃፍታም ነጋዴ *haftam negadi*
type *(n.)* ዓይነት *aynet*
typesetter *(n.)* ኣፋኺሱ *afkisu*
typhoid *(n.)* ተሳሒቡ ካብ ምግቢ ዝወፅእ *teshibu kab mgbi zwese*
typhoon *(n.)* ኣውሎ ንፋስ *awulo nfas*
typhus *(n.)* ተስሓብቲ *tesehabti*
typical *(adj.)* ዝተለመደ *ztelemede*
typify *(v.)* ምሳሌ ዝኮነ *msale zkone*
typist *(n.)* ፀሓፊት *sehafit*
tyrannize *(v.)* ጨቂኑ ገዚኡ *chqinu geziau*
tyranny *(n.)* ኣምባገነንነት *ambagenennet*
tyrant *(n.)* ጨካን ኣምባ ገነን *chekan ambagenen*
tyre *(n.)* ናይ መኪና ጎማ *namekina goma*

U

ubiquitous *(adj.)* ፍቖድኡ *fqodeu*
udder *(n.)* መውዕሎ *mew'ëlo*
ugliness *(n.)* ክፉእ *kfu'e*
ugly *(adj.)* ክፉእ *kfu'e*
ulcer *(n.)* ቁስሊ *qusli*
ulterior *(adj.)* ዝበለፀ *zbeletse*
ultimate *(adj.)* መወዳእታ *mewedaeta*
ultimately *(adv.)* ብመወዳእታ *b'mewedaeta*
ultimatum *(n.)* ናይ መወዳእታ መጠንቀቕታ *nay mewedaeta metenkekta*
ultra *(pref.)* ብጣዕሚ *betaemi*
ultramarine *(n.)* ማያዊ *mayawi*
ultrasonic *(adj.)* ናይ ደምፂ ማዕበል *nay demtsi maebel*
ultrasound *(n.)* ኣልትራሳውንድ *sltrasawnd*
umber *(n.)* ፅልም ዝበለ *tselm zebele*
umbilical *(adj.)* ዕትብቲ *Etbti*
umbrella *(n.)* ፅላል *tselal*
umpire *(n.)* ዳኛ *dagna*
unable *(adj.)* ኣይከኣለን *aykealen*
unaccountable *(adj.)* ኣረማዊ *aremawi*
unadulterated *(adj.)* ዘይተበረዘ *zetebereze*
unalloyed *(adj.)* ዘይተሓወሰ *zeyteHawese*
unanimity *(a.)* ዘይምእዛዝ *zeyme'ezaz*
unanimous *(adj.)* ሓደ ድምፂ *Hade demtsi*
unarmed *(adj.)* ብዘይ ናይ ውግእ መሳርሒ *bzey nay wege'e mesarhi*

unassailable *(adj.)* **ኣይሰርሕን** *ayserhen*
unassuming *(adj.)* **ልዙብ** *lzub*
unattended *(adj.)* **ትጽቢት ዘይተገብረሉ** *tetsbit zaytegeberelu*
unavoidable *(adj.)* **ዘይተርፍ** *zayteref*
unaware *(adj.)* **ብሓፈሻ ፍሉጥ ዝኾነ** *bhafesha emun zeykone*
unbalanced *(adj.)* **ኢሚዛናዊ** *i'mizanawi*
unbelievable *(adj.)* **ዘይእመን** *zey'emen*
unbend *(v.)* **ምቅናዕ** *mqna'e*
unborn *(adj.)* **ዘይተወልደ** *zeytewelde*
unbridled *(adj.)* **ዘይተሓዋውሰ** *zeyteHawese*
unburden *(v.)* **ልግስነት** *lgsnet*
uncalled *(adj.)* **ዘይተፀወዐ** *zeytetsewe'e*
uncanny *(adj.)* **ዘይልሙድ** *zeylmud*
unceremonious *(adj.)* **ኩሉ ግዜ** *kulu gzee*
uncertain *(adj.)* **ዘይርግፀኛ** *zeyregetsegna*
uncharitable *(adj.)* **ጥሙይ** *tmuy*
uncle *(n.)* **ኣኮ** *ako*
unclean *(adj.)* **ዘይፅሩይ** *zeytseruy*
uncomfortable *(adj.)* **ዘይምቹ** *zeymechu*
uncommon *(adj.)* **ዘይልሙድ** *zeylmud*
uncompromising *(adj.)* **ደረቕ** *derek*
unconditional *(adj.)* **ብዘይኩነት** *bzeykunet*
unconscious *(adj.)* **ዘይንቑሕ** *zeynkuh*
uncouth *(adj.)* **ኣማዘን** *amazen*
uncover *(v.)* **ምግላፅ** *mglats*
unctuous *(adj.)* **ዕንዲዳ ጌጽ** *'ëndida geex*
undeceive *(v.)* **ሓቂ** *Haki*
undecided *(adj.)* **ዘይወሰኑ** *zeywesun*
undeniable *(adj.)* **ግልፂ** *gltsi*
under *(prep.)* **ትሕቲ** *thti*
underarm *(adj.)* **ትሕቲ ኢድ** *thti id*
undercover *(adj.)* **ምስጢራዊ** *mistrawi*
undercurrent *(n.)* **ተጻዒኑ** *tetsainu*
undercut *(v.)* **ምቁራፅ** *mkurats*
underdog *(n.)* **ምቁር** *mqur*
underestimate *(v.)* **ነዓቐ** *neaqe*
undergo *(v.)* **ምክዋን** *mkwan*
undergraduate *(n.)* **ተምሃሪ ዩኑቨርስቲ** *temhari yuniversty*
underground *(adj.)* **ትሕቲ መሬት** *thti meriet*
underhand *(adj.)* **ትሕቲ ኢድ** *thti id*
underlay *(n.)* **መኣረምታ** *me'aremta*
underline *(v.t.)* **ኣስመረ** *asmere*
underling *(n.)* **ዝተሰምረ** *ztesemere*
undermine *(v.)* **ነዓቐ** *neaqe*
underneath *(prep.)* **ብትሕቲ** *bthti*
underpants *(n.)* **ሙታንታ** *mutanta*
underpass *(n.)* **መሕለፊ በዓቲ** *mehlegi beati*

underprivileged *(adj.)* ውፁዕ *wxeu'e*
underrate *(v.)* ነዓቐ *neaqe*
underscore *(v.)* ኣስመረ *asmere*
undersigned *(n.)* ፈረመ *fereme*
understand *(v.t.)* ተረድአ *terede'e*
understanding *(n.)* ምርደዳእ *mrdeda'e*
understate *(v.)* ኣትሓተ *athate*
undertake *(v.)* ግዴታ *gdieta*
undertaker *(n.)* ማካየዲ ስራሕ *mekayedi srah*
underwear *(n.)* ሙታንታ *mutanta*
underworld *(n.)* ናይ ለያቡ ዓለም *lay leyabu alem*
underwrite *(v.)* ብታሕቲ ፀሓፈ *btahti tsehafe*
undesirable *(adj.)* ንፁግ *ntsug*
undo *(v.)* ቀልብስ *kelbs*
undoing *(n.)* ምቅልባስ *mqlbas*
undone *(adj.)* ዝተቀልበሰ *ztekelbese*
undress *(v.)* ኣጉልሐ *agulhe*
undue *(adj.)* ዘይርከብ *zeyrekeb*
undulate *(v.)* ዘይዕፀፍ *zey'etsef*
undying *(adj.)* ዘይመውት *zeymewut*
unearth *(v.)* ምኹዓት *mkuat*
uneasy *(adj.)* ከቢድ *kebid*
unemployable *(adj.)* ዘይቁፀር *zeykutser*
unemployed *(adj.)* ሰራሕ ዝፈትሐ *srah zfethe*
unending *(adj.)* ዘይወዳአ *zeywedae*
unequalled *(adj.)* ዝተፈላለየ *ztefelaleye*
uneven *(adj.)* ዘይመጣጠን *zeymetaten*
unexceptionable *(adj.)* ቅቡል *qbul*
unexceptional *(adj.)* ተመሳሳሊ *temesasali*
unexpected *(adj.)* ሃንደበት *handebet*
unfailing *(adj.)* ትኽክል *tkkl*
unfair *(adj.)* ዘይፍትሓዊ *zeyfethawi*
unfaithful *(adj.)* ቅኑዕ ዘይኮነ *qnue zeykone*
unfit *(adj.)* ብቑዕ ዘይኮነ *bku zeykone*
unfold *(v.)* ምቅልዕ *mqlae*
unforeseen *(adj.)* ዘተኣመተ *zeyteamete*
unforgettable *(adj.)* ዘይረሳዕ *zeyresae*
unfortunate *(adj.)* ዘሕዝን *zehzen*
unfounded *(adj.)* ዘይፈለጥ *zeyfelet*
unfurl *(v.)* ምግላሕ *mglah*
ungainly *(adj.)* ዘይጻወር *zeytsawer*
ungovernable *(adj.)* እምቢተኛ *embtegna*
ungrateful *(adj.)* ምስጋና ዘይብሉ *msgana zeybelu*
unguarded *(adj.)* ዘይሕሎ *zeyhlo*
unhappy *(adj.)* ዘይሕጉስ *zeyhgus*
unhealthy *(adj.)* ሕሙም *hmum*
unheard *(adj.)* ዘይሰማዕ *zeysemae*
unholy *(adj.)* ክፉእ *kfue*
unification *(n.)* ሓድነት *hadenet*
uniform *(adj.)* ተመሳሳሊ *temesasali*

unify *(v.)* **ሓደ ምግባር** *hade megbar*
unilateral *(adj.)* **ሓድነት** *hadenet*
unimpeachable *(adj.)* **ክበሃል ዘይክእል** *kbehal zeykel*
uninhabited *(adj.)* **ሰብ ዘይብሉ** *seb zeybelu*
union *(n.)* **ሕብረት** *hbret*
unionist *(n.)* **ማሕበራት** *mahberat*
unique *(adj.)* **ፍሉይ** *fluy*
unisex *(adj.)* **ፆታ ዘይበሉ** *tsota zeybelu*
unison *(n.)* **ሓድነት** *hadenet*
unit *(n.)* **ኣሃዱ** *'ahadu*
unite *(v.)* **ሓደ ምኳን** *hade mekuan*
unity *(n.)* **ሓድነት** *hadenet*
universal *(adj.)* **ናይ ዓለም ኣሕባሪ/ሓቛፊ** *nay alem ahbari/haquafi*
universality *(adv.)* **ዓለምለኻዊነት** *alemlekawinet*
universe *(n.)* **አጽናፈ ሰማይ** *atsenafe semay*
university *(n.)* **ዩኒቨርስቲ** *yuniversty*
unjust *(adj.)* **ዘይፍትሓዊ** *zeyfetHawi*
unkempt *(adj.)* **ጐበጣ** *gWabeẗa*
unkind *(adj.)* **ርጉም** *rgum*
unknown *(adj.)* **ዘይፍሉጥ** *zeyflut*
unleash *(v.)* **ምፍታሕ** *mftah*
unless *(conj.)* **ተዘይኮነ** *tezeykone*
unlike *(prep.)* **ዘይኮነ** *zeykone*
unlikely *(adj.)* **ዘይከውን** *zeykewun*
unlimited *(adj.)* **ዘይውሱን** *zeywusn*
unload *(v.)* **ኣራገፈ** *aragefe*
unmanned *(adj.)* **ሰብ ዘይብሉ** *seb zeybelu*
unmask *(v.)* **ምቕልዐ** *mqlae*
unmentionable *(adj.)* **ክበሃል ዘይክእል** *kbehal zeykel*
unmistakable *(adj.)* **ዘየጋጊ** *zeyegagi*
unmitigated *(adj.)* **ዘይጸወር** *zeytsawer*
unmoved *(adj.)* **ዘይፍቶ** *zeyfeto*
unnatural *(adj.)* **ዘይልሙድ** *zeylmud*
unnecessary *(adj.)* **ዘየድሊ** *zeyedeli*
unnerve *(v.)* **ፈርሐ** *ferhe*
unorthodox *(adj.)* **ዘይቅቡል** *zeyqbul*
unpack *(v.)* **ምርጋፍ** *mrgaf*
unpleasant *(adj.)* **ኣፀያፊ** *atseyafi*
unpopular *(adj.)* **ዘይቅቡል** *zeyqbul*
unprecedented *(adj.)* **ዘይፀቡይ** *zeytsebuy*
unprepared *(adj.)* **ዘይድልው** *zeydeluw*
unprincipled *(adj.)* **ባዕለገ** *baelege*
unprofessional *(adj.)* **ሞያዊ ዘይኮነ** *moyawi zeykone*
unqualified *(adj.)* **ብቑዕ ዘይኮነ** *bku zeykone*
unreasonable *(adj.)* **ደረቕ** *derek*
unreliable *(n)* **ዘየተኣማምን** *zeyeteamamn*
unreserved *(adj.)* **ዘይትሑዝ** *zeythuz*
unrest *(n.)* **ዘይምርግጋዕ** *zeymreggae*

unrivalled *(adj.)* **ዘይተማልአ** *zeytemale*
unruly *(adj.)* **ተለዋዋጥነት** *telewawatnet*
unscathed *(adj.)* **ዘየጎድእ** *zeyg'e*
unscrupulous *(adj.)* **ውሑድ** *wHud*
unseat *(v.)* **ወደቐ** *wedeqe*
unselfish *(adj.)* **ዘይርጉም** *zeyregum*
unsettle *(v.)* **ተረበሸ** *terebeshe*
unshakeable *(adj.)* **ዘይነቓነቕ** *zeyneqaneq*
unskilled *(adj.)* **ዘይክእል** *zeyk'el*
unsocial *(adj.)* **ምስ ሰብ ዘይቀርብ** *ms seb zeyqerb*
unsolicited *(adj.)* **ዘይቅቡል** *zeyqbul*
unstable *(adj.)* **ዘይድልዱል** *zeydeldul*
unsung *(adj.)* **ዘይተዘመረ** *zeytezemere*
unthinkable *(adj.)* **ዘይሕሰብ** *zeyhseb*
untidy *(adj.)* **ብትንትን ዝበለ** *btntn zbele*
until *(prep.)* **ክሳብ** *ksab*
untimely *(adj.)* **ዘይጊዝይዊ** *zeygziyawi*
untold *(adj.)* **ዘይተነግረ** *zeytegebre*
untouchable *(adj.)* **ዘይትንከፍ** *zeytnkef*
untoward *(adj.)* **ተለዋዋጥነት** *telewawatnet*
unusual *(adj.)* **ዘይልሙድ** *zeylmud*
unutterable *(adj.)* **ክበሃል ዘይክእል** *kbehal zeykel*
unveil *(v.)* **ምቕልዕ** *mqlae*
unwarranted *(adj.)* **ፍቓድ ዘይበሉ** *fqad zeyblu*
unwell *(adj.)* **ዘይፅቡቕ** *zeytsbuq*
unwilling *(adj.)* **ብዘይድልየት** *bzeydlyet*
unwind *(v.)* **ዘርገሐ** *zergeḧe*
unwise *(adj.)* **ጮንቀት** *chenqet*
unwittingly *(adv.)* **ሃረርተኛ** *harerteňa*
unworldly *(adj.)* **ዘይልሙድ** *zeylmud*
unworthy *(adj.)* **ብቑዕ ዘይኮነ** *bku zeykone*
up *(adv.)* **ላዕሊ** *la'eli*
upbeat *(adj.)* **ሕጉስ** *Hgus*
upbraid *(adj.)* **ዝኾነ ቦታ** *zḱone bota*
upcoming *(adj.)* **መፃኢ** *metsai*
update *(v.)* **ግዝያዊ** *gziyawi*
upgrade *(v.)* **ምምሕያሽ** *mmhyash*
upheaval *(n.)* **ረብሻ** *rebsha*
uphold *(v.)* **ምልዓል** *mlal*
upholster *(v.)* **ኸደነ** *kedene*
upholstery *(n.)* **ምኽዳን** *mkdan*
uplift *(v.)* **ኣለዓዓለ** *ale'a'ale*
upload *(v.)* **ፀዓነ** *tse'anew*
upper *(adj.)* **ላዕለዋይ** *la'eleway*
upright *(adj.)* **ቅኑዕ** *qnu'e*
uprising *(n.)* **ዓመፅ** *amex*
uproar *(n.)* **ይቕሬታ ሓተተ** *q̈reeta ḧatete*
uproarious *(adj.)* **ይቕሬታ** *yq̈reeta*
uproot *(v.)* **ሱር ሰደድ** *surseded*
upset *(v.)* **ኣቐየመ** *aqyeme*
upshot *(n.)* **ሃዋርያ** *hawarya*
upstart *(n.)* **ጭረት** *čret*

upsurge *(n.)* **እስካሕከሐ** - *askaḧkeḧe*
upturn *(n.)* **መሰርሒ** *mesarḧi*
upward *(adv.)* **ንላዕሊ** *nlaeli*
urban *(adj.)* **ከተማ** *ketema*
urbane *(adj.)* **ብሩህ** *bruh*
urbanity *(n.)* **ምኽታም** *mKtam*
urchin *(n.)* **ምቕልቃል** *mqlqal*
urge *(v.)* **አእመነ** *aemene*
urgent *(adj.)* **አግዳሲ** *agedasi*
urinal *(n.)* **መሸኒ** *mesheni*
urinary *(adj.)* **ቱቦ ሽንቲ** *tubo shennti*
urinate *(v.)* **ሸነ** *shene*
urine *(n.)* **ሽንቲ** *shnti*
urn *(n.)* **ሓሞኽሽቲ** *hamokshti*
usable *(adj.)* **ዝጠቅም** *zTekem*
usage *(n.)* **አጠቓቕማ** *atekakma*
use *(v.t.)* **ምጥቓም** *mtqam'*
useful *(adj.)* **ጠቓሚ** *tekami*
useless *(adj.)* **ዘይጠቅም** *zaytekm*
user *(n.)* **ተጠቃሚ** *teteqami*
usher *(n.)* **ዓጃቢ** *ajai*
usual *(adj.)* **ልሙድ** *lmud*
usually *(adv.)* **ከም ልሙድ** *kem lmud*
usurp *(v.)* **ቈጸራ** *qWexera*
usurpation *(n.)* **ጐዘየ** *gWazeye*
usury *(n.)* **ዚሰማማዕ** *zisemama'ë*
utensil *(n.)* **አቕሓ** *aqha*
uterus *(n.)* **ማህጸን** *mahxen*
utilitarian *(adj.)* **ተገንዘበ** *tegenzebe*
utility *(n.)* **አቕሓ** *aqha*
utilization *(n.)* **አጠቓቕማ** *atekakma*
utilize *(v.)* **ምጥቓም** *mtqam'*
utmost *(adj.)* **ዝበለፀ** *zbeletse*
utopia *(n.)* **ምቹው** *mchuw*
utopian *(adj.)* **ምቹው** *mchuw*
utter *(adj.)* **ዘረባ** *zereba*
utterance *(n.)* **ዘረባ** *zereba*
uttermost *(adj. & n.)* **ዝተዘርበሩ** *ztezerelu*

V

vacancy *(n.)* **ሃህታ** *hahta*
vacant *(adj.)* **ጥርሑ** *ṭrḥu*
vacate *(v.)* **ወጸ** *wexe*
vacation *(n.)* **ዕርፍቲ** *'ërfti*
vaccinate *(v.)* **ከተበ** *ketebe*
vaccination *(n.)* **ክታበት** *ktabet*
vaccine *(n.)* **ክታበት** *ktabet*
vacillate *(v.)* **ተወላወለ** *tewelawele*
vacillation *(n.)* **ውልውል ነግ ፈረግ** *wlwl neg fereg*
vacuous *(adj.)* **ዛህላል** *zahlal*
vacuum *(n.)* **ባዶሽ** *badosh*
vagabond *(n.)* **በጋሚዶ** *begamido*
vagary *(n.)* **ፊንታ** *finta*
vagina *(n.)* **መሸኒት** *meshenit*
vagrant *(n.)* **ከርታት** *kertat*
vague *(adj.)* **ዘይንጹር** *zeynxur*
vagueness *(n.)* **ዘይንጹር** *zeynxur*
vain *(adj.)* **ብላሽ** *blash*
valance *(n.)* **መጋረጃ** *megareğ*
vale *(n.)* **ስንጭሮ** *snçro*
valediction *(n.)* **ስንብታ** *snbta*
valentine *(n.)* **አፍቃሪ** *'afqari*
valet *(n.)* **አላይ ክዳውንቲ** *'alay kdawnti*
valetudinarian *(n.)* **ስልኩይ** *slkuy*

valiant *(adj.)* **ተባዕ** *teba'ë*
valid *(adj.)* **ብቑዕ** *bqu'ë*
validate *(v.)* **ብቕዓት** *bq'ät*
validity *(n.)* **ብቕዓት** *bq'ät*
valise *(n.)* **ባልጃ** *balğa*
valley *(n.)* **ስንጭሮ** *snčro*
valour *(n.)* **ጅግንነት** *ğgnnet*
valuable *(adj.)* **ክቡር** *kbur*
valuation *(n.)* **ኣሻንና** *'ashanna*
value *(n.)* **ዋጋ** *waga*
valve *(n.)* **መፈንቶ** *mefento*
vamp *(n.)* **ስውንዋኖ** *swnwano*
vampire *(n.)* **ምሎክ** *mlok*
van *(n.)* **መኪና** *mekina*
vandal *(n.)* **ኣዕናዊ** *'a'ënawi*
vandalize *(v.)* **ኣበላሸወ** *'abelashewe*
vane *(n.)* **ሓባር ንፋስ** *ḥabar nfas*
vanguard *(n.)* **መሪሕ** *meriḥ*
vanish *(v.)* **ተሸርበ** *tesherbe*
vanity *(n.)* **ትዕቢት** *t'ëbit*
vanquish *(v.)* **ሰዓረ** *se'äre*
vantage *(n.)* **ብልጫ** *blča*
vapid *(adj.)* **ላህዛዝ** *lahzaz*
vaporize *(v.)* **ሃፈፈ** *hafefe*
vapour *(n.)* **ሃተፍተፍ** *hateftef*
variable *(adj.)* **ተቐያያሪ** *teqeyayari*
variance *(n.)* **ፍልልይ** *flly*
variant *(n.)* **ልውጥ** *lwẗ*
variation *(n.)* **ፍልልይ** *flly*
varicose *(adj.)* **ሕቡጥ** *ḥbuṭ*
varied *(adj.)* **ዝተፈላለየ** *ztefelaleye*
variegated *(adj.)* **ጉራማይለ** *guramayle*
variety *(n.)* **ዓይነት ዓሌት** *'äynet 'äleet*
various *(adj.)* **ዝተፈላለየ** *ztefelaleye*
varlet *(n.)* **ተፈላለየ** *tefelaleye*
varnish *(n.)* **ቫርኒች** *varniche*
vary *(v.)* **ተፈላለየ** *tefelaleye*
vascular *(adj.)* **ናይ ሻምብቆ ኣካል** *nay shambqo 'akal*
vase *(n.)* **ባዞ** *bazo*
vasectomy *(n.)* **መጥባሕቲ መትረብ ዘርኢ** *meẗbaḧti metreb zer'i*
vassal *(n.)* **ጊላ** *gila*
vast *(adj.)* **ሰፊሕ** *sefiḥ*
vaudeville *(n.)* **ምርኢት** *mr'it*
vault *(n.)* **ቀስቲ** *qesti*
vaunted *(adj.)* **ቀስቲ** *qesti*
veal *(n.)* **ስጋ ምራኽ** *sga mraḱ*
veer *(n.)* **ኣንፈት ቀየረ** *'anfet qeyere*
vegan *(n.)* **ሓምሊ ዝቕለቡ** *ḧamli zqelebu*
vegetable *(n.)* **ናይ ኣትክልቲ** *nay 'atklti*
vegetarian *(n.)* **በላዕ ሓምሊ** *bela'ë ḥamli*
vegetate *(v.)* **ተረፈ0** *terefe'ë*
vegetation *(n.)* **ቡቕሊ** *buqli*
vehement *(adj.)* **ብርቱዕ** *brtu'ë*
vehicle *(n.)* **መሳርያ ምጉዕዓዝ** *mesarya mgu'ë'äz*
veil *(n.)* **ጉልባብ** *gulbab*
vein *(n.)* **ቨይን** *veyn*
velocity *(n.)* **ፍጥነት** *fṭne*
velour *(n.)* **ቫሎር** *valor*
velvet *(n.)* **ዓለባ ሃሪ** *'äleba hari*
venal *(adj.)* **በላዒ** *bela'ï*
vend *(v.)* **ሸጠ** *sheṭe*
vendetta *(n.)* **ሕነ** *ḥne*
vendor *(n.)* **ሸያጢ** *sheyaṭi*

veneer *(n.)* **መሸፈን ሉሕ** *meshefen luḥ*
venerable *(adj.)* **ዓቢ** *'äbi*
venerate *(v.)* **ኣኽበረ** *'aǩbere*
vengeance *(n.)* **ፍዳ** *fda*
vengeful *(adj.)* **ቂመኛ** *qimeña*
venial *(adj.)* **ዕሽሽ ኪበሃል ዚከኣል** *'ëshsh kibehal zike'al*
venom *(n.)* **ሕንዚ** *ḥnz*
venomous *(adj.)* **ሕንዛም** *ḥnzam*
venous *(adj.)* **ናይ ቨይን** *nay veyn*
vent *(n.)* **መፈንቶ** *mefento*
ventilate *(v.)* **ኣርወሐ** *'arweḥe*
ventilation *(n.)* **ርውሓት** *rwḥat*
ventilator *(n.)* **መርውሓ** *merwḥa*
venture *(n.)* **ፈተነ** *fetene*
venturesome *(adj.)* **ዓንዳሪ** *'ändari*
venue *(n.)* **መራኸቢ ቦታ** *meraǩebi bota*
veracious *(adj.)* **ናይ ብሓቂ** *nay bḥaqi*
veracity *(n.)* **ሓቅነት** *ḥaqnet*
veranda *(n.)* **በረንዳ** *berenda*
verb *(n.)* **ግሲ** *gsi*
verbal *(adj.)* **ናይ ቃላት** *nay qalat*
verbiage *(n.)* **ቃለ-ድርዳረ** *qaledrdar*
verbose *(adj.)* **ቃለ-ድርዳረኣዊ** *qaledrdare'aw*
verbosity *(n.)* **ቃለ-ድርዳረነት** *qaledrdarene*
verdant *(adj.)* **ለምለም** *lemlem*
verdict *(n.)* **ፍርዲ** *frdi*
verge *(n.)* **ጥርዚ** *ṭrzi*
verification *(n.)* **ኣመሳኸረ** *'amesaǩere*
verify *(v.)* **ኣመሳኸረ** *'amesaǩere*
verily *(adv.)* **ብሓቂ** *bḥaqi*
verisimilitude *(n.)* **ሓቂ መሰልነት** *ḥaqi meselne*
veritable *(adj.)* **ሓቀኛ** *ḥaqeña*
verity *(n.)* **ሓቅነት** *ḥaqnet*
vermin *(n.)* **ኣራዊት** *'arawit*
vernacular *(n.)* **ናይታ ሃገር** *nayta hager*
vernal *(adj.)* **ጽድያዊ** *xdyawi*
versatile *(adj.)* **ዋሓለ** *waḥale*
verse *(n.)* **ቤት** *beet*
versed *(adj.)* **ክኢላ** *k'ila*
versify *(v.)* **ገጠመ** *geṭeme*
version *(n.)* **ትርጓም** *trgWam*
verso *(n.)* **ጸጋማይ ገጽ** *xegamay gex*
versus *(prep.)* **ኣንጻር** *'anxar*
vertebra *(n.)* **ገረንገራት** *gerengerat*
vertebrate *(n.)* **ገረንገራዊ** *gerengerawi*
vertex *(n.)* **ጫፍ** *çaf*
vertical *(adj.)* **ዓንዳዊ** *'ändawi*
vertigo *(n.)* **መንጸሮር** *menxeror*
verve *(n.)* **ውዕውዕ ስምዒት** *w'ëw'ë sm'ït*
very *(adv.)* **ኣዝዩ** *'azyu*
vessel *(n.)* **መዕቆሪ** *me'ëqori*
vest *(n.)* **ጅለ** *ǧle*
vestibule *(n.)* **ወገፈ** *wegefe*
vestige *(n.)* **ኣሰር** *'aser*
vestment *(n.)* **ልብሲ** *lbsi*
vestry *(n.)* **ቤተ-ልብሲ** *beetelbsi*
veteran *(n.)* **ወተሃደር ነበር** *wetehader neber*
veterinary *(adj.)* **ንሕማም እንስሳ ዚምልከት** *nḥmam 'ènssa zimlket*
veto *(n.)* **ቀውፊ** *qewfi*
vex *(v.)* **ኣሕረቐ** *'aḥreq̈e*
via *(prep.)* **ብመንገዲ** *bmengedi*

viable *(adj.)* ኪቕጽል ዚኽእል *kiq̈xl zik'èl*
viaduct *(n.)* ድንድል *dndl*
vial *(n.)* ብልቃጥ *blqaṭ*
viands *(n.)* መግቢ *megbi*
vibrant *(adj.)* ተነዝናዚ *teneznazi*
vibrate *(v.)* ተነዝነዘ *tenezneze*
vibration *(n.)* ንዝናዘ *nznaze*
vicar *(n.)* ቆሞስ *qomos*
vicarious *(adj.)* በጃ *beǧa*
vice *(n.)* ሕማቕ ኣመል *ḥmaq̈ 'ame*
viceroy *(n.)* ምስሌነ *msleene*
vice-versa *(adv.)* ተቓወመ *teq̈aweme*
vicinity *(n.)* ቅርበት *qrbet*
vicious *(adj.)* እከይ *'èkey*
vicissitude *(n.)* ምቅይያራት *mqyyarat*
victim *(n.)* ስዋእቲ *meswa'èti*
victimize *(n.)* ኣደደ *'adede*
victor *(n.)* መዋኢ *mewa'i*
victorious *(adj.)* ዕዉት *ëwut*
victory *(n.)* ዓወት *'äwet*
victualler *(n.)* ስንቂ *snqi*
victuals *(n.)* ኣስነቖ *'asneq̈e*
video *(n.)* ቪድዮ *vidyo*
vie *(v.)* ተወዳደረ *tewedadere*
view *(n.)* ምርኣይ *mr'ay*
vigil *(n.)*.ሓለዋ *ḥalewa*
vigilance *(n.)* ትኩርና *tkurna*
vigilant *(adj.)* ጥንቁቕ *ṭnquq̈*
vignette *(n.)* ስልማት ናይ መጽሓፍ *slmat nay mexḥaf*
vigorous *(adj.)* ዝተማልአ *ztemal'e*
vigour *(n.)* ብርታዐ *brta'ë*
vile *(adj.)* ነውራም *newram*
vilify *(v.)* ኣዋረደ *'awarede*
villa *(n.)* ቪላ *vila*
village *(n.)* ቁሸት *qushet*
villain *(n.)* ገበነኛ *gebeneña*
vindicate *(v.)* ሓቅነት ኣረጋገጸ *ḥaqnet 'aregagexe*
vine *(n.)* ተኽሊ ወይኒ *tek'li weyni*
vinegar *(n.)* ኣቸቶ *'acheto*
vintage *(n.)* ቀውዒ ናይ ወይኒ *qew'ï nay weyni*
vintner *(n.)* ሸቃጥ ነቢት *sheqaṭ nebit*
violate *(v.)* ገሃሰ *gehase*
violation *(n.)* ገበን *geben*
violence *(n.)* ዓመጽ *'ämex*
violent *(adj.)* ጎነጻዊ *gonexawi*
violet *(n.)* ሊላ *lila*
violin *(n.)* ቫዮሊን *vayolin*
violinist *(n.)* ስነ-ጠቢብ *sneṫebib*
virago *(n.)* ናግራም ሰበይቲ *nagram sebeyti*
viral *(adj.)* ስሙይ *smuy*
virgin *(n.)* በዱ *bedu*
virile *(adj.)* ጠንካራ *ṭenkara*
virility *(n.)* ሰብእነት *seb'ènet*
virtual *(adj.)* ግብራዊ *gbrawi*
virtue *(n.)* ውርዝውና *wrzwna*
virulent *(adj.)* ሓደገ'ኛ ብርቱዕ *ḥadegeña brtu'ë*
virus *(n.)* ቫይረስ *vayres*
visa *(n.)* ቪዛ *viza*
visage *(n.)* ገጽ *gex*
viscid *(adj.)* ሓፊስ *ḥafis*
viscose *(n.)* ቪስኮዝ *viskoz*
viscount *(n.)* መስፍን *mesfn*
viscous *(adj.)* ሓፊስ *ḥafis*
visibility *(n.)* ተረኣይነት *tere'aynet*

visible *(adj.)* ኪረአ ዚኸኣል *kire'e zike'al*
vision *(n.)* ራእይ *ra'èy*
visionary *(adj.)* ራእያዊ *ra'èyawi*
visit *(v.)* በጽሐ - *bexḥe*
visitation *(n.)* ብጽሖ *bxḥo*
visitor *(n.)* በጻሒ *bexaḥi*
visor *(n.)* ድርዒ ገጽ *dr'ï gex*
vista *(n.)* ትርኢት *tr'it*
visual *(adj.)* ርእየታዊ *r'èyetawi*
visualize *(v.)* ቀረጸ *qerexe*
vital *(adj.)* ምስ ህይወት ዝተኣሳሰረ *ms hywet zte'asasere*
vitality *(n.)* ህይወት *hywet*
vitalize *(v.)* ህይወት ሃበ *hywet habe*
vitamin *(n.)* ቪታሚን *vitamin*
vitiate *(v.)* ኣሕመቐ *'aḥmeq̈e*
viticulture *(n.)* ኵስኰሳ ወይኒ *kuskWasa weyni*
vitreous *(adj.)* ጥርሙዛዊ *ṭrmuzawi*
vitrify *(v.)* ናብ ጥርሙዝ ለወጠ *nab ṭrmuz leweṭe*
vitriol *(n.)* ቪትርዮል *vitryol*
vituperation *(n.)* **shnglaẗ mwxa'è** *ሽንግላጥ ምውጻእ*
vivacious *(adj.)* ህይወታዊ ንጡፍ *hywetawi nṭuf*
vivid *(adj.)* ውዕውዕ *w'ëw'ë*
vivify *(v.)* ህይወት መለሰ *hywet melese*
vixen *(n.)* ዋዕሮ *wa'ëro*
vocabulary *(n.)* ቃላት *qalat*
vocal *(adj.)* ድምጻዊ *dmxawi*
vocalist *(n.)* ደራፊ *derafi*
vocation *(n.)* ሞያ *moya*
vociferous *(adj.)* ወጫጪ *weç̣aç̣i*
vogue *(n.)* ዘመናይ *zemenay*
voice *(n.)* ደሃይ *dehay*
voicemail *(n.)* ምድራዝ *mdraz*
void *(adj.)* ባድም *badm*
voile *(n.)* ሻሽ *shash*
volatile *(adj.)* በናኒ *benani*
volcanic *(adj.)* እሳተ-ጎመራዊ *'èsategomerawi*
volcano *(n.)* እሳተ-ጎመራ *'èsategomera*
volition *(n.)* ዊንታ *winta*
volley *(n.)* መሾምበባ *meshombeba*
volt *(n.)* ቮልት *volt*
voltage *(n.)* ዓቐን ሓይሊ ኤሌክትሪክ *'äq̈en ḧayli 'eeleektrik*
voluble *(adj.)* ክኢላ *k'ila*
volume *(n.)* ቅጺ *qxi*
voluminous *(adj.)* ሰፊሕ *sefiḥ*
voluntary *(adj.)* ወለንታዊ ዊንታዊ *welentawi wintawi*
volunteer *(n.)* ወለንተወ ፍቓደኛ ኮነ *welentewe fq̈adeña kone*
voluptuary *(n.)* ፈታው ምቾት *fetaw mchot*
voluptuous *(adj.)* ስምዒታዊ *sm'ïtawi*
vomit *(v.)* ትፋእ *tfa'è*
voodoo *(n.)* ቩዱ *vudu*
voracious *(adj.)* ሃርጋፍ *hargaf*
vortex *(n.)* ዘራጊቶ *zeragito*
votary *(n.)* መናኒ *menani*
vote *(n.)* ድምጺ ምርጫ *dmxi mrç̣a*
votive *(adj.)* መብጻዓዊ *mebxa'äwi*
vouch *(v.)* ተዋሓሰ *tewaḥase*
voucher *(n.)* ቫውቸር *vawcher*
vouchsafe *(v.)* ለገሰ *legese*

vow *(n.)* መብጽዓ *mebx'ä*
vowel *(n.)* ኣድማጺ *admaxi*
voyage *(n.)* ጉዕዞ *gu'ëzo*
voyager *(n.)* ገያሺ *geyashi*
vulcanize *(v.)* ቨልከነ *velkene*
vulgar *(adj.)* ጽዩፍ *xyuf*
vulgarian *(n.)* በዓለገ *be'älege*
vulgarity *(n.)* መቐረት ዘይብሉ *meq̈eret zeyblu*
vulnerable *(adj.)* ተነቃፊ *teneqaf*
vulpine *(adj.)* ናይ ወኻርያ *nay weḱarya*
vulture *(n.)* ጋም *gam*

W

wacky *(adj.)* ዘይልሙድ *zeylemud*
wad *(n.)* እኩብ *ekub*
waddle *(v.)* ተሳለየ *tesaleye*
wade *(v.)* ተንፋሕኰ *tenfaḥḱWa*
wader *(n.)* ዓይነት ዑፍ *'äynet 'üf*
wadi *(n.)* ሩባ *ruba*
wafer *(n.)* ሕብስተ-ቁርባን *ḥbstequrban*
waffle *(v.)* ኣዕጀውጀወ ለፍለፈ *'a'ëğewğewe leflef*
waft *(v.)* ኣንሳፈፈ *'ansafefe*
wag *(v.)* ኣወጣወጠ *'aweṭaweṭe*
wage *(n.)* ደሞዝ ዓስቢ *demoz 'äsbi*
wager *(n. & v.)* ተወራረደ *tewerarede*
waggle *(v.)* ኣወጣወጠ *'aweṭaweṭe*
wagon *(n.)* ባጎኒ *bagoni*
wagtail *(n.)* ዑፍ *üf*
waif *(n.)* ዘኽታም *zeḱtam*
wail *(n.)* በኸየ *beḱeye*
wain *(n.)* ቃፍላይ *qafla*
wainscot *(n.)* ምሉእ ዘድሊ *mlu'è zedli*
waist *(n.)* መዓጡቕ *me'äṭuq̈*
waistband *(n.)* ቅናት *qnat*
waistcoat *(n.)* ሰደርያ *sederya*
wait *(v.)* ጸንሐ *xenḥe*
waiter *(n.)* ኣሰላፊ *'aselafi*
waitress *(n.)* ኣሰላፊት *'aselafit*
waive *(v.)* ሰሓበ *seḥabe*
wake *(v.)* ተንስአ *tens'e*
wakeful *(adj.)* ጽን በሃሊ *xn behali*
waken *(v.)* ኣለዓዓለ *'ale'ä'äle*
walk *(v.)* ተጓዕዘ *tegWa'ëze*
wall *(n.)* መንደቕ *mendeq̈*
wallaby *(n.)* ንእሽቶ ካንጋሩ *n'èshto kangaru*
wallet *(n.)* ማሕፉዳ *maḥfuda*
wallop *(v.)* ደከረ *dekere*
wallow *(v.)* ኣንገርገረ *'angergere*
Wally *(n.)* ሕሉም *ḥlum*
walnut *(n.)* ጀዝ *ğez*
walrus *(n.)* መጥበዊ *meẗbewi*
waltz *(n.)* ቫልስ *vals*
wan *(adj.)* ምህሙን *mhmun*
wand *(n.)* ከረዛን *kerezan*
wander *(v.)* ኮብለለ *koblele*
wane *(v.)* እናጠፍአት ከደት *'ènaṭef'et kedet*
wangle *(v.)* ሓበለ *ḥabele*
want *(v.)* ደለየ *deleye*
wanting *(adj.)* ድልየት *dlyet*
wanton *(adj.)* ፈኖ *feno*
war *(n.)* ኲናት *kWinat*
warble *(v.)* ዘመረ *zemere*
warbler *(n.)* ስነ-ጠቢብ *sneṭebib*
ward *(n.)* ሓለዋ *ḥalewa*

warden *(n.)* ሓላፊ *ḥalafi*
warder *(n.)* ድጓና *dgWana*
wardrobe *(n.)* ኣርማድዮ ክዳውንቲ *'armadyo kdawnti*
ware *(n.)* ስኑዕ ኣቕሑ *snu'ë 'aq̈ḥu*
warehouse *(n.)* ካዝና *kazna*
warfare *(n.)* ቅዲ ኲናት *qdi kunat*
warlike *(adj.)* ፈታው ኲናት *fetaw kunat*
warm *(adj.)* ልቡጥ *lbu*
warmth *(n.)* ልብጠት *lbṭet*
warn *(v.)* ኣጠንቀቐ *'aṭenqeq̈*
warning *(n.)* መጠንቀቕታ *meṭenqeq̈ta*
warp *(v.)* ደርበየ *derbeye*
warrant *(n.)* ፍቓድ *feqad*
warrantor *(n.)* ዋሕስ *waḥs*
warranty *(n.)* መዝነት *meznet*
warren *(n.)* ስፍራ ማናቲለ *sfra manatile*
warrior *(n.)* ወተሃደር *wetehader*
wart *(n.)* ጡብ ኣድጊ *ṭub 'adgi*
wary *(adj.)* ጥንቁቕ *ṭnquq̈*
wash *(v.)* ሓጸበ *ḥaxebe*
washable *(adj.)* ክሕፀብ ዝኽእል *kHxeb zK'el*
washer *(n.)* ሓጻባይ *ḥaxabay*
washing *(n.)* ምሕጻብ *mḥxab*
wasp *(n.)* ዕኮት *'ëkot*
waspish *(adj.)* ሓራቕ *ḥaraq̈*
wassail *(n.)* ፈንጠዝያ *fenṭezya*
wastage *(n.)* ብኽነት *bḱnet*
waste *(v.)* ኣባኸነ *abaKene*
wasteful *(adj.)* ሸለልተኛ *shelelteña*
watch *(v.)* ተዓዘበ *te'äzebe*
watchful *(adj.)* ዝተበራበረ *zteberabere*
watchword *(n.)* ቃለ-ምስጢር *qalemsṭir*
water *(n.)* ማይ *may*
water *(n.)* ማይ *may*
waterfall *(n.)* መንጫዕጫዕታ *menča'ëča'ëta*
watermark *(n.)* ሕታም *Htam*
watermelon *(n.)* ብርጭቕ *brčq*
waterproof *(adj.)* ማይ ዓገት *may 'äget*
watertight *(adj.)* ማይሰጠም *mayseṭem*
watery *(adj.)* ቀጢን *qeṭin*
watt *(n.)* ኣሃዱ ናይ ኤለትሪካዊ ጉልበት *ahadu nay 'eeletrikawi gulbet*
wattage *(n.)* ኤለትሪክ -መስፈር *'eeletrik- mesfer*
wattle *(n.)* ባዛር ሹቕ *bazar shuq̈*
wave *(v.)* ባዙቃ *bazuqa*
waver *(v.)* ኮነ *kone*
wavy *(adj.)* ናብ ደንደስ ኣጸገዐ *nab dendes 'axege'ë*
wax *(n.)* መና *mena*
way *(n.)* መገዲ *megedi*
waylay *(v.)* ቆርቋር *qorqWAr*
wayward *(adj.)* ቢግል *bigl*
we *(pron.)* ንሕና *nhna*
weak *(adj.)* ድኹም *dKum*
weaken *(v.)* ኣድከመ *adkeme*
weakling *(n.)* ድኹም *dKum*
weakness *(n.)* ድኻም *dKam*
weal *(n.)* ተሸከመ *teshekeme*
wealth *(n.)* ንብረት *nbret*
wealthy *(adj.)* ሃብታም *habtam*
wean *(v.)* እንስሳ *ènssa*
weapon *(n.)* ክላሽ *klash*
wear *(v.)* ተኸድነ *teKedene*
wearisome *(adj.)* ድኻም *dkam*

weary *(adj.)* **ዝደኸመ** *zdekeme'*
weasel *(n.)* **ናይ እንስሳ ሽም** *nay nsesa shm*
weather *(n.)* **ኩነታት ኣየር** *kunetat ayer*
weave *(v.)* **መልክዕ** *melk'ë*
weaver *(n.)* **ቢቨር** *biver*
web *(n.)* **ዓለአ ሳሬት** *aleba sariet*
webpage *(n.)* **ድሕረ ገፅ** *dhde getse*
website *(n.)* **ድሕረ ገፅ** *dhde getse*
wed *(v.)* **ኣመርዓወ** *amerawe*
wedding *(n.)* **መርዓ** *mer'a*
wedge *(n.)* **መንጸፍ** *menxef*
wedlock *(n.)* **ምርዕውነት** *mrewenet*
Wednesday *(n.)* **ረቡዕ** *rebu'e*
weed *(n.)* **ኣረም** *arem*
week *(n.)* **ሰሙን** *semun*
weekday *(n.)* **መዓልቲ ስራሕ** *me'alti srah*
weekly *(adj.)* **ሰሙናዊ** *semunawi*
weep *(v.)* **በኸየ** *beKeye'*
weepy *(adj.)* **በኻዪ** *bekayi*
weevil *(n.)* **ብንጅር** *bnĵr*
weigh *(v.)* **መዘነ** *mezene*
weight *(n.)* **ክብደት** *kbdet*
weighting *(n.)* **ወረደ ኣጋጠመ** *werede 'agaẗeme*
weightlifting *(n.)* **በቕዐ** *beq̈'ë*
weighty *(adj.)* **ኸቢድ** *kebid*
weir *(n.)* **ግድብ** *gdb*
weird *(adj.)* **ዘይልሙድ** *zeylemud*
welcome *(n.)* **እንኳዕ ብደሓን መፃኻ** *enkuae bdehan mexaka*
weld *(v.)* **ዓጸፈ** *axefe*
welfare *(n.)* **ድሕንነት** *dHnenet*
well *(n.)* **ጨለ** *chele*
well *(adv.)* **ጨለ** *chele*
wellington *(n.)* **መጀመርታ** *meĵemerta*
welt *(n.)* **ኣዘናገዐ** *azenage'ë*
welter *(n.)* **ኣብ ክንዲ** *ab kndi*
wen *(n.)* **ገበረ** *gebere*
wench *(n.)* **ጠባይ** *ẗebay*
wend *(v.)* **ቈረጸ** *qWerexe*
west *(n.)* **ምዕራብ** *merab*
westerly *(adv.)* **ምዕራባዊ** *merabawi*
western *(adj.)* **ምዕራባዊ** *merabawi*
westerner *(n.)* **ምዕራባዊ** *meraawi*
westernize *(v.)* **ምዕራባዊ ምግር** *merabawi mgbar*
wet *(adj.)* **ርሑስ** *rhus*
wetness *(n.)* **ርሑስነት** *rhusnet*
whack *(v.)* **ዘይልሙድ** *zeylemud*
whale *(n.)* **ዓሳ ነባሪ** *asa neari*
whaler *(n.)* **ሃዳኒ ዓሳ ነባሪ** *hadani asa neari*
whaling *(n.)* **ምህዳን ዓሳ ነባሪ** *mhdan asa nebari*
wharf *(n.)* **ፋርጎ** *fargo*
wharfage *(n.)* **ናይ መርከብ መሳርሒ** *nay merkeb mesarhi*
what *(pron. & adj.)* **እንታይ** *entay*
whatever *(pron.)* **ዋላ** *wala*
wheat *(n.)* **ስርናይ** *srnay*
wheaten *(adj.)* **ስርናይ** *srnay*
wheedle *(v.)* **ኣውያት** *awyat*
wheel *(n.)* **መኪና** *mekina*
wheeze *(v.)* **ታሪኽ** *tariK*
whelk *(n.)* **ፈጸጋ** *fexega*
whelm *(v.)* **መናፍሕ** *menafH*
whelp *(n.)* **ከብዲ** *kebdi*
when *(adv.)* **ምዓዝ** *meaz*

whence *(adv.)* ግላዊ ኣቕሑ *glawi 'aq̈ḧu*
whenever *(conj.)* ዝኾነ ግዜ *zKone gzie*
where *(adv.)* ኣበይ *abey*
whereabouts *(adv.)* ኣበይ ከምዘሎ *abey kemzelo*
whereas *(n.)* ተኾነውን *tekonewen*
whet *(v.)* ካራ *kara*
whether *(conj.)* ርቦ *rbo*
whey *(n.)* ለወየ *leweye*
which *(pron. & adj.)* ኣየን *ayen*
whichever *(pron.)* ዝኾነ ይኹን *zKone yKun*
whiff *(n.)* ገቢረ-ሰናይ *gebiresenay*
while *(n.)* ክሳብ *ksab*
whilst *(conj.)* ክሳብ *ksab*
whim *(n.)* ቐልዲ *qeldi*
whimper *(v.)* ኣውያት *awyat*
whimsical *(adj.)* ተጻዋታይ *texawatay*
whimsy *(n.)* ጽዋታ *xewata*
whine *(n.)* ብኽያት *bKyat*
whinge *(v.)* ኣንጸርጸረ *anxerxere*
whinny *(n.)* መንጸርጸሪ *menxerxeri*
whip *(n.)* ፈራሕ *ferHe*
whir *(n.)* ፋርጎ *fargo*
whirl *(v.)* ምዝዋር *mzwar*
whirligig *(n.)* ምዝዋር *mzwar*
whirlpool *(n.)* መዝወሪ *mezweri*
whirlwind *(n.)* መዝወሪ ንፋስ *mezweri nfas*
whirr *(v.)* ደንቆሮ *denqoro*
whisk *(v.)* ወቐዐ *weqe*
whisker *(n.)* ጭሕሚ *cheHmi*
whisky *(n.)* ውስኪ *wski*
whisper *(v.)* ሕሹኽሹኽ *hshukshuk*
whist *(n.)* ንፋስ *nfas*
whistle *(n.)* ፋጻ *faxa*
whit *(n.)* ንእሽቶ *aeshto*
white *(adj.)* ጻዕዳ *xaeda*
whitewash *(n.)* መሕጸቢ *meHxei*
whither *(adv.)* ጻዕዳ *xaeda*
whiting *(n.)* ምጽዕዳው *mxedaw*
whittle *(v.)* ጻዕዳ *xaeda*
whiz *(v.)* ኣራዊታዊ እንስሳዊ ጨካን *'arawitawi 'ènssawi čekan*
who *(pron.)* መን *men*
whoever *(pron.)* ማንም ይኹን *manm yekun*
whole *(adj.)* ግኡድጓድ *gudguad*
whole-hearted *(adj.)* ምሉእ ልቢ *mluelbi*
wholesale *(n.)* መሸጣ *mesheta*
wholesaler *(n.)* ቅጥፈት *qẗfet*
wholesome *(adj.)* ዝሓሸ *zḧashe*
wholly *(adv.)* ኣብ መንጎ *'ab mengo*
whom *(pron.)* ንመን *nmen*
whoop *(n.)* ሓጎስ *hagos*
whopper *(n.)* ተሓጓሳይ *tehaguasay*
whore *(n.)* ኣመንዝር *amenzer*
whose *(pron.)* ናይ መን *naymen*
why *(adv.)* ንምንታይ *nmntay*
wick *(n.)* ሰረየ *sereye*
wicked *(adj.)* ክፉእ *kfue*
wicker *(n.)* ሽንጣር *shentar*
wicket *(n.)* ፍርቂ በብዓመት *frqi beb'ämet*
wide *(adj.)* ገፊሕ *gefiH*
widen *(v.)* ኣግፈሐ *agfeHe*
widespread *(adj.)* ውሩይ *wruy*

widow *(n.)* ሰብኣያ ዝሞታ *seaya zemota*
widower *(n.)* ሰብበይቱ ዝሞተቶ *sebeytu zmoteto*
width *(n.)* ስፍሓት *sfHat*
wield *(v.)* ምውፃእ *mwxae*
wife *(n.)* ሰበይቲ *sebeyti*
wig *(n.)* ሽንጣር *shentar*
wiggle *(v.)* ምውዝዋዝ *mwzwaz*
Wight *(n.)* ምስኪን *mskin*
wigwam *(n.)* ጎጆ *gjo*
wild *(adj.)* በረኻ *bereKa*
wilderness *(n.)* በረኻ *bereKa*
wile *(n.)* ምምሻጥ *mmshaẗ*
wilful *(adj.)* ሚስጥረኛ *mistregna*
will *(v.)* ፍቓድ *fqad*
willing *(adj.)* ፍቓደኛ *fqadegna*
willingness *(adj.)* ፍቓድ *fqad*
willow *(n.)* ኦም *om*
wily *(adj.)* ንፉዕ *nfu'e*
wimble *(n.)* ምቕናን *mqnan*
wimple *(n.)* ሻሽ *shash*
win *(v.)* ሰዓረ *seare*
wince *(v.)* ቓንዛ *qanza*
winch *(n.)* ዓረብያ *arebya*
wind *(n.)* ንፋስ *nfas*
windbag *(n.)* ተዛራባይ *tezarabay*
winder *(n.)* ነፋሽ *nefash*
windlass *(n.)* ሊፍት *lift*
windmill *(n.)* ዕፍ ንፋስ *ef nfas*
window *(n.)* መስኮት *meskot*
windy *(adj.)* ንፋስ *nfas*
wine *(n.)* ወይኒ *weyni*
winery *(n.)* ምስራሕ ወይኒ *msraH weyni*
wing *(n.)* ክንፊ *knfi*
wink *(v.)* ጠቐሰ *Teqese*
winkle *(n.)* ሽም እንስሳ *shm enssa*
winner *(n.)* ተዓዋቲ *tawati*
winning *(adj.)* ዓወት *awet*
winnow *(v.)* ንፋስ *nfas*
winsome *(adj.)* ስዕረት *seret*
winter *(n.)* ሓጋይ *ḧagay*
wintry *(adj.)* ኢኮሎጂ *ikoloĵi*
wipe *(v.)* ኣጽረየ *axreye*
wire *(n.)* ሽቦ *shbo*
wireless *(adj.)* መስመር ኣልባ *mesmer albo*
wiring *(n.)* መስመር *msmer*
wisdom *(n.)* ጥበብ *tbeb*
wise *(adj.)* ጠቢብ *tebib*
wish *(v.)* ትምኒት *tmnit*
wishful *(adj.)* ትምኒት *tmnit*
wisp *(n.)* ንእሽቶ *neshto*
wisteria *(n.)* ዘለፋ *zelefa*
wistful *(adj.)* ጥንቁቕ *tnquq'*
wit *(n.)* ቀልዲ *qeldi*
witch *(n.)* ጠንቋሊት *tenqualit*
witchcraft *(n.)* ጥንቆላ *tnqola*
witchery *(n.)* ጥንቆላ *tnqola*
with *(prep.)* ብ *b*
withal *(adv.)* ብተወሳኺ *btewesaKi*
withdraw *(v.)* ምውጻእ *mwxae*
withdrawal *(n.)* ምውጻእ *mwxae*
withe *(n.)* ምስ *ms*
wither *(v.)* ምስ *ms*
withhold *(v.)* ምሕባእ *mhbae*
within *(prep.)* ውሽጢ *wshti*
without *(prep.)* ብዘይ *bzey*
withstand *(v.)* ምቅዃም *mqQuam*
witless *(adj.)* ደረቕ *dereq*
witness *(n.)* ምምስካር *mmskar*
witter *(v.)* ምብስባስ *mbsbas*
witticism *(n.)* ቐልዲ *qeldi*
witty *(adj.)* ባጫ *bacha*
wizard *(n.)* ጠንቋሊ *tenquali*

wizened *(adj.)* ጻዕደወ *xa'ëdewe*
woad *(n.)* ልዙብ *lzub*
wobble *(v.)* ጥርሑ *ẗrḧu*
woe *(n.)* ኮበርታ *koberta*
woeful *(adj.)* ድምጺ *dmxi*
wok *(n.)* ኣተዓሻሸወ *ate'äshashewe*
wold *(n.)* ነትጕ *netgWi*
wolf *(n.)* ተኹላ *tekula*
woman *(n.)* ሰበይቲ *seeyti*
womanhood *(n.)* ሰበይቲ ምኳን *sebeyti mkuan*
womanize *(v.)* ሰበይቲ ምኳን *sebeyti mkuan*
womb *(n.)* ማህጸን *mahxen*
wonder *(v.)* ሓሰበ *hasebe*
wonderful *(adj.)* ጽቡቕ *xbuk*
wondrous *(adj.)* ቃና *qana*
wonky *(adj.)* ኣበር *aber*
wont *(n.)* ኣይከውንን *aykewnn*
wonted *(adj.)* ሓዋወሰ *ḧawawese*
woo *(v.)* ፍቕሪ *fqri*
wood *(n.)* ጣውላ *tawla*
wooded *(adj.)* ጣውላ *tawla*
wooden *(adj.)* ጣውላ *tawla*
woodland *(n.)* ጫካ *chaka*
woof *(n.)* ምንባሕ *mnbah*
woofer *(n.)* ነባሒ *nbahi*
wool *(n.)* ሃሪ *hari*
woollen *(adj.)* ሃሪ *hari*
woolly *(adj.)* ሃሪ *hari*
woozy *(adj.)* ደብዛዝ *dbzaz*
word *(n.)* ቃል *qal*
wording *(n.)* ኣጠቓቕማ ቃል *atekakema qal*
wordy *(adj.)* ቓል ዝበዝሖ *qal zbezho*
work *(n.)* ስራሕ *srah*
workable *(adj.)* ዝስራሕ *zsrah*
workaday *(adj.)* ናይ ስራሕ መዓልቲ *nay srah mealti*
worker *(n.)* ሰራሕተኛ *serahtegna*
working *(n.)* ዝሰርሕ *zserh*
workman *(n.)* ሰራሕተኛ *serahtegna*
workmanship *(n.)* ሰራሕተኛ *serahtegna*
workshop *(n.)* ናይ ስራሕ ቦታ *naysrah bota*
world *(n.)* ዓለም *alem*
worldly *(adj.)* ዓለማዊ *alemawi*
worm *(n.)* ሓሰኻ *haseka*
worried *(adj.)* ጭንቀት *chnqet*
worrisome *(adj.)* ጭኑቕ *chnuq*
worry *(v.)* ተጨነቐ *techeneqe*
worse *(adj.)* ዝኸፍእ *zkefe*
worsen *(v.)* በኣሰ *bease*
worship *(n.)* ምምላኽ *mmlaK*
worshipper *(n.)* ኣምላኺ *amlaKi*
worst *(adj.)* ዝኸፍእ *zKefe*
worsted *(n.)* ኣኽፈእ *aKfe*
worth *(adj.)* ዋጋ *waga*
worthless *(adj.)* ቌንደፈ *qWendefe*
worthwhile *(adj.)* ዋጋ ዘለዎ' *waga zelewo*
worthy *(adj.)* ዓመድ *gWamed*
would *(v.)* ይኸውን *ykewn*
would-be *(adj.)* ይኸውን *ykewn*
wound *(n.)* ቆሰለ *qosele*
wrack *(n.)* ጻህያይ ባሕሪ *xahyay baḥri*
wraith *(n.)* መልኣከ ሞት *mel'ake mot*
wrangle *(n.)* ተጎናፈጠ *tegonafeṭe*
wrap *(v.)* ጠቕለለ *ṭeq̈lele*

wrapper *(n.)* መጎልበቢ *megolbebi*
wrath *(n.)* ቁጠዐ *quṭe'ë*
wreak *(v.)* ገለጸ *gelexe*
wreath *(n.)* ዓንኬል *'änkeel*
wreathe *(v.)* ኣኽበበ *'aḱbebe*
wreck *(n.)* ዕንወት *'ënwet*
wreckage *(n.)* ፍራስ *fras*
wrecker *(n.)* ቀንጻሊ *qenxali*
wren *(n.)* ንእሽቶ ዓይነት ዑፍ *n'èshto 'äynet 'üf*
wrench *(v.)* ምጥዋይን ምስሓብን *mṭwayn msḥabn*
wrest *(v.)* ጠወየ *ṭeweye*
wrestle *(v.)* ተቓለሰ *teq̈alese*
wrestler *(n.)* ተቓላሲ *teq̈alasi*
wretch *(n.)* ቅርሱስ *qrsus*
wretched *(adj.)* ስቅያታዊ *sqyatawi*
wrick *(v.)* ቆጸየ *qoxeye*
wriggle *(v.)* ኣካይዳ ተመን ከደ *'akayda temen kede*
wring *(v.)* ጸመቈ *xemeq̈We*
wrinkle *(n.)* ዓጠረ *'äṭere*
wrinkle *(n.)* ዓጠረ *'äṭere*
wrist *(n.)* ጉንቦ ኢድ *gunbo 'id*
writ *(n.)* ኣዛዚ *'azazi*
write *(v.)* ጸሓፈ *xeḥafe*
writer *(n.)* ጸሓፊ *xeḥafi*
writhe *(v.)* ተፋሕሰ *tefaḥse*
writing *(n.)* ጽሕፈት *xḥfet*
wrong *(adj.)* ግጉይ *gguy*
wrongful *(adj.)* ጽዩፍ *xyuf*
wry *(adj.)* ጎምጻጽ ጠዋይ *gomxax ṭeway*

X

xenon *(n.)* ከቢድ ጋዝ *kebid gaz*
xenophobia *(n.)* ፅልኢ ሓደሽቲ ሰባት *tselei hdeshti sebat*
Xerox *(n.)* መባዝሒኢ ማሽን *mebazHi mashn*
Xmas *(n.)* ልደት *ldet*
x-ray *(n.)* ራጅ *raj*
xylophages *(adj.)* ባልዕ *megarya*
xylophilous *(adj.)* ናይ ዕንጨይቲ ነዋሪ *nay encheyti newari*
xylophone *(n.)* ናይ ዕንጨይቲ ሙዚቃ መሳርሒ *nay encheyti muzika mesarhi*

Y

yacht *(n.)* ጀልባ *jelba*
yachting *(n.)* ናይ ጀልባ ሃበ *nay jelba habe*
yachtsman *(n.)* ናይ ጀልባ ሰብ *nay jelba seb*
yak *(n.)* ብዕራይ *beray*
yam *(n.)* ሽኮር ድንሽ *shkor dnesh*
yap *(v.)* ዘረባ *zereba*
yard *(n.)* መረባ *mereba*
yarn *(n.)* ፈትሊ *fetli*
yashmak *(n.)* መሸፈኒ ሻሽ *meshefeni shash*
yaw *(v.)* ኣምቧሃቐ *ambuahaqe*
yawn *(v.)* ምምቡሃቕ *mmbuhaq*
year *(n.)* ዓመት *amet*
yearly *(adv.)* ዓመታዊ *ametawi*
yearn *(v.)* ሃረር በለ *harer bele*
yearning *(n.)* ናፍቖት *nafqot*
yeast *(n.)* ለቢቶ *lebito*
yell *(n.)* ኣእወየ *aeweye*

yellow *(adj.)* ብጫ *bcha*
yelp *(n.)* ኣእወየ *aeweye*
Yen *(n.)* ሳንቲም *santim*
yeoman *(n.)* ዓኳይ *akuay*
yes *(excl.)* እወ *ewe*
yesterday *(adv.)* ትማሊ *tmali*
yet *(adv.)* ሕጂ *Hji*
yeti *(n.)* ኣብ ሂማልያ ዝነብር እንስሳ *ab himalya zeneber ensesa*
yew *(n.)* ኦም *om*
yield *(v.)* ኣፍረየ *afreye*
yob *(n.)* ናይ ሰገናት *nay segenat*
yodel *(v.)* ምዝማር *mzmar*
yoga *(n.)* ዮጋ *yoga*
yogi *(n.)* ናይ ዮጋ ሰብ *nay yoga seb*
yogurt *(n.)* ርግኦ *rguo*
yoke *(n.)* ኣርዑት *arut*
yokel *(n.)* ናይ ሃገረሰብ *nay hagereseb*
yolk *(n.)* ፃዕዳ ክፋል እንቋቑሖ *tsaeda kfal enquaquho*
yonder *(adj.)* ርሑቕ *rhuQ*
yonks *(n.)* ዮንክስ *yonks*
yore *(n.)* ዘአረገ *ze'erege*
you *(pron.)* ንስኻ *nsKa*
young *(adj.)* ሰገን *segen*
youngster *(n.)* ሰገን *segen*
your *(adj.)* ናትካ *natk*
yourself *(pron.)* ዓርስኻ *arseka*
youth *(n.)* ንእስነት *n'esenet*
youthful *(adj.)* መንእሰይ *men'esey*
yowl *(n.)* በኸየ *beKeye*
yummy *(adj.)* ምቁር *mqur*

Z

zany *(adj.)* ዘይተለመደ *zeytelemde*
zap *(v.)* ኮረንቲ ሓዘ *korenti haze*
zeal *(n.)* ብርቱዕ ድልየት *brtu'e dlyet*
zealot *(n.)* ኣኽራሪ *aKrari*
zealous *(adj.)* ኣዝዩ ህንቁዉ *azyu hnquw*
zebra *(n.)* ኣድጊ በረኻ *adgi bereKa*
zebra crossing *(n.)* ዜብራ መንገዲ *zebra mengedi*
zenith *(n.)* ጫፍ *medegef*
zephyr *(n.)* ህዱእ *hdu'e*
zero *(adj.)* ባዶ *bado*
zest *(n.)* ድልየትን ታሕጓስን *dlyetn taHguasn*
zigzag *(n.)* ስብርባር ሕንፃፅ *sbrbar Hntsats*
zilch *(n.)* ባዶ *bado*
zinc *(n.)* ዚንጎ *zingo*
zing *(n.)* ድልየት *dlyet*
zip *(n.)* ሻርኔራ *sharnira*
zircon *(n.)* ማዕድን *maeden*
zither *(n.)* ሙዚቃ መሳርሒ *muzika mesarhi*
zodiac *(n.)* ሰማያዊ *semayawi*
zombie *(n.)* ዘይሞተ መዉት *zeymote muwut*
zonal *(adj.)* ክልላዊ *kllawi*
zone *(n.)* ክልል *kll*
zoo *(n.)* መካነ እንስሳት *makane enssat*
zoology *(n.)* ስነ-እንስሳ *sne-enssat*
zoom *(v.)* ሸውታ *shewta*

Tigrigna-English

ሀ

ሀምፕ hemp *(n.)* **Cannabis**
ሀርፒስ herpis *(n.)* **Herpes**
ሁንዱፍ hunduf *(adj.)* **impulsive**
ሁጉሬ huguree *(n.)* **bumpkin**
ሁፕላ hupla *(n.)* **hoopla**

ሂ

ሂለል hilel *(n.)* **crescent**
ሂስቶግራም histogram *(n.)* **histogram**
ሂወት hiwet *(n.)* **life**
ሂወት ዘይብሉ hiwet zeyblu *(adj.)* **lifeless**
ሂወት ዘይብሉ ነገር hiwet heyblu neger *(adj.)* **inanimate**
ሃህታ hahta *(n.)* **lacuna**
ሃህታ hahta *(n.)* **vacancy**
ሃለለ halele *(v.)* **bray**
ሃለለ halele *(n.)* **hammock**
ሃለወ halewe *(v.)* **exist**
ሃለዋት halewat *(n., a)* **situation**
ሃለውለው halewlew *(n.)* **blarney**
ሃለውለው halewlew *(n.)* **rigmarole**
ሃለውለው halewlew *(n.)* **tattle**
ሃልሃልታ halhalta *(n.)* **flare**
ሃልሃልታ halhalta *(v.)* **spurt**
ሃልሃልታ halhalta *(n.)* **blaze**
ሃልሃል አበለ halhal abele *(v.)* **inflame**
ሃላይ halay *(adj.)* **crass**
ሃላይ halay *(adj.)* **fatuous**
ሃላይ halay *(n.)* **oaf**
ሃልመት halmet *(n.)* **helmet**
ሃሎጅን halojn *(n.)* **halogen**
ሃመንመን ዝበለ hamenmen zbele *(adj.)* **gaga**
ሃምስተር hamster *(n.)* **hamster**
ሃምበርገር hamberger *(n.)* **hamburger**
ሃምባቆቶ hambaqoto *(n.)* **midriff**
ሃረመ hareme *(v.)* **beat**
ሃረመ hareme *(v.)* **hit**
ሃረመ hareme *(v.)* **kick**
ሃረር በለ harer bele *(v.)* **yearn**
ሃረርተኛ harerteña *(adj.)* **anxious**
ሃረርታ harerta *(n.)* **gluttony**
ሃረፈ harefe *(v.)* **pine**
ሃሪ hari *(n.)* **silk**
ሃሪ hari *(n.)* **wool**
ሃሪ ዝመስል hari zmesl *(adj.)* **silken**
ሃሪ ዝመስል hari zmesl *(adj.)* **woollen**
ሃርሞኑዮም harmunyem *(n.)* **harmonium**
ሃርጋፍ hargaf *(adj.)* **voracious**
ሃርጋፍ hargaf *(n.)* **vulture**
ሃሰሰ hasese *(v.i)* **fade**
ሃሰሰ hasese *(v.)* **tarnish**
ሃሰው በለ hasew bele *(v.)* **grope**
ሃሰየ haseye *(v.)* **disable**
ሃሳስ hasas *(adj.)* **dim**
ሃሳዪ hasayi *(adj.)* **prejudicial**
ሃቀነ haqene *(v.)* **attempt**
ሃበ habe *(v.)* **grant**
ሃበ habe *(v.)* **grant**
ሃበ habe *(v.)* **give**
ሃበ habe *(v.)* **ascribe**
ሃበሬታ ተለዋወጠ habereta *(v.)* **communicate**
ሃብቲ habti *(n.)* **welt**
ሃብቲ habti *(n.)* **affluence**
ሃብቲ habti *(n.)* **mammon**
ሃብታም habtam *(adj.)* **affluent**

ሃብታም habtam *(adj.)* **opulent**
ሃብታም habtam *(adj.)* **wealthy**
ሃብት habt *(n.)* **wealth**
ሃተ'ፈ hatefe *(v.)* **blab**
ሃተፈ/ለፈለፈ hatefe/lefelefe *(v.)* **chatter**
ሃተፍተፍ hateftef *(v.)* **prattle**
ሃተፍተፍ hateftef *(n.)* **vapour**
ሃተውቀጠው hatew qeẗew *(n.)* **eyewash**
ሃነነ hane-ne *(v.)* **gape**
ሃነጸ hanexe *(v.)* **build**
ሃነፀ hanxe' *(v.)* **construct**
ሃናት hanat *(n.)* **scalp**
ሃናጺ hanaxi *(n.)* **architect**
ሃናፂ hanatxi' *(adj.)* **constructive**
ሃንቀዉታ hanqewta *(n.)* **curiosity**
ሃንደበታዊ handebetawi *(adj.)* **haphazard**
ሃንደበታዊ handebetawi *(adj.)* **abrupt**
ሃንደበት handebet *(adj.)* **random**
ሃንደበት handebet *(adj.)* **sudden**
ሃንደበት handebet *(adj.)* **unexpected**
ሃንደፍታ handefta *(n.)* **impulse**
ሃካይ hakay *(adj.)* **slothful**
ሃወኸ haweke *(v.)* **disconcert**
ሃወኸ haweḱe *(v.)* **hurry**
ሃዋህዉ hawahewu *(n.)* **circumstance**
ሃዋህው hawahewu' *(n.)* **context**
ሃዋህዉ hawahw *(n.)* **cosmos**
ሃዋህው hawahw *(n.)* **atmosphere**
ሃዋርያ hawarya *(n.)* **apostle**
ሃዋሲ hawasi *(n.)* **sensor**
ሃዊኹ hawiku *(v.)* **perturb**
ሃውሪ hawri *(adj.)* **arbitrary**
ሃውተተ hawtati *(adj.)* **adrift**
ሃውታቲ hawtati *(adj.)* **discursive**
ሃውታቲ hawtete *(v.)* **yaw**
ሃያሲ hayasi *(n.)* **critic**
ሃይማኖተኛ haymanotegna *(adj.)* **devout**
ሃይማኖተኛ haymanoteña *(adj.)* **godly**
ሃይማኖተኛ haymanotena *(n.)* **piety**
ሃይማኖተኛ haymanptegna *(adj.)* **religious**
ሃይማኖታዊ haymanotawi *(adj.)* **mystical**
ሃይማኖታዊ ቦታታት ዝበጽሕ haymanotawi botatat zbxh *(n.)* **pilgrim**
ሃይማኖታዊ ፅምብል haymanotawi tsmbl *(n.)* **sacrament**
ሃይማኖት haymanot *(n.)* **religion**
ሃይድሮጅን haydrogen *(n.)* **hydrogen**
ሃዲም hadim *(n.)* **fugitive**
ሃዝረጠ hazreẗe *(v.)* **bloat**
ሃዝራጥ hazraẗ *(adj.)* **corpulent**
ሃደመ hademe *(v.)* **flee**
ሃደነ hadene *(v.)* **hunt**
ሃዳኒ ዓሳ ነባሪ hadani asa neari *(n.)* **whaler**
ሃዳኒ እንስሳ hadali ènssa *(n.)* **predator**
ሃዳናይ hadanay *(n.)* **hunter**
ሃዳዳይ hadaday *(n.)* **steed**
ሃገራት ምብራቕ hagerat mbraq *(n.)* **orient**
ሃገር hager *(n.)* **country**
ሃገር hager *(n.)* **state**
ሃገር ቦቆል hager boqol *(adj.)* **endemic**

ሃገር ክሒድካ ምስ ፀላኢ ምሕባር hager kihidka ms selai mhbar ***(n.)*** **treason**
ሃገራዊ hagerawi ***(adj.)*** **inland**
ሃገር ዘመሓድር ጉጅለ hager zemehadr gujele ***(n.)*** **oligarchy**
ሃጓም hagwam ***(adj.)*** **concave**
ሃፀይ haxey ***(n.)*** **emperor**
ሃፅፊ hatzfi ***(n.)*** **gust**
ሃፈፈ hafefe ***(v.)*** **evaporate**
ሃፈፈ hafefe ***(v.)*** **vaporize**
ሃፋ hafa ***(n.)*** **steam**
ሃፍቲ hafti ***(n.)*** **opulence**
ሃፍታም haftam ***(nabob)*** **nabob**
ሃፍታም haftam ***(adj.)*** **rich**
ሃፍታምነት haftamnet ***(n.)*** **richness**
ሃፍታም ነጋዴ haftam negadi ***(n.)*** **tycoon**
ሄሊኮፕተር heel ***(n.)*** **cardamom**
ሄል heelikopter ***(n.)*** **helicopter**
ሄሞግሎቢን hemoglobin ***(n.)*** **haemoglobin**
ሄሮይን heeroyn ***(n.)*** **heroine**
ሄክታር hluw ***(n.)*** **present**

ህ

ህሉው hektar ***(n.)*** **hectare**
ህላወ hlawe ***(n.)*** **entity**
ህላወ hlawe ***(n.)*** **survival**
ህላወ hlawe ***(n.)*** **being**
ህላዌ hlawe ***(n.)*** **presence**
ህልቂት hlqit ***(n.)*** **holocaust**
ህልከኛ hlkegna ***(adj.)*** **obdurate**
ህልኸኛ hlkegna ***(adj.)*** **scrappy**
ህልኸኛ hlkena ***(n.)*** **perversity**
ህልኽ hlk ***(n.)*** **obduracy**
ህልኽ hlk ***(adj.)*** **perverse**
ህልው hlw ***(adj.)*** **immanent**
ህልዉና hlwna ***(n.)*** **existence**
ህመት hmet ***(n.)*** **moment**
ህሩግ ምባል hrug mbal ***(n.)*** **intrusion**
ህሩግ በሃሊ hrug behali ***(adj.)*** **intrusive**
ህሩግ በለ hrug bele ***(v.)*** **intrude**
ህሩድ hrud ***(n.)*** **turmeric**
ህሩፍ hruf ***(adj.)*** **lustful**
ህሩፍ hruf ***(adj.)*** **greedy**
ህርመታዊ hrmetawi ***(adj.)*** **metrical**
ህስየት hsyet ***(n.)*** **detriment**
ህበይ hbey ***(n.)*** **ape**
ህበይ hbey ***(n.)*** **gorilla**
ህበይ hbey ***(n.)*** **monkey**
ህበይ hebeyei ***(n.)*** **chimpanzee**
ህበይ hbey ***(n.)*** **baboon**
ህቡብ ሰብ hbub seb ***(n.)*** **personage**
ህቦብላ hebobla ***(n.)*** **hurricane**
ህቦብላ h-bo-b-la ***(n.)*** **gale**
ህቦብላ ውርጪ hbobla wrči ***(n.)*** **blizzard**
ህንቁዉ hnquw ***(adj.)*** **desirous**
ህንዳዊ hndawi ***(n.)*** **Indian**
ህንጡዉ hntuw ***(adj.)*** **eager**
ህንጡው hnẗuw ***(n.)*** **alacritous**
ህንጡይ hntuy ***(adj.)*** **keen**
ህንጡይ hnẗuy ***(adj.)*** **curious**
ህንጡይ hnẗuy ***(adj.)*** **avid**
ህንጻ hnxa ***(n.)*** **building**
ህንጻ hnxa ***(n.)*** **edifice**
ህንፀት hintsxet' ***(n.)*** **construction**
ህኩይ hkuy ***(adj.)*** **idle**
ህኩይ hkuy ***(adj.)*** **shiftless**
ህዋ hwa ***(n.)*** **space**
ህዋሳዊ hwasawi ***(adj.)*** **sensory**
ህዋሳዊ hwasawi ***(adj.)*** **sensuous**
ህዋስ hwas ***(n.)*** **sense**

ህውተታ hwteta *(n.)* **bathos**
ህዉከት hwuket *(n.)* **chaos**
ህውከተኛ hwketegna *(n.)* **urchin**
ህውከት hwket *(n.)* **commotion**
ህውከት hwket *(n.)* **riot**
ህውከት hwket *(n.)* **rising**
ህውከት ፈጠረ hwket fetere *(v.)* **rampage**
ህዉኽ hwukh *(adj.)* **overwrought**
ህዉኽ hwuk *(adj.)* **raring**
ህውኽ hwḱ *(adj.)* **hasty**
ህያብ hyab *(n.)* **fairing**
ህያው hyaw *(adj.)* **alive**
ህያውነት hyawnet *(n.)* **immortality**
ህያው ገበረ hyaw gebere *(v.)* **immortalize**
ህይሰት hyset *(n.)* **critique**
ህይወት hywet habe *(v.)* **vitalize**
ህይወት ሃበ hywet *(n.)* **vitality**
ህይወት መለሰ hywet melese *(v.)* **vivify**
ህዝቢ hzbi *(n.)* **folk**
ህዝባዊ hzbawi *(adj.)* **public**
ህዱእ hd'u *(adj.)* **quiet**
ህዱእ hdu'e *(adj.)* **restful**
ህዱእ hdu'e *(adj.)* **secure**
ህዱእ hdu'e *(adj.)* **sedate**
ህዱእ hdu'è *(adj.)* **calm**
ህዱእ hdu'e *(adj.)* **still**
ህዱእ he-du-e *(adj.)* **gentle**
ህዱእ hdu'e *(n.)* **zephyr**
ህዱእ ናብራ hdu'e nabra *(n.)* **idyll**
ህዱእ ንፋስ hdu'è nfas *(n.)* **breeze**
ህዱእ ጋልቢት hdu'è galbit *(n.)* **canter**
ህድሁድ hdhud *(adj.)* **fusty**
ህድህድ h'dh'd *(adj.)* **stuffy**
ህድማ h'dma *(n.)* **stampede**
ህድሞ hdmo *(n.)* **bunk**
ህድአት hd'at *(n.)* **sobriety**
ህድኣት hd'at *(n.)* **quietude**
ህገራ hgera *(n.)* **nationalization**
ህጻን hxan *(n.)* **babe**
ህጻን hxan *(n.)* **baby**
ህጻን hrtsan *(n.)* **tot**
ህፀፅ hxex *(n.)* **exigency**
ህፁፅ htzutz *(adj.)* **frantic**
ህፃን htsan *(n.)* **kid**

ሆ

ሆልምየም holmyem *(n.)* **holmium**
ሆሎግራም hologram *(n.)* **hologram**
ሆምየፓተኛ homyepategna *(n.)* **homoeopath**
ሆምየፓቲ homyepati *(n.)* **homeopathy**
ሆርሞን hostel *(n.)* **hostel**
ሆስፒታል hormon *(n.)* **hormone**
ሆስተል hospital *(n.)* **hospital**
ሆባይ hobay *(n.)* **nave**
ሆቴል hoteel *(n.)* **hotel**

ለ

ለሓሰ lehase *(v.)* **lick**
ለሓኾ lehake *(v.)* **seep**
ለመም በለ lemem bele *(v.)* **crawl**
ለመነ lemene *(v.)* **invoke**
ለመነ lemene *(v.)* **beg**
ለመነ lemene *(v.)* **beseech**
ለመጭ lemec *(adj.)* **crafty**
ለመጭ lemech *(adj.)* **soapy**
ለመፀ lemetse *(v.)* **daub**
ለመፀ lemetse *(v.)* **smear**

ለሚን lemin *(n.)* **lemon**
ለሚፅ lemix *(adj.)* **even**
ለማኒ lemani *(adj.)* **mendicant**
ለማኒ lemani *(n.)* **beggar**
ለማሽ lemash *(adj.)* **lank**
ለማዳ እንስሳ lemada enssa *(adj.)* **tame**
ለምለም lemlem *(adj.)* **lush**
ለምለም lemlem *(adj.)* **verdant**
ለምበእ lemba'è *(n.)* **flab**
ለምባጥ lembaẗ *(adj.)* **floppy**
ለሞዕንቲ lemoanti *(adv.)* **today**
ለሞዓንቲ ምሸት lemoanti mshet *(adv.)* **tonight**
ለቀቀ leqeqe *(v.)* **release**
ለቆታ leqota *(n.)* **pod**
ለቓም ፊደል lebeda *(n.)* **epidemic**
ለቐቐ leq̈am fidel *(n.)* **compositor**
ለቖታ-ፍረ leq̈eq̈e *(v.)* **enfranchise**
ለበዳ leq̈otafre *(n.)* **capsule**
ለበዳ lebeda *(n.)* **plague**
ለበጠ lebeẗe *(v.i.)* **galvanize**
ለባም lebam *(adj.)* **magnanimous**
ለባም lebam *(adj.)* **sage**
ለባም lebam *(adj.)* **sensible**
ለኣኸ le'ake *(v.)* **dispatch**
ለኣኸ le'ake *(v.)* **send**
ለካሌካ liekalieka *(n.)* **lolly**
ለካቲት lekatit *(n.)* **February**
ለኾቶ lekhoto *(n.)* **strop**
ለወሰ leweye *(v.)* **bend**
ለወየ lewese *(v.)* **knead**
ለወጠ lewete *(v.)* **change**
ለወጠ lewete *(v.)* **shift**
ለወጠ lewete *(v.)* **transform**
ለወጠ lewete *(v.)* **transmute**
ለወጠ leweẗe *(v.)* **commute**
ለወጠ leweẗe *(v.)* **swap**
ለውጠ ኣልቦነት lewẗe albonet *(n.)* **monotony**
ለዉጢ ገበረ lewẗi gebere *(v.)* **customize**
ለዋህ lewah *(adj.)* **benign**
ለዓለ le'äle *(v.)* **heighten**
ለዓት le'ät *(n.)* **haft**
ለዓት le'ät *(n.)* **knob**
ለዘየ lezeye *(v.)* **slobber**
ለይቲ leyti *(n.)* **night**
ለገመ legeme *(v.)* **shirk**
ለገበ legebe *(v.)* **darn**
ለገሰ legese *(v.)* **donate**
ለገሰ legese *(v.)* **vouchsafe**
ለጋሚ legami *(adj.)* **grudging**
ለጋሲ legasi *(n.)* **donor**
ለጋስ legas *(adj.)* **generous**
ለጋስ legas *(adj.)* **lavish**
ለጋስ legas *(adj.)* **munificent**
ለጋስ legas *(adj.)* **bountiful**
ለጠፈ letefe *(n.)* **paste**
ለጥ ዝበለ leẗ zbele *(n.)* **expanse**
ለፍለፈ leflefe *(v.t.)* **gabble**
ለፍለፈ leflefe *(v.)* **jabber**
ለፍላፊ leflefi *(adj.)* **talkative**
ለፍላፊ leflafi *(n.)* **magpie**
ለፍዐ lef'ë *(v.)* **moil**

ሉ

ሉል lul *(n.)* **pearl**
ሉዑል በዓል ስልጣን lu'el be'al sltan *(adj.)* **magisterial**
ሉዝ luz *(n.)* **almond**

ሊ

ሊሊ lili *(n.)* **lily**
ሊላ lila *(n.)* **lilac**
ሊላ lila *(n.)* **violet**
ሊላ lila *(n.)* **purple**
ሊሎ lilo *(n.)* **kite**
ሊሞዚን limozin *(n.)* **limousine**
ሊቀ መላእክት liqe mela'èkt *(n.)* **archangel**
ሊቀ-ጳጳሳት liqep̌ap̌asat *(n.)* **archbishop**
ሊቀ ፓፓስ liqe papas *(n.)* **primate**
ሊቅ liq *(n.)* **intellect**
ሊብራ lbra *(n.)* **Libra**
ሊትሮ litro *(n.)* **litre**
ሊቺ lichi *(n.)* **lychee**
ሊኖ lino *(n.)* **linen**
ሊኬቶ likieto *(n.)* **padlock**
ሊግ lig *(n.)* **league**
ሊፍት lift *(n.)* **windlass**

ላ

ላህለሀ lahle-he *(v.i)* **gasp**
ላህመት lahmet *(n.)* **cream**
ላሕሚ laȟmi *(n.)* **cow**
ላህማም lahmam *(adj.)* **purblind**
ላህዘዝ በለ lahzez bele *(v.)* **loll**
ላህዛዝ lahzaz *(adj.)* **vapid**
ላህዛዝ lahezaz' *(adj.)* **clumsy**
ላህጃ lahja *(n.)* **dialect**
ላህጃም lahjam *(n.)* **simpleton**
ላሕለሐ laĥleĥe *(v.)* **fray**
ላሕታት lmu'e meriet *(n.)* **oasis**
ላሙዕ መሬት laḥtat *(adj.)* **hoarse**
ላማ lama *(n.)* **blade**
ላማ lama *(n.)* **razor**
ላምባ lamba *(n.)* **kerosene**
ላምባ lamba *(n.)* **paraffin**
ላምባዲና lampadina *(n.)* **flashlight**
ላምብሬታ lambrieta *(n.)* **scooter**
ላምፖን lampone *(n.)* **raspberry**
ላርቫ larva *(n.)* **larva**
ላሳኛ lasagna *(n.)* **lasagne**
ላቂባ መስመር laqeeba mesmer *(n.)* **by-line**
ላንቃ lanqa *(n.)* **larynx**
ላቲትዩድ latityud *(n.)* **latitude**
ላንጋላንጋ langalanga *(adj.)* **equivocal**
ላዕለዋይ la'eleway *(adj.)* **supreme**
ላዕለዋይ la'eleway *(adj.)* **upper**
ላዕለዋይ laëleway *(adj.)* **premier**
ላዕለዋይ ቤት ፍርዲ la'eleway beet frdi *(n.)* **Chancery**
ላዕለዋይ ቀሺ laëleway qeshi *(n.)* **prelate**
ላዕለዋይ ደብሪ መርከብ la'ëleway debri merkeb *(n.)* **deck**
ላዕሊ la'eli *(adv.)* **up**
ላዕሊ la'ëli *(adj.)* **high**
ላውሮ lawro *(n.)* **laurel**
ላዛ ዘይብሉ laza zeyblu *(adj.)* **bland**
ላጉን lagun *(n.)* **lagoon**
ላግፂ lagtsi *(n.)* **ridicule**
ላግፂ lagxi *(n.)* **mockery**
ላግጺ lagxi *(n.)* **burlesque**
ላግፂ lagtzi *(n.)* **hoax**
ላፀየ latseye *(v.)* **shave**
ላቫ lava *(n.)* **lava**
ላቫንዳ lavanda *(n.)* **lavender**
ሌባ leba *(n.)* **robber**

ል

ልሕላሐ lḣlaḣe ***(n.)*** **abrasion**
ልሒኹ lhiku ***(v.)*** **percolate**
ልመና lmena ***(n.)*** **request**
ልሙስ lmus ***(n.)*** **cripple**
ልሙዕ lmu'ë ***(adj.)*** **fertile**
ልሙዕነት lmu'ënet ***(n.)*** **fertility**
ልሙዳዊ lmudawi ***(adv.)*** **ordinarily**
ልሙድ lmud ***(adj.)*** **ordinary**
ልሙድ lmud ***(adj.)*** **accustomed**
ልሙድ lmud ***(adj.)*** **commonplace**
ልሙድ lmud ***(adj.)*** **customary**
ልሙድ lmud ***(adj.)*** **familiar**
ልሙድ lmud ***(adj.)*** **usual**
ልሙድ lmud ***(adj.)*** **workaday**
ልሙድ ምግቢ lmud mgbi ***(n.)*** **diet**
ልሙድነት lmudnet ***(n.)*** **prevalence**
ልሙድ ኮነ lmud kone ***(v.)*** **prevail**
ልሙፅ lmuts ***(adj.)*** **sleek**
ልሙፅ lmuts ***(adj.)*** **slick**
ልሙፅ lmuts ***(adj.)*** **smooth**
ልሙፅ lmutz ***(adj.)*** **glossy**
ልማድ le-mad ***(n.)*** **habit**
ልማድ lmad ***(n.)*** **routine**
ልማድ lmad ***(adj.)*** **wont**
ልምሉም lmlum ***(adj.)*** **supple**
ልምምድ lmmd ***(n.)*** **exercise**
ልምምድ lmmd ***(n.)*** **rehearsal**
ልምዲ lmdi ***(n.)*** **custom**
ልምዲ lmdi ***(n.)*** **experience**
ልምዲ lmdi ***(n.)*** **norm**
ልሳናዊ lsanawi ***(n.)*** **lingual**
ልሳናዊ lsanawi ***(adj.)*** **linguistic**
ልስሉስ lslus ***(adj.)*** **flaccid**
ልስሉስ lslus ***(adj.)*** **lax**
ልስሉስ lslus ***(adj.)*** **silky**
ልስሉስ lslus ***(adj.)*** **soft**
ልስሉስ ክፋል ስኒ lslus kfal sni ***(n.)*** **pulp**
ልቀት lket ***(n.)*** **removal**
ልቃሕ lqah ***(n.)*** **credit**
ልቃሕ ትሕጃ lqaḣ tḣja ***(n.)*** **mortgage**
ልቓሕ lqhah ***(n.)*** **loan**
ልቓሕ lqah ***(n.)*** **overdraft**
ልበ ምሉእ lbe mlu'e ***(adj.)*** **ebullient**
ልቡጥ lbuẗnet ***(n.)*** **moderation**
ልቡጥነት lbu ***(adj.)*** **warm**
ልቢ lebi ***(n.)*** **heart**
ልቢ ምንጥልጣል lbi mntltal ***(n.)*** **suspense**
ልቢ ሰቐለ lbi seqele ***(n.)*** **thrill**
ልቢ ወለድ lbi weled ***(n.)*** **fiction**
ልቢ ዝነክእ lbiznekea ***(adj.)*** **touching**
ልባዊ lebawi ***(adj.)*** **heartfelt**
ልባዊ lebawi ***(adj.)*** **hearty**
ልባዊ lbawi ***(adj.)*** **cordial**
ልብላዕ ዓሳ lblaa asa ***(n.)*** **trout**
ልብምና lbmna ***(n.)*** **sagacity**
ልብሲ lbsi ***(n.)*** **attire**
ልብሲ lbsi ***(n.)*** **vestment**
ልብስታት ጎልፎ lbstat golfo ***(n.)*** **hosiery**
ልብ ወለዳዊ lbe weledawi ***(adj.)*** **factitious**
ልብጠት lbṭet ***(n.)*** **warmth**
ልኡላን l'ulan ***(n.)*** **nobility**
ልኡኻት l'ukat ***(n.)*** **delegation**
ልኡኽ l'uk ***(n.)*** **overseer**
ልኡኽ l'uk ***(n.)*** **agent**
ልኡኽ l'uk ***(n.)*** **delegate**
ልኡኽ l'uḱ ***(n.)*** **ambassador**
ልኡኽ l'uḱ ***(n.)*** **emissary**
ልኡኽ l'uḱ ***(n.)*** **envoy**
ልኡኽ l'uḱ ***(n.)*** **errand**
ልክዕ lkë ***(adj.)*** **precise**

ልክዕ lk'ë ***(adj.)*** **accurate**
ልክዕ lk'ë ***(adj.)*** **just**
ልክዕ lk'ë ***(adj.)*** **right**
ልክዕ lk'ë ***(adj.)*** **correct**
ልክዕነት lkënet ***(n.)*** **precision**
ልክዕነት lk'ënet ***(n.)*** **authenticity**
ልኹፍ lkuf ***(adj.)*** **rabid**
ልኻይ lkay ***(n.)*** **ointment**
ልኽስክስ lḱsks ***(adj.)*** **promiscuous**
ልኽፈተ እሳት lkfete esat ***(n.)*** **pyromania**
ልዓት-ሴፍ le-a-t seef ***(n.)*** **hilt**
ልስሉስ ቆብዕ lslus qob'ë ***(n.)*** **bonnet**
ልዕለ ሓያል l'ele ḧayal ***(n.)*** **superpower**
ልዕለ ባህርያዊ l'elebahryawi ***(adj.)*** **uncanny**
ልዕለ ሰብኣዊ l'ele seb'awi ***(adj.)*** **superhuman**
ልዕለ ተፈጥሮኣዊ l'ele tefetro'awi ***(adj.)*** **supernatural**
ልዕለ ዉራቕ l'ele wuraqhe ***(adj.)*** **superscript**
ልዕለ ድምፃዊ l'ele dmxawi ***(adj.)*** **supersonic**
ልዕሊ መጠን ምጥቃም l'eli meten mtqam ***(v.)*** **overdo**
ልዕሊ ዓቕን ሚዛን ሰብነት leli aqn mizan sebnet ***(n.)*** **obesity**
ልዑላውነት l'ulawnet ***(n.)*** **sovereignty**
ልዑል l'ul ***(adj.)*** **superior**
ልዑል l'ul ***(v.)*** **outclass**
ልዑል l'ül ***(adj.)*** **extreme**
ልዑልነት l'ülnet ***(n.)*** **Highness**
ልዕልና l'elna' ***(n.)*** **superiority**
ልዕልና l'elna' ***(n.)*** **supremacy**
ልዕል ዝበለ lel zbele ***(n.)*** **perch**
ልዕበት l'ëbet ***(n.)*** **adaptation**

ልውጠ-ስም lwẗesm ***(n.)*** **alias**
ልውጠት lwẗet ***(n.)*** **metamorphosis**
ልውጠት lwẗet ***(n.)*** **mutation**
ልዙብ lzub ***(adj.)*** **affable**
ልዙብ lzub ***(adj.)*** **unassuming**
ልዝብ lzb ***(n.)*** **negotiation**
ልደት ldet ***(n.)*** **nativity**
ልደት ldet ***(n.)*** **Xmas**
ልዳት ldat ***(n.)*** **sill**
ልግስነት lgsnet ***(n.)*** **altruism**
ልግስና legesena ***(n.)*** **generosity**
ልጓም lgwam ***(n.)*** **brake**
ልጓም lgwam ***(n.)*** **bridle**

ሎ

ሎብስተር lobster ***(n.)*** **lobster**
ሎተሪ loteri ***(n.)*** **lottery**
ሎንጊ longi ***(n.)*** **slush**
ሎንጊቱድ longitud ***(n.)*** **longitude**
ሎጋሪዝም logarizm ***(n.)*** **logarithm**

ሑ

ሑሩይ heray ***(adj.)*** **okay**
ሑጉስ hugus ***(adj.)*** **lively**
ሑጸ ḥutsa ***(n.)*** **grit**
ሑፃ hutsa ***(n.)*** **sand**

ሒ

ሒላብ ȟilab *(n.)* **nappy**
ሒሳባዊ ȟisabawi *(adj.)* **mathematical**
ሒሳብ ȟisab *(n.)* **mathematics**
ሒሹ hishu *(v.)* **transcend**
ሒቅታ hiqta *(n.)* **hiccup**
ሒእሒእታ ȟi'eȟi'eta *(n.)* **snigger**
ሒዝካዮ እትውልድ ኽእለት hizkayo etwled kh'elet *(adj.)* **innate**
ሒደት hidet *(adj.)* **scanty**
ሒደት ȟidet *(adj.)* **some**

ሓ

ሓለቃ ሓምሳ haleqa hamsa *(n.)* **sergeant**
ሓለቃ መርከብ ȟaleka merkeb *(n.)* **skipper**
ሓልቃም halqam *(adj.)* **scrawny**
ሓለቃ ዓሰርተ ȟleqa 'äserte *(n.)* **corporal**
ሓለቃ ተምሃሮ ȟaleqa temharo *(n.)* **monitor**
ሓለቓ ȟaleq̈a *(n.)* **boss**
ሓለቓ ȟaleq̈a *(n.)* **foreman**
ሓለቓ ደብሪ haleqa debri *(n.)* **dean**
ሓለፈ ȟalefe *(v.)* **elapse**
ሓለፋ ȟalefa *(n.)* **privilege**
ሓላለኸ ȟalaleke *(v. t)* **entangle**
ሓላለኸ ȟalaleḱe *(v.)* **complicate**
ሓላሚ ȟalami *(adj.)* **fanciful**
ሓላኒ ȟalani *(n.)* **aspirant**
ሓላዊ haláwi *(n.)* **guardian**
ሓላዊ ȟalawi *(n.)* **invigilator**
ሓላዊ ȟalawi *(n.)* **keeper**
ሓለወ halewe *(v.)* **tend**
ሓለወ ȟalewe *(adj.)* **invigilate**
ሓለወ ȟalewe *(v.)* **keep**
ሓለዋ halewa *(n.)* **indemnity**
ሓለዋ ḥalewa *(n.)* **ward**
ሓለዋ ḥalewa *(n.)* **vigil**
ሓለዋ ተፈጥሮ haalewa tefetero *(n.)* **conservation**
ሓለዋ ፅርየት halewa tsryet *(n.)* **sanitation**
ሓለዋት halewat *(n.)* **toffee**
ሓለንጊ halengi *(n.)* **scourge**
ሓለንጋይ ȟalengag *(adj.)* **svelte**
ሓላዊ ማዕጾ ḥalawi-ma'ëxo *(n.)* **goalkeeper**
ሓላዊ ቤተ-መፃሕፍቲ halwi biete-metsahft *(n.)* **librarian**
ሓላዊ ነብሲ ȟalawi nebsi *(n)* **bodyguard**
ሓላዊ ገረብ halwi gereb *(n.)* **ranger**
ሓላፊ halafi *(n.)* **chief**
ሓላፊ halafi *(n.)* **director**
ሓላፊ ȟalafi *(n.)* **functionary**
ሓላፊ ḥalafi *(n.)* **warden**
ሓላፍነት ȟalafnet *(n.)* **duty**
ሓላፍነት ȟalafnet *(n.)* **responsibility**
ሓላፍነት ሃበ ȟalafnet habe *(v.)* **entrust**
ሓላፍነት ዘይስምዖ ȟalafnet zeysm'ö *(adj.)* **irresponsible**
ሓልሓሊፉ halhalifu *(adj.)* **occasional**
ሓልሓሊፉ halhalifu *(adv.)* **occasionally**
ሓልዮተኛ ȟalyotegna *(adj.)* **dutiful**
ሓልዮት ȟalyot *(n.)* **solicitude**
ሓሓ ȟaȟa *(n.)* **pelican**
ሓሓሊፉ hahalifu *(adj.)* **infrequent**
ሓሓሊፉ ዝርአ ȟaȟalifu zr'e *(adj.)* **sporadic**
ሓሓሊፍ ዝድጋገም hahalifu zdegagem *(adj.)* **intermittent**
ሓመሰ ȟamese *(v.)* **swim**

ሓመዳይ hameday *(adj.)* **drab**
ሓመድ ȟamed *(n.)* **soil**
ሓሙስ hamus *(n.)* **Thursday**
ሓሙኽሽታይ ḥamuḱshtay *(n.)* **grey**
ሓምበበ hambebe *(v.)* **whiz**
ሓምባሲ ȟambasi *(adj.)* **natant**
ሓምሳ ȟamsa *(adj. & n.)* **fifty**
ሓምሻሺ ȟamshashi *(adj.)* **smashing**
ሓምሸሸ ȟamsheshe *(v.)* **smash**
ሓሙሽተ ȟamushte *(adj. & n.)* **five**
ሓሙሽተ ማንታ hamušte manta *(n.)* **Quinn**
ሓማሲ ȟamasi *(n.)* **swimmer**
ሓማት ȟamat *(n.)* **mother-in-law**
ሓሜት ḥameet *(n.)* **gossip**
ሓምለ ȟamle *(n.)* **July**
ሓምሊ ዝቐለቡ ȟamli zq̈elebu *(n.)* **vegan**
ሓምሓም ḥamḥam *(n.)* **gourd**
ሓምሾኽ hamxok *(v.)* **scrunch**
ሓምተለ ȟamtele *(v.)* **crumple**
ሓሞት hamot *(n.)* **pancreas**
ሓሞት ȟamot *(n.)* **bile**
ሓሞኩሽቲ ȟamokushti *(n.)* **ash**
ሓሞኹሽቲ ዝዕቆረሉ hamokshti zeqorelu *(n.)* **urn**
ሓረረ harere *(v.)* **char**
ሓረረ harere *(v.)* **sear**
ሓረሰ ȟarese *(v.)* **cultivate**
ሓረስታይ ȃarestay *(n.)* **farmer**
ሓረስታይ harestay *(n.)* **tiller**
ሓረስታይ ȃarestay *(n.)* **peasant**
ሓረስታይ ȟarestay *(n.)* **ploughman**
ሓረስቶት ȃarestot *(n.)* **peasantry**
ሓረቐ ȃareqe *(v.)* **resent**
ሓረደ ȟarede *(v.)* **cut**
ሓረግ hareg *(n.)* **phrase**
ሓረግ ȟareg *(n.)* **creeper**
ሓረጣ hareta *(n.)* **usury**
ሓሪም ḥarim *(n.)* **harem**
ሓራቕ ȟaraq̈ *(adj.)* **irate**
ሓራቕ ȟaraq̈ *(adj.)* **irritable**
ሓራቕ ḥaraq̈ *(adj.)* **waspish**
ሓራጅ ȟaraĵ *(n.)* **auction**
ሓራ ኣዉፀአ ȃara awwxe'e *(v. t)* **emancipate**
ሓርማዝ ȃarmaz *(n.)* **elephant**
ሓርሽ ȃarše *(n.)* **rhinoceros**
ሓርበኛ ȟrbegna *(n.)* **militant**
ሓርበኛ harbena *(n.)* **patriot**
ሓርበኛነት harbenanet *(n.)* **patriotism**
ሓርበኛዊ harbenawi *(adj.)* **patriotic**
ሓርነኽ harnekhe *(n.)* **snore**
ሓርናኺ harnakhi *(adj.)* **stertorous**
ሓርአ ȃar'e *(v.)* **defecate**
ሓርገፀ ȟargex *(n.)* **crocodile**
ሓርገፅ ȟargex *(n.)* **alligator**
ሓርፈፈ ȃarfefe *(v.)* **ruffle**
ሓርፋፍ harfaf *(adj.)* **jagged**
ሓርፋፍ ȃarfaf *(adj.)* **rough**
ሓርፋፍ ȃarfaf *(adj.)* **rugged**
ሓሰማ ȟasema *(n.)* **swine**
ሓሰረ ȃasere *(v.)* **depreciate**
ሓሰር ḥaser *(n.)* **hay**
ሓሰር ȟaser *(n.)* **straw**
ሓሰበ haseb *(v.)* **contemplate**
ሓሰበ hasebe *(v.)* **consider**
ሓሰበ hasebe *(v.)* **think**
ሓሰበ ȟasebe *(v.)* **mean**
ሓሳቢ ha'sabi *(adj.)* **considerate**
ሓሳቢ hasbi *(adj.)* **thoughtful**
ሓሳቢ hasabi *(n.)* **thinker**
ሓሳባት hasabat *(n.)* **perspective**
ሓሳባዊ hasabawi *(adj.)* **imaginary**
ሓሳብ ȟsab *(n.)* **proposal**

ሓሳብ ȟsab ***(n.)*** **proposition**
ሓሳብ ḥasab ***(n.)*** **idea**
ሓሳብ hasab ***(n.)*** **contemplation**
ሓሳብ ምቕራብ ȟsab mq̈rab ***(v.)*** **propose**
ሓሳብ ከለሰ hasab kelese ***(v.)*** **theorize**
ሓሳብ ዘመንጪ hasab zemenchi ***(n.)*** **theorist**
ሓሳብ ዝገልፅ ĥasab zgelx ***(adj.)*** **expressive**
ሓሰኻ haseka ***(n.)*** **insect**
ሓሰኻ haseka ***(n.)*** **worm**
ሓሰኻ ሃሪ ĥaseka hari ***(n.)*** **silkworm**
ሓሰኽሰኽ በለ haseksek bele ***(v.)*** **teem**
ሓሰወ hasewe ***(v.)*** **lie**
ሓሰወ hasewe ***(v.)*** **sneak**
ሓሳዊ hasawi ***(n.)*** **liar**
ሓሶት ĥasot ***(n.)*** **deceit**
ሓሶት ȟasot ***(adj.)*** **spurious**
ሓሶት ĥasot ***(adj.)*** **false**
ሓሶትነት ĥasotnet ***(n.)*** **falsehood**
ሓሸማ hashema ***(n.)*** **pig**
ሓሻሺ ĥashashi ***(adj.)*** **extravagant**
ሓሻሺ ȟashashi ***(n.)*** **spendthrift**
ሓሽሽ hshsh ***(n.)*** **opium**
ሓሸዋማ hashewama ***(adj.)*** **sandy**
ሓቀኛ hakegna ***(adj.)*** **truthful**
ሓቀኛ ḥaqeña ***(adj.)*** **veritable**
ሓቀኛ ȟaqeṅa ***(adj.)*** **authentic**
ሓቀኛ ȟaqeṅa ***(adj.)*** **bona fide**
ሓቀኛ ĥakegna ***(adj.)*** **sincere**
ሓቂ haki ***(n.)*** **truth**
ሓቂ haki ***(v.)*** **undeceive**
ሓቂ መሰልነት ḥaqi meselne ***(n.)*** **verisimilitude**
ሓቂ መሳሊ ȟaqi mesali ***(adj.)*** **specious**
ሓቂ ዘይብሉ ȟaqi zeyblu ***(adj.)*** **bogus**
ሓቂዩ በለ haqiyu bele ***(v.)*** **claim**
ሓቃቂ ȟaqhaqi ***(adj.)*** **soluble**
ሓቃቅነት ȟaqhaqnet ***(n.)*** **solubility**
ሓቐኛ ĥaqegna ***(adj.)*** **genuine**
ሓቐቐ ĥaqeqe ***(v.)*** **digest**
ሓቐቐ ĥaqeqe ***(v. t)*** **dissolve**
ሓቅነት ĥaqnet ***(n.)*** **realism**
ሓቅነት ĥaqnet ***(n.)*** **reality**
ሓቅነት ȟaqnet ***(n.)*** **probity**
ሓቅነት ḥaqnet ***(n.)*** **veracity**
ሓቅነት ḥaqnet ***(n.)*** **verity**
ሓቅነት ኣረጋገጸ ḥaqnet 'aregagexe ***(v.)*** **vindicate**
ሓቅነታዊ ĥaqnetawi ***(adj.)*** **realistic**
ሓቆነ haqone ***(v.)*** **churn**
ሓቆነ haqone ***(v.)*** **shake**
ሓቖፈ ȟaqofe ***(v.)*** **cuddle**
ሓቖፈ ȟaqofe ***(v.)*** **nestle**
ሓቈነ ȟaq̈wene ***(v.)*** **jiggle**
ሓቘፈ ȟaq̈ofe ***(v.)*** **enfold**
ሓቘፈ haqo-fe ***(v.)*** **hug**
ሓቘፈ ĥaqofe ***(v.)*** **embrace**
ሓበለ ḥabele ***(v.)*** **wangle**
ሓበላ habela ***(n.)*** **cataract**
ሓበረ habere ***(v.)*** **imply**
ሓበረ habere ***(v.)*** **inform**
ሓበረ ȟabere ***(v.)*** **bode**
ሓበረ ȟabere ***(v.)*** **suggest**
ሓበራዊ መንበሪ ህንፃ haberawi menberi hintsa ***(n.)*** **condominium**
ሓበራዊ ምርድዳእ haberawi merederaoo ***(n.)*** **consensus**
ሓበሬታ habereeta ***(n.)*** **suggestion**
ሓበሬታ ĥabereta ***(n.)*** **data**
ሓበሬታ ĥabereta ***(n.)*** **datum**
ሓበሬታ ȟberieta ***(n.)*** **placard**

ሓበሬታ haberieta *(n.)* **information**
ሓበሬታ ምሕታት haberieta mhtat *(v.)* **inquire**
ሓበሬታ ረኸበ ȟabereeta rekebe *(v.)* **elicit**
ሓበሬታዊ haberietawi *(adj.)* **informative**
ሓበን ȟaben *(n.)* **pride**
ሓበጠ ȟabeẗe *(v.)* **swell**
ሓበጀራይ ȟabejeray *(adj.)* **motley**
ሓበጀራይ ȟabeĵeray *(adj.)* **brindle**
ሓቢርካ ምንባር habireka menebare *(n.)* **coexistence**
ሓቢ ጸሊም ȟabi xelim *(n.)* **jasmine**
ሓባሊ ȟabali *(n.)* **smoothie**
ሓባሪ habari *(n.)* **informer**
ሓባሪ habari *(adj.)* **suggestive**
ሓባሪ ĥabari *(n.)* **dial**
ሓባሪ ḥabari *(n.)* **guide**
ሓባሪ መፅሓፍ habari metsehaf *(n.)* **guidebook**
ሓባ'ሪ ተንሰፋፋይ ȟabari tensefafay *(n.)* **buoy**
ሓባራዊ ȟabarawi *(adj.)* **common**
ሓባር ንፋስ ḥabar nfas *(n.)* **vane**
ሓባሲ habasi *(n.)* **jailer**
ሓባጠ ጎባጥ ቦታ habate gobat bota *(n.)* **tack**
ሓባጥ habat *(adj.)* **puffy**
ሓባጥ ጎባጥ ĥabaẗ gobaẗ *(adj.)* **gnarled**
ሓብለት ȟablet *(n.)* **necklet**
ሓብሓብ ȟabȟab *(n.)* **melon**
ሓብአ habe *(v.)* **withhold**
ሓብአ ȟab'e *(v.)* **conceal**
ሓብአ ȟab'e *(v.)* **stash**
ሓብአ ḥab'e *(v.t)* **hide**
ሓቦ ȟabo *(n.)* **mettle**
ሓቦ ȟabo *(n.)* **morale**
ሓቦ ȟabo *(n.)* **stamina**
ሓቦኛ ȟabogna *(n.)* **mettlesome**
ሓተላ ሓፂን ĥatela ĥatsin *(n.)* **slag**
ሓተመ ȟateme *(v.)* **print**
ሓተተ ĥatete *(v.)* **debrief**
ሓተተ ĥatete *(v.)* **enquire**
ሓተተ ȟatete *(v.)* **interrogate**
ሓተተ ȟatete *(v.)* **ask**
ሓተታ ȟateta *(n.)* **commentary**
ሓተታ ኣቕራቢ ȟateta aqrabi *(n.)* **commentator**
ሓታል ĥatal *(adj.)* **slushy**
ሓታሚት ȟatamit *(n.)* **printer**
ሓትኖ ȟatno *(n.)* **aunt**
ሓነቐ haneqe *(v.)* **choke**
ሓነቐ haneqe *(v.)* **throttle**
ሓነቐ ȟaneqe *(v.)* **strangle**
ሓናኽ hanak *(adj.)* **timid**
ሓናኽ ĥanak *(adj.)* **prudent**
ሓንከሰ hankese *(v.)* **limp**
ሓንካስ ȟankas *(adj.)* **lame**
ሓንኮለ ĥankole *(v.)* **disrupt**
ሓንጎል ȟangol *(n.)* **brain**
ሓንጀ መንጂ ĥanjemenji *(n.)* **frill**
ሓንፈፀ ȟanfex *(n.)* **mulatto**
ሓከመ ḥakeme *(v.)* **heal**
ሓኪም hakim *(n.)* **therapist**
ሓኪም ĥakim *(n.)* **doctor**
ሓኪም ĥakim *(n.)* **physician**
ሓኪም ȟakim *(n.)* **medic**
ሓኪም ኣእምሮ ȟakim aèmro *(n.)* **psychiatrist**
ሓኮረ hakore *(v.)* **creep**
ሓኳሪ እምባ ȟaḱwari emba *(n.)* **mountaineer**
ሓኸለ hakhele *(n.)* **sternum**
ሓወልቲ hawelti *(n.)* **colossus**
ሓወልቲ ĥawelti *(n.)* **effigy**

ሓወልቲ ḧawelti ***(n.)*** **monument**
ሓወልቲ ḧawelti ***(n.)*** **statue**
ሓወልታዊ ḧaweltawi ***(adj.)*** **statuesque**
ሓወልትታት ḧawelt'tat ***(n.)*** **statuary**
ሓወሰ ḧawese ***(n.)*** **meld**
ሓወሰ ḧawese ***(v.)*** **mix**
ሓወየ ĥaweye ***(v.)*** **recuperate**
ሓወየ ĥaweye ***(v.)*** **revive**
ሓዊ ምቅፅፃል hawi mktstsal ***(n.)*** **tinder**
ሓዊ ዝመስል ĥawi zmesl ***(adj.)*** **fiery**
ሓዋላ ĥawala ***(n.)*** **remittance**
ሓዋወሰ ĥawawese ***(v.)*** **obfuscate**
ሓዋወሰ hawawese ***(v.)*** **scramble**
ሓዋወሰ ḧawawese ***(v. t)*** **blend**
ሓዋወሰ ḧawawese ***(adj.)*** **wonted**
ሓው ḧaw ***(n.)*** **brother**
ሓውለለ ḧawlele ***(v.)*** **squint**
ሓውሲ ḧawsi ***(adv.)*** **somewhat**
ሓውሲ ትሮፒካዊ ḧawsi tropikawi ***(adj.)*** **subtropical**
ሓዘ ḥaze ***(v.t)*** **hold**
ሓዘ haze ***(v.)*** **seize**
ሓዘ ĥaze ***(v.)*** **preoccupy**
ሓዘ ḥaze ***(v.t)*** **handle**
ሓዘ haze' ***(v.t.)*** **contain**
ሓዘ ḧaze ***(v.)*** **comprise**
ሓዘነ ḧazene ***(v.)*** **mourn**
ሓዘን ĥazen ***(n.)*** **doldrums**
ሓዘን ḧazen ***(n.)*** **bereavement**
ሓዘን ḧazen ***(n.)*** **heartbreak**
ሓዘን ḧazen ***(n.)*** **sorrow**
ሓዘን ምግላፅ hazen mglats ***(n.)*** **lament**
ሓዘንተኛ ḧazentegna ***(n.)*** **mourner**
ሓዘንተኛ ḧazentegna ***(n.)*** **mourning**
ሓዘ haze ***(v.)*** **occupy**
ሐዚታት hezitat ***(adv.)*** **lately**
ሓየለ ḧayele ***(v.)*** **strengthen**
ሓየረ ḧayere ***(v.)*** **banish**
ሓየከ hayyeke ***(v.)*** **chew**
ሓየኸ ḧayeḱe ***(v.)*** **masticate**
ሓያል ĥayal ***(adj.)*** **energetic**
ሓያል ĥayal ***(adj.)*** **fierce**
ሓያል ĥayal ***(adj.)*** **forceful**
ሓያል ḧayal ***(adj.)*** **mighty**
ሓያል ḧayal ***(adj.)*** **swingeing**
ሓያል ḧeyal ***(adj.)*** **powerful**
ሓያሎ hyalo ***(adj. & pron.)*** **several**
ሓይሊ ḧyli ***(n.)*** **power**
ሓይሊ ĥayli ***(n.)*** **force**
ሓይሊ ḧayli ***(n.)*** **strength**
ሓይሊ ሰብ hayli seb ***(n.)*** **manpower**
ሓይሊ ስሕበት ĥayli sḥbet ***(n.)*** **gravitation**
ሓይሊ ባሕሪ ḧayli baḧri ***(n.)*** **navy**
ሓይሊ ቀነሰ ĥayli qenese ***(v.)*** **disempower**
ሓይሊ ፈረስ ḥayli feres ***(n.)*** **horsepower**
ሓደ ḧade ***(adj.)*** **an**
ሓደ hade ***(n. & adj.)*** **one**
ሓደ ምግባር hade megbar ***(v.)*** **unify**
ሓደ ምኧን hade mekuan ***(v.)*** **unite**
ሓደ ሰብ hade seb ***(pron.)*** **someone**
ሓደ ሺሕ ኪሎ ግራም hade shih kilogram ***(n.)*** **tonne**
ሓደ ወገን hade wegen ***(adj.)*** **unilateral**
ሓደ ዝእዋኑ ḧade z'ewanu ***(adj.)*** **synchronous**
ሓደ ዝደርቡ ገዛ ḧade zderbu geza ***(n.)*** **bungalow**
ሓደገ ĥadega ***(v.)*** **retract**
ሓደገ hadege ***(v.t.)*** **leave**
ሓደገ ĥadege ***(v.)*** **forgo**

ሓደገ ȟadege *(v.)* **forsake**
ሓደገ ȟadege *(v.)* **quit**
ሓደገኛ ȟaadegegna *(adj.)* **risky**
ሓደገኛ ȟadegegna *(adj.)* **dangerous**
ሓደገኛ h'degegna *(adj.)* **malignant**
ሓደገኛ hadegena *(adj.)* **perilous**
ሓደገ'ኛ ḥadegeña *(adj.)* **virulent**
ሓደገ'ኛ ḧadegeṅa *(adj.)* **adventurous**
ሓደጋ hadega *(n.)* **peril**
ሓደጋ ȟadega *(n.)* **danger**
ሓደጋ ȟadega *(n.)* **emergency**
ሓደጋ ȟadega *(n.)* **risk**
ሓደጋ ḥadega *(n.)* **hazard**
ሓደጋ ḧadega *(n.)* **accident**
ሓደ ግዜ hade gizie *(adv.)* **once**
ሓዲድ ȟadid *(n.)* **rail**
ሓዳር ḧadar *(n.)* **marriage**
ሓዳሳይ ȟadasay *(n.)* **reformer**
ሓደ ዓይነት hade aynet *(adj.)* **identical**
ሓደ ድምጺ hade demtsi *(adj.)* **unanimous**
ሓዱሽ ኣማኒ ḧadush amani *(n.)* **neophyte**
ሓዱሽ ክላሲካዊ ḧadush klasikawi *(adj.)* **neoclassical**
ሓድነት hadenet *(n.)* **unification**
ሓድነት hadẹnet *(n.)* **unison**
ሓድነት hadenet *(n.)* **unity**
ሓድነት hadnet *(n.)* **coalition**
ሓድነት ḧadnet *(n.)* **solidarity**
ሓድነት hadnet *(n.)* **oneness**
ሓድ ቋንቋ ብካሊእ ቋንቋ ክፀሓፍ ክሎ hade qnaqa bkalie qanqa ksehaf kelo *(v.)* **transliterate**
ሓድሽ ḧadsh *(adj.)* **new**
ሓድሽ ḧadsh *(n.)* **novelty**
ሓጀር ȟajer *(n.)* **ruby**
ሓጀት ḧajet *(n.)* **accessory**
ሓገል ḧagel *(n.)* **abscess**
ሓገዘ hageze *(v.)* **support**
ሓገዘ ḥageze *(v.)* **help**
ሓገዘ ḧageze *(v.)* **assist**
ሓገዝ ḧagez *(n.)* **assistance**
ሓገዝ ḧagez *(n.)* **backing**
ሓገዝ ḧagez *(n.)* **support**
ሓገዝ ገንዘብ ḧagez genzeb *(n.)* **subsidy**
ሓገገ ȟagege *(v.)* **enact**
ሓጋያዊ hagayawi *(adj.)* **wintry**
ሓጋዚ ḧagazi *(adj.)* **auxiliary**
ሓጋዚ ḥagazi *(adj.)* **helpful**
ሓጋዚ ምሕቃቕ መግቢ hagazi mhqaq megbi *(adj.)* **peptic**
ሓጋዚ ኣልቦ ḥagazi 'albo *(adj.)* **helpless**
ሓጋይ ḧagay *(n.)* **winter**
ሓጎስ hagos *(n.)* **whoop**
ሓጎስ ȟagos *(n.)* **gaiety**
ሓጎደ ȟagode *(v.t)* **forge**
ሓጎፀጎፀ ኣበለ ḧagwaxgwax 'abele *(v.t.)* **jolt**
ሓጐስ ḥagos *(n.)* **happiness**
ሓጐስ ḧagwas *(n.)* **jubilation**
ሓጥያተኛ ȟatyategna *(n.)* **sinner**
ሓጥያት ȟatyat *(n.)* **sin**
ሓጥያት ዝመልኦ ȟatyat zmel'o *(adj.)* **sinful**
ሓጫጪ ḧačači *(adj.)* **ironical**
ሓጸረ ḧaxere *(v.)* **bound**
ሓጸበ ḥaxebe *(v.)* **wash**
ሓጻባይ ḥaxabay *(n.)* **washer**
ሓጺር ፅሁፍ ȟaxir xȟuf *(n.)* **essay**
ሓፁር ȟaxur *(n.)* **fence**
ሓጺር ḧaxir *(adj.)* **brief**
ሓጺርነት ḧaxirnet *(n.)* **brevity**

ሓጺርን ብሩህን ȟaxirn bruhn *(adj.)* **concise**
ሓጺር መግለጺ ȟaxir meglexi *(n.)* **briefing**
ሓጺር ትረኻ haxir traka *(n.)* **parable**
ሓጺር ዕረፍቲ haxir erefti *(n.)* **pause**
ሓጺር ጽሑፍ ȟatsir ts'ȟuf *(n.)* **docket**
ሓፀበ ȟaxebe *(v.)* **swill**
ሓፀበ ȟatsebe *(v.)* **rinse**
ሓፀረ ȟaxere *(v.)* **encase**
ሓፁር ȟaxur *(n.)* **cordon**
ሓፂቡ ኣስታረረ hatzibu astarere *(v.)* **launder**
ሓፂር ȟaxir *(n.)* **compendium**
ሓፂር ኖቨል ȟaxir noveela *(n.)* **novelette**
ሓፂን ȟatsin *(n.)* **iron**
ሓፂር ȟatsir *(adj.)* **short**
ሓፂር ዘረባ ȟaxir zereba *(adj.)* **curt**
ሓፂር ግጥም ȟatsir gtmi *(n.)* **skirmish**
ሓፂር ፈተና ȟatsir fetena *(n.)* **quiz**
ሓፂርን ንፁርን hatsirn ntsurn *(adj.)* **succinct**
ሓፀበ hatsxebe *(v.)* **cleanse**
ሓፅቢ ȟatsbi *(n.)* **dam**
ሓፅቢ ȟatsbi *(n.)* **reservoir**
ሓፈረ hafere *(v.)* **inhibit**
ሓፈረ ȟafere *(v.)* **blush**
ሓፋር hafar *(adj.)* **sheepish**
ሓፋር hafar *(adj.)* **timorous**
ሓፋር ȟafar *(adj.)* **retiring**
ሓፋር ȟafar *(adj.)* **shy**
ሓፋር ȟafar *(adj.)* **coy**
ሓፋር ȟafar *(adj.)* **bashful**
ሓፈሰ ȟafese *(v.)* **condense**
ሓፈሻዊ ȟafeshawi *(adj.)* **general**
ሓፊስ ḥafis *(adj.)* **viscous**
ሓፊስ ḥafis *(adj.)* **viscid**
ሓፊስ ፈሳሲ ሽኮር hafis fesasi sukor *(n.)* **treacle**
ሓፋሽ ȟafash *(n.)* **commoner**
ሓፍቲ ȟaftawi *(adj.)* **sisterly**
ሓፍታዊ ȟafti *(n.)* **sister**
ሓፍ ኮፍ በለ ȟaf kof bele *(v.)* **bob**
ሓፍ ዝበለ ብርኪ ȟaf zbele brki *(n.)* **pinnacle**

ሕ

ሕሉም ḥlum *(n.)* **Wally**
ሕሉፍ hluf *(adj.)* **past**
ሕሉፍ ሰዓት hluf seat *(n.)* **pastime**
ሕሊና hi'lina *(n.)* **conscience**
ሕሊና ምስሓት hilina mesehate *(n.)* **coma**
ሕላስ ȟlas *(n.)* **spear**
ሕላፍ መመረቕታ ȟlaf memereq̈ta *(n.)* **postgraduate**
ሕላፍ ሰዓት ȟlaf seät *(n.)* **curfew**
ሕልሚ ȟlmi *(n.)* **dream**
ሕልሚ ቀትሪ ȟlmi qetri *(n.)* **reverie**
ሕልማዊ hlmawi *(adj.)* **utopian**
ሕልማዊ ȟlmawi *(adj.)* **surreal**
ሕልኽላኽ hlklak *(adj.)* **intricate**
ሕልኽልኽ ȟlḱlḱ *(n.)* **complexity**
ሕልኽልኽ ȟlḱlḱ *(n.)* **complication**
ሕልናዊ ȟlnawi *(adj.)* **moral**
ሕልና ዘይብሉ hlna zeyblu *(adj.)* **unscrupulous**
ሕልፍን ትርፍን hlfn trfn *(adj.)* **superabundant**
ሕልፍን ትርፍን h'lfn t'rfn *(adj.)* **superabundance**
ሕመት himet *(n.)* **coal**
ሕሙም hmum *(n.)* **patient**
ሕሙም hmum *(adj.)* **unhealthy**
ሕሙም ȟmum *(adj.)* **ailing**

ሕሙም ḧmum *(adj.)* **morbid**
ሕሙም ḥmum *(adj.)* **ill**
ሕሙም ĥmum *(adj.)* **sick**
ሕሙም ĥmum *(adj.)* **sickly**
ሕማም hmam *(n.)* **malady**
ሕማም ĥmam *(n.)* **disease**
ሕማም ĥmam *(n.)* **sickness**
ሕማም ḧmam *(n.)* **ailment**
ሕማም ḧmam *(adv.)* **morbidity**
ሕማም ḧmam *(n.)* **syndrome**
ሕማም ḥmam *(n.)* **illness**
ሕማቅ ምሕደራ ḧmaq mḧdera *(n.)* **mismanagement**
ሕማቅ ስምዒት ንሓፅር ግዘ hmaq smiet nhasir gze *(n.)* **twinge**
ሕማቕ hmaq *(adj.)* **disastrous**
ሕማቕ ḥmaq̈ *(adj.)* **horrible**
ሕማቕ ḧmaq̈ *(adj.)* **bad**
ሕማቕ ሃለዋት ĥmaq halewot *(n.)* **plight**
ሕቑፊ-ዕምባባ ḧq̈ufi'ëmbaba *(n.)* **bouquet**
ሕማቕ ጠባይ hmaq tebay *(adj.)* **pettish**
ሕቋን ፀባ ḧqwan xeba *(n.)* **milkshake**
ሕማም ምንፍርፋር ĥmam mnfrfar *(n.)* **epilepsy**
ሕማም ሸሮኽ hemam sheroke *(n.)* **cholera**
ሕማም ኣእምሮ ĥmam aemro *(n.)* **psychosis**
ሕማቅነት hmaqnet *(n.)* **ugliness**
ሕማቅ ኣማሓድራ hmaq ama'hadra *(n.)* **maladministration**
ሕማቅ ኣጋጣሚ ḧmaq agaẗami *(n.)* **misadventure**
ሕማቅ ዕድል ḧmaq ëdl *(n.)* **mischance**
ሕማቕ ኣመል ḥmaq̈ 'ame *(n.)* **vice**
ሕምሕምታ ፈረስ ḧmḧmta feres *(n.)* **neigh**
ሕምባሻ ḧmbasha *(n.)* **baguette**
ሕምባሻ ḧmbasha *(n.)* **bread**
ሕምብሊላይ ḧmbililay *(adj.)* **spiral**
ሕምብሊል በለ ḥmblil bele *(v.)* **gyrate**
ሕምብርቲ h-m-brti *(n.)* **hub**
ሕምየት ĥmyet *(n.)* **rumour**
ሕሩጭ ĥruĉ *(n.)* **flour**
ሕሩጭ ḧruč *(n.)* **powder**
ሕሩቕ ḧruq̈ *(adj.)* **angry**
ሕራነ ĥrane *(n.)* **rage**
ሕርቃን ĥrqan *(n.)* **displeasure**
ሕርቃን ĥrqan *(n.)* **dudgeon**
ሕርቃን ĥrqan *(n.)* **fume**
ሕርቃን ḧrqan *(n.)* **ire**
ሕርሻ hersha *(n)* **husbandry**
ሕርሻ ĥrsha *(n.)* **farm**
ሕርሻ ḧrsha *(n.)* **agriculture**
ሕርሻዊ ḧrshawi *(adj.)* **agricultural**
ሕሰም ḧsem *(n.)* **misery**
ሕሱም hsum *(adj.)* **inimical**
ሕሱም ሰብ ĥsum seb *(n.)* **ruffian**
ሕሱር ĥsur *(adj.)* **disreputable**
ሕሱር ĥsur *(adj.)* **shoddy**
ሕሱር ḧsur *(adj.)* **measly**
ሕሳር hesaree *(adj.)* **cheap**
ሕሳብ ḧsab *(n.)* **account**
ሕስረት hsret *(n.)* **indignity**
ሕስረት ĥsret *(n.)* **disrepute**
ሕሹኽሹኽ hshukshuk *(v.)* **peep**
ሕሹኽሹኽ hshukshuk *(v.)* **whisper**
ሕሽኩለኛ ḧshkulegna *(n.)* **marsupial**
ሕሽ ዝበለ ኣተሓሳስባ ዘለዎ hish zbele atehasasba zelwo *(adj.)* **transcendent**
ሕበጥ hbet *(n.)* **lump**

ሕበጥ ḧbeẗ *(n.)* **bulge**
ሕቡእ hbu'e *(n.)* **oblivion**
ሕቡእ hibuea' *(adj.)* **clandestine**
ሕቡእ hebu'e *(n.)* **obscurity**
ሕቡእ hbu'e *(n.)* **crypt**
ሕቡእ hbu'e *(adj.)* **ulterior**
ሕቡእ ḧbu'e *(n.)* **cache**
ሕቡእ ḧbu'e *(adj.)* **surreptitious**
ሕቡእ ḧbu'e *(adj.)* **covert**
ሕቡእ ምፍርራሕ ḧbu'e mfrraḧ *(n.)* **blackmail**
ሕቡእ ምስጢር ዘለዎ ĥbu'e mistir zelewo *(adj.)* **oracular**
ሕቡእ ትርጉም ዘለዎ hbu'e trgum zelewo *(n.)* **overtone**
ሕቡጥ ḥbuṭ *(adj.)* **varicose**
ሕቢብ በለ hbib bele *(v.)* **whirr**
ሕቢብታ hbibta *(n.)* **whir**
ሕባበት hbabet *(n.)* **scum**
ሕብረ መድያዊ ḧbre medyawi *(n.)* **multimedia**
ሕብረተሰብ hbreteseb *(n.)* **society**
ሕብረት hbret *(n.)* **union**
ሕብሪ hbri *(n.)* **crayon**
ሕብሪ ኣልቦ hbri 'albo *(n.)* **colourless**
ሕብሪ ዋሃዮ hbri wahiyo *(n.)* **pigment**
ሕብራዊ ምረኢት ḧbrawi mreit *(n.)* **pageantry**
ሕብስቲ hbsti *(n.)* **loaf**
ሕብሪ hibri *(n.)* **colour**
ሕብሪ he-bri *(n.)* **hue**
ሕብብር hhbbr *(n.)* **collaboration**
ሕብስተ-ቁርባን ḥbstequrban *(n.)* **wafer**
ሕብጠት hbeẗet *(n.)* **swelling**
ሓታሚ ḧtami *(n.)* **publisher**
ሕታም htam *(n.)* **watermark**
ሕታም ĥtam *(n.)* **edition**
ሕትመት ḧtmet *(n.)* **publication**
ሕቶ hto *(n.)* **inquiry**
ሕቶ hto *(n.)* **query**
ሕቶ hto *(n.)* **question**
ሕነ ĥne *(n.)* **reprisal**
ሕነ ĥne *(n.)* **revenge**
ሕነ ፈደየ ĥne fedeye *(v.t.)* **requite**
ሕነ ፈደየ ĥne fedeye *(v.)* **retaliate**
ሕነ ምፍዳይ ĥne mfday *(n.)* **retaliation**
ሕነ ḥne *(n.)* **vendetta**
ሕኒን በለ ḥenin bele *(v.)* **growl**
ሕናኽ ĥnake *(n.)* **prudence**
ሕንቅሕንቅሊተይ hnqhnqlitey *(v. t)* **conundrum**
ሕንቅሕንቅሊተይ ĥnqlĥnqlitey *(n.)* **riddle**
ሕንዚ ḥnz *(n.)* **venom**
ሕንዚዝ ḧnziz *(n.)* **beetle**
ሕንግድ hngd *(adj.)* **insubordinate**
ሕንግድ ĥngd *(adj.)* **restive**
ሕንጥልጥል hntltl *(n.)* **wattle**
ሕንፍሽፍሽ ĥnfshfsh *(n.)* **disorder**
ሕንፍጽፋጽ ḥnftsefatse *(n.)* **hotchpotch**
ሕክምና hkmna *(n.)* **therapy**
ሕክምና hkmna *(n.)* **treatment**
ሕክምና ማህፀን ĥkmna mahtzen *(n.)* **gynaecology**
ሕክምናዊ hkmnawi *(adj.)* **therapeutic**
ሕክምናዊ ḧkmnawi *(adj.)* **medical**
ሕክምናዊ ḧkmnawi *(n.)* **medicine**
ሕኹራ እምባ ḧḱwura emba *(n.)* **mountaineering**
ሕዙእ ቦታ ĥbu'e bota *(n.)* **reservation**
ሕዋስ ḧwas *(n.)* **mixture**

ሕዋስ ምቁራን ħwas mquran ***(n.)*** **confection**
ሕዋስ ባዚቃ ħwas baziqa ***(n.)*** **amalgam**
ሕዉስ ĥwus ***(n.)*** **extrovert**
ሕዉስነት ħwusnet ***(n.)*** **sociability**
ሕዉስነት ħwusnet ***(adj.)*** **sociable**
ሕውስዋስ ħwswas ***(n.)*** **melange**
ሕውስዋስ ħwswas ***(n.)*** **mosaic**
ሕዉስዋስ መስተ hiwuswas meste ***(n.)*** **cocktail**
ሕውነታዊ ħwnetawi ***(adj.)*** **fraternal**
ሕውነት ĥwnet ***(n.)*** **fraternity**
ሕውነት ħwnet ***(n.)*** **brotherhood**
ሕውየት ĥwyet ***(n.)*** **recovery**
ሕዚ ħzi ***(adv.)*** **now**
ሕያዋይ ĥyaway ***(adj.)*** **debonair**
ሕያዋይ ħyaway ***(adj)*** **benevolent**
ሕያዋይ ħyaway ***(adj.)*** **mild**
ሕያዋይ ħyaway ***(adj.)*** **neighbourly**
ሕያዋይ heya-way ***(adj.)*** **humane**
ሕያዋይ ħyaway ***(adj.)*** **nice**
ሕያዋይነት ħyawaynet ***(n.)*** **benevolence**
ሕያው ħyaw ***(adj.)*** **animated**
ሕዳር ħdar ***(n.)*** **November**
ሕዳግ hdag ***(n.)*** **margin**
ሕድሕድ ĥdĥd ***(adj.)*** **every**
ሕድሕድ ĥdĥd ***(adj.)*** **each**
ሕድሳት ĥdsat ***(n.)*** **renovation**
ሕድገት ħdget ***(n.)*** **concession**
ሕገ መንግስቲ hige mengistii ***(n.)*** **constitution**
ሕጉስ higus' ***(adj.)*** **cheery**
ሕጉስ ĥgus ***(adj.)*** **exuberant**
ሕጉስ ħgus ***(adj.)*** **glad**
ሕጉስ hgus ***(adj.)*** **happy**
ሕጉስ hgus ***(adj.)*** **sportive**
ሕጉስ hgus ***(adj.)*** **upbeat**
ሕጉስ ĥgus ***(adv.)*** **gaily**
ሕጉስ ĥgus ***(adj.)*** **gay**
ሕጉስ ħgus ***(adj.)*** **jolly**
ሕጉስ ħgus ***(adj.)*** **merry**
ሕጉስ ħgus ***(adj.)*** **mirthful**
ሕጉስ ḥgus ***(adj.)*** **joyous**
ሕጉስ ħgus ***(adj.)*** **blithe**
ሕጉስነት hgusnet ***(adv.)*** **joviality**
ሕጊ hgi ***(n.)*** **law**
ሕጊ ĥgi ***(n.)*** **dogma**
ሕጊ ĥgi ***(n.)*** **rule**
ሕጊ ħgi ***(n.)*** **statute**
ሕጊ መፅደቕቲ hgi metsdeqhti ***(n.)*** **legislature**
ሕጊ ምፅዳቕ hgi mtsdaqh ***(n.)*** **legislation**
ሕጊ ኣልቦ hgi albo ***(adj.)*** **lawless**
ሕጊ ኣፅደቐ hgi atsdqh ***(v.)*** **legislate**
ሕጊ ኣፅዳቒ higi atzdaqhi ***(adj.)*** **legislative**
ሕጊ ዝጠሓሰ hgi ztehase ***(n.)*** **malefactor**
ሕጋዊ hgawi ***(adj.)*** **lawful**
ሕጋዊ hgawi ***(adj.)*** **legal**
ሕጋዊ hgawi ***(adj.)*** **legitimate**
ሕጋዊ ĥgawi ***(adj.)*** **dogmatic**
ሕጋዊ ĥgawi ***(adj.)*** **rightful**
ሕጋዊ ስልጣን ħgawi slt̆an ***(n.)*** **jurisdiction**
ሕጋዊነት hgawinet ***(n.)*** **legitimacy**
ሕጋዊነት hgawnet ***(n.)*** **legality**
ሕጋዊ ንክኽዉን ገበረ ĥgawi nknkewn gebere ***(v.)*** **decriminalize**
ሕጋዊ ገበረ hgawi gebere ***(v.)*** **legalize**
ሕግግ በለ h'g'g bele ***(v.t.)*** **snarl**
ሕጡብ ማቶኒ ħt̆ub matoni ***(n.)*** **brick**
ሕጡብ ወርቂ ħt̆ub werqi ***(n.)*** **bullion**
ሕጫጪ ħčače ***(n.)*** **irony**

ሕጭጭታ h'ch'chta ***(n.)* screech**
ሕጹይ ȟxuy ***(n.)* candidate**
ሕጽበት ȟxbet ***(n.)* ablution**
ሕጽኒ ȟxni ***(n.)* bosom**
ሕጽኖት ḥxnot ***(n.)* honeymoon**
ሕፀ ĥxe ***(n.)* engagement**
ሕፁይ ĥxuy ***(n.)* fiancé**
ሕፂፀታ htsitsta ***(n.)* screech**
ሕፀረት ĥtsret ***(n.)* paucity**
ሕፀረት ĥtsret ***(n.)* shortage**
ሕፀረት ምግቢ htsret mgbi ***(n.)* malnutrition**
ሕፀር ምጥን ዝበለ hsr mtn zbele ***(adj.)* terse**
ሕፋኖ hfano ***(n.)* handful**
ሕፍረት hfret ***(n.)* inhibition**
ሕፍረት hfret ***(n.)* shame**
ሕፍረት ዘይብሉ hfret zeyblu ***(adj.)* indiscreet**
ሕፍረት ዘይምህላይ hfret zeymhlay ***(n.)* indiscretion**
ሕፍሰት hfset ***(n.)* consistency**
ሓጓዲ ȟagwadi ***(n.)* blacksmith**
ሓራድ ስጋ ȟarad sga ***(n.)* butcher**
ሕነ ፈደየ ȟne fedeye ***(v.)* avenge**

መ

መተባበዒ temsaṭ ***(n.)* inspiration**
ዓኮር me'äkor ***(n.)* bum**
መዓልቦ me'älbo ***(n.)* destination**
መዓልቲ me'älti ***(n.)* day**
መዓልቲ ዕረፍቲ mealti erefti ***(n.)* Sabbath**
መዓልቲ ስራሕ me'alti srah ***(n.)* weekday**
መዓናጡ me'änaťu ***(n.)* bowel**
መዓንጡ me'änaťu ***(n.)* entrails**
መአንገድ ድርጎኛ me'anged drgoȟa ***(n.)* billet**
መዓንጣ me'änta ***(n.)* gut**
መዓንጣ me'änẗa ***(n.)* intestine**
መዓቀቢ ሬሳ me'äqebi reesa ***(n.)* morgue**
መዓር me'är ***(n.)* honey**
መአረምታ me'aremta ***(n.pl.)* amendment**
መዓርፎ mearfo ***(n.)* terminus**
መዓርፎ ነፈርቲ me'ärfo neferti ***(n.)* aerodrome**
መዓርግ me'ärg ***(n.)* gradation**
መዓርግ ዘለዎ me'ärg zelewo ***(adj.)* honourable**
መዕፀፊ ቦታ measefi bota ***(n.)* turning**
መዓሸጊ መራኽብ me'ashegi merakb ***(n.)* wharf**
መዓስከር me'äsker ***(n.)* camp**
መዓት me'ät ***(adj.)* countless**
መዓት me'ät ***(n.)* disaster**
መዓት me'ät ***(n.)* multitude**
መዓት me'ät ***(n.)* ream**
መዓት me'ät ***(n.)* calamity**
መዐትዐቲ me'ät'ëti ***(n.)* garter**
መዓጡቕ me'äṭuq̈ ***(n.)* waist**
መአዛ me'aza ***(n.)* fragrance**
መአዛ me'aza ***(n.)* nutrient**
መዓዛ me'äza ***(n.)* aroma**
መዓዛ -ፍወሳ me'äza fwesa ***(n.)* aromatherapy**
መአዛ ዘለዎ me'aza zelewo ***(adj.)* delectable**
መአዛ ዘለዎ me'aza zelewo ***(adj.)* nutritious**
መአዛዊ me'azawi ***(adj.)* nutritive**

መአዘዚ መድሃኒት meazezi medhanit *(n.)* **prescription**
መብልዒ እንስሳ ጋቢያ mbl'e anbesa gabiya *(n.)* **manger**
መባእታ meba'eta *(adj.)* **elementary**
መባእታዊ mebaètawi *(adj.)* **primary**
መባኹዕቲ mebakueti *(n.)* **yeast**
መባዝሒኢ ማሽን mebazhi mashn *(n.)* **Xerox**
መበገሲ mebegesi *(n.)* **premise**
መበቆል mebekol *(n.)* **provenance**
መበል ዒስራ mebel aisra *(adj.&n.)* **twentieth**
መበል ዒስራ mebel aisra *(adj.&n.)* **twentieth**
መበል ዓሰርተ ሽድሽተ mebel äserte šdšte *(adj. & n.)* **sixteenth**
መበል ዓሰርተ ሰለስተ mebel aserte seleste *(adj. & n.)* **thirteenth**
መበል ዓሰርተ ትሽዓተ mebel äserte tsh'äte *(adj. & n.)* **nineteenth**
መበል ዓሰርተ ሸውዓተ mebel aserte xew'ate *(adj. & n.)* **seventeenth**
መበል ዓሰርተ ክልተ mebel asertekIte *(adj.&n.)* **twelfth**
መበል ዓሰርተ ክልተ mebel asertekIte *(adj.&n.)* **twelfth**
መበል ሰብዓ mebel seb'a *(adj. & n.)* **seventieth**
መበል ሰላሳ mebel selasa *(adj. & n.)* **thirtieth**
መበል ሰላሳ mebel selasa *(adj. & n.)* **thirtieth**
መዓደ me'äde *(v.)* **advise**
መዓደ me'äde *(v.)* **recommend**
መኣዲ me'adi *(n.)* **serving**
መኣዲ me'adi *(n.)* **helping**
መበል ስሳ mebel ssa *(adj. & n.)* **sixtieth**
መበል ቴስዓ mebel tees'ä *(adj. & n.)* **ninetieth**
መበራትዒ meberat'i *(n.)* **supercharger**
መበረኽያ meberekya *(n.)* **rostrum**
መበፀበፂ mebexbexi *(n.)* **blender**
መበፀበፂ mebexbexi *(n.)* **mixer**
መብኮሪ mebkori *(n.)* **truant**
መብላዕልዒ mebla'ël'ï *(n.)* **reactor**
መብለጭለጪ meblečleči *(adj.)* **flamboyant**
መብልሒ meblhi *(n.)* **sharpener**
መበቆል meboqol *(n.)* **cradle**
መብራህርሂ mebrahrhi *(n.)* **clarification**
መብረዲ mebredi *(n.)* **rasp**
መብሰሊ mebseli *(n.)* **cooker**
መብጽዓ mebx'ä *(n.)* **commitment**
መብዛሕትኡ mebza'ht'u *(n.)* **majority**
መብዛሕቱኡ mebzaḣt'u *(n.)* **most**
መጨረሻ mečeresha *(adj.)* **last**
መዳጎኒ medagoni *(n.)* **cage**
መዳጎኒ medagoni *(n.)* **limbo**
መዳልያተኛ medalyategna *(v.i.)* **medallist**
መዳቀሊት medaqelit *(n.)* **copier**
መዳርግቲ ዘይብሉ medargti zeyblu *(adj.)* **unrivalled**
መዳይ meday *(n.)* **way**
መደብ medeb *(n.)* **programme**
መደብ medeb *(n.)* **schedule**
መደብ medeb *(n.)* **terrace**
መደብ medeb *(n.)* **plan**
መደበ medebe *(v.)* **mete**
መደበር medeber *(n.)* **station**
መደብለ ባህላዊ medeble bahlawi *(adj.)* **multicultural**
መደገፍታ medegefta *(n.)* **splint**

መደገፍታ medegefta *(n.)* **strut**
መደቀሲ ክፍሊ medekesi kfli *(n.)* **dormitory**
መደሎ medelo *(n.)* **gong**
መደምደምታ medemdemta *(n.)* **closure**
መደምደምታ ዘይብሉ medemdemta zeyblu *(adj.)* **inconclusive**
መደምደምያ medemdemya *(n.)* **epilogue**
መደናገሪ medenageri *(adj.)* **deceptive**
መደናገሪ medenageri *(n.)* **knave**
መደናገሪ medenageri *(n.)* **racketeer**
መደንደል medendel *(n.)* **railing**
መደንደል medendel *(n.)* **banisters**
መደንደል medendel *(n.)* **barricade**
መደንዘዚ medenzezi *(n.)* **anaesthetic**
መደቀሲ medeqesi *(n.)* **berth**
መደርብዮ mederbyo *(n.)* **shuttle**
መደርደሪ mederderi *(n.)* **rack**
መደርደርያ mederderya *(n.)* **shelf**
መደረ medere *(n.)* **discourse**
መደረ medere *(n.)* **speech**
መደረ ናእዳ medere naeda *(n.)* **panegyric**
መደረጋሕ mederegaȟ *(n.)* **avalanche**
መደያይቦ medeyaybo *(n.)* **rung**
መደያይቦ medeyaybo *(n.)* **staircase**
መድያየቢ medeyayebi *(n.)* **escalator**
መደያየቢ medeyayebi *(n.)* **scaffold**
መደየቢ medeyebi *(n.)* **ramp**
መደየቢት medeyebit *(n.)* **elevator**
መድፍዕ medf'ë *(n.)* **cannon**
መድገምያ medgemya *(n.)* **rosary**
መድሓኒት medhanit *(adj.)* **purgative**
መድሓኒት medĥanit *(n.)* **drug**
መድሓኒት medȟanit *(n.)* **medication**
መድሃኒታዊ medhanitawi *(adj.)* **pharmaceutical**
መድሓርሓሪ medĥarĥri *(adj.)* **reactionary**
መድሕን medȟn *(n.)* **insurance**
መድሕን medḥn *(n.)* **haven**
መዲተራንያዊ mediteranyawi *(adj.)* **Mediterranean**
መድመጺ እዝን medmexi ezni *(n.)* **headphone**
መድመይቲ medmeyti *(n.)* **haemorrhage**
መድረኽ medrek *(n.)* **dais**
መድረኽ medrek *(n.)* **forum**
መድረኽ medreḱ *(n.)* **platform**
መድረኽ medreḱ *(n.)* **podium**
መድረኽ medreḱ *(n.)* **arena**
መድረኽ medrekh *(n.)* **stage**
መድረቒ medreqi *(n.)* **dryer**
መዕበዪት me'ëbeyit *(n.)* **nanny**
መዐፈኒ me'ëfeni *(n.)* **silencer**
መዐደሊ መድሓኒት me'ëdeli medhanit *(n.)* **dispensary**
መንቀሊ mneqsi *(n.)* **cause**
መንፀባረቒ mntsebareqhi *(adj.)* **luminous**
መቕጻዕቲ mqxaeti *(n.)* **penalty**
መራኸቢ mrakhebi *(n.)* **link**
መራኸቢ mreakhebi *(n.)* **linkage**
መዐገሲ me'egesi *(n.)* **sedative**
መዕገቲ me'ëgeti *(n.)* **restraint**
መዕገቲ ስኒ me'ëgeti sni *(n.)* **ratchet**
መዐቀቢ me'ëkebi *(n.)* **deterrent**
መዕቆቢ me-ekobi *(n.)* **housing**
መዕለበጢ me'ëlebeẗi *(adj.)* **feisty**
መእለዪ me'eleyi *(n.)* **spur**
መዐቀቢ me'ëqebi *(n.)* **preservative**

መዐቀብያ me'eqebya ***(n.)*** **conservatory**
መዕቀሊ me'ëqeli ***(n.)*** **refuge**
መዕቀሊ me'ëqeli ***(n.)*** **shelter**
መዕቆቢ me'eqobi ***(n.)*** **sanctuary**
መዕቆሪ me'ëqori ***(n.)*** **vessel**
መዕረፍ ሄሊኮፕተር me'ëref heelikopter ***(n.)*** **heliport**
መዕረፊ me'ërefi ***(n.)*** **hospice**
መዕረፊ ፀማልያታት me'erefi tsemalyatat ***(n.)*** **sanatorium**
መዕረፊ ፀማልያታት me'erefi tsemalyatat ***(n.)*** **sanatorium**
መእሰሪ me'eseri ***(n.)*** **strap**
መእሰሪ ኸልቢ me'eseri kebi ***(n.)*** **leash**
መእሰሪ me'èseri ***(n.)*** **band**
መእተዊ me'etewi ***(n.)*** **access**
መእተዊ me'etewi ***(n.)*** **entrance**
መእተዊ me'etewi ***(n.)*** **prelude**
መዕጠይጠዪ me'ëteyteyi ***(adj.)*** **reluctant**
መዕፀዊ ዕለት me'ëtsewi ëlet ***(n.)*** **deadline**
መባኸኒ mebakeni ***(adj.)*** **wasteful**
መብጽዓ mebx'ä ***(n.)*** **vow**
መብጻዓዊ mebxa'äwi ***(adj.)*** **votive**
መፋሕፍሒ mefaḥfḥi ***(n.)*** **grater**
መፈንቶ mefento ***(n.)*** **valve**
መፈንቶ mefento ***(n.)*** **vent**
መፍሰል mefsel ***(n.)*** **hinge**
መጋረጃ megareğ ***(n.)*** **valance**
መጋርያ megarya ***(n.)*** **hearth**
መግቢ megbi ***(n.)*** **viands**
መጎልበቢ megolbebi ***(n.)*** **wrapper**
መጓሰ meguase ***(n.)*** **herd**
መንጨዕጨዕታ menča'ëča'ëta ***(n.)*** **waterfall**
መንደቕ mendeq̈ ***(n.)*** **wall**
መረቕ mereq̈ ***(n.)*** **gravy**
መስሓቕ mesḥaq̈ ***(adj.)*** **humorous**
መሸኒት meshenit ***(n.)*** **vagina**
መስርዕ-መዓርግ mesr'ëme'ärg ***(n.)*** **hierarchy**
መጥሓኒ meṭḥani ***(n.)*** **grinder**
መወጠጢ ፈረስ meweṭeṭi feres ***(n.)*** **halter**
መዛወሪ መርከብ mezaweri merkeb ***(n.)*** **helm**
መዝነት meznet ***(n.)*** **warranty**
መእ'ዘኒ me'e'zeni ***(n.)*** **minaret**
መፋሓፍሒ ወረቀት mefahafhi wereqet ***(n.)*** **sandpaper**
መፋሓፍሕቲ mefahafhti ***(n.)*** **sander**
መፋለጢ mefaleẗi ***(adj.)*** **introductory**
መፋጥርቲ mefatrti ***(adj.)*** **inborn**
መፈላለዪ ሕንጻጽ mefelaleyi hentsatse ***(n.)*** **hyphen**
መፈለምታ mefelemta ***(n.)*** **genesis**
መፈንቶ mefento ***(n.)*** **sluice**
መፈረሺ mefereshi ***(n.)*** **stuffing**
መፈተሺ mefeteshi ***(n.)*** **manhole**
መፈጸምታ mefetsmta ***(n.)*** **termination**
መፈጸምታ mefexemta ***(n.)*** **expiry**
መፈጸምታ ዘይብሉ mefexemta zeyblu ***(adj.)*** **perpetual**
መፍለስ mefles ***(n.)*** **boar**
መፍልሒ meflḧi ***(n.)*** **boiler**
መፍረ ኣዕዋፍ mefre aëwaf ***(n.)*** **poultry**
መፍተል meftel ***(n.)*** **spindle**
መፍትሕ mefth ***(n.)*** **key**
መፍትሕ ዳዶ meft'h dado ***(n.)*** **spanner**
መጓዓዝያ megaazya ***(n.)*** **transportation**

መጓዓዝያ megaazya *(n.)* **transporter**
መጋቢት megabit *(n.)* **march**
መጋብር megabr *(n.)* **deed**
መጋረጃ megareja *(n.)* **curtain**
መጋረጃ megareja *(n.)* **pelmet**
መጋረጃ megareja *(n.)* **shutter**
መጋርያ megarya *(n.)* **bonfire**
መጋጥም megatm *(n.)* **joint**
መጋጠሚ megatmi *(n.)* **commissure**
መጋየፂ ወረቀታት megayesi werketat *(n.)* **tinsel**
መጋየፂ megayetzi *(n.)* **jewel**
መጋየፂ ሰራሒ megayetzi serahi *(n.)* **jeweller**
መጋዝ megaz *(n.)* **saw**
መግዳዕቲ ዘለዎ megda'eti zelewo *(n.)* **handicapped**
መገበ megebe *(v.)* **feed**
መገዲ megedi *(n.)* **course**
መገዲ ባቡር megedi babur *(n.)* **railway**
መገዱ ሰሓተ megedu seȟate *(v.)* **straggle**
መገለል megelel *(n.)* **bucket**
መገጣጠሚ megeẗaẗemi *(n.)* **fitting**
መግፈፊ megfefi *(n.)* **rake**
መግሓጢ meghati *(n.)* **scoop**
መግለፂ megletsi *(n.)* **definition**
መግለጺ megletsi *(n.)* **statement**
መግለጺ meglexi *(n.)* **announcement**
መግለፂ meglexi *(n.)* **expression**
መግለጺ ሓጐስ meglexi ȟagwas *(n.)* **congratulation**
መግለጺ ሓጐስ meglexi ȟagwas *(n.)* **felicitation**
መጎተ megote *(n.)* **argument**
መግረፍቲ megrefti *(n.)* **lashings**
መጉዳእቲ meguda'eti *(n.)* **damage**
መጉዳእቲ meguda'eti *(n.)* **strain**
መጉዑዓዝ megueaz *(v.)* **transport**
ምጉጃል megujak *(n.)* **classification**
መጉልሒ megulȟi *(n.)* **amplifier**
መጉልሒ ድምፂ megulȟi dmxi *(n.)* **megaphone**
መጉረምረሚ meguremremi *(adj.)* **querulous**
መጉየዪ meguyeyi *(n.)* **runway**
መጓሰ megwase *(n.)* **flock**
መሓለ meȟale *(v.)* **swear**
መሃንዲስ mehandis *(n.)* **engineer**
መሃንቱስ mehantus *(n.)* **anus**
መሓንዘፍ mehanzef *(n.)* **scythe**
መሃረ mehare *(v.)* **instruct**
መሃረ mehare *(v.)* **teach**
መሓረ meȟare *(v.)* **forgive**
መሓረ meȟare *(adj.)* **spare**
መሓረ meȟare *(v.)* **condone**
መሓረ meȟare *(v.)* **absolve**
መሃሪ mehari *(n.)* **mentor**
መሓወ meĥawe *(v.)* **eradicate**
መሓወ meĥawe *(v.)* **pluck**
መሓውር mehawr *(n.)* **limb**
መሃያ mehaya *(n.)* **emolument**
መሃይም mehaym *(n.)* **illiterate**
መሃይምነት mehaymnet *(n.)* **illiteracy**
መሓዛ meȟaza *(n.)* **pal**
መሃዛይ mehazay *(adj.)* **creative**
መሃዘ mehaze *(v.)* **contrive**
መሃዘ mehaze *(v.)* **devise**
መሃዘ mehaze *(v.)* **improvise**
መሃዘ mehaze *(v.)* **innovate**
መሃዘ mehaze *(v.)* **invent**
መሃዚ mehazi *(n.)* **inventor**
መሕብኢ meĥb'i *(n.)* **den**
መሐለውታ mehelewta *(n.)* **safeguard**

መሐንበቢ meĥenbebi *(n.)* **propeller**
መሐንገጋ meĥengega *(n.)* **gag**
መሕለፊ በዓቲ mehlegi beati *(n.)* **underpass**
መሕነን meȟnen *(n.)* **accelerator**
መሕረቒ mehreqhi *(v.)* **irksome**
መሕረሲ meȟresi *(n.)* **midwife**
መሓሰስያ me'ȟsesya *(n.)* **swab**
መሕተሚ mehtemi *(n.)* **sealant**
መሕፀቢ meĥtsebi *(n.)* **detergent**
መሕፀሪ meĥxeri *(n.)* **fencing**
መሕዘኒት ተዋናዪት mehzednit tewanayit *(n.)* **tragedian**
መሕዘኒ mehzeni *(adj.)* **tearful**
መሕዘኒ mehzeni *(adj.)* **tragic**
መሕዘኒ ኩነታት mehzeni kunetat *(n.)* **tragedy**
መጀመርታ mejemerta *(n.)* **alpha**
መጀመርታ mejemerta *(n.)* **inception**
መጀመርታ mejemerta *(adj.)* **initial**
መጀመርታ meĵemerta *(n.)* **beginning**
መጀነኒ meĵeneni *(n.)* **bandage**
መቃብር mekabr *(n.)* **tomb**
መኻዕታ meḱa'ëta *(n.)* **mirth**
መኳለሊ mekaleli *(n.)* **detour**
መኻን meḱan *(adj.)* **barren**
መካነ መቓብር mekane meqabere *(n.)* **churchyard**
መካነ-መቓብር mekane meq̈abr *(n.)* **graveyard**
መካነ ሙታን mekane mutan *(n.)* **necropolis**
መካኒክ mekanik *(n.)* **mechanic**
መካኒካዊ mekanikawi *(adj.)* **mechanical**
መካኒክስ mekaniks *(n.)* **mechanics**
መካኒክዝም mekanikzm *(n.)* **mechanism**
መካር mekar *(n.)* **sage**
መካርነት mekarnet *(n.)* **aphorism**
መካቲ mekati *(adj.)* **defensive**
መኻይድቲ meḱaydti *(adj.)* **concomitant**
መኻዚኖ mekazino *(n.)* **depot**
መኽበሪ መሰል ሰነድ mekberi mesel sened *(n.)* **patent**
መኽዳድንቲ mekedadnti *(n.)* **furnishing**
መከሓሐሲ mekehahesi *(n.)* **weighting**
መኸኸ mekeke *(v.)* **thaw**
መኸኸ meḱeḱe *(v.)* **melt**
መከላኸሊ ጥንሲ mekelaḱeli ẗnsi *(n.)* **contraceptive**
መከራ mekera *(n.)* **mire**
መከራ mekera *(n.)* **tribulation**
መቀስ mekes *(n.)* **scissors**
መኼት meket *(n.)* **pariah**
መኼታይ meketay *(adj.)* **plebeian**
መከወል mekewel *(n.)* **dashboard**
መኸወሊ mekeweli *(n.)* **screen**
መኸወሊ mekeweli *(n.)* **shield**
መኻን mekhan *(adj.)* **sterile**
መኻንነት mekhan'net *(n.)* **sterility**
መኽደኒ mekhdeni *(n.)* **stopper**
መኸኸ mekhekhe *(v.)* **liquefy**
መኽሰብ mekhseb *(n.)* **lucre**
መኽዘን mekhzen *(n.)* **storage**
መኽዘን mekhzen *(n.)* **store**
መኪና mekina *(n.)* **machine**
መኪና mekina *(n.)* **van**
መኪና በረኻ mekina bereḱa *(n.)* **jeep**
መኪና ቀብሪ mekina qebri *(n.)* **hearse**
መኪና mekina *(n.)* **automobile**

መካነ መቓብር mekne mekabir *(n.)* **cemetery**
መቆንጠጢ mekonteti *(n.)* **tongs**
መኾስተር meḱoster *(n.)* **mop**
መኾስተር meḱoster *(n.)* **besom**
መኾስተር meḱoster *(n.)* **broom**
መኽሰብ mekseb *(n.)* **proceeds**
መኽሰብ meḱseb *(n.)* **profit**
መቕፅዒ mekts'i *(adj.)* **punitive**
መኩሲ mekusi *(n.)* **namesake**
መኹተምያ mekutemya *(n.)* **template**
መኳለሚ mekwalemi *(n.)* **bypass**
መኳንንቲ mekwannti *(n.)* **aristocracy**
መኽዘን mekzen *(n.)* **depository**
መኽዘን mekzen *(n.)* **repository**
መኽዘን meḱzen *(n.)* **bunker**
መኽዘን ምግቢ mekzen mgbi *(n.)* **larder**
መኽዘን meḱzen *(n.)* **barn**
መልአ mel'a *(v.)* **tamp**
መላግቦ melagbo *(adj.)* **conjunct**
መላግቦ melagbo *(n.)* **seam**
መላግቦ ዓፅሚ melagbo atzmi *(n.)* **ligament**
መላግቦ ኣጻብዕቲ melagbo 'axab'ëti *(n.)* **knuckle**
መላገቢ melagebi *(n.)* **stapler**
መላገቢ melagebi *(n.)* **adhesive**
መላገፂ melagetsi *(adj.)* **quizzical**
መላኢ mela'i *(adj.)* **complementary**
መልኣኽ mel'ak *(n.)* **angel**
መልኣከ ሞት mel'ake mot *(n.)* **wraith**
መላለዪ melaleyi *(n.)* **showcase**
መላሚን melamin *(n.)* **melamine**
መላጥ melat *(n.)* **tonsure**
መልአ mel'e *(v.)* **append**
መልአ mel'e *(v.)* **fill**
መልአ mel'e *(v.)* **fulfil**
መልአ mel'e *(n.)* **glut**
መልአ mel'e *(v.)* **imbue**
መለግለጋ meleglega *(n.)* **jelly**
መለግለጋይ ዓሳ meleglegay 'äsa *(n.)* **jellyfish**
መለኛ melegna *(n.)* **tactician**
መረሐ meleh *(v.)* **lead**
መለክዒ melek'i *(n.)* **standard**
መለኪያ melekiya *(n.)* **goblet**
መለኮታዊ melekotawi *(adj.)* **divine**
መለኮታዊ melekotawi *(adj.)* **holistic**
መልእኽተ ሃወርያ mel'ekte hawerya *(n.)* **epistle**
መለለይ ምልክት me'leleyei milikit *(n.)* **chevron**
መለለዪ meleleyi *(n.)* **identification**
መለለዪ ፀባይ meleleyi xebay *(n.)* **characteristic**
መለሳ ቃል melesa qal *(n.)* **synonym**
መለሰ melese *(v.)* **react**
መለሰ melese *(v.)* **refund**
መለሰ melese *(v.)* **restore**
መለስለሲ meleslesi *(n.)* **laxative**
መለጠፊ meleẗfi *(n.)* **plaster**
መለይ meley *(a.)* **nubile**
መለይ meley *(adj.)* **shapely**
መለይ meley *(adj.)* **slender**
መልጎም melgom *(n.)* **stud**
መልጎም melgom *(n.)* **button**
መልሓስ melhas *(n.)* **tongue**
መልሓስ melĥas *(n.)* **repartee**
መልሓሱ ኣልመፀ melĥasu almetse *(v.)* **slurp**
መልሕቕ melḧq *(n.)* **anchor**
መልክዐኛ melkäña *(adj.)* **pretty**
መልክዕ melk'e *(n.)* **texture**
መልክዕ melk'ë *(n.)* **feature**

መልክዕ melk'ë *(n.)* **aspect**
መልክዕ melk'ë *(n.)* **beauty**
መልክዕ melk'ë *(n.)* **splendour**
መልኮታዊነት melkotawinet *(n.)* **divinity**
መልእኽተኛ mel'ḱtegna *(n.)* **messenger**
መልክዑ ቀየረ melk'ü keyere *(v.)* **disguise**
መልመለ melmele *(v.)* **induct**
መልመስቲ melmesti *(n.)* **palsy**
መልቀ melqe *(n.)* **fulcrum**
መልቀ melqe *(n.)* **lever**
መልሰ ተግባር ሃበ melse tegbar habe *(v.)* **respond**
መልሰ-ግብሪ melsegbri *(n.)* **backlash**
መልሲ melsi *(n.)* **answer**
መልሲ melsi *(n.)* **response**
መልሲ ሃበ melsi habe *(v.t.)* **counter**
መልሲ ሃበ melsi habe *(v.)* **reply**
መመሓላለፊ መሳርሒ memahalalefi mesarhi *(n.)* **transmitter**
መማረጺ memaretzi *(adj.)* **fussy**
መማረጺ memarexi *(adj.)* **finicky**
መማፅኢ mema'x'i *(n.)* **matchmaker**
መማዪ memayi *(n.)* **censor**
መማዝንቲ memaznti *(adj.)* **equivalent**
መምሰሊ memeiseli *(n.)* **charlatan**
መመኽነይታ memeḱneyta *(n.)* **justification**
መመላእታ memela'eta *(n.)* **complement**
መመላእታ memela'èta *(n.)* **addendum**
መመላእታ memela'èta *(n.)* **appendage**
መመላኽዒ memelak'e *(n.)* **wainscot**
መመላኽዒ ኬክ memelakh'e cake *(n.)* **icing**
መመልሕቂ memelḧeqi *(n.)* **anchorage**
መመልከቲ memelketi *(n.)* **application**
መመልከቲ memelketi *(n.)* **indicator**
መመቀር ኣፍ memeqer af *(n.)* **dessert**
መመቀሪ memeqeri *(n.)* **sweetener**
መምርሒ memerehii *(n.)* **charter**
መመረቒ ፅሑፍ memereqi tsuĥuf *(n.)* **dissertation**
መመሰሊ memeseli *(n.)* **imposter**
መምህር ቆልዑ memher qoleu *(n.)* **pedagogue**
መምህር memhr *(n.)* **instructor**
መምህር memhr *(n.)* **lecturer**
መምህር memhr *(n.)* **teacher**
መምህር ገዛ memhr geza *(n.)* **governess**
መምለጢ ዘይብሉ memleti zeyblu *(adj.)* **inescapable**
መምልኢ meml'i *(n.)* **charger**
መምልኢ meml'i *(n.)* **filler**
መምልኢ meml'i *(n.)* **intake**
መሞገቲ memogeti *(n.)* **muniment**
መሞቒ memoq̈i *(n.)* **heater**
መምርሒ memrĥi *(n.)* **directive**
መምርሒ memrĥi *(n.)* **guidance**
መምርሒ memrĥi *(n.)* **precept**
መምርሒ memrĥi *(n.)* **regulation**
መምርሒ memrḧi *(n.)* **policy**
መምርሒ memrhi *(n.)* **instruction**
መምፀዪት memtseyit *(n.)* **siphon**
መን men *(pron.)* **who**
መናኣኣሲ mena'a'asi *(adj.)* **dismissive**
መናዓቢ mena'abk *(adj.)* **seditious**

መናብር menabr ***(n.)*** **seating**
መናፍፈሲ ቦታ menafesi bota ***(n.)*** **park**
መናፍሕ menafḧ ***(n.)*** **bellows**
መናገድያ menagedia ***(n.)*** **turnover**
መናን menan ***(adj.)*** **ascetic**
መናን menan ***(adj.)*** **quixotic**
መናኒ menani ***(n.)*** **votary**
መናሸዊ menashewi ***(adj.)*** **derogatory**
መንበሪ ቦታ menberi bota ***(n.)*** **dwelling**
መንበሪ ገዛ menberi geza ***(n.)*** **residence**
መንበሪ ገዛ menberi geza ***(adj.)*** **residential**
መንጫ ጫዕታ mencha chaeta ***(n.)*** **cascade**
መንጨለፍ menchelef ***(n.)*** **ladle**
መንደዲ mendedi ***(n.)*** **burner**
መንደፍ mendef ***(n.)*** **fang**
መንደል mendel ***(n.)*** **chisel**
መንደል mendel ***(n.)*** **drill**
መንደል mendel ***(v.)*** **gouge**
መንደሊ መጋዝ mendeli megaz ***(n.)*** **jigsaw**
መንደቅ mendeq ***(n.)*** **firewall**
መንደቅ እምኒ mendeq emni ***(n.)*** **masonry**
መንደሪኒ menderini ***(n.)*** **tangerine**
መንዲል mendil ***(n.)*** **handkerchief**
መንድቃዊ ቅብኣ mendqawi qb'i ***(n.)*** **mural**
መነባብሮ menebabro ***(n.)*** **livelihood**
መነከዪ ዋሕዚ menekeyi wahzi ***(n.)*** **damper**
መነነ menene ***(v.)*** **abjure**
መነቓቕሒ meneqaqhḧi ***(n.)*** **stimulus**
መንእሰይ men'esey ***(adj.)*** **youthful**
መንእሰይ men'èsey ***(adj.)*** **juvenile**
መነስነሲ menesnesi ***(n.)*** **sprinkler**
መንፈስ menfes ***(n.)*** **ghost**
መንፈስ menfes ***(n.)*** **mood**
መንፈስ menfes ***(n.)*** **spectre**
መንፈስ menfes ***(n.)*** **spirit**
መንፈስ ሰብ menfes seb ***(n.)*** **psyche**
መንፈሳዊ menfesawi ***(n.)*** **mystic**
መንፈሳዊ menfesawi ***(adj.)*** **pastoral**
መንፈሳዊ menfesawi ***(adj.)*** **spiritual**
መንፈሳዊነት menfesawinet ***(n.)*** **mysticism**
መንፈሳውነት menfesawinet ***(n.)*** **spirituality**
መንፊት menfit ***(n.)*** **sieve**
መንገፍ mengef ***(n.)*** **mote**
መንገፊ mengefi ***(n.)*** **flannel**
መንጎኛ mengoȟa ***(n.)*** **intermediary**
መንግስታዊ ምቁጽጻር ናብ ብሕታዊ ምቕያር mengsatawi mquxxar nab bḧtawi mq̈yar ***(n.)*** **privatize**
መንግስተ-ሰማያት mengstesemayat ***(n.)*** **heaven**
መንግስቲ mengsti ***(n.)*** **government**
መንግስቲ ኣልቦ mengsti albo ***(adj.)*** **stateless**
መንጉድ mengud ***(n.)*** **hump**
መንህብ menhb ***(n.)*** **apiary**
መንካዕ menka'ë ***(n.)*** **bat**
መንከስ menkes' ***(n.)*** **chin**
መንከስቲ menkesti ***(n.)*** **sting**
መንነት mennet ***(n.)*** **identity**
መኖከሳዊ menokesawi ***(adj.)*** **monastic**
መንቅብ ዘለዎ menqb zelewo ***(adj.)*** **faulty**
መንቀርቀር menqerker ***(n.)*** **clip**
መንቀርቀር menqerqer ***(n.)*** **clamp**
መንቆርቆር menqorqor ***(n.)*** **funnel**

መንሸራተቲ menšerateti *(n.)* **skate**
መንሸራተቲ ጣውላ menšerateti tawla *(n.)* **skateboard**
መንሸራተቲ mensherateti *(n.)* **cursor**
መንሽሮ menshro *(n.)* **cancer**
መንሹር menshur *(n.)* **pamphlet**
መንሹር menshur *(n.)* **brochure**
መንሸራተቲ menšrateti *(n.)* **sledge**
መንታጋይ mentagay *(n.)* **archer**
መንተፍተፊ menteftefi *(n.)* **spittoon**
መንጠለ mentele *(v.)* **dispossess**
መንጠለ men'tele *(v.)* **snatch**
መንጠለ men'tele *(v.)* **snipe**
መንጠሊና mentelina *(n.)* **cloak**
መንጠሊና menṫelina *(n.)* **cape**
መንጠልጠሊ menṭelṭeli *(n.)* **hanger**
መንጠልጥሎ menteltlo *(n.)* **pendant**
መንፀፍ mentseff *(n.)* **carpet**
መንጸፍ menxef *(n.)* **bedding**
መንጸሮር menxeror *(n.)* **vertigo**
መንዝዐ menz'e *(v.)* **usurp**
መንዘዐ menzeë *(v.)* **expropriate**
መንዘዐ menze'ë *(v.)* **arrogate**
ምዕቃብ m'ëqab *(n.)* **retention**
መቓብር meq̈abr *(n.)* **grave**
መቃብር ከውሒ meqabr kewhi *(n.)* **sepulchre**
መቃጨጪ meqačeči *(n.)* **cynic**
መቓልሕ meq̈alḣ *(n.)* **blip**
መቃልዒ meqali *(n.)* **palmist**
መቃልዒ meqal'i *(adj.)* **inaugural**
መቋመቲ meqamet *(n.)* **scanner**
መቓምጦ meq̈amṭo *(n.)* **habitat**
መቃን meqan *(n.)* **frame**
መቓቐር meq̈aq̈er *(n.)* **bookmark**
መቕድም meqdm *(n.)* **preface**
መቕድም meq̈dm *(n.)* **foreword**
መቕድም meq̈dm *(n.)* **preamble**
መቕድም meq̈dm *(n.)* **prologue**
መቀባጠሪ meqebaťeri *(n.)* **sycophant**
መቐለ meqele *(v.)* **divide**
መቐለስ meq̈eles *(n.)* **axle**
መቐለስያ meqelesya *(n.)* **pivot**
መቀመጫ meqemeča *(n.)* **ass**
መቀመጫ meqemeča *(n.)* **backside**
መቀመጫዊ meqemečawi *(adj.)* **anal**
መቀረ meqere *(v.t.)* **savour**
መቐረት meq̈eret *(n.)* **flavour**
መቐረት ዘይብሉ meq̈eret zeyblu *(n.)* **vulgarity**
መቀፀልታ meqexelta *(n.)* **continuation**
መቀያየዲ meqeyayedi *(n.)* **moorings**
መቓቐለ meqhaqhele *(v.)* **sunder**
መቐረት meqheret *(n.)* **sweetness**
መቐየርታ meqhe'yerta *(n.)* **substitute**
መቐየሪ meqhyeri *(n.)* **switch**
መቓልሕ meqlḣ *(n.)* **echo**
መቆምያ meqomya *(n.)* **scaffolding**
መቅረዝ meqrez *(n.)* **candela**
መቅረዝ meqrez *(n.)* **chandelier**
መቑሹሽ meqshush *(v.)* **perk**
መቁሕ እግሪ mequh 'egri *(n.)* **shackle**
መቁሕ ኢድ mequḧ 'id *(n.)* **handcuff**
መቐረጽ ወረቐት meq̈uretsi wereq̈et *(n.)* **guillotine**
መቑሪ mequri *(n.)* **probe**
መቑሹሽ meq̈ushush *(n.)* **bonus**
መቋደሲ meqwadesi *(adj.)* **indulgent**
መቌለፍ meq̈welef *(n.)* **buckle**
መቐሎ meq̈wulo *(n.)* **griddle**
መቕጻዕቲ meq̈xaëti *(n.)* **punishment**
መቅይሒ meqyḧi *(n.)* **blusher**

መቅይሒ ምዕጉርቲ meqyĥi m'ëgurti *(n.)* **rouge**
መቅዘፊ meqzefi *(n.)* **flipper**
መቕዘፍቲ meq̈zefti *(n.)* **cataclysm**
መቕዘፍቲ meq̈zefti *(n.)* **catastrophe**
መርዓ mer'a *(n.)* **wedding**
መራሕ ብርጌድ meraḧ brgeed *(n.)* **brigadier**
መራሕ መንገዲ meraḧ mengedi *(n.)* **pacemaker**
መራሒ merahi *(n.)* **leader**
መራሒ meraḧi *(n.)* **conductor**
መራሒ መንግስቲ merahi menegeseti *(n.)* **chancellor**
መራሒ ዋኒን meraĥi wanin *(n.)* **entrepreneur**
መራኽቦ meraḱbo *(n.)* **confluence**
መራኽቢ merakebi *(n.)* **rendezvous**
መራኽቢ meraḱebi *(n.)* **junction**
መራኽቢ meraḱebi *(n.)* **juncture**
መራኽቢ ቦታ meraḱebi bota *(n.)* **venue**
መራኽቢ ብዙሓን meraḱebi bzuḧan *(n.)* **media**
መራት merat *(adj.)* **rusty**
መርዓት mer'ät *(n.)* **bride**
መርዓዊ mer'äwi *(v.)* **groom**
መርዓዊ mer'äwi *(n.)* **bridegroom**
መራθሚ meraxemi *(n.)* **bumper**
መራፆ meraxo *(n.)* **constituency**
መራፆ meraxo *(n.)* **electorate**
ምዕራይ m'ëray *(n.)* **rectification**
መርኣያ mer'aya *(adj.)* **earnest**
መርኣያ mer'aya *(n.)* **epitome**
መርኣያ mer'aya *(n.)* **sample**
መርኣያ መንነት mer'aya mennet *(adj.)* **bespoke**
መርኣዪ ፈተነ ምድላው merayi fetene mdlaw *(n.)* **prototype**
መርብብ merbb *(n.)* **grid**
መርበብ merbeb *(n.)* **intranet**
መርበብ merbeb *(n.)* **mesh**
መርበብ merbeb *(n.)* **net**
መርበብ merbeb *(n.)* **netting**
መረበ mereba *(n.)* **foyer**
መረበ mereba *(n.)* **yard**
መረበ mereba *(n.)* **patio**
መረዳእታ mereda'èta *(n.)* **illustration**
መረዳእታ ኣቕረበ mereda'eta aqrebe *(v.)* **corroborate**
መረዳእታ mered'eta *(n.)* **evidence**
መሬት mereet *(n.)* **land**
መረጋገጺ meregagetsi *(n.)* **testament**
መረጋገጺ meregagexi *(n.)* **assurance**
መረጋገጺ meregagexi *(n.)* **proof**
መረን meren *(n.)* **rein**
መረቅ mereq *(n.)* **minestrone**
መረቕ mereq̈ *(n.)* **broth**
መረቀ mereqe *(v.)* **inaugurate**
ምእረራ m'èrera *(n.)* **browser**
መረሸ mereshe *(v.)* **march**
መረፃ meretsa *(n.)* **poll**
መረፃ meretsa *(n.)* **suffrage**
መረθ meretse *(v. t)* **choose**
መረθ meretse *(v.)* **select**
መረፃ merexa *(n.)* **election**
መረθ merexe *(v.)* **elect**
መረጸ merexe *(v.)* **prefer**
መረዘ mereze *(v.)* **intoxicate**
መርፍእ merf'e *(n.)* **needle**
መርፊእ ምውጋእ merfi'e mwga'e *(n.)* **injection**
መርገም mergem *(n.)* **curse**
መርገጺ mergetsi *(n.)* **stance**
መርገፂ mergetzi *(n.)* **footing**

መርጉ mergwi *(n.)* **stucco**
መርሓ ግብሪ merha gbri *(n.)* **prospectus**
መርሐ merĥe *(v.)* **preside**
መርሐ merḧe *(v.)* **conduct**
መሪድያን meridyan *(n.)* **meridian**
መሪሕ meriḥ *(n.)* **vanguard**
መሪሕነት merihnet *(n.)* **leadership**
መሪሕነት merihnet' *(n.)* **chieftain**
መሪር merir *(adj.)* **bitter**
መሪፁ ዝወስድ meritsu zwesd *(adj.)* **selective**
መርጀን merjen *(n.)* **coral**
መርከብ merkeb *(n.)* **cruiser**
መርከብ merkeb *(n.)* **ferry**
መርከብ merkeb *(n.)* **ship**
መርከብ merkeb *(n.)* **shipping**
መርማሪ mermari *(n.)* **coroner**
መርማሪ ገበን mermari geben *(n.)* **detective**
መርማሪ ገበን mermari geben *(n.)* **sleuth**
መርመራ mermera *(n.)* **investigation**
መርመራ ኣስከሬን mermera askegrien *(n.)* **post-mortem**
መርመረ mermere *(v.)* **inspect**
መርሚሩ ፈለጠ mermiru felete *(v.)* **diagnose**
መርቅዒ merq'ë *(n.)* **rivet**
መርሳ mersa *(n.)* **harbour**
መርትዖ ኣቕረበ mert'ö *(v.)* **prove**
መርውሓ merwḥa *(n.)* **ventilator**
መርዛም merzam *(adj.)* **noxious**
መርዛም merzam *(adj.)* **poisonous**
መርዛም merzam *(adj.)* **venomous**
መርዛማ merzama *(adj.)* **toxic**
መርዛማ merzama *(n.)* **toxin**
መርዘን merzen *(n.)* **migraine**
መርዚ ኣወገደ merzi awegede *(v.)* **detoxify**
መሳገሪ mesageri *(n.)* **crossing**
መሳገሪ ሓጹር mesageri hatsur *(n.)* **stile**
መስኣሊት mes'alit *(n.)* **camera**
መሳልል mesall *(n.)* **ladder**
መሳርሒያዊ mesarhawi *(adj.)* **instrumental**
መሳርሒ mesarhi *(n.)* **instrument**
መሳርሒ mesarĥi *(n.)* **device**
መሳርሒ mesarĥi *(n.)* **equipment**
መሳርሒ mesarĥi *(n.)* **gadget**
መሳርሒ mesarḧi *(n.)* **apparatus**
መሳርሒ mesarḧi *(n.)* **hard drive**
መሳርሒ mesarḥi *(n.)* **kit**
መሳርሕቲ mesarḧti *(n.)* **colleague**
መሳርያ ምጉዕዓዝ mesarya mgu'ë'äz *(n.)* **vehicle**
መሳሰዪ mesaseyi *(n.)* **accommodation**
መሳጢ mesati *(v.)* **imposing**
መሳጢ mesati *(adj.)* **scenic**
መሳጢ mesaẗi *(n.)* **cynosure**
መስበኽያ mesbeḱya *(n.)* **pulpit**
መሰጋገሪ mesegageri *(n.)* **gangway**
መሰጋገሪ mesegageri *(n.)* **portage**
መሰገድ mesegodi *(n.)* **gasket**
መስኮት mesekote *(n.)* **casement**
መሰልቸዪ meselchyi *(adj.)* **tedious**
መሰለ mesele *(v.)* **purport**
መሰለ mesele *(v.)* **resemble**
መሰለ mesele *(v.)* **seem**
መሰለ mesele *(v.)* **simulate**
መሰናድኢ mesenad'i *(adj.)* **preparatory**
መሰናኽል mesenakl *(n.)* **drawback**
መሰናኽል mesenaḱl *(n.)* **hurdle**

መሰንበድ ኳኽ mesenbed ka'k ***(n.)*** **scarecrow**
መሰነዪ meseneyi ***(n.)*** **escort**
መሰነዪ meseneyi ***(n.)*** **bouncer**
መሰነይታ meseneyta ***(n.)*** **company**
መሰንገል mesengel ***(n.)*** **rib**
መሰንቀር mesenqer ***(n.)*** **chopstick**
መሰንይቲ mesenyti ***(n.)*** **accompaniment**
መሰረት meseret ***(n.)*** **foundation**
መሰረት meseret ***(n.)*** **rudiment**
መሰረት ኣልቦ meseret 'albo ***(adj.)*** **groundless**
መሰረት ዘይብሉ meseret zeyblu ***(adj.)*** **unfounded**
መሰረታዊ meseretawi ***(adj.)*** **essential**
መሰረታዊ meseretawi ***(adj.)*** **fundamental**
መሰረታዊ ሞገት meseretawi moget ***(adj.)*** **rudimentary**
መሰረተ ኩርናዕ meserete kurn'ë ***(n.)*** **milestone**
መሰረተ ልምዓት meserete lm'at ***(n.)*** **infrastructure**
መሰጠ mesete ***(v.)*** **impress**
መሰጠ meseẗe ***(v.)*** **enthral**
መሰጠ meseẗe ***(v.)*** **fascinate**
መሰጠ meseẗe ***(v.)*** **captivate**
መሰውያ mesewya ***(n.)*** **altar**
መሰየሚ meseyemi ***(n.)*** **denomination**
መስፈዪ mesfeyi ***(n.)*** **suture**
መስፍን mesfn ***(n.)*** **viscount**
መስፍንነት mesfnnet ***(n.)*** **feudalism**
መሽጊ mešgi ***(n.)*** **slat**
መስጊድ mesgid ***(n.)*** **mosque**
መስሓቢ ማሽን meshabi mashn ***(n.)*** **pulley**
መስሓቢ meshabi ***(n.)*** **bait**
መስሓቕ meshaq̈ ***(n.)*** **farce**
መስሓቕ meshaq̈ ***(n.)*** **jest**
መስሓቒን meshaqeen ***(n.)*** **clown**
መስሓቒን mes'haqeen ***(adj.)*** **ludicrous**
መስሓቒን meshaqeen ***(n.)*** **antic**
መስሓቒን meshaq̈een ***(n.)*** **buffoon**
መስሓቒ meshaqhi ***(adj.)*** **laughable**
መሸፈን ሉሕ meshefen luḥ ***(n.)*** **veneer**
መሸፈኒ meshefeni ***(n.)*** **cover**
መሸፈኒ ሻሽ meshefeni shash ***(n.)*** **yashmak**
መሸጋገሪ ቦታ meshegageri bota ***(n.)*** **transit**
መሸጋገሪ፣ናይ ሽግግር ወቕቲ/ግዜ meshegageri,na mshiggar gze ***(n.)*** **transition**
መሸጎሪ meshegori ***(n.)*** **latch**
መሸጐር meshegwar ***(n.)*** **bolt**
መሸሊት ወዲ ተባዕታይ mesheit nay wedi tebaetay ***(n.)*** **penis**
መሸከል meshekel ***(n.)*** **physique**
መሸንበባ በረድ meshenboba bered ***(n.)*** **hail**
መሸኒ mesheni ***(n.)*** **urinal**
መሸንቆቋ meshenqoqa ***(n.)*** **noose**
መሸራሸሪ ህዝቢ mesherasheri hzbi ***(n.)*** **promenade**
መሸጣ mesheta ***(n.)*** **sale**
መሸገጥ meshget ***(n.)*** **locker**
መሸጐራጉር meshgwaragur ***(n.)*** **alley**
መሸሎኺ meshloki ***(n.)*** **hatch**
መሸሎቐ meshloqe ***(v.)*** **scald**
መሸምበባ meshombeba ***(n.)*** **volley**
መሲሕ mesiḧ ***(n.)*** **messiah**

መስከረም meskerem *(n.)* **September**
መስኮት meskot *(n.)* **pane**
መስኮት meskot *(n.)* **window**
መስኮት አፍንጫ meskot afnča *(n.)* **nostril**
መሽኮት በለ meškot bele *(v.)* **slink**
መስመር ጎኒ mesmer goni *(n.)* **sideline**
መስመር መኾስተር mesmer meḱoster *(n.)* **Hoover**
መስመስታ mesmesta *(n.)* **sheen**
መስኖ mesno *(n.)* **irrigation**
መስቀል mesqel *(n.)* **cross**
መስቀላዊ ዘመተ mesqelawi zemete *(n.)* **crusade**
መስቆሪቶ mesqorito *(n.)* **lobe**
መስራቲ mesrati *(n.)* **founder**
መስርዕ mesr'e *(n.)* **train**
መስርዕ mesr'ë *(n.)* **queue**
መስረብያ mesrebya *(n.)* **distillery**
መሰረታዊ ሞገት mesretawi moget *(n.)* **rationale**
መስረተ mesrete *(v.)* **situate**
መስርሕ mesrȟ *(n.)* **process**
መስርሕ ምርካብ mesrȟ mrkab *(n.)* **procurement**
መስርሳ ምግቢ mesrhi mgbi *(n.)* **wok**
መስታ mesta *(adj.)* **coeval**
መስተ meste *(n.)* **beverage**
መስተፋቅራዊ mestefaqrawi *(adj.)* **amatory**
መስተማሰሊ mestemaseli *(adj.)* **maudlin**
መስተማሰሊ meste'maseli *(adj.)* **sullen**
መስተንክር mestenkr *(adj.)* **spectacular**
መስተንክር mestenkr *(adj.)* **swashbuckling**
መስተርእየት mester'eyet *(n.)* **spectacle**
መስተዋድድ mestewadd *(n.)* **preposition**
መስተውዓሊ mestewali *(adj.)* **percipient**
መስተውዐሊ mestew'ali *(adj.)* **sagacious**
መስተውዓሊ mestewäli *(adj.)* **provident**
መስተውዓሊ mestew'äli *(adj.)* **judicious**
መስተውዓሊ mestew'äli *(adj.)* **reasonable**
መስተፃምር mestexamr *(n.)* **conjunction**
መስትዋት mestwat *(n.)* **mirror**
መስዋእታዊ meswa'etawi *(adj.)* **sacrificial**
መስዋእቲ meswa'eti *(n.)* **sacrifice**
መስዋእቲ meswa'èti *(n.)* **victim**
መጣበቒ meẗabeqi *(n.)* **glue**
መታለሊ metaleli *(n.)* **cheat**
መታለሊ metaleli *(adj.)* **cunning**
መታለሊ metaleli *(adj.)* **deceitful**
መታለሊ metaleli *(adj.)* **fraudulent**
መታለሊ metaleli *(adj.)* **illusory**
መታለሊ metaleli *(adj.)* **perfidious**
መታለሊ metaleli *(n.)* **trickster**
መታወር metawer *(n.)* **bar**
መጥባሕቲ meẗbahti *(n.)* **surgery**
መጥባሕቲ መትረብ ዘርኢ meẗbaȟti metreb zer'i *(n.)* **vasectomy**
መጥብሒ metbhi *(n.)* **lancet**
መተዓሻሸዊ ነገር m-ete-a-sha-she-wi neger *(n.)* **gimmick**
መተባበዒ metebab'e *(n.)* **incentive**

መተባብዒ metebab'e *(n.)* **inducement**
መተሓበሪ metehababeri *(n.)* **directory**
መተሓላለፊ metehalalefi *(n.)* **passage**
መተሓፃፀቢ ኣቁሑት metehasasebi akuhut *(n.)* **toiletries**
መተሓፃፀቢ metehatsatsebi *(n.)* **sink**
መተካእታ metekaeta *(n.)* **replacement**
መተካእታ meteka'eta *(n.)* **surrogate**
መተኮራዊ metekorawi *(adj.)* **focal**
መተኮስ ሬሳ metekos resa *(n.)* **pyre**
መጠን meten *(n.)* **proportion**
መጠን meten *(n.)* **rate**
መጠን meẗen *(n.)* **amount**
መጠን ድንገት meten dnget *(n.)* **incidence**
መጠነ ሓለፍ meten ḧalef *(n.)* **surfeit**
መጠን ዝናብ meten znab *(n.)* **rainfall**
መጠነኛ meẗenegna *(adj.)* **middling**
መተንፈሲ metenfesi *(n.)* **respirator**
መጠንከርያ metenkerya *(n.)* **toner**
መጠንቀቕታ metenqekta *(n.)* **caution**
መጠንቀቒ meẗenqeq̈i *(v.)* **portend**
መጠንቀቕታ meẗenqeq̈ta *(n)* **alarm**
መጠንቀቕታ meṭenqeq̈ta *(n.)* **warning**
መጠንጠኒ meẗenẗeni *(n.)* **spool**
መጠቓለሊ meẗeqaleli *(n.)* **summary**
መጠቅለሊ meteqleli *(n.)* **roller**
መጠቕለሊ meẗeq̈leli *(n.)* **package**
መተርኣስ meter'as *(n.)* **cushion**
መተርኣስ meteras *(n.)* **pillow**
መተርኣስ ብርኪ meter'as brki *(n.)* **hassock**

መተረ metere *(v.)* **mince**
መጠርነፍታ meẗernefta *(n.)* **synopsis**
መጠጠ meẗeẗe *(v.)* **stretch**
መጠይቅ meteyk *(n.)* **questionnaire**
መጠፋፍኢ metfaf'ï *(adj.)* **shifty**
መጥፍኢ ጸጉሪ metf'i tseguri *(adj.)* **depilatory**
መጥሓን meẗ'ḧan *(n.)* **mill**
መትሓዚ methazi *(n.)* **container**
መትከል metkel *(n.)* **principle**
መትከል metkel *(n.)* **tenet**
መትከል metkel *(n.)* **theorem**
መትከል ስነ ምግባር metkel sne mgbar *(n.)* **morality**
መትከር metker *(n.)* **hassle**
መትከር metker *(n.)* **nuisance**
መትኮብ metkob *(n.)* **beak**
መጥምቓዊ meẗmq̈awi *(n.)* **Baptist**
መትናዊ metnawi *(adj.)* **nervous**
መትኒ metni *(n.)* **Nerve**
መጥቃዕቲ meẗqa'ëti *(n.)* **aggression**
መጥቃዕቲ meẗq'ëti *(n.)* **assault**
መጠራቀሚ metraqemi *(n.)* **receptacle**
መትረብ metreb *(n.)* **canal**
መትረብ metreb *(n.)* **channel**
መትረብ metreb *(n.)* **ditch**
መትረብ ፍሳስ metreb fsas *(n.)* **sewerage**
መትረብ ግንቢ metreb g'nbi *(n.)* **moat**
መፃኢ metsai *(adj.)* **upcoming**
መጻንሒ metsanhi *(adj.)* **tentative**
መፃረዪ metsareyi *(n.)* **refinery**
መፃወዲ metsawedi *(n.)* **decoy**
መጽሎ metselo *(n.)* **hob**
መፀዋዕታ metsewa'eta *(n.)* **summons**

መፀዋዕታ metsewa'ëta ***(n.)*** **invitation**
መጽሓፍ metshaf ***(n.)*** **textbook**
መፂሄት metsihiet ***(n.)*** **magazine**
መፂፀ metsits ***(adj.)*** **sour**
መፅለሊ metsleli ***(n.)*** **shed**
መፅናዕቲ metsna'eti ***(n.)*** **study**
መፅናዕቲ metsnaëti ***(n.)*** **research**
መፅናዕቲ ምዕባለ ቋንቋታት metsnaeti m'ëbale qanqatat ***(n.)*** **philology**
መፅናንዒ metsna'n'i ***(n.)*** **solace**
መጽንሒ መልእኽቲ metsnhi melekti ***(n.)*** **voicemail**
መፅወድያ metswedya ***(n.)*** **snare**
መጥወዪ meẗweyi ***(n.)*** **crook**
መፃኢ metza'i ***(n.)*** **future**
መፀባበቂ metzebabeqi ***(n.)*** **make-up**
መፀየ metzeye ***(v.)*** **leach**
መዋጮ mewacho ***(n.)*** **kitty**
መዋእል mewa'el ***(n.)*** **standing**
መዋኢ mewa'i ***(n.)*** **victor**
መዋኽር mewaker ***(n.)*** **gazebo**
መዋላይ mewalay ***(n.)*** **financier**
መዋላይ mewalay ***(n.)*** **sponsor**
መዋኽራዊ mewaqhrawi ***(adj.)*** **structural**
መዋኽር mewaqr ***(n.)*** **framework**
መዋቅር mewaqr ***(n.)*** **machinery**
መዋኽር mewaqr ***(n.)*** **structure**
መዋቲ mewati ***(adj.)*** **mortal**
መዋጥር mewatr ***(n.)*** **dilemma**
መውዓይ mew'äy ***(n.)*** **heating**
መወዳእታ mewedaeta ***(adj.)*** **ultimate**
መወዳእታ meweda'èta ***(n.)*** **conclusion**
መወዳእታ meweda'èta ***(adj.)*** **final**
መወዳእታ ዘይብሉ meweda'èta zeyblu ***(adj.)*** **interminable**
መወዳእታ ኣልቦ meweda'ta albo ***(n.)*** **infinity**
መወድስ meweds ***(n.)*** **rhapsody**
መወጅሂ mewejhi ***(n.)*** **conditioner**
መወቃቀቢ mewekakebi ***(n.)*** **decor**
መዉዓሊ ህፃናት mew'eli hxanat ***(n.)*** **crèche**
መውዐሊ ህፃናት mew'ëli hxanat ***(n.)*** **nursery**
መውዕሎ mew'ëlo ***(n.)*** **allowance**
መወልወሊ mewelweli ***(n.)*** **towelling**
መወልወሊ ኣፍ mewelweli a'f ***(n.)*** **napkin**
መወናወኒ mewenaweni ***(n.)*** **allure**
መወስቦኣዊ mewesbo'awi ***(v.t. & i.)*** **conjugal**
መወሰኽታ mewesekhta ***(n.)*** **supplement**
መውቃዕቲ mewqa'ëti ***(n.)*** **concussion**
መውቅዒ mewqe ***(n.)*** **whip**
መውቀጢ mewqeẗi ***(n.)*** **mortar**
መውስቦኣዊ mewsbo'awi ***(adj.)*** **matrimonial**
መዉፅኢ mewx'i ***(n.)*** **exit**
መውጽኢ-ነፍሲ mewx'inefsi ***(n.)*** **alibi**
መጽጻወቲ ቦታ mexaweti bota ***(n.)*** **playground**
መጸ mexe ***(v.)*** **accede**
መጸ mexe ***(v.)*** **arrive**
መፀባበቒ mexebabeqi ***(adj.)*** **cosmetic**
መፀባበቂ ቕብኣት mexebabeqi qb'at ***(n.)*** **cosmetic**
መፅናዕንዒ mexenaee'neeeii ***(n.)*** **consolation**

መፀውዒ mexew''ï *(n.)* **nomenclature**
መጸየ mexeye *(v.)* **absorb**
መጽሓፍ mexḧaf *(n.)* **book**
መጽሓፍ ንጀመርቲ mexḧaf *(n.)* **primer**
መጽሓፍ ቅዱስ mexḧaf qdus *(n.)* **Bible**
መጽሓፍ ሸያጢት mexḧaf sheyaẗit *(n.)* **bookseller**
መጺፅ mexix *(adj.)* **acerbic**
መፅለሊ mexleli *(n.)* **filter**
መጽናዕቲ ድምጺ ልሳን mexnaeti dmxi lsan *(adj.)* **phonetic**
መዛግብቲ mezagbti *(n.)* **archives**
መዛዘሚ mezazemi *(n.)* **finial**
መዛዘሚ mezazemi *(n.)* **selvedge**
መዛዘሚ mezazemi *(n.)* **binding**
መዝበብ mezbeb *(n.)* **spout**
መዘኻኸሪ mezekakeri *(n.)* **reminder**
መዘኻኸሪ mezeḱakeri *(n.)* **memento**
መዘኻኸሪ mezeḱaḱeri *(n.)* **note**
መዘኻኸሪት mezeḱaḱerit *(n.)* **notebook**
መዘከርታ mezekerta *(n.)* **keepsake**
መዘከርታ mezekerta *(n.)* **souvenir**
መዘክር mezekr *(n.)* **memo**
መዘክር mezekr *(n.)* **memorandum**
መዘምራን mezemeran *(n.)* **choir**
መዘምራን mezemeran *(adj.)* **latent**
መዘምራዊ mezemrawi *(adj.)* **choral**
መዘና mezena *(n.)* **counterpart**
መዘና ኣንበ mezena albo *(adj.)* **peerless**
መዘና ኣልቦ mezena albo *(adj.)* **superlative**
መዘና ዘይብሉ mezena zeyblu *(adj.)* **nonpareil**
መዘናግዒ ክፍሊ(ሳሎን) mezenagei kfli *(n.)* **parlour**
መዘናግዒ mezenag'i *(n.)* **entertainment**
መዘናግዒ ቦታ mezenag'ï bota *(n.)* **resort**
መዘነ mezene *(v.)* **weigh**
መዘዘ mezeze *(v.)* **authorize**
መዝገብ mezgeb *(n.)* **dossier**
መዝገብ mezgeb *(n.)* **ledger**
መዝገብ mezgeb *(n.)* **register**
መስመር msmer *(n.)* **line**
መስመር msmer *(n.)* **wiring**
መስርዕ ሕብርታት ናይ ዝተዋህበ ስራሕ msrie hbrtat nay ztewahbe srah *(n.)* **palette**
መጥበውቲ mtbeewti *(n.)* **mammal**
መዝገብ mezgeb *(n.)* **trench**
መዝገበ mezgebe *(v.t.)* **jot**
መዝገበ ቃላት mezgebe kalat *(n.)* **dictionary**
መዝገበ ቃላት mezgebe qalat *(n.)* **lexicon**
መዝገበ-ታሪኽ mezgebe tarik *(n.)* **annals**
መዝሓሊ mezhali *(n.)* **cooler**
መዝሓሊ mezḧali *(n.)* **fridge**
መዝሓሊት mezḧalit *(n.)* **freezer**
መዝሓቀ mezĥaqe *(v.)* **extrude**
መዚ mezi *(n.)* **authority**
መዝሙር mezmur *(n.)* **anthem**
መዝሙር mezmur *(n.)* **chorus**
መዝሙር ዳዊት mezmur dawit *(n.)* **psalm**
መዞሪ mezori *(n.)* **roundabout**
መዞሪ mezori *(n.)* **winder**
መዝረጊ mezregi *(n.)* **spoiler**
መዝረቕ mezreq *(n.)* **skewer**

መዝወሪ ንፋስ mezweri nfas *(n.)* **whirlwind**
መፍረ ሓሰማ mfre hasema *(n.)* **piggery**
መገዛዝኢ mgza'è *(n.)* **governance**
መሓሪ mhari *(adj.)* **clement**
መፀውዒ ሽም qendi *(n.)* **forename**
መኻን mkhan *(adj.)* **infertile**
መልእኽቲ ml'ḱti *(n.)* **message**
መወለዒ mwel'e *(n.)* **lighter**
መዘና mzena *(n.)* **peer**
መሓላ mehala *(n.)* **oath**
መሐብሐቢ ዘኽታም ህፃናት mehebhebi zektam htsanat *(n.)* **orphanage**
መላዘቢ melazebi *(n.)* **overture**
መስርዕ mesr'e *(n.)* **order**
መስዋእቲ meswa'eti *(n.)* **offering**
መርመረ mermere *(v.)* **overlook**
መበቈላውነት mebeqolawinet *(n.)* **originality**
መከራ mekera *(n.)* **ordeal**
መካነ-ትዕዝብቲ mekane-t'ezebti *(n.)* **observatory**
መኰነን mekonen *(n.)* **officer**
መውጽኢ mewts'i *(n.)* **outlet**
መደረ medere *(n.)* **oration**
መዳራይ medaray *(n.)* **orator**
መድሓኒት ልዕሊ መጠን ምውሳድ medhanit l'eli meten mwsad *(n.)* **overdose**
መጀመሪ mejemeri *(n.)* **originator**
መጀመሪ mejemeri *(n.)* **outset**
መጀመርያ mejemerya *(n.)* **onset**
መጥቃዕቲ metqa'ëti *(n.)* **offence**
መጸለዪ ክፍሊ mrtseleyi kfli *(n.)* **oratory**
መጸባበቒ metsebabeqi *(n.)* **ornament**

ሙ

ሙዚቃዊ ቅናት muziqawi qnat *(n.)* **orchestra**
ሙዚቃዊ ቅናት muziqawi qnat *(adj.)* **orchestral**
ሙሉእ ሂወት mlu'e hiwet *(adj.)* **lifelong**
ሙሉእ milu'e *(adj.)* **full**
ሙጒሊ muguili *(n.)* **pus**
ሙሁር muhur *(adj.)* **literate**
ሙቅ muk *(adj.)* **thermal**
ሙቀት እና ደርቅ ኣየር muket ena derq ayer *(n.)* **tropic**
ሙኮራ mukora *(n.)* **trial**
ሙላህ mulah *(n.)* **mullah**
ሙልሳ mulsa *(n.)* **mousse**
ሙሉእ mulu'e *(adj.)* **entire**
ሙሉእ ብሙሉእ mulu'e bmulu'e *(prep.)* **throughout**
ሙሉእ ሓሳብ mulu'e hasab *(n.)* **sentence**
ሙምያ mumya *(n.)* **mummy**
ሙቀት መቆፃፀሪ ብልሃት muqet meqosaser blhat *(n.)* **thermostat**
ሙቀት መጠን muqet meten *(n.)* **temperature**
ሙራለ murale *(n.)* **joist**
ሙስካ muska *(n.)* **musk**
ሙስኪቶ muskito *(n.)* **musket**
ሙስኬተኛ muskitogna *(n.)* **musketeer**
ሙስሊ musli *(n.)* **muesli**
ሙስሊን muslin *(v.)* **muslin**
ሙስታንግ mustang *(n.)* **mustang**
ሙስቴላ musteela *(n.)* **mink**
ሙታንታ mutanta *(n.)* **underpants**
ሙታንታ mutanta *(n.)* **underwear**
ሙታንቲ mutanti *(n.)* **panties**

ሙዝ muz *(n.)* **banana**
ሙዛ muza *(n.)* **muse**
ሙዚቃ መሰርሒ muzika mesarhi *(n.)* **zither**
ሙዚቃ muziqa *(n.)* **music**
ሙዚቃዊ muziqawi *(adj.)* **jazzy**
ሙዚቃዊ muziqawi *(adj.)* **musical**
ሙዚቃዊ ምርኢት muziqawi mr'it *(n.)* **concert**
ሙዚቀኛ muziqegna *(n.)* **musician**

ሚ

ሚዛኑ ሰሓተ mizanu seȟate *(v.)* **overbalance**
ሚዶ/መመሸጥ mido/memesheti *(n.)* **comb**
ሚሽሚሽ mishmishe *(n.)* **apricot**
ሚእታዊት mietawit *(n.)* **percentage**
ሚእቲ mi-eti *(adj.& n.)* **hundred**
ሚሐ miḧe *(n.)* **matrix**
ሚላሳ milasa *(n.)* **molasses**
ሚትራ mitra *(n.)* **mitre**
ሚሊግራም miligram *(n.)* **milligram**
ሚሊሜትር milimeetr *(n.)* **millimetre**
ሚልየን milyen *(n.)* **million**
ሚልየነር milyener *(n.)* **millionaire**
ሚና mina *(n.)* **mine**
ሚኒባስ minibas *(n.)* **minibus**
ሚኒካብ minikab *(n.)* **minicab**
ሚኒም minim *(n.)* **minim**
ሚኒስከርት miniskert *(n.)* **miniskirt**
ሚኒስተር minister *(n.)* **minister**
ሚኒስተራዊ ministrawi *(adj.)* **ministerial**
ሚርቶ mirto *(n.)* **myrtle**
ሚስማር mismar *(n.)* **nail**
ሚስጥራዊ mis̆tirawi *(adj.)* **subtle**
ሚስጢርነት mis̆tirnet *(n.)* **subtlety**
ሚስጥር mis̆tr *(n.)* **mystery**
ሚዛን mizan *(n.)* **scale**
ሚዛናዊ mizanawi *(adj.)* **equitable**
ሚዛናዊ mizanawi *(adj.)* **fair**

ማ

ማዕጠቕ ma'ëťeq *(n.)* **girth**
ማህደረ ቃላት mahdere qalat *(n.)* **glossary**
ማጀንታ maĵenta *(n.)* **magenta**
ማዕክል meee'kele *(n.)* **centre**
ማዕበል maebel *(n.)* **turbulence**
ማዕበል ma'ebel *(n.)* **storm**
ማዕበላዊ maebelawi *(adj.)* **wavy**
ማዕበላዊ ma'ebelawi *(adj.)* **stormy**
ማዕበላዊ ma'ebelawi *(adj.)* **tidal**
ማዕበላዊ ma'ebelawi *(n.)* **tidally**
ማዕበለ ma'ebele *(v.)* **wave**
ማዕበለ ma'ëbele *(v.)* **evolve**
ማዕዳ ma'ëda *(n.)* **recommendation**
ማእዳ ዝግበኦ ma'eda zgbe'o *(adj.)* **meritorious**
ማዕድን maeden *(n.)* **zircon**
ማዕድን ma-e-den *(n.)* **garnet**
ማዕድን ma'edn *(n.)* **talc**
ማእገር ma'eger *(n.)* **shoulder**
ማዕቐፍ ma-ekef *(n.)* **gamut**
ማእኸል ma'eḱel *(adj.)* **midst**
ማእኸላይ ma'eḱelay *(adj.)* **median**
ማእኸላይ ma'eḱelay *(n.)* **medium**
ማእኸላይ ma'eḱelay *(adj.)* **middle**
ማእከላይ ma'èkelay *(adj.)* **intermediate**
ማእኸላይ ሰለዋ ma'ëḱelay selewa *(n.)* **mezzanine**

ማእከላይ ma'èkelay ***(n.)* average**
ማዕከን ma'ëken ***(n.)* granary**
ማዕከን ሓበሬታ ma'ëken ĥabereta ***(n.)* database**
ማእኸል ma'ekhel ***(n.)* locus**
ማእኸል መዘናግዒ ma'ekhel mezanag'e ***(n.)* lounge**
ማዕረ ma'ere ***(n.)* stalemate**
ማዕረ ma'ëre ***(adj.)* equal**
ማዕረ ma'ëre ***(adj.)* quits**
ማዕረ ገበረ ma'ëre gebere ***(v. t)* equalize**
ማዕረ ጌሩ ረአየ ma'ëre gieru re'aye ***(v.)* equate**
ማዕረ ዝርሕቀቱ ma'ëre zrĥqetu ***(adj.)* equidistant**
ማዕረ-ጐድናዊ ma'ëregwadnawi ***(adj.)* equilateral**
ማዕርነት maernet ***(n.)* parity**
ማዕርነት ኩነታት maernet kunetat ***(n.)* par**
ማእሰርቲ ma'eserti ***(n.)* bondage**
ማእሰርቲ ma'eserti ***(n.)* custody**
ማእሰርቲ ma'eserti ***(n.)* detention**
ማእሰርቲ ma'èserti ***(n.)* confinement**
ማዕተብ ma'ëteb ***(n.)* necklace**
ማዕጺድ ma'ëtsid ***(n.)* sickle**
ማዕፆ ma'ëtso ***(n.)* door**
ማዕጾ ርባ ma'ëtso rba ***(n.)* grating**
ማእዘር ma'ezer ***(n.)* spoke**
ማእዘራይ ma'ezeray ***(adj.)* radial**
ማእዝን ma'èzn ***(n.)* bearing**
ማፋ mafa ***(n.)* Louvre**
ማፋ ማይ mafa may ***(n.)* hydrant**
ማፊን mafin ***(n.)* muffin**

ምዕጋት mägat ***(n.)* prevention**
ማግኔት magnet ***(n.)* magnet**
ማግኔታዊ magnetawi ***(adj.)* magnetic**
ማግኔታዊነት magnetawinet ***(n.)* magnetism**
ማሕ በለ maĥ bele ***(v.)* flash**
ማሕበር maȟber ***(n.)* commune**
ማሕበር maȟber ***(n.)* confederation**
ማሕበር maḥber ***(n.)* guild**
ማሕበር ደናግል maĥber denagl ***(n.)* sisterhood**
ማሕበር maȟber ***(n.)* association**
ማሕበራት mahberat ***(n.)* unionist**
ማሕበራዊ mahberawi ***(adj.)* social**
ማሕበራዊ ከባቢ maȟberawi kebabi ***(n.)* milieu**
ማሕበራዊነት mahberawinet ***(n.)* socialism**
ማሕበረ ሰብ maȟbere seb ***(n.)* community**
ማሕበረሰብ ma'hbereseb ***(n.)* sociology**
ማሕበርነታዊ mahbernetawi ***(n. & adj.)* socialist**
ማሕደፍ maĥdef ***(n.)* rudder**
ማህደር mahder ***(n.)* portfolio**
ማህደር mahder ***(n.)* satchel**
ማህደረ ትምህርቲ mahdere tmhrti ***(n.)* scholarship**
ማሕበረሰባዊ mahebresebawi ***(adj.)* civil**
ማሕፉዳ maḥfuda ***(n.)* wallet**
ማሕበራዊ ደረጃ mahiberawi dereja ***(n.)* caste**
ማሕለኻ mahleka ***(n.)* disincentive**
ማህለት mahlet ***(n.)* hymn**
ማሕምም mahmm ***(n.)* chum**
ማሕቋቖ maĥqwaq ***(adj.)* emaciated**
ማሕረዲ mahredi ***(n.)* shambles**
ማሕረሳዊ maȟresawi ***(adj.)* agrarian**

ማሕሲእ mahsi'e ***(n.)*** **lamb**
ማሕተም mahtem ***(n.)*** **seal**
ማሕተም maȟtem ***(n.)*** **stamp**
ማህጸን mahxen ***(n.)*** **uterus**
ማህጸን mahxen ***(n.)*** **womb**
መካነ እንስሳት makane enssatat ***(n.)*** **zoo**
ማእኸላይ ma'ḱelay ***(adj.)*** **moderate**
ማእኸላይ ma'ḱelay ***(adj.)*** **neutral**
ማኪና makina ***(n.)*** **car**
ማማ mama ***(n.)*** **mum**
ማሞዝ mamoz ***(n.)*** **mammoth**
ማና mana ***(n.)*** **manna**
ማንጋኔዝ manganiez ***(n.)*** **manganese**
ማንጎ mango ***(n.)*** **mango**
ማንካ manka ***(n.)*** **spoon**
ማንካ ሙሉእ manka mulu'e ***(n.)*** **spoonful**
ማንም ይኹን manm yekun ***(pron.)*** **whoever**
ማንቋ manqwa ***(n.)*** **rift**
ማንታ manta ***(n.)*** **twin**
ማንቲለ mantile ***(n.)*** **hare**
ማንትለ mantle ***(n.)*** **rabbit**
ማንትራ mantra ***(n.)*** **mantra**
ማኑዋል manuwal ***(n.)*** **handbook**
ማዕበል ባሕሪ maobrl hahi ***(n.)*** **tide**
ማራኺ marakhi ***(adj.)*** **striking**
ማራኺ marakhi ***(adj.)*** **sublime**
ማራኺ maraki ***(n.)*** **captor**
ማራኺ maraki ***(adj.)*** **winsome**
ማራኺ maraḱi ***(adj.)*** **attractive**
ማራኺ maraḱi ***(adj.)*** **interesting**
ማራኺ maraḱi ***(adj.)*** **inviting**
ማራኺ maraḱi ***(adj.)*** **beautiful**
ማራኪ marakii ***(adj.)*** **charming**
ማራቶን maraton ***(n.)*** **marathon**
ማርጋሪን margarin ***(n.)*** **margarine**
ማርጋሪን margarin ***(n.)*** **aubergine**
ማርገሪታ margerita ***(n.)*** **daisy**
ማሪት marit ***(n.)*** **superstition**
ማሪታዊ maritawi ***(adj.)*** **superstitious**
ማርክስነት marksnet ***(n.)*** **Marxism**
ማርማላታ marmalade ***(n.)*** **marmalade**
ማርና marna ***(n.)*** **marl**
ማሮን maron ***(n.)*** **maroon**
ማርስ mars ***(n.)*** **Mars**
ማርሳፓን marsapan ***(n.)*** **marzipan**
ማርሽ marsh ***(n.)*** **gear**
ማርሻቤዲ marshabedi ***(n.)*** **pavement**
ማርሻል marshal ***(n.)*** **marshal**
ማርተሎ martelo ***(n.)*** **hammer**
ማሰነ masene ***(v.)*** **languish**
ማሰኛ masenya ***(n.)*** **bard**
ማስኬራ maskeera ***(n.)*** **mask**
ማታዶር mata'dor ***(n.)*** **matador**
ማይ may ***(n.)*** **water**
ማይ may ***(n.)*** **water**
ማይ ዓገት may 'äget ***(adj.)*** **waterproof**
ማይ ጨው may čew ***(n.)*** **brine**
ማይ ጨባ may cheba ***(n.)*** **whey**
ማይ ምዕጎ may m'ëgo ***(n.)*** **blister**
ማያዊ mayawi ***(n.)*** **ultramarine**
ማያዊ mayawi ***(adj.)*** **aquatic**
ማያዊ mayawi ***(adj.)*** **aqueous**
ማይ መዋህለሊ maye mwaheleli ***(n.)*** **cistern**
ማይካ mayka ***(n.)*** **mica**
ማይክሮ ባዮሎጂ maykro bayoloji ***(n.)*** **microbiology**
ማይክሮ ሰርጀሪ maykro serjeri ***(n.)*** **microsurgery**

ማይክሮቺፕ maykrochip ***(n.)*** **microchip**
ማይክሮፎን maykrofon ***(n.)*** **microphone**
ማይክሮ ሜትር maykromeetr ***(n.)*** **micrometer**
ማይክሮስኮፕ maykroskop ***(n.)*** **microscope**
ማይክሮዌቭ maykroweev ***(n.)*** **microwave**
ማይል mayl ***(n.)*** **mile**
ማዮነዝ mayonez ***(n.)*** **mayonnaise**
ማዮሲን mayosin ***(n.)*** **myosin**
ማይሰጠም mayseṭem ***(adj.)*** **watertight**
ማዘርቦርድ mazerbord ***(n.)*** **motherboard**
ሜዳ mieda ***(n.)*** **field**

ሜ

ሜላ ኣሰራርሓ miela aserarḧa ***(n.)*** **proceedings**
ሜንታ ፐፐሮኒ mienta peperoni ***(n.)*** **peppermint**
ሜዳልያ meedalya ***(n.)*** **medal**
ሜዳልዮን meedalyon ***(n.)*** **medallion**
ሜሎድራማ meelodrama ***(n.)*** **melodrama**
ሜሎድራማዊ meelodramawi ***(adj.)*** **melodramatic**
ሜማ meema ***(n.)*** **censorship**
ሜንታ meenta ***(n.)*** **mint**
ሜርኩሪ meerkury ***(n.)*** **mercury**
ሜስ mees ***(n.)*** **mead**
ሜታቦሊዝም meetabolizm ***(n.)*** **metabolism**
ሜታፊዚካ meetafizika ***(n.)*** **metaphysics**
ሜታፊዚካዊ meetafizikawi ***(adj.)*** **metaphysical**
ሜትር meetr ***(n.)*** **meter**
ሜትር meetre ***(n.)*** **metre**
ሜትሮኣዊ meetro'awi ***(adj.)*** **metric**
ሜትዮር meetyor ***(n.)*** **meteor**
ሜትዮሪካዊ meetyorikawi ***(adj.)*** **meteoric**
ሜትዮሮሎጂ meetyoroloji ***(n.)*** **meteorology**
ሜላ ደላዪ ሰብ mela delayi seb ***(n.)*** **trouble-shooter**
ሜጋ ባይት meega bayt ***(n.)*** **megabyte**
ሜጋ ሀርዝ meega herz ***(n.)*** **megahertz**
ሜጋ ፒክስል meega piksl ***(n.)*** **megapixel**
ሜኑ menu ***(n.)*** **menu**
ሜዳ በረድ meda bered ***(n.)*** **rink**

ም

ምዕዳግ mëdag ***(v.)*** **purchase**
ምውዓል mw'al ***(n.)*** **investment**
ምውዳድ mwdad ***(n.)*** **montage**
ምውዳድ mwdad ***(n.)*** **adjustment**
ምውድዳር mwddar ***(n.)*** **competition**
ምውፋር mwfar ***(n.)*** **sortie**
ምውጋእ mwgai ***(v.)*** **poke**
ምውካስ mwkas ***(n.)*** **reference**
ምውላድ mwlad ***(n.)*** **birth**
ምውልዋል mwlwal ***(n.)*** **polish**
ምውቕ mwq̈ ***(adj.)*** **fervid**
ምውራድ mwrad ***(n.)*** **ebb**
ምውራድ mwrad ***(n.)*** **perversion**

ምውራድ mwrad *(n.)* **landing**
ምውራር mwrar *(n.)* **invasion**
ምውዓይ መግቢ ባክተርያ ንምጥፋእ mwuay megbi bakteriya nmtfae *(adj.)* **pasteurized**
ምዉቅ mwuq *(adj.)* **spirited**
ምዉቕ ዝበለ mwuq zbele *(adj.)* **tepid**
ምዉቕን ምቹዊን mwuqn mchuwn *(adj.)* **cosy**
ምዉቕን ምቹዊን mwuqn mchuwn *(adj.)* **cosy**
ምውሳድ mwusad *(n.)* **takeaway**
ምዉት mwut *(adj.)* **deceased**
ምዉት mwut *(adj.)* **soulless**
ምውጻእ mwxae *(v.)* **withdraw**
ምውጻእ mwxae *(n.)* **withdrawal**
ምጽዓቕ mx'äq *(n.)* **concentration**
ምጽኣት mx'at *(n.)* **advent**
ምፀታይ mxetay *(n.)* **nectarine**
ምጽላም mxlam *(n.)* **calumny**
ምጽላይ mxlay *(v.)* **pray**
ምዝገባ mzgeba *(n.)* **registration**
ምዝማር mzmar *(v.)* **yodel**
ምዝመዛ mzmeza *(n.)* **extraction**
ምዝንጋዕ mzngaë *(n.)* **prank**
ምዝንጋዕ mznga'ë *(n.)* **distraction**
ምዝንጋዕ mznga'ë *(n.)* **evasion**
ምዝንጋዕ mznga'ë *(n.)* **recreation**
ምዝንጋዕ mznga'ë *(n.)* **amusement**
ምዝራብ ዘይኽእል mzrab zeykh'el *(adj.)* **inarticulate**
ምጽናዕ mxnae *(n.)* **persistence**
ምጽንናዕ mxnna'ë *(n.)* **condolence**
ምፅራይ mx'ray *(n.)* **enquiry**
ምፁ mxu *(n.)* **mongoose**
ምጽ'ዋት mxwat *(n.)* **alms**
ምፅያቕ mxyaq *(n.)* **mottle**
ምዩቕ በለ myuq̈ bele *(v.)* **blench**
ምይይጥ myyt *(n.)* **debate**
ምይይጥ myyt *(n.)* **discussion**
ምዝባለ mzbale *(n.)* **deformity**
ምዝባጥ mzbat *(n.)* **smack**
ምዝቡል mzbul *(adj.)* **abnormal**
ምዕዶ m'ëdo *(n.)* **advice**
ምብዓድ mb'ad *(n.)* **sedition**
ምብካል mbkal *(v.)* **pollute**
ምብኻይ mbḱay *(v.)* **blub**
ምብልዕላዕ mbl'ëlaë *(n.)* **reaction**
ምብልሻው mblshaw *(n.)* **blight**
ምብልሻው mblshaw *(n.)* **undoing**
ምብቋል mbqwal *(n.)* **germination**
ምብራድ mbrad *(n.)* **refrigeration**
ምብራህ mbrah *(n.)* **illumination**
ምብርዓን mbr'än *(n.)* **miscarriage**
ምብራቕ mbraq̈ *(n.)* **east**
ምብራቓዊ mbraq̈awi *(adj.)* **eastern**
ምብራር mbrar *(n.)* **expulsion**
ምብራር mbrar *(n.)* **repulsion**
መብረቕ mbreqh *(n.)* **lighting**
መበረቕ mbreqh *(n.)* **lightening**
ምብስባስ mbsbas *(v.)* **witter**
ምብትታን mbttan *(n.)* **rout**
ምቡኺዕ mbukwa'ë *(n.)* **fermentation**
ምብዛሕ mbzah *(n.)* **preponderance**
ምብዛሕ mbzaḧ *(v.)* **populate**
ምብዛሕ mbzaḧ *(n.)* **propagation**
ምጭባጥ mčbaẗ *(n.)* **compression**
ምቾት mchot *(n.)* **comfort**
ምቾት mchot *(n.)* **convenience**
ምቾት mchot *(n.)* **luxury**
ምቹው mchuw *(adj.)* **favourable**
ምቹው mchuw *(adj.)* **luxurious**
ምቹው mchuw *(adj.)* **suitable**
ምቹው mchuw *(n.)* **utopia**
ምቹው mchu'w *(adj.)* **comfortable**

ምቹዊ mchuwi *(adj.)* **convenient**
ምቹው mchuwi *(adj.)* **cuddly**
ምእዙዝ me-ezuz *(adj.)* **genial**
ምዕፋን m'efan *(n.)* **suffocation**
ምጉርምራም mgurmram *(v.i.)* **grunt**
ምሓዝ m-ha-z *(v.)* **grab**
ምሕኩልቲ mḥkulti *(n.)* **hip**
ምህሙን mhmun *(adj.)* **wan**
ምሕናቕ mḥnaq̈ *(n.)* **hanging**
ምንቃሕ mnkah *(v.)* **waken**
ምቕዳሕ mq̈daḥ *(n.)* **imitation**
ምቕማጥ mq̈maṭ *(n.)* **habitation**
ምርኢት mr'it *(n.)* **vaudeville**
ምስክር mskr *(n.)* **voucher**
ምስሌነ msleene *(n.)* **viceroy**
ምስሊ msli *(n.)* **image**
ምስማዕ msma'ë *(n.)* **hearing**
ምጽያቕ mtseyaq̈ *(n.)* **graffiti**
ምውላዕ mwla'ë *(n.)* **ignition**
ምሕረት meherte *(n.)* **clemency**
ምቹውነት mchuwnet *(n.)* **suitability**
ምጭንጓዕ mčnguaë *(n.)* **pump**
ምጭራሕ mĉraĥ *(n.)* **exclamation**
ምድብ mdb *(n.)* **rating**
ምድብ መዘና mdb mezena *(n.)* **peerage**
ምደባ mdeba *(n.)* **placement**
ምደባ mdeba *(n.)* **assignation**
ምድፋር mdfar *(n.)* **molestation**
ምድጋፍ mdgaf *(n.)* **adherence**
ምድጋም mdgam *(n.)* **recurrence**
ምድጋም ፍእምተ ቃል mdgam f'emte qal *(v.)* **alliterate**
ምድግጋም mdggam *(n.)* **reiteration**
ምድሓን mdhan *(n.)* **salvation**
መድሓኒ mdhani *(n.)* **panacea**
ምድህላል mdhlal *(n.)* **diversion**
ምድጃ mdja *(n.)* **stove**
ምድላው mdlaw *(n.)* **bias**
ምድላው mdlaw *(n.)* **composition**
ምድላው mdlaw *(n.)* **partiality**
ምድላው mdlaw *(n.)* **preparation**
ምድላይ mdlay *(n.)* **pursuit**
ምድላይ mdlay *(n.)* **quest**
ምፅመድ mdmas *(n.)* **trap**
ምድንጋር mdngar *(n.)* **elusion**
ምድንጋር mdngar *(n.)* **perplexity**
ምድንጋር mdngar *(n.)* **rigging**
ምድንጓይ mdnguay *(n.)* **procrastination**
ምድቃል mdqal *(n.)* **clone**
ምድራዊ mdrawi *(adj.)* **earthly**
ምድራዊ mdrawi *(adj.)* **secular**
ምልክዑ ቀይሩ melk'u keyru *(v.)* **transfigure**
ምእማን meman *(n.)* **persuasion**
ምእማር m'èmar *(n.)* **conception**
ምምጽዋት meme tse wat *(n.)* **handout**
ምዕራብ merab *(n.)* **west**
ምዕራባዊ merabawi *(adj.)* **western**
ምዕራባዊ ምግባር merabawi mgbar *(v.)* **westernize**
ምድራዝ mdraz *(n.)* **massage**
ምድረ-ማያዊ mdremayawi *(n.)* **amphibian**
ምድሪ mdri *(n.)* **earth**
ምድሪ ዝንቕንቕ ድምጺ mdri z'nqhn'qh dmtsi *(adj.)* **stentorian**
ምዱብ ስራሕ mdub sraḧ *(n.)* **assignment**
ምድያብ mdyab *(n.)* **accession**
ማዓድን me'ädn *(n.)* **mineral**
ምዕጉርቲ meaegurtii *(n.)* **cheek**
ምእላይ meaelayi *(n.)* **clearance**
ማሕደረ እንቋቑሖ mahdere enquaquho *(n.)* **ovary**

ማዕድን ma'adn *(n.)* **ore**
ምዕጋት meegat *(n.)* **containment**
ምዕራፍ mee'eraf *(n.)* **chapter**
ምክልኻል ጥንሲ meihil'hal tinsi *(n.)* **contraception**
ምኩሕ mekuhh *(n. &adj.)* **chauvinist**
ምቁራፅ mekuraxee *(n.)* **cessation**
ምእላይ m'elay *(n.)* **disposal**
ምልክዐ ምድሪ melka mdri *(n.)* **terrain**
ምልክዕ ምቅያር melka mkyar *(n.)* **transfiguration**
ምምራፅ mmrts *(v.)* **opt**
ምስ ዓይኒ ወይ ምርኣይ ዝምልከት ms ayni wey mr'ay zmlket *(adj.)* **optic**
ምስፋር msfar *(n.)* **occupancy**
ምቅዋም mqwam *(n.)* **objection**
ምቅዋም mqwam *(n.)* **opposition**
ምብራቓዊ mbraqawi *(adj.)* **oriental**
ምትዕርራይ mt'ereray *(v.)* **overhaul**
ምቹው mchuw *(adj.)* **opportune**
ምንጩው mnchuw *(v.)* **originate**
ምዕራባዊ m'erabawi *(adj.)* **occidental**
ምዕራብ m'erab *(n.)* **occident**
ምዕባይ m'ebay *(v.)* **outgrow**
ምዕብላል m'eblal *(v.)* **outdo**
ምእዋድ m'ewad *(n.)* **owe**
ምእዋድ m'ewad *(adj.)* **owing**
ምእዙዝ m'ezuz *(adj.)* **obedient**
ምኽሓድ ዝኽእል mkhad zk'el *(adj.)* **objectionable**
ምውናን mwnan *(adj. & pron.)* **own**
ምውካል mwukal *(v.)* **outsource**
ምዓዝ meaz *(adv.)* **when**
ምዕባለ m'ëbale *(n.)* **advancement**
ምዕባለ m'ëbale *(n.)* **progress**
ምዕቡል m'ëbul *(adj.)* **futuristic**
ምዕጥይጣይ m'ëtytay *(n.)* **reluctance**
ምእዋጥር mewatr *(n.)* **jam**
ምእዛዝ m'ezaz *(n.)* **submission**
ምእዙዝ m'ezuz *(adj.)* **complaisant**
ምእዙዝ m'ezuz *(adj.)* **courteous**
ምእዙዝ m'ezuz *(adj.)* **docile**
ምእዙዝ m'ezuz *(adj.)* **submissive**
ምፍዳይ mfday *(n.)* **repayment**
ምፍሕፋሕ mf̂hfaĥ *(n.)* **rub**
ምፍኳስ mfkwas *(n.)* **simplification**
ምፍላጥ mflaẗ *(v.)* **publicize**
ምፍላጥ mflaẗ *(n.)* **introduction**
ምፍልላይ mfllay *(n.)* **parting**
ምፍልላይ mfllay *(n.)* **separation**
ምፍንጫል mfn'chal *(n.)* **schism**
ምፍንጫል mfn'chal *(n.)* **secession**
ምፍንጃር mfnjar *(n.)* **explosion**
ምፍርራሕ mfrrah *(n.)* **intimidation**
ምፍርራስ mfrras *(n.)* **disrepair**
ምፍሳስ mfsas *(n.)* **spillage**
ምፍሳስ ደም mfsas dem *(n.)* **gore**
ምፍሳስ መጉሊ mfsas meguili *(n.)* **pyorrhoea**
ምፍጣር mftar *(n.)* **creation**
ምፍጣጥ m'fẗaẗ *(v.)* **stare**
ምፍታው mftaw *(n.)* **liking**
ምፍትሕታሕ mftĥtaĥ *(n.)* **relaxation**
ምፍጻም mfxam *(n.)* **completion**
ምግባር mgbar *(n.)* **taxation**
ምግቢ mgbi *(n.)* **food**
ምግቢ mgbi *(n.)* **meal**
ምግቢ mgbi *(n.)* **nourishment**
ምግጫው/ስግንጢር mgchaw/sgntir *(n.)* **paradox**
ምግዳድ mgdad *(v.)* **impose**
ምግዳድ mgdad *(n.)* **imposition**
ምግዳ'ድ mgdad *(n.)* **compulsion**

ምግዳፍ mgdaf *(n.)* **cession**
ምግላብ m-glab *(n.)* **gallop**
ምግላል mglal *(n.)* **insulation**
ምግላል mglal *(n.)* **isolation**
ምግላፀ mglats *(v.)* **uncover**
ምግላጽ ምጉት mglax mgut *(v.)* **plead**
ምግናሕ mgnah *(n.)* **manoeuvre**
ምግናን mg'nan *(n.)* **hyperbole**
ምግንዛብ mgnzab *(n.)* **acknowledgement**
ምግታእ mgta'e *(n.)* **restriction**
ምግጥጣም mgẗtam *(n.)* **assemblage**
ምንፋሕ m'nfaḧ *(n.)* **spray**
ምንፍርፋር mnfrfar *(n.)* **seizure**
ምንጋፍ mngaf *(v.)* **rid**
ምንጋጋ mngaga *(n.)* **jaw**
ምንጋር mnggar *(v.)* **talk**
ምንካእ mnka'e *(n.)* **impact**
ምንካይ mnkay *(n.)* **deduction**
ምንካይ mnkay *(n.)* **diminution**
ምንካይ mnkay *(n.)* **reduction**
ምንካይ ኣፅዋር mnkay atswar *(n.)* **disarmament**
ምንቅርፋፍ mnkrfaf *(v.)* **traipse**
ምንቅጥቃጥ mnktkat *(v.)* **twitch**
ምንኩስና mnkusna *(n.)* **monasticism**
ምንም እኳ mnm ekwa *(prep.)* **despite**
ምንም መስተ ዘይሰቲ mnm meste zeyseti *(adj.)* **teetotal**
ምንም መስተ ዘይሰቲ mnm meste zeyseti *(n.)* **teetotaller**
ምንም ዘይምግባር mnm zetmgbar *(n.)* **inaction**
ምንም'ኳ mnmkwa *(conj.)* **although**
ምንቕ በለ mnq̈ bele *(v.)* **budge**
ምንቅስቃስ mnqsqas *(n.)* **locomotion**
ምንቅስቃስ mnqsqas *(n.)* **motion**
ምንቅስቃስ mnqsqas *(n.)* **movement**
ምንቅስቃስ ፈሳሲ ዝጠቅም መሳርሒ mnqsqas fesasi zẗekm mesarḧi *(n.)* **pipette**
ምንቅስቓሳዊ mnqsq̈asawi *(adj.)* **kinetic**
ምንቅጥቃጥ mnqtqat *(n.)* **tremor**
ምንቅጥቃጥ mnqt'qat' *(n.)* **convulsion**
ምንቋት mnq̈uat *(v.)* **plummet**
ምንስፋፍ mnsfaf *(n.)* **buoyancy**
ምንስናስ mn'snas *(n.)* **sprinkling**
ምንጥብጣብ mntbtab *(n.)* **leakage**
ምንተፋ ድንኳን mntefa dnkwan *(n.)* **shoplifting**
ምንጥልጣል mntltal *(n.)* **pendulum**
ምንትራኽ mntrak *(n.)* **quibble**
ምንጻፍ mntsaf *(n.)* **underlay**
ምንፃፍ ምድሪ mntsaf mdri *(n.)* **rug**
ምንፅብራቕ mntsbraq *(n.)* **projection**
ምንዋሕ mnwaḧ *(n.)* **prolongation**
ምንፃፍ mnxaf *(n.)* **mat**
ምንፃግ mnxag *(n.)* **negation**
ምንጻሀ mnxah *(n.)* **purification**
ምንጻል mnxal *(n.)* **abortion**
ምንጽጻር mnxxar *(n.)* **comparison**
ምንዮት mnyot *(n.)* **fancy**
ምንዛዐ mnza'ë *(n.)* **appropriation**
ምንዝርና mnzrna *(n.)* **prostitution**
ምቅባእ mqbaè *(n.)* **paint**
ምቅባእ mqbaè *(n.)* **portrayal**
ምቅባል mqbal *(n.)* **acceptance**
ምቅባል ኣበየ mqbal abeye *(v.)* **disclaim**

ምቅብጣር mqbẗar ***(n.)*** **sycophancy**
ምቕዳሕ mq̈daḧ ***(v.)*** **pour**
ምቕሉል m'qhlul ***(adj.)*** **subservient**
ምቕሉልነት m'qhlulnet ***(n.)*** **subservience**
ምቕናስ mqhnas ***(v.)*** **subside**
ምቕናስ m'qhnas ***(n.)*** **subtraction**
ምቕያር mqhy'yar ***(n.)*** **substitution**
ምቕላዕ mqlae ***(v.)*** **unveil**
ምቅላዕ mqla'e ***(n.)*** **exposure**
ምቅላዕ mqla'ë ***(n.)*** **revelation**
ምቅላል mqlal ***(mitigation)*** **mitigation**
ምቕላል mq̈lal ***(n.)*** **alleviation**
ምቅሊት mqlit ***(n.)*** **dividend**
ምቕልቃል mq̈lqal ***(n.)*** **appearance**
ምቕሉል mq̈lul ***(adj.)*** **compliant**
ምቕሉል mq̈lul ***(adj.)*** **homely**
ምቕሉል mq̈lul ***(adj.)*** **polite**
ምቕማር mq̈mar ***(n.)*** **computation**
ምቕማጥ mq̈maẗ ***(v.)*** **posit**
ምቅናዕ mqna'e ***(v.)*** **unbend**
ምቕናን mqnan ***(n.)*** **wimble**
ምቅቛም mqquam ***(v.)*** **withstand**
ምቕራብ mqrab ***(v.)*** **provide**
ምቕራብ mq̈rab ***(n.)*** **presentation**
ምቕራፍ mqrf ***(n.)*** **peel**
ምቕሶ mq̈so ***(n.)*** **haircut**
ምቅታል mqtal ***(n.)*** **assassination**
ምቁር mqur ***(n.)*** **ambrosia**
ምቁር mqur ***(adj.)*** **delicious**
ምቁር mqur ***(adj.)*** **mellow**
ምቁር mqur ***(adj.)*** **palatable**
ምቁር mqur ***(adj.)*** **saccharine**
ምቁር mqur ***(adj.)*** **succulent**
ምቁር mqur ***(n.)*** **sweet**
ምቁር mqur ***(adj.)*** **sweet**
ምቑር mqur ***(adj.)*** **yummy**
ምቁር ባኒ mqur bani ***(n.)*** **bun**
ምቍራጽ mqurats ***(n.)*** **interception**
ምቁራፅ mqurats ***(n.)*** **interruption**
ምቁራፅ mqurats ***(n.)*** **severance**
ምቁራጽ mqurats ***(n.)*** **stoppage**
ምቀረፅ mqurax ***(n.)*** **excise**
ምቁጣብ mqutab ***(n.)*** **thrift**
ምቕጻዕ mqxae ***(v.)*** **penalize**
ምቕጻዕ mq̈xaë ***(v.)*** **punish**
ምቕያር mqyar ***(n.)*** **conversion**
ምርዕውነት mrewenet ***(n.)*** **wedlock**
ምርጋፍ mrgaf ***(v.)*** **unpack**
ምርግጋእ m'rg'ga'e ***(n.)*** **stabilization**
ምርግጋጽ mrggax ***(n.)*** **confirmation**
ምርግጋጽ mrggax ***(n.)*** **affirmation**
ምርሃጽ mrhax ***(v.t.)*** **perspire**
ምርኢት mr'it ***(n.)*** **exhibition**
ምርኢት mr'it ***(n.)*** **tableau**
ምርኢት ኣጋ ምሸት mr'it aga mshet ***(n.)*** **matinee**
ምርኢት ኣቕራቢ mr'it 'aq̈rabi ***(n.)*** **juggler**
ምርካብ mrkab ***(n.)*** **delivery**
ምርኮ mrko ***(n.)*** **booty**
ምርኩስ mrkus ***(n.)*** **crutch**
ምርመራ mrmera ***(n.)*** **diagnosis**
ምርመራ mrmera ***(n.)*** **examination**
ምርምረ-ሬሳ mrmre reesa ***(n.)*** **autopsy**
ምርቓ mrq̈a ***(n.)*** **blessing**
ምርራው mr'raw ***(n.)*** **lullaby**
ምርሳዕ ኣበየ mrsa'ë abeye ***(v.)*** **rankle**
ምርጥራጥ mr'tra't ***(n.)*** **lurch**
ምሩኽ mruḱ ***(n.)*** **captive**
ምሩኽነት mruḱnet ***(n.)*** **captivity**
ምሩጽ ስእሊ mrux seli ***(adj.)*** **picturesque**
ምርኡይ mr'uy ***(adj.)*** **gaudy**

ምርኡይ mr'uy ***(adj.)*** **notable**
ምርኡይ mr'uy ***(adj.)*** **showy**
ምርኡይ mr'uy ***(adj.)*** **snazzy**
ምስ ባሕሪ ዝተተሓሓዘ ms bahri ztetehahaze ***(adj.)*** **maritime**
ምስ ሓዳር ዝተተሓሓዘ ms hadar ztetehahaze ***(adj.)*** **marital**
ምስ ህጻናት ጾታዊ ርክብ ምፍጻም ዝማረኽ በጽሒ ms hixanat xotawi rkb mfxam zmareḱ bexḧi ***(n.)*** **paedophile**
ምስ ህይወት ዝተኣሳሰረ ms hywet zte'asasere ***(adj.)*** **vital**
ምስ ጡብ ዝተተሓሓዘ ms tub ztetehahaze ***(adj.)*** **mammary**
ምሳሕ msah ***(n.)*** **lunch**
ምሳሕ msah ***(n.)*** **luncheon**
ምሳሌ ዝኮነ msale zkone ***(v.)*** **typify**
ምሳሌ ዘረኢ msalie zereei ***(n.)*** **precedent**
ምስኣን ms'an ***(n.)*** **lack**
ምስባኽ msbaḱ ***(v.)*** **preach**
ምስዳድ msdad ***(n.)*** **consignment**
ምስፋር msfar ***(n.)*** **settlement**
ምስፍሕፋሕ msf̂hfaĥ ***(n.)*** **extension**
መስጋድ msgad ***(n.)*** **prostration**
ምስጋና msgana ***(n.)*** **gratitude**
ምስጋና msgana ***(v.t.)*** **praise**
ምስጋና ኣልቦነት msgana albonet ***(n.)*** **ingratitude**
ምስጋና ዘይብሉ msgana zeybelu ***(adj.)*** **ungrateful**
ምስጋና ዘይብሉ msgana zeyblu ***(adj.)*** **thankless**
ምስጋር msgar ***(adj.)*** **passing**
ምስጉን msgun ***(adj.)*** **decorous**
ምስጉን msgun ***(adj.)*** **glorious**
ምስጓግ msgwag ***(n.)*** **eviction**
ምስጓግ msgwag ***(n.)*** **persecution**
ምስጓግ m'sgwag ***(n.)*** **suspension**
ምስጓም m'sgwam ***(n.)*** **step**
ምሽባን mshban ***(n.)*** **complicity**
ምሸት mshet ***(n.)*** **evening**
ምስሒት msĥit ***(n.)*** **allotment**
ምሽኩንዳር mshkundar ***(n.)*** **harassment**
ምሽምቃቅ ጭዋዳ mshmqaq cwada ***(n.)*** **cramp**
ምሽጥር mshẗr ***(n.)*** **enigma**
ምሽጥር ነገር mshtr negere ***(v.)*** **divulge**
ምሽዋድ mshwad ***(n.)*** **trick**
ምስክር mskr ***(n.)*** **eyewitness**
ምስክር mskr ***(n.)*** **testimony**
ምስክር ወረቀት mskr werket ***(n.)*** **testimonial**
ምስኳዕ mskwa'ë ***(n.)*** **insertion**
ምሰላ msla ***(n.)*** **proverb**
ምስላ msla ***(n.)*** **saying**
ምስላብ mslab ***(n.)*** **infatuation**
ምስላኽ mslakh ***(n.)*** **insinuation**
ምስላዊ mslawi ***(adj)*** **figurative**
ምስላዊ mslawi ***(adj.)*** **proverbial**
ምስሌኣዊ ዛንታ mslee'awi zanta ***(n.)*** **allegory**
ምስሌነ mslene ***(n.)*** **prefect**
ምስሊ ቅዱሳን msli qdusan ***(n.)*** **icon**
ምስሉይነት msluynet ***(n.)*** **affectation**
ምስምማዕ msm'emae ***(n.)*** **transcription**
ምቅይያራት mqyyarat ***(n.)*** **vicissitude**
ምራኽ mraḱ ***(n.)*** **calf**
ምጉዕዓዝ mgu'ë'äz ***(n.)*** **haulage**
ምጉጃል mgujal ***(n.)*** **grouping**
ምጉላሕ mgulaĥ ***(n.)*** **emphasis**
ምጉማድ mgumad ***(n.)*** **mayhem**

ምጉንፋት mgunfat *(n.)* **wrangle**
ምጉስቓል mgusqhal *(n.)* **manhandle**
ምጉት mgut *(n.)* **litigation**
ምጉት mgut *(n.)* **polemic**
ምጓዐዝ mgwa'az *(n.)* **conveyance**
ምሕባር mḧbar *(n.)* **amalgamation**
ምሕባጥ m'hbaẗ *(n.)* **swell**
ምህዳእ mhda'e *(n.)* **stillness**
ምሕዳግ mḧdag *(n.)* **abdication**
ምህዳን ዓሳ ነባሪ mhdan asa nebari *(n.)* **whaling**
ምሕዳስ mĥdas *(adj.)* **renewal**
ምሕዳስ mĥdas *(adj.)* **restoration**
ምሕደራ እንዳ ፖስጣ mḧdera ènda posẗa *(n.)* **postmaster**
ምሒር mĥir *(adj.)* **dire**
ምሒር ማረኸ mĥir mareke *(v.)* **enchant**
ምሒር mḧir *(adj.)* **arrant**
ምሒር mḧir *(adv.)* **sorely**
ምሕላፍ mhlaf *(v.)* **pass**
ምሕላው mhlaw *(n.)* **keeping**
ምሕልዋይ mhlway *(n.)* **jibe**
ምህሙን mhmun *(adj.)* **flimsy**
ምሕናቕ m'ḧnaq *(n.)* **strangulation**
ምሕንዳል m'hndal *(n.)* **malformation**
ምሕንጋድ mḥngad *(n.)* **insubordination**
ምሕንሓን mhnhan *(n.)* **whinny**
ምሕንቃቕ mhnqaq *(v.)* **pamper**
ምህራም mhram *(v.)* **pulsate**
ምሕራስ mḧrasq̈a *(n.)* **plough**
ምሕራይ mhray *(n.)* **selection**
ምሕረት mĥret *(n.)* **remission**
ምሕረት mḧret *(n.)* **abstinence**
ምሕረት mḧret *(n.)* **amnesty**
ምሕረት m'ḧret *(n.)* **mercy**
ምሕረት mhretawi *(n.)* **pardon**
ምሕረታዊ mhretawi *(adj.)* **pardonable**
ምሕረታዊ-ቅትለት mĥretawi qtlet *(n.)* **euthanasia**
ምህርቲ mhrti *(n.)* **production**
ምህርቲ mhrti *(n.)* **takings**
ምሕሳብ mhsab *(n.)* **imagination**
ምሕሳር mĥsar *(n.)* **depreciation**
ምሕታም mḧtam *(v.)* **publish**
ምሕፀና m'ḧtsena *(n.)* **solicitation**
ምሕፃር mhtzar *(n.)* **immure**
ምሁር mhur *(adj.)* **erudite**
ምሁር mhur *(adj.)* **learned**
ምሁር mhur *(n.)* **scholar**
ምሁራዊ mhurawi *(adj.)* **scholarly**
ምሕጻብ mḥxab *(n.)* **washing**
ምሕጻብ mḧxab *(n.)* **bath**
ምሕጻር mḧxar *(n.)* **abbreviation**
ምሕፃር mḧxar *(n.)* **contraction**
ምሕፅንታ mĥxnta *(v. t)* **entreaty**
ምሕያው mḧyaw *(n.)* **animation**
ምሕየሻ mḧyesha *(n.)* **modification**
ምሕዝነታዊ mḧznetawi *(adj.)* **amicable**
ምህዞ mhzo *(n.)* **figment**
ምልጋብ milgab *(n.)* **contagion**
ምኢሳልነት misalnet *(n.)* **idealism**
ምሽጥራዊ ስምምዕ mishtirawi simemeeh *(n.)* **collusion**
ምስጢራዊ mistrawi *(adj.)* **undercover**
ምጥቓም mit; qqam' *(n.)* **consumption**
ምፅባዕ mitsbaee *(prep.)* **contra**
ምጅሃር mĵhar *(adj.)* **pompous**
ምጅማር mĵmar *(n.)* **commencement**
ምርዓም mr'äm *(n.)* **adoption**

ምራን mran ***(n.)*** **thong**
ምራተ mrate ***(n.)*** **rust**
ምርኣይ mr'ay ***(n)*** **look**
ምርኣይ mr'ay ***(n.)*** **view**
ምርባሕ mrbaĥ ***(n.)*** **reproduction**
ምርባሕ mrbaḧ ***(n.)*** **multiplication**
ምርባሕ mrbaḧ ***(n.)*** **proliferation**
ምርባሕ ዓሳ mrbaĥ äsa ***(n.)*** **fishery**
ምርጫ mrča ***(n.)*** **ballot**
ምርጫ mrča ***(n.)*** **preference**
ምርጫ ዘካይድ mrča zekayd ***(n.)*** **pollster**
ምርጫዊ mrčawi ***(adj.)*** **preferential**
ምርጫ mrcca ***(n.)*** **choice**
ምርዳእ mrdae ***(v.)*** **perceive**
ምርዳእ mrda'e ***(n.)*** **fathom**
ምርዳእ mrda'è ***(n.)*** **comprehension**
ምርዳእ mrda'è ***(n.)*** **apprehension**
ምርድዳእ mrdeda'e ***(n.)*** **understanding**
ምቅባእ mkba'e ***(n.)*** **tinge**
ምቅባር mkbar ***(v.)*** **whelm**
ምኽዳን mkdan ***(n.)*** **upholstery**
ምክፋእ mkfa'è ***(n.)*** **aspersions**
ምክፋል mkfal ***(v.)*** **partake**
ምኽፋል mkfal ***(v.)*** **pay**
ምክፍፋል mkffal ***(n.)*** **partition**
ምኽፋል mkhfal ***(n.)*** **liquidation**
ምኽኒት mkhnit ***(v.)*** **excuse**
ምኽንያታዊ mkhnyatawi ***(adj.)*** **logical**
ምኽትል ኣራታዒ mkhtl arta'i ***(v.)*** **subedit**
ምኽክር mkkr ***(n.)*** **deliberation**
ምኽላል mklal ***(n.)*** **enclosure**
ምክልኻል mklkal ***(n.)*** **defence**
ምኽልካል mklkal ***(n.)*** **prohibition**
ምክልኻል mklḱal ***(n.)*** **protection**
ምክንያት mknyat ***(n.)*** **reason**
ምኽንያት mḱn'yat ***(n.)*** **motive**
ምክንያት ዘይብሉ ቁጥዐ mknyat zeyblu qutea ***(n.)*** **tantrum**
ምኽንያቱ mknyatu ***(conj.)*** **because**
ምኽሪ/ማዕዳ mkri/ma'ëda ***(n.)*** **counsel**
ምኽታል mktal ***(n.)*** **pursuance**
ምኽታም mktam ***(n.)*** **urbanity**
ምኽታ'ም mḱtam ***(n.)*** **conurbation**
ምክታት mktat ***(n.)*** **inclusion**
ምክታት mktat ***(v.)*** **incorporate**
ምኽትል mktl ***(n.)*** **deputy**
ምኹምሳዕ mkumsa'ë ***(n.)*** **rumination**
ምኹናን mḱunan ***(n.)*** **condemnation**
ምኩርካዕ mkurka'e ***(v.)*** **tickle**
ምኩሳሕ mkusah ***(n.)*** **inflammation**
ምኩሻም mkusham ***(n.)*** **foreplay**
ምልአተ ጉባኤ ml'ate guba'e ***(n.)*** **quorum**
ምልበዳ mlbeda ***(n.)*** **moulding**
ምልእ ዝበለ ml'e zbele ***(adj.)*** **turgid**
ምልዕዓል ml'ë'äl ***(n.)*** **initiative**
ምልጋብ mlgab ***(n.)*** **patch**
ምልጋፀ mlgatz ***(n.)*** **levity**
ምልህላህ mlhlah ***(v.)*** **pant**
ምልካይ ሕብሪ mlkay hhbri ***(n.)*** **colouring**
ምልክት mlkt ***(n.)*** **crest**
ምልክት mlkt ***(n.)*** **label**
ምልክት mlkt ***(n.)*** **notation**
ምልክት mlkt ***(n.)*** **sign**
ምልክት mlkt ***(n.)*** **signal**
ምልክት mlkt ***(n.)*** **symbol**
ምልክት mlkt ***(n.)*** **token**
ምልክት mlkt ***(n.)*** **track**
ምልክት mlkt ***(n.)*** **mark**

ምልክት ሕማም mlkt ḧmam *(n.)* **symptom**
ምልክት ሕማም ዘለዎ mlkt ḧmam zelewo *(adj.)* **symptomatic**
ምልክት ኮነ mlkt kone *(v.)* **symbolize**
ምልክት መግበሪ mlkt megberi *(n.)* **marker**
ምልክት ምግባር mlkt mgbar *(n.)* **marking**
ምልክት ዝልጠፍ ወይ ዝእሰር mlkt zltef wey z'eser *(n.)* **tag**
ምልክት mlkt *(n.)* **beck**
ምልክት mlkt *(n.)* **beep**
ምልክት mlkt *(n.)* **portent**
ምልክታ mlkta *(n.)* **handbill**
ምልክታ mlkta *(n.)* **notice**
ምልክታ mlkta *(n.)* **notification**
ምልክታዊ mlktawi *(adj.)* **symbolic**
ምልኩዕ mlku'ë *(adj.)* **handsome**
ምልላይ mllay *(v.)* **identify**
ምልማስ mlmas *(v.)* **paralyse**
ምልምል mlml *(v.)* **recruit**
ምልምስና mlmsna *(n.)* **paralysis**
ምሎክ mlok *(n.)* **vampire**
ምልሻ mlsha *(n.)* **militia**
ምልስላስ mlslas *(n.)* **harrow**
ምልጣፍ mlẗaf *(n.)* **post**
ምልፃይ mltsay *(n.)* **shaving**
ምሉእ mlu'e *(adj.)* **utter**
ምሉእ mlu'e *(adj.)* **whole**
ምሉእ mlu'è *(adj.)* **complete**
ምሉእ mlu'è *(adv.)* **wholly**
ምሉእ ክዳን mlu'e kidan *(n.)* **suit**
ምሉእ ልቢ mluelbi *(adj.)* **whole-hearted**
ምልዋጥ mlwat *(n.)* **transformation**
ምምብጻዕ mmbxaë *(n.)* **promise**
ምምጋል m'mgal *(v.)* **suppurate**
ምምሃር mmhar *(n.)* **learning**
ምምሃዝ mmhaz *(n.)* **invention**
ምምሕዳር mmhdar *(n.)* **management**
ምምሕዳር m'mḧdar *(n.)* **superintendence**
ምምሕዳር ገንዘብ mmĥdar genzeb *(n.)* **finance**
ምምሕዳር ወረዳ mmḧdar wereda *(n.)* **borough**
ምምሕዳር mmḧdar *(n.)* **administration**
ምምሕዳራዊ mmhdarawi *(adj.)* **managerial**
ምምሕዳራዊ mmḧdarawi *(adj.)* **administrative**
ምምሕልላፍ mmhllaf *(v.)* **transfer**
ምምሕልላፍ mmḧllaf *(n.)* **giro**
ምምህርና mmhrna *(n.)* **pedagogy**
ምምሕያሽ mmĥyaš *(n.)* **reformation**
ምምሕያሽ mmḧyash *(n.)* **amelioration**
ምምካን mmkan *(n.)* **sterilization**
ምምኽካር mmkkar *(n.)* **consultation**
ምምላእ mmla'e *(n.)* **filling**
ምምላእ mmla'e *(n.)* **infusion**
ምምላኽ mmlak *(n.)* **worship**
ምምላስ mmlas *(n.)* **return**
ምምላጥ m'mlaẗ *(n.)* **squeak**
ምምልካት mmlkat *(n.)* **indication**
ምምልካት mmlkat *(n.)* **pointing**
ምምንጫው mmn'chaw *(n.)* **secretion**
ምምቕራሕ mmq̈raḧ *(n.)* **allocation**
ምምቅራሕ ስልጣን mmqrah sltan *(n.)* **devolution**
ምምራሕ mmrah *(n.)* **lead**
ምምራቕ mmraq *(n.)* **graduate**
ምምራዝ mmraz *(n.)* **intoxication**
ምምርባብ mmrbab *(n.)* **blog**

ምምርሳሕ mmrsaḧ *(n.)* **sophistication**
ምምርሳሕ mmrsaḧ *(n.)* **adulteration**
ምምሳል mmsal *(v.)* **impersonate**
ምምሳል mmsal *(n.)* **impersonation**
ምምሳል mmsal *(n.)* **pretence**
ምምስኻር mmskar *(n.)* **verification**
ምምስካር mmskar *(n.)* **witness**
ምምጣጥ m'mẗaẗ *(n.)* **suction**
ምምፃእ mmtsa'e *(v.)* **import**
ምናልባሽ mnalbash *(adv.)* **perhaps**
ምናልባት mnalbat *(adv.)* **maybe**
ምናልባት mnalbat *(adj.)* **probable**
ምናልባት mnalbat *(adv.)* **probably**
ምናምን mnamn *(n.)* **mediocrity**
ምናት mnat *(n.)* **arm**
ምንባር mnbaar *(n.)* **living**
ምንባብ mnbab *(n.)* **reading**
ምንባሕ mnbah *(n.)* **woof**
ምንጭብጫብ mnčbčab *(n.)* **plaudits**
ምንጪ mnchi *(n.)* **source**
ምንጪ mnĉi *(n.)* **resource**
ምንጪ mnči *(n.)* **fountain**
ምንዳድ mndad *(v.)* **burn**
ምዝዋር mzwar *(v.)* **oscillate**
ምድምሳስ mdemsas *(n.)* **obliteration**
ምግልባጥ mglbat *(v.)* **overturn**
ምግዳፍ mgdaf *(n.)* **omission**
ምስሉይ meslu *(n.)* **hypocrite**
ምስሉይነት mesluynet *(n.)* **hypocrisy**
ምእታዉ m'etaw *(n.)* **entry**
ምጥሓን me-tha-n *(v.)* **grind**
ምዕሪት m'ërit *(n.)* **equation**
ምዕሩግ m'ërug *(adj.)* **graceful**
ምዕሩግነት m'ërugnet *(n.)* **grandeur**
ምዕሩይ m'ëruy *(adj.)* **symmetrical**
ምዕሩዩነት m'ëruynet *(n.)* **symmetry**
ምእሳር m'esar *(n.)* **imprison**
ምስክር ወረቐት mesekir wereqet *(n.)* **certificate**
ምዕሻግ m'ëshag *(n.)* **dock**
ምጽብባቕ mtsbbaq *(n.)* **ornamentation**
ምፍጣር እንቋቕሖ mftar enquaqho *(v.)* **ovulate**
ምስምማዕ msmma'e *(n.)* **acquiescence**
ምስምማዕ msm'maë *(n.)* **pact**
ምስምስ msms *(n.)* **pretext**
ምስንባት msnbat *(n.)* **resignation**
ምስራሕ msrah *(n.)* **making**
ምስራሕ ወይኒ msrah weyni *(n.)* **winery**
ምስራቕ msraq *(v.)* **pilfer**
ምስራቕ msraqh *(n.)* **loot**
ምስስል mssl *(n.)* **resemblance**
ምስታፍ mstaf *(n.)* **participation**
ምስጢራዊ mstiawi *(adj.)* **secret**
ምስጢር mstir *(v.t.)* **puzzle**
ምስጢር mstir *(n.)* **secrecy**
ምስጢር msẗir *(n.)* **mystique**
ምስጢር ኣካፈለ msẗir 'akafele *(v.)* **confide**
ምስጢራዊ msẗirawi *(adj.)* **confidential**
ምስጢራዊ msẗirawi *(adj.)* **esoteric**
ምስጢራዊ msẗirawi *(adj.)* **mysterious**
ምስእጢራዊ መደብ msẗirawi medeb *(n.)* **plot**
ምስጢረኛ mstiregna *(adj.)* **secretive**
ምስትኽካል mstkhkal *(n.)* **improvement**
ምስትንፋስ mstnfas *(n.)* **respiration**

ምስትውዓል mstwu'al ***(n.)*** **sensibility**
ምሱጥ msuẗ ***(n.)*** **enthusiastic**
ምስዮናዊ m'syonawi ***(n.)*** **missionary**
ምትብባዕ mtbba'ë ***(n.)*** **patronage**
ምጥቧብ mẗ'bwab ***(n.)*** **suckling**
ምትእኽኻብ mt'ekkab ***(n.)*** **reunion**
ምትዕርራኽ mt'ërrak ***(n.)*** **intimacy**
ምትእስሳር mt'essar ***(n.)*** **affiliation**
ምትእስሳር mt'essar ***(n.)*** **implication**
ምትእስሳር mt'essar ***(n.)*** **liaison**
ምትእስሳር mt'es'sar ***(n.)*** **nexus**
ምትእስሳር mt'èssar ***(n.)*** **concatenation**
ምትዕፅፃይ mt'etstsaw ***(v.t.)*** **jam**
ምጥፍፋእ mtffa'e ***(n.)*** **scam**
ምትግባር mtgbar ***(v.)*** **perform**
ምትግባር mtgbar ***(n.)*** **implement**
ምጥሓል mtḥal ***(n.)*** **immersion**
ምጥሓስ mẗḧas ***(v.)*** **breach**
ምትሃታዊ m'thatawi ***(adj.)*** **spectral**
ምትሃተ ብርሃን mthate br'han ***(n.)*** **spectrum**
ምትሕብባር mtḧbbar ***(n.)*** **alliance**
ምትሕብባር mtḧbbar ***(n.)*** **cooperation**
ምትሕልላፍ mtḧllaf ***(n.)*** **postponement**
ምትካል እግሪ mtkal egri ***(n.)*** **flotation**
ምትካዝ mtkaz ***(adj.)*** **pensive**
ምትኽኻእ mtkh'kha'e ***(n.)*** **succession**
ምትኳር mtkwar ***(n.)*** **focus**
ምትላል mtlal ***(n.)*** **deception**
ምትላል mtlal ***(n.)*** **delusion**
ምትላል mtlal ***(n.)*** **manipulation**
ምጥምዛዝ mtmzaz ***(n.)*** **torsion**
ምትንባህ mtnbah ***(n.)*** **allusion**
ምትንባይ mtnbay ***(v.)*** **prognosticate**
ምትንኳስ mtnkwas ***(n.)*** **provocation**
ምጥቃም mtqam' ***(v.t.)*** **use**
ምጥቃም mtqam' ***(v.)*** **utilize**
ምጥራር mtrar ***(n.)*** **demarcation**
ምጥርናፍ mẗrnaf ***(n.)*** **packing**
ምፅጋን mtsgan ***(n.)*** **maintenance**
ምፅላም mtslam ***(n.)*** **slander**
ምፅማም mtsmam ***(n.)*** **sufferance**
ምፅቃጥ mtsqat ***(n.)*** **repression**
ምፅራይ mtsray ***(n.)*** **refinement**
ምጹጹላይ mtsutsulay ***(n.)*** **squirrel**
ምጥዋይን ምስሓብን mṭwayn msḥabn ***(v.)*** **wrench**
ምፅልላው mtzllaw ***(n.)*** **interplay**
ምፅንባር mtznbar ***(n.)*** **incorporation**
ምዑዝ m'üz ***(adj.)*** **fragrant**
ምኡዝ ተኽሊ m'uz tekli ***(n.)*** **herb**

ሞ

ሞዴል modeel ***(n.)*** **ideal**
ሞባእ moba'e ***(n.)*** **oblation**
ሞያ moya ***(n.)*** **occupation**
ሞዴል modeel ***(n.)*** **model**
ሞደም modem ***(n.)*** **modem**
ሞደሻ modesha ***(n.)*** **anvil**
ሞጁል mojul ***(n.)*** **module**
ሞቅ ዝበሎ mok zbelo ***(n.)*** **tipsy**
ሞካ moka ***(n.)*** **mocha**
ሞከረ mokr ***(v.)*** **try**
ሞለኩዩል molekuyul ***(n.)*** **molecule**
ሞለኩዩላዊ molekuyulawi ***(adj.)*** **molecular**
ሞልጎሙ ብዕንጨይቲ ዝኮነ ክዳን molgomu bancheyti zteserhe kedean ***(n.)*** **toggle**
ሞልሟል molmwal ***(n.)*** **ellipse**
ሞንጎኛ mongogna ***(n.)*** **middleman**

ሞኖ mono *(n.)* **mono**
ሞኖዲ monodi *(n.)* **monody**
ሞኖግራፍ monograf *(n.)* **monograph**
ሞኖግራም monogram *(n.)* **monogram**
ሞንሱን monsun *(n.)* **monsoon**
ሞራለ morale *(n.)* **lintel**
ሞርፊን morfin *(n.)* **morphine**
ሞርጋናዊ morganawi *(adj.)* **morganatic**
ሞሳ mosa *(n.)* **accolade**
ሞሳሬላ mosareela *(n.)* **mozzarella**
ሞስኮኣዊ mosko'awi *(n.)* **muscovite**
ሞት mot *(n.)* **death**
ሞት mot *(n.)* **decease**
ሞት mot *(n.)* **doom**
ሞት mot *(n.)* **mortality**
ሞተ mote *(v.)* **die**
ሞቴል moteel *(n.)* **motel**
ሞተር moter *(n.)* **engine**
ሞተር moter *(n.)* **motor**
ሞተር mote'r' *(n.)* **chassis**
ሞተር ብሽክሌታ moter bshkleeta *(n.)* **moped**
ሞተር ብሽክሌታ moter bshkleeta *(n.)* **motorcycle**
ሞተር ሃፋ moter hafa *(n.)* **steamer**
ሞተረኛ moteregna *(n.)* **motorist**
ሞያ moya *(n.)* **expertise**
ሞያ moya *(n.)* **profession**
ሞያ moya *(n.)* **vocation**
ሞያ ዘይብሉ moya zeyblu *(n.)* **layman**
ሞያ moya *(n.)* **calling**
ሞያዊ moyawi *(adj.)* **technical**
ሞያዊ moyawi *(adj.)* **utilitarian**
ሞያዊ ስልጣነ ቴክኖሎጂ moyawi sltena teknology *(n.)* **technology**
ሞያዊ ዘይኮነ moyawi zeykone *(adj.)* **unprofessional**
ሞይቱ ዝተወልደ moytu ztewelede *(n.)* **stillborn**
ሞያዊ moyawi *(adj.)* **occupational**

ረ

ረአየ re'eye *(v.)* **look**
ረፋዕ refaë *(n.)* **porter**
ረፋዕ በለ refa'ë bele *(v.)* **slump**
ረፈተ refete *(v.)* **demobilize**
ረፍረፈ refrefe *(v.)* **decimate**
ረጌ rege *(n.)* **reggae**
ረገጸ regetse *(v.)* **stamp**
ረገጸ regetse *(v.)* **tread**
ርግፀኛነት regexegninet *(n.)* **certitude**
ረጊድ regid *(adj.)* **thick**
ረጌድ ዝንጉርጉር ክዳን regid zngurgur kdan *(n.)* **tweed**
ረጎደ regode *(v.)* **thicken**
ረግራግ regrag *(adj.)* **slimy**
ረግረግ regreg *(n.)* **slime**
ረግረግ regreg *(n.)* **sludge**
ረግረግ regreg *(n.)* **swamp**
ረግረግ reg'reg *(n)* **marsh**
ረጉድ reguied *(adj.)* **plump**
ርጉፀ reguxee *(adj.)* **certain**
ረጉድ ጓንቲ regwid gwanti *(n.)* **mitten**
ረጉድ regwid *(adj.)* **beefy**
ረሃፀ rehaxe *(n.)* **sweat**
ረጂቶ rejeeto *(n.)* **bra**
ረጂመንት rejiment *(n.)* **regiment**
ረኸበ rekebe *(v.)* **detect**
ረኸበ rekebe *(v.)* **discover**
ረኸበ rekebe *(v.)* **find**

ረኸበ rekebe *(v.)* **procure**
ርክብ re'ke'be *(n.)* **connection**
ረኸበ reḱebe *(v.)* **acquire**
ረኸበ reḱebe *(v.)* **meet**
ረከመ rekeme *(v.)* **knit**
ረኸበ rekhebe *(v.)* **locate**
ረኺቡ ኣምፀአ rekibu amtse'e *(v.)* **retrieve**
ረክላም reklam *(n.)* **advertisement**
ረኽሳዊ reksawi *(adj.)* **septic**
ረኽሲ reksi *(n.)* **infection**
ረኽሲ reksi *(n.)* **sepsis**
ረኾሰ reḱwase *(v.)* **fester**
ረማስ remas *(n.)* **barge**
ረምቁታ remquta *(n.)* **debacle**
ረምታ remta *(n.)* **barrage**
ረምታ remta *(n.)* **rhythm**
ረምታዊ remtawi *(adj.)* **rhythmic**
ረቋሒ reqahi *(n.)* **denominator**
ረቃቂቶ reqaqito *(n.)* **groin**
ረቂቕ መንፈስ reqiq menfes *(n.)* **phantom**
ረቂቅ ሽፋን reqiq shfan *(n.)* **membrane**
ረቒቕ req̈iq̈ *(adj.)* **abstract**
ረቂቕ reqiqh *(adj.)* **superfine**
ረቋሒ reqwaḧ *(n.)* **criterion**
ረቋሒ reqwaĥi *(n.)* **factor**
ረሳሕ resah *(adj.)* **scruffy**
ረሳሕ resaĥ *(adj.)* **dirty**
ረሳሕ resaĥ *(adj.)* **sleazy**
ረሳሕ resaḧ *(adj.)* **sordid**
ረሳዒ resa'ï *(adj.)* **forgetful**
ረስዐ res'ë *(v.)* **forget**
ረስኒ resni *(n.)* **fever**
ረትዐ ret'ë *(v.)* **confute**
ረተበ retebe *(v.)* **assign**
ረቲና retina *(n.)* **retina**
ረዋዪ rewayi *(adj.)* **satiable**
ረዚን rezin *(adj.)* **leaden**
ረዚን rezin *(adj.)* **staid**
ረይረይ reyrey *(adj.)* **shaky**
ረኺቡ rekibu *(v.)* **obtain**
ረጕድ regiud *(adj.)* **obese**
ረዓመ re'äme *(v.)* **adopt**
ረዓሚ re'ämi *(adj.)* **adoptive**
ረአየ re'aye *(v.)* **see**
ረባሺ rebashi *(adj.)* **troublesome**
ረብሻ rebesha *(n.)* **tumult**
ረብሻ ዘለዎ rebesha zelewo *(adj.)* **tumultuous**
ረበሸ rebeshe *(v.)* **disturb**
ረበሸ rebeshe *(v.)* **pester**
ረበሸ rebeshe *(v.)* **unsettle**
ረብሓ rebha *(n.)* **weal**
ረብሓ rebḧa *(n.)* **benefit**
ረብሓ rebḧa *(n.)* **advantage**
ረብሐ rebḧe *(v.t.)* **advantage**
ረብረበ rebrebe *(v.)* **splash**
ረብሻ rebša *(n.)* **ruckus**
ረብሻ rebsha *(n.)* **upheaval**
ረቡዕ rebu'e *(n.)* **Wednesday**
ረዳኢ reda'i *(adj.)* **beneficial**
ረዳት ሓኪም redat ĥakim *(n.)* **paramedic**
ረዳት redat *(n.)* **assistant**
ረድኤት red'iet *(n.)* **aid**

ሩ

ሩባ ruba *(n.)* **gully**
ሩባ ruba *(n.)* **river**
ሩባ ruba *(n.)* **stream**
ሩለት rulet *(n.)* **roulette**
ሩር በለ rur bele *(v.)* **purr**
ሩዝ ruba *(n.)* **wadi**

ሩበ ra'èy *(n.)* **vision**
ራእይ r'èsi *(n.)* **head**
ርእሲ robra *(n.)* **gull**
ሮብራ ruz *(n.)* **rice**

ሪ

ሪፈረንዶም riferendom *(n.)* **plebiscite**
ሪሕ riĥ *(n.)* **gout**
ሪሕ riḧ *(n.)* **arthritis**
ሪሓን riĥan *(n.)* **basil**
ሪኬትስ rikets *(n.)* **rickets**
ርክብ rikib *(n.)* **contact**
ሪክሻ rikša *(n.)* **rickshaw**
ሪፐፕሊክ ripeplic *(n.)* **republic**
ሪፐፕሊካዊ ripeplikawi *(adj.)* **republican**
ሪት rit *(adv.)* **aft**
ሪቮልቨር rivolver *(n.)* **revolver**
ሪዝ riz *(n.)* **moustache**
ራብዓይ rab'äy *(adj.& n.)* **fourth**
ራዳር radar *(n.)* **radar**
ራድየም radyem *(n.)* **radium**
ራድዮግራፊ radyografi *(n.)* **radiography**
ራድዮሎጂ radyologi *(n.)* **radiology**
ራኢ ዘለዎ ra'e zelewo *(adj.)* **visionary**
ራዕደ ዕብጠት ra'ede ebt't *(n.)* **claustrophobia**
ራዕዲ raedi *(n.)* **panic**
ራዕዲ ra'edi *(n.)* **terror**
ራዕዲ ra'ëdi *(n.)* **jitters**
ራዕዲ መሬት raëdi mereet *(n.)* **earthquake**
ራእይ ra'èy *(n.)* **apocalypse**
ራፋኖ rafano *(n.)* **radish**
ራግቢ ragbi *(n.)* **rugby**
ራህዲ rahdi *(adj.)* **sultry**
ራህረሀ rahrehe *(v.)* **sympathize**
ራሕረሐ raĥreĥe *(v.)* **spurn**
ራሕረሐ raĥreĥe *(v.t.)* **abandon**
ራሕሲ rahsi *(n.)* **dampness**
ራሕሲ raĥsi *(n.)* **moisture**
ራህዋ rahwa *(n.)* **delectation**
ራህዋ rahwa *(n.)* **respite**
ራህያ rahya *(n.)* **pond**
ራጅ raj *(n.)* **x-ray**
ራኬት raket *(n.)* **racket**
ራም ram *(n.)* **rum**
ራሚኖ ramino *(n.)* **rummy**
ረይራይ rayray *(adj.)* **rickety**
ራዛ raza *(n.)* **stork**
ሬድዮ redyo *(n.)* **radio**
ሬሳ reesa *(n.)* **corpse**
ሬሳ ኣቃፀለ reesa aqaxele *(v.)* **cremate**
ሬሳ መቃፀሊ ቦታ reesa meqaxeli bota *(n.)* **crematorium**
ሬሳ ምቅፃል reesa mqxal *(n.)* **cremation**
ሬሳ reesa *(n.)* **cadaver**
ሬሳ reesa *(n.)* **cadaver**
ሬክታንግል rektangl *(n.)* **rectangle**
ሬክታንጉላር rektangular *(adj.)* **rectangular**

ር

ርሁድ rehude *(adj.)* **clammy**
ርእሰ ኸተማዊ r'ese ḱetemawi *(adj.)* **metropolitan**
ርእሰ ኸተማ r'ese ḱtema *(n.)* **metropolis**

ርእሰ መምህር r'ese memhr *(n.)* **headmaster**
ርእሰ ቅትለት r'ese qtlet *(n.)* **suicide**
ርእሰ ቅትለታዊ r'ese qtletawi *(adj.)* **suicidal**
ርእሰ-ማል ገበረ r'èsemal gebere *(v.)* **capitalize**
ርእሰ-ማል r'èsemal *(n.)* **capital**
ርእሰ-ማላዊ r'èsemalawi *(n. &adj.)* **capitalist**
ርእሰ-ማልነት r'èsemalnet *(n.)* **capitalism**
ርእሰምምሕዳራዊ r'èsemmḧdarawi *(adj.)* **autonomous**
ርእሰ-ርጉጽነት r'èserguxnet *(n.)* **aplomb**
ርእሰ-ታሪኽ r'èsetariḱ *(n.)* **autobiography**
ርእሰ-ጽሑፍ r'èsexḧuf *(n.)* **autograph**
ርእሲ ቃንዛ r'èsi qanza *(n.)* **headache**
ርባዕ rba'ë *(n.)* **quadrant**
ርብዒ rb'ï *(n.)* **quarter**
ርቦ rbo *(n.)* **bench**
ርቡዕ ጎናዊ rbu'ë gonawi *(n.)* **quadrilateral**
ርቡዕ ጉጅለ rbuë gujle *(n.)* **quartet**
ርቡዕ ማንታ rbu'ë manta *(n.)* **quadruplet**
ርቡዕ መሓውር rbu'ë meĥawr *(n.)* **quadruped**
ርቡዕ ኩርናዕ rbu'ëkurnaë *(n.)* **quad**
ርቡሽ rbush *(adj.)* **maladjusted**
ርቡፅ rbuts *(adj.)* **rash**
ርቡጽ rbux *(adj.)* **agog**
ርቡፀ rbux *(adj.)* **heady**
ርቺት rwḥat *(n.)* **ventilation**
ርውሓት rchit *(n.)* **squib**
ርደኢት rdeit *(n.)* **perception**
ርደኢት rdeit *(n.)* **purview**
ርዲ rdi *(n.)* **fastness**
ርዱእ rdue *(adj.)* **perspicuous**
ርጡብ retub *(adj.)* **humid**
ርእየት r'eyet *(n.)* **sight**
ርእየታዊ r'èyetawi *(adj.)* **visual**
ርእይቶ ሓዘ r'eyto *(v.)* **deem**
ርእይቶ r'èyto *(n.)* **comment**
ርእይቶ ሃበ r'eyto habe *(v.)* **remark**
ርፍራፍ rfraf *(n.)* **crumb**
ርፍራፍ ምጋዝ rfraf mogaz *(n.)* **sawdust**
ርግኣት rg'at *(n.)* **sangfroid**
ርግኣት rg'at *(n.)* **serenity**
ርግኣት r'g'at *(n.)* **stability**
ርግቢት rgbit *(n.)* **cuckoo**
ርግቢት rgbit *(n.)* **pigeon**
ርጐእ rgo'e *(adj.)* **serene**
ርጉእ r'gu'e *(adj.)* **stable**
ርጉም rgum *(adj.)* **despicable**
ርጉም rgum *(n.)* **scoundrel**
ርጉም rgum *(adj.)* **unkind**
ርግኦ rguo *(n.)* **yogurt**
ርግፀ r'g'x *(adj.)* **sure**
ርግፀነት rgx'net *(n.)* **surety**
ርሃጽ rhax *(n.)* **perspiration**
ርሕቀት ጉዕዞ ዓቃኒት rhket guezo aqanit *(n.)* **pedometer**
ርሆምበስ rhombes *(n.)* **rhombus**
ርሕቀት r̂hqet *(n.)* **distance**
ርሕቀት rḧqet *(n.)* **mileage**
ርህራሀ rhrahe *(n.)* **sympathy**
ርህሩህ rhruh *(adj.)* **merciful**
ርህሩህ rhruh *(adj.)* **sympathetic**
ርሁድ rhud *(adj.)* **muggy**
ርሁድ rhud *(adj.)* **sticky**
ርሑቕ r̂huq *(adj.)* **distant**

ርሑቕ rĥuq *(adv.)* **far**
ርሑቕ rĥuq *(adv.)* **further**
ርሑቕ rĥuq *(adj.)* **remote**
ርሑቕ ግንዛበ rĥuq gnzabe *(n.)* **foresight**
ርሑስ rhus *(adj.)* **damp**
ርሑስ rhus *(adj.)* **wet**
ርሑስነት rhusnet *(n.)* **wetness**
ርካሽ rkash *(adj.)* **inexpensive**
ርክብ rkb *(n.)* **relevance**
ርክብ rkb *(n.)* **communication**
ርከሳ rkesa *(n.)* **gambit**
ርኻብ r'khab *(n.)* **stirrup**
ርኽሰት rkset *(n.)* **sacrilege**
ርሳሕ ፈሳሲ rsah fesasi *(n.)* **sewage**
ርሳስ rsas *(n.)* **pencil**
ረስሓት rsĥat *(n.)* **dirt**
ርስሓት rsĥat *(n.)* **grime**
ርስሓት rsĥat *(n.)* **sleaze**
ርስሓት ወገደ rsĥat wegede *(v.)* **excrete**
ርስቲ rsti *(n.)* **domain**
ርስቲ rsti *(n.)* **manor**
ርሱን rsun *(adj.)* **burning**
ርትዓዊ ሓቂ rt'äwi ĥaqi *(n.)* **fact**
ርትዓውነት rt'äwnwt *(n.)* **rationalism**
ርውየት rwuyet *(n.)* **satiety**
ርውየት rwyet *(n.)* **fulfilment**
ርውየት rwyet *(n.)* **indulgence**
ርእይቶ r'eyto *(n.)* **opinion**
ርእይቶ ሃበ r'eyto hab *(v.)* **opine**
ርእዮት r'eyot *(n.)* **outlook**
ሮቦት robot *(n.)* **robot**
ሮብራ robra *(n.)* **seagull**
ሮድስተር rodster *(n.)* **roadster**
ሮድየም rodyem *(n.)* **rhodium**
ሮኬት roket *(n.)* **rocket**
ሮለር ኮስተር roler koster *(n.)* **rollercoaster**
ሮራ rora *(n.)* **plateau**
ሮስተር roster *(n.)* **roster**
ሮዛ roza *(adj.)* **pink**
ሮዜት rozet *(n.)* **rosette**

ሰ

ሰዓብቲ ወለዶ seäabti weledo *(n.)* **posterity**
ሰፋፊ sefafi *(n.)* **aerial**
ሰፋፊቶ sefafito *(n.)* **glider**
ሰፋራይ sefaray *(n.)* **settler**
ሰፋዪ ክዳን sefayi kdan *(n.)* **tailor**
ሰፈር sefer *(n.)* **neighbourhood**
ሰፈር sefer *(n.)* **nest**
ሰፈር አዕዋፍ sefer aëwaf *(n.)* **roost**
ሰፈር ኣልቦ sefer albo *(adj.)* **numberless**
ሰፈር ኣራዊት sefer 'arawit *(n.)* **lair**
ሰፈር ድኻታት sefer dkatat *(n.)* **slum**
ሰፈር ኳኽ sefer kwak *(n.)* **rookery**
ሰፈር ነፈርቲ sefer neferti *(n.)* **hangar**
ሰፈር ሽጉጥ sefer shguṭ *(n.)* **holster**
ሰፈረ sefere *(v.)* **inhabit**
ሰፈረ sefere *(v.)* **quantify**
ሰፈረ sefere *(v.)* **settle**
ሰፈርተኛ sefertegna *(n.)* **resident**
ሰፈየ sefeye *(v.)* **sew**
ሰፈየ sefeye *(v.)* **stitch**
ሰፊሕ sefih *(adj.)* **loose**
ሰፊሕ sefiĥ *(adj.)* **elaborate**
ሰፊሕ sefiĥ *(adj.)* **roomy**

ሰፊሕ sefiḧ *(adj.)* **ample**
ሰፊሕ sefiḥ *(adj.)* **vast**
ሰፊሕ sefiḥ *(adj.)* **voluminous**
ሰፊሕ sefiḧ *(adj.)* **broad**
ሰፊሕ sefiḧ *(adj.)* **capacious**
ሰፍነግ sefneg *(n.)* **sponge**
ሰጋእ መጋእ በሃሊ sega'è mega'è behali *(adj.)* **hesitant**
ሰጋእጋእ በለ sega'ega'e bele *(v.)* **falter**
ሰጋላይ segalay *(n.)* **astrologer**
ሰግአ seg'e *(v.t)* **dread**
ሰግአ seg'e *(v.)* **misgive**
ሰገባ segeba *(n.)* **scabbard**
ሰገደ segede *(v.)* **bow**
ሰገን segen *(adj.)* **young**
ሰገን segen *(n.)* **youngster**
ሰገነት segenet *(n.)* **balcony**
ሰገጥ በለ segeẗ bele *(v.)* **flinch**
ሰጎደ segode *(v.)* **guzzle**
ሰጎገ segoge *(v.)* **dismiss**
ሰጎመ segome *(v.)* **stride**
ሰሓ seha *(v.i.)* **itch**
ሰሓበ seḧabe *(v.)* **attract**
ሰሓበ seḧabe *(v.)* **pull**
ሰብኣይ sb'ay *(n.)* **man**
ሰሓቢ sehabi *(adj.)* **luscious**
ሰሓቢ seḧabi *(adj.)* **piquant**
ሰሓፊት sehafit *(n.)* **typist**
ሰሓቒ seĥaqi *(adj.)* **risible**
ሰሓተ seḧate *(v.)* **miss**
ሰሓተ seḧate *(v.)* **stray**
ሰሓቕ sehqh *(n.)* **laughter**
ሰሓቐ sehqhe *(v.)* **laugh**
ሰኽራም sekaram *(adj.)* **drunkard**
ሰክረታርየት sekretaryet *(n.)* **secretariat**
ሰኹዐ seḱu'ë *(v.)* **insert**
ሰላሕታ selaḧta *(n.)* **stealth**
ሰላሊ selali *(n.)* **spy**
ሰላም selam *(n.)* **peace**
ሰለም ኣበለ selam abele *(v. i)* **doze**
ሰላም በለ selam bele *(n.)* **greet**
ሰላማዊ selamawi *(n.)* **pacific**
ሰላማዊ selamawi *(adj.)* **peaceable**
ሰላማዊ selamawi *(adj.)* **peaceful**
ሰላማዊ selamawi *(adj.)* **placid**
ሰላማዊ ሰልፊ selamawi selfi *(n.)* **demonstration**
ሰላምታ selamta *(n.)* **greeting**
ሰላምታ selamta *(n.)* **salutation**
ሰላምታ selamta *(n.)* **salute**
ሰላሳ selasa *(adj. & n.)* **thirty**
ሰላሳ selasa *(adj. & n.)* **thirty**
ሰላጠ selaẗe *(n.)* **cove**
ሰልዲ seldi *(n.)* **coinage**
ሰሌዳ መፋትሕ seleeda mefatḥ *(n.)* **keyboard**
ሰሌዳ ምልክታ seleeda mlkta *(n.)* **noticeboard**
ሰሌዳ seleeda *(n.)* **blackboard**
ሰለፍ selef *(n.)* **thigh**
ሰለፍ ሓሰማ selef ḥasema *(n.)* **ham**
ሰለኹ seleḱwa *(v.)* **insinuate**
ሰላማዊ ሰልፊ ጌሩ selemawi selfi gieru *(n.)* **picket**
ሰለመ seleme *(v.)* **stud**
ሰለመ seleme *(v.)* **adorn**
ሰለስተ seleste *(adj. & n.)* **three**
ሰናን senay *(adj.)* **serrated**
ሰናይ ግብሪ senay gbri *(n.)* **succour**
ሰንበደ senbede *(v.)* **appal**
ሰንበት senbet *(n.)* **Sunday**
ሰንበተ senbete *(n.)* **sojourn**
ሰንደል sendel *(n.)* **sandal**
ሰንደልደል በለ sendeldel bele *(v.)* **shamble**

ሰንደቕ sendeq̈ ***(n.)*** **banner**
ሰንደወ sendewe ***(v.)*** **discard**
ሰንደወ sendewe ***(v.)*** **fling**
ሰነ sene ***(n.)*** **June**
ሰለስተ ዕፅፊ seleste asfi ***(n.)*** **triple**
ሰለስተ ግዜ seleste gze ***(adv.)*** **thrice**
ሰለስተ ቅድሕታት seleste kdhtat ***(adj.)*** **triplicate**
ሰለስተ ማናቱ seleste manatu ***(n.)*** **triplet**
ሰለስተ መአዝን seleste meazen ***(n.)*** **triangle**
ሰለስተ ተመሳሳሊ ሓሳብ ዘለዎ seleste temesasali hasab zelewo ***(n.)*** **trilogy**
ሰለስተ ወገን seleste wegen ***(adj.)*** **tripartite**
ስልጣነ seletan ***(n.)*** **civilization**
ሰለይ በለ seley bele ***(v.)*** **trudge**
ሰልፊ selfi ***(n.)*** **array**
ሰታይ setay ***(adj.)*** **alcoholic**
ሰታይ setay ***(n.)*** **dipsomania**
ሰልፊ selfi ***(n.)*** **parade**
ሰልፊ selfi ***(n.)*** **procession**
ሰልፊ ተወጣሕቲ selfi teweẗahti ***(n.)*** **cavalcade**
ሰንፈላል senfelal ***(n.)*** **rut**
ሰንገለ sengele ***(v.)*** **coax**
ሰንገለ sengele ***(v.)*** **comfort**
ሰንገወ sengewe ***(v.)*** **spay**
ሰንካቲ senkati ***(n.)*** **baker**
ሰንከልከል በለ senkelkel bele ***(v.)*** **totter**
ሰንከልከል በለ senkelkel bele ***(v.)*** **wobble**
ሰንከተ senkete ***(v.)*** **bake**
ሰንኬሎ senkielo ***(n.)*** **pail**
ሰንቀ senqe ***(n.)*** **ceiling**
ሰንጣቂት sentaqit ***(n.)*** **diameter**
ሰንጠቀ senteqe ***(v.)*** **rive**
ሰንጠቐ senẗeq̈e ***(v.)*** **intersect**
ሰንጢ senti ***(n.)*** **dagger**
ሰንቲግሬድ sentigreed ***(adj.)*** **centigrade**
ሰንቲሜትር sentimeetr ***(n.)*** **centimetre**
ሰፒኖሬሎ sepinoreelo ***(n.)*** **stickleback**
ሰፕራቶ seprato ***(n.)*** **sprat**
ሰቐለ seq̈ele ***(v.)*** **hoist**
ሰቀላ seqhela ***(n.)*** **loft**
ሰራሒ በርሚል serah̆i bermil ***(n.)*** **cooper**
ሰራሒ ሳእኒ serahi saeni' ***(n.)*** **cobbler**
ሰራሕተኛ serahtegna ***(n.)*** **worker**
ሰራሕተኛ ገዛ serahtegna geza ***(n.)*** **maid**
ሰራሕተኛ መዓድን serah̆tegna me'ädn ***(n.)*** **miner**
ሰራሕተኛታት serah̆tegnatat ***(n.)*** **staff**
ሰራሕተኛታት serahtenatat ***(n.)*** **personnel**
ሰራሕተኛት serahtenyatat ***(n.)*** **crew**
ሰራቒ seraqi ***(n.)*** **thief**
ሰራቒ seraq̈i ***(n.)*** **burglar**
ሰራዊት serawit ***(n.)*** **army**
ሰራዊት ፈረሰኛ serawit fresenya ***(n.)*** **cavalry**
ሰራዪ serayi ***(n.)*** **magician**
ሰራዝ seraz ***(n.)*** **stroke**
ሰርዐ ser'ë ***(v.)*** **align**
ሰርዐ ser'ë ***(v.)*** **rank**
ሰርዐ ser'ë ***(v.)*** **arrange**
ሰርዐ ser'ë ***(v.)*** **systematize**
ሰረገላ seregela ***(n.)*** **carriage**
ሰረገላ seregela ***(n.)*** **coupe**

ሰረገላ በረድ seregela bered *(n.)* **sleigh**
ሰርከስ serekse *(n.)* **circus**
ሰረቀ sereqe *(v.)* **rob**
ሰረቐ sereqhe *(v.)* **steal**
ሰረቐ sereqhe *(v.)* **swipe**
ሰረረ serere *(v.)* **copulate**
ሰረት seret *(n.)* **plinth**
ሰረት seret *(n.)* **basis**
ሰረት ኣልቦ seret'albo *(adj.)* **baseless**
ሰረታዊ seretawi *(n.)* **basic**
ሰረተ serete *(n.)* **base**
ሰረተ serete *(v.)* **embed**
ሰረተ ሓሳብ serete hasab *(n.)* **thesis**
ሰረፀ seretze *(v.)* **infiltrate**
ሰረየ sereye *(v.)* **conjure**
ሰረየ sereye *(v.)* **bewitch**
ሰረዘ sereze *(v.)* **annul**
ሰረዘ sereze *(v.)* **revoke**
ሰረዘ sereze *(v.)* **abrogate**
ሰረዘ sereze *(v.)* **cancel**
ሰርሐ serhe *(v.)* **make**
ሰርሒ መጣምር serhi metamr *(n.)* **saddler**
ሰራሕተኛ serȟtegna *(n.)* **employee**
ሰሪሑ ረኽበ seriȟu rekebe *(v.)* **earn**
ሰሪቕካ ምራይ seriqka mray *(v.)* **peek**
ሰርወ serwe *(n.)* **lath**
ስስዐ ses'ë-a *(n.)* **greed**
ሳዕሰዐ sëse'ë *(v.)* **dance**
ሰሰነ sesene *(v.)* **thrive**
ሰዓረ se'are *(v.)* **overcome**
ሰዓረ se'are *(v.)* **overpower**
ሰገን segen *(n.)* **ostrich**
ሰገደ segede *(n.)* **obeisance**
ሰጎገ segoge *(v.)* **oust**
ሰፋራይ sefaray *(n.)* **occupant**
ሰተኖግራፊ setenografi *(n.)* **stenography**
ሰተፕ setep *(n.)* **steppe**
ሰተየ seteye *(v. t)* **drink**
ሰተየ seteye *(v.)* **imbibe**
ሰጢሙ ዝተኣሰረ setimu zeteasere *(adj.)* **tight**
ሰዓበ seäbe *(v.)* **ensue**
ሰዓበ se'äbe *(v.)* **adhere**
ሰዓበ se'äbe *(v.)* **follow**
ሰኣለ se'ale *(v.)* **depict**
ሰኣለ se'ale *(v.)* **draw**
ሰዓለ se'äle *(v.)* **cough**
ሰኣሊ seali *(n.)* **photographer**
ሰዓመ se'ame *(v.t.)* **kiss**
ሰዓመ se'ame *(v.)* **smooch**
ሰኣነ se'ane *(v.)* **lose**
ሰዓረ seare *(v.)* **win**
ሰዓረ se'äre *(v. t.)* **defeat**
ሰዓረ se'äre *(v.)* **repeal**
ሰዓረ se'äre *(v.)* **surmount**
ሰዓረ se'äre *(v.)* **vanquish**
ሰዓት seat *(n.)* **chronograph**
ሰዓት seat' *(n.)* **clock**
ሰዓት se'ät *(n.)* **hour**
ሰዓት ደወል seat' dewel *(n.)* **chime**
ሰብኣያ ዝሞታ seaya zemota *(n.)* **widow**
ሰብ seb *(n.)* **person**
ሰብ seb *(n.)* **mankind**
ሰበ ስልጣን seb sltan *(n.)* **dignitary**
ሰብ ሰራሕ seb sraȟ *(adj.)* **synthetic**
ሰብ ዘይብሉ seb zeybelu *(adj.)* **uninhabited**
ሰብ ዘይብሉ seb zeybelu *(adj.)* **unmanned**
ሰብ ዝሰርሖ ጸጉሪ seb zserho xeguri *(n.)* **wig**
ሰብዓ seb'a *(adj. & n.)* **seventy**

ሰባበረ sebabere *(v.)* **inflect**
ሰባበረ sebabere *(v.t.)* **shatter**
ሰባኺ sebaḱi *(n.)* **preacher**
ሰባር መርከብ sebar merkeb *(n.)* **shipwreck**
ሰባት sebat *(n.)* **people**
ሰብኣዊ seb'awi *(adj.)* **human**
ሰብኣዊ ኮነ seb'awi kone *(v.)* **humanize**
ሰብኣዊነታዊ seb'awinetawi *(adj.)* **humanitarian**
ሰብኣዊነት ገፈፈ seb'awnet gefefe *()* **dehumanize**
ሰብኣይ ንግስቲ sebeaayi negeseti *(n.)* **consort**
ሰበባ sebeba *(n.)* **moss**
ስብሒ sebehi *(n.)* **cellulite**
ሰበኸ sebeke *(v.)* **sermonize**
ሰብእነት seb'ènet *(n.)* **virility**
ሰበረ sebere *(v.)* **break**
ሰበይታይ sebeytay *(adj.)* **effeminate**
ሰበይቲ sebeyti *(n.)* **woman**
ሰበይቲ ምኳን sebeyti mkuan *(v.)* **womanize**
ሰበይቲ ወዲ sebeyti wedi *(n.)* **daughter-in-law**
ሰበይትነት sebeytnet *(n.)* **womanhood**
ሰበይቱ ዝሞተቶ sebeytu zmoteto *(n.)* **widower**
ሰደደ sedede *(v.)* **consign**
ሰደደ sedede *(v.)* **propel**
ሰደቓ sedeqa *(n.)* **desk**
ሰደቓ sedeqa *(n.)* **diagram**
ሰደረ sedere *(v.)* **lope**
ሰደርያ sederya *(n.)* **waistcoat**
ሰዲድ sedid *(n.)* **footage**
ሰውአ sew'a *(v.)* **sacrifice**
ሰወአ sewe'e *(v.)* **immolate**
ሰውሒ sewhi *(n.)* **lawn**
ሰውሒ sewhi *(n.)* **turf**
ሰውሒ sewḧi *(n.)* **meadow**
ሰውሰወ sewsewe *(v.)* **shrug**
ሰያዒ seya'i *(adj.)* **sexy**
ሰየፈ seyefe *(v.)* **behead**
ሰየፈ seyefe *(v.)* **decapitate**
ሰየመ seyeme *(v.)* **designate**
ሰየመ seb'awnet *(n.)* **humanism**
ሰብኣውነት seḥabe *(v.)* **waive**
ሰሓበ selamta 'id *(n.)* **handshake**
ሰላምታ ኢድ seyeme *(v.)* **nominate**

ሲ

ሲደር cider *(n.)* **cider**
ሲጋር sigar *(n.)* **cigar**
ሲልፎ silfo *(n.)* **sylph**
ሲሊንደር silinder *(n.)* **cylinder**
ሲንዲካቶ sindikato *(n.)* **syndicate**
ሲረና sirena *(n.)* **buzzer**
ሲሶ siso *(adj.)* **third**
ሲትሩስ sitrus *(n.)* **citrus**
ሲትሩሳዊ sitrusawi *(adj.)* **citric**
ሲያናይድ siyanayd *(n.)* **cyanide**
ሲ si *()* **C**

ሳ

ሳዕቤን saëbeen *(n.)* **effect**
ሳዕቤን sa'ëben *(n.)* **repercussion**
ሳዕቤናዊ saëbenawi *(adj.)* **resultant**
ሳዕቤን saebien *(n.)* **upshot**
ሳዕቤን saee'bene *(n.)* **consequence**
ሳእኒ ጎማ sa'eni goma *(n.)* **sneaker**
ሳምሶማ ሳምሶማ *(v.)* **jog**

ሳዕሪ sa'ëri *(n.)* **grass**
ሳዕሪ ኣብልዐ sa'ëri 'abl'ë *(v.)* **graze**
ሳዕሳዒይ sa'ëse'ë *(n.)* **dancer**
ሳፋሪ safari *(n.)* **safari**
ሳጓ sagwa *(n.)* **nickname**
ሳሕቲ sahti *(adv.)* **seldom**
ሳሕቲ saḥti *(adv.)* **hardly**
ሳሕቲ ዝርከብ sahti zrkeb *(adj.)* **scarce**
ሳሕቲ ዝርከብ saĥti zrkeb *(adj.)* **rare**
ሳካሪን sakarin *(n.)* **saccharin**
ሳኬቶ sakieto *(n.)* **sachet**
ሳክስፎን saksfon *(n.)* **saxophone**
ሳልቤታ salbeeta *(n.)* **bib**
ሳልፈር salfer *(n.)* **sulphur**
ሳሎን salon *(n.)* **salon**
ሳልሳ salsa *(n.)* **salsa**
ሳልሳይ ደረጃ salsay dereja *(adj.)* **tertiary**
ሳልቬታ salvieta *(n.)* **serviette**
ሳልቮ salvo *(n.)* **salvo**
ሳምባ samba *(n.)* **lung**
ሳምዕተኛ samëtegna *(n.)* **notary**
ሳምራዊ samrawi *(n.)* **Samaritan**
ሳሙና samuna *(n.)* **soap**
ሳንዱቕ sanaduqe *(n.)* **cist**
ሳንባ መንቀርሳ sanba menkersa *(n.)* **tuberculosis**
ሳንዲ sandi *(n.)* **sundae**
ሳንዱች sanduch *(n.)* **sandwich**
ሳንዱቕ sanduq̈ *(n.)* **box**
ሳንቲም sanetim *(n.)* **cent**
ሳንቲም sanetime *(n.)* **coin**
ሳንጃ sanĵa *(n.)* **bayonet**
ሳንቲም santim *(n.)* **penny**
ሳንቲም santim *(n.)* **Yen**
ሳንቲም ዘይብሉ santim zeyblu *(adj.)* **penniless**

ሳሬት sareet *(n.)* **spider**
ሳሪ sari *(n.)* **sari**
ሳቲን satin *(n.)* **satin**
ሳትላይት satlayt *(n.)* **satellite**
ሳፁን ሬሳ satsun resa *(n.)* **casket**
ሳፁን ሬሳ satsun resa *(n.)* **coffin**
ሳውና sawuna *(n.)* **sauna**
ሳይበር sayber *(comb.)* **cyber**
ሳይበርስፔስ sayberspas *(n.)* **cyberspace**
ሳይኮሎጂካል saykoloĵikal *(adj.)* **psychological**
ሳይኮሎጂካዊ saykoloĵikawi *(n.)* **psychologist**
ሳይኮሎጂ saykoloyĵi *(n.)* **psychology**
ሳይንስ sayns *(n.)* **science**
ሳይንሳዊ saynsawi *(adj.)* **scientific**
ሳይንቲስት saynst *(n.)* **scientist**

ሴ

ሴዳን siedan *(n.)* **sedan**
ሴፍ sief *(n.)* **sabre**
ሴኦል sieol *(n.)* **perdition**
ሴጣን sietan *(n.)* **Satan**
ሴጣናዊ sietanawi *(adj.)* **satanic**
ሴፍ seef *(n.)* **sword**
ሴጋ ገበረ seega gebere *(v.)* **masturbate**
ሴራሚክ seeramik *(n.)* **ceramic**
ሴጋለ segale *(n.)* **rye**
ስጋዊ segawi *(adj.)* **carnal**
ስእላዊ selawi *(adj.)* **photographic**
ስእላዊ መግለፂ s'elawi megletzi *(n.)* **graph**
ስእላዊ መግለጺ selawi meglexi *(n.)* **pictograph**
ሴልሲየስ selcius *(n.)* **Celsius**

ስሙይ ሰብ semuyei sebe *(n.)* **celebrity**
ስነ ከዋክብቲ sene kewakbti *(n.)* **horoscope**
ስነ ስርዓታዊ sene sereaa'tawii *(adj.)* **ceremonial**
ስነ-ጥዕና sene te-ena *(n.)* **hygiene**
ሰነድ sened *(n.)* **document**
ሰነድ ልቓሕ sened lqah *(n.)* **debenture**
ሰነፍ senef *(n.)* **idler**
ሰነፍ senef *(adj.)* **indolent**
ሰነፍ senef *(adj.)* **lazy**
ሰነገ senege *(v.)* **gobble**
ስነ ስርዓት ዘለዎ senei sereat zelewoo *(adj.)* **ceremonious**
ሰንሰለት seneselet *(n.)* **chain**
ሰይጣን seytan *(n.)* **devil**
ሱቕ በሃሊ suq behali *(adj.)* **taciturn**
ሱቖ suqo *(n.)* **gruel**
ሱር sur *(n.)* **root**
ሱር ዝሰደደ sur zsedede *(adj.)* **rooted**
ሱሱዕ susu'ë *(adj.)* **rapacious**
ስእነት s'enet *(n.)* **loss**
ስእነት ዓቕሚ s'enet 'aqmi *(n.)* **incapacity**
ስመ ጽራሕ sme tsrah *(n.)* **onomatopoeia**
ስም ምጥፋእ shem mxfa'e *(n.)* **obloquy**
ስራሕ ኣብዘሐ srah abzahe *(v.)* **overburden**
ስርዐ ser'ë *(v.)* **organize**
ስነ ህላወ sne hlawe *(n.)* **ontology**
ስዉር swr *(n.)* **occult**
ስቪል sevil *(n.)* **civilian**
ስፋይ sfay *(n.)* **stitch**
ስፈ ንህቢ sfe nhbi *(n.)* **honeycomb**
ስፍሓት sfhat *(n.)* **width**
ስፍሓት s'fḧat *(n.)* **stretch**
ስፍሓት sfḧat *(n.)* **amplitude**
ስፍሓት sfḧat *(n.)* **area**
ስፍለት sflet *(n.)* **anomaly**
ስፍራ ባሕተዎት sfra bahtewot *(n.)* **hermitage**
ስፍሪ sfri *(n.)* **quantity**
ስፍሰፋ sfsefa *(n.)* **weightlifting**
ስጋ sga *(n.)* **curry**
ስጋ sga *(n.)* **flesh**
ስጋ sga *(n.)* **meat**
ስጋ በጊዕ sga begi'ë *(n.)* **mutton**
ስጋ ሓሰማ sga ḧasema *(n.)* **pork**
ስጋ ምልባስ sga mlbas *(n.)* **incarnation**
ስጋ ምራኽ sga mraḱ *(n.)* **veal**
ስጋ ሰለወ sga selewe *(v.)* **grill**
ስጋ ዝለበሰ sga zlebese *(adj.)* **incarnate**
ስግኣት sg'at *(n.)* **misgiving**
ስገም sgem *(n.)* **barley**
ስግለት ከዋኽብቲ sglet kewaḱbti *(n.)* **astrology**
ስነ-መግቢ sin-e meg-bi *(n.)* **gastronomy**
ስራሕ sir'ahh *(n.)* **career**
ስቓይ skay *(n.)* **torture**
ስክፍታ skfta *(n.)* **compunction**
ስኽፍታ skfta *(n.)* **premonition**
ስክፍታ skfta *(n.)* **qualm**
ስክፍታ skfta *(n.)* **scruple**
ስኪዞፍረንያ skizofrenia *(n.)* **schizophrenia**
ስኮታዊ skotawi *(v.)* **Scot**
ስኩፍ skuf *(adj.)* **scrupulous**
ስላሴ slasi *(n.)* **trinity**
ስላጣ slata *(n.)* **salad**
ስልበጣ slbeta *(n.)* **recrimination**

ስለ sle ***(n.)*** **sake**
ስለ ጉዕዞ ዘርኢ ፊልሚ sleguazo zerai filmi ***(n.)*** **travelogue**
ሰላሕታዊ s'leḧatawi ***(adj.)*** **stealthy**
ስለላ slela ***(n.)*** **espionage**
ስለመ sleme ***(v.)*** **caparison**
ስለው ፈለው slew felew ***(n.)*** **see-saw**
ስለዚ slezi ***(adv.)*** **accordingly**
ስለዚ slezi ***(adv.)*** **thus**
ስሊከን sliken ***(n.)*** **silicon**
ስልኪ slki ***(n.)*** **telephone**
ስልኪ ኣልቦ slki albo ***(adj.)*** **wireless**
ስልኩይ slkuy ***(n.)*** **valetudinarian**
ስልማት ናይ መጽሓፍ slmat nay mexḥaf ***(n.)*** **vignette**
ስልመ ክንቲት slme kntit ***(n.)*** **plume**
ስልኪ seli ***(n.)*** **phone**
ስእሊ seli ***(n.)*** **photo**
ስእሊ seli ***(n.)*** **photograph**
ስእሊ s'eli ***(n.)*** **drawing**
ስእሊ s'eli ***(n.)*** **picture**
ስእሊ መሬት s'èli mereet ***(n.)*** **landscape**
ስእሊ ዝፈጥር ንሽተይ ነጠብጣብ ኣብ ኮምፒተር sèli zfeẗr nèshtey neẗebẗab nay kompiter ***(n.)*** **pixel**
ስልጣን sltan ***(n.)*** **dominion**
ስልጣን ሃበ slẗan habe ***(v.)*** **empower**
ስልጣን ዝሃዘ sltan zhaze ***(n.)*** **tenure**
ስልጣኑ ኣካፈለ sltanu akafele ***(v.)*** **decentralize**
ስልጣንያ sltanya ***(n.)*** **jar**
ስልታዊ s'ltawi ***(adj.)*** **strategic**
ስልጠና sltena ***(n.)*** **training**
ስልቲ slti ***(n.)*** **strategy**
ስልቲ s'lti ***(n.)*** **stratagem**
ስልቲ ዘውጽእ s'lti zewts'e ***(n.)*** **strategist**
ኣልትራሳውንድ sltrasawnd ***(n.)*** **ultrasound**
ስልጡን sltun ***(adj.)*** **urbane**
ስሉብ slub ***(n.)*** **eunuch**
ስሉም slum ***(n.)*** **tapestry**
ስሉጥ sluẗ ***(adj.)*** **agile**
ስሉጥ sluṭ ***(adj.)*** **handy**
ስሉጥ sluẗ ***(adj.)*** **brisk**
ስም s'm ***(n.)*** **noun**
ስም ኣጥፈአ sm atfe'e ***(n.)*** **denunciation**
ስም ከተማ sm ketema ***(n.)*** **Perry**
ስም ሰብ ዘፀልም sm seb zetselm ***(adj.)*** **scurrilous**
ስምዓት sm'ät ***(n.)*** **audition**
ስምብራት smbrat ***(n.)*** **contusion**
ሽምደዳ šmdeda ***(n.)*** **rote**
ስምዒት sm'eit ***(n.)*** **sensation**
ስምዒት sm'eit ***(n.)*** **sentiment**
ስምዒት ሓዘን smeit hazen ***(n.)*** **pathos**
ስምዒት ዘለዎ sm'eit zelewo ***(adj.)*** **sentient**
ስምዒት ዘንቀሳቕስ smëit zenqesaqs ***(adj.)*** **poignant**
ስምዒታዊ smeitawi ***(adj.)*** **passionate**
ስምዒታዊ sm'eitawi ***(adj.)*** **sentimental**
ስመራግድ smeragd ***(n.)*** **emerald**
ስመ-ስውር smeswr ***(adj.)*** **anonymous**
ስመ-ስውርነት smeswrnet ***(n.)*** **anonymity**
ስምዒ sm'ie ***(n.)*** **wax**
ስሚዒት sm'ït ***(n.)*** **emotion**
ስምዒት sm'ït ***(n.)*** **feeling**
ስምዒት ቀስቀሰ sm'ït qesqese ***(v.)*** **electrify**

ስምዒት ዝመልኦ sm'it zmel'o ***(adj.)*** **soulful**
ስምዒት ዝቅስቅስ sm'ïït zqsqs ***(adj.)*** **emotive**
ስምዒታዊ sm'ïtawi ***(adj.)*** **emotional**
ስምዒታዊ sm'ïtawi ***(adj.)*** **impassioned**
ስምዒታዊ sm'ïtawi ***(adj.)*** **intense**
ስምምዕ smm'e ***(adj.)*** **tacit**
ስምምዕ smm'e ***(a.)*** **unanimity**
ስምምዕ smm'ë ***(n.)*** **agreement**
ስምምዕ smm'ë ***(n.)*** **concord**
ስምምዕ smm'ë ***(n.)*** **concordance**
ስምምዕ smm'ë ***(n.)*** **conformity**
ስምምዕ smm'ë ***(n.)*** **correspondence**
ስምምዕ smm'ë ***(n.)*** **assent**
ስምረት smret ***(n.)*** **realization**
ስምስም smsm ***(n.)*** **sesame**
ስሙይ smuy ***(adj.)*** **eminent**
ስሙይ smuy ***(adj.)*** **famous**
ስናፐር snaper ***(n.)*** **snapper**
ስድስቶ sdsto ***(n.)*** **sextuplet**
ስባር sbar ***(n.)*** **fragment**
ስብኣይነት sb'aynet ***(n.)*** **manhood**
ስብሓት sbĥat ***(n.)*** **reverence**
ስብሒ sbĥi ***(n.)*** **fat**
ስብሒ sbḥi ***(n.)*** **grease**
ስብሒ ምውጋድ sbhi mwgad ***(n.)*** **liposuction**
ስብከት sbket ***(n.)*** **parish**
ስብከት sbket ***(n.)*** **propaganda**
ስብከት sbket ***(n.)*** **sermon**
ስብቅልነት sbqlnet ***(n.)*** **elegance**
ስብቆ sbqo ***(n.)*** **soup**
ስብቁል sbqul ***(adj.)*** **chic**
ስብቁል sbqul ***(n.)*** **dandy**
ስብርባር ሕንፃፅ sbrbar hntsats ***(n.)*** **zigzag**
ስብረት sbret ***(n.)*** **breakage**
ስቡዕ ጐኖ sbu'ë guano ***(n.)*** **heptagon**
ስቡር sbur ***(adj.)*** **broken**
ስድዓት sd'at ***(n.)*** **seduction**
ስደት sdet ***(n.)*** **exile**
ስደተኛ sdetegna ***(n.)*** **refugee**
ስዲ sdi ***(adj.)*** **impertinent**
ስዲ sdi ***(adj.)*** **rude**
ስዲ sdi ***(adj.)*** **unruly**
ስዲ ኸደ sdi ḱede ***(v.)*** **misbehave**
ስዲ ንባብ sdi nbab ***(n.)*** **prose**
ስድነት sdnet ***(n.)*** **asperity**
ስድነግ sdnet ***(n)*** **impertinence**
ስድነት sdnet ***(n.)*** **misbehaviour**
ስድራ sdra ***(n.)*** **span**
ስድራ ቤት sdra biet ***(n.)*** **family**
ስድራቤት sdrabetawi ***(n.)*** **parentage**
ስድራቤታዊ sdrabetawi ***(adj.)*** **parental**
ስንብራት snbrat ***(n.)*** **bruise**
ስንጭሮ snčro ***(n.)*** **vale**
ስነ ኣእምሮ sne aèmro ***(n.)*** **psychiatry**
ስነ ባህለታዊ sne bahletawi ***(adj.)*** **semantic**
ስነ-በረራ sne berera ***(n.)*** **aviation**
ስነ ብሂላዊ sne bhilawi ***(adj.)*** **mythological**
ስነ ብረት sne bret ***(n.)*** **metallurgy**
ስነ ዕዳጋ sne edaga ***(n.)*** **marketing**
ሰነ ሃለዋት sne halewat ***(n.)*** **statistics**
ስነ ሃለዋታዊ sne halewatawi ***(adj.)*** **statistical**
ስነ ሓሸራ sne ĥashera ***(n.)*** **entomology**
ስነ-ሃይማኖት sne haymanot ***(n.)*** **theology**

ስነ ህይወተኛ sne hywetenya *(n.)* **biologist**
ስነ ህዝቢ sne hzbi *(n.)* **demography**
ስነ ምድረኛ sne mdregna *(n.)* **geologist**
ስነ ምድሪ sne mdri *(n.)* **geology**
ስነ ማዓድን sne me'ädn *(n.)* **mineralogy**
ስነ መትኒ sne metni *(n.)* **neurology**
ስነ መዛርዕ sne mezar'ë *(n.)* **morphology**
ስነ ምግባራዊ sne mgbarawi *(n.)* **ethical**
ስነ ምግባረኛ sne mgbaregna *(n.)* **moralist**
ስነ ምግባሩ ኣመሓየሸ sne mgbaru ameȟayeshe *(v.)* **moralize**
ስነ ምሕዳር sne mĥdar *(n.)* **ecology**
ስነ ምንቅስቃስ sne mnqskas *(n.)* **dynamics**
ስነ ነፀብራቅ sne netsebraq *(n.)* **reflexology**
ስነ ቃላዊ sne qalawi *(adj.)* **lexical**
ስን ቕመም sne qe'mem *(n.)* **chemistry**
ስነ ቅርፃቅርፂ sne qrtsaqrtsi *(n.)* **sculpture**
ስነ ቅርፃዊ sne qrtsawi *(adj.)* **sculptural**
ስነ ቁጠባ sne quteba *(n.)* **economics**
ስነ ሴም sne siem *(adj.)* **Semitic**
ስነ ስርዓት sne sr'ät *(n.)* **discipline**
ስነ ስርዓት sne sr'ät *(n.)* **propriety**
ስነ ፅሑፋዊ sne tzhufawi *(adj.)* **literary**
ስነ-ዉሕስና sne- wuhsna *(n.)* **immunology**
ስነ ፅዋ sne xwa *(n.)* **mythology**
ስነ ዜጋ sne zeega *(n.)* **civics**
ስነ-ኣትክልቲ sne'atklti *(n.)* **botany**
ስነ-በረራ sneberera *(n.)* **aeronautics**
ስነ-ዱር snedur *(n.)* **forestry**
ስነ-ዕለታት sne'ëletat *(n.)* **chronology**
ስነ-እንስሳ sne-enssa *(n.)* **zoology**
ስነ-ፈለክ snefelek *(n.)* **astronomy**
ስነ-ሓሳብ sneḥasab *(n.)* **ideology**
ስነ-ሕጊ sneȟgi *(n.)* **jurisprudence**
ስነ-ህንጻ snehnxa *(n.)* **architecture**
ስነ-ህይወት snehywet *(n.)* **biology**
ስነ-ኮኾበኛ snekoḱobenya *(n.)* **astronomer**
ስነ ሞጎት sne-mogot *(n.)* **logic**
ስነ-ቅመም ህይወታውያን sneqmem hywetawyan *(n.)* **biochemistry**
ስነ-ቅርጺ ኣካል sneqrxi 'akal *(n.)* **anatomy**
ስነ-ሰብ sneseb *(n.)* **anthropology**
ስነ-ስርዓት በዓል sne-srät beäl *(n.)* **pageant**
ስነ-ጥበባዊ snetbebawi *(adj.)* **artistic**
ስነ-ጠቢብ snetebib *(n.)* **artist**
ስነ-ጽባቐ snexbaq̈e *(n.)* **aesthetics**
ስንፈተ ግብረስጋ snfete gebresga *(n.)* **impotence**
ስንፈተ ግብረስጋ ዘለዎ snfete gebresga zelewo *(adj.)* **impotent**
ስንፍነት snfnet *(n.)* **idleness**
ስኒ sni *(n.)* **cog**
ስኒ sni *(n.)* **tooth**
ስኒ ኣውፂኡ ን ህፃን sni awsiau nhsan *(v.)* **teethe**
ስኒ ሓርማዝ sni ȟarmaz *(n.)* **ivory**
ስኒት snit *(n.)* **chord**
ስኒት snit *(n.)* **rapprochement**
ስኒት snit *(n.)* **rhyme**

ስንቂ መቅረቢ snqi meqrebi *(n.)* **victualler**
ሽንቅጥ šnqt *(adj.)* **slim**
ስኑከር snuker *(n.)* **snooker**
ሶዳ soda *(n.)* **soda**
ሶደመኛዊት sodemegnawit *(n.)* **lesbian**
ሶዶምነት sodomnet *(n.)* **sodomy**
ሶፋ sofa *(n.)* **sofa**
ሶፍቲ softi *(n.)* **tissue**
ሶኬት sokiet *(n.)* **plug**
ሶኬት sokiet *(n.)* **socket**
ሶሎ solo *(n.)* **solo**
ሶኔት soniet *(n.)* **sonnet**
ሶኑይ sonuy *(n.)* **Monday**
ሶርኖ sorno *(n.)* **sinus**
ፆታ ምቅያር sota mkyar *(n.)* **transsexual**
ስፓም spam *(n.)* **spam**
ስፓንየል spanyel *(n.)* **spaniel**
ስፔይናዊ speeynawi *(n.)* **Spaniard**
ስፔይናዊ speeynawi *(n.)* **Spanish**
ስፒናች spinach *(n.)* **spinach**
ስፖርት sport *(n.)* **sport**
ስፖርታዊ sportawi *(adj.)* **athletic**
ስፖርታዊ sportawi *(adj.)* **sporting**
ሰፖርተኛ sportegna *(n.)* **sportsman**
ስፖርተኛ sporteňa *(n.)* **athlete**
ስፓዳ sppoda *(n.)* **rapier**
ስቃይ sqay *(n.)* **affliction**
ስቃይ sqay *(n.)* **bane**
ስቃይ sq̈ay *(n.)* **agony**
ስቅያታዊ sqyatawi *(adj.)* **wretched**
ስርዓት sräat *(n.)* **procedure**
ስራሕ srah *(n.)* **task**
ስራሕ srah *(n.)* **work**
ስራሕ sraḧ *(n.)* **job**
ስራሕ ኣልቦነት sraĥ albonet *(n.)* **redundancy**
ስራሕ ኣፈፃሚ srah asfetsami *(n.)* **manager**
ሰራሕ ካይላ sraḧ kayla *(v.)* **potter**
ሰራሕ ሸኽላ sraḧ shḱla *(n.)* **porcelain**
ሰራሕ ዝፈትሐ srah zfethe *(adj.)* **unemployed**
ስራሕ ዝክልክል ነገር srah zklkl neger *(v.)* **trammel**
ስራሕቲ ቅርፂ sraḧti qrxi *(n.)* **carvery**
ስርዓት sr'at *(n.)* **manner**
ስርዓት sr'at *(n.)* **mannerism**
ስርዓት sr'at *(n.)* **system**
ስርዓት ኣልቦ sr'ät 'albo *(n.)* **anarchy**
ስርዓት ኣትሓዘ sr'ät atĥaze *(v.)* **regulate**
ስርዓት ቀብሪ sr'ät qebri *(n.)* **funeral**
ስርዓት ዘይተምሃረ sr'at zeytemhare *(n.)* **indiscipline**
ስርዒታዊ s'rätawi *(adj.)* **systemic**
ስርዓተ መንግስቲ sr'äte mengsti *(n.)* **regime**
ስርዓተ መርበብ sr'äte merbeb *(n.)* **network**
ስርዓተ መጽናዕቲ ሕማም srate mxnaeti hmam *(n.)* **pathology**
ስርዓተ ነጥቢ sr'ate netbi *(n.)* **punctuation**
ስርዓተ ንግስና sr'äte ngsna *(n.)* **coronation**
ስርዓተ ትምህርቲ sräte tmhrti *(n.)* **curriculum**
ስራይ sray *(n.)* **charm**
ስራይ sray *(n.)* **glamour**
ስርበተ ደም srbete dem *(n.)* **plethora**
ስረ sre *(n.)* **pants**
ስረ sre *(n.)* **trousers**

ስረ-ግትር sregtr *(n.)* **bloomers**
ስረ-ግትር sregtr *(n.)* **breeches**
ስሬት sret *(n.)* **deliverance**
ስረዛ sreza *(n.)* **cancellation**
ስረዛ sreza *(n.)* **deletion**
ስረዛ sreza *(n.)* **revocation**
ስርሓት ካይላ srḧat kayla *(n.)* **pottery**
ስርኤል sriel *(n.)* **fairy**
ስሪንጋ sringa *(n.)* **syringe**
ስርዒት ፈረስ sr'ït feres *(n.)* **harness**
ስርቂ srki *(n.)* **theft**
ስርናይ srnay *(n.)* **wheat**
ስርቂ srqi *(n.)* **burglary**
ስርቂ srqi *(n.)* **robbery**
ስርቂ srqi *(n.)* **stole**
ሽርተቴ šrtete *(n.)* **ski**
ስሩብ srub *(adj.)* **imminent**
ስሩዕ sru'ë *(adj.)* **formal**
ስሩዕ sru'ë *(adj.)* **regular**
ስሩዕ መዝገብ sru'ë mezgeb *(n.)* **catalogue**
ስርወ መንግስቲ srwe mengsti *(n.)* **dynasty**
ስርወ መንግስቲ srwe-mengsti *(n.)* **kingdom**
ስርየት sryet *(n.)* **absolution**
ስሳ ssa *(adj. & n.)* **sixty**
ስሳነ ህይወት ssane hywet *(n.)* **biodiversity**
ስስዐ ss'ë *(n.)* **avarice**
ስስዐ sseä *(n.)* **cupidity**
ስሓኒ sḧani *(n.)* **basin**
ስሰና ssena *(n.)* **accretion**
ስስዐ ssie *(n.)* **parsimony**
ስሱዕ ssu'e *(adj.)* **selfish**
ስታድየም stadyem *(n.)* **stadium**
ስቴሮፎኒክ steerofonik *(adj.)* **stereophonic**
ስቴሮስኮፒክ steeroskopik *(adj.)* **stereoscopic**
ስተኖግራፈር stenografer *(n.)* **stenographer**
ስተንስል stensel *(n.)* **stencil**
ስተረዮ steryo *(n.)* **stereo**
ስተተስኮፕ steteskop *(n.)* **stethoscope**
ስቲግማታ stigmata *(n.)* **stigmata**
ስትሮቦ strobo *(n.)* **strobe**
ስትሮይድ stroyd *(n.)* **steroid**
ስሑው sḧuw *(adj.)* **sparse**
ስሕተት s'htet *(adj.)* **incorrect**
ስሕተት sĥtet *(n.)* **fault**
ስሕተት sḧtet *(n.)* **mistake**
ስቱዲዮ studyo *(n.)* **studio**
ሱላ sula *(n.)* **barbecue**
ሱላ sula *(n.)* **cutlet**
ሱልጣኒት sulẗanit *(n.)* **sultana**
ሕሱም sum *(prep.)* **notorious**
ስኡን s'un *(adj.)* **destitute**
ስውንዋኖ swnwano *(n.)* **vamp**
ስዉእ swu'e *(n.)* **martyr**
ስዉር swur *(adj.)* **disembodied**
ስዉያ swya *(n.)* **personification**
ስውየት swyet *(n.)* **spasm**
ስውየታዊ swyetawi *(adj.)* **spasmodic**
ስያፍ syaf *(n.)* **bevel**
ስየ sye *(n.)* **palm**
ስየማ syema *(n.)* **nomination**
ስዩም s'èlawi *(adj.)* **graphic**
ስእላዊ selel bele *(v.)* **glide**
ሰለል በለ sem'ë *(v.)* **hear**
ሰምዐ sewasw *(n.)* **grammar**
ሰዋስው sfra manatile *(n.)* **warren**
ስፍራ ማናቲለ sḥbet *(n.)* **gravity**
ስሕበት sm'ïtawi *(adj.)* **voluptuous**

ስምዒታዊ snbta *(n.)* **valediction**
ስንብታ snčro *(n.)* **valley**
ስንጭሮ snu'ë 'aq̈ḥu *(n.)* **ware**
ስኑዕ ኣቕሑ swṭet *(n.)* **insight**
ስውጠት segome *(n.)* **advance**
ሰጎመ sne ïnti *(n.)* **archaeology**
ስነ ጥንቲ sga kebti *(n.)* **beef**
ስጋ ከብቲ xete *(v.)* **sell**

ሸ

ሸጠ xampo *(n.)* **shampoo**
ሻምፖ šadšay *(adj. & n.)* **sixth**
ሻድሻይ xaw'ay *(adj. & n.)* **seventh**
ሻውዓይ xax *(n.)* **shawl**
ሻሽ xew'ate *(adj. & n.)* **seven**
ሸውዓተ xeyati *(n.)* **seller**
ሸያጢ shfta *(n.)* **bandit**
ሽፍታ xfan *(n.)* **sheath**
ሽፋን xto *(n.)* **scent**
ሽቶ xto amezgabi *(n.)* **scorer**
ሽቶ ኣመዝጋቢ sheqaṭ nebit *(n.)* **vintner**
ሸቃጥ ነቢት syum *(n.)* **nominee**
ሸየመ šeyeme *(v.)* **promote**
ሻሂ shahi *(n.)* **tea**
ሻሕኻር shahikar *(adj.)* **coarse**
ሻሕካር shahkar *(adj.)* **scabrous**
ሻለይ shaley *(n.)* **chalet**
ሻምብቆ shamboqo *(n.)* **flute**
ሻምብቆ shambqo *(adj.)* **tubular**
ሻሞት shamot *(n.)* **asparagus**
ሻምፓይን shampayn *(n.)* **champagne**
ሻንቅላ shanqla *(n.)* **nigger**
ሻቕሎት shaqlot *(n.)* **disquiet**
ሻቕሎት shaq̈lot *(n.)* **agitation**
ሻራ shara *(n.)* **conspiracy**
ሻርቢ sharbi *(n.)* **scarf**
ሻርነት ዘይምህላው sharnet zeymhlaw *(n.)* **non-alignment**
ሻሽ shash *(n.)* **sash**
ሻሽ shash *(n.)* **voile**
ሻሽ shash *(n.)* **wimple**
ሻሽ shash *(n.)* **cambric**
ሻጣራ shatra *(adj.)* **tricky**
ስሕበት sḧbet *(n.)* **attraction**
ሽቦ shbo *(n.)* **wire**
ሽብርተኛ shbrtegna *(n.)* **terrorist**
ሽክና ርእሲ škna r'esi *(n.)* **skull**
ሽልሽል šlšl *(n.)* **remit**
ሽልማት šlmat *(n.)* **reward**
ሽብርተኝነት shbrtegnnet *(n.)* **terrorism**
ሽፋሽፍቲ shefashfti *(n.)* **brow**
ሸፋጢ shefati *(adj.)* **devious**
ሸፈነ shefene *(v.)* **dissimulate**
ሸፈነ shefene *(v.)* **envelop**
ሸፈነ shefene *(v.)* **insulate**
ሸፈነ shefene *(v.)* **suffuse**
ሸፈነ/ከወለ shefene/kewele *(v.)* **cover**
ሽፍጢ shefe'ti *(n.)* **chicanery**
ሽጣራ štara *(n.)* **ruse**
ሽጋራ shegara *(n.)* **cigarette**
ሽጎማኖ shegomano *(n.)* **terry**
ሽሓነ shehane *(n.)* **censer**
ሽሓነ shehane *(n.)* **salver**
ሽሓነ shehane *(n.)* **dish**
ሽሓጠ sheḧaẗe *(v.)* **cajole**
ሽሕ'ኳ እንተ she-h-kua ente *(adv.)* **however**
ሽኽላ shekla *(n.)* **crockery**
ሽተኽበተኽ šetekbetek *(n.)* **raffle**
ሽክላ ቆርቆሮ shekla qorqoro *(n.)* **tile**
ሽክሚ shekmi *(n.)* **burden**

ሸኾና shek̍wana *(n.)* **heel**
ሸላጊ shelagi *(n.)* **mortgagee**
ሸለፍ shelef *(n.)* **lap**
ሸለል በለ shelel bele *(v. t)* **disregard**
ሸለል በለ shelel bele *(v.)* **neglect**
ሸለለ shelele *(v.)* **baste**
ሸለልትነት sheleltnet *(n.)* **laxity**
ሸለመ she-leme *(v.)* **garnish**
ሸለመ sheleme *(v.)* **award**
ሸለመ sheleme *(v.)* **bestow**
ሸለን shelen *(n.)* **aniseed**
ሸለውሊዋ መጫወቲ shelewliwa mechaeti *(n.)* **trapeze**
ሸማቲ shemati *(n.)* **consumer**
ሸበጥ šebet *(n.)* **slipper**
ሸፈሕ በለ šefeĥ bele *(v.t.)* **shuffle**
ሸምዳዲ shemdadi *(adj.)* **bookish**
ሸምገለ shemgele *(v.)* **mediate**
ሸሞንተ shemonte *(adj. & n.)* **eight**
ሸምጣጢ shemtati *(adj.)* **sarcastic**
ሸምጢ shemti *(n.)* **loin**
ሸነ shene *(v.)* **urinate**
መሸባረቂ shenkata *(n.)* **trimmer**
ሸንሸነ shenshene *(n.)* **pleat**
ሸቀጥ sheqeẗ *(n.)* **merchandise**
ሸቅሸቅታ sheqsheqta *(n.)* **angina**
ሸራፍ sheraf *(n.)* **dent**
ሸራፍ sheraf *(adj.)* **toothless**
ሸርበጥ sherbeẗ *(n.)* **sorbet**
ሸረፈ sherefe *(v.)* **indent**
ሸረር sherer *(n.)* **whirligig**
ሸርፍራፍ sherifrafe *(n.)* **chip**
ሸርሸረ shershere *(v.)* **erode**
ሸርጣን sherẗan *(n.)* **crab**
ሸታቲ shetati *(adj.)* **smelly**
ሸጠ sheṭe *(v.)* **vend**
ሸሞንተ ወገን shemonte wegen *(n.)* **octagon**
ሽርሽር shrshr *(n.)* **outing**
ሸጠጥ shetet *(n.)* **zip**
ሸወዘ sheweze *(v.)* **annoy**
ሸውሃት shewhat *(n.)* **appetite**
ሸውታ shewta *(v.)* **zoom**
ሸያጣይ sheyatay *(n.)* **salesman**
ሸጠ sheyaṭi *(n.)* **vendor**
ሸያጢ ዕምበባ sheyaẗi ëmbeba *(n.)* **florist**
ሸያጢ ኣሕምልቲ sheyaẗi ĥamli *(n.)* **greengrocer**
ሸያጢ ናውቲ ጽሕፈት sheyaẗi nawti tsĥfet *(n.)* **stationer**
ሸያጢ ቆቢዕ አንስቲ sheyaẗi qobi'ë ansti *(n.)* **milliner**
ሹመት shumet *(n.)* **preferment**
ሹቅ shuq *(n.)* **mart**
ሹሻን shushan *(n.)* **lotus**
ሽፋን shfan *(n.)* **casing**
ሽፋን shfan *(n.)* **coating**
ሽፋን shfan *(n.)* **facing**
ሽፋን shfan *(n.)* **layer**
ሽፌር shfer *(n.)* **driver**
ሽፍጢ shfti *(n.)* **duplicity**
ሽፍጢ shfẗi *(n.)* **fraud**
ሽግር shgr *(n.)* **difficulty**
ሽግር shgr *(n.)* **hardship**
ሽግር shgr *(n.)* **problem**
ሽግር shgr *(n.)* **adversity**
ኣሸጋሪ shgrawi *(adj.)* **problematic**
ሽጉጥ shguẗ *(n.)* **pistol**
ሽሕ ዓመት shĥ ämet *(n.)* **millennium**
ሽሕ 'ኳ shĥ ekwa *(prep.)* **notwithstanding**
ሽሕ'ኳ shĥkwa *(conj.)* **albeit**
ሽሕ shih *(adj. & n.)* **thousand**
ሽርባ/በርበረ shirba/berebre *(n.)* **chilli**

ሽቶ shito *(n.)* **cologne**
ሽድሽተ šdšte *(adj.& n.)* **six**
ሽኻል shkal *(n.)* **peg**
ሽኾና shḱona *(n.)* **hoof**
ሽኮር shkor *(n.)* **sugar**
ሽኮር ድንሽ shkor dnesh *(n.)* **yam**
ሽኮራዊ ምግቢ shkorawi mgbi *(n.)* **sweetmeat**
ሽኮረይ shkorey *(n.)* **sweetheart**
ሽኮርያ shkorya *(n.)* **diabetes**
ሽኩዕኩዕ በለ shku'eku'e bele *(v.)* **snuggle**
ሽኹላል shkulal *(n.)* **roll**
ሽላ shla *(n.)* **buzzard**
ሽላ shla *(n.)* **falcon**
ሽልማት shlmat *(n.)* **decoration**
ሽልማት shlmat *(n.)* **prize**
ሽልማት shlmat *(n.)* **trophy**
ሽም shm *(n.)* **name**
ሽም እንስሳ shm enssa *(n.)* **winkle**
ሽም ስድራ shm sdra *(n.)* **surname**
ሽምዓ shm'ä *(n.)* **candle**
ሽማግለ shmagle *(n.)* **committee**
ሽማግሌ shmagle *(adj.)* **elderly**
ሽመና ማሽን shmena mashn *(n.)* **loom**
ሽመት shmet *(n.)* **promotion**
ሽምገላ shmgela *(n.)* **mediation**
ሽምገላ shmgela *(n.)* **mediation**
ሽምራር shmrar *(n.)* **crease**
ሽምጠጣ shmteta *(n.)* **sarcasm**
ሽታሕ በለ šetah bele *(v.)* **skid**
ሽታሕ በለ šetah bele *(v.)* **slide**
ሽታሕታሕ በለ šetaĥtaĥ bele *(v.)* **slither**
ሽንቅላት ምውጻእ shnqlat mwts'e *(n.)* **vituperation**
ሽንቲ shnti *(n.)* **urine**
ሽንቲ ቤት shnti bet *(n.)* **toilet**
ሽንቲ ቤት shnti biet *(n.)* **latrine**
ሽንቲ ቤት shnti biet *(n.)* **lavatory**
ሽንቲ ቤት shnti biet *(n.)* **loo**
ሽንጥሮ shntro *(n.)* **dale**
ሽንጥሮ shntro *(n.)* **dell**
ሽንጥሮ shnẗro *(v.)* **meander**
ሽመ shome *(v.)* **appoint**
ሽራዕ shra'ë *(v.)* **canvass**
ሽራጥ shraẗ *(n.)* **stripe**
ሽርካ shrka *(n.)* **ally**
ሽርካ shrka *(n.)* **interface**
ሽርክነት shrket *(n.)* **partnership**
ሽርክነት shrknet *(n.)* **cahoots**
ሽርሙጣ shrmuẗa *(n.)* **strumpet**
ሽሮቦ shrobo *(n.)* **syrup**
ሽርሽር shrshr *(n.)* **excursion**
ሽርሽር shrshr *(n.)* **jaunt**
ሽርሽር shrshr *(n.)* **picnic**
ሽሻይ shshay *(n.)* **bonanza**
ሽታ shta *(n.)* **smell**
ሽታ shta *(n.)* **spoor**
ሽጣራ shtara *(n.)* **wile**
ሽጣራ sh'ẗara *(n.)* **subterfuge**
ሽቶል shtol *(n.)* **stiletto**
ሽውሓት ኣልቦነት shwḧat 'albonet *(n.)* **anorexia**
ሽምኒት shmnit *(n.)* **octavo**
ሽታ shta *(adj.)* **odorous**
ሽጉርቲ shegurti *(n.)* **onion**
ሹጉሹግ ssgushug *(n.)* **alcove**
ሽፋን shfan *(adj.)* **overcast**
ሽፍታ shfta *(n.)* **outlaw**

ቀ

ቀባጥ qebaẗ *(adj.)* **capricious**
ቀባፅ qebats *(adj.)* **desperate**
ቀብአ qeb'e *(v.)* **anoint**
ቀበኣይ qebeay *(n.)* **painter**
ቀበረ qebere *(v.)* **bury**
ቀብሪ qebri *(n.)* **burial**
ቀዳድ qedad *(n.)* **slot**
ቀዳዲ ብርሃን qedadi brhan *(n.)* **floodlight**
ቀዳሓይ qedaȟay *(n.)* **mimic**
ቀዳሒ ደም qedaȟi dem *(n.)* **artery**
ቀዳም qedam *(n.)* **Saturday**
ቀዳማይ qedamay *(adj.)* **primal**
ቀዳማይ ፈነወ ፊልሚ qedamay felewe filmi *(n.)* **premiere**
ቀዳማይ መሓውር qedamay meĥawr *(n.)* **foreleg**
ቀዳማይ ምስራዕ qedamay msraë *(n.)* **primacy**
ቀዳማይ ርቦኛ qedamay rbogna *(n.)* **frontbencher**
ቀዳማይ ረድኤት qedamay red'eet *(n.)* **first aid**
ቀዳምነት qedamnet *(adv.)* **primarily**
ቀዳምነት qedamnet *(n.)* **priority**
ቀዳምነት ዝሓዘ qedamnety zhaze *(n.)* **pioneer**
ቀዳሲ qedasi *(n.)* **celebrant**
ቀደም qedem *(adj.)* **erstwhile**
ቀደመ qedem *(v.)* **excel**
ቀደም qedem *(n.)* **yore**
ቀዳምነት qedemanet *(n.)* **precedence**
ቀደሰ qede'se *(v.)* **consecrate**
ቀድሐ qedȟe *(v.)* **copy**
ቀድሐ qedḥe *(v.)* **imitate**
ቀዲምካ ምሕሳብ qedimka mĥsab *(n.)* **premeditation**
ቀዲሙ ሒዙ qedimu ȟizu *(v.)* **pre-empt**
ቀዲሙ ዝተሰርሐ qedimu zteserȟe *(adj.)* **prefabricated**
ቄሳራዊ qeesarawi *(n.)* **caesarean**
ቀሓር qeȟar *(n.)* **heartburn**
ዕግበት qeig'bet *(n.)* **contentment**
ቀጀለ qejele *(v.)* **fantasize**
ቀልቡ ኣጥፊአ qelbu aẗfe'a *(v.)* **swoon**
ቀልደድ qelded *(n.)* **arch**
ቀልደዳዊ qeldedawi *(n.)* **arcade**
ቀልዲ qeldi *(n.)* **quip**
ቐልዲ qeldi *(n.)* **whim**
ቀልዲ qeldi *(n.)* **wit**
ቐልዲ qeldi *(n.)* **witticism**
ቀልዐ qel'e *(v.)* **unfold**
ቀልዐ qel'e *(v.)* **unmask**
ቀልዐ qel'ë *(v.)* **reveal**
ቀለቤት qelebet *(n.)* **ring**
ቀለም qelem *(n.)* **dye**
ቀለም qelem *(n.)* **tint**
ና ቀለም መቅጠኒ ኬሚካል qelem meqteni kemikal *(n.)* **turpentine**
ቀለወ qelewe *(v.)* **roast**
ቀልሃ qeliha *(n.)* **cartridge**
ቀሊል qelil *(adj.)* **easy**
ቀሊል qelil *(adj.)* **facile**
ቀሊል qelil *(adj.)* **portable**
ቀሊል qelil *(adj.)* **simple**
ቀልቀል qelqel *(n.)* **stool**
ቀልጠፈ qeltefe *(v.)* **quicken**
ቀልቀል qelqel *(n.)* **outskirts**
ቀደመ qedeme *(v.)* **outstrip**
ቀዳማዊ qdamawi *(adj.)* **original**
ቀማሚ መድሃኒት qemami medhanit *(n.)* **pharmacist**

ቀማሪት qemarit *(n.)* **calculator**
ቀማሲ qemasi *(n.)* **gourmet**
ቀመም qemem *(n.)* **condiment**
ቀመም qemem *(n.)* **seasoning**
ቀመም qemem *(n.)* **spice**
ቀመም ዝበዝሖ qemem zbezḧo *(adj.)* **spicy**
ቀመር qemer *(n.)* **formula**
ቀመር qemer *(n.)* **calculation**
ቀመረ qemere *(v.)* **formulate**
ቀመረ qemere *(v.)* **calculate**
ቀሚሽ qemish *(n.)* **skirt**
ቀሚሽ qemish *(n.)* **gown**
ቀምቃማይ qemqamay *(n.)* **barber**
ቀምቀመ qemqeme *(v.)* **lop**
ቀምሽ qemš *(n.)* **robe**
ቀምሽ qemsh *(n.)* **frock**
ቀምታ qemta *(n.)* **nap**
ቀምታ qemta *(n.)* **siesta**
ቀናእ qena'e *(adj.)* **envious**
ቀናእ qena'è *(adj.)* **jealous**
ቀንዲ qendi *(n.)* **core**
ቁልቁል ኣፍ ዝተሰጥሐ kulkul afu ztesethe *(adj.)* **prostrate**
ቁልቁለት kulkulet *(n.)* **declivity**
ቁምነገር kum neger *(n.)* **plank**
ቂምታ kimta *(n.)* **pique**
ቅልጡፍ kltuf *(adj.)* **rapid**
ቅኑስ knus *(adj.)* **reductive**
ቅልጣፈ kltafe *(n.)* **rapidity**
ቅርሕንቲ kiri hinti *(n.)* **confrontation**
ቅድመ ኩነት kdme kunet *(n.)* **proviso**
ቅድስተ ቅዱሳን kdste kdusan *(adj.)* **sacrosanct**
ቆርበት korbet *(n.)* **skin**
ቐዳሒ kedahi *(n.)* **imitator**
መፀውዒ ሽም qendi *(n.)* **forename**
ቀንዲ qendi *(adj.)* **intimate**
ቀንዲ qendi *(n.)* **principal**
ቀንዲ qendi *(n.)* **staple**
ቀንዲ ክብደት qendi kbdet *(n.)* **brunt**
ቀንዲ ተዋሳኢ qendi tewasai *(n.)* **protagonist**
ቀንደኛ qenedegna *(adj.)* **classical**
ቀንዲ qenedi *(adj.)* **central**
ቀነነ qenene *(n.)* **gradient**
ቀነነ qenene *(v.)* **tilt**
ቀነሰ qenese *(v.)* **subtract**
ቀንፈዘው በለ qenfezew bele *(v.)* **linger**
ቀንፈዘው በለ qenfezew bele *(v.)* **loiter**
ቀኒሱ qenisu *(v.)* **pare**
ቀኖና qenona *(n.)* **canon**
ቀንጠብጠብ በለ qentebteb bele *(v.)* **tamper**
ቀንጠጠ qentete *(v.)* **denude**
ቐንጠጠ qentete *(v.)* **undress**
ቀንጠወ qenṫew *(v.)* **nip**
ቀንፀለ qentsele *(v.)* **slay**
ቀንጸሊ qal'ë *(n.)* **glade**
ቃልዕ qaledrdare'aw *(adj.)* **verbose**
ቃለ-ድርዳረኣዊ qarsa *(n.)* **hockey**
ቃርሳ qdus *(adj.)* **holy**
ቅዱስ qesqese *(v.)* **instigate**
ቀስቀሰ qeṭin *(adj.)* **watery**
ቀጢን qew'ï nay weyni *(n.)* **vintage**
ቀውዒ ናይ ወይኒ qoretse *(v.)* **hack**
ቆረጸ qosli *(n.)* **wound**
ቆስሊ qoṭqoat *(n.)* **hawthorn**
ቆጥቋጥ qrsus *(n.)* **wretch**
ቅርሱስ quliḧ bele *(v.i.)* **glance**
ቍሊሕ በለ quṭe'ë *(n.)* **wrath**
ቁጠዐ qwanqwagna *(n.)* **idiom**
ቋንቋኛ qxi *(n.)* **volume**

ቅጺ qenxali *(n.)* **wrecker**
ቅእንዘርዘር q'enzerzer *(n.)* **dalliance**
ቅቃሕ qe-qah *(n.)* **husk**
ቀቀኖ qeqeno *(n.)* **swan**
ቀቀብ qeqheb *(n.)* **maple**
ቀራጺቶ qeraxito *(n.)* **crotchet**
ቀረበ qerebe *(v.i.)* **near**
ቀረበ qerebe *(v.)* **approach**
ቀረፈ qerefe *(v.)* **excoriate**
ቅርፍቲ qerefti *(n.)* **hull**
ቀረመ qereme *(v.)* **glean**
ቀረፅ qerets *(n.)* **tariff**
ቀረፀ qeretse *(v.)* **carve**
ቀረጸ qerexe *(v.t.)* **imagine**
ቀረጸ qerexe *(v.)* **visualize**
ቅርሺ qeriishe *(n.)* **cash**
ቀሪሽ qerixe *(n.)* **shark**
ቀርቀብ ኣበለ qerqeb abele *(v.)* **nab**
ቀርጣፊ qertafi *(n.)* **rodent**
ቀስ ኢሉ qes ilu *(adv.)* **slowly**
ቀስ ዝብል qes zbl *(adj.)* **slow**
ቀስብቀስ qesbqes *(adj.)* **gradual**
ቀሰ'በ qesebe *(v.)* **compel**
ቀሰረ qesere *(v.)* **laminate**
ቀሺ qeshi *(n.)* **pontiff**
ቀሺ qeshi *(n.)* **priest**
ቀስቃሲ ስምዒት ኮይኑ ቀረበ qesqasi sm'et koynu qerebe *(v.)* **sensationalize**
ቀስቀሰ qesqese *(v.)* **incite**
ቀስቀሰ qesqese *(v.)* **motivate**
ቀስታ qesta *(n.)* **slowness**
ቀስተ ድመና qeste demena *(n.)* **rainbow**
ቀስቲ qesti *(n.)* **vault**
ቀስቲ qesti *(n.)* **arc**
ቀስቲ qesti *(n.)* **bow**
ቀስቲ qesti *(n.)* **dart**
ቀጥ በለ qet bele *(adj.)* **perpendicular**
ቀጣፊ qeẗafi *(adj.)* **mendacious**
ቀታሊ qetali *(adj.)* **fatal**
ቀታሊ ነፍሲ qetali nefsi *(n.)* **murderer**
ቀታል-ነፍሲ qetalnefsi *(n.)* **assassin**
ቀተለ qetele *(v.)* **kill**
ቀተለ qetele *(v.)* **assassinate**
ቀጠንቲ qeẗenti *(adj.)* **spindly**
ቀጥቀጥ qeteqetw *(v.)* **castrate**
ቀጢን qetin *(adj.)* **tenuous**
ቀጢን qetin *(adj.)* **thin**
ቀጢን ስልኪ qeẗin slki *(n.)* **filament**
ቀጥቀጠ qetqete *(v.)* **geld**
ቀጥቀጠ qeẗqeẗe *(v.)* **belabour**
ቀጥቀጠ qeẗqeẗe *(n.)* **stomp**
ቀራፃይ qetsaray *(n.)* **recorder**
ቀፀላይ qetselayi *(n.)* **coke**
ቀፀለ qetsele' *(v.)* **continue**
ቀፃላይ qetsetay *(adj.)* **continuous**
ቀፅላ qetsla *(n.)* **slab**
ቀፀላ qetsla *(n.)* **slate**
ቀፅሪ መርከብ qetsri merkeb *(n.)* **shipyard**
ቀጥታዊ qettawi *(adj.)* **direct**
ቀጥታዊ qeṭtawi *(adj.)* **immediate**
ቀዋሚ qewami *(n.)* **coefficient**
ቀዋሚ ኣቑሑ qewami aquĥu *(n.)* **fixture**
ቀዋሚ መዓስከር qewami me'äsker *(n.)* **cantonment**
ቀዋምነት qewamnet *(n.)* **permanence**
ቀውፊ qewfi *(n.)* **veto**
ቀውዒ qew'ï *(n.)* **autumn**
ቀዉላል qewlal *(adj.)* **gangling**
ቀፃልነት qexalnet *(n.)* **continuity**
ቀጸላ qexela *(n.)* **ply**

ቀፀረ qexri *(n.)* **cartel**
ቀጽረ qexri *(n.)* **bloc**
ቀሽነት qexri qeshnet *(n.)* **priesthood**
ቀይ ሱር qey sur *(n.)* **beetroot**
ቀያሲ qeyasi *(n.)* **surveyor**
ቀያየረ qeyayere *(v.)* **reshuffle**
ቀይዲ በተኽ qeydi betek *(adj.)* **feral**
ቀይዲበተኽ qeydi betek *(n.)* **rogue**
ቀይድ በተኽ qeydi betek *(adj.)* **unbridled**
ቀየደ qeyede *(v.)* **impound**
ቀየረ qeyere *(v.)* **alter**
ቀየረ qeyere *(v.)* **convert**
ቀይሕ qeyh *(n.)* **crimson**
ቀይሕ qeyĥ *(adj.)* **red**
ቀይሕ qeyĥ *(adj.)* **reddish**
ቀይሕ ፍረ qeyḧ fre *(n.)* **strawberry**
ቀይሕ ሕብረ qeyiha hib're *(n.)* **carmine**
ቀዛሒ qezaȟi *(adj.)* **bleak**
ቀዛሕዛሕ ዝብል qezaĥzaĥ zbl *(adj.)* **frowsty**
ቂም qim *(n)* **grudge**
ቂመኛ qimegna *(adj.)* **spiteful**
ቂመኛ qimeña *(adj.)* **vengeful**
ቂምታ qimta *(n.)* **acrimony**
ቂምታ qimta *(n.)* **spite**
ቁባ quba *(n.)* **dome**
ቁልዕነት qulënet *(adj.)* **puerile**
ቁልፊ qulfi *(n.)* **belt**
ቁልቁል qulqul *(adj.)* **steep**
ቁም ነገር qum neger *(n.)* **merit**
ቁማል qumal *(n.)* **louse**
ቁመት qumet *(n.)* **height**
ቁመት qumet *(n.)* **stature**
ቁምነገረኛ qumnegeregna *(adj.)* **serious**
ቁንጪ qunĉi *(n.)* **flea**
ቁንጩል qunčul *(adj.)* **compendious**
ቁኒን qunin *(n.)* **reel**
ቁኖ quno *(n.)* **plait**
ቛንቋኛዊ qunquñawi *(adj.)* **idiomatic**
ቁራ qura *(n.)* **raven**
ቁራስ quras *(n.)* **bit**
ቁራፅ qurats *(n.)* **slice**
ቁራፅ qurats *(n.)* **stub**
ቁራፅ ጉንዲ qurats gundi *(n.)* **stump**
ቁራፅ qurax *(n.)* **cutting**
ቁርባን qurban *(n.)* **communion**
ቁርፀት ከብዲ quretset kebedi *(n.)* **colic**
ቁረ/ቀዝሒ quri/qezhi *(n.)* **chill**
ቁርማም qurmame *(n.)* **chunk**
ቁርሲ qursi *(n.)* **breakfast**
ቈርጠጠ qurtete *(v.)* **tweak**
ቁርፅራፅ qurtsrats *(n.)* **snippet**
ቁሩብ qurub *(adj.)* **meagre**
ቁሩብ qurub *(n.)* **modicum**
ቁሩብ ፍልልይ qurub fl'ly *(n.)* **nuance**
ቁሳውነት qusawnet *(n.)* **materialism**
ቁሸት qushet *(n.)* **village**
ቁስሊ qusli *(n.)* **blain**
ቁስሊ qusli *(n.)* **ulcer**
ቁጥዐ quẗ'ë *(n.)* **annoyance**
ቁጥዐ quẗ'ë *(n.)* **anger**
ቁጠባ quteba *(n.)* **economy**
ቁጠባ quteba *(n.)* **retrenchment**
ቁጠባዊ qutebawi *(adj.)* **economic**
ቁጥዐ qute-e *(n.)* **huff**
ቁጠዐ quẗe'ë *(n.)* **fury**
ቁጥቋጥ qutqwat *(n.)* **heath**
ቁጥቋጥ qutqwat *(n.)* **shrub**
ቍጽጽር qutstsr *(n.)* **inspection**
ቁፀፀር qutstsr *(n.)* **scrutiny**
ቍጻር quxar *(n.)* **knot**

ቍጽራዊ quxrawi *(adj.)* **arithmetical**
ቁፀሪ quxri *(n.)* **figure**
ቁፅሪ quxri *(n.)* **number**
ቁጽሪ ፖስጣ quxri posẗ *(n.)* **postcode**
ቍጽሪ quxri *(n.)* **arithmetic**
ቁፅፅር quxxr *(n.)* **control**
ቁፅፅር qux'xr *(n.)* **supervision**
ቁዘማ quzema *(adj.)* **plaintive**
ቁጸራ qitsra *(n.)* **tryst**
ቃንጫ qhanca *(n.)* **stalk**
ቐደመ qedeme *(v.)* **overtake**
ቃጭል qačl *(n.)* **bell**
ቃዕታ qaeta *(n.)* **click**
ቃፍላይ qafla *(n.)* **wain**
ቃፍላይ qaflay *(n.)* **caravan**
ቅፍታን qaftan *(n.)* **kaftans**
ቀዘፊ mejelebi *(n.)* **paddle**
ቅድመ ፍጻመ qdme fxame *(n.)* **antecedent**
ቃሕታ qahta *(n.)* **whimsy**
ቃል qal *(n.)* **word**
ቃል ኪዳን qal kidan *(n.)* **covenant**
ቃል ክሱስ qal ksus *(n.)* **plea**
ቃል ምእታው qal mètaw *(n.)* **pledge**
ቓል ዝበዝሖ qal zbezho *(adj.)* **wordy**
ቃላት qalat *(n.)* **vocabulary**
ቃለ ምልልስ qale mlls *(n.)* **dialogue**
ቃለ-ድርዳረ qaledrdar *(n.)* **verbiage**
ቃለ-ድርዳረነት qaledrdarene *(n.)* **verbosity**
ቃለ-ማሕላ qalemaȟla *(n.)* **affidavit**
ቃለ-መጠይቕ qalemeẗeyq̈ *(n.)* **interview**
ቃለ-ምስጢር qalemsṭir *(n.)* **watchword**
ቃልቃል በለ qalqal bele *(adj.)* **aflame**
ቃና qana *(adj.)* **wondrous**
ቃናያይ qanayay *(n.)* **tuner**

ቃንጫ qancha *(n.)* **stem**
ቃንጃ qanja *(n.)* **hamstring**
ቃንዛ qanza *(n.)* **ache**
ቃንዛ qanza *(n.)* **pain**
ቃንዛ ጭዋዳ qanza čwada *(n.)* **myalgia**
ቃቓ qaq̈a *(n.)* **cackle**
ቃቐወ qaqhewe *(v.)* **squawk**
ቃራና qarana *(n.)* **bough**
ቃሬዛ qareeza *(n.)* **bier**
ቃሬዛ qareeza *(n.)* **stretcher**
ቃርፋ qarfa *(n.)* **cinnamon**
ቃርማ qarma *(n.)* **beagle**
ቃታ qata *(n.)* **trigger**
ቃፀሎ qaxelo *(n.)* **combustion**
ቃዝኖት qaznot *(n.)* **melancholia**
ቅብኣ qba *(n.)* **portrait**
ቀብአ qb'a *(v.)* **portray**
ቅብኣ qba *(n.)* **painting**
ቅብኣ ምቅባእ qb'a mqbaè *(n.)* **portraiture**
ቅባለ qbale *(n.)* **approval**
ቅብአት qb'at *(adj.)* **unctuous**
ቅብብል qbbl *(n.)* **relay**
ቅበላ qbela *(n.)* **admission**
ቅበላ qbela *(n.)* **admittance**
ቅበጥ qbeẗ *(n.)* **caprice**
ቅብሊት qblit *(n.)* **receipt**
ቅብፀት qbtset *(n.)* **despair**
ቅቡል qbul *(adj.)* **unexceptionable**
ቅቡል q'bul *(n.)* **stereotype**
ቅጫ qĉa *(n.)* **patty**
ቅጭን qĉn *(adj.)* **elegant**
ቅዳሕ qdah *(n.)* **tracing**
ቅዳሕ qdaḣ *(n.)* **copy**
ቅዳሕ qdaḧ *(n.)* **facsimile**
ቅዳሕ ቅብሊት qdaḧ qblit *(n.)* **counterfoil**

ቅዳሰ ሙታን qdase mutan *(n.)* **requiem**
ቅድድም መሰናኽል q'd'dm mesenakhl *(n.)* **steeplechase**
ቅደኛ qdegna *(n.)* **stylist**
ቅዲ qdi *(n.)* **fashion**
ቅዲ qdi *(n.)* **pattern**
ቅዲ qdi *(n.)* **style**
ቅዲ ብዝለበሰ qdi b'zlebese *(adj.)* **stylized**
ቅዲ ክዳን qdi kdan *(n.)* **guise**
ቅዲ ኩናት qdi kunat *(n.)* **warfare**
ቅዲ ዘለዎ qdi zelewo *(adj.)* **stylistic**
ቅድም qdm *(adv.)* **formerly**
ስልጣን qdme *(n.)* **prerogative**
ቅድመ ዓብላላዊ qdme äblalawi *(adj.)* **predominant**
ቅድመ ዓብላልነት qdme äblalnet *(n.)* **predominance**
ቅድመ ኹነት qdme kunet *(n.)* **precondition**
ቅድመ ምዕብላል qdme mëblal *(v.)* **predominate**
ቅድሚ መርዓ qdme merä *(adj.)* **premarital**
ቅድመ ንጡፍ qdme ntuf *(adj.)* **proactive**
ቅድመ ስም qdme sm *(n.)* **prefix**
ቅድመ ታሪኽ qdme tariḱi *(adj.)* **prehistoric**
ቅድመ ውሳነ qdme wsane *(v.)* **predetermine**
ቅድሚ qdmi *(adj.)* **prior**
ቅድሚ qdmi *(adv.)* **before**
ቅድመ ኹነት qdmi ḱunet *(n.)* **prerequisite**
ቅድሚ_ግዘ qdmi_gze *(adv.)* **ago**
ቅድሚት qdmit *(n.)* **front**
ቅድስና qdsna *(n.)* **sanctity**
ቅርሱስ qrsus *(adj.)* **ominous**
ቅቡል qbul *(adj.)* **orthodox**
ቅናት-ዙረት qnate zuret *(n.)* **orbit**
ቅንዕና qn'ëna *(n.)* **orthodoxy**
ቅጥዒ ዘይብሉ qt'ë zeyblu *(adj.)* **outrageous**
ቅዱስ ፅሑፍ qdus tshuf *(n.)* **scripture**
ቐማሚ qe'mami *(n.)* **chemist**
ቕብኣት qhb'at *(n.)* **lotion**
ቕብኣት qhb'at *(n.)* **lubricant**
ቕብኣት qhb'at *(n.)* **lubrication**
ቕብኣት ቐበአ qhb'at qhbe'e *(v.)* **lubricate**
ቐላይ qhelay *(n.)* **lake**
ቐለም qhelem *(n.)* **ink**
ቐጢን ነዊሕ qhetin newih *(adj.)* **lanky**
ቐፃልነት ዘይብሉ qhetsalnet zeyblu *(adj.)* **inconsistent**
ቕመም qhmem *(n.)* **ingredient**
ቕንድብ qhndb *(v.)* **lash**
ቖፃል ኹብር እምኒ qhotsal khubr emni *(n.)* **jade**
ቖፀሊ qhotsli *(n.)* **leaf**
ቕርፊት መሬት qhrfit meriet *(n.)* **mantle**
ቑቡል qhubul *(adj.)* **justifiable**
ቑልዕነት qhul'enet *(n.)* **infancy**
ቑልፊ qhulfi *(n.)* **lock**
ቑራፅ ዕንፀይቲ qhurats entseyti *(n.)* **log**
ቑጡዕ qhute'e *(adj.)* **indignant**
ቑጠዐ qhute'e *(n.)* **indignation**
ቑጡብ qhutub *(adj.)* **laconic**
ቅልስ qls *(n.)* **duel**
ቅልጥፍነት qltfnet *(n.)* **agility**
ቀልጢፉ ዝኩሪ qltifu zkuri *(adj.)* **temperamental**

ቅልጡፍ qltuf ***(v.)*** **prompt**
ቅልጡፍ qltuf ***(adj.)*** **quick**
ቅልጡፍ qlẗuf ***(adj.)*** **fast**
ቅልጡፍ qlẗuf ***(adj.)*** **swift**
ቅልጡፍ ሳዕስዒት qlẗuf sa'ës'ït ***(n.)*** **jig**
ቅልፅም qltzm ***(n.)*** **forearm**
ቅሉዕ qlu'ë ***(adj.)*** **blatant**
ቅልዉላዉ qlwlaw ***(n.)*** **crisis**
ቅመማዊ ፍወሳ qmemawi fwesa ***(n.)*** **chemotherapy**
ቅሚጦ qmito ***(n.)*** **rick**
ቅሚጦ qmiẗo ***(n.)*** **stack**
ቅሙጥ ገንዘብ qmuẗ genzeb ***(n.)*** **fund**
ቅናት qnat ***(n.)*** **girdle**
ቅናት qnat ***(n.)*** **waistband**
ቅንኣት qn'at ***(n.)*** **envy**
ቅንኣት qn'at ***(n.)*** **jealousy**
ቅንዕና qn'ëna ***(n.)*** **honesty**
ቅንዕና qn'ëna ***(n.)*** **integrity**
ቅንዕና qn'ëna ***(n.)*** **rectitude**
ቅንዕና qn'ëna ***(n.)*** **sincerity**
ቅነሳ qnesa ***(n.)*** **discount**
ቅንፍ qnf ***(n.)*** **bracket**
ቅንፍ qnf ***(n.)*** **parenthesis**
ቅንፍር qnfr ***(n.)*** **clove**
ቅንፍዝ qnfz ***(n.)*** **porcupine**
ቅንጦተኛ qnẗotegna ***(n.)*** **sybarite**
ቅፅበታዊ qxbetawi ***(adj.)*** **automatic**
ቅጽል qxl ***(n.)*** **adjective**
ቅጽጽ ዝበለ qxx zbele ***(adj.)*** **congested**
ቅያ qya ***(n.)*** **saga**
ቅያኖስ qyanos ***(n.)*** **cyan**
ቅያር qyar ***(adj.)*** **alternative**
ቅያዊ ዛንታ qyawi zanta ***(n.)*** **epic**
ቅየዓ qye'ä ***(n.)*** **mimicry**
ቅየዓዊ ተዋስኦ qye'äwi tewas'o ***(n.)*** **mime**
ቅየዓዊ ተዋስኦ qye'äwi tewas'o ***(n.)*** **mime**
ቅየራ qyera ***(n.)*** **alteration**
ቕኑዕ ሓሳብ ዘለዎ qnu'e hasab zelewo ***(adj.)*** **optimistic**
ቅንጥሻራ qnẗshara ***(n.)*** **mushroom**
ቅኑዕ qnu'e ***(adj.)*** **upright**
ቅኑዕ qnu'ë ***(adj.)*** **honest**
ቅኑዕ qnu'ë ***(adj.)*** **righteous**
ቅኑዕ ዘይኮነ qnue zeykone ***(adj.)*** **unfaithful**
ቅኑዕ ዘይኮነ qnue zeykone ***(adj.)*** **unreasonable**
ቅኑዕ ዘይምሕሳብ qnue zeymhsab ***(n.)*** **pessimism**
ቅኑዕ q'nu'ë ***(adj.)*** **straight**
ቅኑዕ ዘይሓስብ qnuo hasab ***(n.)*** **pessimist**
ቅንጹብ ፈረስ qnxub feres ***(n.)*** **pony**
ቅቅል q'ql ***(n.)*** **stew**
ቅራፍ qraf ***(n.)*** **flake**
ቅራፍ qraf ***(n.)*** **bark**
ቅራረት qraret ***(n.)*** **runnel**
ቅርዓት qr'ät ***(n.)*** **concourse**
ቅርበት qrbet ***(n.)*** **vicinity**
ቅርበት qrbet ***(n.)*** **proximity**
ቅርዳድ qrdad ***(n.)*** **shred**
ይቕሬታ ሓተተ q̈reeta ḧatete ***(v.)*** **apologize**
ቅርፍቲ qrfti ***(n.)*** **crust**
ቅርፍቲ qrfti ***(n.)*** **scab**
ቅርሕንቲ qrĥnti ***(n.)*** **discord**
ቅርሕንቲ qrĥnti ***(n.)*** **feud**
ቅርሕንቲ qrĥnti ***(n.)*** **rancour**
ቅርሕንቲ qrĥnti ***(n.)*** **antipathy**
ቅሪት qrit ***(n.)*** **fossil**
ቅርንጫፍ qrnchaf ***(n.)*** **twig**

ቅርሲ qrsi *(n.)* **hangover**
ቅርሲ qrsi *(n.)* **relic**
ቅርሱስ qrsus *(adj.)* **fateful**
ቅርሱስ ዕድል qrsus ëdl *(n.)* **misfortune**
ቅርታ qrta *(n.)* **discontent**
ቅርታ qrta *(n.)* **dissatisfaction**
ቅርታ qrta *(n.)* **grievance**
ቅርታ qrta *(n.)* **resentment**
ቅርጥማት qrtmat *(n.)* **rheumatism**
ቅርፀ ኣልቦ qrtse 'albo *(adj.)* **shapeless**
ቅርፂ qrtsi *(n.)* **shape**
ቅርፂ qrtzi *(n.)* **gerund**
ቑርሱስ qruȟ qrsus *(n.)* **jinx**
ቅርጸ-ኣልቦ qrxe'albo *(adj.)* **amorphous**
ቅሳነት qsanet *(n.)* **composure**
ቅሳነት qsanet *(n.)* **ease**
ቅስመት qsmet *(n.)* **acquisition**
ቅጥዒ qẗ'ï *(n.)* **format**
ቅጥዒ ምስኣን qẗ'i ms'an *(n.)* **superfluity**
ቅጥዒ ዘይብሉ qẗ'i zeyblu *(adj.)* **superfluous**
ቅትለት qtlet *(n.)* **killing**
ቅትለት qtlet *(n.)* **murder**
ቅትለተ-ኣቦ qtlet abo *(n.)* **patricide**
ቅትለተ-ኣደ qtlet ade *(n.)* **matricide**
ቅትለት ንጉስ qtlet ngus *(n.)* **regicide**
ቅትለተ-ሰብ qtleteseb *(n.)* **homicide**
ቅጥቁጥ ብዕራይ qẗquẗ b'ëray *(n.)* **bullock**
ቅፅበታዊ qtsbetawi *(adj.)* **instantaneous**
ቅፅበት qtsbetawi *(adj.)* **instant**
ቅፁዕ qtsu'ë *(adj.)* **prim**
ቅፅበታዊ qtzbetawi *(adv.)* **forthwith**
ቆብዕ qob'ë *(n.)* **hat**
ቆብዕ qob'ë *(n.)* **hood**
ቈጽለ መጽሊ qoetsele metseli *(v.t.)* **greenery**
ቆፎ ሓሰኻ qofo haseka *(n.)* **cocoon**
ቆፎ qofo *(n.)* **bin**
ቆለ qole *(n.)* **craze**
ቆለ qole *(n.)* **quirk**
ቆልዓ qolea' *(n.)* **child**
ቆለበ qolebe *(v.)* **catch**
ኮልዐ qole'ea *(v.)* **gild**
ቁልዕነት qole'enet' *(n.)* **childhood**
ቆማል qomal *(adj.)* **lousy**
ቆሞስ qomos *(n.)* **vicar**
ቆንስል qonesele *(n.)* **consul**
ቆንፀላዊ qonexelawi *(n.)* **consular**
ቖንጆ qonjo *(adj.)* **gorgeous**
ቆንቆር qonqkor *(n.)* **chimney**
ቆንቋን qonqwan *(adj.)* **ramshackle**
ቆንስል qonsl *(n.)* **diplomat**
ቆንስላዊ qonslawi *(adj.)* **diplomatic**
ቆንጠጠ qontete *(v.)* **pinch**
ቆቃዕ qoqa'ë *(n.)* **miser**
ቆራር qorar *(adj.)* **frigid**
ቆራር qorare *(adj.)* **chilly**
ቆራር qorare *(adj.)* **cold**
ቆራፃይ qoratzay *(n.)* **cutter**
ቆርበት ጤል qorbeet ẗeel *(n.)* **suede**
ቆርበት ኣልፍዐ qorbet alf'e *(n.)* **tan**
ቆርበት ፍሓቂ qorbet fehaqi *(n.)* **tanner**
ቆረጸ qoretse *(v.)* **hew**
ቆረፀ qoretse *(v.)* **sever**
ቆሪፁ qorisu *(v.)* **trim**
ቆርቆሮ qorqoro *(n.)* **alloy**
ቆርቋር qorqwar *(adj.)* **beady**

ቆርጠመ qorẗeme *(v.)* **crunch**
ቆርጠምጠማ qorẗemẗema *(n.)* **cartilage**
ቆፃል ድይመንድ qosal dymend *(n.)* **turquoise**
ቆጣቢ qotabi *(adj.)* **economical**
ቆጣቢ qotabi *(adj.)* **thrifty**
ቆጣቢ qoẗabi *(adj.)* **sparing**
ቆጠበ qotebe *(v.)* **retrench**
ቖፃል qotsal *(adj. & n.)* **green**
ቆፀየ qotseye *(v.)* **dislocate**
ቖፃሪ qoxari *(n.)* **employer**
ቆፀራ ህዝቢ qoxera hzbi *(n.)* **census**
ቆፀረ qoxere *(v.)* **count**
ቆፀረ qoxere *(v.)* **employ**
ቆጸየ qoxeye *(v.)* **wrick**
ቆይቆይ በለ qoyqoy bele *(v.)* **scrimp**
ቆዝሞፖሊታዊ qozmopolitawi *(adj.)* **cosmopolitan**
ቋጸረ qua-tse-re *(v.)* **hitch**
ቅዋማዊ qwamawi *(adj.)* **constitutional**
ቀዋሚ qwami *(adj.)* **permanent**
ቋንቋ qwanqwa *(n.)* **language**
ቋንጣ ዓሳ qwanẗa 'äsa *(n.)* **bloater**
ቈብዕ qweb'ë *(n.)* **cap**
ቈላሕታ qwelaḣta *(n.)* **glimpse**
ቈልዓዊ qwel'äwi *(n.)* **immaturity**
ቈልቋል qwelqwal *(n.)* **cactus**
ቈራቢ qwerabi *(n.)* **communicant**
ቈጥቋጥ qweẗqwaẗ *(n.)* **bush**
ቈጸራ qwexera *(n.)* **appointment**
ቈጸረ qwexere *(v.)* **compute**
ቈየቛ qweyeq̈wa *(n.)* **brawl**
ቈይቍ qweyqwi *(n.)* **altercation**

<u>በ</u>

በጃ beğa *(adj.)* **vicarious**
በጋሚዶ begamido *(n.)* **vagabond**
በገና begena *(n.)* **harp**
በጊዕ begi'e *(n.)* **sheep**
በሓጫጨረ beha'cha'chre *(v.)* **scrawl**
በሃም beham *(n.)* **dummy**
በሃም beham *(n.)* **moron**
በሓተ beḣate *(v.)* **monopolize**
ቤላሮባ beilaroba *(v.)* **peddle**
ብዕካክ b'ekak *(n.)* **tartar**
ብዕካክ b'ëkak *(n.)* **plaque**
በኻዪ bekayi *(adj.)* **fretful**
በኻዪ bekayi *(adj.)* **weepy**
በኸኽታ bekekta *(n.)* **puff**
በከለ bekele *(v.)* **contaminate**
በከለ bekele *(v.)* **taint**
በኸየ bekeye *(v.)* **bewail**
በኸየ bekeye *(v.)* **cry**
በኸየ bekeye *(n.)* **yowl**
በኸየ bekeye' *(v.)* **weep**
በኸየ bekheye *(v.)* **sob**
በኾኽ አበለ bekok 'abele *(n.)* **whiff**
በኹዐ beku'ë *(v.)* **ferment**
ብኽያት beḱyat *(n.)* **wail**
በላዕ ሰብ bela'ë seb *(n.)* **cannibal**
በላዕ ስጋ bela'ë sga *(n.)* **carnivore**
በላዒ bela'ï *(adj.)* **venal**
በለ bele *(v.)* **allege**
በለ bele *(n.)* **say**
በለስ ጥልያን beles ẗlyan *(n.)* **fig**
በለሳን belesan *(n.)* **balsam**
በለፀ beletze *(v.)* **surpass**
በለፀ belexe *(v.)* **exceed**
በዓል beaal *(n.)* **celebration**
በዓቲ beaa'ti *(n.)* **cave**
በዓል be'äl *(n.)* **festival**

በዓል ኣስቤዛ be'äl 'asbeza *(n.)* **grocer**
በዓል ቤት beal bet *(n.)* **husband**
በዓል ድንኳን be'äl dnkwan *(n.)* **shopkeeper**
በዓል ገዛ be'äl geza *(n.)* **landlord**
በዓል ግርማ ሞገስ beal grma moges *(adj.)* **charismatic**
ብዓል ሓደራ beal hadera *(n.)* **trustee**
በዓል ሓሙሽተ መኣዝን beal hamushte meazn *(n.)* **pentagon**
በዓል ሓሙሽተ መስመር መስሕቒ ግጥሚ be'al hamushte mesmer msheqhi gtmi *(n.)* **limerick**
በዓል ለዓት መነጽር be'äl le'ät menexr *(adj.)* **binocular**
በዓል ማስኬራ be'äl maskeera *(n.)* **masquerade**
በዓል መኣርግ beal mearg *(adj.)* **titled**
በዓል መዚ be'äl mezi *(adj.)* **authoritative**
በዓል ሞያ beal moya *(n.)* **technician**
በዓል ሞያ beal moya *(n.)* **technologist**
በዓል ሞያ beäl moya *(adj.)* **professional**
በዓል ሙሉእ ጥዕና beal mulu'e t'ena *(adj.)* **lusty**
በዓል ሰለስተ እግሪ መሳርሒ beal seleste agri mesarhi *(n.)* **trident**
ብዓል ሰለስተ እግሪ beal seleste egri *(n.)* **tripod**
በዓል ሰለስተ ጎማ ሳይክል beal seleste goma sycle *(n.)* **tricycle**
በዓል ሰለስተ ሕብሪ ባንደራ beal seleste hbri bandera *(n.)* **tricolour**
በዓል ሰለስተ መኣዝን beal seleste meazn *(adj.)* **triangular**
በዓል ዘመን be'al zemen *(n.)* **upstart**
በሊሕ belih *(adj.)* **clever**
በሊሕ belih *(adj.)* **sharp**
በሊሕ belih *(adj.)* **trenchant**
በሊሕ beliĥ *(adj.)* **edgy**
በሊሕ beliḧ *(adj.)* **brilliant**
በሊሕ beliḧ *(adj.)* **cute**
በሊሕ beliḧ *(adj.)* **apt**
በልሰነ belsene *(v.)* **embalm**
በዓለገ be'älege *(adj.)* **naughty**
በዓለገ be'älege *(n.)* **vulgarian**
ብዕልግና be'älegna *(n.)* **immorality**
በዓልሞያ be'älmoya *(n.)* **expert**
በዓልቲ ገዛ be'älti geza *(n.)* **landlady**
በዓልቲ ሓዳር bealti hadar *(n.)* **housewife**
በኣሰ bease *(v.)* **worsen**
በዓቲ beati *(n.)* **tunnel**
በዓቲ be'äti *(n.)* **grotto**
በብዓይነቱ beb'äynet *(adj.)* **multifarious**
በብዓይነቱ beb'äynetu *(n.)* **assortment**
ብዕብድብድ b'ëbdbd *(adv.)* **amok**
በብቁሩብ bebequrub *(adv.)* **piecemeal**
በብቑሩብ ኣእተወ bebq̈urub 'a'ètewe *(v.)* **instil**
በብቑሩብ ሰተየ bebqurub seteye *(v.)* **tipple**
በናጅር benaĵr *(n.)* **bangle**
በናጅር benaĵr *(n.)* **bracelet**
በናኒ benani *(adj.)* **volatile**
ብእንቡኡ b'enb'u *(adv.)* **shortly**
በንዚን benzin *(n.)* **diesel**
በንዚን benzin *(n.)* **petrol**
በቃቕ beqaqh *(adj.)* **stingy**
በቅዐ beq'ë *(v.)* **qualify**
በቕዐ beq̈'ë *(v.)* **befit**
በቕሊ beqli *(n.)* **mule**

ብቕሊሉ ዝረኣይ beqlilu zereaayii *(adj.)* **conspicuous**
በቖለ beqole *(v.)* **germinate**
በታኒ betani *(adj.)* **improvident**
በታተነ betatene *(v.)* **disintegrate**
ቤተ ክርስቲያን bete kiristian *(n.)* **church**
ቤት መስተ bete meste *(n.)* **saloon**
ቤት መዝገብ bete mezgeb *(n.)* **registry**
ቤት ነገስታት bete' negeseta't *(n.)* **chateau**
ቤት ነገስታት bete negestat *(n.)* **castle**
በተነ betene *(v.)* **disband**
በተነ betene *(v.)* **scatter**
በተነ betene *(v.)* **spread**
በተነ betene *(v.)* **strew**
በጥሐ bet'ĥe *(v.)* **slash**
ብዘይጥርጥር bethzey tiritir *(adv.)* **certainly**
በቲ beti *(prep.)* **along**
በትናሕ betnaĥ *(adj.)* **rancid**
በጥራን beĭran *(n.)* **snob**
በጥራን beĭran *(adj.)* **snobbish**
በትረ መንግስቲ betre mengsti *(n.)* **sceptre**
በትሪ ፖሊስ betri polis *(n.)* **baton**
በፀበፀ betsbetse *(v.)* **dilute**
በጽበጸ betse betse *(v.)* **hydrate**
በፅሐ bets'he *(v.)* **reach**
በጽሐ - bexḥe *(v.)* **visit**
በጽሒ bexḧi *(adj.)* **adolescent**
በየደ beyede *(v.)* **weld**
በየነ beyene *(v.t.)* **adjudge**
በየነ-ዓሌታዊ beyene'äleetawi *(adj.)* **interracial**
በየነ-መንግስታዊ beyenemengstawi *(n.)* **interstate**
በይነ ዕብለላ beyne ëblela *(n.)* **monopoly**
በይነ ቁርቁር beyne qurqur *(n.)* **soliloquy**
በይነ ተዋስኦ beyne tewas'o *(n.)* **monologue**
በይኑ beynu *(adv.)* **alone**
በራድ berad *(n.)* **kettle**
በራድ beradd *(n.)* **cauldron**
በራሕ beraḧ *(adj.)* **bald**
በረንዳ beranda *(n.)* **piazza**
በራቂቶ beraqito *(n.)* **shin**
በራሪ ወረቀት berari wereket *(n.)* **tract**
ብዕራይ beray *(n.)* **yak**
በርበረ berbere *(n.)* **capsicum**
በረድ bered *(n.)* **floe**
በረድ bered *(n.)* **ice**
በረዳም ዝናብ beredam znab *(n.)* **sleet**
በረዳዊ beredawi *(adj.)* **glacial**
በረኻ bereka *(n.)* **wilderness**
በረንዳ berenda *(n.)* **porch**
በረንዳ berenda *(n.)* **veranda**
በረቐ bereqqe' *(n.)* **china**
በረሰ berese *(n.)* **decompose**
በርጋሞት bergamot *(n.)* **bergamot**
በርገር berger *(n.)* **burger**
በርሀ berhe *(v.)* **shine**
በሪ beri *(n.)* **gate**
በሪኽ berikh *(adj.)* **lofty**
በርሚል bermil *(n.)* **barrel**
በርኒሽ bernich *(n.)* **lacquer**
በርቁቕ berquq *(n.)* **plum**
በሳሲዑ besasieu *(v.)* **perforate**
በስበሰ besbese *(v. i)* **decay**
በስበሰ besbese *(v.)* **rot**
በሰላ besela *(n.)* **scar**
በሰለ besele *(v.)* **ripen**

በዳን bedan *(adj.)* **acrid**
በደል bedel *(n.)* **injustice**
በደል bedel *(n.)* **tort**
በደው bedew *(adj.)* **silly**
በዲዶ bedido *(n.)* **smallpox**
በዱ bedu *(n.)* **virgin**
በለጽ belets *(n.)* **opportunism**
በላዪ belayi *(adj.)* **obsolescent**
ቡጭ ኣበለ buch abele *(v.)* **squirt**
ቡዱን budun *(n.)* **team**
ቡፌ bufee *(n.)* **buffet**
ቡለቲን buletin *(n.)* **bulletin**
ቡን bun *(n.)* **coffee**
ቡናዊ ሕመት bunawi hmet *(n.)* **lignite**
ቡናዊ ቀይሕ bunawi qeyh *(n.)* **mahogany**
ቡናዊ bunawi *(n.)* **brown**
ቡቅሊ buqhli *(n.)* **malt**
ቡራኬ burakee *(n.)* **benediction**
ቡሽ bush *(n.)* **bung**
ቡሶላ busola *(n.)* **compass**
ቡስጣ busẗa *(n.)* **envelope**
ቡት but *(n.)* **wellington**
ቡቲክ butik *(n.)* **boutique**
ቢ b *( )* **B**
ባቤል babeel *(n.)* **Babel**
ባጫ bacha *(n.)* **taunt**
ባጫ bacha *(adj.)* **witty**
ባዴላ badeela *(n.)* **spade**
ባዴላ badela *(n.)* **shovel**
ባዴላ/ድስቲ badela/dsti *(n.)* **pan**
ባድሚንተን badminten *(n.)* **badminton**
ባዶ bado *(adj.)* **inane**
ባዶ bado *(n.)* **nil**
ባዶ bado *(adj.)* **zero**
ባዶ bado *(n.)* **zilch**
ባዶ ገበረ bado gebere *(v.)* **nullify**
ባእባእ በለ ba'eba'e bele *(v.)* **fumble**
ባእብእ ba'eb'e *(v.)* **stutter**
ባዕዳዊ ba'ëdawi *(adj.)* **exotic**
ባዕዳዊ ba'ëdawi *(adj.)* **foreign**
ባዕዲ ba'ëdi *(adj.)* **alien**
ባዕዲ ba'ëdi *(n.)* **foreigner**
ባዕዳዊ baeedawi *(adj.)* **colonial**
ባዕላ ba'ëla *(pron.)* **herself**
ባዕለገ baelege *(adj.)* **unprincipled**
ባዕለገ bae'lege' *(adj.)* **cheeky**
ባዕለይ ba'ëley *(pron.)* **myself**
ባዕሊ ba'ëli *(n.)* **ego**
ባዕልነት ba'ëlnet *(n.)* **egotism**
ባዕሎም ba'elom *(pron.)* **themselves**
ባዕሉ ንባዕሉ ዘይስማዕማዕ ba'elu n ba'elu zeysma'ema'e *(adj.)* **incoherent**
ባእሲ baesi *(n.)* **tussle**
ባእሲ ba'esi *(n.)* **infighting**
ባእሲ ba'esi *(n.)* **scrimmage**
ባእሲ ba'esi *(n.)* **strife**
ባእታ ba'eta *(n.)* **element**
ብኣፍንጭኡ ደረዘ b'afn'č'u dereze *(v.)* **nuzzle**
ባጎኒ bagoni *(n.)* **wagon**
ባህገኛ bahgenya *(n.)* **idealist**
ባህጊ bahgi *(adj.)* **wistful**
ባሕጎገ baȟgoge *(v.)* **corrode**
ባህላዊ bahlawi *(adj.)* **cultural**
ባህላዊ መግቢ ላቲን ኣመሪካ bahlawi megbi latin amrica *(n.)* **pastel**
ባህላዊ ዛንታ bahlawi zanta *(n.)* **lore**
ባህሊ bahli *(n.)* **culture**
ባህሊ bahli *(n.)* **ritual**
ባህሊ bahli *(n.)* **tradition**
ባህሊ ዝህሉ bahli zhlu *(n.)* **traditionalist**
ባሕረኛ bahregna *(n.)* **mariner**

ባሕረኛ bahregna *(n.)* **sailor**
ባህረት bahret *(n.)* **instinct**
ባህረታዊ bahretawi *(adj.)* **instinctive**
ባሕሪ bahri *(n.)* **sea**
ባህርያዊ bahryawi *(adj.)* **inherent**
ባህርያዊ bahryawi *(adj.)* **intrinsic**
ባሕታዊ baḥtawi *(n.)* **hermit**
ባሕተላይ baḧtelay *(n.)* **bachelor**
ባጀት baĵet *(n.)* **budget**
ባኮ bako *(n.)* **carton**
ባክተሪያ bakteriya *(n.)* **bacteria**
ባላ bala *(n.)* **stake**
ባላ bala *(n.)* **stanchion**
ባላ እግሪ bala egri *(n.)* **stilt**
ባላባት balabat *(n.)* **baron**
ባልዶንጓ baldongwa *(n.)* **bean**
ባልዕ bale *(adj.)* **xylophages**
ባለይ baley *(n.)* **ballet**
ብኣልኮል ዝብፅበፅ መድሓኒት balkol zbtsbets medhanit *(n.)* **tincture**
ባልሳ balsa *(n.)* **balm**
ባልታዊ baltawi *(adj.)* **satirical**
ባልተኛ baltegna *(n.)* **satirist**
ባልጠጂ balťeĵi *(n.)* **butler**
ባልቲ balti *(n.)* **satire**
ብዓልቲ ቤት b'alti beet *(n.)* **wife**
ባምቡላ bambula *(n.)* **doll**
ባንዴራ bandiera *(n.)* **flag**
ባኒ bani *(n.)* **croissant**
ባንጆ banĵo *(n.)* **banjo**
ባንከኛ bankegna *(n.)* **banker**
ባንኪ banki *(n.)* **bank**
ባንኮኒ bankoni *(n.)* **counter**
ብአንጻሩ bantaru *(adv.)* **vice-versa**
ብኣቕሑት ኣማልአ b'aquĥt amal'e *(v.)* **furnish**
ባራካ baraka *(n.)* **shanty**
ባራካ baraka *(n.)* **barrack**
ባራኩዳ barakuda *(n.)* **barracuda**
ባርባራዊ barbarawi *(n.)* **barbarian**
ባርባራዊ barbarawi *(adj.)* **barbaric**
ባርነት barbebt *(n.)* **slavery**
ባርዕ bar'ë *(n.)* **fire**
ባረኸ bareke *(v.)* **sanctify**
ባረኸ bareḱe *(v.)* **hallow**
ባረኸ bareḱe *(v.)* **bless**
ባርኾት barkot *(n.)* **sanctification**
ባርነት barnet *(n.)* **thrall**
ባርኖስ barnos *(n.)* **locust**
ባሮሜተር baromeeter *(n.)* **barometer**
ባርያ barya *(n.)* **slave**
ባርያ ገበረ barya gebere *(v.)* **enslave**
ባርያዊ baryawi *(adj.)* **slavish**
ባስ bas *(n.)* **bass**
ባስታ basta *(n.)* **pasta**
ባጤራዊ ፖሊሲ baťeerawi polisi *(n.)* **monetarism**
ባተሪ bateri *(n.)* **battery**
ብያቲ bati *(n.)* **tray**
ባጤራ እንግሊዝ baťiera èngliz *(n.)* **pound**
ባቲክ batik *(n.)* **batik**
ብዓውታ b'äwta *(adv.)* **aloud**
ባውዛ bawza *(n.)* **limelight**
ብዓይኒ ዘይረአ b'äyni zeyre'e *(adj.)* **microscopic**
ባዮፕሲ bayopsi *(n.)* **biopsy**
ባይት bayt *(n.)* **byte**
ባይታ bayta *(n.)* **floor**
ባይታ bayta *(n.)* **ground**
ባይቶ bayto *(n.)* **senate**
ባዛር bazar *(n.)* **bazaar**
ባዚሊካ bazilika *(n.)* **basilica**
ባዚቃ baziqa *(n.)* **gramophone**

ባዚቃዊ baziqawi *(adj.)* **mercurial**
ባዝራ bazra *(n.)* **mare**
ባዙቃ bazuqa *(n.)* **bazooka**

ቤ

ቤኮን beekon *(n.)* **bacon**
ቤላሮባ beelaroba *(n.)* **hawker**
ቤት ፍርዲ beet frdi *(n.)* **court**
ቤት ግምጃ beet gmja *(n.)* **bursary**
ቤት ማእሰርቲ beet ma'èserti *(n.)* **jail**
ቤት መዘጋጃ beet mezageja *(n.)* **municipality**
ቤት ምኽሪ beet mkri *(n.)* **council**
ቤት ንህበት beet nhbet *(n.)* **foundry**
ቤት ፅሕፈት beet xḧfet *(n.)* **bureau**
ቤተ ክህነት beete khnet *(n.)* **ministry**
ቤተ መዘክር beete mezekr *(n.)* **museum**
ቤተ ፀሎት beete xelot *(n.)* **chapel**
ቤት ስኒማ bet ciniema *(n)* **cinema**
ቤት ፍርዲ bet frdi *(n.)* **tribunal**
ቤት ግምጃ bet gmja *(n.)* **treasury**
ቤት ሕፅቦ bet htsbo *(n.)* **launderette**
ቤተ መቅደስ bet mekdes *(n.)* **temple**
ቤት መስተ bet meste *(n.)* **pub**
ቤት ምግቢ bet mgbi *(n.)* **restaurant**

ብ

ብዕልኛ b'ëlgna *(n.)* **disrespect**
ብዕልግና b'ëlg'na *(n.)* **misconduct**
ብዕልግቲ b'ëlgti *(n.)* **slut**
ብዕሊ ክንገር ዝግባእ bëli knger zgba'e *(adj.)* **notifiable**
ብ b *(prep.)* **by**
ብ b *(prep.)* **with**
ብገምደ ዝንቀሳቐስ ኣሻንጉሊት b gemed znqesaqhes ashangulit *(n.)* **marionette**
ብሓሳብ b hasab *(adv.)* **ideally**
ብ ቫይረስ b vires *(adj.)* **viral**
ብዓል ዝና ba'al zna *(adj.)* **accredited**
ብኣጋ ኣፍልጦ b'aga 'aflẗo *(n.)* **foreknowledge**
ብህላዊ bahlawi *(adj.)* **traditional**
ብዓል ቤት b'al biet *(n.)* **spouse**
ብዓል ጎባን bäl goban *(n.)* **cuckold**
ብዓል ሕድሪ bäl hdri *(n.)* **custodian**
ብዓል ሞያ b'äl moya *(n.)* **practitioner**
ብዓል ንፅል መነፀር b'äl nxl menexr *(adj.)* **monocular**
ብዓል ስልጣን b'al sltan *(adj.)* **incumbent**
ብባሕሪ ተጓዓዘ bbahri tegu'aze *(v.)* **sail**
ብባህሪኡ bbahri'u *(adv.)* **naturally**
ብበዝሒ bbezĥi *(adj.)* **galore**
ብበዝሒ ምምፃእ bbezhi mmtsa'e *(n.)* **influx**
ብብርቱዕ ሃረፈ bbrtu'ë harefe *(v.)* **hanker**
ብጭጉራፍ ወቕዐ bĉguraf weq'ë *(v.)* **flagellate**
ብጫ bcha *(adj.)* **yellow**
ብጫ እምኒ bcha emni *(n.)* **topaz**
ብጫ ክፋል እንቋቑሖ bcha kfal enquaquho *(n.)* **yolk**
ብጭቃ ዝተሰርሐ bĉqa zteserĥe *(adj.)* **earthen**
ብድብድ bd'bd *(adj.)* **musty**

ብደንቢ bdenbi *(adv.)* **indeed**
ብደቒቃ bdeqiqa *(adv.)* **minutely**
ብድሕሪ bdḧri *(adv.)* **after**
ብድሕሪት ሸነኽ bdĥrit shenek *(adj.)* **posterior**
ብድሕሪት bdḧrit *(prep.)* **behind**
ብድሕሪኡ bdhriu *(adv.)* **then**
ብድሕሪኡ bdhriu *(adv.)* **thence**
ብድሌት bdliet *(adj.)* **voluntary**
ብድንገት ምጭፍላቕ bdnget mchflak *(v.)* **implode**
ብዱቕስካ ምኻድ bdquska mkhad *(n.)* **somnambulism**
ብድቁሱ ዝኸድ bdqusu zkhed *(n.)* **somnambulist**
ብዕሉግ b'elug *(adj.)* **lewd**
ብዕሉግ b'elug *(adj.)* **licentious**
ብዕሉግ b'elug *(adj.)* **wanton**
ብዕሉግ b'ëlug *(adj.)* **amoral**
ብዕሉግ b'ëlug *(adj.)* **discourteous**
ብዕሉግ b'ëlug *(v.)* **pervert**
ብዕሉግ b'ëlug *(adj.)* **surly**
በልጸገ belxege *(v.)* **prosper**
ብእምነት ዘይኮነ ብኩነታት ዝሰርሕ bèmnet zeykone bkunetat zserḧ *(adj.)* **pragmatic**
ብዕሙር ኣገባብ b'ëmur agbab *(adv.)* **richly**
ብጣዕሚ betaemi *(pref.)* **ultra**
ብጣዕሚ ገፊሕ betaemi gefihei *(adj.)* **cavernous**
ብዝለዓለ ጥንቓቐ beze-le-a-le tenkake *(adv.)* **gingerly**
በዘወ bezewe *(v.)* **mortify**
ብዕዘዛ b'ëzeza *(n.)* **somnolence**
በዚ ገይሩ bezi geyru *(adv.)* **hereby**
ብዙሕ bezuhi'h *(adj.)* **considerable**
ብዕዙዝ bëzuz' *(adj.)* **somnolent**
ብዕዙዝ b'ëzuz *(adj.)* **sleepy**
ብዕዙዝ b'ëzuz *(adj.)* **somnolent**
ብፈሳሲ ዝሰርሕ bfesasi zserh *(adj.)* **hydraulic**
ብፍላይ bflay *(adv.)* **especially**
ብፍቕሪ ሓረረ bfqri ĥarere *(v. t)* **enamour**
ብፍጥነት bftnet *(n.)* **trice**
ብጋኔን ኣትሓዘ bganen at'haze *(v.)* **demonize**
ብግቡእ ኣገባብ bgbu'e agbab *(adv.)* **duly**
ብጌጋ ኣንበበ bgeega anbebe *(v.)* **misread**
ብጌጋ ኣርኣየ bgeega 'ar'aye *(v.)* **belie**
ብጌጋ ፈረደ bgeega ferede *(v.)* **misjudge**
ብጌጋ ፊደል ፀሓፈ bgeega fidel xeḧafe *(v.)* **misspell**
ብጌጋ መርሐ bgeega merḧe *(v.)* **mislead**
ብጌጋ ምርዳእ bgeega mrda'e *(n.)* **misunderstanding**
ብጌጋ ቀመረ bgeega qemere *(v.)* **miscalculate**
ብጌጋ ጠቐሰ bgeega ẗeqese *(v.)* **misquote**
ብጌጋ ተረድአ bgeega terd'e *(v.)* **misunderstand**
ብጌጋ ተጠቀመ bgeega teẗeqeme *(v.)* **misuse**
ብጌጋ ትርጉም ሃበ bgeega trgum habe *(v.)* **misconstrue**
ብጌጋ ምግንዛብ bgeegs mg'nzab *(v.)* **misconceive**
ብጌጋ ምርዳእ bgiega mrda'e *(n.)* **misapprehension**
ብጌጋ ተረደአ bgiega terede'e *(v.)* **misapprehend**

ብግመ ዝተሸፈነ bgme zteshefene *(adj.)* **misty**

ብግምት ምውሳን bgmt mwsan ***(n.)*** **presupposition**

ብግምት ወሰነ bgmt wesene ***(v.)*** **presuppose**

ብሓደ bhade ***(adv.)*** **together**

ብሓደ ኩነታት ዝተራከቡ ሰባት bhade kunetat zterakebu sebat ***(n.)*** **turnout**

ብሓደ መዓልቲ ሰለስተ ዉድድር ምሽናፍ bhade mealti seleste gze mshnaf ***(adj.)*** **treble**

ብሓደ ነገር ዘተኮረ ነዊሕ ፅሑፍ bhade neger zetekore newih suhuf ***(n.)*** **treatise**

ብሓዱሽ bḧadush ***(adv.)*** **newly**

ብሓጐስ ፈንጨሐ bḧagwas fenčeḧe ***(v.)*** **enrapture**

ብሃንደበት bhandebet ***(adv.)*** **suddenly**

ብሓንሳብ bĥansab ***(adj.)*** **simultaneous**

ብሓቂ bĥaqi ***(adv.)*** **really**

ብሓቂ bḥaqi ***(adv.)*** **verily**

ብሓቂ bḧaqi ***(adv.)*** **actually**

ብሓርኮትኮቱ ዝሃፍተመ bharkorkotu zhafteme ***(adj.)*** **self-made**

በሃሩር ተሳቐየ bharuṛ tesaqeye ***(v.)*** **swelter**

ብሓሶት መስከረ bĥasot meskere ***(v.)*** **perjure**

ብሓሶት ምምስካር bĥasot mmskar ***(n.)*** **perjury**

ብሓፂሩ bḧatsiru ***(adv.)*** **summarily**

ብሓይሊ ወሰደ bḧayli wesede ***(v.)*** **extort**

ብሕቡእ bhbu'e ***(adj.)*** **underhand**

ብሓደ ግዜ ልዕሊ ሓደ ሰብኣይ ትምርያ ሰበይቲ bḧde gzie lëli ḧade gzie sebay tmräw sebeyti ***(n.)*** **polyandry**

ብሓደ ግዜ ልዕሊ ሓደ ሰብኣይ/ሰበይቲ ምምርዓው bḧde gzie lëli ḧade gzie sebay/sebeti mmräw ***(n.)*** **polygamy**

ብሓደ ግዜ ልዕሊ ሓደ ሰብኣይ/ሰበይቲ ተመርዓዊ bḧde gzie lëli ḧade gzie sebay/sebeti temeräwi ***(adj.)*** **polygamous**

ብሄር bheer ***(n.)*** **nation**

ብሄራዊ bheerawi ***(adj.)*** **national**

ብሕጊ ዝተወሰነ bḧgi ztewesene ***(adj.)*** **statutory**

ብሕጎጋ bḧgoga ***(n.)*** **corrosion**

ብሓባር ተቀመጠ bhhabar teqemete ***(v.)*** **cohabit**

ብሂል bhil ***(n.)*** **dictum**

ብሂል bhil ***(n.)*** **epigram**

ብሒቑ bĥiq ***(n.)*** **dough**

ብህሎ bhlo ***(n.)*** **allegation**

ብሕማቕ bḧmaq̈ ***(adv.)*** **badly**

ብህንጥይና bhnẗyna ***(adv.)*** **avidly**

ብሕቋር bĥqwar ***(n.)*** **groove**

ባህሪ bhri ***(n.)*** **trait**

ብሕታዊ bhtawi ***(adj.)*** **lone**

ብሕታዊ bhtawi ***(adj.)*** **lonely**

ብሕታዊ bhtawi ***(adj.)*** **lonesome**

ብሕታዊነት bhtawinet ***(n.)*** **loneliness**

ብሕትኡ ምኺን ዝመርፅ bht'u mukhun zmerts ***(n.)*** **loner**

ብሕትውና bḧtwna ***(n.)*** **celibacy**

ብህፁፅ ዝተሰርሓ bhuxux zteserḧe ***(adj.)*** **cursory**

ብሕያውነት bḥyawnet ***(adv.)*** **kindly**

ቢጫ ዕንበባ bich enbeba *(n.)* **marigold**
ብኢድ ዝተፃሓፈ b'id ztetzehafe *(n.)* **manuscript**
ቢደ bide *(n.)* **bidet**
ቤት ብልዒ biet bl'ï *(n.)* **eatery**
ቤት ሕብስቲ biet hbsti *(n.)* **pastry**
ቤት ሕብስቲ biet hbsti *(n.)* **patisserie**
ቤት ማሕቡስ biet maḧbus *(n.)* **prison**
ቤት መድሃኒት biet medhanit *(n.)* **pharmacy**
ቤት ምግብን መስተን biet mgbn mesten *(n.)* **tavern**
ቤተ መንግስታዊ biete mengstawi *(adj.)* **palatial**
ቤተ መንግስቲ biete mengsti *(n.)* **palace**
ቤተ-ፈተነ biete-fetene *(n.)* **laboratory**
ቤተ-መፃሕፍቲ biete-metsahft *(n.)* **library**
ቢኪኒ bikini *(n.)* **bikini**
ቡሊምያ bilimiya *(n.)* **bulimia**
ቢልያርዶ bilyardo *(n.)* **billiards**
ቢልዮን bilyon *(n.)* **billion**
ቢራ bira *(n.)* **ale**
ቢራ bira *(n.)* **beer**
ብሪንጃል birinjal *(n.)* **brinjal**
ቢሮ biro *(n.)* **pen**
ቢሮክራሲ birokrasi *(n.)* **bureaucracy**
ቢሮክራት birokrat *(n.)* **bureaucrat**
ቢስተካ bisteka *(n.)* **steak**
ቢቨር biver *(n.)* **beaver**
ቢያቲ biyati *(n.)* **plate**
ብጃማ bĵama *(n.)* **pyjamas**
ብጃንጥላ ዝንቆት bjantla znqot *(n.)* **parachutist**
ብጀካ bjeka *(prep.)* **barring**
ብጀካ bjeka *(prep.)* **except**
ብኽብረት bḱbret *(v.)* **please**
ብከላ bkela *(n.)* **pollution**
ብቐሊሉ ዛእምን bkelilu za'amn *(adj.)* **gullible**
ብክልተ ጎኒ ዝርከብ bklte goni zrkeb *(prep.)* **astride**
ብኽነት bḱnet *(n.)* **wastage**
ብኮፍ ዝግበር bkof zgber *(adj.)* **sedentary**
ብኮፍካ ሸመት bkofka šmet *(n.)* **sinecure**
ብኮምፒዩተር ኣስረሐ bkompyuter asreh *(v.)* **computerize**
ብኮንትሮባንድ ኣእተወ bkontroband a'etewe *(v.)* **smuggle**
ብቆርብት ቀዳድ ርስሓት ምውጋድ bkorbet kedda dshat mray *(v.)* **transpire**
ብኮረንቲ ኣቑሰለ bkorenti aqusele *(v.)* **electrocute**
ብቑዕ ዘይኮነ bku zeykone *(adj.)* **unfit**
ብቑዕ ዘይኮነ bku zeykone *(adj.)* **unqualified**
ብቑዕ ዘይኮነ bku zeykone *(adj.)* **unworthy**
ብኹሉኹሉ bkulukulu *(adv.)* **roundly**
ብኩራት bkurat *(n.)* **absence**
ብኳርያ bkwarya *(n.)* **fox**
ብኽያት bkyat *(n.)* **croak**
ብኽያት bkyat *(n.)* **cry**
ብኽያት bkyat *(n.)* **whine**
ብላዕ ዘይበልዕ bla'e zeybel'e *(adj.)* **incorruptible**
ብልዕሊ ዝግበር blaeli zgber *(n.)* **topping**

ብላክቤሪ blakberi *(n.)* **blackberry**
ብላሽ blash *(n.)* **fiasco**
ብላሽ blash *(adj.)* **vain**
ብላይ blay *(adj.)* **ragged**
ብልጭ ብልጭ በለ blč blč bele *(v.)* **glimmer**
ብልጫ blča *(adj.)* **pre-eminent**
ብልጫዊ blčawi *(n.)* **pre-eminence**
ብልጭታ blchta *(n.)* **spark**
ብልጭልጭ በለ blĉlĉ bele *(v.)* **glitter**
ባልዕ ble *(n.)* **pest**
ብልዕሊ bl'ëli *(prep.)* **above**
ብልሓት blhat *(n.)* **technique**
ብልሓት blĥat *(n.)* **diplomacy**
ብልሓት blĥat *(n.)* **genius**
ብልሓት blḧat *(n.)* **contrivance**
ብልሓት blhat *(n.)* **tact**
ብልሓት blḧat *(n.)* **prowess**
ብልሓተኛ blĥategna *(adj.)* **resourceful**
ብልሓተኛ bl'ḧategna *(adj.)* **methodical**
ብልሒ blhi *(n.)* **tang**
ብልሒ ግምቢ b'lḧi gmbi *(n.)* **steeple**
ብልህነት blhnet *(n.)* **brilliance**
ቢልዮነር blilyoner *(n.)* **billionaire**
ብሎን blon *(n.)* **screw**
ብልቃጥ blqat *(n.)* **phial**
ብልሹነት blshunet *(n.)* **futility**
ብልሹው blshuw *(adj.)* **bent**
ብልሹው blshuw *(adj.)* **dysfunctional**
ብልሽው blshw *(adv.)* **awry**
ብልሹው blshw *(adj.)* **putrid**
ብልጽግና bltsg'na *(n.)* **prosperity**
ብልፁግ bltsug *(adj.)* **prosperous**
ብሉፅ blutz *(adj.)* **superb**
ብሉፅ እዋን blutz ewan *(n.)* **innings**
ብሉፅ blux *(n.)* **ace**
ብሉፅ blux *(adj.)* **classic**
ብሉፅ blux *(n.)* **elite**
ብሉፅ ዕዮ blux ëyo *(n.)* **masterpiece**
ብማዕዶ bma''ëdo *(adv.)* **across**
ብማዕዶ ፈረደ bma'ëdo ferede *(v.)* **prejudge**
ብማእኸል bmaekel *(prep. &adv.)* **through**
ብመድሓኒት ምድቃስ bmedhanit mdqas *(n.)* **sedation**
ብልክዕ ምምልካት bmelke mmlkat *(v.)* **pinpoint**
ብመንፅር bmenxr *(adv.)* **according**
ብመቀስ ቆረፀ bmeqes qoretse *(v.)* **snip**
ብመርከብ ተጓዓዘ bmerkeb tgwaäze *(v.)* **cruise**
ብመርትዖ ደገፈ bmert'o degefe *(v.)* **substantiate**
ብመርትዖ ምድጋፍ bmert'o mdbaf *(n.)* **substantiation**
ብ መሳርሒ ቅርፂ ዘዋፅእ bmesarhi qrsi zwese *(n.)* **turner**
ብመሰረት bmeseret *(n.)* **accordance**
ብመስኖ ማይ ኣስተየ bmesno may 'asteye *(v.)* **irrigate**
ብመጠኑ bmeṫenu *(adv.)* **fairly**
ብመወዳእታ b'mewedaeta *(adv.)* **ultimately**
ብምክሓድ bmkhad *(adj.)* **treacherous**
ብምልምስና ዝሳቐ ሰብ bmlmsna zsaqe seb *(adj.)* **paralytic**
ብምሳሌ ምጥቃም bmsalee mṭqam *(n.)* **imagery**
ብምስጋእ bmsga'e *(conj.)* **lest**
ብምትሓዝ ዝግነ ቅርሺ bmthaz zgne qrshi *(v.)* **tote**

ብሙቀት ዝጥንክር ፕላስቲክ bmuqet ztnker plastik *(adj.)* **thermosetting**
ብምዝንባል bmznbal *(adv.)* **astray**
ብነብሱ ዘይምራሕ bnebsu zeymraḧ *(n.)* **puppet**
ብነጻ bnetsa *(adv. &adj.)* **gratis**
ብንፋስ እትጥሕን መኪና bnfas etthn mekina *(n.)* **windmill**
ብንጅር bnĵr *(n.)* **beet**
ብንፁር ዘይረአ bnuxr zeyr'e *(adj.)* **faint**
ብፖስጣ bposẗa *(adj.)* **postal**
ብፖስታ ዝተገዙኡ bposta ztegez'u *(n.)* **mail order**
ብቕዓት bq'at *(n.)* **credentials**
ብቕዓት bqät *(n.)* **efficiency**
ብቅዓት bq'ät *(n.)* **qualification**
ብቕዓት bq̈'ät *(n.)* **validity**
ብቅዓታዊ bq'ätawi *(adj.)* **qualitative**
ብቕዱስ ዝምራሕ ዓዲ bqdus zmrah adi *(n.)* **theocracy**
ብቀሊሉ bqelilu *(adv.)* **readily**
ብቀሊሉ ክቆፃፀርዎ ዝክእሉ bqelilu kqosaserwa zk'al *(adj.)* **tractable**
ብቐሊሉ ተናዳዲ bqelilu tenadadi *(adj.)* **testy**
ብቐሊሉ ዝነድድ bqelilu znedd *(adj.)* **flammable**
ብቀጥታ bqetta *(adv.)* **directly**
ብቅዓት ዘይብሉ bqha'at zeyblu *(adj.)* **ineligible**
ብቐሊሉ bqhelilu *(adv.)* **lightly**
ብቐሊሉ ዝፅሎ ሰብ bqhelilu ztslo seb *(adj.)* **suggestible**
ብቐሊሉ ዘይሓቅቕ bqhelilu zwyhaqqh *(adj.)* **indigestible**
ብቕጽበት b'qhtsbet *(adv.)* **straightway**
ብቅልጡፍ bqltuf *(adv.)* **quickly**
ብቕልጡፍ bq̈ltuf *(n.)* **ado**
ብቕልጡፍ bq̈lẗuf *(adv.)* **apace**
ብቕሉዕ bq̈lu'ë *(adv.)* **barely**
ብቑዕ bqu'ë *(adj.)* **efficient**
ብቑዕ bqu'ë *(adj.)* **eligible**
ብቁዕ bq̈u'ë *(adj.)* **fit**
ብቑዕ bq̈u'ë *(adj.)* **valid**
ብሑቕ መሰል bque mesl *(n.)* **pasty**
ብቑዕ bq̈u'ë *(adj.)* **appropriate**
ብቋልያ bqwalya *(adj.)* **nascent**
ብር በለ br bele *(v.)* **flush**
ብራድ brad *(n.)* **filings**
ብራኸ braḱe *(n.)* **altitude**
ብራኳ brakwa *(n.)* **jug**
ብራኳ brakwa *(n.)* **pitcher**
ብራንዲ brandi *(n.)* **brandy**
ብርጭቆ brchiqo *(n.)* **tumbler**
ብርጭቕ brčq *(n.)* **watermelon**
ብርጭቆ brčqo *(n.)* **beaker**
ብርእሲ ስሒብካ ዝኽደን ኽዳን brèsi sḧibka zḱden ḱdan *(n.)* **pullover**
ብረት bret *(n.)* **metal**
ብረት bret *(n.)* **weapon**
ብረታዊ bretawi *(adj.)* **metallic**
ብረይል breyl *(n.)* **Braille**
ብርጌድ brgied *(n.)* **legion**
ብርግፀ brg'x *(adv.)* **surely**
ብርሃን brhan *(n.)* **light**
ብርሃን ሃበ brhan habe *(v.)* **irradiate**
ብርሃን ሰማይ brhan semay *(n.)* **skylight**
ብርሃን ወሃቢ br'han wehabi *(n.)* **luminary**
ብርሃን ወርሒ brhan werḧi *(n.)* **moonlight**
ብርሃን ዘሕልፍ brhan zehlf *(adj.)* **translucent**
ብሪ bri *(n.)* **silver**
ብርዒ br'i *(n.)* **stylus**

ብሪጌድ brigeed *(n.)* **brigade**
ብሪቕሪቕ briq̈riq̈ *(n.)* **glazier**
ብሪቕሪቕታ briq̈riq̈ta *(n.)* **gloss**
ብሪጣንያዊ briťanyawi *(adj.)* **British**
ብሪውምሪው በለ briwmriw bele *(v.)* **gibber**
ብርካተ brkate *(n.)* **abundance**
ብርካተ brkate *(n.)* **profusion**
ብርኩት brkut *(adj.)* **numerous**
ብርለ brle *(n.)* **flask**
ብርለ ነቢት brle nebit *(n.)* **decanter**
ብርኒጎ brnigo *(n.)* **quail**
ብሮንዞ bronzo *(n.)* **bronze**
ብሮት brot *(n.)* **mole**
ብርቃሕ brqaḧ *(n.)* **notch**
ብርቒ brqi *(adj.)* **precious**
ብርሰት brset *(v. t)* **decomposition**
ብርሰት brset *(n.)* **destruction**
ብርስን brsn *(n.)* **lentil**
ብርታዐ brta'ë *(n.)* **vigour**
ብርቱዕ brtu'e *(adj.)* **herculean**
ብርቱዕ brtu'e *(adj.)* **vigorous**
ብርቱዕ brtu'ë *(adj.)* **acute**
ብርቱዕ brtu'ë *(adj.)* **ardent**
ብርቱዕ brtu'ë *(adj.)* **dynamic**
ብርቱዕ ጨና brtuë čena *(adj.)* **pungent**
ብርቱዕ ጨና ምህላው brtuë čena mhlaw *(n.)* **pungency**
ብርቱዕ ድሌት brtu'ë dleet *(n.)* **ardour**
ብርቲዕ ድልየት brtu'e dlyet *(n.)* **zeal**
ብርቱዕ ስምዒት brtue smeit *(n.)* **passion**
ብርቱዕ ተምሳጥ brtu'ë temsaẗ *(n.)* **fervour**
ብርቱዕ brtu'ë *(adj.)* **strong**
ብሩህ bruh *(adj.)* **apparent**
ብሩህ bruh *(adj.)* **intelligible**
ብሩህ bruh *(adj.)* **lucent**
ብሩህነት bruhnet *(adv.)* **lucidity**
ብሩኽ bruḱ *(adj.)* **blessed**
ብግዜ ቀዳማይ brzie qedamay *(adj.)* **prime**
ብፅብፅ ዓመፅ bsbs ames *(n.)* **turmoil**
ብሰዓቱ bseatu *(adj.)* **timely**
ብሰላሕታ bsela'ḧta *(adv.)* **stealthily**
ብሰለስተ ዕንጨይቲ ዝተስኣለ ስእሊ bseleste ansyti ztesale seli *(n.)* **triptych**
ብሰንጠረዥ ምስራሕ ምምዳብ bsenterez msrah mmdab *(n.)* **tabulation**
ብሰንጠረዥ ዝተሰርሐ bsenterez zteserhe *(adj.)* **tabular**
ብሰንጠረዥ ኣዘጋጅዩ bsenterz azegaj'u *(v.)* **tabulate**
ብሽክለታ bshkleta *(n.)* **bicycle**
ብሽክለታ bshkleta *(n.)* **bike**
ብሽክሌተኛ bshkliteenya *(n.)* **cyclist**
ብሽኮቲ bshkoti *(n.)* **biscuit**
ብሽኩቲ bshkuti *(n.)* **cracker**
ብስለት bs'let *(n.)* **maturity**
ብስልኪ፣ቲቪ፣ኢንተርኔት ርክብ bslki,tivi,internet rkb *(n.)* **telecommunications**
ብስምምዕነ ት bsmm'enet *(adv.)* **tamely**
ብስናው b-snaw *(n.)* **halitosis**
ብጣዕሚ ቡዙሕ btaami bzuh *(adj.)* **tremendous**
ብጣዕሚ ሓያል btaami hayal *(adj.)* **torrential**
ብጣዕሚ ምህንጣይ btaami mhntay *(n.)* **tenterhook**
ብታዕሚ btaemi *(adv.)* **too**

ብጣዕሚ ዓቡዪ btaemi abyi *(adj.)* **titanic**
ብጣዕሚ ቡዙሕ bta'emi buzuh *(adj.)* **infinite**
ብጣዕሚ ብዙሕ bẗaëmi bzuḧ *(adj.)* **profuse**
ብጣዕሚ ሓያል ንፋስ btaemi hayal nfas *(n.)* **tornado**
ብጣዕሚ ናይ ምድላይ ስሚዒት btaemi namdlay smi'it *(n.)* **temptation**
ብጣዕሚ ፁብቕ bta'emi tsubqh *(adj.)* **magnificent**
ብጣሕ bẗaḧ *(n.)* **nick**
ብትብዓት b-tb-at *(adj.)* **gamely**
ብጥብቂ bẗbqi *(adv.)* **strictly**
ብተደጋጋሚ ምህራም btedegagami mhram *(v.)* **pummel**
ብተኸታታሊ bteketatali *(adv.)* **consecutively**
ብተክኖሎጅይ ዝተሓገዘ bteknology ztehageze *(adj.)* **technological**
ብቴሌቪዥን ተሓላሊፉ btelevizn tehalalifu *(v.)* **televise**
ብተሎ b'telo *(adv.)* **soon**
ብተመሳሳሊ btemesasali *(adv.)* **likewise**
መተንፈሲ btenfesi *(n.)* **inhaler**
ብጠቕላላ bteqlala *(n.)* **totality**
ብተርታ ሰርዐ bterta ser'e *(v.)* **serialize**
ብተስፋ btesfa *(adv.)* **hopefully**
ብተወሳኺ btewesaki *(adv.)* **else**
ብተወሳኺ btewesaki *(adv.)* **furthermore**
ብተወሳኺ btewesaki *(adv.)* **withal**
ብተወሳኺ btewesaḱi *(adv.)* **moreover**
ብጽሒት bẗḧit *(n.)* **portion**
ብትሕቲ bthti *(prep.)* **underneath**
ብጥንቃቐ ኣንቢቡ btnqaqe anbibu *(v.)* **peruse**
ብጥንቃቀ መርመረ btnqaqe mermere *(v.)* **scrutinize**
ብጥንቃቐ ምንባብ btnqaqe mnbab *(n.)* **perusal**
ብትንትን ዝበለ btntn zbele *(adj.)* **untidy**
ብጥራነ bẗrane *(n.)* **snobbery**
ብጥራሽ bẗrash *(adv.)* **never**
ብጥርጣረ ጠመተ bẗrẗare ẗemete *(adv.)* **askance**
ብፀሓይ ዝሰርሕ btseḧay zserh *(adj.)* **solar**
ብፅሒት btshit *(n.)* **share**
ብፅሒት btsĥit *(n.)* **quota**
ብፅሒት btsĥit *(n.)* **quotient**
ብጽሑፍ አስፈረ btshuf asfere *(v.)* **transcribe**
ብፁእተኛ btsu'etegna *(n.)* **puritan**
ብፁእተኛዊ btsu'etegnawi *(adj.)* **puritanical**
ብንፁር bnxur *(adv.)* **clearly**
ቦኽቦኽ boḱboḱe *(v.)* **moulder**
ቦምብ bomb *(n.)* **bomb**
ቦርሳ borsa *(n.)* **bag**
ቦርሳ borsa *(n.)* **purse**
ቦርሳ ኢድ borsa e-i-d *(n.)* **handbag**
ቦታ bota *(n.)* **place**
ቦታ bota *(n.)* **site**
ቦታ ለወጠ bota lewete *(v.)* **relocate**
ቦታ ምሓዝ bota mḥaz *(n.)* **installation**
ቦጦሎኒ boẗoloni *(n.)* **battalion**
ብዙሕ buzuh *(adj.)* **many**
ብዋጋ ዘይትመን bwaga zeytmen *(adj.)* **priceless**
ቧምብላ bwambula *(n.)* **toy**

ብዋኒን ዝተጸምደ bwanin ztexemde *(adj.)* **busy**
ብወግዒ ገሰፀ bweg'ï gesetse *(v.)* **reprimand**
ብወግዒ ተሸመ bweg'ï tesheme *(v.)* **accredit**
ብወቅታዊ ፋሽን ዝክተል bwuqtawi fashn zktel *(adj.)* **trendy**
ብዉሽጢ ማይ ዝጎዓዝ ቦምብ bwushti may zgoaz bomb *(n.)* **torpedo**
ብዉሽጡ ዘርኢ bwushti zer,i *(adj.)* **transparent**
ብዉሽጢ ኣመሓላሊፍካ ምርኣይ bwushty amehalalifka mray *(n.)* **transparency**
ብጻይ bxay *(n.)* **companion**
ብፃይ bxay *(n.)* **fellow**
ብጻይ bxay *(n.)* **comrade**
ብፃይነት bxaynet *(n.)* **fellowship**
ብጻይነት bxaynet *(n.)* **camaraderie**
ብጽሕና bxḧna *(n.)* **adolescence**
ብጽሖ bxḥo *(n.)* **visitation**
ብፁእነት bxu'enet *(n.)* **beatitude**
ብያቲ byati *(n.)* **saucer**
ብዛዕባ bza'ëba *(prep.)* **about**
ብዛዕባ bza'ëba *(prep.)* **concerning**
ብዛዕባ bza'ëba *(prep.)* **regarding**
ብዘስሕቅ መልክዑ ምምሳል bzeshq melkau mmsal *(n.)* **travesty**
ብዘይ bzey *(adj.)* **wanting**
ብዘይ bzey *(prep.)* **without**
ብዘይ ፍርዲ ሓኒቕካ ምቕታል bzey frdi haniqhka mqhtal *(n.)* **lynch**
ብዘይ ጉድኣት bzey gud'at *(adv.)* **scot-free**
ብዘይ ካፈይን bzey kafeyn *(adj.)* **decaffeinated**
ብዘይ ምሕቓቕ ምግቢ ዝመፅእ ቓንዛ ኸብዲ bzey mhqaqh mgbi zmets'e qhanza kebdi *(n.)* **indigestion**
ብዘይ ምንቅስቓስ bzey mnqsq̈as *(n.)* **poise**
ብዘይ ናይ ውግእ መሳርሒ bzeẏ nay wege'e mesarhi *(adj.)* **unarmed**
ብዘይ ታህዋኽ bzey tahwak *(adj.)* **leisurely**
ብዘይተገዳስነት bzey tegedasnet *(adj.)* **unceremonious**
ብዘይ ጥቅሚ ዘዊሩ bzey tkmi zewiru *(v.)* **twiddle**
ብዘይድልየት bzeydlyet *(adj.)* **unwilling**
ብዘየግድስ bzeyegds *(adv.)* **regardless**
ብዘይፍላጥ bzeyflat *(adv.)* **unwittingly**
ብዘይኩነት bzeykunet *(adj.)* **unconditional**
ብዘይምንቅስቓስ bzeymnqsqhas *(adv.)* **statically**
ብዘይምቁራፅ bzeymqurax *(adj.)* **nonstop**
ብዘይተገዳስነት bzeytegedasnet *(adv.)* **anyhow**
ብዝሒ bzĥi *(n.)* **quantum**
ብዝሒ ህዝቢ bzḧi hzbi *(n.)* **population**
ብዝሒ bzḧi *(n.)* **bulk**
ብዝለዓለ bzle'äle *(adv.)* **highly**
ብዙሕ bzuh *(pron.)* **lot**
ብዙሕ bzuĥ *(n.)* **plenty**
ብዙሕ bzuḧ *(n.)* **more**
ብዙሕ bzuḧ *(pron.)* **much**
ብዙሕ bzu'ḧ *(adj.)* **substantial**
ብዙሕ bzuh *(adj.)* **innumerable**

ብዙሕ ህዝቢ ዘለዎ bzuḧ hzbi zelewo *(adj.)* **populous**
ብዙሕ ቅርፁ bzuḧ qrxu *(adj.)* **multiform**
ብዙሕ ቋንቛ ዝዛረብ bzuḧ quanq̈a zzareb *(adj.)* **polyglot**
ብዙሕ ዝዓይነቱ bzuḧ z'äynetu *(adj.)* **multiple**
ብዙሕ ዝጎኑ bzuḧ zgonu *(adj.)* **multilateral**
ብዙሕ ዝሓቆፈ bzuḧ zḧaqofe *(n.)* **multiplex**
ብዙሕ ዝመዳያቱ bzuh zmedayatu *(adj.)* **manifold**
ብዙሕ ዝዛረብ bzuḧ zzareb *(n.)* **jay**
ብዙሕነት bzuĥnet *(n.)* **diversity**
ብዙሕነት bzuḧnet *(n.)* **multiplicity**
ባዶ bado *(adj.)* **void**
ባዶሽ badosh *(n.)* **vacuum**
ባዕሉ ba-e-lu *(pron.)* **himself**
ባህረ-ሓደ bahreḥade *(adj.)* **homogeneous**
ባህረ-ሓደ bahreḥade *(a.)* **homogeneous**
ባልጃ balğa *(n.)* **valise**
ባዞ bazo *(n.)* **vase**
በዓል be-al *(n.)* **holiday**
ቤት beet *(n.)* **verse**
ቤተ-ልብሲ beetelbsi *(n.)* **vestry**
በላዕ ሓምሊ bela'ë ḥamli *(n.)* **vegetarian**
በረዳዊ beredawi *(n.)* **icy**
በጻሒ bexaḥi *(n.)* **visitor**
ብልጫ blç̣a *(n.)* **vantage**
ብልሓት blḥat *(n.)* **knack**
ብልሂ blhi *(adj.)* **imaginative**
ብልቃጥ blqaṭ *(n.)* **vial**
ብመንገዲ bmengedi *(prep.)* **via**
ብርኪ brki *(n.)* **knee**
ብርቱዕ brtu'ë *(adj.)* **vehement**
ብቴሌግራፍ btelegraph *(n.)* **telegraphy**
ቡቕሊ buq̈li *(n.)* **vegetation**
በዓለገ boalege *(adj.)* **obscene**
በዓል መዚ be'al mezi *(adj.)* **official**
በዳሊ bedali *(n.)* **offender**
ቤት-ጽሕፈት biet-tshfet *(n.)* **office**
ብሓሳብ ወሓጠ bhasab wehate *(v.)* **obsess**
ብሓደ ለይቲ bhade leyti *(adv.)* **overnight**
ብስርዓት bsr'at *(adj.)* **orderly**
ብርሃን ዘየሕልፍ brhal zeyehelf *(adj.)* **opaque**
ብርሃን-አልባነት brhal albanet *(n.)* **opacity**
ብቑፅሪ በለፀ bqutsri beletse *(v.)* **outnumber**
ብቓል bqal *(adj.)* **oral**
ብቓል bqal *(adv.)* **orally**
ብቕጽበት bqtsbet *(adv.)* **outright**
ብተደጋጋሚ btedegagami *(adv.)* **often**
ብኣንጻሩ b'antsaru *(adj.)* **opposite**
ብኣጋጣሚ ሰምዐ b'agatami sem'e *(v.)* **overhear**
ብዕሊ b'eli *(adv.)* **officially**
ብዕልግና b'ëlgna *(n.)* **obscenity**
ብዕራይ b'eray *(n.)* **ox**
ብዕድመ በለፀ b'edme beletse *(v.)* **outlast**
ብዕድመ በለፀ b'edme beletse *(v.)* **outlive**
ብኽብደት በለፀ bkbdet beletse *(v.)* **outweigh**
ብኽያት bkyat *(n.)* **outcry**
ብዙሕ ምእማት bzih m'emat *(v.)* **overestimate**

ብድሕሪት bdhrit ***(adv.)* overleaf**
ብጃፓናውያን ዝስራሕ ናይ ወረቐት ቅርፃቕርፂ bjapanawyan zsrah nay wereqet qrtsaqrtsi ***(n.)* origami**
ብጉያ ቐደመ bguya qedeme ***(v.)* outrun**
ብጋህዲ bgahdi ***(adv.)* openly**
ብጠቕላላ bteqlala ***(adj.)* overall**
ብጣዕሚ መሊኡ bta'emi meli'u ***(v.)* overflow**
ብጣዕሚ ኣስተማሰለ bta'emi astemasele ***(v.)* overreact**
ብጣዕሚ ዓብዪ bta'emi abyi ***(adj.)* overgrown**
ብጣዕሚ ፅቡቕ bta'emi tsbuq ***(adj.)* outstanding**
ብፍጥነት ምዝዋር b'ëray bereḱa ***(n.)* bison**
ብዕራይ በረኻ bwsay mqxal ***(n.)* arson**
ብውሰይ ምቅጻል vals *(n.) waltz*

ቨ

ቩዱ bftnet mzwar ***(n.)* overdrive**
ቫልስ varniche ***(n.)* varnish**
ቫርኒቸ vayolin ***(n.)* violin**
ቫዮሊን vayres ***(n.)* virus**
ቫይረስ valor ***(n.)* velour**
ቫሎር velkene ***(v.)* vulcanize**
ቨልከነ veyn ***(n.)* vein**
ቬይን vidyo ***(n.)* video**
ቪድዮ vila ***(n.)* villa**
ቪላ viskoz ***(n.)* viscose**
ቪስኮዝ viskya ***(n.)* mistletoe**
ቪስክያ vitamin ***(n.)* vitamin**
ቪታሚን vitryol ***(n.)* vitriol**
ቪትርዮል viza ***(n.)* visa**
ቪዛ volt ***(n.)* volt**
ቮልት vudu ***(n.)* voodoo**

ተ

ተመልካቲ temelkati ***(n.)* onlooker**
ተመጣጠረ temetatere ***(v.)* overreach**
ተስፈኛ tesfegna ***(n.)* optimist**
ተራ tera ***(adv.)* oft**
ተቓወመ teqaweme ***(v.)* oppose**
ተናሓናሒ tenahanahi ***(adj.)* operative**
ተናሓናሒ tenahanahi ***(n.)* opponent**
ተአዘዘ te'azeze ***(v.)* obey**
ተዓዘበ te'azebe ***(v.)* observe**
ተዓዘበ te'azebe ***(v.)* oversee**
ተኣዛዝነት teazaznet ***(n.)* obedience**
ተደገፈ tdegefe ***(v.)* lean**
ተኣፋፊ teafafi ***(adj.)* queasy**
ተኣፋፊ te'afafi ***(adj.)* fractious**
ተኣፋፊ te'afafi ***(adj.)* sensitive**
ተዓገሰ teagese ***(v.)* tolerate**
ተዓገሰ te'ägese ***(v.)* forbear**
ተኣኻኸበ te'akakebe ***(v.)* converge**
ተኣከበ te'akebe ***(v.)* congregate**
ተኣከበ te'akebe ***(v.)* convene**
ተዓኹለለ teäkulele ***(v.)* curl**
ተኣልየ te'alye ***(v.t.)* shun**
ተኣማማኒ te'amamani ***(adj.)* confident**
ተኣማኒ te'amani ***(adj.)* conceivable**
ተኣማኒ te'amani ***(adj.)* faithful**
ተኣማኒ te'amani ***(n.)* loyalist**
ተኣማኒነት te'amaninet ***(adj.)* fidelity**
ተኣማንነት te'amannet ***(n.)* allegiance**
ተኣመነ te'amene ***(v.)* acknowledge**

ተኣመነ te'amene *(v.)* **admit**
ተኣምር te'amr *(n.)* **miracle**
ተኣምራዊ te'amrawi *(adj.)* **miraculous**
ተኣነነ te'anene *(v.)* **deign**
ተኣነነ te'anene *(v.)* **groan**
ተዓንገለ te'angele *(v.)* **subsist**
ተዓንቀፈ te'änqefe *(v.)* **stumble**
ተአንጠጠ teantete *(v.)* **tiptoe**
ተዓራረኸ te'ärareke *(v.)* **befriend**
ተኣሳሰረ te'asasere *(v.)* **interlink**
ተኣሳሰረ te'asasere *(v.)* **belong**
ተዓፅፉ teasifu *(v.)* **turn**
ተዓፃፃፊ te'atsatsafi *(adj.)* **malleable**
ተዓፃፃፊ te'atsatsefi *(adj.)* **lithe**
ተኣዋዲ te'awadi *()* **debtor**
ተዓወተ te'awete *(v.)* **achieve**
ተዓወተ teäwete *(v.)* **succeed**
ተዓፃፋይ እዋን teäxafay ewan *(n.)* **flexitime**
ተዓዛቢ te'äzabi *(n.)* **spectator**
ተኣዛዝነት te'azaznet *(n.)* **subordination**
ተዓዘብቲ te'äzebti *(n.)* **audience**
ተኣዘዘ te'azeze *(v.)* **comply**
ተባኣሳይ teba'asay *(adj.)* **bellicose**
ተባደለ tebadele *(v.)* **barter**
ተባዕ teba'e *(adj.)* **manful**
ተባዕ teba'ë *(adj.)* **intrepid**
ተባዕ teba'ë *(adj.)* **nervy**
ተባዕ teba'ë *(adj.)* **valiant**
ተባዕ teba'ë *(adj.)* **bold**
ተባዕ teba'ë *(adj.)* **brave**
ተብኣሲ tebaeisu *(adj.)* **truculent**
ተባዕታይ teba'ëtay *(n.)* **male**
ተባዕታይ teba'ëtay *(adj.)* **masculine**
ተባዕታይ ኣድጊ teba'ëtay 'adgi *(n.)* **jackass**
ተባዕታይ ፈረስ teba'etay feres *(n.)* **stallion**
ተባላዒ tebala'i *(adj.)* **caustic**
ተባላዒ tebala'i *(adj.)* **corrosive**
ጠባቒ መልእኽቲ ẗebaqhi mel'ekhti *(n.)* **sticker**
ተባራዒ tebara'i *(adj.)* **inflammable**
ተባረዐ tebare'ë *(adv.)* **ablaze**
ተበኣሰ tebe'ase *(v.t)* **fight**
ተበላሸወ tebelashew *(v.)* **malfunction**
ተበለፀ tebelexe *(v. t)* **exploit**
ተበራበረ teberabere *(v.)* **rouse**
ተበርጠጠ tebertete *(v.)* **condescend**
ተበታኒ ፅሑፍ tebetani tzhuf *(n.)* **leaflet**
ተበታተነ tebetatene *(v.)* **disperse**
ተበተነ tebetene *(v.)* **dissipate**
ትዕቢት t'ëbit *(n.)* **arrogance**
ትዕቢት t'ëbit *(n.)* **conceit**
ትዕቢተኛ t'ëbiteňa *(adj.)* **arrogant**
ተንበልባሊ tebnbelbali *(n.)* **streamer**
ተጨበጠ tecebet'e *(v.)* **cringe**
ተጨበጠ teĉebete *(v.)* **shrink**
ተጨምደደ teĉemdede *(v.)* **shrivel**
ተጨናፈረ teĉenafere *(v.)* **ramify**
ተጨናነቐ teĉenaneqe *(v.t.)* **fret**
ተጨፍለቐ techefleqhe *(v.)* **squish**
ተጨነቐ techeneqe *(v.t.)* **stress**
ተጨነቐ techeneqe *(v.)* **worry**
ተጨቓጫቒ techeqhachaqhi *(n.)* **squabble**
ተደጋጋሚ ምውቃዕ ልቢ tedagagami mwqae lbi *(v.)* **palpitate**
ተዳወበ tedawebe *(v.)* **abut**
ተደጋጋሚ tedegagami *(adj.)* **continual**
ተደጋጋሚ tedegagami *(adj.)* **frequent**

ተደጋጋሚ tedegagami ***(adj.)*** **insistent**
ተደገመ tedegeme ***(v.)*** **recur**
ተደጎለ tedegole ***(v.)*** **huddle**
ተደግሰ tedegse ***(v.)*** **relapse**
ተደላያይ tedelayay ***(adj.)*** **traceable**
ተደላዪ tedelayi ***(adj.)*** **desirable**
ተደማፂ tedemaxi ***(n.)*** **consonant**
ተደመሮ tedemero ***(n.)*** **plus**
ተደናበረ tedenabere ***(v.)*** **bumble**
ተደናጋጽነት tedenagaxnet ***(n.)*** **empathy**
ተደናገረ tedenagere ***(v.)*** **perplex**
ተደቕደቐ tedeq̈deq̈e ***(v.)*** **plunge**
ተደራቢ tederabi ***(n.)*** **lagging**
ተደራቢ tederabi ***(n.)*** **lining**
ተደርዓመ tederame ***(v.)*** **collapse**
ተደራራቢ tederarabi ***(n.)*** **spate**
ተደርባዪ tederbayi ***(adj.)*** **disposable**
ተደሰተ tedesete ***(v.)*** **revel**
ተዓጻጻፊ teëaxaxafi ***(adj.)*** **pliable**
ተዓጻፊ teëaxaxafi ***(adj.)*** **pliant**
ቴስዓ tees'ä ***(adj. & n.)*** **ninety**
ተፍአ tef'a ***(n.)*** **spit**
ተፋሕሰ tefaḥse ***(v.)*** **writhe**
ተፋረየ tefareye ***(v.)*** **reproduce**
ተፍአ tef'e ***(v.)*** **belch**
ተፈዳዳዪ tefedadayi ***(adj.)*** **reciprocal**
ተፈደረ tefeder ***(v.)*** **federate**
ተፈላለየ tefelaleye ***(v.)*** **differ**
ተፈላለየ tefelaleye ***(v.)*** **disagree**
ተፈላሳፊ tefelasafi ***(n.)*** **philosopher**
ተፈላጥነት tefelatnet ***(n.)*** **repute**
ተፈላጥነት tefelaẗnet ***(n.)*** **fame**
ተፈላጥነት tefelaẗnet ***(n.)*** **publicity**
ተፈንጨሐ tefenĉeĥe ***(v.)*** **gloat**
ተፈንጨለ tefen'chele ***(v.)*** **secede**
ተፈንጠረ tefentere ***(v.)*** **recoil**
ተፈንጠረ tefenẗere ***(v.)*** **snap**
ተፈቃሪ tefeqari ***(adj.)*** **lovely**
ተፈራረቐ teferareqe ***(v.t.)*** **alternate**
ተፈታታኒ ሰብ tefetatani seb ***(n.)*** **tempter**
ተፈታተነ tefetatene ***(v.)*** **lure**
ተፈታዊ tefetawi ***(adj.)*** **amiable**
ተፈታዊ tefetawi ***(adj.)*** **favourite**
ተፈታዊ tefetawi ***(adj.)*** **popular**
ተፈታዊ tefetawi ***(adj.)*** **prepossessing**
ተፈታዊ ምግባር tefetawi mgbar ***(v.)*** **popularize**
ተፈታዊ tefetawi ***(adj.)*** **adorable**
ተፈታውነት tefetawnet ***(n.)*** **popularity**
ተፈጥሮኣዊኛ tefeẗro'awegna ***(n.)*** **naturalist**
ተፈጥሮኣዊ tefeẗro'awi ***(adj.)*** **natural**
ተፈጥሮነት tefeẗroneet ***(n.)*** **naturism**
ተፈፃምነት ዘለዎ tefexamnet zelewo ***(adj.)*** **applicable**
ተፈቃሪ tefqari ***(adj.)*** **lovable**
ተፍታትሐ teftatĥe ***(v.)*** **relax**
ተፈታዊ teftawi ***(adj.)*** **likeable**
ተፈጥሮ tefẗro ***(n.)*** **nature**
ተጋጨወ tegaccewe ***(v.)*** **crash**
ተጋጫዊ/ስግንጢራዊ tegachawi sgintrawi ***(adj.)*** **paradoxical**
ተጋጨወ tegachewe ***(v.)*** **collide**
ተጋዳላይ tegadalay ***(n.)*** **fighter**
ተጋደደ tegadede ***(v.)*** **deteriorate**
ተጋገየ tegageye ***(v.)*** **err**
ተጋሕተነ tegaḣtene ***(v.)*** **bestride**
ተጉዕዚ tegaizu ***(n.)*** **traveller**
ተጋሳያይ tegasayay ***(n.)*** **rapist**
ተጋተረ tegatere ***(v.)*** **confront**

ተጋጠመ tegat'me *(v.)* **clash**
ተጋወረ tegawere *(v.)* **adjoin**
ተጋውሖ tegawĥe *(v.)* **resonate**
ተግባር tegbar *(n.)* **function**
ተግባር tegbar *(n.)* **practice**
ተግባር tegbar *(n.)* **action**
ተግባራዊ tegbarawi *(adj.)* **functional**
ተገባበረ tegebabere *(v.)* **interact**
ተገብአ tegeb'e *(v. t.)* **deserve**
ተገዳሚ tegedami *(adj.)* **transverse**
ተገዳር ሓረስታይ tegedar ḥarestay *(n.)* **hawk**
ተገዳሲ tegedasi *(adj.)* **solicitous**
ተገልበጠ tegelbeẗe *(v.)* **flip**
ተገምበወ tegembewe *(v.)* **recline**
ተገምሰሰ tegemsese *(n.)* **repose**
ተገናዛይ tegenazay *(n.)* **sadist**
ተገናዛይነት tegenazaynet *(n.)* **sadism**
ተገንዘበ tegenzebe *(v.)* **realize**
ተገንዘበ tegenzebe *(v.)* **appreciate**
ተገጣጠመ tegetateme *(v.)* **coincide**
ተገጣጠመ tegeẗaẗeme *(v.)* **interlock**
ተገየፅድ tegeyetsd *(v.)* **simper**
ተጒ ምባል tegiue mbal *(v.)* **pop**
ተጓዳኢ tegoda'i *(adj.)* **harmful**
ተጎድአ tegod'e *(v.)* **strain**
ተጎላቲ tegolati *(n.)* **monopolist**
ተጎንባሲ tegonbasi *(adj.)* **servile**
ተጎንባስነት tegonbasnet *(n.)* **servility**
ተጎንበሰ tegonbese *(v.)* **stoop**
ተግሳፅ tegsats *(n.)* **reproof**
ትዕግስቲ tegsti *(n.)* **patience**
ትዕግስቲ t'egsti *(n.)* **tolerance**
ትዕግስቲ t'ëgsti *(n.)* **solitaire**
ትዕግስቲ t'egsti *(n.)* **toleration**
ተጒመፅመፅ tegume-tse-me-tse *(v.)* **gargle**
ተጓዕዘ tegwa'ëze *(v.)* **walk**
ተጓንፎ tegwanefo *(n.)* **coincidence**
ተጓነፀ tegwanetse *(v.)* **dash**
ተጓሳጣይ tegwasaẗay *(n.)* **boxer**
ተጓያቒ tegwayaqi *(adj.)* **quarrelsome**
ተጓየየ tegwayeye *(v.)* **race**
ተጓየየ tegwayeye *(v.)* **rush**
ተሓባባሪ teȟababari *(adj.)* **confederate**
ተሓባበረ tehababere *(v.)* **collaborate**
ተሓብአ teȟab'e *(v.)* **cower**
ተሓበበረ tehabere *(v.)* **cooperate**
ተሃዳናይ tehadanay *(n.)* **quarry**
ተሃዳኒ tehadani *(n.)* **prey**
ተሃድሶ tehadso *(n.)* **reclamation**
ተሃድሶ tehadso *(n.)* **renaissance**
ተሓጎሰ teĥagose *(v.)* **rejoice**
ተሓላፊ tehalafi *(adj.)* **passable**
ተሓላቒ teȟalaq̈i *(n.)* **advocate**
ተሓለቀ teȟaleq̈e *(v.)* **advocate**
ተሓንበበ teȟanbebe *(adj.)* **swish**
ተሓንጋጢ መሳርሒ teȟangati mesarȟi *(n.)* **backpack**
ተሓንጋጢ ሳንጣ teȟangati santa *(n.)* **rucksack**
ተሃንቀወ tehanqewe *(v. t)* **crave**
ተሃቀወ tehaqewe *(v.)* **covet**
ተሓሰበ teha'sebe *(v.)* **constitute**
ተሓሰመ teĥaseme *(v.)* **rebuff**
ተሓሰመ teĥaseme *(v.)* **repudiate**
ተሓታታይ አይኮነን በለ teĥatatay aykonen bele *(v.)* **exonerate**
ተሓታቲ tehatati *(adj.)* **liable**
ተሓታቲ teĥatati *(adj.)* **responsible**
ተሓታቲ teȟatati *(adj.)* **accountable**

ተሓታቲ teȟatati *(adj.)* **amenable**
ተሓታትነት tehatatnet *(n.)* **liability**
ተሓዋወሰ teȟawawese *(v.)* **mingle**
ተሃወኸ tehaweǩe *(v.)* **hasten**
ተሓዝ ገንዘብ teȟaz genzeb *(n.)* **bursar**
ተሓዚ ገንዘብ teȟazi genzeb *(n.)* **purser**
ተሓዚ መዝገብ tehazi mezgeb *(n.)* **registrar**
ተሓዚ ትሕጃ tehazi thja *(n.)* **pawnbroker**
ተኸራኸረ teherakere *(v.)* **contend**
ተኸታታሊ tehe'tata'li *(adj.)* **consecutive**
ትሕተ ምድራዊ ሓዲድ teȟte mdrawi ȟadid *(n.)* **subway**
ትሕትና tehtena *(n.)* **humility**
ትሑት tehut *(adj.)* **humble**
ተጃህረ tejahre *(v.)* **bluff**
ተጃህረ tejahre *(v.)* **swank**
ተጀሃሪ teĵehari *(v.)* **brag**
ኣኻእሎ teka'elo *(n.)* **finesse**
ተኻፋሊ ሚስጢር tekafali mistir *(adj.)* **privy**
ተካል tekal *(adj.)* **dreary**
ተኻረየ teǩareye *(v.t)* **hire**
ተካትዐ tekat'ë *(v. t.)* **debate**
ተክአ tek'e *(v.)* **replace**
ተክአ tek'e *(v.)* **supersede**
ተክአ tek'e *(v.)* **supplant**
ተቀባሊ tekebali *(n.)* **recipient**
ተኸባሲ tekebasi *(adj.)* **reversible**
ተኸደነ tekedene *(v.)* **dress**
ተኸድነ tekedene *(v.)* **wear**
ተከአ teke'e *(v.)* **replenish**
ተኸፋሊ tekefali *(n.)* **payable**
ተኸላኸላይ teǩelaǩalay *(adj.)* **protective**
ተኸላኸለ tekelakele *(v.)* **defend**
ተኽእሎ tek'elo *(n.)* **possibility**
ተኸምበለ tekembele *(v.)* **tumble**
ተኸናኸነ tekenakene *(v.)* **treat**
ተኸሳሲ tekesasi *(n.)* **defendant**
ተኸሳሲ tekesasi *(n.)* **respondent**
ተኸታሊ teketali *(n.)* **follower**
ተኸታሊ teketali *(n.)* **sequel**
ተኸታታሊ teketatali *(adj.)* **serial**
ተኸታተለ teketatele *(v.t.)* **trace**
ተኸታተለ teǩetatele *(v.)* **attend**
ተከታቲሉ teketatilu *(n.)* **trail**
ተኸተለ teketele *(v.)* **pursue**
ተኸወለ tekewele *(v.)* **disappear**
ተኻራዪ tekharayi *(n.)* **lessee**
ተኻራዪ ገዛ tekharayi geza *(n.)* **lodger**
ተኽልከለ tekhelkele *(v.)* **stymie**
ተኽእሎ tekh'elo *(adj.)* **subjunctive**
ተኸታታሊ tekhetatali *(adj.)* **successive**
ተኾርመየ tekhormeye *(v.i.)* **squat**
ተ኿ሳሒ tekhuasahi *(adj.)* **inflammatory**
ተኸላኸለ teǩlaǩele *(v.)* **protect**
ተክሊ tekli *(n.)* **tree**
ተኽሊ teǩli (n.) **plant**
ተኽሊ ወይኒ teǩli weyni *(n.)* **vine**
ተኽሊ ዝተተኸለሉ ቦታ teǩli zteteǩlelu bota *(n.)* **plantation**
ተኽልታት tekltat *(n.)* **flora**
ተኾላተፈ tekolatefe *(v.)* **slur**
ተቆናጅዩ tekonajyu *(v.)* **titivate**
ተኮናኒ tekonani *(adj.)* **damnable**
ተኾናታሪ tekonatari *(n.)* **contractor**
ተኾነውን tekonewen *(conj.)* **whereas**
ተኾርመየ tekormeye *(v.)* **crouch**
ተኾርመየ tekormeye *(v.)* **slouch**

ተኮሰ tekose *(v.)* **shoot**
ተኹላ tekula *(n.)* **wolf**
ተኹሲ tekusi *(n.)* **shooting**
ተኹሲ ቁረፀ teḱusi qurexe *(n.)* **ceasefire**
ተኳዕነነ tekwa'ënene *(v.)* **swagger**
ተኧተኸ teḱwatoḱe *(v.)* **nudge**
ተላበዒ telabaei *(n.)* **pestilence**
ተላዕለ tela'ële *(v.)* **arise**
ተላጋቢ telagabi *(adj.)* **catching**
ተላጋቢ telagabi *(adj.)* **contagious**
ተላመደ telamede *(v.)* **practise**
ተላዘበ telazebe *(v.)* **negotiate**
ተለኣኣኻይ tele'a'akay *(n.)* **courier**
ቴሌግራም telegaram *(n.)* **telegram**
ቴሌግራፍ telegaraph *(n.)* **telegraph**
ተለማመደ telemamede *(v.)* **rehearse**
ተለቅሐ teleqḧe *(v.)* **borrow**
ተለጠፈ teletefe' *(v.)* **cling**
ቴሌቪዥን televizion *(n.)* **television**
ተለዋጣይ telewaẗay *(adj.)* **mutable**
ተለዋጢ telewaẗi *(v.)* **mutative**
ተለዋዋጣይ telewawaẗay *(adj.)* **fickle**
ተለዋዋጢ telewawaẗi *(v.)* **fluctuate**
ተለዋወጠ telewaweẗe *(v. t)* **exchange**
ተለዋወጠ telewaweẗe *(v.)* **interchange**
ተለዋይ ጨንገር ዊሊው teleway chenger wiliw *(n.)* **wicker**
ተለወጠ teleweẗe *(v.)* **mutate**
ተለውየ telewye *(v.)* **shear**
ተልእኾ tel'ḱo *(n.)* **mission**
ተልመዴን telmedeen *(n.)* **amateur**
ተልመዴን telmedeen *(n.)* **apprentice**
ተልመዴናዊ telmedeenawi *(adj.)* **amateurish**
ተማእዛዚ tema'ezazi *(adj.)* **biddable**
ተማጎተ temagote *(v.)* **litigate**
ተማጎተ temagote *(v.)* **argue**
ተማጓታይ temagwatay *(n.)* **litigant**
ተማሓላለፊ temaḧalalefi *(adj.)* **communicable**
ተማሃራይ ዩኒቨርሲቲ ነበር temaharay yuniversiti neber *(n.)* **alumnus**
ተማህለለ temahlele *(v.)* **supplicate**
ተማሕፀነ temahtsene *(v.)* **solicit**
ተማሕፀነ temahtzene *(v.t.)* **implore**
ተማሕፀነ temaĥxene *(v.)* **entreat**
ተማሕፀነ temaḧxene *(v.t.)* **appeal**
ተማራኺሲ temaraḱwasi *(adj.)* **interdependent**
ተማስሎ temaslo *(n.)* **affinity**
ተማዛዛንነት temazazannet *(n.)* **equilibrium**
ተምበርካኺ temberkaki *(n.)* **defeatist**
ተምበርከኸ temberkeḱe *(v.)* **capitulate**
ተመጋቢ temegabi *(n.)* **diner**
ተመጋቢ temegabi *(n.)* **feeder**
ተመገበ temegebe *(v.)* **dine**
ተመሓላለፊ temehalalafi *(adj.)* **transferable**
ተመሃራይ temeharay *(n.)* **pupil**
ተመሃራይ temeharay *(n.)* **student**
ተመካቲ temekati *(adj.)* **defensible**
ትምክሕቲ temekeheti *(n.)* **chauvinism**
ተመላላሲ temelalasi *(adj.)* **recurrent**
ተመላለሰ temelalese *(v.)* **retort**
ተመላሲ temelasi *(adj.)* **resilient**

ተመሊስካ ምስትንታን temeliska mstntan *(n.)* **retrospect**
ተመልካቲ temelkati *(n.)* **toreador**
ተመልካቲ temelkati *(n.)* **bystander**
ተመልከተ temelkete *(v.)* **revere**
ተመልከተ temelkete *(v.)* **concern**
ተመልከተ temelkete *(v.)* **behold**
ተመልሰ temelse *(v.)* **return**
ተመልሰ temelse *(v.)* **revert**
ተመን temen *(n.)* **snake**
ተመነየ temeneye *(v.)* **aspire**
ተመንወ temenwe *(n.)* **pall**
ተመቃላይ temeqalay *(n.)* **numerator**
ተመርዓወ temer'äwe *(v.)* **marry**
ተመርማሪ temermari *(n.)* **examinee**
ተመሳሳሊ temesasali *(adj.)* **alike**
ተመሳሳሊ temesasali *(adj.)* **cognate**
ተመሳሳሊ temesasali *(n.)* **lookalike**
ተመሳሳሊ temesasali *(adj.)* **same**
ተመሳሳሊ temesasali *(adj.)* **similar**
ተመሳሳሊ temesasali *(adj.)* **synonymous**
ተመሳሳሊ temesasali *(adj.)* **analogous**
ተመሳሳሊ temesasali *(adv.)* **unexceptional**
ተመሳሳሊ temesasali *(adj.)* **uniform**
ተመሳሳሊነት temesasalinet *(n.)* **likeness**
ተመሳሳሊነት temesasalinet *(n.)* **similarity**
ተመሳሳልነት temesasalnet *(n.)* **analogy**
ተመሳሰለ temesasele *(v.)* **liken**
ተመሻጠረ temeshatere *(v.)* **conspire**
ተመሻጠረ temesha'tere *(v.)* **connive**
ተመስጦ temesto *(n.)* **impression**
ተመጣጣኒ temetatani *(adj.)* **proportional**
ተመጣጣኒ temetatani *(adj.)* **proportionate**
ተመጣጣኒ temetatani *(adj.)* **tantamount**
ተመጣጣሪ temeẗaẗari *(adj.)* **ambitious**
ተመጣጢ temetati *(adj.)* **elastic**
ተመፃዳቂ temetsadaqi *(adj.)* **sanctimonious**
ተመዛበለ temezabele *(v.)* **deform**
ተመዛዛይ temezazay *(n.)* **drawer**
ተመዛዚ ከብሒ temezazi kebḧi *(n.)* **commode**
ተመዝገበ temezgebe *(v.)* **enrol**
ተመሓላለፊ temhalallefi *(adj.)* **infectious**
ተምሃረ temhare *(v.)* **learn**
ተምሃሪ temhari *(n.)* **learner**
ተምሃሪ ዩኑቨርስቲ temhari yuniversty *(n.)* **undergraduate**
ተሞርከሰ temorkese *(v.)* **depend**
ተሞርከሰ temorkese *(v.)* **rely**
ተዉህቦ twhbo *(n.)* **flair**
ተሰራጨወ tsrachew *(v.)* **circulate**
ቱቦ tubo *(n.)* **duct**
ትቦ tubo *(n.)* **pipe**
ቱቦ tubo *(n.)* **tube**
ቱቦ ፍሳስ tubo fsas *(n.)* **sewer**
ቱቦ ማይ tubo may *(n.)* **hose**
ቱፋሕ tufaḧ *(n.)* **apple**
ትእምርተ እግሪ t'emrete egri *(adj.)* **subscript**
ትእምርትነት t'emrtnet *(n.)* **symbolism**
ተምሳል temsal *(n.)* **semblance**
ተምሳሌት temsaleet *(n.)* **metaphor**
ተምሳጥ temsaẗ *(n.)* **awe**

ተናዳዲ tenadadi *(n.)* **temper**
ተናዳዲ tenadadi *(adj.)* **touchy**
ተናእደ tena'ede *(v.)* **acclaim**
ተናፈረ tenafere *(v.)* **flit**
ተናኸፈ ንምዕራይ tenakefe nm'eray *(v.)* **tinker**
ተናሳሒ tenasaĥi *(adj.)* **repentant**
ተናሳሒ tenasahi *(adj.)* **penitent**
ተናስሐ tenasĥe *(v.)* **repent**
ተናጠረ tenaẗere *(v.)* **splatter**
ተናዘዘ tenazeze *(v.)* **avow**
ተናዘዘ tenazeze *(v.)* **confess**
ተናዘዘ tenazeze *(v.)* **profess**
ተነባቢ tenbabi *(adj.)* **legible**
ተንበልበለ tenbelbele *(v.)* **flaunt**
ተንበርከኸ tenberkeḱe *(v.)* **kneel**
ተንበየ tenbeye *(v.)* **envisage**
ተንበየ tenbeye *(v.t)* **forecast**
ተንበየ tenbeye *(v.)* **foresee**
ተንበየ tenbeye *(v.)* **foretell**
ተንበየ tenbeye *(v.)* **presage**
ተንደልሃፀ tendelhatse *(v.)* **slip**
ተነባዪ tenebayi *(n.)* **forerunner**
ተነበየ tenebeye *(v.)* **predict**
ተነበየ tenebeye *(v.)* **prophesy**
ተነጫናጪ tenecha na chi *(adj.)* **grumpy**
ተነፋሒት ጀልባ tenefaĥit jelba *(n.)* **raft**
ተነቃፊ teneqaf *(adj.)* **vulnerable**
ተነቃፊ teneqafi *(adj.)* **delicate**
ተነቃፊነት teneqafinet *(n.)* **delicacy**
ተንቀሳቃሲ ስልኪ teneqesaqasi seliki *(n.)* **cell phone**
ተነቑተ teneqhte *(v.)* **swoop**
ተነፃሊ tenetsali *(n.)* **separatist**
ተነውነወ tenewnewe *(v.)* **joggle**
ተነጻጻሪ tenexaxeri *(adj.)* **comparative**

ተነዝሐ tenezhe *(v.)* **pervade**
ተነዝነዘ tenezneze *(v.)* **vibrate**
ተንፈኽፈኸ tenfekfeke *(v.)* **simmer**
ተንጎድጊዱ tengedagidu *(v.)* **teeter**
ተንከባለለ tenkebalele *(v.i.)* **roll**
ተንኮል tenkol *(n.)* **malice**
ተንኮል tenkol *(n.)* **mischief**
ተንኮል tenkol *(n.)* **ploy**
ተንኮል tenkol *(n.)* **trickery**
ተንኮለኛ tenkolegna *(adj.)* **disingenuous**
ተንኮለኛ tenkolegna *(adj.)* **malicious**
ተንኮለኛ tenkolegna *(adj.)* **mischievous**
ተንኮለኛ tenkolenya *(n.)* **catty**
ተንኮሰ tenkose *(v.)* **provoke**
ተንኰል tenkwal *(n.)* **guile**
ተንቀሳቃሲ tenqesaqasi *(n.)* **locomotive**
ተንቀሳቃሲ tenqesaqasi *(adj.)* **mobile**
ተንቀሳቃሲ tenqesaqasi *(adj.)* **movable**
ተንቀሳቃሲ tenqesaqasi *(adj.)* **moving**
ተንቀሳቃሲ tenqesaqasi *(adj.)* **roving**
ተንቀሳቃስነት tenqesaqasnet *(n.)* **mobility**
ተንቀሳቀሰ tenqesaqese *(v.)* **move**
ተንቀጥቀጠ tenqetqete *(v.)* **quake**
ተንሳፋፊ tensafafi *(adj.)* **buoyant**
ተንሳፈፈ tensafefe *(v.)* **float**
ተንሳተተ tensatete *(v.)* **scud**
ተንሰአ tense'e *(v.)* **rise**
ጥንሲ ẗensi *(n.)* **gestation**
ተንታኒ tentani *(n.)* **analyst**
ተንጠብጢቡ tentebtibu *(v.)* **trickle**
ተንጠልጠለ tenṭelṭele *(v.i.)* **hang**
ተንተነ tentene *(v.)* **analyse**

ተንቲኑ tentu *(v.)* **parse**
ተቃብሐ teqabhe *(v.)* **clinch**
ተቓዳዊ teq̈adawi *(adj.)* **compatible**
ተቓዳዊ teq̈adawi *(adj.)* **concurrent**
ተቓላዕነት teqala'enet *(n.)* **subjection**
ተቓላዒት teqala'ït *(n.)* **debutante**
ተቓላሲ teq̈alasi *(n.)* **wrestler**
ተቓለሰ teq̈alese *(v.)* **wrestle**
ተቃልዖ teqal'ö *(n.)* **debut**
ተቃፃዊ teqatsawi *(a.)* **shadow**
ተቓዋሚ teqawami *(n.)* **dissident**
ተቃዋሚ teqawami *(adj.)* **resistant**
ተቓዋምነት teq̈awamnet *(n.)* **protestation**
ተቓወመ teqaweme *(v.)* **demur**
ተቓወመ teqaweme *(v.)* **disapprove**
ተቃወመ teqaweme *(v.)* **dissent**
ተቃወመ teqaweme *(v.)* **militate**
ተቃወመ teqaweme *(v.)* **remonstrate**
ተቓወመ teqaweme *(v.)* **resist**
ተቓዉሞ teqawmo *(n.)* **disapproval**
ተቓውሞ teqawmo *(n.)* **exception**
ተቃውሞ teqawmo *(n.)* **resistance**
ተቓውሞ teq̈awmo *(n.)* **protest**
ተቓያቕት ሰበይቲ teqayaqit sebeyti *(n.)* **termagant**
ተቐባላይ teq̈ebalay *(n.)* **addressee**
ተቀባሊ teqebali *(n.)* **receiver**
ተቀባሊ teqebali *(adj.)* **receptive**
ተቀባሊ ጋሻ teqebali gaša *(n.)* **receptionist**
ተቀባሊት ቅርሺ teqebalit qereshi *(n.)* **cashier**
ተቐባልነት ዘለዎ teq̈ebalnet zelewo *(adj.)* **acceptable**
ተቐበለ teqebele *(v.)* **get**
ተቀበለ teqebele *(v.)* **receive**
ተቐበለ teq̈ebele *(v.)* **approve**
ተቐበለ teq̈ebele *(v.)* **accept**
ተቐዳደመ teq̈edademe *(v.)* **compete**
ተቐልቀለ teqelqele *(v.)* **emerge**
ተቐጠበ teq̈ețebe *(v.)* **abstain**
ተቐያያራይ teqeyayaray *(adj.)* **flexible**
ተቐያያሪ teq̈eyayari *(adj.)* **variable**
ተቐያያሪ ሕብርታት teq̈eyayari ḧbrtat *(n.)* **kaleidoscope**
ተቓለሰ teqhalese *(v.)* **struggle**
ተቓጻዊ teqhatsawi *(n.)* **stalker**
ተቐባልነት ዘይብሉ teqhbalnet zeyblu *(adj.)* **immoderate**
ተቐባልነት ዘይብሉ teqhebalnet zeyblu *(adj.)* **inexcusable**
ተቅማጥ teqmat *(n.)* **dysentery**
ተቆጠበ teqotebe *(v.t.)* **refrain**
ተቆፃፃሪ teqotsatsari *(n.)* **regulator**
ተቖፃፃሪ teqoxaxari *(n.)* **controller**
ተቆፃፃሪ teqoxaxari *(adj.)* **monitory**
ተቖፃፃራይ teqoxaxari *(n.)* **supervisor**
ተቖፃፀረ teqoxaxere *(v. t)* **curb**
ተቖፃፃረ teqoxaxere *(v.)* **supervise**
ተቛየቈ teq̈wayeq̈we *(v.)* **bicker**
ተቈጻጻሪ teq̈wetsatsari *(n.)* **inspector**
ተራ tera *(adj.)* **mediocre**
ተራ tera *(adj.)* **prosaic**
ተራ tera *(n.)* **rota**
ተራ tera *(adj.)* **banal**
ተራብሐ terabḧe *(v.)* **proliferate**
ተራድኣዊ terad'awi *(adj.)* **cooperative**
ተራእየ tera'èye *(v.)* **appear**
ተራኻቢ terakabi *(adj.)* **confluent**
ተራኸበ terakebe *(v.)* **liaise**
ተራቓቓይ teraqaqay *(n.)* **pedant**
ተጠርጣሪ teraẗari *(n)* **suspect**

ተርባይን terbayn *(n.)* **turbine**
ተርብዐ terb'ë *(v.)* **lacerate**
ተርበዐ terbe'ë *(v.)* **rip**
ተረበሸ terebeše *(v.)* **rattle**
ተረዳኢ teredaei *(adj.)* **perceptive**
ተረድአ tered'e *(v.)* **grasp**
ተረድአ tered'e *(v.)* **comprehend**
ተረድአ tered'e *(v. t)* **conceive**
ተረድአ tered'e *(v.)* **apprehend**
ተረደአ teredea' *(v.)* **construe**
ተረድአ terede'e *(v.t.)* **understand**
ተረፍ teref *(n.)* **remainder**
ተረፍ ዕፃድ teref ëtsad *(n.)* **stubble**
ተረፍ መረፍ ኣራረየ teref meref arareye *(v.)* **scavenge**
ተረፍ teref *(n.)* **balance**
ተረፈ terefe *(v.)* **fail**
ተረፍ terefe *(n.)* **surplus**
ተረፍመረፍ terefmeref *(n.)* **remnant**
ተረፍመረፍ terefmeref *(n.)* **scrap**
ተርጋጊፁ teregagisu *(v.)* **trample**
ተረጎመ teregome *(v.)* **interpret**
ተረካቢ ይዕደዮ terekabi y'edeyo *(n.)* **scapegoat**
ተረኸ tereke *(v.)* **recount**
ተረቅራቂ ሉሕ tereqraqi luḧ *(n.)* **batten**
ፀረር ዝብል terer zbl *(adj.)* **runny**
ተርእዮ ter'eyo *(n.)* **scenario**
ተርጎመ tergome *(v.)* **translate**
ተሪር terir *(adj.)* **crisp**
ተሪር terir *(adj.)* **drastic**
ተሪር terir *(adj.)* **firm**
ተሪር terir *(adj.)* **hard**
ተሪር terir *(adj.)* **incisive**
ተሪር terir *(adj.)* **rigid**
ተሪር terir *(adj.)* **rigorous**
ተሪር terir *(adj.)* **solid**
ተሪር terir *(adj.)* **stiff**
ተሪር terir *(adj.)* **stringent**
ተሪር terir *(adj.)* **sturdy**
ተሪር ክቡር እምኒ terir kbur 'èmni *(n.)* **agate**
ተሪር ሽፋን terir shfan *(n.)* **hardback**
ተሪር terir *(adj.)* **adamant**
ተሪር terir *(adj.)* **scathing**
ተርከሰ terkese *(v.)* **moisten**
ጎልፎ termin *(n.)* **jumper**
ተሮግሮግ በለ terogrog bele *(v.)* **crackle**
ተርታ terta *(n.)* **row**
ተርታ terta *(n.)* **sequence**
ተርታ terta *(n.)* **series**
ተርታዊ tertawi *(adj.)* **sequential**
ተርተረ tertere *(v.t.)* **slit**
ተሳፋፋይ tesafafay *(adj.)* **navigable**
ተሳሕበ tesaḥbe *(v.)* **gravitate**
ተሳኽዐ tesaḱ'ë *(v.)* **materialize**
ተሳለየ tesaleye *(v.)* **amble**
ተሳለየ tesaleye *(v.)* **waddle**
ተሳናዪ tesanayi *(adj.)* **coherent**
ተሳነየ tesaneyei *(v.)* **cohere**
ተሳነየ ተስማዕሞያም ነበሩ tesany' tesmaemoom neberu *(v.)* **coexist**
ተሳቀየ tesaqeye *(v.)* **afflict**
ተሳቀየ tesaqeye *(v.)* **agonize**
ተሳተፈ tesatefe *(v.)* **indulge**
ተስሳተፈ tesatefe *(v.)* **participate**
ተሳትፎ tesatfo *(n.)* **attendance**
ተሰበረ tesbere *(v.t)* **fracture**
ተሰብአ teseb'a *(v.)* **personify**
ተሰባሪ tesebari *(adj.)* **fragile**
ተሰባሪ tesebari *(adj.)* **brittle**
ተሰደደ tesedede *(v.)* **emigrate**
ተሰሓሒቱ ዘይፈልጥ tesehahitu zeyfelt *(adj.)* **infallible**

ተሰካሚ tesekami *(n.)* **carrier**
ተሰልባጢ teselbati *(adj.)* **reflexive**
ተሰልበ teselbe *(v.)* **infatuate**
ተሰልበጠ teselbete *(v.)* **backfire**
ተሰልበጠ teselbete *(v.)* **rebound**
ተሰማዒ tesema'e *(adj.)* **influential**
ተሰማዒነት tesema'enet *(n.)* **influence**
ተሰማምዐ tesemam'e *(v.)* **acquiesce**
ተሰማምዐ tesemam'ë *(v.)* **agree**
ተሰማምዐ tesemam'ë *(v.)* **concur**
ተሰማምዐ tesemam'ë *(v.)* **conform**
ተሰምዖ tesem'ö *(v.)* **feel**
ተሰናበተ tesenabete *(v.)* **resign**
ተሰነፈ tesenefe *(v.)* **succumb**
ተሰቀለ teseqele *(v.)* **mount**
ተሰራሰረ teserasere *(v.)* **cavort**
ተሰርጓጒት tesergwagwit *(n.)* **submarine**
ተስፋ tesfa *(n.)* **prospect**
ተስፋ ኣልቦ tesfa 'albo *(adj.)* **hopeless**
ተስፋ ሃበ tesfa habe *(v. t.)* **cheer**
ተስፋ ዘይብሉ tesfa zeyblu *(adj.)* **forlorn**
ተስፋ ዘይምግባር tesfa zeymgbar *(adj.)* **pessimistic**
ተስፋ ዝሀብ tesfa zhb *(adj.)* **prospective**
ተስፋ ዝቖረፀ tesfa zqoretse *(adj.)* **despondent**
ተስፋ ዝወሃቦ tesfa zwehabo *(adj.)* **promising**
ተስፋኣዊ tesfa'awi *(adj.)* **auspicious**
ተስፋሕፈሐ tesfahfehe *(adj.)* **widespread**
ተስፈኛ tesfegna *(adj.)* **sanguine**
ተስፈኛ ተዋሳኢት tesfegna tewasa'it *(n.)* **starlet**
ተሻበነ teshabene *(v.)* **intrigue**
ተስሓቢ tes'ĥabi *(n.)* **reptile**
ትእስሓቢ መኪና teshabi mekina *(n.)* **trailer**
ተሻጋሪ teshagari *(adj.)* **transitive**
ተሻጊሩ teshagiru *(v.)* **traverse**
ተሻራኺ tesharaki *(n.)* **partner**
ተሸገረ teshegere *(v.)* **beset**
ተሸካሚ teshekami *(n.)* **trestle**
ተሸኽለ teshekele *(v.)* **dive**
ተሸከመ teshekeme *(n.)* **bear**
ተሸከመ teshekeme *(v.)* **carry**
ተሸምቀቐ teshemqeqe *(v.)* **wince**
ተሸራሸረ tesherashere *(v.)* **stroll**
ተሽከርካሪ teshkerkari *(v.)* **twirl**
ተሽከርካሪ teshkerkari *(n.)* **wheel**
ተሽከርከረ teshkerkere *(v.)* **swivel**
ተሽከርካሪ teškerkari *(adj.)* **rotary**
ተሽከርካሪ teškerkari *(n.)* **rotor**
ተስማምዐ tesmam'e *(v.)* **stipulate**
ተሰማምዕ tesmam'ë *(v.)* **correspond**
ተሳናዪ መደምደምታ tesnayi medemdemta *(n.)* **syllogism**
ተሳቐየ tesqeye *(v.i.)* **suffer**
ተስተብሃሊ testebhali *(adj.)* **noticeable**
ተጣዕሰ teta'ëse *(n.)* **regret**
ተታኸሰ tetakese *(v.)* **drowse**
ተጣላዓይ tetala'äy *(n.)* **punter**
ተጣላዒ teẗala'ï *(n.)* **gambler**
ተጣልዐ teẗal'ë *(v.)* **gamble**
ተጣልዐ teẗal'ë *(v.)* **bet**
ተጣራጣሪ tetaratari *(adj.)* **dubious**
ተጣርዐ teṭar'ë *(v.)* **grumble**
ተታተየ tetateye *(v.)* **toddle**

ተተካኢ ሓኪም teteka'e hakim *(n.)* **locum**
ተተኮስቲ tetekosti *(n.)* **ammunition**
ተጠንቀቅ teťenqeq̈ *(v.)* **beware**
ተጠቃሚ teteqami *(n.)* **user**
ተጠቐመ teteqeme *(v.)* **wield**
ተጠቐመ teťeqeme *(v.)* **exert**
ተጠቕመ teťeq̈me *(v.)* **avail**
ተጣራጣሪ teteratari *(n.)* **sceptic**
ተጣራጣሪ teteratari *(adj.)* **sceptical**
ተጠራጣሪ teťeraťari *(adj.)* **irresolute**
ተጠራጠረ teťeraťere *(v.)* **suspect**
ተጠወየ teťeweye *(v.)* **swerve**
ተትሓሓዚ ተኽሊ tethahazi tekli *(n.)* **wisteria**
ተጻዋታይ ቫየሊን tetsawatay vayelin *(n.)* **violinist**
ተጽጊዑ ሓልፍመስመር tetsegiuzhalf mesmer *(n.)* **tangent**
ተፀላኢ tetsela'i *(adj.)* **disagreeable**
ተፀንበረ tetsenbere *(v.)* **socialize**
ተፀናተወ tetzenatewe *(v.)* **lurk**
ተፀወገ tetzewege *(v.i)* **frown**
ተዋዳዳሪ tewadadari *(n.)* **competitor**
ተዋጋኢ tewagaei *(n)* **combatant**
ተዋገየ tewageye *(n.)* **bargain**
ተዋገየ tewageye *(v.)* **haggle**
ተዋሃደ tewahade *(v.)* **assimilate**
ተዋሓሰ tewaḥase *(v.t)* **guarantee**
ተዋሓሰ tewaḥase *(v.)* **vouch**
ተዋላዋሊ tewalawali *(adj.)* **ambivalent**
ተዋሳኢ tewasa'i *(n.)* **actor**
ተዋሳኢት tewasa'it *(a.)* **actress**
ተዋስኦ tewas'o *(n.)* **acting**
ተዋስኦ tewas'o *(n.)* **drama**
ተወዛወዘ tewazaweze *(v.)* **swing**
ተዋዛይ tewazay *(n.)* **jester**
ተዋዛዪ tewazayi *(n.)* **comedian**
ተዋዛዪ tewazayi *(adj.)* **comic**
ተዋዛዪ tewazayi *(adj.)* **jocose**
ተዋዛዪ tewazayi *(v.t.)* **jocular**
ተዋዘየ tewazeye *(n.)* **joker**
ተዋዘየ tewazeye *(n.)* **banter**
ተወዳዳራይ tewedadaray *(n.)* **rival**
ተወዳዳሪ te'we'dada'rei *(n.)* **contestant**
ተወዳደረ tewedadere *(v. t)* **emulate**
ተወዳደረ tewedadere *(v.)* **vie**
ተወፋራይ tewefaray *(n.)* **serf**
ተወሃሃበ tewehahabe *(v.)* **reciprocate**
ተወካሊ tewekali *(adj.)* **representative**
ተወካልነት tewekalnet *(n.)* **representation**
ተወከለ tewekele *(v.)* **represent**
ተወላዲ teweladi *(n.)* **descendant**
ተወላዲ teweladi *(adj.)* **indigenous**
ተወላዒ tewela'ï *(adj.)* **fluorescent**
ተወላወለ tewelawele *(v.)* **boggle**
ተወልደ tewelde *(adj.)* **born**
ተወለዐ tewele'ë *(v.)* **kindle**
ተወንጫፊ tewenčafi *(n.)* **missile**
ተወንጨፈ tewenĉefe *(v.)* **rifle**
ተወንጨፈ tewenchfe *(v.)* **whirl**
ተወቃሲ teweqasi *(adj.)* **culpable**
ተወራዛዪ tewerazayi *(adj.)* **sententious**
ተወራዛይነት tewerazaynet *(n.)* **sophism**
ተወርሰ tewerese *(v.)* **devolve**
ተወርሶኣዊ tewerso'awi *(adj.)* **hereditary**
ተወሳኺይ tewesakay *(n.)* **additive**
ተወሳከ-ግሲ tewesakegsi *(n.)* **adverb**

ተወሳኺ tewesakhi ***(adj.)* subsidiary**
ተወሳኺ tewesakhi ***(adj.)* supplementary**
ተወሳኺ tewesaki ***(n.)* adjunct**
ተወሳኺ tewesaki ***(adj.)* extra**
ተወሳኺ tewesaḱi ***(adj.)* additional**
ተወሳኺ tewesaḱi ***(n.)* amplification**
ተወሳወሰ tewesawese ***(v.)* limber**
ተወታፊ ፈውሲ tewetafi fewsi ***(n.)* suppository**
ተወጣሓይ tewetâhay ***(n.)* rider**
ተወጣሪ tewetari ***(adj.)* tensile**
ተወጥሐ tewet'ĥe ***(v.)* ride**
ተወጥወጠ teweẗweẗe ***(v.)* protrude**
ተወዛወዘ tewezaweze ***(v.)* nod**
ተወዛወዘ tewezaweze ***(v.)* wiggle**
ተውሓሰ tewhase ***(v.)* underwrite**
ተውህቦ tewhbo ***(n.)* aptitude**
ተውህቦ tewhbo ***(n.)* talent**
ተውላጠ ስም tewlate sm ***(n.)* pronoun**
ትዉልዲ te-wle-di ***(n.)* generation**
ተውሳኸ-ዕጥቂ tewsaḱe'ëẗqi ***(n.)* accoutrement**
ተወሳኺ ግብሪ tewsakhi gbri ***(n.)* surtax**
ተወሳኺ ቋንቋ tewsakhi quanqua ***(n.)* lingua**
ተውሳስ tewsas ***(n.)* ringworm**
ተዉህቦ ዘለዎ tewuhbo zelewo ***(adj.)* gifted**
ተውኒት tewunit ***(n.)* theatre**
ተውኒታዊ tewunitawi ***(adj.)* theatrical**
ተፃበአ texab'e ***(v.)* contradict**
ተጻራፊ texarafi ***(adj.)* abusive**
ተጻራሪ texarari ***(n.)* antagonist**
ተፃራሪ texarari ***(n.)* antithesis**
ተፃራሪ texarari ***(n.)* antonym**
ተፃራሪ ቃል texarari qal ***(n.)* contradiction**
ተጻራርነት texararnet ***(n.)* antagonism**
ተጻረረ texarere ***(v.)* antagonize**
ተፃረረ texarere ***(v.)* contravene**
ተጻረረ texarere ***(v.)* counteract**
ተጻዋታይ texawatay ***(n.)* player**
ተጻዋታይ texawatay ***(adj.)* whimsical**
ተጻዋታይ ፒያኖ texawatay piyano ***(n.)* pianist**
ተፃወረ texawere ***(v.)* cope**
ተፃወረ texawere ***(v.)* endure**
ተጻወተ texawete ***(v.i.)* frolic**
ተጻይ texay ***(n.)* adversary**
ተጸዓኒት texe'änit ***(n.)* freighter**
ተጸባጻቢ texebaxabi ***(n.)* accountant**
ተፀባይ texebayi ***(adj.)* expectant**
ተጸበየ texebeye ***(v.)* anticipate**
ተጸበየ texebeye ***(v.)* await**
ተጸግዐ texeg'ë ***(v.)* affiliate**
ተጸልወ texelwe ***(v.)* bask**
ተፀንበረ texenbere ***(v.)* merge**
ተይፈልጥኻ ዝግበር teyfeltka zgber ***(adj.)* inadvertent**
ትዕይንቲ t'eynti ***(n.)* locale**
ተዛካሪ tezakari ***(adj.)* catchy**
ተዛምዶነት tezamdonet ***(n.)* relativity**
ተዛመደ tezamede ***(v.)* correlate**
ተዛራባይ tezarabay ***(n.)* windbag**
ተዛራቢ tezarabi ***(n.)* speaker**
ተዛረበ tezarebe ***(adj.)* dictate**
ተዛረበ tezarebe ***(v.)* speak**
ተዛታያይ tezatayay ***(n.)* negotiator**
ተዛታዪ tezatayi ***(n.)* interlocutor**
ተዛተየ tezateye ***(v.)* discuss**
ተዛወረ tezawere ***(v.)* ramble**

ትእዛዝ tezaz *(n.)* **writ**
ትእዛዝ t'ezaz *(n.)* **imperative**
ትእዛዝ t'ezaz *(n.)* **mandate**
ትእዛዝ t'ezaz *(n.)* **requisition**
ትእዛዝ ለወጠ t'ezaz leweṫe *(v.)* **countermand**
ትእዛዝ t'èzaz *(n.)* **behest**
ተዛዘመ tezazeme *(v.)* **culminate**
ተዘክሮ tezekro *(n.)* **memory**
ተዘክሮ tezekro *(n.)* **recollection**
ተዘማመደ tezemamede *(v.)* **interrelate**
ተዘርግሐ tezerghe *(v.)* **unfurl**
ተዘዋዋሪ tezewawari *(adj.)* **indirect**
ተዘይኮነ tezeykone *(n.)* **winner**
ተዓዋቲ tawati *(n.)* **paperback**
ተዓጻጻፊ ገበር ዘለዎ መጽሓፍ taxaxafi geber zelewo mxhaf *(v.)* **watch**
ተዓዘበ te'äzebe *(adj.)* **vibrant**
ተነዝናዚ teneznazi *(v.)* **wade**
ተፍአ tef'è *(v.)* **vomit**
ተፈላለየ tefelaleye *(v.)* **vary**
ተኽሊ ሓጹር teḱli ḥatsur *(n.)* **hedge**
ተለኣኣኺ tele'a'aḱi *(n.)* **herald**
ተንስአ tens'e *(v.)* **wake**
ተረኣይነት tere'aynet *(n.)* **visibility**
ተረፈዐ terefe'ë *(v.)* **vegetate**
ተረረ terere *(v.)* **harden**
ተስፋ tesfa *(n.)* **hope**
ተሸርበ tesherbe *(v.)* **vanish**
ተጠማጠመ teṭemaṭeme *(v.t.)* **grapple**
ተጻባኢ tetsaba'i *(adj.)* **hostile**
ተዋዛዪ tewazayi *(n.)* **harlequin**
ተዋዛዪ tewazayi *(n.)* **humorist**
ተወሃሃደ tewehahade *(v.)* **harmonize**
ተወላወለ tewelawele *(v.)* **hesitate**
ተወላወለ tewelawele *(v.)* **vacillate**
ተወራረደ tewerarede *(n. & v.)* **wager**
ተጻዋቲ መሳርሒ texawati mesarhi *(n.)* **instrumentalist**
ተስፋ ቆረፀ taesfa kors *(v.)* **tire**
ታዕታዕ ዘብዝሕ taëtaë zebzh *(adj.)* **rowdy**
ትዕግስተኛ tagstegna *(adj.)* **tolerant**

ታ

ታሕጓስ tahguasn *(n.)* **zest**
ታሕጓስ taĥgwas *(n.)* **festivity**
ታሕጓስ taĥgwas *(n.)* **fun**
ታሕጓስ taḥgwas *(n.)* **gratification**
ታሕጓስ taȟgwas *(n.)* **bliss**
ታሕጓስ taĥhgwas *(n.)* **excitement**
ታሕሳስ tahsas *(n.)* **December**
ታሕታዋይ ዳኛ tahtaway dagna *(n.)* **magistrate**
ታሕታይ taȟtay *(adj.)* **nether**
ታሕታዋይ tahteway *(adj.)* **junior**
ታሕተዋይ taȟteway *(adj.)* **subordinate**
ታሓትዋይ መዓርግ taȟteway me'arg *(n.)* **subaltern**
ታሕተዋይነት tahtewaynet *(n.)* **inferiority**
ታህዋኽ tahwaḱ *(n.)* **haste**
ታሕዋስያን tahwas-eyan *(n.)* **germ**
ታኬላ takela *(n.)* **slough**
ታክሲ taksi *(n.)* **cab**
ታክሲ taksi *(n.)* **taxi**
ታምፖን tampon *(n.)* **tampon**
ታንኒካ tanika *(n.)* **tin**
ታኒካ tanika *(n.)* **can**
ታኒካ tanika *(n.)* **canister**

ታንኪ tanki *(n.)* **tank**
ታንኳ tankwa *(n.)* **canoe**
ታንቴላዊ tanteelawi *(adj.)* **lacy**
ታሪኽ tariḱ *(n.)* **history**
ታሪኽ ሂወት tariḱ hiwet *(n.)* **memoir**
ታሪክ ህይወት tarik hywet *(n.)* **biography**
ታሪኻዊ tariḱawi *(adj.)* **historic**
ታሪኻዊ tariḱawi *(adj.)* **historical**
ታሽዓይ tash'äy *(adj. & n.)* **ninth**
ታተ ዝብለ ህፃን tate zble hsan *(n.)* **toddler**

ት

ትብዓት tb'ät *(n.)* **boldness**
ትብዓት tb'ät *(n.)* **fortitude**
ትብዓት tb'ät *(n.)* **bravery**
ትዕቢት t'ëbit *(n.)* **vanity**ትኽክል ዘይኮነ tkhkl zeykone *(adj.)* **inexact**
ትኩዝ tkuz *(adj.)* **glum**
ትርጓም trgwam *(n.)* **version**
ትርኢት tr'it *(n.)* **vista**
ትዕዝምቲ t'ëzmti *(n.)* **rapture**
ተዝናነየ teznaneye *(v.)* **lounge**
ትፍንያታዊ tfn'yatawi *(adj.)* **subjective**
ትፍስህቲነት tfshtinet *(n.)* **hedonism**
ትፍታፍ tftaf *(n.)* **spittle**
ትግባሬ tgbarie *(n.)* **performance**
ትግበራ tgbera *(n.)* **attainment**
ትጉሕ tguh *(adj.)* **diligent**
ትከግመ theg'me *(n.)* **smog**
ትሕጃ ምሓዝ thja mhaz *(n.)* **lien**
ትሕጃ ምትሓዝ thja mthaz *(n.)* **pawn**
ትሕት ዝበለ tht zbele *(adj.)* **lower**
ትሕተ ምድራዊ tḧte mdrawi *(adj.)* **subterranean**
ትሕተ ውኖኣዊ tḧte wno'awi *(adj.)* **subconscious**
ትሕተ-ቤት tḧtebeet *(n.)* **basement**
ትሕቲ thti *(prep.)* **under**
ትሕቲ መሬት ዝርከብ ክፍሊ tĥti meret zrkeb kfli *(n.)* **dungeon**
ትሕቲ መሬት thti meriet *(adj.)* **underground**
ትሕቲ tḧti *(prep.)* **below**
ትሕቲ tḧti *(adv.)* **beneath**
ትሕትና tĥtna *(n.)* **decorum**
ትሕትና tḧtna *(n.)* **modesty**
ትሕትና ዘይፈልጥ thtna zeyfelt *(adj.)* **impudent**
ትሕትና tḧtna *(n.)* **courtesy**
ትሑት thut *(adj.)* **low**
ትሑት thut *(adj.)* **lowly**
ትሑት thut *(n.)* **underling**
ትሑት tḧut *(adj.)* **inferior**
ትሑት tḧut *(adj.)* **modest**
ተሳፋሪ tsafari *(n.)* **passenger**
ተቛም tqhuam *(n.)* **institution**
ትንታነኣዊ tntane'awi *(adj.)* **analytical**
ትንተና tntena *(n.)* **analysis**
ትራፊክ trafic *(n.)* **traffic**
ትርቢዒት trbi'ët *(a.)* **quadrangle**
ትርቢዒታዊ trbi'ëtawi *(n.)* **quadrangular**
ትርብዒት t'rb'it *(n.)* **square**
ትረኻ treka *(n.)* **tale**
ትርፋማ trfama *(adj.)* **lucrative**
ትርፊ trfi *(n.)* **excess**
ትርፊ ግዘ trfi gize *(n.)* **leisure**
ትርፍራፍ trfraf *(n.)* **remains**
ትርግታ trgta *(n.)* **pulsation**

ትርግታ trgta *(v.)* **throb**
ትርጉም trgum *(n.)* **meaning**
ትርጉም trgum *(n.)* **translation**
ትርጉም አልቦ trgum albo *(adj.)* **senseless**
ትርጉም አልቦ trgum albo *(n.)* **signification**
ትርጉም አልቦ trgum 'albo *(adj.)* **absurd**
ትርጉም አልቦነት trgum 'albonet *(n.)* **absurdity**
ትርጉም ምንጻር trgum mnxar *(v.)* **paraphrase**
ትርጉም ዘይብሉ trgum zeyblu *(n.)* **nonsense**
ትርጉም ዘይብሉ trgum zeyblu *(adj.)* **pointless**
ትርጉም ዘይህብ trgum zeyhb *(adj.)* **insensible**
ትርጉሙ ፈልፈለ trgumu felfele *(v.)* **decode**
ትሪግኖመትሪ trignomietry *(n.)* **trigonometry**
ትሕዝቶ ፅሑፍ tḧzto xḧuf *(n.)* **suppliant**
ትሮፒካዊ muket ena derq ayer *(adj.)* **tropical**
ቴማ tiema *(adj.)* **thematic**
ቴንብር ዓቃቢ tienbr aqabi *(n.)* **philately**
ቲፎ ሕማም tifo hmam *(n.)* **typhus**
ትሕጃ tihija *(n.)* **collateral**
ትሕዝቶ tihizeto *(n.)* **content**
ቲኬት tikiet *(adj.)* **careful**
ትካል tkal *(n.)* **agency**
ትካል tkal *(n.)* **enterprise**
ትካል tkal *(n.)* **establishment**
ትካል tkal *(n.)* **institute**
ትካዊ tkawi *(adj.)* **smoky**
ትኻዋንነት tkawnet *(n.)* **symbiosis**
ትካዘ tkaze *(n.)* **depression**
ትካዘ tkaze *(n.)* **melancholy**
ትኽክል tk'ekl *(adj.)* **true**
ትኻስ tkhas *(n.)* **snooze**
ትኽክል ዘይኮነ tkhkl zeylone *(adj.)* **inaccurate**
ትኹረት ዘይህብ tkhret zeyhb *(adj.)* **inattentive**
ትኪ tki *(n.)* **smoke**
ትኽክል tkkl *(adj.)* **unfailing**
ትኽክለኛ tkklennya *(n.)* **parcel**
ትኽሎኣዊ tkloawi *(v.)* **perpetrate**
ትኹል tkul *(adj.)* **vertical**
ትኩር tkur *(adj.)* **astute**
ትኩርና tkurna *(n.)* **vigilance**
ትኩርና tkurna *(n.)* **acumen**
ትኩስ tkus *(adj.)* **fresh**
ትኩዝ tkuz *(adj.)* **morose**
ትኳዕ tkwa'ë *(n.)* **blotch**
ትኳዕ t'kwa'ë *(n.)* **speckle**
ትኋን tḱwan *(n.)* **bug**
ትልሚ tlmi *(n.)* **project**
ትማሊ tmali *(adv.)* **yesterday**
ትምባኮ tmbako *(n.)* **tobacco**
ትምህርታዊ tmhrtawi *(adj.)* **didactic**
ትምህርታዊ tmhrtawi *(adj.)* **scholastic**
ትምህርተ-ሃይማኖት tmhrtehaymanot *(n.)* **catechism**
ትምህርቲ tmhrti *(n.)* **education**
ትምህርቲ tmhrti *(n.)* **lecture**
ትምህርቲ tmhrti *(n.)* **lesson**
ትምህርቲ ቤት tmhrti bet *(n.)* **school**
ትምህርቲ ቴክኖሎጂ tmhrti tieknoloĵi *(n.)* **polytechnic**
ትምኒት tmnit *(n.)* **fantasy**
ተመነየ tmnit *(v.)* **wish**
ትምኒት tmnit *(adj.)* **wishful**

ትምኒት tmnit *(n.)* **ambition**
ትምኒት tmnit *(n.)* **aspiration**
ትምየና tmyena *(n.)* **forgery**
ትምዩን tmyun *(adj.)* **counterfeit**
ትንባሃዊ tnbahawi *(adj.)* **syllabic**
ትንባሀ tnbahe *(n.)* **syllable**
ትንበያ tnbeya *(n.)* **prescience**
ትንቢት tnbit *(n.)* **prediction**
ትንቢት tnbit *(n.)* **prophecy**
ትንቢታዊ tnbitawi *(adj.)* **prophetic**
ትንፋስ tnfas *(n.)* **breath**
ትንግርቲ tngrti *(n.)* **feat**
ትንግርቲ tn'grti *(adj.)* **splendid**
ትንሳእ tnsa'e *(n.)* **revival**
ትንሳኤ tnsa'ie *(n.)* **Easter**
ተከሰተ tekesete *(v.)* **occur**
ተወሳኺ ሰዓት tewesaki se'at *(n)* **overtime**
ተዘይኮነ ግን tezeykone gn *(adv.)* **otherwise**
ተገደደ tegedede *(v.)* **obligated**
ተፃዋቲ tetsawati *(adj.)* **outgoing**
ቱርኳዊ turkwawi *(n.)* **ottoman**
ተባዕታይ ጣዎስ tabaetay taewa *(n.)* **peacock**
ታቦት tabot *(n.)* **shrine**
ታቦት tabot *(n.)* **ark**
ታህዋስያን tahwasyan *(n.)* **organism**
ትርፊ ክፍሊት trfi kflit *(v.)* **overcharge**
ትዕዝብቲ t'ezebti *(n.)* **observation**
ትፍግእት tfg'et *(n.)* **scenery**
ትርኢት tr'it *(n.)* **riposte**
ትርኽ trk *(n.)* **bauble**
ትርኪምርኪ ስልማት trkimrki slmat *(adj.)* **moist**
ትርኩስ trkus *(adj.)* **soppy**
ትርኩስ trkus *(n.)* **daffodil**
ትሮምቦኖ trombono *(n.)* **absentee**
ትሩፍ truf *(n.)* **participant**
ትሰታፋይ tsatafay *(n.)* **tonsil**
ትጽቢት txbit *(n.)* **anticipation**
ትፅቢት ገበረ txbit gebere *(v.)* **expect**
ትያትር ቆልዑ tyatr qoleu *(n.)* **pantomime**
ትዝታ tzta *(v.)* **reminiscence**
ትዝታዊ tztawi *(adj.)* **reminiscent**
ትዋሕታ twahta *(n.)* **hoot**
ትውልዲ twldi *(n.)* **descent**
ቶንሲል tonsil *(n.)* **lathe**
ቶርንዮ tornyo *(n.)* **orgy**

ቸ

ቸሊዶንያ chelidonya *(n.)* **celandine**
ቸርቻሪ ĉerĉari *(n.)* **retailer**
ቸንዳ chenda *(n.)* **marquee**
ቸክ chek *(n.)* **cheque**
ቻርት chart *(n.)* **chart**
ቼዝ chezz' *(n.)* **chess**
ቸግር chger *(n.)* **inconvenience**
ቸኩል chkul *(adj.)* **impetuous**
ቾክ chok *(n.)* **chalk**

ነ

ነዝዐ nez'ë *(v.i.)* **ooze**
ነገር neger *(n.)* **object**
ነጸገ netsege *(v.)* **overrule**
ነቕዐ neq'ä *(v.)* **crack**
ነቃዕ neqa'ë *(n.)* **fissure**
ነቓዕ neqa'ë *(n.)* **crack**
ነቃፀ neqax *(adj.)* **mulish**
ነቓጽ neqax *(adj.)* **wayward**
ነቀፈ neqefe *(v.)* **castigate**
ነቐፈ neqefe *(v.)* **chide**

ነቐፈ neqefe *(v.)* **criticize**
ነቀፈ neqefe *(v.)* **revile**
ነቐፌታ neqefeeta *(n.)* **criticism**
ነቐለ neqele *(v.)* **depart**
ነቐለ neqele *(v.)* **disconnect**
ነቐለ neqele *(v.)* **trip**
ነቐለ neqele *(v.)* **uproot**
ንዕቐት n'eqet *(n.)* **contempt**
ንዕቀት n'eqet *(n.)* **scorn**
ንዕቐት n'ëqet *(n.)* **disdain**
ንዕቀት ዘለዎ n'eqet zelewo *(adj.)* **scornful**
ነቀወ neqewe *(v.)* **bellow**
ነቐጸ neqexe *(v.)* **wither**
ነቓፀ neqhats *(adj.)* **stubborn**
ነቕሐ neq̈ḧe *(v.)* **awake**
ነቕሐ neq̈ḧe *(v.)* **awaken**

ን

ንቑጽ nequtse *(adj.)* **husky**
ንእስነት n'esenet *(n.)* **youth**
ንእሽተይ n'eshtey *(adj.)* **mini**
ንእሽተይ n'eshtey *(adj.)* **small**
ንእሽተይ n'eshtey *(adj.)* **tiny**
ንእሽተይ በደል n'eshtey bedel *(n.)* **misdemeanour**
ንእሽተይ ድምጺ መጋዉሒ neshtey dmsi megawuhi *(n.)* **tweeter**
ንእሽተይ ጋዜጣ n'eshtey gazieta *(adj.)* **tabloid**
ንእሽተይ ምኽሪ ሃበ n'eshtey mkri habe *(n.)* **tipster**
ንእሽተይ ናይ ኤሊትሪክ ፍሰት መቆፃፀሪ መሳርሒ n'eshtey nay eletric hayli mokosaseri *(n.)* **transistor**
ንእሽተይ ስርቂ n'eshtey srki *(n.)* **pickings**
ንእሽተይን ማራኺን n'eshteyn marakin *(adj.)* **dainty**
ንእሽትሊት n'eshtlit *(adj.)* **miniature**
ንእሽቶ neshto *(n.)* **wisp**
ንእሽቶ n'eshto *(adj.)* **petite**
ንእሽቶ n'eshto *(n.)* **smidgen**
ንእሽቶ በርሚል n'èshto bermil *(n.)* **keg**
ንእሽቶ ደሴት n'èshto deseet *(n.)* **islet**
ንእሽቶ ፊደል n'eshto fidel *(adj.)* **minuscule**
ንእሽቶ ሓወልቲ n'eshto ḧawelti *(n.)* **statuette**
ንእሽቶ ካንጋሩ n'èshto kangaru *(n.)* **wallaby**
ንእሽቶ መጽሓፍ n'èshto mexḧaf *(n.)* **booklet**
ንእሽቶ መጽሓፍ n'èshto mexḧaf *(n.)* **booklet**
ንእሽቶ ምስሊ n'èshto msli *(n.)* **figurine**
ንእሽቶ ነኺል nèshto neḱual *(v.)* **prick**
ንእሽቶ ቁሸት n'èshto qushet *(n.)* **hamlet**
ንእሽቶ ቈልዓ n'èshto qwel'ä *(n.)* **chit**
ንእሽቶ ወሓዚ n'eshto weḧazi *(n.)* **streamlet**
ንእሽቶ ዝሓበጠት neshto zhabetet *(n.)* **wen**
ነስነሰ nesnese *(v.i.)* **sprinkle**
ንእስነት n'èsnet *(n)* **boyhood**
ንእሽቶ n'ešto *(adj.)* **slight**
ነታጕ netagwi *(adj.)* **explosive**
ነፃነት netanet *(n.)* **independence**
ነጥቢ netbi *(n.)* **dot**

ነጥቢ netbi *(n.)* **spot**
ነጥቢ neẗbi *(n.)* **point**
ነትዐ net'ë *(v.t.)* **rupture**
ነተጉ netege *(v.)* **explode**
ነተጕ netegwa *(v.)* **burst**
ነጠረ neẗere *(v.i)* **jump**
ነጠረ neẗere *(v.)* **bounce**
ነትጒ netgwi *(n.)* **blast**
ነተጉ netigu *(v.)* **detonate**
ነቲሕ netiḧ *(n.)* **miasma**
ነቲሕ netiḧ *(n.)* **stench**
ነቶገ netoge *(v.)* **erupt**
ነፃ netsa *(adj.)* **independent**
ነፃ netsa *(adj.)* **liberal**
ነፃ ኣውፃኢ netsa awtsa'e *(n.)* **liberator**
ነፃ ኣውፀአ netsa mwtsa'e *(v.)* **liberate**
ነፃነት netsanet *(n.)* **liberation**
ነፃነት netsanet *(n.)* **liberty**
ነፀብራቅ netsebraq *(n.)* **radiance**
ነፀብራቅ netsebraq *(n.)* **reflection**
ነጸፈት netsefet *(v.)* **wean**
ነፀገ netsege *(v.)* **reject**
ነፀለ netsela *(v.)* **seclude**
ንፁር netsxur *(adj.)* **clear**
ነፀብራቅ netzebrqh *(n.)* **lustre**
ነወመ neweme *(v.)* **hibernate**
ነዊሐ newĥe *(v.)* **elongate**
ነዊሕ newih *(adj.)* **lengthy**
ነዊሕ newih *(adj.)* **long**
ነዊሕ newih *(adj.)* **tall**
ነዊሕ ጭቅጭቅ ዝተሓወሰ ንግግር newih chikchik ztehaweso nggr *(n.)* **tirade**
ነዊሕ ጉዕዞ ብእግሪ newih guazo b'ageri *(n.)* **trek**
ነዊሕ ካልሲ newiḧ kalsi *(n.)* **stocking**
ነዊሕ ልበወለድ newiḧ lbeweled *(n.)* **novel**
ነዊሕ ሳእኒ newiḧ sa'èni *(n.)* **boot**
ነዊሒ ጦር newih tor *(n.)* **javelin**
ነዊሕ ፀጉሪ newih tseguri *(n.)* **tress**
ነዊሕ ጸናሒ newiḧ xenaḧi *(n.)* **protractor**
ንለዊሕ ዝጸንሕ newiḧ zxeniḧ *(adj.)* **protracted**
ነውነወ newnewe *(v.t.)* **jostle**
ነውነውታ newnewta *(n.)* **jerk**
ነውራም newram *(adj.)* **indecent**
ነውራም newram *(adj.)* **nasty**
ነውራም newram *(adj.)* **vile**
ነውራም newram *(n.)* **cad**
ነውሪ newri *(adj.)* **immoral**
ነውሪ newri *(n.)* **indecency**
ነውፂ newtsi *(n.)* **shock**
ነዉጺ newtsi *(adj.)* **turbulent**
ነውሪ newuri *(n.)* **scandal**
ነውፂ መትኒ newxi metni *(n.)* **neurosis**
ነጸገ nexege *(v.)* **forswear**
ነፀገ nexege *(adj.)* **pseudo**
ናይ ሓሶት nay ĥasot *(adj.)* **terrestrial**
ናይ መሬት nay meriet *(adj.)* **vascular**
ናይ ሻምብቆ ኣካል nay shambqo 'akal *(adj.)* **telegraphic**
ናይ ቴሌግራፍ nay telegram *(adj.)* **venous**
ናይ ቨይን nay veyn *(pron.)* **him**
ንዓኡ ne-a-u *(adj.)* **headstrong**
ነቓጽ neq̃atse *(n.)* **wren**
ንእሽቶ ዓይነት ዑፍ n'èshto 'äynet 'üf *(a.)* **grenade**
ንእሽቶ ቦምባ n'èshto bomba *(v.)* **hop**

ነጠረ neṭere *(v.t.)* **hop**

ነጠረ neṭere *(n.)* **underworld**

ናይ ለያቡ ዓለም lay leyabu alem *(n.)* **hemisphere**

ንፍቀ-ክቢ nfqekbi *(v.)* **negate**

ናይ ሙዚቃ ስልቲ ney muzika slti *(n.)* **tempo**

ንፋስ nfas *(n.)* **draught**

ንፋስ nfas *(n.)* **wind**

ንፋስ nfas *(adj.)* **windy**

ንፍቀ ምድሪ nfqe mdri *(n.)* **equator**

ንፍራ nfra *(n.)* **flight**

ንፉዕ nfu'e *(adj.)* **smart**

ንፉዕ nfu'e *(adj.)* **wily**

ንፉዕ nfu'ë *(adj.)* **able**

ንፍዮ nfyo *(n.)* **measles**

ን ግብረ ስጋዊ ግኑኝነት ስሚዕት ምልዕዓል ngbre ssgawi gnugnunet smiait ml'eal *(v.)* **titillate**

ንግዳዊ ngdawi *(adj.)* **commercial**

ንግዳዊ ngdawi *(adj.)* **mercantile**

ንግደት ngdet *(n.)* **pilgrimage**

ንግዲ ngdi *(n.)* **commerce**

ንግዲ ngdi *(n.)* **trade**

ንግሆ ngho *(n.)* **morrow**

ንግስና ngsna *(n.)* **monarchy**

ንግስቲ ngsti *(n.)* **queen**

ንግስቲ ነገስት ngsti negest *(n.)* **empress**

ንጉደት ስምዒት ngudet smi'it *(n.)* **catharsis**

ንጉሆ nguho *(n.)* **morning**

ንጉስ ngus *(n.)* **king**

ንጉስ ngus *(n.)* **monarch**

ንጉስ ngus *(n.)* **sovereign**

ንጉሳዊ ngusawi *(adj.)* **regal**

ንጉሳዊነት ngusawi *(n.)* **royalty**

ንሓደጋ አሳጠሐ nĥadega asaťeeĥe *(v.)* **endanger**

ንሓጺር ግዜ nḧaxir gzee *(adv.)* **awhile**

ንህቢ nhbi *(n.)* **bee**

ንሕማም እንስሳ ዚምልከት nḥmam 'ènssa zimlket *(adj.)* **veterinary**

ንሕማቅ ነገር አውዓለ nḧmaq neger aw'äle *(v.)* **misapply**

ንሕና nhna *(pron.)* **we**

ንህዝቢ ኣርአየ nhzbi ar'aye *(v.)* **exhibit**

ኒከል nikel *(n.)* **nickel**

ኒኮቲን nikotin *(n.)* **nicotine**

ኒርቫና nirvana *(n.)* **nirvana**

ነዊሕ ሂወት niweh hiwet *(n.)* **longevity**

ኒውትሮን niwtron *(n.)* **neutron**

ኒዮሊቲክ niyolitik *(adj.)* **Neolithic**

ኒዮን niyon *(n.)* **neon**

ነኸሰ nkes *(v.)* **clench**

ንከያ nkeya *(n.)* **deflation**

ንከያ nkeya *(n.)* **rebate**

ንኸይወርስ ከልከለ nkeywers kelkele *(v.)* **disinherit**

ንላዕሊ nlaeli *(adv.)* **upward**

ንላዕሊ ምዛር nlaeli mzar *(n.)* **upturn**

ንመሕነቒ ዝጥቀምዎ ዕንጨይቲ n-mehneqi z-tkemwo enchei-ti *(n.)* **gallows**

ንመን nmen *(pron.)* **whom**

ንመገዲ ብቑዕ ዝኮነ nmengedi bqu'ë kone *(adj.)* **roadworthy**

ንምግላፅ ዘፀግም nmglats zetsegm *(adj.)* **indescribable**

ንምምባር ዘይኾን nmmbar zeykhon *(adj.)* **inhabitable**

ንምንባብ ምፅጋም nmnbab mtzgam *(n.)* **illegibility**

ንምንታይ nmntay *(adv.)* **why**

ንነፍሲ ወከፍ nnefsi wekef ***(prep.)*** **per**
ንነዊሕ ግዜ ዝፀንሕ nnewi gzie ztsenh ***(adj.)*** **lasting**
ነከዩ ሸጠ mkurats ***(v.)*** **undercut**
ንእሽተይ ቐላይ mlkt neshtey q̈lay ***(n.)*** **pool**
ናይ ኢድ መሳርሒ ḧrtum ***(n.)*** **tool**
ናይ ሓሶት ጸብጻብ nay ḧasot xebxab ***(n.)*** **canard**
ኖራ nora ***(n.)*** **lime**
ኖራ nora ***(n.)*** **whitewash**
ኖርደታይ nordetay ***(adj.)*** **Nordic**
ንቅድሚት nqdmit ***(adv.)*** **ahead**
ንቕድሚት nq̈dmit ***(adv. &adj.)*** **forward**
ንቅድሚት ኣምርሐ nqdmit amrḧe ***(v.)*** **proceed**
ንቅድሚት ተደርበየ nqdmit tederbeye ***(n.)*** **projectile**
ንቅሎ nqlo ***(n.)*** **departure**
ንቁሕ nquh ***(adj.)*** **dashing**
ንቑሕ nquh ***(adj.)*** **perky**
ብቍሩብ nqurub ***(adv.)*** **slightly**
ንርሑቕ nrḧuq̈ ***(adv.)*** **afar**
ንሳ nsa ***(pron.)*** **her**
ንሳ nsa ***(pron.)*** **she**
ንስሓ nsha ***(n.)*** **penance**
ንስሓ nsĥa ***(n.)*** **repentance**
ንሽሙ nshmu ***(adj.)*** **nominal**
ንፅህና nshna ***(n.)*** **tidiness**
ንስኻ nska ***(pron.)*** **you**
ንስም ብቻ ዝወሃብ መኣርግ nsm bcha zwehab mearg ***(adj.)*** **titular**
ንስሪ nsri ***(n.)*** **eagle**
ንሱ nsu ***(pron.)*** **he**
ንሱ ንሳ nsu nsa ***(pron.)*** **it**
ንሱ ድማ nsu dma ***(n.)*** **namely**
ንጣብ ቀለም nẗab qelem ***(n.)*** **blot**
ንጣብ nẗab ***(n.)*** **blob**
ንጣር n'ẗar ***(n.)*** **speck**
ንጥፈት nẗfet ***(n.)*** **activity**
ነጥረ ነገር ntre neger ***(n.)*** **particle**
ንጥረ ነገር n'ẗre neger ***(n.)*** **substance**
ንፅገት ntsget ***(n.)*** **rejection**
ንፅህና nts'hna ***(n.)*** **purity**
ንፅል ntsl ***(adj.)*** **single**
ንፅል ntsl ***(adj.)*** **singular**
ንፅልነት ntslnet ***(n.)*** **singularity**
ንፅልታ ntslta ***(n.)*** **singlet**
ንፅፅር ntstsr ***(n.)*** **simile**
ንፁግ ntsug ***(adj.)*** **undesirable**
ንፁር ntsur ***(adj.)*** **decided**
ንፁር ntsur ***(adj.)*** **specific**
ንፁር ዘይኮነ ntsur zeykone ***(adj.)*** **indistinct**
ንጡፍ nẗuf ***(adj.)*** **spry**
ንጡፍ nṭuf ***(adj.)*** **vivacious**
ንጡፍ nẗuf ***(adj.)*** **active**
ንፁር ntzur ***(adj.)*** **lucid**
ንፁር ntzur ***(adj.)*** **manifest**
ንኡድ n'ud ***(adj.)*** **excellent**
ኑኡሽተይ nu'eshtey ***(adj.)*** **little**
ኑኡሽተይ ኣረጊት ሆቴል nu'eshtey aregit hotel ***(n.)*** **inn**
ኑጋት nugat ***(n.)*** **nougat**
ኑጉሳዊ nugusawi ***(adj.)*** **imperial**
ኑጉሳዊነት nugusawinet ***(n.)*** **imperialism**
ኑክልየስ nuklyes ***(n.)*** **nucleus**
ኑክልየሳዊ nuklyesawi ***(adj.)*** **nuclear**
ኑቑሕ ዘይኮነ nuqhuh zeykone ***(adj.)*** **inactive**
ንኡስ n'us ***(n.)*** **junior**
ንኡስ n'us ***(adj.)*** **minor**
ንኡስ ኣርእስቲ n'us ar'esti ***(n.)*** **subtitle**
ንኡስ ድምር n'us dmr ***(n.)*** **subtotal**

ንኡስ ውዕል ገበረ n'us w'el gebere *(v.)* **subcontract**
ኑኡሹተይ nu'ushtey *(adj.)* **marginal**
ኑዛዜ nuzazee *(n.)* **confession**
ንወሲብ ዘወናውን nwesib zewenawn *(adj.)* **sensual**
ንውሓት nwhat *(n.)* **length**
ንውሽጢ ምእታው nwsheti metw *(n.)* **penetration**
ንውሽጢ ኣስተንፈሰ nwshti astenfese *(v.)* **inhale**
ንዉፅ ኣእምሮ nwux a'emro *(adj.)* **neurotic**
ንፅፈ ፃግን nxfe xag'n *(n.)* **menopause**
ንፅፍ ፃግናዊ nxfe xag'nawi *(adj.)* **menstrual**
ንፅል ኣምልኾ nxl amlḱo *(n.)* **monolatry**
ንፅል ድምፃዊ nxl dmxawi *(adj.)* **monophonic**
ንፅል ሃዲድ nxl hadid *(n.)* **monorail**
ንፅል ከውሒ nxl kewḧi *(n.)* **monolith**
ንፅል መነፅር nxl menexr *(n.)* **monocle**
ንፅል መውስቦ nxl mewsbo *(n.)* **monogamy**
ንፅል ሲላበል nxl silabel *(n.)* **monosyllable**
ንፅል ዝሕብሩ nxl zḧbru *(n.)* **monochrome**
ንጹህ nxuh *(adj.)* **pure**
ንጹህነት nxuhnet *(n.)* **purist**
ንፁር nxur *(adj.)* **articulate**
ንፁር nxur *(adj.)* **clarion**
ንፁር nxur *(adj.)* **evident**
ንፁር nxur *(adj.)* **explicit**
ንፅፅር nxxr *(n.)* **contrast**
ንየው nyew *(adv.)* **afield**
ንዘልኣለም nzel'alem *(adv.)* **forever**
ንዝናዘ nznaze *(n.)* **vibration**
ን n *(prep.)* **for**
ን ኣሰናዳኢ መልእኽቲ n asenada'i mel'ekti *(adj.)* **editorial**

ና

ናይ ኢኤለትሪክ ሓይሊ ዝቅይር መሳርሒ na eletric hayli zqyir mesarhi *(n.)* **transformer**
ናይ ልቢ na' ae lebii *(adj.)* **cardiac**
ና ኤሜሪካ ደርሆ na america derho *(n.)* **turkey**
ና ዕንበባ ዓይነት na anbeba aynet *(n.)* **tulip**
ናይ ድምፂ ቃና na dmsi kana *(n.)* **tone**
ና ሓደ ስራሕ መረዳድኢ ቋንቋ na hade srah meredadei kanka *(adj.)* **terminological**
ና ሓደ ስራሕ መረዳድኢ ቋንቋ na hade srah meredadei kanka *(n.)* **terminology**
ና ከተማ ኤለትሪክ ባቡር na ketema electric babur *(n.)* **tram**
ና ከዉሒ ጎቦ na kewuhi gobo *(n.)* **tor**
ና መጨረሻ ደረጃ na mecheresha dereja *(adj.)* **terminal**
ናይ መርከብ ፅዕነት ጠቅላላ ክብደት na merkeb teklala s'anet *(n.)* **tonnage**
ና ነዳቂ ማንካ na nedaqi manka *(n.)* **trowel**

ና ፖሊስ ዱላ na polis dula *(n.)* **truncheon**

ናይ ሮማውያን ና ኣወዳት ጃኪት na romawuyan na awedat jaket *(n.)* **toga**

ና ተቅራኒ ክዳን ክክደን ዝፎቲ na teqarani sota kdan kkden zufoti *(n.)* **transvestite**

ና ወይኒ በርሚን na weyni brmin *(n.)* **tun**

ናዓ na'ä *(v.)* **come**

ናዓወት መዓልቲ naawet mealti *(adj.)* **triumphal**

ናዓወት ስሚዒት naawet smait *(adj.)* **triumphant**

ናብ nab *(prep.)* **into**

ናብ nab *(prep.)* **to**

ናብ nab *(prep.)* **towards**

ናብ ብሕቲ መለሰ nab bĥti melese *(v.)* **denationalize**

ናብ ደቡብ nab debub *(adj.)* **southerly**

ናብ ሓደ ገጽ nab ȟade gex *(adv.)* **aside**

ናብ ሕጊ ኣቕረቡ nab ȟgi aq̈ribu *(v.)* **prosecute**

ናብ ሕጊ ምቕራብ nab ȟgi mq̈rab *(n.)* **prosecution**

ናብ ርሑቕ nab rȟuq̈ *(adv.)* **away**

ናብ ሰሜን nab semeen *(adj.)* **northerly**

ናብ ስልጣን መለሰ nab sltan melese *(v.)* **reinstate**

ናብ ጥርሙዝ ለወጠ nab ṭrmuz leweṭe *(v.)* **vitrify**

ናብ ወፃዕ ለኣኸ nab wexa'i le'ake *(v. t.)* **export**

ናብ ዩኒቨርሲቲ ኣተወ nab yuniversiti atewe *(v.)* **matriculate**

ናብ ዝነበሮ ክምለስ ዘይኽእል nab znebro kmles zeyk'el *(adj.)* **irreversible**

ናብ/ካብ ምዕራብ nab/kab m'erab *(adv.)* **westerly**

ና ባሕሪ ኣባ ጋቢየ nabahri aba gabuye *(n.)* **turtle**

ናባያይ nabayay *(n.)* **carer**

ናባዪ nabayi *(n.)* **caretaker**

ናበይ nabey *(adv.)* **whither**

ናብኡ ሸነኽ nab'u shenek *(adv.)* **thither**

ናብዚ nabzi *(adv.)* **hither**

ናቾ nacho *(n.)* **nacho**

ናድራር ክዳን nadrar kdan *(n.)* **tuxedo**

ናይ ኣዕዋፍ ፍፆት naeawaf fsot *(v.)* **twitter**

ናዕቢ na'ëbi *(n.)* **affray**

ናዕቢ na'ëbi *(n.)* **subversion**

ናዕቢ naebi *(n.)* **pandemonium**

ናእዳ na'èda *(n.)* **commendation**

ናእዳ na'èda *(n.)* **compliment**

ናዕናዕ na'ena'e *(n.)* **spearmint**

ናዕዋ na'ëwa *(n.)* **frenzy**

ናፍቆት nafqot *(n.)* **longing**

ናፍቆት nafqot *(n.)* **nostalgia**

ናፍቖት nafqot *(n.)* **yearning**

ናፍጣ nafṫa *(n.)* **naphthalene**

ና ግሊ መምህር nagli memhr *(n.)* **tutor**

ና ጎሳ nagosa *(adj.)* **tribal**

ናግራም ሰበይቲ nagram sebeyti *(n.)* **virago**

ና ሃደን ከልቢ nahaden kelbi *(n.)* **terrier**

ናሓረግ መደገፊ ዕንጨይቲ nahareg medegefi anseyti *(n.)* **trellis**

ና ሓርማዝ ስኒ naharmaz sni *(n.)* **tusk**
ና ሓዘን ደወል nahazen dewel *(n.)* **toll**
ናህሪ nahri *(n.)* **momentum**
ናህሪ ቀነሰ nahri kenese *(v.)* **decelerate**
ናሕሲ naĥsi *(n.)* **roof**
ናሕሲ ኣፍ naȟsi af *(n.)* **palate**
ናሕሲ ምስራሕ naĥsi msraĥ *(n.)* **roofing**
ናይ ክብደት መለክዒ nakbdet melekai *(n.)* **ton**
ናይ መኪና ጎማ namekina goma *(n.)* **tyre**
ናመምሃሪ ክፍሊት namemhari kflit *(n.)* **tuition**
ናምስጋና ንግግር namsgana nggr *(n.)* **tribute**
ናሙና namuna *(n.)* **specimen**
ና ንእሽተይ ዒፍ ድምፂ naneshtey aif dmsi *(v.)* **tweet**
ናርቺዞ narchizo *(n.)* **narcissus**
ናፀሓይ ምዕራብ nasahay marab *(n.)* **twilight**
ናፅዕነት መኪና nas'anet mekina *(n.)* **truck**
ናፅዕነት መኪና ሹፈር nas'anet mekina shuifer *(n.)* **trucker**
ና ስፈት መኪና ፒዳል nasfyet mekina pedal *(n.)* **treadle**
ና ስኒ መጎርገሪ ዕንጨይቲ nasni megorgori anchyti *(n.)* **toothpick**
ናስትሮ nastro *(n.)* **ribbon**
ናስትሮ nastro *(n.)* **tape**
ናታ nata *(pron.)* **hers**
ናተይ natey *(pron.)* **mine**
ናተይ natey *(adj.)* **my**
ናትካ natk *(adj.)* **your**
ናፃ ለቀቀ natsa leqeqe *(v.)* **deregulate**
ናቱ natu *(adj.)* **his**
ናፃ natza *(adj.)* **free**
ናጻ natza *(n.)* **freebie**
ናጻ natza *(adj.)* **gratuitous**
ናፃ ምካድ natza mkad *(n.)* **impunity**
ናፅነት natzanet *(n.)* **freedom**
ናፅነት natzneg *(n.)* **manumission**
ና ወታደር ጃኬት nawetader jaket *(n.)* **tunic**
ናውቲ ጽሕፈት nawti tsȟfet *(n.)* **stationery**
ናውጼን nawxeen *(adj.)* **boisterous**
ናጻ ምልቃቕ naxa mlqaq̈ *(n.)* **acquittal**
ናይ ኣደ nay ade *(adj.)* **maternal**
ናይ ኣደ nay ade *(adj.)* **motherly**
ናይ ኣእምሮ nay a'emro *(adj.)* **mental**
ናይ ኣፍንጫ nay afnča *(adj.)* **nasal**
ናይ ዓሌት nay äleet *(adj.)* **ethnic**
ናይ ኣልኮል መስተ nay alkol meste *(n.)* **liquor**
ናይ ኣመጋግባ ኪኢላ nay amegagba ki'ila *(n.)* **dietician**
ናይ ኣምልኾት ቦታ nay amlkot bota *(n.)* **gurdwara**
ናይ ኣናእሽተይ ጀልባ መዕረፊ nay ana'ushtey jelba me'erefi *(n.)* **marina**
ናይ ዓንዲ ሑቀ nay ändi ȟuqe *(adj.)* **spinal**
ናይ ኣትክልቲ nay 'atklti *(n.)* **vegetable**
ናይ ዓፅሚ ጉንቦ ኢድ nay äxmi gunbo id *(adj.)* **carpal**
ናይ ባሕሪ nay bahri *(adj.)* **marine**

ናይ ባሕሪ ውግእ nay bahri wg'e *(adj.)* **naval**

ናይ ባይቶ nay bayto *(adj.)* **senatorial**

ናይ በዓል nay be'äl *(adj.)* **festive**

ናይ ቤት መዘጋጃ nay beet mezageja *(adj.)* **municipal**

ናይ ፍርዲ ቤት ኽልከላ nay bet ferdi khlkela *(n.)* **injunction**

ናይ ብሓቂ nay bḥaqi *(adj.)* **veracious**

ናይ ብርሃን ጨረር nay brhan cherer *(n.)* **laser**

ናይ ቡቲክ ኣሻንጉሊት nay butik ashangulit *(n.)* **mannequin**

ናይ ደብዳበ መግለጺ nay debdabe mglexi *(n.)* **pigeonhole**

ናይ ደገ ማዕፆ ዘለዎ ክፍሊ ገዛ nay dege ma'etso zelewo kfli geza *(n.)* **maisonette**

ናይ ደቂ ኣንስትዮ ስረ ብርኪ nay deki- anstyo sre brki *(n.)* **knickers**

ናይ ደምፂ ማዕበል nay demtsi maebel *(adj.)* **ultrasonic**

ናይ ደናግል ገዳም nay denagl gedam *(n.)* **convent**

ናይ ዶልሺ ሰራሒ nay dolshi serahi *(n.)* **confectioner**

ናይ ድቂ እንስትዮ ክዳን ዉሽጢ nay dqi anstyo kdan wushti *(n.)* **lingerie**

ናይ ዱር nay dur *(adj.)* **sylvan**

ናይ ዕዳጋ ማእኸል nay edaga ma'ekhel *(n.)* **mall**

ናይ እግረኛ መንግዲ nay egregna mengedi *(n.)* **kerb**

ናይ ዕልቋቅ nay 'elqaq *(adj.)* **seminal**

ናይ ዕምበባ ጌፀ nay embaba ge-tse *(n.)* **garland**

ናይ ዕንጨይቲ ሙዚቃ መሳርሒ nay encheyti muzika mesarhi *(n.)* **xylophone**

ናይ ዕንጨይቲ ነዋሪ nay encheyti newari *(adj.)* **xylophilous**

ናይ እንቃቁሖ ፃዕዳ nay enqaquho xa'eda *(n.)* **albumen**

ናይ እንስሳ ጫፍ ጡብ nay enssa chaf tub *(n.)* **teat**

ናይ እንስሳትን ኣትክልትን ዘፅንዕ nay enssat atkltn zesn'a *(n.)* **taxonomy**

ናይ ዕንፀይቲ nay entseyti *(adj.)* **wooden**

ናይ ፋንጋይ ሕማም nay fangay hmam *(n.)* **thrush**

ናይ ፈረንሳይ nay ferensay *(adj.)* **French**

ናይ ጋማ nay gama *(adj.)* **nuptial**

ናይ ግብረ ስጋ ሉዑል ድልየት ዘለዎ nay gbre sga l'eul dlyet zelewo *(adj.)* **lascivious**

ናይ ግብሪ nay gbri *(adj.)* **fiscal**

ናይ ግድን nay gdn *(adv.)* **necessarily**

ናይ ገባሪ ሰናይ nay gebari senay *(adj.)* **charitable**

ናይ ገበነኛታት፣ሰባት ስብስብ nay gebenegnatat sebeseb *(n.)* **gang**

ናይ ገበነኛ መፅናዕቲ nay gebenenya mexna'eti *(n.)* **criminology**

ናይ ገጠር nay geter *(adj.)* **rural**

ናይ ገጽ nay gex *(adj.)* **facial**

ናይ ገዛ እንስሳ nay geza enssa *(n.)* **pet**

ናይ ጉዕዞ ዉጥን nay go'ezo wutn *(n)* **itinerary**

ናይ ግጥሚ ቤት nay gtmi biet *(n.)* **stanza**

ናይ ጉዕዞ ሻንጣ nay gu'ezo shanta ***(n.)*** **luggage**
ናይ ጉጅለ nay gujle ***(adj.)*** **collective**
ናይ ጉልበት ሰራሕተኛ nay gulbet serahtegna ***(n.)*** **workman**
ናይ ጓል nay gwal ***(adj.)*** **girlish**
ናይ ሓባር nay ḧabar ***(adj.)*** **mutual**
ናይ ሓባር ብልጽግና nay ḧabar blxgna ***(n.)*** **commonwealth**
ናይ ሓደጋ nay ḧadega ***(adj.)*** **accidental**
ናይ ሓደጋ ምርመራ nay hadega mrmera ***(n.)*** **inquest**
ናይ ሃገረሰብ nay hagereseb ***(n.)*** **yokel**
ናይ ሓሶት nay hasot ***(adj.)*** **snide**
ናይ ሓሶት nay ĥasot ***(adj.)*** **fake**
ናይ ሓሶት ክሲ nay hasot ksi ***(n.)*** **libel**
ናይ ሓሶት ሽም nay ĥasot šm ***(n.)*** **pseudonym**
ናይ ሓይሊ nay ḧayli ***(adj.)*** **forcible**
ናይ ሃይማኖት ጠቢብ nay haymanot tebib ***(n.)*** **theologian**
ናይ ሒሳብ ኪኢላ nay ḧisab ki'ila ***(n.)*** **mathematician**
ናይ ሂወት ካብ ሞት ናብ ህያው ምዝዉዋር nay hiwet hab mot nab hyab mshiggar ***(n.)*** **transmigration**
ናይ ሕጂ nay ḧji ***(adj.)*** **present**
ናይ ህንፃ መተሓላለፊ nay hnxa meteḧalalefi ***(n.)*** **corridor**
ናይ ሕርሻ መኪና nay hrsha mekina ***(n.)*** **tractor**
ናይ ሕቶ ቃል nay ḧto qal ***(adj.)*** **interrogative**
ናይ ህዋ nay hwa ***(adj.)*** **spatial**
ናይ ህጻናት ዶክቶር nay hxanat doctor ***(n.)*** **paediatrician**
ናይ ኢድ nay 'id ***(adj.)*** **manual**
ናይ ኢድ ጨዋዳ nay 'id ciwada ***(n.)*** **triceps**
ናይ ጃጃዊ nay jajawi ***(adj.)*** **craven**
ናይ ጀልባ ሃበ nay jelba habe ***(n.)*** **yachting**
ናይ ጀልባ ሰብ nay jelba seb ***(n.)*** **yachtsman**
ናይ ጀልባ ታሕታዋይ ኣካል nay jelba tahtaway alkal ***(n.)*** **keel**
ናይ ካህናት nay kahnat ***(adj.)*** **clerical**
ናይ ክዳውንቲ nay kdawunti ***(adj.)*** **sartorial**
ናይ ከብዲ nay kebdi ***(a.)*** **abdominal**
ናይ ከዋኽብቲ ስብስብ nay kewakbti sebseb ***(n.)*** **galaxy**
ና ክልል ፖሊስ nay kll plis ***(n.)*** **trooper**
ናይ ኮንትራት nay kontrat ***(adj.)*** **contractual**
ናይ ክራይ nay kray ***(n.)*** **rental**
ናይ ክራይ ስምምዕነት nay kray smm'enet ***(n.)*** **lease**
ናይ ክሳድ nay ksad ***(adj.)*** **cervical**
ናይ ቅየሳ መሳርሒ nay kyesa mesarhi ***(n.)*** **theodolite**
ናይ ለይቲ nay leyti ***(adj.)*** **nocturnal**
ናይ ማእኸላይ ዘመን nay ma'ek̍elay zemen ***(adj.)*** **medieval**
ናይ ሜዳ ተኒስ ጨዋታ nay meda tenis chewata ***(n.)*** **tennis**
ናይ መገጣጥም nay megetatm ***(adj.)*** **rheumatic**
ናይ መጀመርታ nay mejemerta ***(adj.)*** **early**
ናይ መጀመርያ nay mejemerya ***(adj.)*** **preliminary**
ናይ ሜለ ገረብ nay mele gereb ***(n.)*** **pear**

ናይ መንፈስ(ኣእምሮ) ርክብ nay menfes aemro rkb *(n.)* **telepathy**
ናይ መቓብር nay meqabr *(adj.)* **sepulchral**
ናይ መርዓ nay mer'ä *(adj.)* **bridal**
ናይ መራኽብ nay meraḱb *(adj.)* **nautical**
ናይ መሬት ኣቀማምጣ nay meret akemamta *(n.)* **topography**
ናይ መሬት ኣቀማምጣ ዘርኢ ካርታ nay meret akemamta zerei karta *(adj.)* **topographical**
ናይ መሬት ኣቀማምጣ ዝፅንዕ ሙሁር nay meret akemamta zesna muhur *(n.)* **topographer**
ናይ መርዚ ፅንዓት nay merzi snat *(n.)* **toxicology**
ናይ መሰረት nay meseret *(adj.)* **radical**
ናይ መጥባሕቲ ሓኪም nay metbahti ȟakim *(n.)* **surgeon**
ናይ መትኒ nay metni *(adj.)* **neural**
ናይ መወዳእታ መጠንቀቕታ nay mewedaeta metenkekta *(n.)* **ultimatum**
ናይ መውስቦ nay mewsbo *(n.)* **spousal**
ናይ መጻኢ ፍልጠት nay mexaei flẗet *(n.)* **precognition**
ናይ መጻኢ ዝጥንቁል nay mexaei zẗnqul *(adj.)* **psychic**
ናይ ምህዞ nay mhzo *(adj.)* **fictitious**
ናይ ሙኳን ዕድል nay mkhuan edl *(n.)* **likelihood**
ናይ ምንቅጥቃጥ መሬት nay mnqtqat meriet *(adj.)* **seismic**
ናይ ምንጎ ግዜ nay mongo gzee *(adv.)* **meantime**
ናይ ሞተር መንቀሳቐሲ nay moter menqesaqesi *(n.)* **tappet**
ናይ ምቅልቃል ባህረ ኣበው nay mqlqal bahre 'abew *(adj.)* **atavistic**
ናይ ምርኣይ ዓቕሚ nay mr'ay 'äqmi *(n.)* **eyesight**
ናይ ምርባሕ nay mrbaȟ *(adj.)* **reproductive**
ናይ ሙቀት መለክዒ መሳርሒ nay muket melek'e mesarhi *(n.)* **thermometer**
ናይ ሙኳን ዕድል nay muḱuan ëdl *(n.)* **probability**
ናይ ሙዚቃ ግጥሚ nay muziqa gtmi *(n.)* **lyric**
ናይ ሙዚቃ ግጥሚ ገጣሚ nay muziqa gtmi getami *(n.)* **lyricist**
ናይ ናሕሲ ኣፍ nay naȟsi af *(adj.)* **palatal**
ናይ ንግዲ ዉዕሊ nay ngdi wualo *(n.)* **transaction**
ናይ ንግሪ ምልክት nay ngdimlkt *(n.)* **trademark**
ናይ እንስሳ ሽም nay nsesa shm *(n.)* **weasel**
ናይ ፓፓስ nay papas *(adj.)* **papal**
ናይ ጳጳስ ዘዉዲ nay papas zewdi *(n.)* **tiara**
ናይ ፕላኔታት nay planatan *(adj.)* **planetary**
ናይ ፖለቲካ nay polotika *(adj.)* **politic**
ናይ ቓላት nay qalat *(adj.)* **verbal**
ናይ ቅድሚት nay qdmit *(adj.)* **fore**
ናይ ቅድሚት መብራህቲ nay qdmit mebrahti *(n.)* **headlight**
ናይ ቀደም nay qedem *(adj.)* **former**
ናይ ቀደም nay qedem *(n.)* **predecessor**

ናይ ቀደም nay qedem ***(adj.)*** **quondam**
ናይ ቀልዲ nay qeldi ***(adj.)*** **facetious**
ናይ ቀልዲ ኣዘራርባ nay qeldi azerazba ***(n.)*** **pleasantry**
ናይ ቀረባ እዋን nay qereba ewan ***(adj.)*** **recent**
ናይ ቆርበት ፋብሪካ nay qorbet fabrika ***(n.)*** **tannery**
ናይ ቆርበት ኖኍል nay qorbet noḱual ***(n.)*** **pore**
ናይ ቋንቋ ሙሁር nay quanqua muhur ***(adj.)*** **linguist**
ናይ ርብዒ ዓመት nay rb'ï amet ***(adj.)*** **quarterly**
ናይ ሰብኣይ nay sb'ay ***(adj.)*** **manly**
ናይ ሰዓል ከረሜላ nay se'al keremiela ***(n.)*** **lozenge**
ናይ ሰገናት nay segenat ***(n.)*** **yob**
ናይሰለስተ ሙዚቃ nay seleste muziqa ***(n.)*** **trio**
ናይ ሰዉነት ጅማት nay sewunet jmat ***(n.)*** **tendon**
ናይ ሻምቦቆ ኣየር nay shamboqo ayer ***(adj.)*** **bronchial**
ናይ ሽንቲ nay shennti ***(adj.)*** **urinary**
ናይ ስኒ nay sni ***(adj.)*** **dental**
ናይ ስኒ ሓኪም nay sni ĥakim ***(n.)*** **dentist**
ናይ ስኒ ሕማም nay sni hmm ***(n.)*** **toothache**
ናይ ስኒ ሳሙና nay sni samuna ***(n.)*** **toothpaste**
ናይ ፁሑፍ ስምምዕነት nay suhuf smm'a ***(n.)*** **treaty**
ናይ ጣቋ ዘረባ nay takwa zereba ***(adj.)*** **rhetorical**
ናይ ቲፎ nay tifo ***(n.)*** **typhoid**
ናይ ፅዕንት መኪና nay ts'ent mekina ***(n.)*** **lorry**
ናይ ትሽትሽ nay tshtsh ***(adj.)*** **underarm**
ናይ ፆታዊ ርክብ ድሌት nay tsotawi rkb dliet ***(n.)*** **libido**
ናይ ውድድር ምርኢት nay wddr mr'it ***(n.)*** **rodeo**
ናይ ወደብ መድረኽ nay wedeb mdreke ***(n.)*** **pier**
ናይ ወዲ ንጉሳዊ nay wedi ngusawi ***(adj.)*** **princely**
ናይ ወዲ ስም nay wedi s'm ***(adj.)*** **Stuart**
ናይ ወኻርያ nay wek̔arya ***(adj.)*** **vulpine**
ናይ ውግእ nay wg'e ***(adj.)*** **martial**
ናይ ውልቀ nay wlqe ***(adj.)*** **solitary**
ናይ ውንዘፋ ጠለብ nay wnzefa teleb ***(n.)*** **caveat**
ናይ ዉሽጢ ዓዲ nay wshti ädi ***(adj.)*** **domestic**
ንይ ውሽጢ ክዳን nay wshti kdan ***(n.)*** **petticoat**
ናይ ውልቀ መምህር nay wulqe memher ***(adj)*** **tutorial**
ናይ ውሽጥኻ ዘይምዝራብ nay wushtkha zeymzrab ***(adv.)*** **insincerity**
ናይ ዉሽጡ ዘይዛረብ nay wushtu zeyzareb ***(adj.)*** **insincere**
ናይ ጻዕዳ ኢድ ጥንቁልና nay xaeda eid tnqulna ***(n.)*** **palmistry**
ናይ ፅዋ nay xwa ***(adj.)*** **mythical**
ናይ የዋህነት ተግባር nay yewahnet tegbar ***(n.)*** **largesse**
ናይ ዮጋ ሰብ nay yoga seb ***(n.)*** **yogi**
ናይ ዘርኢ nay zer'i ***(adj.)*** **genetic**

ንዓይ ዘይብል n'ay zeybl *(adj.)* **selfless**

ናይ ዝናብ ክዳን nay znab kdan *(n.)* **tarpaulin**

ናይ ዝናብ ክዳን nay znab kdan *(n.)* **mackintosh**

ናይ ሓንጎል nayei hanegole *(adj.)* **cerebral**

ናይ ቆልዓ nayei qolea' *(adj.)* **childish**

ናይ ማዕድን ከሰል nayi maeidin kesel *(n.)* **colliery**

ናይ ቆንስል ገዛ nayi qonsele geza *(n.)* **consulate**

ናይሎን naylon *(n.)* **nylon**

ናይ ማይ መትሓዚ ዓብዪ ጎማ naymay methazi abuyi goma *(n.)* **tanker**

ናይ መን naymen *(pron.)* **whose**

ናዮም nayom *(adj.)* **their**

ናይ ስራሕ ቦታ naysrah bota *(n.)* **workshop**

ናይታ ሃገር nayta hager *(n.)* **vernacular**

ናይትሮጅን naytrojn *(n.)* **nitrogen**

ንባዕሉ nba'ëlu *(pron.)* **itself**

ነባሒ nbahi *(n.)* **woofer**

ንብዓት nb'at *(n.)* **tear**

ንበይኑ nbeynu *(adv.)* **solely**

ንብረት nbret *(n.)* **asset**

ንቡር nbur *(adj.)* **normal**

ንቡር ኩነት nbur kunet *(n.)* **normalcy**

ንዝዙሓት ኣማልኽቲ ምምላኽ nbzuȟat amalḱti mm!aḱ *(n.)* **polytheism**

ንብዙሓት ኣማልኽቲ ዘምልኽ nbzuȟat amalḱti zemlḱ *(adj.)* **polytheistic**

ንጫብ n'cha'b *(n.)* **swag**

ንደገ ndege *(adv.)* **forth**

ንደገ ኣተንፈሰ ndege atenfese *(v.)* **exhale**

ንድፋዊ ndfawi *(adj.)* **schematic**

ንድፊ ndfi *(n.)* **design**

ንድፊ ndfi *(n.)* **draft**

ንድፊ ndfi *(n.)* **scheme**

ንድፊ ndfi *(n.)* **sketch**

ንድሕሪት ndȟrit *(adv.)* **aback**

ንድሕሪት ተመልሰ ndȟrit temelse *(v.)* **reverse**

ንድሕሪት ዘኣንፈቱ ndȟrit z'anfetu *(adj.)* **retrograde**

ንድሕሪት ዘይብል ndhrit zeybl *(v.i.)* **persevere**

ንድሕሪት ዝጥምት ndȟrit ztmt *(adj.)* **retrospective**

ንድሕሪት ndȟrit *(adj.)* **backward**

ነኣደ ne'ade *(v.)* **commend**

ነኣደ ne'ade *(v. i)* **compliment**

ነዓቐ neaqe *(v.)* **underestimate**

ነዓቐ neaqe *(v.)* **undermine**

ነዓቐ neaqe *(v.)* **underrate**

ነዓቐ ne'äqe *(v.)* **despise**

ነዓቒ ne'aqi *(adj.)* **contemptuous**

ነብዐ neb'a *(v.)* **tear**

ነባዒ neba'ï *(adj.)* **lachrymose**

ነባር nebar *(adj.)* **chronic**

ነበልባል nebelbal *(n.)* **flame**

ነበረ nebere *(v.)* **dwell**

ነበረ nebere *(v.)* **live**

ነበረ nebere *(v.)* **reside**

ንብረት/ንዋይ neberet/newaye *(n.)* **chattel**

ነበርቲ neberti *(n.)* **inhabitant**

ነብሐ nebhe *(v.)* **yap**

ነቢይ nebie *(n.)* **prophet**

ነብሪ nebri *(n.)* **tiger**

ነብስኻ ምምርማር nebsḱa mmrmar *(n.)* **introspection**
ነብስኻ ምቁጽጻር nebska mqutstsar *(n.)* **temperance**
ነብሱ መርመረ nebsu mermere *(v.)* **introspect**
ነቡላ nebula *(n.)* **nebula**
ነዳድ nedad *(adj.)* **apoplectic**
ነዳድ nedad *(adj.)* **cantankerous**
ነዳዲ nedadi *(adj.)* **combustible**
ነዳዲ nedadi *(n.)* **fuel**
ነዳዲ ዘይቲ nedadi zyti *(n.)* **petroleum**
ነዳ'እ ሓርማዝ neda'e harmaz *(n.)* **mahout**
ነዳቃይ nedaqay *(n.)* **mason**
ነዲ nedi *(n.)* **rubric**
ነድሪ nedri *(n.)* **paddy**
ነድሪ ጭራምዑት nedri čram'ut *(n.)* **appendicitis**
ነድሪ ኮንጃንክቲቫ nedri konjanktiva *(n.)* **conjunctivitis**
ነድሪ ሳንቡእ nedri sanbuè *(n.)* **pneumonia**
ኔክታር neektar *(n.)* **nectar**
ኔፕትዩን neeptyun *(n.)* **Neptune**
ነፋሪት nefarit *(n.)* **aeroplane**
ነፋሪት nefarit *(n.)* **aircraft**
ነፋሪት nefarit *(n.)* **plane**
ነፋሻ nefasha *(adj.)* **airy**
ነፋፂ nefatsi *(adj.)* **skittish**
ነፈረ nefere *(v.i)* **fly**
ነፈሰ nefese *(v.)* **blow**
ነፈየ nefeye *(v.)* **sift**
ነፍሐ nefhe *(v.)* **inflate**
ነፍሐ nefḧe *(v.)* **blare**
ነፍሪ nefri *(n.)* **anthrax**
ነፍሲ nefsi *(n.)* **soul**
ነጋዳይ negaday *(n.)* **dealer**
ነጋዳይ አክስዮን negaday aksyon *(n.)* **stockbroker**
ነጋዳይ negaday *(n.)* **businessman**
ነጋዴ negade *(n.)* **trader**
ነጋዴ negade *(n.)* **tradesman**
ነጋዲ negadi *(n.)* **merchant**
ነገራት negerat *(n.)* **stuff**
ነገረ negere *(v.)* **tell**
ነገረኛ negeregna *(adj.)* **provocative**
ነገረኛ negerenya *(adj.)* **belligerent**
ነገሰ negese *(v.)* **reign**
ነግሒ negĥi *(n.)* **furrow**
ነጎድጓድ negodgad *(n.)* **thunder**
ነጎድጓዳዊ negodgadawi *(adj.)* **thunderous**
ነግራም negram *(n.)* **shrew**
ነግራም negram *(adj.)* **strident**
ነሃባይ nehabay *(n.)* **smith**
ነሃባይ ወርቂ nehabay werqi *(n.)* **goldsmith**
ነሓሰ neḧase *(n)* **August**
ነሓሲ neḧasi *(n.)* **copper**
ነኳል nekal *(n.)* **puncture**
ነኸሰ neḱese *(v.)* **bite**
ነከየ nekeye *(v.)* **decrease**
ነከየ nekeye *(v.)* **diminish**
ነከየ nekeye *(v. t)* **dwindle**
ነከየ nekeye *(v.)* **reduce**
ነኪኡ nekiau *(v.)* **touch**
ነኟል neḱual *(n.)* **hole**
ንዕለቱ ኣቀደመ n'ëletu 'aqedeme *(v.)* **backdate**
ናብ ዓፅሚ ምቕያር nab atsmi mqyar *(v.)* **ossify**
ናብ ደገ nab dege *(adj.)* **outward**
ናትና natna *(adj.)* **our**
ናይ nay *(prep.)* **of**
ናይ ሓደ ሰብ ግዴታ nay hade seb gdieta *(n.)* **onus**

ናይ ሙዚቃ 8ኖታታት በቢ 2 ኖታ ዝፈላለዩ ney muziqa 8notatat bebi 2 nota zfelaleyu ***(n.)*** **octave**

ናይ ዓይኒ nay ayni ***(adj.)*** **ocular**

ናይ ዓይኒ ሓኪም nay ayni hakim ***(n.)*** **optician**

ናይ ዓፅምን መግጣጠምን ሕክምና nay atsmn megetatemin hkmna ***(n.)*** **osteopathy**

ናይ ዕምበባ ዓይነት nay embaba aynet ***(n.)*** **orchid**

ናይ እንቋቑሖ ቅርጺ nay enquaquho qrtsi ***(adj.)*** **oval**

ናይ እንቋቑሖ ቅርጺ nay enquaquho qrtsi ***(adj.)*** **ovate**

ናይ ጀልባ በትሪ nay jelba betri ***(n.)*** **oar**

ንሕና nhna ***(pron.)*** **ourselves**

ንላዕሊ nla'eli ***(prep.)*** **over**

ንቕድሚት nqdmit ***(adv.)*** **onward**

ንትጓ ntuag ***(n.)*** **outburst**

ንድፊ ndfi ***(n.)*** **outline**

ንጹግ ntsug ***(n.)*** **outcast**

አ

ኣብ ስልጣን ኣደየበ 'ab slṭan 'adeyebe ***(v.)*** **install**

ኣበር ዘይብሉ 'aber zeyblu ***(adj.)*** **impeccable**

ኣብነት 'abnet ***(n.)*** **instance**

ኣብዚ 'abzi ***(adv.)*** **here**

ኣቸቶ 'acheto ***(n.)*** **vinegar**

ኣደራሽ 'aderash ***(n.)*** **hall**

ኣድልዎ ዘይብሉ 'adlwo zeyblu ***(adj.)*** **impartial**

ኣዕናዊ 'a'ënawi ***(n.)*** **vandal**

ኣእንጋዲ 'a'èngadi ***(adj.)*** **hospitable**

ኣፍቃሪ 'afqari ***(n.)*** **valentine**

ኣፍራሒ 'afraḥi ***(adj.)*** **horrific**

ኣፍርሐ 'afrḥe ***(v.)*** **horrify**

ኣጉልሐ 'agulḥe ***(v.)*** **highlight**

ኣሓጐሰ 'aḧagwase ***(v.)*** **gladden**

ኣሕመቐ 'aḥmeq̈e ***(v.)*** **vitiate**

ኣካይዳ ተመን ከደ 'akayda temen kede ***(v.)*** **wriggle**

ኣኽበበ 'aḱbebe ***(v.)*** **wreathe**

ኣኽበረ 'aḱbere ***(v.)*** **venerate**

ኣኽበረ 'aḱbere ***(v.)*** **glorify**

ኣልዓለ 'al'äle ***(v.)*** **heave**

ኣላይ ክዳውንቲ 'alay kdawnti ***(n.)*** **valet**

ኣሎዎ... 'alowo ***(v.)*** **have**

ኣመሳኸረ 'amesaḱere ***(v.)*** **verify**

ኣምለጠ amleṫe ***(v.i)*** **escape**

ኣነ 'ane ***(pron.)*** **I**

ኣንፈት ቀየረ 'anfet qeyere ***(v.)*** **veer**

ኣንገርገረ 'angergere ***(v.)*** **wallow**

ኣቕሓ 'aq̈ḧa ***(n.)*** **commodity**

ኣራዊት 'arawit ***(n.)*** **vermin**

ኣረድአ 'ared'e ***(n.)*** **illustrate**

ኣርማድዮ ክዳውንቲ 'armadyo kdawnti ***(n.)*** **wardrobe**

ኣሰላፊት 'aselafit ***(n.)*** **waitress**

ኣሰር 'aser ***(n.)*** **vestige**

ኣሻንና 'ashanna ***(n.)*** **valuation**

ኣሻቐለ 'ashaq̈ele ***(v.)*** **haunt**

ኣተባብዐ 'atebab'ë ***(v.)*** **hearten**

ኣተባብዐ 'atebab'ë ***(v.)*** **inspire**

ኣጠንቀቐ 'aṭenqeq̈ ***(v.)*** **warn**

ኣዋረደ 'awarede ***(v.)*** **vilify**

ኣወጣወጠ 'aweṭaweṭe ***(v.)*** **waggle**

ኣየር ዘየሕልፍ 'ayer zeyeḥlf ***(adj.)*** **hermetic**

ኣዝዩ 'azyu ***(adv.)*** **very**

ኤለትሪክ -መስፈር 'eeletrik- mesfer ***(n.)*** **wattage**

እኽሊ 'èḱli *(n.)* **grain**
እናጠፍአት ከደት 'ènaṭef'et kedet *(v.)* **wane**
እሳተ-ጎመራ 'èsategomera *(n.)* **volcano**
እስትሕጋግ 'èsthgag *(n.)* **gratuity**
ኣብ ምቅርራብ 'ab mqrrab *(adv.)* **afoot**
ኣብ ዙርያ 'ab zurya *(adv.)* **around**
ኣሕነኽ 'aḧneḱe *(adj.)* **abash**
ኣኮኣዊ 'ako'awi *(adj.)* **avuncular**
ኣባጨጓራ aaba'che'guara *(n.)* **caterpillar**
ኣዕለለ/ኣዉገዐ aae'lele/aawugeaa' *(v. i.)* **chat**
ኣገደደ aagedede *(v.)* **constrain**
ኣጓየየ aaguwayeye *(v.)* **chase**
ኣካተተ aakate'te *(v.)* **consist**
ኣማኸረ aamake're *(v.)* **consult**
ኣአንገደ a'anged *(v.)* **entertain**
ኣራኽበ aara'eh'kebe *(v.)* **connect**
ኣታለለ aatalele *(v.)* **cheat**
ኣእትዩ aatyu *(v.)* **tuck**
ኣዋረደ aawarede *(v. t.)* **cheapen**
ኣውቲስታ aawutiseta *(n.)* **chauffeur**
ኣብ ኤስያ ዝርከብ ቤተ ጸሎት ab asya zrkeb bete tselot *(n.)* **pagoda**
ኣብ ባሕሪ ስርቂ ab bahri srqi *(n.)* **piracy**
ኣብ ባይታ 'ab bayta *(adj.)* **aground**
ኣብ ድሕረ መድረኽ ab dḧre medreḱ *(adv.)* **backstage**
ኣብ ዕዳ ዛኣተወ ab eda z'atewe *(adj.)* **indebted**
ኣብ እዋን ab ewan *(prep.)* **during**
ኣብ ፎቅ ዝካረ መንበሪ ab foq zkare menberi *(n.)* **tenement**
ኣብ ገበን ምሽራኽ ab geben mshrak *(adj.)* **complicit**
ኣብ ገምገም ab gemgem *(adv.)* **ashore**
ኣብ ገምገም ባሕሪ ዝርከብ ab gemgem bahiri zirkeb *(n.)* **coaster**
ኣብ ግምት ብዘይምእታው 'ab gmt bzeym'ètaw *(adj.)* **irrespective**
ኣብ ግርዝውና ዝቦቁል ጸጉሪ ab grzwna zboqul xeguri *(adj.)* **pubic**
ኣብ ጐድኒ ab gwadni *(prep.)* **alongside**
ኣብ ሓደ ቦታ ዝተተከለ ናብ ካሊእ ቦታ ነቂልካ ምትካል ab hade bota ztetekele nab kalie bota neklka mtkal *(v.)* **transplant**
ኣብ ሓደጋ ኣውደቐ 'ab ḧadega 'awdeq̈e *(v.)* **jeopardize**
ኣብ ሓደጋ ጠሓለ ab hadega tehale *(v.)* **imperil**
ኣብ ሂማልያ ዝነብር እንስሳ ab himalya zeneber ensesa *(n.)* **yeti**
ኣብ ካፕሱላ ዓጸወ 'ab kapsula 'äxewe *(v.)* **encapsulate**
ኣብ ክክልተ 'ab keklte *(comb.)* **bi**
ኣብ ክክልት ዓመት ab keklte 'ämet *(adj.)* **biannual**
ኣብ ክንዲ ab kndi *(n.)* **behalf**
ኣብ ክንዲ ab kndi *(adv.)* **instead**
ኣብ ክንዲ ab kndi *(n.)* **stead**
ኣብ ክሳድ ዝእሰር ፎቶ ዝሓዘ መጋይፂ ab ksasd zeseer foto zelowo mgayetsi *(n.)* **locket**
ኣብ ኩሎም ኣማልኽቲ ምእማን ab kulom amalkti meman *(n.)* **pantheism**
ኣብ ኩሎም ኣማልኽቲ ዝኣምን ab kulom amalkti zamn *(adj.)* **pantheist**
ኣብ ኩሉ ህልዊ ab kulu hlwi *(adj.)* **omnipresent**

አብ ኩሉ ምህላው ab kulu mhlaw *(n.)* **omnipresence**
አብ ልዕሊ ab la'eli *(n.)* **top**
አብ ላዕሊ ab la'ëli *(adv.)* **above**
አብ ልዕሊ ab l'eli *(prep.)* **on**
አብ ልዕሊ 'ab l'ëli *(adv.)* **aboard**
አብ ማይ ዝነብር እንስሳ ab may znebr ensesa *(n.)* **oyster**
አብ መንጎ ab mengo *(prep.)* **among**
አብ መንጎ 'ab mengo *(prep.)* **amid**
አብ መንጎ 'ab mengo *(adv.)* **between**
አብመንጎ ቤተሰብ ዝግበር ግብረ ስጋ ab mengo beteseb zgber gbre-sga *(n.)* **incest**
አብ መርከብ ab merkeb *(adv.)* **overboard**
አብ መወዳእታ ab meweda'ta *(adv.)* **eventually**
አብ ሞንጎ ab mongo *(adv.)* **midway**
አብ መንጎ መፀ ab mongo mexe *(v.)* **supervene**
አብ ነፍሳት ዝነብሩ ፍጥረት ab nefsat znebru ftret *(n.)* **parasite**
አብ ቀረባ ab qereba *(adv.)* **nigh**
አብ ቀረባ እዋን ab qereba ewan *(adv.)* **recently**
አብ ሰዓቱ ab seätu *(adj.)* **punctual**
አብ ሰዓቱ ዝርከብ ab seätu zrkeb *(n.)* **punctuality**
አብ ስጋ ዝቕባእ ዘይቲ ab sga zqhba'e zeyti *(n.)* **marinade**
አብ ስምምዕ ዘይምብፃሕ ab smmë zeymbtsah *(n.)* **deadlock**
አብ ስራሕ ዝወዓለ ab srah zwe'ale *(adj.)* **operational**
አብ ታሕቲ ab tahti *(adv.)* **down**
አብ ጥቃ ab ẗqa *(adv.)* **near**
አብ ጥቓ ab ẗqa *(prep.)* **beside**
አብ ፅሑፍ ዝሰፈረ ab tshuf zsefere *(n.)* **transcript**
አብ ወሰን ዝርከብ ab wesen zrkeb *(adj.)* **outlying**
አብ ዉሽጢ ab wushti *(prep.)* **in**
አብ ውሽጢ ገዛ ab wushti geza *(adj.)* **indoor**
አብ ዘይቦቱኡ አቀመጠ ab zey bot'u aqemeẗe *(v.)* **misplace**
አብ ዘይቲ አለኸ ab zeyti aleke *(v.)* **marinate**
አብ ዝኾነ ዘይርከብ ab zkone zeyrkeb *(adv.)* **nowhere**
አብ ዝቅፅል ab zqxl *(prep.)* **after**
አብ ዙርያ ab zurya *(adv.)* **about**
አብ ab *(prep.)* **at**
አባ ሸማኔ aba shemanie *(n.)* **leopard**
ዓብዓበ äb'äbe *(v.)* **swaddle**
አባጨወ 'abačewe *(v.)* **jeer**
አባጨወ aba'chewe *(v.i.)* **scoff**
አባደመ abademe *(v.)* **devastate**
አባዕለገ aba'ëlege *(v.)* **deprave**
አባኻኒ abakani *(adj.)* **prodigal**
አባኻኒ abaḱani *(adj.)* **profligate**
አባኸነ abakene *(v.)* **fritter**
አባኸነ abakene *(v.)* **waste**
አባኸነ aba'khene *(v.)* **squander**
አባኾበራ abakobera *(n.)* **cyclone**
አባል abal *(n.)* **member**
አባል ባይቶ abal bayto *(n.)* **senator**
አባል ቤት ምኽሪ abal beet mkri *(n.)* **councillor**
አባል ፈራዶ abal ferado *(n.)* **juror**
አባል ሕጊ አፅዳቒ abal higi atsdaqhi *(n.)* **legislator**
አባል ኮነ 'abal kone *(v.)* **join**
አባል ምንቅስቓስ abal mnqsq̈as *(n.)* **activist**

አባል ፓርላማ abal parlama ***(n.)*** **parliamentarian**
አብዓለ 'ab'äle ***(v.)*** **celebrate**
አባለተ abalete ***(v.)*** **satirize**
አባልገ abalge ***(n.)*** **godfather**
አባልገ abalge ***(n.)*** **godmother**
አባልነት abalnet ***(n.)*** **membership**
አባረረ abarere ***(v.)*** **dispel**
አባረረ abarere ***(v. t)*** **eject**
አባረረ abarere ***(v.)*** **evict**
አባረረ abarere ***(v. t)*** **expel**
አባረረ abarere ***(v.)*** **repulse**
አባረረ abarere ***(v.)*** **sack**
አባዝሐ abazĥe ***(v.)*** **propagate**
አበጋሲ abegasi ***(n.)*** **setter**
አበ-ገዳም 'abegedam ***(n.)*** **abbot**
አበሃህላ abehahla ***(n.)*** **jargon**
አበላሸወ abelashewe ***(v.)*** **mar**
አበላሸወ abelashewe ***(v.)*** **spoil**
አበላሸወ abelashewe ***(v.)*** **undo**
አበላሸወ 'abelashewe ***(v.)*** **vandalize**
አበር ምህላው aber mhlaw ***(n.)*** **imperfection**
አበር ዘለዎ aber zelewo ***(adj.)*** **imperfect**
አበር ዘውፅእ aber zewx'e ***(adj.)*** **censorious**
አበር aber ***(n.)*** **blemish**
አበራበረ aberabere ***(v.)*** **liven**
አበራበረ aberabere ***(v.)*** **arouse**
አበረኛ aberegna ***(adj.)*** **defective**
አበረኸ abereke ***(v.)*** **elevate**
አበርትዐ aberte'ë ***(v.)*** **reinforce**
አበሳጨወ abesaĉewe ***(v.)*** **embitter**
አበሳጨወ abesaĉewe ***(v.)*** **exasperate**
አበሳጨወ abesaĉewe ***(v.)*** **frustrate**
አበው abew ***(n.)*** **ancestor**
አበው abew ***(n.)*** **paisley**
አበዋት abewat ***(n.)*** **ancestry**
አበዋዊ abewawi ***(adj.)*** **ancestral**
አበይ abey ***(adv.)*** **where**
አበይ ከምዘሎ abey kemzelo ***(adv.)*** **whereabouts**
አበየ abeye ***(v.)*** **refuse**
አብለጭሊጩ ablechlichu ***(v.)*** **twinkle**
አብለሐ ableh ***(v.)*** **sharpen**
አብለሐ ablehe ***(v.)*** **whet**
አብነት abnet ***(n.)*** **example**
አብነት abnet ***(n.)*** **quintessence**
አብኖስ a'bnos ***(n.)*** **ebony**
አቦ abo ***(n)*** **dad**
አቦ abo ***(n.)*** **father**
አቦ ጋቡየ abo gabuye ***(n.)*** **tortoise**
አቦወንበር abo' weneber ***(n.)*** **chairman**
አቦአዊ aboawi ***(adj.)*** **paternal**
አቦሓጎ 'aboȟago ***(n.)*** **forefather**
አቦነት abonet ***(n.)*** **paternity**
አብራህረሀ abrahereh ***(v.)*** **clarify**
አብራህረሀ abrahrehe ***(v.)*** **demystify**
አብራህረሀ abrahrehe ***(v. t)*** **elucidate**
አብራህረሀ abrahrehe ***(v.)*** **explain**
አብረሀ abrehe ***(v.)*** **lighten**
አብረሰ abrese ***(v.t.)*** **ravage**
አብርሀ abrhe ***(v.)*** **illuminate**
አብሰለ absele ***(v.)*** **cook**
አብሺቁ abshiqu ***(v.)*** **traduce**
አብቲ ማዕዶ abti maedo ***(adj.)*** **yonder**
አብፀሐ abtseĥe ***(v.)*** **deliver**
አብኡ ab'u ***(adv.)*** **there**
አቡን abun ***(n.)*** **bishop**
አቡቐለም abuqhelem ***(n.)*** **squid**
አብዮታዊ abyotawi ***(adj.)*** **revolutionary**

አብዚ እዋን abzi èwan *(adv.)* **presently**
አብዚ ከባቢ'ዚ abzi kebabizi *(adv.)* **hereabouts**
አብዚሕካ ገንዘብ ምውጻእ abziĥka genzeb mwtsas'e *(v.)* **overdraw**
ኣጨብጨበ ačebčebe *(v.)* **applaud**
ኣጨፈቐ ačefeq̈e *(adj.)* **bedraggled**
ኣጨናነቐ aĉenaneqe *(v.)* **fluster**
ኣጨነቐ ačeneq̈e *(v.)* **ail**
ኣጨንገፈት ačengefet *(v.)* **miscarry**
ኣቻዮ achayo *(n.)* **steel**
ኣቸጋሪ ሰብ achegari seb *(n.)* **tormentor**
ኣጨነቐ ač̣heneq̈e *(v.)* **harass**
ኣጭለምለመ aĉlemleme *(v.t)* **flicker**
ኣዳኸመ adakeme *(v.)* **debilitate**
ኣዳኸመ adakeme *(v.)* **emasculate**
ኣዳኸመ adakeme *(v.)* **enfeeble**
አዳላዊ ቐብሪ adalawi qebri *(n.)* **undertaker**
ኣዳለወ adalewe *(v.)* **discriminate**
ኣዳለወ adalewe *(v.)* **prepare**
ኣዳመፀ adametze *(v.)* **listen**
ኣድቀለ adaqele *(v.)* **replicate**
ኣደራሽ adarash *(n.)* **gallery**
ኣዳራሽ መቃብር adarash meqabr *(n.)* **mausoleum**
አዳራሽ adarashe *(n.)* **chamber**
ኣደ ade *(n.)* **mother**
ኣደበ adebe *(v.)* **chasten**
ኣደዳ adeda *(n.)* **victimize**
ኣደፋፈረ adefafere *(v.)* **abet**
ኣደፋፈረ adefafere *(v.)* **embolden**
ኣደሃሀረ adehahere *(v.)* **enliven**
ኣደኽደኸ adekhdekhe *(v.)* **stunt**
ኣደማምጻ ademamxa *(n.)* **pronunciation**
ኣደመ ademe *(v.)* **revolt**
ኣደመ ademe *(v.)* **boycott**
ኣደናገረ adenagere *(v.)* **confuse**
ኣደናገረ adenagere *(v.)* **discomfit**
ኣደናገረ adenagere *(v.)* **rig**
ኣደናገረ 'adenagere *(v.)* **juggle**
ኣደናጎየ adenagoye *(v.)* **prorogue**
ኣደናጎየ adenagueye *(v.)* **procrastinate**
ኣደነት adeneet *(n.)* **motherhood**
ኣደነቐ adeneq̈e *(v.)* **astonish**
ኣደንጋጽነት adengaxnet *(n.)* **poignancy**
ኣደንጎየ adengoye *(v. t)* **delay**
ኣደንጎየ adengoye *(v.)* **reprieve**
ኣደንጎየ adengoye *(v.)* **temporize**
ኣደንዛዚ adenzazi *(adj.)* **lethargic**
ኣደንዛዚ adenzazi *(adj.)* **stunning**
ኣደንዛዚ ነገር adenzazi neger *(n.)* **narcotic**
ኣደንዘዘ adenzeze *(v.)* **stun**
ኣደንዘዘ adenzeze *(v.)* **stupefy**
ኣደቃሲ adeqasi *(adj.)* **soporific**
ኣድጊ በረኸ adgi bereka *(n.)* **zebra**
ኣድጊ adgi *(n.)* **donkey**
ኣድሓነ adhane *(v.)* **salvage**
ኣድሓነ adhane *(v.)* **save**
ኣድሓነ adĥane *(v.)* **redeem**
ኣድሓነ adĥane *(v.)* **rescue**
ኣድሓኒ adhani *(n.)* **saviour**
ኣድሓርሓረ adĥarĥare *(v.t.)* **retreat**
ዓዲ ወዓለ ädi weale *(v.)* **retire**
ዓዲ ውዒልነት ädi wealnet *(n.)* **retirement**
ኣድካሚ 'adkam *(adj.)* **laborious**
ኣድካሚ adkami *(adj.)* **menial**
ኣድካሚ adkami *(adj.)* **strenuous**
ኣድካሚ adkami *(adj.)* **tiresome**
ኣድካሚ adkami *(adj.)* **trying**

አድካሚ adkami *(adj.)* **arduous**
አድከመ adkeme *(v.)* **exhaust**
አድከመ adkeme *(v.)* **impair**
አድከመ adkeme *(v.)* **weaken**
አድከየ adkeye *(v.)* **impoverish**
አድላይ adlay *(adj.)* **germane**
አድላዪ adlayi *(adj.)* **necessary**
አድላዪ adlayi *(adj.)* **pertinent**
አድላዪ adlayi *(adj.)* **requisite**
አድላዪ adlayi *(n.)* **significant**
አድላዪ ነገር adlayi neger *(n.)* **requisite**
አድላዪነት adlaynet *(n.)* **necessity**
አድላይነት adlaynet *(n.)* **significance**
አድለየ adleye *(v.)* **necessitate**
አድማ adma *(n.)* **mutiny**
አድማዒነት adma'ïnet *(n.)* **efficacy**
አድማሳዊ admasawi *(adj.)* **cosmic**
አድማፂ admatsi *(n.)* **revolution**
አድማፂ adma'txi *(adj.)* **constituent**
አድማጺ admaxi *(n.)* **vowel**
አድመፀ admexe *(v.)* **enunciate**
አድመጸ admexe *(v.)* **pronounce**
አዳሚ admi *(adj.)* **mutinous**
አድሚራል admiral *(n.)* **admiral**
አድናቖት adnakot *(n.)* **wonder**
አድናቒ adnaqi *(n.)* **fan**
አድናቖት adnaq̈ot *(n.)* **admiration**
አድነቐ adneq̈e *(v.)* **admire**
አድንቆ adnqo *(n.)* **astonishment**
አድራሻ adrash *(n.)* **location**
አድራሻ adrasha *(n.)* **domicile**
አድራሻ adrasha *(n.)* **address**
አድሪ adri *(n.)* **mustard**
አዕበየ aëbeye *(v.)* **enlarge**
አዕበየ a'ëbeye *(v.)* **nurture**
አዕደየ a'edeye *(v.)* **levy**
አዕገበ a'egebe *(v.)* **satisfy**
አዐገሰ a'ëgese *(v.)* **relieve**
አዕጀውጀወ ለፍለፈ 'a'ëğewğewe leflef *(v.)* **waffle**
አዕጎምጎመ a'ëgomgome *(v.)* **mutter**
አእካል ዝበልዕ aekal zibel'e *(n.)* **weevil**
አእላፍ aelaf *(n.)* **aeon**
አዕለቕለቐ 'a'ëleq̈leq̈e *(v.)* **inundate**
አእመነ aemene *(v.)* **persuade**
አእመነ aemene *(v.)* **urge**
አእመነ a'emene *(v.)* **convince**
አእምሮ a'emro *(n.)* **mind**
አእምሮአዊ a'emro'awi *(adj.)* **intellectual**
አዕሚቑ ዝሓስብ a'ëmuqu zhasb *(adj.)* **reflective**
አዕናዊ a'ënawi *(n.)* **destroyer**
አዕነወ aenewe *(v.)* **zap**
አዕነወ a'ënewe *(v.)* **demolish**
አዕነወ a'ënewe *(v.)* **destroy**
አአንጋዲ a'engadi *(n.)* **host**
አአንጋዲነት a'engadinet *(n.)* **hospitality**
አአንጋዲት a'engadit *(n.)* **hostess**
አዐንዘዘ ae-nzeze *(v.)* **hypnotize**
አዐንዘዘ a'ënzeze *(v.)* **mesmerize**
አዕረፈ a'ërefe *(v.)* **rest**
አዕረገ 'a'ërege *(v.)* **escalate**
አዐረየ a'ërye *(v.)* **rectify**
አዐርዩ ተዓዘበ aëryu teäzebe *(v.)* **peer**
አዕጠቀ a'ëteqe *(v.)* **equip**
አዕጠይጠየ aëteteye *(v.)* **dally**
አእተወ a'etewe *(v.)* **implant**
አእተወ a'etewe *(v.)* **infuse**
አእተወ a'ètewe *(v.)* **involve**
አዕጠይጠየ a'ëteyteye *(v.)* **dawdle**
አዕወልወለ a'ëwelwele *(v.)* **nauseate**
አእወየ aeweye *(n.)* **yell**

አይዋይ aeweye *(n.)* **yelp**
ኣእወየ a'eweye *(v.)* **scream**
ኣእወየ a'eweye *(v.i.)* **shout**
ኣእወየ a'eweye *(v.)* **shriek**
ኣዕዛዚ a'ëzazi *(n.)* **booster**
ኣዕዘምዘመ a'ëzemzeme *(v.)* **babble**
ኣዕዘዘ a'ëzeze *(v.)* **boost**
ኣዕዘዘ a'ëzeze *(v.)* **maximize**
ኣፍ af *(n.)* **gob**
ኣፍ a'f *(n.)* **mouth**
ኣፍ ጡብ a'f ťub *(n.)* **nipple**
ኣፍ ቱቦ af tubo *(n.)* **nozzle**
ኣፋፍኖት afafenote *(n.)* **clue**
ኣፋኾሰ afakose *(v.)* **simplify**
ኣፋኰሰ afakwase *(v.)* **allay**
ኣፋለጠ afaleťe *(v.)* **acquaint**
ኣፋለጠ afaleťe *(v.)* **introduce**
ኣፋለጠ afaleťe *(v.)* **advertise**
ዓፋን ድምጺ äfan dmxi *(n.)* **muffler**
ኣፍደገ afdege *(n.)* **lobby**
ኣፍደገ afdege *(n.)* **portal**
ኣፍደገ afdege *(n.)* **threshold**
ኣፈ ሙዝ afe muz *(n.)* **muzzle**
ኣፈዳድላ afedadla *(n.)* **spelling**
ኣፈላላይ afelalay *(n.)* **difference**
ኣፈላላይ afelalay *(n.)* **discrepancy**
ኣፈላላይ afelalay *(n.)* **disparity**
ኣፈላላይ afelalay *(n.)* **segregation**
ኣፈራረሐ aferarehe *(v.)* **intimidate**
ኣፈራርሐ aferarhe *(v.)* **threaten**
ኣፈሸለ afeshele *(v.)* **foil**
ኣፍቀረ afkere *(v.)* **dote**
ኣፍኮሰ afkose *(v.)* **slacken**
ኣፍላቒ aflaq̈i *(n.)* **prompter**
ኣፍልቢ aflebi *(n.)* **chest**
ኣፍለጠ aflete *(v.)* **proclaim**
ኣፍለጠ afleťe *(v.)* **apprise**
ኣፍልጦ aflto *(n.)* **recognition**
ኣፍንጫ afnča *(n.)* **nose**
ኣፍቃዲ afqadi *(adj.)* **permissive**
ኣፍቃሪ afqari *(n.)* **lover**
ኣፍቃሪ afqari *(n.)* **soul mate**
ኣፍቀደ afqede *(v.)* **permit**
ኣፍቀረ afqere *(v.t.)* **adore**
ኣፍቀረ af'qere *(v.)* **cherish**
ኣፍራዪ afrayi *(n.)* **producer**
ኣፍራይነት afraynet *(n.)* **productivity**
ኣፍረሐ afreĥe *(v.)* **frighten**
ኣፍረሰ afrese *(v.)* **rescind**
ኣፍረየ afreye *(v.)* **generate**
ኣፍርየ afreye *(v.)* **produce**
ኣፍረየ afreye *(v.)* **synthesize**
ኣፍረየ afreye *(v.)* **yield**
ኣፍርሐ afrhe *(v.)* **unnerve**
ኣፍሪካዊ afrikawi *(adj.)* **African**
ኣፍሸለ afšele *(v.)* **refute**
ኣፍሰሰ a'fsese *(v.)* **spill**
ኣፍሸለ afshele *(v.)* **disprove**
ኣፍጠጠ aftete *(v.)* **ogle**
ኣጋ ምሸት aga mshet *(n.)* **dusk**
ኣጋዕዘየ aga'ëzeye *(v.)* **disarrange**
ኣጋፋሪ 'agafari *(n.)* **chamberlain**
ኣጋገየ agageye *(v.)* **disorientate**
ኣጋገየ agageye *(v.)* **garble**
ኣጋገየ agageye *(v.)* **misdirect**
ኣጋገየ agageye *(v.)* **misguide**
ኣጋላባይ agalabay *(n.)* **jockey**
ኣጋነነ aganene *(v.)* **exaggerate**
ኣጋነነ aganene *(v.)* **overact**
ኣጋር agar *(n.)* **pedestrian**
ኣጋር መንገዲ agar mengedi *(n.)* **path**
ኣጋጣሚ agatami *(n.)* **incident**
ኣጋጣሚ agatami *(n.)* **occasion**
ኣጋዋሒ agawaĥi *(adj.)* **resonant**
ኣጋውሐ agawĥe *(v.)* **reverberate**

አግባባ ዘይብሉ ኣሰራርሓ agbab zeyblu aserarha *(n.)* **malpractice**
አግባብ ዘይብሉ agbaba zeyblu *(adj.)* **improper**
አግባብ ዘይብሉ ፀባይ agbaba zeyblu tsebay *(n.)* **impropriety**
አግባብነት ዘይብሉ agbabnet zeyblu *(adj.)* **inappropriate**
አግደደ agdede *(v.)* **aggravate**
አገባብ agebab *(n)* **ethic**
አገባብ agebab *(n.)* **formality**
አገባብ agebab *(n.)* **means**
አገባብ agebab *(n.)* **method**
አገባብ agebab *(n.)* **mode**
አገባብ ኣዘራርባ agebab azerarba *(n.)* **parlance**
አገባብ ዘይብሉ ጽለኢ agebab zeyblu xlei *(n.)* **prejudice**
አገባባዊነት agebabawineet *(n.)* **modality**
አገዳዲ agedadi *(adj.)* **obliging**
አገዳሲ agedasi *(adj.)* **noteworthy**
አገዳሲ agedasi *(adj.)* **pivotal**
አገዳሲ agedasi *(adj.)* **salient**
አግዳሲ agedasi *(adj.)* **urgent**
አገዳሲ 'agedasi *(adj.)* **momentous**
ናይ ስፖርት ሜዳ agedasi akal *(n.)* **pitch**
አገደደ agedded *(v.)* **coerce**
አገደ agede *(v.)* **prohibit**
አገደ agede *(v.)* **ban**
አገላገለ agelagela *(v.)* **extricate**
አገላትዐ agelat'e *(v.)* **maltreat**
አገላትዐ agelat'ë *(v.)* **mishandle**
አገልጋሊ agelgali *(n.)* **attendant**
አገልጋሊ agelgali *(n.)* **servant**
አገልጋሊ agelgali *(n.)* **varlet**
አገልጋሊ ቤተክርስትያን agelgali bete krstyan *(n.)* **sexton**
አገልገለ agelgele *(v.)* **serve**
አገልግሎት agelglot *(n.)* **service**
አገረመ agereme *(v.)* **amaze**
አገረመ agereme *(v.)* **baffle**
አገጣጣማይ ageẗaẗamay *(n.)* **fitter**
አገጣጠመ ageẗaẗeme *(v.)* **assemble**
አግፈሐ agfehe *(v.)* **dilate**
አግሃደ aghade *(v.)* **declassify**
አግሃደ aghade *(v.)* **evince**
አግለለ aglele *(v.)* **ostracize**
አግለለ 'aglele *(v.)* **isolate**
አጎደ agode *(v.)* **stoke**
አጎልበተ agolbete *(v.)* **foster**
አጎምጅዩ agomjyu *(v.)* **tantalize**
አግሪፎልዮ agrifolyo *(n.)* **holly**
አግጣሚ agẗami *(n.)* **joiner**
አጉባዕብዐ aguba'ëb'ë *(v.)* **hector**
አጉደለ agudele *(v.)* **deduct**
አጉዶ agudo *(n.)* **hut**
አጉሃየ aguhaye *(v.)* **grieve**
አጉል agul *(adj.)* **neuter**
አጉለ agule *(n.)* **truffle**
አጉለሐ agulehe *(v.)* **magnify**
አጉለሐ 'aguleḧe *(v.)* **emboss**
አጉለሐ aguleḧe *(v.)* **accentuate**
አጉልሐ agulḧe *(v.)* **amplify**
አጉረምረመ aguremreme *(v.)* **gripe**
አጉረምረመ aguremreme *(v.)* **mumble**
አጉረምረመ aguremreme *(v.)* **murmur**
አጉረምረመ aguremreme *(v.)* **whimper**
አጉረጠ 'agureẗe *(v.)* **jab**
አጐዓዓዚ agwa'ä'äzi *(n.)* **haulier**
አጓዲ agwadi *(n.)* **stoker**
አጓም agwam *(n.)* **bud**
አጐመ agwame *(v.)* **burgeon**

አጓነፈ agwanefe *(v.)* **encounter**
አጓነየ agwaneye *(v.i.)* **alienate**
አህደአ ahad'e *(v.t.)* **abate**
አህደአ ahad'e *(v.t.)* **abate**
ኣሓደሰ aĥadese *(n.)* **renovate**
ኣሃዱ 'ahadu *(n.)* **unit**
ኣሃዱ ኣምላኸኛ ahadu amlaḱegna *(n.)* **monotheist**
ኣሃዱ ኣምላኽነት ahadu amlaḱnet *(n.)* **monotheism**
ኣሃዱ ናይ ኤለትሪካዊ ጉልበት ahadu nay 'eeletrikawi gulbet *(n.)* **watt**
ኣሓጎሰ 'aĥagwase *(v.)* **exhilarate**
ኣሐየለ ahayl'e *(v.)* **consolidate**
ኣሃዝ ahaz *(n.)* **digit**
ኣሃዝ ahaz *(n.)* **numeral**
ኣሃዛዊ ahazawi *(adj.)* **digital**
ኣሃዛዊ ahazawi *(adj.)* **numerical**
ኣሕበረ a'ĥbere *(v.)* **stir**
አህድአ ahd'e *(v.)* **pacify**
አህድአ ah-dea *(v.i)* **hush**
አህደአ ahde'e *(v.)* **defuse**
አህደአ ahde'e *(v.)* **lull**
አህደአ ahde'e *(v.)* **mollify**
አህደአ ahde'e *(v.)* **quieten**
አህደአ ahde'e *(v.)* **soothe**
ኣሐደሰ ahdese *(v.)* **recondition**
ኣሐደሰ aĥdese *(v.)* **renew**
ኣሐደሰ ahedese *(v.)* **refresh**
ኣሐደሰ aĥedese *(v.)* **recreate**
አሀገረ ahegere *(v.)* **nationalize**
ኣሐጎሰ aĥegose *(v.i)* **excite**
ኣሐጐሰ aḥegwase *(v.)* **gratify**
አሀለኸ aheleke *(v.)* **knacker**
ኣሐንጠሰ aĥenťese *(v.i.)* **sneeze**
አህፈፈ ahfefe *(v.)* **defrost**
ኣሕፈረ aĥfere *(v.)* **embarrass**
ኣሓጎሰ aĥgose *(v. t.)* **delight**
አህላኺ ahlaki *(adj.)* **demanding**
ኣሕለፈ ahlefe *(v.)* **undergo**
ኣሕቃቂ aĥqaqi *(n.)* **solvent**
አህረፈ ahrefe *(v.)* **entice**
ኣሕረቀ aĥreqe *(v.)* **displease**
ኣሕረቐ 'aḥreq̈e *(v.)* **vex**
ኣሕረረ ahrere *(v.)* **scorch**
ኣሕረረ aĥrere *(v.)* **singe**
ኣሕሰረ aĥsere *(v.)* **degrade**
አህተፍተፈ ahteftefe *(v.)* **hallucinate**
አህተፍተፈ ahteftefe *(v.)* **rave**
ኣሕፀረ aĥtsere *(v.)* **shorten**
አህጉር መቋረጺ ahugur meqaresi *(adj.)* **transcontinental**
ኣሕዋት aĥwat *(n.)* **sibling**
ኣሕወየ aĥweye *(v.)* **reimburse**
ኣሕጸረ aĥxere *(v.t)* **abridge**
ኣሕጸረ 'aĥxere *(v.t.)* **abbreviate**
ኣሕየወ aĥyewe *(v.)* **animate**
ኣሕዛኒ aĥzani *(adj.)* **mournful**
ኣሕዘነ ahzene *(v.)* **sadden**
ኣሕዘነ aĥzene *(v.)* **deject**
ኣሕዘነ aĥzene *(v.)* **disappoint**
ኢድ እግሪ ርእሲ ዘይብሉ ኣካል aid agri resi zeyblu akal *(n.)* **torso**
ኣጅቦ ajbo *(n.)* **curd**
ኣጀንዳ aĵenda *(n.)* **agenda**
ኣጅቦ ajobo *(n.)* **cheese**
ኣካባቢ akababi *(n.)* **surroundings**
ኣካቢ akabi *(n.)* **collector**
ኣካደሚ akademi *(n.)* **academy**
ኣካደሚያዊ akademiyawi *(adj.)* **academic**
ኣካፍአ akaf'a *(v.)* **stigmatize**
ኣካፈለ 'akafele *(v.)* **impart**
ኣኻፈየ akafeye *(n.)* **drizzle**
ኣካጁ akaju *(n.)* **cashew**
ኣካል akal *(n.)* **organ**

አካል ዕምበባ akal ëmbeba *(n.)* **stamen**
አካል akal *(n.)* **body**
አካላዊ ተፈጥሮ akalawi tefetro *(adj.)* **physical**
አካላዊ akalawi *(adv.)* **bodily**
አኽኣለ ak'ale *(v.)* **enable**
አቃልዐ akal'ë *(v.)* **debunk**
አካለ ጎደሎ ገበረ akale godelo gebere *(v.)* **mutilate**
አካለ-ስንኩል akalesnkul *(n.)* **invalid**
አካል ምጉዳል akam mgudal *(n.)* **mutilation**
አካራዪ akarayi *(n.)* **lessor**
አካረየ akareye *(v.t.)* **sublet**
አካታቲ akatati *(adj.)* **inclusive**
አካትዒ akat'ë *(adj.)* **debatable**
አካተተ akatete *(v.)* **include**
አካየደ akayede *(v.)* **officiate**
አካይዳ akayida *(n.)* **gait**
አኽባር ሕጊ aḱbar ȟgi *(n.)* **prosecutor**
አኽባሪ akbari *(adj.)* **respectful**
አኽባሪ akbari *(adj.)* **reverent**
አኽበረ aḱbere *(v.)* **commemorate**
አኽበረ aḱbere *(v.)* **comport**
አኽበረ aḱbere *(v.)* **bide**
አኽብሮት aḱbrot *(n.)* **homage**
አኼባ akeba *(n.)* **rally**
አኼባ ዕርቂ akeba eirqi *(n.)* **parley**
አከባቢ akebabi *(n.)* **setting**
አከበ akebe *(v.)* **agglomerate**
አከበ akebe *(v.)* **amass**
አከበ akebe *(v.)* **collate**
አከበ akebe *(v.)* **gather**
አከበ akebe *(v.)* **muster**
አከበ akebe' *(v.)* **collect**
አከዳድና akedadna *(n.)* **dressing**
አኼባ akeeba *(n.)* **convocation**
አኼባ aḱeeba *(n.)* **assembly**
አኬባ aḱeeba *(n.)* **meeting**
አከፋፈለ akefafele *(v.)* **dispense**
አከሓሓስ akeȟaȟase *(v.)* **offset**
አከላበተ akelabete *(v.)* **maul**
አኸለ akele *(v.)* **suffice**
አከራኸሪ akerakari *(adj.)* **controversial**
አከርካሪ ዘይብሎም እንስሳታት akerkari zeyblom anssatat *(n.)* **tentacle**
አከሻሽና akešašna *(n.)* **recipe**
አከሻሽና akeshashna *(n.)* **cuisine**
አክፈለ akfele *(v.)* **charge**
አኻሊ a'khali *(n.)* **sufficiency**
አኽበረ akhbere *(v.)* **solemnize**
አኽሊል aklil *(n.)* **coronet**
አኽሊል aklil *(n.)* **crown**
አኽሊል ብርሃን aḱlil brhan *(n.)* **aura**
አኮ ako *(n.)* **uncle**
አኾምሳዒ akomsa'ï *(n.)* **ruminant**
አኾምሰዐ akomse'ë *(v.)* **ruminate**
አኾምሰዐ aḱomse'ë *(v.)* **munch**
አኽራሪ akrari *(n.)* **zealot**
አክሪሊክ 'akrilik *(adj.)* **acrylic**
አክሮባስያዊ akrobasyawi *(adj.)* **acrobatic**
አክሮባት akrobat *(n.)* **acrobat**
አኽሳቢ aksabi *(adj.)* **gainful**
አክስዮን ak'syon *(n.)* **stock**
አክቲኒየም aktiniyem *(n.)* **actinium**
አኩፓንክቸር akupankcher *(n.)* **acupuncture**
አኩስቲካዊ akustikawi *(adj.)* **acoustic**
አቋራጭ akwaraĉ *(n.)* **shortcut**
አኳርየም akwaryem *(n.)* **aquarium**
አኳሸመ akwasheme *(v.i)* **flirt**
አላገበ alagebe *(v.)* **interconnect**

አላገበ alagebe ***(v.)* staple**
አላገፀ alagetse ***(v.)* deride**
አላገፀ alagetse ***(v.)* gibe**
አላገፀ alagetse ***(n.)* sneer**
አላገጸ alagetse ***(v.)* tease**
አላገፀ alagexe ***(v.)* mock**
አላ'ላዪ alalayi ***(n.)* compère**
አልዓለ alale ***(v.)* pick**
አልዓለ al'ale ***(v.t.)* lift**
አልዐለ al'äle ***(v.)* raise**
አላማይ alamay ***(n.)* weaver**
አላቐቐ alaqeqe ***(v.)* disengage**
ኣላይ ሕሙም alay ḧmum ***(n.)* nurse**
ኣላዪ ኣአጋርን ኣጸብዕቲ ኣአጋርን alayi aearnaxabetn aegarn ***(n.)* pedicure**
ኣላዛቢ alazabi ***(n.)* moderator**
ኣልቦ albo ***(adj.)* devoid**
ኣልቦነት albonet ***(n.)* nihilism**
ኣልቡም 'album ***(n)* album**
ኣለዓዓለ ale'a'ale ***(v.)* uplift**
ኣለዓዓለ ale'ä'äle ***(v.)* precipitate**
ኣለኸ aleḱe ***(v.)* bathe**
ኣለኹ ኣለኹ ኢሉ aleḱu aleḱu eilu ***(n.)* pretension**
ኣለለየ aleleye ***(v.)* discern**
ኣለማመደ alemamede ***(v.)* accustom**
ኣለማሚዱ alemamidu ***(v.)* train**
አለመ aleme ***(v.)* weave**
ኣለመ 'aleme ***(v.)* fabricate**
ኣለቀሐ aleqehe ***(v.)* lend**
ኣለርጂ alerji ***(n.)* allergy**
ኣለርጂነት alerjinet ***(adj.)* allergic**
ኣለስለሰ aleslese ***(v.)* soften**
ኣለዋዊጥካ ምቕማጥ alewawitka mqmat ***(n.)* permutation**
ኣለዋዊጡ ፂሒፉ alewawitu sihifu ***(v.)* transpose**
ኣለሸ alexe ***(v.)* scour**
ኣለየ aleye ***(v.)* avert**
ኣልገበ algebe ***(v.t.)* affix**
ኣልገሰ algese ***(v.)* eliminate**
ኣልገሰ algese ***(v.)* extirpate**
ኣልገሰ algese ***(v.)* remove**
ኣልገሰ algese ***(v.)* obviate**
ኣልጀብራ alĵebra ***(n.)* algebra**
ኣልካሊ alkali ***(n.)* alkali**
ኣልከሚ alkemi ***(n.)* alchemy**
ኣልኮል alkol ***(n.)* alcohol**
ኣልማናክ almanak ***(n.)* almanac**
ኣልማዝ almaz ***(n.)* diamond**
ኣልመደ almede ***(v.t.)* habituate**
ኣልቀቐ alqeqe ***(v.)* evacuate**
ኣልተያ alteya ***(n.)* marshmallow**
ኣሉሚኒዮም aluminiyom ***(n.)* aluminium**
ኣሉታ aluta ***(adj.)* negative**
ኣሉታዊ alutawi ***(adj.)* adverse**
ኣሉታውነት alutawinet ***(n.)* negativity**
ኣማእከለ zamaeekele ***(v.)* centralize**
ኣማዕበለ ama'ëbele ***(v.)* enrich**
ኣማዕደወ ama'edewe ***(v.)* scan**
ኣማዕረገ ama'ërege ***(v.)* dignify**
ኣማጓቲ amagwati ***(adj.)* argumentative**
ኣማጓቲ amagwati ***(adj.)* moot**
ኣመሓዳሪ amaḧadari ***(n.)* curator**
ኣማሃረ amahare ***(v.)* educate**
ኣማኸሪ amaha'ri ***(n.)* consultant**
ኣመሓየሸ amahayeshe ***(v.)* adapt**
ኣማሓየሸ amaḧayeshe ***(v.)* meliorate**
ኣማሓደረ ama'hdere ***(v.)* manage**
ኣማኸሪ amakari ***(n.)* counsellor**
ኣማካሪ amakari ***(n.)* courtier**
ኣማኸረ amakere ***(v.)* counsel**
ኣማኒት amanit ***(n.)* confidant**

አማራፂ amaratsi *(n.)* **option**
አማስሖ amasĥe *(v.)* **allot**
አማወቐ amaweqe *(v.)* **flex**
አማዞን amazon *(n.)* **Amazon**
ኣምባገነንነት ambagenennet *(adj.)* **totalitarian**
ኣምባገነንነት ambagenennet *(n.)* **tyranny**
ኣምቡላንስ ambulans *(n.)* **ambulance**
ኣምዐ am'ë *(n.)* **nettle**
ኣመዓራረየ ame'ärareye *(v. t)* **dispose**
ኣመዓራረየ ame'ärareye *(v.)* **adjust**
ኣመጋግባ amegagba *(n.)* **nutrition**
ኣመሓደረ amehadare *(v.)* **superintend**
ኣመሓዳሪ amehadari *(n.)* **superintendent**
ኣመሓዳሪ amehadari *(adj.)* **administrator**
ኣመሓደረ amehadere *(v.)* **administer**
ኣመሓላለፈ amehalalefe *(v.)* **defer**
ኣመሓላለፈ amehalalefe *(v.)* **refer**
ኣመሓላሊፉ amehalalifu *(v.)* **transmit**
ኣመሓየሸ amehayeše *(v.)* **reform**
ኣመሓየሸ amehayeše *(v.)* **retouch**
አመሓየሸ amehayeshe *(v.)* **upgrade**
ኣመሓየሸ amehayeshe *(v.)* **ameliorate**
ኣመሓየሸ amehayeshe *(v.)* **amend**
አመኬላ amekiela *(n.)* **thistle**
ኣመክሮ amekro *(n.)* **parole**
ኣመክሮ amekro *(n.)* **probation**
ኣመል amel *(n.)* **temperament**
ኣመል ኮይኑዎ amel koynuwo *(n.)* **trifle**
ኣመላኸተ amelakete *(v. t)* **denote**
ኣመልካቲ amelkati *(n.)* **applicant**
ኣመልካቲቶ 'amelkatito *(n.)* **forefinger**
ኣመልክዐ amelk'ë *(v.)* **beautify**
ኣመልከተ amelkete *(v.)* **annotate**
ኣመልከተ amelkete *(v.t.)* **apply**
ኣመልከተ amelkete *(v.)* **indicate**
ኣመልከተ amelkete *(v.)* **notify**
ኣመልከተ amelkete *(v.)* **signify**
ኣመልከተ amelkete *(v.)* **beckon**
ኣመና a'mena *(adj.)* **super**
ኣመና ድሙቕ amena dmu-que *(adj.)* **garish**
ኣመና ልሙድ amena lmud *(adj.)* **hackneyed**
ኣመና ንጡፍ amena nťuf *(adj.)* **hyperactive**
ኣመንጨወ amenĉewe *(v.)* **derive**
ኣመንጨወ amen'chewe *(v.)* **secrete**
ኣመነ amene *(v.)* **concede**
ኣመነ amene *(v.)* **believe**
ኣመንዝር amenzer *(n.)* **whore**
ኣመንዝራ amenzra *(n.)* **prostitute**
ኣመንዝራዊ amenzrawi *(adj.)* **meretricious**
ኣመቐረ ameqere *(v.)* **sweeten**
ኣመራሰሐ ameraseĥe *(v.)* **adulterate**
ኣመራሰሐ ameraseĥe *(v.)* **besmirch**
ኣመራስሐ amerasĥe *(n.)* **sophisticate**
ኣመርዓወ amerawe *(v.)* **wed**
ኣመስጋኒ amesgani *(n.)* **grateful**
ኣመስጋኒ amesgani *(adj.)* **beholden**
ኣመስገነ amesgene *(v.)* **thank**
ኣመሻሽጣ ጸጕሪ ameshashťa tseguri *(n.)* **hairstyle**
ኣመስከረ ameskere *(v.)* **certify**

ኣመስጠረ amesťere *(v.)* **encrypt**
ኣመተ amete *(v.t.)* **allude**
ኣመዛበለ amezabele *(v. t)* **displace**
ኣመዛዛኒ amezazani *(adj.)* **rational**
ኣመዛዘነ amezazene *(v.)* **ponder**
ኣመዛዘነ amezazene *(v.)* **rationalize**
ኣመዝገበ amezgebe *(v.)* **score**
ኣምፊትያትር amfityatr *(n.)* **amphitheatre**
ኣሚዶ amido *(n.)* **starch**
ኣሚዶኣዊ amido'awi *(adj.)* **starchy**
ኣምከነ amkene *(v.)* **sterilize**
ኣመኩሮኣዊ amkuroawi *(n.)* **probationer**
አምላኽ ምእማን amlak m'eman *(n.)* **theism**
ኣምላኽ ጣኦት amlaḱ ṭa'ot *(n.)* **heathen**
አምላኻዊ አስተምህሮ amlakawi astemhro *(n.)* **theosophy**
ኣምላኺ መናፍስቲ amlakhi menafsti *(n.)* **spiritualist**
ኣምላኺ amlaki *(n.)* **worshipper**
አምለከ amleke *(v.)* **idolize**
ኣምለቈ amleq̈we *(v.)* **blurt**
ኣምለሰ amlese *(v.)* **regain**
ኣምለሰ amlese *(v.)* **retch**
ኣምለጠ amlete *(v.)* **elude**
ኣምለጠ amleẗr *(v. t)* **evade**
ኣምልካቲ amlkati *(adj.)* **indicative**
ኣምልኾተ መናፍስቲ amlkhote menafsti *(n.)* **spiritualism**
ኣምልኾ amlko *(n.)* **cult**
ኣምልኾ amlḱo *(n.)* **adoration**
ኣምልኾተ ሴጣን amlkote sietan *(n.)* **Satanism**
እምነት ምግባር amnet mgbar *(n.)* **trust**
እምነት ዝግበረሉ amnet zgberelu *(adj.)* **trustworthy**
ኣምፐር amper *(n.)* **ampere**
ኣምፑል ampul *(n.)* **bulb**
ኣምር amr *(n.)* **concept**
ኣምራቲ amrati *(n.)* **manufacturer**
ኣምረተ amrete *(v.)* **manufacture**
ኣምርሐ amrhe *(v.)* **wend**
ኣምሳሊ amsali *(adj.)* **pretentious**
ኣምሳሊ amsali *(adj.)* **affected**
ኣምሰለ amsele *(v.)* **feign**
ኣምለሰ amsele *(v.)* **reclaim**
ኣምሰሉ amselu *(v.)* **pretend**
ኣምሰሉ amselu *(n.)* **sham**
ኣምሲልካ ምቕራብ amsilka mq̈rab *(n.)* **hype**
ኣምፃኢ amtsa'e *(n.)* **importer**
ኣምፀአ am-tse-a *(v.)* **garner**
ኣምፀአ amxe'e *(v.)* **fetch**
ኣምጸአ amxe'e *(v.)* **bring**
ኣናደደ anadede *(v.)* **infuriate**
ኣናደየ anadeye *(v.)* **search**
ኣናደየ anadeye *(v.i.)* **seek**
ኣናጎንስጢስ anagonsťees *(n.)* **acolyte**
ኣናናስ ananas *(n.)* **pineapple**
ኣናሸወ anashewe *(v.)* **decry**
ኣናሸወ anashewe *(v.)* **denigrate**
ኣናሸወ anashewe *(v.)* **lampoon**
ኣናወፀ anawetse *(v.)* **destabilize**
ኣናውሐ anawḧe *(v.)* **prolong**
ኣንባር anbar *(n.)* **anklet**
ኣንበበ anbebe *(v.)* **read**
ኣንበበ anbebe *(v.t.)* **spell**
ኣንበልበለ anbelbele *(v.)* **brandish**
ኣንበረ anbere *(v.)* **lay**
ኣንበርከኸ anberkeke *(v.)* **quell**
ኣንበሳ anbesa *(n.)* **Leo**

አንበሳ anbesa ***(n.)*** **lion**
አንጨባረቀ anĉebareqe ***(v.)*** **dabble**
አንጭዋ anĉwa ***(n.)*** **rat**
አንጭዋ ančwa ***(n.)*** **mouse**
አንድሮይድ androyd ***(n.)*** **android**
ኣነ a'ne ***(pron.)*** **me**
ኣነዓዓቢ ane'ä'äbi ***(adj.)*** **subversive**
ኣነኣኣሰ ane'a'ase ***(v.)*** **devalue**
ኣንነኣኣሲ aneaasi ***(adj.)*** **pejorative**
ኣነዓበ ane'äbe ***(v.i.)*** **subvert**
ኣነፍነፈ anefnefe ***(v.)*** **snuffle**
ኣነነት anenet ***(n.)*** **narcissism**
ኣነቓቕሐ aneqaqh'he ***(v.)*** **stimulate**
ኣነቓቓሒ aneqhaqhaȟi ***(n.)*** **stimulant**
ኣነፀረ anetsere ***(v.)*** **specify**
ኣነወረ anewere ***(v.)*** **scandalize**
ኣነጻጸረ anexaxere ***(v.)*** **compare**
ኣንፈሰ anfese ***(v.)*** **deflate**
ኣንፈት anfet ***(n.)*** **direction**
ኣንፈት anfet ***(n.)*** **hint**
ኣንፈት ቀየረ anfet qeyere ***(v.)*** **deflect**
ኣንፈት ቀየረ anfet qeyere ***(v. t)*** **divert**
ኣንፈጥፈጠ anfetfete ***(v.)*** **quaver**
ኣንፈጥፈጠ anfetfete ***(v.)*** **shudder**
ኣንፈቱ ቀየረ anfetu qeyere ***(v.)*** **diverge**
ኣንፊ anfi ***(n.)*** **snout**
ኣንጋረ angare ***(n.)*** **leather**
ኣንገብገበ angebgebe ***(v.)*** **flap**
ኣንገሰ angese ***(v.)*** **crown**
ኣንገሰ angese ***(v.)*** **enthrone**
ኣንጉዕ angu'e ***(n.)*** **tallow**
ኣንጓዕ angwa'ë ***(n.)*** **node**
ኣንሃረ anhare ***(v.)*** **accelerate**
አንከባለለ ankebalwle ***(v.)*** **trundle**
ኣንቀጥቀጠ anketkete ***(v.)*** **dither**
ኣንቆልቆለ ankolkole ***(v. t.)*** **decrement**
ኣንኳለ ankwale ***(adj.)*** **broach**
ኣንቀሐ anqeĥe ***(n.)*** **mover**
ኣንቀሳቓሲ anqesaqasi ***(adj.)*** **spastic**
ኣንቀጥቓጢ anqeẗqaẗi ***(v.)*** **quiver**
ኣብ ምቅርራብ 'ab mqrrab ***(adv.)*** **afoot**
ኣብ ዙርያ 'ab zurya ***(adv.)*** **around**
ኣሕነኸ 'aȟneḱe ***(adj.)*** **abash**
ኣኮኣዊ 'ako'awi ***(adj.)*** **avuncular**

ከ

ከቢድ kebid ***(adj.)*** **onerous**
ከቢድ ሓጎስ kebid hagos ***(adj.)*** **overjoyed**
ከቢድ ፅዕነት kebit ts'enet ***(v.)*** **overload**
ከፈለ kefle ***(v.)*** **obtrude**
ኩሉ ምፍላጥ kulu mflat ***(n.)*** **omniscience**
ኩሉ ከኣሊ kulu keali ***(adj.)*** **omnipotent**
ኩሉ ፈላጢ kulu felati ***(adj.)*** **omniscient**
ካልእ kal'e ***(adj. & pron.)*** **other**
ካብ 80-89 ዕድመ ዘለዎ ሰብ kab 80-89 edme zelewo seb ***(n.)*** **octogenarian**
ካብ ልክዕ ንላዕሊ kab lk'e nla'eli ***(adv.)*** **overly**
ካብ ልክዕ ንላዕሊ kab lk'e nla'eli ***(v.)*** **overrate**
ካብ መስመር ወጻኢ kab mesmer wetsa'i ***(adj.)*** **offside**
ካብ መጠን ንላዕሊ kab meten nla'eli ***(v.)*** **overstep**

ካብ መጠን ንላዕሊ ዓርሰ ምትእምማን kab meten nla'eli arse mt'emman *(adj.)* **overweening**

ካብ ርእሲንላዕሊ kab r'esi nla'eli *(adv.)* **overhead**

ካብ ጥረምረ ዝስራሕ ዓይነት ምግቢ kab teremer zsrah aynet mgbi *(n.)* **oatmeal**

ካቦት kabot *(n.)* **overcoat**

ኬላ kela *(n.)* **outpost**

ክስብ ዝፈስስ ዝምልእ ksab zfess zmel'e *(n.)* **overspill**

ክስተት kstet *(n.)* **occurrence**

ክርከብ ዝኽእል krkeb zkel *(adj.)* **obtainable**

ክባዊ ኣካል kbawi akal *(n.)* **orb**

ክፉት kfut *(adj.)* **open**

ክፍተት kftet *(n.)* **opening**

ኮረችያ koretya *(n.)* **oak**

ካርዲ ka'ardi *(n.)* **card**

ካብ kab *(prep.)* **from**

ካብ kab *(prep.)* **since**

ካብ 13-19 ዝርከብ kab 13-19 zrkeb *(adj.)* **teens**

ካብ ኣርእስቲ ወፀ kab ar'esti wetse *(v.)* **digress**

ካብ ቦታ ወጻኢ ምንቅስቓስ kab bot wexaei mnqsq̈as *(n.)* **prolapse**

ካብ ደረቕ ናብ ሃፋ kab dereq nab hafa *(v.)* **sublimate**

ካብ ዕንፀይቲ ዝተሰረሐ መዶሻ kab entseyti ztesreh medisha *(n.)* **mallet**

ካብ እስካብ kab eskab *(n.)* **interval**

ካብ ገዝሚ ወጻኢ ንብረት መርዓት kab gezmi weai nbret mrat *(n.)* **paraphernalia**

ካብ ሃገር ወጻኢ kab hager wexa'i *(adv.)* **abroad**

ካብ ሃሪ ዝተሰርሐ kab hari zterhe *(adj.)* **woolly**

ካብ ሓሰማ ዝርከብ ስብሒ kab hasama zrkeb sbhi *(n.)* **lard**

ኣፅረየ kab ḧaẗyat anxehe *(v.)* **purge**

ካብ ሓጥያት ምንጻሀ kab ḧaẗyat mnxah *(n.)* **purgation**

ካብ ሓደ ንላዕሊ kab ḧde alaëli *(adj.)* **plural**

ካብ ሕጂ ንደሓር kab ḥği ndeḥar *(adv.)* **henceforth**

ካብ ሕልሚ ኣላቀቐ kab ĥlmi alaqeqe *(v.)* **disenchant**

ካብ ኢድ ናብ ኣፍ kab id nab a'f *(n.)* **subsistence**

ካብ ክሳድ ንላዕሊ kab ksad nlaeli *(adj.)* **perfunctory**

ካብ መዓንጣ ንልዕሊ ጥራሕካ ምካን kab meantanlaali trahka mukan *(adj.)* **topless**

ካብ መሃያ ወጻኢ ዝርከብ kab mehaya wexaei zrkeb *(n.)* **perquisite**

ካብ መስመር ዝወጸ kab mesmer zwetse *(n.)* **straggler**

ካብ መስመሩ ኣስሓተ kab mesmeru as'ĥate *(v. t.)* **derail**

ካብ መጥቃዕቲ ንምክልኻል ኣፀጋሚ kab metka'et nmklkhal zetsgm *(adj.)* **indefensible**

ካብ ፅሑፍ kab shuf *(adj.)* **textual**

ካብ ፅሑፍ kab shuf *(adj.)* **textual**

ካብ ስርናይ ዝተሰርሐ kab srnay zteserhe *(adj.)* **wheaten**

ካብ ፃባ ዝስራሕ ጠንካራ ቡን kab tsaba zsrah tenkara bun *(n.)* **latte**

ካባረ kabare *(n.)* **cabaret**

ከበይ kabey *(adv.)* **whence**
ካብስትኖ kabstno *(n.)* **capstan**
ካብ ሕጂ kabz hji *(adv.)* **hence**
ካቻቪተ ka'chavite *(n.)* **screwdriver**
ካደት kadet *(n.)* **cadet**
ካዲ kadi *(n.)* **caddy**
ካድምዩም kadmyum *(n.)* **cadmium**
ካድረ kadre *(n.)* **cadre**
ካዕካዕ ka'ëka'ë *(n.)* **nut**
ካዕካዕታ ka'ëka'ë bele *(n.)* **guffaw**
ካዕካዕታ ka'ëka'ëta *(n.)* **hilarity**
ካዕካዕታዊ ka'ëka'ëtawi *(adj.)* **hilarious**
ካዕካዓዊ ka'ëka'ëwi *(adj.)* **nutty**
ካፋ kafa *(n.)* **shower**
ካፌ kafee *(n.)* **cafe**
ካፊተርያ kafiterya *(n.)* **cafeteria**
ካሓዲ kaĥadi *(n.)* **renegade**
ካሕዳም kahdam *(n.)* **traitor**
ካህናት kahenat' *(n.)* **clergy**
ካህን kahin *(n.)* **cleric**
ካህን kahin' *(n.)* **chaplain**
ካህን kahn *(n.)* **parson**
ካህን kahn *(n.)* **pastor**
ካህን kahn *(adj.)* **reverend**
ካሕሳ kahsa *(n.)* **restitution**
ካሕሳ kaḧsa *(n.)* **atonement**
ካሕሳ kaḧsa *(n.)* **compensation**
ካካው kakaw *(n.)* **cocoa**
ካካው kakaw *(n.)* **cacao**
ካልኣዋይ kal'away *(adj.)* **secondary**
ካልኣይ kal'ay *(adj.)* **second**
ካልእ kal'è *(adj.)* **another**
ካልኣይ/ማዕረ kaleay/maere *(n.)* **paragon**
ካሊእ ሽሙ kali'e shmu *(adv.)* **alias**
ካሎሪ kalori *(n.)* **calorie**
ካልሲ kalsi *(n.)* **sock**
ካልስዩም kalsyum *(n.)* **calcium**
ካምቻ kamcha *(n.)* **blouse**
ካምፎራ kamfora *(n.)* **camphor**
ካምኮርደር kamkorder *(n.)* **camcorder**
ካምፓስ kampas *(n.)* **campus**
ካምሻ kamša *(n.)* **shirt**
ካሙን kamun *(n.)* **cumin**
ካምዮ kamyo *(n.)* **cameo**
ካንጋሩ kangaru *(n.)* **kangaroo**
ካንሸሎ kanshelo *(n.)* **courtyard**
ካንቲና kantina *(n.)* **canteen**
ካፓሲተር kapaciter *(n.)* **capacitor**
ካራ kara *(n.)* **knife**
ካራት kara 't *(n.)* **carat**
ካራሜል karame' el *(n.)* **caramel**
ካርቦሃይድሬት karbohaydreet *(n.)* **carbohydrate**
ካርቦን karbon *(n.)* **carbon**
ካርቦኔት karboneet *(adj.)* **carbonate**
ካርቾፊ karchofi *(n.)* **artichoke**
ካርድዮግራፍ kardyograf *(n.)* **cardiograph**
ካርድዮሎጂ kardyoloĵi *(n.)* **cardiology**
ካሪካቸር karikacher *(n)* **caricature**
ካርማ karma *(n.)* **karma**
ካርኒቫል karnival *(n.)* **carnival**
ካሮሳ karosa *(n.)* **chaise**
ካሮሳ karosa *(n.)* **buggy**
ካርታ karta *(n.)* **map**
ካርተሊና kartelina *(n.)* **postcard**
ካርቶን kartoon *(n.)* **cardboard**
ካርቱን kartun *(n.)* **cartoon**
ካርያ karya *(n.)* **pecan**
ካሳ kasa *(n.)* **crate**
ካሽሚር kashmir *(n.)* **cashmere**
ካስታኖ kastano *(n.)* **chestnut**

ካስታርድ kastard *(n.)* **custard**
ካተድራል katedral *(n.)* **cathedral**
ካትራመ katrame *(n.)* **tar**
ካውካዝያዊ kawkazyawi *(adj.)* **Caucasian**
ካውሎ ፍዮሪ kawlo fyori *(n.)* **broccoli**
ካውሎ kawlo *(n.)* **cabbage**
ካዉሎ ፍዮሪ kawulo fiyorii *(n.)* **cauliflower**
ካዝና kazina *(n.)* **coffer**
ካዚኖ kazino *(n.)* **casino**
ካዝና kazna *(n.)* **safe**
ካዝና kazna *(n.)* **warehouse**
ክባር kbar *(adj.)* **costly**
ክባር kbar *(adj.)* **expensive**
ክባዊ kbawi *(n.)* **spherical**
ክብድብድ ምባል kbd'bd mbal *(n.)* **malaise**
ክብደት kbdet *(n.)* **mass**
ክብደት kbdet *(n.)* **profundity**
ክብደት kbdet *(n.)* **weight**
ክበሃል ዘይክእል kbehal zeykel *(adj.)* **unmentionable**
ክበሃል ዘይክእል kbehal zeykel *(adj.)* **unutterable**
ክቢ kbi *(n.)* **sphere**
ክቢብ kbibe *(adj.)* **circular**
ክቦሳ kbosa *(n.)* **cuff**
ክብረት kbret *(n.)* **gravitas**
ክብረት kbret *(n.)* **prestige**
ኽብሪ kbri *(n.)* **deference**
ክብሪ kbri *(n.)* **dignity**
ኽብሪ kbri *(n.)* **esteem**
ክብሪ kbri *(n.)* **glorification**
ክብሪ kbri *(n.)* **kudos**
ክብሪ kbri *(n.)* **majesty**
ክብሪ kbri *(n.)* **reputation**
ክብሪ kbri *(n.)* **respect**
ክብሪ kbri *(n.)* **glory**
ክብሪ ዝረከበ kbri zrekebe *(n.)* **laureate**
ክብሰት kbset *(n.)* **reversal**
ክቡብ kbub *(n.)* **enclave**
ክቡር kbur *(adj.)* **dear**
ክቡር kbur *(n.)* **Excellency**
ክቡር kbur *(adj.)* **illustrious**
ክቡር kbur *(n.)* **plush**
ክቡር kbur *(adj.)* **respectable**
ክቡር kbur *(n.)* **treasure**
ክቡር kbur *(adj.)* **valuable**
ክቡር እምኒ kbur emni *(n.)* **gem**
ክዳን kdan *(n.)* **apparel**
ኽዳን kdan *(n.)* **garb**
ክዳን kdan *(n.)* **garment**
ክዳን ካህን kdan kahn *(n.)* **cassock**
ክዳን ለይቲ kdan leyti *(n.)* **nightie**
ክዳን ሰበይቲ kdan sebeyti *(n.)* **costume**
ክዳኑ ኣዉፀአ kdanu awtse'e *(v.)* **disrobe**
ክዳውንቲ kdawnti *(n.)* **clothing**
ክዳውንቲ መርዓት kdawnti merat *(n.)* **trousseau**
ክድሕን ዘይኽእል kdhn zeykh'el *(adj.)* **incurable**
ክድነቕ ዝግቦአ kdneqh zgbo'e *(adj.)* **laudable**
ከኣለ ke'ale *(v.)* **can**
ከባብ kebab *(n.)* **kebab**
ከባቢ kebabi *(n.)* **locality**
ከባሂ kebahi *(adj.)* **cloying**
ከብዲ እግሪ kebdi egri *(n.)* **sole**
ከብዲ kebdi *(n.)* **abdomen**
ከብዲ kebdi *(n.)* **belly**
ከበበ kebebe *(v. t)* **encircle**
ከበባ kebebe *(n.)* **siege**
ከበበ kebebe *(v.)* **surround**

ከበበ kebebe *(v.)* **besiege**
ከበሮ kebero *(n.)* **drum**
ከበርቴ kebertee *(n.)* **aristocrat**
ከብሒ ክሽነ kebhi kshne *(n.)* **pantry**
ከብሒ kebḧi *(n.)* **cabinet**
ከቢ kebi *(n.)* **circle**
ከቢብ kebib *(adj.)* **round**
ከቢድ kebid *(adj.)* **profound**
ከቢድ kebid *(adj.)* **terrific**
ከቢድ kebid *(adj.)* **uneasy**
ኸቢድ kebid *(adj.)* **weighty**
ከቢድ ብረት kebid bret *(n.)* **artillery**
ከቢድ ጋዝ kebid gaz *(n.)* **xenon**
ከቢድ ሓዘን kebid hazen *(adj.)* **terrible**
ኸቢድ ኩነታት kebid kuknetat *(n.)* **imbroglio**
ከቢድ ስቃይ kebid skay *(n.)* **throes**
ከቢድ ስቃይ kebid skay *(n.)* **torment**
ከቢድ ኩነታት kebidkunetat *(n.)* **pickle**
ከብቲ kebtei *(n.)* **cattle**
ከቻፕ kechap *(n.)* **ketchup**
ኸዳን kedan *(n.)* **cladding**
ከደ kede *(v.t)* **go**
ከደ kede *(v.)* **betake**
ከድዐ ked'ë *(v.)* **betray**
ኸደነ kedene *(v.)* **upholster**
ከደነ kedene' *(v.)* **clothe**
ከደራይ kederay *(adj.)* **swarthy**
ኬክ keek *(n.)* **cookie**
ከፋሊ kefali *(n.)* **payee**
ከፋት ሸውሃት kefat shewhat *(n.)* **appetizer**
ከፈለ kefele *(v.)* **defray**
ከፈለ kefele *(v.)* **liquidate**
ከፈለ kefele *(v.)* **remunerate**
ካብ ልክዕ ንላዕሊ መኽሰብ ḧadḧdawi mek̸seb *(n.)* **profiteering**

ክእለት k'elet *(n.)* **ability**
ኪምለስ ዚክኣል kimles zike'al *(adj.)* **answerable**
ክልተ ዓመታዊ klte 'ämetawi *(adj.)* **biennial**
ክልቲኡ klti'u *(adj. & pron.)* **both**
ክፍለ አለም kefele ale'm *(n.)* **continent**
ክፍለ አለማዊ kefele alemawii *(adj.)* **continental**
ክፍሊት kefelit *(n.)* **charge**
ክግልገል ዝክእል keglgel zk'el *(adj.)* **serviceable**
ከሓደ keĥade *(v. i.)* **deny**
ከሓደ keĥade *(v.)* **disown**
ከሓዲ keĥadi *(adj.)* **disloyal**
ከሓዲ እምነት keḧadi 'èmnet *(n.)* **apostate**
ከሓሰ keĥase *(v.)* **recompense**
ከሓሰ keĥase *(v.)* **recoup**
ከሓሰ keḧase *(v.)* **compensate**
ከሓሰ keḧase *(v.)* **atone**
ኬክ kek *(n.)* **gateau**
ከከም kekem *(adj.)* **respective**
ከልባዊ kelbawi *(adj.)* **canine**
ከልቢ kelbi *(n.)* **dog**
ከልቢ እለሻ kelbi eleša *(n.)* **retriever**
ከልቢ ሃድን kelbi hadn *(n.)* **greyhound**
ከለለ kelele *(v.)* **enclose**
ከለሰ kelese *(n.)* **review**
ከለሰ kelese *(v.)* **revise**
ክእለት k'elet *(n.)* **facility**
ክእለት k'elet *(n.)* **faculty**
ክእለት k'elet *(n.)* **skill**
ክእለት k'èlet *(n.)* **competence**
ክእለት ዘረባ k'elet zereba *(n.)* **elocution**
ክእለት k'èlet *(n.)* **artifice**

ከእለታዊ k'eletawi *(adj.)* **tactical**
ከልካሊ kelkali *(adj.)* **prohibitive**
ኸለከለ kelkele *(v. t.)* **debar**
ከልከለ kelkele *(v.)* **deprive**
ከልከለ kelkele *(v.)* **disallow**
ኸልከለ kelkele *(v.)* **forbid**
ከም kem *(prep.)* **like**
ከም ብሓዱሽ kem bȟadush *(adv.)* **anew**
ከም ፍጹም ምቑፃር kem fxum mqutsar *(v.)* **idealize**
ከም ገለ kem gele *(adv.)* **somehow**
ከም ልሙድ kem lmud *(adv.)* **usually**
ከም ዝፍቀር ገበረ kem zfqer gebere *(v.)* **endear**
ከም kem *(adv.)* **as**
ከመይ kemey *(adv.)* **how**
ኬሚካል kemikal *(adj.)* **chemical**
ከምኡ kem'u *(n.)* **ditto**
ከምኡ kem'u *(adj.)* **such**
ከምኡ'ውን kem'uwn *(adv.)* **also**
ከባቢ kenabi *(n.)* **environment**
ከንበለ kenbele *(v.)* **topple**
ኬንዳ kenda *(n.)* **tent**
ከንፈር kenfer *(n.)* **lip**
ከንፈር ማንቲለ kenfer mantile *(n.)* **harelip**
ከንፈራዊ kenferawi *(adj.)* **labial**
ከኒና kenina *(n.)* **quinine**
ከኒና kenina *(n.)* **pill**
ከንቲባ kentiba *(n.)* **mayor**
ከንቱ kentu *(adj.)* **futile**
ከንቱ kentu *(n.)* **reprobate**
ከርበ kerebe *(n.)* **myrrh**
ከረሜላ keremeela *(n.)* **candy**
ከረናዊ kerenawi *(adj.)* **alpine**
ክርስትና keresetena *(n.)* **Christianity**
ክርስቶስ keresetos *(n.)* **Christ**
ክርስቲያን keresitiyane *(adj.)* **Christian**
ከረጢት kereẗit *(n.)* **pouch**
ከረዛን kerezan *(n.)* **wand**
ከርፋሕ kerfaḧ *(adj.)* **miserable**
ከርከስ kerkes *(n.)* **ridge**
ከርታት kertat *(n.)* **vagrant**
ከሳሲ kesasi *(n.)* **suitor**
ከሳሳይ kesasy *(n.)* **plaintiff**
ከስዓዊ kes-ä-wi *(adj.)* **gastric**
ከሰበ kesebe *(v.)* **gain**
ከሰረ kesere *(v.)* **forfeit**
ከሰሰ kesese *(v.)* **accuse**
ከሰሰ kesese *(v.)* **indict**
ከሰሰ kesese *(v.t.)* **sue**
ከሻኒ keshani *(n.)* **cook**
ከሽዐ kesh'ë *(n.)* **stomach**
ከሽከሽ ቐሚሽ keshkesh qhemish *(n.)* **kilt**
ከስከስ keskes *(n.)* **reef**
ከተበ ketebe *(v.)* **enlist**
ከተበ ketebe *(v.)* **inoculate**
ከተበ ketebe *(v.)* **inscribe**
ከተበ ketebe *(v.)* **vaccinate**
ከተፈ ketefe *(v.)* **chop**
ከተማ ketema *(n.)* **city**
ከተማ ketema *(n.)* **town**
ከተማ ketema *(adj.)* **urban**
ከተረ ketere *(v.)* **waylay**
ከተተ ketete *(v.)* **mobilize**
ቀጢን ketin *(adj.)* **shrill**
ክእቶ ዝከኣል k'èto zke'al *(adj.)* **accessible**
ከወለ kewele *(v.)* **shade**
ከውሓዊ kewȟawi *(adj.)* **megalithic**
ከውሒ kewĥi *(n.)* **rock**
ቀይ ስር key sr *(n.)* **turnip**

ቀያዲ keyadi *(adj.)* **restrictive**
ኮያፍ keyaf *(n.)* **bristle**
ከየቕለብካሉ እትግንዘቦ keyeqhlebkalu etg'nzebo *(adj.)* **subliminal**
ቀይሕ ሓመድ keyh hamed *(n.)* **terracotta**
ከይሲ keysi *(adj.)* **sly**
ከይሲ keysi *(adj.)* **splenetic**
ከዘራን kezeran *(n.)* **cane**
ክፋእ ዘይብሉ kfa'e zeyblu *(adj.)* **spotless**
ክፋል kfal *(n.)* **instalment**
ክፋል kfal *(n.)* **part**
ክፋል kfal *(n.)* **sector**
ክፋል ዕንባባ kfal onbaba *(n.)* **petal**
ክፋሎ kfalo *(n.)* **segment**
ክፍኣት kf'at *(n.)* **bale**
ክፍኣት kf'at *(n.)* **infamy**
ክፍኣት kf'at *(n.)* **misdeed**
ክፈላለዩ ዘይኽእሉ kfelaleyu zeykh'elu *(adj.)* **inextricable**
ክፍፍል kffl *(n.)* **division**
ክፍፍላዊ kfflawi *(adj.)* **systematic**
ክፍለግዘ kfle gze *(n.)* **session**
ክፍለ ሃገር kfle hager *(n.)* **province**
ክፍለ ሃገራዊ kfle hagerawi *(adj.)* **provincial**
ክፍለ ዝከእል kfle zk'el *(adj.)* **separable**
ክፍሊ kfli *(n.)* **compartment**
ክፍሊ kfli *(n.)* **department**
ክፍሊ kfli *(n.)* **room**
ክፍሊ kfli *(n.)* **section**
ክፍሊት kflit *(n.)* **fee**
ክፍሊት kflit *(n.)* **payment**
ክፍሊት kflit *(n.)* **remuneration**
ክፍሊት ዕሻገ መራኽብ kflit eshage merakb *(n.)* **wharfage**
ክፍሊት ፍትሕ kflit ftḧ *(n.)* **alimony**
ክፍሊት ዝርከቦ kflit zrkebo *(adj.)* **remunerative**
ኽፍተት k-ftet *(n.)* **gap**
ክፉእ kfue *(adj.)* **unholy**
ክፉእ kfue *(adj.)* **wicked**
ክፉእ kfu'e *(adj.)* **infamous**
ክፉእ kfu'e *(adj.)* **malign**
ክፉእ kfu'e *(adj.)* **ugly**
ክፉፍ kfuf *(n.)* **hem**
ክፉት መአከቢ ቦታ kfut makebi bota *(n.)* **plaza**
ክጋገ ዝኽእል kgage zk'el *(adj.)* **fallible**
ኽብደት khbdet *(n.)* **load**
ኽዳን khdan *(n.)* **lid**
ክሕደት khdet *(n.)* **infidelity**
ክሕደት khdet *(n.)* **treachery**
ክሕደት kĥdet *(n.)* **repudiation**
ክሕደት kḧdet *(n.)* **denial**
ኽብድ መጥቃዕቲ ኣብፀሐ khebid metqh'eti eabtsehe *(v.)* **maim**
ኽንዲ khndi *(prep.)* **lieu**
ኽሲ khsi *(n.)* **indictment**
ኽትባት khtbat *(n.)* **inoculation**
ክሕፀብ ዝኽእል khxeb zk'el *(adj.)* **washable**
ኪጭበጥ ዘይከኣል kičbeẗ zeyke'al *(adj.)* **intangible**
ክዳን kidan *(n.)* **cloth**
ክዳዉንቲ kidawunti' *(n.)* **clothes**
ክፋል kifale *(n.)* **component**
ክፍሊ kifeli *(n.)* **class**
ኪኢላ ki'ila *(n.)* **specialist**
ክኢላ ki'la *(adj.)* **talented**
ክኢላ k'ila *(adj.)* **adept**
ኪኢላ k'ila *(adj.)* **skilled**
ክኢላ k'ila *(adj.)* **competent**
ክኢላ ሕጊ k'ila ḧgi *(n.)* **jurist**

ክኢላ ስነ መትኒ k'ila sne metni ***(n.)*** **neurologist**
ክኢላ k'ila ***(adj.)*** **accomplished**
ክኢላ k'ila ***(n.)*** **artisan**
ክኢላ k'ila ***(adj.)*** **capable**
ክኢላ k'ila ***(adj.)*** **deft**
ኪሎ kilo ***(n.)*** **kilo**
ኪሎ ባይት kilo-byt ***(n.)*** **kilobyte**
ኪሎሜትር kilomeeter ***(n.)*** **kilometre**
ክሎሪን kilorin ***(n.)*** **chlorine**
ክንክን kinkin ***(n.)*** **care**
ኪርኪር በለ kir kir bele ***(v.t.)*** **giggle**
ኪርዳእ ዚከኣል kirda'è zike'al ***(adj.)*** **comprehensible**
ኪስማዕ ዚከኣል kisma'ë zike'a ***(adj.)*** **audible**
ኪጠሓስ ዘይብሉ kiťeȟas zeyblu ***(adj.)*** **inviolable**
ኪትካእ ዘይከኣል kitka'è zeyke'al ***(adj.)*** **irreplaceable**
ኪዩብ kiyub ***(n.)*** **cube**
ኪዩቢካዊ kiyubikawi ***(adj.)*** **cubical**
ክኸውን ዝኸእል kḱewn zḱ'èl ***(adj.)*** **feasible**
ክኾን ዘይኽእል kkhon zeykh'eal ***(adj.)*** **improbable**
ክኾን ዝኽእል kkhon zkh'el ***(adj.)*** **likely**
ክላክ klak ***(n.)*** **siren**
ክሌምንታይን klemintaine ***(n.)*** **Clementine**
ክለቅቅ ዝክእል kleqq zk'el ***(adj.)*** **removable**
ክለሳ klesa ***(n.)*** **revision**
ክሊኒክ kliniqk ***(n.)*** **clinic**
ክልኩል klkul ***(adj.)*** **inadmissible**
ክልል kll ***(n.)*** **district**
ክልል kll ***(n.)*** **region**
ክልል kll ***(n.)*** **zone**
ክልላዊ kllawi ***(adj.)*** **regional**
ክልላዊ kllawi ***(adj.)*** **zonal**
ክሎሮፎርም kloroform ***(n.)*** **chloroform**
ክልሰ ሓሳብ klse hasab ***(n.)*** **theory**
ክልሰ ሓሳብ klse ȟasab ***(n.)*** **notion**
ክልሰ ሓሳባዊ klse hasabawi ***(adj.)*** **theoretical**
ክልተ klte ***(adj.&n.)*** **two**
ክልተ ጐድናዊ klte gwadnawi ***(adj.)*** **bilateral**
ክልተ ፔዳለ ዘለዎ ሳይክል klte piedale zelewo siykle ***(n.)*** **tandem**
ክልተ ቕነ klte qne ***(n.)*** **fortnight**
ክምስ በለ kms bele ***(v.)*** **chuckle**
ክምስ በለ kms bele ***(v.)*** **smile**
ክንበብ ዘፀግም knbeb zetzegm ***(adj.)*** **illegible**
ክንፊ knfi ***(n.)*** **wing**
ክንፊ ዓሳ knfi äsa ***(n.)*** **fin**
ክንክን ኣፃብዕቲ kn'kn atzab'eti ***(n.)*** **manicure**
ክኒንያ፣ knnya ***(n.)*** **tablet**
ክንቀፍ ዝግባእ knqef zgba'e ***(adj.)*** **reprehensible**
ክንቲት kntit ***(n.)*** **feather**
ክንቲት ዑፍ kntit ëuf ***(n.)*** **plumage**
ክንቲት ዝመልአ kntit zmel'ö ***(adj.)*** **quilted**
ክንየው knyew ***(adv.)*** **beyond**
ኮዓተ ko'äte ***(v.)*** **dig**
ኮዓተ ko'äte ***(v.)*** **excavate**
ኮባልት kobalt ***(n.)*** **cobalt**
ኮበርታ koberta ***(n.)*** **blanket**
ኮብላሊ koblali ***(adj.)*** **runaway**
ኮብለለ koblele ***(v.)*** **elope**
ኮብለለ koblele ***(v.)*** **roam**
ኮብራ ተመን kobra temen' ***(n.)*** **cobra**

ኮደብ በለ kodeb bele ***(v.)* flounce**
ኮፍ በለ kof bele ***(v.)* sit**
ኮፍ መበሊ kof mebeli ***(n.)* seat**
ኮካርድ kokard ***(n.)* cockade**
ኮኬን kokeen ***(n.)* cocaine**
ኮኾብ kokhob ***(n.)* star**
ኮኾብ መሳሊ kokhob mesali ***(adj.)* starry**
ኮኾባዊ kokhobawi ***(adj.)* stellar**
ኮኾባዊ kok̓obawi ***(adj.)* astral**
ኮላዥ kolazz ***(n.)* collage**
ኮሌጅ koleej ***(n.)* college**
ኮለፈ kolefe ***(v.)* punctuate**
ኮለለ kolele ***(v.)* revolve**
ኮሎኛ koloṅa ***(n.)* heather**
ኮሎኔል kolonele ***(n.)* colonel**
ኮማንደር komander ***(n.)* commander**
ኮማንዶ komando ***(n.)* commando**
ኮማዊ komawi ***(adj.)* communal**
ኮመዲኖ komedino ***(n.)* birch**
ኮሚደረ komidere ***(n.)* tomato**
ኮሚሽነር komishner ***(n.)* commissioner**
ኮምፕዩተር kompyuter ***(n.)* computer**
ኮናዕ kona'ë ***(n.)* buck**
ኮናዕ kona'ë ***(n.)* stag**
ኮንቺልያ kon'chilya ***(n.)* scallop**
ኮነ kone ***(conj.&adv.)* nor**
ኮነ ኢልካ kone eilka ***(adv.)* purposely**
ኮነ kone ***(v.)* be**
ኮነ kone ***(v.)* become**
ኮነነ konene ***(v.)* damn**
ኮኒካዊ konikawi ***(adj.)* conical**
ኮኖ kono ***(n.)* cone**
ኮንሰርትዮም konsertyom ***(n.)* consortium**
ኮንስታብል ሰብነት konstable sebenet' ***(n.)* constabulary**
ኮንስታብል konstablee ***(n.)* constable**
ኮንትሮባንድ kontroband ***(n.)* contraband**
ኮንትሮባንድ መስተ kontroband meste ***(adj.)* bootleg**
ኮራዪ korayi ***(adj.)* tetchy**
ኮረብታ korebta ***(n.)* hill**
ኮረቻ korecha ***(n.)* saddle**
ኮረንቲ korenti ***(n.)* electricity**
ኮረር korer ***(n.)* castor**
ኮረት koret ***(n.)* cobble**
ኮረየ koreye ***(adj.)* henpecked**
ኮርፋፍ korfaf ***(adj.)* moody**
ኮርፋፍ korfaf ***(adj.)* petulant**
ኮሪደዮ korideyo ***(n.)* aisle**
ኮረኪ korki ***(n.)* cork**
ኮርኪዕካዮ ዝስሕቅ korkiakayo zshk ***(adj.)* ticklish**
ኮርነት kornet ***(n.)* cornet**
ኮርቲሶን kortison ***(n.)* cortisone**
ኮስታራይ kostaray ***(n.)* sweeper**
ኮስታሪ kostari ***(n.)* duster**
ኮስተረ kostere ***(v.)* sweep**
ኮኮናት coconat ***(n.)* coconut**
ኮንዶም condom ***(n.)* condom**
ኮቶኛ kotogna ***(n.)* quince**
ኮይከር koyker ***(n.)* Quaker**
ኮዝሞሎጂ kozmoloji ***(n.)* cosmology**
ክቕየር ዘይኽእል ሕመቕ kqhyer zeykh'el hmeqh ***(adj.)* incorrigible**
ክቋረፅ ዘይኽእል kquarets zeykh'el ***(adj.)* inexorable**
ክራባት krabat ***(n.)* cravat**
ክራባታ krabata ***(n.)* tie**
ክራይ kray ***(n.)* rent**
ክራይ kray ***(n.)* tenancy**

ክረምቲ kremti *(n.)* **summer**
ክርሃት krhat *(n.)* **apathy**
ክሪ kri *(n.)* **floss**
ክሪ kri *(n.)* **thread**
ክሪክ krik *(n.)* **jack**
ክሪንኪሕ krinkiḧ *(adj.)* **bumpy**
ክሪኬት krkeet *(n.)* **cricket**
ክርክር krkr *(n.)* **contention**
ኽርክር krkr *(n.)* **controversy**
ክርክራዊ krkrawi *(adj.)* **forensic**
ክርኩር kr'kur *(adj.)* **mealy**
ክሮም krom *(n.)* **chrome**
ክርተና krtena *(n.)* **quarantine**
ክሳብ ksab *(prep.)* **until**
ክሳብ ksab *(n.)* **while**
ክሳብ ksab *(conj.)* **whilst**
ክሳድ ksad *(n.)* **neck**
ክሳራ ksara *(n.)* **deficit**
ክሻ ksha *(n.)* **sack**
ክሽናዊ kshnawi *(adj.)* **culinary**
ክብራዊ kbrawi *(adj.)* **honorary**
ክብሪ kbri *(n.)* **honour**
ከቢድ kebid *(adj.)* **heavy**
ከልቢ ሃድን kelbi hadn *(n.)* **hound**
ከውሒ በረድ kewḥi bered *(n.)* **iceberg**
ከውሒ-በረድ kewḧibered *(n.)* **glacier**
ኪዕቀን ዘይከኣል ki'ëqen zeyke'al *(adj.)* **immeasurable**
ክኢላ k'ila *(adj.)* **versed**
ኪቕጽል ዚኽእል kiq̈xl zik̈'èl *(adj.)* **viable**
ኪረአ ዚከኣል kire'e zike'al *(adj.)* **visible**
ኮብለለ koblele *(v.)* **wander**
ኰነ kone *(v.)* **happen**
ክሳብ ሕጂ ksab ḥği *(adv.)* **hitherto**
ክሽምሽ kshmsh *(n.)* **gooseberry**
ክሲ ksi *(n.)* **impeachment**
ኩጀት kujet *(n.)* **hillock**
ኵሊት kulit *(n.)* **kidney**
ኳሕኵሐ kwaḥkuḥe *(v.)* **knock**
ክሽነ kshne *(n.)* **kitchen**
ክሽየጥ ዝኽእል kshyet zk'el *(adj.)* **saleable**
ክሲ ksi *(n.)* **accusation**
ክስላሕ ዘይኽእል kslah zykh'el *(adj.)* **incalculable**
ክስራሕ ዝኽእል ksrah zkh'el *(adj.)* **manageable**
ክስተኽኸል ዘይኽእል ፀገም kstekhakel zeylh'el tsegem *(adj.)* **insurmountable**
ክስተት kstet *(n.)* **phenomenon**
ክስተታዊ kstetawi *(adj.)* **phenomenal**
ክሱስ ksus *(v.t.)* **accused**
ክታብ ktab *(n.)* **amulet**
ክታበት ktabet *(n.)* **vaccination**
ክታበት ktabet *(n.)* **vaccine**
ክታም ktam *(n.)* **cachet**
ክትዕ kt'ë *(v. i)* **dispute**
ክትዕገሶ ዝካኣል kt'egeso zka'al *(adj.)* **tolerable**
ክትግበር ዘይኽእል ktgber zeykh'el *(adj.)* **inapplicable**
ክትዕ ምውጋድ ktie mwgad *(v.)* **parry**
ክትከላኸለሉ ዝከኣል ktkelakelelu zkeal *(adj.)* **tenable**
ክትላዘበሉ ትኽእል ktlazebelu tk̈'el *(adj.)* **negotiable**
ክትነብረሉ ዚበቅዕ ktnebrelu zibeq'ë *(adj.)* **habitable**
ክትራ ktra *(n.)* **wicket**
ክትጽመሞ ዘይከኣል ktsmemo zeyke'al *(adj.)* **insupportable**

ክትጥቀመሉ ትኽእል ktẗqemelu tḱ'èl *(adj.)* **available**
ኳዕናን kuae'nan *(n.)* **panache**
ኲራ kuara *(n.)* **petulance**
ኩዕሾ ምምንጣል kuausho mmntal *(v.t.)* **tackle**
ኩባያ kubaya *(n.)* **cup**
ኩባያ kubaya *(n.)* **mug**
ኩዕሾ ውርጪ ku'esho wrchi *(n.)* **snowball**
ኩዕሶ ዓይኒ ku'ëso äyni *(n.)* **eyeball**
ኩዕሶ እግሪ ku'ëso egri *(n.)* **football**
ኩዕሶ እግሪ ku'ëso egri *(n.)* **soccer**
ኩዕሶ ku'ëso *(n.)* **ball**
ኩሕለ-ምሕሊ kuḧlemḧli *(n.)* **antiperspirant**
ኩሕሊ kuḧli *(n.)* **mascara**
ኩጆት kujet *(n.)* **hummock**
ኩኽ kuk *(n.)* **peach**
ኩኩምበር kukumber *(n.)* **cucumber**
ኩኩናይ kukunay *(n.)* **cock**
ኩኩናይ kukunay *(n.)* **rooster**
ኩላሶ kulaso *(n.)* **morsel**
ኩላሶ kulaso *(n.)* **mouthful**
ኵላሶ kulaso *(n.)* **brunch**
ኩለምሉ kulemulu *(n.)* **entirety**
ኩልተፋ kultefa *(n.)* **lisp**
ኩሉ kulu *(adj.)* **all**
ኩሉ ግዜ kulu gzee *(adv.)* **always**
ኩሉ ዝኣምን kulu zamn *(adj.)* **trustful**
ኩሉ ዚከኣሎ kulu zike'alo *(adj.)* **almighty**
ኩሉኹሉ kuluḱulu *(adv.)* **altogether**
ኩምር ዝበለ ፀጉሪ kumr zbele tseguri *(n.)* **thatch**
ኩምራ kumra *(n.)* **heap**
ኩምራ kumra *(n.)* **pile**
ኩምራ ሓመድ kumra ḧamed *(n.)* **mound**
ኩናነ kunane *(n.)* **damnation**
ኹናት kunat *(n.)* **combat**
ኩነት kunet *(n.)* **case**
ኩነት kunet *(n.)* **condition**
ኩነት kunet *(n.)* **fettle**
ኩነታት ኣየር kunetat ayer *(n.)* **weather**
ኩነታት ኣየር kunetat ayer' *(n.)* **climate**
ኩነታዊ kunetawi *(adj.)* **conditional**
ኩፖን kupon *(n.)* **coupon**
ኹረሽ kuresh *(n.)* **crochet**
ኩሪፍ በለ kurif bele *(n.)* **snort**
ኩርኩር kurkur *(n.)* **pup**
ኩርኩር kurkur *(n.)* **puppy**
ኩርኩር kurkur *(n.)* **whelp**
ኩርኩር ኣንበሳ kurkur aanbesa *(n.)* **cub**
ኩርምቲ kurmti *(n.)* **molar**
ኩርናዓዊ kurna'äwi *(adj.)* **angular**
ኩርናዕ kurna'ë *(n.)* **nook**
ኵርናዕ ኢድ kurna'ë id *(n.)* **elbow**
ኩርናዕ kurna'ë *(n.)* **angle**
ኹርናዕ kurna'ë *(n.)* **corner**
ኩሩዕ kuru'e *(adj.)* **lordly**
ኩሩዕ kuruë *(adj.)* **proud**
ካሮት carrot *(n.)* **carrot**
ካቶሊክ catholic *(adj.)* **catholic**
ክትግበር ዘይክእል ktgeber zeyk'el *(adj.)* **impracticable**
ኵስኰሳ ወይኒ kuskwasa weyni *(n.)* **viticulture**
ኳኽ kwak *(n.)* **crow**
ኳኽ kwak *(n.)* **rook**
ኳሌታ kwaleta *(n.)* **collar**
ኰነነ kwanene *(v.)* **condemn**
ኳንጎ kwanka *(n.)* **quango**

ኲርክ kwark *(n.)* **quark**
ኲርት kwart *(n.)* **quart**
ኲርትዝ kwartz *(n.)* **quartz**
ኵናት kwinat *(n.)* **war**
ክዉን kwun *(adj.)* **actual**
ክዉንነት kwunnet *(n.)* **surrealism**
ኹሉ ምኽኣል kulu mk'al *(n.)* **omnipotence**
ኽብሪ kdri *(n.)* **observance**
ኽዳን kdan *(n.)* **outfit**

ወ

ወረረ werere *(v.)* **overrun**
ወረርሽኝ werershgn *(n.)* **outbreak**
ወቄት weqet *(n.)* **ounce**
ወይ wey *(conj.)* **or**
ወጥዋጥ wetwat *(adj.)* **oblong**
ዋዕሮ wa'ëro *(n.)* **vixen**
ዋሓለ waḥale *(adj.)* **versatile**
ወዲ wedi *(n.)* **lad**
ወገፈ wegefe *(n.)* **vestibule**
ወልዐ wel'ë *(v.)* **ignite**
ወንጌል wengeel *(n.)* **gospel**
ወርቂ werqi *(n.)* **gold**
ውርሲ wersi *(n.)* **heritage**
ወርወረ werwere *(v.)* **hurl**
ወተሃደር ነበር wetehader neber *(n.)* **veteran**
ውህደት whdet *(n.)* **harmony**
ዊንታ winta *(n.)* **volition**
ውልውል ነግ ፈረግ wlwl neg fereg *(n.)* **vacillation**
ውርደተኛ wrdeteña *(adj.)* **ignominious**
ዋጭዋጭታ wachwachta *(n.)* **squeal**
ዋዕላ wa'ela *(n.)* **convention**
ዋዕሮ wa'ëro *(n.)* **bitch**
ዋዕታ wa'eta *(n.)* **sonority**
ዋዕዋዕ waewae *(adj.)* **uproarious**
ዋዕዋዕ wa'ewa'e *(n.)* **clamour**
ዋዕዋዕ wa'ëwa'ë *(n.)* **noise**
ዋዕዋዕ በለ waëwaë bele *(v.)* **roister**
ዋዕዋዕ ዝበዝሖ wa'ëwa'ë zbezḧo *(adj.)* **noisy**
ዋዕዋዕታ waewaeta *(n.)* **uproar**
ዋጋ waga *(n.)* **fare**
ዋጋ waga *(n.)* **price**
ዋጋ waga *(n.)* **value**
ዋጋ waga *(adj.)* **worth**
ዋጋ ኣዉፀአ waga awxe'e *(v.)* **cost**
ዋጋ ቴንብር waga tienbr *(n.)* **postage**
ዋጋ ዘለዎ' waga zelewo *(adj.)* **worthwhile**
ዋጋ ዘይብሉ waga zeyblu *(adj.)* **feckless**
ዋጋ ዘይብሉ waga zeyblu *(adj.)* **worthless**
ዋሕዲ waĥdi *(n.)* **dearth**
ዋሕዲ waĥdi *(n.)* **deficiency**
ዋሕዲ waĥdi *(n.)* **shortfall**
ዋሕዲ ደም waḧdi dem *(n.)* **anaemia**
ዋህዮ waheyo *(n.)* **cell**
ዋህረም wahrem *(n.)* **banger**
ዋህረም wahrem *(n.)* **pudding**
ዋሕስ waḥs *(n.)* **guarantor**
ዋሕስ waḥs *(n.)* **warrantor**
ዋሕስ waḧs *(n.)* **bail**
ዋህዮኣዊ wahyo'awi *(adj.)* **cellular**
ዋሕዚ waĥzi *(n.)* **rivulet**
ዋሕዚ waḧzi *(n.)* **flux**
ዋዒ wa'ï *(n.)* **heat**
ዋላ wala *(pron.)* **whatever**
ዋላ wala *(conj.)* **whether**
ዋላ ሓደ እኳ wala ḧade ekwa *(adj.)* **neither**
ዋላ ሓደ እኳ wala ḧade ekwa *(pron.)* **nobody**

ዋላ ሓደ እኳ wala ȟade ekwa *(pron.)* **none**

ዋላ ሓደሻዕ wala ȟadeshaë *(adv.)* **ever**

ዋላ ሓንቲ wala ȟanti *(pron.)* **nothing**

ዋላካ እንተኮነ walaka entekone *(conj.)* **though**

ዋልድቢት waldbit *(n.)* **attic**

ዋልድቢት waldbit *(n.)* **garret**

ዋልታዊ waltawi *(adj.)* **polar**

ዋና wana *(adj.)* **main**

ዋና wana *(adj.)* **major**

ዋና wana *(n.)* **proprietor**

ዋና ኣእምሮ wana a'emro *(n.)* **mastermind**

ዋና ኣካል wana alkal *(n.)* **mainstay**

ዋና ጎዳና wana godana *(n.)* **thoroughfare**

ዋና ከሻኒ wana kesha'ni *(n.)* **chef**

ዋና ምምሕዳር wana mmhhdar *(n.)* **headquarters**

ዋና ዘይብሉ wana zeyblu *(adj.)* **unattended**

ዋኒን wanin *(n.)* **business**

ዋኒናት waninat *(n.)* **conjuncture**

ዋንነት wannet *(n.)* **possession**

ዋንነታዊ wannetawi *(adj.)* **proprietary**

ዋርድያ wardiya *(v.)* **patrol**

ዋርድያ wardya *(n.)* **sentry**

ዋርዋርታ warwarta *(n.)* **mirage**

ዋይ ኣነ way 'ane *(conj.)* **alas**

ዋዛ waza *(n)* **comedy**

ዋዛ waza *(n.)* **humour**

ዋዛ waza *(n.)* **lark**

ዋዛ waza *(n.)* **raillery**

ውዳሰ-ከንቱ wdasekentu *(n.)* **adulation**

ውድብ wdb *(n.)* **party**

ውድድር wddr *(n.)* **rivalry**

ውድድራዊ wddrawi *(adj.)* **competitive**

ውዲት ኣለመ wdit aleme *(v.)* **sabotage**

ውድቀት wdqet *(n.)* **demise**

ዉድቀት wdqet *(n.)* **downfall**

ዉድቀት wdqet *(n.)* **failure**

ወጫጪ weçaçi *(adj.)* **vociferous**

ወጬጬ wečeče *(v.)* **bawl**

መርዚ wečeče merzi *(n.)* **poison**

ወዳደሰ wedadese *(v.)* **flatter**

ወዳኢ weda'i *(n.)* **executor**

ወድአ wed'e *(n.)* **conclude**

ወድአ wed'e *(v.)* **consume**

ወደብ wedeb *(n.)* **port**

ወደአ wede'e *(v.)* **deplete**

ወደቀ wedeqe *(v. t.)* **decline**

ወደቐ wedeqe *(v.)* **drop**

ወደቐ wedeqe *(v.)* **fall**

ወደቐ wedeq̈e *(v.)* **expire**

ወደሰ wedese *(v.)* **laud**

ወዲ wedi *(n.)* **bloke**

ወዲ ዓበይቲ wedi äbeyti *(n.)* **nobleman**

ወዲ ዓዲ wedi adi *(adj.)* **local**

ወዲ ዓዲ wedi ädi *(n.)* **native**

ወዲኣኮ wedi 'ako *(n.)* **cousin**

ወዲ ደራፊ ፅብቅ ድምፂ ዘለዎ wedi derafi sbuk dmsi zelewo *(n.)* **tenor**

ወዲ ገጠር ኮነ wedi geter kone *(v.)* **rusticate**

ወዲ ገጠር ምኻን wedi geter mkwan *(n.)* **rustication**

ወዲ ሃገር wedi hager *(n.)* **compatriot**

ወዲ ምዕራብ wedi m'erab *(n.)* **westerner**

ወደ መዝሙር wedi mezmur *(n.)* **disciple**
ወድ ንጉስ wedi ngus *(n.)* **prince**
ወዲ ሰብ wedi seb *(n.)* **humanity**
ወዲ ወፃእ wedi wexa'e *(n.)* **expatriate**
ወዲ wedi *(n.)* **boy**
ወዲ ሰብ wediseb *(n.)* **Wight**
ወድወዶ wedwodo *(n.)* **tomboy**
ወፈያ wefeya *(n.)* **contribution**
ወፈየ wefeye *(v.)* **dedicate**
ወፈየ wefeye *(v.)* **devote**
ወፍሪ wefri *(n.)* **expedition**
ወግአ weg'a *(v.)* **pierce**
ወግአ wega *(n.)* **prickle**
ወጋሕታ wegahta *(n.)* **dawn**
ወጋኢ wega'i *(adj.)* **biting**
ወግዓዊ መልእኽቲ weg'äwi mel'eḱti *(n.)* **missive**
ወግዓዊ ምግዳፍ weg'äwi mgdaf *(n.)* **renunciation**
ወግአ weg'e *(v.)* **inject**
ወግአ we'g'e *(v.)* **stab**
ወግዒ weg'ë *(n.)* **rite**
ወገደ wegede *(v.t.)* **renounce**
ወገደ wegede *(v.)* **avoid**
ወገናዊ wegenawi *(adj.)* **sectarian**
ወገንነት wegen'net *(n.)* **nepotism**
ወግዒ weg'i *(n.)* **conversation**
ወግዒ weg'ï *(n.)* **nicety**
ወሃቢ wehabi *(adj.)* **philanthropic**
ወሓደ wehade *(v.)* **lessen**
ወሓጥ ጒንጺ weḧaẗ gwanxi *(n.)* **buffer**
ወሓጠ weĥate *(v.)* **devour**
ወሓጠ weḧaẗe *(v.)* **engulf**
ወሓጠ weḧaẗe *(v.)* **swallow**
ወሓጠ weḥaṭe *(v.)* **gulp**
ወሓዘ weĥaze *(v.)* **drift**
ወሓለ weĥle *(adj.)* **skilful**
ወጃብ wejab *(adj.)* **seedy**
ወጃብ wejab *(n.)* **slob**
ወጃዕጃዕ በሃሊ wejaëjaë behali *(adj.)* **rumbustious**
ወጅሂ weĵhi *(n.)* **complexion**
ወከለ wekele *(v.)* **depute**
ወኪል wekil *(n.)* **proxy**
ውዕል w'el *(n.)* **indenture**
ውዕል w'ël *(n.)* **contract**
ውዕል w'ël *(n)* **contract**
ውዕል w'ël *(n.)* **deal**
ውዕል w'ël *(n.)* **stipulation**
ውዕል w'ël *(n.)* **bond**
ወላድ welad *(n.)* **maternity**
ወላድ welad *(adj.)* **multiparous**
ወላዲ weladi *(n.)* **parent**
ወላዲት weladit *(n.)* **mother**
ወልዳፍ weldaf *(adj.)* **halting**
ወለደ welede *(v.)* **procreate**
ወለደ welede *(v.)* **beget**
ወለዶ weledo *(n.)* **lineage**
ወለዱ ዝቐተለ weledu zqetele *(n.)* **parricide**
ወልፊ welfi *(n.)* **addiction**
ወንበር wenber *(n.)* **couch**
ወንጭፍ wenĉf *(n.)* **sling**
ወንጨፈ wenchefe *(v.)* **hurtle**
ወንበር weneber *(n.)* **chair**
ወነነ wenene *(v.)* **possess**
ወንጀለ wenjele *(v.)* **attribute**
ወንጀለኛ wenjelegna *(adj.)* **guilty**
ወንጀለኛ wenjelegna *(n.)* **miscreant**
ወቐዐ weqe *(v.)* **whisk**
ወቕዐ weq'ë *(v.)* **strum**
ወቀረ weqere *(v.)* **engrave**
ወቀሰ weqese *(v.)* **blame**
ወቀሰ weqese *(v.)* **censure**

ወቀሰ weqese *(v.)* **deprecate**
ወቀሰ weqese *(v.)* **niggle**
ወቀሰ weqese *(v.)* **reproach**
ወቐሰ weqese *(adj.)* **upbraid**
ወቐሰ weq̈ese *(v.)* **berate**
ወቓዓይ weqha'äy *(n.)* **striker**
ወቕታዊ weqtawi *(adj.)* **seasonable**
ወቕታዊ weqtawi *(adj.)* **seasonal**
ወቕታዊ weqtawi *(adj.)* **topical**
ወቕቲ weqti *(n.)* **season**
ወጋኢ weraei *(n.)* **poker**
ወራሪ werari *(n.)* **marauder**
ወራሪ werari *(adj.)* **rampant**
ወራሲ werasi *(n.)* **successor**
ወራሲ werasi *(n.)* **heir**
ወረዳ wereda *(n.)* **precinct**
ወረዳ wereda *(n.)* **canton**
ወረደ werede *(v.t,)* **abdicate**
ወረደ werede *(v.t.)* **alight**
ወረደ werede *(v.)* **befall**
ወረደ werede *(v.)* **descend**
ወረደ werede *(v.)* **disembark**
ወረጃ ዘኮነ ሰብ wereja zekone seb *(n.)* **gentleman**
ወረንጦ werento *(n.)* **tweezers**
ወረቀት ዕዳ wereqet ëda *(n.)* **bill**
ወረራ werera *(n.)* **foray**
ወረራ werera *(n.)* **incursion**
ወረራ werera *(n.)* **raid**
ወረራ we're'ra *(n.)* **conquest**
ወረረ werere *(v.)* **infest**
ወረረ werere *(v.)* **invade**
ወረረ werere *(v.)* **maraud**
ወረረ were're *(v.)* **conquer**
ወረሰ werese *(v.)* **confiscate**
ወረሰ werese *(v.)* **inherit**
ወረጦ werеẗo *(n.)* **forceps**
ወረጦ wereto *(n.)* **pincer**
ወርሓዊ werhawi *(adj.)* **lunar**
ወርሓዊ werḧawi *(adj.)* **monthly**
ወርሒ werḧi *(n.)* **month**
ወርሒ werḧi *(n.)* **moon**
ወሪርካ ምሓዝ werirka m'ḧaz *(n.)* **subjugation**
ወሪሩ ሓዘ weriru ḧaze *(v.)* **subjugate**
ወርቃዊ werqawi *(adj.)* **golden**
ወረቐት werqet *(n.)* **paper**
ወርቀዘቦ werqezebo *(n.)* **brocade**
ወርጠበ werẗebe *(n.)* **stripling**
ወርዊሩ werwiru *(v.)* **toss**
ወሳናይ wesanay *(adj.)* **decisive**
ወሳኒ wesani *(adj.)* **critical**
ወሳኒ wesani *(n.)* **determinant**
ወሳኒ ግጥም wesani gtm *(n.)* **showdown**
ወሰደ wesede *(v.)* **take**
ወሰኽ wesek *(n.)* **increment**
ወሰኸ weseke *(v.)* **augment**
ወሰኸ weseke *(v.)* **increase**
ወሰን wesen *(n.)* **edge**
ወሰን ከተማ wesen ketema *(n.)* **suburb**
ወሰን ከተማ wesen ketema *(adj.)* **suburban**
ወሰን ከተማ wesen ketema *(n.)* **suburbia**
ወሰናወሰን wesena'wesen *(n.)* **contour**
ወሰነ wesene *(v.)* **confine**
ወሰነ wesene *(v. t)* **determine**
ወሰነ wesesne *(v.)* **decide**
ወሽመጥ weshmeẗ *(n.)* **fjord**
ወሽመጥ weshmeṭ *(n.)* **gulf**
ወሽመጥ weshmt *(n.)* **peninsula**
ወሲብ ዘላዓዕል wesib zela'ä'ël *(adj.)* **erotic**

ወሲብ ዝፈቱ wesib zfetu ***(n.)*** **sensualist**
ወሰኽ ዋጋ weskh waga ***(n.)*** **inflation**
ወስላት weslat ***(n.)*** **rascal**
ወስላት weslat ***(adj.)*** **roguish**
ወስታ westa ***(n.)*** **gesture**
ወታደር wetader ***(adj.)*** **military**
ወታደር wetader ***(n.)*** **soldier**
ወታደራዊ ቤት ማእሰርቲ wetaderawi beet ma'eserti ***(n.)*** **stockade**
ወታእታእ በለ weta'eta'e bele ***(v.)*** **splutter**
ወታእታእ በለ weta'eta'e bele ***(v.)*** **stammer**
ወጣም wetam ***(adj.)*** **inquisitive**
ወጣም weẗam ***(adj.)*** **nosy**
ወጣት ዕድሚኡ 13-19 ዝኾነ wetat edmiu kab 13-19 zkone ***(n.)*** **teenager**
ወተፈ wetefe ***(v.)*** **thrust**
ወተግ weteg ***(n.)*** **nape**
ወተሃደር wetehader ***(n.)*** **warrior**
ወጠነ weẗene ***(v.)*** **intend**
ወጠረ we-ṭe-re ***(v.)*** **heckle**
ወትሩ ሕጉስ wetru higus ***(adj.)*** **cheerful**
ወፃኢ ገበረ wetsa'i gebere ***(v.)*** **disburse**
ውዕውዕ w'ëw'ë ***(adj.)*** **fervent**
ውዕውዕ w'ëw'ë ***(adj.)*** **vivid**
ውዕውዕ ስምዒት w'ëw'ë sm'ït ***(n.)*** **enthusiasm**
ውዕውዕ ስምዒት w'ëw'ë sm'ït ***(n.)*** **verve**
ወፃኢ wexa'i ***(n.)*** **expenditure**
ወፃኢ wexa'i ***(n.)*** **expense**
ወጸ wexe ***(v.)*** **vacate**
ወይ wey ***(adv.)*** **either**
ወይቦ weybo ***(adj.)*** **hepatitis**
ወይቦ weybo ***(n.)*** **jaundice**
ወይና ደጋ weyna dega ***(adj.)*** **temperate**
ወይናይ weynay ***(n.)*** **mulberry**
ወይኒ weyni ***(n.)*** **grape**
ወይኒ weyni ***(n,)*** **wine**
ወይዘሪት weyzerit ***(n.)*** **miss**
ወይዘሮ weyzero ***(n.)*** **dame**
ወይዘሮ weyzero ***(n.)*** **lady**
ወይዘሮ weyzero ***(n.)*** **madam**
ወይዘሮ weyzero ***(n.)*** **matron**
ወዛል wezal ***(adj.)*** **blowsy**
ወዛል wezal ***(adj.)*** **shabby**
ወዛል wezal ***(adj.)*** **slatternly**
ወዝቢ wezbi ***(n.)*** **contingency**
ወዘተረፈ wezeterefe ***(adv.)*** **et cetera**
ዉፋይነት wfaynet ***(n.)*** **dedication**
ውግኣት wgat ***(n.)*** **pang**
ወጋእ wge ***(v.i.)*** **peck**
ዋንነታዊ aganazabi ***(adj.)*** **possessive**
ውግእ ውግእ ኣቢሉ wgè wgè abilu ***(v.)*** **prod**
ውግእ wg'è ***(n.)*** **battle**
ውህደት whdet ***(n.)*** **assimilation**
ውህደት whdet ***(n.)*** **coordination**
ዉህደት whdet ***(n.)*** **fusion**
ውሒጣ wḥiṭa ***(n.)*** **glutton**
ዉሕጅ wĥj ***(n.)*** **flood**
ዉሕጅ wḧj ***(n.)*** **current**
ውሕጃዊ wĥjawi ***(adj.)*** **fluvial**
ውህለላ whlela ***(n.)*** **accumulation**
ውሕልልነት wĥllnet ***(n.)*** **dexterity**
ውሕልና ኣእዳው wĥlna a'edaw ***(n.)*** **sleight**
ውህሉል whlul ***(n.)*** **hoard**
ውሕስነት ዝተወሃቦ wḧsnet ztewehabo ***(adj.)*** **assured**

ውሁድ whud *(n.)* **compound**
ውሁድ whud *(adj.)* **concerted**
ውሑዳን wḧudan *(n.)* **minority**
ዊን ዝበሎ ዝገብር win zbelo zgebr *(adj.)* **madcap**
ውከላ wkela *(n.)* **deputation**
ውከሳ ሙታን wkesa mutan *(n.)* **necromancy**
ውክልና wklna *(n.)* **commission**
ውልቀኛ wkqegna *(n.)* **maverick**
ውላድ ድሙ wlad dmu *(n.)* **kitten**
ውልደታዊ wldetawi *(adj.)* **natal**
ውልቃዊ wlqawi *(adj.)* **private**
ዉልቃዊነት wlqawinet *(n.)* **individualism**
ዉልቃዊነት wlqawinet *(n.)* **individuality**
ውልቃውነት wlqawnet *(n.)* **privacy**
ዉልቀ wlqe *(adj.)* **individual**
ውልቀ ምልኪ wlqe mlki *(n.)* **autocracy**
ውልቀኛ w'lqegna *(n.)* **soloist**
ውልቀ-መላኺ wlqemelaḱi *(n.)* **autocrat**
ውልውል wlwl *(n.)* **quandary**
ውቅዒት wq'it *(v.)* **strike**
ውርጪ wrchi *(n.)* **snow**
ዉርደት wrdet *(n.)* **disgrace**
ዉርደት wrdet *(n.)* **dishonour**
ውርደት wrdet *(n.)* **ignominy**
ውርዲ wrdi *(n.)* **breadth**
ውረዛ wreza *(n.)* **courtship**
ውሪግሪግ በለ wrigrig bele *(v.)* **shimmer**
ውርሳ wrsa *(n.)* **confiscation**
ውርሻ wrsha *(n.)* **bequest**
ውርሻዊ wrshawi *(adj.)* **congenital**
ውሩይ wruy *(adj.)* **noted**
ውሩይ wruy *(adj.)* **prestigious**
ውርወራ wrwera *(n.)* **lunge**
ውርዝውና wrzwna *(n.)* **virtue**
ዉሳነ wsane *(n.)* **decision**
ውሳነ ህዝቢ wsane hzbi *(n.)* **referendum**
ወሳኒ wsani *(adj.)* **indispensable**
ውሰኸ wseḱa *(n.)* **addition**
ውሻል wshal *(n.)* **wedge**
ውሻጠ wshate *(n.)* **cellar**
ውሽማ wshma *(n.)* **concubine**
ውሽጣዊ wshtawi *(adj.)* **inmost**
ውሽጣዊ wshẗawi *(adj.)* **interior**
ውሽጣዊ wshẗawi *(adj.)* **internal**
ውሽጣዊ wshẗawi *(adj.)* **inward**
ውሽጣዊ መዘራረቢ wshẗawi mezerarebi *(n.)* **intercom**
ውሽጣዊ ሰንጣቒት wshẗawi senẗaqit *(n.)* **calibre**
ውሽጢ wshti *(prep.)* **within**
ውሽጢ wshẗi *(n.)* **inside**
ውሽጢ ምእታው wshti metaw *(v.)* **penetrate**
ውስኪ wski *(n.)* **whisky**
ውሱን wsun *(adj.)* **exclusive**
ውትረት wtret *(n.)* **tension**
ውፅእ እትው ምባል wts'e 'etuw mbal *(n.)* **sally**
ውጽእ እትው wts'e e'tw *(v.)* **undulate**
ውፅኢት wts'it *(n.)* **result**
ዉድድር wuddr *(n.)* **tournament**
ዉድድር wudi'dir *(n.)* **contest**
ዉዲተኛ wuditenya *(n.)* **conspirator**
ዉገዳ wugeda *(n.)* **avoidance**
ውገዳ wugeda *(n.)* **disqualification**
ዉህብቶ wuhbto *(n.)* **gift**
ውህለላ wuhlela *(n.)* **savings**
ውሁሉል wuhlul *(adj.)* **cumulative**
ውሕስነት wuhsnet *(n.)* **security**

ዉሕስነት wuhsnet *(n.)* **immunity**
ውሕስነት ሃበ wuhsnet habe *(v.)* **immunize**
ዉሑድ wuhud *(adj.)* **scant**
ዉሑድ wuĥud *(adj.)* **few**
ዉሑጅ wuhuj *(n.)* **torrent**
ዉሕስ wuhus *(adj.)* **immune**
ዉሑስ wuhus *(adj.)* **safe**
ዉላድ wulad *(n.)* **progeny**
ውልደ ኦም wulde om *(n.)* **sapling**
ዉሉድ wulud *(n.)* **son**
ዉሉፍ wuluf *(n.)* **addict**
ዉሉፍ wuluf *(adj.)* **addicted**
ዉሉፍ wuluf *(adj.)* **dependent**
ውንታ wunta *(n.)* **déjà vu**
ዉንዘፋ wunzefa *(n.)* **abeyance**
ዉንዙፍ ስራሕ wunzuf sraḧ *(n.)* **backlog**
ዉቃጦ wuqato *(n.)* **tattoo**
ዉቅያኖስ ዘቋርፅ wuqyanos zeqars *(adj.)* **transatlantic**
ዉርጫም wurĉam *(adj.)* **frosty**
ውርጫዊ wurchawi *(adj.)* **snowy**
ዉርጪ wurĉi *(n.)* **frost**
ውርሲ wursi *(n.)* **inheritance**
ዉርሲ wursi *(n.)* **legacy**
ውርይነት wuruynet *(n.)* **renown**
ውሻጠ wushate' *(n.)* **closet**
ውሽጣዊ wushtawi *(adj.)* **inner**
ውሽጣዊ wushtawi *(adj.)* **innermost**
ውሽጣዊ ዋሕዚ wushtawi wahzi *(n.)* **undercurrent**
ዉፂኢታማ wusieitama *(adj.)* **telling**
ዉስተዘ wustez *(n.)* **pun**
ዉሱን wusun *(adj.)* **definite**
ዉሱን wusun *(adj.)* **finite**
ዉሱን wusun *(n.)* **term**
ዉጥሚት wutmit *(n.)* **tab**
ዉፅኣት wuts'at *(n.)* **diarrhoea**
ውፅኢት wutsieiit *(adj.)* **consequent**
ውፅኢት wuts'it *(n.)* **score**
ውፁእ wutsu'e *(adj.)* **distinct**
ዉጡን wutun *(adj.)* **intentional**
ዉዑይ wu'uy *(adj.)* **sprightly**
ውዑይ w'üy *(adj.)* **hot**
ዉዝምበሩ ዝዎየ wuzmbru zwese *(adj.)* **tempestuous**
ውፁዕ wxeu'e *(adj.)* **underprivileged**
ዉፅኢታዊ wxi'itawi *(adj.)* **effective**
ዉዝወዛ wz'waze *(n.)* **swing**
ወጻኢ ገንዘብ wetsa'i genzeb *(n.)* **outlay**
ዋና wana *(n.)* **owner**
ዋንነት wannet *(n.)* **ownership**
ውላድ wlad *(n.)* **offspring**
ውሻጠ wshate *(n.)* **outhouse**
ውቅያኖሳዊ wqyanosawi *(adj.)* **oceanic**
ውቅያኖስ wqyanos *(n.)* **ocean**
ውደሳ wudesa *(n.)* **ode**
ውድብ wudb *(n.)* **organization**
ውፅኢት wts'it *(n.)* **outcome**
ውፅኢት wts'it *(n.)* **output**
ዑደት xudet *(n.)* **goose**

ዓ

ዓመታዊ 'ämetawi *(n.)* **circulation**
ዓዓ 'ä'ä *(adj.)* **annual**
ዓቢ 'äbi *(adj.)* **great**
ዓጋቲ 'ägati *(n.)* **impasse**
ዓጀብቲ äjebti *(n.)* **entourage**
ዓለባ ሃሪ 'äleba hari *(n.)* **velvet**

ዓለምለኻዊ 'älemleǩawi *(adj.)* **global**
ዓማል ämal *(adj.)* **fallow**
ዓንቀፈ 'änqefe *(v.)* **impede**
ዓንቀጸ anqe-tse *(v.)* **hinder**
ዓቃቢ ንዋይ äqabi nway *(n.)* **exchequer**
ዓቀበ 'aqebe *(v. t)* **conserve**
ዓርሱ ተኸናኸነ ärsu tekenakene *(v.)* **fend**
ዓጠረ 'äṭere *(n.)* **wrinkle**
ዓጠረ 'äṭere *(n.)* **wrinkle**
ዓይኒ መፍትሕ 'äyni mefth *(n.)* **keyhole**
ዕቤት 'ëbeet *(n.)* **growth**
ዕብላለ 'ëblale *(n.)* **hegemony**
ዕቡ'ይ 'ëbuy *(n.)* **immodest**
ዕቡ'ይነት 'ëbuynet *(a.)* **immodesty**
ዕኮት 'ëkot *(n.)* **wasp**
ዕንደራ ëndera *(n.)* **escapade**
ዕንክሊል 'ënklil *(n.)* **hoop**
ዕረፍቲ ዘይብሉ 'ërefti zeyblu *(adj.)* **hectic**
ዕሽሽ ኪበሃል ዚከኣል 'ëshsh kibehal zike'al *(adj.)* **venial**
ዕዮ 'ëyo *(n.)* **labour**
ዓመታዊ 'ämetawi *(adj.)* **annual**
ዓቀቅ በለ aaqeq bele *(v.)* **creak**
ዓቀቅታ aaqeqta *(n.)* **creak**
ዓራት ቆልዓ aarat qol'aa *(n.)* **crib**
ዓባስ äbas *(adj.)* **dumb**
ዓባስ äbas *(adj.)* **mute**
ዓባሲ äbasi *(adj.)* **styptic**
ዓባይ ኣፃብዕቲ እግሪ abay asabati egry *(n.)* **toe**
ዓባይቶ abayto *(n.)* **thumb**
ዕብዳን abdan *(n.)* **tomfoolery**
ዓበድበድ äbedbed *(n.)* **furore**
ዓበቅ abeq *(n.)* **scabies**
ዓበሰ äbese *(v.)* **muffle**
ዓበጠ äbete *(v.)* **repress**
ዓበጠ äbete *(v.)* **smother**
ዓበየ äbeye *(v.)* **develop**
ዓበየ äbeye *(v.i.)* **grow**
ዓቢ a'bi *(n.)* **whopper**
ዓቢ 'äbi *(adj.)* **venerable**
ዓቢ ድኳን äbi dkhwan *(n.)* **supermarket**
ዓቢ ድኳን äbi dkhwan *(n.)* **superstore**
ዓቢ ማዕበል äbi ma'ëbel *(v.)* **billow**
ዓቢ äbi *(adj.)* **big**
ዓብይ መኣንጣ abiy meanta *(n.)* **colon**
ዓብላላይ äblalay *(adj.)* **dominant**
ዓብላሊ äblali *(adj.)* **prevalent**
ዓብላሊ äblali *(adj.)* **overbearing**
ዓብለለ ablele *(v.)* **override**
ዓብለለ äblele *(v.)* **dominate**
ዓብለለ äblele *(v.)* **overshadow**
ዓብይ ሹቕ äby shuq *(n.)* **delicatessen**
ዓብዪ abyi *(adj.)* **senior**
ዓብዪ abyi *(adj.)* **outsize**
ዓብይ äbyi *(adj.)* **elder**
ዓብዪ äbyi *(adj.)* **grand**
ዓብዪ äbyi *(adj.)* **noble**
ዓብዪ ገዛ abyi geza *(n.)* **mansion**
ዓብዪ ሞደሻ äbyi modeša *(n.)* **sledgehammer**
ዓብዪ ሳንጣ a'byi santa *(n.)* **holdall**
ዓብዪ ጦር abyi tor *(n.)* **lance**
ዓዳጊ ädagi *(n.)* **buyer**
ዓዳላይ ädalay *(n.)* **distributor**
ዓዳሊ መንሹር adali menshur *(n.)* **pamphleteer**
ዓደለ ädele *(v.)* **allocate**
ዓደለ ädele *(v.)* **confer**

ዓደለ ädele *(v. i)* **deal**
ዓደለ ädele *(v.)* **distribute**
ዓደየ ädeye *(v.)* **expiate**
ዓበድበድ aebedbed *(n.)* **hysteria**
ዓሌት ae-leet *(n.)* **heredity**
ዓፈነ äfene *(v.)* **asphyxiate**
ዓፈነ äfene *(v.)* **stifle**
ዓፈነ äfene *(v.)* **suffocate**
ዓፈነ äfene *(v.)* **suppress**
ዓፈረ äfere *(v.)* **fizzle**
ዓፍራ afra *(n.)* **lather**
ዓፍራ äfra *(n.)* **foam**
ዓፍራ äfra *(n.)* **froth**
ዓፍራ äfra *(n.)* **spume**
ዓፍራ äfra *(n.)* **bubble**
ዓገተ agete *(v.)* **obstruct**
ዓገተ ägete *(v.)* **curtail**
ዓገተ ägete *(v.)* **restrain**
ዓገተ ägete *(v.)* **occlude**
ዓጋፎ ägafo *(n.)* **mob**
ዓጋፎ ägafo *(n.)* **rabble**
ዓጋቲ agati *(n.)* **insulator**
ዓጋቲ ägati *(adj.)* **preventive**
ዓጋዜን ägazeen *(n.)* **antelope**
ዓጋዜን ägazen *(n.)* **deer**
ዒስራ aisra *(adj.&n.)* **twenty**
ዓጃቢ ajabi *(n.)* **outrider**
ዓጀበ äĵebe *(v.)* **accompany**
ዓጀብቲ äjebti *(n.)* **retinue**
ዓጀውጀው äjewjew *(n.)* **delirium**
ዓካር akar *(n.)* **tubercle**
ዓካር äkar *(n.)* **crystal**
ዓቐን aken *(n.)* **gauge**
ዓከሰ äkese *(v.)* **misfire**
ዓኽታ äkhta *(n.)* **sputum**
ዓኳይ akuay *(n.)* **yeoman**
ዓላ a'la *(adj.)* **jovial**
ዓላቕ älaq̈ *(n.)* **bully**
ዓለባ aleba *(n.)* **coir**
ዓለባ ሳሬት aleba sareet *(n.)* **cobweb**
ዓለባ ሳሬት aleba sariet *(n.)* **web**
ቀንዲ aleba saret *(adj.)* **foremost**
ዓለም alem *(n.)* **world**
ዓለም älem *(n.)* **globe**
ዓለም ለኻዊነት älem lekawinet *(n.)* **globalization**
ዓለማዊ alemawi *(adj.)* **worldly**
ዓለማዊ älemawi *(adj.)* **mundane**
ዓለመ aleme *(v.i.)* **aim**
ዓለመኛ ዘይኮነ alemenga zekone *(adj.)* **unworldly**
ዓለምለኻዊ alemlekawi *(adj.)* **universal**
ዓለም-ለኻዊ 'älemlek̍awi *(adj.)* **international**
ዓለምለኻዊነት alemlekawinet *(adv.)* **universality**
ዓለቕቲ aleqti *(n.)* **leech**
ዓሌት alet *(n.)* **clan**
ዓሌት älet *(n.)* **race**
ዓሌታዊ äletawi *(adj.)* **racial**
ዓሌታውነት äletawnwt *(n.)* **racialism**
ዓማፂ ämatsi *(adj.)* **dastardly**
ዓማፂ ämatsi *(adj.)* **rebellious**
ዓማጺ ämaxi *(adj.)* **aggressive**
ዓምበበ ämbebe *(v.)* **bloom**
ዓመደ ሙታን ämde mutan *(n.)* **obituary**
ዓምዲ amdi *(n.)* **pillar**
ዓምዲ ሞስኮት ämdi moskot *(n.)* **mullion**
ዓመፀኛ amesegna *(n.)* **thug**
ዓመት amet *(n.)* **year**
ዓመታዊ ametawi *(adv.)* **yearly**
ዓመታዊ መልዕሎ ämetawi mel'ëlo *(n.)* **annuity**
ዓመተ ämete *(v.)* **blindfold**

ዓመፅ ämets *(n.)* **rebellion**
ዓምፅ ametse *(n.)* **insurrection**
ዓመፀ ämetse *(v.)* **rebel**
ዓመፀኛ ämetsgna *(adj.)* **pushy**
ዓመፅ amex *(n.)* **uprising**
ዓመጽ 'ämex *(n.)* **violence**
ዓመጸ ämexe *(v.)* **abuse**
ዓሚል amil *(n.)* **client**
ዓሚል ämil *(n.)* **customer**
ዓሚል ኮነ ämil kone *(v.)* **subscribe**
ዓሚል ሙኳን ämil mkhwan *(n.)* **subscription**
ዓሚቅ ämiq *(adj.)* **deep**
ዓሚቕ ስንጭሮ ämiq̈ snčro *(n.)* **canyon**
ዓምረረ ämrere *(v.)* **pounce**
ዓንዳሪ 'ändari *(adj.)* **venturesome**
ዓንደረ andere *(v.)* **gambol**
ዓንደረ andere *(v.t.)* **scamper**
ዓንደረ ändere *(v.)* **romp**
ዓንደረ 'ändere *(v.)* **frisk**
ዓንዲ ändi *(n.)* **mast**
ዓንዲ ሑቀ ändi ḧuqe *(n.)* **spine**
ዓንዲ-ሕቖ ändiḧq̈o *(n.)* **backbone**
ዓንዲ anedi *(n.)* **column**
ዓንቀፅ aneqetse *(n.)* **clause**
ዓንቀፀ änqets *(v.)* **remand**
ዓንቀጸ anqetse *(v.)* **thwart**
ዓንቀፀ änqetze *(v.)* **forestall**
ዓንቀጽ anqex *(n.)* **paragraph**
ዓንቀፅ änqex *(n.)* **article**
ዓንገለ ängele *(v.)* **nourish**
ዓንጃል änjal *(adj.)* **daft**
ዓንጃል änjal *(n.)* **fool**
ዓንጃል änjal *(adj.)* **ridiculous**
ዓንጃል änjal *(n.)* **stooge**
ዓንጃል änĵal *(adj.)* **foolish**
ዓንጃል änĵal *(adj.)* **asinine**
ዓንካር änkar *(n.)* **granule**
ዓንካር-ዓንካሪቶ änkar'änkarito *(n.)* **ankle**
ዓንኬል 'änkeel *(n.)* **wreath**
ዓንኬል ankiel *(n.)* **loop**
ዓንቃሪቦ änqaribo *(n.)* **hook**
ዓንቃሪቦ änqaribo *(n.)* **barb**
ዓንቀር ጠበንጃ änqer ťebenĵa *(n.)* **breech**
ዓቃበ-ህንጻ äqabehntsa *(n.)* **janitor**
ዓቀበ aqebe *(v.)* **maintain**
ዓቀበ aqebe *(v.)* **uphold**
ዓቀበ äqebe *(v.)* **deter**
ዓቀበ äqebe *(v.t.)* **perpetuate**
ዓቀበ äqebe *(v.)* **preserve**
ዓቀበ äqebe *(v.)* **reserve**
ዓቀበ äqebe *(v.i.)* **retain**
ዓቀን äqen *(n.)* **dimension**
ዓቀን ä'qen *(a.)* **measure**
ዓቀን ä'qen *(n.)* **measurement**
ዓቐን ፈውሲ äqen fewsi *(n.)* **dose**
ዓቐን ሓይሊ ኤሌክትሪክ 'äq̈en ḧayli 'eeleektrik *(n.)* **voltage**
ዓቀናዊ äqenawi *(adj.)* **quantitative**
ዓቀነ ä'qene *(v.)* **measure**
ዓቐን aqhen *(n.)* **magnitude**
ዓቐን ዘይብሉ ድልየት aqhen zeyblu dlyet *(adj.)* **insatiable**
ዓቕሚ ዘይብሉ aqhmi zeyblu *(adj.)* **incompetent**
ዓቅመ ኣዳም ዝበፅሐ äqme adam betzḧe *(adj.)* **marriageable**
ዓቕሚ äqmi *(n.)* **potency**
ዓቕሚ äqmi *(adj.)* **potential**
ዓቕሚ ዘይብሉ aqmi zeyblu *(adj.)* **incapable**
ዓቕሚ äq̈mi *(n.)* **capability**
ዓቕሚ äq̈mi *(n.)* **capacity**

ዕሽነት ዝትምሎኦ ዉሳኔ arabĥe *(adj.)* **injudicious**
ዓራት ärat *(n.)* **bed**
ዓራት ቆልዓ ärat qol'ä *(n.)* **cot**
ዓራት ዘይሓዘ ተሓካሚ arat zeyhaze tehakami *(n.)* **outpatient**
ዓርቢ 'ärbi *(n.)* **Friday**
ዓረብ äreb *(n.)* **Arab**
ዓረበታይ ärebetay *(n.)* **Arabian**
ዓረብያ arebia *(n.)* **cart**
ዓረብያ/ሰረገላ arebiya/seregela *(n.)* **chariot**
ዓረብኛ ärebnya *(n.)* **Arabic**
ዓረብያ arebya *(n.)* **winch**
ዓረደ 'ärede *(v.)* **fortify**
ዓረነ ärene *(n.)* **snail**
ዓረነ ärene *(n.)* **slug**
መበየዲ mebeyedi *(n.)* **solder**
ዓረር ärer *(n.)* **bullet**
ቢምቦ bimbo *(v.)* **plumb**
ዓርከይ arkey *(n.)* **kith**
ዓርኪ ärki *(n.)* **friend**
ዓርክ ärki *(n.)* **mate**
ዓርማም ärmam *(adj.)* **raucous**
ዓርሞሸሽ ärmoshesh *(n.)* **giant**
ዓርሰ arse *(pron.)* **oneself**
ዓርስኻ arseka *(pron.)* **yourself**
ዓሳ äsa *(n.)* **fish**
ዓሳ ነባሪ asa neari *(n.)* **whale**
ዓሳ ዝምግብ እንስሳ asa zmgb ensesa *(n.)* **otter**
ዓሳው äsaw *(adj.)* **dank**
ዓሰርተ asert *(adj. & adv.)* **ten**
ዓሰርተ ዓመት äserte ämet *(n.)* **decade**
ዓሰርተ ኣርባዕተ 'äserte 'arba'ëte *(adj.& n.)* **fourteen**
ዓሰርተ ሓደ äserte ĥade *(adj. & n.)* **eleven**
ዓሰርተ ሓሙሽተ 'äserte ĥamushte *(adj. & n.)* **fifteen**
ዓሰርተ ክልተ aserte klte *(adj.&n.)* **twelve**
ዓሰርተ ክልተ ዜሮ ዘለዋ ቁፅሪ aserte klte zero zelewo kqutsri *(adj & n.)* **trillion**
ዓስርተ ሽድሽተ äserte šdšte *(adj. & n.)* **sixteen**
ዓሰርተ ሰለስተ aserte seleste *(adj. & n.)* **thirteen**
ዕሰር ሰለስተ aserte seleste *(adj. & n.)* **thirteen**
ዓሰርተ ሸሞንተ äserte shomonte *(adj. & n.)* **eighteen**
ዓሰርተ ትሽዓተ äserte tsh'äte *(adj. & n.)* **nineteen**
ዓሰርተ ሸውዓተ aserte xew'ate *(adj. & n.)* **seventeen**
ዓሻ asha *(adj.)* **unwise**
ዓሻ asha *(adj.)* **witless**
ዓሻ äsha *(adj.)* **stupid**
ዓሻ 'äsha *(n.)* **idiot**
ዓሻኹ äshakwi *(adj.)* **spiky**
ዓሸራ ashara *(n.)* **imprint**
ዓሽከር äshker *(n.)* **minion**
ዓሽከር 'äshker *(n.)* **lackey**
ዓሶ aso *(n.)* **malaria**
ዓስራይ asray *(adj. & n.)* **tenth**
ዓረብያ garebya *(n.)* **trolley**
ዓጓ ägwa *(n.)* **beige**
ዓፃዳይ ätsaday *(n.)* **reaper**
ዓጸዲ ätsadi *(n.)* **harvester**
ዓፀወ atsewe *(adj.)* **close**
ዓፀወ ätsewe *(v.)* **shut**
ዓፀፋ ምላሽ ätsfa mlaš *(n.)* **rejoinder**
ዓጽሚ ሕቑ ዘለዎ atsmi hqe zelewo *(n.)* **vertebrate**
ዓፀረ ሕቀት ätsre ĥqet *(n.)* **dyspepsia**

ዓፅረ ንባብ ätsre nbab *(n.)* **dyslexia**
ዓፀፈ ätzefe *(v.t)* **fold**
ጠቐለለ ťeqlele *(v.)* **furl**
ዓዉ ኢሉ ተዛረበ äw elu tezarebe *(v.)* **declaim**
ዓው ዝበለ aw zbl *(adj.)* **loud**
ዓዋን awan *(adj.)* **idiotic**
ዓዋን awan *(n.)* **sap**
ባስታ መረቕ basta mereq *(n.)* **noodles**
ዓውደ ፍፃመ awde ftsame *(n.)* **scene**
ዓውደ መፅናዕቲ awde metsna'eti *(n.)* **seminar**
ዓውደ መፅናዕቲ äwde mexna'ëti *(n.)* **symposium**
ዓውደ-ኣዋርሕ äwde'awarḧ *(n.)* **calendar**
ዓወለ äwele *(v.)* **rove**
ዓወት awet *(n.)* **achievement**
ዓወት awet *(n.)* **triumph**
ዓወት awet *(adj.)* **winning**
ዓወት äwet *(n.)* **success**
ዓወት 'äwet *(n.)* **victory**
ዓፀደ äxede *(v.)* **mow**
ዓጽሚ äxmi *(n.)* **bone**
ዓይንዳ äynda *(n.)* **acorn**
ዓይነ ስዉር äyne swur *(adj.)* **blind**
ዓይነ ስዉርነት äyne swurnet *(n.)* **blindness**
ዓይነት aynet *(n.)* **type**
ዓይነት äynet *(n.)* **form**
ዓይነት äynet *(n.)* **sort**
ዓይነት äynet *(n.)* **kind**
ዓይነት ዓሌት 'äynet 'äleet *(n.)* **variety**
ዓይነት ባእታ äynet baeta *(n.)* **platinum**
ዓይነት ብሽኩቲ äynet bškuti *(n.)* **pretzel**
ዓይነት ጨርቂ äynet čerqi *(n.)* **poplin**
ዓይነት ዶልሺ äynet dolshi *(n.)* **strudel**
ዓይነት ፍረምረ äynet fremre *(n.)* **pomegranate**
ዓይነት ሕክምና aynet hkmna *(n.)* **orthopaedics**
ዓይነት ቕብኣት aynet kibat *(n.)* **gel**
ዓይነት ማዓድን aynet ma'adn *(n.)* **onyx**
ዓይነት ማዓድን aynet ma'adn *(n.)* **opal**
ዓይነት መዓድን äynet me'ädn *(n.)* **phosphorus**
ዓይነት ንእሽቶ ዓሳ aynet neshto asa *(n.)* **whiting**
ዓይነት ንእሽቶ ዑፍ aynet neshto 'uf *(n.)* **warbler**
ዓይነት ጥረምረ aynet teremer *(n.)* **oat**
ዓይነት ፀወታ äynet tseweta *(n.)* **Sudoku**
ዓይነት ዑፍ 'äynet 'üf *(n.)* **wader**
ዓይኒ äyni *(n.)* **eye**
ዓይኒ ዓተር ayni ater *(n.)* **chickpea**
ዓይኒ ዓተር ayni ater *(n.)* **pea**
ዓይኒ ማይ ayni may *(n.)* **geyser**
ዓይኒ ርግቢ ayni rgbi *(n.)* **lattice**
ዓይኒ ዘይብሉ መርፍእ ayni zeyblu mefe *(n.)* **pin**
ዓዘፍ a-zaf *(adj.)* **garrulous**
ዓዝዓዝ äz'äz *(adj.)* **haggard**
ዓዘቕቲ äzeqti *(n.)* **bog**

ዕ

ዕባራ ebara *(adj.)* **scraggy**
ዕባራ ëbara *(adj.)* **gaunt**
ዕብደት e'bdet *(n.)* **lunacy**
ዕብደት ëbdet *(n.)* **dementia**
ዕብደት ከልቢ ëbdet kelbi *(n.)* **rabies**
ዕብደት ebdt *(n.)* **insanity**
ቁጽጽር ዘይብሉ quxxr zeyblu *(adj.)* **hysterical**
ስንኩለ-ኣእምሮ snkule'a'èmro *(adj.)* **insane**
ጽሉል xlul *(n.)* **lunatic**
ዕቡድ ëbud *(adj.)* **demented**
ዕቡይ ëbuy *(adj.)* **haughty**
ዕቡይ ëbuy *(adj.)* **supercilious**
ዕብየት ebyet *(n.)* **seniority**
ዕብየት ëbyet *(n.)* **development**
ዕዳ ëda *(n.)* **debit**
ዕዳ ëda *(n.)* **debt**
ዕዳ ንምኽፋል ዓቕሚ ምስኣን eda nmkhfakl akmi ms'an *(n.)* **insolvency**
ዕዳ ëda *(n.)* **arrears**
ዕዳጋ ገይሮም edaga girom *(v.)* **transact**
ዕዳጋ edega *(n.)* **market**
ዕደጋ ëdega *(n.)* **shopping**
ዕድል edl *(n.)* **luck**
ዕድል edl *(n.)* **opportunity**
ዕድል ëdl *(n.)* **fortune**
ዕድል ኣልባ edl albo *(adj.)* **luckless**
ዕድል ናይ ምሕዋይ ëdl nay mȟway *(n.)* **prognosis**
ዕድለኛ edlegna *(adj.)* **lucky**
ዕድለኛ ëdlegna *(adj.)* **fortunate**
ዕድለኛ ëdleṅa *(adj.)* **providential**
ዕድመ ëdme *(n.)* **age**
ዕድመ ëdme *(n.)* **duration**
ዕዳኡ ኪኽፍል ዘይከኣለ ed'u kkefel zeyke'ale *(adj.)* **insolvent**
ዕቡድ eebudd *(adj.)* **certifiable**
ዕቡይ eebuy; *(adj.)* **cocky**
ዕድል eedil *(n.)* **chance**
ዕፈና ëfena *(n.)* **suppression**
ዕፍሪት e'frit *(n.)* **crane**
ዕፉን ëfun *(n.)* **corn**
ዕጋት ማይ ëgat may *(n.)* **backwater**
ዕግበት egbet *(n.)* **satisfaction**
ዕግርግር ዘለዎ egereger zelewo *(adj.)* **chaotic**
ዕግርግር e-gerger *(n.)* **hubbub**
ዕገታ ëgeta *(n.)* **obstruction**
ዕግርግር ëgrgr *(n.)* **bedlam**
ድብል-ቕልቕ dblq̈lq̈ *(n.)* **confusion**
ብታነ btane *(n.)* **disarray**
መንገዲ mengedi *(n.)* **route**
ዕግታ ëgta *(n.)* **blockage**
ዕጉብ ëgub *(adj.)* **complacent**
ቅሱን qsun *(adj.)* **smug**
ዕጉስ egus *(adj.)* **patient**
ዕኮት ëkot *(n.)* **hornet**
ዕኳር ekuar *(n.)* **pellet**
ዕኹላል ekulal *(n.)* **coil**
ዕኹላል ዛውያ ëkulal zawya *(n.)* **ringlet**
ዕኳር ወርቂ ëkwar werqi *(n.)* **nugget**
ዕላማ elama *(n.)* **target**
ዕላማ ëlama *(n.)* **goal**
ዕላማ ëlama *(n.)* **intent**
ዕላማ ëlama *(n.)* **intention**
ዕላማ ëlama *(n.)* **purpose**
ዕላማ eïama *(n.)* **aim**
ዕላማ ኣልቦ eïama albo *(adj.)* **aimless**

ዕላማ እና ፖሊሲ ዝሓዘ ፁሑፍ elama ena polisi zhaze tsuhuf *(n.)* **manifesto**
ዕላመት ëlamet *(n.)* **hallmark**
ዕላመት ëlamet *(n.)* **brand**
ዕላምኡ ሓለፈ ëlam'u ĥalefe *(v.)* **overshoot**
ዕላዊ ገበረ ëlawi gebere *(v.)* **disclose**
ዕለት ëlet *(n.)* **date**
ዕለታዊ eletawi *(adj.)* **daily**
ዕለታዊ ማስታወሻ ëletawi mastawesha *(n.)* **diary**
ዕለቱ ዝሰሓተ ëletu zseĥate *(n.)* **anachronism**
ዕልቋቅ elqaq *(n.)* **semen**
ዕስለ else *(n.)* **troop**
ዕልዋ መንግስቲ ëlwa mengsti *(n.)* **coup**
ዕማም ëmam *(n.)* **stint**
ዕምባባ ëmbaba *(n.)* **blossom**
ዕምበባዊ ëmbabawi *(adj.)* **flowery**
ዕምባባዊ 'ëmbabawi *(adj.)* **floral**
ዕምበባ ëmbeba *(n.)* **flower**
ዕምበባ ኒል embeba nil *(n.)* **woad**
ዕምኹ ëmkwa *(n.)* **fist**
ዕምቁት ëmqet *(n.)* **depth**
ዕንጨይቲ ëncheyti *(n.)* **stick**
ዕንዲዳ ጌጽ ëndida geex *(n.)* **amber**
ዕነ ëne *(n.)* **muck**
ዕንፍሩር ënfrur *(v.)* **dapple**
ዕንጓል ëngwal *(adj.)* **mucous**
ዕንቅፋት enqefat *(n.)* **hindrance**
ዕንቅፋት enqfat *(n.)* **obstacle**
ዕንቅፋት ጸገም 'ënqfat xegem *(n.)* **handicap**
ዕንቅፋት ënqfat *(n.)* **snag**
ዕንቅፋት 'ënqfat *(n.)* **impediment**
ዕንቅፋት ënqfat *(n.)* **barrier**
ዕንቆ ënqo *(n.)* **bead**
ዕንቅርቢት enqrbit *(n.)* **scorpion**
ዕንፀይቲ entseyti *(n.)* **wood**
ዕንጨይቲ ሰንደል entseyti sendel *(n.)* **sandalwood**
ዕኑድ ënud *(adj.)* **besotted**
ዕንወት ënwet *(n.)* **havoc**
ዕንወት ënwet *(n.)* **ruin**
ዕንወት 'ënwet *(n.)* **wreck**
ዕንዛዘ enzaze *(n.)* **trance**
ዕንዛዘ ënzaze *(n.)* **hypnosis**
ዕንዚራ e'nzira *(n.)* **lyre**
ዕቋር ëqar *(n.)* **deposit**
ዕቀባ ëqeba *(n.)* **preservation**
ዕቅን e'qn *(adj.)* **snug**
ዕቅን ዘይኮነ ëqn zeykone *(n.)* **misfit**
ዕቁን ë'qun *(adj.)* **measured**
ዕቑር ዓቕሚ ëqur äqmi *(n.)* **potentiality**
ዕራቆት ëraqot *(n.)* **nudity**
ዕራቆተኛ ëraqotegna *(n.)* **nudist**
ዕራቁ ëraqu *(adj.)* **nude**
ዕርደ-ከተማ 'ërdeketema *(n.)* **citadel**
ዕርዲ ërdi *(n.)* **fort**
ዕርዲ ërdi *(n.)* **rampart**
ዕርዲ 'ërdi *(n.)* **fortress**
ዕርዲ ërdi *(n.)* **bastion**
ዕርዲ ërdi *(n.)* **bulwark**
ዕረፍቲ ërefti *(n.)* **adjournment**
ሃጓፍ መንደቕ hagwaf mendeq̈ *(n.)* **recess**
ዕረፍቲ መንጎ ërefti mengo *(n.)* **interlude**
ዕረፍቲ 'ërefti *(n.)* **intermission**
ዕርፍቲ 'ërfti *(n.)* **vacation**
ዕርገት ërget *(n.)* **ascent**
ዕርክነት ërknet *(n.)* **amity**
ዕርቂ erqi *(n.)* **sciatica**
ዕርቂ ërqi *(n.)* **reconciliation**

ዕርቆቱ ërqotu ***(adj.)*** **naked**
ዕሩድ ërud ***(adj.)*** **embattled**
ዕሳው ësaw ***(n.)*** **mould**
ዕስለ ësel ***(n.)*** **melee**
ዕሰል ësel ***(n.)*** **bevy**
ዕሸል eshel ***(n.)*** **infant**
ዕሸል ምቕታል eshel mqhtal ***(n.)*** **infanticide**
ዕሸላዊ e'shelawi ***(adj.)*** **infantile**
ዕሽነት ëshnet ***(n.)*** **folly**
ዕሽነት ëshnet ***(n.)*** **stupidity**
ዕሽነት 'ëshnet ***(n.)*** **idiocy**
ዕሾክ eshok ***(n.)*** **thorn**
ዕሽሽታ ëshshta ***(n.)*** **negligence**
ዕስለ ësle ***(n.)*** **shoal**
ዕስለ ësle ***(n.)*** **swarm**
ዕሽሽ በለ ëšš bele ***(v.)*** **relent**
ዕሱብ ësub ***(adj.)*** **mercenary**
ዕጣን etan ***(n.)*** **incense**
ዕትብቲ etbti ***(adj.)*** **umbilical**
ዕጥቂ ኣፍተሓ ëtki aftehe ***(v.)*** **disarm**
ዕትሮ ëtro ***(n .)*** **pot**
ዕቱብ e'tub ***(adj.)*** **solemn**
ዕቱብነት e'tubnet ***(n.)*** **solemnity**
ዕጡቅ ë'ťuq ***(adj.)*** **militant**
ዑደት ëudet ***(n.)*** **cycle**
ዑደታዊ ëudetawi ***(adj.)*** **cyclic**
ዕዋላ ëwala ***(n.)*** **hooligan**
ኮብላሊ koblali ***(n.)*** **rover**
ዕወጃ eweja ***(v.t.)*** **illusion**
ዕውልና ëwlna ***(n.)*** **debauchery**
ዕውልውል ምባል ëwlwl mbal ***(n.)*** **nausea**
ዕዉት ëwut ***(adj.)*** **fruitful**
ዕዉት ëwut ***(adj.)*** **successful**
ዕዉት ëwut ***(adj.)*** **victorious**
ዕፃድ ቦታ ëxad bota ***(n.)*** **swathe**
ዕፅፍፃፍ ëxfxaf ***(adj.)*** **corrugated**
ዕያግ ጎቦ eyag gobo ***(n.)*** **tarn**
ዕያገነዳ e'yageneda ***(n.)*** **lymph**
ዕዮ ፅርግያ ëyo tsrgya ***(n.)*** **roadwork**
ዕዙም ëzum ***(adj.)*** **spellbound**
ዒባ ïba ***(n.)*** **dung**
ዒባራ ïbara ***(adj.)*** **skinny**
ዒፍ ያሬድ ïf yared ***(n.)*** **nightingale**
ዒላ ila ***(n.)*** **well**
ዕላማ oe'lama ***(adj.)*** **objective**
ዑደት üdet ***(n.)*** **sightseeing**
ዑደት 'üdet ***(n.)*** **circuit**
ዑደታዊ udetawi ***(adj.)*** **orbital**
ዑፍ üf ***(n.)*** **fowl**
ዑፍ üf ***(n.)*** **bird**
ዑና üna ***(adj.)*** **dilapidated**
ዑና üna ***(n.)*** **hovel**
ዑቕባ üqba ***(n.)*** **aegis**
ዑቕባ üqba ***(n.)*** **asylum**

ዘ

ዘምባል zembal ***(adj.)*** **oblique**
ዘቐይም zeqeym ***(adj.)*** **offensive**
ዘኽታም zektam ***(n.)*** **orphan**
ዝዓበየ ና ምርምር መፅሓፍ zabeye namrmr meshaf ***(n.)*** **tome**
ዛብያ zabya ***(n.)*** **axis**
ዛብያ zabya ***(n.)*** **pike**
ዛብያ zabya ***(n.)*** **shaft**
ዛዕጎል zaëgol ***(n.)*** **shell**
ዛዕጎል za'ëgol ***(n.)*** **conch**
ዛዕዛዕታ za'ëza'ëta ***(n.)*** **dew**
ዝዓገበ z'agebe ***(adj.)*** **sated**
ዛጊት zagit ***(adv.)*** **already**
ዝሓበረ zaȟabere ***(adj.)*** **corporate**
ዛሕተለ zaȟtele ***(v.)*** **stagnate**
ዛሕዛሕ ዝበለ zaȟ'zaȟ zbele ***(n.)*** **mess**

ዝዓነወ z'änewe *(adj.)* **rundown**
ዛንታ zanta *(n.)* **narrative**
ዛንታ zanta *(n.)* **story**
ዛንታ ፍቅሪ zanta fqri *(n.)* **romance**
ዛራ zara *(n.)* **brook**
ዛርቲ zarti *(n.)* **elf**
ዛወነ zawene *(v.)* **saunter**
ዘይጠቅም zaytekm *(adj.)* **useless**
ዘይተርፍ zayteref *(adj.)* **unavoidable**
ዛዛሚ zazami *(n.)* **finalist**
ዛዘመ zazeme *(v.)* **finish**
ዝባሕተወ zbaĥtewe *(adj.)* **celibate**
ዝባን zban *(n.)* **surface**
ዝባን ኢድ zban 'id *(n.)* **backhand**
ዝባን zban *(n.)* **back**
ዝበደነ zbedene *(adj.)* **defunct**
ዝበለፀ zbeletse *(adj.)* **deluxe**
ዝበለፀ zbeletse *(adj.)* **utmost**
ዝበለጸ zbelexe *(adj.)* **best**
ዝበልሐ ዕንጸይቲ ሓጹር zbelhe enxeyti haxur *(n.)* **paling**
ዘበን zbene *(n.)* **century**
ዝበቅዕ zbeqe *(adj.)* **worthy**
ዝበረሰ zberese *(adj.)* **decadent**
ዝበስበሰ zbesbese *(adj.)* **rotten**
ዝበሰለ zbesele *(adj.)* **ripe**
ዝበዝሐ zbezhe *(v.)* **preponderate**
ዝብላዕ zblaë *(adj.)* **edible**
ዝብላዕ zbla'ë *(adj.)* **eatable**
ዝቦኾረ zboḱore *(adj.)* **absent**
ዝብስብስ zbsbs *(adj.)* **biodegradable**
ዝጨኑ zĉenu *(adj.)* **redolent**
ዝጭበጥ zchbet *(adj.)* **palpable**
ዝጭበጥ zchbet *(adj.)* **tangible**
ዝደኸመ zdekeme' *(adj.)* **weary**
ዝደቀሰ zdekese *(adj.)* **quiescent**
ዝደሊ zdeli *(adj.)* **needful**
ዝደንፀዎ zdenxewo *(adj.)* **nonplussed**
ዝደንፀዎ zdenxewo *(adj.)* **nonplussed**
ዝድህሰስ ነገር zdhses neger *(adj.)* **tactile**
ዘየስተውዕል ze yestewu 'el *(adj.)* **careless**
ዝዓገበ zea'gebe *(adj.)* **content**
ዘብዐኛ zeb'agna *(n.)* **sentinel**
ዘባህርር ሕልሚ zebahr'r ḧlmi *(n.)* **nightmare**
ዘባል zebal *(adv.)* **askew**
ዘበበ zeḅebe *(v.)* **slope**
ዘዕበድብድ zëbedbd *(adj.)* **berserk**
ዘብዐኛ zeb-egna *(v.)* **guard**
ዝብኢ zeb-ei *(n.)* **hyena**
ዘበለ zebele *(v.)* **slant**
መዋእል mewa'èl *(n.)* **epoch**
ዘበን zeben *(n.)* **era**
ዘበን አምፀኦ zeben amxe'o *(n.)* **fad**
ዘበናዊ zebenawi *(adj.)* **fashionable**
ዘበስር zebesr *(n.)* **precursor**
ዘበተ zebete *(v.)* **trounce**
ዘቢብ zebib *(n.)* **currant**
ዘቢብ zebib *(n.)* **raisin**
ዘብለጭልጭ zeblechlch *(adj.)* **tawdry**
ዘብለጭልጭ zeble'chl'ch *(adj.)* **scintillating**
ዘብለጭልጭ zebleĉlĉ *(adj.)* **shiny**
ዜብራ መንገዲ zebra mengedi *(n.)* **zebra crossing**
ዘጨንቕ zechenq *(adj.)* **tense**
ዘደንግጽ zedengx *(adj.)* **pathetic**
ዘደንግጽ zedengx *(adj.)* **pitiful**
ዘደንጹ zedenxu *(n.)* **prodigy**
ዘደንዝዝ zedenz'z *(n.)* **stunner**
ዘዕግብ ze'egb *(adj.)* **satisfactory**

ዜግነት zeeg'net ***(n.)*** **nationality**
ዜግነት ሃበ zeegnet habe ***(v.)*** **naturalize**
ዜግነት ምሃብ zeeg'net mhab ***(n.)*** **naturalization**
ዜግነታዊ zeegnetawi ***(adj.)*** **civic**
ዘዕግብ ze'eigib ***(adj.)*** **cogent**
ዘዕጀውጅው ze'ëjewjw ***(adj.)*** **delirious**
ዜማዊ zeemawi ***(adj.)*** **melodic**
ዜማዊ zeemawi ***(adj.)*** **melodious**
ዜማዊ zeemawi ***(n.)*** **melody**
ዜና zeena ***(n.)*** **news**
ዘዕኑ ze'ënu ***(adj.)*** **ruinous**
ዘዐንዝዝ ze'ënzz ***(adj.)*** **mesmeric**
ዜሮ zeero ***(n.)*** **nought**
ዘዕወልውል ze'ëwelwl ***(adj.)*** **nauseous**
ዘፍ በለ zef bele ***(v.)*** **flop**
ዘፈፍታ zefefta ***(n.)*** **residue**
ዘፈንፍን zefenfn ***(adj.)*** **repulsive**
ዘፈር zefer ***(n.)*** **fringe**
ዘፍራን zefran ***(n.)*** **saffron**
ዘፍታ zefta ***(n.)*** **grout**
ዘፍጣጥ zeftat ***(n.)*** **paunch**
ዘፍዘፈ zefzefe ***(v.)*** **souse**
ዜጋ zega ***(n.)*** **citizen**
ዘግድድ zegdd ***(adj.)*** **compulsive**
ዘገዳማዊ zegedamawi ***(adj.)*** **wild**
ዘገምተኛ zegemtegna ***(adj.)*** **tardy**
ዜግነት zegenet ***(n.)*** **citizenship**
ዘገርም zegerm ***(adj.)*** **fantastic**
ዘጉሂ zeguhi ***(adj.)*** **deplorable**
ዘጉሂ zeguhi ***(adj.)*** **grievous**
ዘጉሂ zeguhi ***(adj.)*** **rueful**
ዘጓጥጥ zegwaẗt ***(n.)*** **menace**
ዘሓጠ zeȟaẗe ***(v.)*** **lag**
ዘሓጢ zeĥati ***(adj.)*** **recessive**
ዘሕፍር zehfr ***(adj.)*** **shameful**
ዘሕጉስ zeĥgus ***(adj.)*** **delightful**
ዘሕስብ ነገር zeȟsb neger ***(n.)*** **preoccupation**
ዘሕዝን zehzen ***(adj.)*** **unfortunate**
ዘሕዝን zeĥzn ***(adj.)*** **dismal**
ዘሕዝን zehzn ***(adj.)*** **lamentable**
ዘሕዝን zeḧzn ***(adj.)*** **piteous**
ዘይቲ ጉልዒ zeiti gul'i ***(a.)*** **castor oil**
ዘከረ zekere ***(v.)*** **recall**
ዘከረ zekere ***(v.)*** **recollect**
ዘከረ zekere ***(v.)*** **remember**
ዘኽስብ zeksb ***(adj.)*** **profitable**
ዘኽስስ zeḱss ***(adj.)*** **actionable**
ዘልኣለማዊ zel'alemawi ***(adj.)*** **eternal**
ዘልኣለማዊነት zel'alemawinet ***(n.)*** **eternity**
ዘላሊ zelali ***(n.)*** **jumper**
ዘላን zelan ***(n.)*** **nomad**
ዘላናዊ zelanawi ***(adj.)*** **nomadic**
ዘላቒ zelaqi ***(adj.)*** **sustainable**
ዘለኣለማዊ zele'alemawi ***(adj.)*** **monumental**
ዘለፋ zelefa ***(n.)*** **affront**
ዘለለ zelele ***(v.)*** **leap**
ዘለለ zelele ***(v.)*** **skip**
ዜማ zem ***(n.)*** **tune**
ዜማ zema ***(n.)*** **chant**
ዘማ zema ***(n.)*** **nephew**
ዘማዓሪ zema'äri ***(adj.)*** **normative**
ዘምበዐ zembe'ë ***(v.)*** **deviate**
ዘምበየ zembeye ***(v.i.)*** **soar**
ዘመድ zemed ***(n.)*** **kin**
ዘመድ zemed ***(adj.)*** **relative**
ዝእመን z'emen ***(adj.)*** **plausible**
ዘመን ኣምፀኦ zemen amxe'o ***(adj.)*** **modish**
ዘመናዊ zemenawi ***(adj.)*** **modern**

ዘመናዊ zemenawi *(adj.)* **stylish**
ዘመናዊ ኣረኣእያ zemenawi are'a'eya *(n.)* **modernism**
ዘመናውነት zemenawnet *(n.)* **modernity**
ዘመረ zemere *(v.)* **warble**
ዘመስግን zemesgn *(adj.)* **thankful**
ዘይመጣጠን zemetaten *(adj.)* **disproportionate**
ዘመተ zemete *(n.)* **campaign**
ዜና zena *(n.)* **tidings**
ዜና መዋልዕ zena mewalee *(n.)* **chronicle**
ዘምቢል zenbil *(n.)* **trug**
ዘንቢል zenbil *(n.)* **basket**
ዘነኣእስ zene'a'es *(adj.)* **sardonic**
ዘነቓቕሕ መድሓኒ zenekakh medhanit *(n.)* **tonic**
ዝድነቕ zeneqh *(adj.)* **impressive**
ዘንጊ zengi *(n.)* **rod**
ዝንጅብል zenjebel *(n.)* **ginger**
ዘንቀትቅት zenqetqt *(adj.)* **tremulous**
ዝነቐጸ zenqexe *(adj.)* **parched**
ዘንሳፈፈ zensafefe *(adj.)* **afloat**
ዘንሰፋለለት zensefalelet *(adj.)* **becalmed**
ዘንፀባርቅ zentsebarq *(adj.)* **refulgent**
ዘንፀባርቅ zentsebarq *(n.)* **sparkling**
ዘንፀራረዎ zentserarewo *(adj.)* **giddy**
ዘቀላ zeqela *(n.)* **skit**
ዘቀመጠሉ ቦታ ረስዐ zeqemeẗelu bota res'ë *(v.)* **mislay**
ዘቀንዙ zeqenzu *(adj.)* **painful**
ዘቀሓሕር zeqkeha'hir *(adj.)* **contentious**
ዘቕንእ zeqn'e *(adj.)* **enviable**
ዘቛቒት ቡን zequaqit bun *(n.)* **percolator**
ዘቈጥዕ zeq̈uẗ'ë *(n.)* **aggravation**
ዘራእቲ zera'eti *(n.)* **crop**
ዘራፍ zeraf *(n.)* **giraffe**
ዘራጊቶ zeragito *(n.)* **vortex**
ዘራጊቶ ማይ zeragito may *(n.)* **whirlpool**
ዘርአ ነገስት zer'e negest *(n.)* **royal**
ዘረባ zereba *(v.)* **gab**
ዘረባ zereba *(n.)* **utterance**
ዘረባ አልቦ ተዋሳኣይ zereba albo tewasa'ay *(n.)* **mummer**
ዘርዕድ zer'ed *(adj.)* **scary**
ዘፍርህ zefrh *(adj.)* **awesome**
ዘርዕድ zer'ëd *(adj.)* **macabre**
ዘርዕድ zer'ëd *(adj.)* **redoubtable**
ዘረፈ zerefe *(v.)* **plunder**
ኣስኣነ 'as'ane *(v.)* **bereaved**
ዘረፍረፍ zerefref *(n.)* **lace**
ዘረጋግእ zeregag'e *(adj.)* **emollient**
ዘረገ zerege *(v.)* **muddle**
ዘርገሐ zergeḧe *(v.)* **unwind**
ዘርግሐ zergḧe *(v. t)* **broadcast**
ዘርኢ zer'i *(n.)* **spore**
ዘርኢ ተባዕታይ zer'i teba'etay *(n.)* **sperm**
ዘርዘረ zerzere *(v. t)* **enumerate**
ዘስድዕ zesd'e *(adj.)* **seductive**
ዘስደምም zesdem'm *(adj.)* **staggering**
ዘሰንብድ zesenbd *(adj.)* **horrendous**
ዘሰንብድ zesenbd *(adj.)* **shattering**
ዘሰንብድ zesenbd *(adj.)* **shocking**
ዘሰንብድ zesenbd *(n.)* **startling**
ዘሰቅቕ zeseqq *(adj.)* **ghastly**
ዘስገድግድ zesgedgd *(adj.)* **horrid**
ዘስሕቕ zesĥq *(adj.)* **funny**

ዘስካሕክሕ zeskaĥkĥ ***(adj.)*** **gruesome**
ዘስካሕክሕ zeskaḧkḧ ***(adj.)*** **monstrous**
ዘስካሕክሕ zeskaḧkḧ ***(adj.)*** **awful**
ዘጣዕስ zeta'ës ***(adj.)*** **regrettable**
ዘተ zete ***(n.)*** **conference**
ዘተኣማምን zeteamamn ***(adj.)*** **potent**
ዘተባብዕ zetebab'e ***(adj.)*** **heartening**
ዘይተበረዘ zetebereze ***(adj.)*** **unadulterated**
ዘጠንቅቕ zetenqq ***(adj.)*** **cautionary**
ዘጠራጥር zeteratr ***(adj.)*** **questionable**
ዘጠጠ zetete ***(v.)*** **sag**
ዝተኸደነ zetkdn ***(adj.)*** **clad**
ዘጥንታዊ zeẗntawi ***(adj.)*** **antiquarian**
ዘፅልም zetslm ***(adj.)*** **slanderous**
ዘፅምም zetsmm ***(adj.)*** **deafening**
ዘዋራይ zewaray ***(adj.)*** **voluble**
ዘዋሪ ኮኾብ zewari koḱob ***(n.)*** **pulsar**
ዘውደኛ zewdegna ***(n.)*** **royalist**
ዘወንበለ zewenbele ***(v.)*** **maunder**
ማኒኮ maniko ***(v.)*** **crank**
ዘወረ zewere ***(v.)*** **drive**
ዘወረ zewere ***(v.)*** **steer**
ዘይ ተግበራዊ zey tegberawi ***(adj.)*** **impractical**
ዘይኣግባባዊ zeyagbabawi ***(adj.)*** **informal**
ዘይዓገበ zey'ägebe ***(adj.)*** **disaffected**
ዘይዓገቡ zey'agebu ***(n.)*** **malcontent**
ዘይኣክል zeyakl ***(adj.)*** **inadequate**
ዘይኣክል zey'akl ***(adv.)*** **scarcely**
ዘይዓሚቕ zey'amiq ***(adj.)*** **shallow**
ዘያኣርግ zey'arg ***(adj.)*** **durable**
ዘይበላሾ zeybelasho ***(adj.)*** **foolproof**
ዘይበቕዕ zeybeqe ***(adj.)*** **paltry**
ዘይ በሰለ zeybesele ***(adj.)*** **immature**
ዘይብቑዕ zeybqu'e ***(adj.)*** **inefficient**
ዘይደሃል zeydehak ***(adj.)*** **dauntless**
ዘይድልዱል zeydeldul ***(adj.)*** **unstable**
ዘይደሊ zeydeli ***(adj.)*** **loath**
ዘይድልው zeydeluw ***(adj.)*** **unprepared**
ዘይድፈር zeydfer ***(adj.)*** **formidable**
ዘይድንግጽ zeydngts ***(adj.)*** **unmoved**
ዘየድሊ zeyedeli ***(adj.)*** **unnecessary**
ዘይዕድለኛ zey'ëdleña ***(adj.)*** **hapless**
ኣድላዪ ዘይኰነ 'adlayi zeykwane ***(adj.)*** **dispensable**
ዘየድሊ zeyedli ***(adj.)*** **needless**
ዘየድሊ zeyedli ***(adj.)*** **redundant**
ዘይግቡእ zeygbu'è ***(adj.)*** **undue**
ዘየድሊ ድፍረት zeyedli dfret ***(n.)*** **temerity**
ዘየድሊ ትንተና zeyedli tntena ***(n.)*** **trivia**
ዘየድምዕ zeyedm'e ***(adj.)*** **ineffective**
ዘይእዱብ zey'edub ***(adj.)*** **impolite**
ዘየእንግድ zeye'engd ***(adj.)*** **inhospitable**
ዘየጋጊ zeyegagi ***(adj.)*** **unmistakable**
ዘየግድስ zeyegds ***(adj.)*** **negligible**
ዘይዕጉስ zey'ëgus ***(adj.)*** **impatient**
ዘየሕልፍ zeyeḥlf ***(adj.)*** **impassable**
ዘየከራኽር zeyekerakr ***(adj.)*** **indisputable**
ዘይእኹል ናብራ zeyèḱul nabra ***(adv.)*** **poorly**
ዘየማትእ zeyemat'è ***(adj.)*** **emphatic**
ዘይእመን zey'emen ***(adj.)*** **faithless**
ዘየእመን zey'emen ***(adj.)*** **implausible**

ዘይእመን zey'emen ***(adj.)*** **unbelievable**
ዘይእመን zey'èmen ***(adj.)*** **fabulous**
ዝእየናሕሲ zeyenahsi ***(adj.)*** **implacable**
ዘየናሕሲ zeyenaĥsi ***(adj.)*** **relentless**
ዘየቋርፀ zeyeqarts ***(adj.)*** **perennial**
ዘየቋርጽ zeyeqwarx ***(adj.)*** **ceaseless**
ዘየቋርፀ zeye'qwerexe' ***(adj.)*** **constant**
ዘየስርፅ zeyesrtz ***(adj.)*** **impervious**
ዘየተኣማምን zeyeteamamn ***(adj.)*** **precarious**
ዘየተኣማምን zeyeteamamn ***(n)*** **unreliable**
ዘየጠራጥር zeyeteratr ***(adj.)*** **unimpeachable**
ዘይዕቱብ zey'ëtub ***(adj.)*** **frivolous**
ዘየዝሙዉ zeyezemuwue ***(adj.)*** **chaste**
ዘይእዙዝ zey'èzuz ***(adj.)*** **involuntary**
ዘይፈለጠ zeyfelete ***(adj.)*** **unaware**
ዘይፈልጥ zeyfeleṭe ***(adj.)*** **ignorant**
ዘይፈሊ zeyfeli ***(adj.)*** **indiscriminate**
ዘይፈርሕ zeyferĥ ***(adj.)*** **fearless**
ዘይፍትሓዊ zeyfethawi ***(adj.)*** **unfair**
ዘይፍትሓዊ zeyfethawi ***(adj.)*** **unjust**
ዘይፍለጥ zeyflet ***(adj.)*** **inexplicable**
ዘይፍለጥ ጸገም zeyflet xegem ***(n.)*** **pitfall**
ዘይፍሉጥ zeyflut ***(adj.)*** **unaccountable**
ዘይፍሉጥ zeyflut ***(adj.)*** **unknown**
ዘይግቡእ ኪዳን zeygbu'e kidan ***(n.)*** **misalliance**
ዘይግደስ zeygdes ***(adj.)*** **negligent**
ዘይግደስ zeygdes ***(adj.)*** **nonchalant**
ዘይሓስብ zeyḧasb ***(adj.)*** **inconsiderate**
ዘይግደስ zeygdes ***(adj.)*** **mindless**
ሃንዳፍ handaf ***(adj.)*** **reckless**
ዘየጎድእ zeyg'e ***(adj.)*** **unscathed**
ዘይግራሕ zeygraḧ ***(adj.)*** **intractable**
ዘይግታእ zeygta'e ***(adj.)*** **indomitable**
ዘይጊዜኡ zeygzi'u ***(adj.)*** **untimely**
ዘይሓንኽ zeyhank ***(adj.)*** **shameless**
ዘይሓቂ zeyḧaqi ***(adj.)*** **hollow**
ዘይሓቕቕ zeyḥaqq̈ ***(adj.)*** **insoluble**
ዘይሓርር zeyḧarr ***(adj.)*** **ageless**
ዘይሓስብ zeyhasb ***(adj.)*** **thoughtless**
ዘይሕጋዊ zeyḥgawi ***(adj.)*** **illegitimate**
ዘይሕጋዊ zeyḥgawi ***(adj.)*** **illicit**
ዘይሕጋዊ zeyḥgawi ***(adj.)*** **illegal**
ዘይሕጉስ zeyhgus ***(adj.)*** **unhappy**
ዘይሕለል zeyhlel ***(adj.)*** **sedulous**
ዘይሕሎ zeyhlo ***(adj.)*** **unguarded**
ዘይሀሰ zeyhse ***(adj.)*** **invulnerable**
ዘይሕሰብ zeyhseb ***(adj.)*** **unthinkable**
ዘይቅዱስ zeykdus ***(adj.)*** **profane**
ዘይቅዱስ zeykdus ***(adj.)*** **sacrilegious**
ዘይክእል zeyk'el ***(adj.)*** **unskilled**
ዘይኸውን zeykewn ***(adj.)*** **preposterous**
ዘይከውን zeykewun ***(adj.)*** **unlikely**
ዘይኽፈል zeykhfel ***(adj.)*** **indivisible**
ዘይኮነ zeykone ***(prep.)*** **unlike**
ዘይቁፀር zeykutser ***(adj.)*** **unemployable**
ዘይልሙድ zeylemud ***(adj.)*** **wacky**
ዘይልሙድ zeylemud ***(adj.)*** **weird**
ዘይለዋወጥ zeylewaweẗ ***(adj.)*** **invariable**
ዘይተራእየ zeytera'èye ***(adj.)*** **strange**
ተቓውሞ teq̈awmo ***(adj.)*** **uncommon**
ዘይልሙድ zeylmud ***(adj.)*** **unnatural**
ዘይልሙድ zeylmud ***(adj.)*** **unusual**

ዘይልወጥ zeylweẗ *(adj.)* **irrevocable**
ዘይልወጥ zeylweẗ *(adj.)* **monotonous**
ዘይ ምድማፅ zeymdmats *(v.)* **ignore**
ዘይምቹ zeymechu *(adj.)* **uncomfortable**
ዘይምእሙእ zeym'èmu'è *(adj.)* **harsh**
ዘይመጣጠን zeymetaten *(adj.)* **lopsided**
ዘይመጣጠን zeymetaten *(adj.)* **uneven**
ዘይመውት zeymewut *(adj.)* **immortal**
ዘይመውት zeymewut *(adj.)* **undying**
ዘይምግዳስ zeymgdas *(n.)* **nonchalance**
ዘይምሕር zeymḧr *(adj.)* **brutal**
ዘይምካእል zeymk'al *(n.)* **inability**
ዘይምኽእል zeymkh'al *(n.)* **impossibility**
ዘይከእል zeymkh'al *(adj.)* **impossible**
ዘይምምጣን zeymmṭan *(n.)* **imbalance**
ዘይምኖ zeymno *(adj.)* **racy**
ዘይሞተ zeymote *(n.)* **zombie**
ዘይምርግጋዕ zeymreggae *(n.)* **unrest**
ዘይምርዑውቲ zeymr'ëwti *(n.)* **spinster**
ዘይምስምዕማዕ zeymsm'ëma'ë *(n.)* **disagreement**
ዘይምትእምማን zeymt'emman *(n.)* **insecurity**
ዘይሙቹ zeymuchu *(adj.)* **inopportune**
ዘይምሉእ zeymulue *(adj.)* **partial**
ዘይምውሳን zeymwsan *(n.)* **indecision**
ዘይንቡር zeynbur *(adv.)* **singularly**
ዘይንቡር መውቃዕቲ ልቢ zeynbur wqaeti lbi *(n.)* **palpitation**
ዘይነቓነቕ zeyneqaneq *(adj.)* **unshakeable**
ዘይነፃፀል zeynetsatsel *(adj.)* **inseparable**
ዘይንኪ zeynki *(adj.)* **unmitigated**
ዘይንቑሕ zeynkuh *(adj.)* **unconscious**
ዘይንቀሳቀስ zeynqesaqes *(adj.)* **motionless**
ዘይንቀሳቐስ zeynqesaqhes *(adj.)* **static**
ቀዋሚ qewami *(adj.)* **stationary**
ዘይንፀል ኣካል zeyntsel 'akal *(adj.)* **integral**
ዘይንጡፍ zeyntuf *(adj.)* **passive**
ዘይንጹህ zeynutsuh *(adj.)* **impure**
ዘይንጹህና zeynutsuhna *(n.)* **impurity**
ዘይንጹር zeynxur *(adj.)* **ambiguous**
ዘይንጹርነት zeynxurnet *(n.)* **ambiguity**
ዘይቅቡል zeyqbul *(adj.)* **unorthodox**
ዘይቅቡል zeyqbul *(adj.)* **unpopular**
ዘይተጠልበ zeyteẗelbe *(adj.)* **unsolicited**
ዘይቅቡል ገበረ zeyqbul gebere *(v.)* **invalidate**
ዘይቕየር zey'qeyer *(adj.)* **consistent**
ዘይቐሪ ነገር zeyqheri neger *(adj.)* **inevitable**
ዘይቅኑዕ zeyqnu'ë *(adj.)* **dishonest**
ዘይቅኑዕ እምነት zeyqnu'ë emnet *(n.)* **misbelief**
ዘይቅየር zeyqyer *(adj.)* **immutable**
ዘይርደኦ zeyrde'o *(n.)* **dullard**
ሓተላ ብረታት ḧatela bretat *(n.)* **dross**

ንኡስ n'us ***(adj.)*** **petty**
ዘይረብሕ ሰብ zeyrebḧ seb ***(n.)*** **scamp**
ዘይረብሕ zeyrebh ***(adj.)*** **trivial**
ንጸይ ጸጉሪ nxay xeguri ***(n.)*** **fluff**
ዘይጠቅም zeyẗeqm ***(adj.)*** **nugatory**
ዘይረብሕ zeyrebḥ ***(adj.)*** **insignificant**
ዘይረብሕ ምኳን zeyrebḥ mkwan ***(n.)*** **insignificance**
ዘይረአ zeyre'e ***(adj.)*** **invisible**
ዘይርግፀኛ zeyregetsegna ***(adj.)*** **uncertain**
ዘይርጉም zeyregum ***(adj.)*** **unselfish**
ዘይረሳዕ zeyresae ***(adj.)*** **unforgettable**
ዘይርጉጽ zeyrguts ***(adj.)*** **wonky**
ዘይርኹብ zeyrḱub ***(adj.)*** **needy**
ዘይርሳዕ zeyrsa'ë ***(adj.)*** **memorable**
ዘይርስዕ zeyrs'ë ***(adj.)*** **mindful**
ዘይርታዕ zeyrta'ë ***(adj.)*** **irrefutable**
ዘይርትዓዊ zeyrt'äwi ***(adj.)*** **irrational**
ዘይሳገር zeysager ***(adj.)*** **intransitive**
ዘይሳነ ሽም zeysane shm ***(n.)*** **misnomer**
ዘይስዓር zeys'är ***(adj.)*** **invincible**
ዘይሰዓቢ zeyse'äbi ***(n.)*** **nonconformist**
ዘይሰኽረ zeysekhere ***(adj.)*** **sober**
ዘይሰማዕ zeysemae ***(adj.)*** **unheard**
ዘይሰምር zeysemr ***(adj.)*** **pious**
ዘይሰርሕ zeyserh ***(adj.)*** **inoperative**
ዘይስሕብ zeyshb ***(adj.)*** **inconspicuous**
ዘይስሕብ zeyshb ***(adj.)*** **inert**
ትሕተ-ድምጻው tḧtedmxaw ***(adj.)*** **subsonic**
ዘይስማዕ zeysma'e ***(adj.)*** **inaudible**
ዘይስማማዕ zeysma'ëma'ë ***(adj.)*** **discordant**
ዘይስማዕማዑ zeysma'ema'u ***(adj.)*** **incompatible**
ዘይስነ-መጐታዊ zeysnemegwatawi ***(adj.)*** **illogical**
ዘይስንገል zeysngel ***(adj.)*** **inconsolable**
ዘይፅዕር zeys'r ***(adj.)*** **tireless**
ሳሕቲ ዝርኤ saḧti zr'ee ***(adj.)*** **anomalous**
ዘይስሩዕ zeysru'ë ***(adj.)*** **erratic**
ሓባጥ-ጐባጥ ḧabaẗgwabaẗ ***(adj.)*** **irregular**
ዘይስሩዕነት zeysru'ënet ***(n.)*** **irregularity**
ዘይሳኻዕ zeyssakha'e ***(adj.)*** **inauspicious**
ዘይስተኻኸል zeystekhakel ***(adj.)*** **irredeemable**
ዘየተኣማመን zeyte'amamen ***(adj.)*** **insecure**
ዘተኣመተ zeyteamete ***(adj.)*** **unforeseen**
ዘይተዓረቕ zeyte'äreq̈ ***(adj.)*** **irreconcilable**
ዘይተፈርደ zeyteferde ***(adj.)*** **sub judice**
ዘይተነግረ zeytegebre ***(adj.)*** **untold**
ዘይተገዳስነት zeytegedasnet ***(n.)*** **profligacy**
ዘይተጎደኤ zeytegode'e ***(adj.)*** **intact**
ዘይተሓረሰ መሬት zeyteḧarese mereet ***(n.)*** **moor**
ዘይጠሓስ zeytehas ***(adj.)*** **impenetrable**
ዘይተሓስበ zeyteḧasbe ***(n.)*** **surprise**
ዘይተሓሰበሉ zeytehasebelo ***(adj.)*** **casual**

ዘይተሓወሰ zeytehawese ***(adj.)*** **unalloyed**
ዘይተሓዝ zeyteḥaz ***(adj.)*** **impalpable**
ዘይተላገበ zeytelagebe ***(adj.)*** **disjointed**
ዘይተለምደ zeytelemde ***(adj.)*** **unsocial**
ዘይተለመደ zeytelemde ***(adj.)*** **zany**
ዘይጥዕም zeyt'em ***(adj.)*** **insipid**
ዘይጥዕም zeyt'em ***(adj.)*** **tacky**
ዘይተመስገነ zeytemesgene ***(adj.)*** **unsung**
ዘይተመጣጣንነት zeytemeẗaẗannet ***(n.)*** **mismatch**
ዘይተቐየረ zeyteqeyere ***(adj.)*** **pristine**
ዘይጠቅም zeyẗeqm ***(n.)*** **nonentity**
ዘይጠቅም ሽልማት zeyteqm shlmat ***(n.)*** **trinket**
ዘይተፀወዐ zeytetsewe'e ***(adj.)*** **uncalled**
ዘይተዋደደ zeytewadede ***(adj.)*** **frenetic**
ዘይተወደአ zeytewede'e ***(adj.)*** **incomplete**
ዘይተወልደ zeytewelde ***(adj.)*** **unborn**
ዘይተወጠረ zeytewetere ***(adj.)*** **slack**
ዘይጥሓስ zeythas ***(adj.)*** **unassailable**
ዘይትሑዝ zeythuz ***(adj.)*** **unreserved**
ዘይትንከፍ zeytnkef ***(adj.)*** **untouchable**
ዘይትርድኦ ቋንቋ zeytrd'o quanqua ***(n.)*** **lingo**
ዘይፃወር zeytsawer ***(adj.)*** **intolerant**
ዘይፅቡቕ ዝተሰመዖ zeytsbuq ztesemeo ***(adj.)*** **unwell**
ዘይፅቡይ zeytsebuy ***(adj.)*** **unprecedented**
ዘይፅሩይ zeytseruy ***(adj.)*** **unclean**
ዘይፅወር zeytswer ***(adj.)*** **intolerable**
ዘይጥዑም zeyt'um ***(adj.)*** **untoward**
ዘይቱን zeytun ***(n.)*** **guava**
ዘይውዳእ zeywda'e ***(adj.)*** **inexhaustible**
ዘይወዳደሩ zeywedaderu ***(adj.)*** **incomparable**
ዘይወዳአ zeywedae ***(adj.)*** **unending**
ዘይወግዓዊ zeyweg'awi ***(adj.)*** **colloquial**
ዘይወሱን zeywesun ***(adj.)*** **undecided**
ዘይውልቃዊ zeywlqawi ***(adj.)*** **impersonal**
ዘይውርዙይ zeywrzuy ***(adj.)*** **ignoble**
ዘይውሱን zeywusn ***(adj.)*** **unlimited**
ዘይጾታዊ ርክብ zeyxotawi ckb ***(adj.)*** **platonic**
ዘይዛመድ zeyzamed ***(adj.)*** **irrelevant**
ዘይዛረብ zeyzareb ***(adj.)*** **speechless**
ዘዘንበለ zezenbele ***(adj.)*** **tendentious**
ዝፈልጥ ዝመስል zfelt zmesl ***(adj.)*** **knowing**
ዝፈርሐ zferḧe ***(adj.)*** **afraid**
ዝፍፈት zffet ***(n.)*** **dialysis**
ዝፍቀድ zfqed ***(adj.)*** **permissible**
ዝፍወስ zfwes ***(adj.)*** **curable**
ዝፍውስ zfws ***(adj.)*** **curative**
ዝፍውስ zfws ***(adj.)*** **remedial**
ዝገርም zgerm ***(adj.)*** **marvellous**
ዝግለፀሉ መንገዲ zgletselu mengedi ***(n.)*** **manifestation**
ዝግመት zgmet ***(adj.)*** **putative**
ዝግናነ zgnane ***(n.)*** **revulsion**
ዝጎደሎ zgodelo ***(prep.)*** **minus**

ዝጎሃየ zgohaye *(adj.)* **disconsolate**
ዝግታ zgta *(adj.)* **residual**
ዝሓፈረ zḧafere *(adj.)* **ashamed**
ዝሓጀጀ zḧaĵeĵe *(n.)* **hajji**
ቀደም qedem *(adj.)* **bygone**
ኣቐዲሙ ዝተገልጸ 'aq̈edimu ztegelxe *(adj.)* **foregoing**
ዝሓለፈ zḧalefe *(adj.)* **previous**
ዝሓመመ zhameme *(adj.)* **indisposed**
ዝሓሸ ኣተሓሰስባ zhashe atehasasba *(adj.)* **transcendental**
ዝሓሸ zḧashe *(adj.)* **advisable**
ዝሓሸ zḧashe *(adj.)* **better**
ዝሓሸ zḧashe *(adj.)* **wholesome**
ዝሓዘነ zhazene *(adj.)* **sad**
ዝሓዘነ zḧazene *(adj.)* **sorry**
ዝሕታለ zĥtale *(n.)* **retardation**
ዝሕታለ zḧtale *(n.)* **stagnation**
ዝሕጠት zĥtet *(n.)* **recession**
ዝሕፀቡ ክዳውንቲ zhtsebu kdawnti *(n.)* **laundry**
ዝሕቱል zḧtul *(adj.)* **stagnant**
ዝሑል zhul *(adj.)* **cool**
ዝሑል zhul *(adj.)* **parky**
ዝሑል ምንቅስቓስ zḧul mnqsqas *(v.)* **plod**
ዝሁም zhum *(adj.)* **lukewarm**
ዝድነቕ zidneq *(adj.)* **wonderful**
ዜዴ ziede *(n.)* **tactic**
ዚፍቀድ zifqed *(adj.)* **admissible**
ዚነኣድ zine'ad *(adj.)* **admirable**
ዚነኣድ zine'ad *(adj.)* **commendable**
ዚንጎ zingo *(n.)* **zinc**
ዝረገአ ደም ziregeaa' dem' *(n.)* **clot**
ዚሰማማዕ zisemama'ë *(adj.)* **agreeable**
ዚሰማማዕ zisemama'ë *(adj.)* **apposite**
ዝስማዕማዕ zismaemae tsemaexmeaa *(adj.)* **congruent**
ዝተዛዘመ ziteza'zeme' *(n)* **checkmate**
ዚወሃሃድ ziwehahad *(adj.)* **congenial**
ዚጽላእ zixla'è *(adj.)* **abominable**
ዚዝ በለ ziz bele *(v.)* **hum**
ዚዛመድ zizamed *(adj.)* **akin**
ዚዝታ zizta *(n.)* **buzz**
ዘረገ tserege *(n.)* **puddle**
ዛህላል zahlal *(adj.)* **vacuous**
ዘጨንቕ zeçenq *(adj.)* **harrowing**
ዘኽታም zeḱtam *(n.)* **waif**
ዘመናይ zemenay *(n.)* **vogue**
ዘንበየ zenbeye *(v.)* **hover**
ዘይእኹል zey'èḱul *(adj.)* **insufficient**
ዘይጎድእ zeygod'è *(adj.)* **harmless**
ዘይምፍላጥ zeymflaṭ *(n.)* **ignorance**
ዘይቀሳቀስ zeynqesaqhes *(adv.)* **immovable**
ዘይንጹር zeynxur *(adj.)* **vague**
ዘይንጹርነት zeynxurnet *(n.)* **vagueness**
ዘይቀዋሚነት zeyqewaminet *(n.)* **instability**
ዘይረብሕ zeyrebḥ *(adj.)* **immaterial**
ዝተፈላለየ ztefelaleye *(adj.)* **heterogeneous**
ዝተፈላለየ ztefelaleye *(adj.)* **varied**
ዝተመረፀ ztemerxe *(adj.)* **elective**
ዝከኣል zkeal *(adj.)* **possible**
ዝኸበበ zkebebe *(adj.)* **rounded**
ዝኸፍእ zkefe *(adj.)* **worse**
ዝቖትል zketl *(adj.)* **deadly**
ዝኾነ zḱone *(adj.)* **any**
ዝኾነ ቦታ zḱone bota *(adv.)* **anywhere**

ዝኾነ ግዜ zkone gzie ***(conj.)*** **whenever**
ዝኾነ ኮይኑ zkone koynu ***(a.)*** **nonetheless**
ዝኾነ ነገር zḱone neger ***(pron.)*** **anything**
ዝኾነ ሰብ zḱone seb ***(pron.)*** **anyone**
ዝኾነ ይኹን zkone ykun ***(pron.)*** **whichever**
ዝክር zkr ***(n.)*** **commemoration**
ዝክረ-ዓመት zkre'ämet ***(n.)*** **anniversary**
ዝክረ-ዘመን zkrezemen ***(n.)*** **centenary**
ዝክረ ዘመን zkrezemen ***(n.)*** **centennial**
ዝኽሪ zkri ***(n.)*** **remembrance**
ዝኽሪ zḱri ***(n.)*** **memorial**
ዝኽሪ ክልተ ሚኢቲ ዓመት zkri klte mi'iti ämet ***(n.)*** **bicentenary**
ዝለዓለ zleale ***(adj.)*** **paramount**
ዝለአለ zleale ***(adj. & n.)*** **uttermost**
ዝለዓለ zle'äle ***(n.)*** **maximum**
ዝለዓለ ክፋል ቕሽነት zleale kfal qshnet ***(n.)*** **patriarch**
ዝለዓለ ሽልማት zle'ale shlmat ***(n.)*** **jackpot**
ዝማዕበለ zma'ëbele ***(adj.)*** **mature**
ዝማርኽ zmark ***(adj.)*** **sensational**
ዝምድና zmdna ***(n.)*** **correlation**
ዝምድና zmdna ***(n.)*** **kinship**
ዝምድና zmdna ***(n.)*** **relation**
ዝምድና zmdna ***(n.)*** **relationship**
ዝምድና መጠን zmdna meten ***(n.)*** **ratio**
ዝመሓላለፍ ነገር zmehalalef nege ***(n.)*** **transmission**
ዝመኸኸ zmeḱeḱe ***(adj.)*** **molten**
ዝመልአ zmel'e ***(adj.)*** **replete**
ዝመሳሰል zmesasel ***(adj.)*** **analogue**
ዝሞተ zmote ***(adj.)*** **dead**
ዝምስገን zmsgen ***(adj.)*** **creditable**
ዝምስጥ zmst ***(adj.)*** **thriller**
ዝሙት zmut ***(n.)*** **adultery**
ዝና zna ***(n.)*** **eminence**
ዝናብ znab ***(n)*** **rain**
ዝናብ ዘለዎ znab zelewo ***(adj.)*** **rainy**
ምቕናን mq̈nan ***(n.)*** **inclination**
ዝንባለ znbale ***(n.)*** **tendency**
ዝንባለ znbale ***(n.)*** **trend**
ዝንባለ znbalie ***(n.)*** **proclivity**
ዝንበላ znbela ***(n.)*** **aberration**
ዝንቡል znbul ***(adj.)*** **aberrant**
ዝነኣሰ zne'ase ***(adj.& pron.)*** **least**
ዝውሓደ zwḧade ***(adj.)*** **lesser**
ዝዘነቖጸ ፕሮኞ zneq̈ete proňo ***(n.)*** **prune**
ዝንጋዐነት znga'ënet ***(n.)*** **amnesia**
ዝንቀሳቀስ ሕይሊ znqesaqes hyli ***(n.)*** **traction**
ዝንቀሳቀስ ነገር ምልክት ዳሓደገ ዝከድ znqesaqes neger mlkt na hadege zked ***(n.)*** **trajectory**
ዝንተዋ zntewa ***(n.)*** **narration**
ዞረ zore ***(v.)*** **rotate**
ዝቀንዐ zqen'ë ***(adj.)*** **erect**
ዝቀረበ zqerebe ***(adj.)*** **impending**
ዝቀረበ zqerebe ***(adj.)*** **nearest**
ዝቐረበ zqerebe ***(adj.)*** **proximate**
ዝቀውሰ zqewese ***(adj.)*** **deranged**
ዝቕትል zqhtl ***(adj.)*** **lethal**
ዝቖንቖነ zqonqone ***(adj.)*** **decrepit**
ዝቆሰለ zqosele ***(adj.)*** **sore**
ዝቅፀል zqxl ***(adj.)*** **next**
ዝራግ zrag ***(adj.)*** **turbid**
ዝርዳእ zrdae ***(adj.)*** **perceptible**

ዝረአየሉ ኣጋጣሚ zre'ayelu agatami *(n.)* **sighting**
ዝረሓቀ zreĥaqe *(adj.& adv.)* **furthest**
ዝረስሐ ፀጉሪ zreshe seguri *(v.)* **tousle**
ዝርጋሐ zrgahe *(n.)* **scope**
ዝርጋሐ zrgaĥe *(n.)* **extent**
ዝርጋሐ zrgaĥe *(n.)* **range**
ዝርገጽ መቆጻጻሪ ማሺን zrgex mekoxaxeri mashen *(n.)* **pedal**
ዝርጉሕ ቀጽላ zrguḧ qetsla *(n.)* **spreadsheet**
ዝሩግ zrug *(adj.)* **murky**
ዝርዝር zrzr *(n.)* **detail**
ዝርዝር zrzr *(n.)* **index**
ዝርዝር zrzr *(n.)* **tally**
ዝርዝር zr'zr *(n.)* **list**
ዝርዝር z'rz'r *(n.)* **specification**
ዝርዝር ዓሌት zrzr alet *(n.)* **pedigree**
ዝርዝራዊ ፍቕዲ zrzrawi fq̈di *(n.)* **inventory**
ዝርዝረ-ጽሑፋት zrzrexḧufat *(n.)* **bibliography**
ዝሳዕረረ zsa'ërere *(adj.)* **rife**
ዝሰዓበ zse'äbe *(adj.)* **due**
ዝስዕብ zs'ëb *(adj.)* **forthcoming**
ዝስዕብ z's'ëb *(adj.)* **subsequent**
ዝሰሓግ zseḧag *(adj.)* **moribund**
ዝሰምበደ zsembede *(adj.)* **aghast**
ዝሰርሕ zserh *(adj.)* **working**
ዝሰርሕዎ ስራሕ ምፍራሕ zserhwo srah mfrah *(n.)* **trepidation**
ዝስማዕማዕ zsma'ëma'ë *(v.)* **accord**
ዝስራሕ zsrah *(adj.)* **workable**
ዝስረዝ zsrez *(adj.)* **revocable**
ዝተዓፈነ ድምጺ zteafene dmsi *(adj.)* **throaty**
ዝተኣሳሰር zte'asaser *(adj.)* **relevant**
ዝተኣሳሰረ zte'asasere *(adj.)* **tied**
ዝተባህለ ztebahle *(n.)* **dictation**
ዝተበላሸወ z-tebela-shewe *(adj.)* **gammy**
ዝተበራበረ zteberabere *(adj.)* **watchful**
ዝተበሳጨወ ztebesaĉewe *(adj.)* **disgruntled**
ዝተበታተነ ztebetatene *(adv.)* **asunder**
ዝተጨነቐ ztečeneq̈e *(adj.)* **beleaguered**
ዝተጨነቐ ztecheneke *(adj.)* **worried**
ዝተዳኸመ ztedakeme *(adj.)* **effete**
ዝተዳለወ ztedalewe *(adj.)* **biased**
ዝተደናገረ ztedenagere *(adj.)* **bemused**
ዝተደርበየ ztederebye *(n.)* **casting**
ዝተፋላለየ ztefalaleye *(adj.)* **assorted**
ዝተፋትሐ ztefat'ĥe *(n.)* **divorcee**
ዝተራሓሓቐ zteraḧaḧaq̈e *(adv.)* **apart**
በብዓይነቱ beb'äynetu *(adj.)* **sundry**
ዝተፈላለየ ztefelaleye *(adj.)* **unequalled**
ዝተፈላለየ ztefelaleye *(adj.)* **various**
ዝተፈላለዩ ztefelaleyu *(adj.)* **diverse**
ዝተፈለየ ናይ በዓል ክዳን ምክዳን ztefely nay beal kdan mkdan *(n.)* **tog**
ዝተፈቐደሉ ztefeqhedelu *(n.)* **licensee**
ዝተጋፍሐ ztegafĥe *(v.)* **diffuse**
ዝተጋገየ ztegageye *(adj.)* **mistaken**
ዝተጋነነ zteganene *(adj.)* **stilted**
ዝተገደበ ztegedebe *(adj.)* **limited**
ዝተገፍተነ ztegeftene *(adv.)* **ajar**
ዝተገንዘበ ztegenzebe *(adj.)* **aware**

ዝተጎዝጎዘ ztegozgoze *(adv.)* **nearby**
ዝተሃነቀ ztehakene *(adj.)* **deliberate**
ዝተሓላለኸ zteȟalaleǩe *(adj.)* **complex**
ዝተሓላለኸ zteḥalaleǩe *(adj.)* **knotty**
ዝተሓላለኸ ነገር ፈትሐ zteȟalaleke neger fet'he *(v.)* **disentangle**
ዝተሓለወ ztehalewe *(adj.)* **guarded**
ዝተሃሰየ ztehaseye *(adj.)* **disabled**
ዝተሓተ zteȟate *(n.)* **bottom**
ዝተሓተ ቦታ zteȟate bota *(n.)* **nadir**
ዝተሓትመ ወረቐት zteȟatme wereq̈et *(n.)* **printout**
ዝተሓዋወሰ zteȟawawese *(adj.)* **miscellaneous**
ዝተጃህረሉ ztejahrelu *(adj.)* **vaunted**
ፍቱሕ ztekelbese *(adj.)* **undone**
ዝተኸልከለ ነገር ztekelkele neger *(n.)* **taboo**
ዝጠቅም ztekem *(adj.)* **usable**
ዝተከዘ ztekeze *(adj.)* **saturnine**
ዝተላፀየ ztelatseye *(adj.)* **shaven**
ዝተለመደ ztelemede *(adj.)* **typical**
ዝጥዕም ድምፂ zt'ëm dmtsi *(adj.)* **sibilant**
ዝተማሕረ ztemaȟre *(adj.)* **exempt**
ዝተማልአ ztemal'e *(adj.)* **exhaustive**
ዝተሰነየ zteseneye *(adj.)* **fraught**
ዝተመልከ ztemelke *(adj.)* **revered**
ዝተመንጠለ ztementele *(adj.)* **rapt**
ዝተመንወ ztemenwe *(adj.)* **trite**
ዝተመንዘዐ ztemenze'ë *(adj.)* **bereft**
ዝተመራስሐ ztemerasȟe *(adj.)* **sophisticated**
ዝተመስከረሉ ztemeskerelu *(adj.)* **chartered**
ዝተናወጸ ztenawexe *(adj.)* **addled**
ዝተናዘዘ ztenazeze *(adj.)* **testate**
ዝተነፀለ ztenexele *(adj.)* **estranged**
ዝተጠልጠለ ztenteltele *(adj.)* **pendent**
ዝተቓልዐ zteqal'e *(adj.)* **susceptible**
ዝተቓልዐ zteqal'ë *(adj.)* **prone**
ዝተቀደሰ zteqedese *(adj.)* **sacred**
ዝተቐደሰ zteq̈edese *(adj.)* **halal**
ዝተቀናበረ ሙዚቃ zteqenabere muziqa *(n.)* **symphony**
ዝተቐረፀ ፁሑፍ zteqhretse tsuhuf *(n.)* **inscription**
ዝተቖራረፀ zteqorarexe *(adj.)* **fitful**
ዝተራሕረሐ zteraȟreȟe *(n.)* **castaway**
ዝተሳእነ ztesa'ene *(adj.)* **missing**
ዝተሰቕለ zteseq̈le *(adv.)* **aloft**
ዝተሻቐለ zteshaq̈ele *(adj.)* **apprehensive**
ዝተጠበሰ ztetbese *(n.)* **toast**
ዝተተሓባበሩ zteteȟababeru *(adj.)* **allied**
ዝተጠምማዘዘ ztetemazeze *(adj.)* **tortuous**
ዝተጠምዘዘ ztetemazeze *(v.)* **twist**
ዝተጠቕዐ zteẗeqh'ë *(adj.)* **stricken**
ዝተፅዓነ ztets'ane *(n.)* **laden**
ዝተዋሃሃደ ztewahahade *(adj.)* **composite**
ዝተወሃበ ztewehabe *(adj.)* **given**
ዝተወሃሃደ ztewehahade *(adj.)* **harmonious**
ዝተወርሰ መሰል ztewerse mesel *(n.)* **patrimony**
ዝተወጠረ ztewetere *(adj.)* **riddled**
ዝተወጠረ ztewetere *(adj.)* **taut**
ዝተዘርገ ztezerge *(adj.)* **muzzy**
ዝፀልመተ ztselmete *(adj.)* **dark**
ዝፀነሐ ztsenehe *(adj.)* **ingrained**
ዙፋን zufan *(n.)* **throne**
ዙረት zuret *(n.)* **hike**

ምብርራይ mbrray *(n.)* **rotation**
ዙርያ zurya *(n.)* **circumference**
ዙርያዊ zuryawi *(adj.)* **ambient**
ዝወዳደቐ ጓሓፍ zwedeqe guahaf *(n.)* **litter**
ዝወሓደ zwehade *(adj. & pron.)* **less**
ዝወሓደ zweḧade *(adj.)* **minimal**
ዝወሓደ zweḧade *(n.)* **minimum**
ዝወተረ zwetere *(adj.)* **tumescent**
ዝፃነተ zxanete *(adj.)* **extinct**
ዝፀለለ zxelele *(n.)* **filtrate**
ዝፅላእ zxla'e *(adj.)* **averse**
ዝያዳ ክፍሊት zyda kflit *(n.)* **surcharge**
ዘየሕጉስ zyehigus' *(adj.)* **cheerless**
ዝዛረብ ሰብ ኣቋረፀ zzareb seb aqaretse *(v.)* **interject**
ዝዝርጋሕ ዓራት zzrgaḧ 'ärat *(n.)* **couchette**
ዘየሐጉስ zeyehegus *(adj.)* **obnoxious**
ዘየዳልው zeyedalw *(adv.)* **objectively**
ዘይልሙድ zeylmud *(adj.)* **odd**
ዘይቲ zeyti *(n.)* **oil**
ዘይቲ ለከየ zeyti lekeye *(v.)* **oil**
ዘይቲ ዝበዝሖ zeyti zbezho *(adj.)* **oily**
ዘይንጹር zeyntsur *(adj.)* **obscure**
ዘይግልፂ zeygltsi *(adj.)* **ostensible**
ዘይግልፂ zeygltsi *(n.)* **ostentation**
ዘይጠቅም heteqm *(adj.)* **otiose**
ዙረት zuret *(n.)* **oscillation**
ዚረስዕ zres'o *(adj.)* **oblivious**
ዝሐሸ zĥeshe *(adj.)* **optimum**
ዝሐሸ ገበረ zĥheshe gebere *(v.)* **optimize**
ዝለዓለ ክፍሊት ምቕራብ zle'ale kflit mqrab *(v.)* **outbid**
ዝተጋነነ zteganene *(adj.)* **overblown**
ዝተጸባበቐ ztetsebabeqe *(adj.)* **ornate**
ዝንጋዐ znga'e *(n.)* **oversight**
ዝኣረገ z'arege *(adj.)* **outmoded**
ዝዓግት zagt *(adj.)* **obstructive**
ዝዕዘብ z'ezeb *(adj.)* **observant**
ዝያዳ በለጸ zyada blelexe *(v.)* **outshine**
ዝገድድ zegeded *(v.)* **oblige**

የ

የማን yeman *(n)* **right**
የዋህ yewah *(n.)* **tender**
የዋህ yewah *(adj.)* **tender**
የዋህነት yewahnet *(adv.)* **credulity**
የዋህነት yewahnet *(n.)* **goodness**
ያዕያዕታ ya'ëyaëta *(n.)* **rumpus**
ያዕያዕታ ya'ëya'ëta *(n.)* **jazz**
ይኣኽለኒ ዘይብሃል y'akleni zeybhal *(adj.)* **irresistible**
ያታ yata *(n.)* **legend**
ያታዊ yatawi *(adj.)* **legendary**
ይግባእ ygba'e *(v.)* **must**
ይግባእ ygba'e *(v.)* **shall**
ይግባእ ygba'e *(v.)* **should**
ይግበአኒ በሃላይ yigbeani behalayi *(n.)* **claimant**
ይኽእል yḱ'el *(v.)* **might**
ይኽእል y'ḱ'el *(v.)* **may**
ይቕር ንክብል ምእማን yker nkbl m'eman *(v.)* **intercede**
ይኸውን ykewn *(adj.)* **would-be**
ዮጋ yoga *(n.)* **yoga**
ዮንክስ yonks *(n.)* **yonks**
ይቕሬታ yq̈reeta *(n.)* **apology**
ዩኒቨርስቲ yuniversty *(n.)* **university**
ዩሮ yuro *(n.)* **euro**

ይጽናሕ ዝተባህለ yxnah ztebahle *(adj.)* **pending**
ደምሰሰ demsese *(v.)* **obliterate**
ደረቕ dereq *(adj.)* **obstinate**
ደረቕነት dereqnet *(n)* **obstinacy**
ደገ dege *(adv.)* **out**
ደገ dege *(adj.)* **outdoor**
ደገ dege *(n.)* **outside**
ደጋዊ degawi *(adj.)* **outer**
ደጋዊ degawi *(adv.)* **outwardly**
ድልድል dldl *(n.)* **overpass**
ዳኛ daagna *(n.)* **referee**
ዳዶ dado *(n.)* **dice**
ዳዕሮ da'ëro *(n.)* **sycamore**
ዳፍላ dafla *(n.)* **quiff**
ደጋል dagal *(adj.)* **dingy**
ዳጌት dageet *(n.)* **chivalry**
ዳጌተኛ dageetenya *(adj.)* **chivalrous**
ዳገት daget *(n.)* **quay**
ዳጌፋ dagiefa *(n.)* **prop**
ዳግም ኣሐተመ dagm aĥeteme *(v.)* **reprint**
ዳግም ኣሐየለ dagm aĥeyele *(v.)* **regenerate**
ዳግም ኣህገረ dagm ahgere *(v.)* **repatriate**
ዳግም ኣማዕረገ dagm amaërege *(v.)* **rehabilitate**
ዳግም ኣረጋገፀ dagm aregagetse *(v.)* **reaffirm**
ዳግም ኣዋፈረ dagm awafere *(v.)* **redeploy**
ዳግመ ፍርዲ dagm frdi *(n.)* **retrial**
ዳግም ገምገመ dagm gemgeme *(v.)* **reassess**
ዳግም ገምገመ dagm gemgeme *(v.)* **reconsider**
ዳግም ግምገማ dagm gmgema *(n.)* **reappraisal**
ዳግም ጎበዘ dagm gobeze *(v.)* **rejuvenate**
ዳግም ጉብዝና dagm gubzna *(n.)* **rejuvenation**
ዳግም ሃነፀ dagm hanetse *(v.)* **rebuild**
ዳግም ሃነፀ dagm hanetse *(v.)* **reconstruct**
ዳግም ሃነፀ dagm hanetse *(v.)* **revamp**
ዳግም ሓሰበ dagm ĥasebe *(v.)* **rethink**
ዳግም ሓዘ dagm ĥaze *(v.)* **recapture**
ዳግመ ሕውየት dagm ĥwyet *(n.)* **rehabilitation**
ዳግመ ህያው dagm hyawe *(n.)* **revivalism**
ዳግም ልደት dagm ldet *(n.)* **rebirth**
ዳግም መልአ dagm mel'e *(v.)* **refill**
ዳግም ምጅማር dagm mjmar *(n.)* **resumption**
ዳግም ምኳን dagm mkwan *(v.)* **reoccur**
ዳግም ምልዕዓል dagm ml'ëäl *(a.)* **resurgence**
ዳግም ምጥጣዕ dagm mtta'ë *(n.)* **regeneration**
ዳግም ቀፀለ dagm qetsele *(v.)* **resume**
ዳግም ሰርዐ dagm ser'ë *(v.)* **rearrange**
ዳግም ሰወለ dagm sewele *(v.)* **retread**
ዳግም ስጋ ኣልበሰ dagm sga albese *(v.)* **reincarnate**
ዳግም ተለማመደ dagm telemamede *(v.)* **readjust**
ዳግም ተራኣየ dagm tera'aye *(v.)* **reappear**

ዳግም ተፀንበረ dagm testenbere ***(v.)*** **rejoin**
ዳግም ተጠቀመ dagm teteqeme ***(v.)*** **reuse**
ዳግም ወደበ dagm wedebe ***(v.)*** **reconstitute**
ዳግም ወደበ dagm wedebe ***(v.)*** **reorganize**
ዳግም ወነነ dagm wenene ***(v.)*** **repossess**
ዳግም ዝለዓዓል dagm ztela'ääle ***(adj.)*** **resurgent**
ዳግም ኣተንሰአ dagm ztense'e ***(v.)*** **resurrect**
ዳግመ ህግረት dagme hgret ***(n.)*** **repatriation**
ዳግም ተፃወተ dagmtetsawete ***(v.)*** **replay**
ዳኛ dagna ***(n.)*** **umpire**
ዳጎነ dagone ***(v.)*** **intern**
ዳጉሻ dagusha ***(n.)*** **millet**
ደሓነ daĥane ***(v.)*** **recover**
ዳህናው dahnaw ***(adj.)*** **stale**
ዳሕራዋይ dahraway ***(adj.)*** **latter**
ዳሕረዋይ መነፃፀሪ dahreway menetzatzeri ***(n.)*** **hindsight**
ዳህሳሲ dahsasi ***(n.)*** **globetrotter**
ዳህሳሲ dahsasi ***(n.)*** **navigator**
ዳህሳሲ dahsasi ***(n.)*** **scout**
ዳህሰሰ dahsese ***(v.)*** **explore**
ዳህሰሰ dahsese ***(v.t.)*** **survey**
ዳኛ daǹa ***(n.)*** **judge**
ዳኛ daǹa ***(n.)*** **arbitrator**
ዳንደልዮን dandelyon ***(v.)*** **dandelion**
ዳነየ daneye ***(v.)*** **arbitrate**
ዳንጋ danga ***(n.)*** **shank**
ዳንኬራ dankiera ***(n.)*** **fanfare**
ዳኝነት daǹnet ***(n.)*** **arbitration**
ዳርጋ darga ***(adv.)*** **almost**
ዳርጋ darga ***(adv.)*** **nearly**
ዳርጋ darga ***(adv.)*** **rather**
ዳርጋ ኣብ መወዳእታ darga ab mewedet a ***(adj.)*** **penultimate**
ኣጉዶ 'agudo ***(n.)*** **shack**
ኣዳራሽ 'adarash ***(n.)*** **pavilion**
ዳስ das ***(n.)*** **arbour**
ዳስ das ***(n.)*** **bower**
ዳይኖሰር daynoser ***(n.)*** **dinosaur**
ዳይረክተር dayrekter ***(adj.)*** **principal**
ድባብ dbab ***(n.)*** **canopy**
ድብዳቤ dbdabie ***(n.)*** **letter**
ድበት dbet ***(n.)*** **silt**
ድቢ dbi ***(n.)*** **panda**
ድቢ dbi ***(v.t)*** **bear**
ድብልቅልቅ dbl'ql'q ***(n.)*** **medley**
ድብያ dbya ***(n.)*** **ambush**
ደብዛዝ dbzaz ***(adj.)*** **woozy**
ደዓኸ deä'ḱe ***(v.t)*** **mash**
ድብልቕላቕ debaleq̌e ***(n.)*** **jumble**
ደባን deban ***(adj.)*** **dull**
ደበስ debas ***(n.)*** **retribution**
ደባይ ተዋጋኢ debay tewaga'i ***(n.)*** **guerrilla**
ደብዳብ debdab ***(n.)*** **bombardment**
ደብዳቢት debdabit ***(n.)*** **bomber**
ደብደበ debdebe ***(v.)*** **bombard**
ደበና debena ***(n.)*** **nimbus**
ደበና መሰል debena mesel ***(adj.)*** **nebulous**
ደበናማ debenama ***(adj.)*** **cloudy**
ደበንገረ debengere ***(n.)*** **gloom**
ደበ'ሰ debese ***(v.)*** **condole**
ደብለቐ debleq̌e ***(v.)*** **amalgamate**
ደበና debna' ***(n.)*** **cloud**
ደብራዊ debrawi ***(adj.)*** **parochial**
ደብሪ debri ***(n)*** **deck**
ደብሪ debri ***(n.)*** **sanctum**

በርቃዊ መጥቃዕቲ berqawi meẗqa'ëti *(n.)* **blitz**
ደቡብ debub *(n.)* **south**
ደቡባዊ debubawi *(adj.)* **southern**
ደብዛዝ debzaz *(adj.)* **sketchy**
ዴሲቤል decibel *(n.)* **decibel**
ዴሲማል decimal *(adj.)* **decimal**
ደድሕረ ሞት dedḧri mot *(adj.)* **posthumous**
ዴስነት deesnet *(n.)* **communism**
ደፍአ defae *(v.)* **push**
ኣህረረ 'ahrere *(v.)* **tempt**
ደፋፍአ defaf'a *(v.)* **tout**
ደፋፈአ defafe'a *(v.)* **actuate**
ደፋር defar *(adj.)* **daring**
ውዱቕ ፍናን መሽኳት wduq̈ fnan meshkwat *(adj.)* **nerveless**
ደፋር defar *(adj.)* **saucy**
ደፍደፈ defdefe *(v.)* **dab**
ደፍአ def'e *(v.)* **encroach**
ደፍአ def'e *(v.)* **goad**
ደፍአ def'e *(v.)* **hunch**
ደፈነ defene *(n.)* **default**
ደፈረ defere *(v.)* **dare**
ደፈረ defere *(v.)* **molest**
ደፈረ defere *(v.)* **rape**
ደፍጢጡ፣ገሊፁ deftitu,gelisu *(v.)* **tramp**
ደጋፊ degafi *(n.)* **devotee**
ደጋፊ degafi *(n.)* **exponent**
ደጋፊ degafi *(n.)* **partisan**
ደጋፊ degafi *(n.)* **patron**
ደጋፊ ሙኳን degafi mukwan *(v.)* **patronize**
ደጋፊ ሰላም degafi selam *(n.)* **pacifist**
ደጋፊ degafi *(n.)* **aide**
ጥምሮ ïmro *(n.)* **truss**
ደጋገመ degageme *(v.)* **iterate**
ደጋገመ degageme *(v.)* **reiterate**
ደጋዊ degawi *(adj.)* **external**
ደጋዊ ትረኢት degawi treit *(n.)* **physiognomy**
ደገፍ degef *(n.)* **recourse**
ደገፍ degef *(n.)* **reinforcement**
ደገፍ ረኸበ degef rek̗ebe *(v.)* **conciliate**
ደገፈ degefe *(v.)* **endorse**
ደገፈ degefe *(v.)* **sustain**
ብዝርዝር ገለጸ bzrzr gelexe *(v.)* **recite**
ደገመ degeme *(v.)* **recycle**
ደገመ degeme *(v.)* **repeat**
ደጊሙ መልአ degimu mel'e *(v.)* **recharge**
ደጎመ degome *(v.)* **subsidize**
ደጉሐ deguhe *(v. t.)* **dazzle**
ደጉሐ deguḧe *(v.i)* **glare**
ደጐላጽ degwalax *(adj.)* **bulky**
ደሃለ dehale *(v.)* **daunt**
ደሃለ dehale *(v.)* **demoralize**
ደሃለ dehale *(v.)* **discourage**
ደሃለ dehale *(v.)* **dishearten**
ደሓን ኩን deȟan kun *(interj.)* **farewell**
ደሓን ኩን deȟan kun *(n.)* **adieu**
ደሓረ deȟare *(v.)* **regress**
ደሃይ dehay *(n.)* **voice**
ደሃይ dehay *(n.)* **audio**
ደካሊ dekali *(adj.)* **conclusive**
ድኻም dekam *(adj.)* **tired**
ደኽዳኽ dekdak *(n.)* **dwarf**
ድቂሱ ዝሕከም dekisu zhkem *(n.)* **inpatient**
ሚሊሽያ milishya *(n.)* **monger**
ደላ'ላይ delalay *(n.)* **broker**
ደለበ delebe *(v.t.)* **accrue**
ደለል delel *(n.)* **sediment**
ደልየ deleye *(v.)* **need**

ደለየ deleye *(v.)* **require**
ደለየ deleye *(v.)* **want**
ደልሃመት delhamet *(n.)* **murk**
ደልሃመት delhamet *(n.)* **abyss**
ደልሃመታዊ delhametawi *(adj.)* **abysmal**
ዴልታ delta *(n.)* **delta**
ደም ምፍሳስ dem mfsas *(n.)* **bloodshed**
ደም ምሃብ dem mhab *(v.)* **transfuse**
ደም ና ምሃብ ተግባር dem na mhab tegbar *(n.)* **transfusion**
ደም dem *(n.)* **blood**
ደማሚት demamit *(n.)* **dynamite**
ብደም ዝተለቕለቐ bdem zteleq̈leq̈e *(adj.)* **gory**
ደማዊ demawi *(adj.)* **sanguinary**
ደማዊ demawi *(adj.)* **bloody**
ደምበ dembe *(n.)* **stall**
ደምበ ላሕሚ dembe laḧmi *(n.)* **byre**
ደምቢ dembi *(n.)* **etiquette**
ደምደመ demdeme *(v.)* **deduce**
ደምደመ demdeme *(v.)* **infer**
ደመኛ demegna *(n.)* **nemesis**
ደመቐ demeq̈e *(v.)* **brighten**
ወሰኸ weseḱe *(v.)* **add**
ደመየ demeye *(v.)* **bleed**
ደሚቕ ብጫ demiq bicha *(adj.)* **gilt**
ደሞተራ demotera *(n.)* **centipede**
ደሞዝ demoz *(n.)* **salary**
ደሞዝ demoz *(n.)* **stipend**
ደሞዝ demoz *(n.)* **wage**
ደምሰሰ demsese *(v. i)* **delete**
ደምሰሰ demsese *(v.)* **erase**
ሰረዘ sereze *(v.)* **quash**
ደምሰሰ demsese *(v.)* **raze**
ሰረዘ sereze *(v.t)* **abolish**
ድሙ demu *(n.)* **cat**
ደንበ denbe *(n.)* **ranch**
ደንቢ denbi *(n.)* **code**
ደንቢሩ ጢሒሱ denbiru thisu *(v.)* **transgress**
ድንጋፀ denegaxe' *(n.)* **consternation**
ደነነ denene *(v.)* **droop**
ደንፈዐ denfe'ë *(v.)* **flourish**
ደንገፀ dengexe *(v.)* **commiserate**
ደንጎላ dengola *(n.)* **boulder**
ደንቆሮ denqoro *(n.)* **ignoramus**
ደንቆሮ denqoro *(n.)* **berk**
ደንፀወ denxewe *(v.)* **mystify**
ደንጸዎ denxewo *(v.t)* **bewilder**
ደንዘዘ denzeze *(adj.)* **befuddled**
ደንዘዘ denzeze *(v.)* **daze**
ድቓላ deqala *(n.)* **hybrid**
ደቃሲ deqasi *(n.)* **sleeper**
ደቀባት deqebat *(n.)* **gentry**
ደቀሰ deqese *(v.)* **slumber**
ደቂ ባት deqi bat *(n.)* **populace**
ደቂቕ deqiq *(adj.)* **minute**
ውሑድ ሀያብ wḧud hyab *(n.)* **mite**
ደቂቕ ፊልሚ deqiq filmi *(n.)* **microfilm**
ደቂቃ deqiqa *(n.)* **minute**
ደራፊ derafi *(a.)* **singer**
ደራፊ derafi *(n.)* **songster**
ደራፊ derafi *(n.)* **vocalist**
ደራርዕ derar'ë *(v.)* **nudge**
ደራረዘ derareze *(v.)* **caress**
ደራረዘ derareze *(v.)* **fondle**
ደራሲ ወራቢ derasi werabi *(n.)* **composer**
ደሓን ኩን deḥan kun *(excl.)* **goodbye**
ደከረ dekere *(v.)* **wallop**
ደርገፍገፍ በለ dergefgef bele *(v.)* **hobble**
ድጓና dgwana *(n.)* **warder**

ድርዒ ገጽ dr'ï gex *(n.)* **visor**
ደራሲ derasi *(n.)* **author**
ደራዚ derazi *(n.)* **masseur**
ደርበየ derbeye *(v.)* **cast**
ምድረበዳ mdrebeda *(v.)* **desert**
ደርበየ derbeye *(v.)* **throw**
ደርበየሉ derbeyelu *(v.)* **pelt**
ደርቢ derbi *(n.)* **storey**
ደርቢ derbi *(n.)* **stratum**
ደርዐ der'ë *(v.)* **recap**
ደረበ derebe *(v.)* **stratify**
ደረበ derebe *(v.)* **superimpose**
ደረፈ derefe *(v.)* **sing**
ደርሆ dereho *(n.)* **chicken**
ደረጃ dereja *(n.)* **grade**
ደረጃ dereja *(n.)* **level**
ብሩህ ክፍሊ ናይ ወርሒ bruh kfli nay werḧi *(n.)* **phase**
ደረጃ dereja *(n.)* **rank**
መሳልል mesall *(n.)* **stair**
ደረጃ dereja *(n.)* **status**
ደረጃ ኣትሓዘ dereja at'ḧaze *(v.)* **standardize**
ደረጃ ምትሓዝ dereja m'tḧaz *(n.)* **standardization**
ደረኽ derek *(adj.)* **uncompromising**
ደረኸ dereke *(v.)* **incline**
ደረቕ dereq *(n.)* **bigot**
ደረቐ dereqe *(adj.)* **dry**
ደረቀኛ dereqegna *(adj.)* **impious**
ደረቓኛ dereq̈eňa *(adj.)* **flippant**
ደረቓኛ dereq̈eňa *(adj.)* **brash**
ድርቀት dere'qe't *(n.)* **constipation**
ደረቕ dereqh *(adj.)* **inflexible**
ደረት ትርኢት deret tr'it *(n.)* **horizon**
ደረት deret *(n.)* **bust**
ደረት-ኣልቦ deret'albo *(adj.)* **boundless**
ደረተ derete *(v.)* **localize**
ደርፊ derfi *(n.)* **carol**
መዝሙር mezmur *(n.)* **song**
ደርገፍገፍ በለ dergefgef bele *(v.)* **waver**
ደርጊ ስኒ dergi sni *(n.)* **denture**
ደርጎስታ dergosta *(n.)* **smattering**
ደርጓጉ መርከብ derguag merkeb *(n.)* **hulk**
ደርጓዕጓዕ በለ dergwa'ëgwaë bele *(v.)* **rumble**
ደርሆ derho *(n.)* **hen**
ደርሆ ማይ derho may *(n.)* **duck**
ደሮና derona *(n.)* **dust**
ደርቀኛ ጓል derqegna gwal *(n.)* **minx**
ደርዘን derzen *(n.)* **dozen**
ደስ ብዝብል des bzbl *(adv.)* **quaintly**
ደስ ዝብል des zbl *(adj.)* **quaint**
ደስ ዘይብል des zeybl *(adj.)* **seamy**
ደሴት deseet *(n.)* **island**
ደሴት deseet *(n.)* **isle**
ኣቶል 'atol *(n.)* **atoll**
ደሴታዊ desietawi *(adj.)* **insular**
ደስከለ deskele *(v.)* **freeze**
ደስታ desta *(n.)* **glee**
ደስታ desta *(n.)* **joy**
ደው በለ dew bele *(v.)* **stand**
ደወለ dewele *(v.)* **ring**
ጩልጩል በለ člčl bele *(v.)* **tinkle**
ደወለ dewele *(v.)* **call**
ደያቢ deyabi *(adj.)* **ascendant**
ደየበ deyebe *(v.i)* **climb**
ኣብ መርከብ ተሰቕለ 'ab merkeb teseq̈le *(v. t)* **embark**
ደየበ deyebe *(v.)* **ascend**
ድፍፍእ dff'e *(n.)* **scuffle**
ድፍኢት df'it *(n.)* **motivation**
ደገፈ degefe *(n.)* **favour**

ድጋፍ ሃበ dgaf habe ***(v.)*** **espouse**
ድጋፍ dgaf ***(n.)*** **brace**
ድጋም ፍእምተ ቃል dgam f'emte qal ***(n.)*** **alliteration**
ምቕላሖ mq̈laȟe ***(n.)*** **assonance**
ድግግም dggm ***(n.)*** **frequency**
ድግማ dgma ***(n.)*** **repetition**
ድግማ dgma ***(n.)*** **encore**
ድግስ dgs ***(n.)*** **banquet**
ድግስ dgs ***(n.)*** **feast**
ድሕረ ገፅ dhde getse ***(n.)*** **webpage**
ድሕረ ገፅ dhde getse ***(n.)*** **website**
ድህናወ d'hnawe ***(n.)*** **staleness**
ድሕነት dĥnet ***(n.)*** **redemption**
ድሕንነት dhnnet ***(n.)*** **safety**
ድሕንነት dhnnet ***(n.)*** **welfare**
ድሕር ዘይምባል dhr zeymbal ***(n.)*** **perseverance**
ድሕረ ባይታ dȟre bayta ***(n.)*** **backdrop**
ድሕረ ባይታ dȟre bayta ***(n.)*** **background**
ድሑረ ንጡፍ dĥre ntuf ***(adj.)*** **retroactive**
ድሕረ ጥብቆ d'hre tbqo ***(n.)*** **suffix**
ድሕሪ dȟri ***(conj.)*** **after**
ድሕሪ ሕጂ dḥri ḥğı ***(adv.)*** **hereafter**
ድሕሪ መወዳእታ ዛንታ dȟri mewedaèta zanta ***(n.)*** **postscript**
ድሕሪት dĥrit ***(n.)*** **rear**
ድሕሪት dĥrit ***(adj.)*** **retro**
ድሕሪት ምቕራይ dhrit mqhray ***(n.)*** **laggard**
ድህሰሳ dhsesa ***(n.)*** **exploration**
ድህሰሳ dhsesa ***(n.)*** **navigation**
ድሁል dhul ***(adj.)*** **dispirited**
ድሁል dhul ***(adj.)*** **haunted**
ድሑር dĥur ***(adj.)*** **primitive**
ድሑር dȟur ***(adj.)*** **antiquated**
ድዱዕ diduee' ***(n.)*** **cockroach**
ዲግሪ digri ***(n.)*** **degree**
ዲሞክራሲ dimokrasi ***(n.)*** **democracy**
ዲሞክራሲያዊ dimokrasiyawi ***(adj.)*** **democratic**
ዲናሞ dinamo ***(n.)*** **dynamo**
ዲኦድራንት di'odrant ***(n.)*** **deodorant**
ዲፕሎማ diploma ***(n.)*** **diploma**
ዲስክ disc ***(n.)*** **disc**
ዲስኮ disco ***(n.)*** **disco**
ዲቫኖ divano ***(n.)*** **settee**
ዲያስፖራ diyaspora ***(n.)*** **Diaspora**
ድኻ dka ***(n.)*** **pauper**
ድኻ dḱa ***(adj.)*** **poor**
ድኻም dkam ***(n.)*** **debility**
ድኻም dkam ***(n.)*** **fatigue**
ድኻም dkam ***(adj.)*** **wearisome**
ድኻም dkham ***(n.)*** **lethargy**
ምግደራ mgdera ***(n.)*** **disability**
ጉድለት gudlet ***(n.)*** **failing**
ድኽመት dkmet ***(n.)*** **infirmity**
ድኽመት dkmet ***(n.)*** **weakness**
ድኽነት dḱnet ***(n.)*** **poverty**
ስእነት s'ènet ***(n.)*** **privation**
ድኹዒ dḱu'ï ***(n.)*** **compost**
ድኹዒ dḱu'ï ***(n.)*** **fertilizer**
ድኹም dkum ***(adj.)*** **feeble**
ድኹም ሓቦ ዘይብሉ dḱum ȟabo zeyblu ***(adj.)*** **flabby**
ዘይርጉእ zeyrgu'è ***(adj.)*** **groggy**
ምሱን msun ***(adj.)*** **infirm**
ውጹዕ wxu'ë ***(n.)*** **underdog**
ሰንኮፍ senkof ***(adj.)*** **weak**
ድኹም dḱum ***(adj.)*** **frail**
ንእሽቶን ድኹምን n'èshton dḱumn ***(adj.)*** **puny**
ድልድል dldl ***(n.)*** **bridge**

ደልዳላ ሓያል ብርቱዕ deldala ḧayal brtu'ë *(adj.)* **robust**
ሶርኖ sorno *(n.)* **serge**
ድልዱል dldul *(adj.)* **stout**
ቂምቂም qimqim *(n.)* **ticking**
ድሉው dluw *(adj.)* **ready**
ድልየት dlyet *(n.)* **desire**
ድልየት dlyet *(n.)* **interest**
ድልየት dlyet *(n.)* **zing**
ድልየት ዘይብሉ dlyet zeyblu *(adj.)* **indifferent**
ድልየት ዘይምህላው dlyet zeymhlaw *(n.)* **indifference**
ድማ dma *(n.)* **ampersand**
ድማ dma *(conj.)* **and**
ድምበጃን dmbejan *(n.)* **carboy**
ድምደማ dmdema *(n.)* **induction**
ድምደማ dmdema *(n.)* **inference**
ድምር dmr *(n.)* **aggregate**
ድምር dmr *(adj.)* **gross**
ድምር d'mr *(n.)* **sum**
ድምር ፀዓት dm'r xe'ät *(n.)* **synergy**
ድምሰሳ dmsesa *(v.)* **abolition**
ድምሰሳ dmsesa *(n.)* **annihilation**
ድምፃዊ dmtsawi *(adj.)* **sonic**
ድምፂ dmtsi *(n.)* **sound**
ድምፂ ዘየሕልፍ dmtsi zeyeḧlf *(adj.)* **soundproof**
ድሙቅ dmuq *(adj.)* **lurid**
ድሙቅ dmuq *(adj.)* **refulgence**
ድሙቅ ቀይሕ dmuq qeyh *(n.)* **scarlet**
ድሙቅ ሰማያዊ ሕብሪ dmuq semayawi hbri *(n.)* **sapphire**
ድሙቕ ውራይ dmuq̈ wray *(n.)* **pomp**
ድሙቕ dmuq̈ *(adj.)* **bright**
ድምጻዊ dmxawi *(adj.)* **vocal**
ድምፀት dmxet *(n.)* **accent**
ድምጺ ደርሆ ማይ dmxi derho may *(n.)* **honk**
ድምጺ ደወል dmxi dewel *(n.)* **peal**
ድምጺ ምርጫ dmxi mrča *(n.)* **vote**
ድምጺ ትርግታ dmxi trgta *(n.)* **pulse**
ድንበር ምጥሓስ dnber mthas *(n.)* **transgression**
ድንደላ dndela *(n.)* **blockade**
ድንደና ኣረጋውያን dndena 'aregawyan *(n.)* **ageism**
ድንድል dndl *(n.)* **viaduct**
ድንጋጸ dngaxe *(n.)* **compassion**
ድንጋጸ dngaxe *(n.)* **pity**
ድንጋጸ ዘይብሉ dngaxe zeyblu *(adj.)* **pitiless**
ድንጋዘ dngaze *(n.)* **sloth**
ድንገታዊ dngetawi *(adj.)* **incidental**
ድንገተኛ dngeteňa *(adj.)* **hazardous**
ድንግልና dnglna *(n.)* **chastity**
ድንግርግር dngrgr *(n.)* **welter**
ድንግርግር dn'gr'gr *(n.)* **maze**
ድንጉር dngur *(n.)* **rubble**
ድንጉይ dnguy *(adj.)* **late**
ድንጉይ dnguy *(adj.)* **belated**
ድንጉዝ dnguz *(adj.)* **retarded**
ድንኪ dnki *(n.)* **midget**
ድንኪ dnki *(n.)* **pigmy**
ድንኪ dnki *(n.)* **pygmy**
ድንኩል ሰውሒ dnkul sewhi *(n.)* **sod**
ድንኳን dnkwan *(n.)* **shop**
ድንሽ dnsh *(n.)* **potato**
ድንፃወ dntsawe *(n.)* **disbelief**
ድንዛዘ dnzaze *(n.)* **stupor**
ድንዛዘ dnzaze *(n.)* **anaesthesia**
ድንዙዝ dnzuz *(adj.)* **numb**
ኣዳግ 'adag *(adj.)* **stolid**
ድንዙዝ dnzuz *(adj.)* **impassive**
ዶብ dob *(n.)* **frontier**

ዶብ dob *(n.)* **border**
ዶብ dob *(n.)* **boundary**
ዶጭዳጭ dochdach *(n.)* **stockist**
ዶጭዳጭ dochdach *(adj.)* **stocky**
ዶክተርነት doctoret *(n.)* **doctorate**
ዶኩመንታዊ dokumentawi *(n.)* **documentary**
ዶላር dolar *(n.)* **dollar**
ዶልሺ dolshi *(n.)* **flapjack**
ዶልሺ dolshi *(n.)* **cake**
ዶሶ doso *(n.)* **buttock**
ድቃል dqal *(adj.)* **inbred**
ድቃል dqal *(n.)* **replica**
ድቃላ ከልቢ dqala kelbi *(n.)* **mongrel**
ድቓላ dq̈ala *(n.)* **bastard**
ድቃስ dqas *(n.)* **sleep**
ድቀ መሳርሒት dqe mesarȟit *(n.)* **microprocessor**
ድቂ dqi *(n.)* **embryo**
ድቁስ dqus *(adj.)* **asleep**
ድራብነት drabnet *(n.)* **plurality**
ድራጎን dragon *(n.)* **dragon**
ድራማዊ dramawi *(adj.)* **dramatic**
ድራር drar *(n.)* **dinner**
ድራር drar *(n.)* **supper**
ድራውሊኮ drawliko *(n.)* **plumber**
ድርብ drb *(adj.)* **double**
ድርብ drb *(adj.)* **dual**
ድርብ drb *(n.)* **duplex**
ድርብ መርዓ drb mer'ä *(n.)* **bigamy**
ድርብ ጠርጊቶ drb ẗergito *(n.)* **biceps**
ድርብ ፆታዊ drb xotawi *(adj.)* **bisexual**
ድርብ-ልሳናዊ drblsanawi *(adj.)* **bilingual**
ድርዳር drdar *(n.)* **sheaf**
ድረታ dreta *(n.)* **limitation**
ድርዕቶ dr'ëto *(n.)* **duvet**
ድርዕቶ dr'ëto *(n.)* **quilt**
ድርዒ ሓጺን dr'ï ȟaxin *(n.)* **armour**
ድርጅት drjt *(n.)* **corporation**
ድርኪት drkit *(n.)* **impetus**
ድሮ d'ro *(n.)* **eve**
ድርቂ drqi *(n.)* **drought**
ድርቅና drqna *(n.)* **bigotry**
ድርቅና drqna *(n.)* **gall**
ድርሰት drset *(n.)* **literature**
ድርፃን drtsan *(n.)* **gum**
ድስቡጣ dsbuta *(n.)* **despot**
ድስቲ dsti *(n.)* **casserole**
ሕጉስ ȟgus *(adj.)* **convivial**
ሕጉስ dsut *(adj.)* **joyful**
ሕጉስ dsut *(adj.)* **jubilant**
ዱባ duba *(n.)* **pumpkin**
ዱብታ dubta *(n.)* **thud**
ዱኹም dukhum *(adj.)* **listless**
ዱኽዒ duk'i *(n.)* **manure**
ድዑል d'ül *(n.)* **ram**
ዱር dur *(n.)* **forest**
ዱር dur *(n.)* **rainforest**
ዱር ኣብረሰ dur abrese *(v.)* **deforest**
ዱውየት duwyet *(n.)* **leprosy**
ድውሶ dwso *(n.)* **batter**
ደው ኣበለ dwuo aabele *(v.)* **cease**
ዱዊይ dwuy *(n.)* **leper**
ድንጋገ dngage *(n.)* **ordinance**
ጀርመን ger-man *(n.)* **German**
ጀነረተር generater *(n.)* **generator**
ጂኦሜትሪ geo-met-ery *(n.)* **geometry**
ጃህራ ĵahra *(v.)* **boast**
ጃጃዊ jajawi *(n.)* **coward**
ጃኬት ĵakeet *(n.)* **jacket**
ጃኬት ĵakeet *(n.)* **blazer**
ጃኬት ዝናብ jaket znab *(n.)* **raincoat**

ጃልባ መትሓዚ ዓሳ jalba methazi asa *(n.)* **trawler**
ጃልባ ĵalba *(n.)* **boat**
ጃምላ jamla *(n.)* **wholesale**
ጃንጥላ jantla *(n.)* **parachute**
ጀብጀ ብ jebjeb *(n.)* **tassel**
ጀግና jegna *(adj.)* **gallant**
ጅግና jegna *(n.)* **hero**
ጅግንነት jegninet *(n.)* **gallantry**
ጅግንነታዊ jegn-netawi *(adj.)* **heroic**
ጀላቲ jelati *(n.)* **ice-cream**
ጀልባ jelba *(n.)* **yacht**
ጀልፋፍ jelfaf *(adj.)* **unkempt**
ጀልጋድ jelgad *(adj.)* **slovenly**
ጀማሊ jemali *(n.)* **wholesaler**
ጀማራይ jemaray *(n.)* **starter**
ጀማሪ jemari *(n.)* **novice**
ጀመረ jemere *(v.)* **launch**
ጀመረ jemere *(v.)* **start**
ጀመረ ĵemere *(v.)* **begin**
ጀምር jemr *(v.)* **initiate**
ጀኦግራፊ ĵe'ografi *(n.)* **geography**
ጀራግዐ jerag'ë *(v.)* **bungle**
ጀርባዶ jerbado *(n.)* **rectum**
ጀርዲን jerdin *(n.)* **garden**
ጅግና jgna *(adj.)* **courageous**
ጅግና ĵgna *(adj.)* **gutsy**
ጅግንነት jgnnet *(n.)* **courage**
ጃህራ ĵhra *(n.)* **pomposity**
ጅምላ ቅጥለት jimla qtlet *(n.)* **massacre**
ጅኢምናስት jimnast *(n.)* **gymnast**
ጅኢምናስቲካዊ jimnastikawi *(n.)* **gymnastic**
ጂምናዝየም jimnazyem *(n.)* **gymnasium**
ጂንስ ĵins *(n.)* **jeans**
ጂኦግራፈኛ ji'ografi'gna *(n.)* **geographer**
ጂኦግራፍያዊ ji'ografiyawi *(adj.)* **geographical**
ጂኦሜትራዊ ji'omeetrawi *(adj.)* **geometric**
ጂፕሲ jipsi *(n.)* **gypsy**
ጅለ-ሰበይቲ ĵlesebeyti *(n.)* **bodice**
ጅምናስቲክ መስርሒ ዕራት jmnastic mesrhi arat *(n.)* **trampoline**
ጅነ jne *(n.)* **quid**
ጅራታም ኮኾብ ĵratam *(n.)* **comet**
ጅርባ ĵrba *(n.)* **canvas**
ጁባ juba *(n.)* **coat**
ጀመረ ĵemere *(v.)* **commence**
ጁባ ĵuba *(n.)* **pocket**
ጁዶ ĵudo *(n.)* **judo**
ጁፒተር ĵupiter *(n.)* **Jupiter**
ጃኩዚ ǧakuzii *(n.)* **Jacuzzi**
ጀሆ ǧeho *(n.)* **hostage**
ጀለብያ ዘመስል ናይ ጃፓን ክዳን ǧelebya zimesl nay japan kdan *(n.)* **kimono**
ጁት ĵut *(n.)* **jute**
ጅግንነት ǧgnnet *(n.)* **valour**
ጅለ ǧle *(n.)* **vest**
ጅውታ ማይ jwta may *(n.)* **downpour**

ገ

ገለጸ gelexe *(v.)* **wreak**
ገዛ geza *(n.)* **house**
ገልበጠ gelbete *(v.)* **overthrow**
ገደፈ gedefe *(v.)* **omit**
ገድላዊ ጉዕዞ gedlawi gu'ëzo *(n.)* **odyssey**
ግማ'ድ gmad *(n.)* **hunk**

ጎንዶላ gondola *(n.)* **gondola**
ጎሮሮ gororo *(n.)* **gullet**
ጉድኣት gud'at *(n.)* **harm**
ጉልባብ gulbab *(n.)* **veil**
ጉራማይለ guramayle *(adj.)* **variegated**
ጉዑር gu'ür *(n.)* **gravel**
ገዚፍ ዓይነት ከልቢ gezif 'äynet kelbi *(n.)* **bulldog**
ገፅታ trfi *(n.)* **profile**
ጉንጓ gungua *(n.)* **owl**
ጊዜ ዘሕለፈ gizie zehlefe *(adj.)* **overdue**
ጊዜ ዝሓለፎ gizie zhalefo *(adj.)* **outdated**
ጋሕጣጥ gahtat *(adj.)* **obtuse**
ግልጺ gltsi *(adj.)* **overt**
ንጹር nxur *(adj.)* **obvious**
ግልፂ ርእይቶ gltsi r'eyto *(adj.)* **outspoken**
ግምገም ባሕሪ gemgem bahri *(adj.)* **offshore**
ግርምቢጥ grmbit *(n.)* **oddity**
ግዚኡ ዝሓለፈ gziu zhalefe *(adj.)* **obsolete**
ግዳማዊ gdamawi *(adj.)* **outlandish**
ግዳማዊ ሃገር gdamawi hager *(adv.)* **overseas**
ግዴታ gdeta *(n.)* **obligation**
ግዴታ gdeta *(adj.)* **obligatory**
ግዴታ ዘይኮነ gdieta zeykone *(adj.)* **optional**
ጋዓዝ ga'äz *(n.)* **baggage**
ኮክፒት kokpit *(n.)* **cockpit**
ጋቢያ gabiya *(n.)* **hutch**
ጋቢያ ሰፈር ከልቢ gabiya sefer kelbi *(n.)* **kennel**
ጋብላ gabla *(n.)* **trough**
ጋድም gadm *(adj.)* **horizontal**
ጋእ በለ ga'e bele *(v.)* **baulk**
ጋዕጋዕ gaëgaë *(adj.)* **foul**
ጋዕጋዕ ga'ëgaë *(n.)* **slattern**
ጋእጋእ በለ ga'ega'e bele *(v.)* **flounder**
ጋእታ ga'eta *(n.)* **reflex**
ጋዕዘየ ga'ëzeye *(n.)* **corrupt**
ጋዕዘየ ga'ëzeye *(v.)* **debauch**
ጓሓፍ gahaf *(n.)* **trash**
ጋህዲ gahdi *(adj.)* **real**
ጋሕግሐ gahghe *(v.)* **snarl**
ጋሕማጥ gaĥmat *(adj.)* **disorganized**
ጋሕማጥ gaḧmaẗ *(adj.)* **awkward**
ጋሕር gaĥr *(adj.)* **rocky**
ጋህሲ gahsi *(n.)* **sepulchre**
ጋሌጣ galeta *(n.)* **Rusk**
ጋሎን galon *(n.)* **gallon**
ጋማ gama *(n.)* **matrimony**
ጋኔን ganeen *(n.)* **hobgoblin**
ጋኔን ganeen *(n.)* **bogey**
ጋኔን ganen *(n.)* **demon**
ጋንታ ganeta *(n.)* **club**
ጋንስላ gansla *(n.)* **panther**
ጋንታ ganta *(n.)* **squad**
ጋንታ ወታደራት ganta wetaderat *(n.)* **platoon**
ጓንቲ ganti *(n.)* **thimble**
ጋንፅላ gantsla *(n.)* **sail**
ጋራዲ garadi *(n.)* **blinkers**
ጋራጅ gara-j *(n.)* **garage**
ጋርዘ garze *(n.)* **gauze**
ጓሰሰ gasese *(v.)* **scuff**
ጋሻ gasha *(n.)* **guest**
ጋሻ gasha *(n.)* **stranger**
ጋጽ gats *(n.)* **stable**
ጋውሕታ gawhta *(n.)* **jackal**
ጋዝ gaz *(n.)* **gas**
ጋዜጣ gazeeẗa *(n.)* **journal**

ጋዜጠኛ gazeeṫeṅa *(n.)* **journalist**
ጋዜጠኛነት gazeeṫeṅanet *(n.)* **journalism**
ጋዜጣ gazeta *(n.)* **gazette**
ግቢ gbi *(n.)* **premises**
ግብራዊ gbrawi *(adj.)* **practical**
ግብራዊ gbrawi *(adj.)* **virtual**
ግብራዊ ዝኾነ gbrawi zḱone *(adj.)* **practicable**
ግብራውነት gbrawnet *(n.)* **practicability**
ፕራግማትነት pragmatnet *(n.)* **pragmatism**
ግብረ ሰናይ gbre senay *(n.)* **philanthropy**
ግብረ ስጋ gbre sga *(n.)* **intercourse**
ኮርፎ korfo *(n.)* **shag**
ግብረ-ኣበር gbre'aber *(n.)* **accomplice**
ግብረ-ሰዶመኛ gbresedomeña *(n.)* **homosexual**
ግብረ ሰናያዊ gbresenayawi *(n.)* **philanthropist**
ግብሪ gbri *(n.)* **tax**
ግብሪ ዝክፈለሉ gbri zkfelelu *(adj.)* **taxable**
ግብሪ gbri *(n.)* **capitation**
ግብታ gbta *(n.)* **blackout**
ግብጣን gbṫan *(n.)* **captain**
ግብጣኒ gbṫani *(n.)* **captaincy**
ግብታዊ g'btawi *(adj.)* **spontaneous**
ግብታውነት g'btawinet *(n.)* **spontaneity**
ግቡእ gbuè *(adj.)* **proper**
ግብዝና gbzna *(n.)* **cant**
ግጭት gcct *(n.)* **collision**
ግጭት gčt *(n.)* **conflict**
ግዳማዊ gdamawi *(adj.)* **superficial**
ግዳማዊ ኣደጎ gdamawi adego *(n.)* **epidermis**
ግዳማዊ ትሪኢት gdamawi tr't *(n.)* **facade**
ግዳማይ gdamay *(adj.)* **exterior**
ግድዓት gd'ät *(n.)* **jeopardy**
ግድብ gdb *(n.)* **weir**
ግድድፍ gddf *(n.)* **compromise**
ግደ gde *(n.)* **role**
ግዲ ዘይብሉ gdi zeyblu *(adj.)* **phlegmatic**
ግዲ ዘይብሉ gdi zeyblu *(adj.)* **remiss**
ግዴታ gdieta *(adj.)* **mandatory**
ግዴታ gdieta *(v.)* **undertake**
ግድን ምባል gdn mbal *(n.)* **insistence**
ግድነት gdnet *(adv.)* **perforce**
ግድነታዊ gdnetawi *(adj.)* **compulsory**
ግዱስ gdus *(adj.)* **responsive**
ገዓረ ge'äre *(v.)* **rap**
ገዓት geät *(n.)* **porridge**
ገዓት ge'ät *(n.)* **mush**
ገብ ኣበለ geb abele *(v.)* **slam**
ገባር-ሰናይ gebar senay *(adj.)* **beneficent**
ገባሪ ዉሕጅ gebari wuhj *(n.)* **tributary**
ገበል gebel *(n.)* **python**
ገበል gebel *(n.)* **serpent**
ገበላ gebela *(n.)* **portico**
ገበን geben *(n.)* **crime**
ገበን geben *(n.)* **guilt**
ገበናዊ gebenawi *(adj.)* **penal**
ገበነኛ gebenegna *(n.)* **dacoit**
ገበነኛ geben-egna *(n.)* **gangster**
ገበነኛ gebeneña *(n.)* **villain**
ገበነኛ gebenenya *(n.)* **convict**
ገበነኛ gebenenya *(n.)* **criminal**
ገበነኛ gebenenya *(n.)* **culprit**

ገበነኛ gebenenya *(n.)* **felon**
ገበንነኛ ኣብ ባሕሪ ዝዝርፍ gebenn̈a ab baḧri zzrf *(n.)* **pirate**
ገበረ gebere *(v.)* **act**
ገበረ gebere *(v.)* **do**
ገበረ gebere *(v.)* **render**
ገበረ gebere *(v.)* **behave**
ገበጣ gebeta *(n.)* **skittle**
ገበተ gebete *(v.)* **sequester**
ገብገብ ኣበለ gebgeb abele *(v.)* **flutter**
ገቢረ-ሰናይ gebiresenay *(n.)* **benefactor**
ገዳም gedam *(n.)* **abbey**
ገዳም gedam *(n.)* **cloister**
ገዳም gedam *(n.)* **minster**
ገዳም gedam *(n.)* **monastery**
ገዳም gedam *(n.)* **nunnery**
ገዛ ኣበምኔት geza 'abemneet *(n.)* **priory**
ገደብ gedbb *(n.)* **constraint**
ገደብ gedeb *(n.)* **limit**
ገደበ gedebe *(v.)* **circumscribe**
ገደፈ gedefe *(v.)* **relinquish**
ገደል gedel *(n.)* **scarp**
ገድላ gedla *(adj.)* **arable**
ጌጋ geega *(n.)* **error**
ጌጋ geega *(n.)* **lapse**
ጌጋ ሓበሬታ ነገረ geega ḧabereeta negere *(v.)* **misinform**
ጌጋ ስልሒት geega slḧit *(n.)* **miscalculation**
ጌጋ ትርጉም ሃበ geega trgum habe *(v.)* **misinterpret**
ጌጋ ፀብፃብ ሃበ geega xebxab habe *(v.)* **misrepresent**
ጌጋ ግንዛበ geege gnzabe *(n.)* **misconception**
ገፋፍ gefaf *(adj.)* **sluggish**
ገፋፍ ዓሳ gefafi äsa *(n.)* **fisherman**
ገፈፈ gefefe *(v.t.)* **strip**
ገፈሐ gefeĥe *(v.)* **expand**
ገፍሐ gefhe *(v.)* **widen**
ገፊሕ gefih *(adj.)* **wide**
ገፊሕ gefiḧ *(adj.)* **spacious**
ገፊሕ በዓቲ gefihe beatii *(n.)* **cavern**
ገፍላው geflaw *(adj.)* **baggy**
ጌጋ gega *(n)* **demerit**
ግዕጋዕ g'ëga'ë *(n.)* **filth**
ሸልቍ shelqwi *(adj.)* **torrid**
ገሃነም gehanem *(n.)* **hell**
ገሃንማዊ gehanmawi *(adj.)* **infernal**
ገሃሰ gehase *(v.)* **violate**
ገሃጸ gehatse *(v.)* **gnaw**
ገሃጸ gehaxe *(v.)* **browse**
ገጅፍ ዝዓይነቱ geĵf z'äynetu *(adj.)* **jumbo**
ገጂፍ gejif *(adj.)* **massive**
ገላጺ ዓንቀፅ gelatsi änqets *(n.)* **predicate**
ገልበጠ gelbeẗe *(v.)* **capsize**
ገልዒ gel'e *(n.)* **shard**
ገለ ቦታ gele bota *(adv.)* **somewhere**
ገለ ነገር gele neger *(pron.)* **something**
ገለ ሰብ gele seb *(pron.)* **somebody**
ገለፈ gelefe *(v.)* **disqualify**
ገለፃ geletsa *(n.)* **description**
ገለፀ geletse *(v.)* **define**
ሓንጸጸ ḧanxexe *(v.)* **delineate**
ገለፀ geletse *(v.)* **describe**
ግልፅነት geletsinet *(n.)* **clarity**
ኣፍለጠ 'afleẗe *(v.)* **announce**
ኣበጻጽሐ 'abexaxḧe *(v.)* **convey**
ገለፀ gelexe *(v.)* **express**
ገልተው geltew *(n.)* **bobble**
ገምቢ ge'mbi *(n.)* **carcass**

መዳወር medawer *(n.)* **cable**
ገመድ gemed *(n.)* **rope**
ገመድ gemed *(v.)* **strand**
ገመድ gemed *(n.)* **string**
ድባራ ፍሕሶ dbara fȟso *(n.)* **twine**
ገመድ ባንዴራ gemed bandeera *(n.)* **halyard**
ገመድ ገረብ gemed gereb *(n.)* **withe**
ገመድ መሰል gemed mesel *(adj.)* **stringy**
ገመድ ሳእኒ gemed sa'eni *(n.)* **shoestring**
መእሰር ናይ መርከብ me'èser nay merkeb *(n.)* **bollard**
ገመል gemel *(n.)* **beam**
ምቕልልና gemel *(n.)* **politeness**
ገመሰ gemese *(v.)* **bisect**
ግምታዊ ሓሳብ gemetawi hasabe *(n. &v.)* **conjecture**
ግምት gmt *(v.i)* **guess**
ገመተ gemete *(v.)* **presume**
ቀመረ qemere *(v.t.)* **reckon**
ገመተ gemete *(v.)* **suppose**
ገመተ gemete *(v.t.)* **surmise**
ገመተ gemete *(v.)* **assume**
ገመተ gemete *(v.)* **speculate**
ገመየ gemeye *(v.t.)* **sprain**
ገምጋሚ gemgami *(n.)* **actuary**
ደንደስ dendes *(n.)* **embankment**
ገምገም gemgem *(n.)* **shore**
ገምገም ባሕሪ gemgem bahiriyi *(n.)* **coast**
ገምገም ባሕሪ gemgem baȟri *(n.)* **beach**
ገምገመ gemgeme *(v.)* **assess**
ገምገመ gemgeme *(v. i)* **evaluate**
ገምገመ gemgeme *(v.)* **appraise**
ገምራዊ gemrawi *(n.)* **intuitive**
ገምሪ gemri *(n.)* **fluke**
ገምሪ gemri *(n.)* **intuition**
ገምጠለ gemẗele *(v.)* **invert**
ገንጫር genchar *(adj.)* **stroppy**
ገነት genet *(n.)* **paradise**
ገንሐ genhe *(v.)* **scold**
ገንሐ genĥe *(v.t.)* **rebuke**
ገንሐ genĥe *(v.)* **reprove**
ገንዘብ genzeb *(n.)* **currency**
ገንዘብ genzeb *(n.)* **money**
ገንዘብ አኽፋሊ genzeb akfali *(n.)* **teller**
ገንዘብ ሕድሪ ምብላዕ genzeb ȟdri mbla'ë *(v.)* **misappropriation**
ገንዘብ ሰብ ሓሸሸ genzeb seb ȟasheshe *(v.)* **misappropriate**
ገንዘብ ወፈየ genzeb wefeye *(v.)* **endow**
ገንዘባዊ genzebawi *(adj.)* **financial**
ገንዘባዊ genzebawi *(adj.)* **monetary**
ገራሚ gerammi *(adj.)* **incredible**
ገረፈ gerefe *(v.)* **flog**
ገረፈ gerefe *(v.)* **thrash**
ገረንገራት gerengerat *(n.)* **vertebra**
ገረዘ gereze' *(v.)* **circumcise**
ገርሂ gerhi *(adj.)* **artless**
ገርሂ gerhi *(adj.)* **innocent**
ግርማ ሞገስ gerima moges *(n.)* **charisma**
ገርናው gernaw *(adj.)* **senile**
ግሩም ፀባይ gerum tse-bay *(n.)* **gentility**
ስንቀን snqen *(v.)* **snuff**
ገሰፀ gesexe *(v.)* **chastise**
ገሰጸ gesexe *(v.)* **admonish**
ገስጋስ gesgas *(adj.)* **progressive**
ገሸ geshe *(v.t.)* **perambulate**
ዘይጽፉፍ zeyxfuf *(n.)* **lout**
ገስረጥ gesret *(adj.)* **sloppy**
ገስረጥ gesreẗ *(adj.)* **messy**

ገጣሚ geẗami *(n.)* **poet**
ገታር getar *(adj.)* **insolent**
ገታር getar *(adj.)* **wilful**
ግእታርነት getarnet *(n.)* **insolence**
ዓገተ gete *(v.)* **prevent**
ገትአ get'e *(n.)* **restrict**
ገጠመ geṭeme *(v.)* **versify**
ገጠራዊ geterawi *(adj.)* **rustic**
ገጠራዊነት geterawnet *(n.)* **rusticity**
ገጽ gets *(n.)* **page**
ገፅ ከልአ gets kel'e *(v.)* **snub**
ገፀበ getsebe *(v.)* **spatter**
ገዋድ gewad *(n.)* **frump**
ገውታ gewta *(n.)* **bang**
ገፅ gex *(n.)* **face**
ገጽ gex *(n.)* **visage**
ገፅ ሰብ gex seb *(n.)* **countenance**
ገጸ ባህሪ gexe bahri *(n.)* **persona**
ገያሺ geyashi *(n.)* **voyager**
ገያሺት ሰረገላ geyashit seregela *(n.)* **stagecoach**
ጌይፂ geysi *(n.)* **trimming**
ገይፂ geytzi *(n.)* **jewellery**
ጀዝ ĵez *(n.)* **walnut**
ገዛ geza *(n.)* **abode**
ገዛ geza *(n.)* **home**
ገዛ ገጠር geza geṭer *(n.)* **grange**
ገዛ ርእሲ geza r'esi *(n.)* **self**
ገዛኢ geza'i *(n.)* **governor**
ገዛኢ geza'i *(n.)* **ruler**
ገዛኢት እኖ geza'it eno *(n.)* **matriarch**
ገዝአ gez'e *(v.)* **govern**
ግዝአ gez'e *(v.)* **rule**
ዓደገ 'ädege *(v.)* **buy**
ገዝገዘ gezgeze *(v.)* **saw**
ገዚፍ gezif *(adj.)* **enormous**
ገዚፍ gezif *(adj.)* **gigantic**
ገዚፍ gezif *(adj.)* **huge**
ገዚፍ gezif *(adj.)* **prodigious**
ገዚፍ gezif *(adj.)* **sizeable**
ገዚፍ gezif *(adj.)* **stupendous**
ገዚፍ እንስሳ ባሕሪ gezif 'ensssa bahri *(n.)* **walrus**
ገዚፍ ከውሒ gezif kewḧi *(n.)* **megalith**
ገዚፍ gezife *(adj.)* **colossal**
ገዚፍ gezife *(adj.)* **large**
ገዚፍን ብርቱዕን gezifn brtu'ë *(adj.)* **hefty**
ግዕዝም g'ezm *(n.)* **sausage**
ግዕዝም ጀርመን g'ëzm jermen *(n.)* **frankfurter**
ገዝሚ gezmi *(n.)* **dowry**
ግዕዙይ g'ëzuy *(adj.)* **corrupt**
ግዕይዝና g'ëzyna *(n.)* **corruption**
ግፋዕ በረድ gfa'ë bered *(n.)* **moraine**
ግፍዒ gf'i *(n.)* **atrocity**
ግጉይ gguy *(adj.)* **amiss**
ኮብላሊ koblali *(adj.)* **errant**
ግጉይ gguy *(adj.)* **erroneous**
ግጉይ gguy *(adj.)* **wrong**
ግጉይ gguy *(adj.)* **wrongful**
ግጉይ ሓሳብ gguy ĥasab *(n.)* **fallacy**
ግጉይ ማሕተም gguy maȟtem *(n.)* **misprint**
ግህሰት ghset *(n.)* **violation**
ግሁድ ghud *(adj.)* **flagrant**
ግሁድ ghud *(adj.)* **candid**
ጊዲ gidi *(n.)* **mascot**
ጊጋባይት gigabayt *(n.)* **gigabyte**
ጊላ gila *(n.)* **vassal**
ግንዛበ ginizabe *(n.)* **cognizance**
ግንዛበ ዘለዎ giniza'be zelewo *(adj.)* **conscious**
ጊንጢ ginti *(adj.)* **eccentric**
ጊንጢ ginẗi *(n.)* **freak**

ጊታር gitar *(n.)* **guitar**
ጊታር ዝመስል መሳርሒ ሙዚቃ gitar zmesl mesarhi muziqa *(n.)* **lute**
ጊዮሶ giyoso *(n.)* **gudgeon**
ጊዜዊ gizawi *(n.)* **interim**
ጊዜዊ መምበሪ gizawi menberi *(n.)* **lodging**
ግዜያዊ giziyawi *(adj.)* **temporal**
ግዜያዊ giziyawi *(adj.)* **temporary**
ጎጆ gjo *(n.)* **wigwam**
ግላዕ gla'ë *(n.)* **block**
ግላዕ gla'ë *(n.)* **stave**
ግላዊ glawi *(adj.)* **personal**
ግላዊ ኣቕሑ glawi 'aq̈ḧu *(n.)* **belongings**
ግልባ ዝሰልጠነ glba zseltene *(n.)* **trotter**
ግልግል glgl *(n.)* **riddance**
ግሊሰሪን gliserin *(n.)* **glycerine**
ክልተ ግዜ glte gze *(adv.)* **twice**
ግልጺ gltsi *(adj.)* **straightforward**
ግልፂ gltsi *(adj.)* **undeniable**
ግልፂ ዘይኮነ gltsi zeykone *(adj.)* **indefinite**
ግልፂ ዘይኮነ ሰብ gltsi zeykone seb *(n.)* **introvert**
ግልፂ gltzi *(adj.)* **frank**
ግሉኮዝ glukoz *(n.)* **glucose**
ግሉል glul *(adj.)* **aloof**
ግሉል glul *(n.)* **recluse**
ግሉል glul *(adj.)* **secluded**
ግልፅነት glxnet *(n.)* **candour**
ግመ gme *(n.)* **fog**
ግመ gme *(n.)* **mist**
ግመኣዊ gme'awi *(adj.)* **hazy**
ግመል gmel *(n.)* **camel**
ግምገማ gmgema *(n.)* **assessment**
ግምሱስ gmsus *(adj.)* **recumbent**
ግምት gmt *(v. t)* **estimate**
ግምት gmt *(n.)* **supposition**
ግምት g'mt *(n.)* **speculation**
ግምት gmt *(n.)* **presumption**
ግምት ብምሃብ gmt bmhab *(prep.)* **considering**
ግምት gmt *(n.)* **assumption**
ግምታዊ gmtawi *(adj.)* **approximate**
ግምታዊ gmtawi *(adj.)* **notional**
ግምጡል gmẗul *(adj.)* **inverse**
ግምየት gmyet *(n.)* **refraction**
ግን gn *(conj.)* **but**
ግናዕ ኢድ gnae ide *(n.)* **paw**
ኛው gnaw *(v.)* **mew**
ግናይ gnay *(adj.)* **hideous**
ግናይ gnay *(adj.)* **ungainly**
ግንባር gnbar *(n.)* **forehead**
ግምባረኛ ነገር gnbaregna neger *(n.)* **talisman**
ግንቦት g'n'bot *(n.)* **May**
ግነት gnet *(n.)* **exaggeration**
ግንፋለ gnfale *(n.)* **upsurge**
ግንፋለ g'nfale *(n.)* **surge**
ጎኒጎኒ ዝከይድ ጎብጋብ ርቡዕጎናዊ gni goni zkeyd gobgab rubue kurnawi *(n.)* **parallelogram**
ግምጀኛ gnjegna *(n.)* **treasurer**
ግንዮት gnyot *(n.)* **discovery**
ግንዛበ gnzabe *(n.)* **appreciation**
ጎባጥ gobaẗ *(n.)* **curve**
ጎባይ gobay *(n.)* **buffalo**
ጎበጠ gobet'e *(v.)* **warp**
ጎበዝ gobez *(n.)* **guy**
ጎበዝ ጨማቲ gobez chemati *(n.)* **marksman**
ጎብለል goblel *(n.)* **champion**
ጎብናዪ gobnayi *(n.)* **tourist**
ጎብነይቲ ምስትእንጋድ gobneyti mstengad *(n.)* **tourism**
ጎዳኢ goda'e *(adj.)* **injurious**

ጉዳኢ goda'i *(adj.)* **deleterious**
ጎድአ god'e *(v.)* **hurt**
ጎድአ god'e *(v.)* **injure**
ጎደሎ godelo *(adj.)* **deficient**
ጎደና godena *(n.)* **street**
ጎድጋድ ሸሓነ godgad shehane *(n.)* **tub**
ጎድናዊ-ምርጫ godnawimrča *(n.)* **by-election**
ጎድነ-ጎድኒ godnegodni *(adv.)* **abreast**
ጎፍጓፍ gofgwaf *(adj.)* **bushy**
ጎሓፍ go-haf *(n.)* **garbage**
ጎሓፍ goĥaf *(n.)* **refuse**
ጎሓፍ goĥaf *(n.)* **rubbish**
ጎሃየ gohaye *(v.)* **rue**
ጎጀለ gojele *(v.)* **classify**
ጎጀለ goje-le *(v.)* **categorize**
ጋቢና gabina *(n.)* **cabin**
ጎጆ gojo *(n.)* **lodge**
ጎጆ ንህቢ gojo nehbi *(n.)* **hive**
ጎጆ goĵo *(n.)* **booth**
ጐልዓመ golame *(v.)* **truncate**
ጎልፎ gole 'foo *(n.)* **cardigan**
ጎልፍ golf *(n.)* **golf**
ጎልፎ golfo *(n.)* **jersey**
ጎልፎ golfo *(n.)* **sweater**
ጎልጎል golgol *(adj.)* **plain**
ጎልጎል ሳዕሪ golgol saëri *(n.)* **paddock**
ጎልሓጥ golĥaẗ *(adj.)* **gawky**
ጎሎ golo *(n.)* **haunch**
ጎሎ golo *(n.)* **pelvis**
ጎልጠመ golteme *(v.)* **quaff**
ጎማ goma *(n.)* **rubber**
ጎመድ gomed *(n.)* **cudgel**
ጎመድ gomed *(n.)* **bludgeon**
ጎምጠጥ gomẗeẗ *(n.)* **berry**
ጐናነጸ gonanetse *(v.)* **hustle**
ጎነጸ gonetse *(v.)* **shove**
ጎነጻዊ gonexawi *(adj.)* **violent**
ሽምጢ shmẗi *(n.)* **flank**
ጎኒ goni *(n.)* **side**
ጎኒ ባሕሪ goni bahri *(n.)* **seaside**
ጎኒጎኒ gonigoni *(n.)* **parallel**
ጎንፂ gonxi *(n.)* **bump**
ጎራዕራዕ በለ gora'ëraë bele *(v.)* **gurgle**
ጥበበኛ ẗbebeĥa *(adj.)* **shrewd**
ጎራሕ goraḧ *(adj.)* **artful**
ጎረንዳዮ gorandayo *(n.)* **gutter**
ጎረቤት gorebeet *(n.)* **neighbour**
ጎርጎረ gorgore *(v.)* **ransack**
ጎርጎረ gorgore *(v.)* **rummage**
ጎሮሮ gororo *(n.)* **throat**
ወሺፍ weshif *(n.)* **damsel**
ሳዱላ sadula *(n.)* **maiden**
ጓልሕድርትና gwalḧdrtna *(n)* **nymph**
ጎርዞ gorzo *(n.)* **wench**
ጎሳ gosa *(n.)* **tribe**
ጎታት gotat *(adj.)* **languid**
ጎተተ gotete *(v. t)* **drag**
ጎተተ gotete *(v.)* **tow**
መርከብ እትስሕብ ጃልባ merkeb 'ètsḧb ĵalba *(v.)* **tug**
ጎቲም gotim *(adj.)* **blunt**
ጐያዪ goyayi *(n.)* **runner**
ጎያዪ ኣትለት goyayi atlet *(n.)* **sprinter**
ጎየየ goyeye *(v.)* **run**
ጎይቋ goyqwa *(n.)* **quarrel**
ጎይታ goyta *(n.)* **liege**
ጎይታ goyta *(n.)* **lord**
ጎይታ goyta *(n.)* **master**
ጎይታቲ goytati *(adj.)* **bossy**
ጎይታይ goytay *(n.)* **sir**
ጎዞሞ gozomo *(n.)* **chopper**

ግራጭ grach *(n.)* **spike**
ግራፋይት grafayt *(n.)* **graphite**
ግራም gram *(n.)* **gram**
ግራመ grame *(n.)* **amazement**
ግራት መቐለቢ ጥሪት grat meqlebi trit *(n.)* **pasture**
ግራዘ graze *(n.)* **cubicle**
ግርደት grdet *(n.)* **eclipse**
ግረባ greba *(n.)* **afforestation**
ግርጉርነት grgurnet *(n.)* **notoriety**
ግርህነት grhnet *(n.)* **innocence**
ግርህነት grhnet *(n.)* **naivety**
ተራ ምኳን tera mḱwan *(n.)* **simplicity**
ግርማ ሞገስ ዘለዎ grma moges zelewo *(adj.)* **dignified**
ግርምቢጥ grmbiẗ *(adj.)* **grotesque**
ግርምብያለ grmbyale *(n.)* **smock**
ግርምብያለ grmbyale *(n.)* **apron**
ግርንውና grnwuna *(n.)* **senility**
ግርሳም grsam *(adj.)* **myopic**
ግርሳመ grsame *(n.)* **myopia**
ግሩም grum *(adj.)* **majestic**
ግሩም grum *(v.i)* **marvel**
ግሩም grum *(adj.)* **posh**
ግርዝውና grzwna *(n.)* **puberty**
ግስጋሰ gsgase *(v.)* **advance**
ግስጋሰ gsgase *(n.)* **going**
ግሲ gsi *(n.)* **verb**
ግስሩጥ gsrut *(adj.)* **squalid**
ግጥም g-tim *(n.)* **game**
ግጥም g'ẗ'm *(n.)* **match**
ግጥ'ም gẗm *(n.)* **bout**
ግጥማዊ gtmawi *(adj.)* **lyrical**
ግጥሚ ወይ ደርፊ gẗmi wey derfi *(n.)* **ballad**
ግጥሚ gẗmi *(n.)* **poem**
ጓዳ guada *(n.)* **panel**
ጓሂ guahi *(n.)* **heartache**
ጓል gual *(n.)* **puss**
ጓል ንጉስ gual ngus *(n.)* **princess**
ጓንቲ ብረት gua-nti bret *(n.)* **gauntlet**
ጉዕዞ guazo *(n.)* **tour**
ጉዕዞ guazo *(v.)* **travel**
ጉባኤ guba'ee *(n.)* **congress**
ጉቦ gubo *(v. t.)* **bribe**
ጉዳም gudam *(adj.)* **queer**
ጉድኣት gudat *(n.)* **trauma**
ሓደጋ ḧadega *(n.)* **casualty**
ዘይምቹእ ኩነት zeymchu'è kunet *(n.)* **disadvantage**
ጉድኣት gud'at *(n.)* **fatality**
ጉዳይ guday *(n.)* **affair**
ጉዳይ guday *(n.)* **issue**
ጉዳይ guday *(n.)* **matter**
ጉድጓድ gudgad *(n.)* **pit**
ጉድጓድ gudgwad *(n.)* **burrow**
ጉድለት gudlet *(n.)* **defect**
ጉድለት gudlet *(n.)* **flaw**
ሕጽረት ḧxret *(n.)* **shortcoming**
ጉድለት ምሕደራ gudlet mḧdera *(n.)* **misrule**
ጉድለት ተሞክሮ gudlet temokro *(n.)* **inexperience**
ጉድኣት gudu'at *(n.)* **injury**
ጉዕዞ gu'ëzo *(n.)* **journey**
መገሻ megesha *(n.)* **voyage**
ጉጅለ guge-le *(n.)* **category**
ጉሕ guḧ *(n.)* **niche**
ጉሒላ ኣፍቃሪ guḧila afqari *(n.)* **Casanova**
ጉጅለ gujele *(n.)* **group**
ጉጂ guji *(n.)* **cottage**
ዕሙር 'ëmur *(n.)* **cluster**
ጉጅለ gujle *(n.)* **squadron**
ጉጅለ gujle *(n.)* **troupe**

ጉልባብ gulbab *(n.)* **shroud**
ጉልበት gulbet *(n.)* **energy**
ጉልበተኛ gulbetegna *(adj.)* **strapping**
ጉልቻ gulcha *(n.)* **trivet**
ጉለ gule *(n.)* **udder**
ጉልሓጥሓጥ በለ gulḥaṭḥaṭ bele *(n.)* **goggle**
ጉልተኛ gultegna *(n.)* **squire**
ምምሕዳር ሰበኻ mmḧdar sebeḱa *(n.)* **benefice**
ጉልቲ gulti *(n.)* **estate**
ጉሉሕ guluĥ *(adj.)* **prominent**
ጉሉሕነት guluĥnet *(n.)* **prominence**
ጉንቦ ኢድ gunbo 'id *(n.)* **wrist**
ጉንዲ gundi *(n.)* **timber**
ጉንዲ gundi *(n.)* **trunk**
ጉንዲ gundi *(n.)* **bole**
ጉርሒ gurḧi *(n.)* **prude**
ጉርዒ gur'ï *(n.)* **ravine**
ጉርዞ ባሕሪ gurzo baḧri *(n.)* **mermaid**
ጉስጢ gusẗi *(n)* **boxing**
ጉስጢ gusẗi *(v.)* **punch**
ጉስያዊ gusyawi *(adj.)* **evasive**
ጉያ guya *(n.)* **run**
ጉያ guya *(v.)* **sprint**
ጉዚ guzi *(n.)* **fraction**
ጐደና gwadena *(n.)* **avenue**
ጐደና gwadena *(n.)* **boulevard**
ጐድኒ gwadni *(n.)* **facet**
ጐሓፍ gwaḧaf *(n.)* **junk**
ጐሃረ gwahare *(v.)* **glow**
ጓሃየ gwahaye *(v.)* **bemoan**
ጓሂ gwahi *(n.)* **grief**
ጓሂ/ሕርቃን gwahi /ḧrkan *(n.)* **dejection**
ጓሂ gwahi *(n.)* **anguish**
ጓል gwal *(n.)* **daughter**

ጓል gwal *(n.)* **girl**
ፍቕርቲ fq̈rti *(n.)* **lass**
ናይ ክርስትና ውላድ gwal blgna *(n.)* **godchild**
ጓል ሓው gwal ḧaw *(n.)* **niece**
ጓልጓሎ gwalgwalo *(n.)* **sissy**
ጓንጓ gwangwa *(n.)* **cavity**
ጓንቲ gwanti *(n.)* **glove**
ጐራዕራዕ በለ gwara'ëra'ë bele *(v.)* **burble**
ጐራሕ gwaraḣ *(adj.)* **canny**
ጐርጐሐ gwargwaḧe *(v.)* **bore**
ጓሳ ኣባጊዕ gwasa abagi'ë *(n.)* **shepherd**
ጓዘመ gwazeme *(v.)* **roar**
ጐዘየ gwazeye *(v.t.)* **apportion**
ጐዘየ gwazeye *(n.)* **usurpation**
ጓዝማ gwazma *(n.)* **roar**
ጓና guana *(n.)* **outsider**
ጐፍ በለ gwof bele *(v.)* **accost**
ግይፀታ gytsta *(v.)* **smirk**
ግዛዕ gza'e *(n.)* **thing**
ግዝኣት gzat *(n.)* **territory**
ግዝኣት gz'at *(n.)* **colony**
ኣውራጃ awraĵa *(n.)* **county**
ንግስነት ngsnet *(n.)* **empire**
ዓውዲ 'äwdi *(n.)* **realm**
ግዝኣታዊ gzatawi *(adj.)* **territorial**
ግዝፊ gzfi *(n.)* **immensity**
ግዝፊ gzfi *(n.)* **size**
ግዜ gzie *(n.)* **time**
ግዜኡ ዘይበጽሐ gzieeu zeybexḧe *(adj.)* **premature**
ግዜያዊ gziyawi *(adj.)* **transitory**
ግዝያዊ ሓፀር gziyawi hatzur *(n.)* **hoarding**
ግዜያዊ gziywi *(adj.)* **transient**
ግዙእ gzu'e *(n.)* **retainer**
ግዝዋ gzwa *(n.)* **moth**

ግዜያዊ ፈጻሚ gzeeyawi fexami *(adj.)* **acting**
ግዝያዊ gzyawi *(adj.)* **provisional**
ህሞታዊ hmotawi *(adj.)* **momentary**
ግዝያዊ ተኹሲ-ዕጾ gzyawi tek̔usi'ëxo *(n.)* **armistice**
ጎድናዊ godnawi *(adj.)* **outboard**

ጠ

ጠርጠረ ṭerṭere *(v.)* **impeach**
ጠቕለለ ṭeq̈lele *(v.)* **wrap**
ጠንካራ ṭenkara *(adj.)* **virile**
ጠንቋሊ ẗenqwali *(adj.)* **fey**
ጠንቋሊት ṭenqwalit *(n.)* **hag**
ጠሊ ṭeli *(n.)* **humidity**
ጠጥዐ ẗeẗ'e *(v.)* **sprout**
ጠረጴዛ terebeza *(n.)* **table**
ጠርዐ ẗer'ë *(v.)* **complain**
ጠቕጠቐ teqteqe *(v.)* **cram**
ጠራዓይ teraay *(n.)* **petitioner**
ጠወየ ṭeweye *(v.)* **wrest**
ጠባዊ ẗbawi *(n.)* **sucker**
ጠበቓ tbeqha *(n.)* **lawyer**
ጠምበርበር በለ ẗemberber bele *(n.)* **blunder**
ጠዓሞት ẗe'ämot *(n.)* **snack**
ጠዓየ ẗe'aye *(v.)* **survive**
ሰብኣዊ መንነት seb'awi mennet *(n.)* **personality**
ጠባይ ẗebay *(n.)* **conduct**
ቀመማዊ qememawi *(n.)* **hexogen**
ጠባይ ẗebay *(n.)* **behaviour**
ጠበንጃ tebenja *(n.)* **rifle**
ጠበንጃ ṭebenja *(n.)* **gun**
ጠበቃ ẗebeqa *(n.)* **solicitor**
ጠበቓ ẗebeq̈a *(n.)* **attorney**
ጠበቓ ẗebeq̈a *(n.)* **barrister**
ጠበቕ tebeqh *(n.)* **lizard**
ጠባብሐ tebabhe *(v.)* **dissect**
ጠበሰ ẗebese *(v.)* **fry**
ጠቕላላ ርእዮት teqlala r'eyot *(n.)* **overview**
ጠብላቕ teblaq *(adj.)* **officious**
ጠፊኡ tefiu *(adv.)* **off**
ጣኦት ta'ot *(n.)* **oracle**
ጥራይ tray *(adv.)* **only**
ጥርዚ-ስምዒት trzi sm'it *(n.)* **orgasm**
ጥቅምቲ tkemti *(n.)* **October**
ጥፍኣታት tfatat *(n.)* **onslaught**
ጠፍ ኣበለ ẗef abele *(v.)* **flick**
ጠፍአ tef'a *(v.)* **decamp**
ጠበወ ẗebewe *(v.)* **suck**
ጠብሒ tebhi *(n.)* **sauce**
ጠቢብ tebib *(adj.)* **wise**
ጥንሰ-ሓሳብ tebse hasab *(n.)* **hypothesis**
ጤረር ሞገድ teerer moged *(n.)* **surf**
ጠፋኢ tefa'i *(adj.)* **perishable**
ጠፍሐ tef'e *(v.)* **skim**
ጠፈረ-ህዋ ẗeferehwa *(n.)* **aerospace**
ጠፈርተኛ ẗeferteǹa *(n.)* **astronaut**
ጠፊኡ tefi'u *(v.)* **perish**
ጠፍታ ẗefta *(n.)* **spat**
ጠፍጠፈ ẗefẗefe *(v.)* **spank**
ጠገለ ዝሰኣነ መደረ ẗegele zse'ane medere *(adj.)* **fulsome**
ጠገለ-ኣልቦ ẗegele'albo *(n.)* **boor**
ጠሓለ teĥale *(v.)* **drown**
ጠሓለ teĥale *(v.)* **sink**
ጠሓለ ẗehale *(v.)* **submerge**
ጠሓለ ẗehale *(v.)* **submerse**
ጠሓሊ ẗeĥali *(adj.)* **submersible**
ጠሓሰ tehase *(v.)* **infringe**
ጠሓሰ tehase *(v.)* **trespass**
ጠቓሚ tekami *(adj.)* **useful**
ጠቕላላ teklala *(n.)* **total**

ጠቅላላ teklala *(adj.)* **total**
ጠማሪ temari *(adj.)* **cohesive**
ጠልቀየ ẗelqeye *(v.)* **soak**
ጠማዕ tema'e *(n.)* **scrooge**
ጥንቁቕ ẗnquq̈ *(adj.)* **frugal**
በቃቕ beqaq̈ *(adj.)* **miserly**
ጠማዕ ẗema'ë *(n.)* **niggard**
ጠማዕ ẗema'ë *(adj.)* **niggardly**
ኣተወ 'atewe *(v. t)* **dip**
ጠመረ ẗemere *(v.)* **belay**
ጠመረ ẗemere *(v.)* **bind**
ጠመተ temete *(v.)* **regard**
ጠመተ ሃበ temete habe *(v.)* **emphasize**
ጠመየ ẗemeye *(v.)* **starve**
ጠጠመ ẗeẗeme *(v.)* **nibble**
ጠጠው በለ ṭeṭew bele *(v.)* **halt**
ጠጠው ምባል ẗeẗew mbal *(v.)* **pose**
ጠጠው ምባል ẗeẗew mbal *(n.)* **standstill**
ጐራሕ gwaraḧ *(adj.)* **crooked**
ጠዋይ ṭeway *(adj.)* **wry**
ጠዋይ ṭeway *(n.)* **kink**
ጠስሚ ẗesmi *(n.)* **butter**
ጠረዘ tereze *(v. t)* **deport**
ጠርነፈ ẗernefe *(v.)* **compile**
ጠቐነ ẗeqhene *(n.)* **stigma**
ጠቅለለ teqlele *(v.)* **rewind**
ጠቀር ẗeqer *(n.)* **soot**
ጠቀሰ teqese *(v.)* **quote**
ጽቕጠት ዓይኒ xq̈ẗet 'äyni *(v.)* **wink**
ጠቀሰ ẗeqese *(v.)* **mention**
ጠቐሰ ẗeq̈ese *(v.)* **adduce**
ጠቓሚ teqhami *(adj.)* **important**
ጠቓምነት teqhamnet *(n.)* **importance**
መሓጐስ meḧagwas *(n.)* **boon**
ጠቓሚ ẗeq̈ami *(adj.)* **expedient**
ጠቓሚ ሙኳን teqami mukwan *(v.)* **pertain**
ጠቓሚ ẗeq̈ami *(adj.)* **advantageous**
ጠቓሚ ẗeq̈ami *(adj.)* **productive**
ጠርጠረ ẗerẗere *(v.)* **mistrust**
ጠርጣሪ ẗerẗere *(adj.)* **suspicious**
ጠርዚ ẗerzi *(n.)* **striation**
ጠረፍ ẗeref *(n.)* **brink**
ጠንቋሊ tenqali *(n.)* **seer**
ጠንቃዊ ẗenqawi *(adj.)* **causal**
ጠንካራ tenkaara *(adj.)* **tough**
ጠንካራ ṭenkara *(adj.)* **hardy**
ጠንካራ ዕርዲ ẗenkara ërdi *(n.)* **stronghold**
ጠንካራ ናይ ኣሞራ ጭፍሪ tenkara nay amora chifri *(n.)* **talon**
ጠንከረ tenkere *(v.)* **toughen**
ጠቐሰ tekese *(v.)* **cite**
ጠላዕ telae *(n.)* **whist**
ጠላዕ ẗela'ë *(n.)* **camber**
ጠላለፈ telalefe *(v.t.)* **tangle**
ጠላም telam *(adj.)* **slippery**
ጠለብ teleb *(n.)* **demand**
ጠንቋሊ ẗenqwali *(n.)* **sorcerer**
ጠለብ teleb *(n.)* **requirement**
ጠንቂ tenqi *(adj.)* **pernicious**
ጠንቂ ኣለርጂ ẗenqi alerji *(n.)* **allergen**
ጠንቅነት ẗenqnet *(n.)* **causality**
ጠንቋሊ tenquali *(n.)* **wizard**
ጠንቋሊት tenqualit *(n.)* **witch**
ጡብ ኣድጊ ṭub 'adgi *(n.)* **wart**
ጡብ ẗub *(n.)* **breast**
መኣዛዊ me'azawi *(adj.)* **savoury**
ጥዑም t'um *(adj.)* **tasteful**
ጥዑም t'um *(adj.)* **tasty**
ሕያዋይ ጸጋዊ ḧyaway xegawi *(adj.)* **gracious**

ጥዑም ነገር ዝሓዘ ብያቲ t'um neger zhaze byati *(n.)* **tart**
ጡንኩር ዘይኮነ tunkur zeykone *(adj.)* **lenient**
ጡንኩር ዘይኮነ ኣተሓሳስባ tunkur zeykone atehasasba *(n.)* **leniency**
ጡረታ ẗureta *(n.)* **superannuation**
ጡጥ ẗuẗ *(n.)* **cotton**
ዘይጽሉል zeyxlul *(adj.)* **sane**
ጥዑይ ẗ'uy *(adj.)* **hale**
ጥውይዋይ twuyway *(adj.)* **serpentine**
ጥውይዋይ twyway *(adj.)* **sinuous**
ጣኦት ẗa'ot *(n.)* **fetish**
ጣልቃ ኣተወ ẗalqa 'atewe *(v.)* **intervene**
ጣልያናዊ talyanawj *(adj.)* **italic**
ጣሕሸም በለ taĥšem bele *(v.)* **rustle**
ጣንጡ ẗanẗu *(n.)* **mosquito**
መለኮታዊ ባህርይ melekotawi bahry *(n.)* **deity**
ጣኦት ẗa'ot *(n.)* **goddess**
ጣኦት ṭa'ot *(n.)* **idol**
ጣኦት ኣምልኾ ṭa'ot 'amlḱo *(n.)* **idolatry**
ጣዕሚ ta'emi *(n.)* **taste**
ጣዕሚ ዘይብሉ ta'emi zeyblu *(adj.)* **tasteless**
ጣዕሳ ta'ësa *(n.)* **remorse**
ጣቋ ẗaq̈ua *(n.)* **proficiency**
ጣቋ ዘረባ taqwa zereba *(n.)* **rhetoric**
ጣፍያ ẗafya *(n.)* **spleen**
ጣሻ tasha *(n.)* **thicket**
ጣጥያ tatya *(n.)* **shingle**
ቲክ tik *(n.)* **teak**
ጣውላ tawla *(adj.)* **wooded**
ኣርማዲዮ 'armadiyo *(n.)* **cupboard**
ጣውላ እግሪ tawla egri *(n.)* **skirting**
ጣውላ ẗawla *(n.)* **board**
ጤል ṭeel *(n.)* **goat**
ጥዕና ṭ'ëna *(n.)* **health**
ጥረ tre *(adj.)* **uncouth**
ዘይበሰለ zeybesele *(adj.)* **crude**
ጉዕ gu'ë *(adj.)* **callow**
ጥረ-ሕጡብ ẗreĥẗub *(n.)* **adobe**
ጥሪ ẗri *(n.)* **January**
ጥርሑ ṭrḥu *(adj.)* **vacant**
ጥርሑ ẗrĥu *(adj.)* **empty**
ጥርሑ ẗrĥu *(adj.)* **bare**
ጥርሑ ẗrĥu *(adj.)* **blank**
ጥርዓን tran *(n.)* **petition**
ጥርዓን ẗr'än *(n.)* **complaint**
ጥርሙዝ ẗrmuz *(v.t.)* **glass**
ጥርሙዝ ẗrmuz *(n.)* **bottle**
ጥርሙዛዊ ṭrmuzawi *(adj.)* **vitreous**
ጥርንቕ ዘብል ስረ trnqh zble sre *(n.)* **leggings**
ጥርኑፍ ẗrnuf *(adj.)* **compact**
ጥራይ ẗ'ray *(adj.)* **mere**
ጥሜት ẗmiet *(n.)* **famine**
ጥምጥም tmtam *(n.)* **turban**
ጥንግንግ ṭngng *(n.)* **labyrinth**
ጥንቁቕ ṭnquq̈ *(adj.)* **wary**
ጥቕላል ፈትሊ ṭq̈lal fetli *(n.)* **hank**
ጥቅሰ ሳምዕ ẗqse sam'ë *(n.)* **epitaph**
ጥቕሲ ẗqsi *(n.)* **excerpt**
ጥቅላል ẗqlal *(n.)* **bundle**
ጥቕላል ẗq̈lal *(n.)* **packet**
ጥቅላል ብራና tqlal brana *(n.)* **scroll**
ጠቓምነት ẗeq̈amnet *(n.)* **utility**
ጥቕሚ ẗq̈mi *(n.)* **pro**
ጥቅሚ ዘለዎ tqmi zelewo *(adj.)* **salutary**
ጥቅሲ tqsi *(n.)* **quotation**
ጥቅሲ ẗ'q'si *(n.)* **maxim**
ጥንቁቕ ẗnquq̈ *(adj.)* **chary**
ጥቁብ tqub *(adj.)* **reticent**

ጥቁው ẗquw *(adj.)* **proficient**
ጥቃ ẗqa *(adj.)* **adjacent**
ጥቓንጥቓ tqaneteqa' *(adj.)* **contiguous**
ጥበብ tbeb *(n.)* **wisdom**
ጥበብ ስእሊ tbeb seli *(n.)* **photography**
ጥበብ ẗbeb *(n.)* **art**
ጥበበኛ tbebegna *(adj.)* **tactful**
ጥበበኛ tbebenya *(n.)* **craftsman**
ጥብቂ tbki *(adj.)* **thorough**
ጥብቀት ẗbqet *(n.)* **attachment**
ጥብቂ ẗbqi *(adj.)* **strict**
ጥብቂ ሰብ ẗbqi seb *(n.)* **stickler**
ጥብቂ ẗbqi *(adj.)* **austere**
ጥብጥብ በለ tbtb bele *(v. i)* **drip**
ጥብጥታ tbtbta *(n.)* **tap**
ጥብጠባ ẗbẗeba *(adj.)* **spanking**
ጥቡቕ tbuk *(adj.)* **tenacious**
ጥቡቅ ርክብ tbuq rkb *(n.)* **rapport**
ጥሩምባ trumba *(n.)* **trumpet**
ጥሩምባ ṭrumba *(n.)* **horn**
ጥሩምባ ẗrumba *(n.)* **bugle**
ጥሮታ trota *(n.)* **pension**
ጥሮተኛ trotena *(n.)* **pensioner**
ጥርጣረ trtare *(n.)* **distrust**
ጥርጣረ trtare *(n.)* **doubt**
ጥርጣረ ẗr'ẗare *(n.)* **suspicion**
ጥርዛዊ trzawi *(adj.)* **peaky**
ዝለዓለ ነጥቢ zle'äle neẗbi *(n.)* **peak**
ወሰን ዓንኬል wesen 'änkeel *(n.)* **rim**
ጥርዚ ṭrzi *(n.)* **verge**
ጥርዝያ ẗrzya *(n.)* **banishment**
ጥንሲ ẗnsi *(n.)* **pregnancy**
ጥንስቲ ẗnsti *(adj.)* **pregnant**
ጥንታዊ tntawi *(adj.)* **primeval**
ወደባት wedebat *(adj.)* **aboriginal**
ጥንታዊ ẗntawi *(n.)* **antique**
ጥንታዊ ẗntawi *(adj.)* **ancient**
ጥንታዊ ẗntawi *(adj.)* **archaic**
ጥንቲ ẗnti *(n.)* **antiquity**
ጦብሎቕ በሃሊ ẗobloq̈ behali *(n.)* **interloper**
ጦፍታ ẗofta *(n.)* **fillip**
ጥንቁቅ tenquq *(adj.)* **cautious**
ጥሙይ temuy *(adj.)* **hungry**
ጥዕና አእምሮ t'ena a'emro *(n.)* **sanity**
ጥዑም ግዜ ṭ'üm gzee *(n.)* **heyday**
ጥዑይ ṭ'üy *(adj.)* **healthy**
ጥንካረ tenkara *(n.)* **tenacity**
ጥንካሬ tenkara *(n.)* **toughness**
ጥራጥረ teraterre *(n.)* **cereal**
ጥማር ẗmar *(n.)* **bunch**
ጥሜት ẗmeet *(n.)* **starvation**
ጥምቀት ẗmqet *(n.)* **baptism**
ጥምረት tmret *(n.)* **cohesion**
ጥሙይ tmuy *(adj.)* **skimp**
ጥምየት ṭmyet *(n.)* **hunger**
ጥንቢ ክንቲት tnbi kntit *(n.)* **shuttlecock**
ጥንካረ ẗnkare *(n.)* **stringency**
ጥንቆላ tnkola *(n.)* **tarot**
ጥንቃቓዊ ẗnqaq̈awi *(adj.)* **precautionary**
ጥንቃቐ ẗnqaq̈e *(n.)* **precaution**
ጥንቃቒ ዘይፈልጥ tnqaqhie zeyfelt *(adj.)* **imprudent**
ጥንቅልዕሸው ẗnql'ëshew *(n.)* **somersault**
ጥንቆላ tnqola *(n.)* **witchcraft**
ጥንቆላ tnqola *(n.)* **witchery**
ጥንቆላ ẗnqola *(n.)* **sorcery**
ስቱር stur *(adj.)* **discreet**
ንጥንቁቕን ትኽክልን nẗnquq̈n tḱkln *(adj.)* **meticulous**
ጥንቁቕ ẗnquq̈ *(adj.)* **alert**

ጥንቁቕ ẗnquq̈ *(adj.)* **attentive**
ጥንቁቕ ẗnquq̈ *(adj.)* **painstaking**
ጥንቁቕ ẗnquq̈ *(adj.)* **prudential**
ጥንቁቕ ṭnquq̈ *(adj.)* **vigilant**
ጥልቀት ẗlqet *(n.)* **anti-climax**
ጥልቀት ኣልቦነት ẗlqet albonet *(n.)* **superficiality**
ጥልቂ ẗlqi *(adj.)* **abstruse**
ጥልቁይ t'lquy *(adj.)* **soggy**
ጥልቁይ ẗlquy *(adj.)* **sopping**
ጥማር timar *(n.)* **ticket**
ጥንቁቅ tinkuq *(n.)* **combination**
ጥሪት trit *(n.)* **property**
ጥቕላል tklal *(adj.)* **exact**
ጥልፊ tlfi *(n.)* **embroidery**
ሪካሞ rikamo *(n.)* **sampler**
ሳላሚ salami *(n.)* **motif**
ጥልመት ẗlmet *(n.)* **betrayal**
ጥሑል ẗḧul *(adj.)* **sunken**
ጥሕሰት thset *(n.)* **infringement**
ጥፈሻ ẗfesha *(n.)* **bankruptcy**
ጥፉሽ ẗfush *(adj.)* **bankrupt**
ጥፉሽ ẗfush *(adj.)* **broke**

ጨ

ጨቆነ ĉeqone *(v.)* **oppress**
ጸቓጢ xeq̈aẗi *(adj.)* **oppressive**
ጨቋኒ čeqwani *(n.)* **oppressor**
ጨና chena *(n.)* **odour**
ጨንፈር ĉenfer *(n.)* **offshoot**
ጫፋቱ ተደራረበ chafatu tederarebe *(v.)* **overlap**
ጭቆና cheqona *(n.)* **oppression**
መወዳእታ meweda'èta *(n.)* **end**
ጫፍ čaf *(n.)* **acme**
ጫፍ čaf *(n)* **apex**
ጫፍ ብርዒ čaf br'ï *(n.)* **nib**
ጫፍ čaf *(n.)* **brim**
ጫሕጫሕ ኣበለ čaḧčaḧ 'abele *(n.)* **jingle**
ጫካ čaka *(n.)* **jungle**
ጫማ ĉama *(n.)* **shoe**
ጫቑት čaqwit *(n.)* **nestling**
ጫዉጫዉታ ĉawĉawta *(n.)* **din**
ጭበጣ ĉbeta *(n.)* **shrinkage**
ጭቡጥ čbuẗ *(n.)* **concrete**
ጫፍ ccaf *(n.)* **climax**
ጭፍራ ከዋኽብቲ ccfra ke'wakib'ti *(n.)* **constellation**
ጩቕ በለ cchuq' bel'le *(v.)* **chirp**
ጭልታ cclta *(n.)* **clink**
ጨዳድ cdade *(n.)* **cleft**
ጨዓይ ጸጉሪ ዘለዎ ĉe'äy xeguri zelewo *(adj.)* **blonde**
ጨብጨባ čebčeba *(n.)* **applause**
ጨበጠ čebeẗe *(v.)* **compress**
ጨብረቕረቕ ĉebreqreq *(n.)* **ripple**
ጨካን ĉekan *(adj.)* **ferocious**
ኣረመን 'aremen *(n.)* **fiend**
ጨካን ĉekan *(adj.)* **ruthless**
ጨካን čekan *(adj.)* **cruel**
ጨካን ፍጥረት čekan fẗret *(n.)* **harpy**
ጨካን čekan *(n.)* **behemoth**
ጨለ čele *(adj.)* **adroit**
ጨማደደ ĉemadede *(v.)* **rumple**
ጨናዊ ĉenawi *(adj.)* **funky**
ጨነወ ĉenewe *(v.)* **reek**
ጨንፈር ĉenfer *(n.)* **ramification**
ጨንፈር ሕክምና ህጻናት ĉenfer ḧkmna hxanat *(n.)* **paediatrics**
ጨንፈር čenfer *(n.)* **branch**
ጨቓዊት čeq̈awit *(n.)* **brood**
ጨቕጨቀ čeqčeqe *(v.t.)* **nag**
ጨራዕራዕ በለ ĉera'ëraë bele *(v.)* **sizzle**

ጨረር ĉerer *(n.)* **ray**
ጨረርታ ĉererta *(n.)* **radiation**
ጨርሔ ĉerĥe *(v.)* **exclaim**
ጨርቂ ĉerqi *(n.)* **rag**
ጨርቂ ሽንቲ ĉerqi shnti *(n.)* **diaper**
ጨወየ ç̣ewey *(v.)* **kidnap**
ጨወየ čeweye *(v.t.)* **abduct**
ጭፍራ čfra *(n.)* **fleet**
ሕዳግ ḧdag *(n.)* **ledge**
ጫፍ čaf *(n.)* **tip**
ዝለዓለ ነጥቢ zle'äle neẗbi *(n.)* **zenith**
ጫፍ ch'af *(n.)* **summit**
ጫሕገረ chaḧgere *(adj.)* **streaky**
ጫካ chaka *(n.)* **woodland**
ጪካ ዝተሸፈነ ገቦ chaka ztexefene gebo *(n.)* **wold**
ጭቡጥ ch'buẗ *(adj.)* **substantive**
ምጭባጥ mčbaẗ *(v.)* **clasp**
ጨበጠ chebeẗe *(v.)* **squeeze**
ዓትዓተ 'ät'äte *(v.)* **grip**
ጨጫፍ chechaf *(n.)* **periphery**
ቸኮላታ checolata *(n.)* **chocolate**
ጨደደ chedede *(v.)* **cleave**
ጨደረ che-dere *(n.)* **howl**
ጨፋለቀ chefaleqe *(v.)* **mangle**
ጨፍለቐ chefleqhe *(v.)* **squash**
ጨጓር čheguar *(adj.)* **hairy**
ጨጉሪ ኣምበሳ ወይ ፈረስ cheguri ambesa wey feres *(n.)* **mane**
ጭሕሚ ድሙ chehmi *(n.)* **whisker**
ኣረመናዊ 'aremenawi *(adj.)* **savage**
ንቑጽ nq̈ux *(adj.)* **stark**
ጨካን chekan *(adj.)* **uncharitable**
ጨካን ç̣hekan *(adj.)* **heartless**
ጨካን ኣምባ ገነን chekan ambagenen *(n.)* **tyrant**
ጨለ chele *(adv.)* **well**
ጨምዳድ chemdad *(adj.)* **wizened**
ጨና chena *(n.)* **perfume**
ጨና ምልካይ chena mlkay *(adv.)* **perfume**
ጨነወ chenewe *(v.)* **stink**
ጨንፈር chenfer *(n.)* **sprig**
ጨረት cheret *(n.)* **tick**
ጨርቃ ጨርቂ cherka cherki *(n)* **textile**
ጨው chew *(n.)* **salt**
ጨዋም chewam *(adj.)* **saline**
ጨዋም chewam *(adj.)* **salty**
ጨዋምነት chewamnet *(n.)* **salinity**
ጭሕጋር čḧgar *(n.)* **comma**
ጭጋረት chgaret *(n.)* **livery**
ጭጋረት chgaret *(n.)* **species**
ጨሓጋገረ chhagagere *(v.)* **scrabble**
ጭሕጋር ch'ḧgar *(n.)* **streak**
ጭፍጨፋ chif'chefa *(n.)* **carnage**
ጭኮንበሳ chikonbesa *(n.)* **cheetah**
ጭቃ chiqa *(n.)* **clay**
ጭካነኣዊ chkane-awi *(adj.)* **heinous**
ጭከና chkena *(n.)* **savagery**
ጭሕሚ čḧmi *(n.)* **beard**
ጭንጫ ch'ncha *(adj.)* **stony**
ጭንቀት chnqet *(n.)* **stress**
ጭንቂ chnqi *(n.)* **woe**
ጭንቂ ዝመልኦ chnqi zmelo *(adj.)* **woeful**
ጭኑቕ chnuq *(adj.)* **strained**
ኣጨናቒ ačenaq̈i *(adj.)* **worrisome**
ጭሖሎ čḧolo *(n.)* **bowl**
ጨቊኑ chqinu *(v.)* **tyrannize**
ጭራ chra *(n.)* **tail**
ጭራም chram *(n.)* **piece**
ጭርቃን chrqan *(n.)* **parody**
ጭሩ chru *(n.)* **wagtail**

ጭሩ ገበላ chru gebela *(n.)* **sparrow**
ጩቅ በለ chuqk' bele *(n.)* **cheep**
ጩራ chu-ra *(n.)* **girder**
ጭካነ čkane *(adv.)* **cruelty**
ጭንጫ ĉnĉa *(n.)* **detritus**
ጭንፋር ቀርኒ čnfar qerni *(n.)* **antler**
ኛኽ ምባል ǹaḱ mbal *(n.)* **fuss**
ምሽቓል mshq̈al *(n.)* **anxiety**
ጭንቂ ĉnqi *(n.)* **distress**
ጭንቁራዕ ĉnqura'ë *(n.)* **frog**
ጫፍ çaf *(n.)* **vertex**
ጨካን ĉekan *(adj.)* **evil**
ጭፍራ çfra *(n.)* **horde**
ጭፉን ĉfun *(n.)* **fanatic**
ጨንገር ምድ'ቓል çhenger mdq̈al *(n.)* **graft**
ጨወየ cheweye *(v.)* **hijack**
ጭኑቕ ĉnuq *(adj.)* **febrile**
ጭራሮ በረድ çraro bered *(n.)* **icicle**
ጭቃ čqa *(n.)* **bailiff**
ሓመዳይ[ንሕብሪ] ዝተደናገረ ȟamedaynȟbri ztedenagere *(n.)* **mud**
ጭራምዑት čram'ut *(n.)* **appendix**
ጭራዋጣ ĉrawaẗa *(n.)* **fiddle**
ቸርቸራ ĉrĉera *(n.)* **retail**
ጭርጭርታ cr'crta *(n.)* **trill**
ጭረት čret *(n.)* **apostrophe**
ጭርሖ ĉrȟo *(n.)* **slogan**
ጭርሖ črȟo *(n.)* **motto**
ጭርታ črta *(n.)* **aperture**
ጩራ ĉura *(n.)* **radius**
ልዙብ lzub *(adj.)* **genteel**
ጭዋ ĉ'wa *(adj.)* **decent**
ጭዋዳ čwada *(n.)* **muscle**
ጭዋዳዊ čwadawi *(adj.)* **muscular**
ጭውነት ĉ'wnet *(n.)* **decency**
ጭውያ čwya *(n.)* **abduction**
ጭብጨባ ĉbĉeba *(n.)* **ovation**
ጭንቀት chenqet *(n.)* **obsession**
ጭካነ abi wenjel *(n.)* **outrage**

ጰ

ጲጵታ ̈pipta *(n.)* **bleep**
ጳጳስ ṕaṕas *(n.)* **pope**
ጴራቅሊጦስ peeraqlitos *(n.)* **whit**
ጵጵስና ppsna *(n.)* **papacy**

ጸ / ፀ

ጸላዕላዕ tsela'ela'e *(adj.)* **sunny**
ጸዕዳ xaeda *(adj.)* **white**
ጸዕደወ xa'ëdewe *(v.)* **blanch**
ጸዕቂ xa'ëqi *(n.)* **congestion**
ጸዕረኛ xa'ëreǹa *(adj.)* **assiduous**
ጸላም-ዓይኒ tselam'äyni *(n.)* **liver**
ጸህያይ xahyay *(n.)* **weed**
ጸጸ xaxe *(n.)* **ant**
ጸጸ መጺጽ xaxe mexix *(adj.)* **antacid**
ጽባቐ xbaq̈ *(n.)* **prettiness**
ጽባቐ ጽሕፈት xbaq̈e xȟfet *(n.)* **calligraphy**
ጽባቐኣዊ xbaq̈e'awi *(adj.)* **aesthetic**
ጽብቕቲ xbq̈ti *(n.)* **belle**
ፅቡቕ xbuq *(adj.)* **fine**
ጽዱይ xduy *(adj.)* **aseptic**
ጽድያዊ xdyawi *(adj.)* **vernal**
ጸዓደ xe'äde *(v.)* **assert**
ፀዓረ xe'äre *(v.)* **endeavour**
ፀባ xeba *(n.)* **milk**
ፀባ መሰል xeba mesel *(adj.)* **milky**
ፀባይ xebay *(n.)* **character**

ፀብሒ xebhi *(n.)* **chutney**
ፀቢብ xebib *(adj.)* **narrow**
መሳፍሒ ዘይብሉ mesafȟi zeyblu *(adj.)* **poky**
ፀብለልታ xeblelta *(n.)* **excellence**
ናይ ተጻባጻቢ ሞያ nay texabaxabi moya *(n.)* **accountancy**
ጸብጻብ xebxab *(n.)* **audit**
ፀብፃቢ xebxabi *(n.)* **correspondent**
ፅምብል xeembil *(n.)* **ceremony**
ፀፍዐ xef'ë *(v.)* **swat**
ፀፍዒ xef'ï *(n.)* **flurry**
ፀፊሕ xefiȟ *(adj.)* **flat**
ጸፊሕ ሸሓኒ xefiȟ sheȟani *(n.)* **platter**
ፀገም xegem *(n.)* **mishap**
ፀገነ xegene *(v.)* **mend**
ፀጉሩ ረገፈ xeguru regefe *(v.)* **moult**
ጸሓፊ xeḥafi *(n.)* **writer**
ፀሓፊ ኖቬላ xeȟafi noveela *(n.)* **novelist**
ጸሓፊ ቲያትር xeȟafi tyatr *(n.)* **playwright**
ጽዕነት xëinet *(n.)* **pack**
ፀላኢ xela'i *(n.)* **enemy**
ፀላኢ xela'i *(n.)* **foe**
ፀላም xelam *(n.)* **negress**
ጸልአ xel'e *(v.)* **abominate**
ጸለቑ xeleq̈wu *(v.)* **abscond**
ጸለወ xelewe *(v.)* **affect**
ፀሊም xelim *(n.)* **negro**
ጸሊም መዝገብ xelim mezgeb *(n.)* **blacklist**
ፀሊም ሞሉስኮ xelim molusko *(n.)* **mussel**
ጸሊም ጸጉሪ xelim xeguri *(n.)* **brunette**
ጸሊም xelim *(adj.)* **black**
ጸሎት xelot *(n.)* **prayer**
ጸመቔ xemeq̈we *(v.)* **wring**
ጸመቔ xemeq̈we *(v.)* **brew**
ጸምሪ xemri *(n.)* **fleece**
ጸምሪ xemri *(n.)* **fur**
ፀንበረ xenbere *(v.)* **annex**
ጸንዐ xene *(v.)* **persist**
ጸንዐ xen'ë *(v.i)* **abide**
ፅዕነት x'ënet *(n.)* **cargo**
ጸቕጢ xeq̈iẗu *(n.)* **pressure**
ጸቕጣዊ xeq̈ẗawi *(v.)* **pressurize**
ጸረ xere *(n.)* **anti**
ጸረ ባልዕ xere ble *(n.)* **pesticide**
ጸረ-ጓና ኣካል xere gwana 'akal *(n.)* **antibody**
ጸረ-ሕንዚ xere ȟnzi *(n.)* **antidote**
ጸረ-ምቅፅፃል xere mqxxal *(n.)* **antioxidant**
ጸረበ xerebe *(v.)* **whittle**
ጸረ-ማሕበራዊ xeremaȟberawi *(adj.)* **antisocial**
ጸረ-ነፍሳት xerenefsat *(n.)* **antibiotic**
ጸረ-ቃንዛ xereqanza *(n.)* **analgesic**
ጸረ-ረኽሲ xererek̓si *(adj.)* **antiseptic**
ጽሪጉ xerigu *(v.)* **pave**
ጸቒጡ xeẗiẗu *(v.)* **press**
ፅዋዕ xewaee *(n.)* **chalice**
ጸወታ xeweta *(v.i.)* **play**
ጸጸር xexer *(n.)* **pebble**
ጸህያይ ባሕሪ xahyay baḥri *(n.)* **wrack**
ጸጋማይ ገጽ xegamay gex *(n.)* **verso**
ጸሓፈ xeḥafe *(v.)* **write**
ጸንሐ xenḥe *(v.)* **wait**
ጽሕፈት xḥfet *(n.)* **writing**
ጽን በሃሊ xn behali *(adj.)* **wakeful**
ጽቡቕ tsebuq̈ *(adj.)* **good**
ጽኪ tseki *(n.)* **gland**
ጽርግያ tsergya *(n.)* **highway**
ጽፍዒት xf'it *(v.)* **whack**

ፅፉፍ xfuf ***(adj.)*** **natty**
ፅፉፍ xfuf ***(adj.)*** **neat**
ፅግዕ xg'ë ***(n.)*** **mumps**
ጽገ ዕንበባ xge ënbaba ***(n.)*** **pollen**
ጽግዕተኛ xg'ëteňa ***(adj.)*** **ancillary**
ፅሕዲ xĥdi ***(n.)*** **fir**
ፅሕዲ ሊባኖስ xhdi libanos ***(n.)*** **cedar**
ፅሕዲ ቆጽሮስ xḧdi qopros ***(n.)*** **cypress**
ፅሕፍቶ xĥfto ***(n.)*** **fate**
ጽሕፍቶ xḧfto ***(n.)*** **predestination**
ፅሕጊ xĥgi ***(n.)*** **fibre**
ጺጽ በለ xix bele ***(v.)*** **wheeze**
ጽላል xlal ***(n.)*** **parasol**
ጽልኣት xl'at ***(n.)*** **aversion**
ጽልኢ xl'i ***(n.)*** **animosity**
ፅልኢ xl'i ***(n.)*** **enmity**
ፅሉል xlul ***(adj.)*** **crazy**
ፅልዋ xlwa ***(n.)*** **ambit**
ፅማቕ xmaq̈wu ***(n.)*** **juice**
ጽምብላሊዕ xmblali'ë ***(n.)*** **butterfly**
ፅምዳዊ xmdawi ***(adj.)*** **binary**
ጽምደ-ሰልፋዊ xmdeselfawi ***(adj.)*** **bipartisan**
ጽምደ-ትኹረታዊ xmdetḱuretawi ***(adj.)*** **bifocal**
ፅምዲ xmdi ***(n.)*** **couple**
ጽምዲ xmdi ***(n.)*** **pair**
ፅምዲት xmdit ***(n.)*** **couplet**
ጽምሉው xmluw ***(adj.)*** **pale**
ፅመራ xmra ***(n.)*** **synthesis**
ፅንዓት xn'at ***(n.)*** **consolidation**
ፅንበራ xnbera ***(n.)*** **annexation**
ፅንብል xnbl ***(n.)*** **fete**
ፅንበራ x'nera ***(n.)*** **merger**
ፅንፈኛ xnfenya ***(n.)*** **extremist**
ጽኑዕ xnue ***(adj.)*** **persistent**
ፅኑዕ ክትትል xnu'e kt'tl ***(n.)*** **surveillance**
ዘይውዳእ zeywda'è ***(adj.)*** **abiding**
ፅንፅሕለ xnxĥle ***(n.)*** **flint**
ፆታ ኣልቦ xota 'albo ***(adj.)*** **asexual**
ጽዖታዊ x'ötawi ***(adj.)*** **callous**
ፅርግያ ተሽከርከርቲ xrgya teshkerkerti ***(n.)*** **motorway**
ጽዋ xwa ***(n.)*** **anecdote**
ፅውፅዋይ xwxway ***(n.)*** **fable**
ፅውፅዋይ xwxway ***(n.)*** **myth**
ጽያቕ xyaq̈ ***(v.)*** **blur**
ፅዩፍ xyuf ***(adj.)*** **abhorrent**
ጽዩፍ xyuf ***(adj.)*** **vulgar**
ፀጥ ዝበለ ነገር set zbele neger ***(adj.)*** **tranquil**
ፀጥታ setta ***(n.)*** **tranquillity**
ፃድቅ tsadk ***(n.)*** **saint**
ፃድቃዊ tsadkawi ***(adj.)*** **saintly**
ፃዕዳ ሽጉርቲ tsa-e-da sh-gur-ti ***(n.)*** **garlic**
ሕፍሰት ḧfset ***(n.)*** **density**
ፃዕቂ tsa'ëqi ***(n.)*** **intensity**
ፃዕራም tsa'eram ***(adj.)*** **industrious**
ጻዕረኛ xa'ëreňa ***(adj.)*** **studious**
ፃውዒት ዝርዝር ሽም tsaw'ït zrzr šm ***(adj.)*** **sanitary**
ፅባሕ tsbah ***(adv.)*** **tomorrow**
ፍሕሹው fḧshuw ***(adj.)*** **pleasant**
ጽቡቕ tsbuq ***(adj.)*** **twee**
ንፕሮግራም nprogram ***(v.)*** **download**
ፀዓነ tse'anew ***(v.)*** **download**
ፀዓቐ tse'äqe ***(v.)*** **intensify**
ፀዓረ tseare ***(v.i.)*** **toil**
ፀዓረ tse'äre ***(v.)*** **strive**
ፀቢብ መተሓላለፎ tsebib meteḧalalfo ***(n.)*** **stricture**

ዝርዝር ጸብጻብ zrzr xebxab *(n.)* **recital**
ፀብፃብ tsebtsab *(n.)* **record**
ፀብፃብ ሃበ tsebtsab habe *(v.)* **report**
ፀብፃብ ዜና tsebtsab zena *(n.)* **reportage**
ጸዳል tsedal *(v.)* **gleam**
ፀፍዐ tsef'ë *(v.t.)* **slap**
ጸፍዒ tsef'i *(n.)* **squall**
ጸጋ tsega *(n.)* **grace**
ፀጋም tsegam *(n.)* **left**
ጸግዒ tseg'e *(n.)* **tutelage**
ዘይምቻው zeymchaw *(n.)* **discomfort**
ጸቢብ xebib *(n.)* **strait**
ሰኪዐት seki'ët *(n.)* **toils**
ጸገሙ አካፈለ tsegemu 'akafele *(v.)* **unburden**
ፀገነ tsegene *(v.)* **refit**
ፀገነ tsegene *(v.)* **repair**
ጸጓር tseguar *(adj.)* **hirsute**
ጸጉሪ tseguri *(n.)* **hair**
ፀሓፋይ tsehafay *(n.)* **scribe**
ጸሓፊ tsehafe *(n.)* **secretary**
ፀሓፊ tsehafi *(n.)* **clerk**
ፀሓፊ ተዋስኦ tsehafi tewas'o *(n.)* **dramatist**
ፀሓታተረ tsehatatere *(v.)* **scribble**
ፀሓይ tse'ḧay *(n.)* **sun**
ፀሓይ ተፀልወ tse'ḧay tetselwe *(v.)* **sun**
ፀሓያማ tse'ḧayama *(n.)* **effort**
ፃዕሪ xa'ëri *(n.)* **menstruation**
ፃግነ xag'n *(n.)* **cornea**
ፃዕዳ አይኒ xa'ëda ayni *(n.)* **tingle**
ፅላል tselal *(n.)* **umbrella**
ፀላም ኸብዲ tselam kebdi *(n.)* **coriander**
ፃቅዳ xaqda *(n.)* **iris**
ፀልአ tsel'e *(v.)* **detest**
ፀልአ tsel'e *(v.)* **dislike**
ጸልአ tsel'e *(v.t.)* **hate**
ጽልኢ tsel-ei *(n.)* **hostility**
ፅልኢ ሓደሽቲ ሰባት tselei hdeshti sebat *(n.)* **xenophobia**
ፀለመ tseleme *(n.)* **defamation**
ፀለቕ tseleq *(n.)* **ransom**
ፀሊም tselim *(adj.)* **stygian**
ጸሊም እምኒ tselim 'èmni *(n.)* **granite**
ፀሊም ሊላዊ tselim lilawi *(n.)* **indigo**
ፅልም ዝበለ tselm zebele *(n.)* **umber**
ፀልማት tselmat *(n.)* **darkness**
ጽልሙት tselmut *(adj.)* **gloomy**
ፀሎት tselot *(n.)* **invocation**
ጽሉእ tselu'è *(adj.)* **hateful**
ፀማም tsemam *(adj.)* **deaf**
ፅምብል በዓል tse-m-bel be-al *(n.)* **gala**
ፀረ ምንግስቲ tse-mengsti *(n.)* **insurgent**
ፀንበረ tsenber *(v.)* **combine**
ፀንበረ tsenbere *(v.)* **conflate**
ኣእተወ 'a'ètewe *(v.)* **subsume**
ፅዕነት ts'ënet *(n.)* **shipment**
ፀንሐ tsenhe *(v.)* **remain**
ጸንሐ tsenḧe *(v.)* **stay**
ጽንጽያ tsentseya *(n.)* **gnat**
ጸቕጢ-ደም ምቕናስ tseqti dem mqnas *(n.)* **hypotension**
ጸቕጢ-ደም ምውሳኽ tseqti dem mwsak *(n.)* **hypertension**
ፀራቢ tserabi *(n.)* **carpenter**
ቀራጺ qeraxi *(n.)* **sculptor**
ፀረ ዕፈና tsere ë'fena *(n.)* **decongestant**

ፀረ ለዉጢ tsere lewuti ***(adj.)*** **conservative**
ጸረ ቃንዛ tsere qanza ***(n.)*** **painkiller**
ፀረ_ባልዕ tsere-bal'e ***(n.)*** **insecticide**
ፀረበ tserebe ***(v.)*** **sculpt**
ፀረፈ tserefe ***(v.t.)*** **insult**
ፀረገ ንጡፍ tserege ntuf ***(adj.)*** **radioactive**
ፀርፊ tserfi ***(n.)*** **invective**
ፀጥ ዝበለ tset zbele ***(adj.)*** **silent**
ፀጥታ tsetta ***(n.)*** **silence**
ጸዋግ tsewag ***(adj.)*** **stern**
ፀዋግ ገፅ tsewag getse ***(n.)*** **scowl**
ጸዋር tsewar ***(n.)*** **stoic**
ፀዉዐ tsew'e ***(v.)*** **summon**
ፀወዐ tsewe'ë ***(v.)*** **invite**
ፀየቐ tseyeqe ***(v.)*** **deface**
ጸየቐ tseyqhe ***(v.t.)*** **stain**
ፅፍፈት tsffet ***(n.)*** **quality**
ፈጣን ንጡፍ feẗan nẗuf ***(adj.)*** **dapper**
እሩም 'èrum ***(adj.)*** **suave**
ፅገሬዳ tsgereda ***(n.)*** **rose**
ፅገሬዳዊ tsgeredawi ***(adj.)*** **rosy**
ተጸጋዒ texega'ï ***(n.)*** **dependant**
ፅግዕተኛ tsg'ëtegna ***(n.)*** **protectorate**
ፅግዕተኛነት tsg'ëtegnanet ***(n.)*** **dependency**
ትሽዓተ tshäte ***(adj. & n.)*** **nine**
ፅሕፈት ኢድ tshfet 'id ***(n.)*** **script**
ፅሕፍቶ ts'ĥfto ***(n.)*** **destiny**
ፅሑፍ tshuf ***(n.)*** **text**
ፅያፍ tzyaf ***(n.)*** **gaffe**
ፅፍሪ txefri ***(n.)*** **claw**
ፅርበት tsirbet ***(n.)*** **carpentry**
ጺጽ በለ tsi-tse bele ***(v.i)*** **hiss**
ፅኪ ጉዕጉዕቲ tski gu'egu'eti ***(n.)*** **thyroid**
ፅላል tslal ***(n.)*** **shade**
ፅላል ዘለዎ tslal zelewo ***(adj.)*** **shady**
ፅላሎት መሳሊ tslalo mesali ***(adj.)*** **shadowy**
ፅላሎት tslalot ***(n.)*** **shadow**
ፅላሎት tslalot ***(n.)*** **silhouette**
ፅላኣት tsleat ***(n.)*** **repugnance**
ዘይተፈታውነት zeytefetawnet ***(n.)*** **disfavour**
ፅልኢ tsl'i ***(n.)*** **disgust**
ፅልኢ tsl'i ***(n.)*** **distaste**
ጽልሙት tslmut ***(adj.)*** **sombre**
ፅሉል tslul ***(n.)*** **psychopath**
ፅማቕ ፅሑፍ tsmaq tsĥuf ***(n.)*** **precis**
ፅምደ ዜማ tsmde zema ***(n.)*** **duet**
ፅምዲ tsmdi ***(n.)*** **duo**
ፅምኢ tsm'i ***(n.)*** **thirst**
ፅምሉው tsmluw ***(adj.)*** **sallow**
ፅሙእ tsmu'e ***(adj.)*** **thirsty**
ባድም badm ***(adj.)*** **desolate**
ብሕቱው bȟtuw ***(n.)*** **seclusion**
ብሕት'ነት bȟtnet ***(n.)*** **solitude**
ወሳኒነት wesaninet ***(v. t)*** **determination**
ውሳነ ብይን wsane byn ***(n.)*** **resolution**
ጽንዓት ts'n'ät ***(n.)*** **steadiness**
ጽንሰ-ሓሳባዊ tsnsehasabawi ***(adj.)*** **hypothetical**
ጽንኩር xnkur ***(adj.)*** **severe**
ጉልቡት gulbut ***(adj.)*** **stalwart**
ጽኑዕ tsnu'e ***(adj.)*** **steady**
ነቕ ዘይብል neq̈ zeybl ***(adj.)*** **resolute**
ፅኑዕ ምኽን tsnu'ë mkwan ***(n.)*** **rigour**
ጽኑዕ tsnu'ë ***(adj.)*** **steadfast**
ፅኑዕነት tsnu'enet ***(n.)*** **severity**
ፆታ tsota ***(n.)*** **sex**

ፆታ ዘይበሉ tsota zeybelu ***(adj.)*** **unisex**
ፆታዊ tsotawi ***(adj.)*** **sexual**
ፆታዊ ኣድልዎ tsotawi 'adlwo ***(n.)*** **sexism**
ፆታውነት tsotawnet ***(n.)*** **sexuality**
ጽቐጥቅጥ tsqtqt ***(n.)*** **throng**
ፅርበ እምኒ መቃብር tsrbe 'emni meqabr ***(n.)*** **sarcophagus**
ፅርግያ tsrgya ***(n.)*** **road**
ፅሩይ tsruy ***(adj.)*** **tidy**
ጥስጠሳ tstesa ***(n.)*** **saturation**
ፁብቕ tsubuqh ***(adj.)*** **luxuriant**
ፁሉል tsulul ***(adj.)*** **mad**
ፁሉል tsulul ***(n.)*** **maniac**
ፅዑቕ ts'üq ***(adj.)*** **dense**
ፅዑቕ ts'üq ***(adj.)*** **intensive**
ፁሩይ tsury ***(adj.)*** **immaculate**
ፅቡቕ ድልየት tzbuq dlyet ***(n.)*** **goodwill**
ፀጋምተኛ tzegamtegna ***(n.)*** **leftist**
ፀገም tzegem ***(n.)*** **masochism**
ፀሓፊ ታሪኽ tzehafi tarik ***(n.)*** **historian**
ፀንበረ tzenbere ***(v.)*** **fuse**
ፅዕነት tz'ënet ***(n.)*** **freight**
ፀዋግ tzewag ***(adj.)*** **grim**
ፅላለ tzlale ***(n.)*** **mania**
ፅልዋ tzlwa ***(n.)*** **leverage**
ፅምኢ tzm'i ***(n.)*** **lust**
ፅሙድ tzmud ***(adj.)*** **hooked**
ፅሟቕ ለሚን tzmwaq lemin ***(n.)*** **lemonade**
ፆታ tzota ***(n.)*** **gender**
ጹረት tsuret ***(n.)*** **octroi**
ፅልኣት tsl'at ***(n.)*** **odium**

ፈ

ፈላሚ felami ***(n.)*** **origin**
ፊትንፊት fitnfit ***(n.)*** **obverse**
ፋል fal ***(n.)*** **omen**
ፍልልይ flly ***(n.)*** **odds**
ፋብሪካ fabrika ***(n.)*** **factory**
ፋዱስ fadus ***(n.)*** **noon**
ፋእሚ fa'emi ***(n.)*** **skein**
ፋሓም faḧame ***(n.)*** **charcoal**
ፋሕፋሒ fah̆fah̆i ***(adj.)*** **abrasive**
ፋሕፍሐ fahfhe ***(v.)*** **scrub**
ፋሕፍሐ faĥfĥe ***(v.)*** **rub**
ሓግሓገ ḧagḧage ***(v.)*** **scrape**
ሓንጠጠ ḧanẗeẗe ***(v.t.)*** **scratch**
ፋጅ faj ***(n.)*** **fudge**
ፋጅዮ fajyo ***(n.)*** **beech**
ፋክስ faks ***(n.)*** **fax**
ፋክቱር faktur ***(n.)*** **invoice**
ፋሉላዊ falulawi ***(n.)*** **anarchist**
ፋሉልነት falulnet ***(n.)*** **anarchism**
ሰማፎሮ semaforo ***(n.)*** **beacon**
ሽግ shg ***(n.)*** **torch**
ፋንጋይ fangay ***(n.)*** **fungus**
ፋንጣ fanẗa ***(n.)*** **grasshopper**
ፋኑስ fanus ***(n.)*** **lamp**
ፋኑስ fanus ***(n.)*** **lantern**
ፋርዳ farda ***(n.)*** **singleton**
ፋረንሃይት farenhayt ***(n.)*** **Fahrenheit**
ፋርኬታ farkeeta ***(n.)*** **fork**
ፋስ fas ***(n.)*** **hatchet**
ፋስ fas ***(n.)*** **axe**
ፋሽስትነት fashstnet ***(n.)*** **fascism**
ፋሽያ fashya ***(n.)*** **fascia**
ፋጻ faxa ***(n.)*** **whistle**
ፋይል fayl ***(n.)*** **file**
ፋይቶት faytot ***(n.)*** **courtesan**
ፍድፉድ fdfud ***(v.t.)*** **abundant**

ፈጬጭ በለ feĉeĉ bele *(v.)* **fizz**
ፈደየ fedeye *(v.)* **acquit**
ገንዘብ መለሰ genzeb melese *(v.)* **repay**
ፈድፈደ fedfede *(v.i.)* **abound**
ፌስታዊ ኣኼባ feestawi 'akeeba *(n.)* **jamboree**
ፈሓረ fehare *(v.)* **delve**
ፈኸም በለ fekhem bele *(v.)* **smoulder**
ፈኲስ ቢራ fekwis bira *(n.)* **lager**
ፈላሳይ felasay *(n.)* **migrant**
ፈላስፋ felasfa *(n.)* **sophist**
ፈላሲ felasi *(n.)* **monk**
ፈላሲት felasit *(n.)* **nun**
ፈላጥ felaẗ *(n.)* **geek**
ፈላጥ felaẗ *(n.)* **nerd**
ፈላጥ felat' *(adj.)* **conversant**
ፈለኽለኽ በለ felekhlekh *(v.)* **squirm**
ፈለማ felema *(adj. & n.)* **first**
ፈለሰ felese *(v.)* **immigrate**
ፈለሰ felese *(v.)* **migrate**
ፈለጠ felete *(v.i.)* **recognize**
ፈለጥኩ በሃሊ feletku bhali *(adj.)* **pedantic**
ነጸለ nexele *(v.)* **detach**
ፈለየ feleye *(v. t)* **distinguish**
መለሰ melese *(v.)* **refund**
ኣግለለ 'aglele *(v.)* **segregate**
ዝተኸፋፈለ ztekefafele *(v.)* **separate**
ፈለየ feleye *(v.)* **thresh**
ፈልፋሊ felfali *(n.)* **font**
ፈልፋሊት felfalit *(v.)* **spring**
ፈልፈለ felfele *(v.)* **incubate**
ፈልሐ felḧe *(v.i.)* **boil**
ፍእምቶ ኣሰናዳዊ f'emto asenadawi *(n.)* **blurb**
ፈንጨጨ fencheche *(v.)* **splay**
ዕጀባ 'ëĵeba *(n.)* **convoy**
ፈነወ fenewe *(v.)* **emit**
ጸልአ xel'e *(v.)* **loathe**
ፈንፈነ fenfene *(v.)* **abhor**
ፈንጊ fengi *(n.)* **faction**
ፈንቀለ fenqele *(v.)* **dislodge**
ፈንጠጋር fenẗegar *(adj.)* **bizarre**
ፈንጠዝያ fentezya *(n.)* **spree**
ሃሰየት haseyet *(n.)* **euphoria**
ፈንጠዝያ fenṭezya *(n.)* **wassail**
ፈንጠዝያ fenẗezya *(n.)* **binge**
ፈንጢስካ ምእታው fenẗiska m'ètaw *(n.)* **irruption**
ፈንፀሐ fentseḧe *(v.)* **split**
ፈቓድ feqad *(n.)* **franchise**
ብቕዓት bq'ät *(n.)* **warrant**
ስምምዕ smm'ë *(n.)* **consent**
ፈቃር feqar *(adj.)* **affectionate**
ህኑን hnun *(adj.)* **fond**
ፈቀደ feqede *(v.t.)* **consent**
ፈቀደ feqede *(v.)* **let**
ፈቐደ feq̈ede *(v.)* **allow**
ፈራዲ feradi *(n.)* **arbiter**
ፈራዶ ferado *(n.)* **judiciary**
ነባሮ nebaro *(n.)* **jury**
ዘፍርህ zefrh *(adj.)* **fearful**
ሃድእ had'e *(adj.)* **meek**
ብዘይ -ዓንዲሕቖ bzey-'ändiḧq̈o *(adj.)* **spineless**
ፈራሕነት ferahnet *(n.)* **timidity**
ፈራሚ ferami *(n.)* **signatory**
ፈራረሰ ferarese *(v.)* **crumble**
ፈራዪ ferayi *(adj.)* **prolific**
ፈረደ ferede *(v.)* **adjudicate**
ፈረደ ferede *(v.)* **convict**
ፈረመ fereme *(n.)* **undersigned**
ፈረቐ fereq̈e *(v.)* **halve**
ፈረስ feres *(n.)* **horse**

ፈረስ ጋለቢ feres galabi *(adj.)* **equestrian**
ፈረሰኛ ወተሃደር fereseňa wetehader *(n.)* **knight**
ፈረሰኛ feresenya *(adj.)* **cavalier**
ፈርፈረ ferfere *(v.t)* **grate**
ፈርሀ ግብረ-ሰዶመኛ ferhe gbresedomeňa *(n.)* **homophobia**
ፈርሎንግ ferlonga *(n.)* **furlong**
ፈርን fern *(n.)* **fern**
ፈሳሲ fesasi *(n.)* **fluid**
ፈሳሲ fesasi *(n.)* **liquid**
ፈሳሲ ኮላ fesasi kone *(n.)* **mucilage**
ፈሳዊ fesawi *(adj.)* **flatulent**
ፈሰመ feseme *(v.)* **discolour**
ፈሰሰ fesese *(v.i)* **flow**
ፈስፋስ fesfas *(n.)* **sluggard**
ፈሲሕ fesiḧ *(v.)* **swanky**
ፈታላይ fetalay *(n.)* **spinner**
ፍጡን fťun *(adj.)* **nimble**
ቀዝሓዊ qezḧawi *(adj.)* **nippy**
ሓራቕ ḧaraq̈ *(adj.)* **snappy**
ፈጣን feťan *(adj.)* **speedy**
ፈጣን ጎደና feťan godena *(n.)* **speedway**
ፈታናይ fetanay *(n.)* **Trier**
ፈጣሪ fetari *(n.)* **creator**
ፈጣሪ fetari *(n.)* **innovator**
ፈታተሐ fetatĥe *(v.)* **dismantle**
ፈታው መጽሓፍ fetaw mexḧaf *(n.)* **bibliophile**
ፈታዊ ሃገር fetawi hager *(n.)* **nationalist**
መርመራ mermera *(n.)* **exam**
ፈተና fetena *(n.)* **test**
ፈተ'ነ fetene *(v.)* **attempt**
ብድሆ bdho *(n.)* **challenge**
ምኮራ mkora *(n.)* **experiment**
ኣቐዲሙ ረኣየ 'aq̈edimu re'aye *(n.)* **preview**
ምሕዳስ mḧdas *(n.)* **innovation**
ንምትላል ፈጠረ nmtlal feťere *(n.)* **trump**
ፈጠራ feťera *(n.)* **concoction**
ፈጠረ fetere *(v.)* **create**
ለቐቐ leq̈eq̈e *(v.)* **unleash**
ፈትሐ fet'ĥe *(v.)* **decipher**
ፈትሐ fetḧe *(v.)* **solve**
ፈንጢሑ ተንተነ feti'ĥu tentene *(v.)* **deconstruct**
ፈትሊ fetli *(n.)* **yarn**
ፈትሊ ሽምዓ fetli shm'a *(n.)* **wick**
ፈፀጋ ዓይኒ fetsega äynj *(n.)* **sty**
ፈፀጋ fetzega *(n.)* **freckle**
ፈዋሳይ fewasay *(n)* **quack**
ፈዋሲ fewasi *(adj.)* **medicinal**
ፈወሰ fewese *(v. t.)* **cure**
ፈውሲ fewsi *(n.)* **remedy**
ፈውሲ ዓሻ fewsi äsha *(n.)* **nostrum**
ፈፃሚ fexami *(n.)* **executive**
ፈፀጋ fexega *(n.)* **acne**
ፈጸጋ fexega *(n.)* **pimple**
ፈጸመ fexeme *(v.)* **commit**
ረሸነ reshene *(v.)* **execute**
ዛዘመ zazeme *(v.)* **accomplish**
መልአ mel'e *(v.)* **consummate**
ኣጸቢቑ ዘይበሰለ 'axebiq̈u zeybesele *(adj.)* **sodden**
ነዋሚ newami *(adj.)* **torpid**
ፈዘዘ fezeze *(v.)* **glaze**
ፍግረት fgret *(n.)* **erosion**
ፍሕፍሕ fĥfĥ *(n.)* **friction**
ፍሒኛ fḧinya *(n.)* **balloon**
ፍሒሩ አውጽአ fhiru awts'a *(v.)* **unearth**
ፍሕኛ fḧna *(n.)* **bladder**
ፍሕኛ fḧnyawi *(n.)* **cyst**

ፍሕኛዊ fḧnyawi *(adj.)* **cystic**
ፍሕሶ fḧso *(n.)* **cord**
ፍሕሶ ጸምሪ fhso tsemri *(n.)* **worsted**
ፊደል fidel *(n.)* **alphabet**
ብናይ ፊደላት ተርታ bnay fidelat terta *(adj.)* **alphabetical**
ፊደላዊ fidelawi *(adj.)* **literal**
ፌደራላዊ fiederalawi *(adj.)* **federal**
ፈደረሽን fiedereshn *(n.)* **federation**
ፌንግ ሽዊ fieng shwi *(n.)* **feng shui**
ፊፍ በለ fif bele *(v.)* **sniffle**
ፊሕታ fiḧta *(n.)* **boom**
ፊልሚ filmi *(n.)* **film**
ፊልሚ filmi *(n.)* **movies**
ፊሎሎጅየኛ filolojgna *(n.)* **philologist**
ፊሎሎጅያዊ filolojyawi *(adj.)* **philological**
ፊኖክዮ finokyo *(n.)* **fennel**
ፊንታ finta *(n.)* **vagary**
ፊርማ firma *(n.)* **signature**
ፊስቶ fiseto *(n.)* **cask**
ፊተውራሪ fitewrari *(n.)* **spearhead**
ፊዚክስ fizkis *(n.)* **physics**
ፊዝዮተራፒ fizyoterapi *(n.)* **physiotherapy**
ፍኩስ ጽፍዒት fkus xfeit *(v.)* **pat**
ፍላቅ flaq *(adj.)* **derivative**
ፍላጻ flaxa *(n.)* **arrow**
ፍልፍል fl'fl *(n.)* **spa**
ፍልሖ flho *(n.)* **termite**
ፍሊልታ flilta *(n.)* **jet**
ፍሊት flit *(n.)* **aerosol**
ፍልልይ flly *(n.)* **distinction**
ምልውዋጥ mlwwaẗ *(n.)* **variation**
ፍሎራይድ florayd *(n.)* **fluoride**
ፍልቀት flqet *(n.)* **evolution**
ፍልቀተ-ቃል flqeteqal *(n.)* **etymology**
ፍልሰት flset *(n.)* **migration**
ፍልስፍና flsfna *(n.)* **philosophy**
ፍልስፍናዊ flsfnawi *(adj.)* **philosophical**
ፍልጠት flẗet *(n.)* **mastery**
ፍሉ flu *(n.)* **flu**
ፍሉጥ flut *(adj.)* **renowned**
ዘየማትእ ሓቂ zeyemat'è ḧaqi *(n.)* **truism**
ዝተፈልየ ztefelye *(adj.)* **different**
ዝተቖራረጸ zteq̈orarexe *(adj.)* **discrete**
ፍሉይ fluy *(adj.)* **especial**
ዘይተለምደ zeytelemde *(adj.)* **extraordinary**
ዓጃባዊ 'äĵabawi *(adj.)* **remarkable**
ፍሉይ fluy *(adj.)* **special**
ዝተፈልየ ztefelye *(adj.)* **unique**
ልውጥ lwẗ *(n.)* **variant**
ፍሉይ fluy *(adj.)* **particular**
ናይ ፍላይ nay flay *(adj.)* **peculiar**
ፍሉይ ግዳሰ fluy gdase *(n.)* **hobby**
ፍሉይ ክእለት fluy k'elet *(n.)* **forte**
ውሕልነት wḧlnet *(n.)* **specialization**
ፍሉይ ክእለት ኣጥረየ fluy k'elet aẗreye *(v.)* **specialize**
ፍሉይ ጠባይ fluy ṭebay *(n.)* **idiosyncrasy**
ፍሉይ ፆታዊ fluy tzotawi *(adj.)* **heterosexual**
ፍሉይነት fluynet *(n.)* **speciality**
ፍልየት flyet *(n.)* **detachment**
ፍንጫል fnchal *(n.)* **splinter**
ፍንጫል ምእመናን fn'chal m'emenan *(n.)* **sect**
ፍንጪ fnči *(n.)* **cue**
ፍንጫልጫል fnĉlĉal *(n.)* **shrapnel**
ፊነክስ fneks *(n.)* **phoenix**
ፍንፈና fnfena *(n.)* **abhorrence**

ፍንፉን fnfun *(adj.)* **loathsome**
ፍዳ fda *(n.)* **vengeance**
ፈላሲ felasi *(n.)* **immigrant**
ፈለጠ feleṭe *(v.)* **know**
ፈታው ኩናት fetaw kunat *(adj.)* **warlike**
ፈታው ምቾት fetaw mchot *(n.)* **voluptuary**
ፈታው መግቢ fetaw megbi *(n.)* **gourmand**
ፈተነ fetene *(n.)* **venture**
ፍልልይ flly *(n.)* **variance**
ፍልሰት flset *(n.)* **immigration**
ፍልጠት flṭet *(n.)* **knowledge**
ፈኩስ ግመ fokis gme *(n.)* **haze**
ፍቓደኛ fq̈adeña *(n.)* **volunteer**
ፍጥነት fṭnet *(n.)* **velocity**
ፍንጉፀ fnguts *(adj.)* **deviant**
ፎልዮ folyo *(n.)* **folio**
ፎቅ foq *(n.)* **tower**
ፎረፎር forefor *(n.)* **dandruff**
ፎርኖ forno *(n.)* **toaster**
ፎጣ fota *(n.)* **towel**
ፍቶ ኮፒ foto kopi *(n.)* **photocopy**
ፎቶ ኮፒ foto kopi *(n.)* **photostat**
ፍቭያ fovya *(n.)* **phobia**
ፎዝፌት fozfeyet *(n.)* **phosphate**
ፍቓድ fqad *(n.)* **permission**
ፍቓድ fqad *(v.)* **will**
ፍቓደኛ fq̈adeǹa *(adj.)* **willing**
ፍቓድ ዘይበሉ fqad zeyblu *(adj.)* **unwarranted**
ፍቓደኛ fqadegna *(adj.)* **willing**
ፍቓድ ኣምላኽ fq̈d amlaḱ *(n.)* **providence**
ፍቓድ fqhad *(n.)* **licence**
ፍቕሪ fqhri *(n.)* **love**
ፍቖድኡ fq̈odeu *(adj.)* **ubiquitous**
ፍቕራዊ fqrawi *(n.)* **paramour**
ፍቅራዊ fqrawi *(adj.)* **romantic**
ፍቕራዊ fq̈rawi *(adj.)* **amorous**
ፍቕሪ fqri *(n.)* **devotion**
ፍቅሪ ሃገር fqri hager *(n.)* **nationalism**
ፍቕሪ ክምስርት ፈተነ fqri kmsrt fetene *(v.)* **woo**
ፍቕሪ መግለፂ ቃል fqri meglexi qal *(n.)* **endearment**
ፍቑር fq̈ur *(adj.)* **beloved**
ፍራስ fras *(n.)* **wreckage**
ፍርዳዊ frdawi *(adj.)* **judicial**
ከም ገበነኛ ምፍራድ kem gebeneǹa mfrad *(n.)* **conviction**
ፍርዲ frdi *(n.)* **judgement**
ፍርዲ frdi *(n.)* **ruling**
ፍርዲ frdi *(n.)* **verdict**
ፍረ fre *(n.)* **fruit**
ፈረየ fereye *(n.)* **seed**
ፍረ ዓካት fre 'äkat *(n.)* **kernel**
ፍረ ካስታኖ fre kastano *(n.)* **conker**
ፍረ ነገር fre neger *(n.)* **essence**
ፍረ ነገር fre neger *(n.)* **gist**
ፍረ ነብሲ frenebsi *(n.)* **testicle**
ፍረ ነብሲ frenebsi *(n.)* **testis**
ፍርሓት frḧat *(n.)* **cowardice**
ፍርሃታዊ frhatawi *(adj.)* **reverential**
ምፍርራሕ mfrraḧ *(n.)* **threat**
ጭንቀት čnqet *(n.)* **dismay**
ፈርሀ ferhe *(n.)* **fear**
መሰንበዲ mesenbedi *(n.)* **fright**
ፍርሒ frḥi *(n.)* **horror**
ፍሪጅ frij *(n.)* **refrigerator**
ፍሪቅሪቅ ዝብል friqriq bele *(adj.)* **fizzy**
ፍርናሽ frnash *(n.)* **mattress**
ፍርናሽ frnash *(n.)* **pad**
ጉዝጓዝ guzgwaz *(v.)* **padding**
ፍርናሽ ሓሰር frnash haser *(n.)* **pallet**

ፍርቀ ክቢ frqe kebi *(n.)* **semicircle**
ፍርቀ ኽረምቲ frqe ḱremti *(adj.)* **midsummer**
ፍርቀ ለይቲ frqe leyti *(n.)* **midnight**
ፍርቀ መዓልቲ frqe me'älti *(n.)* **midday**
ፍርቂ frqi *(adj.)* **mid**
ፍርቁ frqu *(adv.)* **partly**
ፍርሰት frset *(n.)* **nullification**
ፍርስራስ frsras *(n.)* **debris**
ፍርትት ዝብል frtt zbl *(adj.)* **friable**
ፍሩስ frus *(adj.)* **null**
ፍሩሽካ frushka *(n.)* **fodder**
ፍርያት fryat *(n.)* **product**
ፍርያት ግጥሚ fryat gẗmi *(n.)* **poetry**
ፍሰሃ fseha *(n.)* **ecstasy**
ፍሰሃ fseha *(n.)* **felicity**
ፍሰት fset *(n.)* **creek**
ፍስሃ fsha *(n.)* **pleasure**
ፍሽኽታ fshḱta *(v.)* **grin**
ፍሹል fshul *(adj.)* **abortive**
ፍሽለት fšlet *(n.)* **refutation**
ፍሱሕ fsuh *(adj.)* **jaunty**
ፍታሕ ftaḧ *(n.)* **solution**
ፍታሕ ሃበ ftaĥ habe *(v.)* **resolve**
ፍትሕ ft'ĥ *(n.)* **divorce**
ፍትሓዊ ft'ĥawi *(adj.)* **dispassionate**
ፍትሒ ftĥi *(n.)* **equity**
ፍትሒ ftḧi *(n.)* **impartiality**
ፍትሒ ftḧi *(n.)* **justice**
ፍጥነት ftnet *(n.)* **pace**
ፍጥነት fẗnet *(n.)* **speed**
ፍትነት ማሽን መዐቀኒ ftnet mashn me'eqeni *(n.)* **tachometer**
ፍጥረት ftret *(n.)* **creature**
ፍጻመ ftsame *(n.)* **happening**
ፍፁም ftsum *(adj.)* **sheer**
ፍፁም ለወጠ ftsum lewete *(v.)* **revolutionize**
ፍትወት ftwet *(n.)* **penchant**
ፍትወት ftwet *(n.)* **affection**
ፍትወተ ስጋ ftwete sga *(n.)* **sensuality**
ፍፁም ftzum *(adj.)* **implicit**
ፉል ful *(n.)* **peanut**
ፉሉይ fuluy *(adj.)* **inimitable**
ፉርዳ furda *(n.)* **bay**
ፉት በለ fut bele *(v.)* **sip**
ፍወሳ ሕማም ኣእምሮ fwesa ḧmam aèmro *(n.)* **psychotherapy**
ፍፃመ fxame *(n.)* **episode**
ፍጻሜ fxamee *(n.)* **event**
ምርሻን mrshan *(n.)* **execution**
ፍጻሜ fxamee *(n.)* **accomplishment**
ፍጹም fxum *(adj.)* **categorical**
ምሉ'እ mlu'è *(adj.)* **perfect**
ኣውቶክራት 'awtokrat *(adj.)* **autocrat**
ዘዋርድ zeward *(adj.)* **abject**
ፍፁም መላኪ fxum melaki *(adj.)* **absolute**
ፍጹምነት fxumnet *(n.)* **perfection**
ፍንፉን fnfun *(adj.)* **odious**
ፎርኖ forno *(n.)* **oven**

ፐ

ፐንጉን pengyun *(n.)* **penguin**
ፐፐሮኒ peperoni *(n.)* **pepper**
ፑርጋቶርዮ purgatoryo *(n.)* **purgatory**
ፒንሳ pinsa *(n.)* **pliers**
ፒራሚድ piramid *(n.)* **pyramid**
ፒሳ pisa *(n.)* **pizza**
ፒስቶን piston *(n.)* **piston**

ፒያኖ piyano *(n.)* **piano**
ዋልታ-ምድሪ waltamdri *(n.)* **pole**
ፖሎ palo *(n.)* **polo**
ፓንኬክ pankek *(n.)* **pancake**
ፓንታሎኒ pantaloni *(n.)* **pantaloons**
ፓፓጋሎ papagalo *(n.)* **parrot**
ፓራመተር parameter *(n.)* **parameter**
ፓርላማዊ parlamawi *(adj.)* **parliamentary**
ፓርላማ parlma *(n.)* **parliament**
ፓሮ paro *(n.)* **leek**
ፓስፖርት pasport *(n.)* **passport**
ፓይ pay *(n.)* **pie**
ፓይሎት paylot *(n.)* **pilot**
መራሕ ነፋሪት meraḧ nefarit *(n.)* **aviator**
ፔርሙዝ permuz *(n.)* **thermos**
ፕላኔት planiet *(n.)* **planet**
ፕላተሌት planiet *(n.)* **platelet**
ፕላስቲክ plastik *(n.)* **plastic**
ፕራላይን pralayn *(n.)* **praline**
ፕራንያ pranya *(n.)* **pram**
ፕሬዝደንት presdent *(n.)* **president**
ፕሬዝደንታዊ presdentawi *(adj.)* **presidential**
ፕሪዝም prizm *(n.)* **prism**
ፕሮፌሰር profieser *(n.)* **professor**
ፕሮጀክቶር proĵecter *(n.)* **projector**
ፕሮስተይት prosteyt *(n.)* **prostate**
ፕሮቲን protin *(n.)* **protein**
ፕላንተይን planteyn *(n.)* **plantain**
ፖድካስት podkast *(n.)* **podcast**
ፖለቲከኛ poletikegna *(n.)* **statesman**
ፖለቲከኛ poletikeňa *(n.)* **politician**
ፖለቲቻዊ ጥርናፈ poletikeňawi ẗrnafe *(n.)* **polity**
ፖለቲክስ poletiks *(n.)* **politics**
ፖሊግራፍ poligraf *(n.)* **polygraph**
ፖሊስ polis *(n.)* **police**
ፖሊስ polis *(n.)* **policeman**
ፖሊሳዊ ምርመራ polisawi mrmera *(n.)* **inquisition**
ፖለቲካዊ polotikawi *(adj.)* **political**
ፖርኖግራፊ pornografi *(n.)* **pornography**
ፖስታ posta *(n.)* **mail**
ፖስጣ ቤት posẗa biet *(n.)* **post office**
ፖስተር poster *(n.)* **poster**
ፖፕላር potlar *(n.)* **poplar**